STATISTICA™

Volume I:
GENERAL CONVENTIONS & STATISTICS I

Volume I: CONVENTIONS & STATISTICS I
Volume II: GRAPHICS
Volume III: STATISTICS II
Volume IV: INDUSTRIAL STATISTICS
Volume V: LANGUAGES: BASIC and S

STATSOFT SINGLE USER LICENSE AGREEMENT

The following constitutes the terms of the License Agreement between a single user (User) of this software package, and the producer of the package, StatSoft, Inc. (called Statsoft hereafter). By opening the package, you (the User) are agreeing to become bound by the terms of this agreement. If you do not agree to the terms of this agreement do not open the package, and contact the StatSoft Customer Service Department (or an authorized StatSoft dealer) in order to obtain an authorization number for the return of the package. This License Agreement pertains also to all third party software included in or distributed with StatSoft products.

License

Unless explicitly stated on the program disks, the enclosed software package is sold to be used on one computer system by one user at a time. This License Agreement explicitly excludes renting or loaning the package. Unless explicitly stated on the program disks, this License Agreement explicitly excludes the use of this package on mulituser systems, networks, or any time sharing systems. (Contact StatSoft concerning Multiuser License Programs.) The user is allowed to make a backup copy for archival purposes and/or to install the software package on a hard disk. However, the software will never be installed on more than one hard disk at a time. The documentation accompanying this software package (or any of its parts) shall not be copied or reproduced in any form.

Disclaimer of Warranty

Although producing error free software is obviously a goal of every software manufacturer, it can never be guaranteed that a software program is actually free of errors. Business and scientific application software is inherently complex (and it can be used with virtually unlimited numbers of data and command settings, producing idiosyncratic operational environments for the software); therefore, the User is cautioned to verify the results of his or her work. This software package is provided "as is" without warranty of any kind. StatSoft and distributors of StatSoft software products make no representation or warranties with respect to the contents of this software package and specifically disclaim any implied warranties or merchantability or fitness for any particular purpose. In no event shall StatSoft be liable for any damages whatsoever arising out of the use of, inability to use, or malfunctioning of this software package. StatSoft does not warrant that this software package will meet the User's requirements or that the operation of the software package will be uninterrupted or error free.

Limited Warranty

If within 30 days from the date when the software package was purchased (i.e., the StatSoft invoice date), the program disks are found to be defective (i.e., they are found to be unreadable by the properly aligned disk drive of the computer system on which the package is intended to run), StatSoft will replace the disks free of charge. After 30 days, the User will be charged for the replacement a nominal disk replacement fee. If within 90 days from the date when the software package was purchased (i.e., invoice date), the software package was found by the User not capable of performing any of its main (i.e., basic) functions described explicitly in promotional materials published by StatSoft, StatSoft will provide the User with replacement disks free of defects, or if the replacement cannot be provided within 90 days from the date when StatSoft was notified by the User about the defect, the User will receive a refund of the purchasing price of the software package.

Updates, Corrections, Improvements

The User has a right to purchase all subsequent updates, new releases, new versions, and modifications of the software package introduced by StatSoft for an update fee or for a reduced price (depending on the scope of the modification). StatSoft is not obligated to inform the User about new updates, improvements, modifications, and/or corrections of errors introduced to its software packages. In no event shall StatSoft be liable for any damages whatsoever arising out of the failure to notify the User about a known defect of the software package.

Chapter 1:
GENERAL CONVENTIONS

Table of Contents

Detailed Table of Contents

StatSoft®

StatSoft®

Chapter 1:

GENERAL CONVENTIONS

USER-INTERFACE IN *STATISTICA* (OVERVIEW)

Most of the topics discussed in this chapter are also included in the *Quick Reference* manual, which contains a review of the features and options of *STATISTICA* in a question and answer format. This chapter provides a reference guide with descriptions of individual dialogs.

General Features

Customized Operation

There are several ways in which the *STATISTICA* system can be controlled. The following sections summarize the features of the four main alternative user-interfaces of the program: (1) interactive interface, (2) macros, (3) *SCL* command language, and (4) control from within other Windows applications. However, note that:

- many aspects of those user-interfaces do not exclude each other, thus depending on your specific applications and preferences, you can combine them;
- the *Auto Task Buttons* facility (a floating or docked toolbar with user-defined buttons which can be assigned to specific tasks, custom-designed procedures, or sequences of keystrokes) can be used to integrate the alternative user-interfaces and, for example, to provide quick access to batch programs or commonly used files; and
- almost all features of those alternative user interfaces represent only default settings which can be customized (leading to different appearance and behavior of the program); it is usually recommended to customize your system in order to take full advantage of *STATISTICA*'s potential to meet your preferences and optimal requirements of the tasks which you need to accomplish (see the section on *Customizing the user-interface*, page 1017).

Alternative Access to the Same Facilities; Custom Styles of Work

Even without any customization, the default settings of *STATISTICA* offer alternative user-interface means and solutions to achieve the same results. The "alternative access" principle present in every aspect of its user-interface allows *STATISTICA* to support different styles of work. For example, most of the commonly-used tools of the interactive user-interface in *STATISTICA* can be accessed alternatively from:

- traditional pull-down menus,
- via keyboard shortcuts,
- by using the toolbars ("ribbons") and the clickable fields on the status bar,
- via *Auto Task Buttons* (a floating toolbar with buttons which can be assigned to user-specified tasks or sequences of keystrokes), and
- from the flying menus associated with specific objects (cells, graphic objects, parts of graphs) and called by clicking the right-mouse-button on the object (context-sensitive menus, see below).

StatSoft

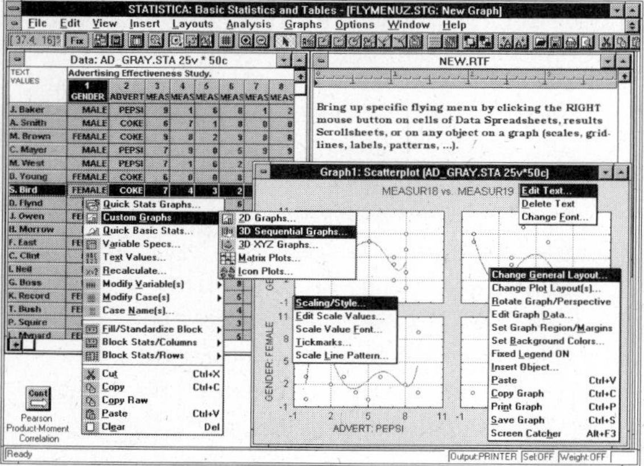

It is suggested that you explore the alternative user-interface facilities of *STATISTICA* before becoming "attached" to one style or another.

1. Interactive User-Interface

Overview

Main components of the interactive user-interface in *STATISTICA*. Although the interactive user-interface of *STATISTICA* is not the only one available (see the sections on the alternative user-interfaces 2, 3, and 4, below), it is in most cases the easiest and most commonly used.

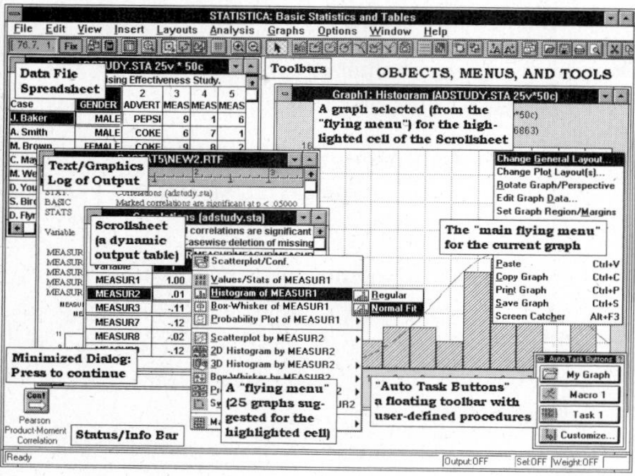

The diagram above illustrates the main components of the screen (note that usually you would not see simultaneously all of the facilities and tools shown in the diagram). Most of the tools and facilities shown above are described in the subsequent sections of this manual (those sections are organized around the specific toolbar options accompanying each of those facilities).

Modular Structure

Modules. *STATISTICA* consists of modules, each containing a group of related procedures. When you switch modules, you can either keep *STATISTICA* down to one application window only, or alternatively, you can keep the previously used modules open, because each of them can be run in a separate window (as a separate Windows application, as described below).

When you run the modules of *STATISTICA* as separate applications, you will find all "general purpose" facilities (such as the data spreadsheet, *BASIC*, *SCL*, and all graphics procedures) available in every module and at every point of analysis.

This architecture of *STATISTICA*, coupled with its support for multitasking, allows you not only to easily compare results from different analyses but also to run them simultaneously in different application windows.

You can quickly switch modules by:

- clicking on their icons on the desktop,
- bringing up their respective application windows (if they are already open), or
- selecting them in the *STATISTICA Module Switcher*, which can be customized to facilitate quick access to the procedures you use most often.

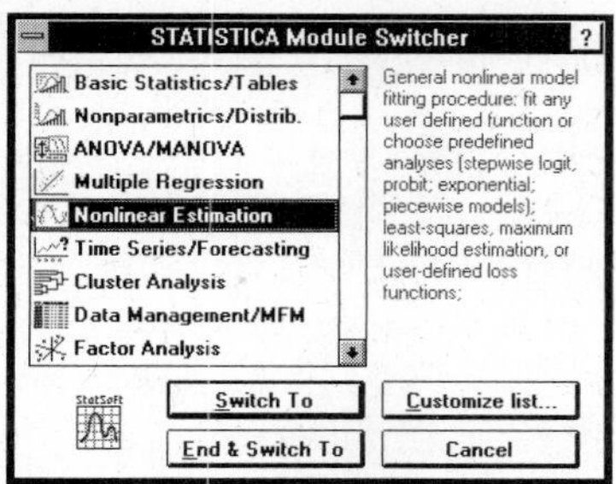

The *Module Switcher*. The *Switcher* works in a manner similar to the Windows *Task Switcher* (which is called by double-clicking anywhere on the empty space on the Windows desktop). It can also be invoked in a similar way, by double-clicking anywhere on the empty space within the *STATISTICA* application window. You can also call it by pressing the first (leftmost) button on every toolbar or by selecting the option *Other Statistics* in the pull-down menu *Analysis*.

The *Module Switcher* may open new modules into the same or new application windows (see page 1018 for an overview of the two ways in which the *Module Switcher* may operate).

Icons representing *STATISTICA* modules. When you first install *STATISTICA*, *Setup* creates a group of applications on your desktop called *STATISTICA*, and sets up icons for the *Module Switcher* (see the icon *STATISTICA*, the first icon in the group, below), the *Basic Statistics and Tables* module, and some other programs (e.g., *Help*, *Setup*).

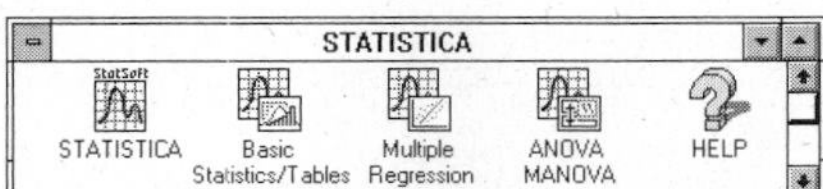

As mentioned above, you may prefer to start some modules by clicking on their respective icons on the desktop (instead of using the *Moaule Switcher*); thus, you may want to create icons for more modules than those automatically created by *Setup*. To create an icon for an application in a group, follow the standard Windows conventions (choose *New* in the *File* menu in *Program Manager* and create a new *Program Item*).

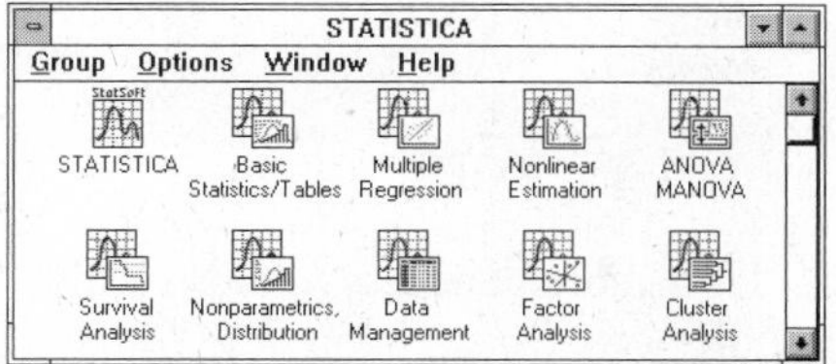

Note that when you create a new *Program Item* (icon) in a group, *Program Manager* will automatically create the respective icon for the module and label it with an abbreviated name (no wider than the icon). If you find that some of those names are not sufficiently clear, you may edit or expand the name in the *Description* field of the Windows *Program Item Properties* dialog.

Custom icon setups. You can also customize the setup of application icons by associating them with specific data files (enter the data file name into the *Command Line* field of the Windows *Program Item Properties* dialog), so that a particular data file will be open whenever you click on the module icon.

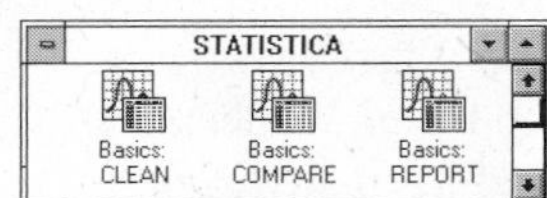

You can also create multiple icons for the same module, as shown above, each associated with a different input data file (the differences may be represented by different custom names which you can assign to the icons in their respective Windows *Program Item Properties* dialog, see the field *Description*).

The "Flow" of Interactive Analysis

Startup panel. When a module opens, a respective startup panel appears, for example:

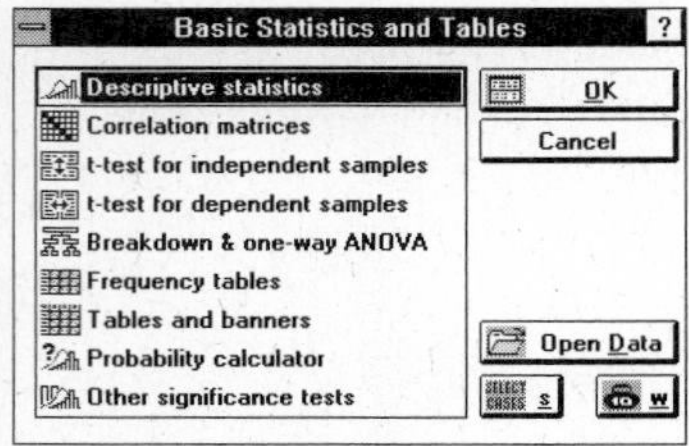

The panel provides a shortcut access to those pull-down menu facilities of the current module which the users will most likely use first. The panel saves you from having to access the menus, which usually requires additional steps. (Our tests indicate that startup panels considerably reduce the number of operations necessary in a typical *STATISTICA* session, especially if it involves performing a variety of analyses.) If you prefer to use the traditional interface and would rather access the pull-down menus *Analysis* or *File* (which contain all options of the startup panel), you can use them anyway because the startup panel is a modeless dialog box and clicking anywhere outside the panel will automatically iconize it (you can also suppress displaying it altogether, see page 1017).

The *Auto Task Buttons* alternative to Startup panel. The *Auto Task Buttons* floating toolbar (see Chapter 6) can be set up as an alternative, customized startup panel. Unless you suppress it, this floating toolbar normally appears when you start a module; thus you can define its buttons (use the *Customize...* button) to contain the tasks you are most likely to perform first. Those tasks may be defined either by specifying a desired sequence of keystrokes, or by entering a set of respective task commands using *SCL* (*STATISTICA Command Language*).

"Analysis definition" and "output selection" dialogs. When the desired analysis and (when requested) a new data file are selected in the startup panel, the analysis definition dialog will appear, where you can select the variables to be analyzed and other options and features of the task to be performed.

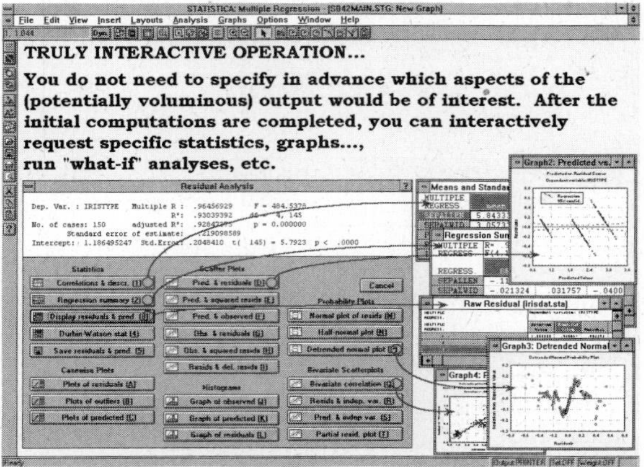

In some simple analyses (such as descriptive statistics, as shown on the sample screen below), the analysis definition dialog also serves as an output selection dialog where you can request the type and format of the output (e.g., some specific Scrollsheets or graphs).

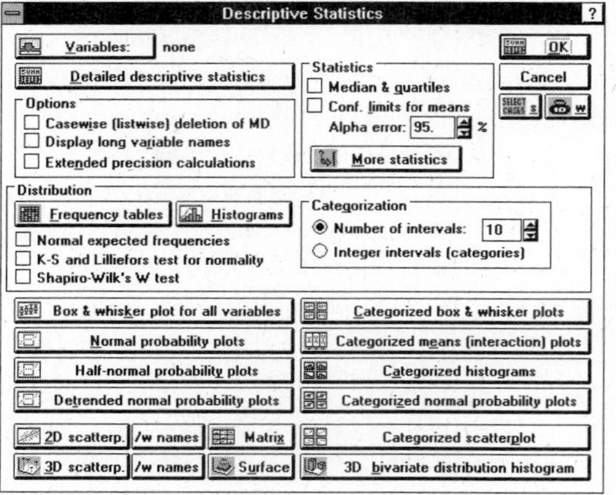

Output (queues of Scrollsheet and graph windows). Consecutive output Scrollsheets and graphs appear in separate windows which form queues of a fixed length and are managed (i.e., automatically closed) on a first-in-first-out basis.

The default length of each of the two queues is 3. In other words, when the fourth Scrollsheet (or graph) is created, then the first one is closed. You can adjust the length of each queue (temporarily in the pull-down menu *Window* or permanently in the pull-down menu *Options*).

Regardless of the length of the queue, you can also *lock* individual windows to "remove" them from the queue (use the two *Manager* options in the pull-down menu *Window*), so that they will not close as long as you do not exit the program. Scrollsheets and graphs are managed by the same respective queues regardless of how they were produced (e.g., both Scrollsheet and graph windows can be generated automatically by the program or by you directly from spreadsheets, Scrollsheets, menus, or dialogs).

Automatic Generation of Reports (Text and Graphs) and Automating Interactive Analyses

In addition to the macro- and command-based alternative user-interfaces offered in *STATISTICA* (see below), a variety of facilities are provided to automate conducting sequences of similar analyses and/or to automatically produce reports and printouts without having to specifically send each part of the output (Scrollsheets, graphs) to the printer or report window (or file).

Auto Task Buttons. This floating or docked toolbar (see page 1014) contains user-defined buttons assigned to standard tasks, operations, or custom-defined procedures (use the *Customize...* button to assign to new buttons: *STATISTICA Command Language* (*SCL*) tasks, *STATISTICA BASIC* programs, or simply editable sequences of keystrokes). Then, pressing a button will execute a task or a series of tasks of practically unlimited complexity.

Internal batch processing mode. Whenever applicable, *STATISTICA* offers the *internal batch processing mode* option for relevant analyses. This mode is usually invoked simply by selecting a list of variables to be processed, rather than a single variable. Then, the same, currently specified design or requested comparison is automatically repeated by the program for each of the selected variables (for example, the same design of multiple regression, breakdowns, *t*-test, or the Kruskal-Wallis test can be repeated for each variable in a list of dependent variables). Such procedures also offer *Internal batch processing and printing* options which will perform the requested sequence of analyses without requiring any user input and automatically send the reports to the printer, *Text/output Window*, or disk file.

Auto-reports and automatic printing of Scrollsheets. Regardless of whether the subsequent analyses are automatically invoked by the internal batch options (mentioned in the previous paragraph) or interactively requested by the user, you can select the *Auto-report* option (see the pull-down menu *Options* or the clickable *Output* field on the status bar, Chapter 2). These options allow you to have the contents of every output window (that will be produced in the course of subsequent analyses) sent to the printer or report window (or file) without requiring any user-action.

The option to automatically produce such a record of each Scrollsheet and/or graph generated on-screen is useful even if you do not intend to keep a permanent record of the output; for example, in exploratory data analyses, it is sometimes useful to be able to return to some earlier results of a long sequence of explorations. For that purpose, instead of printing, the entire output (both Scrollsheets and graphs) can be directed to the temporary, scrollable *Text/output Window* and later printed, saved, or copied into word processor files (see Chapter 5).

Automatic printing of graphs. The option to automatically print every graph that is displayed on the screen (see the clickable *Output* field on the status bar; see Chapter 2) is mostly useful as a batch graph printing facility. In most circumstances, producing hard copies of graphs is relatively time-consuming. Thus, it is useful to use this option if you intend to print a series ("cascade") of graphs generated by a particular analysis (e.g., a long series of graphs necessary to visualize the configuration of means for a higher-order interaction in ANOVA or a cascade of 3D bivariate histograms for a multi-way table).

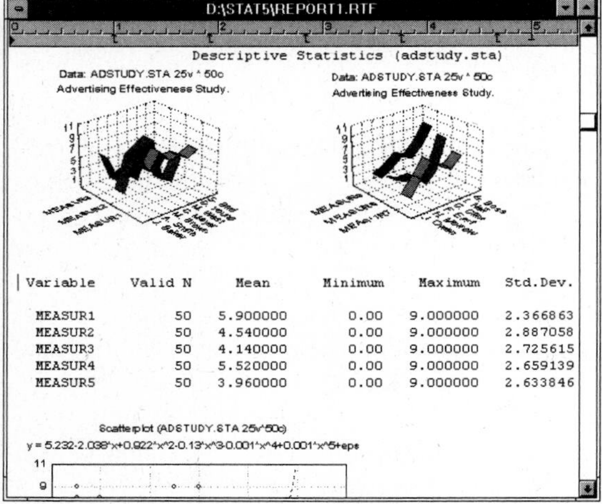
D:\STAT5\REPORT1.RTF

Descriptive Statistics (adstudy.sta)

Data: ADSTUDY.STA 25v * 50c
Advertising Effectiveness Study.

Data: ADSTUDY.STA 25v * 50c
Advertising Effectiveness Study.

Variable	Valid N	Mean	Minimum	Maximum	Std.Dev.
MEASUR1	50	5.900000	0.00	9.000000	2.366863
MEASUR2	50	4.540000	0.00	9.000000	2.887058
MEASUR3	50	4.140000	0.00	9.000000	2.725615
MEASUR4	50	5.520000	0.00	9.000000	2.659139
MEASUR5	50	3.960000	0.00	9.000000	2.633846

Scatterplot (ADSTUDY.STA 25v*50c)
y = 5.232-2.038*x+0.922*x^2-0.13*x^3-0.001*x^4+0.001*x^5+eps

It is much faster however, to direct multiple graphs generated in an analysis to the *Text/output Window* (see Chapter 5). (Note that there is also a batch printing facility for printing previously-saved graphs and Scrollsheets; select *Print Files...* from the pull-down menu *File*, see Chapter 3.)

"Automatic pressing" of the *Continue* button to speed up the batch output. When, instead of reviewing the output on-screen, you need to quickly produce a hard copy of a series of graphs or tables (or send it to the *Text/output Window*), then it is advantageous to select the option *Auto-Exit from Scrollsheets and Graphs* (see Chapter 3) in the *Page/Output Setup* dialog. If that option is selected, *STATISTICA* will "internally" press the *Continue* button on every graph and Scrollsheet, thus allowing you to print (or send to the *Text/output Window*) long sequences of Scrollsheets and graphs without having to press the *Continue* button at the end of every "queue-full" of documents (by default every third graph or third Scrollsheet).

Document Windows in *STATISTICA*

Four main types of *document windows* in *STATISTICA* (MDI). *STATISTICA* follows the standard MDI (*Multi Document User-Interface*) conventions. Each of its output windows is treated as a separate *document*, and the contents of each *document* can be managed in a variety of standard ways including editing, saving, and opening. There are four main types of documents supported in *STATISTICA*:

- data spreadsheets
- output Scrollsheets
- graphs
- *Text/output Windows* (containing reports consisting of text and graphs)

(as shown in the diagram at the beginning of this section).

Integration between the *documents*. Each of the four main types of *STATISTICA* document-windows manages different types of "data." However, they are closely integrated not only via the optimized Clipboard support (allowing you to automatically convert one type of data into another) but also via a variety of methods to "convert" one entire document into another. For example, all text and numeric documents (or their selected subsets) can be converted into graphs in a variety of ways. Text can be incorporated into graphs, and graphs

can be converted into text (i.e., numeric) representations. This architecture of *STATISTICA* coupled with its support for *DDE* (the Windows-specific data integration mechanisms) and a comprehensive *OLE* client and server support (including nested graphic compound documents) offers countless options to creatively explore the data, verify hypotheses, and present the results.

Toolbars related to types of active document-windows. Each of the main types of *STATISTICA* document-windows (see above) manages different types of data, and thus offers different customization and management options. These differences are reflected in the toolbars which accompany each type of window. Toolbar options for each of the four main types of windows are described in the respective following sections:

- data spreadsheets (see Chapter 3),
- output Scrollsheets (see Chapter 4),
- *Text/output Windows* (see Chapter 5), and
- graphs (see Volume II of the manual).

2. Macros

STATISTICA supports the creation of two types of macros: editable sequences of keystrokes and recorded actions (mouse movements and/or keyboard activity).

Both types of macros can be created either by using the *Macros* option in the pull-down menu *Options*, or by pressing the *Customize* button on the floating *Auto Task Buttons* toolbar (see page 1014).

Editable sequences of keystrokes. Sequences of keystrokes can be entered in a text format (and edited) and assigned to buttons on the floating *Auto Task Buttons* toolbar (see page 1014). This easy to use method allows the user to automate execution of tasks of any degree of complexity (from simple ones, such as entering a specific selection of variables, to complex graph customizations, data transformations, or long batches of procedures). Existing macros can be easily modified or combined in a designated editor featuring *quick-entry* buttons. Also, recorded macros (see the next paragraph) can be opened and edited in this editor.

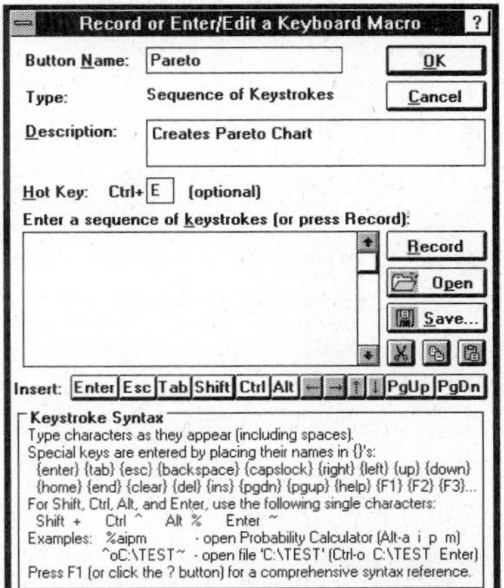

Recording actions. In addition to the support for editable sequences of keystrokes (mentioned in the previous paragraph) which can be assigned to buttons on the floating *Auto Task Buttons* toolbar (see Chapter 6), *STATISTICA* offers an internal macro recording system,

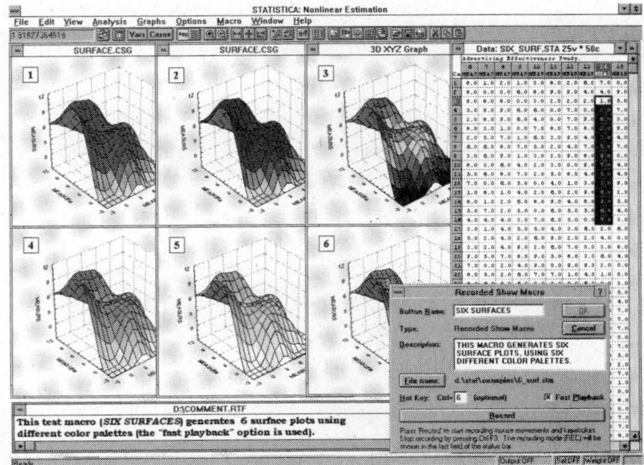

which supports not only keyboard actions but also mouse actions which optionally can be played back

at the speed at which they were recorded, thus they can be used to create slide-show style presentations, training materials, etc.

The macro management facilities are available from the *Macros* option in the *Options* pull-down menu, by pressing CTRL+F3, or by pressing the *Customize...* button on the floating *Auto Task Buttons* toolbar (see Chapter 6).

Applications. These facilities (accessible at every point of your work) provide an alternative or supplement to the interactive user-interface because they allow you to specify even complex tasks which can then be executed repeatedly (to automate routinely-performed operations). These macros can also be used to augment the interactive user-interface; for example, a macro (initiated with a single mouse click on an *Auto Task Button* or a keystroke) may contain a long variable list, a repeatedly executed graph, or an embedding operation, etc.

3. *STATISTICA* Command Language (*SCL*)

Entering and Executing *SCL* Programs

STATISTICA can also be run in a "true" batch mode as a command-driven system using its built-in *SCL* (*STATISTICA Command Language*) application control language, available in every module from the pull-down menu *Analysis*. You can type in sequences of plain-English commands to perform specific operations and then repeatedly execute them in batch.

Alternatively, you can use the *Wizard* (shown below) to quickly select the desired commands.

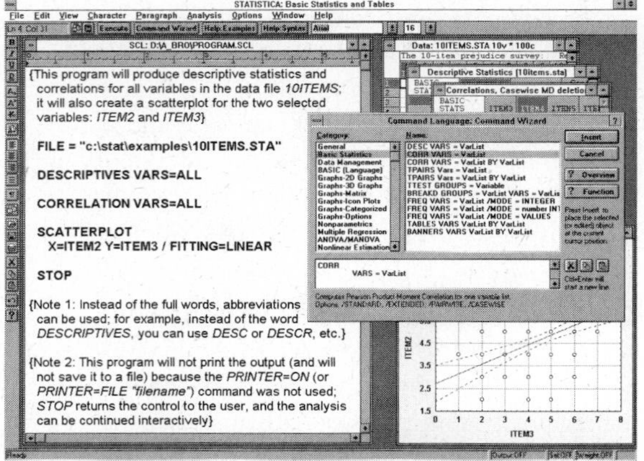

An integrated environment is provided to write and debug "batches" of *SCL* commands. The environment includes a text editor integrated with the *Wizard* (shown above; see the *Command Wizard* button on the *Command Language* toolbar), syntax-help with examples, and a set of integrated verification facilities (available in the pull-down menu *Options*).

Verification facilities of the *SCL* editor. While writing *SCL* programs, you can verify not only the formal correctness of your commands, but also their consistency with the contents of the data files that are to be processed (see the options available in the pull-down menu *Options*). For example, while writing an *SCL* program, you can verify on-line whether the requested variable names or text values exist in the specified data sets to be processed (for details, see the on-line documentation by pressing F1 or the ? button in the toolbar, or double-clicking on the status bar on the bottom of the window).

Interrupting execution of *SCL* programs. Execution of *SCL* programs can be interrupted by clicking the mouse (either left or right button) or pressing either the ESC or CTRL+BREAK keys. *STATISTICA* will ask you for confirmation before the program is halted.

Custom Extensions to *SCL*

Your *SCL* programs can include not only the predefined commands and options to perform specific statistical, data management, and graphics operations (see the toolbar *Help:Examples* and *Help:Syntax* buttons), but can also be expanded to include your own "commands" defined via the *Send Keys* facility (following the MS Visual BASIC conventions).

For example, your own extensions to *SCL* can perform Clipboard operations (e.g., *Copy*, *Paste*), change the default output from specific procedures, etc.

SCL programs can also include programs and procedures written in *STATISTICA BASIC* (the *STATISTICA* data transformation, data management and graphics programming language available in every module, see the *Electronic Manual*). For example, custom-defined *STATISTICA BASIC* graphs or computational procedures can be executed as part of *SCL* batches of commands.

Run-time User-Interface for *SCL* Programs

Although the *SCL* command language does not offer (directly) a designated run-time user-interface, you can use *STATISTICA BASIC* programs (to be called from an *SCL* command program) to design dialog boxes and other elements of the user-interface which will allow users of the *SCL* program to select variables, data files, etc. in run-time (see the examples in the *Electronic Manual*).

"Turn-key" Execution of *SCL* Programs

The *STATISTICA Run Module*. The *Command Language* also includes a *STATISTICA Run module* allowing you to develop "turn-key" applications which can be executed by clicking on the respective "custom application" icons on the Windows desktop.

This option is useful when the same analysis or series of analyses is executed repeatedly, and it allows your *SCL* programs to be used by persons unfamiliar with *STATISTICA* conventions.

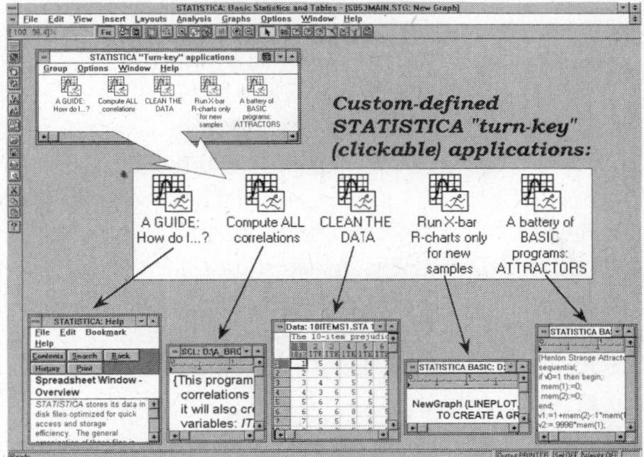

In order to produce such a turn-key application, first write an *SCL* program to be executed and save it as usual (e.g., as *Program1.scl*). Then use your Windows *Program Manager* to create an icon for the *STATISTICA Run* application called *Sta_run.exe* (this application resides in your *STATISTICA* directory).

In the optional command field for the icon, specify the name of the *SCL* program to be executed (e.g., *d:\data\program1.scl*). Now, whenever you click on the icon, that program (e.g., *Program1.scl*) will be executed. You can create as many of such custom-*STATISTICA*-application icons as you need, and by using the *Program Manager* you can assign meaningful names to them:

representing the tasks or analyses that they perform.

Assigning *SCL* programs to *Auto Task* Buttons. Alternatively, you can assign *SCL* programs to buttons on the customizable *Auto Task Buttons* floating toolbar (see below).

4. Controlling *STATISTICA* from within Other Windows Applications

Because *STATISTICA* supports the Microsoft Windows *DDE*/API interface standard, you can also build *SCL* (*STATISTICA Command Language*, see the previous section) commands or entire *SCL* scripts into macros created within and run from other Windows applications (e.g., MS Excel, MS Word).

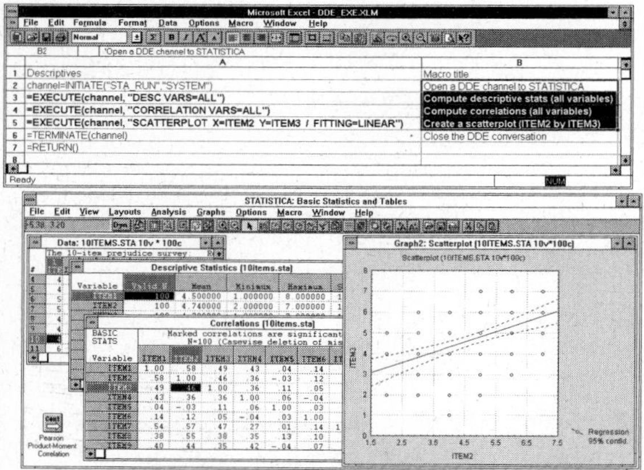

This compatibility of *STATISTICA*'s *Command Language*, coupled with *STATISTICA*'s support of *DDE* for exchange of data (see Chapters 3 and 7), *OLE* (client/server, nested compound graphics, see Volume II), and compatibility with the standard Windows file, Clipboard, and graph formats allows you to achieve a high level of integration between different Windows applications.

For example, as shown above, an Excel macro may include *SCL* commands which will call *STATISTICA* from within Excel, perform a specified set of analyses, and then transfer and integrate specific parts of the output and/or graphs created by *STATISTICA* into your current Excel worksheet or workbook.

The *Auto Task* Buttons Floating or Docked Toolbar

The *Auto Task Buttons* facility is a floating, customizable toolbar (you can toggle the display of the toolbar by pressing CTRL+M).

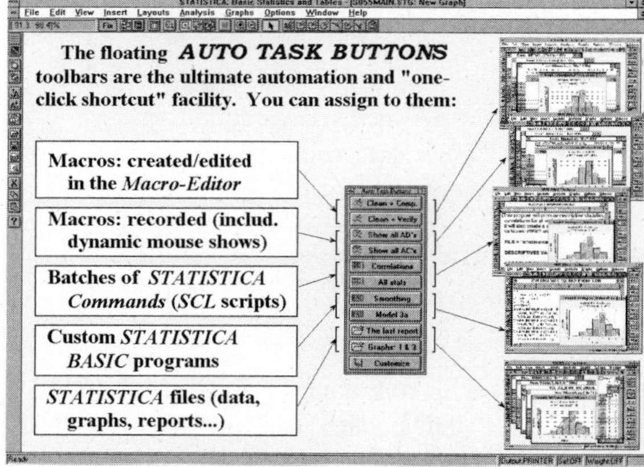

The buttons of the toolbar can be defined/reassigned by pressing the *Customize...* button (or by pressing the respective button while holding down the CTRL key). In the subsequent dialog, you can select and assign to new (or existing) buttons:

- sequences of standard *STATISTICA* tasks and operations defined using the *STATISTICA Command Language* (*SCL*, see page 1012);

- custom-designed procedures written in *STATISTICA BASIC* (this may include new computational procedures, data transformations, data management operations, custom graphic procedures, as well as procedures written in other programming languages and called from *STATISTICA BASIC* which provides support for external *DLL*s, see the *Electronic Manual*);
- data files or any supplementary *STATISTICA* files (e.g., graphs, reports, Scrollsheets), which you commonly use (e.g., for reference) and thus which could be made conveniently accessible by assigning them to *Auto Task Buttons*; and
- editable sequences of keystrokes representing commonly used procedures, tasks or customizations. These editable macros can be entered in text format (following the standard Microsoft *Sendkeys* conventions) and later modified.

The definition of the *Auto Task Buttons* toolbar can be saved (in the same *Customize...* dialog);

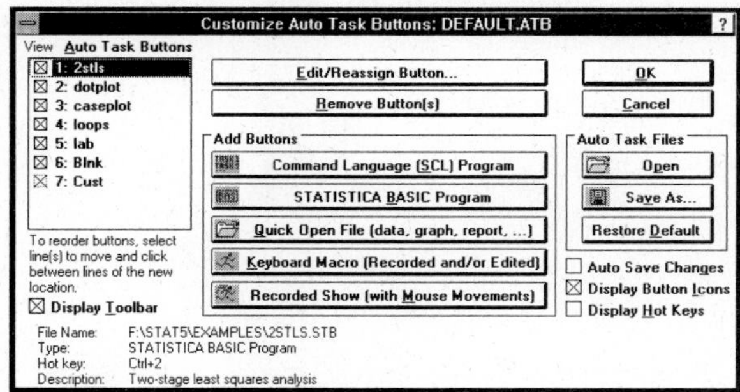

the toolbar can be global, or local – associated with specific modules or specific projects (the name of the current toolbar is displayed in the title bar of the dialog, see above), and may contain large libraries of custom tasks and procedures.

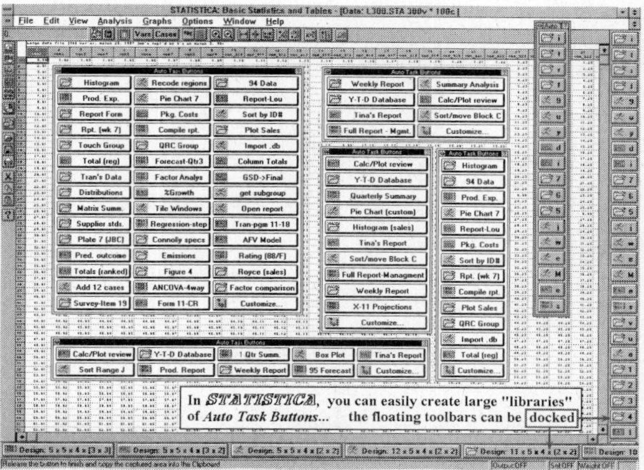

The *Auto Task Buttons* toolbar can be used as a convenient "front end" for user-specified extensions of standard procedures,

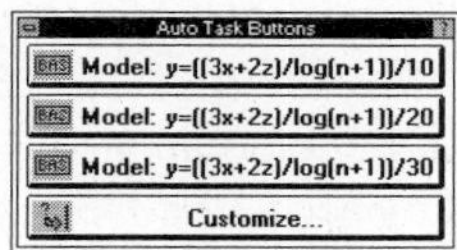

and it can be easily customized to take very little space on the screen.

The toolbars can be resized with the mouse:

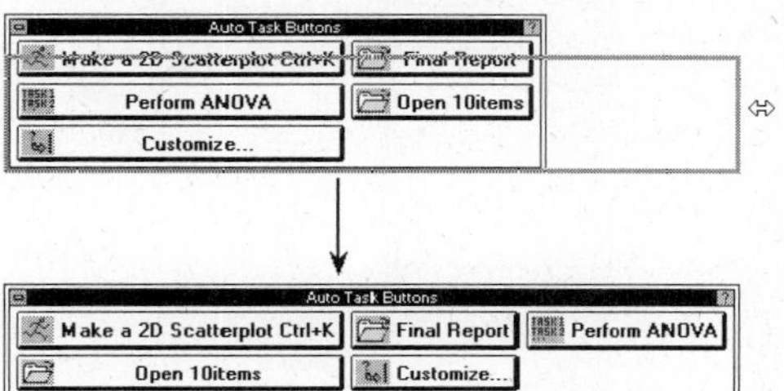

and can also be docked by dragging it to a border of the *STATISTICA* application window (as shown below).

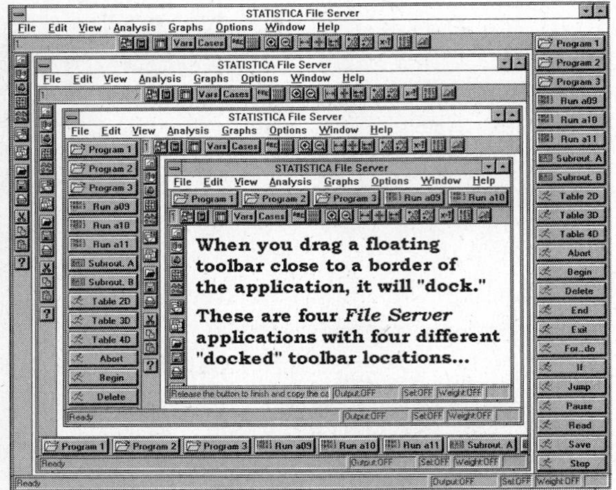

As mentioned before, the buttons of the *Auto Task Buttons* toolbar can be customized or reassigned in the global *Customize Auto Task Buttons* dialog (accessible by pressing the *Customize...* button on the toolbar). However, individual buttons can also be customized and/or reassigned by accessing their respective customization dialogs directly; specifically, you can click on the respective button with the mouse while holding down the CTRL key:

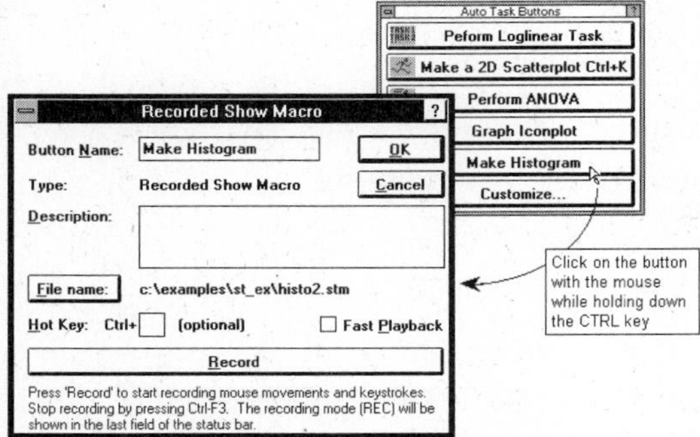

and the respective customization dialog (for this button) will open.

Note that you can quickly switch between different, previously saved *Auto Task Buttons* toolbars by selecting the last option in the flying menu, accessible by clicking anywhere on the toolbar with the right mouse button.

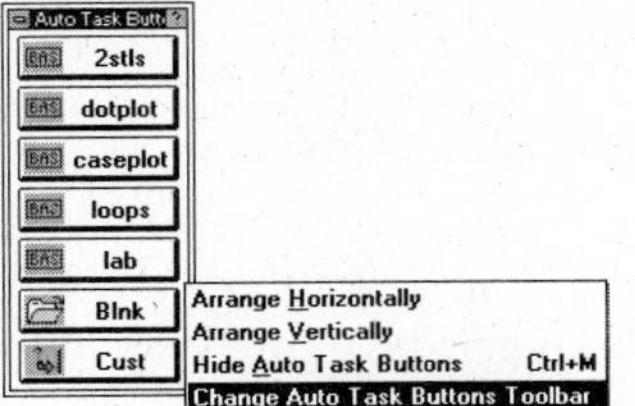

For more information on the *Auto Task Buttons* facility in *STATISTICA*, see Chapter 6.

CUSTOMIZING THE OPERATION AND APPEARANCE OF *STATISTICA*

Customization of the User-Interface

The behavior and appearance of *STATISTICA* can be customized by the user and the user-interface of the program may be changed and become more "elaborate" as the user's needs change.

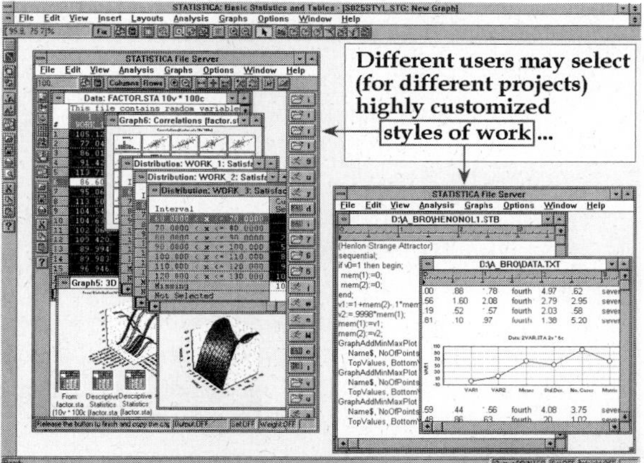

Depending on the requirements of the tasks to be performed, as well as your personal preferences for particular "modes" of work (and aesthetic choices), you can, for example:

> suppress all icons, toolbars, status bars, long menus, floating *Auto Task Buttons* toolbars, Workbook facilities, *Drag-and-Drop* facilities, dynamic (automatic) links between graphs and data, 3D effects in tables, 3D effects in dialog boxes, and request "bare-bones" sequential output with simple, paper-white Scrollsheets (output tables) and monochrome graphs, and set the system to automatically maintain no more than one simple output window at a time (see the left panel on the screen, below);

or alternatively, you could:

> define elaborate local and global *Auto Task Buttons* floating toolbars, take full advantage of all special tools and controls, icons, toolbars, macros (e.g., assign particular tasks to specific keys), Workbook facilities, *Drag-and-Drop* facilities, establish multiple dynamic (automatic) links between graphs and data and internal *OLE* links between graphical objects, customize the output windows with colors, special fonts, and highlights, adjust the default graph styles and their display modes, extend the number of simultaneous output windows and/or *lock* "reference" graphs and Scrollsheets to create an elaborate, multilayered data analysis environment facilitating the exploration of complex data sets and allowing you to compare different aspects of the output (see the right panel on the screen, below).

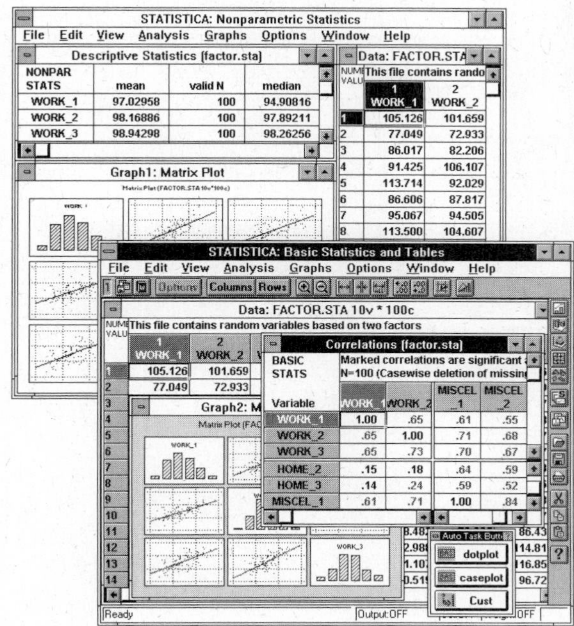

StatSoft

Running *STATISTICA* in One Application Window vs. Multiple Application Mode

One of the global system customizations of *STATISTICA* allows you to select whether, by default, the program will run in a single application window or as multiple applications (in their separate windows). The most immediate consequence of this setting applies to the way in which the *Module Switcher* works (see Chapter 2): double-clicking on the name of a module in the *Switcher* will either open the new module replacing the current one, or will open a new application window for the new module without closing the previous one.

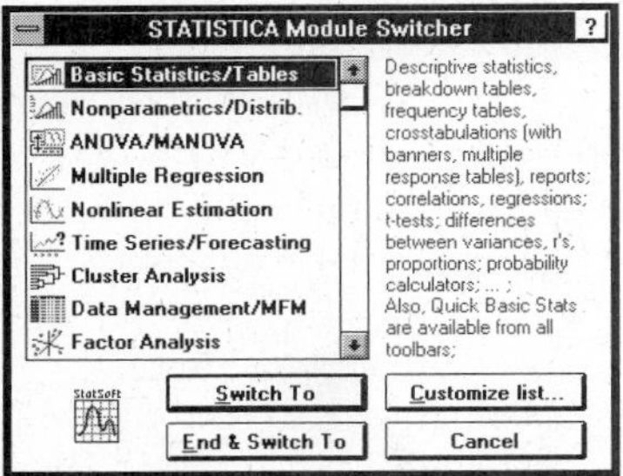

The selection of this operating mode can be made using the *Module Switching: Single Application Mode* setting, in the *Defaults: General* dialog (accessible from the pull-down menu *Options*).

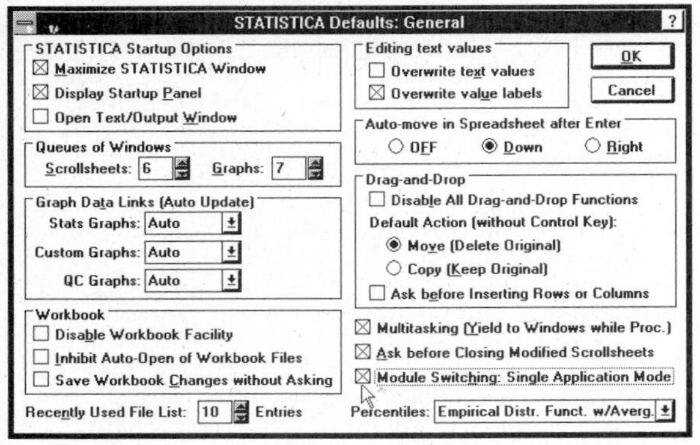

If the check box is marked, then *STATISTICA* will run in the single-application mode.

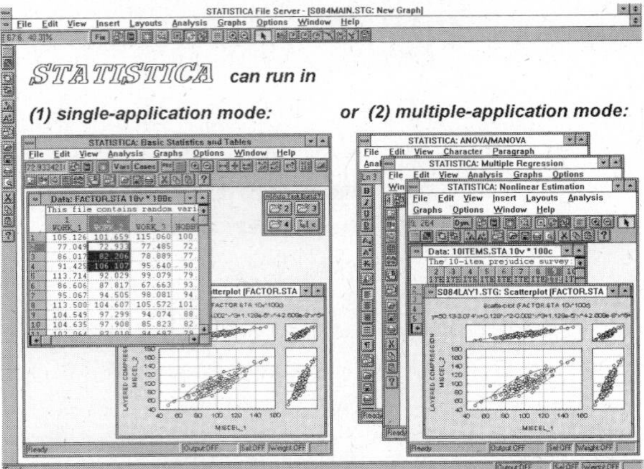

(1) Single application mode. When you select the single application window mode, then switching between modules during a *STATISTICA* session will not open new application windows. Each new module will be opened into the same window replacing the module used before. Some users will like this "simple" mode because it keeps all analyses in a single application-window location and limits the number of programs opened on the desktop to a minimum.

Note that a similar effect can be achieved by pressing the *End & Switch To* button in the *Module Switcher*; the application window of the current module will close, but it will not be replaced by the new one; instead, the new module will open in the "next" application window.

(2) Multiple application mode. The main advantage of the multiple application mode is that you can run different analyses (modules) simultaneously in different, simultaneously-open application windows. You can switch between the modules without closing the previous ones and take advantage of independent queues of Scrollsheets and graphs in different module application windows. This mode has clear advantages for most types of analyses allowing the user to use (and compare results of) different analytic tools.

Local vs. Permanent Customizations (Pull-down Menus: *View* vs. *Options*)

Many aspects of the appearance of the program can be adjusted both in the pull-down menus *View* and *Options*.

Pull-down menu *View*. The difference between the two is that the changes requested in the pull-down menu *View* will affect the current appearance of the program (e.g., hide the toolbar) or the current document-window (e.g., change font in the spreadsheet).

Pull-down menu *Options*. Many of those options are also included in the pull-down menu *Options* where they can be adjusted as permanent program defaults. Note, however, that those options (in the *Options* menu) which are applicable to the document-windows of a particular type (e.g., a graph or a spreadsheet) will not change that document; instead, they will only be stored as program defaults which will affect the creation of the *next* (i.e., *new*) object of the respective type.

For example, if you set the spreadsheet appearance defaults in the pull-down menu *Options*, you will see them only when you create a new file (via *New Data...* or *Import*). These defaults will not, however, affect any files opened from the disk because those files will always be brought in with the specific appearance with which they were previously saved (use the pull-down menu *View* to customize the existing objects). Typically, the defaults set for Scrollsheets and graphs will have more immediate, noticeable effects, as the program creates *new* Scrollsheets and graphs during the course of any analysis.

General Default Settings and Graph Default Settings

Customization of the general system defaults. The general default settings can be adjusted at any point in the program. They control:

- the general aspects of the behavior of the program (such as maximizing *STATISTICA* on startup, Workbook facilities, *Drag-and-Drop* facilities, automatic links between graphs and data, or enabling the multitasking mode, etc.),
- the way in which the output is produced (e.g., automatic printing of Scrollsheets or graphs, format of reports, buffering, etc.),
- the general appearance of the application window (icons, toolbars, etc.), and
- the appearance of document windows (colors, font),

and each of them can be adjusted in the respective dialogs accessible in the pull-down menu *Options*. Two of these dialogs are shown below.

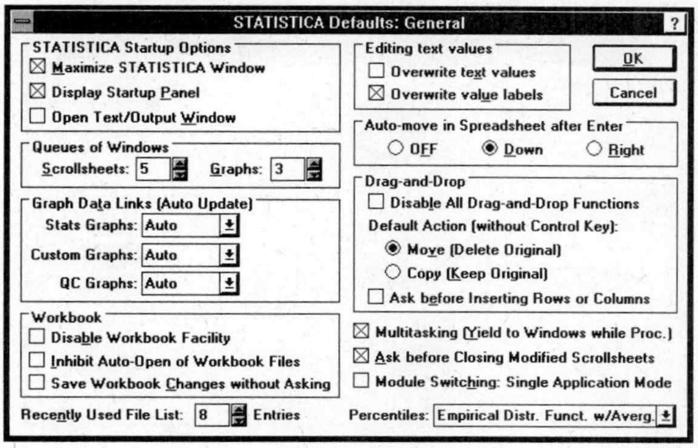

STATISTICA Defaults: General
STATISTICA Startup Options
☒ Maximize STATISTICA Window
☒ Display Startup Panel
☐ Open Text/Output Window
Queues of Windows
Scrollsheets: 5 Graphs: 3
Graph Data Links (Auto Update)
Stats Graphs: Auto
Custom Graphs: Auto
QC Graphs: Auto
Workbook
☐ Disable Workbook Facility
☐ Inhibit Auto-Open of Workbook Files
☐ Save Workbook Changes without Asking
Recently Used File List: 8 Entries
Editing text values
☐ Overwrite text values
☒ Overwrite value labels
OK
Cancel
Auto-move in Spreadsheet after Enter
○ OFF ◉ Down ○ Right
Drag-and-Drop
☐ Disable All Drag-and-Drop Functions
Default Action (without Control Key):
◉ Move (Delete Original)
○ Copy (Keep Original)
☐ Ask before Inserting Rows or Columns
☒ Multitasking (Yield to Windows while Proc.)
☒ Ask before Closing Modified Scrollsheets
☐ Module Switching: Single Application Mode
Percentiles: Empirical Distr. Funct. w/Averg.

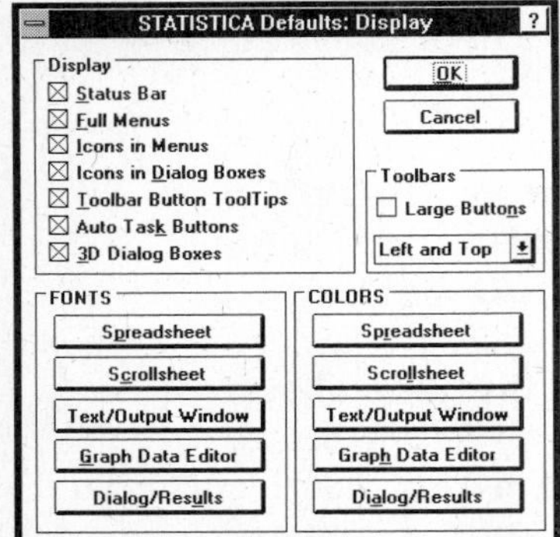

All these and other general settings are accessible regardless of the type of the document window which is currently active (e.g., a Scrollsheet or a graph).

Customization of the graphics default settings. The graphics facilities of *STATISTICA* also allow you to set permanent defaults; they affect practically all aspects of the appearance of the graphs (a total of over 500 settings).

Because many of these default adjustment options are specific for particular types of graphs and they offer shortcuts to globally copy all graph settings to or from the *current* graph, the dialogs allowing you to adjust these and other graph default settings are accessible from the same pull-down menu (*Options*) only when a graph window is active.

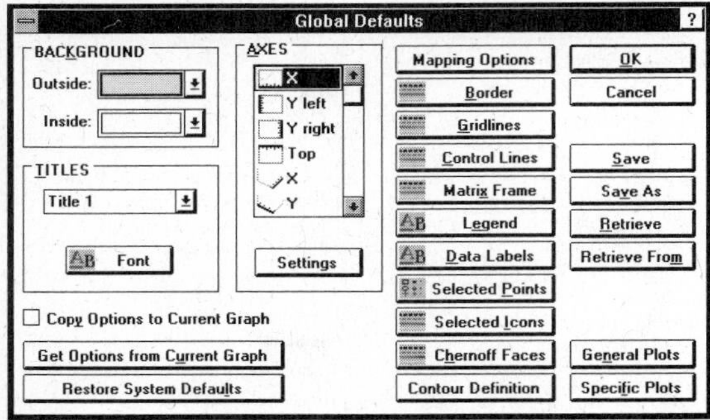

The only exception is the dialog controlling the general conventions for accessing data by *Stats Graphs* (the option *Stats Graphs Options*),

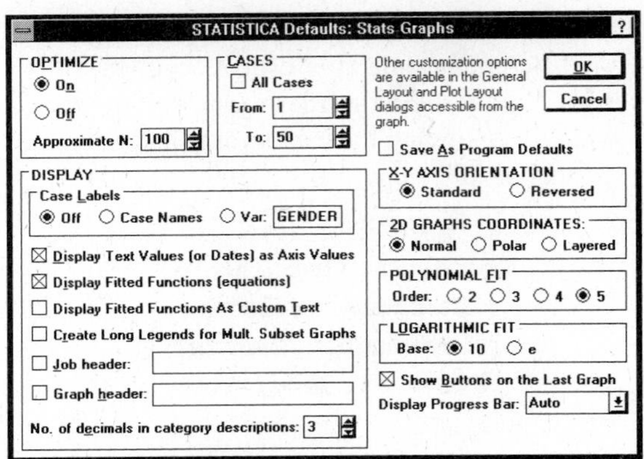

which is always available in this menu because these options may need to be changed before any graphs are produced.

Please refer to Volume II (*Graphics*) for descriptions of these options.

Maintaining Different Configurations of *STATISTICA*

Unless you otherwise instruct the program, *STATISTICA* stores all current settings and defaults, including the *Auto Task Buttons* floating toolbar definitions in the directory from which you start the program (most of those settings are stored in a file called *statist.ini*, see the *Electronic Manual* for more information about that file).

The fact that the configuration information is stored in the directory from which you started *STATISTICA* allows you to maintain different configurations of the program for different projects or types of your work. For example, you can call *STATISTICA* from different disk directories, each of them associated with a different set of document files and in each of them, *STATISTICA* could be configured with a different set of output settings, graph defaults, etc. Alternatively, you could set up different *STATISTICA* icons in different application groups on the Windows desktop (each representing a project or type of job), and in each of them, specify a different *Working Directory* field (using the Windows *Program Item Properties* dialogs).

Customized Configurations for Individual Users on a Network

The same principle (see the previous paragraph) applies to network installations of *STATISTICA*. On a network, the program is installed in only one location (on a server disk drive), but each user can still configure the program differently because the appropriate configuration settings depend on the (local) disk drive from which the program is called. Note that you need to choose the *Network Installation* option of the *STATISTICA Setup* program in order to install it properly on a non-local drive (network server); then run the *reinst.exe* program from each workstation (to configure the workstations).

Note that a network version of *STATISTICA* is necessary to assure its reliable operation when used by more than one user at a time.

SELECTING/REVIEWING VARIABLES AND VALUES

Selecting Variables for Analyses

When you need to select one or more variables for an analysis in *STATISTICA*, a variable selection dialog will open.

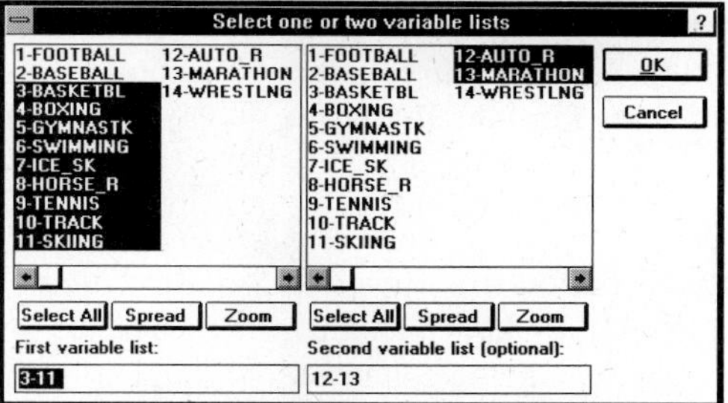

There are three types of variable selection dialogs (see below) that may open, depending on the analysis: (1) dialogs for selecting a single list of variables, (2) dialogs for selecting multiple lists of variables, and (3) dialogs for selecting a single variable.

Selecting Variables

Variables can be selected either by highlighting them in the list or by entering their variable number in the dialog edit window. In most cases (where applicable), when you mark a block of data in the spreadsheet and then enter into either the *Selecting a Variable from a Single List* or *Selecting a Variable from a Double (or Multiple) List* dialog for the first time, the highlighted variables in the block will be suggested to you in the dialog (i.e., "pre-selected"). The range of the block of variables will be displayed and highlighted in the dialog edit window. In order to edit the variable number in the edit window, simply type over the highlighted numbers (you do not have to delete the numbers first).

The SHIFT and CTRL selection. If you choose to select the variables by highlighting them in the list, you can select a continuous block of variables by holding down the left-mouse-button and dragging the cursor over the variables that you want to highlight. You can also highlight a continuous block of variables by clicking on the first variable name that you want to select, and while holding down the SHIFT key, clicking on the last variable name that you want to select. This method will select the first and last variables and all variables in-between. You can select discontinuous blocks of variables by holding down the CTRL key and then clicking on each variable that you want to select.

Shortcut Method to Select one Variable and Exit

When you need to select only one variable in the single variable list, simply double-click on the variable name to select it and close the dialog box. Double-clicking in a variable selection dialog with more than one selection list will not change the previously selected variables; therefore, when you need to select only one variable in one of the lists, first select all of the other variables in the other lists, then simply double-click on the single variable name in the last list to select all of the highlighted variables and close the dialog box.

De-selecting Previously Selected Variables

You can de-select discontinuous or continuous blocks of previously selected variables by holding down the CTRL key and then clicking on each variable that you want to de-select. Alternatively, you can de-select variables by deleting the respective variable number(s) from the edit window.

Note. For information on the respective analysis (or graph) designs and the way in which the selected variables are used in the respective procedures, refer to the respective chapter for the dialog from which this selection window originates. For specific information on each variable selection dialog, see below.

Selecting Variables from a Single List

This dialog opens whenever you are requested to select variables from a single list.

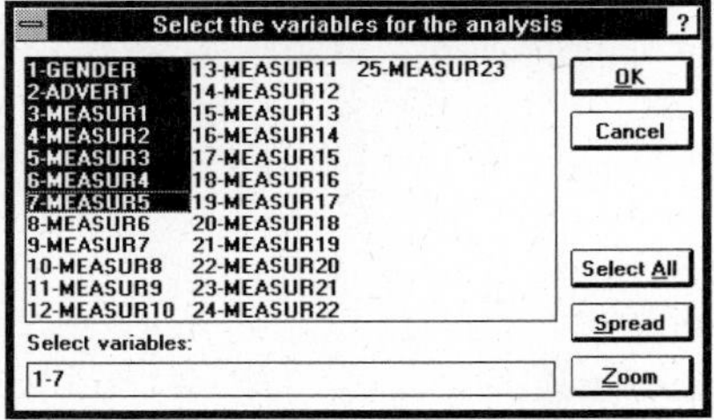

If the list of variables is too large for the display window, then the list will be scrollable.

Selecting Variables

Select variables in this dialog either by highlighting them or entering the variable number in the edit window and then clicking on the *OK* button (see above for more information on selecting and de-selecting variables).

Select All

Click this button to automatically select all of the variables in the list. Alternatively, you can enter an * (asterisk) in the edit window to select the entire list of variables.

Spread/Shrink

When you click on this button, any long variable names associated with each variable will be displayed.

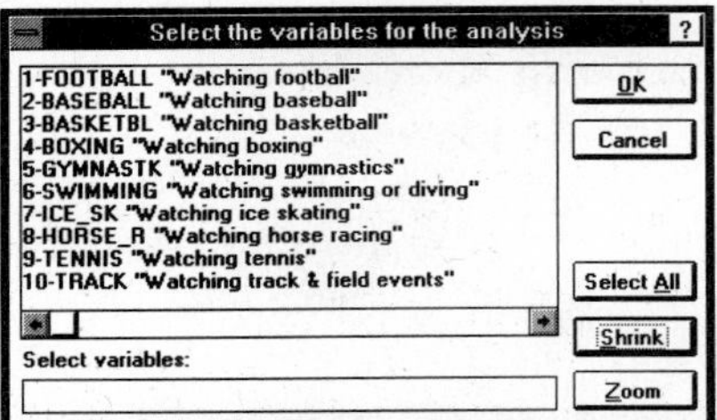

Click on this button again to remove the long variable names from the list.

Zoom

Clicking this button will open the *Variable Values Window* (for the first of the highlighted variables, see below) in which you can browse through a scrollable sorted list of the data values (numeric and text equivalents).

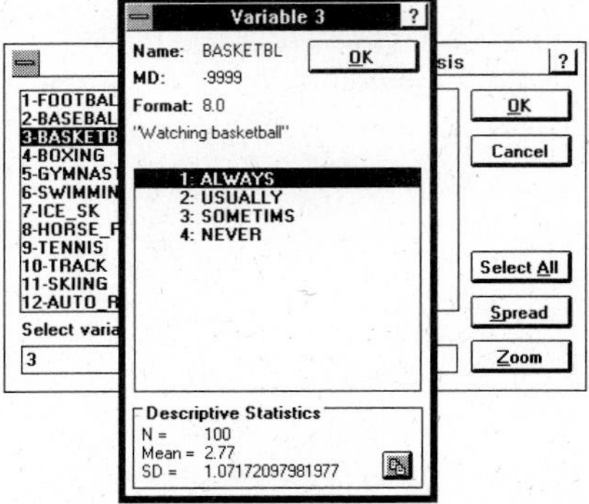

The bottom section of the dialog displays descriptive statistics for the variable (which can be copied to the Clipboard by pressing the *Copy* button).

Selecting Variables from a Double (or Multiple) List

Some analyses may require you to select variables from more than one list of variables (e.g., one list for independent variables and another for dependent variables).

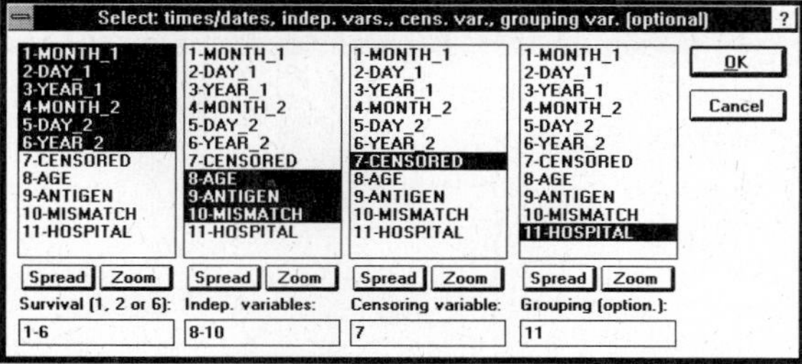

When this is the case, a dialog will open displaying two (or more) list boxes containing the variables from which you can make your selection.

Selecting Variables

Select variables in each list by highlighting the desired variables or by entering the variable numbers in the edit window of each list and then clicking on the *OK* button (see above for more information on selecting and de-selecting variables).

Select All

Click this button in the appropriate list to automatically select all of the variables in that list. Alternatively, you can enter an * (asterisk) in the edit window to select all available variables in that particular list.

Spread/Shrink

When you click on this button, any long variable names associated with each variable will be displayed (as shown in the section on the *single list*, above). Click on this button again to remove the long variable names from the list.

Zoom

Clicking this button will open the *Variable Values Window* (for the first of the highlighted variables, see below) in which you can browse through a scrollable, sorted list of the data values (numeric and text equivalents), as shown in the section on the *single list*, above.

Selecting a Single Variable from a List

This dialog opens whenever you are requested to select one variable from a list of variables.

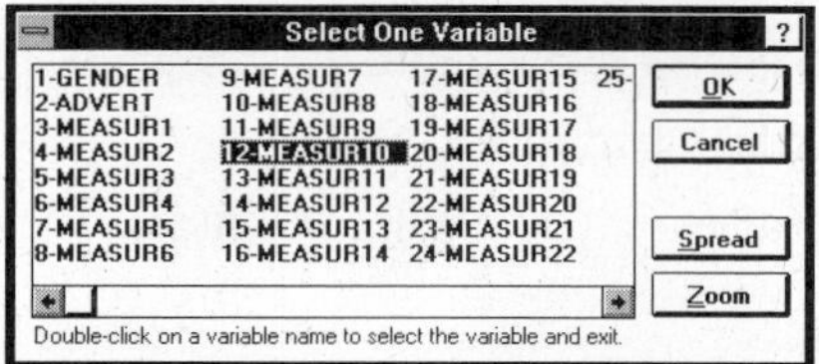

If the list of variables is too large for the display window, then the list will be scrollable.

Selecting Variables

Select a variable in this dialog either by double-clicking on the variable name or by highlighting it (clicking once on the variable name) and then clicking on the *OK* button.

Spread/Shrink

When you click on this button, the long variable names (if there are any) associated with each variable in the list will be displayed (as shown in the section on the *single list*, above). Click on this button again to remove the long variable names from the list.

Zoom

Clicking this button will open the *Variable Values Window* in which you can browse through a scrollable, sorted list of the data values (numeric and text equivalents, see below), as shown in the section on the *single list*, above.

Reviewing Variables from a List

This dialog opens whenever you request to review the names of variables as well as other variable attributes.

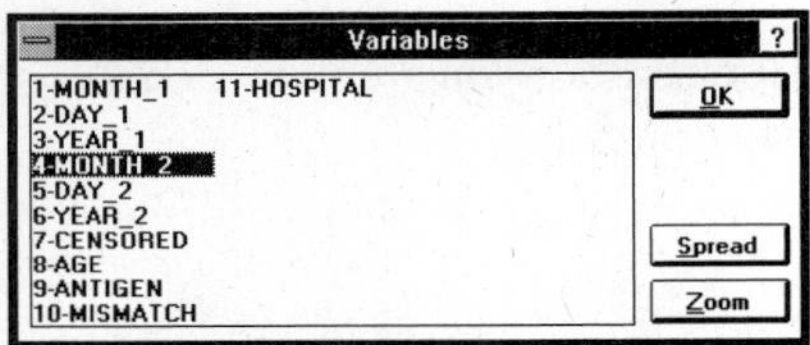

If the list of variables is too large for the display window, then the list will be scrollable.

Spread/Shrink

When you click on this button, the long variable names (if there are any) associated with each variable in the list will be displayed (as shown in the section on the *single list*, above). Click on this button again to remove the long variable names from the list.

Zoom

Clicking this button will open the *Variable Values Window* in which you can browse through a scrollable, sorted list of the data values (numeric and text equivalents), as shown below.

Variable Values Window

This window (accessible by clicking on the *Zoom* button in the variable selection windows, see above, or by selecting the *Quick Stats Graphs - Values of ...* option from the right-mouse-button flying menu) allows you to examine the values of a variable, its name, missing data value, format and long variable name (if there is one), and some descriptive statistics for that variable (see below).

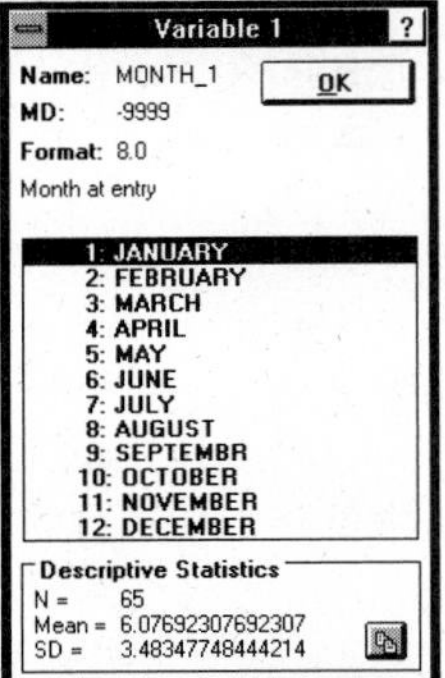

Variable Values

The variable values are presented in a scrollable, sorted list through which you can browse. If the variable has any text values, then these are displayed next to their numeric equivalents in the list.

Descriptive Statistics

The descriptive statistics for the variable include the sample size (*N*), mean, and standard deviation. You can copy the variable name and these statistics to the Clipboard (press on the *Copy* button in this part of the dialog) in order to paste it into a graph or text window, or to use it in another Windows application (e.g., Microsoft Word for Windows).

Selecting Codes

The *Codes* dialog will open whenever you have to select codes for grouping variables (i.e., specific values of a variable to be used to identify group membership of cases or observations). The dialog will display the grouping variable name and then prompt you to enter the codes for that variable (e.g., 1, *Male*, "#52").

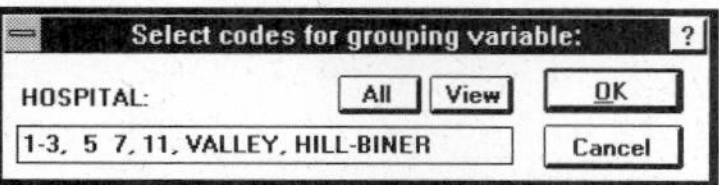

You may either type specific codes in the window, or enter an * (asterisk) to accept all of the codes available for the variable. When entering text codes in this window, you can save time by typing the codes in the edit field with lower case letters and *STATISTICA* will automatically convert them to upper case letters (e.g., *smith* will be converted to *SMITH*). However, since *STATISTICA* distinguishes between lower and upper case letters in codes, be sure to place any code that needs to remain in lower case letters in single or double quotes (e.g., 'Smith', "Pepsi", "StatSoft", see below).

The following conventions apply when entering code names:

- If codes consist of only uppercase letters and numbers (e.g., *ITEM9*, *MALE*) but not starting with a number, then the code will be displayed in the edit field without single or double quotes around them.
- Codes which have been entered in the spreadsheet in upper *and* lower case or *only* lower case letters (e.g., '*Male*', "*test1*") need to be displayed in quotes (single or double) in this edit window in order to preserve the upper and lower case character formatting.
- Codes which start with a number or a character other than a letter (e.g., "*=shift3*", '*39lbs*', "*49°C*", "*15-Apr*") need to be displayed in quotes (single or double).
- Date values will be displayed in quotes (single or double) if the variable's format is set to *Date* (see *Edit Variable (Current) Specs*, Chapter 3).

Shortcut. If you leave all fields in this dialog empty (blank) and click *OK*, then *STATISTICA* will identify and automatically use all available codes (for the previously specified grouping variables). Also, the same effect will be achieved if you do not enter this dialog but click the *OK* button in the previous (design specification) dialog, without explicitly specifying any codes.

Drag-and-Drop Operations in *STATISTICA*

STATISTICA supports the complete set of standard spreadsheet (Excel-style) *Drag-and-Drop* facilities, as summarized below.

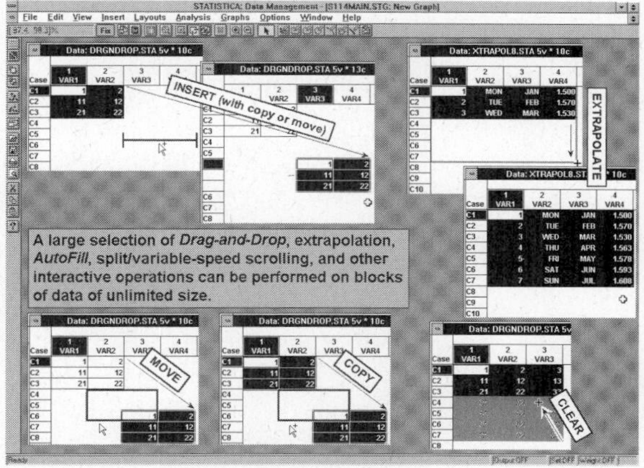

Scrollsheets support the same *Drag-and-Drop* facilities with the exception of inserting.

For detailed information on the *Drag-and-Drop* facilities in *STATISTICA*, see Chapter 3.

KEYBOARD INTERFACE

Keyboard combinations can be used as Hot Keys in order to access various *STATISTICA* procedures. Hot Keys can be classified as global (available in every window) or local (for specific windows or *Auto Task Buttons*). You can assign a Hot Key to a macro via the *Auto Task Buttons* (see Chapter 6). A complete listing of the global and local Hot Keys are given below.

Global Hot Keys

The following Hot Keys are available in all document windows.

File I/O:	Open file of the current type	CTRL+O
	Save	CTRL+S
	Save As	F12
Open Other:	New Data	CTRL+N
	Data File	CTRL+F12
	Graph File	SHIFT+F3
	Scrollsheet	CTRL+F11
Toolbars:	Auto Task Buttons	CTRL+M
Printing:	Print	CTRL+P, F4
	Page/Output Setup	SHIFT+F4
Edit:	Undo	CTRL+Z or ALT+BACKSPACE
	Select All (see *Note*)	CTRL+A
	Clear Selection	DEL
Clipboard:	Cut	CTRL+X
	Copy	CTRL+C
	Paste	CTRL+V
	Screen Catcher	ALT+F3
Analyses:	Startup Panel	CTRL+T
	Resume Analysis	CTRL+R
	Case Selection Conditions	F8
	Weighting Variable	F7
Macros:	Record macro	CTRL+F3
	Run macro	CTRL+KEY
Windows:	Cascade	SHIFT+F6
	Tile Horizontally	ALT+F6
	Tile Vertically	ALT+SHIFT+F6
	Help	F1
	Close	CTRL+F4
	Close all unlocked Windows but data file	CTRL+L
	Exit	ALT+F4
	Switch to	CTRL+ESC

Note. In the *Graph* window, all contents of the window are always "selected" in that the entire graph will be copied to the Clipboard when you press CTRL+C. Pressing CTRL+A (the global "select all" hot key), will select consecutive custom objects; pressing SHIFT+CTRL+A will go back down the list of objects.

Local Hot Keys

Spreadsheet Window

In addition to the common (global) keys available in every window, the following keyboard combinations are specific to the spreadsheet window.

Convert:	Convert to Scrollsheet	F11
Recalculate:	Recalculate All Formulas	F9

Edit:	Undo	CTRL+Z or ALT+BACKSPACE
	Edit Cell	F2
	Edit Current Specs	CTRL+F2
	Expanding Blocks	SHIFT-cursor
	[or position the cursor in one corner of the block to be selected, scroll to the location of the opposite (diagonal) corner and click in that corner location while holding down the SHIFT key].	
Customization:	View Font	CTRL+F9
	Customize Colors	SHIFT+F9
Graphs	Quick Stats Graphs	F3

Scrollsheet Window

The following keyboard combinations (local Hot Keys) are specific to the Scrollsheet window.

Edit:	Edit Cell	F2
	Column Specs	CTRL+F2
	Row Name	ALT+F2
	Expanding Blocks	SHIFT-cursor
	[or position the cursor in one corner of the block to be selected, scroll to the location of the opposite (diagonal) corner and click in that corner location while holding down the SHIFT key].	
Customization:	View Font	F9
	Customize Colors	SHIFT+F9
Graphs	Quick Stats Graphs	F3

Text/output, STATISTICA BASIC, or SCL Windows

The following keyboard combinations (local Hot Keys) are specific to the *Text/output Window* (see Chapter 5), *STATISTICA BASIC* window, or *SCL* window.

Edit:	Undo	CTRL+Z or ALT+BACKSPACE
	Find	CTRL+F
	Find Next	CTRL+ALT+F
	Replace	CTRL+H
	Go To	F5
	Insert Bitmap from File	F3
	Object Size	SHIFT+ F 3
	Colors	SHIFT+F9
	Insert page break	CTRL+ENTER
Characters:	Regular	CTRL+0 (zero)
	Bold	CTRL+B
	Italic	CTRL+I
	Underline	CTRL+U
	Double Underline	CTRL+D
	Font	F9
Wizard (applicable to *SCL* and *STATISTICA BASIC*)		ALT+I

Graph Window

The following keyboard combinations (local Hot Keys) are specific to the Graph window.

Edit:	Undo	CTRL+Z
	Select All	CTRL+A (see below)
Object Properties:	Object Properties	ALT+ENTER

Object Alignment:	Alignment Grid	CTRL+G
	Snap to Grid	hold TAB

Select all. In the Graph window, all contents of the window are always "selected" in that the entire graph will be copied to the Clipboard when you press CTRL+C. Therefore, pressing CTRL+A (the global "select all" hot key), will select consecutive custom objects; pressing SHIFT+CTRL+A will go back down the list of objects.

Rotating text using cursor keys. Select the added text and use the PAGE DOWN and PAGE UP hot keys to rotate text objects selected in the graph clockwise or counterclockwise, respectively, in 5° increments.

To rotate in 1° increments, hold down the CTRL key while pressing PAGE DOWN and PAGE UP.

Moving and resizing objects using cursor keys. Select an object and position the cursor on the object (to resize or move it), then use the keyboard cursor keys to drag a shadow of the selected graph object to a new position.

Hold down the CTRL key for fine (1 pixel only) dragging movements. Press ENTER to complete the action.

Graph Data Editor Window

The following keyboard combinations (local Hot Keys) are specific to the *Graph Data Editor* window (see Volume II).

Edit:	Edit Cell	F2
	Edit Current Specs	CTRL+F2
Customization:	View Font dialog	F9
	Customize Colors	SHIFT+F9

Megafile Manager Window

The following keyboard combinations (local Hot Keys) are specific to the *Megafile Manager* window (see Volume III of the manual).

Edit:	Edit Cell	F2
Customization:	View Font	F9
	Customize Colors	SHIFT+F9

MOUSE CONVENTIONS

In addition to the standard, Windows-system related applications, the mouse provides shortcuts to specific features in *STATISTICA*.

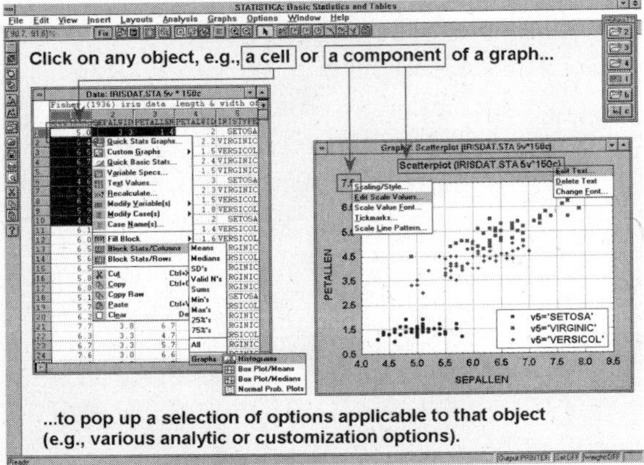

See below for an overview of these mouse conventions and functions.

Smart *MicroScrolls*

New, *Smart MicroScrolls* are now implemented in all *edit fields* for entering numeric values (e.g., 10). The following example illustrates how the *MicroScrolls* can be controlled with the left- and right-mouse-buttons.

PRESS WITH:

LEFT-MOUSE-BUTTON: 11, 12, 13, 14, ...
RIGHT-MOUSE-BUTTON: 20, 30, 40, 50, ...

LEFT-MOUSE-BUTTON: 40, 39, 38, 37, ...
RIGHT-MOUSE-BUTTON: 31, 21, 11, 1, ...

Our tests indicate that *STATISTICA*'s implementation of this facility greatly increases the efficiency of the user-interface.

Unlike the simple *MicroScrolls* supported in some other applications, in *STATISTICA*, all *MicroScrolls* automatically adjust to the current content of the field and they increment or decrement the last significant digit.

The right-mouse-button can be used to increment or decrement the next-to-last digit (e.g., clicking on the *MicroScroll* with the left-mouse-button increments *.15* to *.16*, then *.17*, *.18*, etc.; if you click on the right-mouse-button, *0.15* will change to *0.25*, then to *.35*, *.45*, etc.).

Right- and Left-Mouse-Buttons

Left-Mouse-Button

The left-mouse-button is used for selecting (e.g., an option in a dialog), highlighting (e.g., a block of data in a spreadsheet), and dragging (e.g., dragging a block in a spreadsheet or dragging an object in a graph; see below). Double-clicking on an object with the left-mouse-button provides a direct shortcut to some of the most commonly used dialogs in *STATISTICA*.

For example, double-clicking with the left-mouse-button on a spreadsheet or Scrollsheet cell, header, column name, etc., will bring up a dialog allowing you to edit the respective feature, while double-clicking with the left-mouse-button on a graph object, title, point marker, etc., will bring up the respective dialog allowing you to edit that part of the graph. In this way, you save a step whenever you want to access a commonly-used option. In addition, double-clicking on the background of *STATISTICA* will bring up the *Module Switcher*.

Right-Mouse-Button

When you click on an object (e.g., a cell in a spreadsheet) with the right-mouse-button, a dynamic flying menu will come up.

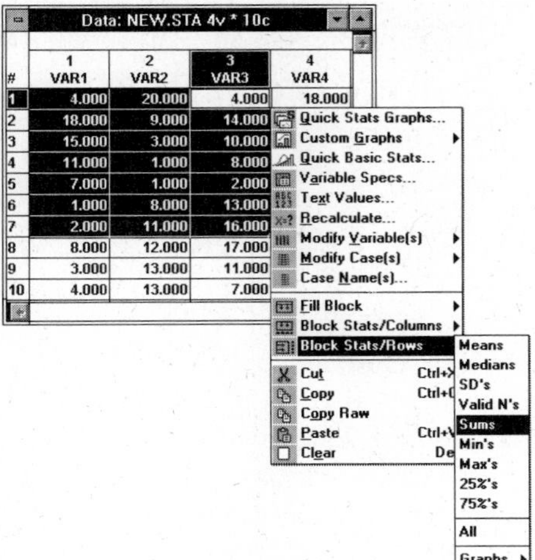

These flying menus allow easy access to some commonly-used options in every window in *STATISTICA* (e.g., graph window, spreadsheet window, *Text/output Window*, etc.).

For example, if you click with the right-mouse-button on a spreadsheet cell, a flying menu of graph options, statistics options, Clipboard operations, and others will come up (see above), allowing you to quickly perform the desired operation. Clicking on the background of *STATISTICA* with the right-mouse-button will bring up the *Module Switcher*.

Selecting Items from Multiple-Selection Lists

You can select items in a multiple-selection list in the following manners:

- Click on an item to select (highlight) it. Clicking OK in the dialog will accept the selection.
- Double-click on an item to select it and accept the selection (close the dialog).
- In order to select a continuous list of items, you can (1) hold down the left-mouse-button and drag the cursor over the items that you want to highlight or (2) highlight the first item and then while holding down the SHIFT key, click on the last item that you want to select.
- In order to select a discontinuous list of items, hold down the CTRL key and click on the desired items.

Using the SHIFT and CTRL Keys with the Mouse

For some applications of the mouse, holding down the CTRL or SHIFT key will modify the default mouse actions. For example,

- You can quickly highlight a block of values in a spreadsheet or Scrollsheet by clicking on a cell to define the beginning of the block and then (e.g., after scrolling with the scrollbars) while holding down the SHIFT key, click on a cell that will define the end of the block (the SHIFT-click convention). All of the values in-between will be highlighted.
- Holding down the CTRL key when you click on an *Auto Task Button* (see page 1014 and Chapter 6) will open the respective dialog for editing the contents of the button.
- Holding down the CTRL key while pressing either the *Graphics* window *Increase Font* or *Decrease Font* toolbar buttons will achieve a small (4% instead of the default 16%) increase or decrease in the mapping base (see Chapter 2).
- Holding down the CTRL key while pressing on the spreadsheet window toolbar button will switch to the value label display in the spreadsheet (see Chapter 2).
- Hold down on the SHIFT key while you are dragging the mouse in the *Graphics* window in

order to make a square, squared rounded rectangle, circle, or quarter arc (see Chapter 2).

Specific applications are given below.

Other Applications

In addition to the applications mentioned above, you can perform the following using the mouse:

- *Drag-and-Drop*: The mouse provides shortcuts for moving, copying, deleting, inserting, extrapolating, etc. a block of values in the spreadsheet or Scrollsheet (see 3).

Data: NEW.STA 6v * 10c

#	1 VAR1	2 VAR2	3 VAR3	4 NEWVAR4	5 NEWVAR5	6 NEWVAR6
1	4.000	20.000	4.000			
2	18.000	9.000	14.000			
3	15.000	3.000	10.000			
4	11.000	1.000	8.000			
5	7.000	1.000	2.000	4.000	20.000	4.000
6	1.000	8.000	13.000	18.000	9.000	14.000
7	2.000	11.000	16.000	15.000	3.000	10.000
8	8.000	12.000	17.000			

- Increase/decrease column width: Adjust the spreadsheet or Scrollsheet column width by dragging the right column border to the desired width (see Chapter 3).

Data: ADSTUDY.STA 25v * 50c

Advertising Effectiveness Study.

Case	1 GENDER	2 ADVERT	3 MEAS	4 MEAS	5 MEAS	6 MEAS	7 MEAS
J. Baker	MALE	PEPSI	9	1	6	8	1
A. Smith	MALE	COKE	6	7	1	8	0
M. Brown	FEMALE	COKE	9	8	2	9	8
C. Mayer	MALE	PEPSI	7	9	0	5	9
M. West	MALE	PEPSI	7	1	6	2	8
D. Young	FEMALE	COKE	6	0	0	8	3
S. Bird	FEMALE	COKE	7	4	3	2	5

The new width of the column is indicated by a dashed line (as shown in the illustration above).

- Split Scrolling (in spreadsheets and Scrollsheets): Split the spreadsheet or Scrollsheet window (i.e., split scrolling; see Chapter 3) by dragging the split box (the black rectangle at the top of the vertical scrollbar or to the left of the horizontal scrollbar).

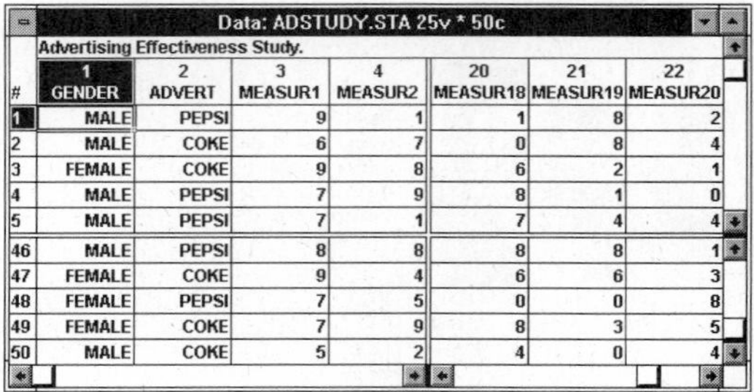

Data: ADSTUDY.STA 25v * 50c

Advertising Effectiveness Study.

#	1 GENDER	2 ADVERT	3 MEASUR1	4 MEASUR2	20 MEASUR18	21 MEASUR19	22 MEASUR20
1	MALE	PEPSI	9	1	1	8	2
2	MALE	COKE	6	7	0	8	4
3	FEMALE	COKE	9	8	6	2	1
4	MALE	PEPSI	7	9	8	1	0
5	MALE	PEPSI	7	1	7	4	4
46	MALE	PEPSI	8	8	8	8	1
47	FEMALE	COKE	9	4	6	6	3
48	FEMALE	PEPSI	7	5	0	0	8
49	FEMALE	COKE	7	9	8	3	5
50	MALE	COKE	5	2	4	0	4

- Variable speed scrolling: Controls the speed at which you scroll (1 line at a time by moving the cursor a short distance away or one page at a time by moving the cursor further away) when you extend a block outside the spreadsheet or Scrollsheet (see Chapter 3).

- *MicroScrolls* 1.11 : Enable you to increase or decrease the value in a numeric edit field incrementally, by either the last digit (click on the micro scroll with the left-mouse-button, e.g., 1.11, 1.12, 1.13, ...) or the last digit by a factor of 10 (click on the micro scroll with the right-mouse-button, e.g., 1.11, 1.21, 1.31, ...; see page 1032).

- Toolbar configuration: Double-clicking on the space between the buttons of the toolbar will toggle between four toolbar configurations (1 line, 2 lines, right & top, and left & top; see Chapter 2).

- *Auto Task Buttons*: Holding down the CTRL key while clicking on an *Auto Task Button*,

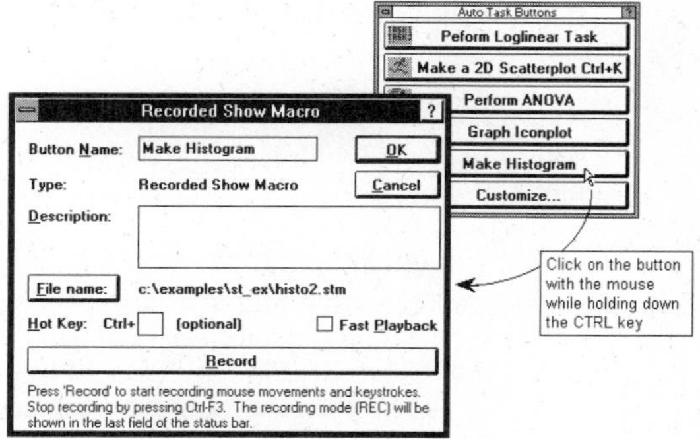

will open a dialog allowing you to edit the *Auto Task Buttons* contents (see Chapter 6).

- *Auto Task Buttons* toolbar: Double-clicking on the space between the buttons of the *Auto Task Buttons* toolbar with the left-mouse-button will resize it (alternatively, you can drag this toolbar's border with the mouse to resize it).

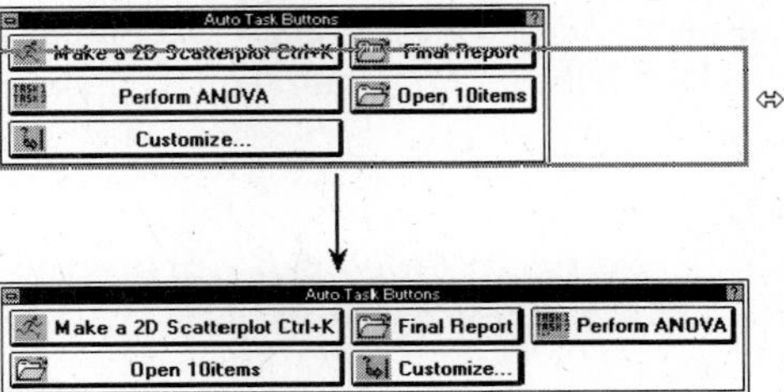

Clicking with the right-mouse-button will bring up a flying menu of options. You can "dock" the toolbar by dragging it to an area of the *STATISTICA* window (above the toolbar, below the status bar, or to either side of the window) where the toolbar will change configuration and remain in that position until you drag it to a different area of the window (see Chapter 6).

- Reordering items in a list: You can reorder items in a list (e.g., Workbook, *Auto Task Buttons*, *Multiple-Graph AutoLayout Wizard*, etc.) by highlighting one or more (in a continuous or dis-continuous list) items and then moving the mouse cursor to the desired position (the cursor will change to a ⇕). Clicking the left-mouse-button will then move the highlighted item(s) to the insertion point.

Graph Applications

The following applications apply to the *Graphics* window in *STATISTICA*. Note that the current mouse coordinates (or angle of rotation, see below) will be displayed in the *Change Show* window of the *Graphics* toolbar.

For more information on each of these applications, see Volume II.

- *OLE*: Link or embed foreign document files to *STATISTICA* documents by dragging them with the mouse directly from *File Manager* (across application windows) and dropping them onto *STATISTICA* graphs.
- *Brushing*: Highlight data points from the graph by clicking on them with the brushing tool.
- *Zoom in* and *Zoom out* tools: Zoom in ("magnifies") or zooms out ("shrinks"), respectively, the selected area of the graph.
- Drawing tools: Add rectangles, ovals (or circles), polylines and free-hand drawings, arrows, etc. to a graph. Hold down on the SHIFT key while you are dragging the mouse in order to make a square, squared rounded rectangle, circle, or quarter arc.
- Resizing and moving: Resize (drag on a "black selection square," ↔) or moves (drag the entire object, ✥) selected graph objects. For fine adjustments, see *Controlling the mouse with the keyboard in graphs*, below.
- Editing polyline objects: Reshape individual segments of the polyline drawing by dragging with the mouse on either the object area black selection squares or any of the black selection squares that mark the line segments. For fine adjustments, see *Controlling the mouse with the keyboard in graphs*, below.
- Rotating text: You can interactively rotate custom text by selecting it in the graph and then dragging one of the object handles (small black squares) in the desired direction [the angle (in degrees) will be displayed in the *Change Show* window of the *Graphics* toolbar].

For fine adjustments (1 degree movements), see *Controlling the mouse with the keyboard in graphs*, below.

- *Snap to Grid*: Align drawing objects with the drawing grid, an invisible network of lines that covers the drawing area.
- *Graph Mapping Base*: Clicking on the or toolbar buttons will change the value of the *Graph Mapping Base* by ±16%, respectively. Holding down the CTRL key while pressing either of these buttons will achieve a smaller (4%) increase or decrease in the mapping base.
- *Controlling the mouse with the keyboard in graphs*: You can also emulate the mouse with the keyboard in order to move or resize an object by selecting the object, placing the mouse over the object, and then using the keyboard cursor keys to move or resize the object. Hold down the CTRL key for fine (1 pixel only) movements and press ENTER to complete the action.

Note that the mouse cursor will change to the appropriate tool to match the application for which it is being used. Clicking on the ESC key will return the mouse to the default mode.

You can also use the mouse (press on the left-mouse-button) to interrupt a current action (e.g., redrawing of a graph, processing of an *SCL* program, etc.; for more information, see below.

Breaking, Stopping, or Interrupting the Current Action

Sometimes it may be necessary to stop, break, or interrupt the current action or analysis. In this case, you can do so in the following manners:

Analysis. Click on the CANCEL button on the *Progress Bar* to interrupt the task in progress.

Graph redraw. Graph redraw may be interrupted by a click of the mouse (anywhere on the screen) or by pressing any key.

Brushing (in a graph). You can deactivate the brushing tool by clicking on the *Point Tool* toolbar button or by pressing the ESC key.

Printing. You can interrupt the printing of spreadsheets, Scrollsheets, graphs, text output, etc., by clicking on the CANCEL button on the *Printing* dialog.

STATISTICA BASIC. Click on the ESC key or the CANCEL button on the *Progress Bar* in order to interrupt the execution of the *STATISTICA BASIC* program.

SCL. You can interrupt execution of the *SCL* program at any point by clicking the mouse or pressing the ESC or CTRL+BREAK keys.

MML. Click on the ESC key or the CANCEL button on the *Progress Bar* in order to interrupt the execution of the *MML* program.

Macros. To stop recording a macro, press CTRL+F3. To break a macro playback, click on the mouse button, or press the ESC or CTRL+BREAK keys.

OTHER DIALOGS, OPTIONS

Windows System Menu

You can use the *System Menu* options described below to perform various *Window* functions. To open this menu, click on the button in the upper left-hand corner of the *STATISTICA* window or on the minimized *STATISTICA* icon.

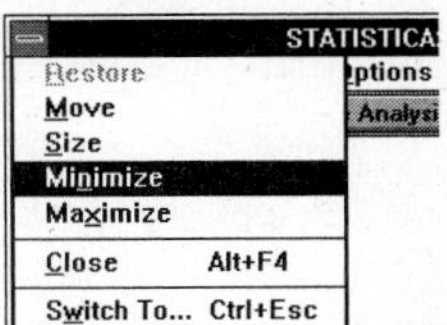

Restore

This option restores the window to its previous size after it has been maximized or minimized.

Move

This option will enable you to use the keyboard to move the window to another position.

Size

With this option you can enable the keyboard to change the size of the window.

Minimize

This option reduces the window to an icon.

Maximize

Selecting this option will enlarge the window to its maximize size.

Close

Selecting this option will close the current *STATISTICA* module.

Switch To

This option will open the *Task List* dialog from which you can select between running applications and rearrange their windows and icons.

Reopen File Saved in Another Module

This dialog box is displayed when you run two (or more) *STATISTICA* modules simultaneously, modify the same file in both modules, and then try to save it in one of the modules.

For example:

1. You are using and have modified file *A.sta* in *Basic Statistics and Tables.*
2. You are using and have modified file *A.sta* in *Data Management.*
3. You request *Save* in *Data Management.*

In such a case, after saving the file in *Data Management*, the program will ask you if you wish to reopen the new (saved) version of *A.sta* in *Basic Statistics and Tables.*

If you answer *Yes*, the file will be reopened to reflect the result of the *Save* operation performed in *Data Management*. If you answer *No*, then the changes you made in *Basic Statistics and Tables* will be maintained.

Note that a similar situation will occur when in one module you perform a *Save As* operation and specify the name of a file that has been modified but not saved in another module.

For example:

1. You are using and have modified the file *A.sta* in *Basic Statistics and Tables*.
2. You are using file *B.sta* in *Data Management*.
3. You request *Save As* in *Data Management*, and specify *A.sta* as a new name for the saved file.

In such a case, *STATISTICA* will first warn you that *A.sta* already exists and will be overwritten. Then, after saving the file in *Data Management*, the program will ask you if you wish to reopen the new (saved) version of *A.sta* in *Basic Statistics and Tables*.

If you answer *Yes*, the file will be reloaded to reflect the result of the *Save As* operation performed in *Data Management*. If you answer *No*, the changes you made in *Basic Statistics and Tables* will be maintained.

Save Modified File before Opening it in Another Module

This dialog box is displayed when you run two (or more) *STATISTICA* modules simultaneously and in one module try to open a file that is currently in use and has been modified (but not saved) in another module.

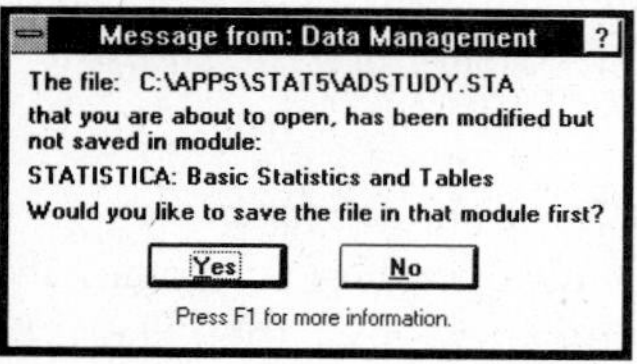

For example:

1. You are using and have modified the file *A.sta* in *Basic Statistics and Tables*.
2. You request *Open* in *Data Management* and specify *A.sta* as the file to be opened.

In such a case, the program will ask if you want to save the changes you made in *Basic Statistics and Tables* before opening the file in *Data Management*.

If you answer *Yes*, *Basic Statistics and Tables* will automatically save the file, and the new version will be opened in *Data Management*. If you answer *No*, *Data Management* will open the original version of *A.sta*.

Note that a similar situation will occur when you use and modify (but not save) a file in one module and then try to run another *STATISTICA* module.

For example:

1. You are using and have modified file *A.sta* in *Basic Statistics and Tables*.
2. You bring up *STATISTICA Module Switcher* and select *Data Management*.

When *Data Management* is opening, it tries to open *A.sta* as its data file. After determining that *A.sta* has been modified but not saved in *Basic Statistics and Tables*, the program will perform the same action as described in the example above.

STATISTICA FILE SERVER

The *STATISTICA File Server* is a small, rapidly loading module of *STATISTICA*

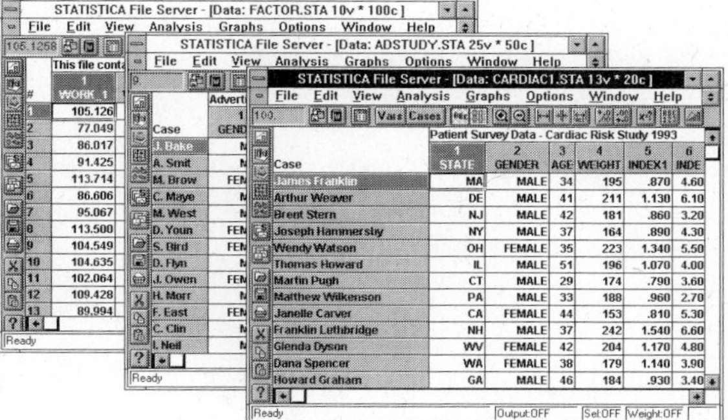

which provides facilities for accessing and modifying all *STATISTICA* files, including data files (file name extension **.sta*), Scrollsheet files (file name extension **.scr*), graphics files (file name extension **.stg*), *SCL* files (file name extension **.scl*) and *STATISTICA BASIC* files (file name extension **.stb*). A *STATISTICA* file may be opened directly into the *STATISTICA File Server* by simply double-clicking on its file name in the Windows *File Manager*.

In addition, the *STATISTICA File Server* application provides *OLE* support for *STATISTICA* files in other applications (if there is not any other module of *STATISTICA* currently running).

Also, you may have as many instances of the *File Server* open at one time as your operating system will allow, permitting you to review and edit many data files at once.

Custom-designing New Modules of *STATISTICA*

You can use the *File Server* application as a foundation to develop your own "specialized *STATISTICA* modules" or "*STATISTICA* applications" written in *STATISTICA BASIC* or a combination of *SCL* (*STATISTICA Command Language*) and *BASIC*.

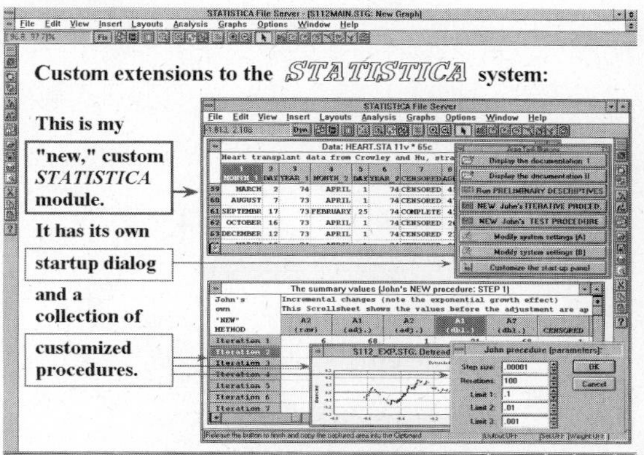

The *Auto Task Buttons* toolbar (see Chapter 6) can be used as a convenient startup panel for the new module. Each button on the toolbar can be set up to execute a different, custom-designed computational, graphics, or data management procedure.

INDEX

A

B

C

D

E

F

G

I

K

L

M

N

O

P

Q

R

S

T

V

W

Chapter 2:
TOOLBARS

Table of Contents

Detailed Table of Contents

Chapter 2:
TOOLBARS

INTRODUCTORY OVERVIEW

This section contains brief descriptions of the functions which can be requested by pressing the toolbar buttons. The name of each button is displayed in a *ToolTip* as you point to the button (see the illustration below).

For a comprehensive reference on each of these functions, access the on-line *Electronic Manual* (press the F1 key, double-click on the status bar on the bottom of the *STATISTICA* window, or press the *Help* ? toolbar button). Note that most functions accessible through the toolbar buttons are also accessible through other controls. For example, they are accessible through the flying menus (which can be activated by pressing the right-mouse-button or via keyboard shortcuts) and from the pull-down menus.

Customizing toolbars. All toolbars in *STATISTICA* can be customized using the *Toolbars* option in the pull-down menu *Options* or a flying menu available by pressing the right-mouse-button in the toolbar.

For example, some toolbars contain more buttons than can fit on the standard VGA (640x480) screen; thus they can be split and repositioned.

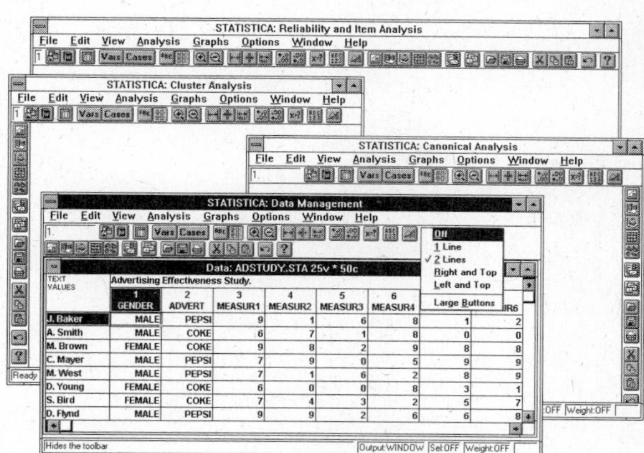

You may toggle between four configurations of the toolbar by double-clicking on the toolbar outside any of the buttons.

In addition to the spreadsheet, Scrollsheet, *Text/output Window* and graph toolbars, *STATISTICA* offers *Auto Task Buttons*, a floating (or docked), user-defined toolbar that allows you to quickly access most of *STATISTICA*'s task automation facilities.

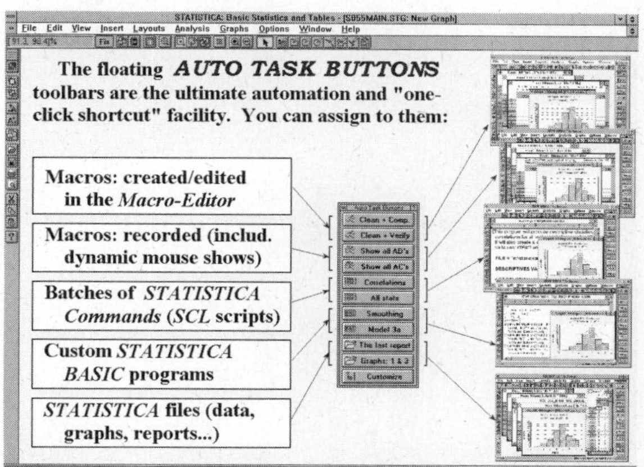

For more information on *Auto Task Buttons*, refer to Chapter 6.

DATA SPREADSHEET TOOLBAR

The spreadsheet window allows you to edit the input data, and it offers a variety of data base management and data transformation/recoding operations.

The *STATISTICA* spreadsheet also supports split display and/or split and variable-speed scrolling and the extended set of standard (MS Excel-style) block *Drag-and-Drop* and intelligent block extension operations.

STATISTICA: Basic Statistics and Tables

File Edit View Analysis Graphs Options Window Help

Recalculate Variable(s)

Data: ADSTUDY.STA 25v * 50c

Advertising Effectiveness Study.

TEXT VALUES	1 GENDER	2 ADVERT	3 MEAS	4 MEAS	5 MEAS	6 MEAS	7 MEAS	8 MEAS	9 MEAS	23 MEAS	24 MEAS	25 MEAS
J. Baker	MALE	PEPSI	9	1	6	8	1	2	1	3	3	7
A. Smith	MALE	COKE	6	7	1	8	0	0	6	8	0	7
M. Brown	FEMALE	COKE	9	8	2	9	8	8	0	0	2	6
C. Mayer	MALE	PEPSI	7	9	0	5	9	9	6	3	7	6
M. West	MALE	PEPSI	7	1	6	2	8	9	6	7	9	9
D. Young	FEMALE	COKE	6	0	0	8	3	1	0	4	4	8
S. Bird	FEMALE	COKE	7	4	3	6	7	1	1	9	4	3
D. Flynd	MALE	PEPSI	9	9	2	9	8	2	7	0	7	8
J. Owen	FEMALE	PEPSI	7	8	2	7	9	0	1	3	8	5
H. Morrow	MALE	PEPSI	6	6	2	8	3	6	4	9	4	4
F. East	FEMALE	PEPSI	4	6	6	5	6	8	7	0	2	5
C. Clint	MALE	COKE	7	3	3	7	0	6	5	3	4	5
I. Neil	MALE	PEPSI	6	2	3	1	8	1	4	6	8	6

Ready | Output:OFF | Sel:OFF | Weight:OFF

Some other specialized data management and data transformation facilities are available in the *Data Management* module.

The spreadsheet toolbar provides quick access to the most commonly used data management facilities and graphs based on raw data. All facilities accessible via the toolbar buttons listed below are also available by using other program controls (see above).

3.12 0. The Show Field

The *Show Field* displays the value of the currently highlighted cell at a higher precision than will fit in the respective columns of the spreadsheet. The width of the *Show Field* can be adjusted (toggled) by clicking on it with the mouse

or by clicking on the *Change Show* option in the pull-down menu *View*.

1. Module Switcher

Brings up the *STATISTICA Module Switcher* (the first button in all toolbars). The *Switcher* gives you quick access to all "modules" (i.e., groups of analytic procedures) available in your version of *STATISTICA*. The *Switcher* works in a manner similar to the Windows *Task Switcher* (available by double-clicking on the Windows desktop) and can be opened by double-clicking anywhere on the background of the *STATISTICA* window.

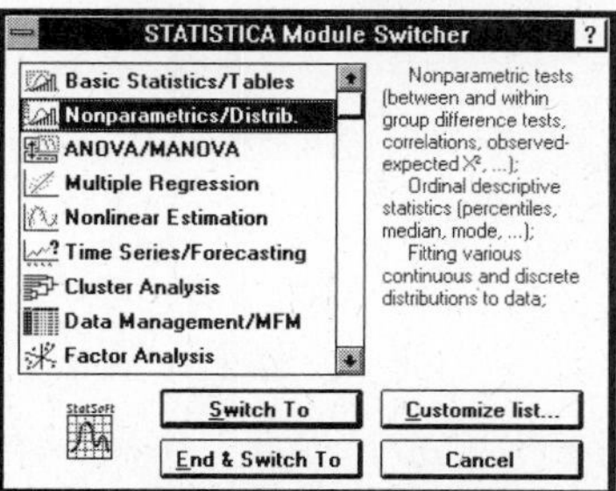

Depending on the current configuration, the *Switcher* may open new modules into the same or new application windows.

Note that although the list of modules in the *Switcher* can be scrolled, it is convenient to have the modules most commonly used in your specific work listed on the top and thus not requiring scrolling; the order of modules listed can be customized by pressing the *Customize list...* button (on the *Module Switcher*).

2. Workbook Management

Brings up the *Data File Header, Notes and Workbook Info* dialog (the second button on all toolbars). This dialog allows you to enter a one-line *File Header* which appears at the top of the spreadsheet, detailed file information or notes about the data set's contents, source, etc., and to manage all supplementary files (e.g., graphs, reports, programs) used with the current data set.

Workbooks (overview). *STATISTICA* data set files can be considered to be "Workbooks" of files because they contain (automatically store) information about all supplementary files (e.g., graphs, reports, programs) used with the current data set. A log of these files can be reviewed by pressing the *Workbook* toolbar button or by double-clicking on the title area (header) of the data spreadsheet.

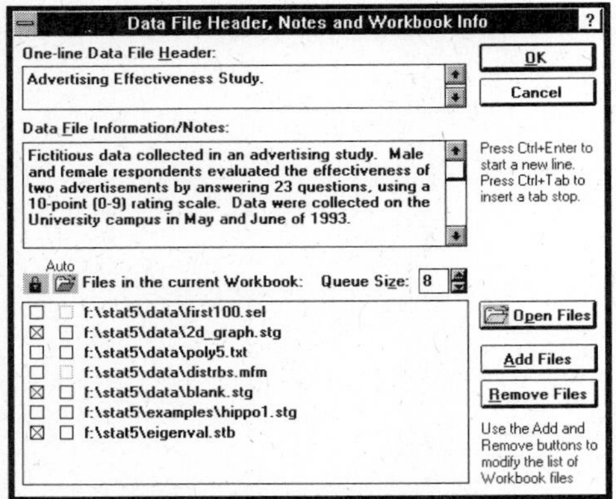

Specific files (from the list of workbook files) can be marked to be opened automatically when you open the data file by checking the box next to the file name below the *Auto Open* icon (Auto).

Queue of Workbook files. A list of the most recently opened or created supplementary files is maintained in a "queue" where older files are removed from the list as new graphs, reports, and programs are saved. Files are removed from the queue on a first-in-first-out basis. The length of this queue is saved with the data set and may be changed by the user (the default length is 32 files) in the *Data File Header, Notes and Workbook Info* dialog shown above. Regardless of the length of the queue, individual files may be "locked" (i.e., "removed" from the queue) by checking the box next to the file name below the *Lock* icon.

The list of supplementary (Workbook) files associated with the current data set is also available in all *Open/Save* dialogs in *STATISTICA* (see the bottom part of the dialog shown below).

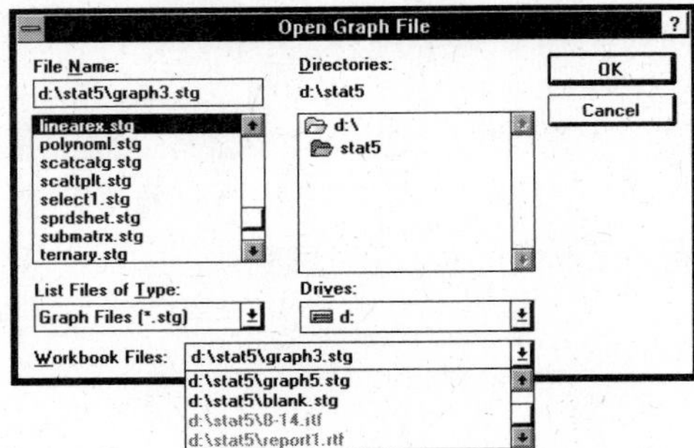

The relevant (for the current *Open/Save* dialog) file names are not dimmed in the list and can be selected by double-clicking.

3. Variable Specification Window (for All Variables)

Brings up the combined *Variable Specification* window; this window allows you to review/edit a table of all variable specifications (names, formats, missing data values, long labels, formulas or links, etc. defining individual variables).

Variables: NEW.STA 12v * 11c

Var	Name	MD Code	Format	Long Name (label, formula or link)
1	D_ENTRY	-9999	DATE1	Date of Entry
2	T_ENTRY	-9999	TIME1	Time of Entry
3	D_EXIT	-9999	DATE2	Date of Exit
4	T_EXIT	-9999	TIME2	Time of Exit
8	SUM_SCOR	-9999	8.3	= V5 + V6 + V7 ; Total Score
9	AV_SCORE	-9999	8.3	= (V5 + V6 + V7) / 3 ; Mean Score
10	%CHANGE	-9999	8.3	= (V7 - V5) / V7 ; Percent Change Du
11	DURATION	-9999	8.3	= V3 - V1 ; Duration of Exposure
12	ALPHA_Z	-9999	9.4	Alpha characteristic (derived)

Cut Ctrl+X
Copy Ctrl+C
Paste Ctrl+V
Clear Del
Fill Block Down

Note that detailed variable specifications for each individual variable can be accessed by double-clicking on the variable name in the spreadsheet, which brings up a dialog containing the specifications of the selected variable.

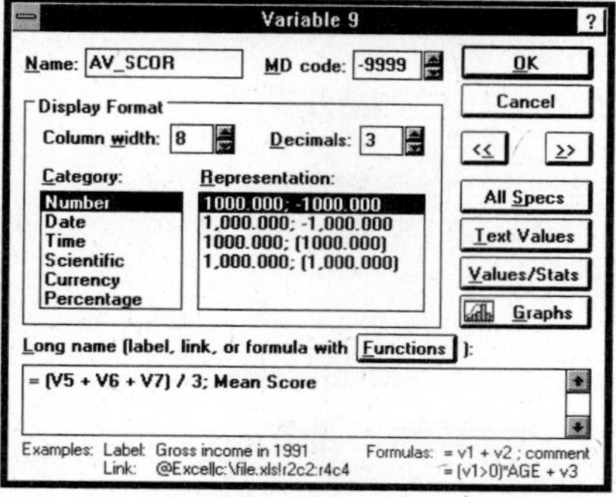

From this individual variable specifications dialog you can also go back to the combined table of specifications of all variables by pressing the *All Specs* button.

4. Global Operations on Variables

Brings up a menu of global *Variable* editing and restructuring options: *Add*, *Move*, *Copy*, *Delete*, edit *Current Specs*, edit *All Specs* (see the button, above), edit *Text Values*, *Date Values*, *Recalculate*, *Shift (lag)*, *Rank*, *Recode*.

***Global* vs. *Clipboard* operations on variables.** Unlike the Clipboard operations of cutting, copying, and pasting blocks of data (or contents of entire columns), these operations will affect not only the contents of the columns of data but also the columns themselves (where applicable). For example, the *Delete* operation will remove not only the contents of the selected range of columns but the columns themselves as well.

Also, note the difference between these global operations performed on variables (treated as logical units of the *STATISTICA* data files) and all Clipboard spreadsheet operations which work the same way as in all standard spreadsheets (e.g., MS Excel).

For example, the global operations of copying, deleting, or moving variables available from this menu will not depend on the current location of the cursor or block (highlight), other than by the fact that the highlighted variable names will be suggested to you in the respective dialogs (thus offering a shortcut method of selecting variables to be affected by the operation). The operations will always be performed on all cases of selected variables, regardless of whether or not all cases or only a subset of cases are currently highlighted for the respective variables.

On the other hand, in the case of Clipboard operations, only the segment of data which is highlighted will be copied, and (following the common spreadsheet conventions) pasting will always begin from the current cursor position, and proceed down.

Thus, even when you (a) highlight and copy an entire variable, (b) highlight another (entire) column and then (c) intend to paste the Clipboard content to that new location ("replacing" the previous values) -- the operation will be performed as intended only if you have placed the cursor at the top of the new column. If you placed it somewhere in the middle, then the pasting will start from that point down.

***Drag-and-Drop* operations.** Note that all *Drag-and-Drop with Insert* (press the SHIFT key) operations will change the size of the data file; the same is true of simple dragging blocks outside the boundaries of the current data file. However, dragging (without *Insert*) within the current data file boundaries produces results identical to using the Clipboard (except that the Clipboard is not used).

Cases 5. Global Operations on Cases

Brings up a menu of global *Case* editing/restructuring options: *Add*, *Move*, *Copy*, *Delete*, edit/manage case *Names*.

STATISTICA: Basic

File Edit View Analysis Graphs

Add... Move... Copy... Delete... Names...

Case	1 GENDER	2 ADV		4 MEAS
J. Baker	MALE	PEP		1
A. Smith	MALE	COKE	6	7
M. Brown	FEMALE	COKE	9	8
C. Mayer	MALE	PEPSI	7	9
M. West	MALE	PEPSI	7	1
D. Young	FEMALE	COKE	6	0

***Global* vs. *Clipboard* operations on cases.** Unlike the Clipboard operations of cutting, copying, and pasting blocks of data (or contents of entire rows, that is, cases), these operations will affect not only the contents of the rows of data, but the rows themselves.

For example, the *Delete* operation will remove not only the contents of the selected range of rows but the rows, too (see the previous section on the Vars button for more explanation and examples of the differences between the global and Clipboard operations and the *Drag-and-Drop* operations).

6. Text/numeric Value Display (Hold Down CTRL to Display Value Labels)

Toggles between displaying text values in the data spreadsheet:

Data: ADSTUDY.STA 25v * 50c — Advertising Effectiveness Study.

TEXT VALUES	1 GENDER	2 ADVERT	3 MEAS	4 MEAS	5 MEAS	6 MEAS	7 MEAS	8 MEAS
J. Baker	MALE	PEPSI	9	1	6	8	1	2
A. Smith	MALE	COKE	6	7	1	8	0	0
M. Brown	FEMALE	COKE	9	8	2	9	8	8
C. Mayer	MALE	PEPSI	7	9	0	5	9	9

displaying their numeric equivalents:

Data: ADSTUDY.STA 25v * 50c — Advertising Effectiveness Study.

NUMERIC VALUES	1 GENDER	2 ADVERT	3 MEAS	4 MEAS	5 MEAS	6 MEAS	7 MEAS	8 MEAS
J. Baker	1	1	9	1	6	8	1	2
A. Smith	1	2	6	7	1	8	0	0
M. Brown	2	2	9	8	2	9	8	8
C. Mayer	1	1	7	9	0	5	9	9

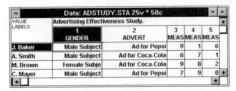

and displaying their value labels (hold down the CTRL key while clicking on the button to display value labels):

Data: ADSTUDY.STA 25v * 50c — Advertising Effectiveness Study.

VALUE LABELS	1 GENDER	2 ADVERT	3 MEAS	4 MEAS	5 MEAS
J. Baker	Male Subject	Ad for Pepsi	9	1	6
A. Smith	Male Subject	Ad for Coca-Cola	6	7	1
M. Brown	Female Subje	Ad for Coca-Cola	9	8	2
C. Mayer	Male Subject	Ad for Pepsi	7	9	0

STATISTICA supports "double notation" of values where each value may have two "identities:" numeric (e.g., *1*) and text (e.g., *MALE*); see also the *Text Values Manager*, button, below.

Value labels. Note that each value may also have a long label/comment attached to it; these labels are used automatically in reports (depending on the report style setting). These long value labels/comments can be displayed and edited either in the spreadsheet (hold down the CTRL key while clicking on the button to display the value labels), or they can be edited and managed in the *Text Values Manager*.

7. Case Names Display (toggle)

Toggles between displaying case names in the data spreadsheet display:

Data: ADSTUDY.STA 25v * 50c

TEXT VALUES	Advertising Effectiveness Study. 1 GENDER	2 ADVERT	3 MEAS	4 MEAS	5 MEAS	6 MEAS	7 MEAS	8 MEAS
J. Baker	MALE	PEPSI	9	1	6	8	1	2
A. Smith	MALE	COKE	6	7	1	8	0	0
M. Brown	FEMALE	COKE	9	8	2	9	8	8
C. Mayer	MALE	PEPSI	7	9	0	5	9	9
M. West	MALE	PEPSI	7	1	6	2	8	9
D. Young	FEMALE	COKE	6	0	0	8	3	1

and displaying case numbers:

Data: ADSTUDY.STA 25v * 50c

TEX VAL	Advertising Effectiveness Study. 1 GENDER	2 ADVERT	3 MEAS	4 MEAS	5 MEAS	6 MEAS	7 MEAS	8 MEAS	9 MEAS	10 MEAS
1	MALE	PEPSI	9	1	6	8	1	2	1	3
2	MALE	COKE	6	7	1	8	0	0	6	8
3	FEMALE	COKE	9	8	2	9	8	8	0	3
4	MALE	PEPSI	7	9	0	5	9	9	6	6
5	MALE	PEPSI	7	1	6	2	8	9	6	4
6	FEMALE	COKE	6	0	0	8	3	1	0	7

In order to enter, edit, or manage (e.g., change the width, copy from a variable, etc.) the current case names, double-click on any case name in the spreadsheet.

If the current data set contains no case names, you can create them by double-clicking on the case number column or re-sizing the case number column with the mouse.

8. Zoom-in

Zooms-in (increases the font size and proportionately increases all parts of the spreadsheet).

Data: ADSTUDY.STA 25v * 50c

TEXT VALUES	Advertising Effectiveness Study. 1 GENDER	2 ADVERT	3 MEASUR1	4 MEASUR2
J. Baker	MALE	PEPSI	1	1
A. Smith	MALE	COKE	2	7
M. Brown	FEMALE	COKE	3	8
C. Mayer	MALE	PEPSI	4	9
M. West	MALE	PEPSI	5	1

9. Zoom-out

Zooms-out (decreases the font size and proportionately decreases all parts of the spreadsheet).

Data: ADSTUDY.STA 25v * 50c

TEXT VALUES	Advertising Effectiveness Study. 1 GENDER	2 ADVERT	3 MEASUR1	4 MEASUR2	5 MEASUR3	6 MEASUR4	7 MEASUR5	8 MEASUR6
J. Baker	MALE	PEPSI	1	1	6	8	1	2
A. Smith	MALE	COKE	2	7	1	8	0	0
M. Brown	FEMALE	COKE	3	8	2	9	8	8
C. Mayer	MALE	PEPSI	4	9	0	5	9	9
M. West	MALE	PEPSI	5	1	6	2	8	9
D. Young	FEMALE	COKE	6	0	0	8	3	1
S. Bird	FEMALE	COKE	7	4	3	2	5	7
D. Flynd	MALE	PEPSI	9	9	2	6	6	8
J. Owen	FEMALE	PEPSI	7	8	2	3	6	9
H. Morrow	MALE	PEPSI	6	6	2	8	3	6
F. East	FEMALE	PEPSI	4	6	6	5	6	8

10. Increase the Column Width

Increases the width of the current column (i.e., the column marked by the current cursor position). The same effect can be achieved by dragging the right border line of the column header (name) with the mouse.

Data: ADSTUDY.STA 25v * 50c

TEXT VALUES	Advertising Effectiveness Study. 1 GENDER	2 ADVERT	3 MEAS	4 MEAS	5 MEAS	6 MEAS	7 MEAS
J. Baker	MALE	PEPSI	9	1	6	8	1
A. Smith	MALE	COKE	6	7	1	8	0
M. Brown	FEMALE	COKE	9	8	2	9	8
C. Mayer	MALE	PEPSI	7	9	0	5	9
M. West	MALE	PEPSI	7	1	6	2	8
D. Young	FEMALE	COKE	6	0	0	8	3
S. Bird	FEMALE	COKE	7	4	3	2	5

The new width of the column is indicated by a dashed line (as shown in the illustration above).

11. Decrease the Column Width

Decreases the width of the current column (i.e., the column marked by the current cursor position). The same effect can be achieved by dragging the right border line of the column header (name) with the mouse (see the previous topic).

12. Adjust the Global Column Width

Adjusts the width of all columns of the spreadsheet (global column width adjustment).

This setting will affect the display formats of all variables in the current data file.

13. Add One Decimal

Adds one decimal place to the value display format of the current variable (for example, after pressing this button, the value *12.23* will be displayed as *12.234*).

14. Remove One Decimal

Removes one decimal place from the value display format of the current variable (for example, after pressing this button, the value *12.234* will be displayed as *12.23*).

15. Recalculate

Recalculates the current variable or, optionally, all variables defined by formulas in the current data file (you may also press F9 in the spreadsheet to skip this dialog and recalculate all valid formulas).

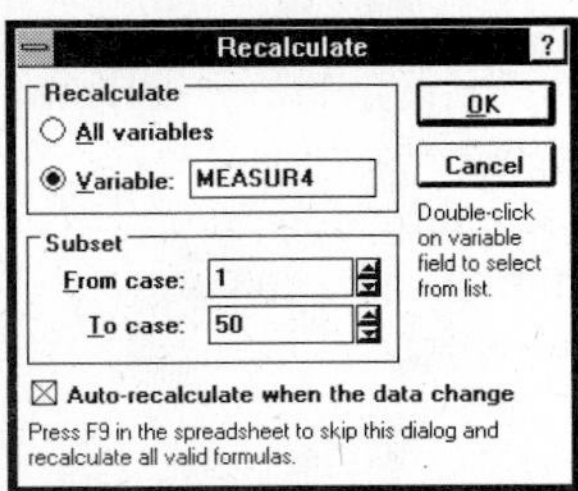

Those formulas can be entered as part of the variable specifications -- to enter/edit the specifications, double-click on the variable name in the spreadsheet or press the *Variable Specifications* toolbar button (see the button, above).

Note that if the intended result of the transformation is recoding of values (rather than performing arithmetic operations), there is a designated recoding facility available from the spreadsheet Vars button.

16. Text Values Manager

Brings up the *Text Values Manager* with all text values and long value labels/comments for the current variable.

The *Text Values Manager* can be used to edit and manage (e.g., sort, copy between variables, fill, rearrange) the assignments between text and numeric values and their labels.

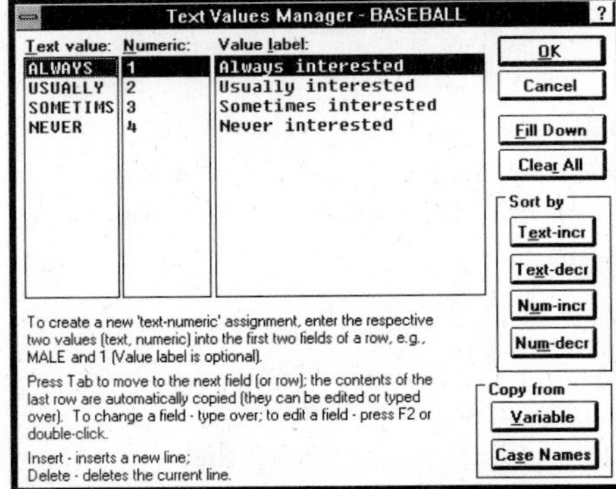

You can also access the *Text Values Manager* by clicking on the *Text Values* button in the individual variable specifications dialog (see page 1053) or from the *Current Specs* option in the Vars toolbar menu.

17. Quick Basic Stats

These procedures include a selection of basic statistics which can be performed on long lists of variables (e.g., correlation matrices for all variables in the data set), and all analyses can be performed *by groups*, for every value (i.e., code) of a selected grouping variable.

Data: IRISDAT.STA 5v * 150c

Fisher (1936) iris data: length & width of sepals and petals,

	1 SEPALLEN	2 SEPALWID	3 PETALLEN	4 PETALWID	5 IRISTYPE
1	5.0	3.3			
2	6.4	2.8			
3	6.5	2.8			
4	6.7	3.1			
5	6.3	2.8			
6	4.6	3.4			
7	6.9	3.1			
8	6.2	2.2			
9	5.9	3.2			
10	4.6	3.6	1.0	.2	SETOSA
11	6.1	3.0	4.6	1.4	VERSICOL

Descriptives of PETALLEN-PETALWID
Correlations of PETALLEN-PETALWID
Frequencies of PETALLEN-PETALWID
Descriptives by...
Correlations by...
Frequencies by...
Probability Calculator
More...

The *Quick Basic Stats* options are also available from the spreadsheet right-mouse-button flying menu and from the *Analysis* pull-down menu of any module of *STATISTICA* (as well as from Scrollsheets, see page 1070). *Quick Basic Stats* can be invoked at any point of your data analysis (e.g., to provide supplementary information when you review output from any *STATISTICA* module).

For a detailed discussion of *Quick Basic Stats*, see Chapter 10.

"Quick" selection of variables in *Quick Basic Stats.* One of the main advantages of *Quick Basic Stats* is that usually they do not require that you select the variables for the analysis via the standard variable selection dialogs – instead, the variables are automatically chosen from the block currently highlighted in the spreadsheet or Scrollsheet. *STATISTICA* will prompt you to select variables only if the block does not contain a sufficient number of variables or if a grouping variable is required.

In all spreadsheets (and those Scrollsheets which involve only one list of variables rather than two lists or one grouping variable and a list), the flying menu will have the following format:

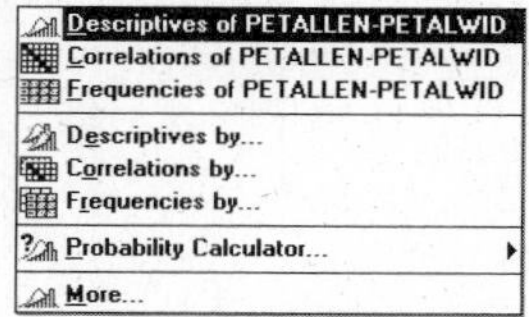

If you select any of the analyses involving a grouping variable (*by...*), *STATISTICA* will open the standard *Select Variable* dialog from which you may select the variable by which to perform the analysis.

From Scrollsheets having a matrix format, or a format where the cursor position may indicate two variables rather than one, predefined analyses *by groups* are available from the *Quick Basic Stats* menu (and *STATISTICA* will not ask you for the selection of the "*by...*" variable for the analysis).

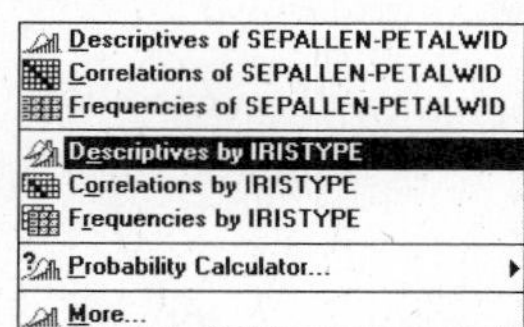

If no variables are indicated by the current cursor position, then selecting any of the *Quick Basic Stats* will prompt you to select a variable(s) from a list. Additional statistics and graphs are available by selecting the *More...* option on the *Quick Basic Stats* menu.

From this dialog, you may also override the default selection of variables (based on the currently highlighted block of data).

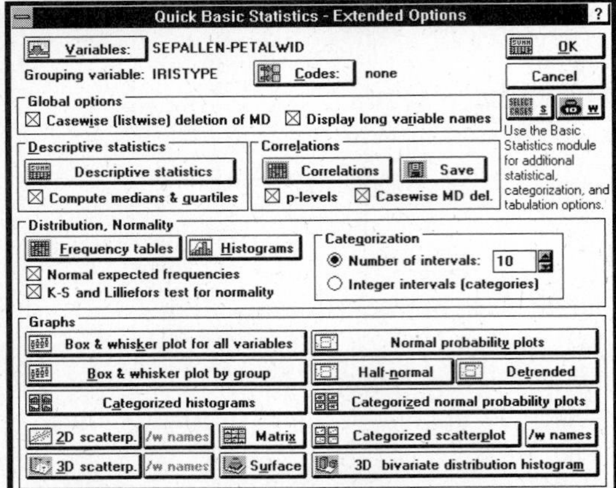

As the *Quick Basic Statistics* are computed, *STATISTICA* will take into account the current case selection and weighting conditions for the variables being analyzed (case selection and weighting conditions may also be changed from the *Quick Basic Statistics - Extended Options* dialog).

See also *Block Stats* (see Chapter 3), which produce descriptive statistics and statistical graphs for data in the currently highlighted block.

Probability Calculator. Selecting this option opens the *Probability Distribution Calculator* with interactive graphs of density and distribution functions which update automatically as you change the parameters.

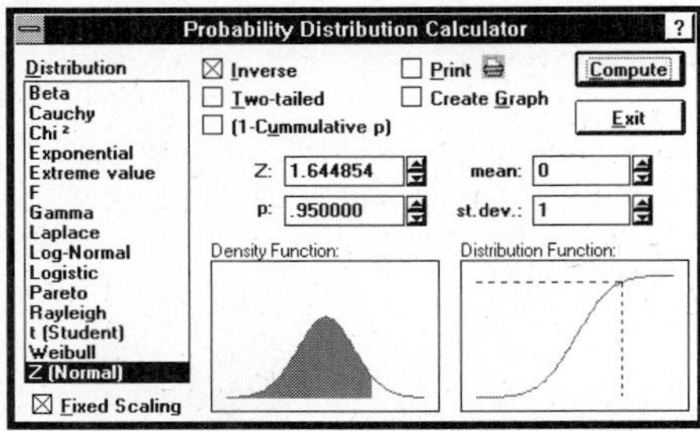

This flexible tool can be used to explore and examine shapes of a variety of theoretical distributions. Also, it offers procedures to compute probabilities for various test statistics as well as critical values (e.g., critical value of *Chi-square* significant at the *p=.05* level for a specific number of *df*).

18-23. Spreadsheet Graph Buttons

The spreadsheet graphics options accessible by pressing any of the next six buttons are similar to those also available for all results Scrollsheets (see the next toolbar, page 1067) except for minor differences as described in the following sections.

The text of the one-line data file header (displayed in the title area of the spreadsheet) is transferred to the first title field of the respective *Custom* (but not *Stats*) graphs (it can be interactively edited, customized or removed).

Dynamic links to data. All of these (currently displayed) graphs are automatically updated whenever you change the corresponding data in the spreadsheet (or the data are changed via *DDE*). The automatic links can be changed to *manual* (or disabled) for specific graphs (use the pull-down menu *Graphs*, option *Graph Data Links*), or this entire graph update facility can be customized or disabled (use the pull-down menu *Options*). Also, when saved, each of these graphs is automatically added to the Workbook list; in the *Workbook* dialog (see page 1052) the graph file can be marked as "auto-open," and the updated graph will automatically open when you open the data file.

18. Custom 2D Graphs (from the Spreadsheet)

Brings up the *Custom 2D Graphs* definition dialog allowing you to custom-define a wide variety of 2D graphs from any combinations of cases and/or variables (or their subsets) in the current spreadsheet.

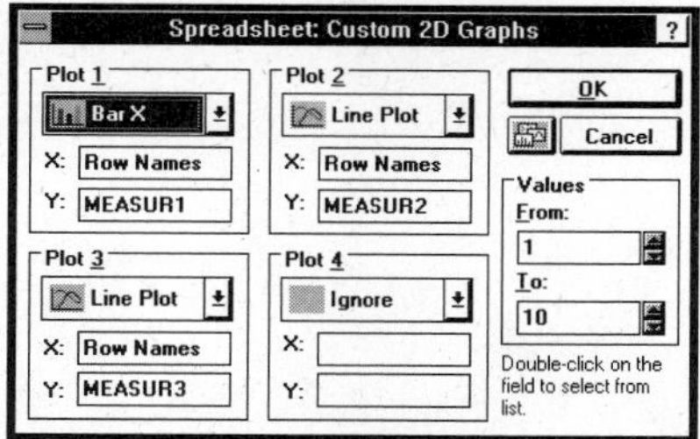

Note that not only cases and variables, but also case names and variable names can be used to define the graphs; thus not only *true-XY* (i.e., "scientific") but also simple *sequential* (i.e., "business") graphs can be defined using this facility.

Depending on the type of graph requested, case names and/or variable names are used by default to label either the axes (in true-XY graphs) or consecutive points on the axes (in sequential graphs).

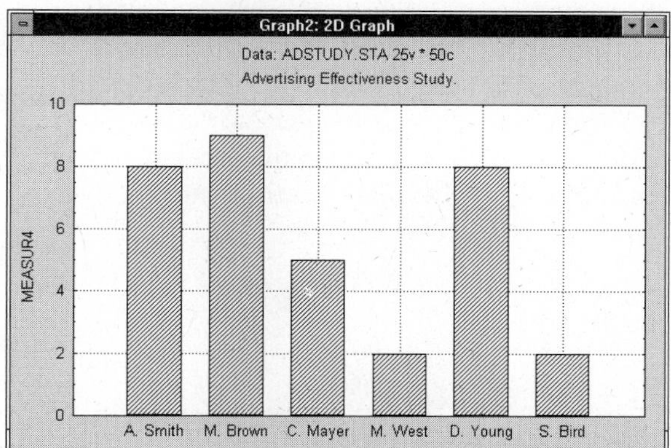

The data layout for the graph suggested by the program when the dialog appears depends on the current cursor position and/or block (highlighted) in the current spreadsheet. By default, data from the highlighted block will be plotted.

See page 1058 for information on auto-links to the data file.

19. Custom 3D Sequential Graphs (from the Spreadsheet)

Brings up the *Custom 3D Sequential Graphs* definition dialog allowing you to custom-define 3D sequential graphs from any combinations of rows and/or columns (or their subsets) in the spreadsheet.

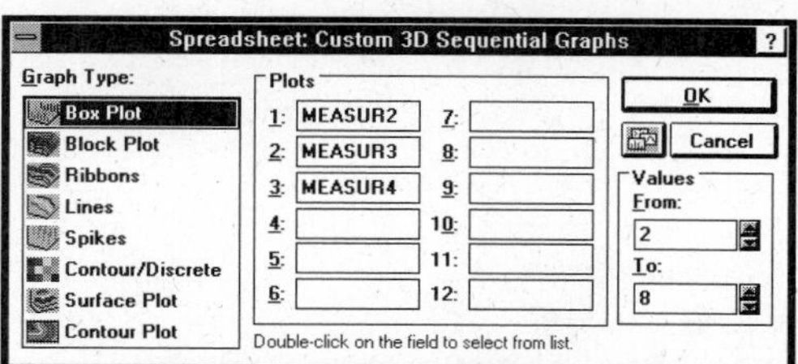

Unlike the *3D XYZ Graphs* (see the next button) where data are interpreted as triplets of *X*, *Y*, and *Z* values representing coordinates of individual observations (or units of data) in three-dimensional space, the sequential graphs provide 3D visualizations of simple sequences of values of the selected series of data (e.g., in the form of the blocks, boxes, or ribbons).

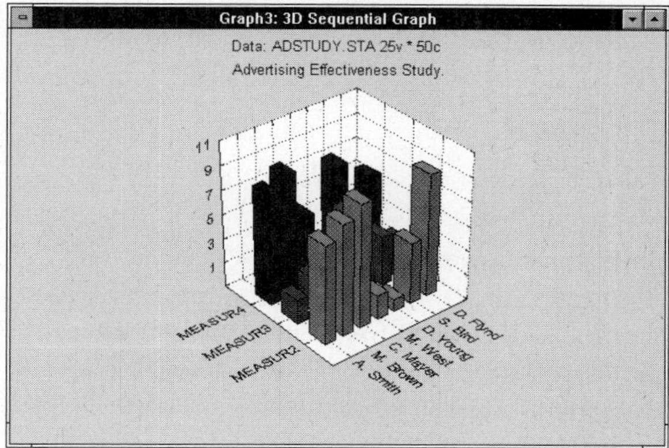

Case names or variable names (depending on whether sequences of cases or variables are plotted) are used to label the consecutive sequences of data on the *Y*-axis (e.g., *Measur2*, *Measur3*, *Measur4*).

StatSoft

The consecutive numbers of individual values in the plotted sequences of data (or case names) are represented on the *X*-axis. The actual values (represented by the "heights" of points) are plotted against the *Z*-axis. The data layout for the graph suggested by the program depends on the current cursor position and/or block (highlighted) in the current spreadsheet; by default, data from the highlighted block will be plotted.

See page 1058 for information on auto-links to the data file.

20. Custom 3D XYZ Graphs (from the Spreadsheet)

Brings up the *Custom 3D XYZ Graphs* definition dialog allowing you to custom-define 3D scatterplots and surface plots from any combinations of rows and/or columns (or their subsets) in the spreadsheet.

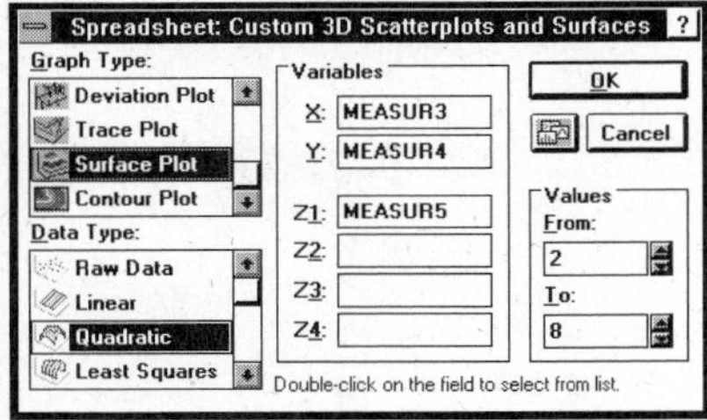

Unlike the *3D Sequential Graphs* (see the previous button) where simple sequences of data are visualized, in *3D XYZ* graphs, data are interpreted as triplets of *X*, *Y*, and *Z* (or multiple *Z*'s) values representing coordinates of individual observations (or units of data) in three-dimensional space.

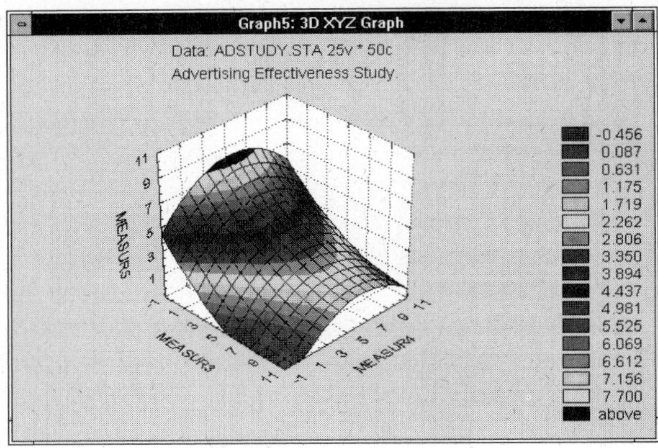

Not only cases and variables, but also case names and variable names can be used to define the *X*- and *Y*-scales (i.e., they can be defined as sequential scales). Thus, depending on the type of graph requested, case names and/or variable names are used by default to label either the (*X*- and/or *Y*-) axes or consecutive points on those axes. The *Z*-axis must represent values of the plotted cases or variables. The data layout for the graph suggested by the program depends on the current cursor and/or block (highlighted) in the current spreadsheet. By default, data from the highlighted block will be plotted.

See see page 1058 for information on auto-links to the data file.

21. Custom Matrix Graphs (from the Spreadsheet)

Brings up the *Custom Matrix Graphs* definition dialog allowing you to custom-define a variety of matrix graphs from any combinations of rows and/or columns (or their subsets) in the current spreadsheet.

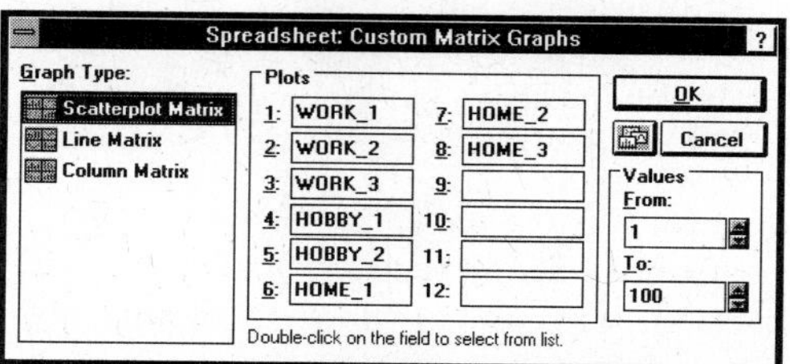

For the selected matrix plot, the selected series of data (i.e., cases or variables in the spreadsheet) are treated as "variables" in the graph and plotted against each other (depending on the type of the graph).

Note that this graph allows you to visualize correlations not only between variables (columns of data), but also between cases (rows of data).

22. Custom Icon Graphs (from the Spreadsheet)

Brings up the *Custom Icon Graphs* definition dialog allowing you to custom-define a variety of icon graphs from any combinations of rows and/or columns (or their subsets) in the current spreadsheet.

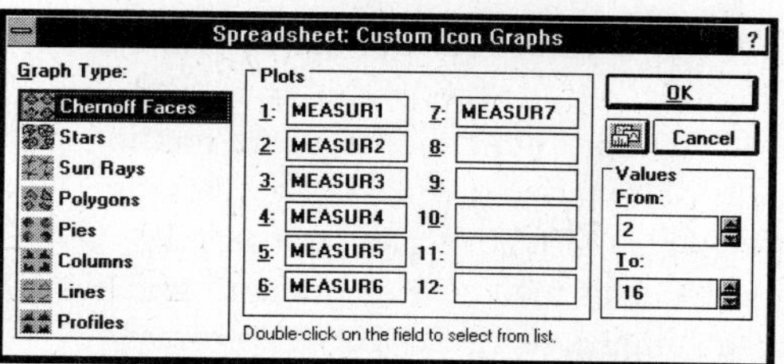

For the selected icon plot, the consecutive icons represent configurations of values of the cases or variables (selected for the graph), and they are labeled with the names of the consecutive cases or variables (respectively).

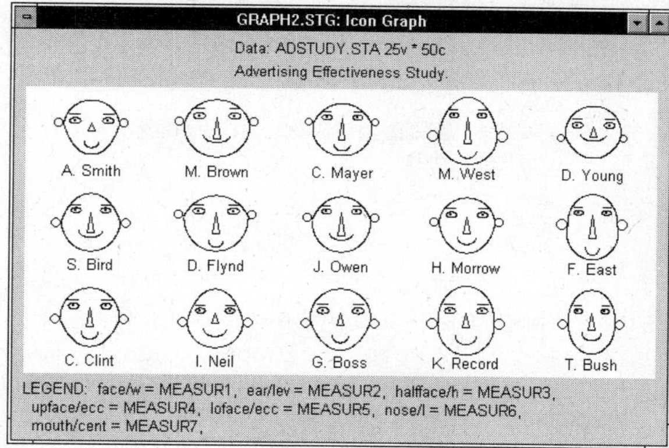

The data layout for the graph suggested by the program depends on the current cursor position and/or block (highlighted) in the current spreadsheet. By default, data from the highlighted block will be plotted.

See page 1058 for information on auto-links to the data file.

23. Quick Stats Graphs (from the Spreadsheet)

Brings up a menu of *Quick Stats Graphs* (that is, statistical graphs) for the current variable (i.e., the column where the cursor is located). Unlike *Custom Graphs* (see the previous five buttons), which provide general tools to visualize numerical

output and allow you to custom-define graphs, *Quick Stats Graphs* are predefined statistical graphs. They represent either standard methods to graphically summarize raw data (e.g., various scatterplots, histograms, or plots of central tendencies such as medians) or standard graphical analytic techniques (e.g., categorized normal probability plots, detrended probability plots, or plots of confidence intervals of regression lines).

Data: IRISDAT.STA 5v * 150c

Fisher (1936) iris data: length & width of sepals and petals,

#	1 SEPALLEN	2 SEPALWID	3 PETALLEN	4 PETALWID	5 IRISTYPE
1	5.0				SETOSA
2	6.4				VIRGINIC
3	6.5				VERSICOL
4	6.7				VIRGINIC
5	6.3				VIRGINIC
6	4.6				SETOSA
7	6.9				VIRGINIC
8	6.2				
9	5.9				
10	4.6				
11	6.1	3.0	4.6	1.4	VERSICOL
12	6.0	2.7	5.1	1.6	VERSICOL
13	6.5	3.0	5.2	2.0	VIRGINIC
14	5.6	2.5	3.9	1.1	VERSICOL

Values/Stats of SEPALWID
Histogram of SEPALWID
Box-Whisker of SEPALWID
Probability Plot of SEPALWID
Scatterplot by...
2D Histogram by...
3D Histogram by...
Box-Whisker by...
Probability Plot by...
Matrix Scatterplot...

Normal Probability
Half-Normal Prob.
Detrended

If the selected graph requires more than one variable (e.g., all categorized graphs, where the currently selected variable is plotted *across* levels of some other variable, see the next graph), a variable selection dialog will appear allowing you to select the missing variable.

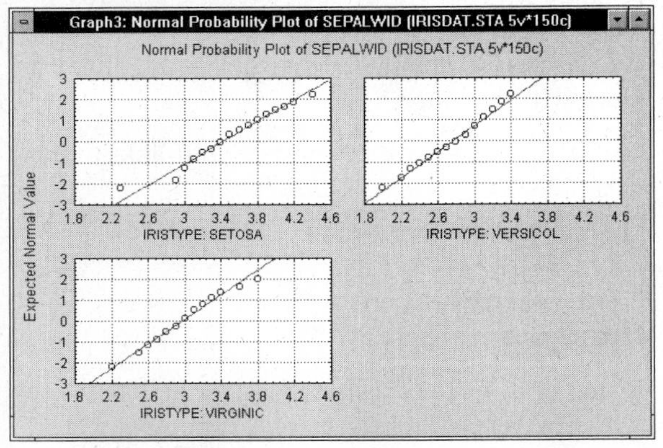

These graphs process and represent data taking into account the currently defined case selection conditions and case weights (see the *Sel: OFF* and *Weight* fields on the status bar on the bottom of the *STATISTICA* window).

The same selection of *Quick Stats Graphs* is also accessible from all Scrollsheets, but in most Scrollsheets, the selection of variables for all bivariate *Quick Stats Graphs* is automatically determined by the program to provide meaningful visualizations of the respective results (e.g., categorized graphs).

***Quick Stats Graphs* vs. *Stats Graphs*.** *Quick Stats Graphs* are easily accessible from the toolbars (as shown here) or flying menus in spreadsheets and Scrollsheets, and they include the most commonly used types of *Stats Graphs* (*Stats Graphs* are available only from the *Graphs Gallery* (see the next button) or the pull-down menu *Graphs*). Although *Quick Stats Graphs* do not offer as many options as *Stats Graphs*, they are quicker to select. Unlike *Stats Graphs*:

- *Quick Stats Graphs* can be called from flying menus and toolbars (and they do not require any pull-down menu selections),
- *Quick Stats Graphs* do not require the user to select variables (the variable selection is determined by the current cursor position within a Scrollsheet or spreadsheet), and
- *Quick Stats Graphs* do not require the user to select options from intermediate dialogs (default formats of the respective graphs are produced).

See page 1058 for information on auto-links to the data file.

***Block Stats Graphs*.** These graphs (not accessible from the toolbar but from the flying menu) produce statistical summary graphs for data in columns or rows of the currently selected block.

24. *STATISTICA* Graphs Gallery

This button (which is also available in the graph definition dialog for each graph) opens the *STATISTICA Graphs Gallery* dialog,

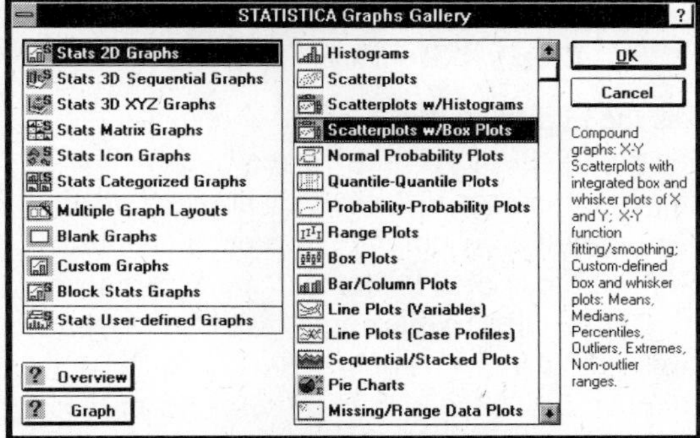

from which you can quickly and easily access all *Stats Graphs*, *Custom Graphs*, *Blank Graphs*, and *Stats User-defined Graphs*. To select the highlighted graph, double-click on its name (or press the *OK* button).

25. Open Data File

Opens the file selection window allowing you to select a data file (file name extension *.*sta*) and then opens the selected file in the spreadsheet window (replacing the current window). *STATISTICA* data files can also be opened directly from the *File Manager* by double-clicking on the respective file name.

Note that a list of recently-used data files is automatically appended to the pull-down menu *File*, as shown below.

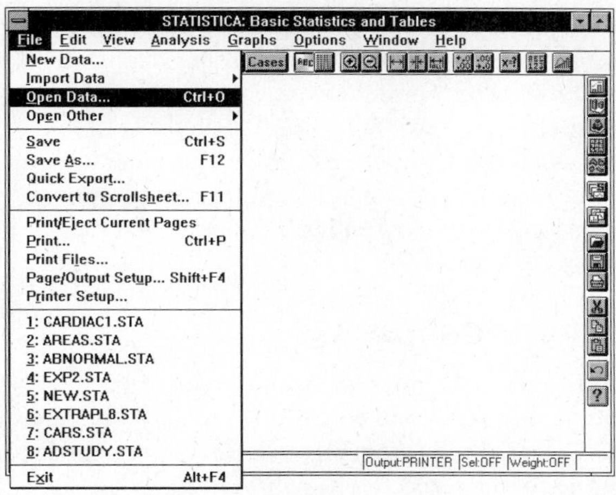

The length of this list can be configured in the *General Defaults* dialog, accessed from the *Options* pull-down menu.

26. Save Data File

Saves the current data file under the same or a different file name (the default data file name extension is *.*sta*). If an existing file is being overwritten, then, by default, the previous file is renamed into a backup file (file name extension *.*bak* instead of *.*sta*).

27. Print Data File (or Highlighted Block)

Prints data from the current spreadsheet. This is a shortcut method to send the current data file to an output channel: printer, disk file, or the *Text/output Window* (depending on the current setting of the output, see the clickable *Output* field on the status bar on the bottom of the *STATISTICA* window, page 1106).

Unlike the *Print...* (or CTRL+P) option available in the pull-down menu *File*, pressing this shortcut button will not open the *Print Data* options dialog (containing options to customize the format and contents of the data listing). Instead, the entire file (or a highlighted block, if one is selected) will be sent to the output. The format of the data listing will follow the current *Print...* settings (accessible from the pull-down menu *File*). See the section on the status bar (*Output* field, page 1106) for information about report styles, formatting options, adjusting margins, printing gridlines, and other output options.

28. Cut (Block)

Cuts (removes) the contents of the currently highlighted cells and copies them to the Clipboard. The cleared cells are replaced with the missing data values of the respective variables.

***Clipboard* operations vs. *Global* operations on cases or variables.** Note that unlike the *Global* operations performed on ranges of cases or variables and treating them as logical units (see the buttons Vars and Cases, pages 1053 and 1054, respectively) the Clipboard operations follow the standard spreadsheet conventions and apply only to the contents of the selected cells. They depend entirely on the current block (highlight) and cursor position.

For example, note that the *Global* operation of deleting or moving variables (see the button Vars, page 1053) will affect (remove) not only the contents of the respective columns but also the columns themselves; thus they will change the structure of the data file (and those operations will always be performed on entire variables regardless of whether all cases or only a subset of cases is currently highlighted in the selected variables). In the case of Clipboard operations, however, only the segment of data which is highlighted will be cut, and (following the common spreadsheet conventions) pasting will always begin from the current cursor position, and proceed down.

Thus, for example, if in order to move a variable, you (a) highlighted and cut an entire column, (b) highlighted another (entire) column and then (c) pasted the Clipboard contents to that new location (intending to "replace" the previous values) -- the operation will be performed as intended only if you have placed the cursor at the top of the new column. If you have placed it somewhere in the middle, then the pasting will start from that point down.

29. Copy (Block)

Copies the highlighted part of the spreadsheet to the Clipboard (to select the entire spreadsheet, click on the upper left corner of the spreadsheet). Selecting this option will copy not only the contents in the highlighted block of cells but also the case names (or numbers) and variable names associated with the highlighted cells (use *Copy Raw* from the pull-down menu *Edit* to copy only the contents of the highlighted block of cells without the corresponding case and variable names).

Data: ADSTUDY.STA 25v * 50c

Advertising Effectiveness Study.

NUMERIC VALUES	3 MEASUR1	4 MEASUR2	5 MEASUR3	6 MEASUR4	7 MEASUR5
J. Baker	9	1	6	8	1
A. Smith	6	7	1	8	0
M. Brown	9	8	2	9	8
C. Mayer	7	9	0	5	9
M. West	7	1	6	2	8
D. Young	6	0	0	8	3
S. Bird	7	4	3	2	5
D. Flynd	9	9	2	6	6
J. Owen	7	8	2	3	6

Copy:

	MEASUR2	MEASUR3	MEASUR4
A. Smith	7	1	8
M. Brown	8	2	9
C. Mayer	9	0	5
M. West	1	6	2
D. Young	0	0	8
S. Bird	4	3	2

Copy Raw:

7	1	8
8	2	9
9	0	5
1	6	2
0	0	8
4	3	2

Note that blocks copied from *STATISTICA* spreadsheets are tab-delimited. Thus, if pasted into a word processor document, they will appear as tab-

delimited tables (compatible with table generators in Windows word processors, e.g., MS Word).

Technical Note. In order to increase compatibility with other applications, *STATISTICA* automatically produces a variety of special Clipboard formats. For example, spreadsheet formats are produced and will be used when you paste the contents of the Clipboard (copied from *STATISTICA*) into a spreadsheet document in MS Excel or Lotus for Windows.

30. Paste (Block)

Pastes the current contents of the Clipboard into the spreadsheet starting at the current cursor position. See the section on the *Cut* operation (button, above) for a description of differences between *Global* operations on cases and variables (which treat them as logical units, see the buttons Vars and Cases, pages 1053 and 1054, respectively), and Clipboard operations which follow the standard spreadsheet Clipboard conventions. For example, when you intend to copy (via the Clipboard) an entire variable to a new location, make sure that the cursor is placed at the top of the destination column, because the data will always be pasted from the cursor down (even if the entire destination column is highlighted).

Clipboard operations in the spreadsheet. When you copy or move a block in the spreadsheet (e.g., via *Drag-and-Drop*), the values which are copied will depend on the display mode of the spreadsheet. If the spreadsheet is displaying numeric values (or value labels) when the block is copied to the Clipboard, then only those numeric values (or value labels) will be copied. If the spreadsheet is displaying text values when the block is copied to the Clipboard, then not only are the text values copied to the Clipboard, but also the corresponding numeric values and value labels (if any). This may result in the assignment of text values to numeric values that did not previously have text value equivalents (see below).

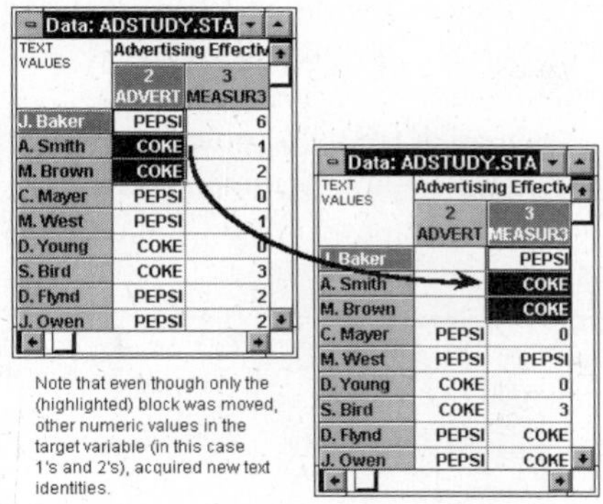

Note that even though only the (highlighted) block was moved, other numeric values in the target variable (in this case 1's and 2's), acquired new text identities.

Dates (and times). In *STATISTICA* data files, value display formats are properties of variables and not individual cells. Therefore, if you paste into *STATISTICA* a block of data containing formatted date (or date/time) values (e.g., from MS Excel), the dates will appear as Julian (integer) values (e.g., *34092* instead of *May 3, 1993*) unless you set the format of the appropriate variables to *Date*in the *Variable Specs* dialog.

31. Undo

Select this option in order to reverse (undo) the last specific command or action in the spreadsheet (such as editing, moving or copying blocks, random fill, recoding or ranking variables, etc.). The *STATISTICA* spreadsheet supports multi-level undo (with 16 buffers); therefore, you can undo multiple actions by selecting this option consecutively (up to 16 times).

Keyboard shortcut: CTRL+Z (or ALT+BKSP)

 32. Help

This button accesses the *STATISTICA* on-line *Electronic Manual* (the last button on all toolbars). *STATISTICA* provides comprehensive on-line documentation for all program procedures and all options available in a context-sensitive manner by pressing the F1 key or the help button [?] on the toolbar or the caption bar of all dialog boxes (there is a total of over 10 megabytes of compressed documentation included). Due to its dynamic Hyper-text organization (and various facilities allowing you to customize the help system), it is usually faster to use the on-line documentation (*Electronic Manual*) than to look for information in the printed manuals.

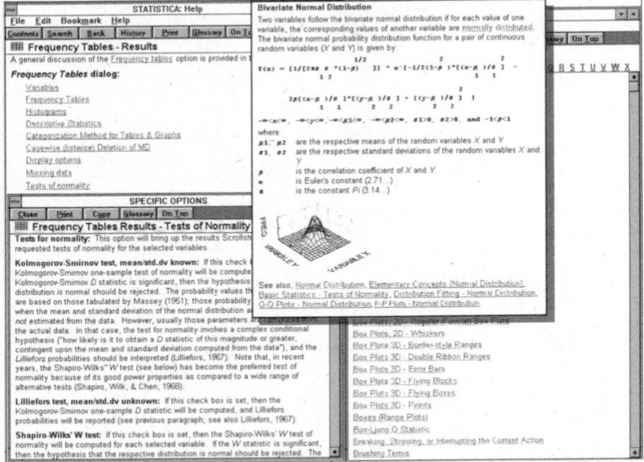

Help is also available by double-clicking anywhere on the help message area of the status bar on the bottom of the *STATISTICA* window (the status line also displays short explanations of the pull-down menu options or toolbar buttons, available when an option is highlighted or a button pressed). For more information on any option, you may press the help key (F1) when the option is highlighted or selected.

Statistical Advisor. A *Statistical Advisor* facility is built into the on-line help system. When you select the *Advisor* option from the pull-down menu *Help*, the program will ask you a set of simple questions about the nature of the research problem and the type of your data, and then it will suggest to you the statistical procedures which appear most relevant (and tell you where to look for them in the *STATISTICA* system).

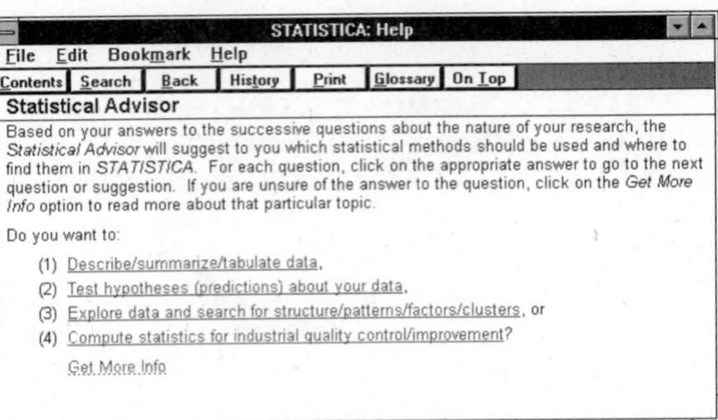

SCROLLSHEET (SCROLLABLE OUTPUT WINDOW) TOOLBAR

Scrollsheets are "spreadsheet-like" tables used in *STATISTICA* to display the numeric and text output. Scrollsheets can hold anywhere from a short line to megabytes of output, and they offer a variety of options to facilitate reviewing the results, visualizing them in predefined and custom-defined graphs, and converting them into presentation-quality reports. Scrollsheets support *Drag-and-Drop* operations, block extrapolation of values, and split and variable-speed scrolling (split scrolling is shown below).

STATISTICA: Basic Statistics and Tables

File Edit View Analysis Graphs Options Window Help

1.29749615479183 Columns Rows

Decrease Decimal Tool

Descriptive Statistics (adstudy.sta)

Variable	Mean	Confid. -95.000%	Confid. +95.000%	Variance	Std.Dev.
GENDER	1.440000	1.297496	1.582504	.251429	.501427
ADVERT	1.460000	1.316919	1.603081	.253469	.503457
MEASUR1	5.900000	5.227345	6.572655	5.602041	2.366863
MEASUR2	4.540000	3.719507	5.360493	8.335102	2.887058
MEASUR3	4.140000	3.365389	4.914611	7.428980	2.725615
MEASUR4	5.740000	4.991800	6.488200	6.931020	2.632683
MEASUR17	4.480000	3.612575	5.347425	9.315918	3.052199
MEASUR18	4.540000	3.717501	5.362499	8.375918	2.894118
MEASUR19	4.080000	3.290989	4.869011	7.707755	2.776284
MEASUR20	4.300000	3.516418	5.083582	7.602041	2.757180
MEASUR21	4.440000	3.570828	5.309172	9.353469	3.058344
MEASUR22	5.080000	4.301504	5.858496	7.503673	2.739283
MEASUR23	4.640000	3.851156	5.428844	7.704490	2.775696

Data: ADSTUDY.STA 25v * 50c   Cont Descriptive Statistics

Ready   Output:OFF   Sel:OFF   Weight:OFF

The Scrollsheet toolbar provides quick access to the most commonly used output management facilities and graphs of the Scrollsheet data.

All program control facilities that are accessible via the toolbar buttons listed below are also available from menus and via the keyboard (thus, they can be recorded into mouse-independent macros). The layout of toolbars can be customized (see page 1049).

0. The Show Field

The *Show Field* displays the value of the currently highlighted cell at a higher precision than will fit in the current column widths.

1.2   1.234567   1.23456789012346

The width of the *Show Field* can be adjusted (toggled) by clicking on it with the mouse or by using the *Change Show* option in the pull-down menu *View*.

1. Module Switcher

Brings up the *STATISTICA Module Switcher* (this button is common to all toolbars). The *Switcher* gives you quick access to all "modules" (i.e., groups of analytic procedures) available in your version of *STATISTICA*. Depending on the current configuration, the *Switcher* may open new modules into the same or new application windows.

2. Workbook Management

Brings up the *Workbook* dialog (this is always the second button on all toolbars); this dialog allows you to enter a one-line *File Header* which appears at the top of the spreadsheet, detailed file information or notes about the data set's contents, source, etc., and to manage all supplementary files (e.g., graphs, reports, programs) used with the current data set. See page 1052 for more information on managing workbooks of files.

3. Zoom-in

Zooms-in (increases the font size and proportionately increases all parts of the Scrollsheet).

Descriptive Statistics (adstudy.sta)

Variable	Valid N	Mean	Conf -95.00
GENDER	50	1.440000	1.297
ADVERT	50	1.460000	1.316
MEASUR1	50	5.900000	5.227

4. Zoom-out

Zooms-out (decreases the font size and proportionately decreases all parts of the Scrollsheet).

Descriptive Statistics (adstudy.sta)

Variable	Valid N	Mean	Confid. -95.000%	Confid. +95.000%	Median	Sum
GENDER	50	1.440000	1.297496	1.582504	1.000000	72.0000
ADVERT	50	1.460000	1.316919	1.603081	1.000000	73.0000
MEASUR1	50	5.900000	5.227345	6.572655	6.000000	295.0000
MEASUR2	50	4.540000	3.719507	5.360493	5.000000	227.0000
MEASUR3	50	4.140000	3.365389	4.914611	3.500000	207.0000
MEASUR4	50	5.520000	4.764281	6.275719	6.000000	276.0000
MEASUR5	50	3.960000	3.211469	4.708531	4.500000	198.0000
MEASUR6	50	4.840000	3.981898	5.698102	4.500000	242.0000
MEASUR7	50	4.660000	3.950704	5.369296	5.000000	233.0000
MEASUR8	50	3.720000	2.922263	4.517737	3.000000	186.0000
MEASUR9	50	4.160000	3.294248	5.025752	4.000000	208.0000
MEASUR10	50	3.940000	3.072252	4.807748	4.000000	197.0000

This option may be particularly useful to review large tables where data which meet particular criteria (e.g., significant correlation coefficients) are marked (see the button, below).

5. Increase the Column Width

Increases the column width (incrementally). The same effect can be achieved by dragging any border line between Scrollsheet column headers (names) with the mouse.

Descriptive Statistics (adstudy.sta)

Variable	Valid N	Mean	Confid. -95.000%	Confid. +95.000%
GENDER	50	1.4400	1.2975	1.5825
ADVERT	50	1.4600	1.3169	1.6031
MEASUR1	50	5.9000	5.2273	6.5727
MEASUR2	50	4.5400	3.7195	5.3605
MEASUR3	50	4.1400	3.3654	4.9146
MEASUR4	50	5.5200	4.7643	6.2757
MEASUR5	50	3.9600	3.2115	4.7085

Note that the column width, as well as the margin width, value display format and column names can also be adjusted in the *Scrollsheet Column Specifications* dialog. This dialog is accessible by double-clicking on the respective column name in the Scrollsheet (analogous to double-clicking on variable names in the spreadsheet).

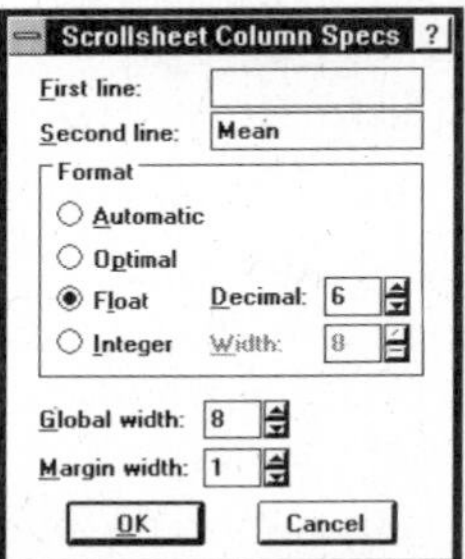

For example, the above dialog is displayed when you double-click on the column (*Mean*) highlighted in the Scrollsheet shown in the previous section.

6. Decrease the Column Width

Decreases the column width (incrementally, see also the previous button). The same effect can be achieved by dragging any border line between Scrollsheet column headers (names) with the mouse.

7. Adjust Column Widths, Margins

Adjusts the column width, margin width and the width of the row name (first) column in the Scrollsheet by a specified amount of space.

The margins (which can be adjusted in this dialog) separate the active display field from the gridlines.

8. Add One Decimal

Adds one decimal place to the value display format of the current variable (for example, after pressing this button, the value *12.23* will be displayed as *12.234*).

9. Remove One Decimal

Removes one decimal place from the value display format of the current variable (for example, after pressing this button, the value *12.234* will be displayed as *12.23*).

10. Mark Cells

Marks (or un-marks) individual values or a block of values (if one is currently selected) in the Scrollsheet to make them stand out from the rest. The marked Scrollsheet values will be identified by a color other than the default data value color (by default, marked values appear red, but the color can be changed by using the pull-down menu *View*, or the *Display...* option in the pull-down menu *Options*). When printed, the marked cells will be identified with an * (asterisk) next to the value (other options to handle marked cells in printed or saved reports are available and can be selected in the *Print Scrollsheet* dialog, allowing you to customize various aspects of the Scrollsheet printing).

Cells marked by *STATISTICA*. Many procedures in *STATISTICA* automatically mark specific cells or blocks in Scrollsheets in order to "highlight" some results (e.g., unusually high frequencies in a frequency table, statistically significant correlation coefficients in a correlation matrix, or statistically significant effects in an ANOVA table of all effects). For example, in the following Scrollsheet, note that (among others) the correlation between *Gender* and *Measur7*, and between *Advert* and *Measur9* are marked in a different color (indicating significance at $p<.05$):

Correlations (adstudy.sta)

BASIC STATS — Marked correlations are significant at p < .05000
N=50 (Casewise deletion of missing data)

Variable	GENDER	ADVERT	MEASUR 1	MEASUR 2	MEASUR 3	MEASUR 4	MEASUR 5	MEASUR 6
MEASUR6	.05	-.15	-.01	.15	.14	-.16	.23	1.00
MEASUR7	-.37	.05	-.12	.05	.04	.01	-.05	.12
MEASUR8	-.04	-.02	-.02	-.08	-.19	.01	-.19	-.33
MEASUR9	-.15	.38	-.12	-.21	.21	.10	-.47	-.27
MEASUR10	.04	.03	-.15	.05	-.09	-.24	-.07	.13
MEASUR11	-.24	.06	.18	-.21	-.02	.09	-.01	-.15
MEASUR12	-.10	-.27	.03	-.01	-.11	-.01	.11	.04
MEASUR13	-.19	.27	-.21	.14	-.14	-.12	-.03	.00
MEASUR14	.07	-.25	-.04	-.21	-.22	.14	.17	.03
MEASUR15	.02	-.05	-.08	-.00	.30	-.21	.03	.21
MEASUR16	.06	.04	-.07	.07	-.16	.11	.43	.20

Such Scrollsheets usually offer an option to change the criterion used to select the cells to be highlighted (e.g., the *p*-level for correlation coefficients) via the **Options** button on the toolbars of the Scrollsheets, which are initially displayed with marked cells.

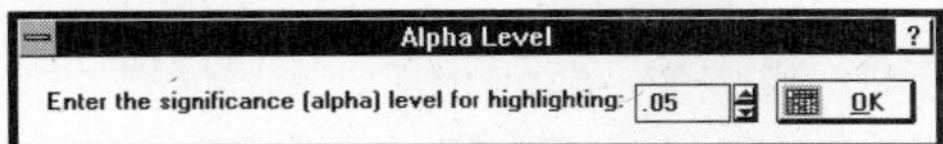

Highlighted values in the *Graph Data Editor*. The *Graph Data Editor* is a special type of Scrollsheet associated with each graph, which contains the specific values displayed in the graph. The values highlighted in that *Editor* (i.e., displayed in a different color) are those which are *selected* using the interactive *Brushing* tool in the graph (see the graph toolbar button, page 1085).

Note that the term *highlighted* has a specific meaning when used in the context of brushing data points in the graph. There, data points which are *highlighted* (in the graph) are those which are only identified with the mouse but still not *marked*, *labeled*, or *turned off*, as long as a brushing *Action* (e.g., labeling or marking) is not executed.

11. Quick Basic Stats

As in spreadsheets (see page 1057), pressing this toolbar button brings up a flying menu of *Quick Basic Stats* for the variables in the current Scrollsheet.

Correlations (irisdat.sta)

BASIC STATS — Marked correlations are significant at p < .05000; N=150 (Casewise deletion of missing data)

Variable	SEPALLEN	SEPALWID	PETALLEN	PETALWID	IRISTYPE
SEPALLEN	1.00	-.12	.87	.82	.78
SEPALWID	-.12	1.00	-.43	-.37	-.43
PETALLEN	.87	-.43	1.00	.96	.95
PETALWID	.82				.96
IRISTYPE	.78				1.00

Descriptives of SEPALLEN-PETALWID
Correlations of SEPALLEN-PETALWID
Frequencies of SEPALLEN-PETALWID
Descriptives by IRISTYPE
Correlations by IRISTYPE
Frequencies by IRISTYPE
Probability Calculator...
More...

Refer to page 1057 for details about the selection of variables listed in the *Quick Basic Stats* menu.

12-17. Scrollsheet Graph Buttons

The Scrollsheet graphics options accessible by pressing any of the next six buttons are similar to those available for data spreadsheets (see the previous toolbar) except for minor differences as described in the following sections.

The text of the Scrollsheet titles is transferred to the title fields of the respective *Custom* (but not *Stats*) graphs (it can be interactively edited, customized or removed).

12. Custom 2D Graphs (from the Scrollsheet)

Brings up the *Custom 2D Graphs* definition dialog allowing you to custom-define a wide variety of 2D graphs from any combinations of rows and/or columns (or their subsets) in the current Scrollsheet.

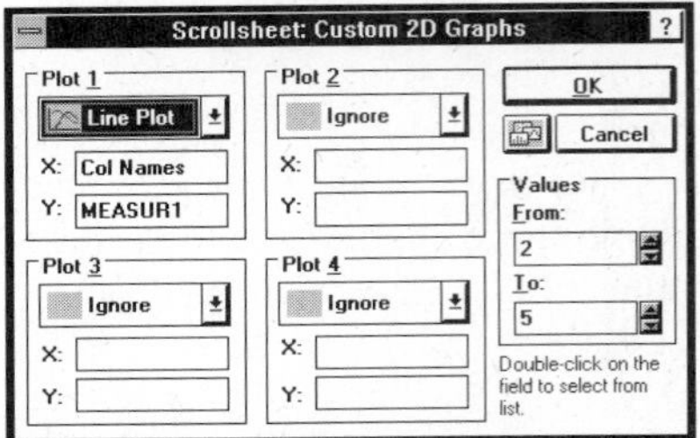

Note that not only rows and columns, but also row names and column names can be used to define the graphs; thus not only *true-XY* (i.e., "scientific") but also simple *sequential* (i.e., "business") graphs can be defined using this facility. Depending on the type of graph requested, row names and/or column names are used by default to label either the axes (in true-XY graphs) or consecutive points on the axes (in sequential graphs).

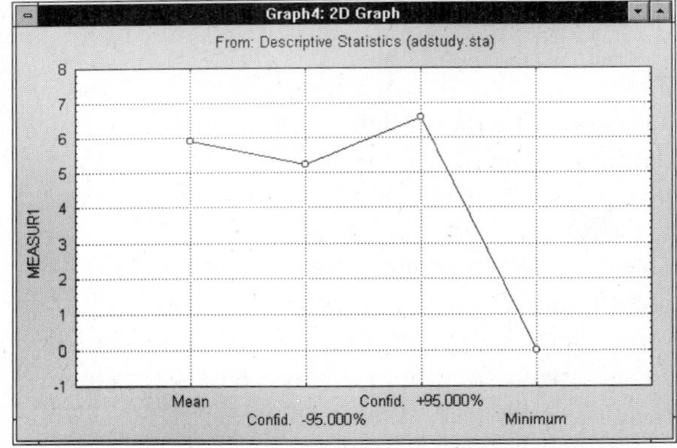

The data layout for the graph suggested by the program when the dialog appears depends on the current cursor position and/or block (highlighted) in the current Scrollsheet. By default, data from the highlighted block will be plotted.

13. Custom 3D Sequential Graphs (from the Scrollsheet)

Brings up the *Custom 3D Sequential Graphs* definition dialog allowing you to custom-define 3D sequential graphs from any combination of rows and/or columns (or their subsets) in the current Scrollsheet.

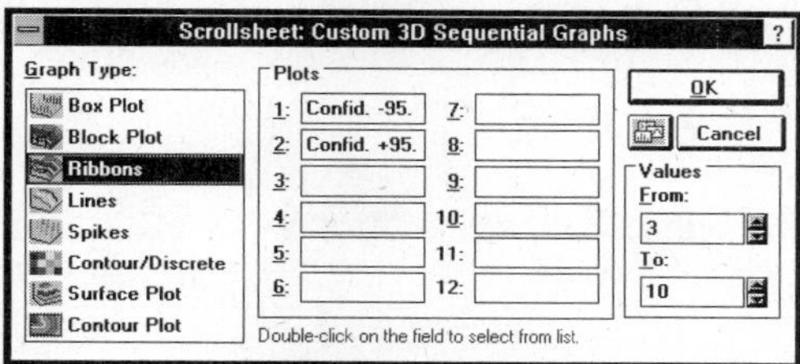

Unlike the *3D XYZ Graphs* (see the next button) where data are interpreted as triplets of *X*, *Y*, and *Z* values representing coordinates of individual observations (or units of data) in three-dimensional space, the sequential graphs provide 3D visualizations only of simple sequences of values of the selected series of data (e.g., in the form of blocks, boxes, or ribbons).

Scrollsheet row names or column names (depending on whether sequences of rows or cases are plotted) are used to label the consecutive sequences of data on the *Y*-axis. The consecutive numbers of individual values in the plotted sequences of data are represented on the *X*-axis. The actual values (represented by the "heights" of points) are plotted against the *Z*-axis.

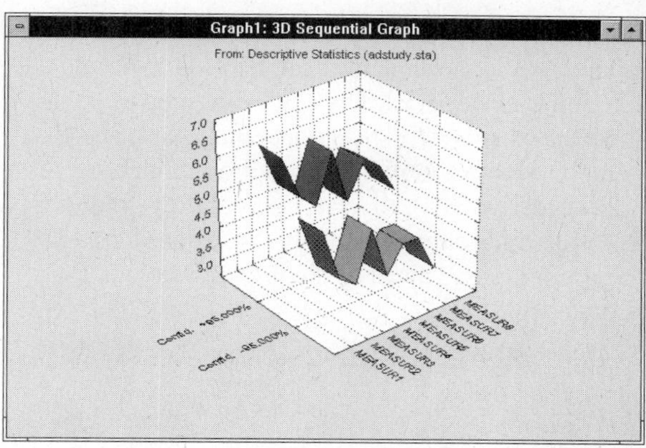

The data layout for the graph suggested by the program depends on the current cursor position and/or block (highlighted) in the current Scrollsheet. By default, data from the highlighted block will be plotted.

14. Custom 3D XYZ Graphs (from the Scrollsheet)

Brings up the *Custom 3D XYZ Graphs* definition dialog allowing you to custom-define 3D scatterplots and surface plots from any combinations of rows and/or columns (or their subsets) in the current Scrollsheet.

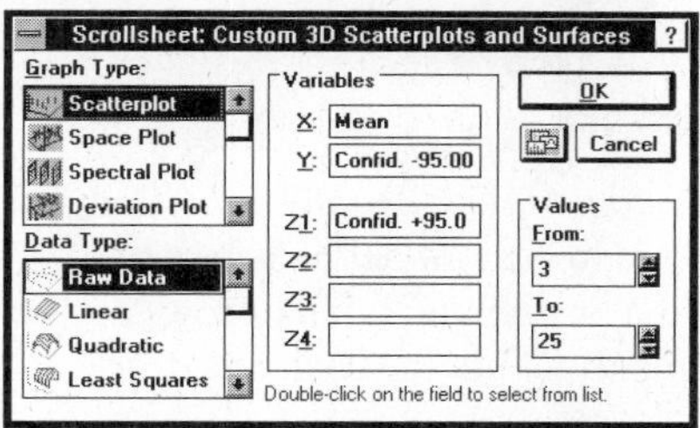

Unlike the *3D Sequential Graphs* (see the previous button) where simple sequences of data are visualized, in the 3D XYZ graphs data are interpreted as triplets of *X*, *Y*, and *Z* (or multiple *Z*'s) values representing coordinates of individual observations (or units of data) in three-dimensional space. Not only rows and columns, but also row names and column names can be used to define the *X*- and *Y*-scales (i.e., they can be defined as sequential scales). Thus, depending on the type of graph requested, row names and/or column names are used by default to label either the (*X*- and/or *Y*-) axes or consecutive points on those axes. The *Z*-axis represents values of the plotted rows or columns.

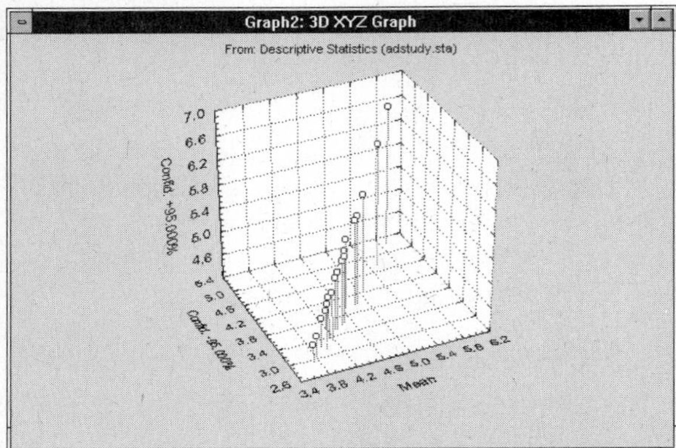

The data layout for the graph suggested by the program depends on the current cursor and/or block (highlighted) in the current Scrollsheet. By default, data from the highlighted block will be plotted.

15. Custom Matrix Graphs (from the Scrollsheet)

Brings up the *Custom Matrix Graphs* definition dialog allowing you to custom-define a variety of matrix graphs from any combination of rows and/or columns (or their subsets) in the current Scrollsheet.

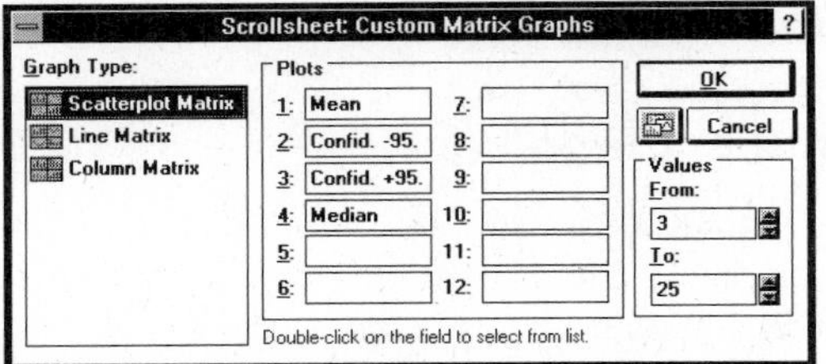

For the requested type of matrix plot, the selected series of data (i.e., rows or columns in the Scrollsheet) are treated as "variables" in the graph and plotted against each other (depending on the type of the graph).

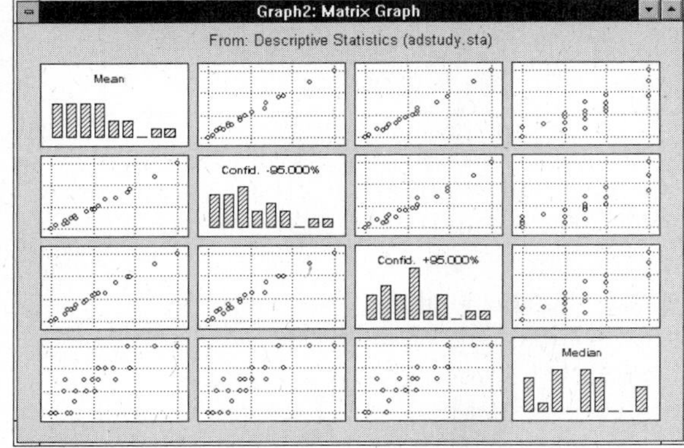

Note that either columns or rows of values in the Scrollsheet can be represented as "variables" plotted in the graph.

16. Custom Icon Graphs (from the Scrollsheet)

Brings up the *Custom Icon Graph* Icon definition dialog allowing you to custom-define a variety of icon graphs from any combination of rows and/or columns (or their subsets) in the current Scrollsheet.

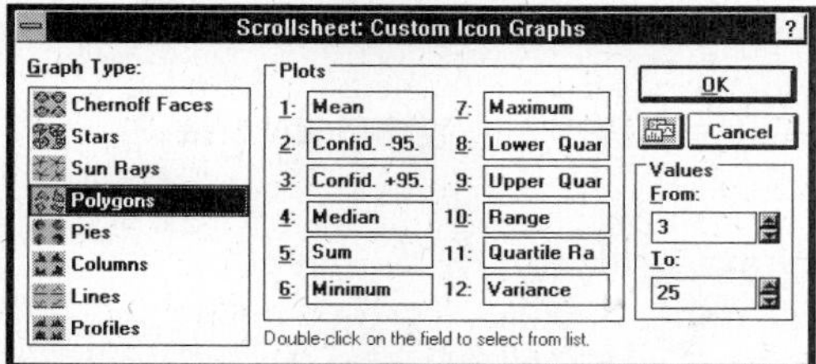

For the selected icon plot, the consecutive icons represent configurations of values of the rows or columns (selected for the graph), and they are labeled with the names of the consecutive rows or columns (depending on whether rows or columns are plotted).

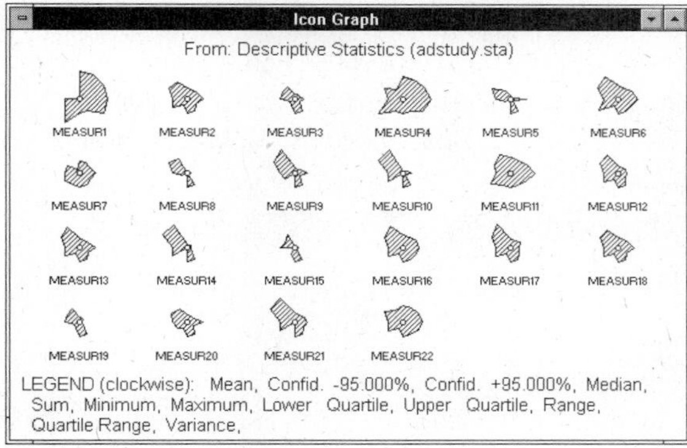

The data layout for the graph suggested by the program depends on the current cursor position and/or block (highlighted) in the current Scrollsheet; by default, data from the highlighted block will be plotted.

17. Quick Stats Graphs (from the Scrollsheet)

Brings up a menu of *Quick Stats Graphs* (that is, statistical graphs) for the current Scrollsheet.

Correlations (adstudy.sta)

Continue...

Marked correlations are significant at p < .05000
N=50 (Casewise deletion of missing data)

Variable	MEASUR4	MEASUR5	MEASUR6	MEASUR7	MEASUR8
MEASUR8	.0090	-.1948	-.3305	.0531	1.0000
MEASUR9	.0953	-.4672			
MEASUR10	-.2374	-.0663			
MEASUR11	.0945	-.0051			
MEASUR12	-.0101	.1078			
MEASUR13	-.1171	.0315			
MEASUR14	.1387	.1655			
MEASUR15	-.2083	.0298			
MEASUR16	.1058	.4318			
MEASUR17	.2477	-.0255			
MEASUR18	.0025	.1635			
MEASUR19	.0578	-.0191			

Scatterplot/Conf.
Values/Stats of MEASUR5
Histogram of MEASUR5
Box-Whisker of MEASUR5
Probability Plot of MEASUR5
Scatterplot by MEASUR9
2D Histogram by MEASUR9
3D Histogram by MEASUR9
Box-Whisker by MEASUR9
Probability Plot by MEASUR9
Swap MEASUR5 and MEASUR9
Matrix Scatterplot...
Normal Probability
Half-Normal Prob.
Detrended

Unlike *Custom Graphs* (see the previous five buttons), which provide a general tool to visualize numerical output and allow you to custom-define graphs, *Quick Stats Graphs* are predefined statistical graphs. They offer either graphical methods which are specific for the type of results displayed in the current Scrollsheet (e.g., icon plots of residuals), or they represent standard methods to graphically summarize and analyze raw data (e.g., various scatterplots, histograms, or plots of central tendencies such as medians, categorized normal probability plots, detrended probability plots). Some Scrollsheets offer non-standard graphs; in most Scrollsheets, however, the variables which will be represented in the graph (see the menu, above) depend on the current cursor position in the Scrollsheet and the type of the Scrollsheet.

For example, in descriptive statistics Scrollsheets, the variable represented by the row where the cursor is located will be suggested for graphs. For the graphs which require more than one variable (e.g., scatterplots or all categorized graphs, where the currently selected variable is plotted across levels of some other variable), the second variable will also be suggested based on the current cursor position, or the global categorical variable applicable to multiple rows and/or columns of this Scrollsheet (depending on the contents of the Scrollsheet).

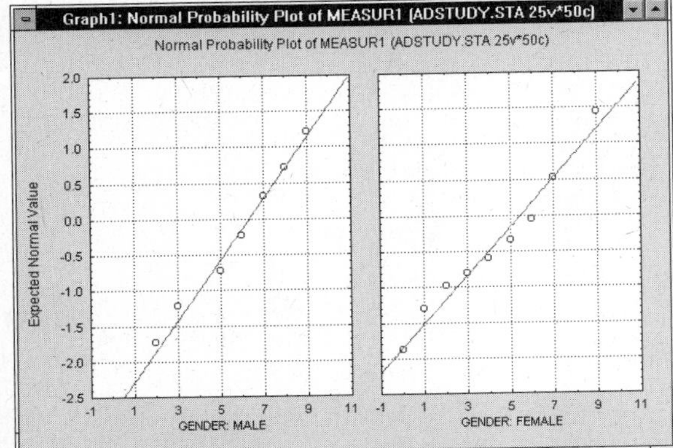

In cases when the secondary variable cannot be derived from the contents of the current Scrollsheet (or from the design of the analysis), a variable selection dialog will appear allowing you to select the missing variable.

Note that these graphs process and represent data taking into account the currently defined case selection conditions and case weights (see the *Sel: OFF* and *Weight* fields on the status bar on the bottom of the *STATISTICA* window).

Quick Stats Graphs vs. Stats Graphs. *Quick Stats Graphs* are easily accessible from the toolbars (as shown here) or flying menus in spreadsheets and Scrollsheets, and they include the most commonly used types of *Stats Graphs* (*Stats Graphs* are available only from the *Graphs Gallery* (see the next button) or the pull-down menu *Graphs*). Although *Quick Stats Graphs* do not offer as many options as *Stats Graphs*, they are quicker to select. Unlike *Stats Graphs*:

- *Quick Stats Graphs* can be called from flying menus and toolbars (they do not require any pull-down menu selections),
- *Quick Stats Graphs* do not require the user to select variables (the variable selection is determined by the current cursor position within a Scrollsheet or spreadsheet), and
- *Quick Stats Graphs* do not require the user to select options from intermediate dialogs (default formats of the respective graphs are produced).

Block Stats Graphs. These graphs (not accessible from the toolbar but from the flying menu or the *Graphs Gallery*) produce statistical summary graphs for data in columns or rows of the currently selected block.

18. *STATISTICA* Graphs Gallery

This button (which is also available in the graph definition dialog for each graph) opens the *STATISTICA Graphs Gallery* dialog, in which you can quickly and easily access all *Stats Graphs*, *Custom Graphs*, *Blank Graphs*, and *Stats User-defined Graphs*.

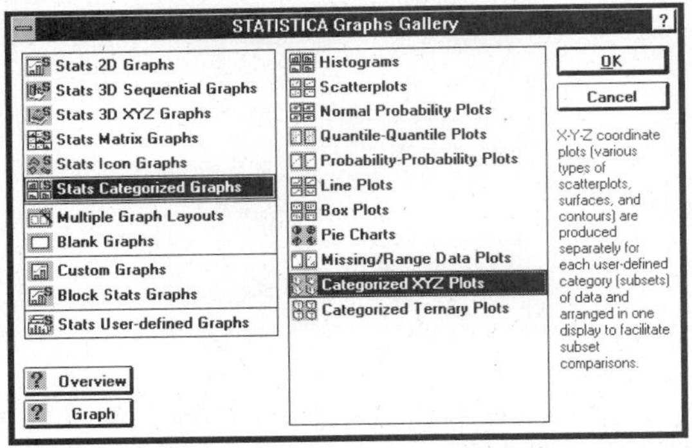

The same selection of graphs is also available in the pull-down menu *Graphs*. To select the highlighted graph, double-click on its name (or press the *OK* button)

19. Open Scrollsheet File

Opens the file selection window allowing you to select a Scrollsheet file (file name extension **.scr*) and then opens the selected file in a new Scrollsheet window.

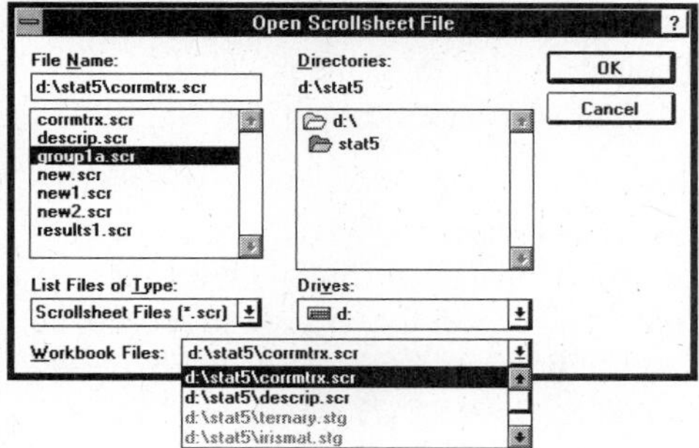

Note that every file *Open/Save* dialog in *STATISTICA* features easy access to the list of all files used with the current data set (see information on Workbooks, page 1052). Therefore, any file (of the relevant type) from the Workbook list can be easily located and selected by double-clicking on it. Workbook files which cannot be opened in the current dialog are dimmed.

20. Save Scrollsheet File

Saves the current Scrollsheet under the same file name (if one exists) or a new file name (the default Scrollsheet file name extension is **.scr*). See the previous button for information on accessing the list of Workbook files from all *Open/Save* dialogs. While saving, any Workbook file name can be selected from the list if you wish to overwrite it.

21. Print Scrollsheet (or Highlighted Block)

Prints data from the current Scrollsheet. This is a shortcut method to send the contents of the current Scrollsheet to an output channel: printer, disk file, and/or the *Text/output Window* (depending on the current setting of the output, see the clickable *Output* field on the status bar on the bottom of the *STATISTICA* window; see page 1106); the relevant dialog is shown below.

Unlike the *Print...* (or CTRL+P) option available in the pull-down menu *File*, pressing this shortcut button will not open the *Print Scrollsheet* options dialog (containing Scrollsheet printing options). Instead, the entire Scrollsheet (or a highlighted block, if one is selected) will be sent to the output channel. The format of the printout will follow the current *Print...* settings (accessible from the pull-down menu *File*).

Automatic printing. Note that if you need to keep a complete log of all Scrollsheets (and/or graphs, see page 1106) which are displayed on the screen without having to manually press the *Print* button for each Scrollsheet, select the *Automatically Print All Scrollsheets* option in the *Page/Output Setup* dialog (accessible by double-clicking on the *Output* field on the status bar at the bottom of the *STATISTICA* window, see page 1106).

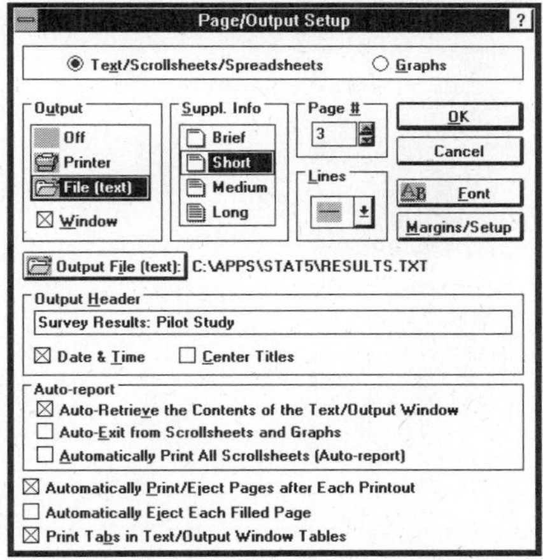

In the same dialog, you will be able to specify where to direct the output: printer, a disk text-output file, or a scrollable *Text/output Window* (see Chapter 5). You may also specify where to direct graphics output, which may be automatically included in the log of Scrollsheets (see page 1106 for details).

See the section on the status bar *Output* field (page 1106) for information about report styles, formatting options, printing gridlines, adjusting margins, and other output options.

22. Cut (Block)

Cuts (removes) the contents of the currently highlighted cells and copies them to the Clipboard.

23. Copy (Block)

Copies the highlighted part of the Scrollsheet to the Clipboard (to select the entire Scrollsheet, click on the upper left corner of the Scrollsheet). Selecting this option will copy not only the contents in the highlighted block of cells but also the row names and column names associated with the highlighted cells (use the option *Copy Raw* from the pull-down menu *Edit* to copy only the contents of the highlighted block of cells without the corresponding row and column names).

Correlations (adstudy.sta)

BASIC STATS — Marked correlations are significant at p < .05000
N=50 (Casewise deletion of missing data)

Variable	MEASUR1	MEASUR2	MEASUR3	MEASUR4	MEASUR5	MEASUR6
MEASUR1	1.00000	.01404	-.10534	.19326	.03536	-.01371
MEASUR2	.01404	1.00000	-.05908	.00521	.07805	.14824
MEASUR3	-.10534	-.05908	1.00000	-.08909	-.21242	.13917
MEASUR4	.19326	.00521	-.08909	1.00000	.09627	-.16227
MEASUR5	.03536	.07805	-.21242	.09627	1.00000	.22757
MEASUR6	-.01371	.14824	.13917	-.16227	.22757	1.00000
MEASUR7	-.11643	.04583	.03714	.00873	-.05178	.11992
MEASUR8	-.02273	-.08421	-.18683	.00897	-.19477	-.33046
MEASUR9	-.11945	-.21423	.20617	.09533	-.46720	-.27007
MEASUR10	-.15052	.05468	-.09216	-.23738	-.06628	.12954
MEASUR11	.18364	-.20835	-.02379	.09450	-.00509	-.14969
MEASUR12	.02565	-.01010	-.11361	-.01008	.10776	.03633
MEASUR13	-.20505	.13800	-.14355	-.11714	-.03154	.00118
MEASUR14	-.03683	-.21365	-.22139	.13867	.16546	.02665

Copy:

	MEASUR2	MEASUR3	MEASUR4
MEASUR2	1.00000	-.05908	.00521
MEASUR3	-.05908	1.00000	-.08909
MEASUR4	.00521	-.08909	1.00000
MEASUR5	.07805	-.21242	.09627
MEASUR6	.14824	.13917	-.16227
MEASUR7	.04583	.03714	.00873

Copy Raw:

1.00000	-.05908	.00521
-.05908	1.00000	-.08909
.00521	-.08909	1.00000
.07805	-.21242	.09627
.14824	.13917	-.16227
.04583	.03714	.00873

Note that blocks copied from *STATISTICA* Scrollsheets are tab-delimited. Thus, if pasted into a word processor document, they will appear as tab-delimited tables (compatible with table generators in Windows word processors, e.g., MS Word).

Technical Note: In order to increase compatibility with other applications, *STATISTICA* automatically produces a variety of special Clipboard formats. For example, spreadsheet formats are produced, and will be used when you paste the contents of the Clipboard (copied from *STATISTICA*) into a spreadsheet document in MS Excel or Lotus for Windows.

24. Paste (Block)

Pastes the current contents of the Clipboard into the Scrollsheet starting at the current cursor position.

25. Help

This button accesses the *STATISTICA* on-line *Electronic Manual* (the last button on all toolbars). *STATISTICA* provides comprehensive on-line documentation for all program procedures and all options available in a context-sensitive manner by pressing the F1 key or the help button ? on the toolbar (or caption bars of all dialog boxes).

TEXT/OUTPUT WINDOW TOOLBAR

The *Text/output Window* works in a manner similar to a word processor; it is *RTF*-compatible (*R*ich *T*ext *F*ormat), it supports formatted text and graphs, and allows you to manage text/graphics reports of practically unlimited size. It can be used:

(1) to review/edit a log of output which was displayed in consecutive Scrollsheets and/or graphs in the course of analyses (options are provided to automatically direct all text and/or graphics output to this report facility);

(2) to open (and review/edit) output files or any other text or text and graphics (*RTF*) files; and

(3) as a local text and graph notepad.

Each of these three applications is briefly described in the following paragraphs.

(1) Log of some or all Scrollsheets and graphs. In order to open a *Text/output Window* for output, check the *Text/output Window* option in the pull-down menu *View*. The window will open, and then whenever you direct a spreadsheet, graph, Scrollsheet, or a selected block of cells to the output, it will appear in the window. This output channel can also be requested in the *Page/Output Setup* dialog (accessible by double-clicking on the *Output* field on the status bar at the bottom of the *STATISTICA* window, see page 1106). If the *Printer* or *File* output is also selected in that dialog, the output will be directed simultaneously to the *Text/output Window* and that other channel. Alternatively, you could select one of the *Auto-report* options (see page 1106), and then as each Scrollsheet and/or graph is displayed on the screen, it will simultaneously be sent to the currently specified output channels, and thus, also to the *Text/output Window* (if one is open).

(2) Reviewing text files. Independent of the current *Text/output Window* which was opened for output (see the previous paragraph), previously-saved text files can be opened in new text windows by choosing the *Text/output...* option in the sub-menu of the option *Open Other* (pull-down menu *File*). All text (ASCII) files and formatted (**.rtf*) files with graphics can be edited.

(3) Notepads. Regardless of how a *Text/output Window* was opened (see the previous two paragraphs), it can always be used as a notepad (you can enter/edit text or paste text and graphs or other artwork via the Clipboard).

Format of tabular output. All table-formatted output in the *Text/output Window* is tab-delimited (by default), and thus it can be copied and pasted to spreadsheets (as values, not as text) and to word processors (as input for table formatting).

Toolbar. The *Text/output Window* toolbar provides quick access to the most-commonly used text output management facilities.

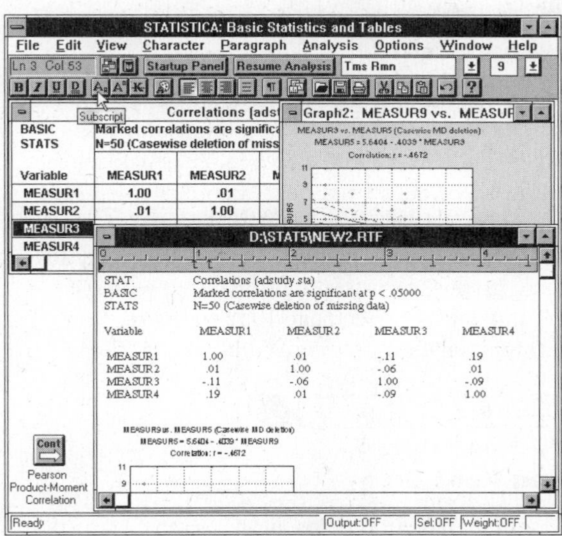

All of the options accessible via the toolbar buttons listed below are also available from menus and via

StatSoft

the keyboard (thus, they can be recorded into mouse-independent macros).

1. The Show Field

The *Show Field* in the *Text/output Window* toolbar indicates the position (line and column) of the cursor within the window. The width of the *Show Field* can be toggled by clicking on it with the mouse.

2. Module Switcher

Brings up the *STATISTICA Module Switcher* (this button is common to all toolbars). The *Switcher* gives you quick access to all "modules" (i.e., groups of analytic procedures) available in your version of *STATISTICA*. Depending on the current configuration, the *Switcher* may open new modules into the same or new application windows.

3. Workbook Management

Brings up the *Workbook* dialog (this is always the second button on all toolbars); this dialog allows you to enter a one-line *File Header* which appears at the top of the spreadsheet, record detailed file information or notes about the data set's contents, source, etc., and to manage all supplementary files (e.g., graphs, reports, programs) used with the current data set. See page 1052 for more information on managing Workbooks of files.

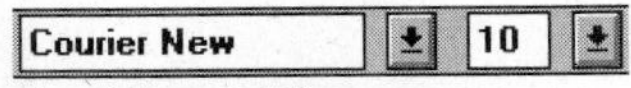

4. Font Name and Font Size

The *Font Selection* fields allow you to change the font and font size of new text or selected text.

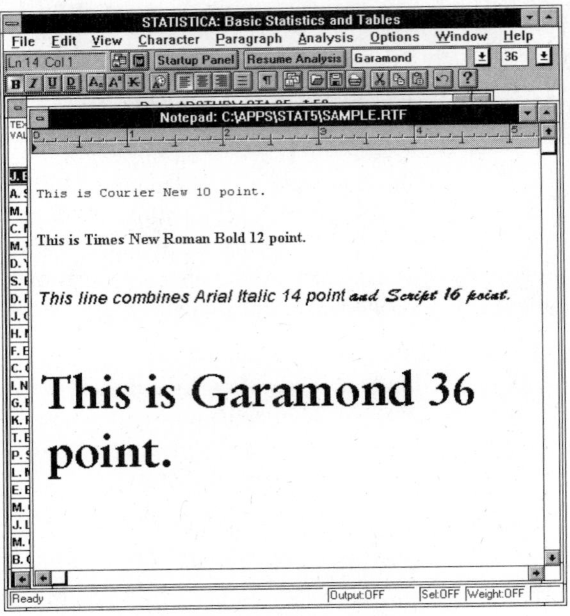

Fonts, font sizes, and character attributes can be mixed within each line of text.

5. Character Formatting

These buttons allow you to set character formatting for selected text (keyboard shortcuts are also available for formatting options):

- **Bold** text (keyboard: CTRL+B);
- *Italic* text (keyboard: CTRL+I);
- Underline text (keyboard: CTRL+U);
- Double Underline text (keyboard: CTRL+D);
- *Subscript* text (sub$_{\text{script}}$);
- *Superscript* text (super^{script});
- *Strikethrough* (~~strikethrough~~);
- Opens the *Color* dialog permitting the selection of color for new or selected text.

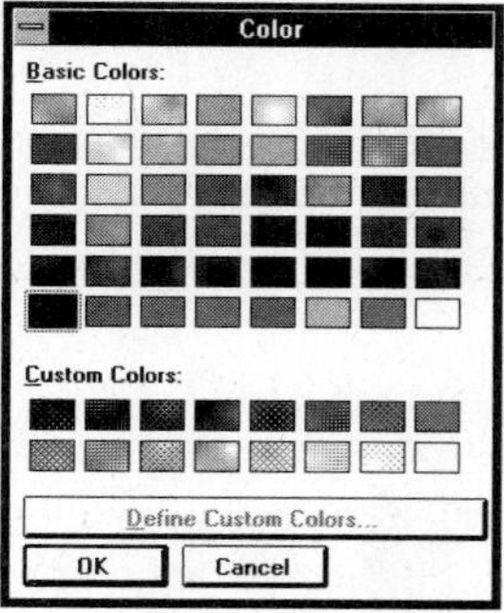

Note that the default font and color for the text in the *Text/output Window* can be specified in the *STATISTICA Defaults - Display* dialog, accessible from the *Options* pull-down menu.

6. Paragraph Formatting

This group of buttons controls the format of new or selected paragraphs:

- *Left-justifies* (left-margin aligns) text and graphs;
- *Centers* text or graphics between margins;
- *Right-justifies* (right-margin aligns) text;
- Toggles between single and double *Line Spacing*;
- Toggles between showing and hiding paragraph marks (¶) and hidden text in the window.

7. Startup Panel

Brings up the *Startup Panel*, which is the first analysis selection or analysis definition dialog of the current module (the same as pressing CTRL+T, or selecting the *Startup Panel* option from the pull-down menu *Analysis*).

For example, this is the startup panel of the *Basic Statistics and Tables* module:

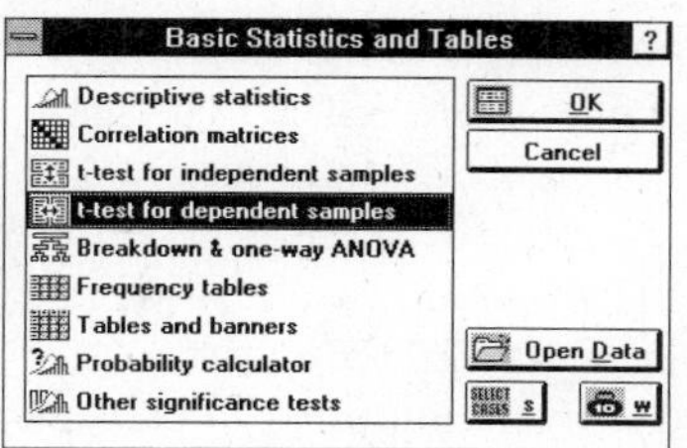

If an analysis is already in progress, and thus by starting over you would lose some of the previous selections, *STATISTICA* will ask you for confirmation. Alternatively, instead of starting over, you can resume the current analysis (see the next button).

Resume Analysis

8. Resume Analysis

Resumes the current analysis by bringing to the top the last-used analysis definition or output selection window [the same as pressing CTRL+*R*, selecting the *Resume Analysis* option from the pull-down menu *Analysis*, or pressing the floating *Cont* (continue) button].

9. Print Block

Prints the contents of the currently selected (i.e., highlighted) block of text (including graphics) from the *Text/output Window*.

Note that as an output facility, the *Text/output Window* has a different status than spreadsheets and Scrollsheets:

> One can say that the *Text/output Window* is both an on-screen "output-review tool" (like Scrollsheets or graph windows) and an "output channel" (like printer or disk-output files) where you can direct output from analyses by pressing the print button.

Printing from the *Text/output Window*. Due to its different status, printing from that facility is configured differently than printing from spreadsheets or Scrollsheets. When you press the

Print button, the entire contents of the *Text/output Window* (or a block, if one is selected) will be sent directly to the printer, regardless of the current setting of the *Output* field on the status bar (on the bottom of the *STATISTICA* window), e.g., it will be sent to the printer even if the *Printer* output is turned *Off* or directed to an output file. If you want to save the *Text/output Window* contents (including graphs, your notes, pasted text, etc.), use the *Save* option (see the button, below).

If you intend to keep a complete, permanent log of all output which is displayed on the screen, the quickest way to do so is to select some of the *Auto-report* options (see the clickable *Output* field on the status bar on the bottom of the *STATISTICA* window, page 1106). This will automatically direct the contents of all displayed output Scrollsheets and/or graphics windows to the *Text/output Window*. See the section on the status bar (page 1106) for information about formatting options, printing gridlines, and other output options.

10. *STATISTICA* Graphs Gallery

This button (which is also available in the graph definition dialog for each graph) opens the *STATISTICA Graphs Gallery* dialog,

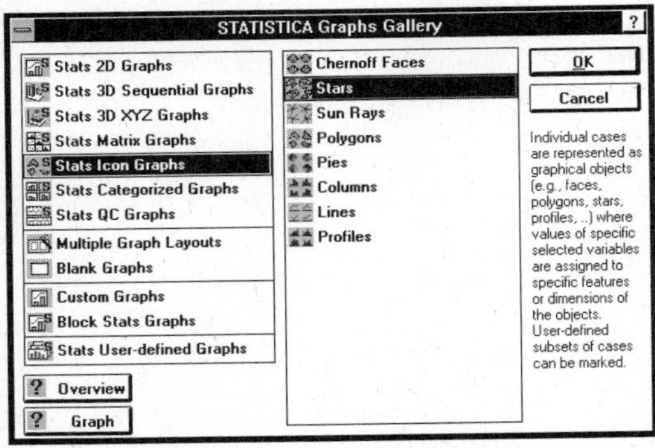

from which you can quickly and easily access all *Stats Graphs*, *Custom Graphs*, *Blank Graphs*, and *Stats User-defined Graphs*.

11. Open Report File

Opens a report file [the default file name extension is **.rtf* (*R*ich *T*ext *F*ormat) or **.txt*] of your choice in the *Text/output Window*.

Note that every *Open/Save* dialog in *STATISTICA* features easy access to the list of all files used with the current data set (see information on Workbooks, page 1052), allowing any file (of the relevant type) from the Workbook list to be easily located and selected by double-clicking on the file's name.

12. Save Report File

Saves the contents of the current *Text/output Window* (text and graphs) to a report file (the default file name extension is **.rtf*); see the *Print* button (, above) for more information about printing and saving the text/output files.

See the previous button for information on accessing the list of Workbook files from all *Open/Save* dialogs. While saving, any Workbook file name can be selected from the list if you wish to overwrite it.

13. Cut Block of Text and/or Graphs

Cuts the selected (i.e., highlighted) block of text and/or graphs and puts it on the Clipboard (see the next button for information on the supported Clipboard data formats).

14. Copy Block of Text and/or Graphs

Copies the selected (i.e., highlighted) block of text to the Clipboard.

Technical Note: One of the formats of the copied items (text and graphs) created by *STATISTICA* in the Clipboard is *RTF* (*R*ich *T*ext *F*ormat); thus all

text formatting information can be easily transferred to word processors and other applications which support the *RTF* format.

15. Paste Text and/or Graphs

Pastes the text and/or graphics contents of the Clipboard to the *Text/output Window* starting at the current cursor location.

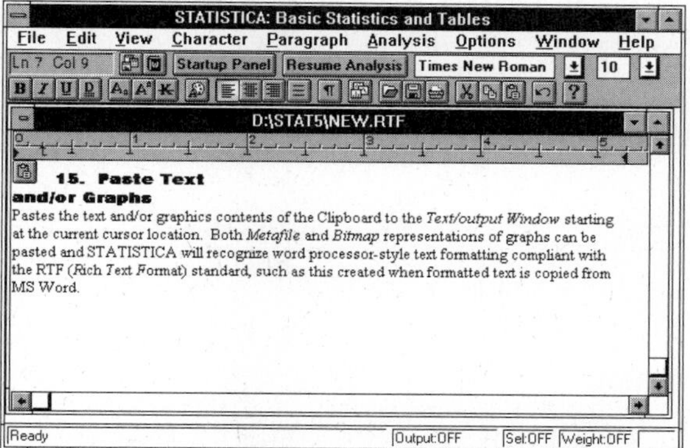

Both *Metafile* and *Bitmap* representations of graphs can be pasted, and *STATISTICA* will recognize word processor-style text formatting compliant with the *RTF* (*R*ich *T*ext *F*ormat) standard (as illustrated above, created with formatted text copied from MS Word).

16. Undo

Clicking this button allows you to reverse the last change made to the report in the *Text/output Window*.

17. Help

This button accesses the *STATISTICA* on-line *Electronic Manual* (the last button on all toolbars). *STATISTICA* provides comprehensive on-line documentation for all program procedures and all options available in a context-sensitive manner by pressing the F1 key or the help button ? on the toolbar.

GRAPH TOOLBAR

The toolbar which accompanies the graphics window offers a selection of drawing, graph customization and multigraphics management options (e.g., linking, embedding graphs and artwork).

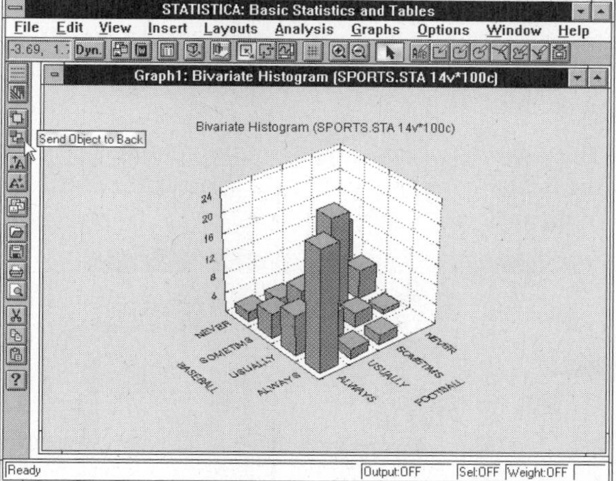

Most of the graph control and customization facilities accessible via the toolbar buttons listed below are also available from menus (thus, they can be recorded into mouse-independent macros). All toolbars can be customized to adjust the number and order of buttons in the toolbar (see page 1049).

1.023, 0.930

0. The Show Field

The *Show Field* in the graphics toolbar displays the current coordinates of the cursor in the graph window (in spreadsheets and Scrollsheets, it displays the contents of the highlighted cell, see the sections on the previous two toolbars). It acts as a "screen reader" which is dynamically updated whenever the cursor (mouse) is moved over the current (active) graph window, and it displays the graph coordinate values. By default (i.e., in the *Dynamic* mode, see below), the coordinates represent the values corresponding to the *X*- and *Y*-axes of the current graph. You can switch to the *Fixed* mode by pressing the button next to the *Show Field* (see below), and then the field will display the absolute (%) window coordinates which are independent of the graph scale: *[0, 0]%* represents the lower-left corner of the window and *[100, 100]%* represents the upper-right corner. Also, when you rotate text on-screen (by dragging its corner), the *Show Field* displays the angle by which the text is rotated.

The width of the *Show Field* can be toggled by clicking on it with the mouse, or by selecting the *Change Show* option on the pull-down menu *View*.

Dyn. / Fix 1. Dynamic-/Fixed Mode (toggle)

Toggles between the *Dynamic* and *Fixed* mode for graphic object customization (see the previous paragraph for these two modes of displaying the graphics cursor coordinates).

***Dynamic* mode.** In the *Dynamic* (default) mode, all custom objects placed anywhere on the graph (e.g., drawings, arrows, text, embedded or linked graphs or other artwork) will be anchored against the current *X*- and *Y*-axis scale coordinates.

1.023, 0.930 Dyn.

Thus, they will be dynamically attached to specific "logical" graph locations (and not absolute positions within the graph window). When the graph is re-scaled or moved within its window, the relations between the custom (*Dynamic*) objects and the respective graph components will not change (e.g., an arrow will still mark the same point on a line graph even when the graph is re-scaled and this point is now in a different place in the window).

***Fixed* mode.** In the *Fixed* mode, however, all custom objects will always remain in their absolute positions, anchored only against the proportions of the window.

For example, if you add a footnote at the bottom of the graph, it will always remain on the bottom even if the graph is re-scaled.

Status indicator. This button can be used as a status indicator for individual custom graphic objects -- when you highlight an object (e.g., click on a custom text label), the position of the button will reflect the object's status (*Dynamic* or *Fixed*).

Changing status of objects. The button can also be used to change the status of an object: after highlighting an object, press the button and the status of the object will adjust accordingly.

2. Module Switcher

Brings up the *STATISTICA Module Switcher* (this button is common to all toolbars). The *Switcher* gives you quick access to all "modules" (i.e., groups of analytic procedures) available in your version of *STATISTICA*. Depending on the current configuration, the *Switcher* may open new modules into the same or new application windows.

3. Workbook Management

Brings up the *Workbook* dialog (this is always the second button on all toolbars); this dialog allows you to enter a one-line *File Header* which appears at the top of the spreadsheet, detailed file information or notes about the data set's contents, source, etc., and to manage all supplementary files (e.g., graphs, reports, programs) used with the current data set. See page 1052 for more information on managing Workbooks of files.

4. Graph Data Editor

Brings up the *Graph Data Editor* containing all data which are displayed in the current graph. In *STATISTICA*, all values represented in every graph can be reviewed and edited directly.

In other words, regardless of whether the graph represents raw data from the data spreadsheet, parts of a Scrollsheet output, or a set of calculated or derived scores (e.g., in a probability plot), these values are always accessible in the internal *Graph Data Editor*.

The *Editor* is organized into multi-column segments representing individual plots (i.e., series of data) from the current graph.

Graph Data for Graph1: 2D Graph

Data: ADSTUDY.STA 25v * 50c
Advertising Effectiveness Study.

	MEASUR2 Bar X		MEASUR3 Line Plot		MEASUR4 Step Plot	
	X	Y	X	Y	X	Y
1	1.00	1.00	1.00	6.00	1.00	8.00
2	2.00	7.00			2.00	8.00
3	3.00	8.00			3.00	9.00
4	4.00	9.00			4.00	5.00
5	5.00	1.00			5.00	2.00
6	6.00	0.00			6.00	8.00
7	7.00	4.00			7.00	2.00
8	8.00	9.00			8.00	6.00
9	9.00	8.00			9.00	3.00
10	10.00	6.00			10.00	8.00
11	11.00	6.00			11.00	5.00
12	12.00	3.00			12.00	7.00
13	13.00	2.00			13.00	1.00
14	14.00	2.00			14.00	8.00

Add Plot
Add Rows
Cut Ctrl+X
Copy Ctrl+C
Paste Ctrl+V
Clear Del
Plot Layout
General Layout
Point Label/ID Info
Mark Block
Label Block
Turn off Block
Highlight Block
De-select Block
Selected Data (All)

In mixed graphs, each multi-column segment may represent a different type of plot (e.g., line plot, scatterplot), and these types are marked by icons in the column name areas of the *Editor*. The multi-column segments may consist of single, double, triple or quadruple columns of values (depending on the type of the respective plot). The contents of the editor can be expanded, combined with other data, saved to a file, etc. (for more information, press the F1 key in the *Editor*). When you save the graph, the complete contents of the *Editor* are also stored in the graphics file, so that later you can continue interactive data analyses (e.g., brushing, see the next button). The *Editor* also contains options to manage the data points which have been marked via brushing (see the next button); for example, you can selectively copy them to the Clipboard, transfer to a new plot, etc.

5. Brushing Tool

Activates the *Brushing* mode and brings up the interactive *Brushing* dialog. When this mode is activated, the cursor changes to a "gunsight-style" cross-hair (rectangle and lasso brushes are also available, see the *Brushing* dialog), and the program will allow you to highlight data points from the graph by clicking on them with the cross-hair (or enclosing them in the rectangle or lasso).

STATISTICA features a comprehensive selection of brushing facilities, including a variety of tools for manipulation of data points on screen, as well as the management of brushed (selected) data points.

How *Brushing* works: The difference between highlighting data and *Updating* the *Action*. Highlighting data points in a graph is a precursor to performing an *Action*. This is analogous to highlighting in word processors, where highlighting text is a precursor to performing an action (e.g., applying a font attribute such as boldface or italic). In a similar fashion, "pointing to" (highlighting) specific data in a graph amounts to "telling the program" on which data points you will execute the specified *Action*.

No changes are made to the graph as long as you do not *Update* the graph (i.e., execute the currently specified *Action*). When the desired points are highlighted, pressing the *Update* button in the *Brushing* dialog (see below) will execute the current brushing *Action* (as specified in the *Action* section of the dialog). As a result of the *Action*, the highlighted points can be *Marked* (with a different marker), *Labeled*, or *Turned off* (that is, temporarily eliminated from the graph, e.g., to explore the influence of outliers on a fitted function).

One more action that is available, *De-Select*, allows you to remove all attributes (*marked*, *labeled*, *turned off*, or *highlighted*) due to previous actions performed on the selected points of the current plot (or on all plots if the *All Plots* option is chosen, see the combo box in the brushing dialog).

De-select All. Pressing this button will remove all attributes (e.g., *marked*, *labeled*, *turned off*, or *highlighted*) from all selected points of all plots (regardless of the current plot setting in the combo box) and restore their default, unselected status.

Auto Update. For graphs which are redrawn quickly, it is useful to select the *Auto Update* option which will cause the graph to automatically update (i.e., execute the current *Action*) after each application of the brushing tool. Thus, in the *Auto Update* mode, data points are never highlighted but become immediately *marked*, *labeled*, etc.

Reverse. Pressing this button inverts all *Actions*; you may choose to *Un-Mark*, *Un-Label*, or *Turn ON* highlighted points.

Animation. If the current brush type is *Rectangle* or *Lasso*, then the animated brushing mode can be enabled (check the *Animation* box).

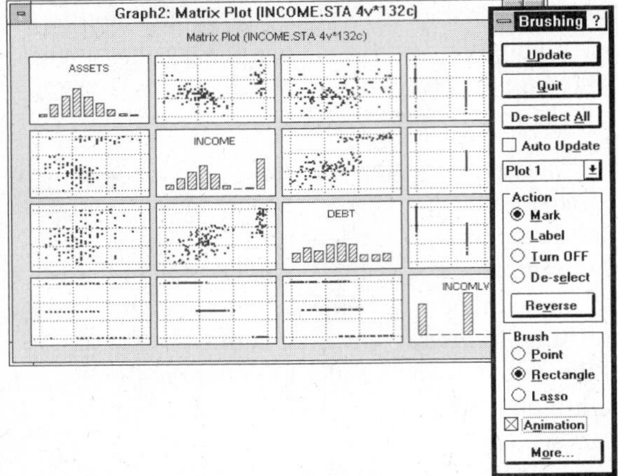

This option will automatically move the brush over the graph under interactive control of the *Animation* dialog settings.

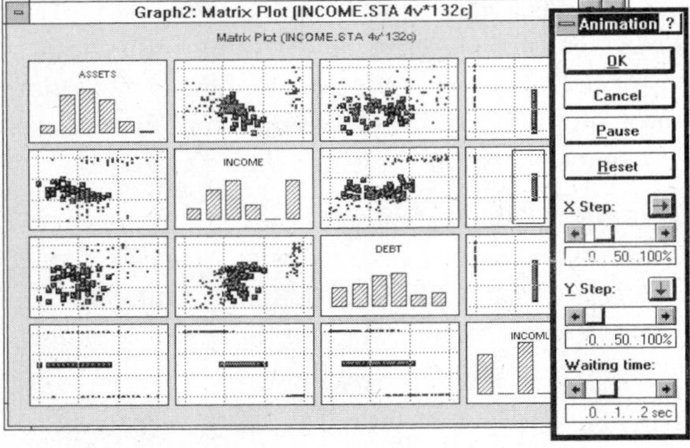

This technique is particularly useful in exploratory data analyses using matrix plots.

More... Pressing the *More...* button in the initial *Brushing* dialog will bring up the *Brushing - Extended Options* dialog containing options to *Highlight* (or *De-highlight* or *Swap* the highlight attribute) points by specifying the value range coordinates of selected variables, or by reference to attributes of previously selected points. All *Extended Options* work in conjunction; that is, points may be selected by ranges of values *and* by attributes and/or combinations of attributes.

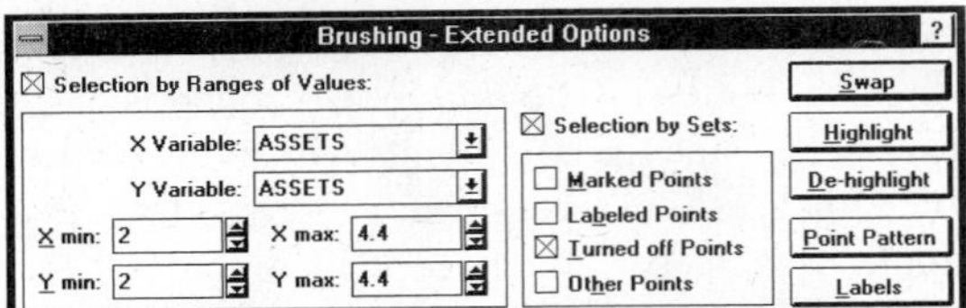

Points *Highlighted* via the *Extended Options* dialog will have the *Action* specified in the *Brushing* dialog applied to them when the *Update* button in that dialog is pressed. For example, you may choose to *Highlight* points which have previously been *Marked* (i.e., had their point markers changed) by checking *Marked Points* in the *Extended Options* dialog and clicking *Highlight*; you may then temporarily remove them from the display (and from fitted functions) by selecting *Turn OFF* in the *Brushing* dialog.

Note that in the *Auto Update* mode (see above), when highlighting is not available (because all *Actions* are instantly updated), the *Highlight* and *De-highlight* buttons in this dialog are not available (dimmed), and pressing the *OK* button carries out the action.

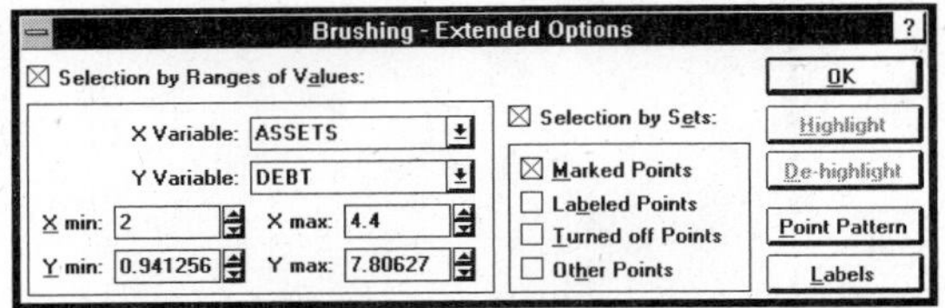

Exiting the brushing mode. The *Brushing* tool is deactivated by clicking on the *Point Tool* (the default mode, see button below), or by pressing the ESC key. Note that when you exit the *Brushing* mode, *highlighting* of points on which an *Action* has not been executed (i.e., which have not been *marked, labeled*, etc.) will not be displayed until you re-enter the *Brushing* mode for this graph.

Managing the selected data points (applications). Brushing is typically used in exploratory data analysis (EDA) to interactively explore the contribution of specific data points to

patterns of relations between variables (e.g., in scatterplot matrices) or to identify (e.g., label) outliers. However, it is often necessary to manage the selected data points (for example, to selectively copy them to the Clipboard or to create a new column of data consisting of the selected data points). These operations can be performed in the *Graph Data Editor*.

6. Maintain Graph Aspect Ratio (*MAR* Mode)

Enables the default, *MAR* (*Maintain Aspect Ratio*) mode for graph window re-sizing.

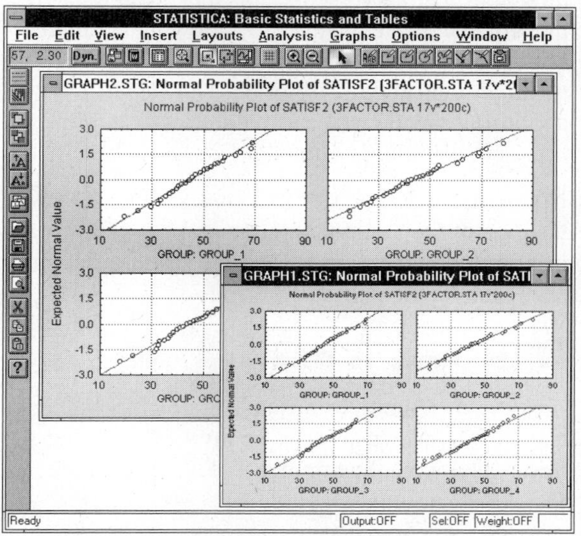

In this mode, the graph aspect ratio is maintained as you re-size the window so that the graph proportions are not distorted.

Maintaining a customized aspect ratio. By default, this button is pressed; it becomes de-selected when you switch to a different mode (e.g., in order to adjust the graph proportions, see the next button). Note that after the graph proportions are modified (see the next button), pressing the *MAR* re-sizing mode button will not restore the original proportions but will "freeze" the current proportions; that is, it will allow you to automatically maintain the current graph aspect ratio when the graph window is re-sized.

The default graph aspect ratio. The default graph aspect ratio can be modified in the *Graph Mapping Options* dialog, accessible from the pull-down menu *View*; e.g., you can set the default graph proportions to *1:1* instead of the standard screen proportions.

7. Change Graph Aspect Ratio (Non-*MAR* Mode)

Enables the free (non-proportional) graph window re-sizing mode. In this mode, the graph can be "stretched" or "squeezed" in either direction, changing the proportions between the X and Y coordinates of 2D displays and other relations between graph components. (Note that this mode allows interactive adjustment of graph proportions; this adjustment can also be made in the *Graph Mapping Options* dialog, see pull-down menu *View*.)

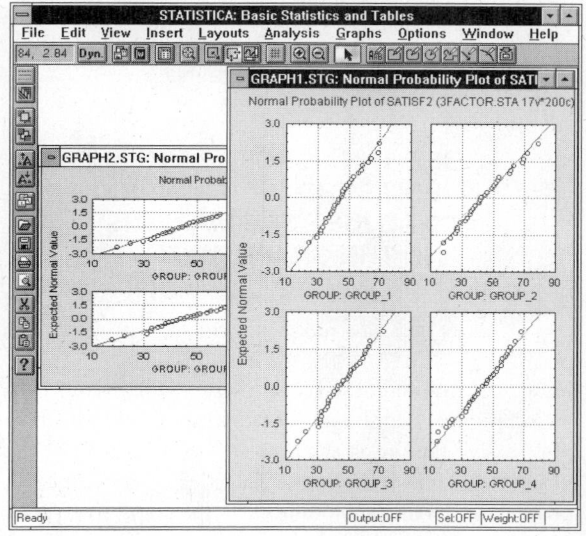

The modified proportions of the graph will also be reflected in the printout (as can be examined using the *Print Preview* facility, use the *Print Preview* toolbar button or select *Print Preview* from the pull-down menu *File*). After the proportions are adjusted, you can make them permanent for this graph by switching back to the default *MAR* re-sizing mode (*Maintain the graph Aspect Ratio*), see the previous button; the new proportions will then be maintained as the graph window is re-sized. See the previous topic for information on adjusting the default graph aspect ratio (e.g., to *1:1*).

8. Adjust Graph Area and Margins

Enables the *graph area and margins adjustment* mode. When you enter this mode, scroll-bars will appear around the graph window, allowing you to move the graph position within the graph area.

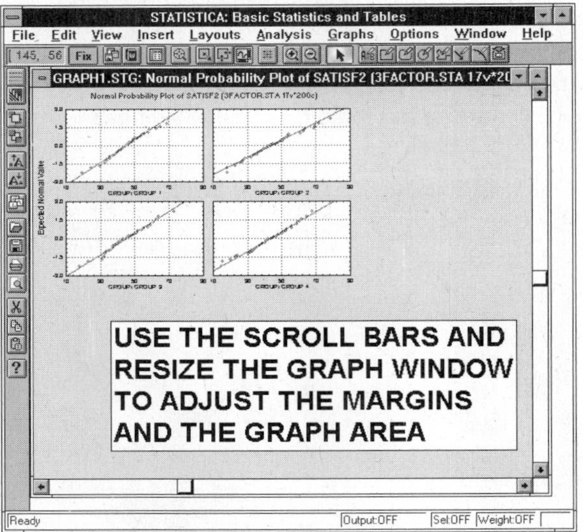

However, unlike in the two previous window re-sizing modes (see the previous two buttons), when you re-size the graph window in this mode, the graph itself will remain unaffected (i.e., its size or proportions will not change). At the same time, re-sizing of the window will result in adding (or subtracting) space to or from the area around the graph. This way, you can, for example, adjust the margins or add extra space on one side of the graph in order to type in or paste some text, embed or link another graph, etc.

Note that in this mode, the *STATISTICA* application window serves as a frame of reference for all those plot area adjustment operations; thus the position of the graph window within the *STATISTICA* window and the relative size of the graph window will affect the available range of movement of the graph and the amount of extra space which can be added. In order to increase the space available in all directions, before you enter this mode and re-size the window, place the graph window in the middle of the *STATISTICA* application window and keep it no larger than about 25% of the *STATISTICA* application window (see also the *Blank Graph* option in the pull-down menu *Graphs*).

Note that the default size of all margins (i.e., the position of the graph within the graph window) can be adjusted in the *Graph Mapping Options* dialog, accessible in the pull-down menu *View*.

9. Snap to Grid

Pressing this button brings up a dialog in which you can enable (and customize) an invisible drawing grid to help you align drawn objects (e.g., lines, rectangles, inserted graphics or text objects).

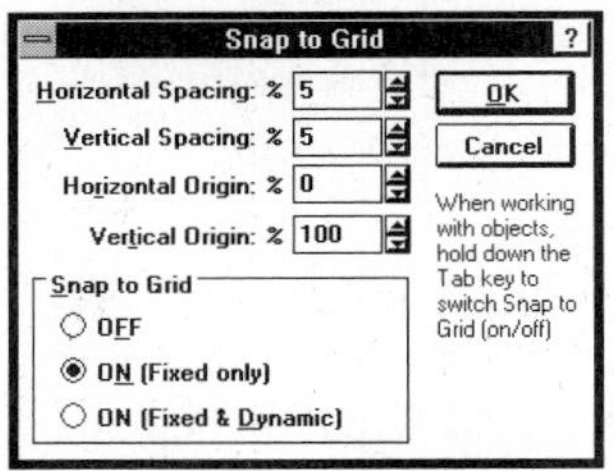

By default, the object is pulled into alignment with the nearest intersection of gridlines (as if the

resolution of the screen were "decreased"). This is the so-called snap-to-grid effect.

The display of the alignment grid itself in the graph may be toggled on and off by pressing CTRL+G, or selecting the option *Alignment Grid* from the *View* pull-down menu.

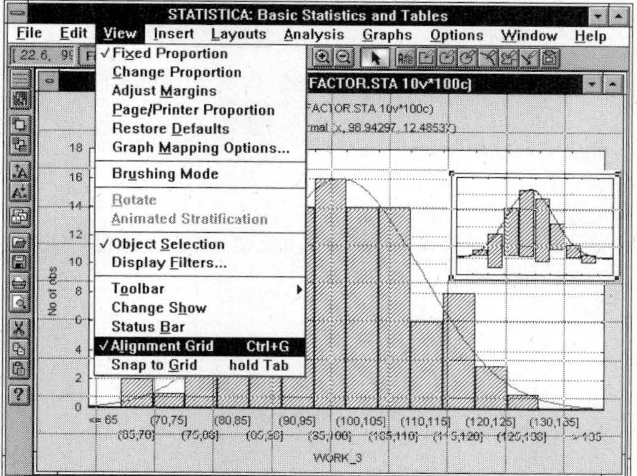

If the *Snap to Grid* option is turned off, the grid no longer affects drawn objects. The snap-to-grid facility may be toggled while placing individual objects by holding down the TAB key (e.g., even if the *Snap to Grid* facility is turned off, it can be enabled by holding down the TAB key). To display the grid, select the option *Alignment Grid* from the *View* pull-down menu. The *Snap to Grid* facility may be enabled only for objects placed in *Fixed* mode, or for objects placed in either *Fixed* or *Dynamic* mode (see page 1083 for details on the two modes of placing objects in the graph).

Applications. A typical application of the *Snap to Grid* facility is when you need to align objects (e.g., a series of custom text objects, independent segments of a legend, or embedded graphs); it is also useful while drawing diagrams, flow charts, etc.

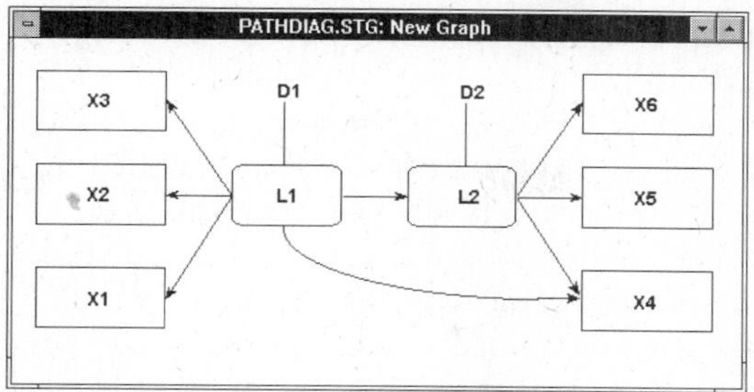

10. Zoom-in

Zooms-in (magnifies) the selected area of the graph. When you select this option (and enter the *Zoom In* mode), the mouse cursor will become a "magnifier," 🔍, enabling you to proportionally enlarge the current graph. Place the magnifier over the area of the graph that you want to view and click once on the left-mouse-button.

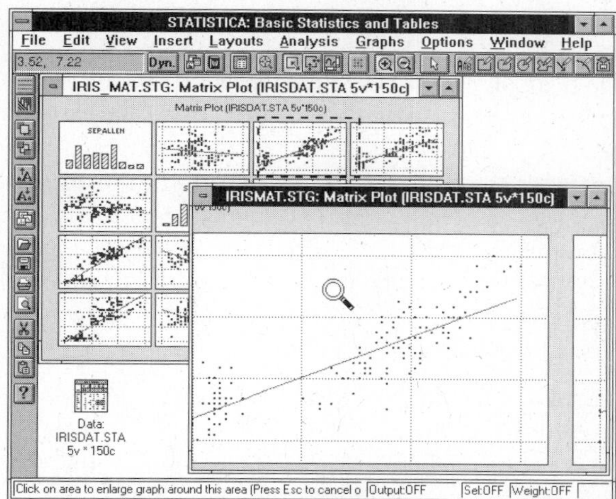

This will result in a magnified view of the specified area; the point where you click (the focal point of magnification) will become the center of the new graph window. Each time you click the mouse when you are in this mode (while the cursor looks like a magnifier), the graph area will be magnified by a factor of approximately 2; you may press it up to 5 times to achieve a magnification ratio of approximately 32:1.

Logical zoom vs. "mechanical stretching." Note that this tool offers more than just "mechanical stretching" of the picture. Specifically, it provides a logical magnification of the selected area while maintaining the sizes of point markers, fonts, and width of all lines. Thus, the *Zoom In* tool effectively increases the "functional resolution" of the display, allowing you to inspect areas of the graph which in normal (1:1) mode were not readable due to overlapping markers or point labels. In contrast, if the zoom was "mechanical" and not logical, and the size of point markers was increased with the magnification ratio, then one would not be able to see the details (e.g., overlapping points) revealed in the illustration above.

Custom vs. default graph mapping. Note that, by default, the size of fonts, markers, and spacing between the components of the graph will remain the same as you *Zoom In* (to allow for truly logical zooming—revealing more details, and not mechanical stretching). However, the size of fonts, markers, and spacing will be proportionately reduced as you *Zoom Out* (see next topic), to allow for true reduction of the entire graph area. This can be adjusted in the *Graph Mapping Options* dialog from the pull-down menu *View*, and fonts, markers, and spacing may be forced to rescale or to stay the same for both *Zoom In* and *Zoom Out*.

Drawing in zoom mode. Because the *Zoom In* tool provides logical magnification (see the previous paragraph), the black editing/re-sizing squares (for an illustration, see *Proportional vs. nonproportional* re-sizing, page 1094) will maintain their size independent of the zoom ratio; therefore, the zoom mode can be used to make precise modifications to freehand drawings.

Scrolling the graph in the zoom mode (moving a "magnifying glass" over the graph). Because the zoom mode in *STATISTICA* is based on a *virtual plot area* technology (and not "partial redrawing"), you can use the *Zoom In* tool in conjunction with the *graph area and margins adjusting* mode (see the previous button).

By enabling that mode, you will place scroll-bars around the graph (see below), allowing you to scroll the magnified area in the graph window. This way of examining a graph resembles moving a "magnifying glass" over the graph.

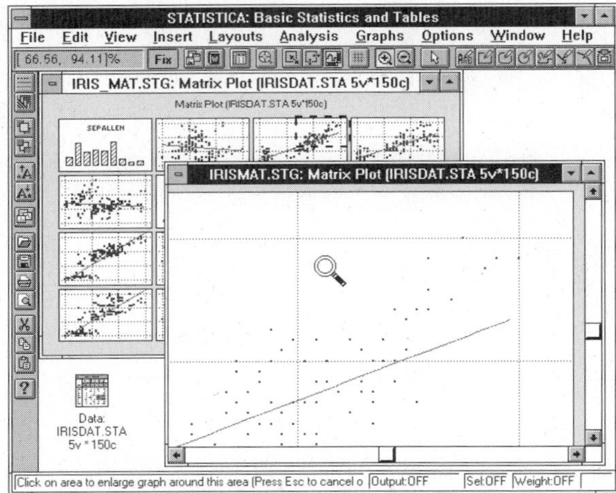

Reversing the zoom operation. You can also decrease the graph "size" (in the same increments that you increased it) using the *Zoom Out* tool (see the next button). Note that unless you select exactly the same focal points for the *Zoom Out* operation as those you had used for *Zoom In*, the original location of the graph in the window will not be restored. In order to restore the original graph position (as well as the default margins and the magnification ratio), use the *Restore Original Settings* option from the graph pull-down menu *View*.

11. Zoom-out

Zooms-out (reduces the size of) the selected area of the graph. The *Zoom Out* tool works in a manner analogous to the *Zoom In* tool (see the previous button).

This option is useful when the details of the graph do not need to be salient, but you need a lot of extra space around the graph, in order, for example, to embed some artwork or paste text for a poster or a compound graphics document. (See also the *Blank Graph* option, pull-down menu *Graphs*)

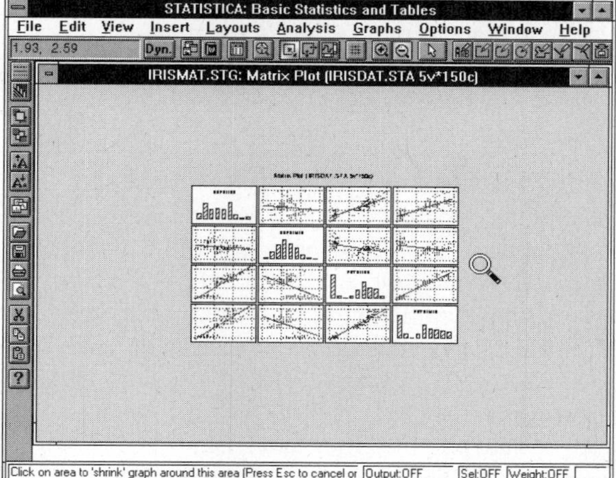

Custom vs. default graph mapping. Note that, unlike the *Zoom In* mode (see the previous topic), the size of fonts, markers, and spacing will be proportionately reduced as you *Zoom Out* to allow for true reduction of the entire graph area. This can be adjusted in the *Graph Mapping Options* dialog from the pull-down menu *View*, and fonts, markers, and spacing may be forced to rescale or to stay the same for both *Zoom In* and *Zoom Out*.

12. Point Tool (Default Mode)

Enables the *Point Tool*, which is the default mode for all graph windows (indicated when the wide button is depressed). This mode will allow you to use the left-mouse-button to select graph objects (e.g., arrows, embedded or linked objects, etc.) or different parts of the graph (e.g., titles, scales, gridlines, etc.) for customization, editing, or interactive analysis (e.g., "X-raying layers" of 3D sequential graphs). You will temporarily exit from this selection mode whenever you choose one of the interactive graph customization options (e.g., brushing, add text, draw arrows and other objects, embed graphs). Clicking on the *Point Tool* button will return *STATISTICA* to the default selection mode of operation.

Pressing ESC. Also, pressing ESC to exit a drawing, embedding, or brushing mode will return to this default mode. Note that the current mode (or any active graphic object manipulation operation) is always briefly referenced in the help area of the status line on the button of the *STATISTICA* window.

13. Graphic Text Editor

Opens the *Graphic Text Editor* -- a facility to enter, edit, and format custom text (e.g., notes, comments, or larger portions of text) in *STATISTICA* graphs and drawings.

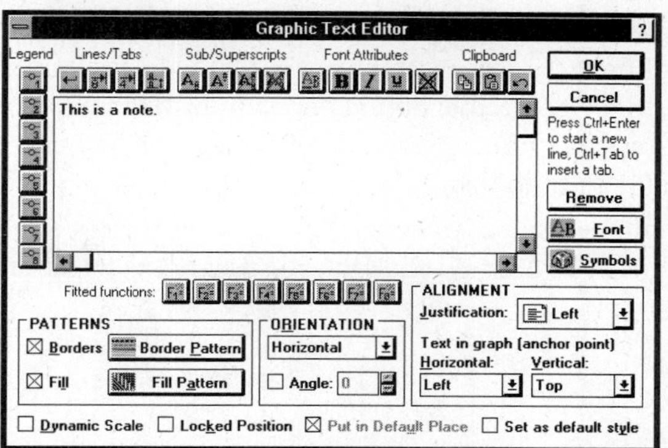

Text entered or pasted into the editor can be edited or formatted and then placed into the graph by pressing *OK* (the editor will close and the cursor will change into the editor-style cursor; move the cursor to the desired location on the graph and then click the left-mouse-button to place the text). The text can later be selected in the standard manner (by a mouse click) and moved (i.e., dragged) like every

StatSoft

other graphic object. Double-clicking on an existing custom text object will open the *Graphic Text Editor*, allowing you to edit or change the attributes of the existing text. Depending on the current status of the *Dynamic/Fixed* switch (see page 1083), the new text will be positioned on the graph dynamically (i.e., its location will adjust to all future graph changes) or in a fixed window position (e.g., always in the bottom left corner, 10% of the window width from the left). This can be changed using the *Dynamic Scale* option in the editor, the default setting in the *Text Objects Style* dialog (accessible from the pull-down menu *Insert*), or by highlighting the text and clicking on the Dyn./Fix toolbar button (see page 1083).

Formatting, Control Characters, mini-toolbar. The *Graphic Text Editor* offers a variety of text formatting, positioning and alignment options, including multiple levels of subscripts and superscripts, legend symbols (corresponding to patterns of consecutive plots in the current graph), and many others. The simplest way to use the text attributes (e.g., italics, superscripts, etc.) is to highlight the part of text to be formatted and then press the respective button on the mini-toolbar (see below for a brief description of each of the buttons on the mini-toolbar).

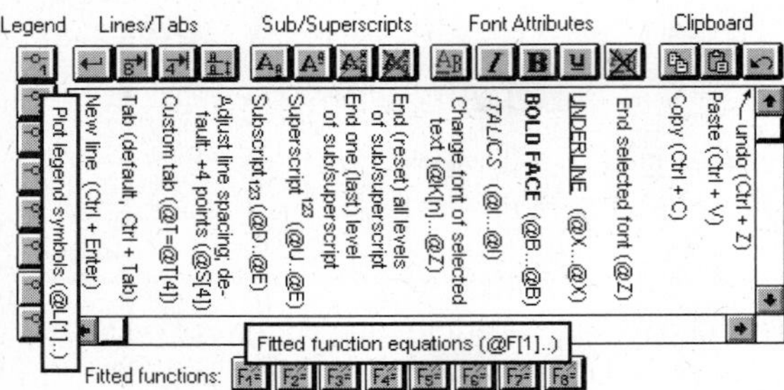

STATISTICA will then insert the appropriate Control Characters into the text. However, you can also enter the Control Characters directly into the text. For example, @B marks the beginning and end of the bold character format (thus @BTEXT@B will appear as **TEXT**).

Control Characters. The same Control Characters are supported in all edit fields which are used to enter graphic text in *STATISTICA* (e.g., titles, scale values, value labels, category names and values, legends, etc.); thus, all graphic text can be customized. Also, text customized in the *Graphic Text Editor* can be copied and then pasted into all text components of *STATISTICA* graphs. For more details and examples, refer to the *Electronic Manual* by pressing ? or the F1 key in the *Graphic Text Editor*.

Advanced text formatting, formulas. In addition to the most-commonly used text formatting options accessible from the mini-toolbar of the *Graphic Text Editor*, a variety of advanced text formatting facilities are accessible by using the Control Characters (e.g., formulas can be entered and edited). For example, custom tab stops and line spacing can be controlled in small increments; options are provided to obtain legend symbols for particular values of variables plotted in contour and surface graphs, or to automatically place in legends the values (of the plotted variable) corresponding to specific shading levels of the graph. For more details and examples, refer to the *Electronic Manual* by pressing ? or the F1 key in the *Graphic Text Editor*.

Combining text and graphs. Practically unlimited amounts of text can be entered (or pasted and then edited and formatted) into *STATISTICA* graphs, allowing you to produce documents combining text, formulas, and pictures.

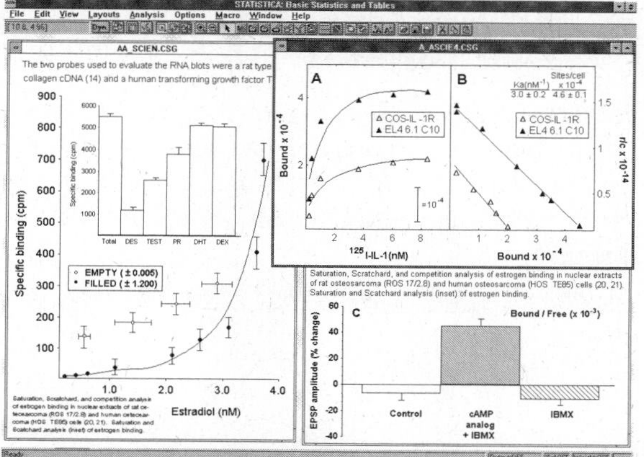

As mentioned before, you can access the *Graphic Text Editor* and customize any existing custom text in *STATISTICA* graphs by double-clicking on the text (left-mouse-button) or clicking on it with the right-mouse-button and then selecting the appropriate text customization operation from the flying menu which will pop up. This also applies to movable legends which have the same status as custom text.

14. Draw Rectangles

Enters the *rectangle drawing mode*. After pressing the button, the cursor will change into a cross-hair allowing you to draw rectangles by dragging the mouse on the graph.

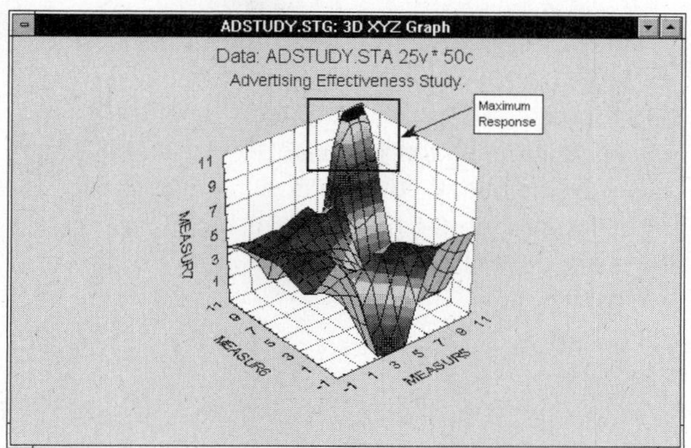

Drawing squares. If you hold down the SHIFT key while drawing, a square is produced (equal height and width proportions are maintained).

Exit. To exit from the drawing mode, click on the *Point Tool* (see the button, page 1091) or press ESC.

Patterns. The line and fill patterns depend on the current default settings (as determined in the *Shape Objects Style* dialog from the pull-down menu *Insert*) but can be changed later by clicking on the rectangle with the right-mouse-button and selecting the feature to be customized from the flying menu which will pop-up. Alternatively, you can later select the rectangle by clicking on it (the black selection squares will surround the rectangle) and then adjust its appearance by pressing the line or fill pattern customization buttons (see the respective buttons, pages 1098 and 1098, respectively).

Dynamic/fixed. Depending on the current setting of the *Dynamic Scale* check box in the *Shape Objects Style* dialog (from the pull-down menu *Insert*), each new rectangle will be positioned on the graph dynamically (i.e., its location will adjust to all graph changes) or in a fixed window position (e.g., in the bottom left corner of the window, 10% of the window width from the left).

15. Draw Rounded Rectangles

Enters the *rounded rectangle drawing mode* (see the summary on drawing and customizing rectangles, above).

Drawing rounded squares. If you hold down the SHIFT key while drawing, a rounded square is produced (equal height and width proportions are maintained).

16. Draw Ovals

Enters the *oval drawing mode* (see the summary on drawing and customizing rectangles, above).

Drawing circles. If you hold down the SHIFT key while drawing, a circle is produced (equal height and width proportions are maintained).

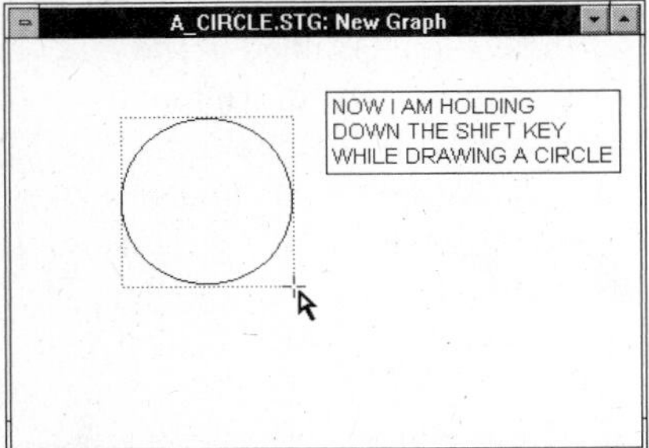

17. Draw Arcs

Enters the *arc drawing mode* (see the summary on drawing and customizing rectangles, above). After pressing the button, the cursor will change into a cross-hair allowing you to draw arcs by dragging the mouse on the graph. The arc is drawn as one-quarter of an ellipse and can be controlled as illustrated below.

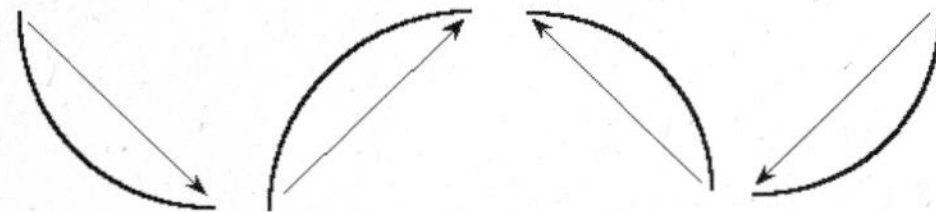

Specifically, the proportions of the ellipse depend on the angle of mouse movement (45° will produce a quarter-circle arc; alternatively, hold down the SHIFT key while drawing).

The orientation of the arc (concave vs. convex) will depend on the direction of the movement (up or down, respectively; see the illustration above).

18. Draw Freehand, Polylines

Enters the *freehand/polyline/polygon drawing mode* (see the summary on drawing and customizing rectangles, above). After pressing the button, the cursor will change into a "brush" with a pointed tip (see below).

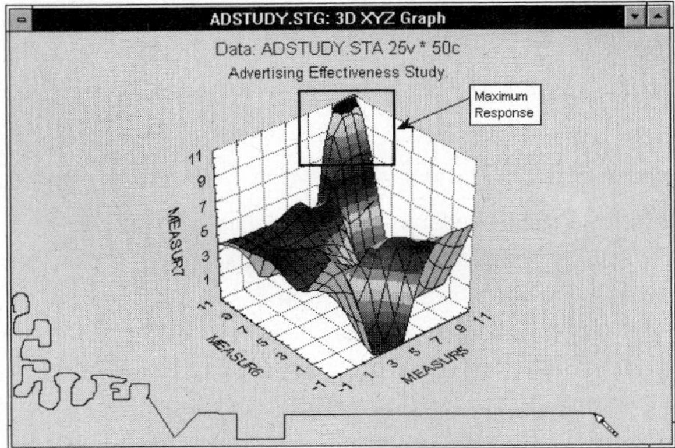

Freehand lines. In order to produce freehand drawings, press the left-mouse-button and drag the brush.

Straight lines. To draw a straight segment of a line, place the tip of the brush on the starting point of the segment and click the mouse; then (after releasing the button), move the tip of the brush to the endpoint of the segment, and click again. To finish drawing the object, double-click the mouse.

Filled shapes. Filled shapes are produced when the fill pattern is enabled (see the fill pattern customization, button, page 1098); note that the shape of the line or polyline does not have to be closed in order to be filled as long as it forms at least one cove (i.e., when it is not straight), as shown below.

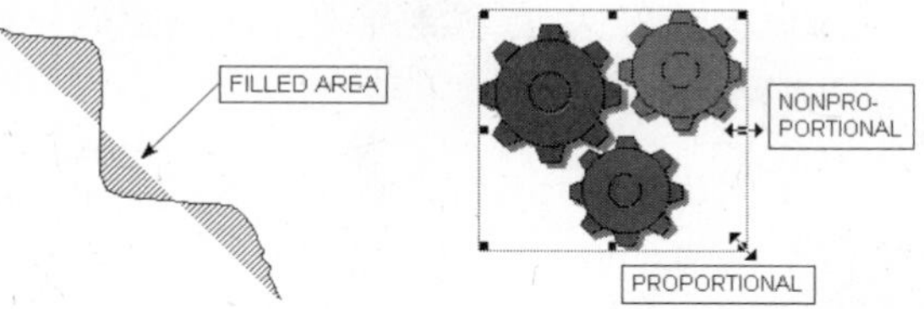

Proportional vs. nonproportional re-sizing. In addition to the standard graphic object customization facilities (see the summary on drawing and customizing rectangles, button , above), several line-drawing specific features are supported. When the object is selected, it is surrounded by 8 (instead of the standard 4) black re-sizing squares. Dragging by a corner-square will allow you to proportionately-re-size the drawing, whereas dragging by the middle-side-squares will allow you to re-size (i.e., stretch or squeeze) the object in only one direction.

The re-sizing mode is indicated by the shape of the arrow to which the cursor will change when you move it over the re-sizing squares. For example, in the following graph the cursor is positioned over the upper-right re-sizing square. Its diagonal, double-headed appearance indicates that dragging this re-sizing square will proportionately re-size the object.

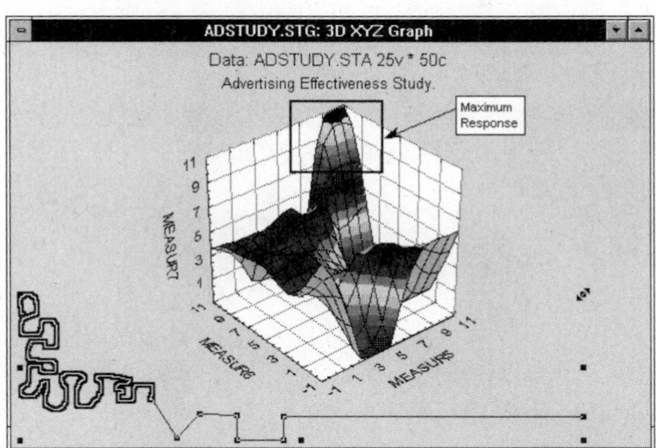

Line shape editing. Additionally, when you select a line drawing, you can edit the details of the *shape* of the line. A black rectangle will appear in every point of the line drawing where the line changes its direction (see the above illustration) -- you can now drag any one of them with the mouse to modify the local shape of the drawing.

Editing in Zoom mode. True freehand drawings will be densely covered by the squares, because they consist of many very short segments. In order to edit such densely curved shapes, zoom-in on the drawing (see the *Zoom-in* button , page 1089).

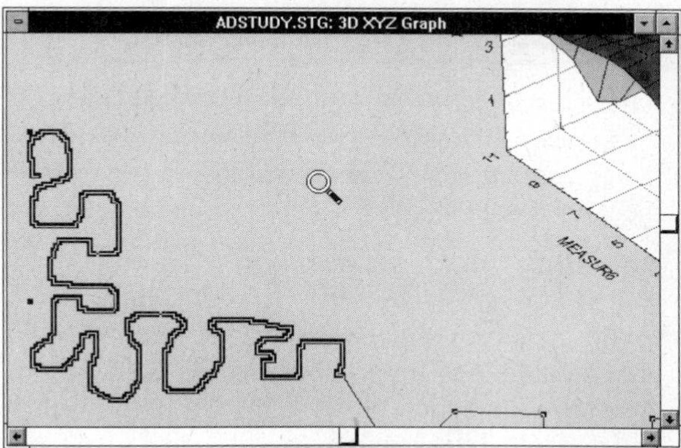

Drawings can consist of large numbers of independent or overlapping segments, and the order in which they will be redrawn (and, consequently, overwrite each other) can be controlled using *Redraw order control* tools (*Bring to Front* and *Send to Back*, see the respective buttons and , page 1098). Drawing and all other graph customization options (e.g., embedding) can be performed in every graph re-sizing mode, including the zoom-in mode (which can be used to increase the drawing precision, as shown in the illustration above).

19. Draw Arrows, Custom Error Bars

Enters the *arrow and error bar drawing mode*. After pressing the button, the arrow style customization dialog will appear. A number of

StatSoft

predefined arrow styles can be selected and countless custom arrow and error bar styles can be custom-designed using this arrow customization facility.

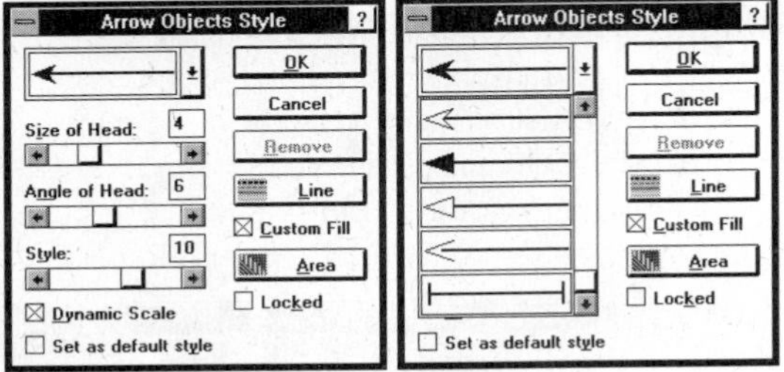

After pressing *OK* to accept the arrow style, move the mouse to the starting point (head) of the arrow, then press and drag the mouse to the position where the tail will be located.

Adjusting the arrow position. The style, as well as the precise size and location, of the arrow (or the error bar) can also be adjusted later: Click on it with the right-mouse-button to select an arrow customization option from the flying menu which will pop up. To reposition an arrow, first select the arrow by clicking on it (the black re-sizing squares will appear on its ends); drag either of the squares to adjust the length and/or the angle of the arrow. To drag the entire arrow, place the mouse anywhere on its body (the cursor will change to the four-arrow icon) and then drag the entire object.

20. Insert Objects (*OLE*)

Enters the *object embedding* or *linking* mode. After pressing the button, the *Insert* dialog (also available from the pull-down menu *Insert*) will appear allowing you to combine into one display different objects (text, spreadsheets, metafiles, bitmaps, *STATISTICA* graphs, etc.).

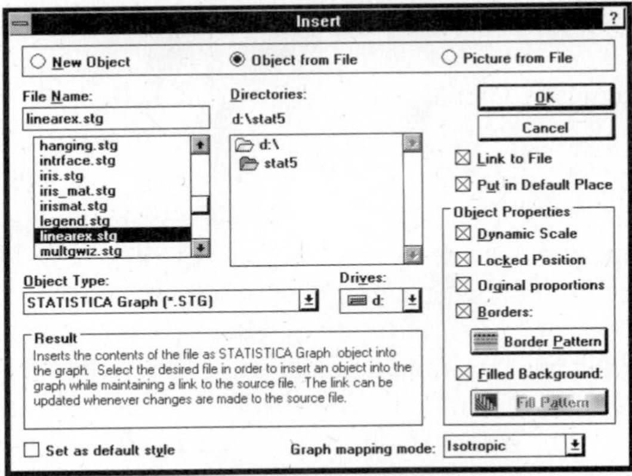

Object types. When *New Object* is selected, you may choose the type of object to be created from a list of Windows applications which support *OLE*. After selecting the object type and clicking *OK*, the application will open allowing you to create the new object. When *Object from File* is selected, you may select the type of object to be inserted from a list of Windows applications which support *OLE*; selecting the object type will display all previously saved files for that application. When *Picture from File* is selected, you may insert non *OLE*-compliant objects saved in standard Windows graphics formats: metafile format (file name extension **.wmf*) or bitmap format (file name extension **.bmp*). For more information, press ? or the F1 key to access the *Electronic Manual*.

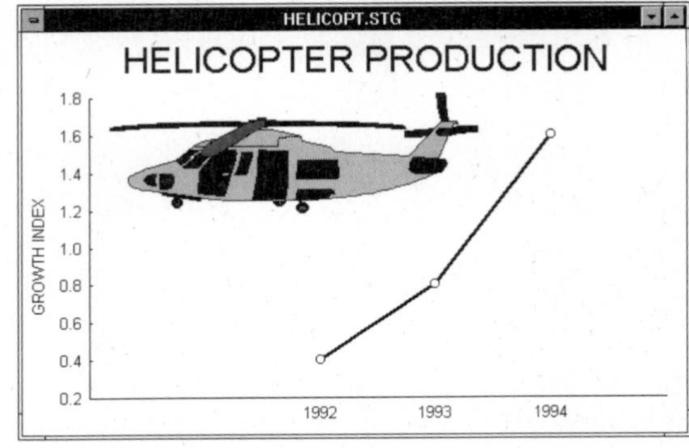

Linking vs. Embedding (overview). *STATISTICA* supports *OLE* (*O*bject *L*inking and

*E*mbedding) in both the server and client mode. That is, not only can *STATISTICA* graphs be dynamically updated in other applications (server mode), but foreign (*OLE*-compliant) objects (e.g., graphs, worksheets) and *STATISTICA*'s own objects can be built into *STATISTICA* graphs and later be dynamically updated. In other words, you can incorporate external objects in *STATISTICA* graphs not only by pasting them (see button, page 1102), but also by accessing the objects directly from disk files (e.g., by dragging them with the mouse directly from the *File Manager*, across application windows, and placing them onto *STATISTICA* graphs).

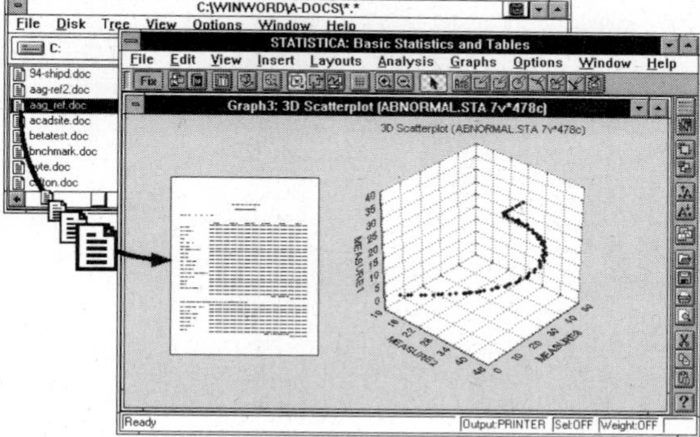

STATISTICA supports both linked (i.e., dynamically related) and embedded (i.e., statically "built in") objects, and those objects can be accessed from any files created by Windows applications, including files in the *STATISTICA* native graphics format (file name extension **.stg*). Also, *STATISTICA* can act simultaneously as an *OLE* server and client, and one of the unique features of *STATISTICA*'s *OLE* implementation is that it supports *nested compound documents* (up to fourth order); that is, *STATISTICA* documents with embedded documents can be embedded in other *STATISTICA* documents.

Note that each of the two methods of incorporating artwork from external sources into *STATISTICA* graphs (*linking* and *embedding*) has its advantages and disadvantages.

Linked objects. Graphs with linked objects are redrawn somewhat slower because their redrawing may involve updating links to external files; however, updating such graphs can be automatic (the status of links can be adjusted in the *Links...* dialog accessible from the graph pull-down menu *Edit*),

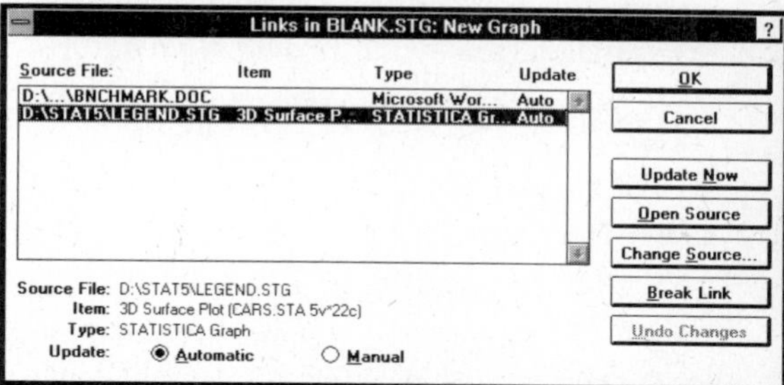

and this allows you to easily create compound documents which include "always current" contents of other files.

Embedded objects. Graphs with embedded objects may be redrawn faster (than graphs with linked objects), because they include no links to external files which need to be updated. The relations between those objects and other applications are limited to the editing option: the server application is called when you double-click on the object; however, embedded objects can be updated only by manually replacing or modifying them.

All characteristics of the foreign objects (whether *linked* or *embedded*) and their relation to other components of the current graph can be adjusted later from the *Edit* pull-down menu (or by clicking on it with the right-mouse-button which will open a flying menu of available object-customization choices). The only exception is the mode for incorporating an object (*linking* or *embedding*) which can be determined at the point of incorporating the file (later, only linked objects can be changed into embedded, see option *Convert to Embedded* from the pull-down menu *Edit*).

Automatic rescaling and adjustment of inserted *STATISTICA* graphs. If the inserted object is a *STATISTICA* graph, it is automatically rescaled/adjusted such that the sizes of all fonts, markers, and spacing between graph components are optimal for the relative size of the object (with the client window). This feature can be controlled by using the *Graph Mapping Mode* options in the *Insert* dialog (see the *Electronic Manual* for details).

21. Adjust Line Pattern

Allows you to select the line style (pattern, color combination, size, measurement units and mode) for the currently-selected custom graphic object. If no object is selected, then pressing this button will have no effect [in order to adjust the patterns for the new (subsequent) objects to be entered, use the *Object Styles* dialog in the pull-down menu *Insert*].

The line pattern customization dialog shown above is used not only for custom graphic objects, but it is also common to customizations of many other line-components of *STATISTICA* graphs (e.g., it will appear whenever you double-click on any line or curve in any graph).

Special line customization features. In addition to the common line-customization options, this dialog offers some unique features, such as support for two-color line patterns (e.g., select any of the non-continuous line patterns, set the line to non-transparent, and choose a desired "background color" which will fill the breaks in the line pattern). The line thickness can be adjusted either in units of device-dependent pixels (and these settings will apply to pixels of any size on the screen, printer, or recorder) or in device-independent point-units (1 point = $^1/_{72}$ of an inch) in quarter-point increments (i.e., $^1/_{288}$ of an inch). Note that to achieve the desired effects when hard copies are produced, and to avoid the common "too thin" one-pixel-wide lines printed by default on laser printers, a global minimum width for all printed lines can be adjusted in the *Print Options* dialog (see button, below).

22. Adjust Fill Pattern

Allows you to select the fill pattern style (pattern design, color combination, and mode) for the currently selected. If no object is selected, then pressing this button will have no effect [in order to adjust the patterns for the new (subsequent) objects to be entered, use the *Object Styles* dialog in the pull-down menu *Insert*].

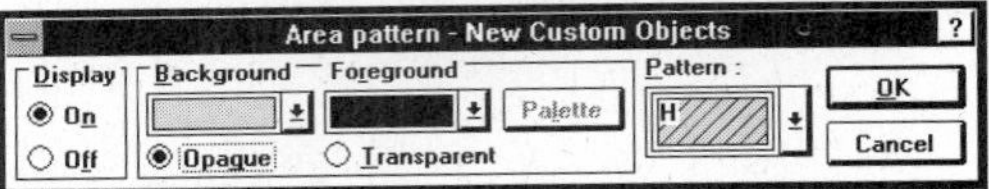

The pattern customization dialog shown above is used not only for custom graphic objects, but it is also common to customizations of many other components of *STATISTICA* graphs which involve filled areas.

Special area customization features. In addition to the common area-customization options, this dialog offers some unique features, such as "transparent hatch" fill patterns or support for two-color fill patterns (e.g., set the fill-pattern to non-transparent and not solid, then choose a desired "background color" which will fill the breaks in the pattern).

23. Bring to Front

Brings the currently selected custom graphic object to the "front." The *Bring to Front* operation allows you to place a custom graphic object "on top" of all others by changing the object redrawing order such that the current object is redrawn last and thus will

remain not covered by any other objects (see also the next button, *Send to Back*).

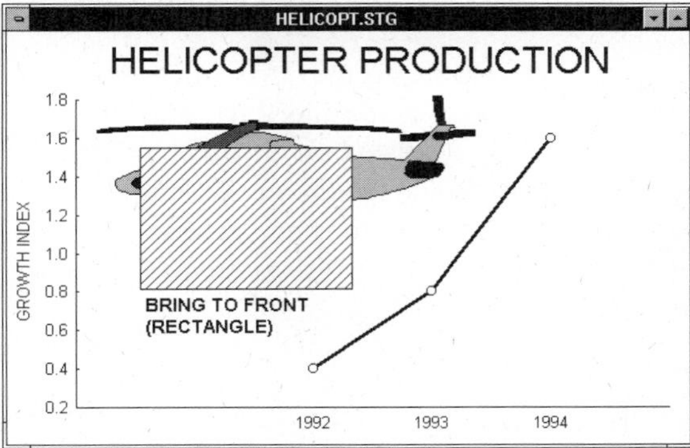

For example, if you intended to place a text object on top of some artwork which was drawn (or embedded) later, you would highlight the text and press the *Bring to Front* button (alternatively, you could highlight the background object and press the *Send to Back* button, see below).

24. Send to Back

Sends the currently-selected custom graphic object to the "back." In other words, it will be redrawn first, so that it can be covered by other custom graphic objects, which are redrawn later.

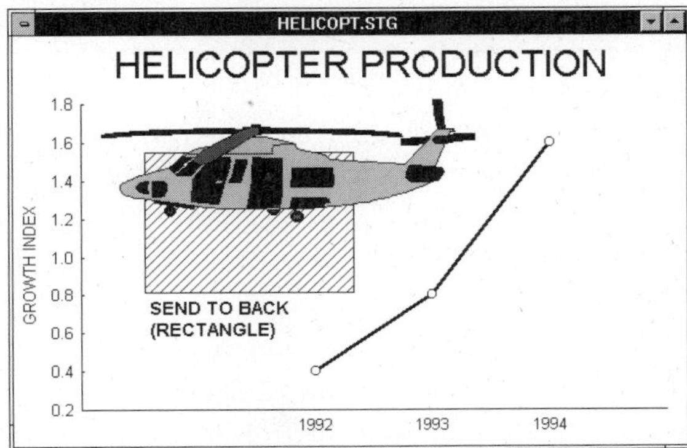

This *Send to Back* operation is analogous (i.e., opposite) to the one initiated by pressing the *Bring to Front* button (see the previous button).

25. Increase All Fonts, Markers, Widths by 16% (CTRL - 4%)

Proportionately increases the size of all fonts (as well as markers and all distances and spacing defined in points or related to font and marker sizes) in the graph. Pressing the button once will increase all those sizes by 16%; hold down the CTRL key while pressing this button to achieve a smaller (4%) increase rate.

This *Global Font Increase* tool is useful in cases when a small graph is to be produced (e.g., for publication) and when the size of all fonts relative to the body of the graph needs to be different than in graphs of standard size.

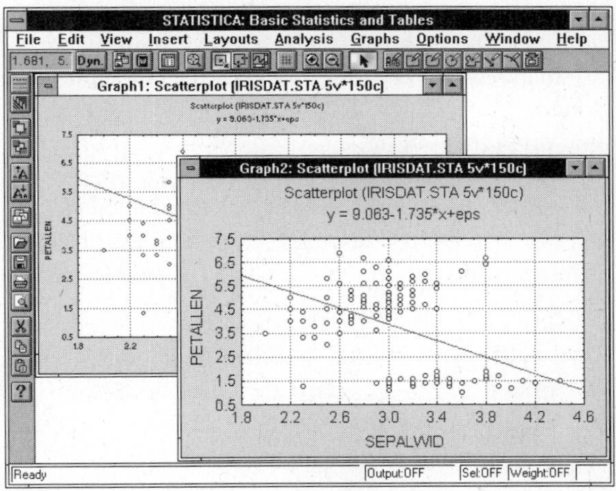

The lower graph in the screen above is the result of pressing the *Global Font Increase* button (the upper graph uses the default font).

Technical Note: *logical* vs. *physical* font sizes (mapping font sizes onto plot regions of different sizes). Technically speaking, this tool controls the *Graph Mapping Base* factor (also accessible in the *Graph Mapping Options* dialog from the pull-down menu *View*, where default settings can be changed). In *STATISTICA*, all graph displays and printouts can be continuously

StatSoft

scaled along with their fonts. Unless you change the *Graph Mapping Base* factor (as provided by the current button), the fonts will appear printed in their actual *physical* size (as set in points; 1 point = $^1/_{72}$ of an inch) if letter-size paper is used, if portrait orientation with the default (1 inch) margins on all sides is specified, and if the default graph proportions are not modified (the *Graph Mapping Base* setting can be modified in the *Graph Mapping Options* dialog, accessible from the pull-down menu *View*).

The shortcut font size adjustment enabled by pressing this button allows you to effectively increase or decrease all fonts (both on the screen and in graph printouts) not by changing the specific font size settings (e.g., not by changing a 12-point setting into a 14-point setting) but by globally adjusting the manner in which the logical font sizes are mapped into the plot region of the screen or the printout (i.e., *Graph Mapping Base*). Thus, after you press this button, a text object in the graph which was set to size 10 (points) will remain set to 10, but this size (10) will now be represented by approximately 16% larger letters when displayed or printed, as determined by the new *Graph Mapping Base* factor.

Embedded or linked graphs. Note that if the mapping mode in an inserted (i.e., embedded or linked) graph is set to *Fixed Size Font* (i.e., it is tied to the *Mapping Base* setting of the master document, see the *Object Properties* dialog for the child graph), then clicking the *Global Font Increase* button will also affect font sizes in the inserted graph.

Default settings. The default setting of the *Graph Mapping Base* (see above) can be adjusted in the *Graph Mapping Options* dialog (pull-down menu *View*).

26. Decrease All Fonts, Markers, Widths by 16% (CTRL - 4%)

Proportionately decreases the size of all fonts (as well as markers and all distances and spacing defined in points or related to font and marker sizes) in the graph (the *Global Font Decrease* tool). This tool works in a manner analogous (i.e., opposite) to the *Global Font Increase* tool (see the previous button).

27. *STATISTICA* Graphs Gallery

This button (which is also available in the graph definition dialog for each graph) opens the *STATISTICA Graphs Gallery* dialog,

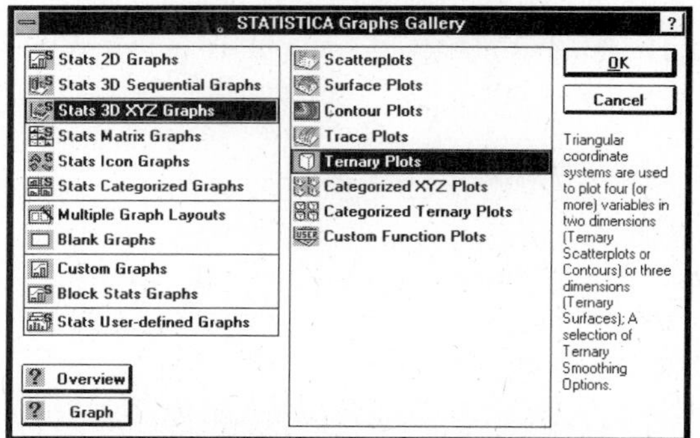

from which you can quickly and easily access all *Stats Graphs*, *Custom Graphs*, *Blank Graphs*, and *Stats User-defined Graphs*.

28. Open Graph File

Opens a *STATISTICA* graphics file (the default file name extension is **.stg*). The new graph will be opened in a separate window. Note that *STATISTICA* graph files can also be opened directly from the *File Manager* by double-clicking on the respective file name.

In order to access a graph or artwork in a different graphics format, use the *Insert* facility which allows you to access Windows graphics metafiles (file name extension **.wmf*), bitmap graphics files (file name extension **.bmp*), and many other formats of graphics and other files (see the *Insert Objects* button, above).

Note that every *Open/Save* dialog in *STATISTICA* features easy access to the list of all files used with the current data set (see information on Workbooks, page 1052), allowing any file (of the relevant type) from the Workbook list to be easily located and selected by double-clicking on the file's name.

29. Save Graph File

Saves the current graph into a *STATISTICA* graphics file (the default graph file name extension is **.stg*). The file will contain the graph with a complete set of all customizations and options, including the current set of all data displayed in the graph (as can be seen in the *Graph Data Editor*, see button, above). If an existing file is being overwritten, then *STATISTICA* will give you an option to rename that graph file into a backup file (file name extension **.bak* instead of **.stg*).

See the previous button for information on accessing the list of Workbook files from all *Open/Save* dialogs. While saving, any Workbook file name can be selected from the list if you wish to overwrite it.

30. Print Graph

Prints the current graph. This is a shortcut method to print the graph to the currently selected output channel (*Printer* and/or the *Text/output Window*) following the default graph printout settings (or settings as they were last modified in the *Page/Output Setup* dialog). If you need to modify any graph printout settings, use the *Page/Output Setup* dialog or the *Print* option in the pull-down menu *File*. Unlike the *Print* button on the toolbar, using the menu option will not initiate the printing immediately, but will first display an intermediate dialog (*Print Options*) allowing you to adjust various printout and printer settings. Use the *Print Preview* option (press the toolbar button or use the pull-down menu *File*) to see how the graph will appear on the page and to adjust the margins. Note that there is also a batch printing facility available by selecting the *Print Files...* option from the pull-down menu *File*.

You may also request that all graphs be automatically printed and/or added to the analysis log in the *Text/output Window*; see page 1106 for details.

31. Print Preview

Displays the graph as it will appear on the page, allowing you to modify the print area and margins of the printout.

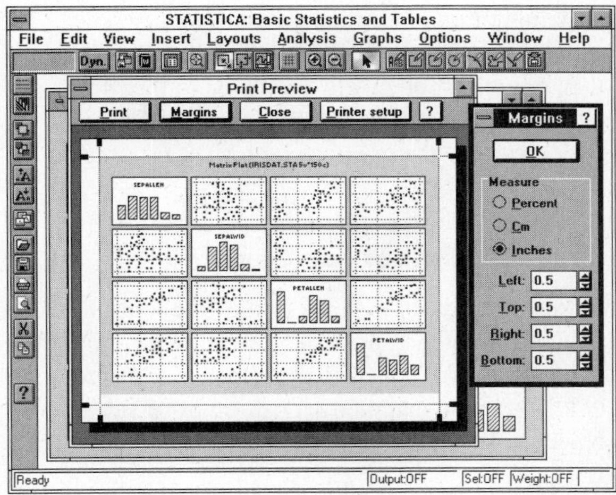

The *Print Preview* window is re-sizable; thus you can see details of the graph as they will appear on the printout. The margins can be adjusted (after pressing the *Margins* button) by dragging the margin lines or entering specific printout size

measurements (in inches, centimeters, or percentages).

32. Cut Graphic Object

Cuts (i.e., removes) the currently selected (i.e., highlighted) graphic object (such as text, label, drawing, or embedded/linked graphs and other objects) and copies it to the Clipboard (the same as pressing CTRL+X). In order to increase compatibility with other Windows applications, in addition to a copy of the object in the native *STATISTICA* format, metafiles, bitmaps, and also text representations of the cut object are copied to the Clipboard.

33. Copy Graph, Graphic Object, or Text

Copies a selected object or the entire *STATISTICA* graph to the Clipboard (the same as pressing CTRL+C). If a graphic object (such as text, label, drawing, or an embedded graph linked or other artwork) is currently selected (i.e., highlighted), then only that object will be copied to the Clipboard. The same formats as in the *Cut* operation (see the previous button) are supported.

34. Paste Graph, Graphic Object, or Text

Pastes the current contents of the Clipboard in default format (see *Technical Note*, below) into the upper-left corner of the graph (the same as pressing CTRL+V). You can then reposition or re-size the object accordingly.

Technical Note (*Paste Special*): Options for pasting objects into *STATISTICA* graphs. The *Paste Special* option from the graphics *Edit* pull-down menu will allow you to select the format, frame, and location for the Clipboard object when it is pasted in a *STATISTICA* graph, and optionally allow you to establish a link to the source file.

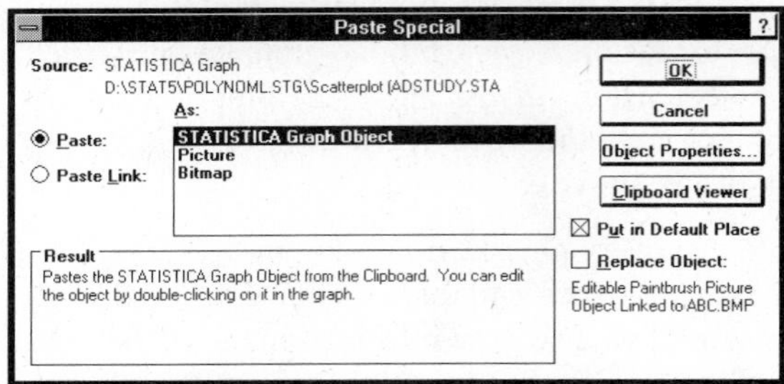

The *Paste Link* option is available only if the source application is running, and if the source file from which the object was copied has been saved.

The following options are available in this dialog:

Source: Lists the source of the Clipboard object.

Paste: Selecting *Paste* and accepting the default format selection is the same as selecting *Paste* from the *Edit* pull-down menu (or pressing the toolbar button or CTRL+V). Specify the desired format (see *As:*, below) in order to paste the Clipboard object into the current graph in a non-default format.

Paste Link: Pastes the Clipboard object into the current graph while maintaining a link to the source document file (the same as selecting *Paste Link* from the *Edit* pull-down menu).

As: Select the format of the Clipboard object to be pasted.

Replace Object: Select this option in order to paste over (i.e., replace) the currently selected object in the *STATISTICA* graph. This option is available only when an object is selected.

Put in Default Place: Select this option to paste the Clipboard object in the upper-left-hand corner of the graph (the default location; the object can be moved or re-sized after pasting). If this option is deselected, the location and size of graph area in which to paste the Clipboard

object must be specified with the cursor (i.e., the object will be pasted only after you "draw" the rectangle and release the mouse).

Object Properties: Click on this button in order to bring up the *Object Properties* dialog and select from several options for the newly pasted object.

Clipboard Viewer: Clicking this button will open the Windows *Clipboard Viewer*, allowing you to preview the Clipboard object.

Technical Note: Mapping of pasted *STATISTICA* graphs. If the pasted object is a *STATISTICA* graph, several graph mapping options are available, and they can be adjusted in the *Object Properties* dialog [accessible from the *Paste Special* dialog, before the graph is pasted, or later from the right-mouse-button flying menu for the object or by pressing ALT+ENTER (*Object Properties*) when the object is selected]. For example, if you select the *Fixed Size Font* (*Mapping mode*) setting, then the physical size of the font in the object graph will be tied to the *Mapping Base* of the master window, and thus, it will be automatically adjusted when you press the *Global Font Size* buttons (see page 1099) for the graph.

Text. Note that *Text* pasted into *STATISTICA* graphs from the Clipboard can later be edited and customized in the *Graphic Text Editor* (see button, above).

35. Help

This button accesses the *STATISTICA* on-line *Electronic Manual* (the last button on all toolbars). *STATISTICA* provides comprehensive on-line documentation for all program procedures and all options available in a context-sensitive manner by pressing the F1 key or the toolbar help button.

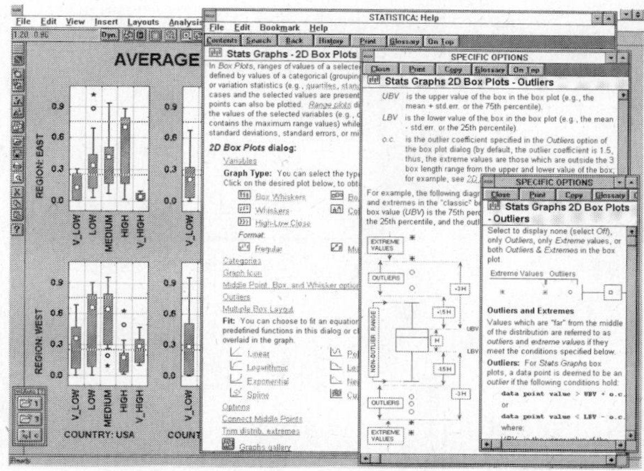

Other buttons on graphics toolbars. The following buttons appear only on toolbars for graphs which display three-dimensional representations of data.

36. Perspective and Rotation

Brings up the *Perspective and Rotation* window (see below) allowing for rotation, spinning (for analytic or exploratory purposes) and interactive adjustment of the point of view for three-dimensional displays.

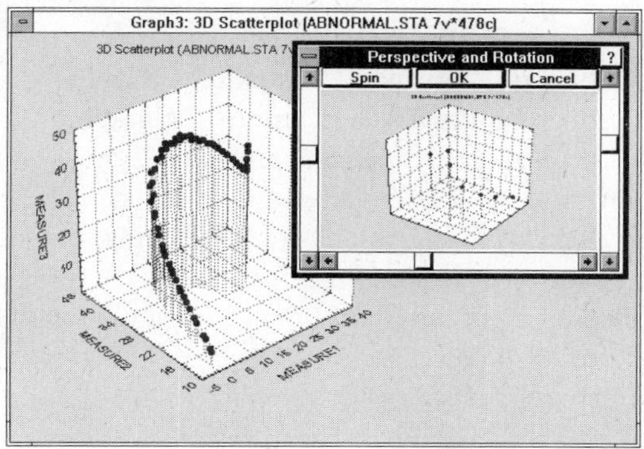

By clicking on the *Spin* button, the display can be set into continuous rotation in clockwise or counter-clockwise directions.

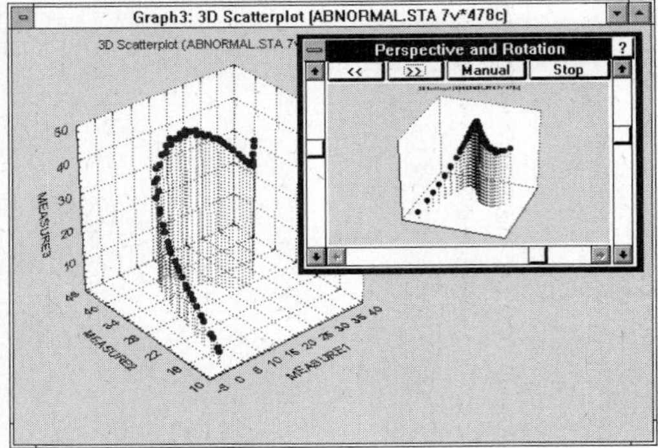

A simplified representation of the graph data is displayed initially (to reduce the redrawing time). All data points will be shown, however, if you request the *Spin* function, so that the complete pattern of data can be explored.

Note that specific adjustments of the viewpoint and perspective (e.g., for an exact reproduction of a display) can also be made by editing the numeric viewpoint parameters accessible by pressing the *More Options...* button in the *General Layout* dialog (use the pull-down menu *Layouts* or double-click on an empty area of the graph outside the axes).

37. Animated Stratification

Initiates the *Animated Stratification* graph redrawing mode. This analytic mode, available for all 3D sequential graphs, will redraw the graph by layers ("slice by slice") pausing after displaying each "cross-section" (e.g., a layer of a surface, a ribbon, a series of range blocks or boxes) to allow you to examine the image. The process is controlled by a pop-up panel (displayed at the top of the screen, see below).

Every time you press the *Continue* button, the next "slice" is drawn. Pressing the *Break* button will complete redrawing the graph scales and labels without completing the remaining layers (e.g., allowing you to print the current cross section). Pressing the *Cancel* button will exit the animated stratification mode and redraw the entire (complete) graph.

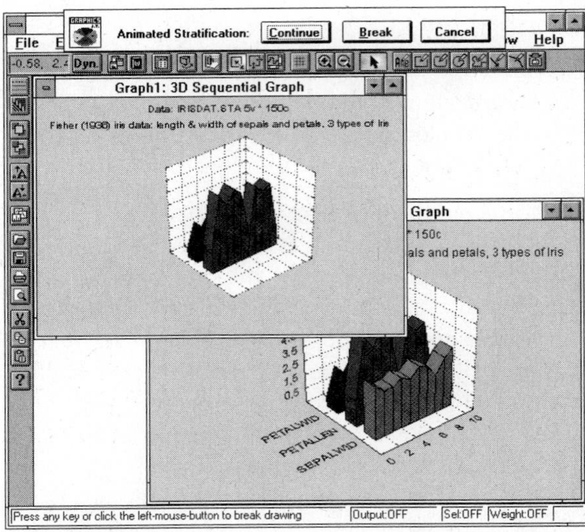

StatSoft

STATUS BAR (AT THE BOTTOM OF THE *STATISTICA* WINDOW)

The status bar, located on the bottom of the *STATISTICA* application window, is used to display short help messages and explanations, and also provides quick access to some of the most-commonly used system facilities.

STATISTICA: Basic Statistics and Tables

File Edit View Analysis Graphs Options Window Help

105.125882490914

Data: FACTOR.STA 10v * 100c

This file contains random variables based on two factors

	1 WORK_1	2 WORK_2	3 WORK_3	4 HOBBY_1	5 HOBBY_2	6 HOME_1	7 HOME_2
1	105.126	101.659	115.060	100.998	95.184	100.281	101.667
2	77.049	72.933	77.485	72.744	61.563	93.854	95.392
3	86.017	82.206	78.889	77.951	91.705	86.773	108.070
4	91.425	106.107	95.640	90.901	111.466	100.248	86.080

Brings up the starting dialog box for the current data analysis | Output:OFF | Sel:OFF | Weight:OFF

Time:00:04 | Cancel

0. Progress Bar with Timer

The status bar changes into a progress bar with a timer whenever data are processed. The *Cancel* button at the end of the bar allows you to interrupt the current processing.

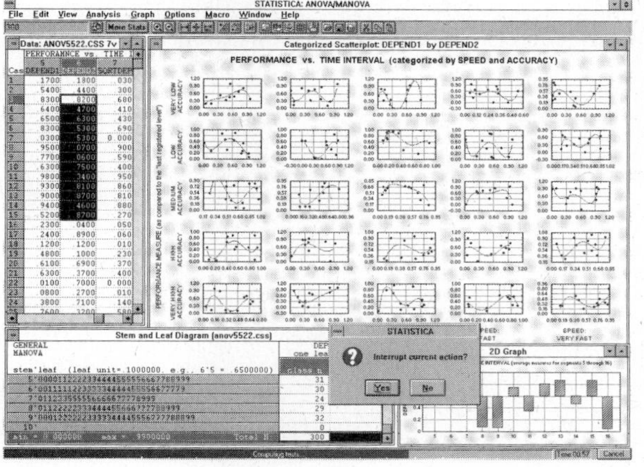

Interrupting Analyses

The timer displays the time that has elapsed from the point when the processing began. If you interrupt the processing temporarily, the timer will continue advancing, but it will automatically adjust for the length of the break if you decide to continue the processing (i.e., answer *No* to the prompt shown above).

Interrupting redraws of graphs. Note that redraws of graphs which are not accompanied by the display of the progress bar can be stopped by pressing any key or clicking with the mouse (anywhere on the screen).

Interrupting execution of *SCL* programs. Execution of *SCL* (*STATISTICA Command Language*) programs can be interrupted by clicking the mouse or pressing the ESC or CTRL+BREAK keys.

Multitasking

STATISTICA supports multitasking (between its modules or other applications).

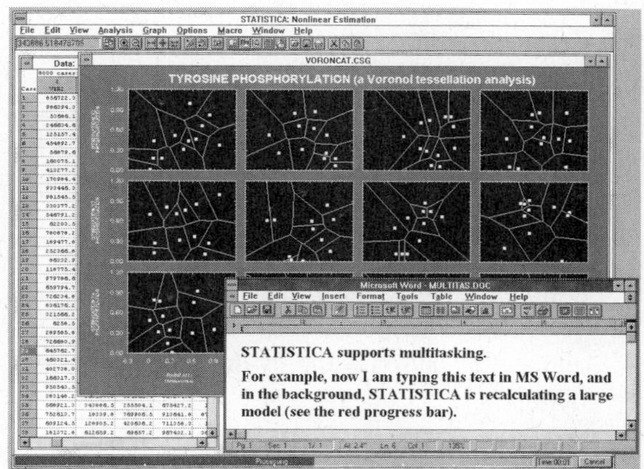

In cases when an unusually large data set or analysis design is being processed, you can switch to another *STATISTICA* module (or other Windows

StatSoft

applications) and the processing will continue in the background.

Clickable Control Fields on the Status Bar

As mentioned before, when the data are not being processed, the status bar is used to display short help messages and explanations, and it provides quick access to some of the most-commonly used facilities which control the output (e.g., printer, output file, *Text/output Window*; report style) and the processing of data (case selection, case weights). It also displays the status of the *STATISTICA* macro recording or execution.

All program control facilities accessible via those status bar shortcuts are also available from menus and via the keyboard (thus, they can be recorded into keyboard macros).

Ready

1. The Message Area

The Message Area of the status bar may serve as a "help button" -- when you double-click on it, the help index window will be brought up. This area is also used to display:

- Brief explanations of the currently highlighted menu choices or the toolbar buttons that are pressed, as shown above (to get a short description of a toolbar button without initiating the respective operation, keep the button pressed to read the message, then, before you release the mouse button, drag the mouse outside the button and only then release the button);
- Status information about the currently performed operation (e.g., *Extracting factors...*, *Operation in Progress...* or *Computing residuals...*);
- Brief instructions relevant to the current stage of analysis or the operation that is being performed (e.g., when a large graph is being redrawn or updated, the message reads: *Press any key or click the mouse to stop redrawing*; after pressing the *Rectangle drawing tool*, the message reads: *Drag in graph to create a rectangle (to cancel, press Esc or click the Point Tool)*).

Output:OFF

2. Output Control

The clickable *Output: OFF* field displays the current status of the output channel (e.g., *PRINTER* instead of *OFF*). It also acts as a button: by double-clicking on it, you can access the *Page/Output Setup* dialogs for printing Scrollsheets/spreadsheets and graphs. These dialogs are also displayed when you request output (e.g., by pressing the *Printer* button on the toolbar) at a point when no output channel (printer, disk file, or the on-screen *Text/output Window*) is specified. You can also access the dialogs from the *Page/Output Setup* option in the pull-down menu *File*. There are two related (layered) dialogs, one for *Text* and another for *Graphs*, which may be accessed from one another by selecting the respective option.

Printing Text/Scrollsheets/Spreadsheets. The options in this layer of the *Page/Output Setup* dialog affect the printing of all text (non-graphics) output displayed in Scrollsheets, data spreadsheets, produced by *STATISTICA BASIC*, etc.

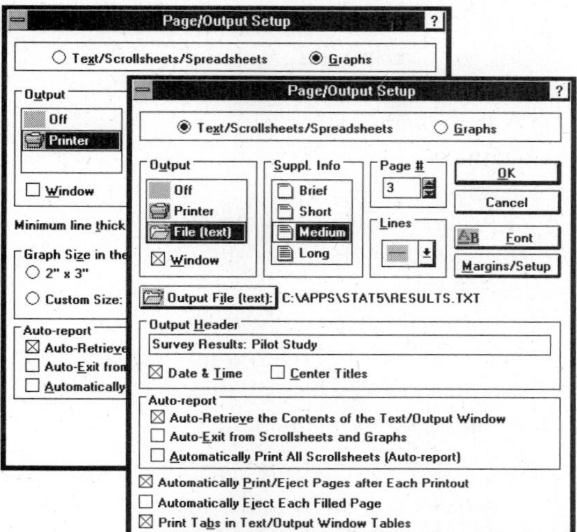

Output channel. In this dialog, you can direct the output to the *Printer*, disk *File*, and/or the optional *Window* (an on-screen text/graphics report log of output; for information on the *Text/output Window*, see the section on the *Text/output Window Toolbar*, page 1077).

Report styles. You can also choose between four different *Report styles,* determining the amount of supplementary information about the current file and the selected variables that will be automatically included with the output Scrollsheets (*Brief*, *Short*, *Medium*, and *Long*; press the help button ? or the F1 key in this dialog for descriptions of the styles).

Margins/Setup. Pressing the *Margins/Setup* button opens the dialog controlling the margins of the text output.

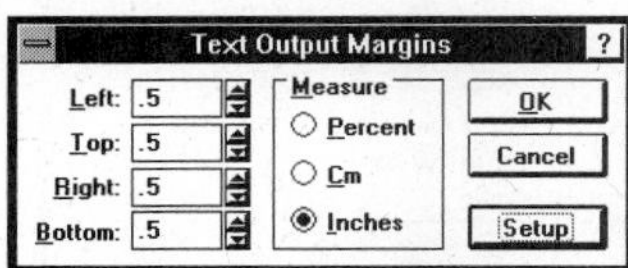

To control the paper orientation (portrait vs. landscape) for the text output, press the *Setup* button (this is the same as selecting the *Printer Setup* option from the pull-down menu *File*).

Note that the margins (as well as the page orientation, etc.) for the graphics printouts can be controlled independently (see below).

Other settings. You can also adjust other aspects of the printout, such as the starting page number and whether to print gridlines in the output tables (spreadsheets and Scrollsheets), and adjust the gridline style (see below), the font used, as well as the text of the optional output header to be printed on the top of each page, date, time, and centering of titles. Finally, this dialog allows you to set the page eject mode and auto-report mode (see below).

Gridlines in output and the speed of printing. Note that gridlines are printed as high-resolution graphics; thus the output is printed faster when the gridlines are suppressed (select the empty field in the list box *Lines*).

Auto-report options. The following *Auto-report* options allow you to automatically create a log (e.g., a text/graphics report) of all analyses performed (see page 1109 for auto-reporting options for graphics).

Auto-Exit from Scrollsheets and Graphs. When Scrollsheets (and/or graphs, see below) are created in batch as the result of an analysis (e.g., frequency tables for a series of variables), you can select this option to suppress the display of the *Continue* button in Scrollsheets when the queue is full. Now when you select the option *Automatically Print All Scrollsheets*, the Scrollsheets will be printed in batch, without interruption.

Automatically Print All Scrollsheets. This switch allows you to automatically generate a text-log of all Scrollsheets displayed on the screen, releasing you from having to press the *Printer* button to print individual Scrollsheets. The contents of every Scrollsheet generated on the screen are automatically sent to the current output channel (printer, disk file, and/or *Text/output Window*) following the report style and conventions defined in this dialog and in the *Print Scrollsheet* options dialog (see Chapter 4). When printing to the *Text/output Window* and used in conjunction with the *Automatically Print All Graphs* option (see printing graphs, page 1109), a combined text/graphics report of all text and graphics results produced during analyses can be created. Note that there is also a batch printing facility which can be used to print previously-saved Scrollsheet files (file name extension **.scr*) in batch, available by selecting the *Print Files...* option from the pull-down menu *File*, see page Chapter 3.

Auto-Retrieve the Contents of the Text-/Output Window. You may check this option in order to automatically open the most recently saved report file in the new *Text/output Window* (e.g., in order to append the current output to the results of a previous analysis). When this option is un-checked, then a blank *Text/output Window* will be opened from the *Page/Output Setup* dialog.

Automatically Print/Eject Pages after Each Printout. When this option is enabled, then after each text output is produced by the program (e.g., when requested via the *Print Data* or *Print Scrollsheet* options or the *Print* toolbar button), the page(s) will be ejected to the printer (or output file). Thus, each printout (table) will start on a new page. If your typical output is very short (e.g., a small Scrollsheet), but you generate a lot of them, then this option may slow you down, because the process of printing will be initiated very often (for each small part of the output); however, the advantage of this mode is that it generates hard copies as soon as they are requested.

Automatically Eject Each Filled Page. When this option is enabled, then each page of the printout will be finalized (ejected) as soon as the page is full. This mode is somewhat slower overall, as the process of printing is initiated separately for each filled page. However, the advantage of this setting is that it automatically produces hard copies of the output as your analysis progresses. Alternatively, when this switch is turned off (and the *Auto Print/Eject* switch is turned off, see the previous paragraph), then all output is accumulated in an internal buffer and sent to the printer all at once at the end of the session (or whenever you select the *Print/Eject Current Pages* option in the pull-down menu *File*, which allows you to "flush out" the output buffer at any point).

Print Tabs in Text Output Tables. When this option is selected, columns in Scrollsheets will be separated by tabs when printed to the *Text/output Window* (this is the default setting). Text tables formatted in this way may be easily converted to tables in word processors (e.g., MS Word).

Printing Graphs. The options in this layer of the *Page/Output Setup* dialog affect the printing of graphs.

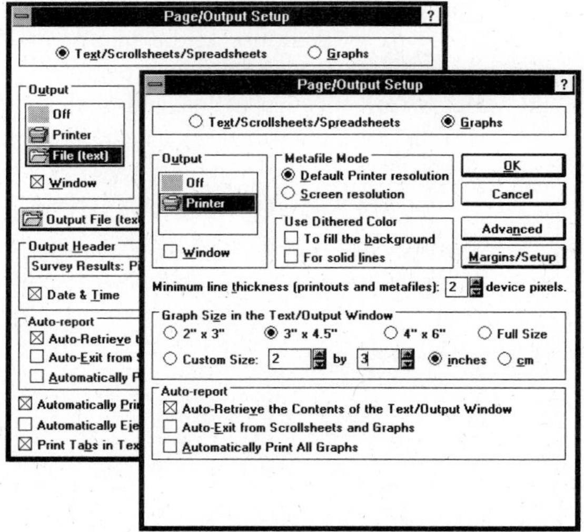

Output channel. In this dialog, you can direct the output to the *Printer*, and/or the optional *Window* (an on-screen text/graphics report log of

output; for information on the *Text/output Window*, see the section on the *Text/output Window Toolbar*, page 1077).

Metafile Mode. All graphics metafiles produced in *STATISTICA*, including Clipboard representations, saved metafiles, and graphs printed to the *Text/output Window* may be represented either in printer resolution (which produces the highest-quality output but uses more memory or disk space), or in screen resolution (which produces better on-screen appearance).

Dithered Color. These options control the use of dithered colors in filling the graph background and the background of custom text, legend, embedded objects, etc. (by default, this option is deselected to allow for optimal appearance of the graph when printed), and in printing solid lines (this option may be useful when the lines are very thick; otherwise the lines may appear "broken").

***Advanced* options.** Pressing the *Advanced* button opens a dialog with additional, less often used, options controlling creation of graphic output including graphic *OLE* objects.

***Margins/Setup*.** Pressing the *Margins/Setup* button opens the dialog controlling the margins of the graphics output.

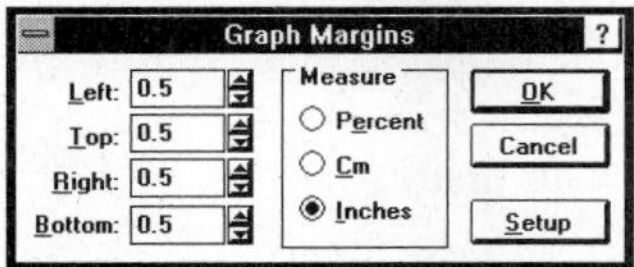

To control the paper orientation (portrait vs. landscape), printer resolution, etc. for the graphics output, press the *Setup* button (this is the same as selecting the *Printer Setup* option from the pull-down menu *File*).

Note that the margins (as well as the page orientation, etc.) for text printouts can be controlled independently (see above).

Minimum line thickness. Specify here the minimum line thickness for printouts and metafiles (in printer or other device pixels). This option is particularily relevant when using a high resolution output device (e.g., 1200 DPI where single-pixel lines are too thin) and also when you set the default size of a graph in the *Text/output Window* to a small size (e.g., 2x3, see the option *Graph Size in Text/output Window*, below).

Unless you increase the default setting of this option (2 printer pixels), the width of all lines printed by *STATISTICA* is determined either by the individual settings of the line width for specific graph components (by default .5 points) or by 2 (device) pixels, whichever is greater. This option allows you to determine the minimum printed line thickness; e.g., if you set it to 3, then all printed lines will be at least 3 printer pixels wide even if they are set to a smaller setting in some *Points/Lines/Area Patterns* dialogs.

If the setting of the *Graph Size in Text/output Window* option is set to a size smaller than *Full*, then the line thickness will be proportionally thinner. You may need to adjust the minimum line thickness in order to compensate.

Graph Size. In this dialog, you may select the default size at which graphs will appear when printed to the *Text/output Window* (graphs may be re-sized after printing).

Auto-report options. The following *Auto-report* options allow you to automatically create a log (e.g., a text/graphics report) of all analyses performed (see above for auto-reporting options for Scrollsheets/spreadsheets).

***Auto-Retrieve the Contents of the Text-/Output Window*.** You may check this option in order to automatically open the most recently saved report file in the new *Text/output Window* (e.g., in order to append the current output to the results of a previous

analysis). When this option is un-checked, then a blank *Text/output Window* will be opened from the *Page/Output Setup* dialog.

Auto-Exit from Scrollsheets and Graphs. When graphs (and/or Scrollsheets, see above) are created in batch as the result of an analysis (e.g., the *Categorized Scatterplots* option in the *Descriptive Statistics* dialog), you can select this option to suppress the display of the *Next* button in graphs when the queue is full. Now when you select the option *Automatically Print All Graphs*, the graphs will be printed in batch, without interruption.

Automatically Print All Graphs. This switch allows you to automatically generate printouts of all graphs that are displayed on the screen. The output will be sent to the currently selected output channel (printer and/or *Text/output Window*). The current printout setup (e.g., printer, options, margins, paper orientation, etc., as selected in the graphics window *Printer Setup* dialog) will be used. Note that there is also a batch printing facility which can be used to print previously-saved graphs (file name extension **.stg*) in batch, available by selecting the *Print Files...* option from the pull-down menu *File*, see Chapter 3.

When printing to the *Text/output Window* and used along with the *Automatically Print All Scrollsheets* option (see above), a combined text/graphics report of all analyses can be automatically created. See page 1077 for more information about options available to format reports in the *Text/output Window*.

Sel:OFF

3. Case Selection Conditions

The clickable *Sel: OFF* field displays the current status of the *Case Selection Conditions*, that is, optional user-defined conditions (or "filters") which can be used to select a particular subset of cases for an analysis.

Normally, all cases encountered in the data file are processed (as long as they do not have missing data). However, you may define temporary subsets of data and temporarily limit an analysis to those subsets only (e.g., only females older than 60, who either have a high cholesterol level or high blood pressure). The *Sel: OFF* field also acts as a button: by double-clicking on it, you can bring up the *Case Selection Conditions* status panel, displaying the currently-specified conditions (if any were defined).

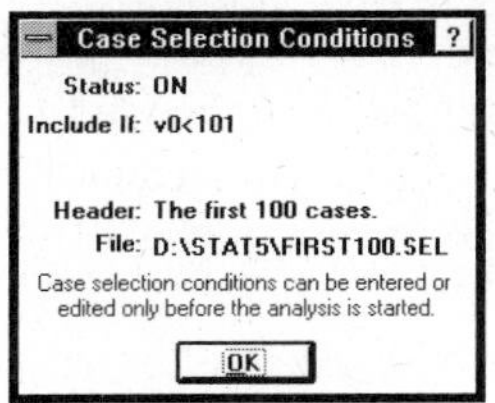

If the conditions were accessed from a file, then information about that file is also displayed in the dialog (e.g., a comment). Unless you are at the beginning of the analysis, only the status information on *Case Selection Conditions* is displayed with no option to change them because otherwise different stages of computations would be based on different subsets of data. However, if you double-click on the status bar field at any point when the conditions can be adjusted (e.g., before an analysis is started), a different window will appear allowing you to enter or edit the text of the conditions.

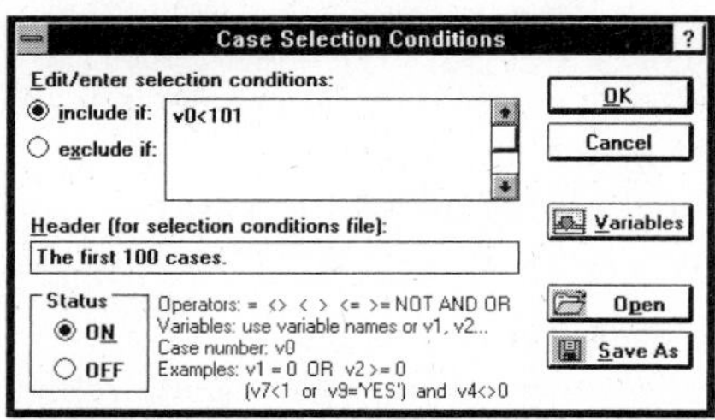

StatSoft

The syntax of those conditions is very simple (note the examples in the help area of the dialog).

You can refer to variables by their numbers (e.g., *v1*, *v2*, *v3*, ...; note that *v0* is the case number) or names (e.g., *Income*, *Profit*). Thus, for example, the condition:

Include if: `v0<101 and v1=1`

will include in the analysis only cases from the first 100 (i.e., case number has to be less than *101*) and where the value of variable number 1 (i.e., *v1*) is *1*. Note that if the name of variable number 1 was *Gender*, and for this particular variable, *1* was equivalent to the text value *MALE* (see the section on text/numeric "double notation" of values in *STATISTICA*, Chapter 7), the same case selection condition could be alternatively entered as:

Include if: `v0<101 and GENDER = 'MALE'`

The syntax of the conditions supports parentheses and various operators and allows you to specify case selection conditions of practically unlimited complexity.

The currently-specified conditions can be preserved even if you turn off the computer (when you exit the program, *STATISTICA* will ask you if you want to preserve the current conditions).

Other applications for the *Case Selection Conditions*. The conditions can also be saved and used with other data sets or for different purposes in *STATISTICA*. The latter is possible because the same syntax and conventions are used in all facilities of the *STATISTICA* system which require or allow you to custom-define subsets of cases. For example, the same conventions apply to the data *Recoding* facility (available by pressing the Vars spreadsheet button, see page 1053), data verification facilities (available in the *Data Management* module, see Chapter 7), or all procedures which allow you to custom-define multiple subsets of data (such as frequency tables, or graphs which display multiple-subsets of data).

Case selection conditions can also be specified by pressing the *Select Cases* button. This button is included on all startup panels and all analysis definition dialogs which are displayed before the data processing begins.

Weight:OFF

4. Case Weights

The clickable *Weight: OFF* field displays the current status of the *Case Weight* option, that is, an option to treat values of a selected variable as (integer) case multipliers when processing data. The weights can be used either for analytic purposes (e.g., some observations may be measurably more "important" and this importance can be represented by some weight scores) or to economize data storage (e.g., in some large data sets, such as some aspects of census or survey data, many cases may be identical, and thus can be represented by one case with an appropriate case weight attached to it).

The *Weight: OFF* field also acts as a button: By double-clicking on the *Weight* field, you can bring up the *Case Weight* status panel, displaying the weight variable (if one was defined).

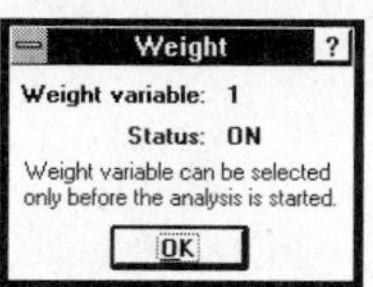

Unless you are at the beginning of the analysis, only the status information on the case weight is displayed with no option to change it, because otherwise different stages of computations would be based on different configurations of data. However, if you double-click on the status bar field at any point when the weight can be adjusted (e.g., before an analysis is started), a different window will

StatSoft

appear, allowing you to specify a weighting variable:

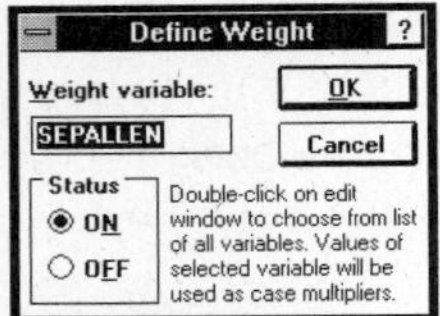

Case weights can also be specified by pressing the *Case Weight* button: . This button is included on all startup panels and all analysis definition dialogs which are displayed before the data processing begins.

5. Macros (Current Status)

The *macro* status field (the last field of the status bar) is normally empty unless the currently performed operation involves a recorded macro. When you are recording a macro, then the *REC* sign flashes in the *Macro* status field.

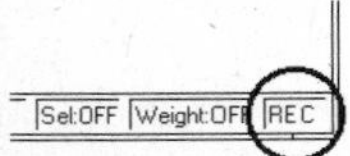

Press CTRL+F3 to stop the recording.

Two types of macros are supported in *STATISTICA*: editable sequences of keystrokes and recorded actions (sequences of mouse movements and/or keyboard activity). Recorded macros can also be opened and edited in the keystroke sequence editor. See Chapter 6 for more information on both types of macros.

StatSoft

INDEX

StatSoft

Chapter 3:

SPREADSHEET WINDOW: MENUS, DIALOGS, OPTIONS

Table of Contents

Detailed Table of Contents

StatSoft

StatSoft

StatSoft

StatSoft

Chapter 3:

SPREADSHEET WINDOW: MENUS, DIALOGS, OPTIONS

DRAG-AND-DROP AND *AUTOFILL* IN SPREADSHEETS

The *Drag-and-Drop* Facilities

STATISTICA supports the complete set of standard spreadsheet (Excel-style) *Drag-and-Drop* facilities, as summarized below.

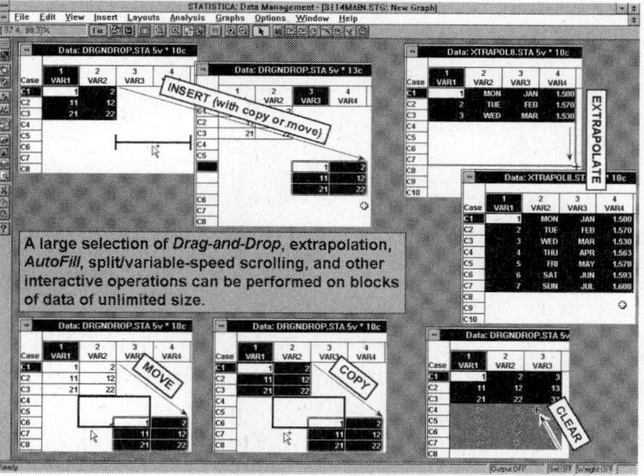
INSERT (with copy or move)
EXTRAPOLATE
A large selection of Drag-and-Drop, extrapolation, AutoFill, split/variable-speed scrolling, and other interactive operations can be performed on blocks of data of unlimited size.
MOVE
COPY
CLEAR

Scrollsheets support the same *Drag-and-Drop* facilities with the exception of inserting.

Note that the *Drag-and-Drop* operations can be disabled by selecting the *Disable All Drag-and-Drop Functions* option in the *STATISTICA Defaults: General* dialog (see page 1213).

Selecting a Block

Blocks may be selected by (1) drag-selecting (holding down the left-mouse-button) with the mouse, (2) clicking in one corner of the block to be highlighted, then scrolling to the desired opposite corner (the original cell will remain selected) and pressing the SHIFT key while clicking in that cell (SHIFT-click), or (3) holding down the SHIFT key while using the cursor keys on the keyboard.

To expand a previously selected block, you may use the SHIFT-cursor key, or scroll the display with the mouse and press the SHIFT key while clicking in the desired corner of the block.

To highlight a large block in "split-pane" mode (as shown below), click in a cell in one pane, then scroll to display the diagonally opposite corner in another pane and use SHIFT-click to select the block.

Data: FACTOR.STA 10v * 100c

This file contains random variables based on two factors

NUME VALU	1 WORK_1	2 WORK_2	3 WORK_3	8 HOME_3	9 MISCEL_1	10 MISCEL_2
1	105.126	101.659	115.060	85.553	104.035	110.278
2	77.049	72.933	77.485	88.609	70.115	72.000
3	86.017	82.206	78.889	93.348	86.021	70.688
4	91.425	106.107	95.640	93.822	101.224	82.665
5	113.714	92.029	99.079	69.621	82.820	70.022
6	86.606	87.817	67.663	108.622	91.400	79.776
95	89.763	99.258	101.209	79.894	79.874	83.703
96	94.618	117.866	103.155	109.056	115.109	115.603
97	84.764	97.653	91.380	115.453	106.268	109.385
98	138.876	117.427	112.185	114.626	138.351	149.032
99	95.370	89.835	107.429	110.570	108.448	105.657
100	106.050	120.708	119.815	93.385	109.357	83.794

Once a block is selected in a spreadsheet or Scrollsheet, you can perform one of the following *Drag-and-Drop* operations.

Moving a Block

A selected block of data may be moved by pointing to the border of the selection (the cross-cursor will change to an arrow) and dragging the block to the new location.

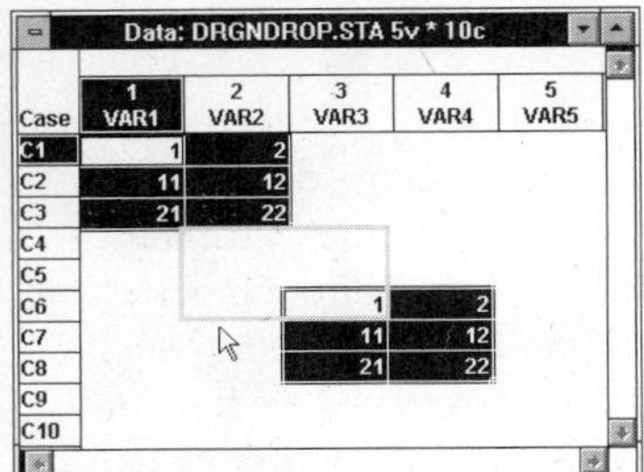

When the block of data is moved, missing values will be placed in those cells. See also, *Moving or copying values in the spreadsheet*, below.

Copying a Block

A block may be copied by pointing to the border of the selection (the cross-cursor will change to an arrow) and pressing the CTRL key (a "plus" sign will appear next to the cursor) while dragging a copy of the block to the new location.

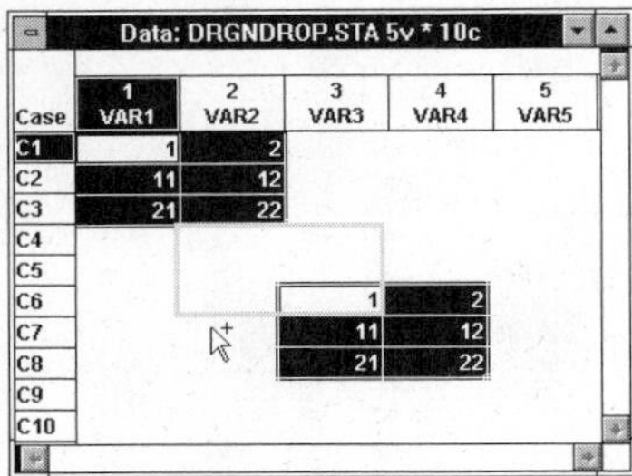

The default action which occurs when dragging a block without pressing the CTRL key may be changed from moving to copying in the *STATISTICA Defaults: General* dialog (see page 1213).

Moving or copying values in the spreadsheet. When you copy or move a block in the spreadsheet via *Drag-and-Drop*, the values which are copied or moved will depend on the display mode of the spreadsheet. If the spreadsheet is displaying numeric values (or value labels) when the block is copied or moved, then only those numeric values (or value labels) will be copied or moved. If the spreadsheet is displaying text values when the block is copied or moved, then not only are the text values copied or moved, but also the corresponding numeric values and value labels (if any).

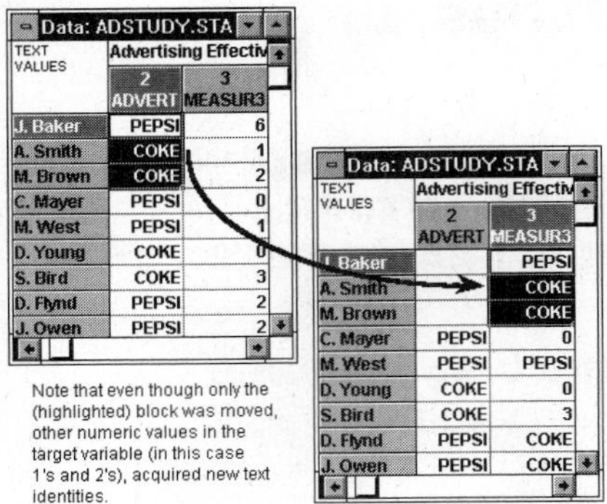

Note that even though only the (highlighted) block was moved, other numeric values in the target variable (in this case 1's and 2's), acquired new text identities.

This may result in the assignment of text values to numeric values that did not previously have text value equivalents (as shown in the illustration above).

Inserting a Block

You may insert a block between rows or columns by pressing the SHIFT key while dragging the block and pointing the cursor between rows or columns (if you also press the CTRL key, the block will be *copied and inserted* instead of *moved and inserted*; a plus will appear next to the arrow-cursor as in the *Drag-and-Drop* copy operation, as shown in the illustration below).

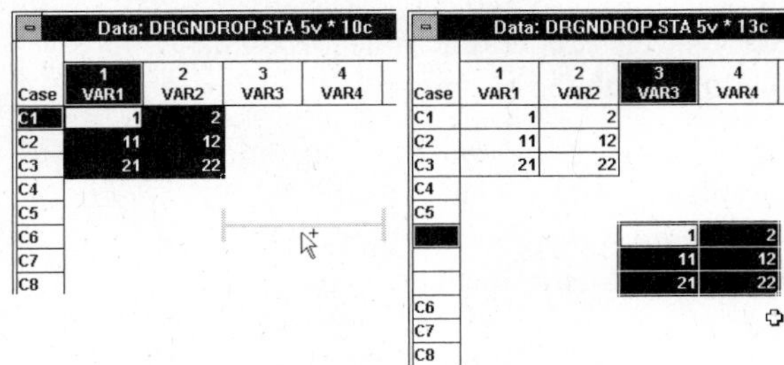

Note that all *Drag-and-Drop with Insert* (press the SHIFT key) operations will change the size of the data file (the *Insert* operation is not available in Scrollsheets); the same is true of simple dragging of blocks outside the boundaries of the current data file. However, dragging (without *Insert*) within the current data file boundaries produces results identical to using the Clipboard (except that the Clipboard is not used).

Clearing a Block

A portion of a (or an entire) block can be cleared by dragging within a selected block.

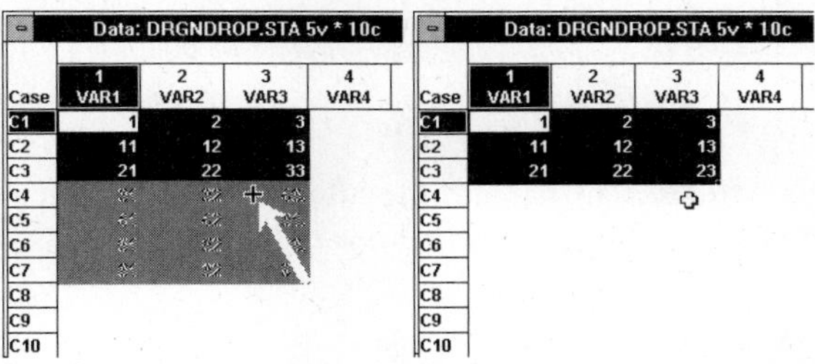

After highlighting the block, move the cursor to the lower-right corner of the block displaying the *Fill Handle*. When it changes to a "plus sign," hold down on the left-mouse-button and drag within the selected block. As you are dragging, the values within the block will become dimmed. When you release the left-mouse-button, the dimmed values will be deleted.

Expanding the Data File using *Drag-and-Drop*

If you drag a block past the current boundary of the spreadsheet, the data file will expand to make room for the new data.

Data: NEW.STA 6v * 10c

#	1 VAR1	2 VAR2	3 VAR3	4 NEWVAR4	5 NEWVAR5	6 NEWVAR6
1	4.000	20.000	4.000			
2	18.000	9.000	14.000			
3	15.000	3.000	10.000			
4	11.000	1.000	8.000			
5	7.000	1.000	2.000	4.000	20.000	4.000
6	1.000	8.000	13.000	18.000	9.000	14.000
7	2.000	11.000	16.000	15.000	3.000	10.000
8	8.000	12.000	17.000			

You can also expand the spreadsheet by using the *Insert* operation (see page 1126). This operation will insert the block between cases or variables, thereby increasing the size of the spreadsheet.

Note that whether you move, copy, or insert new cases or variables, when only part of the variables or cases are to be moved, copied, or inserted beyond the current boundary of the spreadsheet, then *STATISTICA* will fill the remaining values in the variable/case with missing data (see above).

Also note that if you work with large data files (e.g., more than 10 megabytes), you may wish to enable the option to *Ask before inserting rows or columns* in the *STATISTICA Defaults: General* dialog (see page 1213).

Extrapolating a Block (*AutoFill*)

A horizontal or vertical series in a block can be extrapolated by dragging the block *Fill Handle* (a small solid square located on the lower-right corner of the block). Note that if you highlight an entire row or column, then *Fill Handle*s will be displayed both at the top and bottom of the columns or at the beginning and end of the rows.

STATISTICA can create series of values such as sequential numbers, linear extrapolations, and dates (e.g., you can extend a series such as *1*, *2*, *3* to include *4*, *5*, *6*, ...).

Data: XTRAPOL8.STA 5v * 10c

Case	1 VAR1	2 VAR2	3 VAR3	4 VAR4
C1	1	MON	JAN	1.500
C2	2	TUE	FEB	1.570
C3	3	WED	MAR	1.530
C4				
C5				
C6				
C7				
C8				
C9				
C10				

Data: XTRAPOL8.STA 5v * 10c

Case	1 VAR1	2 VAR2	3 VAR3	4 VAR4
C1	1	MON	JAN	1.500
C2	2	TUE	FEB	1.570
C3	3	WED	MAR	1.530
C4	4	THU	APR	1.563
C5	5	FRI	MAY	1.578
C6	6	SAT	JUN	1.593
C7	7	SUN	JUL	1.608
C8				
C9				
C10				

You can extrapolate (*AutoFill*) a block in the following manners:

- If the initial selection contains repeated values, these values will be duplicated in the extended block.
- Non-identical values are extended by linear regression to compute extrapolated values for the series.
- If the block contains text values, then the text value in the last cell will be copied into the extended block.
- If a variable in the block contains dates (i.e., the variable format is set to *Dates* in the *Current Specs* dialog, see page 1161), then based on the pattern of dates, *STATISTICA* will extrapolate the dates appropriately.
- If a variable in the block contains text names (i.e., not dates) of months (e.g., *JAN*, *FEB*, *MAR*, ...), days (e.g., *MON*, *TUE*, *WED*, ...), or quarters (e.g., *Q1*, *Q2*, ...), then *STATISTICA* will extrapolate (in the desired direction) the rest of the names in the series (e.g., *APR*, *MAY*, ..., *DEC*; *THR*, *FRI*, *SAT*, *SUN*; *Q3*, *Q4*, respectively). The syntax for specifying these names is given below (note that it does not matter whether you use upper case or lower case letters; however you need to be consistent throughout the series; e.g., use *Jan*, *Feb*, *Mar*, ..., not *Jan*, *feb*, *Mar*, ...):

Months. The names of months can be spelled out or abbreviated in the following manner (note that the names are limited to 8 characters; therefore, "September" is shortened to "Septembe"):

- *January*, *February*, *March*, *April*, *May*, *June*, *July*, *August*, *Septembe*, *October*, *November*, *December*
- *Jan*, *Feb*, *Mar*, *Apr*, *May*, *Jun*, *Jul*, *Aug*, *Sep*, *Oct*, *Nov*, *Dec*

Days. The names of the days can be spelled out, or abbreviated in the following manner (note that the names are limited to 8 characters; therefore, "Wednesday" is shortened to "Wednesda"):

- *Monday*, *Tuesday*, *Wednesda*, *Thursday*, *Friday*, *Saturday*, *Sunday*
- *Mon*, *Tue*, *Wed*, *Thu*, *Fri*, *Sat*, *Sun*
- *M*, *Tu*, *W*, *Th*, *F*, *Sa*, *Su*

Quarters. The names of quarters of the year can be specified as follows in the variable:

- *Q1*, *Q2*, *Q3*, *Q4*

Extrapolating (*AutoFill* ing) a block upwards or to the left. In the same manner as extrapolating a block down or right, a block may be extrapolated by dragging the *Fill Handle* up or to the left past the original start of the block. Note that if you drag the *Fill Handle* up or to the left and stop within the original selection without going past the top or left side of the selection, you will delete data within the selection (data to be deleted are indicated in gray as you drag within the selection, see page 1127).

Note that you can use the *Fill Block* commands on the pop-up menu or *Edit* pull-down menu to copy the first row or the first column of cells in the block to adjacent cells within the currently selected block.

Variable-speed of Block Highlighting

You can control the speed at which you scroll when you extend a block outside the current display window. By moving the cursor a short distance away from the spreadsheet (or Scrollsheet), you can scroll one line at a time when a block is selected; scroll one page at a time by moving the cursor further away from the spreadsheet (or Scrollsheet).

SPLIT SCROLLING IN SPREADSHEETS AND SCROLLSHEETS

Spreadsheets and Scrollsheets can be split into up to four sections (panes) by dragging the split box (the black rectangle at the top of the vertical scrollbar or to the left of the horizontal scrollbar). This is useful if you have a large amount of information and you want to review results from different parts of the spreadsheet or Scrollsheet.

Data: ADSTUDY.STA 25v * 50c

Advertising Effectiveness Study.

Case	1 GENDER	2 ADVERT	3 MEASUR1	4 MEASUR2	5 MEASUR3	6 MEASUR4
J. Baker	MALE	PEPSI	9	1	6	8
A. Smith	MALE	COKE	6	7	1	8
M. Brown	FEMALE	COKE	9	8	2	9
C. Mayer	MALE	PEPSI	7	9	0	5
M. West	MALE	PEPSI	7	1	6	2
D. Young	FEMALE	COKE	6	0	0	8
S. Bird	FEMALE	COKE	7	4	3	2
D. Flynd	MALE	PEPSI	9	9	2	6
J. Owen	FEMALE	PEPSI	7	8	2	3
H. Morrow	MALE	PEPSI	6	6	2	8

To split a spreadsheet or Scrollsheet window vertically or horizontally, point with the mouse to the vertical or horizontal "split box" (a solid black region just above the upper vertical scroll arrow or next to the left horizontal scroll arrow) and drag the "split cursor" (↔ or ↕) to the row or column where you want the split to occur. You can split the spreadsheet or Scrollsheet into two (see above) or four (see below) "panes."

Data: ADSTUDY.STA 25v * 50c

Advertising Effectiveness Study.

#	1 GENDER	2 ADVERT	3 MEASUR1	4 MEASUR2	20 MEASUR18	21 MEASUR19	22 MEASUR20
1	MALE	PEPSI	9	1	1	8	2
2	MALE	COKE	6	7	0	8	4
3	FEMALE	COKE	9	8	6	2	1
4	MALE	PEPSI	7	9	8	1	0
5	MALE	PEPSI	7	1	7	4	4
46	MALE	PEPSI	8	8	8	8	1
47	FEMALE	COKE	9	4	6	6	3
48	FEMALE	PEPSI	7	5	0	0	8
49	FEMALE	COKE	7	9	8	3	5
50	MALE	COKE	5	2	4	0	4

Note that vertically split panes scroll together when you scroll vertically, while horizontally split panes scroll together when you scroll horizontally.

To remove a split pane from a spreadsheet or Scrollsheet, drag the split box between the scroll arrows to either end of the scroll bar.

To highlight a large block in "split-pane" mode, click in a cell in one pane, then scroll to display the diagonally opposite corner in another pane and use SHIFT-click (see *Selecting a Block*, below) to select the block. You can then use *STATISTICA*'s block operations (i.e., *Drag-and-Drop*, see below, and *Block Stats/Columns/Rows/Graphs*, see page 1189) on the selected block.

The split-pane display is also available in the *Graph Data Editor*,

Graph Data for Graph3: Histogram (ADSTUDY.STA 25v*50c)

Histogram (ADSTUDY.STA 25v*50c)

	MEASUR1 Bar X		MEASUR2 Bar X		MEASUR5 Bar X	
	X	Y	X	Y	X	Y
1	-0.40	1.00	-0.20	4.00	0.40	5.00
2	0.60	2.00	0.80	5.00	1.40	8.00
3	1.60	3.00	1.80	8.00	2.40	5.00
4	2.60	3.00	2.80	3.00	3.40	4.00
6	4.60	7.00	4.80	5.00	5.40	10.00
7	5.60	8.00	5.80	6.00	6.40	5.00
8	6.60	14.00	6.80	5.00	7.40	5.00
9	7.60	1.00	7.80	5.00	8.40	4.00
10	8.60	9.00	8.80	5.00	9.40	1.00

Megafile Manager, and other Scrollsheet-based windows.

DYNAMIC DATA EXCHANGE (*DDE*)

Overview

STATISTICA supports the *Dynamic Data Exchange* (*DDE*) conventions; thus, you can dynamically link a range of data in the spreadsheet to a subset of data in another (Windows) application.

Creating Links

You can establish a *DDE* (Dynamic Data Exchange) link between a "source" (or server) file (e.g., an Excel spreadsheet) and a *STATISTICA* data file (the "client" file), so that when changes are made to the data in the source file, the data will be automatically updated in the *STATISTICA* spreadsheet (client file).

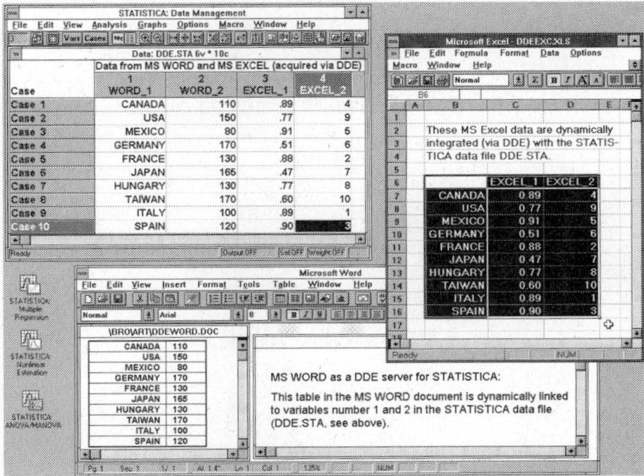

A common application for dynamically linking two files would be in industrial settings, where the *STATISTICA* data file would be dynamically linked with a measurement device (e.g., in order to automatically update specific measurements hourly).

DDE links can be established using the quick, "paste-like" *Paste Link* option in the spreadsheet pull-down menu *Edit* (see below), or by entering a definition of the link into the *Long name (label, formula, link):* field of the *Current Specs* dialog, and they can be managed in the *Link Manager* (see page 1192). You can also use the *DDE* link along with *STATISTICA Command Language* (via the *Run Module*, see below) in order to utilize *STATISTICA* output in another Windows application (e.g., Excel). You can dynamically link a source file with a *STATISTICA* data file in three ways, described in the following sections.

Paste Link

This option (available from the *Edit* pull-down menu, see *Paste Link*, page 1184) is the fastest and easiest way to establish a *DDE* link.

Step 1. Open the source file and copy to the Clipboard the block of data (or text) that you want to link with the client (*STATISTICA*) file. Now, leaving this server file open, switch to the desired *STATISTICA* module.

Step 2. In the *STATISTICA* spreadsheet, designate (highlight) the cell that will "anchor" the data to be pasted into the spreadsheet (the data will be pasted down and to the right of this "anchor" cell).

Step 3. Click on the *Paste Link* option to establish the link. *STATISTICA* will automatically write the *DDE* path (see below) and store it in the *variable long name* (see below) and in the *Links Manager* (see page 1192).

Long Variable Name

DDE links are stored and can be established (and edited) in the *Long Name* option of the *Current Specs* dialog.

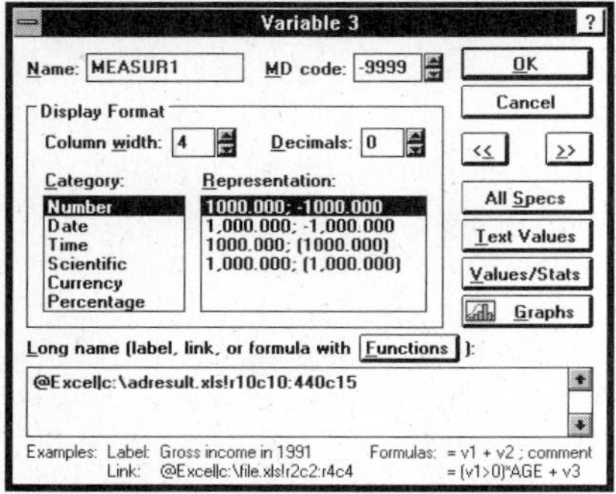

To establish a *DDE* link here, type in the link statement (*DDE* path). The link statement (e.g., *@Excel|c:\Excel\File.xls!r2c2:r4c4;c1;r1*) parts are described below.

(1) @Source Application| . Specify first the source (or server) application (in the above example, the source application is Excel). The *Source Application* must be separated from the rest of the link statement by a "|". You also need to designate whether the *DDE* link is "hot" (place an "@" in front of the *Source Application* to indicate that the client file will be updated whenever the server file is changed) or "cold" (place a "^" in front of the *Source Application* to indicate that the client file will be updated only when the user requests it or changes it back to "hot").

(2) Topic! . The *Topic* designates the name (and path) of the file in the source application and must be separated from the rest of the link statement by a "!" (be sure to establish the full path name for the file). In the above example, the *Topic* (*c:\Excel\File.xls!*) designates not only the name of the Excel file (*File.xls*) but also the drive and directory that the file is in (e.g., *c:\Excel*). How you identify the source file depends on the source application that you are using (refer to your source application for information on how to designate the *Topic*; when you use the *Paste Link* option (see above), this will automatically be designated for your specific application).

(3) Item; . Specify here the cell, range, named range, or some other name specific to your source application followed by a ";" (to separate it from the rest of the *DDE* path). What you specify here is dependent upon the source application (refer to your source application for information on how to designate the Item).

When you use the *Paste Link* option, see above, this will automatically be designated for your specific application). In the above example, a range in the Excel spreadsheet is defined (e.g., *r2c2:r4c4;* specifies the block "from row number 2, column number 2 to row number 4, column number 4").

(4) Column;row . This part of the *DDE* path is optional; by default (when no starting row or column is specified), *STATISTICA* places the first value in the range of linked data into the first cell (row) of the highlighted variable in the spreadsheet and continues placing values down and to the right of this "anchor" cell. If you wish to "anchor" the linked data in a different cell (area) of the spreadsheet, you can designate the column number and row number (separated by a ";") to identify the position of that cell. Alternatively, you can designate only the column (variable) number and *STATISTICA* will use the first cell (row) in that column as the "anchor." Because this portion of the *DDE* path is optional, it is not automatically designated when you use *Paste Link* (see above).

Links Manager

When a link is established, it can be managed using the *Links Manager* (accessible via the *Links...* option in the spreadsheet pull-down menu *Edit*).

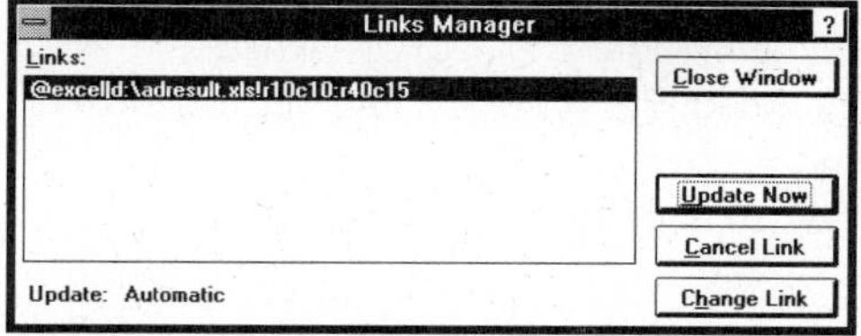

Links. This window displays all the *DDE* links in *STATISTICA*. You can edit a link by highlighting it in this window and then clicking on the *Change Link* button (see below).

Update. Displays the status of the *DDE* link that is currently highlighted in the *Links* window. *DDE* links can be either "hot" (*automatic* status, the "@" symbol precedes the link statement) or "cold" (*manual* status, the "^" symbol precedes the link statement). *Automatic* status means that the linked data in the *STATISTICA* spreadsheet (client file) will automatically be updated whenever any changes are made to the data in the server application. *Manual* status means that the *DDE* link is temporarily disabled and that you will have to manually update the client file using the *Update Now* button or by changing the status back to "hot" (using the *Change Link* button).

Update Now. Click on this button to manually update the *DDE* link (that is currently highlighted in the *Links* window) in the client file (*STATISTICA* spreadsheet data file).

Cancel Link. Click on this button to temporarily disable the currently highlighted *DDE* link. NOTE: When you are about to run an analysis on the linked data file, be sure to use this option to temporarily disable the link so that the data are not changing as the analysis is running. You can resume the link by clicking on the *Update Now* button.

Change Link. Click on this button to open the *Current Specs* dialog in which you can edit the *DDE* link in the *Long Name-Link* option (see *Creating Links (Dynamic Data Exchange)* for detailed information concerning the parts of the *DDE* path).

There are also other applications for the *DDE* data integration facilities in *STATISTICA*; see the *Electronic Manual* on *DDE* for details.

DDE Links, *STATISTICA* *Command Language*, and the Run Module

You can build *STATISTICA Command Language* (*SCL*) commands or entire *SCL* programs into macros created within and run from other Windows applications (e.g., Excel, MS Word, Ami Pro, Quattro Pro). See below for an example of an Excel macro that uses *SCL* commands and the *STATISTICA Run Module* in order to compute some descriptive statistics.

```
Excel macro DDE_EX.XLM:
channel=INITIATE("STA_RUN","SYSTEM")
=EXECUTE(channel, "DESC VARS=ALL")
=TERMINATE(channel)
=RETURN()
```

Line 1. Opens a *DDE* channel to *STATISTICA* (specifically the *Run Module*). Note that *STATISTICA* needs to be on the path, or *Sta_run.exe* needs to be running in order to open a *DDE* channel.

Line 2. Tells *STATISTICA* to execute the *SCL* command "*DESC VARS=ALL*" (i.e., compute descriptive statistics on all variables).

Line 3. Tells Excel to close the *DDE* conversation.

Line 4. Returns to the source application.

This simple example illustrates how you can open a *STATISTICA* module, run a program and then return to the other Windows application. You can also include in the macro commands to copy the *STATISTICA* text output and/or graphs to the Clipboard and then paste it back to the Windows application so that the output can be used in that application (e.g., as part of a report in MS Word).

Note. You can temporarily disable a link in the *Links Manager* (see above) in order to run an analysis using the linked data file. If you do not disable the link and the data are updated while it is

being analyzed in *STATISTICA*, then the resulting analysis may not be meaningful.

SPREADSHEET *FILE* PULL-DOWN MENU

The following dialogs and options are available from the spreadsheet *File* pull-down menu.

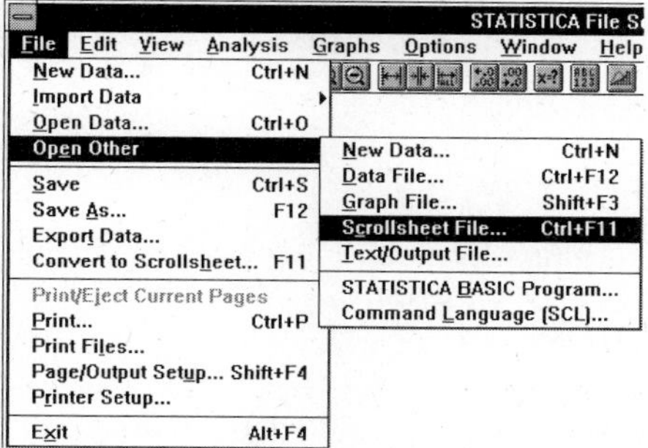

Each of these options are discussed below.

New Data

This option (from the *File* pull-down menu) will enable you to open a new file in which you can enter data. When you select this option, the *New Data*: *Specify File Name* dialog (see below) will open, allowing you to select a file name under which to save the new spreadsheet. After selecting the file name, a 10 variables by 10 cases spreadsheet will be created.

Data: NEW.STA 10v * 10c

NUM VAL	1 VAR1	2 VAR2	3 VAR3	4 VAR4	5 VAR5	6 VAR6	7 VAR7	8 VAR8	9 VAR9	10 VAR10
1										
2										
3										
4										
5										
6										
7										
8										
9										
10										

You can now enter data into the spreadsheet, add/delete cases and variables, edit the variable names and specifications (see *Spreadsheet Edit (Current) Specs*, page 1160) or case names (see *Spreadsheet Edit Case Names*, page 1179), as well as perform other spreadsheet operations (see *Spreadsheet Edit Menu*, page 1157).

You can also create a new data file according to your detailed file specifications [specify the number of variables and cases, automatically create specific sequential variable numbers, define the defaults (e.g., formats), or get the complete set of file definition specifications from another data file, (including the numeric-text value assignments and value labels)] in the *Data Management* module (see Chapter 7).

Spreadsheet Open Other...

This sub-menu is common to all menus (spreadsheet, Scrollsheet, graph, *Text/output Window*), allowing access to all types of *STATISTICA* files.

Open Other
Save Ctrl+S
Save As... F12
Export Data...
Convert to Scrollsheet... F11
Print/Eject Current Pages
Print... Ctrl+P
New Data... Ctrl+N
Data File... Ctrl+F12
Graph File... Shift+F3
Scrollsheet File... Ctrl+F11
Text/Output File...
STATISTICA BASIC Program...
Command Language (SCL)...

These options allow you to open a *New Data* file (page 1135), *Data File* (page 1136), *Graph File* (page 1136), *Scrollsheet File* (page 1136), *Text/output File* (page 1137), *STATISTICA BASIC Program* or *Command Language (SCL)* program file (see the *Electronic Manual* for more information on these last two options). When you select the *New Data* option, the *New Data: Specify File Name* dialog (page 1137) will open, from which you can select a file name under which the new spreadsheet will be saved. After selecting the file name, a 10 variables by 10 cases spreadsheet will be created.

Selecting any of the other options listed above will open the respective *File Open/Save As* dialog (page 1137) in which you can select the file name to open.

Open Data File

Selecting this option from the *File* pull-down menu will bring up the *Open Data File* dialog (see above) from which you can select a *STATISTICA* data file (file with the extension **.sta*) to open. *STATISTICA* data files contain data values and also labels and formats (see: *Spreadsheet Edit (Current) Specs*, page 1160), headers and notes (see: *File Header*, page 1180) and other information. In order to open a non-*STATISTICA* format data file (e.g., Excel, Lotus, Quattro, dBASE, Paradox, ASCII, and others), use the *Import Data* option in the same menu (see page 1138).

Opening multiple data files. Only one data file can be open in a module at one time; however, you can open multiple files (e.g., and copy and paste between them) in different modules or using the *STATISTICA File Server* application. Multiple *File Server* applications can run simultaneously, each with a different data file open.

Toolbar button. See also the spreadsheet window toolbar button.

Keyboard shortcut. CTRL+O

Open Graph File

Selecting this option from the *File* pull-down menu will bring up the *Open Graph File* dialog (see below) from which you can select a *STATISTICA* graph file (file with the extension **.stg*) to open. The *STATISTICA* graph files contain not only the graph (in the *STATISTICA* Graph format) but also all customizations (e.g., drawings, embedded objects, etc.) and the data values represented in the graph. The data can be edited or manipulated after the graph file is opened.

STATISTICA graphs are *OLE* objects, and therefore you cannot simultaneously open more than one instance of the same object by the system (either in the same or different modules). For that reason, if you attempt to open a graph file that is currently open in any module, then a copy of that graph will be opened and the title bar of the duplicate graph will refelect this status (e.g., "*Copy of Hist.stg: ...*").

Keyboard shortcut. SHIFT+F3

Open Scrollsheet File

Selecting this option from the *File* pull-down menu will bring up the *Open Scrollsheet* dialog (see below) from which you can select a Scrollsheet file (file with the extension **.scr*) to open. Scrollsheet files contain the output data and all formatting and customization information (e.g., highlights, custom colors, etc.).

Keyboard shortcut. CTRL+F11

Open Text-/output File

Selecting this option from the *File* pull-down menu will bring up the *Open Text File* dialog (see below) from which you can select a text file (file name extension **.txt*) or *RTF* file (file name extension **.rtf*) to open. The text file that you select here will be opened in the *Text/output Window* (see page 1198).

Open *STATISTICA BASIC* Program

Selecting this option from the *File* pull-down menu will bring up the *Open STATISTICA BASIC File* dialog (see below) from which you can select a *STATISTICA BASIC* file (file name extension **.stb*) to open. The program file that you select here will be opened in the *STATISTICA BASIC Window* (see the *Electronic Manual* for details).

Open Command Language (*SCL*)

Selecting this option from the *File* pull-down menu will bring up the *Open SCL File* dialog (see below) from which you can select a *Command Language* (*SCL*) file (file name extension **.scl*) to open. The program file that you select here will be opened in the *SCL Window* (see the *Electronic Manual* for details).

File Open/Save As Dialog

You can open (options *New Data*, *Open Data*, *Open Other*) or save (options *Save*, *Save As*) a new spreadsheet, Scrollsheet, graph, or Text/output file in this dialog.

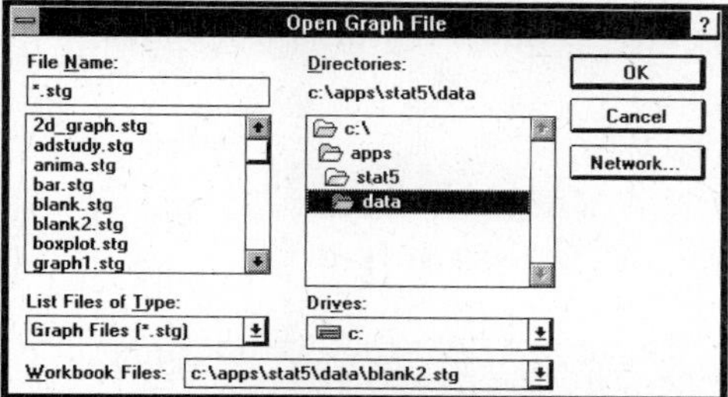

A similar dialog also opens each time you need to select a file to save or open. Each of the above pull-down menu options will open the respective *File Open/Save As* dialog with the following options.

Opening files. *STATISTICA* files can be opened in one of several ways:

- Select the appropriate *Open* option from the *File* pull-down menu or click on the toolbar button to bring up the *File Open/Save As* dialog (described below).
- Double-click on the file name in the Windows *File Manager* in order to open the file in the *STATISTICA File Server* application.
- Drag a file from the Windows *File Manager* and drop it on a *STATISTICA* module icon in order to open that module with the desired file.
- Set the desired files to *Auto Open* in the *Data File Header, Notes, and Workbook Info* dialog. When the associated data file is opened, these files will then open automatically.

File Name

Select from the list or enter the file name here. The main types of files used by *STATISTICA* have the following extensions (see *STATISTICA File Name Extensions* in the *Electronic Manual* for a complete up-to-date listing of the file name extensions):

- Spreadsheet--*STATISTICA* system data files (includes data, variable names, long labels, formulas and links, case names, text values, variable specifications, file notes, and other information); file name extension: **.sta*.
- Scrollsheet--*STATISTICA* output windows (includes the formatted output table); file name extension: **.scr*.
- Graph (includes graphs, graph customizations, embedded graphic objects, links, and graph data); file name extension: **.stg*.
- Text (such as text files created or used in the *Text/output Window* and saving *Graphic Text Editor* data as text files); file name extension: **.txt*.
- Rich Text Format (such as *RTF* files created or used in the *Text/output Window*); file name extension: **.rtf*.
- *STATISTICA BASIC;* file name extension: **.stb*.
- *Megafile Manager;* file name extension: **.mfm*.

List Files of Type

Choose to list in the *File Name* section all the files of a specific type (i.e., spreadsheet/Scrollsheet-/Graph files, backup files, *Megafile Manager* files, or all files). In order to open a non-*STATISTICA* format data file (e.g., Excel, Lotus, Quattro, dBASE, Paradox, ASCII, and others), use the *Import Data* option in the same menu (see below).

Directories

Specify the *Directory* in which the file is located.

Drives

Specify the *Drive* in which the file is located.

Workbook Files

Click on this combo box in order to select a file from a list of supplementary files (e.g., graph files, **.ini* files, import/export files, Scrollsheet files, etc.) associated with the current data file (a log of all supplementary files associated with the current data file is maintained in the *STATISTICA Workbook*). For easy access to a desired file, this list is sorted by file type (e.g., **.scr* file) that you would like to open/save. Files which are not relevant for the current open/save operation are dimmed (they are included for reference only).

Save as Text

This option is only applicable to the *Text/output Window* [including *STATISTICA BASIC* program files, *Command Language* (*SCL*) program files, *SEPATH* command files, and all other applications of the *Text/Output Window*].

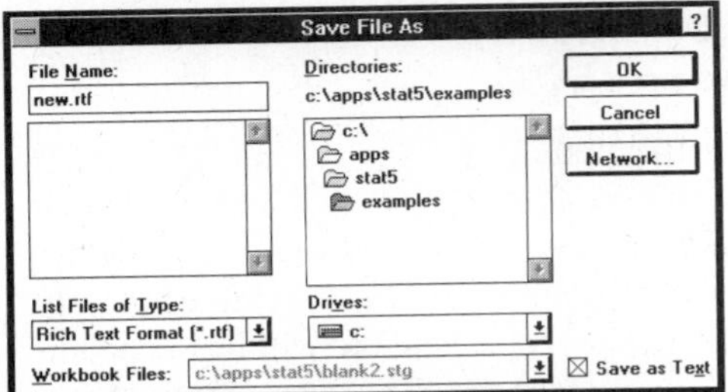

Select this option in order to save the contents of the *Text/output Window* in the standard ASCII text format (file name extension **.txt*). If this option is *not* selected, *STATISTICA* will save the file in the *RTF* format to preserve all special formatting (font, spacing, graphs, etc.). The default (*RTF*) format is normally preferable, but the resulting file cannot be edited with programs which do not support the *RTF* format. If you save it as text, the file can be processed by virtually any program; however, all formatting information and graphs will not be preserved.

Import Data - Quick Import

Importing data to *STATISTICA* by converting foreign data files (e.g., worksheets or data bases) is one of several ways (offered in *STATISTICA*) of accessing data from other applications. Other methods include establishing dynamic *DDE* links between data files and using the Clipboard (which in *STATISTICA* recognizes special Clipboard formatting conventions used by other Windows applications such as Excel or Lotus).

This option will allow you to quickly import files from spreadsheet and data base programs and from ASCII (text) files. *STATISTICA* also features an interface to a wide variety of data base formats via the *ODBC* option and an additional set of specialized data import facilities in the *Data Management* module, which support a large selection of data file formats and offer some additional options for specialized data transfers (e.g., options to split/merge data values and their labels while transferring data to/from file formats which do not support labeled values). The *Quick Import* and *ODBC* options are available from the *File* pull-down menu of every *STATISTICA* module.

When you click on the *Quick Import* option in the *File* pull-down menu and select the desired file to import, the *Quick Import from ...* dialog will open.

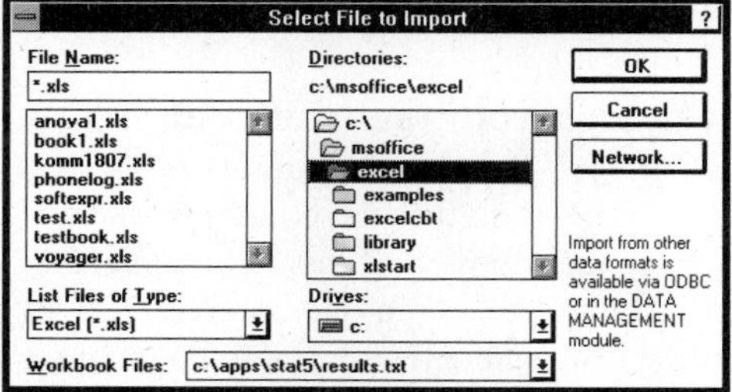

Importing text values longer than 8 characters. If the text values imported using the *Quick Import* options are longer than 8 characters, then value labels will be created to store the long text values in their entirety; the first 8 characters of each value will be used to create the respective *STATISTICA* text values. Note that if this would produce text values which are not uniquely related to the long labels (i.e., create a situation when the same text value would be accompanied by different value labels in different cases), then the last character(s) of the text values will be replaced by digits to create unique text values for the respective value labels.

For example, if the values in the source data set (to be imported) are:

```
Arizona, the south region
Arizona, the north region
Arizona, the central part
```

then those values will be stored as value labels, and the corresponding (unique) 8-character text values will be created as:

```
Arizona1
Arizona2
Arizona3
```

The same conventions apply when you import data to the *STATISTICA* spreadsheet via the Clipboard [e.g., by copying a block of values in a foreign spreadsheet (highlight a block in the spreadsheet and press CTRL+C) and pasting them to the *STATISTICA* spreadsheet (place the cursor in the desired position and press CTRL+V)]. If the text values are longer than 8 characters, then they will be interpreted as *STATISTICA* value labels, and the respective (short) text values will be created from the first 8 characters of each long text (as illustrated above).

Quick Import - Spreadsheet Files

The following options are available in this dialog if you are importing a Lotus, Excel, or Quattro file. Note that if the selected spreadsheet file includes multiple worksheets, then *STATISTICA* will display a list in which you can select the desired worksheet to import.

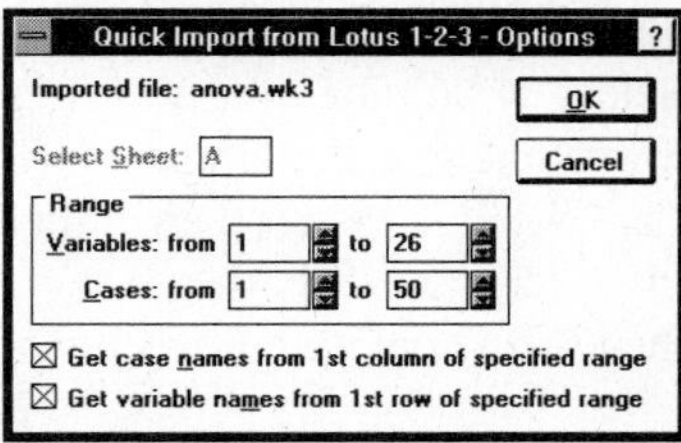

Imported file. The name of the selected file to import will be displayed here.

Select sheet. Specify the desired sheet to be imported here. This option is only available if a Lotus 1-2-3 (Release 3 or later) file or a Quattro file is being imported. If an Excel file is imported, the selection of sheets is available in the subsequent dialog.

StatSoft

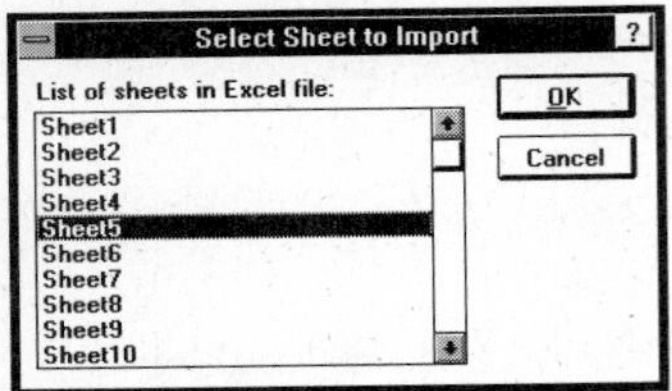

Range. This option permits selection of a specific range of cases and/or variables to be imported.

Variables: Specify the range of variables (columns) to be imported (*From* which variable, *To* which variable, inclusive).

Cases: Specify the range of cases (rows) to be imported (*From* which case, *To* which case, inclusive).

Get case names from 1st column of specified range. Select this option in order to import case names from the first column of the specified range (see above). If this field contains more than 20 characters, then only the first 20 will be used as the case name. If this column contains numeric values instead of text, the case names will be created as "text images" of these values.

Get variable names from 1st row of specified range. Select this option to use the labels from the first row of the specified import range (see above). If any label is longer than eight characters, it will be truncated and only the first eight characters will be used as the variable name.

Quick Import - Data Base Files

The following options are available in this dialog if you are importing a dBASE, Paradox, or Access file.

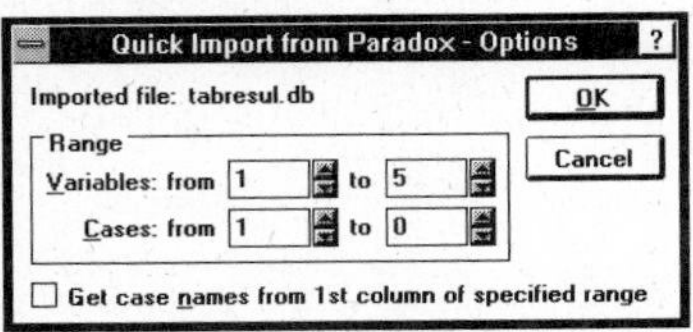

Imported file. The name of the selected file to import will be displayed here.

Range. This option permits selection of a specific range of cases and/or variables to be imported.

Variables: Specify the range of variables (columns) to be imported (*From* which variable, *To* which variable, inclusive).

Cases: Specify the range of cases (rows) to be imported (*From* which case, *To* which case, inclusive).

Get case names from 1st column of specified range. Select this option in order to import case names from the first column of the specified range (see above). If this field contains more than 20 characters, then only the first 20 will be used as the case name. If this column contains numeric values instead of text, the case names will be created as "text images" of these values.

Quick Import - Text Files

The following options are available in this dialog if you are importing a text file.

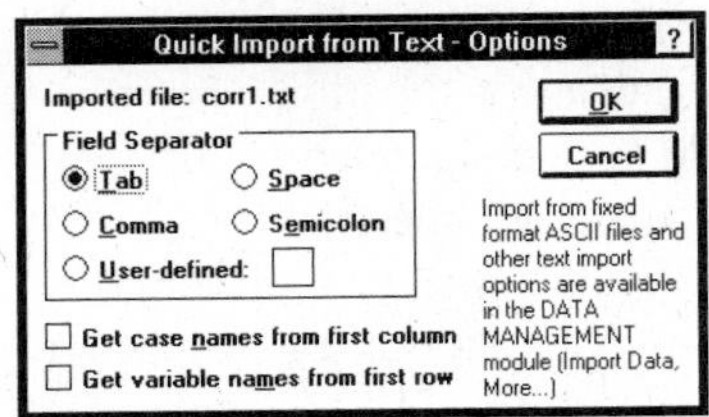

As *STATISTICA* imports the file via the *Quick Import* facility, it will create as many rows as there are lines in the ASCII file. *STATISTICA* will also search for the longest record in the ASCII file. The length of this record will determine the number of variables in the *STATISTICA* data file. For any record in the ASCII file that is smaller than this record, *STATISTICA* will fill the values with missing data (up to the length of the longest record).

Imported file. The name of the selected file to import will be displayed here.

Field separator. Specify the character which is used in the input file as the delimiter. You can select the type of delimiter used from four pre-defined separators (*Tab*, *Space*, *Comma*, or *Semicolon*) or specify the separator via the *User-defined* edit field. For more extensive field separator options, see *Import ASCII Free File* in the *Data Management* module.

Get case names from first column. Select this option in order to create case names from the first field of each record in the ASCII file. If this field contains more than 20 characters, then only the first 20 will be used as the case name. If this field contains numeric values instead of text, then the case names will be created as "text images" of these values.

Get variable names from first row. Select this option in order to create variable names from the first record in the ASCII file. If any field in the first record is longer than eight characters, it will be truncated, and only the first eight characters will be used as the variable name.

Import - *ODBC*

This option will allow you to easily import data from a wide variety of data bases [including many large system data bases (Oracle, Sybase, etc.) using Microsoft Open Data Base Connectivity (*ODBC*)] conventions. The *ODBC* import facilities in *STATISTICA* support multiple data base tables; specific records (rows of tables) can be selected by entering *SQL* query statements. The steps necessary to import data via *ODBC* are outlined below:

- When you select the *Import Data - ODBC* option from the *File* pull-down menu of any module, you will first be prompted to select the data source (name of the server or directory on which the data resides, e.g., dBASE) in the resulting Windows *SQL Data Sources* dialog.

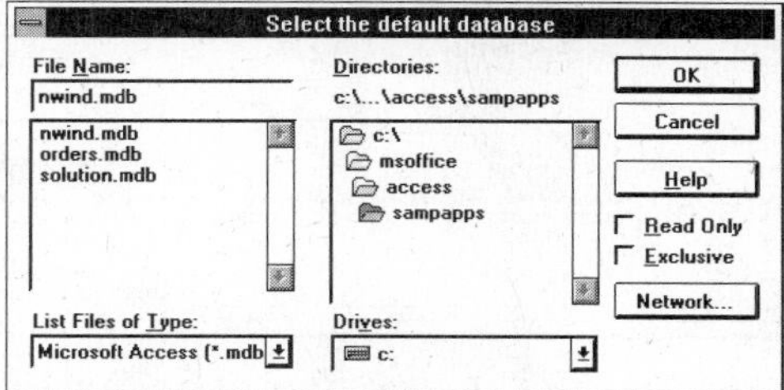

- Next, specify the name and location of the file containing the data in the standard Windows *Select Directory* dialog.
- Now, the *ODBC Import - Select Fields and Specify Conditions for Row Selection* dialog will open, in which you can specify the desired tables, fields, rows, etc. to be imported.

Note that in order to use this option, the *ODBC* drivers (appropriate for the data format to be accessed) need to be installed on your system. The list of currently installed drivers (including those installed by *STATISTICA*) is displayed in the *SQL Data Sources* dialog. If the driver for the data base you intend to access is not included in the list, please contact the respective data base manufacturer.

Select Fields and Specify Conditions for Row Selection

When you select the *Import - ODBC* option from the *File* pull-down menu and select the data source, this dialog will open. Here, you can specify the desired tables, fields, rows, etc. to be imported.

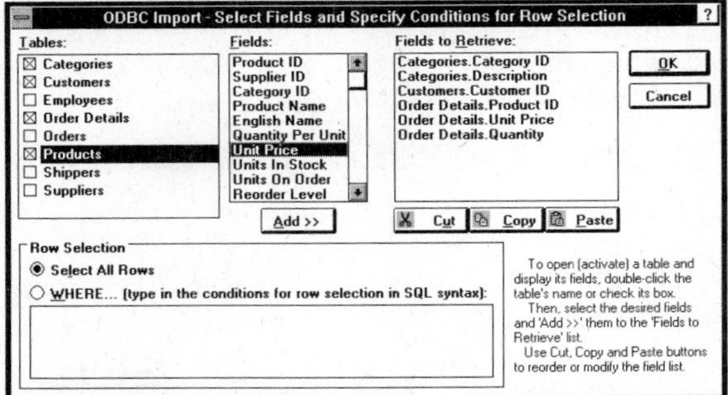

Tables. This area of the *ODBC Import - Select Fields and Specify Conditions for Row Selection* dialog displays all of the tables in the previously selected data base directory. Click on the checkbox ☒ next to the desired table in order to open (activate) the table and display the names of *Fields* (columns) in that table. Alternatively, you can double-click on the *Table* name or press the space bar to cycle through the available tables.

If only one *Table* is available in the directory, then when you open this dialog, the table will automatically be activated and its *Fields* will be displayed.

Fields. Once you select the desired *Table* in the *ODBC Import - Select Fields and Specify Conditions for Row Selection* dialog, the names of *Fields* (columns) associated with that table will be displayed in this area of the dialog. Select the desired fields by highlighting them [continuously or dis-continuously (by holding down the CTRL key while clicking on the names)] in this box and then clicking on the *Add>>* button to transfer the selected field names to the *Fields to Retrieve* box (where they can be managed).

Fields to Retrieve. This area of the dialog represents the fields to be imported from the selected *Tables*. Here, you can manage previously selected *Fields* (columns): You can delete, cut, copy, and/or paste the field names in order to rearrange the list of fields. Note that the order in which the fields are displayed here will be the order in which they will appear in the resulting *STATISTICA* data file.

Row Selection. Specify here either all rows (*Select all Rows*) or a subset of rows (*WHERE...*) to be imported. If you specify the option *Select all Rows*, then when importing data via *ODBC*, *STATISTICA* will create a *SELECT* statement in order to retrieve all user-specified fields from the respective tables. If you want to import only a subset of rows, select the *WHERE...* option and write a correct *SQL WHERE* statement. For *SQL* syntax, please consult an *SQL* manual.

Spreadsheet Save

Save a spreadsheet data file with this option from the *File* pull-down menu. If the file has not been saved before, then the *Save File As* dialog (page 1137) will open in which you can specify the file name and disk location for it to be saved. Once the file name and location have been specified, whenever you select *Save*, the spreadsheet will automatically be saved, overwriting the previous copy of the file. If you want to change the name or location of the file, select the *Save As* option.

Toolbar button. See also the spreadsheet window toolbar button.

Keyboard shortcut. CTRL+S

Spreadsheet Save As

Every time you select this option, the *Save File As* dialog (page 1137) will open in which you can save a spreadsheet data file. By default, the current file name and disk location will be displayed in this dialog. You can save the data file under a new file name or edited default name or specify a different disk location for the spreadsheet data file.

Keyboard shortcut. F12

Quick Export

This option will allow you to export files to Excel, Quattro, Lotus 1-2-3, ASCII (text), and *STATISTICA* 4.5 file formats. *STATISTICA* features a selection of specialized data export facilities in the *Data Management* module, which support a large selection of data file formats and offer some additional options for specialized data transfers (e.g., options to split/merge data values and their labels while transferring data to/from file formats which do not support labeled values). However, the *Quick Export* option is available from the *File* pull-down menu of all *STATISTICA* modules.

When you click on the *Quick Export* option in the *File* pull-down menu, the *Quick Export* dialog will open.

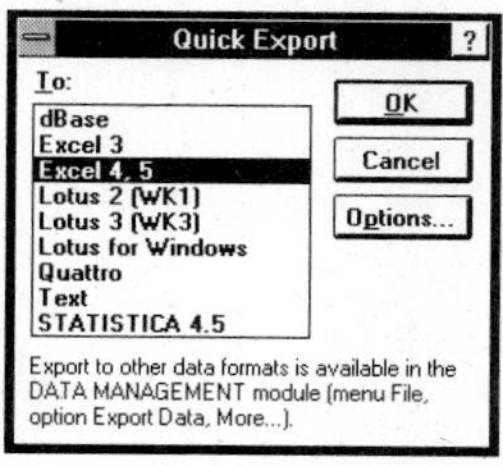

To. The *STATISTICA* file will be exported in the file format that you select here. For other format options, see Chapter 7, *Data Management*.

***Options* button.** Click on this button to bring up a dialog of export options specific to the file format selected above. Please note that there are no options available when exporting to *STATISTICA* 4.5, and the options button will be deselected. Selecting *STATISTICA* 4.5 will save the current data file in a *STATISTICA* 4.5 format. Because certain variable specification categories (time, scientific, currency, percentage) are not available in *STATISTICA* 4.5, variables using these specification categories will be saved as numeric values. Also, the *STATISTICA* 4.5 format only supports data sets with up to 300 variables. You will not be able to export a data set (to *STATISTICA* 4.5 format) with more than 300 variables.

Excel/Lotus/Quattro Quick Export Options

Pressing the *Options* button in the *Quick Export* dialog will open the *Quick Export... - Options* dialog.

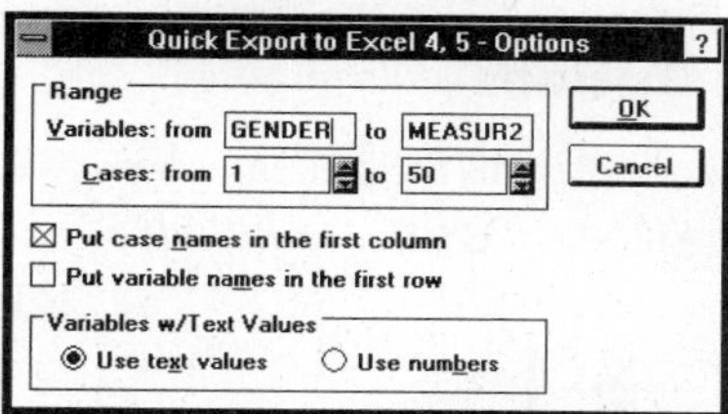

Range. This option permits selection of a specific range of cases and/or variables to be exported.

Variables: Specify the range of variables to be exported (*From* which variable, *To* which variable, inclusive).

Cases: Specify the range of cases to be exported (*From* which case, *To* which case, inclusive).

Put case names in the first column. Select this option in order to put the case names into the first column of the exported file.

Put variable names in the first row. Select this option in order to put the variable names in the first row of the exported file.

Variables w/text values. These options allow you to export either text or numeric values.

Use text values. Select this option if you want to export the text values of variables.

Use numbers. Select this option if you want to export the numeric equivalents of text values of variables.

In order to export both text values and their numeric equivalents and/or export their labels, use the comprehensive export facility available in *Data Management*, which also offers options to store value labels and/or double-notation pairs as values in file formats which do not support labels as double-notation.

Value labels can also be transferred to the applications via the Clipboard (see *Spreadsheet View Text Values*).

Text (ASCII) File Quick Export Options

Pressing the *Options* button in the *Quick Export* dialog will open the *Quick Export... - Options* dialog.

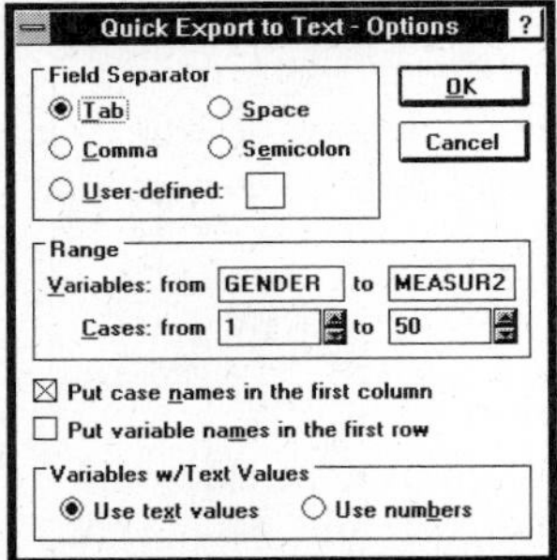

Field Separator. Select the type of delimiter that will be used in the output file. You can specify one of four pre-defined separators (*TAB*, *SPACE*, *COMMA*, or *SEMICOLON*), or a *User-defined* separator. For more extensive field separator options, use the *Data Management Export* facility.

Range. This option permits selection of a specific range of cases and/or variables to be exported.

Variables: Specify the range of variables to be exported (*From* which variable, *To* which variable, inclusive).

Cases: Specify the range of cases to be exported (*From* which case, *To* which case, inclusive).

Put case names in the first column. Select this option in order to put the case names into the first field of each record of the exported file.

Put variable names in the first row. Select this option in order to put the variable names in the first record of the exported file.

Variables w/text values. These options allow you to export either text or numeric values.

Use text values: Select this option if you want to export the text values of variables

Use numbers: Select this option if you want to export the numeric equivalents of text values of variables.

In order to export both text values and their numeric equivalents and/or export their labels, use the comprehensive export facility available in *Data Management* which also offers options to store value labels and/or double-notation pairs as values in file formats which do not support labels as double-notation. Value labels can also be transferred to other applications via the Clipboard.

Convert to Scrollsheet

Create a Scrollsheet from the current spreadsheet (data file) with this option. When you choose this option, the *Select Subset for Scrollsheet* dialog will open.

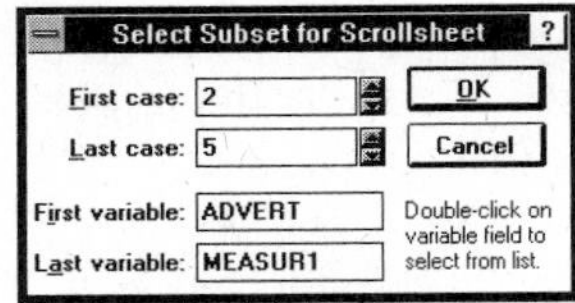

You can specify the range of the data file (by default, either all of the data or the currently highlighted block of data) to include in the Scrollsheet.

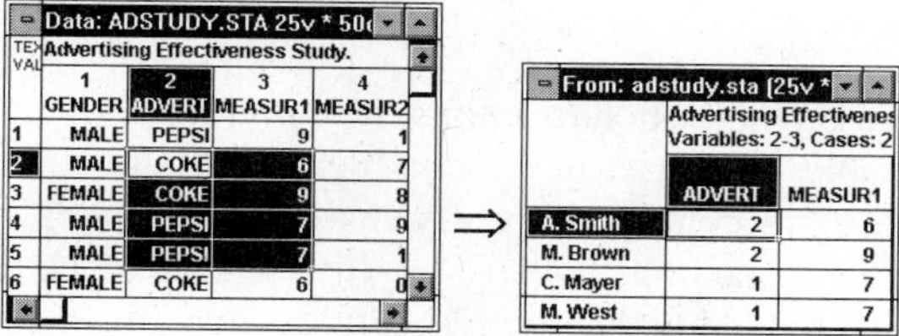

Variable names and case names will become the Scrollsheet column and row names (respectively); the file name, file header and the range (subset) of data selected will become the Scrollsheet titles.

Keyboard Shortcut. F11

First Case

Specify the first case number (inclusive) in the range of cases to be included in the Scrollsheet.

Last Case

Specify the last case number (inclusive) in the range of cases to be included in the Scrollsheet.

First Variable

Specify the first variable name or number (inclusive) in the range of variables to be included in the Scrollsheet. Double-click on the variable edit field to select a variable from a list of current variables in the spreadsheet.

Last Variable

Specify the last variable name or number (inclusive) in the range of variables to be included in the Scrollsheet. Double-click on the variable edit field to select a variable from a list of current variables in the spreadsheet.

Print/Eject Current Pages

When you run an analysis and the *Output* is set to *Printer* or *File* (in the *Page/Output Setup* dialog, see page 1148), *STATISTICA* will internally store the output either until the output fills a page (if the *Automatically Eject Each Filled Page* option is selected in the *Page/Output Setup* dialog) or until the analysis is complete (if the *Automatically Eject Each Filled Page* option is de-selected in the *Page/Output Setup* dialog) before sending it to the printer or output file. The *Print/Eject Current Pages* option will override this internal storage and immediately print (or send to an output file) whatever output has accumulated (technically, a "form feed" will be issued).

Note that this option does not apply to the *Text/output Window* (see page 1198).

Print Data

This option prints the active spreadsheet either to an output file (for later printing), to the printer (for immediate printing), or to the *Text/output Window*, as designated in the *Page/Output Setup* dialog (page 1148). When you select the *Print* option, the *Print Data Dialog* will open.

Shortcut. Click on the *Print* Toolbar button to bypass the *Print Data* dialog (i.e., the previously selected settings or the default settings will be used) and print the spreadsheet. Note that if a block is selected in the spreadsheet, then that block will be printed; otherwise, the entire spreadsheet is printed.

Keyboard shortcut. CTRL+P or F4

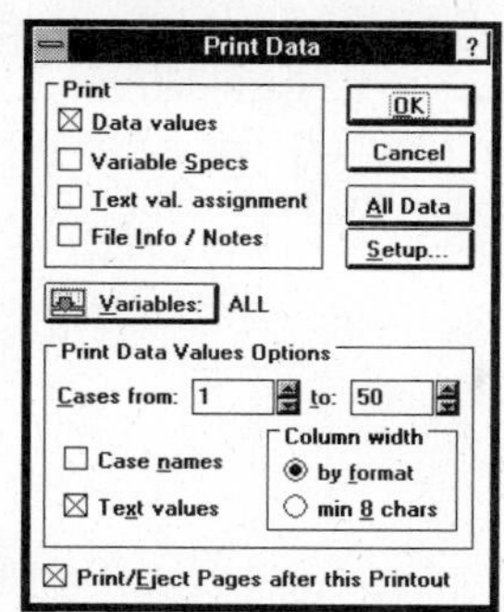

Print

You can choose the parts of the spreadsheet to print by clicking on each option to select or de-select it. Note that whatever parts of the spreadsheet that you manually choose to print here will override your selection of output style in the *Page/Output Setup* dialog (page 1148) if the two choices conflict. For example, if you choose the *Brief* output style in the *Page/Output Setup* dialog and then select all of the printing options described below, then the selections in the *Print Data* dialog will be used when printing the spreadsheet.

Data values. Click this (normally selected) option to include the spreadsheet contents (data values) from the output.

Variable specs. Clicking this option will include a table of all of the variable specifications (name, missing data code, format and long variable name as designated in the *Spreadsheet Edit (Current) Specs* dialog) in the output.

Text value assignment. Clicking this option will include a separate table of text value assignments (text values, numeric equivalents, and value labels as designated in the *Text Values Manager* dialog, see page 1167) in the output.

File info/notes. Click on this option to include the file header and file info/notes (see *File Header*, page 1180) in the output.

Variables

Select the spreadsheet variables to be included in the output (by default: *All*, or the variables in the current block if one is selected in the spreadsheet). Clicking this button will open the *Select Vars for Printing* dialog, from which you can make the variable selection.

All Data

Click on this button to automatically select all variables and cases in the data file. This button provides a shortcut to quickly change the selection of block data in this dialog (in effect when a block is highlighted in the spreadsheet) to all variables and cases.

Print Data Value Options

Cases. You can define a subset of cases to be included in the output by specifying the range of cases that you want printed (*From* what case, *To* what case, inclusive).

Case names. Click on this option to include the case names in the output.

Text values. Click on this option to print the text values instead of numeric values of variables in the spreadsheet.

Column width. Choose the spreadsheet column width to be either the formatted width (*By Format*) or the minimum 8 character width (*Min 8 Char*); the latter will allow you to print full variable names (regardless of the current value formats which may be shorter than the full variable name length).

Print/Eject Pages after this Printout

When selected, this option will cause the requested printout to automatically be sent to the printer or output file when you click *OK* in this dialog or when you press the *Print* button on the toolbar (any other text previously left in the internal buffer will also be printed). Thus, each requested printout (table) will start on a new page. If this option is de-selected, then output will be stored in the internal buffer and sent to the printer depending on the current setting of the check box *Automatically Eject Each Filled Page* (either whenever there is enough to fill one page or all at once later, e.g., when you

exit the module or when you empty the buffer by using the option *Print/Eject Current Pages*). Note that this option will only apply locally (temporarily) to the current *STATISTICA* module and the current session, whereas selecting the *Print/Eject Pages after Each Printout* option in the *Page/Output Setup* dialog (page 1148) will apply globally (permanently).

Setup

Click on this button to open the *Text Output Printer Setup* dialog in which you can select the quality (i.e., resolution) of the printout and the number of copies (see below). The selected printer is also displayed in this dialog and can be changed by clicking on the *Setup* button to open the *Print Setup* dialog (see below), in which you can make the printer selection or change the page orientation or paper size and source.

Text Output Printer Setup

This dialog (accessible from the *Print Data* dialog, see above, via the *Setup* button) allows you to select the print quality (i.e., resolution) and number of copies for the text output.

The selected printer is also displayed in this dialog and can be changed by clicking on the *Setup* button to open the *Print Setup* dialog (see page 1156).

In the *Print Setup* dialog, you can choose a printer from among those installed on your computer, select the print orientation, and specify paper size and source for printing graphs and text output.

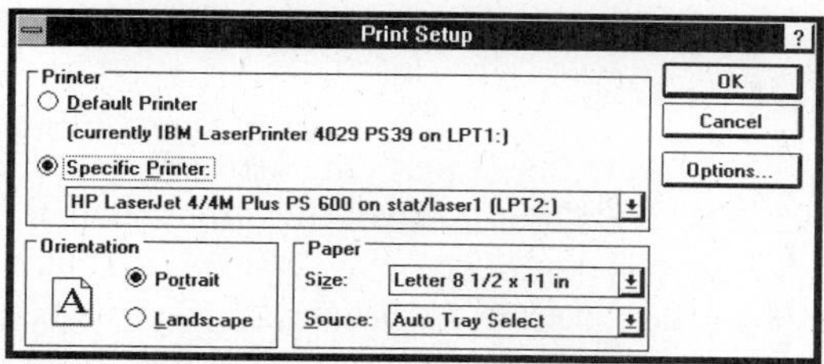

Note that the margins of text output can be adjusted in the *Text Output Margins* dialog (accessible by clicking on the *Margins* button in the *Page/Output Setup* dialog, see below).

Print Graph and Scrollsheet Files

This option (available from the *File* pull-down menu) allows you to print previously saved graphs and Scrollsheets in batch. This option is useful if you want to batch print graphs and Scrollsheets at a later time. You simply save the graphs or Scrollsheets (via the *Scrollsheet Save* or *Save Graph* options, see page 1137) after you make them, then at a later time open this dialog,

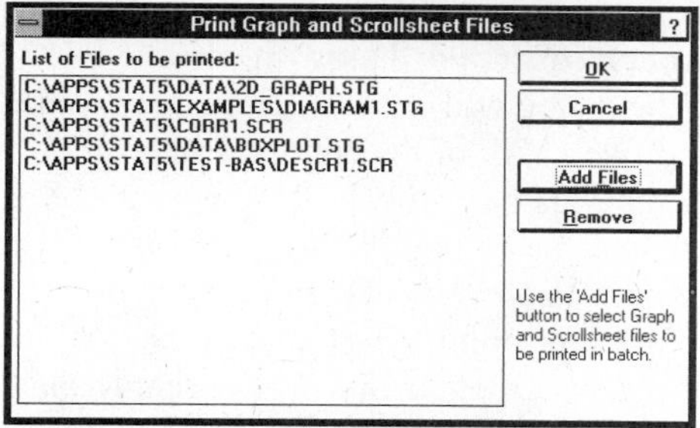

select the desired graphs and Scrollsheets (see above) and click *OK* to begin the batch printing process.

When you click *OK* in this dialog, all of the selected graphs will be printed first (on separate pages, in the order in which they are selected), and then all of the Scrollsheets will be printed together (in the order in which they are selected).

List of Files to be Printed

This area of the dialog displays the list of files to be printed. You can add or remove files from this list using the buttons described below. Once a graph or Scrollsheet file is sent to the printer, its file name is removed from the *List of Files to be Printed*.

Add Files

When you click on this button, the *Select File to be Printed* dialog will open (see page 1137) in which you can select the graph or Scrollsheet files to be printed. Press on the CTRL button in order to select multiple files (continuously or discontinuously) from the list. Once selected, the name of the file will be placed in the *List of Files to be Printed* (see above).

Remove

Click on this button to remove the highlighted file(s) from the *List of Files to be Printed*.

Cancel

When you click *OK* in this dialog, the printing begins but the dialog will continue to be displayed in the background. All of the buttons will be dimmed except this *Cancel* button. You can interrupt the batch printing by clicking on the *Cancel* button. When you click on the *Cancel* button, the batch printing will stop after the printing of the last graph or Scrollsheet sent to the printer buffer is complete.

You can also interrupt the printing of an individual graph or Scrollsheet (rather than interrupting the batch printing) by clicking on the *Cancel* button in the Windows *Printing* status dialog.

Page/Output Setup (Text/Scrollsheets-/Spreadsheets)

This multi-layer dialog allows you to specify the output destination, amount of supplemental information, margin settings, and other options and can be accessed either by double-clicking the *Output* field of the window status bar, selecting the *Page/Output Setup* option in the *File* pull-down menu, or selecting the *Print* option in the *Options* pull-down menu. All of the selections that you make here will become default selections and will be applied globally whenever you open a *STATISTICA* module.

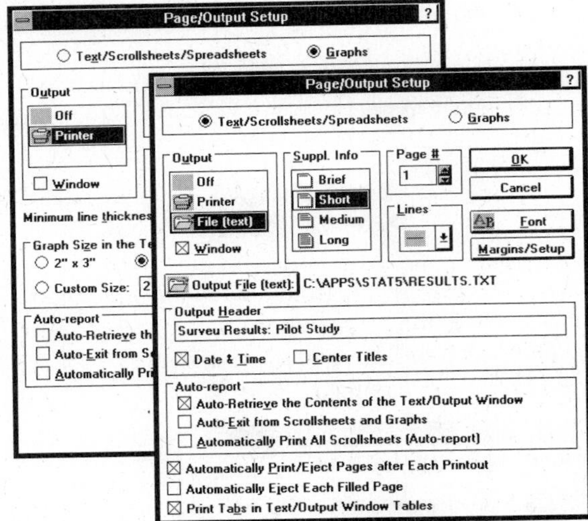

Before printing the text, spreadsheet, or Scrollsheet, select the destination (printer, output file, and/or *Text/output Window* in the *Text/Scrollsheets-/Spreadsheets* layer, or printer and/or *Text/output Window* in the *Graphs* layer) for the output as well as other options from the respective layer of the *Page/Output Setup* dialog.

The following options are available if you select *Text/Scrollsheets/Spreadsheets* as the source of output.

Keyboard shortcut. SHIFT+F4

Output

Select the output destination here.

Off. If this option is selected, then no text output will be printed or sent to an output file.

File (text). Choose to send the contents of a Scrollsheet or spreadsheet to a user-selected output (text) file. When you select this option and then click *OK*, the *Specify Output File* dialog will open (see page 1137), allowing you to name the output file. Alternatively, after selecting this option, you can click on the *Output File (Text)* button to specify a file under which the output will be saved

Printer. When selected, this option sends the contents of the spreadsheet or Scrollsheet to the printer.

Window. When you select this option, then independent of the output destination selected above (i.e., *File* or *Printer*), the output requested from Scrollsheets or spreadsheets will be sent to the *Text/output Window* (see page 1198). Note: The most recently saved *Text/output Window* will be opened when you select this option. To save the output in this window, use the *Save* option from the *File* pull-down menu or click CTRL+S.

Supplementary Information

Select the amount of supplementary information to be printed here.

Brief. Select this most "economical" output style if you want to print only the contents of the selected spreadsheets or Scrollsheets (i.e., no page headers, job headers, or any information about the variables or conditions specified for the analyses will be output).

Short. This output style will include the page header [name of the module, date/time (if requested, see below), page number], current data file name, information on *Case Selection Conditions* and *Case Weights* (if any were specified, see pages 1211 and 1212, respectively), the *Output Header* (see below), the spreadsheet or Scrollsheet contents, a list of (short) names of all variables selected for each analysis, and missing data values.

Medium. This report format is more space-consuming, including (in addition to the Scrollsheet or spreadsheet) all information from the *Short* format and, additionally, the long variable labels (e.g., formulas), reserving one line of output for each variable selected for the current analysis.

Long. The *Long* report style provides the most comprehensive information on each variable selected for analysis. In addition to all information included in the *Medium* report format, it also includes a complete list for each selected variable of all its "double" values, that is, values that have both numeric and text components, and/or values that have value labels.

Note that while printing spreadsheets, whatever parts of the spreadsheet data file that you manually choose to print in the *Print Data* dialog (page 1145) will override your selection of output style here if the two choices conflict. For example, if you choose the *Brief* output style here and then select all of the printing options in the *Print Data* dialog, the selections in the *Print Data* dialog will be used when printing the spreadsheet.

Output File (Text)

This button is available when you select *File* as the output destination and dimmed otherwise. When you click on this button, the *Specify Output File* (see page 1137) dialog will open. Here, you will be able to specify the filename (file name extension **.txt*) under which the text (ASCII) output from Scrollsheets or spreadsheets will be saved. These output files can later be opened in the *Text/output*

Window in order to review, print, or edit the output. Note, however, that unlike the report files generated by directing output to the *Text/output Window*, these disk ASCII text files contain no graphs and no formatting information (font, margins, page layout, etc.).

Page

Specify the page number of the first page of text output here. The following pages will be numbered sequentially, based on the page number here (useful when you continue an existing report). Note that pages cannot be numbered sequentially if you run more than one module of *STATISTICA* simultaneously (i.e., not in the single application mode, see *STATISTICA Module Switcher*, page 1205), and those modules interchangeably produce output.

Lines

Choose one of several line thicknesses (or no lines) for the lines in the output tables. If you do not want any borders around or lines in the output tables, select the blank box in this option. Now, whenever you print a Scrollsheet or spreadsheet, the border lines will be suppressed, and the printing will go much faster.

Output Header

Specify the output header here. This header will be included as the title on every printed page (see the *Short* output heading, above).

Date and Time

Click this option if you want to include the date and time as part of the page header (see the *Short* output setting, above).

Center Titles

Click this option if you want to center (instead of left-justify) the *Output Header*.

Font

Clicking this button will open the *Font* dialog (page 1195) from which you can select the font and font size of the printed output.

Margins

Click on this button in order to open the *Text Output Margins* dialog (see below), in which you can specify the page margins for the printed text from Scrollsheets, Spreadsheets, or the *Text/output Window*. You can specify the margins for printed graphs in either the *Print Preview* or *Page Setup* dialogs, accessible from the graph pull-down menu *File* (see Volume II of the manual).

Automatically Print/Eject Pages after Each Printout

When selected, this option will cause the requested printout to automatically be sent to the printer or output file when you click *OK* in the *Print Data* or *Print Scrollsheet* dialogs (pages 1145 and Chapter 4, respectively) or when you press the *Print* button on the toolbar (any other text previously left in the internal buffer will also be printed). Thus, each requested printout (table) will start on a new page. If this option is de-selected, then output will be stored in the internal buffer and sent to the printer depending on the current setting of the check box *Automatically Eject Each Filled Page* (either whenever there is enough to fill one page or all at once later, e.g., when you exit the module or when you empty the buffer by using the option *Print/Eject Current Pages*, see page 1145).

Automatically Eject Each Filled Page

When this option is selected, *STATISTICA* will store the results of an analysis in its internal buffer only until there is enough to fill one page. When the page is full, it will be sent to the printer or output file (whichever destination you selected in the *Output* option above). *STATISTICA* will continue storing the results and sending the output to the printer or output file one page at a time. You can use the *Print/Eject Current Pages* option from the *File* pull-down menu (see page 1145) at any point in the analysis to immediately send whatever output has accumulated to the printer or output file.

When this option is de-selected, printing will take less time overall: *STATISTICA* will store all of the results of an analysis and will not print or send it to an output file until you either close the active module or select the *Print/Eject Current Pages* option from the *File* pull-down menu (see page 1145). Use the *Print/Eject Current Pages* option at any point in the analysis to immediately send whatever output has accumulated to the printer or output file.

Auto-report Options

The following *Auto-report* options allow you to automatically create a log (e.g., a text/graphics report) of all analyses performed (see page 1153 for auto-reporting options for graphics).

Auto-Retrieve the Contents of the Text-/Output Window. You may check this option in order to automatically open the most recently saved text (file name extension **.txt*) or *R*ich *T*ext *F*ormat (file name extension **.rtf*) file in the new *Text/output Window* (e.g., in order to append the current output to the results of a previous analysis). When this option is un-checked, then a blank *Text/output Window* will be opened from the *Page/Output Setup* dialog.

Auto-Exit from Scrollsheets and Graphs. When Scrollsheets (and/or graphs, see below) are created in batch as the result of an analysis (e.g., frequency tables for a series of variables), you can select this option to suppress the display of the *Continue* button in Scrollsheets when the queue is full. Now when you select the option *Automatically Print All Scrollsheets*, the Scrollsheets will be printed in batch, without interruption.

Automatically Print All Scrollsheets (Auto-Report). If this mode of printing is selected, then in addition to the supplementary information (the amount depends on the current report format setting selected in the *Supplementary Information* option), all output from analyses will automatically be printed either to the printer or to the output file (and/or *Text/output Window*). This mode of printing is useful when you want to maintain a complete log of all output displayed during the course of the analysis.

If you choose to de-select the *Auto-report (Automatically Print All Scrollsheets)* option, then Scrollsheets (or their parts) are printed only upon request by selecting the *Print* option from the *File* pull-down menu (or click the button).

Automatically Print/Eject Pages after Each Printout

When this option is enabled, then after each text output is produced by the program (e.g., when requested via the *Print Data* or *Print Scrollsheet* options or the *Print* toolbar button), the page(s) will be ejected to the printer (or output file). Thus, each printout (table) will start on a new page. If your typical output is very short (e.g., a small Scrollsheet), but you generate a lot of them, then this option may slow you down because the process of printing will be initiated very often (for each small part of the output); however, the advantage of this mode is that it generates hard copies as soon as they are requested.

Automatically Eject Each Filled Page

When this option is enabled, then each page of the printout will be finalized (ejected) as soon as the page is full. This mode is somewhat slower overall, as the process of printing is initiated separately for each filled page. However, the advantage of this setting is that it automatically produces hard copies of the output as your analysis progresses. Alternatively, when this switch is turned off (and the *Auto Print/Eject* switch is turned off, see the previous paragraph), then all output is accumulated in an internal buffer and sent to the printer all at once at the end of the session (or whenever you select the *Print/Eject Current Pages* option in the pull-down menu *File*, which allows you to "flush out" the output buffer at any point).

Print Tabs in Text Output Tables

When this option is selected, columns in Scrollsheets will be separated by tabs when printed to the *Text/output Window* (this is the default setting). Text tables formatted in this way may be easily converted to tables in word processors (e.g., MS Word).

Page/Output Setup (Graphs)

The options in this layer of the *Page/Output Setup* dialog affect the printing of graphs.

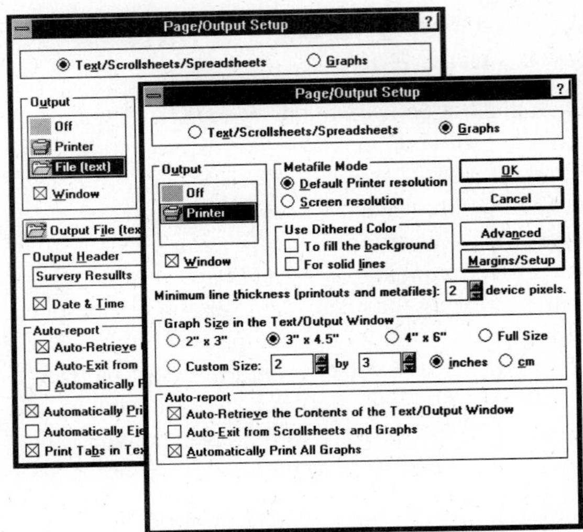

Output Channel

In this dialog, you can direct the output to the *Printer*, and/or the optional *Window* (an on-screen text/graphics report log of output; for information on the *Text/output Window*, see Chapter 5).

Metafile Mode

All graphics metafiles produced in *STATISTICA*, including Clipboard representations, saved metafiles, and graphs printed to the *Text/output Window* may be represented either in printer resolution (which depends on the current printer driver and produces the highest-quality output, but uses more memory or disk space), or in screen resolution (which produces better on-screen appearance).

Dithered Color

These options control the use of dithered colors in filling the graph background and the background of custom text, legend, embedded objects, etc. (by default, this option is deselected to allow for optimal appearance of the graph when printed), and in printing solid lines (this option may be useful when the lines are very thick, otherwise the lines may appear "broken").

Margins/Setup

Pressing the *Margins/Setup* button opens the dialog controlling the margins of the graphics output.

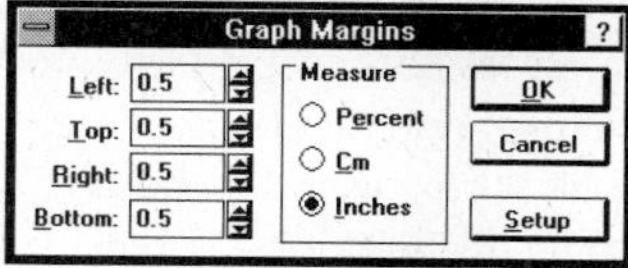

To control the paper orientation (portrait vs. landscape), printer resolution, etc. for the graphics output, press the *Setup* button (this is the same as selecting the *Printer Setup* option from the pull-down menu *File*).

Note that the margins (as well as the page orientation, etc.) for text printouts can be controlled independently (see above, also page 1155).

Minimum Line Thickness

Specify here the minimum line thickness for printouts and metafiles (in printer or other device pixels). This option is particularly relevant when using a high resolution output device (e.g., 1200 DPI where single-pixel lines are too thin) and also when you set the default size of a graph in the *Text/output Window* to a small size (e.g., 2x3, see the option *Graph Size in Text/output Window*, below).

Unless you increase the default setting of this option (2 printer pixels), the width of all lines printed by *STATISTICA* is determined either by the individual settings of the line width for specific graph components (by default .5 points) or by 2 (device) pixels, whichever is greater. This option allows you to determine the minimum printed line thickness; e.g., if you set it to 3, then all printed lines will be at least 3 printer pixels wide even if they are set to a smaller setting in some *Points/Lines/Area Patterns* dialogs.

If the setting of the *Graph Size in Text/output Window* option is set to a size smaller than *Full*, then the line thickness will be proportionally thinner. You may need to adjust the minimum line thickness in order to compensate.

Graph Size

In this dialog, you may select the default size at which graphs will appear when printed to the *Text/output Window* (graphs may be re-sized after printing).

Auto-report Options

The following *Auto-report* options allow you to automatically create a log (e.g., a text/graphics report) of all analyses performed (see above for auto-reporting options for Scrollsheets/spreadsheets).

Auto-Retrieve the Contents of the Text-/Output Window. Check this option in order to automatically open the most recently saved text (file name extension **.txt*) or Rich Text Format (file name extension **.rtf*) file in the new *Text/output Window* (e.g., in order to append the current output to the results of a previous analysis). When this option is un-checked, then a blank *Text/output Window* will be opened from the *Page/Output Setup* dialog.

Auto-Exit from Scrollsheets and Graphs. When graphs (and/or Scrollsheets, see above) are created in batch as the result of an analysis (e.g., the *Categorized Scatterplots* option in the *Descriptive Statistics* dialog), you can select this option to suppress the display of the *Next* button in graphs when the queue is full. Now when you select the option *Automatically Print All Graphs*, the graphs will be printed in batch, without interruption.

Automatically Print All Graphs. This switch allows you to automatically generate printouts of all graphs that are displayed on the screen. The output will be sent to the currently selected output channel (printer and/or *Text/output Window*). The current printout setup (e.g., printer, options, margins, paper orientation, etc., as selected in the graphics window *Printer Setup* dialog) will be used. Note that there is also a batch printing facility which can be used to print previously-saved graphs (file name extension **.stg*) in batch, available by selecting the *Print Files...* option from the pull-down menu *File*, see page 1147.

When printing to the *Text/output Window* and used along with the *Automatically Print All Scrollsheets* option (see above), a combined text/graphics report of all analyses can be automatically created.

Advanced Options

This dialog will open whenever you click on the *Advanced* button in the *Page/Output Setup - Graphs* dialog.

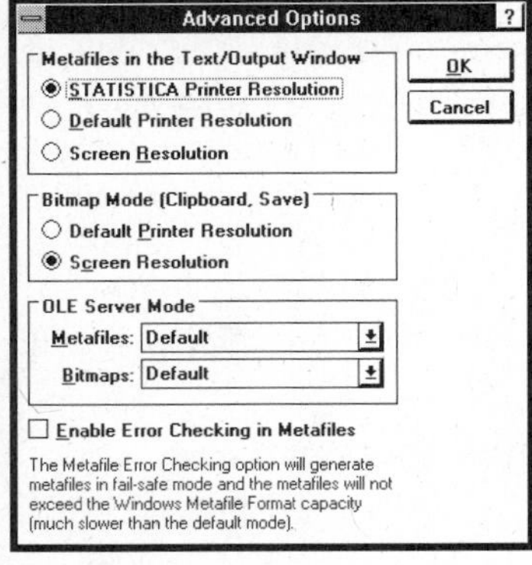

Metafiles in the Text/output Window

These options control the resolution and representation (colors) of all graphics metafiles created by *STATISTICA* which are sent to the *Text/output Window*.

STATISTICA Printer Resolution. When this option is selected and a graph is sent to the *Text/output Window*, the metafile representation created in the *Text/output Window* will depend on the print options in effect for the current *STATISTICA* session.

Default Printer Resolution. When this option is selected and a graph printed to the *Text/output Window*, the metafile (Picture) representation created in the *Text/output Window* will depend on the current (default) settings of the printer driver. (It will not be affected by the driver options changed in the current *STATISTICA* session.)

Screen Resolution. When the *Screen Resolution* option is selected and a graph is sent to the *Text/output Window*, the metafile (Picture) representation created in the *Text/output Window* will depend on the current screen driver.

Bitmap Mode (Clipboard, Save)

These options control the resolution and representation (colors) of all graphics bitmaps created by *STATISTICA* by either copying to the Clipboard or saving as a bitmap.

Default Printer Resolution. When this option is selected, the bitmap representation will depend on the current printer driver.

Screen Resolution. When the *Screen Resolution* option is selected, the bitmap representation will depend on the current screen driver.

OLE Server Mode

These options control the resolution and representations (colors) of all graphics created by *STATISTICA* which are then embedded in another application using *OLE*.

Metafiles/bitmaps. The same three options are available in each combo box: default, printer resolution, and screen resolution. The default mode uses the resolution requested by the client. When printer resolution is selected, the representation will depend on the current printer driver. When screen resolution is selected, the representation will depend on the current screen driver.

Enable Error Checking in Metafiles

Checking this box will enable the Metafile Error Checking option. This option ensures that metafiles will not exceed the Windows Metafile Format capacity; however, it is slower than the default mode.

Text Output Margins

In this dialog (accessible from the *Text-/Scrollsheets/Spreadsheets* layer of the *Page/Output Setup* dialog, see above), you can position the desired text (e.g., from spreadsheets, Scrollsheets, or the *Text/output Window*) on the printed page by adjusting the margins (specify the *Left*, *Top*, *Right*, and *Bottom* margin widths) according to a specific measure (*Percent*, *Centimeter*, or *Inch*). Note that these margin settings are independent of the margin settings for the graphics output (which can be adjusted in the *Print Preview* or *Graph Margins* dialogs, see Volume II of the manual).

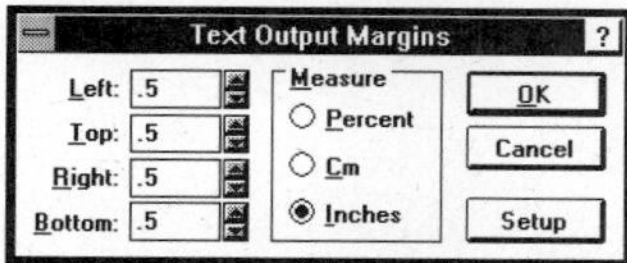

To adjust the paper size and orientation (portrait or landscape) use the *Printer Setup* option in the pull-down menu *File*.

Graph Margins

In this dialog, you can position the graph on the printed page by adjusting the margins (specify the *Left*, *Top*, *Right*, and *Bottom* margin widths) according to a specific measure (*Percent*, *Centimeter*, or *Inch*).

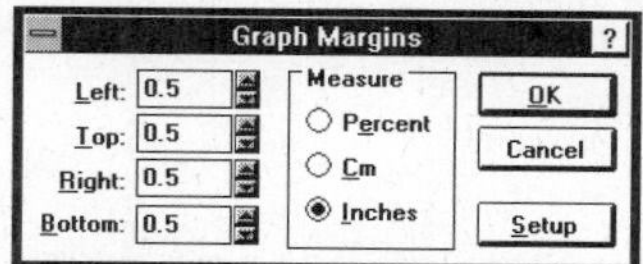

Click on the *Setup* button in the *Graph Margins* dialog to display a dialog of printer options, specific to the printer you chose in the *Select Printing Devices* dialog. Here, you can select the printer settings that will be used as default settings whenever you print a graph to that printer. These printer settings will vary depending on the type of printer that you have chosen; therefore, the dialog resulting from the *Setup* button will appropriately reflect your choice of printer. The margins can also be adjusted interactively in the *Print Preview* dialog, accessible by pressing [button] in the graph toolbar (see Chapter 2).

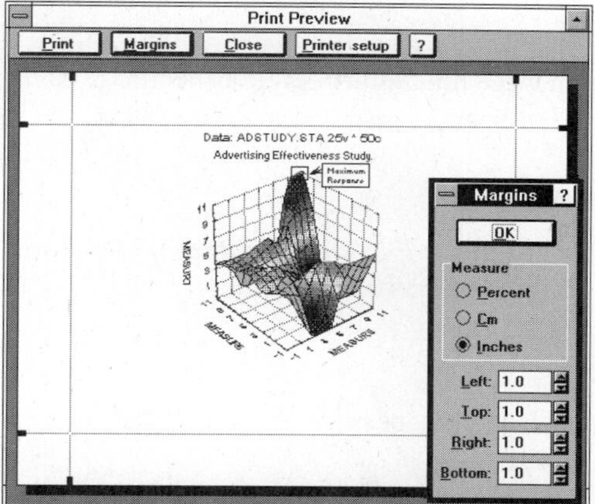

To adjust the paper size and orientation (portrait or landscape) use the *Printer Setup* option in the pull-down menu *File*.

Printer Setup

Selecting this option from the *File* pull-down menu will open the *Print Setup* dialog, in which you can choose a printer, the print orientation, and paper size and source for printing graphs and text output.

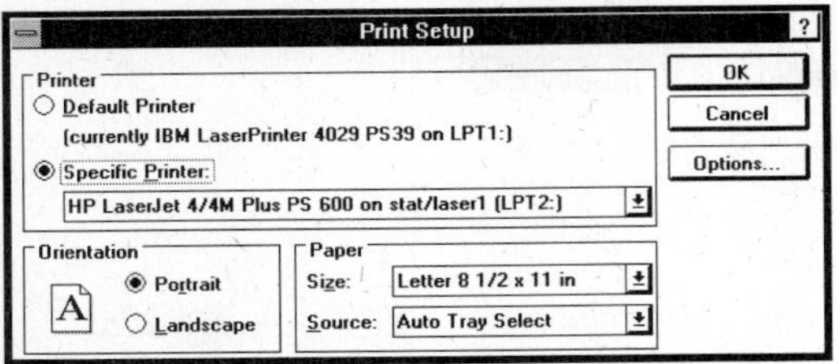

Note that you can maintain separate print selections for graphs and text output (i.e., output from Scrollsheets or spreadsheets).

For example, you can select a *Landscape* page orientation for printing text output in the *Print Setup* dialog accessible from the spreadsheet or Scrollsheet window *File* pull-down menu, and a *Portrait* page orientation for printing graphs in the *Print Setup* dialog accessible from the graph window *File* pull-down menu.

Printer

Select either the default printer or a specific printer from a list of printers installed in your system.

Orientation

Select either *Landscape* or *Portrait* page orientation for printing the graph or text output.

Paper

You can select the paper size and source in these combo boxes.

Options

When you click on this button, a dialog (specific to the selected printer, see above) will open in which you can choose from several printing options (e.g., printing area, margins, scaling amount, etc.).

Exit

Select this option to end your *STATISTICA* session. If you have made any changes to spreadsheets, Scrollsheets, text, or graphs and *Exit* before saving them, *STATISTICA* will prompt you to save the modified objects.

Keyboard Shortcut. ALT+F4

SPREADSHEET *EDIT* PULL-DOWN MENU

The following dialogs and options are available from the spreadsheet *Edit* pull-down menu.

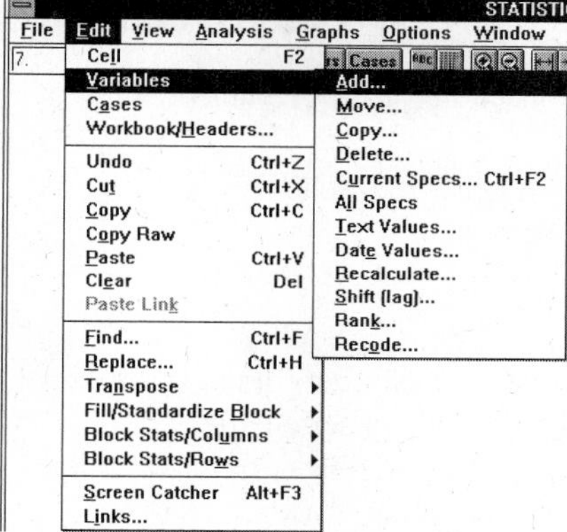

Each of these options are described below.

Spreadsheet Edit Cell

The *Edit Cell* option from the spreadsheet *View* pull-down menu allows you to edit the currently highlighted cell in the spreadsheet without overwriting it. You can start editing either by selecting this option, pressing F2, typing over the highlighted cell, or by typing over the entry. While editing, this option is dimmed.

Keyboard shortcut: F2

Spreadsheet Add Variables

Add variables to the spreadsheet by designating the number of new variables to add, as well as where to add them (after which variable) in the *Add Variables* dialog (accessible from the spreadsheet *Edit - Variables* pull-down menu, the spreadsheet flying menu, or the Vars toolbar button).

You can double-click on the variable edit field in the *Add Variables* dialog to bring up the list of variables in the current spreadsheet and select a variable that the new variable(s) will be placed after.

Number of Variables to Add

Choose the desired number of variables to add to the current spreadsheet. You may include up to 4,092 variables in the *STATISTICA* data spreadsheet or up to 32,000 variables (with up to 255 characters per variable) in *Megafile Manager* (see *Data Management*, Chapter 7).

Insert After Which Variable

Designate the location (variable) in the spreadsheet that the new variable(s) will be added after. The new variables will be added to the right of the variable specified here. You can click on the variable edit field in the *Add Variables* dialog to bring up the list of variables in the current spreadsheet in order to select a variable that the new variable(s) will be placed after.

How to insert before variable number 1. One way to move and insert the values of a variable or block of variables before variable 1 is to use the *Drag-and-Drop* facilities in *STATISTICA*. To do this, first highlight the desired block. Then, move the cursor to one of the borders of the block where it will change into an arrow. Now, to move and insert the block, press SHIFT while dragging the block. Next, position the insertion bar between the case

name column and the first variable column and release the mouse-button to complete the insert. Note that this method does not move the selected variable(s) (i.e., their long value labels, formats, assignments of text/numerical values, etc.) but only the values of the selected block.

An alternative way to move and insert an entire variable or block of variables before variable 1, is to first move the variable(s) after variable number 1 and then move variable number 1 to the right of the moved variable(s) (you can also use the *Spreadsheet Copy Variables* option to first copy the variables and then move them, see page 1159).

Spreadsheet Move Variables

Unlike the Clipboard operations of cutting and pasting the contents of a highlighted range or block of values in the spreadsheet, this option will remove both the contents of the column(s) and the column(s) itself (regardless of whether or not all cases or only a subset of cases are currently highlighted for the respective variables) and insert the columns in the designated position in the spreadsheet; thus the size of the file will remain the same. You can move one or more variables in the spreadsheet by designating the range (inclusive) of variables to be moved and the location (variable to insert after) in the *Move Variables* dialog (accessible from the spreadsheet *Edit - Variables* pull-down menu or the Vars toolbar button).

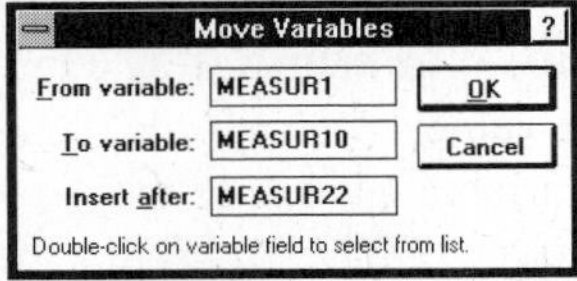

You can easily replace the selection of one variable name with another by double-clicking on the variable edit field in the *Move Variables* dialog to bring up the list of variables in the current spreadsheet from which you can select the desired variable.

From Variable

Designate the first variable (inclusive) in the block of variables to be moved. (Note that if you are moving only one variable, then designate the same variable in both the *From Variable* and *To Variable* lists.)

To Variable

Designate the last variable (inclusive) in the block of variables to be moved.

Insert After

Designate the location (variable) in the spreadsheet that the variable(s) will be inserted after (you cannot insert a block of variables *after* a variable that is included in the range of variables to be moved). The block of variables will be "cut" from their current spreadsheet location and moved to the right of the variable specified here.

How to move before variable 1. One way to move and insert the values of a variable or block of variables before variable 1 is to use the *Drag-and-Drop* facilities in *STATISTICA*. To do this, first highlight the desired block. Then, move the cursor to one of the borders of the block where it will change into an arrow. Now, to move and insert the block, press SHIFT while dragging the block. Next, position the insertion bar between the case name column and the first variable column and release the mouse-button to complete the insert. Note that this method does not move the selected variable(s) (i.e., their long value labels, formats, assignments of text/numerical values, etc.) but only the values of the selected block.

An alternative way to move and insert an entire variable or block of variables before variable 1, is to first move the variable(s) after variable number 1

and then move variable number 1 to the right of the moved variable(s) (you can also use the *Spreadsheet Copy Variables* option, see below, to first copy the variables and then move them).

Spreadsheet Copy Variables

Unlike the Clipboard operations of copying and pasting the contents of a highlighted range or block of values in the spreadsheet, this option will copy both the contents of the columns and the columns themselves (regardless of whether or not all cases or only a subset of cases are currently highlighted for the respective variables) in the designated position, thus the size of the file will increase. You can place a copy of the specified variable(s) at a designated location by specifying the range (inclusive) of variables to be copied and the spreadsheet location (insert after which variable) in the *Copy Variables* dialog (accessible from the spreadsheet *Edit - Variables* pull-down menu).

The copy will include not only the data but also the format, long name, formulas, the numeric-text value assignment, etc. You can easily replace the selection of one variable name with another by double-clicking on the variable edit field in the *Copy Variables* dialog to bring up the list of variables in the current spreadsheet from which you can select the desired variable.

From Variable

Designate the first variable (inclusive) in the block of variables to be copied. (If you are copying only one variable, then designate the same variable in both the *From Variable* and *To Variable* lists.)

To Variable

Designate the last variable (inclusive) in the block of variables to be copied.

Insert After

Designate the location (variable) in the spreadsheet that the variable(s) will be placed after copying (you cannot insert a block of variables *after* a variable that is included in the range of variables to be copied). The copied variables will be located to the right of the variable specified here.

How to copy before variable 1. One way to copy and insert the values of a variable or block of variables before variable 1 is to use the *Drag-and-Drop* facilities in *STATISTICA*. To do this, first highlight the desired block. Then, move the cursor to one of the borders of the block where it will change into an arrow. Now, to copy and insert the block, press SHIFT while dragging the block. Next, position the insertion bar between the case name column and the first variable column and release the mouse-button to complete the insert. Note that this method does not copy the selected variable(s) (i.e., their long value labels, formats, assignments of text/numerical values, etc.) but only the values of the selected block.

An alternative way to copy and insert an entire variable or block of variables before variable 1, first copy the variable(s) after variable number 1 and then move variable number 1 to the right of the copied variable(s) using the *Spreadsheet Move Variables* option (see above).

Spreadsheet Delete Variables

One or more variables can be deleted from the current spreadsheet when you designate the range (inclusive) of variables to be deleted in the *Delete Variables* dialog (accessible from the spreadsheet

Edit - Variables pull-down menu or the Vars toolbar button). You can easily replace the selection of one variable name with another by clicking on the variable edit field in the *Delete Variables* dialog to bring up the list of variables in the current spreadsheet; then select the desired variable.

Unlike deleting (clearing) the contents of a highlighted range or block of values in the spreadsheet, this option will remove both the contents of the column(s) and the column(s) itself; thus the subsequent variables will be moved to the left and the size of the file will decrease.

From Variable

Designate the first variable (inclusive) in the block of variables to be deleted. (Note that if you are deleting only one variable, then designate the same variable in both the *From Variable* and *To Variable* lists.)

To Variable

Designate the last variable (inclusive) in the block of variables to be deleted.

Spreadsheet Edit (Current) Specs

Specifications of the currently highlighted variable (i.e., variable name and format, missing data value, and label, formula or link) can be edited in the *Spreadsheet Edit (Current) Specs* dialog.

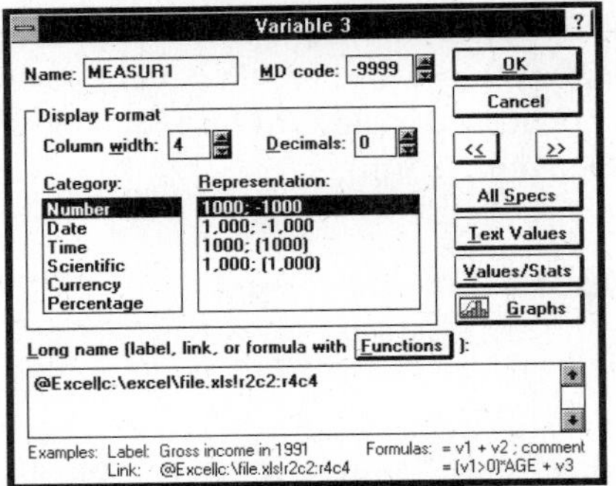

This dialog is accessible from the spreadsheet *Edit - Variables* pull-down menu or the Vars toolbar button option *Current Specs*; it can also be accessed by double-clicking on the variable name in the spreadsheet.

Name

Edit the variable name here. Variable names can be up to 8 characters long, cannot start with the characters: period (.), minus (-), plus (+), or a digit (i.e., *0-9*), and cannot contain spaces, unprintable characters, or the keyboard characters used in data transformations and *STATISTICA* programming languages (" # & ' ( ) + * , - . / ; : < = > [ ] ^ \ { } ~). If any of these characters appear in a variable name, then *STATISTICA* will replace them with an underscore [except in the case when a period (.), minus (-), or plus sign (+) is used as the first character, then this name will be considered invalid and an error message will be issued]. The program does not differentiate between upper and lowercase letters entered in text values (all letters are converted to uppercase).

MD Code

Enter a value for the missing data code (value of the variable that indicates data points for which no data are available) or accept the default code of -9999. Missing data values are displayed as blanks in the cells of the spreadsheet (the value can be viewed in

the spreadsheet toolbar *Show Field* (see Chapter 2) when a blank cell is highlighted) and are ignored in all data analyses.

Format

Column Width. Edit the width (from 1 to 30) of the column here. The default format width is 8 characters. The display format affects only the way in which values are displayed in the spreadsheet and other data listings, and not the internal storage precision of the number.

Decimals. Specify the number of decimal places (less than the column width) to be displayed in the spreadsheet and other data listings (applicable to *Number*, *Scientific*, *Currency*, and *Percentage* categories, see below). The default format is 3 decimal places. The display format affects only the way in which values are displayed in the spreadsheet and other data listings, and not the internal storage precision of the number. For variables containing single *Date* values (see *Date Operations*, page 1169), specifying a *Number* format will display the dates as Julian values (e.g., as *24858* instead of *1/21/1968*). For variables containing *Time* values, specifying a *Number* format will display the time as a decimal value (e.g., as *24858.9375* instead of *1/21/1968 10:30 PM*, or as *.78125* instead of *18:45*)

Category/Representation. For each *Category* that you choose, you can also choose a *Representation* by which to display the values of the current variable.

Number. Select this format if the values of the variable are numeric or numeric with text equivalents. When you select this category, you can specify the number of decimal places to be displayed in the spreadsheet via the *Decimals* option (see above).

Representation. These values are represented in decimal format with or without commas (e.g., *1000* or *1,000*). Negative values of the variable can be represented either with a negative sign (e.g., *-1000*) or with parentheses enclosing the number (e.g., *(1000)*). There are four representations available under this category:

1000.00	-1000.00
1,000.00	-1,000.00
1000.00	(1000.00)
1,000.00	(1,000.00)

Note that a European representation (e.g., 1,20) is supported by *STATISTICA* if you select this style in the Windows *Control Panel*. If this style is not selected in the *Control Panel* and you enter a comma in the decimal place, *STATISTICA* will treat the value as a text value.

Date. Select this variable format in order for variables to be interpreted as dates (e.g., variables containing Julian date values imported or pasted from Excel). Note that in order to be displayed as a valid date, all values in the variable must be correct dates or explicitly defined text values (see also, *Date Operations*, page 1169).

Representation. Select the desired date representation from the list of date formats. In the *View Variable Specs* window (see page 1167), the various *Date* representations are represented by the following keywords (which can also be entered directly in the *Format* column of this window):

3/6/87	DATE1
03/06/1987	DATE2
6-Mar-87	DATE3
6-Mar	DATE4
Mar-1987	DATE5
06/03/87	DATE6
Currently Selected Windows Format	DATE7

Note that if the *Windows Format* is selected, *STATISTICA* will format the date display using the specifications given in the *International* dialog

(Windows 3.1) or the *Regional Settings* dialog (Windows 95) of the *Control Panel.*

Time. This category will display the values of the variables in one of several time formats. Time values of variables are stored in the data as (optional) decimal values representing the fraction of the day since midnight; for example, *6:00AM* is stored as *0.25*. Time values stored in this manner can be used in subsequent analyses and transformed using arithmetic operations; at the same time, they can be displayed as times in reports or graphs (e.g., used to label scale values). *STATISTICA* will format the display of time values according to the current settings in the *International Time Format* option of the Windows *Control Panel.*

Representation. Time can be represented in one of several formats. You can choose from a date-time combination [with either 24-hour time or 12-hour (AM/PM) time format], or just time [either a 24-hour time or 12-hour (AM/PM) time format] in hours and minutes or hours, minutes, and seconds. You could also select the *Windows Format* which will use the current settings in the *International* dialog (Windows 3.1) or the *Regional Settings* dialog (Windows 95) of the *Windows Control Panel.* In the *View Variable Specs* window, the various *Time* representations are represented by the following keywords (which can also be entered directly in the *Format* column of this window):

3/6/87 10:30 PM	TIME1
87/3/6 22:30	TIME2
10:30 PM	TIME3
22:30	TIME4
10:30:25 PM	TIME5
22:30:25	TIME6
Currently Selected Windows Format	TIME7

Scientific. This category allows you to display the values of the variable in scientific notation. When you select this category, you can specify the number of decimal places to be displayed in the spreadsheet via the *Decimals* option (see above).

Representation. The first representation (standard scientific notation) will display all numbers in the column in scientific notation according to the following rules:

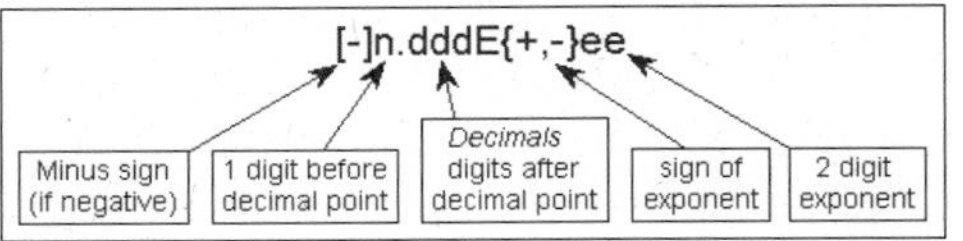

For example, 1.2345E-02 or -3.2100E+08.

The second representation will apply the scientific format only to those (small) values of the variable which would be displayed as 0 (zero) in *Number* format [i.e., they are from the interval (-1,1) and the significant digits start after the position specified by the *Decimals* edit field]. For example, if *Decimals* = 4, and the value is 0.0000123, then in *Number* format, the value would be displayed as 0.0000; whereas, in the second *Scientific* representation, the number would be displayed as 1.230E-5 (displaying 4 digits before E).

Currency. Select this category in order to display the values of the variable in a currency format. When you select this category, you can specify the number of decimal places to be displayed in the spreadsheet via the *Decimals* option (see above).

Representation. Currency values are displayed with a currency symbol before or after the number (depending on the configuration specified on the user's computer; e.g., $, DM, etc., see the Windows *Control Panel*). You can choose to represent negative values of the variable either with a negative sign (e.g., $-*1,000*) or with parentheses enclosing the number (e.g., *($1,000)*).

Percentage: Selecting this format will display the values of the variable as percentages. When you select this category, you can specify the number of decimal places to be displayed in the spreadsheet via the *Decimals* option (see above). The

percentage is based on the fraction of 1 that the value of the variable represents. For example, the value 0.23 will be translated to 23% while 23.4 will be translated to 2340%.

Representation. Percentages are represented with a % character at the end of the number.

Long Name - Label

For each variable, you can assign a long variable name up to 128 characters long. The label can contain notes, including any printable characters.

Long Name - Formula

Variable formulas must start with an equal sign. When you enter a label that starts with an equal sign, *STATISTICA* will assume that it is a formula and will verify it for formal correctness. If the formula is formally correct, you will then be given the choice to recalculate the variable now or later (via the *Recalculate* dialog, page 1172). You can use variable formulas to verify data, transform a variable, recode a variable or create values of the variable based on logical conditions (e.g., *=(v0<=100)*1 + (v0>100)*2* will assign a value of *1* to cases number *1* through *100* and *2* to cases above *100*). Refer to variables by their names (e.g., *Test1*, *Income*) or numbers (e.g., *v1*, *v2*, *v3*, ...); *v0* is the case number. A comment may be added to a formula following a semicolon. For a detailed formula syntax summary see *Summary of STATISTICA Formula Syntax* (page 1165).

Examples:

The following formula computes the average of the first 3 variables.

```
=(v1+v2+v3)/3
```

The following formula recodes cases 1-10 as *1*, and the rest of the cases as *2* (it is followed by a comment).

```
= (v0<=10)*1+(v0>10)*2; this is a comment
```

Note that you can click on the **Functions** button in this dialog in order to open the *Function Wizard* dialog. From this dialog, you can choose the desired part of the formula (e.g., an operator, distribution, math function). When you click *OK* in this dialog, the selection will be pasted in the current cursor position in the edit field.

Long Name - Link

In addition to *notes* and *formulas*, the long variable names can also contain *DDE* link specifications. Following the MS Windows *DDE* (Dynamic Data Exchange) conventions, you can link a variable (or block of data) in *STATISTICA* to a variable (or block) in a spreadsheet in another program, allowing you to automatically update the spreadsheet whenever the "source" (server) file changes. The most common way to establish a *DDE* link between another application and *STATISTICA* is the standard Windows *Paste Link* (page 1184) and *Links* (page 1192) options in the *Edit* pull-down menu. However, a link statement can also be entered directly into the *Long Name* option of this dialog [see *Creating Links (Dynamic Data Exchange)*, Chapter 7, for detailed steps on establishing a *DDE* link using this option, syntax conventions, and *Links Manager* for information on managing *DDE* links].

An example of a link statement (to link a block of data in *STATISTICA* with a block of data in Excel) is: *@Excel|c:\file.xls!r2c2:r4c4*. This example statement establishes a dynamic link with the block "from row number 2, column number 2 to row number 4, column number 4" in the Microsoft

Excel Spreadsheet file *File.xls* (be sure to establish the full path for the file when specifying the file name in the link statement, i.e., *c:\Excel\File.xls*).

All Specs

Clicking on this button will close this dialog (saving any changes) and bring up the *View Variable Specs* dialog (page 1167), which displays the specifications for all variables in the data file.

Text Values

Pressing this button will close this dialog (saving any changes) and bring up the *Text Values Manager* dialog (page 1167).

Values/Stats

Click on this button to open the *Variable Values Window*

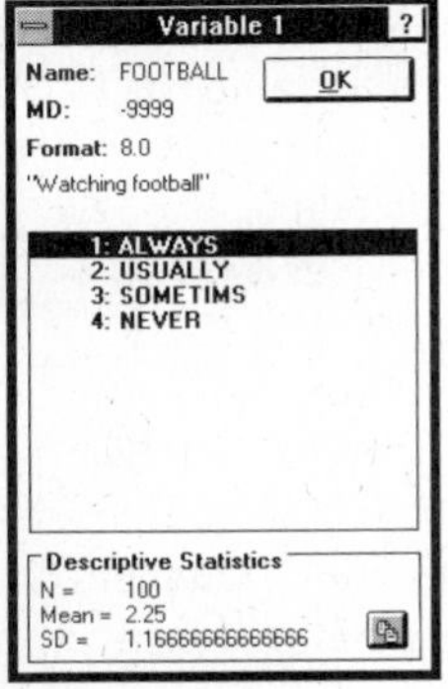

in which you can view the values of the variable as well as some descriptive statistics (*n*, mean, and standard deviation) for that variable.

Graphs

Pressing this button will close this dialog (saving any changes) and bring up a menu of *Quick Stats Graphs* options (see page 1207 in this chapter for an overview; see Volume II of the manual for more information).

[<<], [>>] Buttons

Click on these buttons in order to bring up the *Current Specs* dialog for the previous ([<<]) variable or for the next ([>>]) variable. Note that when you click on either of these buttons, *STATISTICA* will first implement the changes made for the current variable before going to the dialog for the next or previous variable. If you do not want to implement any changes before going to the next or previous dialog, *Cancel* the current dialog, then bring up the *Current Specs* dialog for the desired variable.

Spreadsheet Formulas: Function Wizard

When you click on the [Functions] button in the *Current Specs* dialog (see page 1160), the *Spreadsheet Formulas: Function Wizard* dialog will open. Here you can highlight a *Category* in the first list which will then give the *Name* of the items available under that *Category* in the second list.

When you highlight a *Name* in the second list, the item and a brief description of that item will be given in the lower part of this dialog (see below).

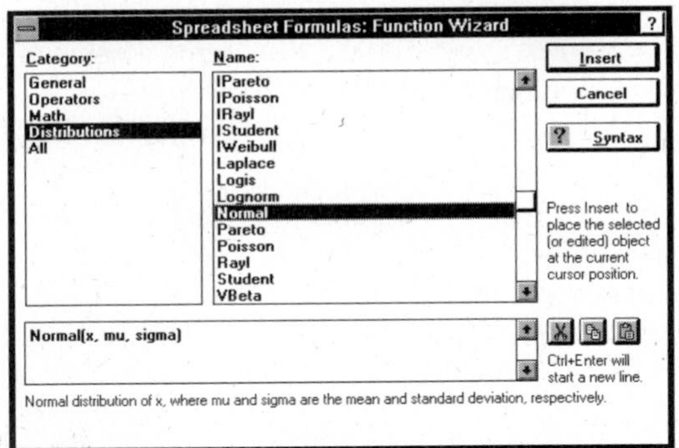

When you click *OK* in this dialog, the selected item will be pasted at the current cursor position in the edit field of the *Current Specs* dialog.

The following *Categories* are available in this dialog (for more detailed information on specific

formula items available in this dialog, see *Syntax Summary*, below):

General:	=, *Vxxx*, *V0*
Operators:	<, >, <>, <=, >=, +, -, *, /, **, ^, *and*, *not*, *or*
Math:	*Abs*, *ArcSin*, *ArcCos*, *ArcTan*, *Cos*, *CosH*, *Exp*, *Euler*, *Hypot*, *Log*, *Log10*, *Log2*, *Max*, *Min*, *Normal*, *Pi*, *Poisson*, *Rnd*, *Round*, *Sign*, *Sin*, *SinH*, *Sqrt*, *Tan*, *TanH*, *Trunc*, *Uniform*
Distributions:	*Beta*, *iBeta*, *vBeta*, *Binom*, *iBinom*, *Cauchy*, *iCauchy*, *vCauchy*, *Chi2*, *iChi2*, *vChi2*, *Expon*, *iExpon*, *vExpon*, *Extreme*, *iExtreme*, *vExtreme*, *F*, *iF*, *vF*, *Gamma*, *iGamma*, *vGamma*, *Geom*, *iGeom*, *Laplace*, *iLaplace*, *vLaplace*, *Logis*, *iLogis*, *vLogis*, *Lognorm*, *iLognorm*, *vLognorm*, *Normal*, *iNormal*, *vNormal*, *Pareto*, *iPareto*, *vPareto*, *Poisson*, *iPoisson*, *Rayleigh*, *iRayleigh*, *vRayleigh*, *Student*, *iStudent*, *vStudent*, *Weibull*, *iWeibull*, *vWeibull*
All:	gives a listing of all of the above items.

Summary of *STATISTICA* Formula Syntax

The following is a summary of syntax conventions for the spreadsheet formulas (which can be entered into the *Spreadsheet Edit (Current) Specs* dialog).

Variable names in formulas. Refer to variables either by their numbers or name (*v0* is the case number). For example:

```
= v1 - v2
= Retail - Cost
```

Comments in formulas. A semicolon in the formula starts a comment. For example:

```
= v1 + v2 ; this is a comment
```

Conditional statements. Logical expressions may be entered into spreadsheet formulas. A logical expression evaluates to *1* if it is true and to *0* if it is false. Therefore, conditional statements may also be created by including a logical expression, contained within parentheses. For example,

```
=(v0<=10)*1 + (v0>10)*2
```

recodes cases 1-10 as *1*, and the rest as *2*. The following logical operators can be used in conditional statements:

`AND, &`	logical AND
`OR, |`	logical OR
`NOT, ~`	logical NOT

For example,

```
=((v1=1) AND (v2=5))*5
```

returns a value of *5* if v1=1 *and* v2=5, and *0* otherwise.

```
=(((v1=1) OR (v2=5))<>0)*5
```

returns the value of *5* if either *or* both conditions hold, and *0* otherwise.

List separators. Some functions in the spreadsheet formulas require more than one parameter (e.g., *Normal(x,0,1)*), and they are separated with *list separators*. *STATISTICA* will use the list separator selected in the *International* dialog from the Windows *Control Panel*. For example, the most commonly used list separator in the United States is a comma (,). Therefore, you would separate a list of numbers, names, etc., with a comma. For example, consider the following spreadsheet formula where the parameters of the Normal distribution are separated by a comma:

```
=normal(v2,0,1)
```

If the list separator is changed (e.g., to reflect one used in another country):

International

Country: Germany | OK
Language: German | Cancel
Keyboard Layout: German | Help
Measurement: Metric
List Separator: ;
Date Format: 10.02.1995, Friday, 10. February 1995 | Change...
Currency Format: 1,22 DM, -1,22 DM | Change...
Time Format: 12:27:30 | Change...
Number Format: 1.234,22 | Change...

then the above spreadsheet formula would be written as:

```
=normal(v2;0;1)
```

When changing the list separator, be sure to use one that is different from the decimal place holder.

Operators. The operators that can be used in spreadsheet formulas are listed below in order of their precedence (order of execution), from the lowest to the highest (parentheses may be used to change the order of operation):

`=, <, >, <>, <=, >=`	- relational operators
`+`	- addition
`-`	- subtraction
`*`	- multiplication
`/`	- division
`**, ^`	- exponentiation

Constants. The following constants are supported in spreadsheet formulas:

`Pi`	- π (3.14159265358979)
`Euler`	- *e* (2.71828182845905)

Functions. Functions supported in spreadsheet formulas include:

`Abs(x)`	- Absolute value of *x*
`Arcsin(x)`	- Arc sine of *x*
`Cos(x)`	- Cosine of *x*
`Exp(x)`	- *e* to the power of *x*
`Log(x)`	- Natural logarithm of *x*
`Log2(x)`	- Binary logarithm of *x*
`Log10(x)`	- Common logarithm of *x*
`Rnd(x)`	- Random number from a uniform distribution in range of *0* to *x*
`Sign(x)`	- Sign of *x*: if *x*>0 then *+1*, if *x*<0 then *-1*, if *x*=0 remains *0*
`Sin(x)`	- Sine of *x*
`Sinh(x)`	- Hyperbolic sine of *x*
`Sqrt(x)`	- Square root of *x*
`Tan(x)`	- Tangent of *x*
`Trunc(x)`	- Truncates *x* to an integer

Distribution functions, their integrals and inverse distribution functions. *STATISTICA* provides a broad selection of pre-defined distribution functions, their integrals and inverse distribution functions that can be used in spreadsheet formulas like all other functions (shown below). For a complete listing of all available distributions and their formulas, see *Appendix I* to this volume of the manual.

Distri-bution	Density or Probability Function	Distribution Function	Inverse Distribution Function
Beta	beta(x,ν,ω)	ibeta(x,ν,ω)	vbeta(x,ν,ω)
Binomial	binom(x,p,n)	ibinom(x,p,n)	
Cauchy	cauchy(x,η,θ)	icauchy(x,η,θ)	vcauchy(x,η,θ)
Chi-square	chi2(x,ν)	ichi2(x,ν)	vchi2(x,ν)
Exponential	expon(x,λ)	iexpon(x,λ)	vexpon(x,λ)
Extreme	extreme(x,a,b)	iextreme(x,a,b)	vextreme(x,a,b)
F	F(x,ν,ω)	iF(x,ν,ω)	vF(x,ν,ω)

Gamma	gamma(x,c)	igamma(x,c)	vgamma(x,c)
Geometric	geom(x,p)	igeom(x,p)	
Laplace	laplace(x,a,b)	ilaplace(x,a,b)	vlaplace(x,a,b)
Logistic	logis(x,a,b)	ilogis(x,a,b)	vlogis(x,a,b)
Lognormal	lognorm(x,μ,σ)	ilognorm(x,μ,σ)	vlognorm(x,μ,σ)
Normal	normal(x,μ,σ)	inormal(x,μ,σ)	vnormal(x,μ,σ)
Pareto	pareto(x,c)	ipareto(x,c)	vpareto(x,c)
Poisson	poisson(x,λ)	ipoisson(x,λ)	
Rayleigh	rayleigh(x,b)	irayleigh(x,b)	vrayleigh(x,b)
Student's	student(x,df)	istudent(x,df)	vstudent(x,df)
Weibull	weibull(x,b,c,θ)	iweibull(x,b,c,θ)	vweibull(x,b,c,θ)

Spreadsheet View (All) Variable Specs

View the variable specifications for all variables in a Scrollsheet when you select this option (accessible from the spreadsheet *Edit - Variables* pull-down menu or the Vars toolbar button).

Data: EXP.STA 9v * 48c

	Name	MD Code	Format	Long Name (label, form
1	GROUP	-9999	9.0	Experimental or control group subject
2	GENDER	-9999	8.0	Subjects' gender
3	DATE	-9999	DATE1	Date of testing
4	TIME	-9999	Cut Ctrl+X	...ction of reward
5	PAID	-9999	Copy Ctrl+C	not subject was offered money
6	STRESS_R	-9999	Paste Ctrl+V	...d stress
7	CORRECT1	-9999	Clear Del	solutions to first problem
8	CORRECT2	-9999	Fill Block Down	solutions to second problem

Included in the Scrollsheet are each variable's number and name, its missing data code, the value format and long variable name or formula. You can edit the variable specifications either here or in the *Spreadsheet Edit (Current) Specs* dialog (page 1160).

Toolbar button. This window can also be called by pressing the spreadsheet window toolbar button.

Spreadsheet Edit Text Values

The *Text Values Manager* is used to edit text values (and their equivalent numeric representations) of the variable that is currently highlighted in the spreadsheet. It is accessible from the spreadsheet *Edit - Variables* pull-down menu, the Vars toolbar button, or the *Text Values* button in the *Spreadsheet Edit (Current) Specs* dialog (see page 1160). In this dialog, the correspondence between the numeric data, text data, and value labels can be managed. Values can be entered, sorted, modified, copied from variable to variable, and more.

Shortcuts. Double-click on a variable (column) name, then click on the *Text Values* button in the resulting dialog; click on the right-mouse-button and select the *Text Values* option from the flying menu; press the (*Text Values Manager*) button on the spreadsheet toolbar.

Example. The text values (*Male* and *Female*) will be edited in the variable called *Gender* in this example.

Step 1. Click on the right-mouse-button on any value of the variable *Gender* in the spreadsheet and then select the *Text Values* option from the flying menu to open the *Text Values Manager* dialog.

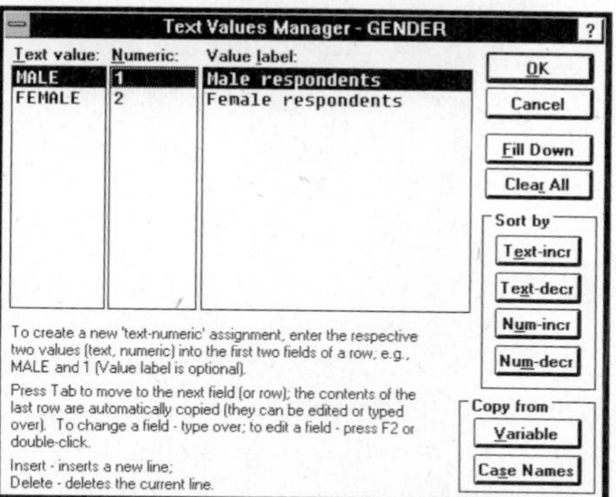

Step 2. To change the text value *Male* to *Boys*, click on *Male* in the *Text Values Manager* dialog and type in the value *Boys*.

Step 3. Press TAB to move to the next field (the numeric value associated with *Boys*) and again to move to the *Value Label* field. Now you can type in a short label describing the value *Boys* (e.g., type in the text string *Boys in single parent homes*).

Step 4. Now that you have edited a text value and entered a value label, click on the *OK* button to exit this dialog and implement the changes to the variable.

Create a New "Text-Numeric" Assignment

Enter the respective two values (text, numeric) into the first two fields of a row, e.g., *MALE* and *1* (the *Value Label* is optional).

Editing a "Text-Numeric" Assignment

Press TAB to move to the next field (or row); the contents of the last row are automatically copied (they can be edited or typed over). To change a field, type over it; to edit a field, press F2 or double-click on it. Use the INSERT key to insert a new line after the current line and the DELETE key to delete the current line.

Text Value

You can manage text values here. Text values can be up to 8 characters long and may contain all characters. Note that leading and trailing blanks will be removed from the text values by the program. *STATISTICA* will distinguish between upper and lowercase letters (e.g., "Smith" is not equivalent to "SMITH").

You can switch between viewing text values or their numeric equivalents in the spreadsheet by pressing the [ABC] button on the spreadsheet toolbar

Numeric

You can manage numeric values that are assigned to text values here. With this unique double notation of variables (where each value can have simultaneously both numeric and text representations), if a variable containing text data is selected for an analysis that requires numeric data, then its numeric values are automatically used.

Value Label

Each text value of a variable can have a label assigned to it. You can enter and manage that label here. Value labels can be up to 40 characters long and contain notes including any printable characters. Value labels are automatically used in the output of all analyses which involve individual values (e.g., frequencies, crosstabulations, breakdowns, etc.).

To display value labels in the spreadsheet, press the [ABC] button while holding down the CTRL key or select the *Text Values - Value Labels* option in the spreadsheet *View* pull-down menu.

Value labels can be printed along with the spreadsheet data by selecting the *Text Value Assignment* option in the *Print Data* dialog or by selecting the *Long* format of supplementary information in the *Page/Output Setup* dialog (see page 1148).

Fill Down

This button automatically assigns consecutive integers (based on the numeric value associated with the first text value in the table) to text values. For example, if you wanted numeric equivalents from *5* to *7* to be associated with three text values, first assign a value of *5* in the number field

associated with the first text value, then press *Fill Down* to automatically assign the next two text entries numeric values of *6* and *7*, respectively.

Clear All

This button will clear all the entries in all fields in the *Text Value Manager* dialog.

Sort by Text-incr

Sorts the *Text*, *Numeric*, and *Value Labels* in the *Text Value Manager* dialog in increasing order alphabetically using the *Text Values* as a sorting key.

Sort by Text-decr

Sorts the *Text*, *Numeric*, and *Value Labels* in the *Text Value Manager* dialog in decreasing order alphabetically using the *Text Values* as a sorting key.

Sort by Num-incr

Sorts the *Text*, *Numeric*, and *Value Labels* in the *Text Value Manager* dialog in increasing order numerically using the *Numeric Values* as a sorting key.

Sort by Num-decr

Sorts the *Text*, *Numeric*, and *Value Labels* in the *Text Value Manager* dialog in decreasing order numerically using the *Numeric Values* as a sorting key.

Copy from

Variable. This option will bring up a standard variable selection dialog, where you can select the variable from which the text-numeric assignments are to be copied.

Case names. This button is only available (active) if the current data file has case names. This option will copy those case names to the *Text value* column of the *Text Values Manager* dialog, and assign consecutive integers in the *Numeric* column.

Date Operations

You can create a single date variable from two or three variables (containing the month and year, day and month, or month, day, and year) or split a single date variable into two or three variables (one each for the month and year, day and month, or month, day, and year) using the *Date Operations* dialog.

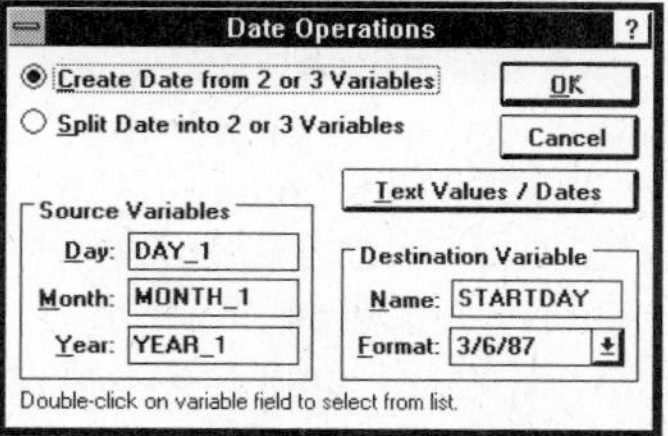

This dialog is accessible from the *Date Values* option in the spreadsheet *Edit - Variables* pull-down menu or the Vars toolbar button (see below for examples).

Create Date from 2 or 3 Variables

Select this option if you want to create single date values (in a new variable) from day, month, and year values in three existing variables or from the month and year values or day and month values in two existing variables.

Split Date into 2 or 3 Variables

Select this option if you want to split single date values (from an existing variable) into separate values for the day, month, and year, in three (previously created) new variables or into separate

values for either the month and year or day and month, in two (previously created) new variables.

Text Values/Dates

Click on this button to open the *Text Values/Dates* dialog (see below). In this dialog, you can change the dates to text labels (e.g., in order to use the date variable as a categorical variable) and vice versa (see page 1171 for more information).

Source Variables

The variable(s) that you select here will depend on whether you are creating a single date or splitting a single date.

Create date from 2 or 3 variables. When you select this option, you will need to specify as the *Source Variables* the three variables containing the *Day*, *Month*, and *Year* values (see *Example 1*, below), or the two variables containing either the *Day* and *Month* (*STATISTICA* will enter the current year as the year value) or the *Month* and *Year* (*STATISTICA* will enter the first day of the month as the day value).

Split date into 1, 2, or 3 variables. When you select this option, you will need to specify as the *Source Variable* the variable containing the single date values.

Destination Variables

The variable(s) that you select here will depend on whether you are creating a single date, or splitting a single date.

Create date from 2 or 3 variables. When you select this option, you will need to specify as the *Destination Variable* a single variable name in which the new date values will be placed (see *Example 1*, below). You will also need to specify the date format by selecting the desired format from the *Format* combo box.

Split date into 1, 2, or 3 variables. When you select this option, you will need to specify as the *Destination Variables*, the previously created variables in which the *Day*, *Month*, and *Year* values (for 3 variables, see *Example 2*, below), the *Day* and *Month* or *Month* and *Year* values (for 2 variables), or the *Day, Month,* or *Year* values (for 1 variable) will be placed.

Example 1 (Create a Single Date)

In this example, a single date variable will be created from three variables using the *STATISTICA* example data file *Heart.sta*. You can access the *Date Operations* dialog by selecting the *Variables - Date Values* option from the *Edit* pull-down menu or by clicking on the Vars Toolbar button and selecting the *Date Values* option.

Step 1. You will first need to create a new variable that will contain the single dates. To do this, select the *Variables - Add* option from the *Edit* pull-down menu and specify 1 new variable to be added to the data file.

For more information on adding variables, see *Add Variables*, page 1157; for more information on changing the variable name and other specifications, see *Spreadsheet Edit (Current) Specs*, page 1160.

Step 2. Now, open the *Date Operations* dialog (see above) and select the option *Create Date from 3 Variables*.

Step 3. In the *Date Operations* dialog, specify the 3 variables with the dates (*Source Variables*) by double-clicking on the *Day*, *Month*, and *Year* variable edit fields and then selecting the appropriate variable from the list of variables in the data file (for more information on selecting

variables, see *Selecting a Single Variable from a List*, Chapter 1).

Step 4. Specify the variable name in which the single date values will be placed (the *Destination Variable*) and also the value format for the single dates. First, double-click on the variable edit field and select the new variable that you previously created as the destination file. Next, select the desired value format from the *Format* combo box (you can later change the date value format in the *Spreadsheet Edit (Current) Specs* dialog 1160).

Step 5. Click *OK* in the *Date Operations* dialog to complete the creation of one date variable from the three variables.

Example 2 (Split a Date Variable)

In this example, three variables with the month, day and year will be created from a single date variable using the *STATISTICA* example data file *Heart.sta* and the new date variable that was created in *Example 1*, above.

Step 1. You will need to create three new variables that will be used as the *Destination Variables* (see below) and will contain the day, month, and year values, respectively (see *Example 1*, *Step 1* for information on creating new variables).

Step 2. Open the *Date Operations* dialog (see above) and select the option *Split Date into 3 Variables*.

Step 3. In the *Date Operations* dialog, the *Source Variable* is now a single variable (instead of three as in the above example). Double-click on this variable edit field to select the variable with the date values from a list of variables in the data file (see *Example 1*, *Step 3*).

Step 4. Specify the *Destination Variables* by double-clicking on the *Day*, *Month*, and *Year* variable edit fields and selecting each of the previously created variables (see *Step 1*).

Step 5. Click *OK* in the *Date Operations* dialog to complete the splitting of the single date variable into three variables.

Text Values-/Dates

In some circumstances it may be useful to create text values with date information (e.g., when using a date variable as a coding variable).

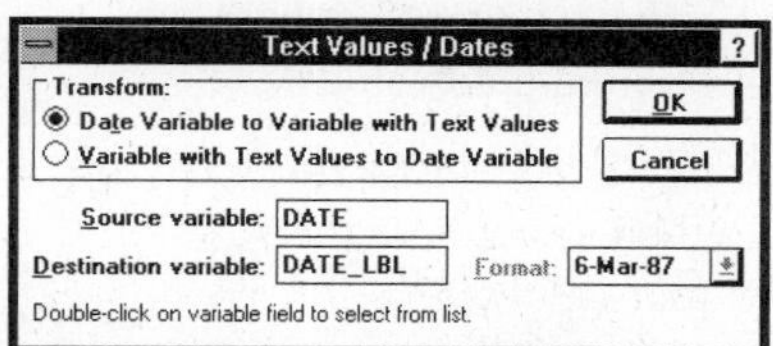

In the *Text Values/Dates* dialog, you can transform the date variable into a variable containing date text values with numeric equivalents in a range that will allow *STATISTICA* to use them as grouping codes (i.e., numeric values less than 32,000). You can also transform a variable containing date text values into a date variable with the desired date format.

Transform

Select the type of variable transformation here.

Date variable to variable with text values. Select this option if you want to transform a date variable (see *Date Operations*, above) into a variable containing dates as text values. The resulting date text values will be of the format MMMDD_YY. For example, the date value *6-Jan-68* (with the Julian value of *24843*) will be transformed to the text value *JAN06_68* (with the numeric equivalent of *4843*).

Variable with text values to date variable. This option allows you to transform variables with dates as text values into date variables. For example, the date text value *MAY25_80* will be transformed into the pre-specified date format of *05/25/80*. In order for *STATISTICA* to recognize the date text value, it must be entered in the MMMDD_YY format. When you transform this text value into a date value, you will be able to select the desired date format (see below).

Source Variable

The variable that you select here will depend on the type of transformation that you are performing:

If you are transforming a *Date Variable to a Variable with Text Values*, then select here the variable with the formatted date values.

If you are transforming a *Variable with Text Values to a Date Variable*, then select here the variable containing the date text values.

Destination Variable

You can select as the destination variable (where the transformed values will be placed) either the source variable (i.e., the transformed values will replace the original values) or a different variable in which the transformed variables will be placed.

Format

When you are transforming a variable with text date values into a variable containing date values, you will be able to select the format for the resulting transformed dates from this combo box.

Spreadsheet Recalculate

You can recalculate a variable (or group of variables) based on the formulas entered in the *Spreadsheet Edit (Current) Specs* dialog (see page 1160) of each variable. This dialog is accessible from the spreadsheet *Edit - Variables* pull-down menu or the Vars toolbar button.

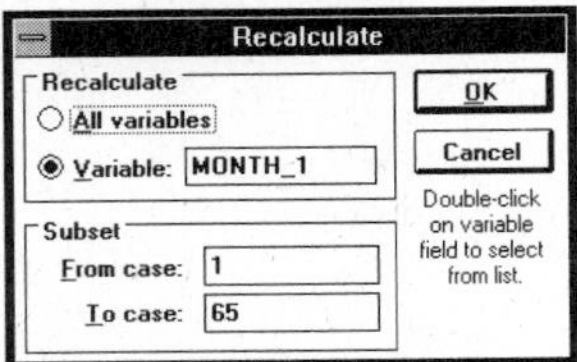

Toolbar button. Spreadsheet window toolbar button x=?.

Keyboard shortcut. Press F9 in the spreadsheet in order to bypass this dialog and recalculate all valid formulas in the current data set (this is the standard spreadsheet *recalculate* key).

All Variables

Use this option to simultaneously recalculate all variables containing formulas.

Variable

You can recalculate a single variable by specifying its name here. Double-click on the variable edit field to select a variable from a list of current variables in the spreadsheet.

Subset

By default, all cases will be recalculated (the first and last case numbers in the data set will be automatically entered below), or if a block is highlighted in the spreadsheet, only the cases included in the block will be recalculated (the first and last case numbers in the block will automatically be entered below).

However, should you want to recalculate a block of cases that is different from the default entries, enter the case numbers in the *From Case* and *To Case* windows.

From case. Specify the first case (inclusive) in the block of cases to be recalculated.

To case. Specify the last case (inclusive) in the block of cases to be recalculated.

Auto-recalculate When the Data Change

Select this option in order to automatically recalcuate all of the spreadsheet formulas when the data are changed in the spreadsheet.

Spreadsheet Shift (Lag) Variables

Use this option (accessible from the spreadsheet *Edit - Variables* pull-down menu or the Vars toolbar button) to shift a selected variable *backward* ("up") or *forward* ("down"), relative to the other variables in the file, by a specified number of cases (*lag*).

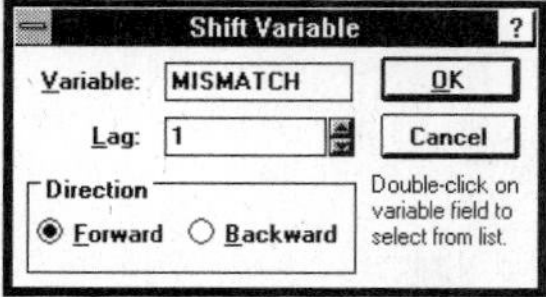

STATISTICA will add blank cases to the remaining variables in the file either before the first case (if the selected variable is shifted *backward*) or after the last case of the data file (if the selected variable is shifted *forward*).

Variable

Select the variable to be shifted here. Double-click on the variable edit field to select a variable from a list of current variables in the spreadsheet.

Lag

Specify the magnitude of the shift (i.e., the number of cases by which to move the variable).

Direction

Choose to either move the variable *forward* ("down") or *backward* ("up") by clicking on the appropriate option button.

Spreadsheet Rank Values

Rank the values of one or more variables in this dialog (accessible from the spreadsheet *Edit - Variables* pull-down menu or the Vars toolbar button).

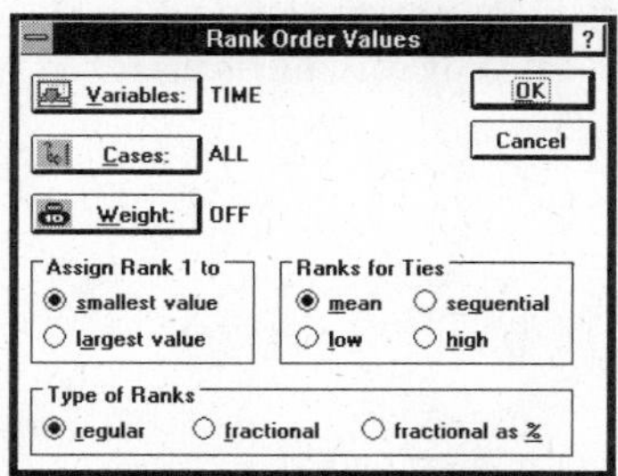

You are given several different options by which to perform the ranking. The values of the variable in the spreadsheet will be replaced with the rankings of those values.

If you want to preserve the original values of the variable, make a copy of this variable (using the *Copy Variables* option, see above, or by *Drag-and-Drop*, holding down the CTRL key) and perform the ranking on the duplicated variable.

Variables

Clicking on this button will bring up the *Select Variables* dialog from which you can select one or more variables to rank.

Cases

Click on this button to open the *Case Selection Conditions* dialog (page 1211). Here you can specify a subset of cases to be ranked. The condition specified here will apply to every variable selected above.

Weight

Before ranking, you can weight the variables selected above by another variable in the spreadsheet. When you click on this button, the *Define Weight* dialog will open (page 1212) from which you can select the weighting variable.

Assign Rank 1 to

You can choose to rank the values in ascending (smallest value of variable is assigned a rank of 1) or descending (largest value of variable is assigned a rank of 1) order.

Ranks for Ties

There are four options available to assign ranks to tied values.

- *Mean*: Assign the ranks of tied values the mean of those ranks.
- *Sequential*: Rank each tied value sequentially (ignore ties).
- *Low*: Assign the lowest rank of the values in the tie as the rank for each value in the tie.
- *High*: Assign the highest rank of the values in the tie as the rank for each value in the tie.

Type of Ranks

Choose the type of rank that you want to perform by clicking on the appropriate option button.

- *Regular*: Rank range is from *1* to *n*.
- *Fractional*: Rank range is from *0* to *1*.
- *Fractional %*: Ranks are percentages based on the fractional ranking of the values of variables.

Spreadsheet Recode Values

You can recode or "translate" the original values of the currently highlighted variable into some new values (dependent upon the values of any variables in the current data set) in the *Recode Values of Variable* dialog (accessible from the spreadsheet *Edit - Variables* pull-down menu or the Vars toolbar button).

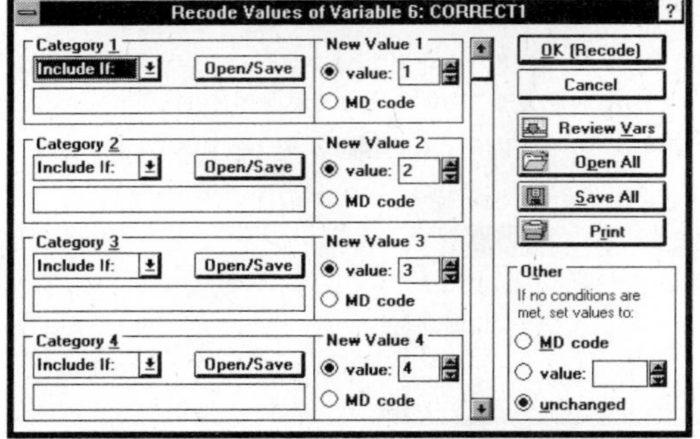

Using this facility, you can recode values of the variable into up to 17 "category" values (16 defined categories and "undefined" values). This "quick recode" facility (available from the spreadsheet at any point of an analysis) can be used to assign codes (or "category values," typically small integers) to a variable. A typical application of this tool is to create values of a new "grouping" variable in order to identify subsets of data as groups to be compared in subsequent analyses. For example, "assign the value of *1* to subjects older than 17, and *2* to subjects younger than 18" or "assign the value of *1* to male subjects, 18 to 25 years old with cholesterol levels below 200; *2* to male subjects 18 to 25 years old with cholesterol levels above 200; and assign the missing data value to all other subjects." In order to recode data in a way that requires that the values of the target variable are not fixed but calculated following some specific formulas (e.g., as an average of values of some other variables), use the spreadsheet *Formulas* (page 1160) or the user-defined recoding functions in the *STATISTICA BASIC* programming language (see the *Electronic Manual*).

Example:

Category 1 Include if: `v1>=0` *New Value:* `1`

Category 2 Include if: `v1<0` *New Value:* `-1`

This set of (two) recoding conditions will convert ("translate") all cases (observations) in the currently highlighted variable into *1* (if the value of variable number 1 for those cases is positive or zero) or into *-1* (if the value of variable number 1 for those cases is negative).

Note that recoding conditions may be defined such that the new values of the current variable do not depend on the old values of that variable, but only on values of some other variables in the data set. In other words, the currently highlighted variable does not have to be included in the text of the recoding conditions. For instance in this example, the currently highlighted variable could be variable number 3, and its new ("recoded") values would depend only on values of variable number 1. If the currently highlighted variable was variable number 1, then its values would be "translated" into new ones (positive values would "become" *1* and negative values would "become" *-1*).

Category

Use up to 16 scrollable categories to recode a variable.

Include/Exclude if. When you choose *include if* and the recode condition evaluates to true, the original values of the recoded variable for cases (observations) that meet the condition will be replaced with the *New Value* (see below) that you have specified. *Exclude if* will assign the *New Value* to the original values for cases (observations) that do not meet the specified recode condition.

Recode condition. Specify the recode condition in the edit field *Category* following the standard *STATISTICA Case Selection Conditions* (see page 1211).

- Operators: =, <>, <, >, <=, >=, *NOT*, *AND*, *OR*
- Variable Names: Specify either variable numbers (e.g., *v1*, *v2*, *v3*, . . .) or variable names (e.g., *GENDER*, *Date*, *time*, . . .)
- Case Number: *v0*
- Examples: *v1=0 OR v2>=0*

  (v1<1 OR v9='YES') AND v4<>0
- Note: Be sure to use single quotation marks to reference the text values of variables, e.g., *'Yes'*

Open/Save button. Use this option to open (and use for recoding) an existing standard *STATISTICA Case Selection Condition* file (those which can be used to select/filter cases for all analyses in the program) as well as save the current condition in each *Category*. Clicking on the *Open/Save* button will open the *Case Selection Condition* dialog (page 1211) where you can edit, save or open case selection conditions (these are the same conditions which are used for processing subsets of cases throughout the program). Case selection conditions saved in this dialog are saved under the file name extension **.sel*. These case selection conditions can

later be used as regular case selection conditions for data analyses when you click *OK* in the *Case Selection Condition* dialog (page 1211).

New value. Specify the new value to replace the original values here. You can choose either a specific value (*Value* option button) or the missing data value (*MD code* option button) as the new value.

Variables

Clicking this button will open the *Variables* dialog from which you can view the variables in the spreadsheet.

Open All

This button opens the *Open Recode Conditions File* dialog from which you can select a file (containing all of the recode categories) to open into the *Recode Values of Variables* dialog. Files opened from this dialog are text files with the file name extension **.txt*. Conditions used for verifying data (see *Verify Data*, Chapter 7, *Data Management*), *Frequency* and *Graph* categorizations (see *Basic Statistics and Tables*, Chapter 9 of this volume, and Volume II of the manual, respectively), and all other facilities in *STATISTICA* which allow you to define multiple case selection conditions are compatible with the conditions that can be specified here. You can use this option to open those previously saved selection conditions for use here.

Save All

This button opens the *Save Recode Conditions File* dialog from which you can designate a file into which to save all of the recode conditions. This file will be saved in text file format (**.txt* extension). These selection conditions are compatible with the conditions used for verifying data (see *Verify Data*, in *Data Management*, Chapter 7), *Frequency* and *Graph* categorizations (see *Basic Statistics and Tables*, Chapter 9 of this volume, and Volume II of the manual, respectively), and all other facilities in *STATISTICA* which allow you to define multiple case selection conditions. The recode conditions that you save via this option can then be used as selection conditions for these other *STATISTICA* applications.

Print

Clicking this button will print the contents of all currently defined recode conditions. You can send the contents of this dialog either to a printer file or to the printer and/or *Text/output Window* depending on your selection in the *Page/Output Setup* dialog (page 1148).

Other

If no conditions are met by a case (observation) when the variable is recoded, you can choose to either set the original values of the recoded variable to missing (click on the *MD code* option button), designate an alternative value (click on the *Value* option button then enter a value), or leave the original values as they are (click on the *Unchanged* option button).

Spreadsheet Add Cases

Add cases to the spreadsheet by designating the number of new cases to add, as well as where to add them (after which case) in the *Add Cases* dialog.

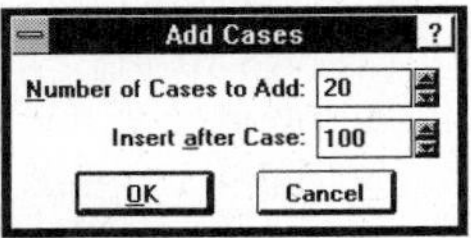

This dialog is accessible from the spreadsheet *Edit - Cases* pull-down menu, spreadsheet right-mouse-button flying menu, or the Cases toolbar button.

Number of Cases to Add

Choose the desired number of cases to add to the current spreadsheet. The number of cases that you can add to a spreadsheet is unlimited.

Insert After Case

Designate the case number after which the new case(s) will be added. The added cases will be located after the case specified here.

How to insert before case 1. One way to copy and insert the values of a case or block of cases before case 1 is to use the *Drag-and-Drop* facilities in *STATISTICA*. To do this, first highlight the desired block. Then, move the cursor to one of the borders of the block where it will change into an arrow. Now, to move and insert the block, press SHIFT while dragging the block. Next, position the insertion bar between the variable names and the first row of the spreadsheet and release the mouse-button. Note that this method does not copy the selected case(s) (i.e., the case names will not be copied) but only the values of the selected block.

In order to copy the entire case or block of cases before case 1, use the copy option (accessible via the Cases toolbar button) and enter case *0* in the *Insert After* edit field. Not only will the values of the selected block be moved, but also the case names.

Spreadsheet Move Cases

Move one or more cases (rows) in the spreadsheet by designating the range (inclusive) of cases to be moved and the location (case to insert after) in the *Move Cases* dialog.

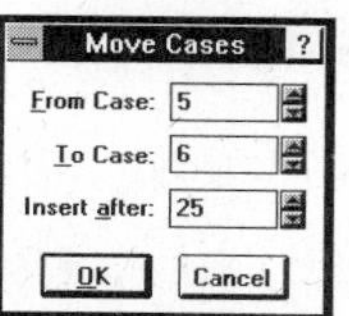

This dialog is accessible from the spreadsheet *Edit - Cases* pull-down menu, spreadsheet right-mouse-button flying menu, or the Cases toolbar button.

From Case

Designate the first case (inclusive) in the block of cases to be moved. (Note that if you are moving only one case, then designate the same case in both the *From Case* and *To Case* lists.)

To Case

Designate the last case (inclusive) in the block of cases to be moved.

Insert After

Designate the location (case) in the spreadsheet that the case(s) will be moved after. The moved cases will be located after the case specified here.

How to insert before case 1. One way to move and insert the values of a case or block of cases before case 1 is to use the *Drag-and-Drop* facilities in *STATISTICA*. To do this, first highlight the desired block. Then, move the cursor to one of the borders of the block where it will change into an arrow. Now, to move and insert the block, press SHIFT while dragging the block. Next, position the insertion bar between the variable names and the first row of the spreadsheet and release the mouse-button. Note that this method does not move the selected case(s) (i.e., the case names will not be moved) but only the values of the selected block.

In order to move the entire case or block of cases before case 1, use the move option (accessible via the Cases toolbar button) and enter case *0* in the *Insert After* edit field. Not only will the values of

the selected block be moved, but also the case names.

Spreadsheet Copy Cases

Unlike the Clipboard operation of copying the contents of a highlighted range or block of values in the spreadsheet, this option will copy both the contents of the row(s) and the row(s) itself (regardless of whether or not all variables or only a subset of variables are currently highlighted for the respective cases). The subsequent cases will be inserted (see *Insert After*, below) into the spreadsheet resulting in an increase in the size of the file. You can place a copy of the specified case(s) at a designated location by specifying the range (inclusive) of cases to be copied and the spreadsheet location (insert after which case) in the *Copy Cases* dialog.

This dialog is accessible from the spreadsheet *Edit - Cases* pull-down menu, the spreadsheet right-mouse-button flying menu, or the *Cases* toolbar button.

From Case

Designate the first case (inclusive) in the block of cases to be copied. (Note that if you are copying only one case, then designate the same case in both the *From Case* and *To Case* lists.)

To Case

Designate the last case (inclusive) in the block of cases to be copied.

Insert After

Designate the location (case) in the spreadsheet that the case(s) will be placed after copying. The copied cases will be located after the case specified here.

How to copy before case 1. One way to copy and insert the values of a case or block of cases before case 1 is to use the *Drag-and-Drop* facilities in *STATISTICA*. To do this, first highlight the desired block. Then, move the cursor to one of the borders of the block where it will change into an arrow. Now, to copy and insert the block, press SHIFT while dragging the block. Next, position the insertion bar between the variable names and the first row of the spreadsheet and release the mouse-button. Note that this method does not copy the selected case(s) (i.e., the case name will not be copied) but only the values of the selected block.

In order to copy a case or block of cases before case 1, use the copy option (accessible via the Cases toolbar button) and enter case *0* in the *Insert After* edit field. Not only will the values of the selected block be copied and inserted before case 1, but also the case names.

Spreadsheet Delete Cases

One or more cases (rows) can be deleted from the current spreadsheet when you designate the range (inclusive) of cases to be deleted in the *Delete Cases* dialog (accessible from the spreadsheet *Edit - Cases* pull-down menu, the spreadsheet right-mouse-button flying menu, or the *Cases* toolbar button).

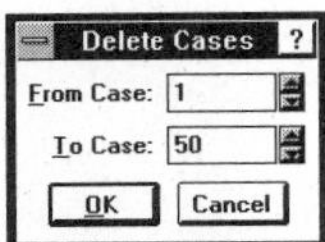

Unlike deleting (clearing) the contents of a highlighted range or block of values in the spreadsheet, this option will remove both the contents of the row(s) and the row(s) itself (regardless of whether or not all variables or only a subset of variables are currently highlighted for the respective cases); thus the subsequent cases will be moved up and the size of the file will decrease.

From Case

Designate the first case (inclusive) in the block of cases to be deleted. (Note that if you are deleting only one case, then designate the same case in both the *From Case* and *To Case* lists.)

To Case

Designate the last case (inclusive) in the block of cases to be deleted.

Spreadsheet Edit Case Names

The *Case Name Manager* dialog (accessible from the spreadsheet *Edit - Cases* pull-down menu, the spreadsheet right-mouse-button flying menu, the Cases toolbar button, or by double-clicking on the case name that you want to edit) lists the case names in a scrollable table where you can review or edit them.

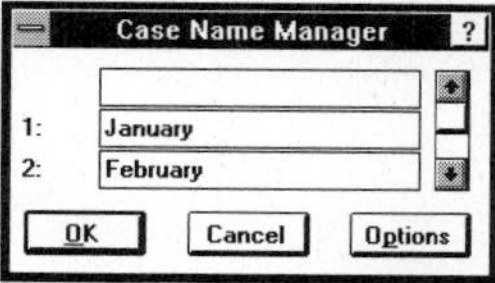

Case names are used as labels only (and not as text values); thus they can contain all printable characters (the same as value labels, see *Text Values Manager*, page 1167).

Case Names

Edit case names in the scrollable table in the *Case Name Manager* dialog. The middle field of three fields in the table is editable. When you first open this dialog, the case name currently highlighted in the spreadsheet will appear in the editing (middle) field with the equivalent case number along side of it. After you edit this name, you can scroll up or down (using the scrollbar or arrow keys) to place a different name in the editing field and the case numbers will scroll with the names.

Options

Clicking this button will open the *Case Names Options* dialog (see below) where you can adjust the case name width, get the case names from the entries in another variable or perform Clipboard operations on case names.

Spreadsheet Case Name Options

When you are editing case names in the *Case Name Manager* dialog (see above), you can open the *Case Names Options* dialog for more editing options.

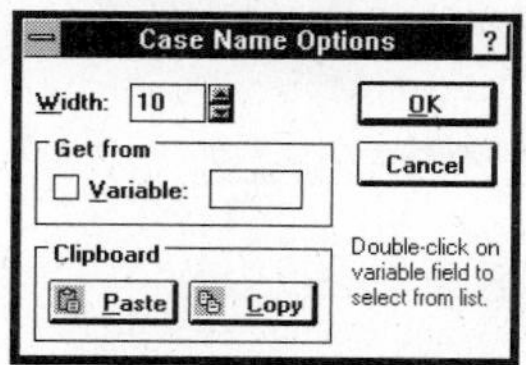

Width

Adjust the case name width here (maximum width is 20 characters). Note that unlike the *Variable Width* (a "display format," see page 1160), which affects only the display of data and not data themselves, the current setting of the case name width will affect the amount of space reserved in the data file for case names. Thus, decreasing the

width will "cut" (delete) parts of the case names which do not fit the new width setting. If you set the width to *0*, then the case names will be deleted.

Get From

If you want, you can get the case names from values of a variable in the current data set. Click on the option *Variable* and then specify the variable number that you want the case names taken from.

Clipboard

You can select the following Clipboard operations to manage case names.

Paste. Clicking this option will paste the contents of the Clipboard into the case names column (from the currently highlighted case on down).

Copy. Clicking this option will copy case names (from the currently highlighted case on down) from the spreadsheet to the Clipboard.

Data File Header, Notes, and Workbook Info

Make notes or comments about the current data file in the *Data File Header, Notes and Workbook Info* dialog.

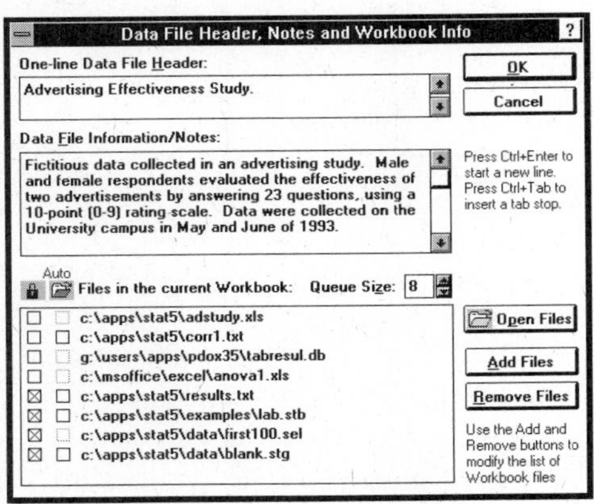

This dialog allows you to enter a one-line *File Header* which appears at the top of the spreadsheet, detailed file information or notes about the data set's contents, source, etc., and to manage the Workbook file list, that is, the list of all supplementary files (e.g., graphs, reports, programs) used with the current data set.

One-Line Header

Enter one line (up to 77 characters) of comment about the file here. The *One-line Header* is saved as part of the file and is printed along with the spreadsheet data file when the *File Info/Notes* option is selected in the *Print Data* dialog (page 1145) or along with the output of analyses when either a *Short*, *Medium* or *Long* report style is selected in the *Page/Output Setup* dialog (page 1148). The header is also included in the title area of all *Custom Graphs* produced from the current data set (see Volume II).

File Information/Notes

Make a comment about the spreadsheet data file here. These notes can be up to 512 characters in length and can include any printable characters. To start a new line in this edit box, press CTRL+ENTER, to enter a tab stop, press CTRL+TAB.

The *File Information/Notes* are printed along with the spreadsheet data file when the *File Info/Notes* option is selected in the *Print Data* dialog (page 1145).

Workbook

STATISTICA data set files can be considered to be "Workbooks" of files because they contain lists of all supplementary files related to the data sets.

This area of the *Data File Header, Notes, and Workbook Info* dialog contains the Workbook management options. Workbooks help to organize sets of supplementary files (e.g., Scrollsheets,

graphs, text/graphics reports, user programs, recodes, etc.) which have been created or used (e.g., reviewed) during the analysis of a data set.

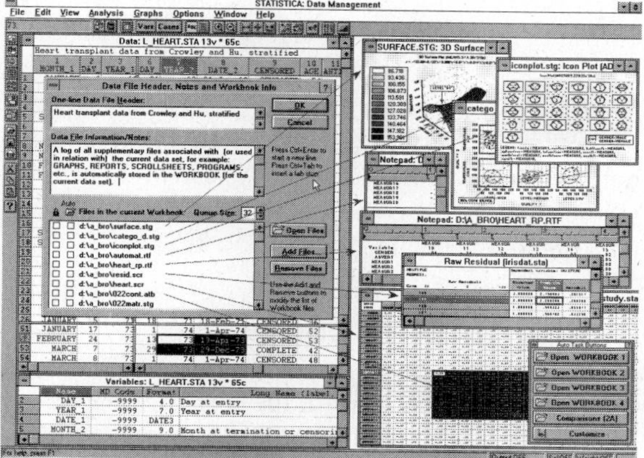

Whenever you open or save a file (e.g., a graph), its name is automatically added to the queue of files in the Workbook file list box. The length of this queue (by default 16) can be changed; when the queue is full, the oldest files are dropped from the list (unless they are locked, see below) as new files are added. An updated list of these files is automatically saved with the data file (this option can be changed in the *STATISTICA Defaults: General* dialog; see also *When the Workbook Facility should be Disabled*, below).

The Workbook list of files is also accessible in every *Open/Save* dialog in *STATISTICA*, so that you can easily select them (when you are opening a file) or overwrite them (when you are saving a file).

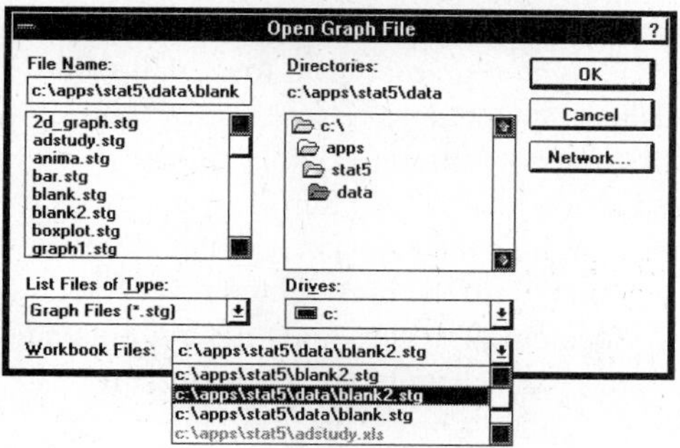

Supplementary files (from the list of Workbook files) can be opened in the following ways:

(1) Double-click on the desired file name in the list of supplementary files. The selected file will open behind the *Data File Header, Notes, and Workbook Info* dialog.

(2) Select (highlight) one or more files to open in the list box and then click on the *Open Files* button (in the *Data File Header, Notes, and Workbook Info* dialog). The *Data File Header, Notes, and Workbook Info* dialog will close and the selected file(s) will open in sequence.

(3) Use the Auto option to select files that will automatically open whenever the current data file is opened (see below).

The Workbook is accessible by double-clicking on the title area of the spreadsheet, by pressing the Workbook toolbar button, or by selecting the *Header...* option in the pull-down menu *Edit*.

The Workbook options are described below:

Lock. Supplementary files can be locked by checking the box next to the file name below the *Lock* icon so that they will not be removed from the Workbook list as the queue is updated or changed.

Auto. Select up to 9 supplementary files in order to automatically open them when you open the data file (so that all supplementary information, e.g., graphs or reports from a previous stage of the analysis, is available whenever you open the data file). When this check-box is dimmed, then these files cannot be automatically opened or opened by double-clicking on them in this list (e.g., this applies to foreign data files as well as all non-document files such as axis definition, surface/contour specifications, etc.).

Note that you can cycle through the checkboxes in the Workbook list using the space bar to select (or

deselect) files to be locked and/or automatically opened.

Files in the current Workbook. A log of all of the supplementary files used with or created from the current data file is given in this area of the dialog. The queue is managed on a first-in-first-out basis, that is, when the queue is full, the oldest file will be removed from the list as a new file is added (unless the file is locked, see above). The types of supplementary files listed here include previously saved graphs, Scrollsheets, reports, programs (e.g., *STATISTICA BASIC* or *SCL* programs), import/export files, case selection conditions, etc.

Queue Size. Specify here, the number of files to be maintained in the supplementary files list. The maximum number of files that can be maintained in this list is 32. The queue is managed on a first-in-first-out basis, that is, when the queue is full, the oldest file will be removed from the list as a new file is added (unless the file is locked, see above).

Add Files. Click on this button in order to open a multiple file selection dialog in which you can select one or more previously saved files to add to the supplementary list of files. You can select the multiple files in this dialog in either a continuous (drag) or discontinuous (press the CTRL key) list.

Remove Files. Click on this button in order to remove (i.e., delete) highlighted files from the *Files in Current Workbook* list.

Open Files. When you click on this button, the files highlighted in the *Files in Current Workbook* list will be opened sequentially after the *Data File Header, Notes, and Workbook Info* dialog closes. To open a file while leaving this dialog open, double-click on the file name in the list.

When the Workbook facility should be disabled. Normally, the Workbook facility works in an automatic manner which is transparent for the user. Data files are sometimes saved upon exiting the program (or changing the data file) even if you did not change (edit) the data set so that the Workbook information in the data file can be updated. However, unless the data set is extremely large, this does not cause any noticeable delay. The only circumstance when it is recommended to disable the Workbook facility (use the *STATISTICA Defaults: General* dialog, see page 1213), is when the data set is extremely large and saving it causes a noticeable delay; then, disabling the Workbook facility will suppress the automatic saving of the data file to update the Workbook list.

Cut

Cut removes the contents of the currently highlighted cells, text, or graph object and copies them to the Clipboard. This action deletes the data values in the Scrollsheet or spreadsheet and replaces them with missing data until new values are entered or pasted in. Highlighted text is simply deleted from the *Text/output Window*. *Cut* replaces the previous contents of the Clipboard with the deleted values, objects, or text.

Toolbar button. See the [X] toolbar button in the spreadsheet and Scrollsheet windows.

Keyboard shortcut. CTRL+X or SHIFT+DEL

Copy

This option copies the contents of the currently highlighted cells or text in the Scrollsheet, spreadsheet, or *Text/output Window* or of the currently highlighted graph object to the Clipboard. For Scrollsheets or spreadsheets, selecting this option will copy not only the contents in the highlighted block of cells in a Scrollsheet or spreadsheet, but also the row names and column names associated with the highlighted cells [use *Copy Raw* (see below) to copy only the highlighted Scrollsheet or spreadsheet block without the row and column names]. *Copy* replaces the previous

contents of the Clipboard with the contents of the highlighted cells, text, or graph object.

Toolbar button. See the toolbar button in the spreadsheet and Scrollsheet windows.

Keyboard shortcut. CTRL+C or CTRL+INS

Copy Raw

Select this option from the spreadsheet *Edit* pull-down menu in order to copy only the data highlighted in the spreadsheet or Scrollsheet to the Clipboard. Unlike the *Copy* option (see above), this option does not copy the row names or column names associated with the highlighted data. *Copy Raw* replaces the previous contents of the Clipboard with the highlighted contents of the spreadsheet or Scrollsheet. See Chapter 2, *Toolbars*, for an example comparing the options *Copy* and *Copy Raw*.

Paste

This option pastes (inserts) the current contents of the Clipboard to the *STATISTICA* Spreadsheet, Scrollsheet, graph, or *Text/output Window*.

When you use this operation in *STATISTICA* spreadsheet, Scrollsheets, or *Text/output Windows*, the current position of the cursor designates the starting place (the upper left-hand corner) for the pasting to begin. *Paste* will then fill the area until everything in the Clipboard is pasted. This option is not available (dimmed) if the Clipboard is empty (or contains an incompatible format, e.g., a picture when you are pasting into a Scrollsheet).

Toolbar button. See the toolbar button in the spreadsheet and Scrollsheet windows.-

Keyboard shortcut. CTRL+V or SHIFT+INS

Pasting in Graphs

When you paste a graphic object in a *STATISTICA* graph using the *Paste* option, the object will be pasted in the upper-left corner of the graph. You can then reposition or resize the object accordingly (see *Resizing an Object*, Volume II of the manual).

Clipboard and graphic objects (technical note). When an object is copied to the Clipboard from *STATISTICA*, these graphic representations (formats) of the object will be created in the Clipboard, in the following order of priority (hierarchy): *STATISTICA Graph* (i.e., *STATISTICA* format), *Metafile* (i.e., picture), and then *Bitmap* and for text objects, the order is, *STATISTICA Graph*, *Metafile*, *Raw text*, and then *Bitmap*. When an object (or text) is copied from another application (e.g., Excel), the order may not be the same as that listed above because both the selection of Clipboard formats produced by an application and the order of these formats is determined by the source application. Therefore, when you use the *Paste* option, the format that is used may not be the best or desired format for the object. In this situation, it is best to use the *Paste Special* option (see Volume II, *Options Common to all Graphs*) which will allow you to select the most applicable graphic format for the Clipboard object.

For example, if you want to paste a large piece of artwork (e.g., a 256 color bitmap) from another application, you would first copy that artwork (from within that application) to the Clipboard (the resulting hierarchy of formats available in the Clipboard would be determined by the source application; in this example, assume that the hierarchy is: Bitmap and then Metafile). Now, when you click on the *Paste* option in *STATISTICA*, the artwork would be pasted in as a bitmap (since this is the highest priority format in the Clipboard); however, the Metafile format may be more suitable for customizations which you are planning and more efficient (in terms of required storage space).

If the *Paste Special* option is used, then you could elect to paste the artwork in the *STATISTICA* graph as a Metafile.

***OLE* pasting.** Please refer to Volume II (*Options Common to all Graphs*) for information on the Windows *OLE* (*O*bject *L*inking and *E*mbedding) facilities supported by *STATISTICA* when pasting graphs into other applications.

Clear

This option deletes text or the contents of the currently highlighted cells. In the Scrollsheet or spreadsheet, the deleted values are replaced with missing data until new values are entered or pasted in. Unlike the *Cut* option (see above), *Clear* does not copy the text or contents of the cells to the Clipboard; therefore, it will not affect the contents of the Clipboard. Note that cells may also be cleared via *Drag-and-Drop* (see page 1127).

Keyboard shortcut. DEL

Paste Link

Use this option to establish a *DDE* (Dynamic Data Exchange) link between another application (the source or server) and *STATISTICA* (the client) using the standard Windows *Paste Link* option. With this option, you can paste cells copied from a Windows application to a block of cells in a *STATISTICA* spreadsheet (from the highlighted cell down and to the right), permanently linking the data in the spreadsheet with the source of the data (server).

When you use this option, the *DDE* link is created and stored in the *Long Name* of the current variable (see *Spreadsheet Edit (Current) Specs* dialog, page 1160). You can also edit a *DDE* link in the *Links Manager* dialog (see page 1192). For more information on *DDE* links, see *Creating Links (Dynamic Data Exchange)*, in Chapter 7, *Data Management*.

Follow the steps outlined below to establish a *DDE* link using the *Paste Link* option.

Step 1. Open the source file and copy to the Clipboard the block of data (or text) that you want to link with the client (*STATISTICA*) file. Now, leaving this server file open, switch to the desired *STATISTICA* module.

Step 2. In the *STATISTICA* spreadsheet, designate (highlight) the cell that will "anchor" the data to be pasted into the spreadsheet (the data will be pasted down and to the right of this "anchor" cell).

Step 3. Click on the *Paste Link* option to establish the link. *STATISTICA* will automatically write the *DDE* path (see *Creating Links (Dynamic Data Exchange)* in Chapter 7, *Data Management*) and store it in the *variable long name* (see page 1160) and in the *Links Manager* (page 1192).

DDE Error

This dialog will open whenever *STATISTICA* needs to re-establish a remote (Dynamic Data Exchange) link -- that is whenever the server is closed and inactive, or the *DDE* topic is not opened.

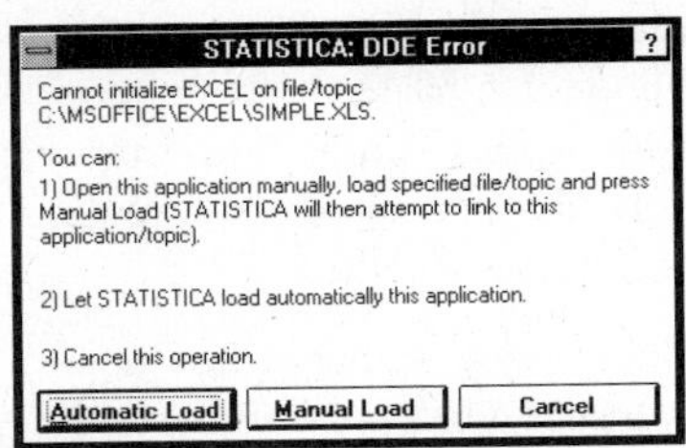

Automatic Load

Click on this button when you want to re-establish the remote link and automatically open the source application file/topic (listed at the top of this dialog; see *Creating Links (Dynamic Data Exchange)*, in Chapter 7, *Data Management*, for more information on the *DDE*). Note that the application must be on the DOS path and the file/topic must be loadable by command line.

Manual Load

Use this option to manually open the specified file/topic. In order to use this option, follow the steps outlined below.

Step 1. Once you have decided to manually open the specified file/topic (but before you click on the *Manual Load* button), switch to the Windows Program Manager (or equivalent) and open the source application (e.g., Excel).

Step 2. Open the appropriate file in the source application.

Step 3. Switch back to the *STATISTICA* module and click on the *Manual Load* button to manually open the file/topic.

Cancel

Click on this button to temporarily disable the link.

Find Value

The *Find* dialog (accessible from the spreadsheet *Edit* pull-down menu) will enable you to search for a specific data value (in the currently highlighted variable) or case name in the spreadsheet, or for a specific text or number in the *Text/output Window*.

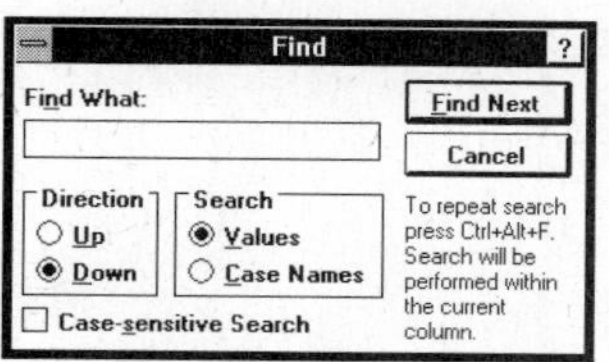

Find What

Specify the variable value (text or numeric) or the case name that you want to search for in the spreadsheet, or the text or number that you want to search for in the *Text/output Window*.

Direction

Find will search either above (select the *Up* option button) or below (select the *Down* option button) the currently highlighted cell, but will stop the search when it reaches the top or bottom of the file.

Search

Choose to search for *Values* in the current variable or for *Case Names* (this option is only applicable to spreadsheets).

Find Next

After you have specified the above options, click on this button to begin the search. When there is more than one match, *Find* will pause so that you can either exit (via the *Cancel* button) the dialog, or click *Find Next* to search for the next match.

Shortcut. You can repeat the search by pressing CTRL+F.

Replace Value

The *Replace* dialog is accessible from the spreadsheet *Edit* pull-down menu.

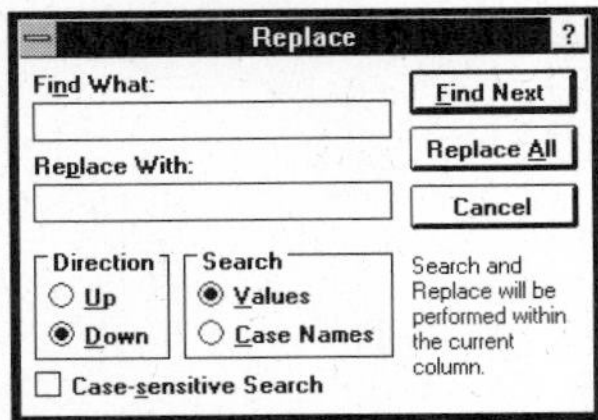

This dialog will enable you to search for a specific data value in the currently highlighted variable (or for a specific case name) and replace it with a different value, or search for a specific text or number in the *Text/output Window*, and replace it with a different text or number.

Find What

Specify the variable value (text or numeric) or the case name that you want to search for and replace.

Replace With

Specify the value (text or numeric) here that will be used to replace the value, text, or case name that you are searching for.

Direction

Replace will search either above (select the *Up* option button) or below (select the *Down* option button) the currently highlighted cell or text, but will stop the search when it reaches the top or bottom of the file.

Search

Choose to search for *Values* in the current variable or for *Case Names* (this option is only applicable to spreadsheets).

Find Next

After you have specified the above options, click on this button to begin the search. When *STATISTICA* has found the specified text, value, or case name, you will be given the following choices to replace it:

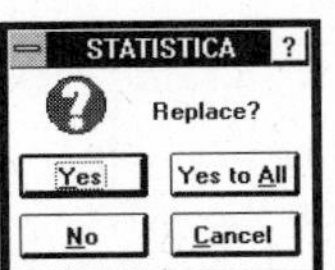

Yes. Click this button to replace the text or value with your specified replacement.

No. Click this button to skip over this value (it will not be replaced).

Yes to all. Click this button to replace all matching text or values without asking for confirmation.

Cancel. Click this button to quit the search and leave the dialog.

Replace All

Click this button instead of the *Find Next* button to replace all values or text that match. You will not be prompted to accept or reject each replacement.

Shortcut. Repeat the search by pressing CTRL+H.

Spreadsheet Transpose Block

Transpose a square block of data in the spreadsheet by highlighting the block in the spreadsheet and then selecting the *Transpose - block* option from the spreadsheet *Edit* pull-down menu. This option will only transpose the data values defined by the highlight and not the data file (see *Transpose Data File*, below).

Before transposing highlighted block:

Data: 10ITEMS.STA 10v * 100c

The 10-item prejudice survey: Results for 40 college students

NUME VALU	1 ITEM1	2 ITEM2	3 ITEM3	4 ITEM4	5 ITEM5	6 ITEM6	7 ITEM7
1	4	5	4	6	4	7	4
2	4	3	4	5	5	4	4
3	4	4	3	5	7	5	3
4	4	3	6	5	4	2	5
5	4	6	7	5	5	3	4
6	5	6	6	8	4	5	6
7	5	5	5	5	6	6	5
8	4	3	2	5	5	5	3

After transposing highlighted block:

Data: 10ITEMS.STA 10v * 100c

The 10-item prejudice survey: Results for 40 college students

NUMERIC VALUES	1 ITEM1	2 ITEM2	3 ITEM3	4 ITEM4	5 ITEM5	6 ITEM6	7 ITEM7
1	4	5	4	6	4	7	4
2	4	3	4	5	5	4	4
3	4	4	3	6	7	6	3
4	4	3	5	5	5	8	5
5	4	6	7	4	5	4	4
6	5	6	5	2	3	5	6
7	5	5	5	5	6	6	5
8	4	3	2	5	5	5	3

Spreadsheet Transpose Data File

By selecting the *Transpose - Data File* option from the spreadsheet *Edit* pull-down menu, you can turn cases into variables and variables into cases by transposing the spreadsheet data file. (You can transpose a square block of data when you select the *Transpose Block* option, see above.)

Before transposing data file:

Data: CARS.STA 5v * 22c

Performance, fuel economy, and approximat

NUMERIC VALUES	1 PRICE	2 ACCELE	3 BRAKIN	4 HANDLI	5 MILAGE
Acura	-.521	.477	-.007	.382	2.079
Audi	.866	.208	.319	-.091	-.677
BMW	.496	-.802	.192	-.091	-.154
Buick	-.614	1.689	.933	-.210	-.154
Corvette	1.235	-1.811	-.494	.973	-.677
Chrysler	-.614	.073	.427	-.210	-.154
Dodge	-.706	-.196	.481	.145	-.154
Eagle	-.614	1.218	-4.199	-.210	-.677
Ford	-.706	-1.542	.987	.145	-1.724
Honda	-.429	.410	-.007	.027	.369
Isuzu	-.798	.410	-.061	-4.230	1.067

After transposing data file:

Data: CARS.STA 22v * 5c

Performance, fuel economy, and approximate price for various automo

NUMERIC VALUES	1 ACURA	2 AUDI	3 BMW	4 BUICK	5 CORVETTE	6 CHRYSLER
PRICE Approxima	-.521	.866	.496	-.614	1.235	-.614
ACCELER Accelerat	.477	.208	-.802	1.689	-1.811	.073
BRAKING Breaking	-.007	.319	.192	.933	-.494	.427
HANDLING Road hold	.382	-.091	-.091	-.210	.973	-.210
MILAGE Miles per	2.079	-.677	-.154	-.154	-.677	-.154

Text value equivalents in the data file will be lost when the file is transposed, because the text-/numeric assignments are specifications of variables (i.e., columns) and not cases (i.e., rows) in *STATISTICA* data files.

Case names (if any) from the original file will become *Long Variable Names*, created from the former (8 character) variable names and up to 12 characters of the former *Long Variable Names* (for a total of 20 characters).

Spreadsheet Fill/Standardize Block - Fill Random Values

This option will fill the highlighted block with random values (in the range of 0 to 1) following the uniform distribution.

Before:

Data: FILL.STA 10v * 10c

NUMERIC VALUES	1 VAR1	2 VAR2	3 VAR3	4 VAR4	5 VAR5	6 VAR6
1						
2						
3						
4						
5						
6						
7						
8						
9						
10						

After:

Data: FILL.STA 10v * 10c

NUMERIC VALUES	1 VAR1	2 VAR2	3 VAR3	4 VAR4	5 VAR5	6 VAR6
1						
2		.001	.564	.193	.809	
3		.585	.480	.350	.896	
4		.823	.747	.174	.859	
5		.711	.514	.304	.015	
6		.091	.364	.147	.166	
7		.989	.446	.119	.005	
8		.009	.378	.532	.571	
9		.602	.607	.166	.663	
10						

To copy down rows, see *Fill/Copy Down* (below); to copy across columns, see *Fill Right* (below). Note that you can also use the *Drag-and-Drop* facility (see page 1125) to copy a block of values or to extrapolate values across a block.

Spreadsheet Fill/Standardize Block - Fill/Copy Down

This option (accessible from the spreadsheet *Edit* pull-down menu, or the spreadsheet right-mouse-button flying menu) will copy the entries in the first row of a highlighted block of cells in the spread-

sheet down the entire block (i.e., into the remaining cells in the block).

Before:

Data: FILL.STA 10v * 10c

	1 VAR1	2 VAR2	3 VAR3	4 VAR4	5 VAR5	6 VAR6
1						
2		1.00	2.00	3.00	4.00	
3						
4						
5						
6						
7						
8						
9						
10						

After:

Data: FILL.STA 10v * 10c

	1 VAR1	2 VAR2	3 VAR3	4 VAR4	5 VAR5	6 VAR6
1						
2		1.00	2.00	3.00	4.00	
3		1.00	2.00	3.00	4.00	
4		1.00	2.00	3.00	4.00	
5		1.00	2.00	3.00	4.00	
6		1.00	2.00	3.00	4.00	
7		1.00	2.00	3.00	4.00	
8		1.00	2.00	3.00	4.00	
9						
10						

If you need to copy a value to consecutive cases of one variable only, highlight a one-column block; its first ("top") value will be copied down to the end of the highlight. (To copy across variables, see the *Fill Right* option, below.) You can also use the *Drag-and-Drop* facility (see page 1125) to copy a block of values or to extrapolate values from a block. Use *Fill Random Values* (see above) in order to fill the cells in the block with random values (following the uniform distribution).

Spreadsheet Fill/Standardize Block - Fill/Copy Right

This option (accessible from the spreadsheet *Edit* pull-down menu) will copy the entries in the first column of a highlighted block of cells in the spreadsheet, across the entire block (to the right of the first column), into the remaining cells in the block.

Before:

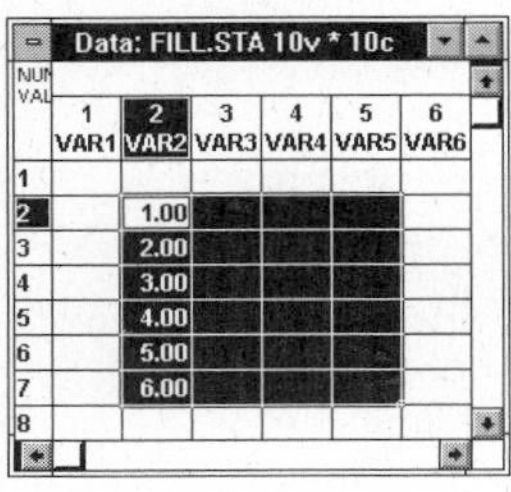
Data: FILL.STA 10v * 10c

	1 VAR1	2 VAR2	3 VAR3	4 VAR4	5 VAR5	6 VAR6
1						
2		1.00				
3		2.00				
4		3.00				
5		4.00				
6		5.00				
7		6.00				
8						

After:

Data: FILL.STA 10v * 10c

	1 VAR1	2 VAR2	3 VAR3	4 VAR4	5 VAR5	6 VAR6
1						
2		1.00	1.00	1.00	1.00	
3		2.00	2.00	2.00	2.00	
4		3.00	3.00	3.00	3.00	
5		4.00	4.00	4.00	4.00	
6		5.00	5.00	5.00	5.00	
7		6.00	6.00	6.00	6.00	
8						

If you need to copy a value to consecutive cells (variables) of one case only, highlight a one-row block; its first (leftmost) case will be copied to all consecutive cells of the case. (To copy down rows, see the *Fill Down* option, above.) You can also use the *Drag-and-Drop* (see page 1125facility to copy a block of values or to extrapolate values from a block. Use *Fill Random Values* (see above) in order to fill the cells in the block with random values (following the uniform distribution).

Spreadsheet Fill/Standardize Block - Standardize Columns

This option (accessible from the spreadsheet *Edit* pull-down menu) will standardize the values in each column of the highlighted block.

Before:

Data: FILL.STA 10v * 10c

	1 VAR1	2 VAR2	3 VAR3	4 VAR4	5 VAR5	6 VAR6
1	1.00	1.00	1.00	1.00	1.00	1.00
2	2.00	2.00	2.00	2.00	2.00	2.00
3	3.00	3.00	3.00	3.00	3.00	3.00
4	4.00	4.00	4.00	4.00	4.00	4.00
5	5.00	5.00	5.00	5.00	5.00	5.00
6	6.00	6.00	6.00	6.00	6.00	6.00
7	7.00	7.00	7.00	7.00	7.00	7.00
8	8.00	8.00	8.00	8.00	8.00	8.00
9	9.00	9.00	9.00	9.00	9.00	9.00
10	10.0	10.0	10.0	10.0	10.0	10.0

After:

Data: FILL.STA 10v * 10c

	1 VAR1	2 VAR2	3 VAR3	4 VAR4	5 VAR5	6 VAR6
1	1.00	1.00	1.00	1.00	1.00	1.00
2	2.00	-1.4	-1.4	-1.4	-1.4	2.00
3	3.00	-.93	-.93	-.93	-.93	3.00
4	4.00	-.46	-.46	-.46	-.46	4.00
5	5.00	0.00	0.00	0.00	0.00	5.00
6	6.00	.463	.463	.463	.463	6.00
7	7.00	.926	.926	.926	.926	7.00
8	8.00	1.39	1.39	1.39	1.39	8.00
9	9.00	9.00	9.00	9.00	9.00	9.00
10	10.0	10.0	10.0	10.0	10.0	10.0

The standardized values are computed as follows:

```
Std. Value = (raw value - mean of
highlighted column) / std. deviation
```

You can standardize the values in highlighted rows via the option *Standardize Rows* (see below). You can also standardize selected variables via the *Data Management* option *Standardize Variables* (that procedure works independent of the currently selected block but takes into account the current case selection conditions and weights).

Spreadsheet Fill/Standardize Block - Standardize Rows

This option (accessible from the spreadsheet *Edit* pull-down menu) will standardize the values in each row of the highlighted block.

Before:

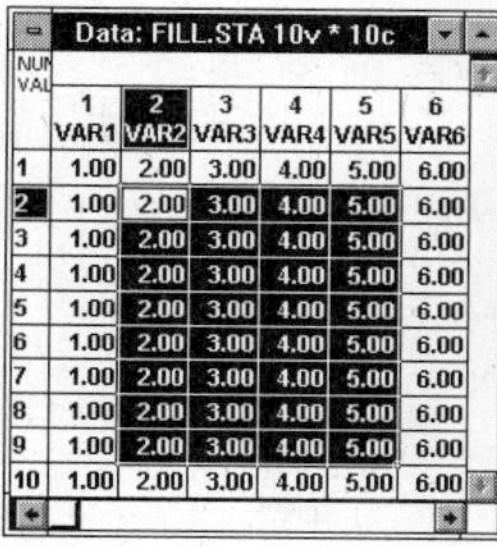

Data: FILL.STA 10v * 10c

	1 VAR1	2 VAR2	3 VAR3	4 VAR4	5 VAR5	6 VAR6
1	1.00	2.00	3.00	4.00	5.00	6.00
2	1.00	2.00	3.00	4.00	5.00	6.00
3	1.00	2.00	3.00	4.00	5.00	6.00
4	1.00	2.00	3.00	4.00	5.00	6.00
5	1.00	2.00	3.00	4.00	5.00	6.00
6	1.00	2.00	3.00	4.00	5.00	6.00
7	1.00	2.00	3.00	4.00	5.00	6.00
8	1.00	2.00	3.00	4.00	5.00	6.00
9	1.00	2.00	3.00	4.00	5.00	6.00
10	1.00	2.00	3.00	4.00	5.00	6.00

After:

Data: FILL.STA 10v * 10c

	1 VAR1	2 VAR2	3 VAR3	4 VAR4	5 VAR5	6 VAR6
1	1.00	2.00	3.00	4.00	5.00	6.00
2	1.00	-1.2	-.39	.387	1.16	6.00
3	1.00	-1.2	-.39	.387	1.16	6.00
4	1.00	-1.2	-.39	.387	1.16	6.00
5	1.00	-1.2	-.39	.387	1.16	6.00
6	1.00	-1.2	-.39	.387	1.16	6.00
7	1.00	-1.2	-.39	.387	1.16	6.00
8	1.00	-1.2	-.39	.387	1.16	6.00
9	1.00	-1.2	-.39	.387	1.16	6.00
10	1.00	2.00	3.00	4.00	5.00	6.00

The standardized values are computed as follows:

```
Std. Value = (raw value - mean of
highlighted row) / std. deviation
```

You can standardize the values in highlighted columns via the option *Standardize Columns* (see above). You can also standardize selected variables via the *Data Management* option *Standardize Variables* (that procedure works independent of the currently selected block but takes into account the current case selection conditions and weights).

Block Stats-/Columns

Click on this option from the spreadsheet or Scrollsheet *Edit* pull-down menu (or flying menu) in order to calculate either the *means*, *medians*, *standard deviations*, *valid n's*, *sums*, the *min*imum value, the *max*imum value, the *25*th percentile, or the *75*th percentile of the values of the variables (columns) in the highlighted block, or choose to calculate *All* of the above statistics.

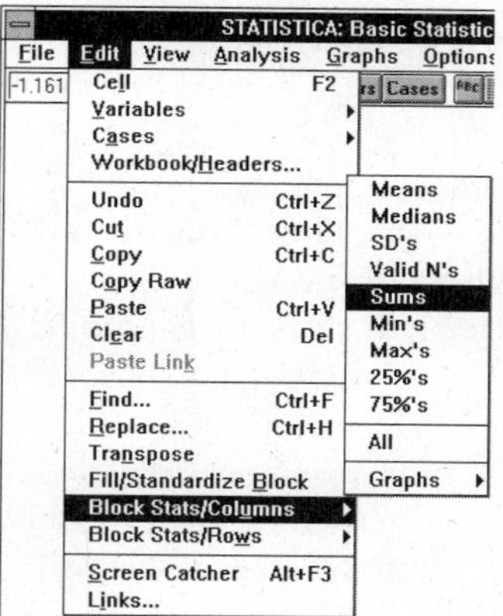

The calculated values will be added after the last row of the spreadsheet or Scrollsheet in new rows (*STATISTICA* will create case names with the names of the statistics and case numbers in the selected block).

Data: CARS.STA 5v * 23c

Performance, fuel economy, and approximat

NUMERIC VALUES	1 PRICE	2 ACCELE	3 BRAKIN	4 HANDLI	5 MILAGE
Mazda	.126	.679	-.133	.500	-1.724
Mercedes	1.051	.006	.120	-.091	-.154
Mitsub.	-.614	-1.003	.084	.382	.718
Nissan	-.429	.073	-.007	.263	.997
Olds	-.614	-.734	.409	.382	2.114
Pontiac	-.614	.679	.536	.145	.195
Porsche	3.454	-2.215	-.296	.618	-1.026
Saab	.588	.679	.246	.263	.021
Toyota	-.059	1.218	.228	.736	-.851
VW	-.706	-.128	.102	.382	.195
Volvo	.219	.612	.138	-.210	.369
MEAN case 2-12		.031	-.141	-.296	

You can also create several types of statistical graphs for the data in the highlighted block (see *Block Stats Graphs*); raw data from the block can be plotted using the *Custom Graphs* facilities.

Note: If your data file is very large (e.g., over 10 megabytes), you may want to set the *Ask before inserting rows and columns* option in the *STATISTICA Defaults: General* dialog so that *STATISTICA* will ask for confirmation before expanding the data file.

Block Stats-/Rows

Click on this option from the spreadsheet or Scrollsheet *Edit* pull-down menu (or flying menu) in order to calculate either the *means*, *medians*, *standard deviations*, *valid n's*, *sums*, the *min*imum value, the *max*imum value, the *25*th percentile, or the *75*th percentile of the values of the cases (rows) in the highlighted block, or choose to calculate *All* of the above statistics. The calculated values will be added after the last column of the spreadsheet or Scrollsheet in new columns

Data: CARS.STA 6v * 22c

NUMERIC VALUES — Performance, fuel economy, and approximate p

	2 ACCELE	3 BRAKIN	4 HANDLI	5 MILAGE	6 MEDIAN
Acura	.477	-.007	.382	2.079	
Audi	.208	.319	-.091	-.677	.263
BMW	-.802	.192	-.091	-.154	.050
Buick	1.689	.933	-.210	-.154	.362
Corvette	-1.811	-.494	.973	-.677	.239
Chrysler	.073	.427	-.210	-.154	-.068
Dodge	-.196	.481	.145	-.154	-.025
Eagle	1.218	-4.199	-.210	-.677	-.412
Ford	-1.542	.987	.145	-1.724	-.280
Honda	.410	-.007	.027	.369	
Isuzu	.410	-.061	-4.230	1.067	
Mazda	.679	-.133	.500	-1.724	

The variable name will contain the name of the selected statistics.

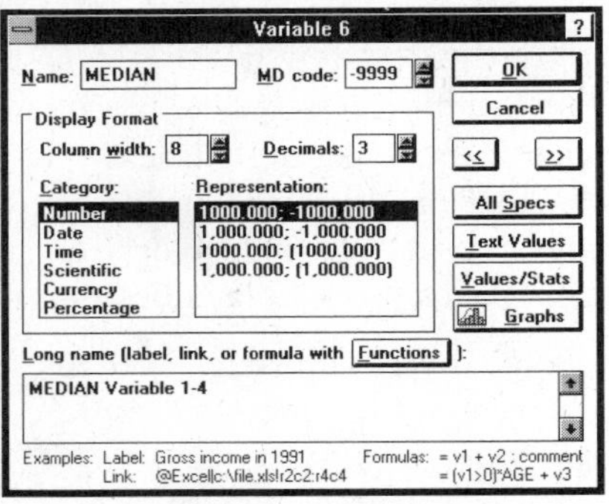

You can also create several types of statistical graphs for the data in the highlighted block (see *Block Stats Graphs*, below); raw data from the block can be plotted using the *Custom Graphs* facilities.

Note: If your data file is very large (e.g., over 10 megabytes), you may want to set the *Ask before inserting rows and columns* option in the *STATISTICA Defaults: General* dialog so that *STATISTICA* will ask for confirmation before expanding the data file.

Block Stats Graphs

Block Stats Graphs are similar to *Custom Graphs* in that they convert values from a selected part (block) of the Scrollsheet or spreadsheet into graphs. However, unlike *Custom Graphs* which allow you to visualize any combination of *raw* values from a Scrollsheet or spreadsheet, *Block Stats Graphs* produce *statistical summary graphs*; these graphs allow you to compare distributions of values in columns (or rows) of the selected block by plotting representations of all columns (or rows) in a single graph. Also, these graphs offer an effective means of exploring (and efficiently summarizing) numeric output from analyses displayed in Scrollsheets (e.g., histograms of *Monte Carlo* output scores in the *SEPATH* module, or a box plot of aggregated means from a multivariate multiple classification table in the *ANOVA/MANOVA* module.

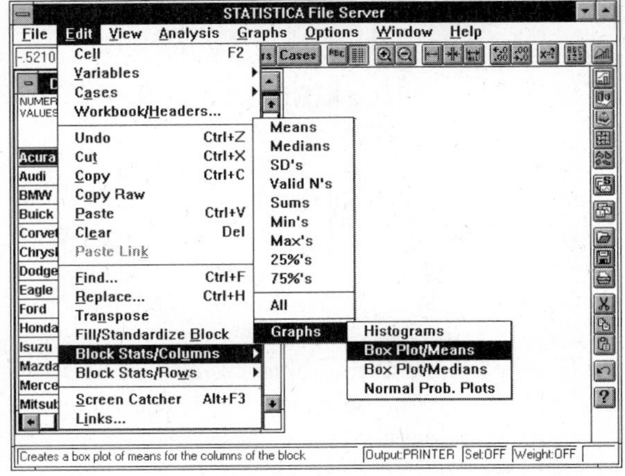

Block Stats Graphs can also be called from the flying menu, *Graphs* pull-down menu, or the *Graphs Gallery* dialog.

If the *Block Stats Graphs* are called from the *Graphs Gallery*, and a Scrollsheet is currently selected, then the highlighted block from the Scrollsheet will be processed. For all other cases (e.g., when a graph or *Text/output Window* is current), then the spreadsheet will be brought to the front of the window and the highlighted block will be processed.

When a *Block Stats Graph* is created from the spreadsheet, then whenever the spreadsheet data are updated, the Block Stats Graph will automatically be updated (see *STATISTICA Defaults: General*).

Histograms

When you select the *Block Stats/Columns* option, a 2D histogram with a fitted normal curve will be created for each column of the block, and plotted in one graph (a multiple histogram) to allow for comparisons between the frequency distributions of values in block columns.

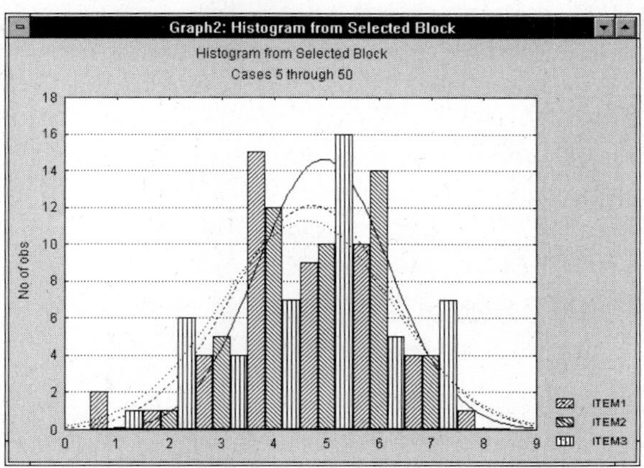

In order to create a univariate histogram, select a block containing only one column.

Similarly, if you select the *Block Stats/Rows* option, then a 2D histogram will be created for each row of the block, and plotted in one graph (a multiple histogram) to allow for comparisons between the frequency distributions of values in block rows. In order to create a univariate histogram, select a block containing only one row.

Notes. If the *Block Stats Graphs* are called from the *Graphs Gallery*, and a Scrollsheet is current, then the highlighted block from the Scrollsheet will be processed. For all other cases (e.g., when a graph or *Text/output Window* is current), then the spreadsheet will be brought to the front of the window and the highlighted block will be processed.

When a *Block Stats Graph* is created from the spreadsheet, then whenever the spreadsheet data are updated, the *Block Stats Graph* will automatically be updated (see *STATISTICA Defaults: General*).

Screen Catcher

This option (accessible from the spreadsheet *Edit* pull-down menu and also at any point in the program by pressing ALT+F3) invokes the *Screen Catcher*, a utility which allows you to select any rectangular area of the screen (or the entire screen) and copy it as a bitmap to the Clipboard.

After selecting this option (or pressing ALT+F3), position the cursor in one corner of the area that you want to copy. Now, while holding down the left-mouse-button, drag the cursor over the area that you want to copy (note that you can drag across different application windows).

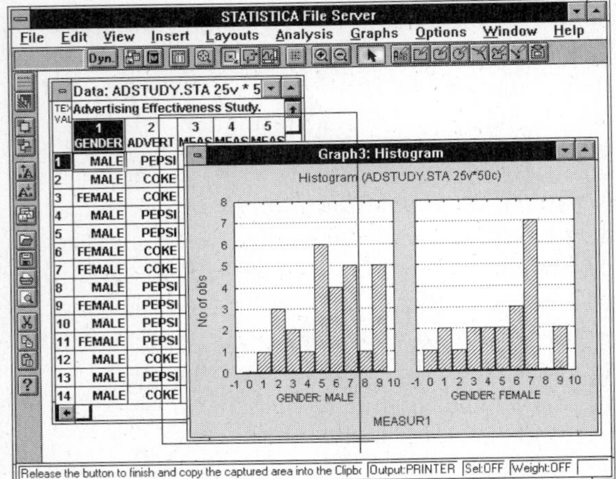

When you release the mouse button, the selected area will be copied to the Clipboard (shown below in the Clipboard Viewer).

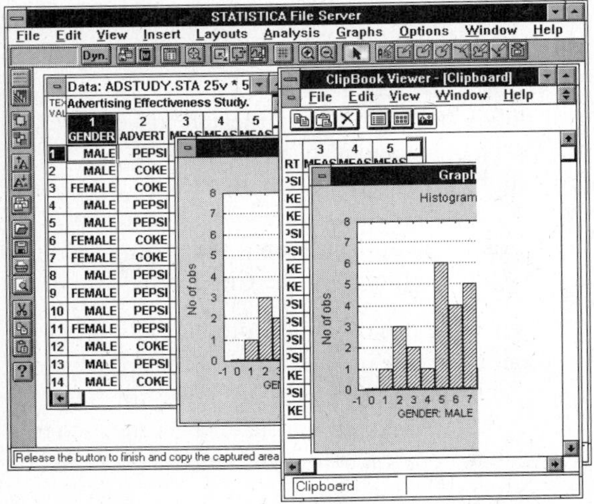

The copied area may contain graphs, Scrollsheets, spreadsheets, or even screens from other applications (if they are currently displayed on the screen). The copied bitmap may then be pasted into *STATISTICA* graphs, or any other application which supports bitmaps.

Note that when selecting the area to be captured, you can rotate by 180°, and/or reverse (produce a mirror image of) the area captured to the Clipboard by choosing one of four directions of dragging the mouse.

The following four examples illustrate the rotation effects which can be achieved by dragging the mouse in different directions over the area to be captured:

AB AB
AB ꓭ∀
AB ꓭA
AB ∀B

This feature can be used in graphical data analysis (e.g., to compare parts of contour graphs) and to create special presentation effects.

Keyboard shortcut. ALT+F3

Spreadsheet Links

This option opens the *Links Manager* dialog from which you can edit the *DDE* (Dynamic Data Exchange) link(s) between a source (or server) application and *STATISTICA* (the client application). These links are stored (and can also be edited) in the *Long Name* option of the *Spreadsheet Edit (Current) Specs* dialog (page 1160). You can also establish a link using the *Paste Link* option (page 1184). For more information on establishing *DDE* links, see *Creating Links (Dynamic Data Exchange)*, in Chapter 7, *Data Management*.

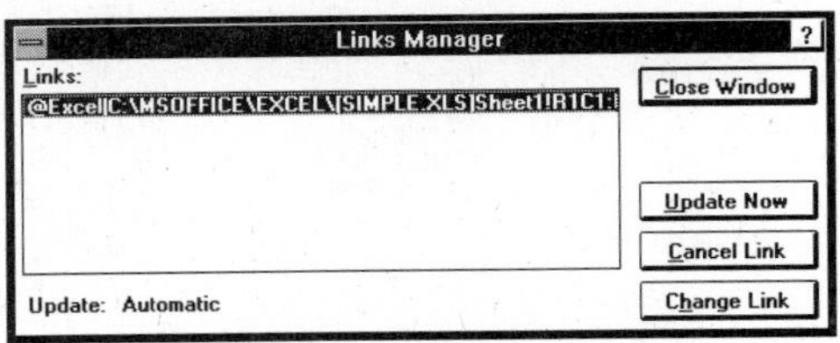

Links

This window displays all the *DDE* links in *STATISTICA*. You can edit a link by highlighting it in this window and then clicking on the *Change Link* button (see below).

Update

Displays the status of the *DDE* link that is currently highlighted in the *Links* window. *DDE* links can be either "hot" (*automatic* status, the "@" symbol precedes the link statement) or "cold" (*manual* status, the "^" symbol precedes the link statement). *Automatic* status means that the linked data in the *STATISTICA* spreadsheet (client file) will automatically be updated whenever any changes are made to the data in the server application. *Manual* status means that the *DDE* link is temporarily disabled and that you will have to manually update the client file using the *Update Now* button or by changing the status back to "hot" (using the *Change Link* button).

Update Now

Click on this button to manually update the *DDE* link (that is currently highlighted in the *Links* window) in the client file (*STATISTICA* spreadsheet data file).

Cancel Link

Click on this button to temporarily disable the currently highlighted *DDE* link. Note: When you are about to run an analysis on a data file linked to a file which may change (e.g., on a network), be sure to use this option to temporarily disable the link so that the data are not changing as the analysis is running. You can resume the link by clicking on the *Update Now* button.

Change Link

Click on this button to open the *Spreadsheet Edit (Current) Specs* dialog (page 1160) dialog in which you can edit the *DDE* link in the *Long Name-Link* option (see *Creating Links (Dynamic Data Exchange)*, in Chapter 7, *Data Management*, for detailed information concerning the parts of the *DDE* path).

SPREADSHEET *VIEW* PULL-DOWN MENU

The following dialogs and options are available from the spreadsheet *View* pull-down menu.

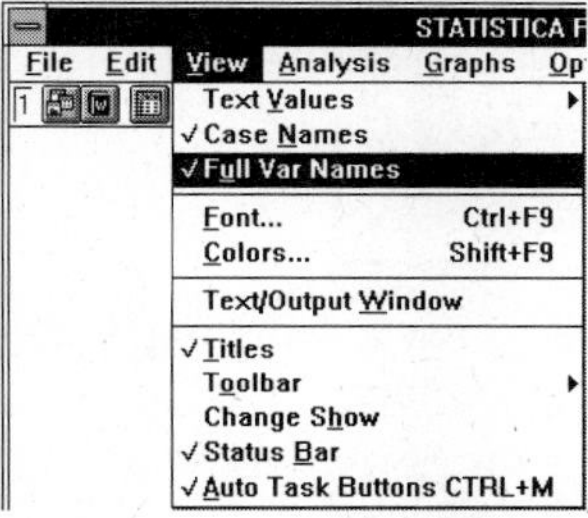

Each of these options are discussed below.

Spreadsheet View Text Values

This option (accessible from the spreadsheet *View* pull-down menu) will toggle between displaying text, numeric equivalent values and value labels (if any) of all variables with text values in the spreadsheet data file. You can switch between the different displays by clicking on the toolbar button (hold down the CTRL key while clicking on the button to display value labels).

Spreadsheet View Case Names

This option (accessible from the spreadsheet *View* pull-down menu) will toggle between displaying case names or case numbers in the spreadsheet data file. When checked, the default setting for the spreadsheet will be to display case names; otherwise (when unchecked), only the case numbers will be displayed.

Toolbar button. See the spreadsheet window toolbar button.

Spreadsheet View Full Variable Names

When the format width of the values of a variable (as specified in the *Spreadsheet Edit (Current) Specs* dialog, page 1160) is less than 8 characters (the maximum width of a variable name), then the displayed variable name is "cut" to the formatted width of its values. In order to view (display) the entire variable name, select the *Full Var Names* option from the spreadsheet *View* pull-down menu. When this option is checked, if any columns are set (formatted) to less than the length of their respective variable name, then the width of this column will be automatically increased to allow the display of the full variable name.

Define Font Dialog

Selecting the *Font* option from the *View* pull-down menu will bring up the *Font* dialog. You can select the type of font, the font style, and the font size in the spreadsheet, Scrollsheet, or other *STATISTICA* facilities. As you make your selections, you can view a sample text in the *Sample* window of this dialog.

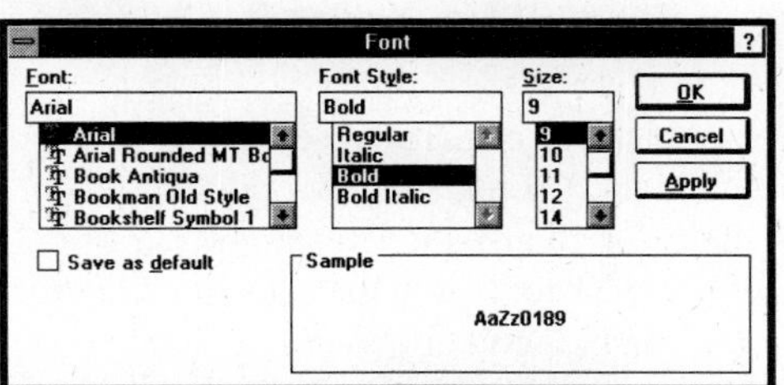

Spreadsheets and Scrollsheets are saved along with their specific font and color settings.

Keyboard shortcut. CTRL+F9

Font

Specify the name of the font that you want to use here. Click on the font type to select it.

Font Style

The available font styles depend on the type of font that you select. First select the font type, then click on the font style that you want to select.

Font Size

The available font sizes depend on the type of font that you select. First select the font type, then click on the font size that you want to select.

Save as Default

Click on this option to save the font settings as the default settings for the spreadsheet/Scrollsheet (different defaults can be selected for spreadsheets and Scrollsheets).

Apply

Use this option when you are entering a font size that may not be supported by the font type. You can view the results of the font size in the view box before using it in *STATISTICA*.

Define Colors for Scrollsheet-/Spreadsheet

Customizes the colors of Scrollsheets and spreadsheets in the *Customize Colors* dialog. You can view the color changes in the sample Scrollsheet/spreadsheet below the selections in this dialog before finalizing your choices.

Each of the options available in this dialog will open the standard *Color* dialog (page 1197), where you can select colors from a standard color palette or customize a color (via the *Define Custom Colors* button).

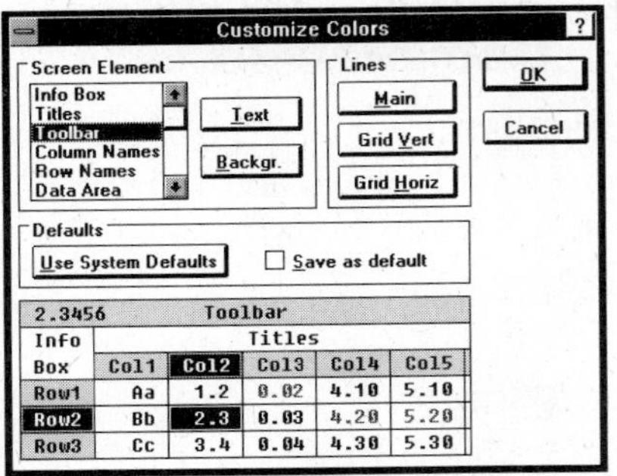

Spreadsheets and Scrollsheets are saved along with their (custom-defined, if any) colors.

Keyboard shortcut: SHIFT+F9

Example. In this example, the color of the Scrollsheet titles will be customized.

Step 1. Select the *Colors* option from the *View* pull-down menu.

Step 2. Now change the color of the Scrollsheet titles by selecting the screen element *Titles*. Click on the *Text* button and select the color that you want the text in the titles to be (say, blue). Now choose a contrasting color for the title background by clicking on the *Backgr.* button selecting a color in the *Color* dialog. You can repeat *Step 2* for every screen element that you want to change the color for.

Step 3. Click on the *OK* button to close the *Customize Colors* dialog and change the colors in the current Scrollsheet.

Screen Element

Select the Scrollsheet/spreadsheet element that you would like to customize (see below for a list of these elements). Each Scrollsheet/spreadsheet element is customized separately, and for each element you can customize only the text foreground (*Text*

button), only the background (*Backgr.* button), or both. Only solid colors are available for *Text*; if a patterned color is selected, then *STATISTICA* will use the solid color closest to the selected patterned color.

- Info Box (i.e., the upper left corner of the sheet)
- Titles
- Toolbar
- Column Names
- Row Names
- Data Area
- Highlight

Lines

Customizes the colors of the lines in the Scrollsheet/spreadsheet.

Main. Changes the color of the lines separating the row names and column names in the Scrollsheet or spreadsheet.

Grid vert. Changes the color of the vertical lines separating the data values in the Scrollsheet or spreadsheet.

Grid horiz. Changes the color of the horizontal lines separating the data values in the Scrollsheet or spreadsheet.

Defaults

You can choose to make your customized colors the default colors if you click on the *Save as Default* option. To restore *STATISTICA*'s default color selections, click on the *Use System Defaults* button.

Color Dialog

The following two dialogs are accessed within the *Customize Colors* dialog whenever you select an element of the spreadsheet/Scrollsheet to customize.

Basic color palette. Click on a color to select it for the Scrollsheet/spreadsheet element in this color palette.

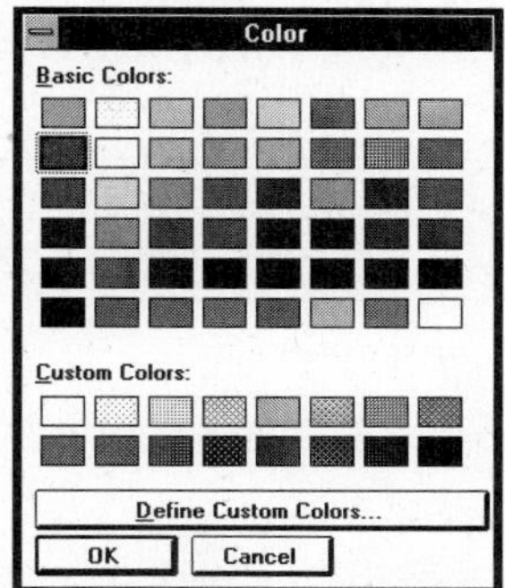

Custom colors. Click the *Define Custom Colors* button to bring up the *Color Refiner Box* from which you can create a customized color and add it to the *Custom Colors Palette*.

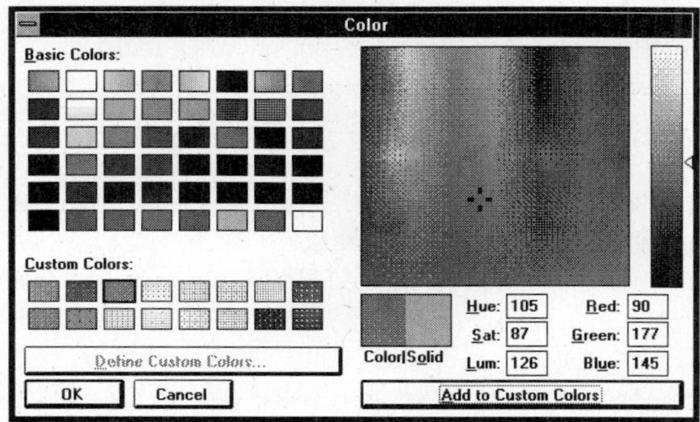

You can create a color by adjusting its *Hue*, saturation (*Sat*) and luminosity (*Lum*) manually, by specifying its *Red*, *Green* and *Blue* component values manually, or by dragging the cursor to the desired color in the *Color Refiner Box* and adjusting the *Luminosity Bar*.

Click on the *Add to Custom Colors* button to add the new color to the selected square in the *Custom Colors Palette*.

Text/output Window

When you select this option from the *View* pull-down menu, the *Text/output Window* will open (see Chapter 5 for more information about this window). All printed output will be directed to this window (regardless of whether or not you are also printing to the printer or disk file).

If you set any of the *Auto-Report* options (e.g., *Automatically Print All Scrollsheets*) in the *Page/Output Setup* dialog (page 1148), then the respective output (e.g., graphs or contents of each Scrollsheet displayed on the screen) will also be automatically directed to the *Text/output Window* (i.e., there is no need to use the print button when this option is enabled). You can also open the *Text/output Window* by selecting the *Window* option in the *Page/Output Setup* dialog (page 1148).

Note that opening this window by either method will result in the printer output from analyses being sent to this window as well as optionally to the printer or file (whichever you choose in the *Page/Output Setup* dialog). You can edit the text in this window as well as paste some additional information there [formatted (*RTF*) text and graphics either from *STATISTICA* or other Windows applications] using the standard *Copy* and *Paste* operations (page 1182).

When running multiple analyses, any "new" results will be appended to the previous analysis results, producing a continuous log of the results of analyses. If you want to permanently store a complete log of analyses, then select the *File Output* option. If you want to permanently store the text and/or graphs from the *Text/output Window* (including your notes or inserts pasted to the window), then use the *Save As Text File* option. You can also use the *Text/output Window* as a "notepad" in order to maintain records or notes. When the *Text/output Window* is open and active, it will have its own toolbar and pull-down menus (see Chapter 5).

Technical note. When a spreadsheet or Scrollsheet is printed to the *Text/output Window*, the font that is defined in the *Page/Output Setup* dialog for spreadsheet and Scrollsheet output will be used as the default font in the *Text/output Window*. Therefore, if you want to print the spreadsheet or Scrollsheet in the *Text/output Window* using a special font, you will need to set that font style in the *Page/Output Setup* dialog. If you are pasting text from another application, select *RTF* as the format in the *Paste Special* dialog in order to paste the text into the *Text/output Window* using the source font style.

Spreadsheet View Titles

With this option, you can choose to display the spreadsheet with a title (when checked, a one line title will be included in the spreadsheet display):

Data: ADSTUDY.STA 25v * 50c

Advertising Effectiveness Study.

	1 GENDER	2 ADVERT	3 MEASUR1	4 MEASUR2	5 MEASUR3	6 MEASUR4	7 MEASUR5
1	MALE	PEPSI	1	1	6	8	1
2	MALE	COKE	2	7	1	8	0
3	FEMALE	COKE	3	8	2	9	8
4	MALE	PEPSI	4	9	0	5	9
5	MALE	PEPSI	5	1	6	2	8
6	FEMALE	COKE	6	0	0	8	3

or without a title (*Title* will appear unchecked in the *View* pull-down menu).

Data: ADSTUDY.STA 25v * 50c

	1 GENDER	2 ADVERT	3 MEASUR1	4 MEASUR2	5 MEASUR3	6 MEASUR4	7 MEASUR5
1	MALE	PEPSI	1	1	6	8	1
2	MALE	COKE	2	7	1	8	0
3	FEMALE	COKE	3	8	2	9	8
4	MALE	PEPSI	4	9	0	5	9
5	MALE	PEPSI	5	1	6	2	8
6	FEMALE	COKE	6	0	0	8	3

The data file header (managed in the *Data File Header, Notes, and Workbook Info* dialog, page 1180) is used as the spreadsheet title. De-selecting the titles will only suppress the display (i.e., it will not delete the *File Header*). You can edit the title by double-clicking on the title area of the spreadsheet (or select the *Header* option from the *Edit* pull-down menu) to open the *Data File Header, Notes and Workbook Info* dialog (see page 1180).

Spreadsheet View Toolbar

When you click on this option from the *View* pull-down menu, you will be able to select from several ways to display the toolbar (described below) in the window or you can toggle between displaying the toolbar and hiding it.

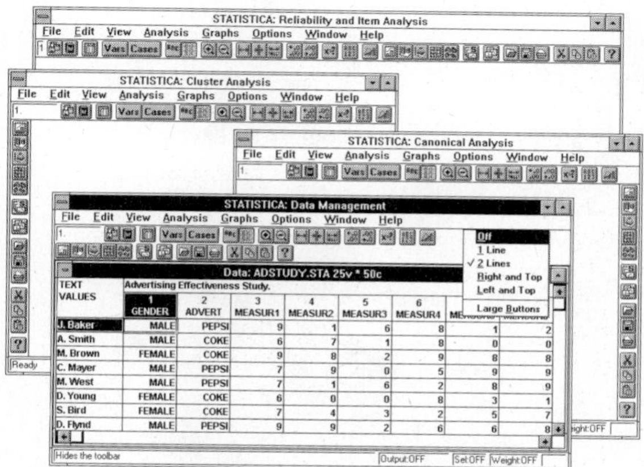

Off. Select this option to temporarily remove the toolbar from the window. (In order to once again display the toolbar, select one of the options described below.)

1 line. When you select this option, the toolbar will be displayed in one line in the spreadsheet window.

2 lines. Select this option to display the toolbar buttons in two lines.

Right & Top. This option will display half of the toolbar at the top of the window and the other half along the right side of the window.

Left & Top. This option will display half of the toolbar at the top of the window and the other half along the left side of the window.

Large Buttons. Select this option to toggle between displaying normal and large buttons in the toolbar (when checked, large toolbar buttons will be displayed, which may be desirable when using higher resolutions, e.g., 1024x768, on a small monitor).

Normal buttons:

Large buttons:

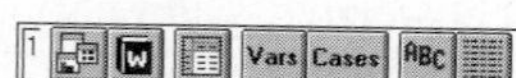

Shortcut. Double-click on the toolbar to rotate through the different configurations. You can also access the toolbar configuration menu by clicking on the toolbar background with the right-mouse-button.

Change Show

Change Show displays the contents of the currently highlighted cell (or cursor position or text rotation angle in graphs or line and column number in the *Text/output Window*) in the *Show* field. Click on this option to toggle between the 3 sizes (lengths) of the *Show* field.

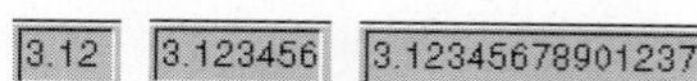

When the display width of the values of a variable (as specified in the *Spreadsheet Edit (Current) Specs* dialog, page 1160) is less than necessary to see all significant digits, use this option to adjust the *Show* field length and view the full length of a value of a variable. Alternatively, click on the *Show* field with the mouse.

StatSoft

View
Status Bar

Toggle between displaying the spreadsheet window status Bar (the bar at the bottom of the screen; see Chapter 2) and hiding it with this option. When checked, the status Bar will be displayed.

While executing a task, *STATISTICA* will use the status bar to display the progress of the task (see *Progress Bar*, below).

Comment

This area of the status bar is reserved for a brief (one line) description of the highlighted pull-down or cell-related menu or option. When nothing is highlighted (data are not being processed and *STATISTICA* is waiting for the next command), the word *Ready* is displayed. Double-click on the comment area in the status bar to open the main *Help* menu.

Output

Displays the current destination (as specified in the *Page/Output Setup* dialog, page 1160) for the output of an analysis. Double-click on *Output* in the status bar to open the *Page/Output Setup* dialog from which you can select the output destination (*Off*, *File*, *Printer* and/or *Window*) and other output options.

Sel

Displays the current status (*On* or *Off*) of the case selection conditions. Double-click on *Sel* in the status bar to open the *Case Selection Conditions* dialog from which you can review and/or specify the case selection conditions (see page 1211).

Weight

Displays the current status (*On* or *Off*) of the variable weighting conditions. Double-click on *Weight* in the status bar to open the *Define Weight* dialog from which you can specify the variable weighting conditions (see page 1212).

REC

This message will flash in the right-hand side of the status bar when you are recording a macro (either a sequence of keystrokes or mouse movements). For more information on recording macros, see Chapter 6, *Auto Task Buttons*.

Progress Bar

When a task is being executed in *STATISTICA*, the status bar (see above) will display the progress of the analysis.

Progress

This area of the progress bar is reserved for displaying the amount of task completed.

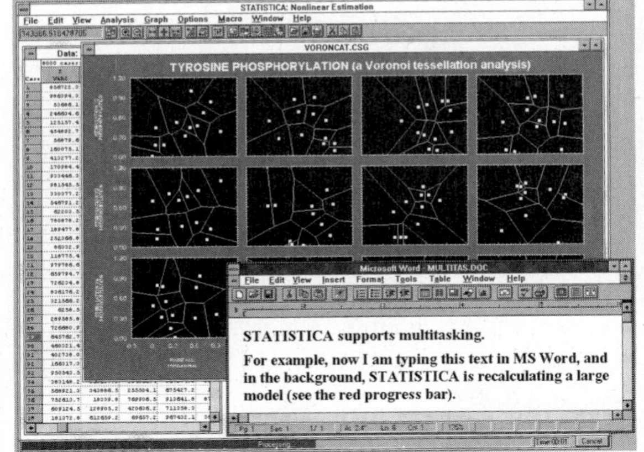

Elapsed Time

STATISTICA displays the elapsed time in seconds since the beginning of the task.

Cancel

Click on this button to interrupt the task in progress; graph redraw may be interrupted by a click of the mouse (anywhere on the screen).

You can control the display of the *Progress Bar* for *Stats Graph* and *Quick Stats Graph* procedures via the *STATISTICA Defaults: Stats Graphs* dialog.

SPREADSHEET *ANALYSIS* PULL-DOWN MENU

The following dialogs and options are available from the spreadsheet *Analysis* pull-down menu. Note that the list of options other than the *Startup Panel, Resume Analysis*, *STATISTICA BASIC*, *Command Language*, *Quick Basic Stats*, and *Other Statistics* options will vary depending on the module. For more information on those options, see the specific chapter for that module. The following *Analysis* pull-down menu is from the *File Server* module, and depicts the options common to all modules of *STATISTICA*.

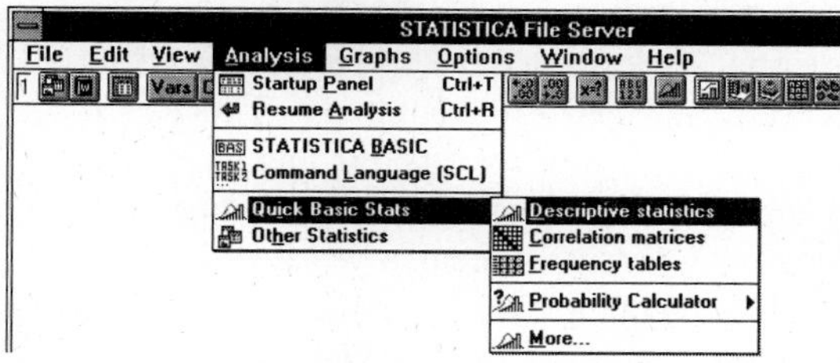

The options common to all *Analysis* pull-down menus are discussed below.

Startup Panel

When you select this option from the *Analysis* pull-down menu, a window will open in which you can select an analysis from those available in the active *STATISTICA* module. Select the analysis by double-clicking on the respective option or by highlighting it and then clicking the *OK* button. Other options available in this window are discussed below. The following startup panel is from the *Basic Statistics and Tables* module.

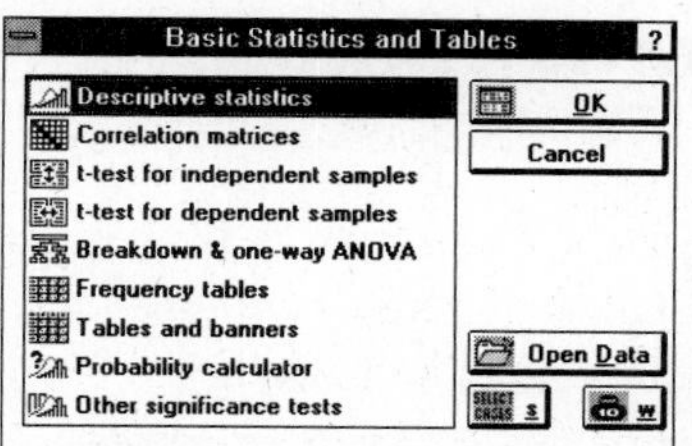

Keyboard shortcut. CTRL+T

Open Data

Clicking on this button will open the standard *Open Data File* dialog (page 1137), from which you can select a data file for the analysis. This is the same option which is also available from the *File* pull-down menu (see page 1136) and from the *Open* toolbar button.

Select Cases

This button will bring up the standard *Case Selection Conditions* dialog (page 1211). Use this dialog to specify a subset of cases in the open data file on which to perform the analysis.

Define Weight (W)

Click on this button to open the *Define Weight* dialog (page 1212), from which you can specify the case weighting conditions for the open data file.

Resume Analysis

When the analysis that you are performing is still active, but the current analysis control dialog is minimized (the analysis icon appears in the lower left-hand corner of the screen), select this option to resume the analysis (open the analysis dialog) from the last dialog. Alternatively, you can double-click on the icon to resume the analysis or (in most cases) click on the *Continue* button in the upper left corner of the current Scrollsheet or graph window.

Keyboard shortcut. CTRL+R.

STATISTICA BASIC

Selecting the *STATISTICA BASIC* option from the spreadsheet *Analysis* pull-down menu will open the *STATISTICA BASIC* program editor window.

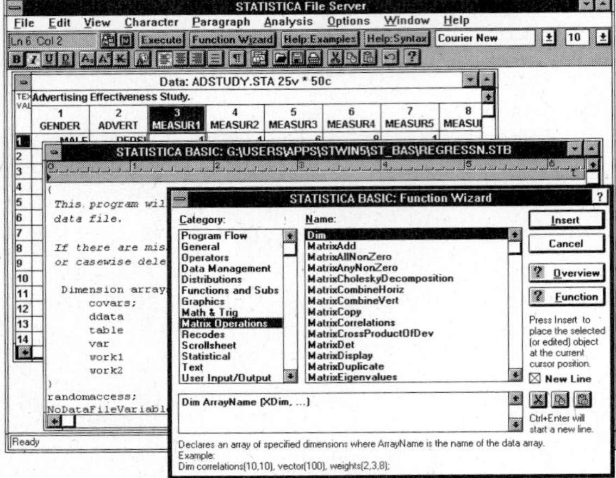

STATISTICA BASIC is a simple to use but powerful programming language which can be used for a variety of types of applications ranging from simple data transformations (e.g., whenever you need to do more than can be done using the spreadsheet formulas, e.g., loops, recoding functions) to building custom, complex, permanent extensions to computational, graphics, and data management procedures of *STATISTICA*.

For more information on *STATISTICA BASIC*, please refer to the *Electronic Manual*.

Command Language

Selecting the *Command Language* option from the spreadsheet *Analysis* pull-down menu will open the *STATISTICA Command Language (SCL)* program editor window.

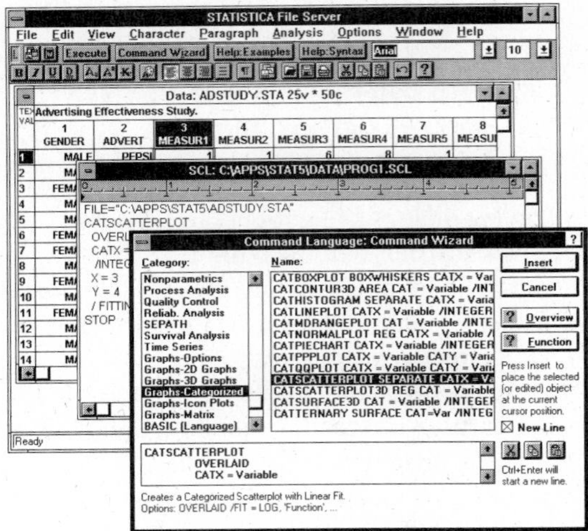

The *STATISTICA Command Language* (*SCL* for short) allows you to run *STATISTICA* in batch mode, that is, you can develop "programs" that will instruct *STATISTICA* in what to do. Those *SCL* programs can then be executed in any module of *STATISTICA* without requiring any additional input. *SCL* programs can also be saved for later repeated use via the *Save As* option in the *File* pull-down menu. You can use the *STATISTICA Command Language* as a "turn-key" system in order to speed up invoking already tested or repeatedly executed *SCL* programs or to develop "fail-safe" programs for persons unfamiliar with *STATISTICA*. Alternatively, you can assign *SCL* programs to buttons on the customizable *Auto Tasks Buttons* floating toolbar (see Chapter 6).

For more information on the *STATISTICA Command Language*, please refer to the *Electronic Manual*.

Quick Basic Stats

The *Quick Basic Stats* options are available from either the spreadsheet or Scrollsheet right-mouse-button flying menu or from the *Analysis* pull-down menu of any module of *STATISTICA*. *Quick Basic*

Statistics can be used at any point of your data analysis (e.g., to provide supplementary information when you review output from any *STATISTICA* module).

These procedures include a selection of basic statistics which can be performed on long lists of variables (e.g., correlation indices for *all* variables in the data set), and all analyses can be performed *by groups*, for every value (i.e., code) of a selected grouping variable.

If *Quick Basic Stats* are called from the spreadsheet pull-down menu *Analysis*, then the variables to be analyzed are selected via subsequent variable selection dialogs.

If *Quick Basic Stats* are called from a right-mouse-button flying menu, then *STATISTICA* will not ask for variables to be analyzed because the selection of variables to be analyzed depends on the current cursor/block location in the spreadsheet or Scrollsheet; *STATISTICA* will ask for variables only if the option *More...* is chosen, or if the currently selected block does not contain enough variables (e.g., if it contains only one variable for *Correlation Matrices*, or one list of variables for an analysis to be performed *by...* groups).

For more information about *Quick Basic Stats*, refer to Chapter 10.

Other Statistics (*STATISTICA* Module Switcher)

Selecting the *Other Statistics* option in the spreadsheet *Analysis* pull-down menu will bring up the *STATISTICA Module Switcher* dialog. This dialog contains a list box of all the *STATISTICA* modules to which you can transfer. Whenever you highlight a module, a brief description of that module appears in the dialog. This dialog also contains some options described below.

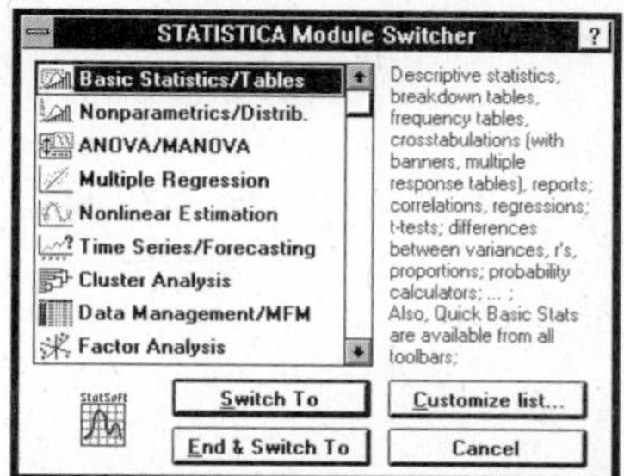

Toolbar button. See the button in the spreadsheet toolbar.

Shortcut. Click the right-mouse-button on the application background in order to bring up this global flying menu. You can also double-click on the application background (analogous to double-clicking on the desktop in order to open the *Windows Task Switcher*).

Switch To

After you have selected (highlighted) the module to which you want to transfer, click on this button to switch to that module. Depending on your selection of single or multiple application mode in the *STATISTICA Defaults: General* dialog (see page 1213), the currently open module (if there is one) will either remain open (de-select the *Single Application Mode*), or will close (select the *Single Application Mode*) when the desired module opens. Alternatively, you can double-click on the module name in this dialog in order to switch to it (keeping the current module open or closing it, see the explanation of single and multiple application modes in Chapter 1, *General Conventions*).

End & Switch To

Use this button to close the module that you are currently using and switch to the module highlighted in this dialog. The effect of using this button when running *STATISTICA* in the *Multiple Application Mode* (see Chapter 1, *General Conventions*, for an explanation of single and

multiple application modes) is similar to running *STATISTICA* in the *Single Application Mode*; the application window of the current module will close but it will not be replaced by the new one; instead the new module will open in the "next" application window.

Customize List

This button will open the *Customize List of Modules* dialog (see below) from which you can customize (rearrange, or reduce) the list of modules. In the *Customize List of Modules* dialog, you can either *Replace* the entire list of modules with only selected modules (most likely the modules that you would use the most) or *Append* selected modules to the end of the Module Switcher list (essentially rearranging the list by moving the modules that you use the least to the end of the list).

Customize List of Modules

The *Customize List of Modules* dialog is used to customize the selection of modules available from the *STATISTICA Module Switcher* (see above).

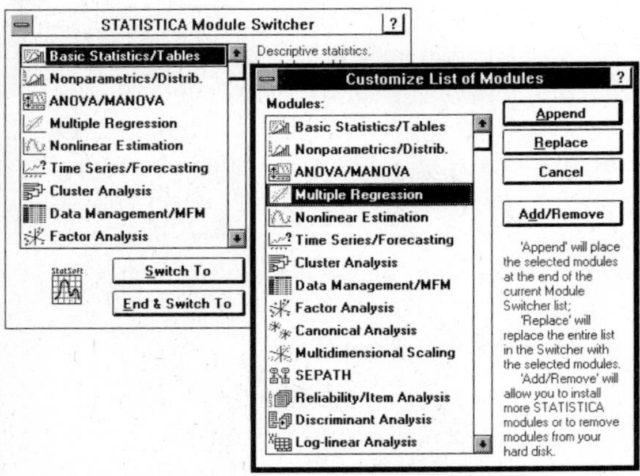

The *Customize List of Modules* dialog contains a list box of all of the modules that have been installed in *STATISTICA* and three other options listed below.

Append

In this mode, the module(s) highlighted in the list will be appended to the end of the *Module Switcher* list.

Replace

In this mode, all modules currently selected in the list will replace the list in the *Module Switcher*.

In order to create a new, specific order of modules in the *Module Switcher* list, *Replace* the first module (this will also remove the previous selection in the *Module Switcher*); then *Append* subsequent modules in the desired order (one at a time).

Add/Remove

Press this button to change the *STATISTICA* configuration. This button starts the *Reinst.exe* program (located in your *STATISTICA* program directory). This utility allows you to install any modules of *STATISTICA* which were not selected during a previous installation, to remove (delete) any previously installed modules, or if you are on a workstation and will use *STATISTICA* from a network file server, you may create your own customized working directory for *STATISTICA*.

SPREADSHEET *GRAPHS* PULL-DOWN MENU

The graphic options in the *Graphs* pull-down menu are discussed in detail in Volume II of the manual.

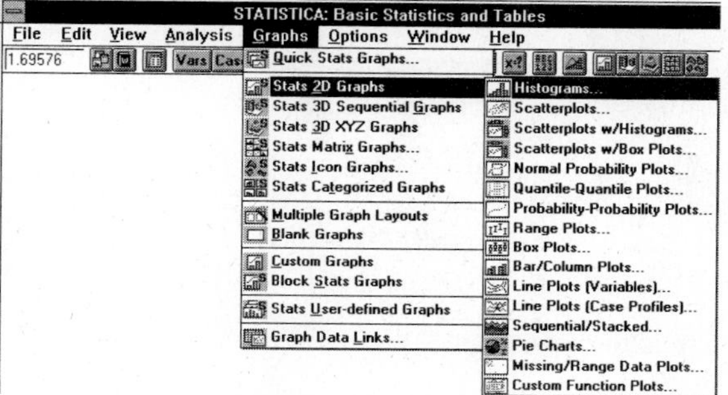

The following paragraphs summarize only the general types of graphs available in *STATISTICA*. Note that all of these graph types are also accessible from the *Graphs Gallery* toolbar button (see Chapter 2).

In addition to the specialized graphs which are available from the output dialogs of all statistical procedures, there are two general categories of graphs accessible from menus and toolbars of all Scrollsheets and spreadsheets:

- *Custom Graphs*, and
- *Stats Graphs* (and *Quick Stats Graphs*).

They differ in terms of the source of data which they visualize; the differences are summarized in the following sections.

Custom Graphs. *Custom Graphs* allow you to visualize any custom-defined combination of values from Scrollsheets and spreadsheets (from rows, columns or both, and/or their subsets). When you select one of the five global types of these graphs (*Custom 2D Graphs*, *Custom 3D Sequential Graphs*, *Custom 3D XYZ Graphs*, *Custom Matrix Graphs* or *Custom Icons Graphs*), a respective dialog will open allowing you to specify the parts of the current Scrollsheet or spreadsheet to be plotted. The layout of this dialog depends on the global type of the *Custom* graph which you have selected (e.g., *Custom 2D Graphs*). The initial selection of the data to be plotted (suggested in that dialog) depends on the current block (or cursor) position in the current Scrollsheet or spreadsheet. Each of these *Custom* graph definition dialogs allow you to select the specific types of graph (within the global type). However, as described below, the graph type can also be adjusted later, after the graph is created (via the *General Layout* or *Plot Layout* dialogs accessible by clicking on the graph background or from the graph pull-down menu *Layouts*).

Each of these *Custom* graph types is also available from the toolbar (see Chapter 2).

Stats Graphs. Unlike *Custom Graphs* (which provide general tools to create custom visualizations of numerical Scrollsheet output, or spreadsheet data, see above), *Stats Graphs* are pre-defined statistical graphs. They are available from the *STATISTICA Graphs Gallery* accessible by pressing the *Graphs Gallery* toolbar button (see Chapter 2) or from the pull-down menu *Graphs*:

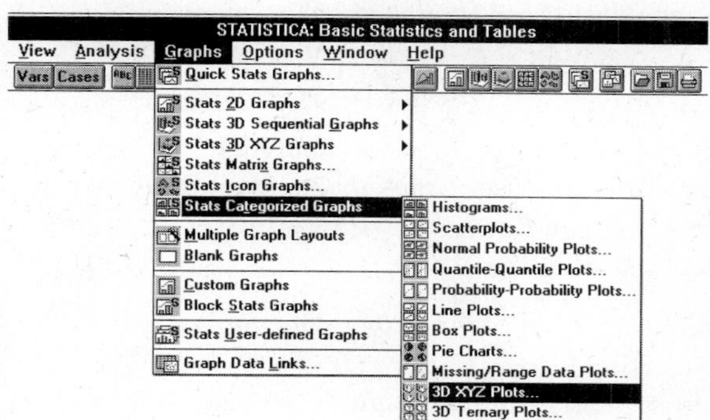

StatSoft

and offer hundreds of types of graphical representations and analytic summaries of data. They are not limited to the values in the current Scrollsheet, and they do not depend on highlighted blocks or the current cursor position; instead, they process data directly from the current data file. They represent either standard methods to graphically summarize raw data (e.g., various scatterplots, histograms, or plots of central tendencies such as medians) or standard graphical analytic techniques (e.g., categorized normal probability plots, detrended probability plots, or plots of confidence intervals of regression lines). As the *Stats Graphs* are generated, *STATISTICA* will take into account the current case selection and weighting conditions (see pages 1211 and 1212 , respectively) for the variables selected to be plotted.

Quick Stats Graphs. *Quick Stats Graphs* include the most-commonly used types of *Stats Graphs* (which are available from the pull-down menu *Graphs*, see the previous paragraph). *Quick Stats Graphs* do not offer as many options as *Stats Graphs*, however, they are quicker to select because unlike *Stats Graphs*:

- *Quick Stats Graphs* can be called from flying menus and toolbars (and they do not require any pull-down menu selections),
- *Quick Stats Graphs* do not require the user to select variables (the variable selection is determined by the current cursor position within a Scrollsheet or spreadsheet), and
- *Quick Stats Graphs* do not require the user to select options from any intermediate dialogs (default formats of the respective graphs are produced).

Clicking on the button on the toolbar, or selecting the *Quick Stats Graphs* option (either from the right-mouse-button flying menu, or the pull-down menu *Graphs*) will open a menu from which you may choose one of the statistical graphs applicable to the current variable, that is, to the variable indicated by the current cursor position in the Scrollsheet or spreadsheet.

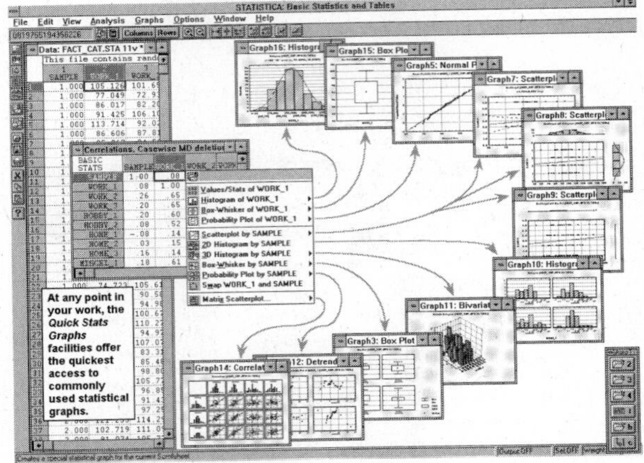

In all spreadsheets and those Scrollsheets which involve only one list of variables (and not two lists or one grouping variable and a list), the flying menu will have the following format (where the "secondary" variable is not specified, see the blank *by...* fields in the lower part of the menu).

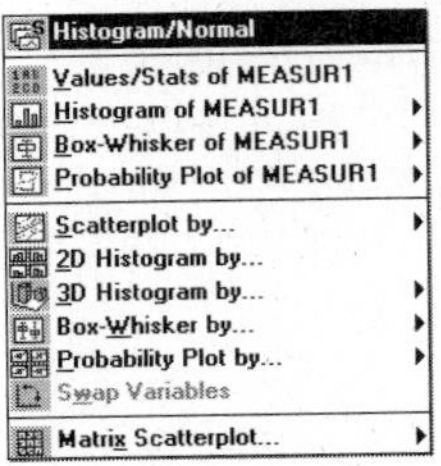

If the Scrollsheet has a matrix format or a format where a cursor position may indicate not one but two variables, then pre-defined bivariate graphs for the specified pair of variables will be available from the *Quick Stats Graphs* menu (and *STATISTICA* will not ask you for the selection of the "second" variable for the bivariate graphs).

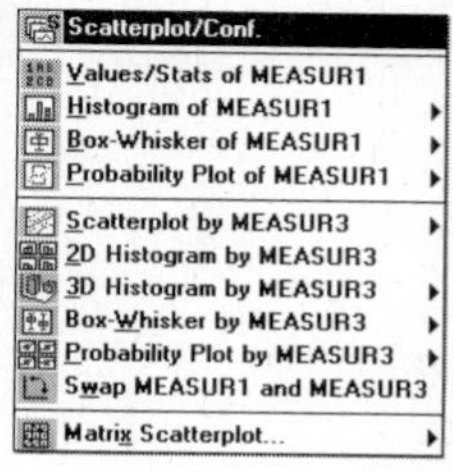

If no variables are indicated by the current cursor position, then selecting any of the *Quick Stats Graphs* will prompt you to select a variable from a list. As the *Quick Stats Graphs* are generated, *STATISTICA* will take into account the current case selection and weighting conditions (see pages 1211 and 1212 , respectively) for the variables that are being plotted.

Block Stats Graphs. These (custom) graphs are available from the *Block Stats/Columns* and *Block Stats/Rows* (see page 1189) flying menu options, or from the *STATISTICA Graphs Gallery*.

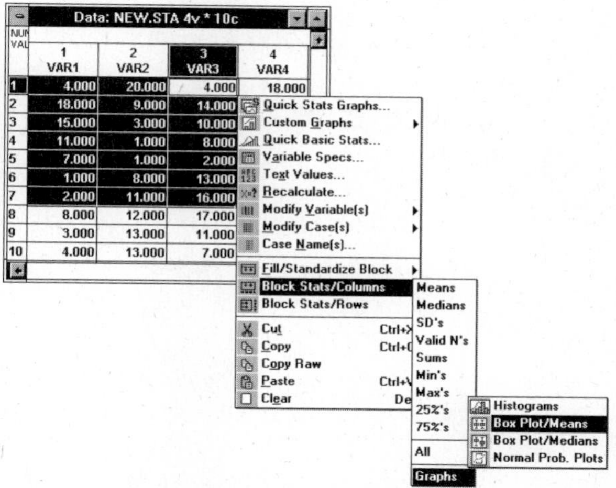

Selecting one of these options will produce the respective statistical summary graph allowing you to compare the values in each row (if *Block Stats/Rows* was selected) or each column (if *Block Stats/Columns* was selected) of the currently highlighted block in the spreadsheet or Scrollsheet. Note that these graphs produce statistical summary graphs for data (rows or columns) in the current block; in this respect, they are similar to *Custom Graphs* (see page 1207) which visualize raw data from the current block.

Other specialized graphs. In addition to the standard selection of *Quick Stats Graphs* (see page 1208), some Scrollsheets also offer other, more specialized statistical graphs (e.g., icon plots of regression residuals, time sequence plots in *Time Series*, or contour plots in *Cluster Analysis*). As mentioned before, other specialized statistical graphs which are related, not to a specific Scrollsheet, but to a type of analysis (e.g., plots of means [e.g., interactions] in *ANOVA/MANOVA*, plots of fitted functions in *Nonlinear Estimation*) are accessible directly from results dialogs (i.e., the dialogs which contain output options from the current analysis).

SPREADSHEET *OPTIONS* PULL-DOWN MENU

The following dialogs and options are available from the spreadsheet *Options* pull-down menu.

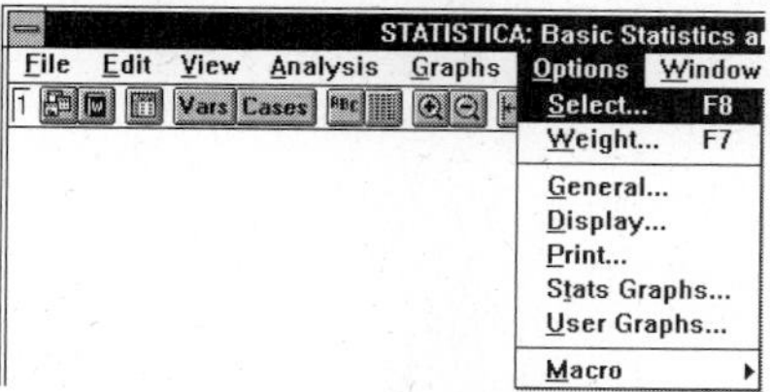

With the exception of the *Stats Graphs* and *User Graphs* options (which are discussed in Volume II of the manual) and *Macros* (which are discussed in Chapter 6, *Auto Task Buttons*), each of these options are discussed below.

Case Selection Conditions

Use *Case Selection Conditions* when you want to include only a subset of cases in an analysis (i.e., use "case filters").

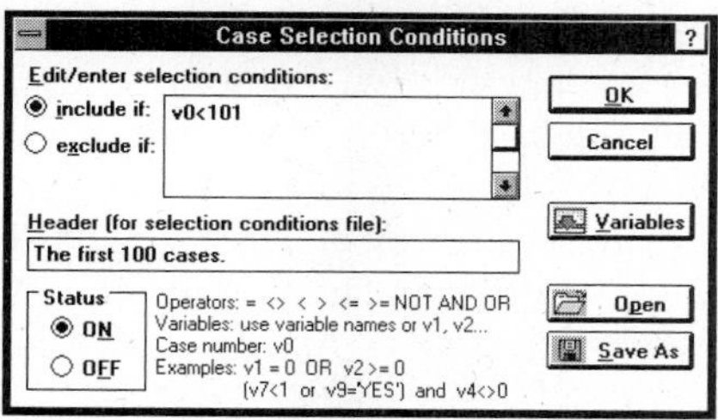

You can access the *Case Selection Conditions* dialog either by clicking on the *Sel* option from the status bar (see Chapter 2), clicking on the [SELECT CASES] *Select Cases* button on the *Startup Panel* or an analysis definition dialog, or by selecting the *Select* option from the *Options* pull-down menu.

Keyboard shortcut. F8

Edit/Enter Selection Conditions

You can enter new or edit existing logical conditions in the edit window. The selection conditions that you specify here will determine whether or not a particular case will be *included in* the analysis (i.e., cases satisfying the logical conditions will be analyzed if the default *include if* option is used) or *excluded from* the analysis (i.e., cases satisfying the logical conditions will be excluded from the analysis when you choose the *exclude if* option).

Examples

The following selection condition will include only cases 1 through 50 in the analysis.

Include If: `v0 <= 50`

The next selection condition will include in the analysis only the cases where the value of variable 1 is equal to *1*.

Include if: `v1 = 1`

You can also use the text values of a variable in case selection conditions. Note that whenever you use text values, be sure to include them in single quotation marks (as shown below).

Include if: `v1 = 'MALE'`

The condition below would exclude from an analysis those cases where the value of *v1* was less than or equal to *10 or* those cases where the values of *v2* equaled *v3*.

Exclude if: `(v1 <= 10) OR (v2 = v3)`

Syntax Summary

The following is a summary of syntax conventions for the case selection conditions. The same

conventions apply to all instances where user-defined case selection conditions are entered in *STATISTICA*.

- Refer to variables either by their numbers (e.g., *v1 = 1*) or their names (e.g., *Gender = 1*); note that you can type variable names in either upper or lower case letters (i.e., *'GENDER'* is equivalent to *'gender'*).
- Enclose text values of a variable in single quotation marks (e.g., *v1 = 'MALE'*); note that the case is ignored by the interpreter; you can type text values in either upper or lower case letters (i.e., *'Yes'* is equivalent to *'YES'*).
- Use parentheses to specify complex logical conditions (see the example above) or change the default precedence of operators.
- Logical Operators:

`=`	- equal
`# , <>, ><`	- not equal
`<`	- less than
`>`	- greater than
`<=`	- less than or equal to
`>=`	- greater than or equal to
`NOT, ~`	- logical NOT
`AND, &`	- logical AND
`OR, !`	- logical OR

Header

Enter one line (up to 77 characters) of comment about the case selection conditions file here (to be saved along with the conditions). The header will be included in the output of analyses when either a *Short*, *Medium* or *Long* report style is selected in the *Page/Output Setup* dialog (page 1148).

Status

The status of this dialog is displayed in the window status bar and identifies whether the case selection condition will affect the processing of data (*On*) or not (*Off*).

Variables

Click on this button to open the *Review Variable* dialog from which you can review the variable names.

Open

When you click on this button, the *Open Selection Conditions Files* dialog (page 1137) will open allowing you to open a previously saved case selection condition file.

Save As

Save case selection conditions in a file when you click on this button to bring up the *Save Selection Conditions* dialog (page 1137). Case selection conditions can later be reopened using the *Open* button (see above).

The case selection conditions entered here are used to select cases for analysis, and if saved to a file, they are stored along with their header in a compressed file format. However, the saved conditions can also be used in (i.e., opened into) all those dialogs where multiple sets of case selection conditions are entered to identify multiple subsets of data (e.g., *Recode*, *Verify Data*, and *Multiple Subset Graphs*).

Selecting a Weighting Variable

This option will allow you to "adjust" the contribution of individual cases to the outcome of an analysis by "weighting" those cases in

proportion to the values of a selected variable. Selecting this option (either by clicking on the *Weight* option on the spreadsheet status bar (see Chapter 2), the *Weight* button on the *Startup Panel* or an analysis definition menu, or by selecting this option from the *Options* pull-down dialog) will open the *Define Weight* dialog in which you can specify the weighting variable.

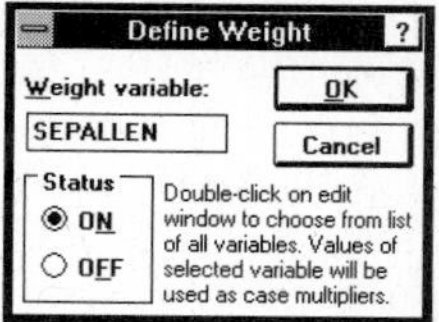

Some statistical procedures can use fractional weights, and in those cases, specific weighting information is described in the sections on those *STATISTICA* modules. Unless specified otherwise, the values of the weights are rounded to the nearest integer and used as "multipliers of cases" when the file is processed.

Keyboard shortcut. F7

Weight Variable

Type in the variable name that you want to be used as the weighting variable or double-click on this variable edit field to open the *Select Variable* dialog. The *Select Variable* dialog will display a list of spreadsheet variables from which you can select the weighting variable.

Status

The status of this dialog is displayed in the window status bar and identifies whether the weighting variable is in use (*On*) or not (*Off*).

STATISTICA Defaults: General

You can customize the general display and operation of *STATISTICA* by selecting (or de-selecting) several options offered in the *STATISTICA Defaults: General* dialog.

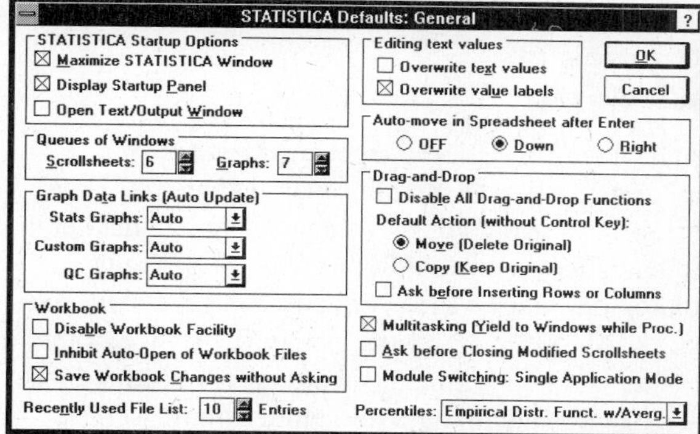

The selections that you make in this dialog will then be used as the default operating conditions whenever you open *STATISTICA*.

STATISTICA Startup Options

The following options will be implemented at startup of a *STATISTICA* module.

Maximize *STATISTICA* window. Select this option if you want the *STATISTICA* window to be maximized at startup. When this option is de-selected, *STATISTICA* will be run in windowed mode.

Display startup panel. Select this option if you want the *STATISTICA* module startup panel to be displayed whenever the module is opened. If this option is de-selected, then the startup panel will not be displayed upon entry into a module (but will be accessible, as usual, via the *Startup Panel* option of the *Analysis* pull-down menu or via the keyboard shortcut CTRL+T). Note that suppressing the startup panel will have only visual and not functional consequences, as it is a modeless dialog box and clicking anywhere outside the panel will automatically iconize it.

Open *Text/output Window*. Select this option if you want the *Text/output Window* to automatically come up whenever a *STATISTICA* module opens.

Queues of Windows

In *STATISTICA*, Scrollsheets and graphs are automatically managed in separate "queues" on a "first-in-first-out" basis. You can change the depth of each queue here, or in the *Window Manager* dialog (see page 1223). Specify a number between 0 and 20; however, if you specify *0*, the size of the queue will be unlimited (then you will need to close windows manually to avoid cluttering the screen and exhausting the memory resources of the computer).

Number of Scrollsheets. Specify here the maximum number of unlocked Scrollsheets to keep on screen. See the *Window Manager* dialog, page 1223, for more information on locking and unlocking Scrollsheets.

Number of graphs. Specify here the maximum number of unlocked graphs to keep on screen. (See the *Window Manager* dialog (page 1223) for more information on locking and unlocking graphs.)

Graph Data Links (Auto Update)

When you create either a *Stats Graph*, *Quick Stats Graph*, *Block Stats Graph*, or *Custom Graph* from a spreadsheet, the spreadsheet data may remain linked with the graph data in the *Graph Data Editor*. When the data are linked, you can make changes to the spreadsheet data and the respective graph(s) will automatically be updated to reflect those changes.

These options control the default settings for links between graphs of respective categories and their data sets. The four settings: *Auto*, *Manual*, *Locked*, and *No link* correspond to the options controlled (for individual graphs) in the *Graph Data Links - Update* dialog.

Stats/Quick Stats Graphs. Select this option to set the default data link status for *Stats Graphs* and *Quick Stats Graphs*.

Custom/Block Stats Graphs. Select this option to set the default data link status for *Custom Graphs* and *Block Stats Graphs*.

QC Graphs. Select this option to set the default data link status for *Quality Control* charts.

Note that embedded graphs (e.g., *Scatterplots w/Histograms*, *Scatterplots w/Box Plots*, embedded graphs created with the *Multiple-Graph AutoLayout Wizard*, or compound graphs created in the *Quality Control* module) can also be updated automatically.

You can manage links between the spreadsheet and current *Stats*, *Quick Stats*, *Block Stats*, *Custom*, or *Quality Control* graphs or embedded graphs, in the *Graph Data Links* dialog (accessible from the graph window *Graphs* pull-down menu); for example, links can be temporarily disabled to allow for extensive data editing without interruption by updating all graphs after every edit action.

Workbook

The following options allow you to control *STATISTICA*'s Workbook facility. For more information on the Workbook facility and its options, see *Data File Header, Notes, and Workbook Info*.

Disable Workbook Facility. The Workbook facility maintains a log of supplementary files for the current data file and offers several options for managing those files. When this option is selected, the Workbook facility will be disabled. See *When* *the Workbook Facility should be Disabled* in the *Toolbars* section of this chapter.

Inhibit Auto-Open of Workbook Files. The Workbook facility allows you to select up to 9 supplementary files to open automatically whenever the associated data file is opened (see *Data File Header, Notes, and Workbook Info* in the *Toolbars* section of this chapter). When you select this option, the Auto option will be inhibited and no supplementary files will open when the data file is opened.

Save Workbook Changes without Asking. When the current data file is saved, all Workbook changes are automatically saved along with it. However, if you close a data file without saving it, the program will either prompt you to save the Workbook changes (deselect this option) or it will automatically save the Workbook changes without prompting you (select this option), depending on the current setting of this option. The manual confirmation of saving Workbook changes can be useful when the data set is extremely large (and thus saving it is time consuming); see also *When the Workbook Facility should be Disabled* in the *Toolbars* section of this chapter.

Recently Used File List

Specify here the number (up to 16) of recently used files that will be displayed in the *File* pull-down menu.

Editing Text Values

Overwrite text values. When this option is de-selected, then when you enter a new text value over an existing one, a new numeric equivalent will be assigned to the new text value; that is, the entry of a new text value will not affect other text values for this variable (the associations between text and numeric values will not change for the current variable). This is the default data entry mode.

When this option is selected, then when a new text value is entered over an existing one, the newly entered text value will replace the existing text value in the table of relations (assignments) between text and numeric values, and the existing numeric equivalent (i.e., numeric value in the current cell) will be reassigned to the new text value. This will cause all cells of the current variable which contain the original text value to be overwritten by the new text value.

Note that this "double-notation" of values can be managed in the *Text Values Manager* dialog.

Overwrite value labels. When this option is selected, then when a new value label is entered over an existing value label (when the spreadsheet is in *Value Label* display, press CTRL while clicking on the spreadsheet toolbar button), the new label will replace the existing one and the text value and numeric equivalent will remain the same as before. This is the default mode, where value labels are treated as "comments" assigned to values (see also the next paragraph).

When this option is de-selected, then when a new value label is entered over an existing one, *STATISTICA* will first try to match it with an existing value label (for the current variable). If there is a match, then that text value and numeric equivalent will be used. If there is no match, then a new text value will be generated from the first 8 characters and a new numeric value will be assigned to this text value (in either case, the numeric value for the cell, and the text value associated with it will change). Note that if the resulting text value is not unique, then a number will be placed at the end to make it unique (e.g., *STATE2*). This is a non-default mode, where value labels are treated as "extensions of values" and not merely as "comments" assigned to values.

Auto-move in Spreadsheet after ENTER

When you enter or edit data in the spreadsheet, this option will allow you to control the movement of the cursor after you press on the ENTER key. You can choose to have the cursor move *down* to the next cell in the column (or to the top of the next column if you are in the last cell in the column), move *right* to the next cell in the row (or to the beginning of the next row if you are in the last cell of the row), or *off* (the cursor does not move after you hit ENTER).

Drag-and-Drop

The following options allow you to control *STATISTICA*'s *Drag-and-Drop* facility.

Disable All *Drag-and-Drop* Functions. When selected, this option will disable all *Drag-and-Drop* functions in the spreadsheet and Scrollsheet. You will still be able to edit spreadsheets and Scrollsheets using the standard editing features for cases and variables from the *Edit* pull-down menu, however, you will not be able to use any of the block operations specific to the *Drag-and-Drop* facility.

Default Action (without Control Key). The mode that you select here determines the default function of the *Drag-and Drop* facility.

Move (Delete Original): If you select this mode, then when the block is selected and you drag it to a different location in the spreadsheet or Scrollsheet, it will be *moved* to the new location (i.e., the block will be cut from the original position and pasted into the new position). In this mode, if you hold down on the CTRL key while dragging the block, the block will be *copied* to the new location. (This is the standard Excel-style of the *Drag-and-Drop* facility.)

Copy (Keep Original): If you select this mode, then when the block is selected and you drag it to a different location in the spreadsheet or Scrollsheet, it will be *copied* to the new location (i.e., the original block will remain and only a copy will be pasted into the new position). In this mode, if you hold down on the CTRL key while dragging the block, the block will be *moved* to the new location. (This is a non-standard style, however, it often proves to be useful in the management of data-base-format data sets when copying blocks is often a more common operation than moving blocks.)

Ask before inserting rows and columns. Select this option in order to have *STATISTICA* prompt you before inserting any rows or columns during a *Drag-and-Drop* or *Block Statistics* operation. The prompt will ask you if you want to insert a specified number of rows/columns and you can click *Yes* to complete the action or *No* to cancel it. When this option is de-selected, the insert action will be completed without any prompt from *STATISTICA*.

Multitasking Mode (Yield to Windows while Processing)

Selecting this option will allow you to switch between Windows applications or different *STATISTICA* modules (use the CTRL+ESC keys to bring up the *Task List* dialog, or ALT+TAB to toggle between applications) whenever *STATISTICA* is processing data. If you are processing a large data file that may require some time, then this option will free you to use another program while you are waiting. However, if this option is de-selected, then the data may be processed somewhat faster. Note that when *STATISTICA* is not processing data, you will always be able to switch between Windows applications or different *STATISTICA* modules.

Note also that when this option is disabled, you will not be able to interrupt redrawing of graphs by clicking the mouse or pressing a key.

Ask Before Closing a Modified Scrollsheet

Select this option if you want a warning message to appear each time you close a modified Scrollsheet. This message will also give you an opportunity to save the modified Scrollsheet (under the filename extension **.scr*) before closing it. If this option is de-selected, then the warning will not appear whenever you close a modified Scrollsheet.

Module Switching: Single Application Mode

When you select this option (choose *Single Application* mode), then switching between modules (by double-clicking on a new module name in the *Module Switcher*, see page 1205) during a *STATISTICA* session will not open new application windows. Each new module will be opened into the same window, replacing the module used before. If this option is de-selected (*Multiple Module Application Windows* mode), then you will be able to switch between *STATISTICA* modules (using the *Module Switcher*, page 1205) without closing the previous ones. Note that in the *Multiple Module* mode, you can also switch in the *Single Application* manner if you press the *End & Switch To* button on the *Module Switcher* (instead of double-clicking on the module name).

Percentiles

This option allows you to select from among six methods for computing percentile values, including medians (50th percentile) and quartiles (25th and 75th percentiles). The method that you select here will apply to every place in the *STATISTICA* program where medians, quartiles, or percentiles are computed, for example, to the computation of:

- percentiles in the *Nonparametrics & Distributions* module;
- medians and quartiles in the *Basic Statistics* module;
- medians and quartiles in *2D* and *3D Box Plots*;
- medians and quartiles in box-whisker plots in *Reproducibility and Repeatability* studies;
- medians and quartiles in box-whisker plots in *Discriminant Analysis*, *Reliability and Item Analysis*, *Basic Statistics*, *Multiple Regression*, and all other modules of *STATISTICA* that offer box-whisker plots as an option from the dialog.

For the following methods, let n be the number of cases, and p be the percentile value divided by 100 (e.g., *50/100* = *.5* for the median). Then, the available choices for computing percentiles are:

Weighted average at X_{np} method. (Weighted average centered at X_{np}). Express np (n times p) as $np=j+g$ where j is the integer part of np, and g is the fractional part of np; then compute:

$$PercentileValue = (1-g)x_j + gx_{j+1}$$

Note that X_0 in the above computation is replaced by X_1 (e.g., if $j = 0$, then the above formula would be $(1-g)x_1 + gx_{(0+1)}$).

Example: Consider the following sorted data: 1, 2, 4, 7, 8, 9, 10, 12, 13

Here, $n = 9$ and let $p = .25$ (the 25th percentile). Express np (n times p) as:

$$np = 9*.25 = 2.25 = j + g$$

therefore, $j = 2$ and $g = .25$. Now compute the 25th percentile as:

$$\begin{aligned}25th\ Percentile &= (1-.25)x_2 + .25x_3\\ &= (.75)2 + (.25)4\\ &= 2.5\end{aligned}$$

Weighted average at $X_{(n+1)p}$ method.

(Weighted average centered at $X_{(n+1)p}$). Express $(n+1)p$ as $(n+1)p=j+g$ where j is the integer part of $(n+1)p$, and g is the fractional part of $(n+1)p$; then compute:

$$PercentileValue = (1-g)x_j + gx_{j+1}$$

Note that X_{n+1} in the above computation is replaced by X_n (e.g., if $j = n$, then the above formula would be $(1-g)x_n + gx_n$).

Example: Consider the following sorted data: 1, 2, 4, 7, 8, 9, 10, 12, 13

Here, $n = 9$ and let $p = .25$ (the 25th percentile). Express *np* (*n* times *p*) as:

$$(n+1)p = 10*.25 = 2.5 = j + g$$

therefore, $j = 2$ and $g = .5$. Now compute the 25th percentile as:

$$\begin{aligned} \text{25th Percentile} &= (1-.5)x_2 + .5x_3 \\ &= (.5)2 + (.5)4 \\ &= 3.0 \end{aligned}$$

Empirical distribution function method.

Express *np* (*n* times *p*) as $np=j+g$ where j is the integer part of *np*, and g is the fractional part of *np*; then choose the percentile value as:

$$PercentileValue = x_j \quad \text{if } g=0$$

$$PercentileValue = x_{j+1} \quad \text{if } g>0$$

Example: Consider the following sorted data: 1, 2, 4, 7, 8, 9, 10, 12, 13

Here, $n = 9$ and let $p = .25$ (the 25th percentile). Express *np* (*n* times *p*) as:

$$np = 9*.25 = 2.25 = j + g$$

therefore, $j = 2$ and $g = .25$. Now, since $g>0$, compute the 25th percentile as:

$$\begin{aligned} \text{25th Percentile} &= x_3 \\ &= 4.0 \end{aligned}$$

Empirical distribution function with averaging method.

Express *np* (*n* times *p*) as $np=j+g$ where j is the integer part of *np*, and g is the fractional part of *np*; then compute the percentile value as:

$$PercentileValue = (x_j + x_{j+1})/2 \quad \text{if } g=0$$

$$PercentileValue = x_{j+1} \quad \text{if } g>0$$

Example: Consider the following sorted data: 1, 2, 4, 7, 8, 9, 10, 12, 13

Here, $n = 9$ and let $p = .25$ (the 25th percentile). Express *np* (*n* times *p*) as:

$$np = 9*.25 = 2.25 = j + g$$

therefore, $j = 2$ and $g = .25$. Now, since $g>0$, compute the 25th percentile as:

$$\begin{aligned} \text{25th Percentile} &= x_3 \\ &= 4.0 \end{aligned}$$

Empirical distribution function with interpolation (MS Excel) method.

Express $(n-1)p$ ($(n-1)$ times p) as $(n-1)p=j+g$ where j is the integer part of $(n-1)p$, and g is the fractional part of $(n-1)p$; then compute the percentile value as:

$$PercentileValue = x_{j+1} \quad \text{if } g=0$$

$$PercentileValue = x_{j+1} + g(x_{j+2} - x_{j+1}) \quad \text{if } g>0$$

Example: Consider the following sorted data: 1, 2, 4, 7, 8, 9, 10, 12, 13

Here, $n = 9$ and let $p = .25$ (the 25th percentile). Express *np* (*n* times *p*) as:

$$(n-1)p = 8*.25 = 2.0 = j + g$$

therefore, $j = 2$ and $g = 0$. Now, since $g=0$, compute the 25th percentile as:

$$\begin{aligned} \text{25th Percentile} &= x_3 \\ &= 4.0 \end{aligned}$$

Closest observation method. (Observation closest to *np*). Compute *j* as the integer part of *np+1/2*, then compute:

```
PercentileValue = xj
```

Example: Consider the following sorted data: 1, 2, 4, 7, 8, 9, 10, 12, 13

Here, $n = 9$ and let $p = .25$ (the 25th percentile). Express *np* (*n* times *p*) as:

```
np + 1/2 = (9*.25) + .5 = 2.75 = j + g
```

therefore, $j = 2$. Now, compute the 25th percentile as:

```
25th Percentile = x2
                = 2.0
```

STATISTICA Defaults: Display

You can customize *STATISTICA*'s window display by selecting (or de-selecting) several options offered in the *STATISTICA Defaults: Display* dialog. The selections that you make here will then be used as the default window display whenever you open *STATISTICA*.

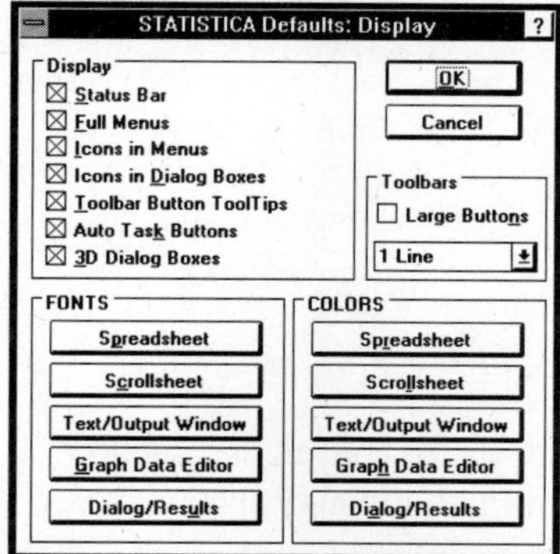

Note that the color and font settings that you select here will not affect the current spreadsheet or Scrollsheets (use the respective *View* options instead, see page 1195) but will only affect the configuration used by *STATISTICA* when creating new spreadsheets (via *New Data*, page 1135) or Scrollsheets.

Show Status Bar

When you select this option, the window status bar (the bar at the bottom of the screen, see Chapter 2) will be displayed. If this option is de-selected, then the status bar will be hidden.

Full Menus

With this option, you can choose between viewing full menus (when selected, names of options and their respective keyboard shortcuts, if any, will be displayed) or short menus (when de-selected, only the names of options will be displayed) in all pull-down menus.

Icons in Menus

Choose to display icons with *STATISTICA* menus items when you select this option. If de-selected, then the icons on menus resulting from the right-mouse-button option, toolbar buttons, and pull-down menus will not be displayed (after de-selecting this option, you may need to close the module and reopen it before the pull-down menu icons are removed).

Icons in Dialog Boxes

Icons are also used in dialog boxes to help identify what options are available (select this option). If you prefer, you can remove these icons from the display by de-selecting this option.

Toolbar Button ToolTips

When you select this option, the *ToolTips* (a balloon-style help for toolbar buttons in *STATISTICA*) will be displayed when you point to a

toolbar button. If this option is de-selected, then the *ToolTips* will not be displayed when you point to a toolbar button.

Auto Task Buttons

When you select the *Auto Task Buttons* option in this dialog (or from the pull-down menu *View*), the *Auto Task Buttons* toolbar (see Chapter 6) will (by default) be displayed in the *STATISTICA* window. If this option is de-selected, then the *Auto Task Buttons* toolbar will be hidden. Note that any Hot Keys assigned to *Auto Task Buttons* can be used regardless of the display setting of the toolbar.

Keyboard shortcut. Press CTRL+M to toggle on/off the *Auto Task Buttons* toolbar.

3D Dialog Boxes

By default, dialog boxes in *STATISTICA* feature 3D effects to improve readability of dialog options. If you prefer, you can remove the 3D effects by de-selecting this option.

Fonts

You can change the default font of entries in the *Scrollsheet*, *Spreadsheet*, *Graph Data Editor*, or *Dialog/Results* (the summary section of results dialogs) by clicking on the appropriate button.

Colors

Change the color of *Spreadsheets*, *Scrollsheets*, and the *Graph Data Editor* by clicking on the appropriate button to bring up the *Customize Color* dialog. You can click on the *Dialog/Results* button to open the *Results Text - Colors* dialog (see below) in which you can select the colors for the specific results components.

Toolbars

This option allows you to select the default way in which to display (or hide) the toolbar in the window.

Large Buttons. Set this check box in order to display large toolbar buttons; this option is useful when a high-resolution (e.g., 800x600 or 1024x768) is used on a small size monitor. If this check box is not set, then standard size toolbar buttons will be displayed.

Toolbar display. Select the desired display style for the toolbar.

Off. Select this option to temporarily remove the toolbar from the window. (In order to once again display the toolbar, select one of the options described below.)

1 line. When you select this option, the toolbar will be displayed in one line in the spreadsheet window.

2 lines. Select this option to display the toolbar buttons in two lines.

Right & Top. This option will display half of the toolbar at the top of the window and the other half along the right side of the window.

Left & Top. This option will display half of the toolbar at the top of the window and the other half along the left side of the window.

Results Text - Colors

This dialog will allow you to change the colors of specific components of the summary section of results dialogs.

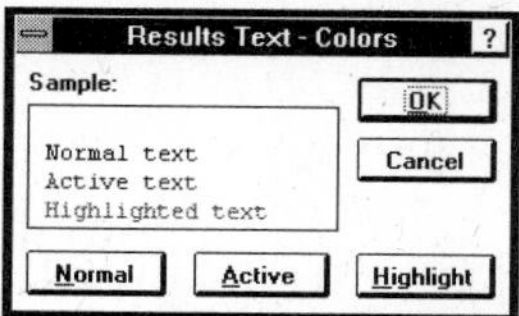

When you click on the appropriate button, a *Colors* dialog will open (page 1196) in which you can select a color for the *Normal* text (the text that describes the names of individual fields), the *Active* text (the text that describes the values of fields), or the *Highlighted* text (the text color in specialized dialogs such as in *Multiple Regression - Results*, which is used to indicate significance). You can view the changes in the dialog *Sample* box after they are made, but before you exit the dialog.

STATISTICA Defaults: Print

When you select the *Print* option from the spreadsheet *Options* pull-down menu, the *Page/Output Setup* dialog will open. The options which can be configured in this dialog are discussed in detail on page 1148. Please refer to that discussion for more details on this option.

Spreadsheet Options - Macro

The following options are available from the *Macro* option on the spreadsheet *Options* pull-down menu.

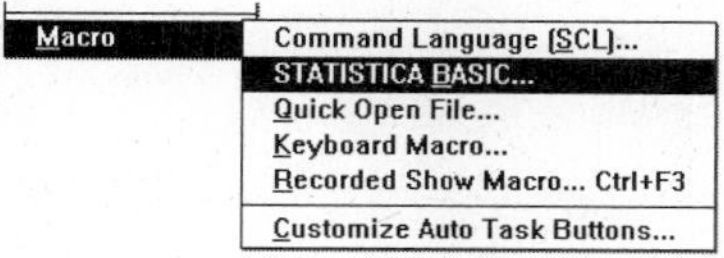

Selecting one of these options will open the respective *Auto Task Buttons* dialog for creating the selected type of macro. Refer to Chapter 6 for compete information on the *Auto Task Buttons* floating or docked toolbar facility.

Command Language (SCL)

Select this option from the *Options* pull-down menu to open the *Edit the Auto Task Buttons Item* dialog. Here you can select a *STATISTICA* Command Language (*SCL*) file to assign to an *Auto Task Button*.

STATISTICA BASIC

When you select this option from the *Options* pull-down menu, the *Edit the Auto Task Buttons Item* dialog will open in which you can select a *STATISTICA BASIC* file to assign to an *Auto Task Button*.

Quick Open File

When you select this option from the *Options* pull-down menu, the *Edit the Auto Task Buttons Item* dialog will open in which you can select a spreadsheet, Scrollsheet, graph, or report file to assign to an *Auto Task Button*.

Keyboard Macro

Select this option from the *Options* pull-down menu to open the *Record or Enter/Edit a Keyboard Macro* dialog. Here you can enter or record a new keyboard macro or open a previously saved keyboard macro file and assign it to an *Auto Task Button*.

Recorded Show Macro

When you select this option from the *Options* pull-down menu, the *Recorded Show Macro* dialog will open in which you can record a new macro or open a previously saved macro file and assign it to an *Auto Task Button*.

Customize Auto Task Buttons

When you select this option from the *Options* pull-down menu, the *Customize Auto Task Buttons* dialog will open in which you can define and edit the buttons assigned to the *Auto Task Buttons* toolbar.

SPREADSHEET *WINDOW* PULL-DOWN MENU

The following dialogs and options are available from the spreadsheet *Window* pull-down menu.

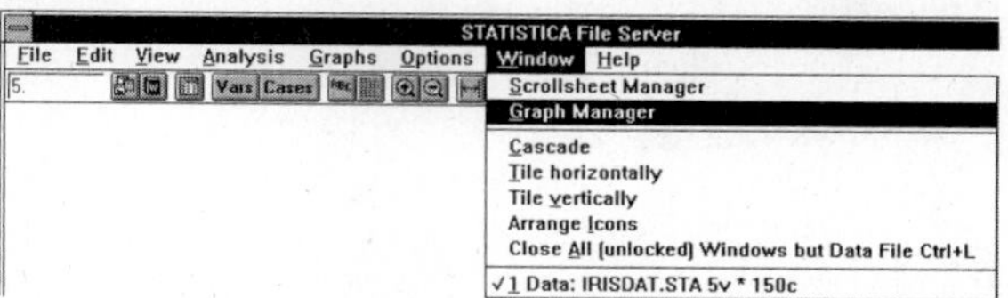

Each of these options are described below.

Scrollsheet and Graph Manager Dialogs

Selecting one of these options will allow you to manage the number of (unlocked, see below) Scrollsheets or graphs that can be displayed on the screen at one time.

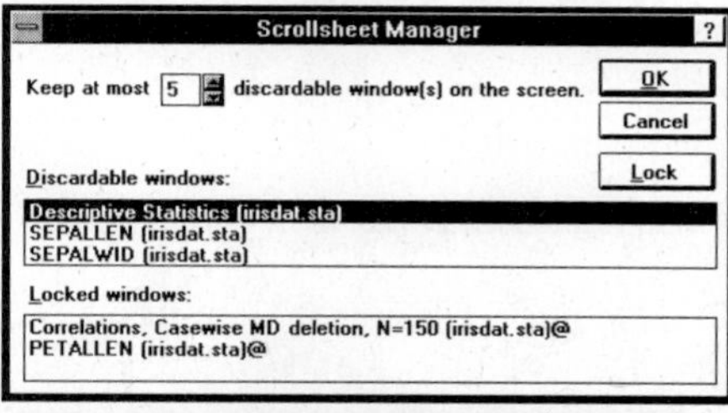

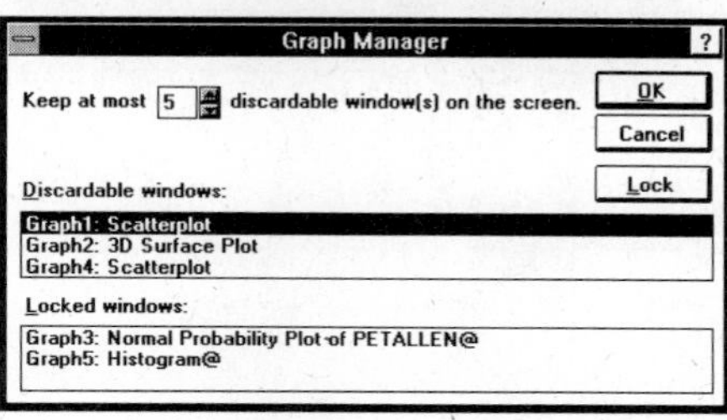

In *STATISTICA*, Scrollsheets and graphs are automatically managed in separate "queues" on a "first-in-first-out" basis.

For example, if the Scrollsheet queue depth is set to 3, then when the fourth Scrollsheet is created, the first one will close automatically. There is no one recommended depth of the queue; the number of entries should be adjusted according to the type of analysis, size of the screen and individual preferences. You can change the depth of the queue in the *Window Manager* dialog, or in the *STATISTICA Defaults: General* dialog (page 1213); you can also control the number of windows (Scrollsheets or graphs) in the screen either by locking them or closing them manually.

Queue

Specify here the maximum number of unlocked windows to keep on screen. You can specify a number between 0 and 20; however if you specify 0, the size of the queue will be unlimited (then you will need to close windows manually to avoid cluttering the screen and exhausting the memory resources of the computer).

Discardable Windows

This is a list of all the unlocked (discardable) windows on screen. When you highlight a window in this list and click on the *Lock* button (see below), you will lock the window, removing it from the queue.

Locked Windows

This is a list of all the locked windows on screen. You can add a window to this list by highlighting its name in the *Discardable Window* list (see above) and then clicking on the *Lock* button (see below); in order to remove a locked window, close it manually.

Lock

Individual windows may be removed from the queue by locking them via the *Lock* button in this dialog. To lock a window, first highlight its name in the *Discardable Window* list (see above) and then click on the *Lock* button. Locked windows (marked with the "@" character at the end of the title) will remain on screen as long as you do not close them manually or exit the module or *STATISTICA*.

Cascade

Select this option to arrange the open *STATISTICA* windows in an overlapping pattern so that the title bar of each window is visible.

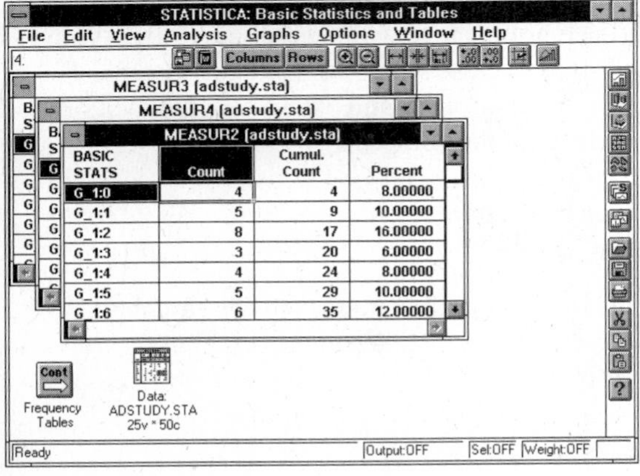

Tile Horizontally

This option will arrange the open *STATISTICA* windows in a horizontal (side by side) pattern.

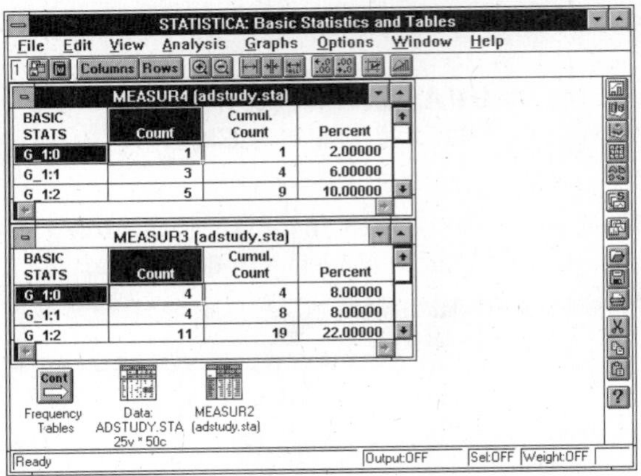

When you select this option, *STATISTICA* will automatically optimize the display of the open windows (with the preference given to tiling horizontally). Graphics windows will maintain their original proportions unless you have de-selected the *Fixed Proportions* option from the graphics window *View* pull-down menu (see Volume II of the manual).

Tile Vertically

This option will arrange the open *STATISTICA* windows in a vertical pattern.

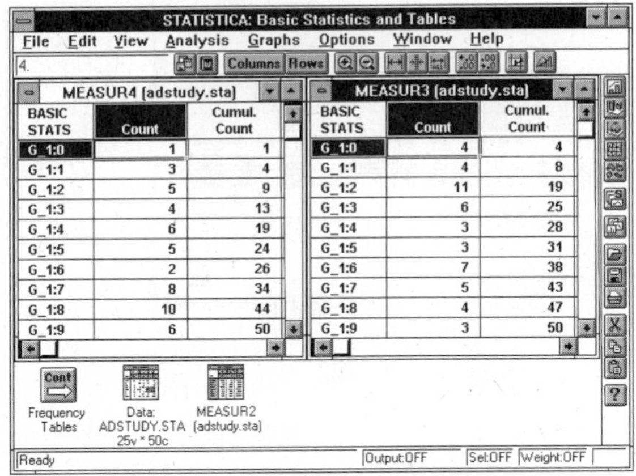

When you select this option, *STATISTICA* will automatically optimize the display of the open windows (with the preference given to tiling vertically).

Graphics windows will maintain their original proportions unless you have de-selected the *Fixed Proportions* option from the graphics window *View* pull-down menu (see Volume II of the manual).

Keyboard shortcut. ALT+SHIFT+F6

Arrange Icons

Select this option to arrange all iconized windows into rows.

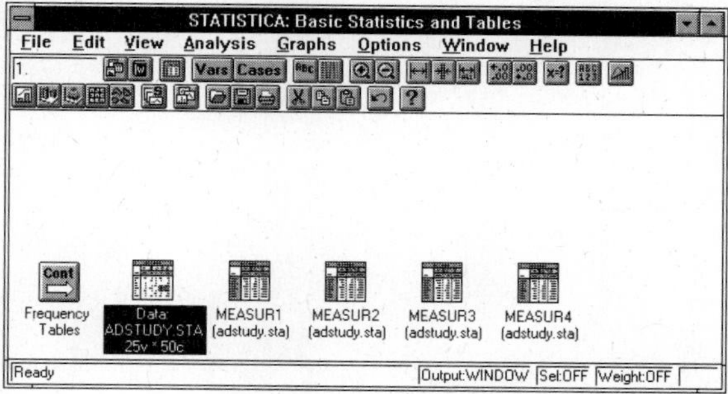

Close All (unlocked) Windows but Data File

This option will close all open (and unlocked) Scrollsheets, graphs, and related windows (e.g., graph data) in *STATISTICA*; the data spreadsheet will remain open. This option is useful when you need to "clear" the screen to start a new analysis. Note that windows opened from files are automatically locked, and will be unaffected by this option.

Keyboard shortcut. CTRL+L

SPREADSHEET *HELP* PULL-DOWN MENU

The following dialogs and options are available from the spreadsheet *Help* pull-down menu, and they allow you to access various parts of the *STATISTICA Electronic Manual.*

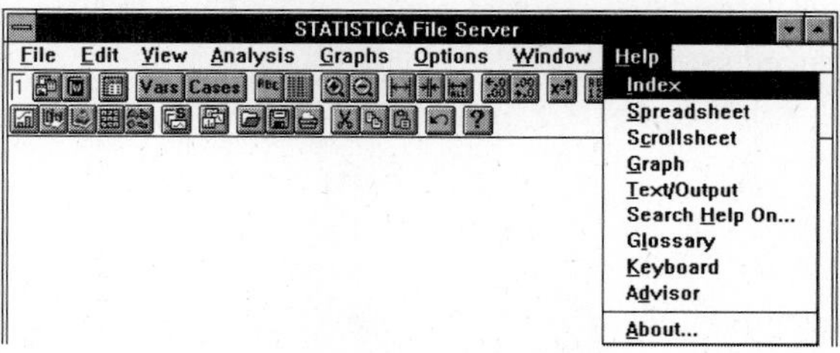

Each of these options opens a *Help* window with information concerning the general topic (see below).

Help Menu - Index

When you select this option, the *STATISTICA Help Index* window will open.

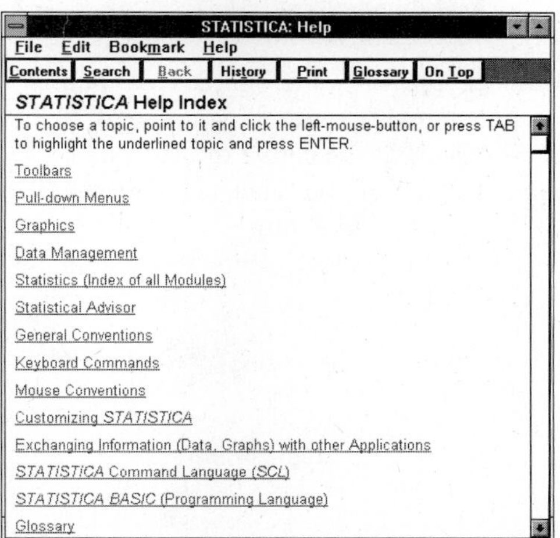

This *Index* provides a listing of the most commonly used *Help* topics. Simply click on a topic name to obtain more information concerning that topic.

Help Menu - Spreadsheet

Selecting this option will open the section of the *Electronic Manual* in which a list of spreadsheet window menus and other options is given. To obtain more information on each topic listed in this window, click on the topic name.

Help Menu - Scrollsheet

Similar to the *Spreadsheet* option, selecting this option will open the section of the *Electronic Manual* in which a list of Scrollsheet window menus and other options is given. To obtain more information on each topic listed in this window, click on the topic name.

Help Menu - Graphs

When you click on this option, the section of the *Electronic Manual* in which a list of graph window menus and other options is given, will open. To obtain more information on each topic listed in this window, click on the topic name.

Help Menu - Text/output

When you click on this option, the section of the *Electronic Manual* in which a list of *Text/output Window* menus and other options is given will open. To obtain more information on each topic listed in this window, click on the topic name.

Help Menu - Search Help On

This standard Windows dialog will open when you select this option from the *Help* pull-down menu.

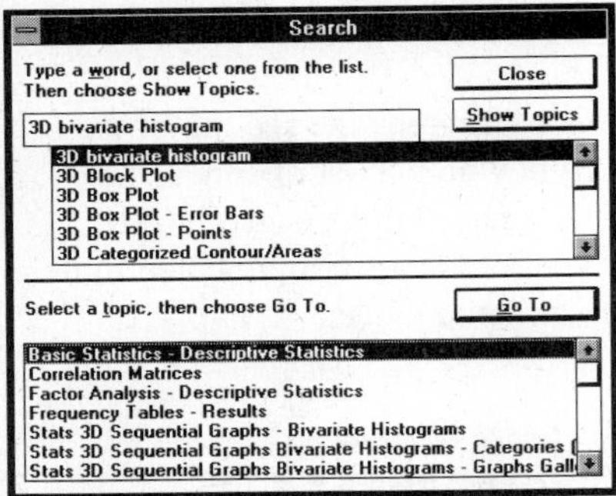

You can utilize this dialog to search for specific topics in *STATISTICA*'s *Electronic Manual* (i.e., on-line help) by entering keywords and then selecting from among the topics associated with those keywords.

Help Menu - Glossary

When you click on this option, the section of the *Electronic Manual* containing an alphabetical listing of all *STATISTICA* glossary entries will open.

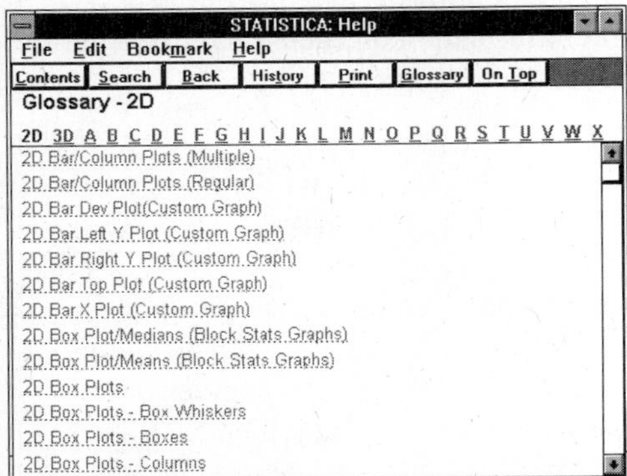

Click on a specific glossary entry in this window to open a pop-up window of information on that topic.

Help Menu - Keyboard

Selecting this option will open the section of the *Electronic Manual* with keyboard combinations of *STATISTICA* options which can be used as "shortcuts" in order to access various *STATISTICA* procedures.

Help Menu - Advisor

Selecting this option will bring up *STATISTICA*'s *Statistical Advisor*.

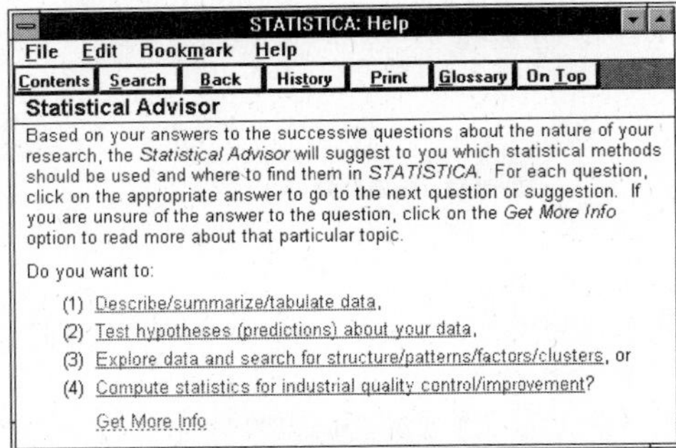

When you select the *Advisor* from the *Help* pull-down menu, the program will ask you a set of simple questions about the nature of the research problem and the type of your data, and then it will suggest to you the statistical procedures which appear most relevant (and tell you where to look for them in the *STATISTICA* system).

Help Menu - About

When you select this option, the *STATISTICA* version, copyright notice and license information is displayed in a window (see below).

The name of the owner/user and institutional affiliation information displayed in this dialog is recorded at the point when the copy of *STATISTICA* is first installed.

Citation of *STATISTICA*

When you click on this button in the *About STATISTICA* dialog, a window will open in which the citation information for *STATISTICA* is displayed

By pressing the button, this information will be copied to the Clipboard for easy access when referencing *STATISTICA*.

INDEX

STATISTICA

StatSoft

S

T

V

W

Chapter 4:

SCROLLSHEET WINDOW: MENUS, DIALOGS, OPTIONS

Table of Contents

Detailed Table of Contents

StatSoft

Chapter 4:

SCROLLSHEET WINDOW: MENUS, DIALOGS, OPTIONS

DRAG-AND-DROP AND AUTOFILL IN SCROLLSHEETS

The *Drag-and-Drop* Facilities

STATISTICA supports the complete set of standard spreadsheet (Excel-style) *Drag-and-Drop* facilities, as summarized below.

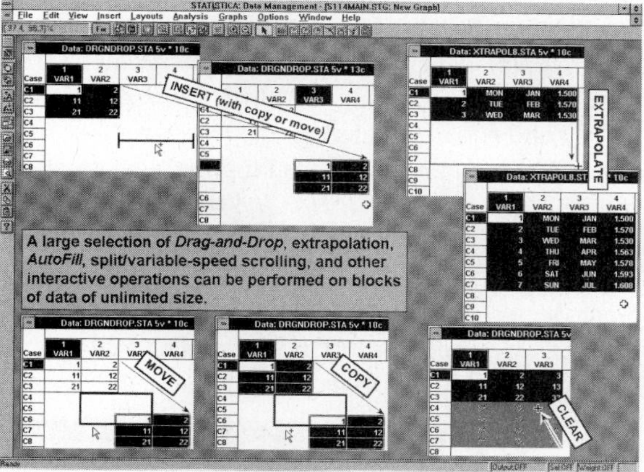
INSERT (with copy or move)
EXTRAPOLATE
A large selection of Drag-and-Drop, extrapolation, AutoFill, split/variable-speed scrolling, and other interactive operations can be performed on blocks of data of unlimited size.
MOVE
COPY
CLEAR

Scrollsheets support the same *Drag-and-Drop* facilities with the exception of inserting. Note that the *Drag-and-Drop* operations can be disabled by selecting the *Disable All Drag-and-Drop Functions* option in the *STATISTICA Defaults: General* dialog (see Chapter 3).

Selecting a Block

Blocks may be selected by (1) drag-selecting (holding down the left-mouse-button) with the mouse, (2) clicking in one corner of the block to be highlighted, then scrolling to the desired opposite corner (the original cell will remain selected) and pressing the SHIFT key while clicking in that cell (SHIFT-click), or (3) holding down the SHIFT key while using the cursor keys on the keyboard.

To expand a previously selected block, you may use the SHIFT-cursor key, or scroll the display with the mouse and press the SHIFT key while clicking in the desired corner of the block.

To highlight a large block in "split-pane" mode (as shown below), click in a cell in one pane, then scroll to display the diagonally opposite corner in another pane and use SHIFT-click to select the block.

Correlations (adstudy.sta)

BASIC STATS — Marked correlations are significant at p < .05000
N=50 (Casewise deletion of missing data)

Variable	MEASUR 5	MEASUR 6	MEASUR 7	MEASUR 8	MEASUR 17	MEASUR 18	MEASUR 19	MEASUR 20
MEASUR6	.23	1.00	.12	-.33	.27	-.07	-.16	.12
MEASUR7	-.05	.12	1.00	.05	.04	.22	.17	-.01
MEASUR8	-.19	-.33	.05	1.00	-.19	.14	.00	-.11
MEASUR9	-.47	-.27	.03	.00	.02	-.29	.03	-.10
MEASUR10	-.07	.13	-.08	.23	.22	-.16	-.02	.05
MEASUR11	-.01	-.15	-.07	.09	.15	-.11	.11	.16
MEASUR12	.11	.04	.09	-.09	.09	.06	-.07	.34
MEASUR16	.43	.20	.17	.09	.07	.06	.19	-.08
MEASUR17	-.03	.27	.04	-.19	1.00	-.18	.11	.29
MEASUR18	.16	-.07	.22	.14	-.18	1.00	-.02	-.11
MEASUR19	-.02	-.16	.17	.00	.11	-.02	1.00	-.29
MEASUR20	-.08	.12	-.01	-.11	.29	-.11	-.29	1.00
MEASUR21	-.08	.04	-.04	.30	.05	.11	.08	-.10
MEASUR22	.15	.24	.08	-.36	-.06	-.07	.01	.08

Once a block is selected in a spreadsheet or Scrollsheet, you can perform one of the following *Drag-and-Drop* operations.

Moving a Block

A selected block of data may be moved by pointing to the border of the selection (the cross-cursor will change to an arrow) and dragging the block to the new location.

Correlations (adstudy.sta)

BASIC STATS — Marked correlations are significant at p < .05000; N=50 (Casewise deletion of missing data)

Variable	MEASUR 1	MEASUR 2	MEASUR 3	MEASUR 4	MEASUR 5	MEASUR 6	MEASUR 7
MEASUR1	1.00	-.01	-.04				
MEASUR2	-.01	1.00	-.06				
MEASUR3	-.04	-.06	1.00				
MEASUR4	.05	.01	.09				
MEASUR5				1.00	-.01	-.04	
MEASUR6				-.01	1.00	-.06	
MEASUR7				-.04	-.06	1.00	
MEASUR8				.05	.01	.09	
MEASUR9							

When the block of data is moved, missing values will be placed in those cells. See also, *Moving or copying values in the Scrollsheet*, below.

Copying a Block

A block may be copied by pointing to the border of the selection (the cross-cursor will change to an arrow) and pressing the CTRL key (a "plus" sign will appear next to the cursor) while dragging a copy of the block to the new location.

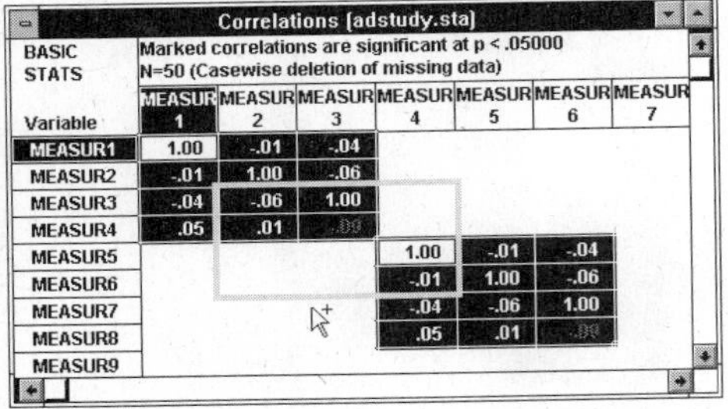

The default action which occurs when dragging a block without pressing the CTRL key may be changed from moving to copying in the *STATISTICA Defaults: General* dialog (see Chapter 3).

Clearing a Block

A portion (or an entire) block can be cleared by dragging within a selected block.

Correlations (adstudy.sta)

Variable	MEASUR 1	MEASUR 2	MEASUR 3
MEASUR1	1.00	-.01	-.04
MEASUR2	-.01	1.00	-.06
MEASUR3	-.04	-.06	1.00
MEASUR4	.05	.01	.09
MEASUR5			
MEASUR6			
MEASUR7			
MEASUR8			
MEASUR9	-.16	-.21	.21
MEASUR10	-.17	.05	-.09

After highlighting the block, move the cursor to the lower-right corner of the block displaying the *Fill Handle*. When it changes to a "plus sign," hold down on the left-mouse-button and drag within the selected block. As you are dragging, the values within the block will become dimmed. When you release the left-mouse-button, the dimmed values will be deleted.

Extrapolating a Block (*AutoFill*)

A horizontal or vertical series in a block can be extrapolated by dragging the block *Fill Handle* (a small solid square located on the lower-right corner of the block). Note that if you highlight an entire row or column, then *Fill Handles* will be displayed both at the top and bottom of the columns or at the beginning and end of the rows. *STATISTICA* can create series of values such as sequential numbers or linear extrapolations (e.g., you can extend a series such as *1*, *2*, *3* to include *4*, *5*, *6*, ...).

Descriptive Statistics (irisdat.sta)

BASIC STATS	Mean	Minimum	Maximum
SEPALLEN	5.8433	1.0000	7.9000
SEPALWID	3.0573	2.0000	4.4000
PETALLEN	3.7580	3.0000	6.9000
PETALWID	1.1993	4.0000	2.5000
5	.1567	5.0000	2.0000
6	-1.166	6.0000	.6300
7	-2.490	7.0000	-.7400
8	-3.813	8.0000	-2.110
9			

You can extrapolate (*AutoFill*) a block in the following manners:

- If the initial selection contains repeated values, these values will be duplicated in the extended block.
- Non-identical values are extended by linear regression to compute extrapolated values for the series.

Extrapolating (*AutoFill* ing) a block upwards or to the left. In the same manner as extrapolating a block down or right, a block may be extrapolated by dragging the *Fill Handle* up or to the left past the original start of the block. Note that if you drag the *Fill Handle* up or to the left and stop within the original selection without going past the top or left side of the selection, you will delete data within the selection (data to be deleted are indicated in gray as you drag within the selection, see page 1240). Note that you can use the *Fill Block* commands on the pop-up menu or *Edit* pull-down menu to copy the first row or the first column of cells in the block to adjacent cells within the currently selected block.

Variable-speed of Block Highlighting

You can control the speed at which you scroll when you extend a block outside the current display window. By moving the cursor a short distance away from the Scrollsheet, you can scroll one line at a time when a block is selected; scroll one page at a time by moving the cursor further away from the Scrollsheet.

SPLIT SCROLLING IN SPREADSHEETS AND SCROLLSHEETS

Spreadsheets and Scrollsheets can be split into up to four sections (panes) by dragging the split box (the black rectangle at the top of the vertical scrollbar or to the left of the horizontal scrollbar). This is useful if you have a large amount of information and you want to review results from different parts of the spreadsheet or Scrollsheet.

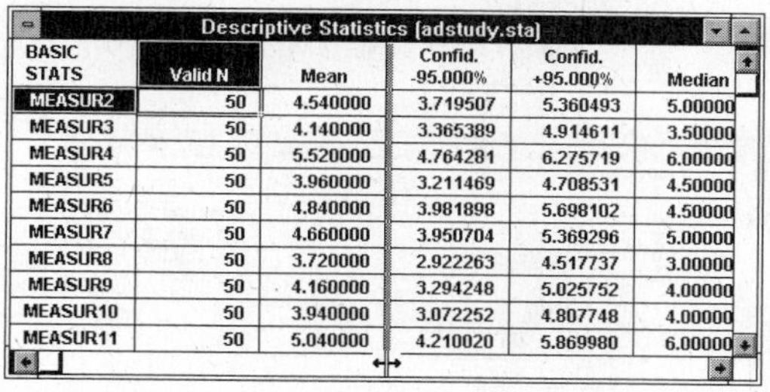

Descriptive Statistics (adstudy.sta)

BASIC STATS	Valid N	Mean	Confid. -95.000%	Confid. +95.000%	Median
MEASUR2	50	4.540000	3.719507	5.360493	5.00000
MEASUR3	50	4.140000	3.365389	4.914611	3.50000
MEASUR4	50	5.520000	4.764281	6.275719	6.00000
MEASUR5	50	3.960000	3.211469	4.708531	4.50000
MEASUR6	50	4.840000	3.981898	5.698102	4.50000
MEASUR7	50	4.660000	3.950704	5.369296	5.00000
MEASUR8	50	3.720000	2.922263	4.517737	3.00000
MEASUR9	50	4.160000	3.294248	5.025752	4.00000
MEASUR10	50	3.940000	3.072252	4.807748	4.00000
MEASUR11	50	5.040000	4.210020	5.869980	6.00000

To split a spreadsheet or Scrollsheet window vertically or horizontally, point with the mouse to the vertical or horizontal "split box" (a solid black region just above the upper vertical scroll arrow or next to the left horizontal scroll arrow) and drag the "split cursor" (↔ or ↕) to the row or column where you want the split to occur. You can split the spreadsheet or Scrollsheet into two (see above) or four (see below) "panes."

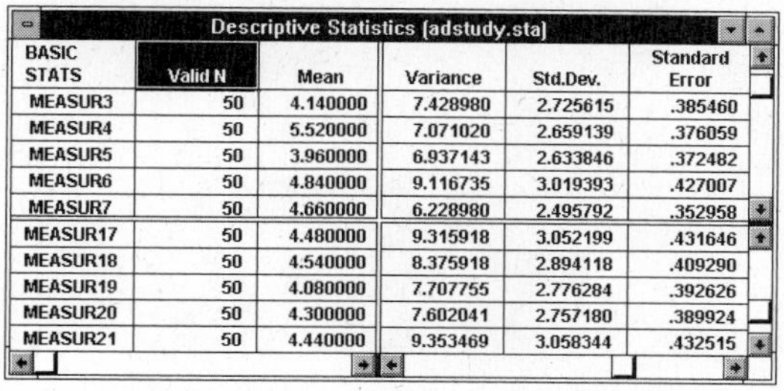

Descriptive Statistics (adstudy.sta)

BASIC STATS	Valid N	Mean	Variance	Std.Dev.	Standard Error
MEASUR3	50	4.140000	7.428980	2.725615	.385460
MEASUR4	50	5.520000	7.071020	2.659139	.376059
MEASUR5	50	3.960000	6.937143	2.633846	.372482
MEASUR6	50	4.840000	9.116735	3.019393	.427007
MEASUR7	50	4.660000	6.228980	2.495792	.352958
MEASUR17	50	4.480000	9.315918	3.052199	.431646
MEASUR18	50	4.540000	8.375918	2.894118	.409290
MEASUR19	50	4.080000	7.707755	2.776284	.392626
MEASUR20	50	4.300000	7.602041	2.757180	.389924
MEASUR21	50	4.440000	9.353469	3.058344	.432515

Note that vertically split panes scroll together when you scroll vertically, while horizontally split panes scroll together when you scroll horizontally.

To remove a split pane from a spreadsheet or Scrollsheet, drag the split box between the scroll arrows to either end of the scroll bar.

To highlight a large block in "split-pane" mode, click in a cell in one pane, then scroll to display the diagonally opposite corner in another pane and use SHIFT-click (see *Selecting a Block*, below) to select the block. You can then use *STATISTICA*'s block

operations (i.e., *Drag-and-Drop*, see above, and *Block Stats/Columns/Rows/Graphs*, see page 1252) on the selected block.

The split-pane display is also available in the *Graph Data Editor*, *Megafile Manager*, and other Scrollsheet-based windows.

Graph Data for Graph3: Histogram (ADSTUDY.STA 25v*50c)

Histogram (ADSTUDY.STA 25v*50c)

	MEASUR1 Bar X		MEASUR2 Bar X		MEASUR5 Bar X	
	X	Y	X	Y	X	Y
1	-0.40	1.00	-0.20	4.00	0.40	5.00
2	0.60	2.00	0.80	5.00	1.40	8.00
3	1.60	3.00	1.80	8.00	2.40	5.00
4	2.60	3.00	2.80	3.00	3.40	4.00
6	4.60	7.00	4.80	5.00	5.40	10.00
7	5.60	8.00	5.80	6.00	6.40	5.00
8	6.60	14.00	6.80	5.00	7.40	5.00
9	7.60	1.00	7.80	5.00	8.40	4.00
10	8.60	9.00	8.80	5.00	9.40	1.00

StatSoft

SCROLLSHEET *FILE* PULL-DOWN MENU

The following dialogs and options are available from the Scrollsheet *File* pull-down menu.

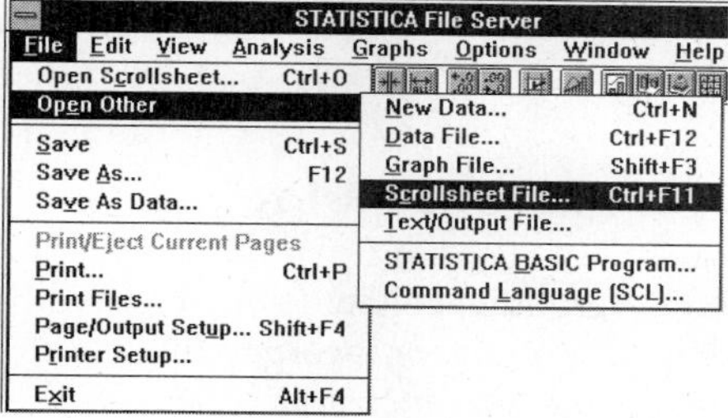

Each of these options are discussed below.

Open Scrollsheet

Selecting this option will bring up the *Open Scrollsheet* dialog from which you can select a Scrollsheet file (with the file name extension **.scr*) to open. Scrollsheet files contain the output data and all formatting and customization information (e.g., highlights, custom colors, etc.).

Toolbar button. See the [button] button in the *Scrollsheet Window* toolbar.

Keyboard shortcut. CTRL+F11

Scrollsheet Open Other File

This sub-menu is common to all menus (spreadsheet, Scrollsheet, graph, *Text/output Window*), allowing access to all types of *STATISTICA* files. These options allow you to open a *New Data* file, an existing *Data File*, *Graph File*, *Scrollsheet File*, *Text/output File*, *STATISTICA BASIC Program* or *Command Language (SCL)* program file (see the *Electronic Manual* for more information on these last two options). When you select the *New Data* option, the *New Data: Specify File Name* dialog will open, from which you can select a file name under which the new spreadsheet will be saved. After selecting the file name, a 10 variables by 10 cases spreadsheet will be created.

Selecting any of the other options listed above will open the respective *File Open/Save As* dialog in which you can select the file name to open.

Scrollsheet Save

Save a Scrollsheet with this option (file name extension **.scr*). If the current Scrollsheet has not been saved before (i.e., it has no file name yet), then the *Save File As* dialog will open in which you can specify the file name and disk location in which to save it. Once the file name and location have been specified, whenever you select *Save,* the Scrollsheet will be automatically saved under the same file name, overwriting the previous copy of the file. If you want to change the name or location of the file, select the *Save As* option.

Toolbar button. See the [button] button in the *Scrollsheet Window* toolbar.

Keyboard shortcut. SHIFT+F12

Scrollsheet Save As

Save a Scrollsheet with this option. Every time you select this option, the *Save File As* dialog will open, in which you can specify the file name and disk location for the Scrollsheet.

Keyboard shortcut. F12

Scrollsheet Save As Data

In *STATISTICA*, output from all analyses (Scrollsheets and graphs) can be converted into input data. Selecting this option will bring up the *Save Scrollsheet As* dialog, in which you can save the contents of the Scrollsheet in spreadsheet (data file) format (files with the file name extension **.sta*), thus allowing you to use the contents of the output Scrollsheet as input for an analysis, or to export it to another file format. When *STATISTICA* makes a spreadsheet out of a Scrollsheet, it uses the Scrollsheet *Row Names* column as the spreadsheet *Case Names* and assigns the Scrollsheet *Column Headings* as the spreadsheet *Variable Names* and *Long Variable Labels* (corresponding to the first and the second line of Scrollsheet column names, respectively). *STATISTICA* also uses the Scrollsheet *Title* as the spreadsheet *File Header*.

Printing Options from the Scrollsheet *File* Pull-down Menu

The following options are available both from the spreadsheet and Scrollsheet *File* pull-down menus and are briefly reviewed on the following pages. For more information about each of these options, please refer to Chapter 3.

Print/Eject Current Pages

When you run an analysis and the *Output* is set to *Printer* or *File* (in the *Page/Output Setup* dialog, see page 1246), *STATISTICA* will internally store the output either until the output fills a page (if the *Automatically Eject Each Filled Page* option is selected in the *Page/Output Setup* dialog) or until the analysis is complete (if the *Automatically Eject Each Filled Page* option is de-selected in the *Page/Output Setup* dialog) before sending it to the printer or output file. The *Print/Eject Current Pages* option will override this internal storage and immediately print (or send to an output file) whatever output has accumulated (technically, a "form feed" will be issued).

Note that this option does not apply to the *Text/output Window* (see Chapter 5).

Scrollsheet Print

Prints the active Scrollsheet either to an output file (for later printing, revising, or incorporating into other documents), to the printer (for immediate printing) and/or to the *Text/output Window* as designated in the *Page/Output Setup* dialog (page 1246). When you select the *Print* option from the Scrollsheet *File* pull-down menu, the *Print Scrollsheet* dialog will open.

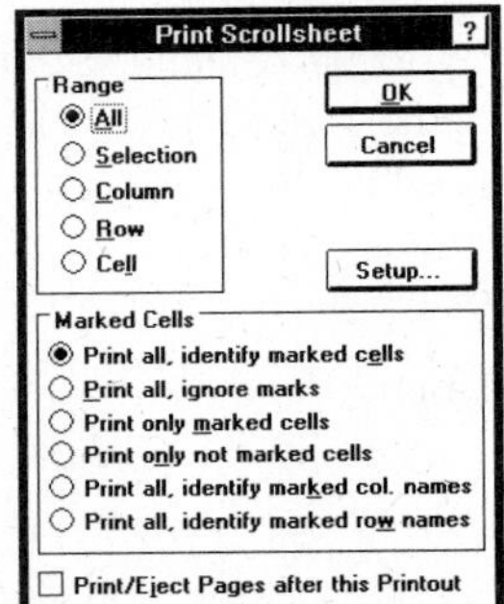

Shortcut. Click on the *Print* toolbar button (see below) to bypass the *Print Data* dialog (i.e., the previously selected settings or the default settings will be used) and print the Scrollsheet. Note that if a block is selected in the Scrollsheet, then that block will be printed; otherwise, the entire Scrollsheet is printed.

Toolbar button. See the [button] button in the *Scrollsheet Window* toolbar.

Keyboard shortcut. CTRL+P

Range

Choose the range of the Scrollsheet to be printed.

All. Print all of the active Scrollsheet.

Selection. Print only the highlighted block of cells in the active Scrollsheet.

Column. Print only the column in which the cursor is located.

Row. Print only the row in which the cursor is located.

Cell. Print only the cell in which the cursor is located.

Marked Cells

The following options are printing options for marked cells in the Scrollsheet. Marked cells are cell entries that are manually marked using the *Mark Selection* option (page 1255) or cell entries that are marked by a *STATISTICA* analysis (i.e., in the case of a correlation analysis, significant correlations are marked).

Print all, identify marked cells. This option will print all of the selected Scrollsheet range (see above) and place an asterisk (*) to the right of each marked cell in the printout.

Print all, ignore marks. Print all of the selected Scrollsheet range (see above), but do not identify any of the marked cells.

Print only marked cells. Prints only the marked cells in the Scrollsheet. All of the column and row headings will be printed, but the unmarked cells will be empty (i.e., no entries in these cells).

Print all, identify marked column names. When there are marked cells in the selected Scrollsheet range (see above), choose this option to mark in the output only the *Column Name* associated with a marked cell instead of marking each individual cell.

Print all, identify marked row names. When there are marked cells in the selected Scrollsheet range (see above), choose this option to mark in the output only the *Row Name* associated with a marked cell instead of marking each individual cell.

Print/Eject Pages after this Printout

When selected, this option will cause the requested printout to automatically be sent to the printer or output file when you click *OK* in this dialog or when you press the *Print* button on the Scrollsheet toolbar (any other text previously left in the internal buffer will also be printed). Thus, each requested printout (table) will start on a new page. If this option is de-selected, then output will be stored in the internal buffer and sent to the printer depending on the current setting of the check box *Automatically Eject Each Filled Page* (either whenever there is enough to fill one page or all at once later, e.g., when you exit the module or when you empty the buffer by using the option *Print/Eject Current Pages*, see page 1244). Note that this option will only apply locally (temporarily) to the current *STATISTICA* module and the current session whereas, selecting the *Print/Eject Pages after Each Printout* option in the *Page/Output Setup* dialog (see page 1246), will apply globally (permanently).

Setup

Click on this button to open the *Text Output Printer Setup* dialog (see below) in which you can select the quality (i.e., resolution) of the printout and the number of copies.

Text Output Printer Setup

This dialog (accessible from the *Print Data* dialog, see above, via the *Setup* button) allows you to select the print quality (i.e., resolution) and number of copies for the text output.

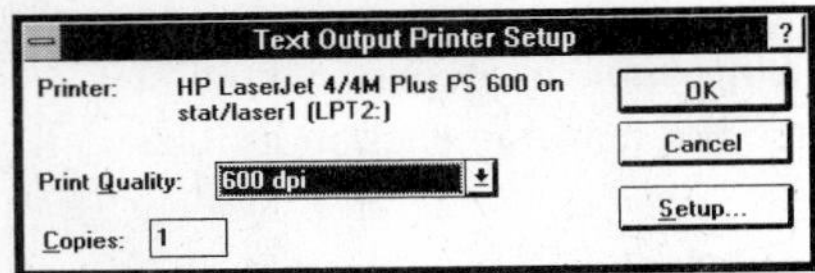

The selected printer is also displayed in this dialog and can be changed by clicking on the *Setup* button to open the *Print Setup* dialog (see page 1247).

In the *Print Setup* dialog, you can choose a printer from among those installed on your computer, select the print orientation, and paper size and source for printing graphs and text output.

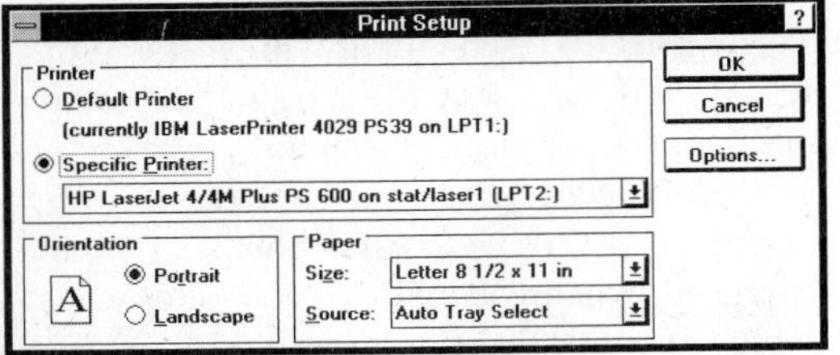

Note that the margins of text output can be adjusted in the *Text Output Margins* dialog (accessible by clicking on the *Margins* button in the *Page/Output Setup* dialog, see below).

Print Graph and Scrollsheet Files

This option (available from the *File* pull-down menu) allows you to print previously saved graphs and Scrollsheets in batch. This option is useful if you want to batch print graphs and Scrollsheets at a later time. You simply save the graphs or Scrollsheets (via the *Scrollsheet Save* or *Save Graph* options, see page 1243) after you make them, then at a later time open this dialog, select the desired graphs and Scrollsheets (see above) and click *OK* to begin the batch printing process.

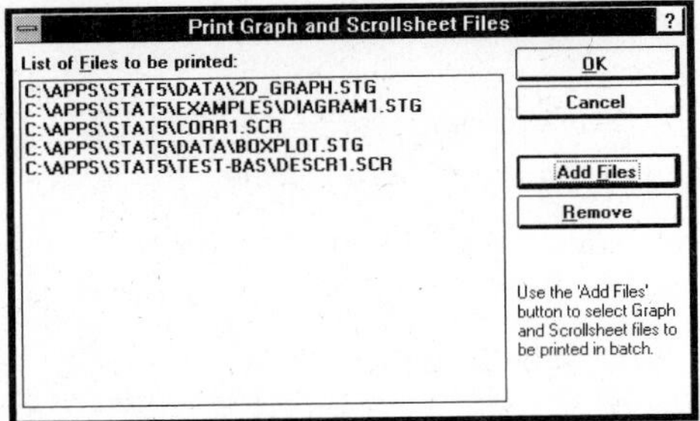

When you click *OK* in this dialog, all of the selected graphs will be printed first (on separate pages, in the order in which they are selected), and then all of the Scrollsheets will be printed together (in the order in which they are selected).

For more information on this option, refer to Chapter 3.

Page/Output Setup

This multi-layer dialog allows you to specify the output destination, amount of supplemental information, margin settings, and other options and can be accessed either by double-clicking the *Output* field of the window status bar, from the *Page/Output Setup* option of the *File* pull-down menu, or from the *Print* option of the *Options* pull-down menu. All of the selections that you make here will become default selections and will be applied globally whenever you open a *STATISTICA* module.

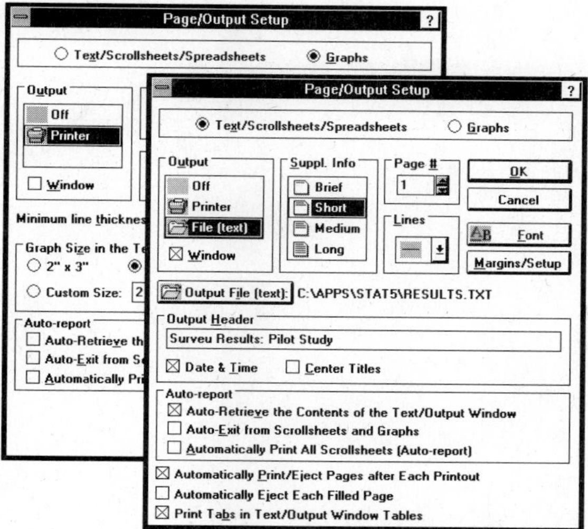

Before printing the text, spreadsheet, or Scrollsheet, select the destination (printer, output file, and/or *Text/output Window* in the *Text/Scrollsheets-/Spreadsheets* layer, or printer and/or *Text/output Window* in the *Graphs* layer) for the output as well as other options from the respective layer of the *Page/Output Setup* dialog.

For more information on this option, refer to Chapter 3.

Printer Setup

Selecting this option from the *File* pull-down menu will open the *Print Setup* dialog in which you can choose a printer, the print orientation, and paper size and source for printing graphs and text output.

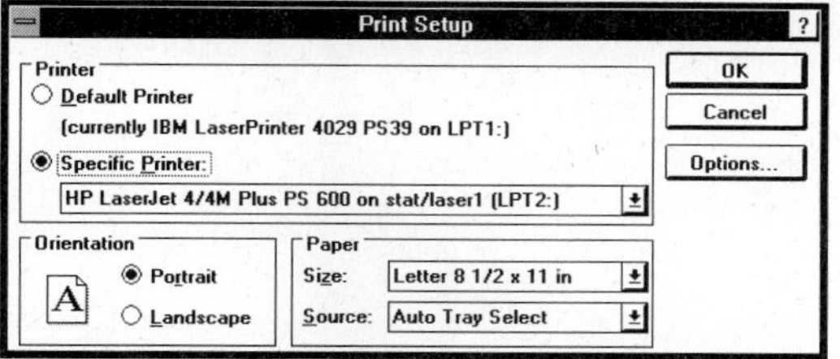

Note that you can maintain separate print selections for graphs and text output (i.e., output from Scrollsheets or spreadsheets).

For more information on this option, refer to Chapter 3.

Exit

Select this option to end your *STATISTICA* session. If you have made any changes to spreadsheets, Scrollsheets, text, or graphs and *Exit* before saving them, *STATISTICA* will prompt you to save the modified objects.

Keyboard Shortcut. ALT+F4

SCROLLSHEET *EDIT* PULL-DOWN MENU

The following dialogs and options are available from the Scrollsheet *Edit* pull-down menu.

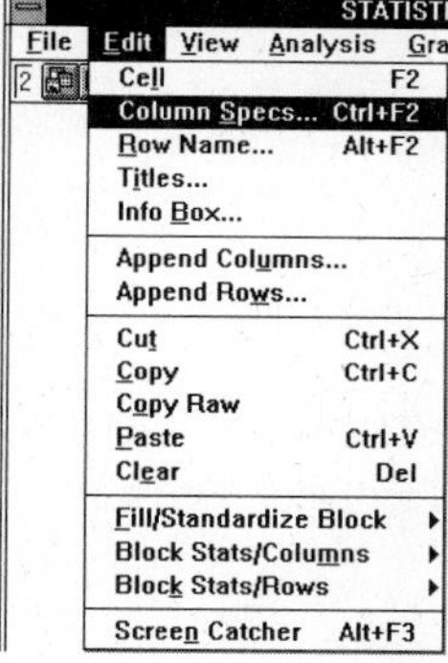

Each of these options is described below.

Scrollsheet Edit Cell

The Scrollsheet *Edit Cell* option allows you to edit the currently highlighted cell in the Scrollsheet without overwriting it. After selecting it, this option is dimmed until you have completed editing the cell.

Keyboard shortcut: F2 or double-click on the cell.

Scrollsheet Edit Column Specs

Edit the column specifications of the currently highlighted column by selecting the *Column Specs* option from the Scrollsheet *Edit* pull-down menu (or, alternatively, double-click on the *Column Name*) to bring up the *Scrollsheet Column Specs* dialog.

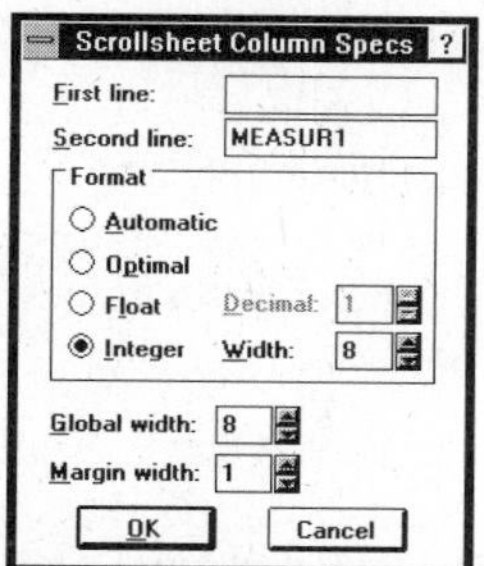

Each column's specifications are edited separately from the others [with the exception of the *Global Width* and *Margin Width* options (see below) which apply to all of the columns in the Scrollsheet].

Keyboard shortcut. CTRL+F2

First Line

Enter the first line of the column heading here. The length of each line of the column heading is limited to the current column width (see *Global Width* below) and can contain any printable characters. If the second line (see below) is empty and the text of the first line is larger than the current column width, then the text will continue to the second line (when displayed in the Scrollsheet), but it will still be edited in this field.

Second Line

Enter the second line of the column heading here. Again, the length is limited to the current column width, and the column heading can contain any printable characters.

Format

Format the display of the Scrollsheet column values using one of the options described below.

Automatic. This option will automatically line up all of the numbers in the column according to the largest number (whether positive or negative) so that the decimal point is in the same position in every cell in the column.

Optimal. The column values will not be aligned by the decimal point if this option is selected, but instead each cell will be adjusted separately to be "optimally" displayed. Based on the *Global Width* and *Margin Width* specifications, the column values will fill the width of the column.

Float. When this option is selected, you can specify the number of decimal points for the values in that column. The minimum number of decimal points is 1 and the maximum number is 15.

Integer. This option will round off any decimal values to integers. Specify the width (minimum = 1, maximum = current column width) to define the display of the integer values.

Global Width

The value entered here (minimum = 1, maximum = 80) determines the width of every column in the Scrollsheet. (This is a global operation, i.e., whatever value you specify here will be applied to every column in the Scrollsheet.) This option can also be accessed in the *Customize Width* dialog (page 1253).

Margin Width

The values in each column can have a pre-specified margin on both sides in order to separate the values in one column from those in another. This option will allow you to specify the width of the margin (minimum = 0, maximum = 10) for every column in the Scrollsheet. (This is a global operation, i.e., whatever value you specify here will be applied to every column in the Scrollsheet.) This option can also be accessed in the *Customize Width* dialog (page 1253).

Scrollsheet Edit Row Name

You can edit the currently highlighted Scrollsheet *Row Name* by selecting this option (or double-clicking on the *Row Name* in the Scrollsheet) to bring up the *Scrollsheet Row Name* dialog.

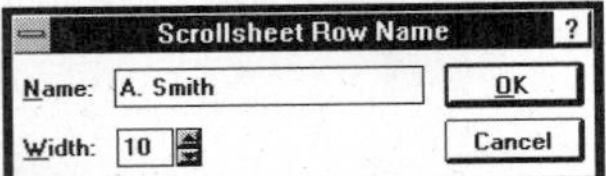

Keyboard shortcut. ALT+F2

Name

Enter/edit the *Row Name* here. The *Row Name* can be up to 40 characters in length and can contain any printable characters.

Width

Enter here a number (minimum = 1, maximum = 40) that will specify (globally) the width of the *Row Names* in the Scrollsheet. You can also specify the global width of *Row Names* in the *Customize Width* dialog (page 1253).

Scrollsheet Edit Titles

Edit Scrollsheet titles in the *Scrollsheet Titles* dialog, accessed either from the *Edit* pull-down menu or by double-clicking on the title area of the Scrollsheet.

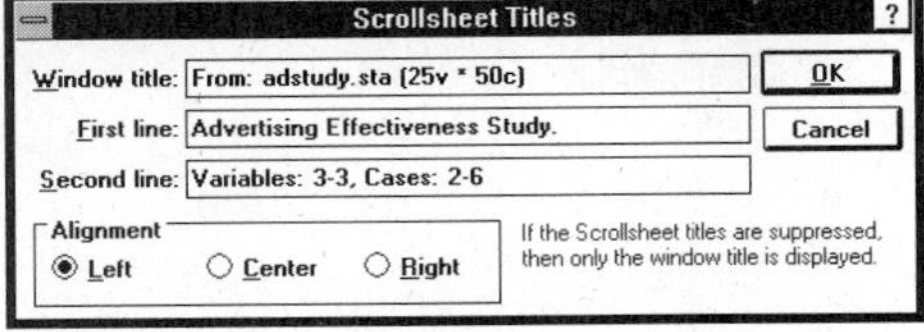

Window Title

By default, the *Window Title* will contain the name of the analysis performed as well as the data file name. You can edit those entries here.

First Line

In addition to the *Window Title*, you are allowed two more lines of Scrollsheet titles. Enter the first title (up to 63 printable characters) for the Scrollsheet here.

Second Line

Enter the second line (up to 63 printable characters) of the Scrollsheet title here. You do not have to use two lines of titles for the Scrollsheet; however, the area reserved in the Scrollsheet for the titles will not be reduced if only one title line is used. Note that when the *Titles* option of the *View* pull-down menu (page 1255) is unchecked (de-selected), then these two titles will not be displayed in the Scrollsheet.

Alignment

Choose to *Center* the *First* and *Second Titles*, or *Left*- or *Right*-justify them in the Scrollsheet.

Scrollsheet Edit Info Box

The *Info Box* is an area to the left of the *Titles* (sometimes temporarily under the *Continue* button) in the Scrollsheet that can be used to further customize the Scrollsheet. You can edit entries in the *Info Box* in the *Scrollsheet Info Box* dialog.

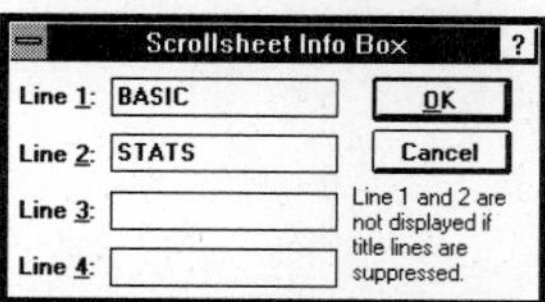

Enter up to 4 lines of Scrollsheet information here. Each of the 4 line entries can only be as long as the current row width (as specified in the *Row Name Width* dialog (page 1250).

Line 1

By default, *STATISTICA* records the statistics module that you are in on this line and continues it (if necessary) in *Line 2*.

Line 2

This line is, by default, a continuation of the module name from *Line 1*. Note that if the Scrollsheet title is suppressed (i.e., *Titles* is de-selected in the *View* pull-down menu, see page 1255), then *Lines 1* and *2* are not displayed in the *Info Box*.

Line 3

By default, this line is left blank in most Scrollsheets.

Line 4

This last line is reserved (by default) for the *Row Names* heading: e.g., *Variables*.

You may edit the text in each of the 4 lines.

Scrollsheet Append Columns/Rows

The *Append Columns* and *Append Rows* options will allow you to add blank columns or rows after the last column or row in the current Scrollsheet.

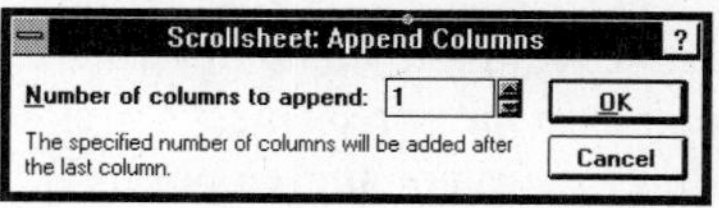

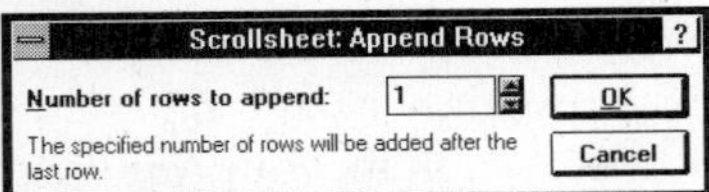

When you click on the appropriate option from the Scrollsheet *Edit* pull-down menu, the resulting dialog will ask you to specify the number of columns or rows that you want to add. Click *OK* in the dialog to add the specified number of rows or columns to the Scrollsheet. The new space can be used for notes or information copied from Scrollsheets or other screens.

Scrollsheet Clipboard Operations

The *Cut*, *Copy*, *Copy Raw*, *Paste*, and *Clear* Clipboard operations are similar to those available in the spreadsheet window. For more information on these operations, see Chapter 3.

Fill/Standardize Blocks

The operations available from this menu option, *Fill Random Values*, *Fill/Copy Down*, *Fill/Copy Right*, *Standardize Rows*, and *Standardize Columns* are similar to those available in the spreadsheet window.

For more information on these options, see Chapter 3.

Block Stats/Rows and Columns

The operations available from this menu option are similar to those available in the spreadsheet window. For more information on these options, see the Chapter 3.

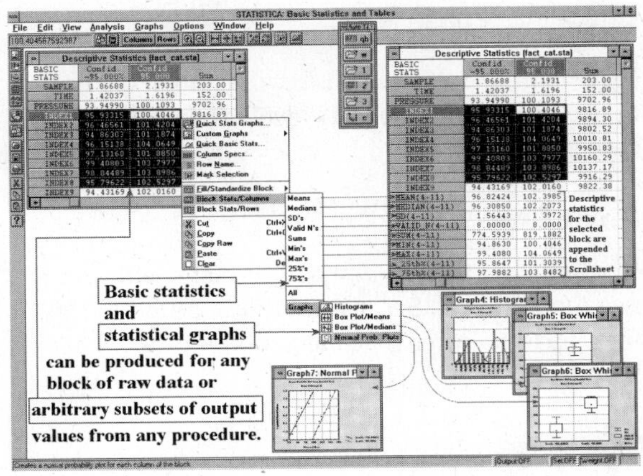

Screen Catcher

This option (accessible from the Scrollsheet *Edit* pull-down menu and also at any point in the program by pressing ALT+F3) invokes the *Screen Catcher*, a utility which allows you to select any rectangular area of the screen (or the entire screen) and copy it as a bitmap to the Clipboard. The copied area may contain graphs, Scrollsheets, spreadsheets, or even screens from other applications (if they are currently displayed on the screen). The copied bitmap may then be pasted into *STATISTICA* graphs or any other application which supports bitmaps. Please refer to Chapter 3 for more information and examples.

SCROLLSHEET *VIEW* PULL-DOWN MENU

The following dialogs and options are available from the Scrollsheet *View* pull-down menu.

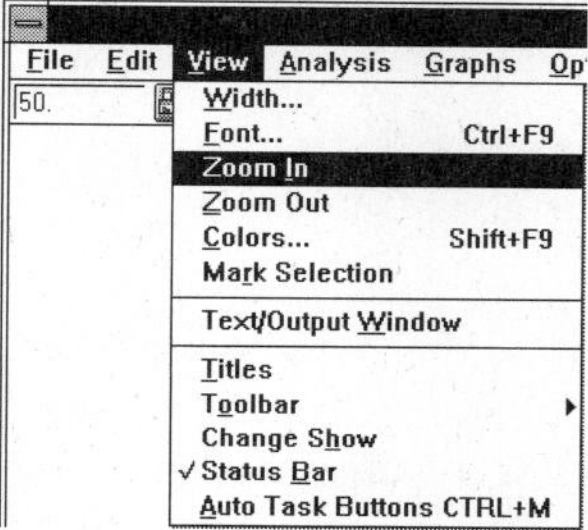

Each of these options are described below.

Scrollsheet View Width

Selecting this option from the *View* pull down-menu will open the *Customize Width* dialog in which you can edit the Scrollsheet *Column Width*, *Row Name Width*, and *Margin Width*. These options are global operations (i.e., the selections you make here will effect every column, row, or margin in the Scrollsheet).

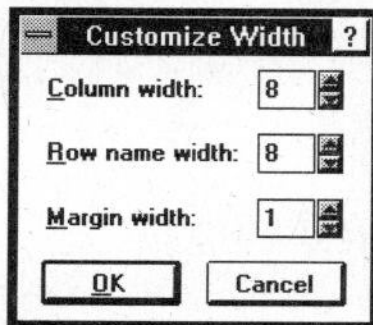

The *Column Width* and *Margin Width* can also be edited in the *Scrollsheet Column Specs* dialog (page 1249).

Toolbar button. See the button in the *Scrollsheet Window* toolbar.

Column Width

The value entered here (minimum = 1, maximum = 80) determines the width of every column in the Scrollsheet.

Row Name Width

Enter here a number (minimum = 1, maximum = 40) that will specify (globally) the width of the Row Names in the Scrollsheet. The Row Name width can also be specified in the *Scrollsheet Row Name* dialog (page 1250).

Margin Width

The values in each column can have a pre-specified margin on both sides in order to separate the values in one column from those in another. This option will allow you to specify the width of the margin (minimum = 0, maximum = 10) for every column in the Scrollsheet.

Note that the column width can also be adjusted interactively by dragging the border between column names or by pressing the and toolbar buttons.

Scrollsheet Font

Selecting the *Font* option from the *View* pull-down menu will bring up the Font dialog. You can edit the type of font, the font style, and the font size in the current Scrollsheet. As you make your selections, you can view a sample of text in the *Sample* window of this dialog. This same dialog is displayed when selecting the display font for spreadsheets; see Chapter 3 for details.

To select a default font for all new Scrollsheets, select *Display* from the *Options* pull-down menu (see page 1261)

Scrollsheet Zoom In

This option allows you to increase the Scrollsheet font (in increments defined by the font type) by clicking the Scrollsheet toolbar button (see below) to incrementally increase the font size.

Descriptive Statistics (adstudy.sta)

Variable	Valid N	Mean	Confid. -95.000%
MEASUR1	50	5.440000	4.743484
MEASUR2	50	4.540000	3.719507
MEASUR3	50	4.140000	3.365389

When you first click on this button, the *Zoom Options* dialog (see below) may open (depending on the type of font in the Scrollsheet), warning you that the current font may not zoom (scale) continuously and offering you the option to change to a different font.

You can also decrease the font (see *Scrollsheet Zoom Out*, below) in the Scrollsheet in the same increments that you increased it.

Toolbar button. See the button in the *Scrollsheet Window* toolbar.

Scrollsheet Zoom Out

This option allows you to decrease the Scrollsheet font (in increments defined by the font type) by clicking the Scrollsheet Toolbar button (see below) to incrementally decrease the font size.

Descriptive Statistics (economic.sta)

Variable	Valid N	Mean	Minimum	Maximum	Std.Dev.
PRIME_RT	7	8.483	6.250	10.870	1.7688
G_D_P	7	4829.929	4540.000	5088.200	170.4904
INFLATN	7	4.043	3.000	5.400	.8696

When you first click on this button, the *Zoom Options* dialog (see below) may open (depending on the type of font in the Scrollsheet), warning you that the current font may not zoom (scale) continuously and offering you the option to change to a different font.

You can also increase the fonts (see *Scrollsheet Zoom In*, above) in the Scrollsheet in the same increments by which they were decreased.

Toolbar button. See the button in the *Scrollsheet Window* toolbar.

Zoom Options Dialog

When you first click on either the *Zoom In* or *Zoom Out* toolbar buttons (see Chapter 2), or select either the *Scrollsheet Zoom In* or *Scrollsheet Zoom Out* option (see above), the *Zoom Options* dialog will open if the current font will not zoom (scale) continuously.

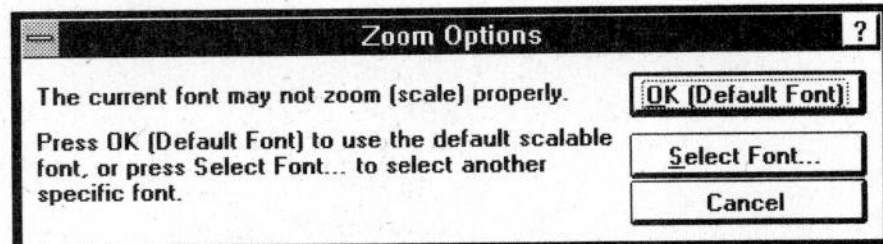

Some fonts do not scale continuously, but only in relatively large increments.

OK (Default Font)

Click this button to accept the default font and exit this dialog in order to increase the font.

Select Font

Click on this button to open the *Font* dialog in order to select a different font for the Scrollsheet or spreadsheet.

Scrollsheet Colors

Customizes the colors of the current Scrollsheets and spreadsheets in the *Customize Colors* dialog. You can view the color changes in the sample

Scrollsheet/spreadsheet below the selections in this dialog before finalizing your choices. Each of the options available in this dialog will open the standard *Color* dialog, where you can select colors from a standard color palette or customize a color (via the *Define Custom Colors* button). This same dialog is displayed when selecting the display colors for spreadsheets; see Chapter 3 for details.

To select default colors for all new Scrollsheets, select *Display* from the *Options* pull-down menu (see page 1261)

Mark Selection

This option (available also from the toolbar and the pop-up right-mouse-button menu from every cell) allows you to mark (or un-mark) individual values or a block of values in the Scrollsheet to make them stand out from the rest. Highlight the cells in the Scrollsheet with the cursor and then select the *Mark Selection* option from the *View* pull-down menu. The marked Scrollsheet values will be identified by a color other than the default data value color (by default, marked values appear red, see *Options - Display*, page 1261) in the *STATISTICA* window and when printed, by default, will be identified with an * (asterisk) next to the value (other options to handle marked cells in printed or saved reports are available and can be selected in the *Print Scrollsheet* dialog, page 1244).

Specific cells or blocks appear already marked in many Scrollsheets (at the point when they are initially generated) in order to "highlight" statistically significant results (e.g., correlation coefficients). Such Scrollsheets usually offer an option to change the criterion used to select the cells to be highlighted (e.g., the significance level) via the *Options* button on the Scrollsheet toolbar (see below).

Toolbar button. See the button in the *Scrollsheet Window* toolbar.

Options Scrollsheet Toolbar Button

This Scrollsheet toolbar button will allow you to change (or select) a specific option (depending on the *STATISTICA* module you are using) that will affect the results in the Scrollsheet.

Options

For example, in some correlation matrices, this button will open a dialog allowing you to set the threshold significance level for correlation coefficients which will be marked in the Scrollsheet (by default $p = .05$).

Text/output Window

Similar to the *Text/ouput Window* option in the spreadsheet *View* pull-down menu, selecting this option will open the *Text/output Window* in which the printed output (text and graphs) can be directed or notes can be taken. For more information, see Chapter 5.

Scrollsheet View Titles

With this option, you can choose to display the Scrollsheet with a title (when checked, a one- or two-line title will be included in the Scrollsheet display), or without a title (*Title* will appear unchecked in the *View* pull-down menu).

De-selecting the titles will only suppress the display (i.e., it will not delete the title information). You can edit the title by double-clicking on the title area of the Scrollsheet (or select the *Titles* option from the *Edit* pull-down menu) to open the *Scrollsheet Titles* dialog (page 1250).

Scrollsheet View Toolbar

When you click on this option from the *View* pull-down menu, you will be able to select from several ways to display the toolbar (described below) in the window or you can toggle between displaying the toolbar and hiding it.

Off. Select this option to temporarily remove the toolbar from the window. (In order to once again display the toolbar, select one of the options described below.)

1 line. When you select this option, the toolbar will be displayed in one line in the spreadsheet window.

2 lines. Select this option to display the toolbar buttons in two lines.

Right & Top. This option will display half of the toolbar at the top of the window and the other half along the right side of the window.

Left & Top. This option will display half of the toolbar at the top of the window and the other half along the left side of the window.

Large Buttons. Select this option to toggle between displaying normal and large buttons in the toolbar (when checked, large toolbar buttons will be displayed, which may be desirable when using higher resolutions, e.g., 1024x768).

Shortcut. Double-click on the toolbar to rotate through the different configurations.

Change Show

Change Show displays the contents of the currently highlighted cell (or cursor position in graphs) in the *Show* field. Click on this option to toggle between the 3 sizes (lengths) of the *Show* field (see Chapter 2).

When the display width of the columns (as specified in the *Scrollsheet Column Specs* dialog, page 1249) is less than necessary to see all significant digits, use this option to adjust the *Show* field length and view the full length of the value. Alternatively, click on the *Show* window with the mouse.

Scrollsheet View Status Bar

Toggle between displaying the Scrollsheet window status bar (the bar at the bottom of the screen, see Chapter 2) and hiding it with this option. When checked, the status bar will be displayed. While executing a task, *STATISTICA* will use the status bar to display the progress of the task.

Comment

This area of the status bar is reserved for a brief (one line) description of the highlighted pull-down or cell-related menu or option. When nothing is highlighted (data are not being processed and *STATISTICA* is waiting for the next command), the word *Ready* is displayed. Double-click on the comment area in the status bar to open the main *Help* menu.

Output

Displays the current destination (as specified in the *Page/Output Setup* dialog, page 1246) for the output of an analysis. Double-click on *Output* in the status bar to open the *Page/Output Setup* dialog from which you can select the output destination (*Off*, *File*, *Printer*, and/or *Window*) and other output options.

Sel

Displays the current status (*On* or *Off*) of the case selection conditions. Double-click on *Sel* in the

status bar to open the *Case Selection Conditions* dialog from which you can specify the case selection conditions (see Chapter 2).

Weight

Displays the current status (*On* or *Off*) of the variable weighting conditions. Double-click on *Weight* in the status bar to open the *Define Weight* dialog from which you can specify the variable weighting conditions (see Chapter 2).

REC

This message will flash in the right-hand side of the status bar when you are recording a macro (either a sequence of keystrokes or mouse movements). For more information on recording macros, see Chapter 6, *Auto Task Buttons*

Scrollsheet Auto Task Buttons

This option allows you to toggle on and off the display of the *Auto Task Buttons* toolbar. Note that any Hot Keys assigned to *Auto Task Buttons* can be used regardless of the display setting of the toolbar.

Keyboard shortcut. CTRL+M.

Please refer to Chapter 6 for more information on *Auto Task Buttons*.

SCROLLSHEET *ANALYSIS* PULL-DOWN MENU

The following dialogs and options are available from the Scrollsheet *Analysis* pull-down menu.

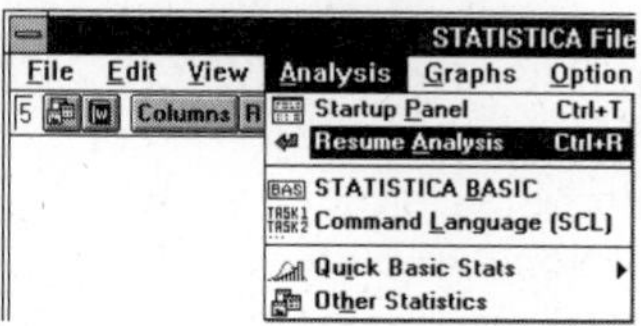

These options are discussed below.

Startup Panel

When you select this option from the *Analysis* pull-down menu, a window will open in which you can select an analysis from those available in the active *STATISTICA* module. The specific contents of the startup panel depend on the module (the example below shows the startup panel for the *Basic Statistics and Tables* module).

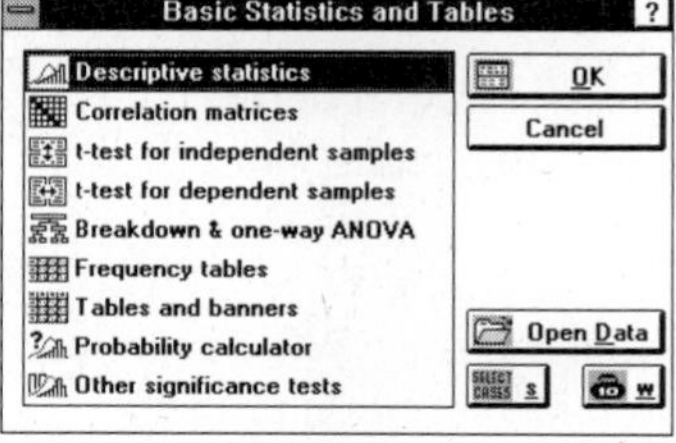

Select the desired analysis by double-clicking on it or by highlighting it and then clicking the *OK* button.

Keyboard shortcut. CTRL+T

Resume Analysis

When the analysis that you are performing is still active, but the current analysis control dialog is minimized (the analysis icon appears in the lower left-hand corner of the screen), select this option to resume the analysis (open the analysis dialog). Alternatively, you can double-click on the [Cont] icon to resume the analysis or (in most cases) click on the *Continue* button (see below) in the upper-left corner of the current Scrollsheet or graph window.

Keyboard shortcut. CTRL+R

Scrollsheet *Continue* Button/Option

Data analysis sometimes results in several Scrollsheets of results. When the number of Scrollsheets produced is greater than the Scrollsheet queue (see *Scrollsheet Manager*, in Chapter 3), a *Continue* button will appear on the last Scrollsheet displayed. Clicking this button will continue the queue and open the next Scrollsheet of results.

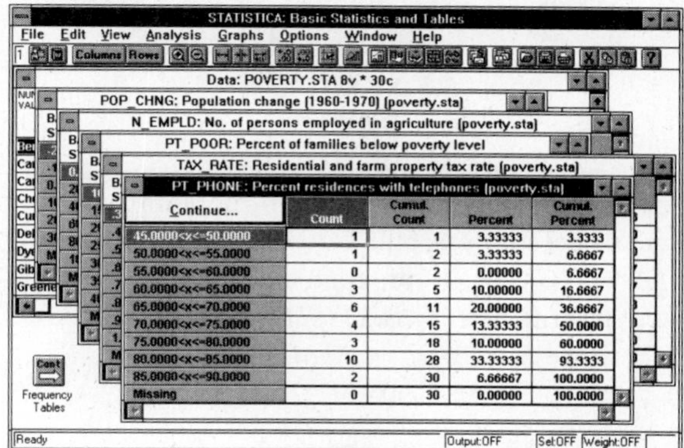

Continue...	Count	Cumul. Count	Percent	Cumul. Percent
45.0000<x<=50.0000	1	1	3.33333	3.3333
50.0000<x<=55.0000	1	2	3.33333	6.6667
55.0000<x<=60.0000	0	2	0.00000	6.6667
60.0000<x<=65.0000	3	5	10.00000	16.6667
65.0000<x<=70.0000	6	11	20.00000	36.6667
70.0000<x<=75.0000	4	15	13.33333	50.0000
75.0000<x<=80.0000	3	18	10.00000	60.0000
80.0000<x<=85.0000	10	28	33.33333	93.3333
85.0000<x<=90.0000	2	30	6.66667	100.0000
Missing	0	30	0.00000	100.0000

If only one Scrollsheet is produced from an analysis (or if it is the last Scrollsheet in the queue), clicking on the *Continue* button will bring up the previous analysis dialog.

Note that you can also re-open the analysis dialog and suppress displaying any additional Scrollsheets which may be waiting in the queue by double-clicking on the analysis icon in the lower corner of the *STATISTICA* window.

Scrollsheet *Continue* and "Floating" *Cont*

There is no difference between the functions of these two buttons as long as the number of Scrollsheets or graphs generated in one sequence by an analysis is not longer than the current "length of the queue" of Scrollsheets or graphs (by default 3). However, when more document windows are about to be generated than can fit in the current queue, then:

- pressing the *Continue* button on the Scrollsheet or graph will proceed with generating the consecutive Scrollsheets and graphs which are waiting in the sequence, while
- pressing the "floating" *Cont* button on the bottom of the screen -- which, in fact, represents the iconized output selection dialog -- will bring up the dialog, breaking the sequence of consecutive Scrollsheets or graphs.

STATISTICA BASIC

Selecting the *STATISTICA BASIC* option from the Scrollsheet *Analysis* pull-down menu will open the *STATISTICA BASIC* program editor window. For more information on *STATISTICA BASIC*, please refer to the *Electronic Manual.*

Command Language

Selecting the *Command Language* option from the spreadsheet *Analysis* pull-down menu will open the *STATISTICA Command Language (SCL)* program editor window. For more information on the *STATISTICA Command Language*, please refer to the *Electronic Manaul.*

Quick Basic Stats

The *Quick Basic Stats* options are available from either the spreadsheet or Scrollsheet right-mouse-button flying menu or from the *Analysis* pull-down menu of any module of *STATISTICA*. *Quick Basic Statistics* can be used at any point of your data analysis (e.g., to provide supplementary information when you review output from any *STATISTICA* module). These procedures include a selection of basic statistics which can be performed on long lists of variables (e.g., correlation indices for *all* variables in the data set), and all analyses can be performed *by groups*, for every value (i.e., code) of a selected grouping variable.

If *Quick Basic Stats* are called from the Scrollsheet pull-down menu *Analysis*, then the variables to be analyzed are selected via subsequent variable selection dialogs.For more information on *Quick Basic Stats*, see Chapter 10.

Other Statistics (*STATISTICA* Module Switcher)

Selecting the *Other Statistics* option in the Scrollsheet *Analysis* pull-down menu will bring up the *STATISTICA Module Switcher* dialog. This dialog contains a list box of all the *STATISTICA* modules to which you can transfer. Whenever you highlight a module, a brief description of that module appears in the dialog.

Toolbar button. See the [button] button in the Scrollsheet toolbar.

Shortcut. Click the right-mouse-button on the application background in order to bring up this global flying menu. You can also double-click on the application background (analogous to double-clicking on the desktop in order to open the *Windows Task Switcher*).

SCROLLSHEET *GRAPHS* PULL-DOWN MENU

The graphic options in the *Graphs* pull-down menu are discussed in detail in Volume II of the manual.

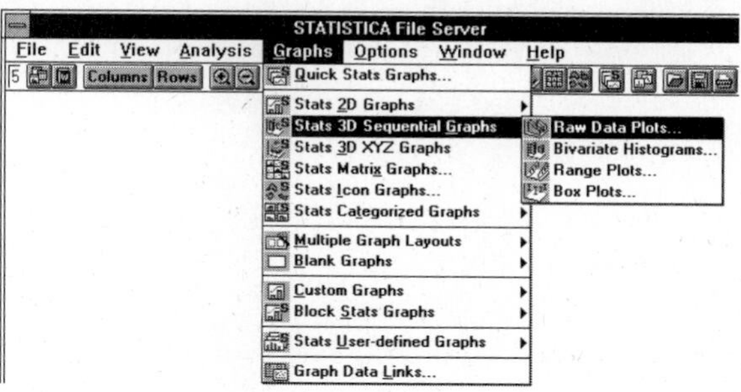

A brief overview of these graphics options is included in Chapter 2.

SCROLLSHEET *OPTIONS* PULL-DOWN MENU

The following dialogs and options are available from the Scrollsheet *Options* pull-down menu.

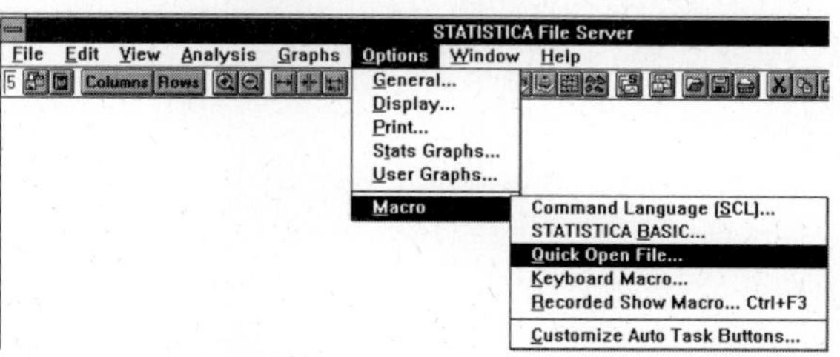

With the exception of the *Stats Graphs* and *User Graphs* options (which are discussed in Volume II of the manual), each of these options are discussed in detail in Chapter 3.

SCROLLSHEET *WINDOW* PULL-DOWN MENU

The following dialogs and options are available from the Scrollsheet *Window* pull-down menu.

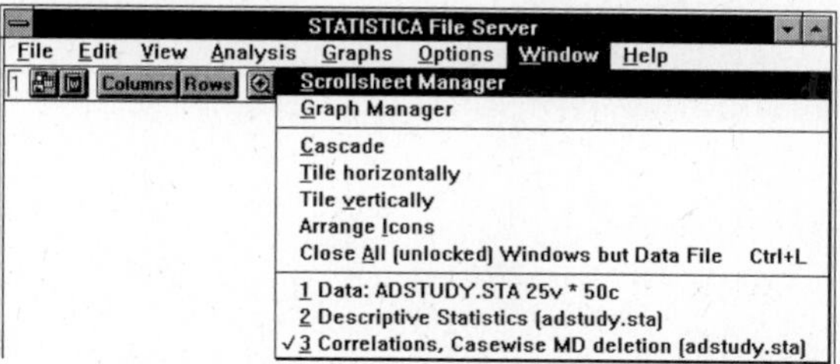

Each of these options are described in Chapter 3.

SCROLLSHEET *HELP* PULL-DOWN MENU

The following dialogs and options are available from the Scrollsheet *Help* pull-down menu.

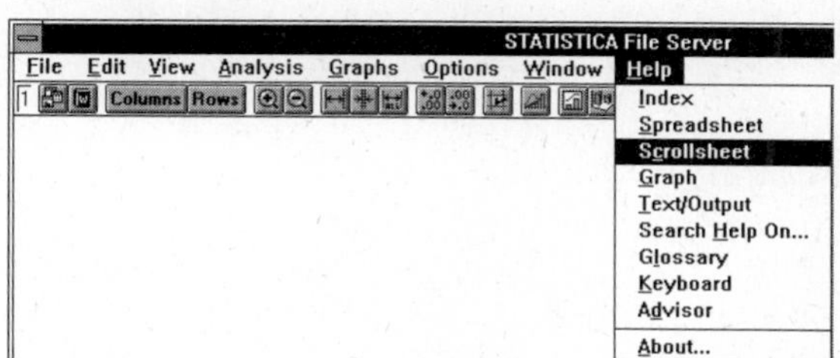

Each of these options opens a *Help* window with information concerning the general topic (see Chapter 3 more information on each topic).

INDEX

V

Z

Chapter 5:

TEXT/OUTPUT WINDOW: MENUS, DIALOGS, OPTIONS

Table of Contents

Detailed Table of Contents

StatSoft®

StatSoft

Chapter 5:

TEXT/OUTPUT WINDOW: MENUS, DIALOGS, OPTIONS

INTRODUCTORY OVERVIEW

The *Text/output Window* works in a manner similar to a word processor; it is *RTF*-compatible (*R*ich *T*ext *F*ormat, it supports formatted text and graphs, see page 1271), and allows you to manage text/graphics reports of practically unlimited size.

The *Text/output Window* can be used:

(1) to review/edit a log of output which was displayed in consecutive Scrollsheets and/or graphs in the course of analyses (options are provided to automatically direct all text and/or graphics output to this report facility, see page 1271);

(2) to open (and review/edit) output files or any other text or text and graphics (*RTF*) files; and

(3) as a local text and graph notepad.

Each of those three applications is briefly described in the following paragraphs.

Log of Selected (or All) Scrollsheets and Graphs

In order to open a *Text/output Window* for output, check the *Text/output Window* option in the pull-down menu *View*. The window will open and then whenever you direct a spreadsheet, graph, Scrollsheet, or a selected block of cells to the output, it will appear in the window.

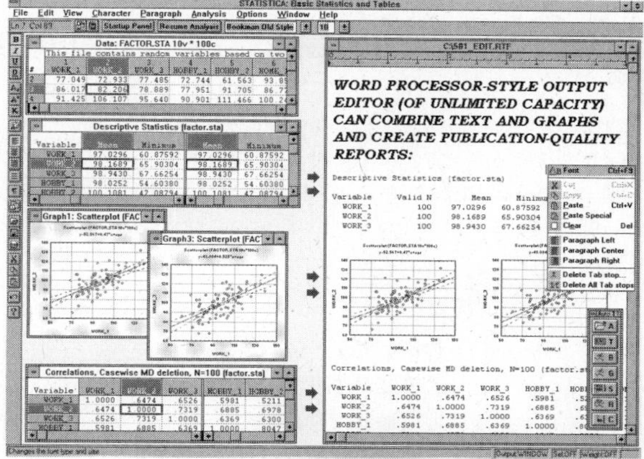

This output channel can also be requested in the *Page/Output Setup* dialog (accessible by double-clicking on the *Output* field on the status bar at the bottom of the *STATISTICA* window, or from the *Print* option in the *Options* pull-down menu).

If the *Printer* or *File* output is also selected in that dialog, the output will be directed simultaneously to the *Text/output Window* and that other channel. Alternatively, you could select one of the *Auto-report* options (see Chapter 6), and then as each Scrollsheet and/or graph is displayed on the screen it will simultaneously be sent to the currently specified output channels, and thus, also to the *Text/output Window* (if one is open).

Reviewing Text Files

Independent of the current *Text/output Window* which was opened for output (see the previous paragraph), previously-saved text files can be opened in new text windows by choosing the *Text/output...* option in the sub-menu of the option *Open Other* (pull-down menu *File*). All text (ASCII) files and formatted (**.rtf*) files with

graphics can be opened in a *Text/output Window* and edited.

Notepads

Regardless of how a *Text/output Window* was opened (see the previous two paragraphs), it can always be used as a notepad (you can enter/edit text or paste text and graphs or other artwork via the Clipboard).

OPENING THE *TEXT/OUTPUT* WINDOW

STATISTICA provides several ways in which to open the *Text/output Window*. After opening, you can direct all output and graphs to this window.

If you set any of the *Auto Report* options (e.g., *Automatically Print All Scrollsheets*) in the *Page/Output Setup* dialog (see Chapter 3), then the respective output (e.g., graphs or contents of each Scrollsheet displayed on the screen) will also be automatically directed to the *Text/output Window*.

Opening via the *STATISTICA Defaults: General* Dialog

Select the *Open Text/output Window* option from the *STATISTICA Defaults: General* dialog in order to automatically open a *Text/output Window* each time a *STATISTICA* module opens (see the third check box in the *STATISTICA Startup Options* group).

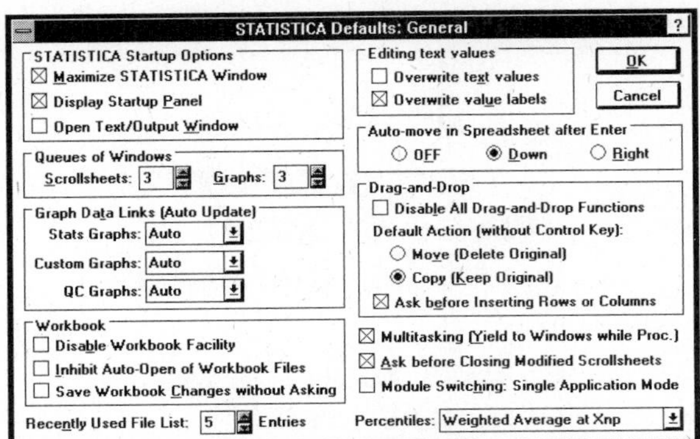

Once selected, this option will become the system default until you de-select it in this dialog.

Open Text File

You can open a previously saved text file (file name extension **.txt*) or *RTF* file (file name extension **.rtf*)

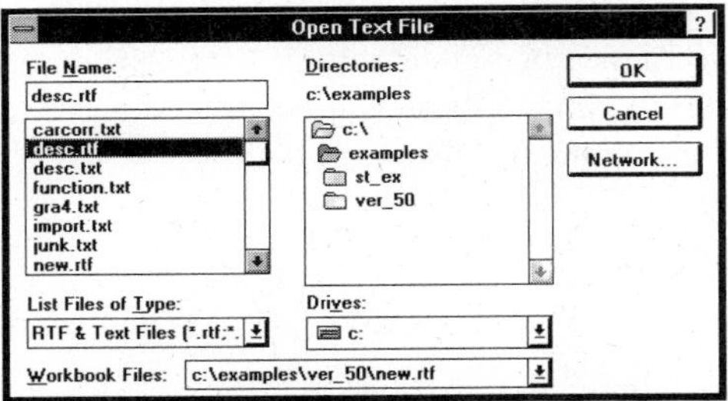

in the *Text/output Window* by selecting the *Open Text* option from the *File* pull-down menu, clicking on the toolbar button, or pressing CTRL+O to bring up the *Open Text File* dialog.

Text/output Window (from the *View* Menu)

When you select this option from the *View* pull-down menu, the most recently saved *Text/output Window* will open. All printed output will be

directed to this window (regardless of whether or not you are also printing to the printer or disk file).

Opening the *Text/output Window* from the *Page-/Output Setup* Dialog

Window

You can also open the *Text/output Window* by selecting the *Window* option in the *Page/Output Setup* dialog (see also Chapter 3).

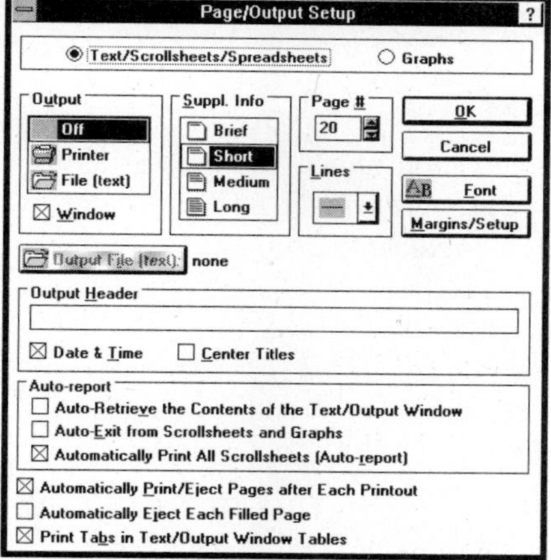

When you select this option, then independent of the output destination selected in this dialog (i.e., *File* or *Printer*), the output requested from Scrollsheets or spreadsheets will be sent to the *Text/output Window*. If the *Automatically Print All Scrollsheets/Graphs (Auto-report)* option is also selected in this dialog, then the output from analyses will automatically be "printed" to the *Text/output Window* (see below).

Auto-retrieve the contents of the *Text/output Window*

When you check this option in the *Page/Output Setup* dialog, *STATISTICA* will automatically open the most recently saved text (file name extension **.txt*) file or *R*ich *T*ext *F*ormat (file name extension **.rtf*) file in the new *Text/output Window* (e.g., in order to append the current output to the results of a previous analysis).

When this option is unchecked, then a blank *Text/output Window* will be opened from the *Page/Output Setup* dialog (when *Window* is selected, see above).

Automatically Print All Scrollsheets/Graphs (Auto Report)

If this mode of printing is selected in the *Page/Output Setup* dialog, then all output from analyses and/or graphs will automatically be printed either to the printer or to the output file and/or *Text/output Window* (if *Window* is selected in this dialog). This mode of printing is useful when you want to maintain a complete log of all output displayed during the course of the analysis. For more information, see Chapter 3.

SAVING *TEXT/OUTPUT WINDOW* FILES

The contents of the *Text/output Window* can be edited to include formatted text and graphics either from *STATISTICA* or other Windows applications. This information can be saved in two formats: as text files or *RTF* files. These two formats are described below.

RTF Files

RTF (*R*ich *T*ext *F*ormat) files are standard, formatted text and graphics files used in *STATISTICA* to store reports (i.e., output from the *Text/output Window*). When files are saved in Rich Text Format (**.rtf*), all of the file formatting is preserved so that it can be read and interpreted by other *RTF*-compatible applications (e.g., MS Word). The Rich Text Format (*RTF*) is a Microsoft standard method of encoding formatted text and graphics for easy transfer between applications.

Text Files

Unlike *RTF* files, when the contents of the *Text/output Window* are saved as a text file (file name extension **.txt*; use the *Save as Text* option, described below), none of the file formatting will be preserved. Therefore, the resulting file will not contain any graphs or formatting information (e.g., font, margins, page layout, etc.); however, it will be compatible with applications which do not support the *RTF* standard.

If you want to permanently store the text and/or graphs from the *Text/output Window* (including your notes or inserts pasted to the window), use the following options from the *File* pull-down menu.

Save

When you select this option, or click on the toolbar button, *STATISTICA* will save the contents of the *Text/output Window* under the current file name and extension (i.e., **.rtf* or **.txt*) without any intermediate dialog. In order to save the contents of the *Text/output Window* under a different file name or extension, use the *Save As* option described below.

Shortcut. Press CTRL+S.

Save As

Selecting this option (or pressing F12) will bring up the *Save File As* dialog

Shortcut. Press F12.

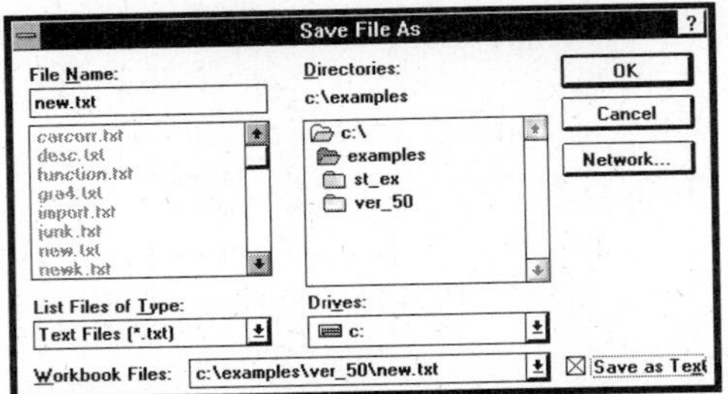

in which you can save the contents of the *Text/output Window* as a text file (file name extension **.txt*; use the *Save as Text* option, described below) or in *RTF* format (file name extension **.rtf*).

Save as Text

This option is only applicable to the *Text/output Window* [including *STATISTICA BASIC* program files, *Command Language* (*SCL*) program files, *SEPATH* command files, and all other applications of the *Text/output Window*]. Select this option in order to save the contents of the *Text/output Window* in the standard ASCII text format (file name extension **.txt*).

If this option is *not* selected, *STATISTICA* will save the file in the *RTF* format to preserve all special formatting (font, spacing, graphs, etc.). The default (*RTF*) format is normally preferable, but the resulting file cannot be edited with programs which do not support the *RTF* format. If you save it as text, the file can be processed by virtually any program; however, all formatting information and graphs will not be preserved.

PRINTING FROM THE *TEXT/OUTPUT WINDOW*

Due to its different status, printing from this facility is configured differently than printing from spreadsheets or Scrollsheets. When you press the *Print* button, press CTRL+P, or select the *Print*

All option from the *Text/output Window File* pull-down menu, the entire contents of the *Text/output Window* will be sent directly to the printer [regardless of the current setting of the *Output* field on the status bar (on the bottom of the *STATISTICA* window)], e.g., it will be sent to the printer even if the *Printer* output is turned *Off* or directed to an output file.

To print only a highlighted block of text from the *Text/output Window*, use the *Print Selection* option (see below). If you intend to keep a complete, permanent log of all output which is displayed on the screen, the quickest way to do so is to select some of the *Auto-report* options (available via the *Page/Output Setup* dialog, see Chapter 3). This will automatically direct the contents of all displayed output Scrollsheets and/or graphics windows to the *Text/output Window*.

Print Selection

Use this option from the *Text/output Window File* pull-down menu to print only the selected (highlighted) block of text in the *Text/output Window*.

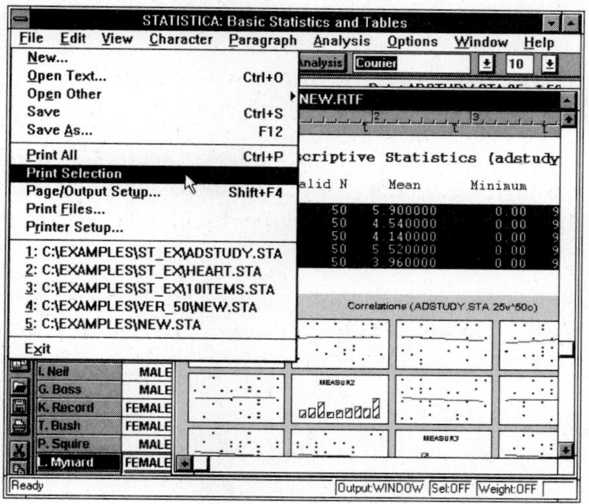

To print all of the text, use the *Print All* option from the *File* pull-down menu.

Text Output Margins

In this dialog (accessible by selecting the *Margins/Setup* option in the *Page/Output Setup* dialog), you can position the desired text (e.g., from the *Text/output Window*, or spreadsheets or Scrollsheets) on the printed page by adjusting the margins (specify the *Left*, *Top*, *Right*, and *Bottom* margin widths) according to a specific measure (*Percent*, *Centimeter*, or *Inch*).

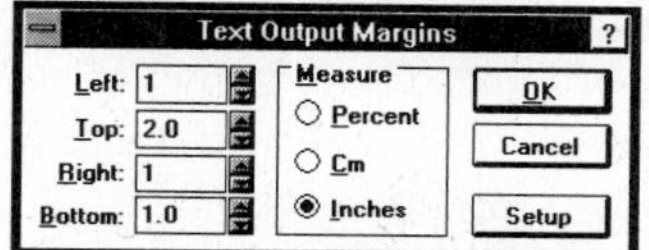

Note that these margin settings are independent of the margin settings for the graphics output (which can be adjusted in the *Print Preview* or *Graph Margins* dialogs).

To adjust the paper size and orientation (*portrait* or *landscape*) use the *Printer Setup* option in the pull-down menu *File*.

FORMATTING TEXT IN THE *TEXT/OUTPUT WINDOW*

The output from analyses as well as added text can be formatted to include specialized fonts or font attributes, specialized paragraph formatting, or embedded graphics or other objects. In order to save the formatted text in this window, save it as an *RTF* (*R*ich *T*ext *F*ormat) file (see page 1271).

Character Formatting

The following options control the format of characters in the *Text/output Window*. These options are accessible from the *Character* pull-down menu or, in some cases, from the *Text/output Window* toolbar (see *Text/output Window Toolbar Buttons*, Chapter 2). Where applicable, the keyboard shortcuts and toolbar buttons for these options are also given.

Font Size and Style

The *Font Selection* dialog (accessible by selecting *Font* in the *Character* pull-down menu or by pressing CTRL+F9) will allow you to change the font style (*Face Name*) and *Size* for either the highlighted text or new text in the *Text/output Window*.

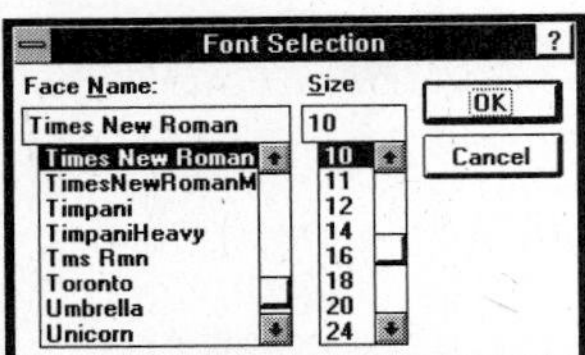

Alternatively, you can use the *Font Selection* field (see below) on the *Text/output Window* toolbar to select the desired font style and size.

Note that if the currently highlighted block of text in the *Text/output Window* contains different fonts, then the font type whose name is displayed in the *Font* field of the *Text/output Window* toolbar will be used if you insert new text or replace the block with new text.

Setting the default font. When a spreadsheet or Scrollsheet is printed to the *Text/output Window*, the font that is defined in the *Page/Output Setup* dialog (see Chapter 3) for spreadsheet and Scrollsheet output will be used as the default font in the *Text/output Window*. Therefore, if you want to print the spreadsheet or Scrollsheet in the *Text/output Window* using a special font, you will need to set that font style in the *Page/Output Setup* dialog.

If you are pasting text from another application, select *RTF* as the format in the *Paste Special* dialog (see page 1277) to paste the text into the *Text/output Window* using the source font style.

Font Attributes

The following font attributes are available in the *Text/output Window*.

Regular font. Select this option from the *Character* pull-down menu [or press CTRL+0 (zero)] to return the font to a regular character formatting (e.g., not italicized).

Bold font. Select this option (click on the B toolbar button or press CTRL+B) in order to make subsequent or highlighted characters **bold**.

Italic font. Select this option (click on the I toolbar button or press CTRL+I) in order to make *italicize* characters.

Underline. Select this option (click on the U toolbar button or press CTRL+U) in order to underline subsequent or highlighted characters.

Double underline. Select this option (click on the D toolbar button or press CTRL+D) in order to double underline subsequent or highlighted characters.

Subscript. Select this option (or click on the toolbar button) in order to subscript subsequent or highlighted characters (e.g., sub$_{\text{script}}$).

Superscript. Select this option (or click on the toolbar button) in order to superscript subsequent or highlighted characters (e.g., super^{script}).

Strikethrough. Select this option (or click on the toolbar button) in order to ~~strikethrough~~ subsequent or highlighted characters.

Hidden. Select this option from the *Character* pull-down menu in order to make subsequent or highlighted characters hidden. You can toggle on/off the display of hidden characters by pressing the ¶ toolbar button or selecting the *Show Hidden* option from the pull-down menu *View*.

Font Color

Select this option (or click on the toolbar button or press SHIFT+F9) in order to change the font color (via the standard Windows *Color* dialog).

Paragraph Formatting

The following options will allow you to control the formatting of paragraphs in the *Text/output Window*. Each of these options are available from the pull-down menu *Paragraph*. In addition, you can change the paragraph alignment and spacing by clicking on the respective toolbar button (see below). Note that you can toggle between showing and hiding the paragraph marks (¶) and hidden text in the window via the ¶ toolbar button or the *Show Hidden* option from the pull-down menu *View*.

Normal

Select this option to return the paragraph formatting to the default style (i.e., align left, single space).

Align Left

Select this option (or click on the toolbar button) to align the paragraph at the left indent (see the highlighted text below).

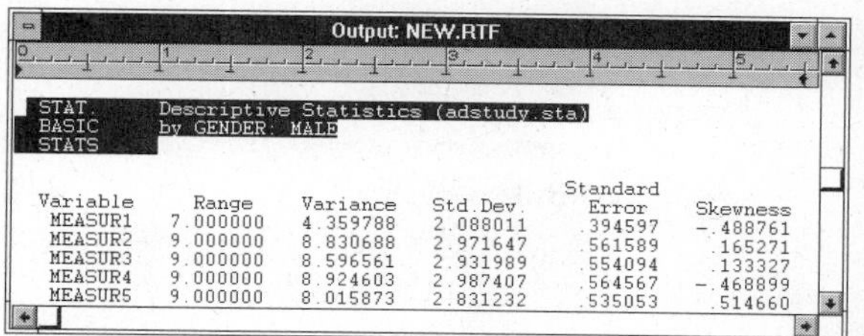

Output: NEW.RTF

STAT. BASIC STATS — Descriptive Statistics (adstudy.sta) by GENDER: MALE

Variable	Range	Variance	Std.Dev.	Standard Error	Skewness
MEASUR1	7.000000	4.359788	2.088011	.394597	-.488761
MEASUR2	9.000000	8.830688	2.971647	.561589	.165271
MEASUR3	9.000000	8.596561	2.931989	.554094	.133327
MEASUR4	9.000000	8.924603	2.987407	.564567	-.468899
MEASUR5	9.000000	8.015873	2.831232	.535053	.514660

Center

Select this option (or click on the toolbar button) to center the paragraph in the middle of the page.

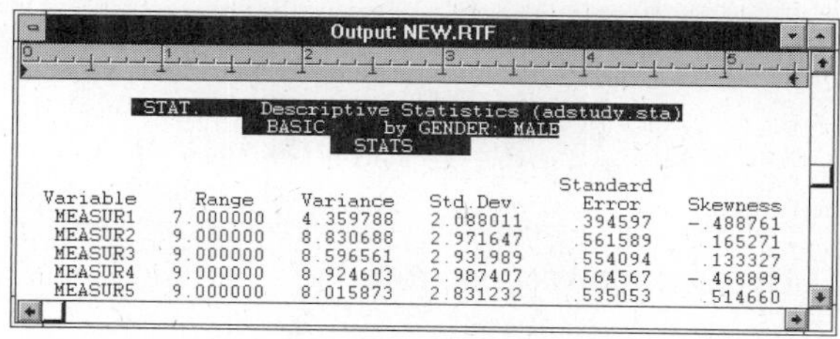

Output: NEW.RTF

STAT. BASIC STATS — Descriptive Statistics (adstudy.sta) by GENDER: MALE

Variable	Range	Variance	Std.Dev.	Standard Error	Skewness
MEASUR1	7.000000	4.359788	2.088011	.394597	-.488761
MEASUR2	9.000000	8.830688	2.971647	.561589	.165271
MEASUR3	9.000000	8.596561	2.931989	.554094	.133327
MEASUR4	9.000000	8.924603	2.987407	.564567	-.468899
MEASUR5	9.000000	8.015873	2.831232	.535053	.514660

Align Right

Select this option (or click on the toolbar button) to align the paragraph at the right indent.

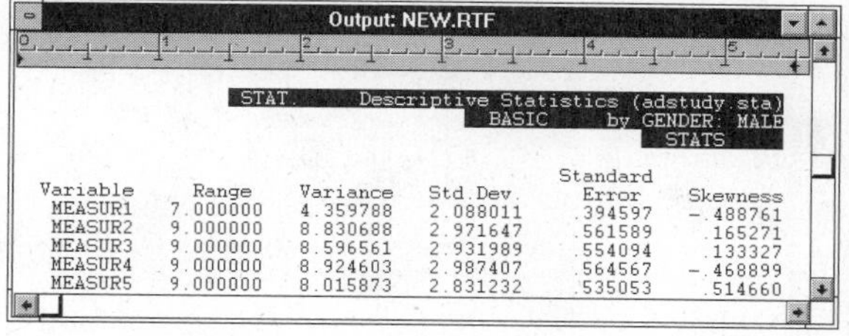

Output: NEW.RTF

STAT. BASIC STATS — Descriptive Statistics (adstudy.sta) by GENDER: MALE

Variable	Range	Variance	Std.Dev.	Standard Error	Skewness
MEASUR1	7.000000	4.359788	2.088011	.394597	-.488761
MEASUR2	9.000000	8.830688	2.971647	.561589	.165271
MEASUR3	9.000000	8.596561	2.931989	.554094	.133327
MEASUR4	9.000000	8.924603	2.987407	.564567	-.468899
MEASUR5	9.000000	8.015873	2.831232	.535053	.514660

Single Space

Select this option (or click on the toolbar button) to set the paragraph spacing to one line.

Double Space

Select this option (or click on the toolbar button) to set the paragraph spacing to two lines.

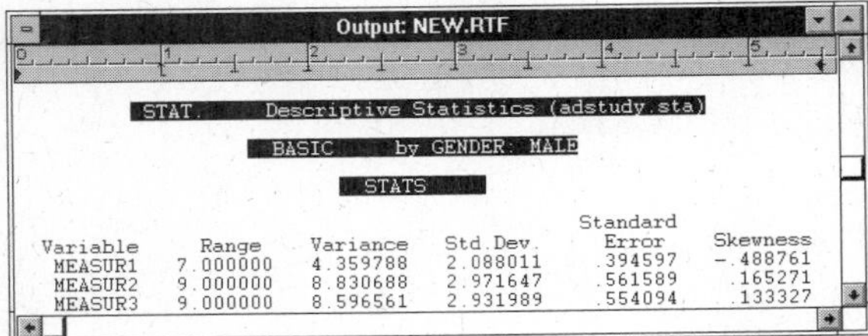

Left Indent

This option allows you to set the left indent in the paragraph (see the highlighted text below).

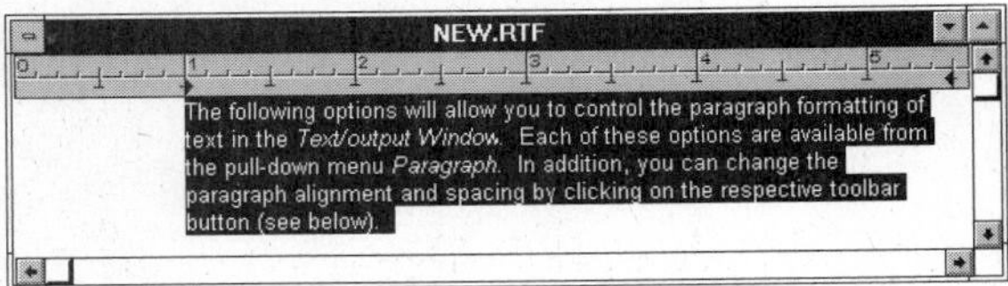

Each click on this option from the *Paragraph* pull-down menu will move the left indent by increments of .5 inches.

Right Indent

This option allows you to set the right indent in the paragraph.

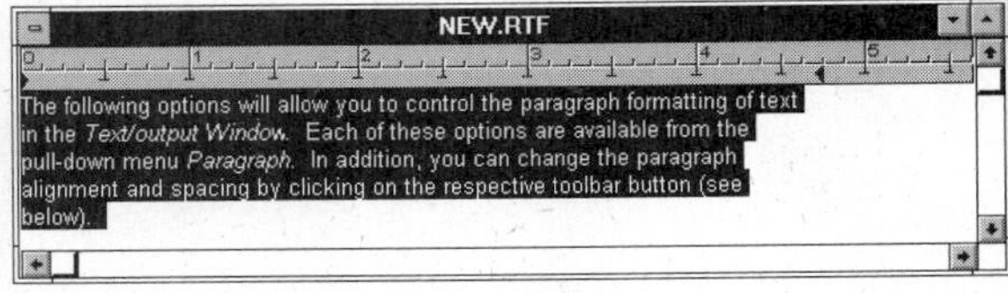

Each click on this option from the *Paragraph* pull-down menu will move the right indent by increments of .25 inches.

Hanging Indent

This option allows you to set the hanging indent (i.e., the indentation of the second and subsequent lines in the paragraph).

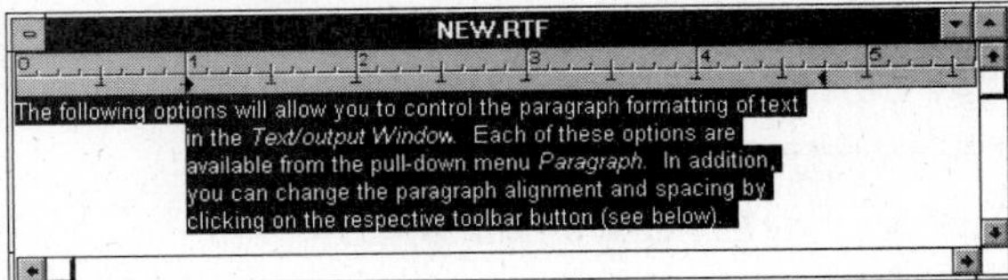

Each click on this option from the *Paragraph* pull-down menu will move the hanging indent by increments of .5 inches.

Ruler

This option toggles between displaying and hiding the Ruler in the *Text/output Window*. The Ruler is used as a measurement scale and is displayed at the top of the *Text/output Window*.

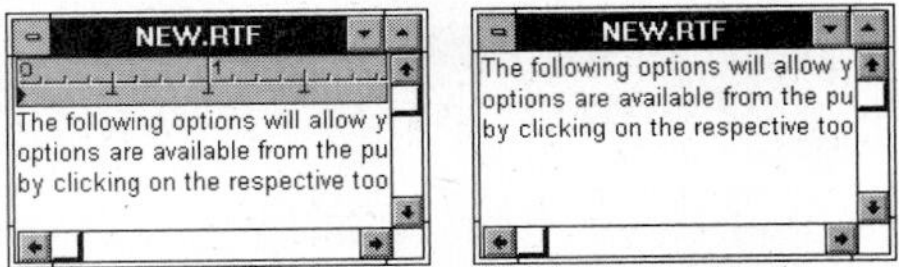

You can click on the ruler with the mouse in order to set Tab stops (see below).

Setting Tab Stops in the *Text/output* Window

You can set Tab stops in the *Text/output Window* by clicking on the Ruler with the left-mouse-button. The Tab stop will be indicated by an arrow on the Ruler (see below).

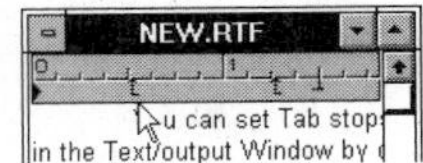

Deleting Tab Stops

To delete a single Tab stop, select the *Delete Tab Stop* option from the right-mouse-button flying

menu. The *Delete Tab Stop* dialog will open in which you can select the desired Tab stop to delete.

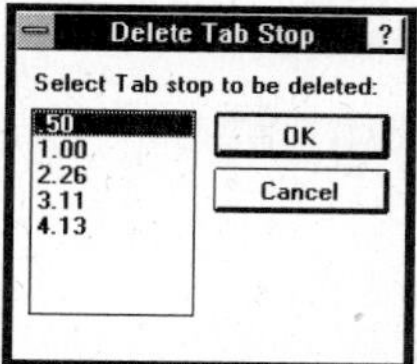

Note that you can also delete a Tab stop by clicking on the Tab stop arrow on the *Text/output Window* Ruler.

To delete all Tab stops in the document, select the *Delete All Tab Stops* option from the right-mouse-button flying menu.

Printing Tabs in Text Output Tables

When the *Print Tabs in Text Output Tables* option is selected in the *Page/Output Setup* dialog (see Chapter 3), *STATISTICA* will print tab-delimited text in the output tables of the *Text/output Window*.

Note that when tabs are used in text output tables, it allows you to use non-proportional fonts (e.g., Times Roman) when pasting the table into a word processor program (e.g., MS Word). Also you can paste the table into a spreadsheet such that each value will be placed in a different cell.

For more information on this option, see *Page/Output Setup*, Chapter 3.

Page Break

Use the *Insert Page Break* option from the *Character* pull-down menu (or alternatively, press CTRL+ENTER) in order to insert a manual (hard) page break where ever you want in the *Text/output Window*. This break will appear as a solid horizontal line in the Window.

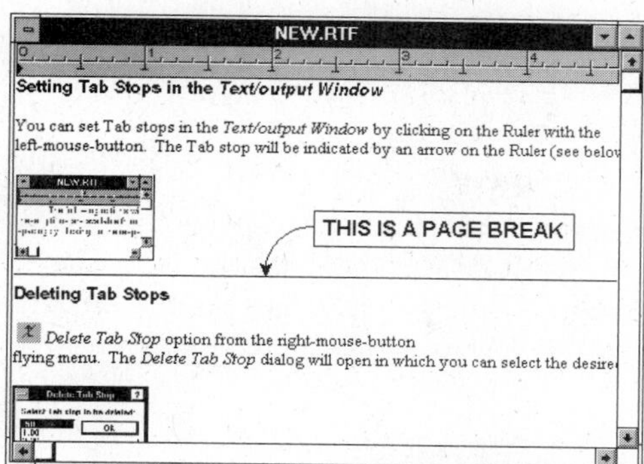

You can use manual page breaks to force text or objects onto a new page, keep paragraphs together, place an object or text at the top of the page, etc.

OTHER *TEXT/OUTPUT WINDOW* PULL-DOWN MENU OPTIONS

In addition to the options described above (see *Opening the Text/output Window*, page 1270, *Saving the Text/output Window*, page 1271, *Printing the Text/output Window*, page 1272, and *Formatting Text in the Text/output Window*, page 1273), the following new options are available from the pull-down menus in the *Text/output Window*.

New Window

Select this option from the *Text/output Window* pull-down menu *File* in order to clear all text in the current *Text/output Window*.

Paste Special

When you select this option, you will be able to choose the desired format (e.g., *R*ich *T*ext *F*ormat, text, or picture, depending on the current Clipboard contents) in which the Clipboard object will be pasted in the *Text/output Window*.

StatSoft

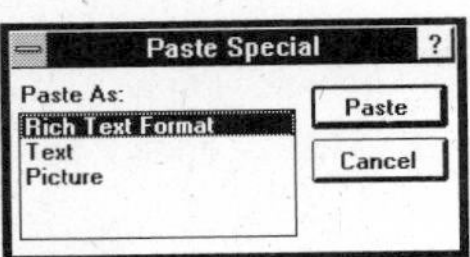

Note that if you are pasting text from another application, select *RTF* as the format in the *Paste Special* dialog in order to paste the text into the *Text/output Window* using the source font style.

Find Value

When you select *Find* from the *Edit* pull-down menu or press CTRL+F, the *Find* dialog will open, enabling you to search for a specific text or number in the *Text/output Window*.

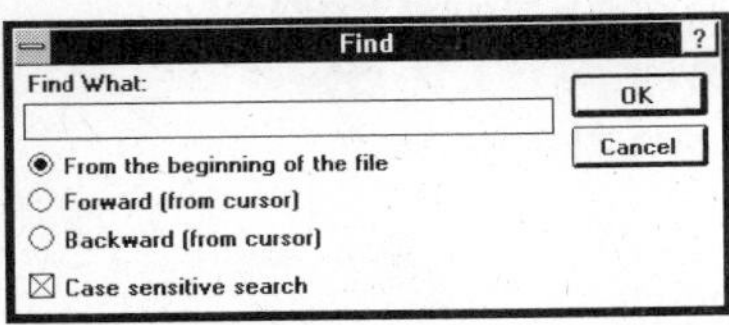

Each of the options in this dialog are discussed below.

Find What

Specify in this edit field the text or number that you want to search for in the *Text/output Window*.

Direction

Find will search either *From the beginning of the file*, or from the current cursor position (*Forward* or *Backward*).

Case Sensitive Search

When you select this option, *STATISTICA* will search for the same upper/lowercase occurrence of the text.

Find Next

A *Find Next* option is available from the *Text/output Window* pull-down menu *Edit*.

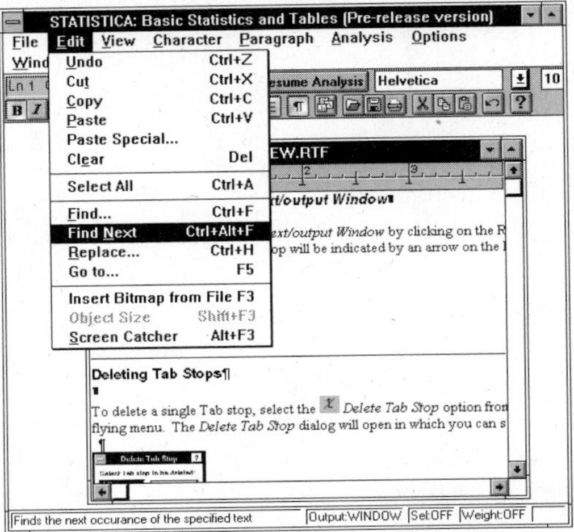

After *STATISTICA* has found the specified text or value, you can continue searching the *Text/output Window* by selecting the *Find Next* option from the *Edit* pull-down menu (or by pressing CTRL+ALT+F) instead of re-opening the *Find* dialog and clicking on the *Find Next* button.

Replace Value

The *Replace* dialog (accessible from the *Edit* pull-down menu or by pressing CTRL+H) will enable you to search for a specific text or number in the *Text/output Window* and replace it with a different text or number.

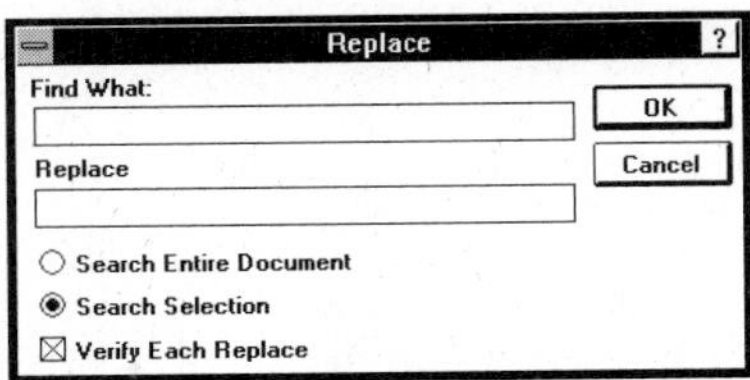

The following options are available in this dialog.

Find What

In this edit field, specify the text or number that you want to search for in the *Text/output Window*.

Replace

In this edit field, specify the text or number that will be used to replace the text or number for which you are searching.

Search

You can choose to search the *Entire Document* or only the *Selection* highlighted by the cursor.

Verify Each Replace

When you set this check box, *STATISTICA* will prompt you to verify the replacement. When the specified text or value is located, the verification dialog will allow you to skip the replacement (click *No*) or complete the replacement (click *Yes*) for each instance found, or to *Cancel* the replacement procedure.

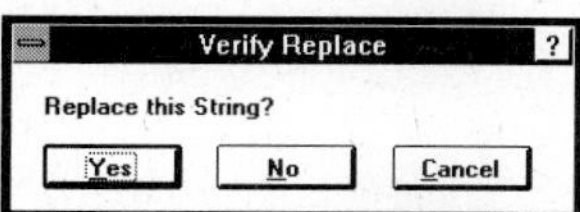

When this option is de-selected, then all occurrences of the text or number specified in the *Find* edit field will be replaced.

Select All

Click on this option from the *Edit* pull-down menu or press CTRL+A in order to select all of the text and objects in the *Text/output Window*.

Go To

Select this option from the *Edit* pull-down menu or press F5 in order to move to the specified location (*Line Number*) in the text.

After entering the desired line number, click *OK* to go to that line of the text.

Text/output Window Undo Option

Click on this option from the *Edit* pull-down menu, click on the toolbar button, or press CTRL+Z (or ALT+BACKSPACE) in order to reverse (undo) the last specific command or action. This option applies to the following types of command or actions:

- Cut, paste, clear;
- the last entry (text or numeric) typed into the *Text/output Window*.

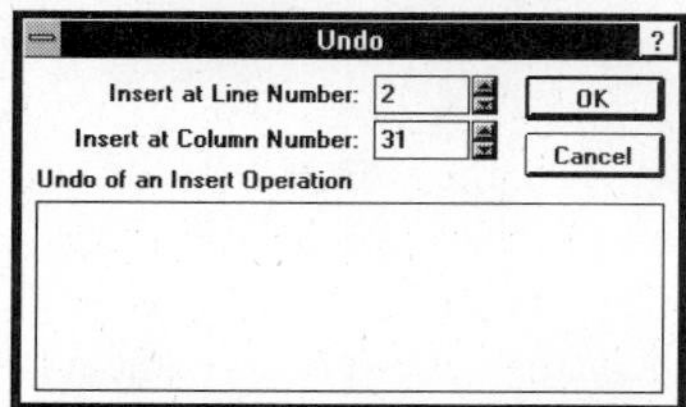

The resulting *Undo* dialog displays the type of *Undo* operation and allows you to specify the location (line and column number) where the *Undo* operation will be performed.

Appending Results

When checked, this option (available from the *Options* pull-down menu) will append (add) the

results of analyses to the end of any existing text in the *Text/output Window*. This is useful if you want a continuous log of output from analyses. However, sometimes you may want to use this *Text/output Window* as a "notepad" in which you can keep notes. If this is the case, then you can temporarily disable the *Append* mode of operation by de-selecting the *Append Results* option (click on this option once again in order to return to the *Append* mode of operation.

Insert Bitmap from File

Selecting this option from the *Edit* pull-down menu or pressing F3 will allow you to insert an object from a file into the text document in the *Text/output Window*. When you select this option, the *File Open/Save As* dialog will open in which you can choose the desired file. When you click *OK* in that dialog, the object will be placed in the graph at the current cursor position.

Object Size

This dialog (accessible from the *Edit* pull-down menu, by pressing SHIFT+F3, or from the right-mouse-button flying menu option *Custom Size*) will allow you to change the size of the selected object in the *Text/output Window*.

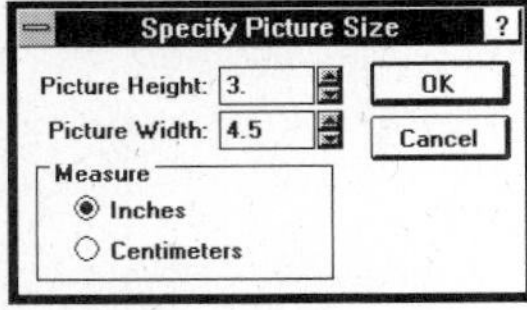

The following options are available in this dialog:

Picture Height/Width

You can specify the height and width (according to the specified measure, see below) of the selected picture with these options.

Measure

Choose to measure the picture size (height and width) in either *inches* or *centimeters* with these options.

Changing the Object Size

In addition to the above option in which you can enter a user-specified object size, the following object sizes are available from the right-mouse-button flying menu when an object is selected in the *Text/output Window*.

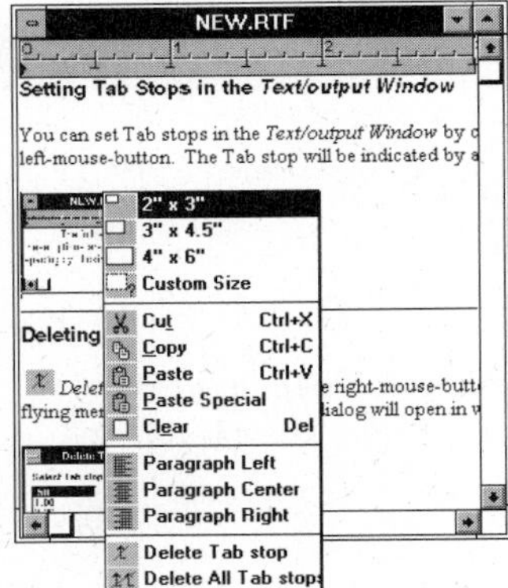

These options allow you to quickly select a different size for the object.

2x3 Object Size

Select this option in order to change the size of the selected object to 2x3 (height x width) inches. See the note about the minimum line width setting, below.

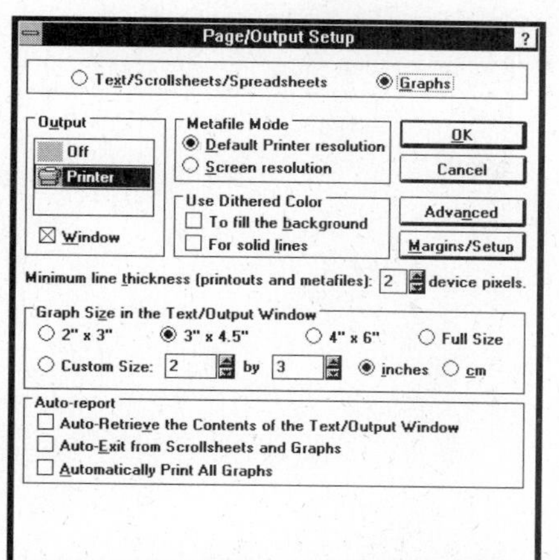

3x4.5 Object Size

Select this option in order to change the size of the selected object to 3x4.5 (height x width) inches. See the note about the minimum line width setting, below.

4x6 Object Size

Select this option in order to change the size of the selected object to 4x6 (height x width) inches. See the note about the minimum line width setting, below.

Custom Size

Clicking on this option will open the *Object Size* dialog in which you can enter the desired size for the object (see page 1281). See the note about the minimum line width setting, below.

Graphic Object Size and the Minimum Line Setting

Note that when you reduce the *STATISTICA* graph in the *Text/output Window* (for example to 2x3), then some lines may appear too thin (in the printout). Therefore, you may want to adjust the minimum line thickness setting in the *Page/Output Setup* dialog (see Chapter 3) to a respectively larger setting.

INDEX

U

V

Chapter 6:

AUTO TASK BUTTONS

Table of Contents

The *Detailed Table of Contents* follows on the next page.

Detailed Table of Contents

StatSoft

Chapter 6: AUTO TASK BUTTONS

INTRODUCTORY OVERVIEW

Auto Task Buttons: User-defined, "One-click Shortcuts"

The *Auto Task Buttons* is a floating (or docked), user-defined toolbar that allows you to quickly access most of *STATISTICA*'s task automation facilities.

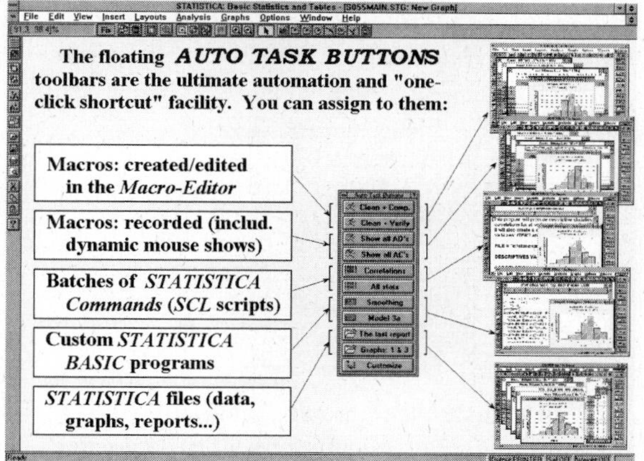

To simplify and speed up access to user-specified procedures, you can define the buttons on the *Auto Task Buttons* toolbar by assigning to them:

- macros created by recording keystrokes and mouse actions;
- macros created by entering sequences of keystrokes (or by editing pre-recorded macros);
- batches of *STATISTICA* procedures specified using *SCL* (*STATISTICA* Command Language);
- user-defined procedures and programs written in *STATISTICA BASIC* (e.g., new graphs, new computational procedures, data transformations, etc.);
- specific *STATISTICA* files (data, graphs, reports, etc.) to which you need quick access.

Procedures assigned to *Auto Task Buttons* can also be invoked with user-specified hot keys. In addition, the *Auto Task Buttons* assigned to macros can be utilized when a dialog is open.

For example, you can create a keyboard macro that will select specific options in a commonly-used dialog (e.g., a *Stats Graph* dialog). Then, when that dialog is open, all you have to do is press the *Auto Task Button* (or optionally use the user-specified Hot Key combination) to run the macro that will select the options for that dialog. (See *Hints*, page 1299, for some useful hints for entering keyboard macros.)

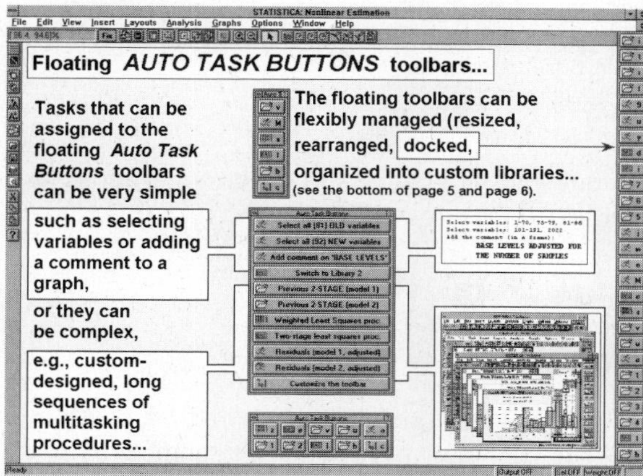

Floating AUTO TASK BUTTONS toolbars...
Tasks that can be assigned to the floating Auto Task Buttons toolbars can be very simple
The floating toolbars can be flexibly managed (resized, rearranged, docked, organized into custom libraries...
(see the bottom of page 5 and page 6).
such as selecting variables or adding a comment to a graph,
or they can be complex,
e.g., custom-designed, long sequences of multitasking procedures...

Note that the display of the *Auto Task Buttons* toolbar can be toggled on and off by pressing CTRL+M.

Custom Extensions to *STATISTICA*

Because user-defined procedures of any type can be assigned to *Auto Task Buttons*, these floating toolbars also provide an efficient user-interface to your custom extensions of the *STATISTICA* system.

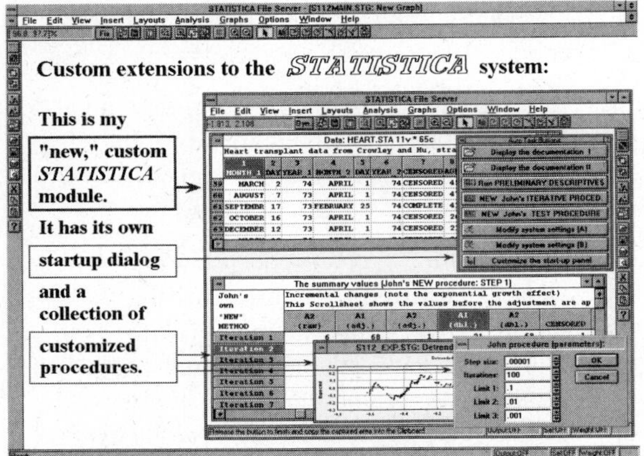

For example, they may contain a list of user-defined regression models,

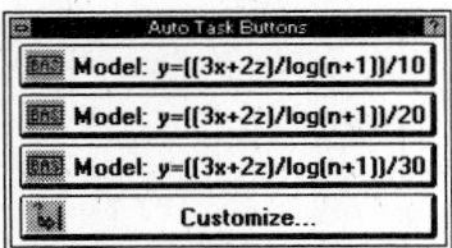

custom types of graphs or graph customizations (defined via macros or *STATISTICA BASIC*).

Large Libraries of *Auto Task Buttons*

You can define any number of *Auto Task Buttons* toolbars (and they may contain any number of buttons).

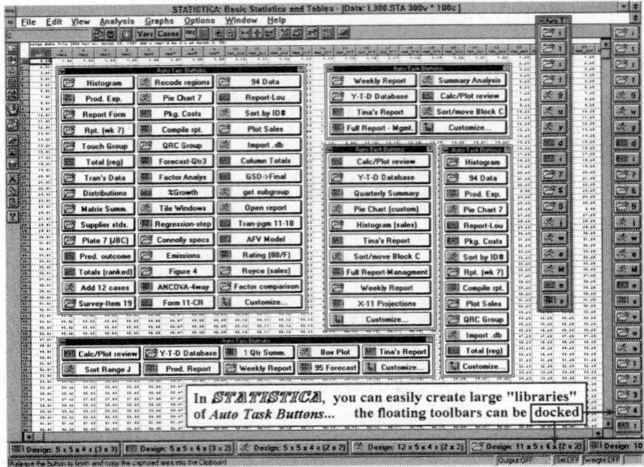

Also, these floating toolbars can be set up as *global* (accessible in every module), or *local* (related to a specific module or project), see page 1293.

You can maintain libraries of those lists of custom procedures. For example, they may contain routinely generated reports, long sequences of analyses, or series of programs that you use to transform or clean data. Alternatively, they may contain "menus" of your custom-designed tests,

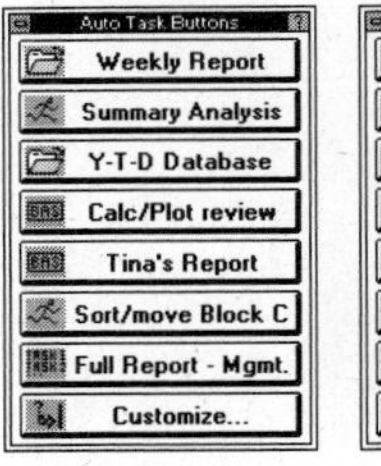

or specific customized graphs, diagrams, or drawings (e.g., dynamically related to data values from a *STATISTICA* data set).

CUSTOMIZING THE *AUTO TASK BUTTONS*

The contents of the *Auto Task Buttons* toolbar can be customized by modifying (e.g., reassigning), adding or removing buttons and also by resizing the

menu (drag the toolbar border with the left-mouse-button), and can be saved. When you press on the *Customize* button on the *Auto Task Buttons* toolbar, the *Customize Auto Task Buttons* dialog will open in which you can add, remove, edit, or review the contents of the *Auto Task Buttons*.

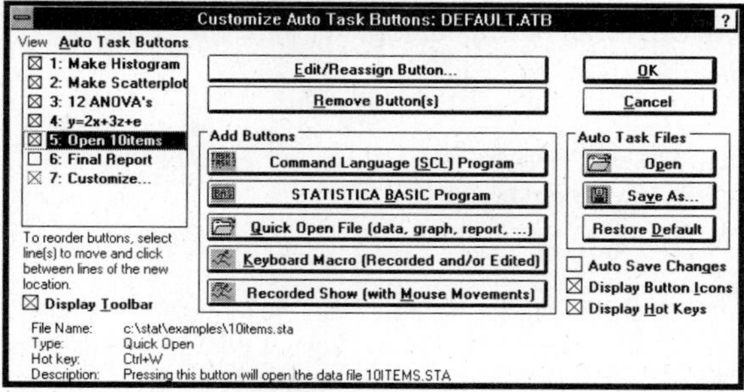

The options available on the *Customize Auto Task Buttons* dialog are discussed below.

View *Auto Task Buttons* List and Description

This area of the dialog displays the names of the buttons available to the current *Auto Task Buttons* toolbar. Only those buttons which are checked in this list (see *View*, below) are displayed in the toolbar. When a button is highlighted in this list, the associated file name, type of file, Hot Key (if specified), and previously entered description of the button is displayed below this area of the dialog (see the illustration above).

View

You can select the buttons to be displayed in the *Auto Task Buttons* toolbar by setting the respective check box in this area of the dialog. Un-checked buttons will not be displayed on the toolbar but will remain in this list, and their actions can still be accessed using the respective Hot Keys (if one is assigned). In this way, you can further customize the *Auto Task Buttons* toolbar by displaying only the desired buttons.

Changing the Order of Buttons

To change the order of the buttons in the toolbar, first highlight one or more of the button names in this area of the dialog, then move the cursor to the desired position in the list, and when the cursor changes to a ‡, click on the left-mouse-button to complete the move.

Editing a Button

To edit the button name, description, Hot Key, or contents, you can

(1) Highlight the desired button name in the buttons list in the *Customize Auto Task Buttons* dialog and then click on the *Edit/Reassign* button (see below) to open the appropriate dialog for editing the button,

(2) Double-click on the desired button name in the list of buttons in the *Customize Auto Task Buttons* dialog, or

(3) Outside this dialog, hold the CTRL key down and click on the desired button on the *Auto Task Buttons* toolbar.

Each of these ways will open the appropriate dialog for editing.

Display Toolbar

De-select this option in order to hide the *Auto Task Buttons* toolbar. Alternatively, you can toggle the toolbar on/off by pressing CTRL+M or via the *View* pull-down menu option *Auto Task Buttons*.

Note that if you assign Hot Keys to specific buttons, their respective actions can still be accessed with

the keyboard even if the *Auto Task Buttons* toolbar is not displayed.

Edit/Reassign Button

Click on this button in the *Customize Auto Task Buttons* dialog in order to edit the highlighted button name, description, file name, Hot Key, and other options.

Remove Button(s)

When you click on this button, all of the highlighted buttons in the *Auto Task Buttons* area of the dialog will be removed from the list of *Auto Task Buttons*. (Note that this option only removes the highlighted buttons from the list and does not delete the associated files.)

Add Button(s)

This area of the dialog provides options for adding new buttons to the *Auto Task Buttons* toolbar. Clicking on each of these buttons opens the appropriate dialog (see below) in which you can define a new button and select the desired action to be assigned to the new button.

Command Language (*SCL*) Program

When you click on this button, the *Edit the Auto Task Buttons* dialog will open in which you can assign an *SCL* program file (file name extension **.scl*) to an *Auto Task Button*. For more information on other options in this dialog, see *Edit the Auto Task Buttons Item*, page 1294.

STATISTICA BASIC Program

This button brings up the *Edit the Auto Task Buttons Item* dialog in which you can select a previously saved *STATISTICA BASIC* file (file name extension **.stb*). For more information on other options in this dialog, see *Edit the Auto Task Buttons Item*, page 1294.

Quick-Open File (Data, Graph, Report, ...)

This button opens the *Edit the Auto Task Buttons Item* dialog (see page 1294) which allows you to select a file from among the many types of *STATISTICA* files (e.g., a data file, graph file, Scrollsheet file, text file, *RTF* file, etc.); the selected file will then be easily available by pressing the respective *Auto Task Button*.

Keyboard Macro (Recorded and/or Edited)

Click on this button to open the *Record or Enter/Edit a Keyboard Macro* dialog in which you can open, enter, or record a keyboard macro. A keyboard macro is an editable macro that is either entered directly (using the standard Microsoft *Sendkeys* conventions) or recorded. You can also open a text file containing a previously-saved sequence of keystrokes. For more information on editable macros and the *Sendkeys* syntax, see the *Record or Enter/Edit a Keyboard Macro* dialog (page 1296).

Recorded Show (with Mouse Movements)

When you click on this button, the *Recorded Show Macro* dialog will open in which you can define

and initiate recording mouse movements as well as keystrokes. When you play back the *Recorded Show* macro, the recorded mouse movements and/or keystrokes will be replayed (the recorded macros can be played back at the speed at which they were recorded or in the *Fast Playback* mode).

Note that macros containing recorded mouse movements are "context-dependent," and they may not produce the same results if the size of the window or its position on the screen changes. Use keystroke-based macros whenever possible for better reproducibility (all menu and dialog box buttons in *STATISTICA* have their own keyboard equivalents).

Note also that recorded mouse movements in macros are not editable. However, if you record any keystrokes using the *Recorded Show* option, you can easily import those keystrokes into the *Record or Enter/Edit a Keyboard Macro* dialog (see page 1296).

Auto Task Files

The following options allow you to change or save the *Auto Task Buttons* configuration file. The name of the current *Auto Task Buttons* file is given in the title area of this dialog. Note that you can also quickly switch between configuration files via the right-mouse-button flying menu option *Change Auto Task Buttons Toolbar* (see page 1304).

Open

Click on this button in order to access the *Open an Auto Task Buttons File* dialog and select a previously-saved *Auto Task Buttons* configuration file. When the selected configuration file (file name extension **.atb*) is opened, it becomes assigned to the current module in the *Statist.ini* file (see the *Electronic Manual* for information on the *Statist.ini* file), and the name of the current module is removed from the module assignment for the previous configuration file (if one was established).

Note that you can also open a previously-saved *Auto Task Buttons* configuration file by clicking on the toolbar with the right-mouse-button and selecting *Change Auto Task Buttons Toolbar* from the flying menu (see page 1304).

Save As

Click on the *Save As* button in order to open the *Save an Auto Task Buttons File* dialog and save the *Auto Task Buttons* configuration under the default name (*Default.atb*) or a new name (file name extension **.atb*). When you save the *Auto Task Buttons* configuration, the file name, path, and associated module will be specified in the *Statist.ini* file (see the *Electronic Manual* for information on the *Statist.ini* file).

Global vs. local *Auto Task Buttons*. An *Auto Task Buttons* configuration file can be assigned to several modules (i.e., global; each time you open the respective file in a module, it becomes assigned to that module in the *Statist.ini* file); however, each module can have only one *Auto Task Buttons* configuration associated with it (i.e., local; either save the configuration in the current module or open a previously-saved configuration file in a module in order for it to be assigned to that module).

For example, the *Default.atb* configuration file will open in every module with which it is associated in the *Statist.ini* file [by default, it is (globally) associated with every module in *STATISTICA*]. If you make changes to this default file and save it under the same path and name, then it will still be associated with each of the modules with which it was previously associated.

Now, if you make changes to the *Default.atb* configuration and save it under a different name or path (e.g., *New.atb*), then the new configuration file

will be assigned (locally) to the current module, and the current module's name will be removed from the list of modules associated with *Default.atb*. However, *Default.atb* will still be assigned to the remaining modules in *STATISTICA*.

Restore Default

When you click on this button, the *Default.atb* (*Auto Task Buttons* configuration) file will be opened and reassigned to the current module.

Auto Save Changes

Select this option in order to skip the default confirmation request (issued by *STATISTICA*) and automatically save any changes to the current *Auto Task Buttons* configuration file.

Display Button Icons

When you de-select this option, icons representing the type of *Auto Task Button* will not be displayed on the button face to the left of the button names (see below).

Button icons: ON

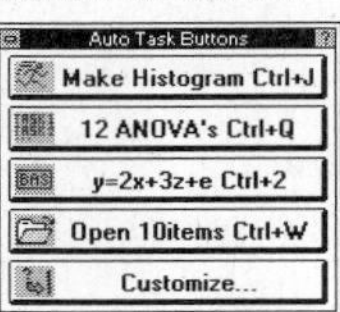

Button icons: OFF

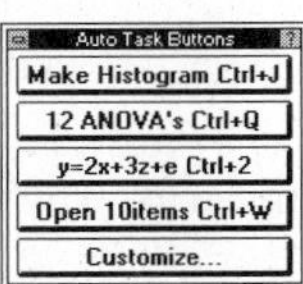

Note that this option can be used if you wish to save space covered by the *Auto Task Buttons* toolbar, and, for example, identify buttons by single letters.

Display Hot Keys

Select this option in order to display Hot Keys (which may have been assigned to an *Auto Task Button*) after the name on the button.

Display Hot Keys: ON Display Hot Keys: OFF

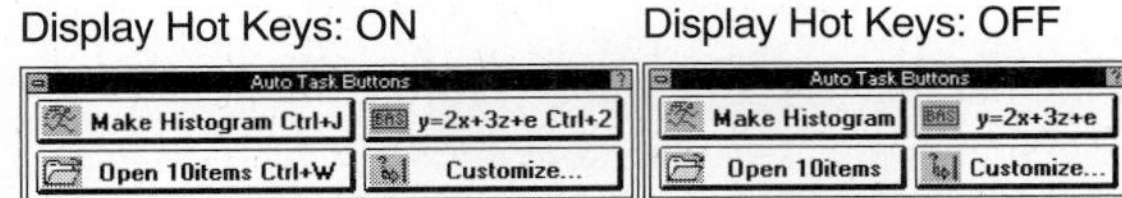

Note that the Hot Keys can be used regardless of their display setting.

EDIT THE *AUTO TASK BUTTONS* ITEM

This dialog is used to create new *Auto Task Buttons* (see *Customize Auto Task Buttons*, page 1290) or to edit existing buttons. Here you can assign a previously saved file (e.g., an *SCL* or *STATISTICA BASIC* program file, or a data, Scrollsheet, graph, or report file) to an *Auto Task Button*.

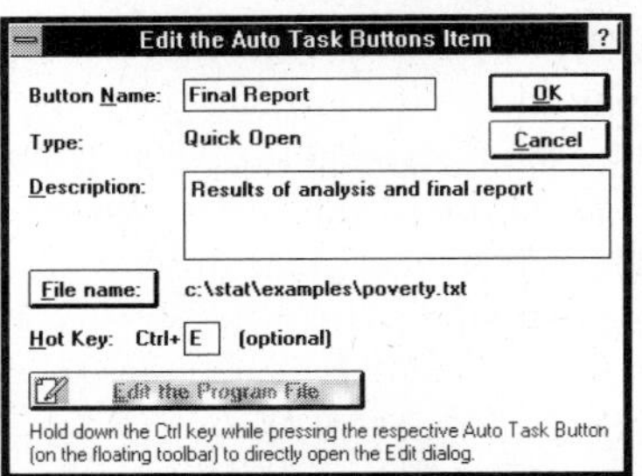

The *STATISTICA BASIC* and *SCL* program files can also be edited from this dialog (see *Edit the Program File* option, below).

Shortcut. You can also access this dialog by double-clicking on the appropriate button name in the list of *Auto Task Buttons* or by holding down the CTRL key and clicking on the appropriate *Auto Task Button* in the toolbar.

Button Name

Enter/edit the name of the *Auto Task Button* (up to 30 characters) here.

Type

This area shows the type of *Auto Task Button* that you have selected. You can enter or edit the button name, description, Hot Key, etc., in this dialog for the following three types of *Auto Task Buttons*:

- *SCL* (*STATISTICA* Command Language);
- *STATISTICA BASIC* program files;
- Quick-open files (e.g., data, Scrollsheet, graph, *RTF*, etc.).

Description

You can edit the description of the button (up to 128 characters) in this edit field. The description that you enter here is displayed in the description area of the *Customize Auto Task Buttons* dialog (see page 1290) when the respective button name is highlighted.

File Name

Click on the *File Name* button in order to change the file associated with this *Auto Task Button*.

Hot Key

If desired, you can assign a Hot Key to this *Auto Task Button*. If you specify a currently assigned Hot Key here [i.e., a system Hot Key (see below) or one currently assigned to an *Auto Task Button*], *STATISTICA* will detect it

and will give you the opportunity to either change the Hot Key or override the current assignment.

System Global Hot (CTRL) Keys

The following Hot Keys (using the CTRL+character key combinations) are global in that they are available in every window (e.g., spreadsheet window, Scrollsheet window, graph window, etc.) in *STATISTICA*.

Open, Save, Print, New Data	CTRL+O, S, P, N
Clipboard	CTRL+C, V, X
Undo	CTRL+Z
Startup Panel, Resume Analysis	CTRL+T, R
Auto Task Buttons (on/off)	CTRL+M
Select All (table, text) or Object (graphs)	CTRL+A
Close All Output Windows	CTRL+L

System Local Hot (CTRL) Keys

The following Hot Keys (using the CTRL+character key combinations) are local in that they are available only in specific windows in *STATISTICA*.

Find, Replace (data, text)	CTRL+F, H
Font Attributes (in text editors)	CTRL+0 (zero), B, I, U, D
Graph Alignment Grid (on/off)	CTRL+G

For a more complete listing of local and global Hot Keys, see *Keyboard Interface* (Chapter 1).

Edit the Program File

Click on this button in order to edit an *SCL* or *STATISTICA BASIC* program file (this option is dimmed when the current button is assigned to a quick open file). When you click on this button, the respective type of *Text/output Window* will open with the respective file for editing (see Chapter 5).

RECORD OR ENTER/EDIT A KEYBOARD MACRO

This dialog allows you to enter, record, edit and save (in a text file) a sequence of keystrokes (an editable macro) that can later be executed by clicking on the designated button in the *Auto Task Buttons* toolbar. A keyboard macro is an editable macro that is either entered directly (using the standard Microsoft *Sendkeys* conventions) or recorded.

You can also open a previously recorded show macro file (file name extension **.stm*, see page 1301), or a text file containing a previously saved sequence of keystrokes for editing here.

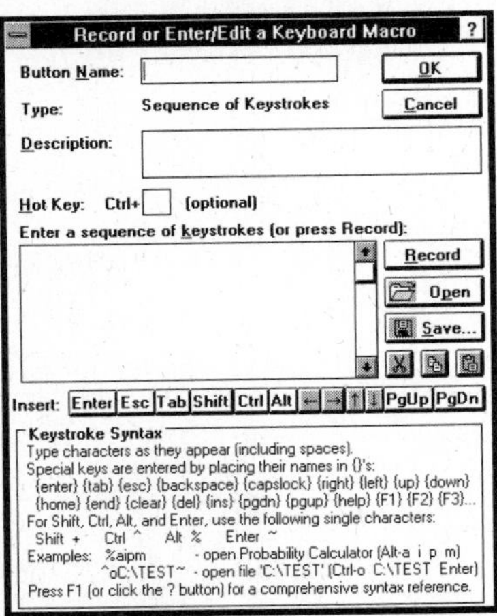

You can enter/record a new keyboard macro in this dialog by clicking on the *Keyboard Macro (Recorded and/or Edited)* button. To edit an existing keyboard macro, highlight the respective button name and click on the *Edit/Reassign* button in the *Customize Auto Task Buttons* dialog. You can also use this dialog to open a previously entered or recorded macro for editing.

Shortcut. You can also access this dialog by double-clicking on the appropriate button name in the list of *Auto Task Buttons* or by holding down the CTRL key and clicking on the appropriate *Auto Task Button* in the toolbar.

Button Name/Type

The *Button Name* edit field allows you to enter or edit (up to 30 characters) the name of this *Auto Task Button*. Immediately below this edit field is displayed the type of *Auto Task Button*.

Description

You can enter a description (up to 128 characters) for this button in the *Description* area of the dialog. The description that you enter here is displayed in the description area of the *Customize Auto Task Buttons* dialog (see page 1290) when the respective button name is highlighted.

Hot Key

If desired, you can assign a Hot Key to this *Auto Task Button*. If you specify a currently assigned Hot Key here (i.e., a system Hot Key or one currently assigned to an *Auto Task Button*), *STATISTICA* will detect it and will give you the opportunity to either change the Hot Key or override the current assignment.

For a listing of global and local Hot Keys, see pages 1295 and 1295, respectively.

Enter a Sequence of Keystrokes (or press Record)

In this area of the dialog, you can enter, record, or edit a sequence of keystrokes (editable macro) which will be executed whenever you click on the respective button in the *Auto Task Buttons* toolbar. The Microsoft *Sendkeys* conventions are used to represent the keystrokes in this macro. You can enter the keystrokes manually or by recording the keystrokes via the *Record* button. Both of these methods are discussed below.

Entering/Editing a Sequence of Keystrokes

You can directly enter or edit the keystrokes using the *Sendkeys* syntax in this edit field. Several *Quick Entry Buttons* are available in order to quickly add commonly-used keystrokes to the sequence (see below). A quick keystroke syntax reference is given in this dialog. For a complete syntax reference of the keystrokes (which closely follow that of the Microsoft *Sendkeys* conventions), see *Keyboard Macros Syntax Reference*, page 1298.

Note that if you are editing a sequence of keystrokes, any additional keystrokes will be inserted at the current cursor position in this edit field. If you highlight a series of keystrokes and enter, record, or insert from a file additional keystrokes, then those keystrokes will replace the highlighted keystrokes.

Record

Instead of manually entering the keystrokes, you can click on the *Record* button in order to begin recording a series of keystrokes (to record mouse movements, use the *Recorded Show Macro* option in the *Customize Auto Task Buttons* dialog, see page 1301). When you click on this button, *REC* will flash in the *Status Bar* to remind you that you are recording.

To stop recording, press CTRL+F3. This recorded macro can be edited as described above (the keystrokes will be displayed in the edit field). Note that if the recording is executed in order to produce a sequence of keystrokes for future editing, you should not use the mouse while recording (because recorded mouse movements cannot be edited).

Quick Entry Buttons

Use the quick entry buttons in the *Record or Enter/Edit a Keyboard Macro* dialog to quickly enter the respective keystrokes in the macro. The quick entry buttons (shown below next to the respective keyboard character) and the codes used to represent specific keyboard characters are listed below (note that the curly brackets `{}` are part of the code).

Quick Entry Buttons	Keyboard Characters	Code
Alt	ALT	`%`
Ctrl	CTRL	`^`
Shift	SHIFT	`+`
Enter	ENTER	`~` or `{Enter}`
Esc	ESCape	`{Esc}`
PgDn	PAGE DOWN	`{Pgdn}`
PgUp	PAGE UP	`{Pgup}`
Tab	TAB	`{Tab}`

↓	Down	`{Down}`
↑	Up	`{Up}`
←	Left	`{Left}`
→	Right	`{Right}`

Open

Click on this button in order to open the *Open an Auto Task Buttons File* dialog in which you can select a previously saved text file (**.txt*) or a recorded macro file (**.stm*) containing a sequence of keystrokes (editable macro). If you open a *Recorded Show Macro* file, then only the keystrokes will be displayed in this editor (mouse movements will be ignored).

Save

Click on this button in order to open the *Save an Auto Task Buttons File* dialog in which you can save the sequence of keystrokes (editable macro) in a text file (**.txt*).

Clipboard Operations (Cut, Copy, Paste)

You can use these buttons to perform the Clipboard operations cut, copy, and paste in this editor.

Keyboard Macros Syntax Reference

The syntax described here follows the same logic as that used in other Windows applications (e.g., Excel, Word for Windows). Note that you can use the *Quick Entry Buttons* (see page 1297) to quickly enter some of the commonly-used keystrokes.

Entering Regular Characters

Each keyboard key is represented by one or more characters. To specify a single keyboard character, use the character by itself. For example, to specify the text "ABC", type **ABC** in the edit field. The keyboard characters **+** (plus sign), **^** (caret), **%** (percent), **~** (tilde), and **()** (parentheses) are used as short-cuts for specific keys (see below). To use these characters as part of a sequence of keystrokes, enclose the character in curly brackets **{}**. For example, to specify the plus sign as part of the "ABC" text string, type **ABC{+}**. To use a curly bracket (**{}**) as part of a sequence of keystrokes, enclose them in curly brackets as well (i.e., use **{{}** and **{}}**).

Entering Special Keyboard Keys

The syntax for keyboard macros allows you to specify keyboard keys that are not displayed when you press on them (e.g., ENTER or TAB) and keys that represent actions rather than characters (e.g., UP or RIGHT). For those keys, use the *Sendkeys* code shown below (note that the curly brackets are part of the code).

Keyboard Character	Use the Code:
ALT	`%`
BACKSPACE	`{Backspace}`
BREAK	`{Break}`
CAPS LOCK	`{Capslock}`
Clear	`{Clear}`
CTRL	`^`
DELETE	`{Del}`
Double quotes	`" "`

Down	`{Down}`
END	`{End}`
ENTER	`~` or `{Enter}`
ESCape	`{Esc}`
F1, ..., F12	`{F`number`}` (e.g., `{F11}`)
Help	`{Help}`
HOME	`{Home}`
INSERT	`{Insert}`
Keyboard Character	type in that key (e.g., `abc@!`)
Left	`{Left}`
PAGE DOWN	`{Pgdn}`
PAGE UP	`{Pgup}`
PRINT SCREEN	`{Prtsc}`
Right	`{Right}`
SHIFT	`+`
Single quotes	`' '`
TAB	`{Tab}`
Up	`{Up}`

Order of Keystrokes

The keystrokes will be processed in the order in which you type them into the editor. For example, if you enter the keystrokes `+EC`, then *STATISTICA* will first press SHIFT followed by the letters *E* and *C*. You can use parentheses, brackets, or curly brackets to define the order of keystrokes.

For example, if you want to hold down the CTRL key while pressing the SHIFT and C keys, specify this "string" as: `^(+C)`. To hold down the SHIFT *and* CTRL keys while pressing two other keys, specify this string as: `+(^(AB))`.

Repeating Keystrokes

You can instruct *STATISTICA* to repeat specific key sequences by specifying the number of times that you want it repeated (use the form `{key number}`). For example, `{LEFT 42}` means press the left arrow key 42 times; `{h 10}` means press the *H* key 10 times. (Note: be sure to leave a space between the code word and the number.)

WAIT Command

You can use the `{WAIT}` command in order to pause the keyboard macro for the specified number of milliseconds (1 second = 1,000 milliseconds).

For example, entering `{WAIT 15000}` will cause the macro to "wait" for 15 seconds before processing the next keystrokes. If no parameter is entered here, then by default, the macro will "wait" for 1 second.

Hints for Entering Keyboard Macros

The following hints may be useful when entering a keyboard macro (see the following example for an illustration of most of these hints).

- Use `{Esc}` at the beginning of the macro if you intend to exit any open dialog boxes. (Note that you should not include this keystroke if you want to perform a keyboard macro from within an open dialog.)
- Use the *Window* pull-down menu to bring the spreadsheet or another type of window to the top to make it current.
- Use the underlined letters in dialog boxes (i.e., so-called accelerators) to specify the option you

wish to select instead of "moving" down, right, etc.

- In list boxes, use **{Home}** in order to position the cursor at the beginning of the list each time, then specify the number of positions **{Down}** to select the desired option.
- Use **%o** (ALT+O) to accept and close dialog boxes (i.e., click *OK*).

Example: Entering a Sequence of Keystrokes Macro

You can execute the following keystrokes in order to make a 2D Scatterplot by entering them in the *Record or Enter/Edit a Keyboard Macro* dialog (page 1296). The keystrokes and their descriptions are given below. Note that you can use the *Quick Entry Buttons* to enter some of the keystrokes used below (see page 1297).

Also note that often the easiest method to create an editable macro is to record it (via the *Record* button in the *Record or Enter/Edit a Keyboard Macro* dialog). See the *Hints* section above for useful information on entering a keyboard macro.

Step 1. Enter the following keystrokes in the *Enter a sequence of keystrokes* area of the *Record or Enter/Edit a Keyboard Macro* dialog:

```
{ESC 3}%w1%g2{DOWN}~v1{TAB}2%of{HOME}
{DOWN 5}%O
```

where

{ESC 3}	Pressing ESC at the beginning of the macro will ensure that any open dialogs will be closed.
%w1	ALT+W followed by 1 opens the *Window* pull-down menu and selects the current data file (to ensure that the spreadsheet is on top; note that the spreadsheet is always the first window file listed in this menu).
%g	ALT+G pulls down the *Graphs* menu.
2	Selects the *Stats 2D Graphs* option in this pull-down menu.
{DOWN}	Moves DOWN 1 line to select the *2D Scatterplots* sub-option in this menu.
~	Presses ENTER to bring up the *2D Scatterplots* dialog.
v	Opens the *Variables* dialog so that you can specify the variables for the plot.
1	Selects variable 1 by entering *1* in the variable selection edit field of the dialog.
{TAB}	TABs to the second list.
2	Selects variable 2 by entering *2* in the variable selection edit field of the dialog.
%o	Presses ALT+O to exit this dialog (i.e., click *OK*) and returns to the *2D Scatterplots* dialog.
f{HOME}	Moves to the *Fit* area of the dialog and places the cursor to the top of the list,
{DOWN 5}	and moves 5 lines DOWN to select the *Polynomial* fit).
%o	Presses ALT+O to exit this dialog (i.e., click *OK*) and create the graph.

Step 2. If you have not already done so, enter a name for this button and description and then save these keystrokes in a text file (file name extension **.txt*).

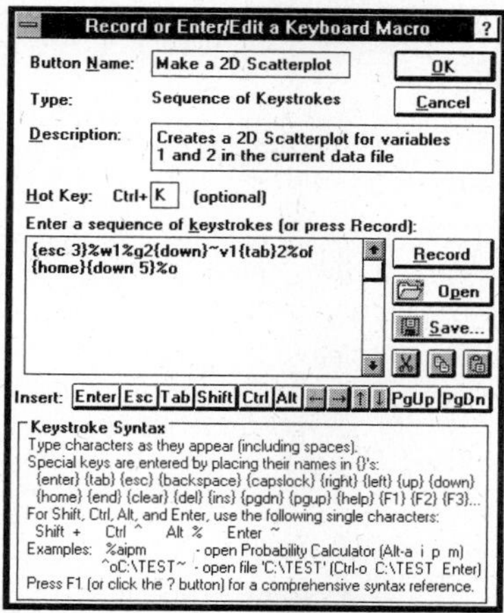

Step 3. Click *OK* to return to the *Customize Auto Task Buttons* dialog (page 1290) where the button name will be added to the list of *Auto Task Buttons*.

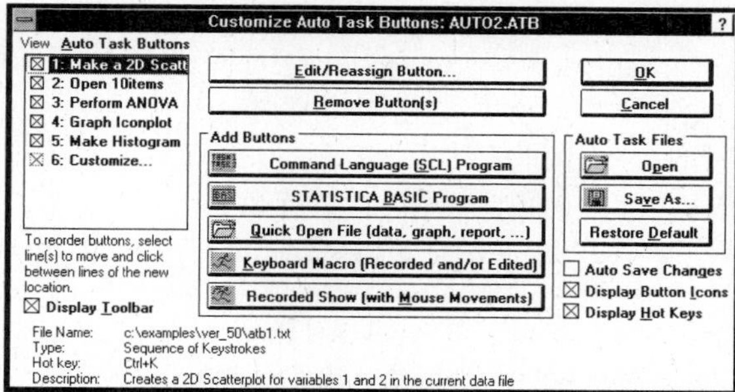

Click *OK* in this dialog to place the button on the *Auto Task Buttons* toolbar.

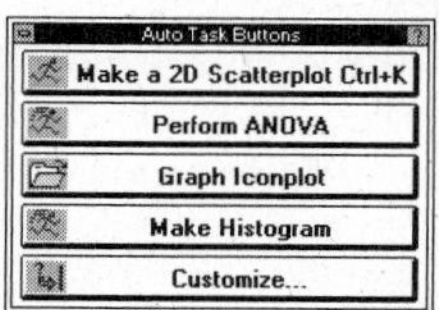

Now, click on this button to create the graph (for example, using the data file *10items.sta*).

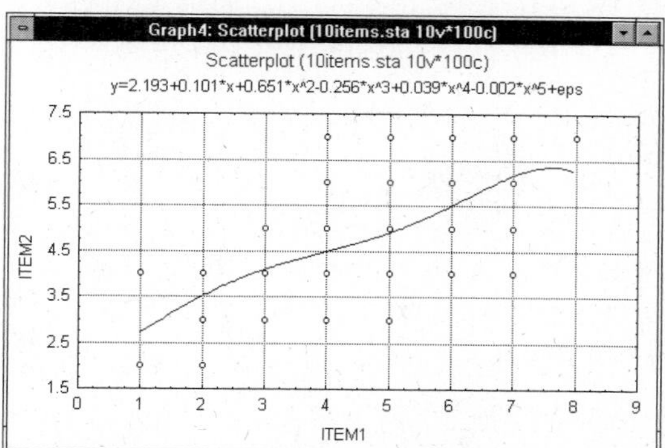

As mentioned before, recording keystrokes is normally the most efficient way to create keyboard macros, and the editor is typically used to expand or edit existing keyboard macros (e.g., by merging).

RECORDED SHOW MACRO

This dialog is accessible by clicking on the *Recorded Show (with Mouse Movements)* button (to record a new macro) or the *Edit/Reassign* button (if the name of an *Auto Task Button* of this type is highlighted) in the *Customize Auto Task Buttons* dialog (see page 1290).

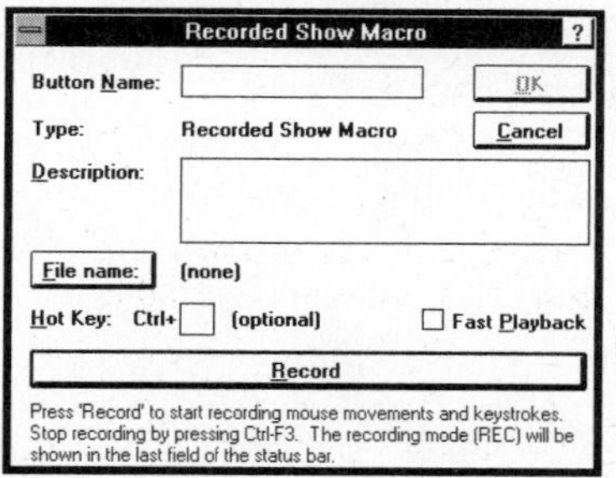

Here you can specify a button name, description, and optionally, a Hot Key for the macro. This type of macro can record mouse movements (which can be played back at the rate at which they were recorded or fast speed) and keystrokes (which can later be edited in the *Record or Enter/Edit a*

Keyboard Macro dialog, page 1296). However, note that macros containing recorded mouse movements are "context-dependent," and they may not produce the same results if the size of the window or its position on the screen changes. Therefore, use keystroke-based macros whenever possible for better reproducibility (all menu and dialog box buttons in *STATISTICA* have their own keyboard equivalents).

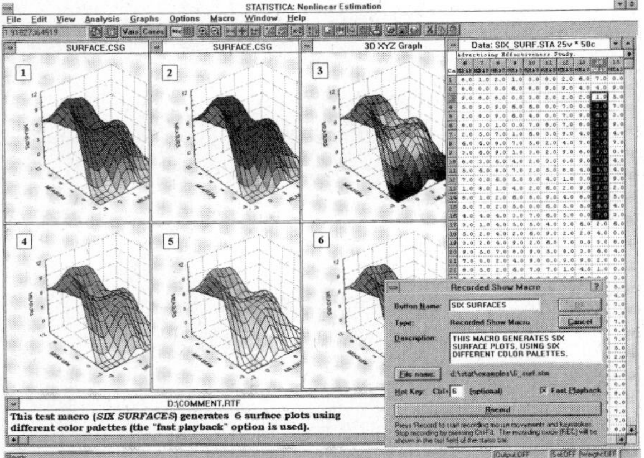

Shortcut. You can also access this dialog by double-clicking on the button's name in the list of *Auto Task Buttons* or by holding down the CTRL key and clicking on the *Auto Task Button* in the toolbar.

Button Name/Type

The *Button Name* edit field allows you to enter or edit (up to 30 characters) the name of this *Auto Task Button*. Immediately below this edit field is displayed the type of *Auto Task Button*.

Description

You can enter/edit the description of the *Auto Task Button* (up to 128 characters) in this edit field. The description that you enter here is displayed in the description area of the *Customize Auto Task Buttons* dialog (page 1290) when the respective button name is highlighted.

File Name

Click on this button to open the *Add a Recorded Show Macro* dialog in which you can select a file name (**.stm*) under which to save the macro.

Hot Key

If desired, you can assign a Hot Key to this *Auto Task Button*. If you specify a currently assigned Hot Key here (i.e., a system Hot Key or one currently assigned to an *Auto Task Button*), *STATISTICA* will detect it and will give you the opportunity to either change the Hot Key or override the current assignment. For a list of global and local Hot Keys, see pages 1295 and 1295, respectively. For a complete list of system Hot Keys, see Chapter 1.

Fast Playback

You can designate the speed of the macro playback here. When you select this option, the macro will be played back very quickly (i.e., with no recorded delays or pauses); otherwise, it is played back at the same rate at which it was recorded. Note that *Recorded Show Macros* which are executed at the rate at which they were recorded (i.e., de-select *Fast Playback*) can be used for demonstration purposes.

Interrupt playback. To halt the macro playback, click on the mouse button, or press the ESC or CTRL+BREAK keys.

Record

When you click on the *Record* button, the program will start recording your mouse movements (and

associated keystrokes). While the program is recording, *REC* will flash in the last field of the *Status Bar*.

Press CTRL+F3 to stop the recording.

Note that macros containing recorded mouse movements are "context-dependent," and they may not produce the same results if the size of the window or its position on the screen changes. Use keystroke-based macros (see *Record or Enter/Edit a Keyboard Macro*, page 1296) whenever possible for better reproducibility (all menu and dialog box buttons in *STATISTICA* have their own keyboard equivalents).

ARRANGING THE *AUTO TASK BUTTONS* TOOLBAR

The following right-mouse-button flying menu options allow you to change the display of the buttons on the *Auto Task Buttons* toolbar. Alternatively, you can change the display format by dragging the borders of the toolbar,

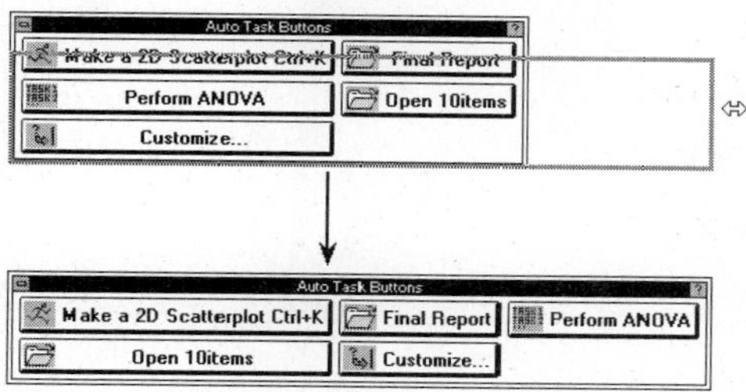

or by double-clicking on the *Auto Task Buttons* toolbar title area.

Arrange horizontally. This right-mouse-button flying menu option will arrange the *Auto Task Buttons* horizontally in the toolbar.

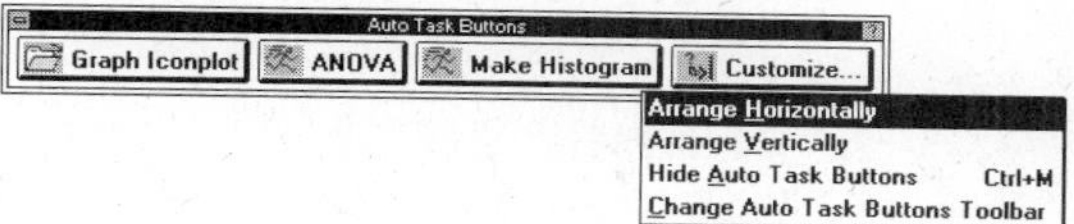

Arrange vertically. This right-mouse-button flying menu option will arrange the *Auto Task Buttons* vertically in the toolbar.

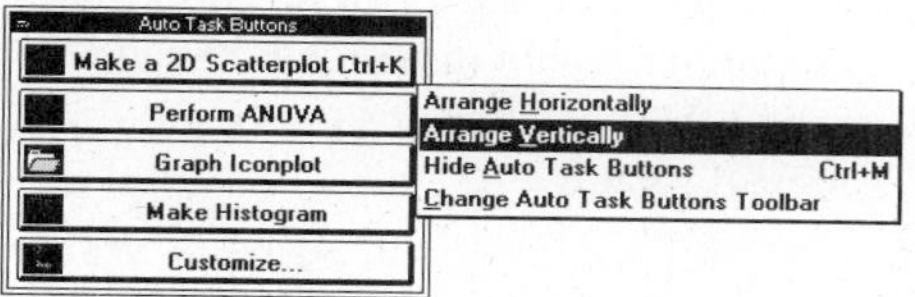

Docking the *Auto Task Buttons* Toolbar

You can "dock" the toolbar by dragging it to an area of the *STATISTICA* window (above the toolbar, below the status bar, or to either side of the window),

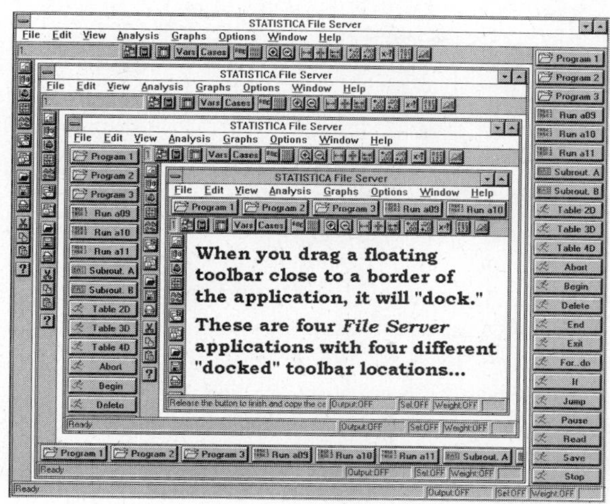

StatSoft

where the toolbar will change configuration and remain in that position until you drag it to a different area of the window.

CHANGE *AUTO TASK BUTTONS* TOOLBAR

When you click on this option from the right-mouse-button flying menu, the *Open an Auto Task Buttons File* dialog will open in which you can select a different *Auto Task Buttons* toolbar to open (file name extension **.atb*). See also, *Auto Task Files*, page 1293.

HOT KEYS IN USE

This dialog will come up whenever the Hot Key that you have selected is currently assigned either to a system operation (see below) or another *Auto Task Button*.

Click *Yes* to reassign the specified Hot Key to the current *Auto Task Button* (overriding any previous assignment). If you do not want to override the existing assignment, click *No* and you will be returned to the previous dialog where you can change the Hot Key. For a listing of global and local Hot Keys, see pages 1295 and 1295, respectively. For a complete listing of system Hot Keys, see Chapter 1.

INDEX

A

C

D

E

G

H

I

K

L

M

StatSoft

O

P

Q

R

S

T

Chapter 7:
DATA MANAGEMENT

Table of Contents

The *Detailed Table of Contents* follows on the next page.

Detailed
Table of Contents

StatSoft

STATISTICA

StatSoft

Chapter 7:
DATA MANAGEMENT

INTRODUCTORY OVERVIEW

In this overview of the *Data Management* module, we will discuss the basic data file organization (that is common to *STATISTICA* and many other programs, e.g., most data base management applications), as well as some unique features supported by *STATISTICA*.

General Organization of *STATISTICA* Data Files

STATISTICA stores its data in disk files that are optimized for quick access and storage efficiency. The general organization of those files is the same as in data base management programs; one can think of each file as a "table," where rows represent *records* (e.g., patients) and each record consists of the same number of *fields* (for example, five types of data available about each of the patients).

Cases (records). In statistical data analysis, records are often referred to as *cases* (rows in the spreadsheet data editor). They represent the elementary "units" of analysis (e.g., patients, subjects in an experiment, days in a time series analysis, measurements in a quality control study, etc.).

Variables (fields). Fields are referred to as *variables* (columns in the spreadsheet). Each variable stores a particular type of information that applies to each case. In other words, each case consists of a set of values, one for each variable in the data set. For example, if cases represented patients, and for each patient five types of data were registered [gender (*Gender*), age (*Age*), education (*Educat*), white cell count (*WCC*), and cholesterol level (*Chol*)], then there would be 5 variables in this data file. The data file could look like this:

```
Case Name     GENDER    AGE  EDUCAT   WCC   CHOL
----------    ------  ----- ------  -----  ------
John Brown      MALE     21   HIGH      7    190
Mary White    FEMALE     19   HIGH      9    205
Adam Smith      MALE     32    LOW     12    217
Judy Jones    FEMALE     31    LOW      6    231
Tom Hill        MALE     19    LOW      4    222
.                  .      .      .      .      .
.                  .      .      .      .      .
.                  .      .      .      .      .
```

Here is how this data file would appear in the *STATISTICA* spreadsheet.

Data: CHOLEST.STA 5v * 20c

TEXT VALUES	1 GENDER	2 AGE	3 EDUCAT	4 WCC	5 CHOL
John Brown	MALE	21	HIGH	7	190
Mary White	FEMALE	19	HIGH	9	205
Adam Smith	MALE	32	LOW	12	217
Judy Jones	FEMALE	31	LOW	6	231
Tom Hill	MALE	19	LOW	4	222
Brian Anderson	MALE	33	HIGH	5	214
Judy Pike	FEMALE	25	HIGH	8	215
Francis Horrowitz	FEMALE	27	LOW	9	200
Jay Stone	MALE	31	LOW	12	203
Sam Sipes	MALE	24	HIGH	11	208
Frank Lester	MALE	28	HIGH	14	194
Henry Roediger	MALE	27	LOW	10	97
Susan deVeer	FEMALE	26	LOW	5	89
Peter Ford	MALE	25	HIGH	8	205

Converting cases into variables (transposing data files). In most statistical analyses, the distinction between cases and variables is very important. Almost all *STATISTICA* analyses compute statistics from values of variables *across cases* (for example, comparing the means of *variables* calculated in different *groups of cases*, etc.). Sometimes, however, you need to do the opposite; specifically, you need to treat variables as cases.

For example, instead of computing the significance of the difference between two groups of subjects (i.e., groups of cases) on one test (i.e., one variable), you may need to compute a difference between the average score in two groups of tests (i.e., groups of variables) in one subject (i.e., one case). In order to

StatSoft®

do that, you need to *transpose* (in a sense, "rotate by +90 degrees") the file, so that cases become variables and variables become cases.

1	2	3
11	12	13
111	112	113

after transposing becomes

1	11	111
2	12	112
3	13	113

Transposing is available as an option on the *Edit* pull-down menu (you can either *Transpose Block* or *Transpose Data File*, see *Spreadsheet Window*, Chapter 3). Another typical application for transposing is when you import a spreadsheet file which is not organized in a standard "data base-like" manner and in which columns (and not rows) represent cases or "observations." After importing such data, first you need to transpose them so that they are interpreted correctly in subsequent analyses.

Before transposing:

Data: TEST.STA 6v * 10c

	1 VAR1	2 VAR2	3 VAR3	4 VAR4	5 VAR5	6 VAR6
1	1.0	1.0	1.0	1.0	1.0	1.0
2	2.0	2.0	2.0	2.0	2.0	2.0
3	3.0	3.0	3.0	3.0	3.0	3.0
4	4.0	4.0	4.0	4.0	4.0	4.0
5						
6						
7						
8						
9						
10						

After transposing:

Data: TEST.STA 10v * 6c

	1 CASE1	2 CASE2	3 CASE3	4 CASE4	5 CASE5	6 CASE6	7 CASE7	8 CASE8	9 CASE9	10 CASE10
VAR1	1.0	2.0	3.0	4.0						
VAR2	1.0	2.0	3.0	4.0						
VAR3	1.0	2.0	3.0	4.0						
VAR4	1.0	2.0	3.0	4.0						
VAR5	1.0	2.0	3.0	4.0						
VAR6	1.0	2.0	3.0	4.0						

Note that when you transpose a file, case names become variable names and variable names become case names (for details, press the F1 key to access the *Electronic Manual*).

Values of Variables

The example data file *Cholest.sta* on the previous page illustrates different types of data that can be stored in variables. In more technical terms, variables can differ regarding the types of measurement scales that their values represent (see *Elementary Concepts*, Chapter 8).

Categorical data (grouping variables). For example, the variable *Gender* does not contain "true" measurements (such as cholesterol level), but merely *codes* or names of categories (*MALE*, *FEMALE*) that indicate group membership of individual cases. In the example, the first case belongs to the group of *MALE*s, while the second belongs to *FEMALE*s. Variable *Educat* has exactly the same status. Those types of variables are often called *grouping* variables because they allow you to identify cases that belong to each group (e.g., those with *HIGH* vs. *LOW* education) and later perform analyses in which the groups would be compared.

In this example, both grouping variables contain text (alphanumeric) data, but their values could also be numeric (e.g., *1=MALE*, *2=FEMALE*). In fact, due to the flexible, so-called *double notation* of variables in *STATISTICA*, both numeric and text values can be used interchangeably to reference values in the same variable (see page 1317 in this overview).

Continuous variables. Other variables in this example data file (e.g., age or cholesterol level), contain values that are measured on *continuous* scales (see *Elementary Concepts*, Chapter 8). Unlike the categorical variables described in the previous paragraph, those are "typical" variables that can be used to compute means, standard deviations and other statistics.

For example, in a simple data analysis one could compare the cholesterol level in males and females. In order to do that, the program would first identify males and females in the data set (based on values of

the grouping variable *Gender*) and then it would calculate the mean of variable *Chol* in each group.

Using continuous variables as grouping variables. The difference between those two elementary types of variables is only in how one instructs the program to use and interpret them (they are not "declared" as such in any permanent way in *STATISTICA*). Moreover, continuous variables can also be used to identify group membership. In order to do that, they are typically *recoded*; the spreadsheet in *STATISTICA* offers a quick on-line recoding facility which can be used to convert *continuous* variables into grouping variables (see below).

For example, based on the values of cholesterol level, you could create a new variable (e.g., called *Ch_level*) in which the value *HIGHCHOL* (or numeric value of *2*) would be assigned to each case where the cholesterol level is above 200, and *LOWCHOL* (or numeric value of *1*) if it is equal or below 200.

Missing data (MD). It often happens that the data set is not perfectly complete and in some cases there is no data available for some variables (e.g., no *WCC* data are available for one of the patients). In those instances some cells in the "table" are blank. Those *missing data* (*MD*'s) are marked in the data file by a reserved value (by default it is *-9999*). Values of a variable that are assigned such *missing data codes* are ignored in all analyses; in the *STATISTICA* spreadsheet, the respective cells containing those values will appear blank ("empty"). When you create a new data file, initially all of its values are empty (technically, they are filled with missing data codes).

Display format vs. storage precision. One of the attributes that can be set separately for each variable is its *display format* (see Chapter 3). For example, *1.005* can be displayed as *1.005000000000* or as *1.* (in the latter case the fractional part cannot be seen). Display formats affect only the way in which values of the variable will appear in the spreadsheet editor. Those formats do not affect the internal representation (i.e., storage precision) of the values and they can be adjusted without affecting the actual values stored in the file.

The default internal storage precision in *STATISTICA* standard data files is *double precision*, which allows for 15 significant digits (e.g. 1.23456789012345), regardless of the display format set by the user. Alternative (more economical in terms of disk space used) storage precisions are available in the *Megafile Manager* data files (see page 1329 and Volume III).

Numeric vs. Text (Alphanumeric) Values

Usually in data base management programs, each field (variable) is defined as either *numeric* or *text* type. In *STATISTICA*, every variable in the data set can be *simultaneously* of numeric and text type, and when you view your data in the spreadsheet editor you can toggle between the numeric and text "identity" of variables (use the option *Text Values* from the spreadsheet *View* pull-down menu or click on the ABC spreadsheet toolbar button).

Example. This simple example illustrates the so-called double notation of values in *STATISTICA*. The following spreadsheet shows a simple data file containing exclusively numeric data:

Data: SIMPLE.STA 3v * 1

	1 GENDER	2 AGE	3 EDUCAT
1	1	21	1
2	2	19	1
3	1	32	2
4	2	31	2
5	1	19	2
6	1	33	1
7	2	25	1
8	2	27	2
9	1	31	2
10	1	24	1

Those variables do not have any text values. You may add one. Highlight (click on) the first value of the first case (currently *1*) and type in *MALE*; then press *Enter*. In this way, you will inform the program that the numeric value *1* corresponds to the text value *MALE*. Not only will the (newly typed) value change to *MALE*, but all values of *1* in this variable will change.

Data: SIMPLE.STA 3v * 1

	1 GENDER	2 AGE	3 EDUCAT
1	MALE	21	1
2	2	19	1
3	MALE	32	2
4	2	31	2
5	MALE	19	2
6	MALE	33	1
7	2	25	1
8	2	27	2
9	MALE	31	2
10	MALE	24	1

What happens when you enter a text value in a field that does not have any numeric values yet? Will it have any numeric equivalent? Yes, every text value in *STATISTICA* data files has a numeric equivalent; in that case, the program would create it automatically (as consecutive integers, starting with *100*). Note that you can enter new or edit existing text values in the *Text Values Manager* dialog (see *Spreadsheet Window*, Chapter 3).

Advantages of double (text/numbers) notation. This unique feature of *STATISTICA* data files facilitates data entry and helps to store and manage data in the most informative terms of plain English words, while maintaining their numeric components (necessary to compute statistics). Note that at the same time, those text values are "true" text values and not merely value labels (used to label the output). For example, you can use them for specifying levels of variables, group codes, selection conditions (e.g., select if *v1 = 'MALE'*), etc.

How *Dates* are Represented in *STATISTICA* Data Files:

Date values of variables are internally stored in Julian format, that is, as a single integer value that represents the number of days that have passed since January 1, 1900; for example, a date entered and displayed as *1/21/1968* will be stored as the Julian date *24,858*; the (optional) decimals are interpreted as time (see the next topic). Date values stored in this manner can be used in subsequent analyses (e.g., in *Survival Analysis* in order to calculate survival times, see below) and transformed using arithmetic operations; at the same time, they can be displayed as dates in reports or graphs (e.g., used to label scale values).

Julian date values can be displayed in the spreadsheet in numeric (Julian) format or in one of several pre-defined date display formats (e.g., *1/6/64*, *6-Jan-64*, *Jan-1964*, *01/06/64*, *01/06/1964*, *6-Jan*).

To change the date display format, select the *Date* format option in the *Current Specs* dialog (accessible by double-clicking on the variable name in the spreadsheet or from the spreadsheet *Edit* pull-down menu) and choose one of the pre-defined display formats.

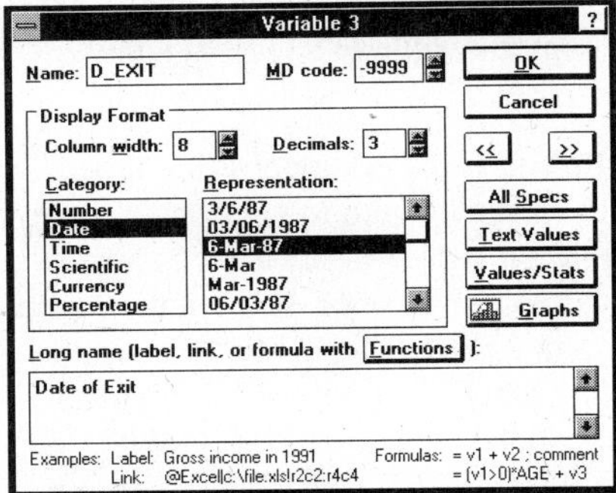

When entering dates into a new variable, you will first need to change the variable display format from *Number* (the default format) to *Date* in the *Current Specs* dialog and select the desired date display format. Now, you can enter the dates in any of the pre-defined date display formats (i.e., enter the dates in the format that is easiest to key in, even if it is different than the desired display format) and *STATISTICA* will recognize those formats, convert the display to the desired date format, and internally store the date values in Julian format. Please refer to the on-line *Electronic Manual* for more detailed information on entering new or pasting copied date values into the data file.

You can create a single date variable from two (month, year or day, month) or three (day, month, year) variables as well as split a single date variable into two or three variables in the *Date Operations* dialog accessible from the *Date Values* option in the spreadsheet **Vars** pull-down menu (see below).

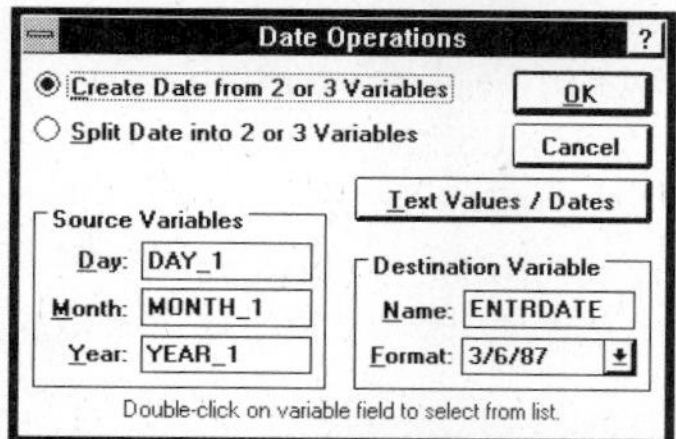

Please refer to the on-line *Electronic Manual* (click **?** or press the F1 key in the dialog shown above) for examples of creating date variables from numeric variables and splitting date variables into numeric variables.

How *Time* is Represented in *STATISTICA* Data Files:

Time values of variables are stored as (optional) decimal values representing the fraction of the day since midnight; for example, *6:00AM* is stored as *0.25*. Time values stored in this manner can be used in subsequent analyses and transformed using arithmetic operations; at the same time, they can be displayed as times in reports or graphs (e.g., used to label scale values).

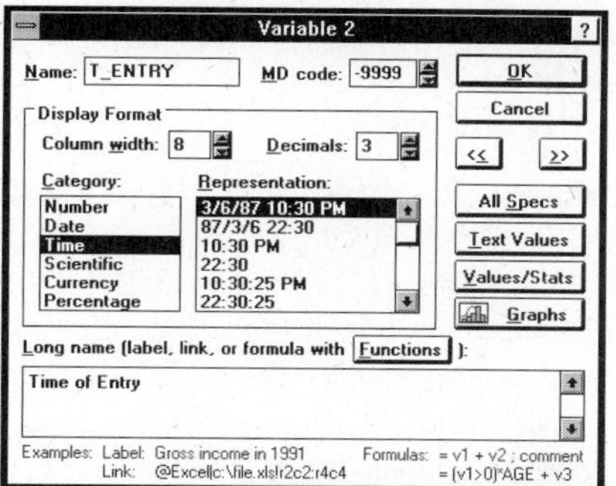

STATISTICA will format the display of time values according to the current settings in the *International - Time Format* option of the Windows *Control Panel*.

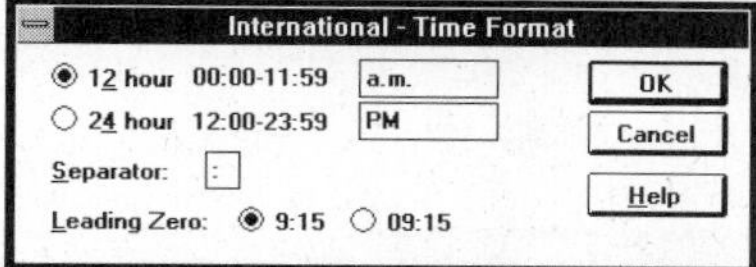

Please refer to the on-line *Electronic Manual* (click **?** or press the F1 key in the *Variable Specifications* dialog) for examples of creating time variables from numeric variables and splitting time variables into numeric variables.

How to use *Date* Values as Codes (e.g., as Values of Grouping Variables):

Some procedures in *STATISTICA* require that values of grouping variables (codes) be less than 32,000, i.e., less than the Julian values of some dates [this does not apply to grouping codes used in all *Stats* (and *Quick Stats*) *Graphs* procedures, *Quick Basic Stats*, *Quality Control*, *Experimental Design*, *Process Analysis*, and other procedures]. In order to use date values as codes smaller than 32,000, convert them into text values using the facility described below.

How to Convert *Date* Values into Text Values and Vice-Versa:

In some circumstances it may be useful to create text values with date information (e.g., when using a date variable as a coding variable with codes smaller than 32,000, see the previous topic). In this case, you can transform the date variable into a variable containing date text values with numeric equivalents in a range that will allow them to be used as codes by all procedures of *STATISTICA* (i.e., numeric values less than 32,000). Use the *Text Values/Dates* dialog to convert dates into codes.

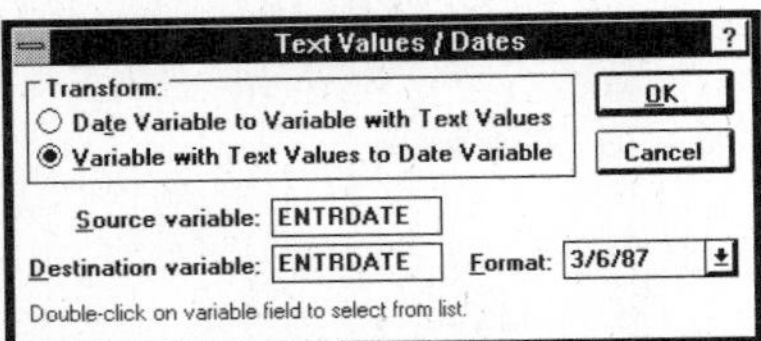

This dialog is accessible by pressing the *Text Values/Dates* button in the *Date Operations* dialog (see page 1319).

Creating Data Files, Entering Data

Data files can be *created* by *importing* them from other formats or applications (see below) or entering them directly into the spreadsheet. Each data file has a fixed number of variables and cases (although it can be changed easily in the spreadsheet window), and other general characteristics (e.g., variable names, comment line, and many others, see *Spreadsheet Window*, Chapter 3).

When you import data to *STATISTICA* from some other file format, usually those characteristics of the new data file are automatically determined by the features of the imported data set. If you create a file "by hand," you need to enter those characteristics directly (or accept the default settings suggested by the program). In *STATISTICA*, data can also be accessed via the *Dynamic Data Exchange* (*DDE*) facilities (see below).

Importing Data from Other Applications

Clipboard. The quickest, and in many cases easiest way to access data files from other Windows applications (e.g., spreadsheets) is to use the Clipboard, which in *STATISTICA* supports special Clipboard data formats generated by applications such as MS Excel or Lotus 1-2-3 for Windows. For example, *STATISTICA* will properly interpret formatted cells (such as *1,000,000* or *$10*) and text values.

File import facilities. Data files from a wide variety of Windows and non-Windows applications can also be accessed and translated into the *STATISTICA* format using the file import facilities (in the *Data Management* module) which also include options to access formatted and free-format text (ASCII) files.

The main advantages of using the file import facilities (over the Clipboard) are that:

- They allow the user to specify the exact way in which the translation is to be performed (e.g., access named ranges in the foreign data files, decide whether or not to import variable names, text values, and case names, and how to interpret them); and
- They allow the user to access types of data which are not (or not easily) accessible to Clipboard operations (such as long value labels, special missing data codes) or multiple components of such compound data files as 3D worksheets of Lotus 1-2-3 for Windows.

***DDE* links.** Finally, *STATISTICA* supports the *Dynamic Data Exchange* conventions, thus you can dynamically link a range of data in its spreadsheet to a subset of data in other (true Windows)

applications. The procedure is in fact much simpler than it might appear, and may be easily employed without technical knowledge about the mechanics of *DDE*, especially when you use the *Paste Link* (instead of the script-entry) method (for details, see Chapter 3, or the *Electronic Manual*).

Formats of *Date* values. In *STATISTICA* data files (which follow a "data-base style" organization), value display formats apply to entire variables and not individual cells (like in Excel). Therefore, values which were formatted as dates in Excel will be displayed in *STATISTICA* as Julian (integer) values (e.g., *34,092* instead of *May 3, 1993*) unless the format of the appropriate variables is set to *Date* (see *Spreadsheet Window*, Chapter 3).

Exporting Data to Other Applications

The Clipboard and data file translation facilities described in the previous topic in the context of importing foreign file formats can also be used to export data from *STATISTICA* to other formats. A similar selection of formats and data types is supported when importing data to and exporting them from *STATISTICA* (see the previous topic).

The Dynamic Data Exchange (*DDE*) Facility

You can establish *DDE* (*Dynamic Data Exchange*) links between a "source" (or server) file (e.g., a MS Excel spreadsheet or a document written in MS Word) and a *STATISTICA* data file (the "client" file), so that when changes are made to the data in the source file, the data will be automatically updated in the *STATISTICA* spreadsheet (client file).

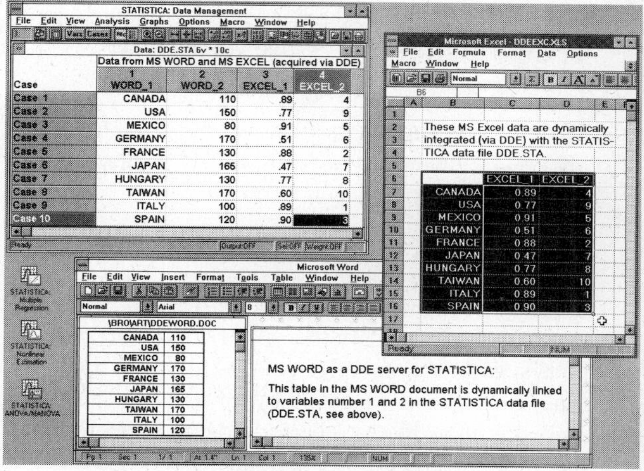

For example, the *STATISTICA* data file shown above is dynamically linked to the data in the MS Excel worksheet and also to the data in the MS Word table.

A common application for dynamically linking two files would be in industrial settings, where the *STATISTICA* data file would be dynamically linked with a measurement device (e.g., in order to automatically update specific measurements hourly). *DDE* links can be established using the quick, "paste-like" *Paste Link* option in the spreadsheet pull-down menu *Edit*, or by entering a definition of the link into the *Long name (label, formula, link)* field of the *Spreadsheet Edit (Current) Specs* dialog (refer to page 1341 for details and examples).

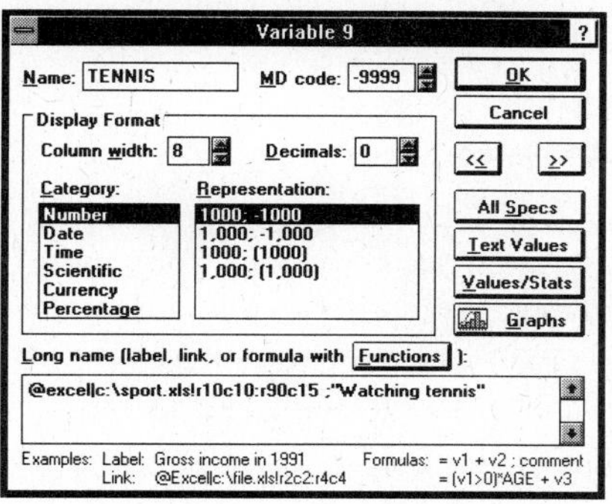

When a link is established, it can be managed using the *Links Manager* (accessible via the *Links...* option in the spreadsheet pull-down menu *Edit*).

There are also other applications for the *DDE* data integration facilities in *STATISTICA*; see the on-line documentation on *DDE* for details.

Verification of Data

Once the data (entered or imported) are in the file, one may need to verify their integrity (logical consistency) and completeness. Although some types of errors in the data may never be trapped, there are many ways to perform data verification based on general criteria that the data should meet.

For example, the verification can be as simple as checking whether values in a variable are "legal" (e.g., only *1* and *2* might be allowed for *Gender*) or whether they fall within allowed ranges of values (e.g., *Age* must be more than *0* and less than *200*). It can also be as complex as checking multiple logical conditions that each value must meet in relation to other values in the same file or in another file (a relatively simple example of conditional verification: if a person is a male *or* less than a certain age, then the number of pregnancies for that person cannot be more than zero. *STATISTICA* contains flexible facilities to perform verification of data using criteria of practically unlimited complexity. For more information on this facility, see page 1366.

Data Editing and Restructuring

Data editing involves not only entering or changing individual values; often one needs to perform more global operations such as reordering variables or cases, moving, copying, or changing the overall size of the data file by adding or deleting cases and variables.

There are two general types of data restructuring operations in *STATISTICA*: (1) standard spreadsheet-type Clipboard based operations, and (2) global data restructuring operations.

(1) Clipboard based operations on cases or variables. Unlike the *Global* operations performed on ranges of cases or variables and treating them as logical units (see below), the Clipboard operations follow the standard spreadsheet conventions and apply only to the contents of the selected cells. They depend entirely on the current block (highlight) and cursor position.

For example, note that the *Global* operations of deleting or moving variables (see below) will affect (remove) not only the contents of the respective columns but also the columns themselves, thus they will change the structure of the data file (and those operations will always be performed on entire variables regardless of whether all cases or only a subset of cases is currently highlighted in the selected variables).

In the case of Clipboard operations, however, only the segment of data which is highlighted will be cut, and (following the common spreadsheet conventions), pasting will always begin from the current cursor position, and proceed down.

Thus, for example, if in order to move a variable, you (a) highlighted and cut an entire column, (b) highlighted another (entire) column and then (c) pasted the Clipboard contents to that new location (intending to "replace" the previous values) -- the operation will be performed as intended only if you have placed the cursor at the top of the new column. If you have placed it somewhere in the middle, then the pasting will start from that point down.

(2) Global operations on cases or variables. Unlike the Clipboard operations of cutting, copying, and pasting blocks of data (or contents of entire columns or rows), the operations offered from the spreadsheet *Edit-Variables* or

Edit-Cases pull-down menu or the spreadsheet *Vars* or *Cases* toolbar buttons (e.g., *Add*, *Move*, *Copy*, etc.), will affect not only the contents of the columns or rows of data but also the columns or rows themselves (where applicable). For example, the *Delete* operation will remove not only the contents of the selected range of columns (or rows) but the columns (or rows), too.

Also, note the difference between these global operations performed on variables or cases (treated as logical units of the *STATISTICA* data files) and all Clipboard spreadsheet operations which work the same way as in all standard spreadsheets (e.g., MS Excel). For example, the global operation of copying, deleting, or moving variables (or cases) available from this menu will not depend on the current location of the cursor or block (highlight), other than by the fact that the highlighted variable names (or case names) will be suggested to you in the respective dialogs (thus offering a shortcut method of selecting variables or cases to be affected by the operation). Global operations on variables will always be performed on all cases of selected variables, regardless of whether or not all cases or only a subset of cases are currently highlighted for the respective variables.

On the other hand, in case of Clipboard operations, only the segment of data which is highlighted will be copied, and (following the common spreadsheet conventions) pasting will always begin from the current cursor position, and proceed down.

Clipboard Operations in the Spreadsheet

When you copy or move a block in the spreadsheet (e.g., via *Drag-and-Drop*, see Chapter 3), the values which are copied will depend on the display mode of the spreadsheet.

Numeric values or value labels. If the spreadsheet is displaying numeric values (or value labels) when the block is copied to the Clipboard, then only those numeric values (or value labels) will be copied.

Text values. If the spreadsheet is displaying text values when the block is copied to the Clipboard, then not only are the text values copied to the Clipboard, but also the corresponding numeric values and value labels (if any). This may result in the assignment of text values to numeric values that did not previously have text value equivalents (see below).

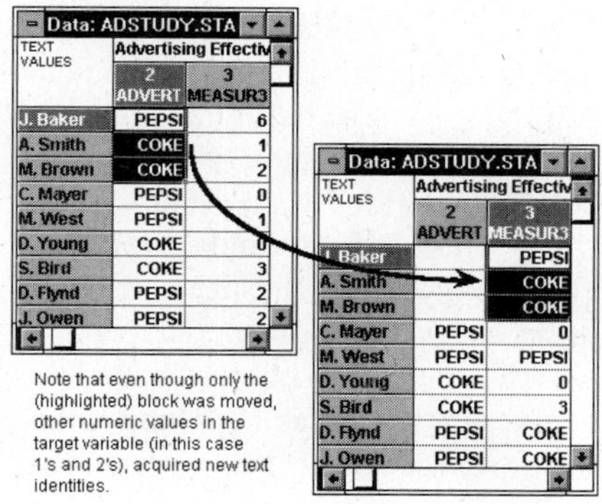

Note that even though only the (highlighted) block was moved, other numeric values in the target variable (in this case 1's and 2's), acquired new text identities.

Data Transformations

Some of the most common data management operations used in statistical data analysis are transformations and recoding of data. Specifically, instead of analyzing raw values of variables that have been entered or imported, you may need to compute new values based on some combinations or arrangements of raw measurements.

Example. Imagine that you need to create a variable that would contain a total test score for each person as an average of his/her scores on 3 test scales. If data from those test scales are stored in variables *v1* through *v3*, then you would need to compute a new variable (e.g., *v4*), defined as:

```
= (v1+v2+v3)/3
```

This is a typical example of a data transformation formula performed for each case in the data file.

Data transformations in *STATISTICA*. As mentioned before, *STATISTICA* data files are organized by cases. Unless you request otherwise, every transformation formula that you specify (see the example above) will be executed for each case in the data file. There are two ways of specifying transformations.

(1) Simple, one-line transformation formulas can be entered directly into the *Spreadsheet Edit (Current) Specs* dialog (see *Spreadsheet Window*, Chapter 3). The quickest way to access that dialog is to double-click on the variable name in the spreadsheet. The formula then becomes, in a sense, a "definition" of a variable. For example, variable *Testmean* in the example above was defined as an average of 3 other variables. Thus, those formulas work differently than in typical spreadsheet applications because a formula entered in a *STATISTICA* variable affects not just a single cell but all values in that variable (column), that is, all cases (row of the spreadsheet), unless you explicitly specify otherwise.

(2) *STATISTICA BASIC* is a programming language accessible from the *Analysis* pull-down menu in every module of *STATISTICA* (see page 1354). *STATISTICA BASIC* is a simple to use but powerful programming language which can be used for a variety of types of applications ranging from simple data transformations (for example, whenever you need to do more than can be done using the spreadsheet formulas, e.g., loops, recoding functions) to building custom, complex, permanent extensions to computational, graphics, and data management procedures of *STATISTICA*.

Other transformations. In addition to spreadsheet formulas and *STATISTICA BASIC*, *STATISTICA* offers a selection of pre-defined, specialized transformations which are accessible from menus and dialogs of specific modules (e.g., the *Time Series* module features a large selection of specialized data smoothing and filtering transformations).

Data Recoding

Recoding of data involves the "translation" of original values into some new values. For example, you can recode values of cholesterol levels in the range of *below 170*, *171* to *200*, and *above 200*, into *1*, *2*, and *3* (or *LOW*, *MEDIUM*, and *HIGH*), respectively. Recoding functions of practically unlimited complexity can be custom-defined in *STATISTICA BASIC* (for the complete most up-to-date syntax reference, refer to the *Electronic Manual*) and used repeatedly in your data transformation programs. However, a quick on-line recoding facility can also be accessed directly from the spreadsheet at any point (see the spreadsheet toolbar button Vars, Chapter 2). The scrollable *Recode Values* dialog which will be displayed, allows you to define new values of the current variable (see the fields *New Value 1*, *New Value 2*, *New Value 3*, etc., below) depending on the specific conditions, which you define (see the fields *Category 1*, *Category 2*, *Category 3*, etc., below).

When specifying the conditions, follow the standard syntax conventions which are common in *STATISTICA* to all those procedures which involve any operation of "selecting cases" based on their values (see *Status Bar*, Chapter 2).

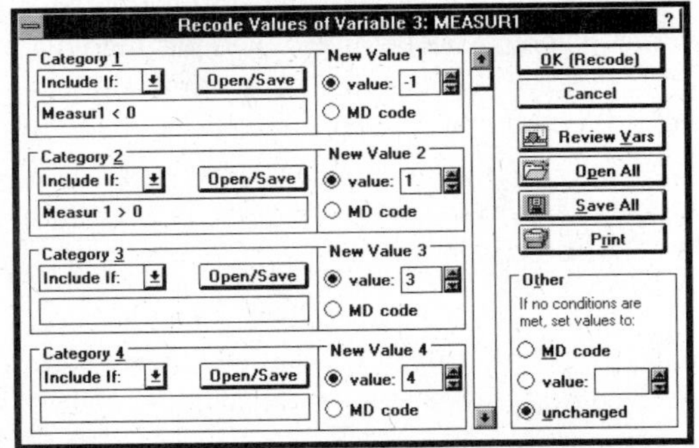

For example, the recoding conditions specified above would "translate" the negative values of the current variable (*Measur1*) into *-1* and positive values into *1*. Note that the *0*'s (the only value which is not included in the two recoding conditions) would be left unchanged, as set using the radio button *unchanged* (see the box *Other* in lower right corner of the dialog).

You can also use here *Case Selection Conditions* that have been specified somewhere else and saved to disk files (either as individual conditions or sets). Note that recoding conditions may be much more complex (see the on-line documentation by pressing F1 in this dialog), and they can be defined such that the new values of the current variable do not depend on the old values of that variable, but only on values of some other variables in the data set. Thus, this facility can be used not only to recode existing data, but also to create values of a new variable based on conditions met by other variables (as illustrated below).

Using the Recoding facility to create new variables. You can use any of the data transformation facilities: spreadsheet formulas or *STATISTICA BASIC* to create values of a new variable based on conditions met by other variables. However, often the quickest way to do it would be to use the on-line data recoding facility described in the previous paragraph, which is accessible at any point from the data spreadsheet (see the spreadsheet toolbar button Vars, Chapter 2). As mentioned in the previous paragraph, the currently highlighted variable does not even have to be included in the text of the recoding conditions. Thus, you can use this facility to create values of a variable based on conditions met by other variables.

For example, you can add a new (empty) variable to the data file, and then use this facility to create the new values. For instance, the recoding conditions could be used to assign *1*'s to the new variable for all "male subjects, 18 to 25 years old with cholesterol levels below 200;" assign *2*'s to "male subjects 18 to 25 years old with cholesterol levels above 200;" and assign the missing data value to all other subjects.

Splitting and Merging Data Files

Splitting data files. All *STATISTICA* data analyses require you to select the variables that will be analyzed; all analyses also support case selection conditions (i.e., filters allowing you to include only selected cases in the analysis, e.g., exclude if *v1='MALE'*; see *Status Bar*, Chapter 2). Thus, every analysis can be based on only a selected subset of data. However, it is sometimes useful to permanently split a data file into subsets. For example, small data files are processed somewhat faster, or if only variables of interest are included in the data file, then you can use the quick *Select All* button convention when selecting variables. In those cases, you can define a subset of data and save it under a separate file name. Subsets can be created by selecting the *Subset* option from the *Analysis* pull-down menu in the *Data Management* module.

Merging data files. There are many circumstances where one needs to merge files. For example, data from more subjects could be collected and then you need to *append* more cases to the end ("bottom") of the existing data file (i.e., merge it with another file that contains the same variables). You could also perform more tests (additional variables) on cases from an existing data file.

merging cases:

1st file
2nd file

merging variables:

1st file	2nd file

A file containing those new variables would be appended at the end ("right side") of the existing data file (i.e., merged with another file that contains

the same cases). The *Merge* option is available from the *Analysis* pull-down menu of the *Data Management* module.

Relational merge. A common problem that arises when merging variables (see the second example above) is that the number and order of cases in the two data files must be precisely the same. If at least one case is missing in the second data file (or there is one case that has no equivalent in the first file), then all subsequent data will be merged with the wrong cases. The solution to this potential problem is to use the *relational merge*. When relationally merging cases from two files, you need to specify a *key* (case identifier) variable in each data set; then for each case, the program will check the values of this key in both data files and merge the cases only if their respective keys match. *STATISTICA* offers comprehensive options to perform relational merge of files.

PROGRAM OVERVIEW

The *Data Management* Module

The *Data Management* module is a comprehensive statistical data base management system that offers a variety of data editing, transformation, and file restructuring facilities.

Spreadsheet. The *STATISTICA spreadsheet window* (accessible not only in the *Data Management* module but also at any point in the program) offers a wide selection of data editing and restructuring options, including: data entry facilities; a complete selection of *Drag-and-Drop* operations; integrated formulas for transforming values of variables; integrated data recoding facility; search and replace facilities; quick movement to specified locations in the file; block operations (copy, move, delete, transpose, standardize); quick fill operations (random value fill); facilities to perform global restructuring operations on the data file (e.g., add, delete, copy, and move ranges of cases and variables, shift variables, etc.); facilities to rank values, manage text values and labels; and many other options.

***STATISTICA* data files.** The *STATISTICA* system data files are optimized for access time and storage efficiency. They can be considered Workbooks, since they also store information about all supplementary files (graphs, Scrollsheets, reports, programs, etc.) used with the current data set, and these files can be opened automatically. *STATISTICA* data files support case names, text and numeric data values, date and time values, short and long variable labels with formulas and *DDE* links to other files, long value labels, and other specifications such as headers, notes, fonts, colors, etc. (see *Spreadsheet Edit (Current) Specs*, Chapter 3). Variables can be defined with spreadsheet formulas and recalculated with a single keystroke (see *Spreadsheet Edit (Current) Specs*, Chapter 3). There can be a practically unlimited number of cases and up to 4,092 double (text + numbers) variables in one data file. Files with up to 32,000 variables can be processed in *Megafile Manager*, accessible from the *Data Management* module (see below, see also Volume III).

Double notation (numeric/text) of values. *STATISTICA* supports a unique *double notation* of variables, where each value can simultaneously have a numeric and text identity. You can use and refer to either the numeric or text identity of these values in all *STATISTICA* modules. For example, if *1* is equivalent to *MALE* in the data file, then in the *Selection Conditions* dialog, you can either enter: exclude if *v1=1*, or the more meaningful, exclude if *v1='MALE'*. A *Text Values Manager* is provided to manage both text values and long value labels and allows you to take full advantage of this flexible data structure with a minimum number of keystrokes. The *STATISTICA* double notation of values is supported by all *STATISTICA* modules to facilitate specification of designs and description of results (Scrollsheets and graphs), even when the analyses are performed exclusively on numeric data. When you view your data in the spreadsheet you can toggle between the numeric and text "identity" of variables using the ABC toolbar button. Also, long value labels are supported; they can be review/edited in the spreadsheet by pressing the CTRL key while clicking on the ABC toolbar button.

Import/export. In addition to the comprehensive Clipboard-based data exchange facilities (*STATISTICA* supports special Clipboard data formats allowing for proper interpretation of data shared with spreadsheets and other applications) and the support to *Dynamic Data Exchange* (*DDE*), *STATISTICA* features a selection of comprehensive data import/export facilities (see *Import Files* and *Export Files*, pages 1375 and 1390, respectively).

You can import/export files in a variety of file formats, including the recent versions of Microsoft Excel, Lotus 1-2-3, all versions of Symphony, Quattro, dBASE III+, IV, and V, Paradox, STG (*STATISTICA* graphics format), mainframe portable file format (compatible with SPSS), and ASCII free- and fixed-format data files. Also, a comprehensive *ODBC* (Open Data Base Connectivity) facility (see Chapter 3) offers a convenient interface to practically all major data base management systems (including Oracle and Sybase). In addition, you can access a variety of free-format text files (sequential, matrix, incomplete matrix, etc.). While importing formatted data, *STATISTICA* will recognize the structure of the file, value labels, text and logical variables, blank cells or fields, and convert them into *STATISTICA* file format equivalents. A variety of import/export options (e.g., named ranges in spreadsheets) are available in the specific import-/export dialogs to facilitate the data conversion process.

Data transformations. Data transformation facilities (see *Spreadsheet Edit (Current) Specs*, Chapter 3) are integrated into the *STATISTICA* spreadsheet and allow you to define variables using formulas. All or selected formulas can be recalculated at once by clicking on the *Recalculate* toolbar button (also, an auto-recalculate option is supported that recalculates all formulas affected by any changes to the data file). The spreadsheet formulas support logical operators and can be used not only for computing new values, but also for simple recoding and data verification. A designated data recoding facility can also be accessed directly from the spreadsheet at any point in the program. In addition, a programming language (*STATISTICA BASIC*) is integrated within every module and can be used to perform data transformations and recoding of unlimited complexity.

***STATISTICA BASIC*.** *STATISTICA BASIC* is a simple to use but powerful programming language which can be used for a variety of types of applications ranging from simple data transformations (for example, whenever you need to do more than can be done using the spreadsheet formulas, e.g., loops, recoding functions) to building custom, complex, permanent extensions to computational, graphics, and data management procedures of *STATISTICA*.

Data verification. An interactive data verification and cleaning facility in the *Data Management* module allows you to specify data integrity or internal consistency criteria of practically unlimited complexity. Data verification can be performed interactively and every case which does not meet the specified conditions can be identified and marked and/or corrected by the user.

Other operations. Facilities are provided to split files into *Subsets* following user-specified criteria. A selection of file *Merge* operations are supported (including the relational and hierarchical relational merge). Data files can be *Sorted* in a number of ways (including multiple nested sort). File headers with labels, formulas and alphanumeric specifications can be merged or transferred to new files. Variables can be *Shifted* (lagged against each other), converted into ranks (in a variety of ways), *Standardized*, and *Missing Values* can be replaced by means. Formatted listings of data specifications, data files, and subfiles can be printed according to user specifications.

Common Spreadsheet Options vs. Options of the *Data Management* Module

As mentioned before, most of the commonly-used data management facilities are integrated with the spreadsheet and available from the data spreadsheet in every module (from the toolbar, *Edit* pull-down menu, or the flying menus). These commonly-available facilities include all spreadsheet operations on cases and variables, data transformations through the spreadsheet formulas, *STATISTICA BASIC* programming language, the on-line recoding facilities, ranking, filling ranges, shifting, *DDE* (*Dynamic Data Exchange*), management of text values, date/time values, long value labels, and many other options (including direct import/export functions and import via *ODBC*).

The *Data Management* module includes all of these options and, in addition, some more specialized data management facilities, such as interactive data verification and cleaning facility, and specialized import/export facilities (e.g., allowing import/export of double notation of values to file formats which normally do not support double notation).

Access to *Megafile Manager* facilities. The *Data Management* module of *STATISTICA* also provides access to all facilities of the *Megafile Manager* data base system (not available in *Quick STATISTICA*), which offers options to access and process data in unusual data formats (e.g., data organized into extremely large records or data with very long text values). A unique feature of *Megafile Manager* is that it can process data with extremely long records (up to 8 megabytes per record). *Megafile Manager* can also be used as an archival data base system to store data combined from various sources (preserving their original formats). Easy-to-use and flexible facilities are provided in the *Data Management* module to move data in and out, between *STATISTICA* data files and archival *Megafile Manager* data bases. Because of the extensive capabilities of *Megafile Manager*, these facilities are discussed in detail in a separate chapter (see Volume III).

Data Management Operations via the *STATISTICA Command Language*

Data management operations can also be performed by specifying the respective commands in the *STATISTICA Command Language* (accessible in every module in the pull-down menu *Analysis*).

Data Management Operations and Custom Procedures via *STATISTICA BASIC*

STATISTICA BASIC (accessible in every module in the pull-down menu *Analysis*) contains a comprehensive selection of specialized functions for data base management.

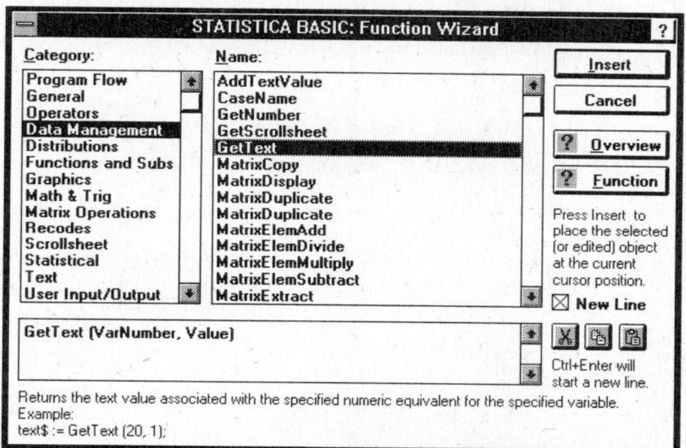

Note that *BASIC* programs can be included in batches of *SCL* (*STATISTICA Command Language*, see above) commands.

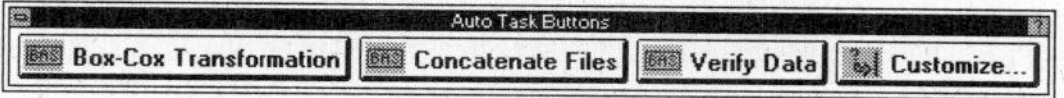

Also, specific custom data base management operations developed in *STATISTICA BASIC* can be assigned to buttons on the *Auto Task Buttons* toolbars and used as permanent extensions of the *STATISTICA* system.

What is *Megafile Manager*?

Overview

Megafile Manager is a specialized data base management system accessible from the *Data Management* module of *STATISTICA*. Its unique feature is that it can manage and directly process types of data which need to be transformed, aggregated, extracted, or cleaned before they can be

directly accessed by statistical or graphics procedures (e.g., data organized into extremely long records or data embedded inside very long text values).

Megafile Manager can process extremely large records of data (*rows*): up to 32,000 columns with up to 255 characters each (up to 8 megabytes per row). Data organized in such long records can, for example, be produced by some automated quality control measurement devices or other data acquisition or monitoring equipment. Also, such files are sometimes useful in maintaining integrated, large archival data banks consisting of numerous merged or concatenated files.

Megafile Manager Data: FREQUEN.MFM 6v * 220c

DATA ON THE RELATIVE FREQUENCY OF USING COGNITIVE TERMS IN JOURNAL ARTICLES

#	1 JOURNAL Text	2 VOLUME Int	3 QUOTE_01 Text
1	Journal of Experimental Psychology: Human Learning and Memory	6	The nature
2	Journal of Experimental Psychology: General	108	Nonanalytic concept formation
3	Journal of Personality and Social Psychology	34	Joint influence of prior
4	Journal of Experimental Psychology: Human Learning and Memory	7	Biased use of statistically relevant i
5	Journal of Personality and Social Psychology	35	The additive nature of chronic and tem
6	Journal of Abnormal Psychology	87	Individual differences multidimensiona
7	Journal of Personality and Social Psychology	35	Autobiographical memor
8	Journal of Experimental Psychology: Human Learning and Memory	8	The inheritance of personality and abi
9	Journal of Personality and Social Psychology	36	Accessibility of negative constructs w
10	Journal of Abnormal Psychology	88	The acquisition of syntax
11	Journal of Experimental Psychology: Human Learning and Memory	9	The effect of sibling relationship on
12	Journal of Personality and Social Psychology	37	Shock-associated words
13	Journal of Abnormal Psychology	89	Biased questions in judgme
14	Journal of Experimental Psychology: Human Learning and Memory	10	Believing anot
15	Journal of Personality and Social Psychology	38	Behaviors mak
16	Journal of Abnormal Psychology	90	Autonomic responses to shock- associat
17	Journal of Personality and Social Psychology	39	Expectancy confirmation processes aris
18	Journal of Experimental Psychology: Human Learning and Memory	11	On consciousness in syntac
19	Journal of Personality and Social Psychology	40	Accuracy of brightness discrimination
20	Journal of Abnormal Psychology	91	The role of context in interp

Data: FREQUEN.STA 6v * 220c

DATA ON THE RELATIVE FREQU

Case	1 JOURNAL	2 VOLUME	3 QUOTE_01
Journal of Experimen	JEP_LMC	6	32
Journal of Experimen	JEP_G	108	76
Journal of Personali	JPSP	34	23
Journal of Experimen	JEP_LMC	7	56
Journal of Personali	JPSP	35	54
Journal of Abnormal	JAP	87	35
Journal of Personali	JPSP	35	65
Journal of Experimen	JEP_LMC	8	23
Journal of Personali	JPSP	36	56
Journal of Abnormal	JAP	88	72
Journal of Experimen	JEP_LMC	9	65
Journal of Personali	JPSP	37	32
Journal of Abnormal	JAP	89	34
Journal of Experimen	JEP_LMC	10	56
Journal of Personali	JPSP	38	34
Journal of Abnormal	JAP	90	34
Journal of Personali	JPSP	39	65
Journal of Experimen	JEP_LMC	11	32
Journal of Personali	JPSP	40	12
Journal of Personali	JAP	91	23

Megafile Manager raw input data (with long text values)

extracted STATISTICA data file (ready for statistical analyses)

Megafile Manager and other *STATISTICA* Facilities

Most likely, the majority of common data processing needs can be easily addressed with the standard procedures available in every module of *STATISTICA*. Therefore, *Megafile Manager* will typically be used only when there is a need for facilities to handle very unusual data importing, management, and pre-processing needs, for example, in order to maintain very large data bases, or perform pre-processing of imported long text values, etc. Note that the standard procedures (offered in every module of *STATISTICA*) can also handle large size and very complex tasks; for example:

- to compute descriptive statistics or correlation matrices for very many variables (e.g., over 1,000) in a single run, use the *Quick Basic Stats* facilities available in every module via the *Analysis* pull-down menu or the toolbar button (see Chapter 10 for details);
- to perform complex recoding and aggregation of data, extensive operations on text values, or complex cleaning and verification of data, use *STATISTICA BASIC*, available in every module of *STATISTICA* from the *Analysis* pull-down menu;
- to import large files from other applications (e.g., Excel, Lotus, Quattro Pro, Paradox, etc.), use the *Import* options available from the pull-down menu *File* in every module of *STATISTICA* (see Chapter 3);
- to perform sequential, hierarchical, or relational merging of files, use the *Merge* option from the *Analysis* pull-down menu in the *Data Management* module, or use the functions available in *STATISTICA BASIC* for accessing external files (and then use the available powerful *STATISTICA BASIC*

functions to merge data via simple or complex user-defined algorithms).

Unique Features of *Megafile Manager*

Maintaining large, archival data banks; hierarchical relations between data bases. *Megafile Manager* offers options for aggregating data sets from other applications and setting up very large (e.g., 8 megabytes per record), efficient archival data bases. It also supports links between related (and hierarchically organized) data sets. Subsets of columns from such archival data banks can be extracted and used with other applications (such as *STATISTICA,* Excel, or Paradox).

Preprocessing large records of raw data. Another unique application of *Megafile Manager* is at the stage of analysis when raw data need to be aggregated or preprocessed before meaningful indices are obtained for use in data analysis. Such raw data sets (e.g., from automated quality control measurement devices or other data acquisition equipment) may feature records that are too long to fit into any standard application (e.g., 32,000 measures per row). *Megafile Manager* can be used to access such data sets, convert them into meaningful indices, and transfer to another application (such as *STATISTICA* or Excel) for further analysis. Such raw data often need to be cleaned and verified before they can be preprocessed. Custom-designed data verification (and interactive correction) can be performed in *Megafile Manager* using its integrated programming language which features specialized functions for interactive data editing and verification.

Data processing, analysis. Thus, *Megafile Manager* not only offers facilities to aggregate, store, and maintain long-record files, but it can also efficiently process them. Its integrated programming language (*MML*) features a variety of data analytic options and a library of functions. *Megafile Manager* also includes basic statistics facilities that can process data regardless of the record size. For example, it can tabulate data, compute descriptive statistics, or generate correlation matrices of practically unlimited size (the size of correlation matrices that could be generated by *Megafile Manager* exceeds the capacity of any existing storage device).

Long text values. Another specific feature of *Megafile Manager* is its ability to process very long text values. Also, its integrated programming language (*MML*) offers a comprehensive selection of functions to manipulate text data.

Exchanging data with *STATISTICA* data files. *Megafile Manager* uses a specialized file format optimized for its specific applications (e.g., maintaining data types from a variety of programs). However, easy to use and flexible facilities are provided in the *Data Management* module to move data in and out between *STATISTICA* data files and archival *Megafile Manager* data bases. For more information about *Megafile Manager*, please refer to Volume III.

STATISTICA DATA FILE FORMAT

General Format

Cases and Variables

The *STATISTICA standard data files* (also referred to as *raw data files*) are organized by *cases* (records, or rows in the spreadsheet) and *variables* (fields, or columns in the spreadsheet). The number of cases in a data file is essentially unlimited. Each file may have 4,092 variables, each of which may have a "double identity" (text/numeric) and long value labels. In unusual applications when this limit needs to be exceeded, then *Megafile Manager* files can be used which support up to 32,000 variables per file (see Volume III).

File Header /Comment

A one-line header (up to 77 characters) may be stored with each *STATISTICA* data file. In addition, a comment of up to 512 characters may also be stored with the file in the *Data File Header, Notes, and Workbook Info* dialog.

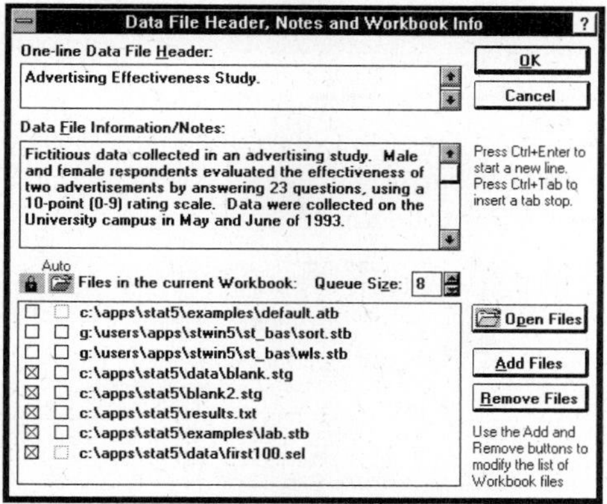

The *Data File Header, Notes and Workbook Info* dialog is accessible by pressing the [button] button on the toolbar, double-clicking on the file header area of the spreadsheet or by clicking on the *Header* option from the *Edit* pull-down menu.

Printing comments/headers. The *One-line Data File Header* and comment (*File Information/Notes*) are saved as part of the file and are printed along with the spreadsheet data file when the *File Info/Notes* option is selected in the *Print Data* dialog (accessible via the *Print* option in the *File* pull-down menu); the one-line header is printed along with the output of analyses when either a *Short*, *Medium* or *Long* report style is selected in the *Page/Output Setup* dialog (see Chapter 3). In addition, you can specify an *output header* to be printed on every page of the output in the *Page/output Setup* dialog (Chapter 3).

Workbook File List

Specific files (from the list of Workbook files) can be opened from this dialog or check-marked to open automatically (Auto [icon]) when you open the data set file, so that all supplementary information (e.g., graphs or reports from a previous stage of the analysis) is available whenever you open the data set.

Case Names

Individual cases in the data file (rows in the spreadsheet) can be labeled with case names up to 20 characters long.

Data: ADSTUDY.STA 25v * 50c

Advertising Effectiveness Study.

TEXT VALUES	1 GENDER	2 ADVERT	3 MEASUR1	4 MEASUR2	5 MEASUR3	6 MEASUR4
J. Baker	MALE	PEPSI	9	1	6	8
A. Smith	MALE	COKE	6	7	1	8
M. Brown	FEMALE	COKE	9	8	2	9
C. Mayer	MALE	PEPSI	7	9	0	5
M. West	MALE	PEPSI	7	1	6	2
D. Young	FEMALE	COKE	6	0	0	8
S. Bird	FEMALE	COKE	7	4	3	2
D. Flynd	MALE	PEPSI	9	9	2	6

Case names can contain any printable characters (including spaces and those characters that are illegal in variable names and text values; see below). Case names have a distinctive status in *STATISTICA* data files (different than text values). They are always displayed in the first column of the spreadsheet (i.e., *before* the first variable), and they stay on the screen when data in the editor are scrolled horizontally. Case names are used by default to label all *STATISTICA* output (Scrollsheets and graphs) that involves listing cases (e.g., contents of clusters in cluster analysis, residuals from regression analysis, factor scores from factor analysis).

Case names are entered into the case names column of the spreadsheet (via the *Case Name Manager* dialog, see *Spreadsheet Window*, Chapter 3), or they can be imported (e.g., from the first column of an Excel or ASCII file) or from a user-specified variable (text or numeric) in the current data file.

All case name management operations (creating, copying, importing, changing the width) are handled in the *Case Name Manager* dialog (accessible by double-clicking on the case name area of the spreadsheet). Because case names may occupy a large portion of the spreadsheet, their display may be toggled on and off through the spreadsheet window *View Case Names* toolbar button (see *Toolbars*, Chapter 2).

Missing Data Code

The missing data code is a reserved value (by default *-9999*) that indicates data points (cells in the spreadsheet) for which no data are available. Missing data values are displayed as blanks in the spreadsheet. Newly created data files are initially filled with missing data. You can enter a missing data code into a cell (i.e., overwrite the current value with missing data) by typing in the specific missing value (e.g. *-9999*), or simply by deleting the contents of the cell and leaving it blank. A user-defined missing data value can also be specified in the *Spreadsheet Edit (Current) Specs* dialog (see *Spreadsheet Window*, Chapter 3).

Variable Specifications

Summary. As mentioned before, due to the flexible "double notation" of all values in *STATISTICA*, there is no distinction between "text" and "numeric" variables. Every variable can contain both numeric and text values. Each variable in a *STATISTICA* data set features (a) a consecutive number, (b) a name up to 8 characters long, (c) a display format, and (d) an optional long variable name, script defining a *DDE* link, or formula. Double-clicking on the variable's name in the spreadsheet opens the *Spreadsheet Edit (Current) Specs* dialog in which the specifications for the variable may be entered or changed.

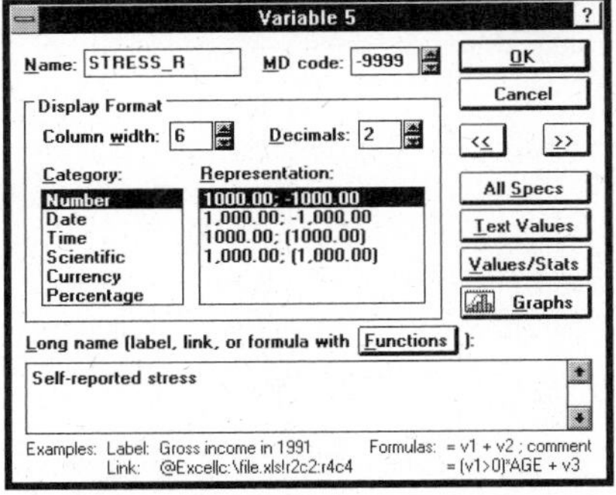

A combined table of specifications of all variables in the current data set can be reviewed/edited by pressing the *All Specs* button in this dialog.

Variables: EXP.STA 8v * 48c

	Name	MD Code	Format	Long Name (label,
1	GROUP	-9999	9.0	Experimental or control group subject
2	GENDER	-9999		ender
3	TIME	-9999		uction of reward
4	PAID	-9999		ot subject was offered money
5	STRESS_R	-9999		ed stress
6	CORRECT1	-9999		solutions to first problem
7	CORRECT2	-9999	8.0	No. correct solutions to second problem
8	CORRECT3	-9999	8.0	No. correct solutions to third problem

Cut Ctrl+X
Copy Ctrl+C
Paste Ctrl+V
Clear Del
Fill Block Down

These features are described in detail below. For an explanation of the *Missing data code*, see above.

Variable Names

STATISTICA variable names can be up to 8 characters long, cannot start with a digit, cannot contain spaces, unprintable characters, or the keyboard characters that are used in data transformations (`" # & ' ( ) * + , - . / ; : < = > [ ] ^ \ { } ~`). The program does not differentiate between upper and lowercase letters entered in variable names; all letters are converted to uppercase.

Display Format: Number

Select this format if the values of the variable are numeric or numeric with text equivalents. When you select this category, you can specify the number of decimal places to be displayed in the spreadsheet via the *Decimals* option.

Numeric representation. Numeric values are represented in decimal format with or without commas (e.g., *1000* or *1,000*). Negative values of the variable can be represented either with a negative sign (e.g., *-1000*) or with parentheses enclosing the number (e.g., *(1000)*).

Data: FORMAT1.STA 10v * 10c

	1 NUM_1	2 NUM_2	3 NUM_3	4 NUM_4
1	1285.0593	1,285.06	1285.06	1,285.06
2	-975.8812	-975.88	(975.88)	(975.88)
3	-2095.368	-2,095.37	(2095.37)	(2,095.37)
4	728.0752	728.08	728.08	728.08
5	-2323.992	-2,323.99	(2323.99)	(2,323.99)
6	1865.8062	1,865.81	1865.81	1,865.81
7	289.3570	289.36	289.36	289.36
8	1408.2665	1,408.27	1408.27	1,408.27
9	1248.6915	1,248.69	1248.69	1,248.69
10	1386.0878	1,386.09	1386.09	1,386.09

There are four representations available under this category:

1000.00; -1000.00 (see variable *NUM_1*, above)

1,000.00; -1,000.00 (see variable *NUM_2*, above)

1000.00; (1000.00) (see variable *NUM_3*, above)

1,000.00; (1,000.00) (see variable *NUM_4*, above)

Note that a European representation (e.g., 1,20 instead of 1.20 or 1.000.000 instead of 1,000,000) is supported by *STATISTICA* if you select this style in the Windows *Control Panel* (shown below).

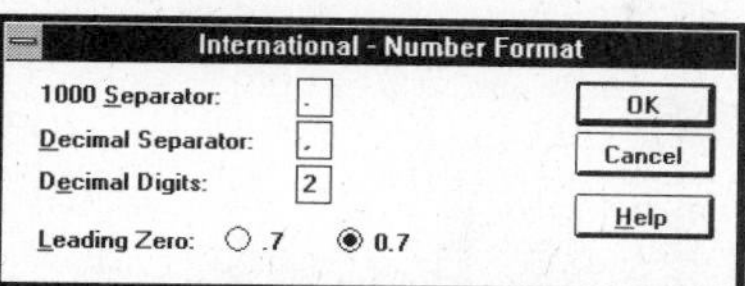

If this style is not selected in the *Control Panel* and you enter a comma in the decimal place, then *STATISTICA* will treat the value as a text value.

Display Format: Date

Date values of variables are internally stored in Julian format (i.e., as a single integer value that represents the number of days that have passed since January 1, 1900). For example, a date entered and displayed as *1/21/1968* will be stored as the Julian date *24,858*; the (optional) decimals are interpreted as time (see the next display format). Date values stored in this manner can be used in subsequent analyses (e.g., in *Survival Analysis* in order to calculate survival times) and transformed using arithmetic operations; at the same time, they can be displayed as dates in reports or graphs (e.g., used to label scale values). In order for variables to be interpreted as dates (e.g., variables containing Julian date values imported or pasted from Excel), select this display format. Note that in order to be displayed as a valid date, the respective values in the variable must be correct dates or explicitly defined text values.

Date representation. Select the desired date representation from the list of date formats:

3/6/87 (see variable *DATE_1*, below)

03/06/1987 (see variable *DATE_2*, below)

6-Mar-87	(see variable *DATE_3*, below)
6-Mar	(see variable *DATE_4*, below)
Mar-1987	(see variable *DATE_5*, below)
06/03/87	(see variable *DATE_6*, below)
Windows Format	(see variable *DATE_7*, below)

Data: DATE.STA 7v * 65c

Date formats for variables.

#	1 DATE_1	2 DATE_2	3 DATE_3	4 DATE_4	5 DATE_5	6 DATE_6	7 DATE_7
1	1/6/68	01/06/1968	6-Jan-68	6-Jan	Jan-1968	06/01/68	1968/01/06
2	5/2/68	05/02/1968	2-May-68	2-May	May-1968	02/05/68	1968/05/02
3	8/31/68	08/31/1968	31-Aug-68	31-Aug	Aug-1968	31/08/68	1968/08/31
4	8/22/68	08/22/1968	22-Aug-68	22-Aug	Aug-1968	22/08/68	1968/08/22
5	9/9/68	09/09/1968	9-Sep-68	9-Sep	Sep-1968	09/09/68	1968/09/09

In the *View Variable Specs* window,

Variables: DATE.STA 10v * 10c

	Name	MD Code	Format	Long Name (label, form
1	DATE_1	-9999	DATE1	First Date Display Format
2	DATE_2	-9999	DATE2	Second Date Display Format
3	DATE_3	-9999	DATE3	Third Date Display Format
4	DATE_4	-9999	DATE4	Fourth Date Display Format
5	DATE_5	-9999	DATE5	Fifth Date Display Format
6	DATE_6	-9999	DATE6	Sixth Date Display Format
7	DATE_7	-9999	DATE7	Current Windows Date Display Format

the various *Date* representations are represented by the following keywords (which can also be entered directly in the *Format* column of this window):

DATE1	3/6/87
DATE2	03/06/1987
DATE3	6-Mar-87
DATE4	6-Mar
DATE5	Mar-1987
DATE6	06/03/87
DATE7	Current Windows Date Format as selected in the *Windows Control Panel*

Note that the *Fill Down* option (from the right-mouse-button flying menu) can be used to quickly copy a format to a range of rows (variables).

Display Format: Time

This category displays the values of the variables in one of several time formats. Time values are stored in the data as (optional) decimal values representing the fraction of the day since midnight; for example, *6:00AM* is stored as *0.25*. Time values stored in this manner can be used in subsequent analyses and transformed using arithmetic operations; at the same time, they can be displayed as times in reports or graphs (e.g., used to label scale values).

Time representation. Time can be represented in one of the following formats:

3/6/87 10:30 PM	(see variable *TIME_1*, below)
87/3/6 22:30	(see variable *TIME_2*, below)
10:30 PM	(see variable *TIME_3*, below)
22:30	(see variable *TIME_4*, below)
10:30:25 PM	(see variable *TIME_5*, below)
22:30:25	(see variable *TIME_6*, below)
Windows Format	(see variable *TIME_7*, below)

You can choose from a date-time combination [with either 24-hour time or 12-hour (AM/PM) time format], or just time [either a 24-hour time or 12-hour (AM/PM) time format] in hours and minutes or hours, minutes, and seconds.

Data: TIME.STA 7v * 5c

Time Formats for Variables

	1 TIME_1	2 TIME_2	3 TIME_3	4 TIME_4	5 TIM_E_5	6 TIME_6	7 TIME_7
1	1/6/68 7:50 AM	68/1/6 7:50	7:50 AM	7:50	7:50:00 AM	7:50:00	7:50:0 AM
2	5/2/68 10:23 PM	68/5/2 22:2	10:23 PM	22:23	10:23:00 PM	22:23:00	10:23:0 PM
3	8/31/68 8:30 AM	68/8/31 8:3	8:30 AM	8:30	8:30:00 AM	8:30:00	8:30:0 AM
4	8/22/68 9:00 PM	68/8/22 21:	9:00 PM	21:00	9:00:00 PM	21:00:00	9:0:0 PM
5	9/9/68 6:15 AM	68/9/9 6:15	6:15 AM	6:15	6:15:00 AM	6:15:00	6:15:0 AM

In the *View Variable Specs* window,

Data: TIME.STA 7v * 5c

	Name	MD Code	Format	Long Name (label,
1	TIME_1	-9999	TIME1	First Time Display Format
2	TIME_2	-9999	TIME2	Second Time Display Format
3	TIME_3	-9999	TIME3	Third Time Display Format
4	TIME_4	-9999	TIME4	Fourth Time Display Format
5	TIM_E_5	-9999	TIME5	Fifth Time Display Format
6	TIME_6	-9999	TIME6	Sixth Time Display Format
7	TIME_7	-9999	TIME7	Current Windows Time Display Format

the various *Time* representations are represented by the following keywords (which can also be entered directly in the *Format* column of this window):

TIME1	3/6/87 10:30 PM
TIME2	87/3/6 22:30
TIME3	10:30 PM
TIME4	22:30
TIME5	10:30:25 PM
TIME6	22:30:25
TIME7	Current Windows Time Format as selected in the *Windows Control Panel*

Note that the *Fill Down* option (from the right-mouse-button flying menu) can be used to quickly copy a format to a range of rows (variables).

Display Format: Scientific

This category allows you to display the values of the variable in scientific notation.

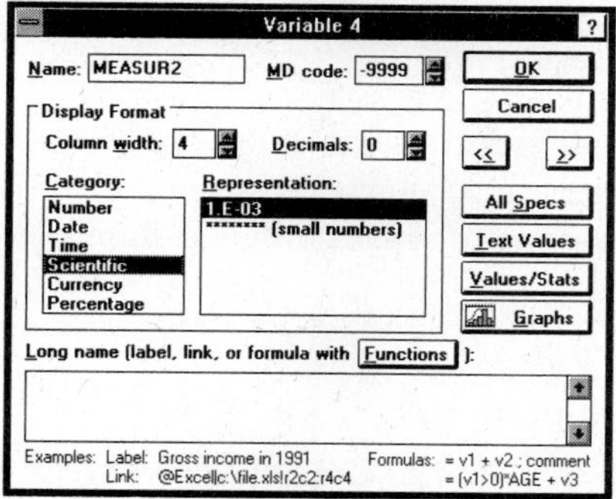

When you select this category, you can specify the number of decimal places to be displayed in the spreadsheet via the *Decimals* option.

Scientific representation. The first representation (standard scientific notation, see above) will display all numbers in the column in scientific notation according to the following rules:

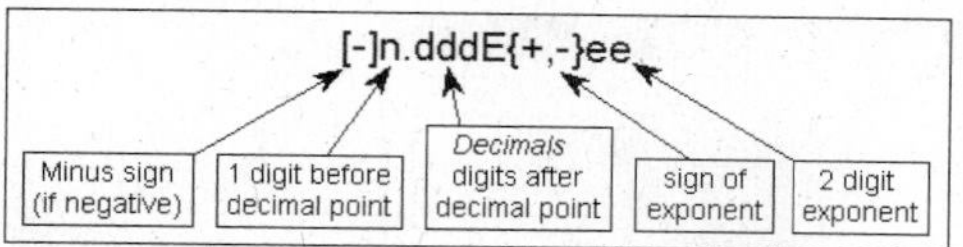

For example, *1.2345E-02* or *-3.2100E+08*.

The second representation will apply the scientific format only to those (small) values of the variable which would be displayed as 0 (zero) in *Number* format [i.e., they are from the interval (-1,1) and the significant digits start after the position specified by the *Decimals* edit field].

For example, if *Decimals = 4*, and the value is *0.0000123*, then in *Number* format, the value would be displayed as *0.0000*, whereas, in the second *Scientific* representation, the number would be displayed as *1.230E-5* (displaying 4 digits before *E*).

Display Format: Currency

Select this category in order to display the values of the variable in a currency format. When you select this category, you can specify the number of decimal places to be displayed in the spreadsheet via the *Decimals* option.

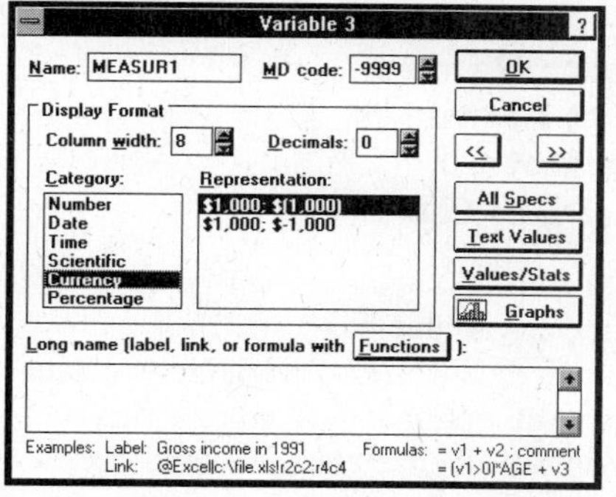

STATISTICA will format the display of currency values according to the current settings in the *International Currency Format* option of the Windows *Control Panel* (shown below).

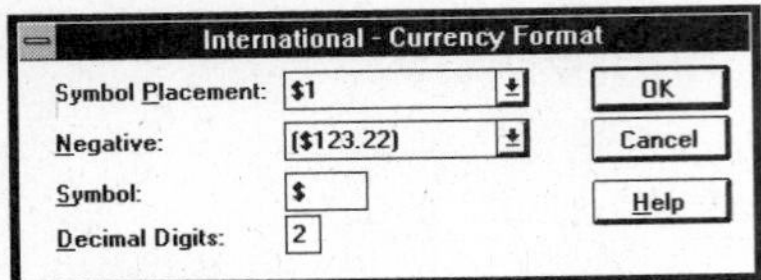

Currency representation. Currency values are displayed with a currency symbol before or after the number (depending on the configuration specified on the user's computer; e.g., *$*, *DM*, etc., see the *Symbol* edit field in the *International - Currency Format* dialog, above). You can choose to represent negative values of the variable either with a negative sign (e.g., *$-1,000*) or within parentheses enclosing the number (e.g., *($1,000)*).

Display Format: Percentage

Selecting this format will display the values of the variable as percentages. The percentage is based on what fraction of 1 the value of the variable represents. For example, the value *0.23* will be translated to *23%* while *23.4* will be translated to *2340%*.

Percentage representation. Percentages are represented with a % sign at the end of the number.

Long Variable Names, Spreadsheet Formulas or Dynamic Data Exchange (*DDE*) Links

Long variable names. In addition to the standard 8 character variable name which is displayed in the spreadsheet, each variable in a data file may also have an optional *long name*. These names may be up to 128 characters long and may contain notes or comments, including any printable characters. The labels can also contain the text of formulas used to compute values of the variable or specifications of *DDE* (Dynamic Data Exchange) links to other Windows application data files.

Spreadsheet formulas. A data transformation or recoding formula can be entered directly into the *Long Name* field in the *Spreadsheet Edit (Current) Specs* dialog. When this is done, the formula becomes, in a sense, a "definition" of the variable.

These formulas work differently than in typical spreadsheet applications: A formula entered into a *STATISTICA* variable affects not just a single cell, but rather all values in that variable (unless explicitly specified otherwise, see conditional statements, below). As mentioned before, system data files in *STATISTICA* are organized into records (as in data base management programs), therefore these formulas will process data sequentially (i.e., across records or cases).

To enter a transformation formula into the variable label, begin the formula with an equal sign, for example:

```
= (v2+v3)/2
```

(following the Excel convention, formulas must have an equal sign as the first character). Comments, if desired, may be added to the formulas by preceding them with a semicolon, for example:

```
= (v1+v2+v3)/3 ; this is a comment
```

Variable names in formulas. Instead of using the short *v#* (letter *v* and a number) convention, specific variable names may be used in the formulas, for example:

```
= (profit1+profit2)/2
```

Case numbers in formulas. You may also create values depending on the case number, which is referred to as *v0* (variable *zero*, which precedes variable 1). For example, the equation

```
= v0+99
```

would assign consecutive integer values (to consecutive cases of the currently specified variable), starting at 100. Note that the case number can be used in conditional statements (see the next paragraph); they can also be used to create a

categorical variable based on the sequential position of the case within the data file. For example, the equation

```
= trunc(((v0-1)/10)+1)
```

will fill the variable with consecutive integers starting with 1 being assigned to consecutive subsets of 10 cases (i.e., *1* will be assigned to cases 1 through 10, *2* will be assigned to cases 11 through 20, and so on).

Conditional statements. Logical expressions may be entered into spreadsheet formulas; they evaluate to *1* if the condition is met, and to *0* if it is false. Therefore, conditional statements may also be created by including a logical expression, contained within parentheses, for example:

```
= (v0<=100)*1 + (v0>100)*2
```

This formula would assign a value of *1* for cases *1* through *100*, and 2 to cases beyond *100*. (Note that in this example formula, the logical conditions have been underlined.) A logical condition (such as *v0>100*) is evaluated as being equivalent to *1* if it is true (i.e., if the case number is greater than *100*), and equivalent to *0* if it is false. Therefore, for the first 100 cases, the equation above will evaluate to *1*1+0*2,* which is equal to *1*, and for all cases above *100*, will evaluate to *0*1+1*2*, which is equal to *2*.

Operators, constants and functions. The operators, constants, and functions that are supported in spreadsheet formulas are a subset of those supported in the *STATISTICA BASIC* programming language (see the *Electronic Manual* for the most up-to-date list of available functions). The operators that can be used in spreadsheet formulas are listed below in order of their precedence (order of execution), from the lowest to the highest (parentheses may be used to change the order of operation).

`=, <, >, <>, <=, >=`	- relational operators
`+ - * /`	- arithmetic operators
`or, |`	- inclusive disjunction
`and, &`	- conjunction
`**, ^`	- exponentiation
`not, ~`	- negation

The following constants are supported in spreadsheet formulas:

`Pi`	- π (3.14159265358979)
`Euler`	- *e* (2.71828182845905)

Functions supported in spreadsheet formulas include:

`Abs(x)`	- Absolute value of *x*
`Arcsin(x)`	- Arc sine of *x*
`Cos(x)`	- Cosine of *x*
`Exp(x)`	- Exponential function (*e* to the *x*)
`Log(x)`	- Natural log of *x* (base *e*)
`Log2(x)`	- Binary logarithm of *x* (base 2)
`Log10(x)`	- Common log of *x* (base 10)
`Rnd(x)`	- Random real number from a uniform istribution in the range from *0* to *x*
`Sign(x)`	- Returns the sign of *x* ($x<0 \rightarrow -1$; $x=0 \rightarrow 0$; $x>0 \rightarrow 1$)
`Sin(x)`	- Sine of *x*
`Sinh(x)`	- Hyperbolic sine of *x*
`Sqrt(x)`	- Square root of x
`Trunc(x)`	- Truncates *x* to an integer

Other specialized functions are available in *STATISTICA BASIC* (the *STATISTICA* programming language).

Distributions and their integrals. The following distribution functions are supported in spreadsheet formulas:

Distri-bution	Density or Probability Function	Distribution Function	Inverse Distribution Function
Beta	beta(x,ν,ω)	ibeta(x,ν,ω)	vbeta(x,ν,ω)
Binomial	binom(x,p,n)	ibinom(x,p,n)	
Cauchy	cauchy(x,η,θ)	icauchy(x,η,θ)	vcauchy(x,η,θ)

Distributions and their integrals (continued)

Distri-bution	Density or Probability Function	Distribution Function	Inverse Distribution Function
Chi-square	chi2(x,ν)	ichi2(x,ν)	vchi2(x,ν)
Exponential	expon(x,λ)	iexpon(x,λ)	vexpon(x,λ)
Extreme	extreme(x,a,b)	iextreme(x,a,b)	vextreme(x,a,b)
F	F(x,ν,ω)	iF(x,ν,ω)	vF(x,ν,ω)
Gamma	gamma(x,c)	igamma(x,c)	vgamma(x,c)
Geometric	geom(x,p)	igeom(x,p)	
Laplace	laplace(x,a,b)	ilaplace(x,a,b)	vlaplace(x,a,b)
Logistic	logis(x,a,b)	ilogis(x,a,b)	vlogis(x,a,b)
Lognormal	lognorm(x,μ,σ)	ilognorm(x,μ,σ)	vlognorm(x,μ,σ)
Normal	normal(x,μ,σ)	inormal(x,μ,σ)	vnormal(x,μ,σ)
Pareto	pareto(x,c)	ipareto(x,c)	vpareto(x,c)
Poisson	poisson(x,λ)	ipoisson(x,λ)	
Rayleigh	rayleigh(x,b)	irayleigh(x,b)	vrayleigh(x,b)
Student's	student(x,df)	istudent(x,df)	vstudent(x,df)
Weibull	weibull(x,b,c,θ)	iweibull(x,b,c,θ)	vweibull(x,b,c,θ)

For more information on these distributions, see the *Appendix I.*

Random numbers. Using the uniform random number generator and the inverse distribution functions (where available) you can generate random numbers that follow the respective distributions described above. For example, the spreadsheet formula:

```
= vweibull(rnd(1), 1, 2, 0)
```

will produce random numbers that follow the Weibull distribution with scale parameter *1*, shape parameter *2*, and location parameter 0. For additional details, see Evans, Hastings, and Peacock (1993, pages 23-24).

Missing data. If the value of any of the variables in a spreadsheet formula is missing, then the respective missing data value will be assigned to the target variable in the current case. For example, consider the transformation formula:

```
= v2 + v3 + v4 + v5
```

If any value of variables *V2*, *V3*, *V4*, or *V5* is missing, the missing data value will be assigned to the variable containing this formula in the current case. Note that the *STATISTICA BASIC* programming language (see the *Electronic Manual*) includes specific functions for handling missing data, such as counts and sums which automatically adjust for missing data.

Illegal functions. If a spreadsheet formula cannot be computed because of illegal values (e.g., square root of a negative number, logarithm of a negative number), the missing data value will be assigned to the target variable.

Division by zero. In general, the missing data value will be assigned to the target variable when division by zero occurs. However, *zero divided by zero evaluates to zero* (0/0 = 0).

Recalculating the spreadsheet. Whenever you enter or edit a spreadsheet formula, you are given the option to recalculate the values of the respective variable now (click *Yes*) or later (click *No*).

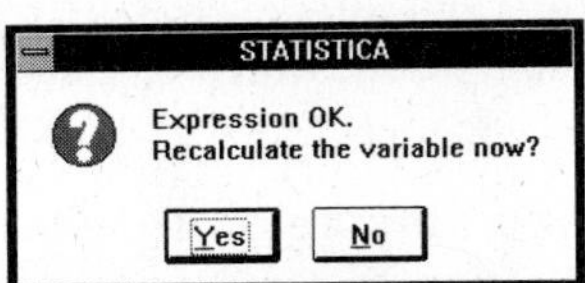

If you choose to recalculate the formulas later, you can do so by clicking on the toolbar button to bring up the *Recalculate* dialog.

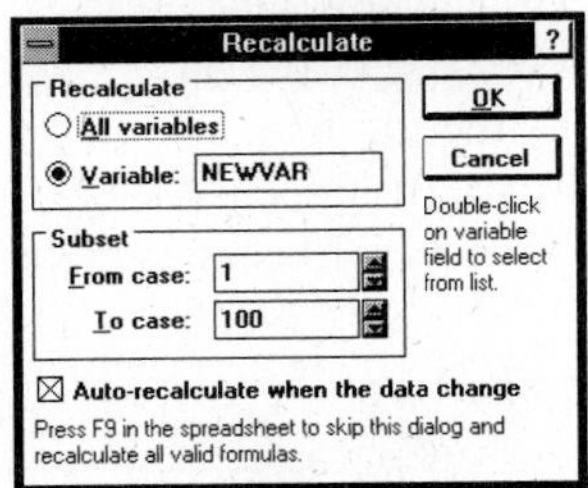

Alternatively, you can press F9 in order to bypass this dialog and recalculate all valid formulas in the current data set.

Auto-recalculate when the data change. Many times, a spreadsheet formula will depend upon the values of other variables in the spreadsheet (e.g., =*v1*+*v2*). *STATISTICA* will detect this interdependency among variables and if the *Auto-recalculate when the data change* option is selected in the *Recalculate* dialog (see above), will recalculate the values of the respective variable(s).

If this option is de-selected, then you will need to press F9 or click on the [x=?] button to update the spreadsheet formulas.

***DDE* (Dynamic Data Exchange) link.** *DDE* links are stored and can be established (and edited) in the *Long Name* option of the *Spreadsheet (Edit) Current Specs* dialog (see *Spreadsheet Window*, Chapter 3). To establish a *DDE* link here, type in the link statement (*DDE* path). (Note that you can also use the *Paste Link* option from the spreadsheet *Edit* pull-down menu to link the files and automatically write the link statement in the *Spreadsheet Edit (Current) Specs* dialog.) For more information, see *Spreadsheet Window*, Chapter 3.

The four parts of the link statement (e.g., *@Excel|c:\Excel\File.xls!r2c2:r4c4;c1;r1*) are described below.

> ***@Source Application|.*** Specify first the source (or server) application (in the above example, the source application is Excel). The Source Application must be separated from the rest of the link statement by a "|". You also need to designate whether the *DDE* link is "hot" (place an "@" in front of the Source Application to indicate that the client file will be updated whenever the server file is changed) or "cold" (place a "^" in front of the Source Application to indicate that the client file will be updated only when the user requests it or changes it back to "hot").

Topic!. The Topic designates the name (and path) of the file in the source application and must be separated from the rest of the link statement by a "!" (be sure to establish the full path name for the file). In the above example, the Topic (*c:\Excel\File.xls!*) designates not only the name of the Excel file (*File.xls*) but also the drive and directory where the file is located (e.g., *c:\Excel*).

How you identify the source file depends on the source application that you are using (refer to your source application for information on how to designate the Topic; when you use the *Paste Link* option from the spreadsheet *Edit* pull-down menu, this will automatically be designated for your specific application, see Chapter 3).

Item;. Specify here the cell, range, named range, or some other name specific to your source application followed by a ";" (to separate it from the rest of the *DDE* path). What you specify here is dependent upon the source application (refer to your source application for information on how to designate the Item; when you use the *Paste Link* option from the spreadsheet *Edit* pull-down menu, this will automatically be designated for your specific application).

In the above example, a range in the Excel spreadsheet is defined (e.g., *r2c2:r4c4*; specifies the block "from row number 2, column number 2 to row number 4, column number 4").

Column;row. This part of the *DDE* path is optional; by default (when no starting row or column is specified), *STATISTICA* places the first value in the range of linked data into the first cell (row) of the highlighted variable in the spreadsheet and continues placing values down and to the right of this "anchor" cell. If you wish to "anchor" the linked data in a different cell (area) of the spreadsheet, you can designate the column number and row number (separated by a ";") to identify the position of that cell.

Alternatively, you can designate only the column (variable) number and *STATISTICA* will use the first cell (row) in that column as the "anchor." Because this portion of the *DDE* path is optional, it is not automatically designated when you use the *Paste Link* option.

Printing/saving long variable names, spreadsheet formulas, or *DDE* links. The long variable name, spreadsheet formula, or *DDE* link is saved as part of the file and is printed (to the printer, output window, or an output file) along with the spreadsheet data file when the *Variable Specs* option is selected in the *Print Data* dialog,

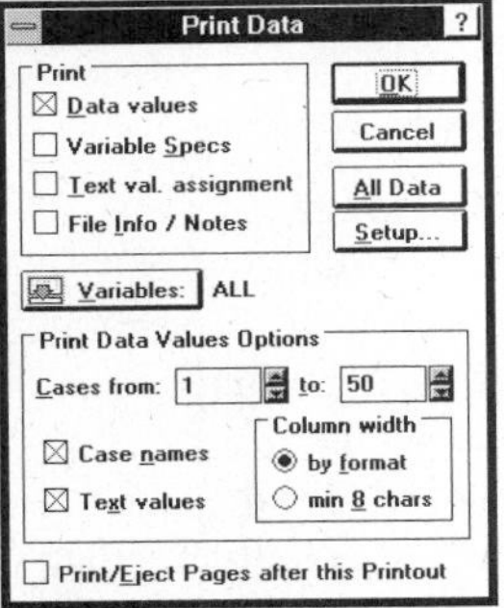

or along with the output of analyses when either a *Short*, *Medium* or *Long* report style is selected in the

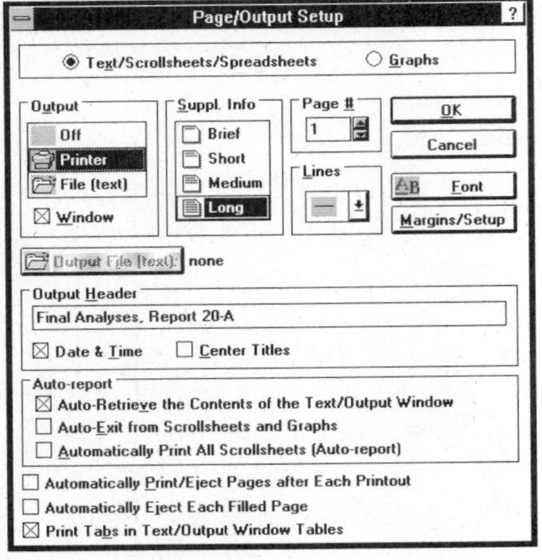

Page/Output Setup dialog (accessible by clicking on the *Print* option in the *Options* pull-down menu, or by double-clicking on the *Output* field of the Status Bar).

Numeric vs. Text Values

What is the "double-notation" (text/numeric) of values? In *STATISTICA*, each value may have two identities: Numeric (e.g., *1*) and text (e.g., *Male*). This double-notation simplifies the use of text values. For example, when entering data, you could enter the values *1* and *2* in variable *Gender* to refer to males and females, respectively. Later, you can type *Male* into any cell containing a *1*, and at the point when you complete the entry, all *1*'s in this column will automatically change to *Male*. In other words, because *1* did not have a text equivalent, the program will understand that you intended to assign the text value *Male* to *1* in this variable. You can repeat the same steps for *2* and *Female*. This feature simplifies entering text values; at the same time you do not lose any advantages of using the numeric data (they can still be used in subsequent numeric analyses). Additionally, each unique text value may have a long value label assigned to it (see the *Text Values Manager* dialog, in the *Spreadsheet Window* chapter, Chapter 3.

How to switch between displaying text and numeric values and value labels in the data spreadsheet. As explained above, *STATISTICA* supports a double-notation of values, where each value of a particular variable can simultaneously have a numeric and text identity. You can switch between displaying text or numeric values or value labels (if any exist) using the spreadsheet toolbar button ABC; hold down the CTRL key while clicking on the ABC button to display value labels.

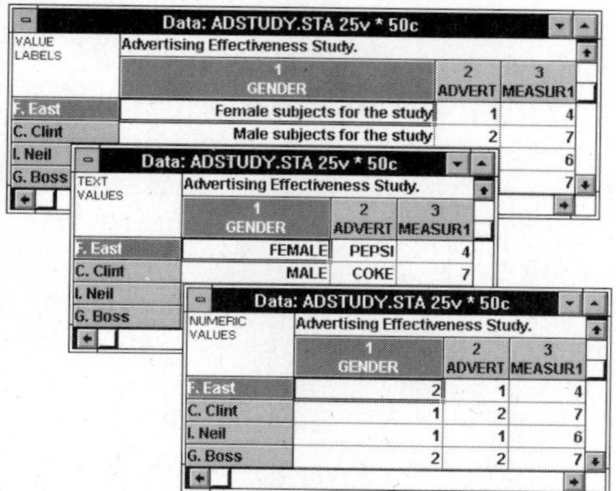

How to enter/edit the assignments between numeric and text values. You can enter/edit text and numeric values in any of the following ways:

- Click on the toolbar button to open the *Text Values Manager* dialog (where the text/numeric assignments can be made, as well as managed, i.e., sorted, selectively transferred from other variables, etc.; see Chapter 3 for details).

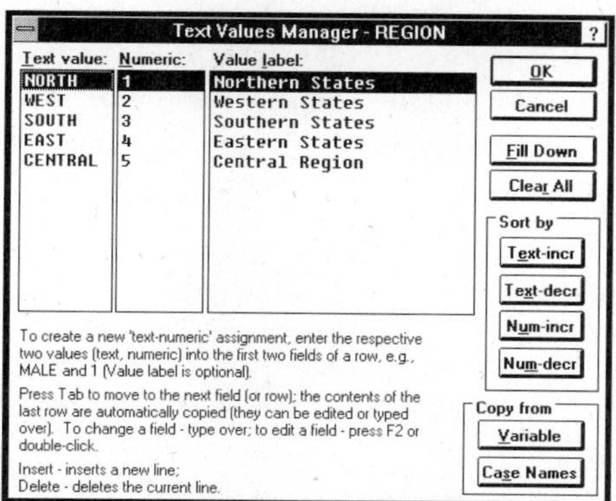

The *Copy from* options in the this dialog allow you to copy to the current variable the text values from other variables or from case names. When you need to copy the numeric/text value assignments and long value labels from one file to another, use the *Merge Files* facility (see page 1359). One of the merge options allows you to concatenate or replace text values with values from another file.

- Click on the button to switch the spreadsheet display to numeric or text values and enter/edit the respective values (hold down the CTRL key while clicking on the button to display value labels).

- You can paste text or numeric values from another variable or another application into the spreadsheet (be sure the spreadsheet display mode matches the values that you are pasting into the spreadsheet; e.g., display text values in the spreadsheet before pasting text values into the spreadsheet). Note that if you copy to the Clipboard a block of spreadsheet data, then the contents of the copied block depends on the current display mode (e.g., to copy text values, be sure to set the display mode to *Text Values*). The only exception are Clipboard operations within the *STATISTICA* spreadsheet (when text values or value labels are displayed), where the copied (or cut) block that is to be pasted to another location of the *STATISTICA* spreadsheet will always contain the full representation of the selected data (i.e., numeric values, text values, and their value labels, if any).

- You can create text values in the spreadsheet by importing them (see the *Quick Import* options, Chapter 3).

Importing Text Values Longer than 8 Characters. If the text values imported using the *Quick Import* options (see Chapter 3) are longer than 8 characters, then value labels will be created to store the long text values in their entirety; the first 8 characters of each value will be used to create the respective *STATISTICA* text values. Note that if this would produce text values which are not uniquely related to the long labels (i.e., create a situation when the same text value would be accompanied by different value labels in different cases), then the last

character(s) of the text values will be replaced by digits to create unique text values for the respective value labels. For example, if the values in the source data set (to be imported) are:

```
Arizona, the south region
Arizona, the north region
Arizona, the central region
```

then those values will be stored as value labels, and the corresponding (unique) 8-character text values will be created as:

```
Arizona1
Arizona2
Arizona3
```

The same conventions apply when you import data to the *STATISTICA* spreadsheet via the Clipboard [e.g., by copying a block of values in a foreign spreadsheet (highlight a block in the spreadsheet and press CTRL+C) and pasting them to the *STATISTICA* spreadsheet (place the cursor in the desired position and press CTRL+V)]. If the text values are longer than 8 characters, then they will be interpreted as *STATISTICA* value labels and the respective (short) text values will be created from the first 8 characters of each long text (as illustrated above).

Value Labels

Value labels are comments or descriptions (up to 40 characters long) that can be assigned to specific text/numeric values in *STATISTICA* data sets, for example:

Text value:	Numeric:	Value label:
Arizona1	1	Arizona, the south regio
Arizona2	2	Arizona, the north regio
Arizona3	3	Arizona, the central reg

Value labels can be displayed and edited directly in the spreadsheet (as well as in the *Text Values Manager* dialog; see Chapter 3). If any values in the current data set have value labels, then the *Text/Numeric Value* display toolbar button, allows you to toggle over three display settings: *Numeric Values*, *Text Values*, and *Value Labels* (hold down the CTRL key while clicking on the button to display value labels). Additionally, you can select the display mode from the spreadsheet *View* pull-down menu. The current display mode is indicated by the text in the upper-left corner of the spreadsheet. Note that text values and value labels will be displayed only for those variables with text values. If no text values exist for the data file, then clicking on the toolbar button (or optionally, selecting the *View - Text Values* pull-down menu option) will bring up the message: *No text values in this data file*.

Text data as variable specifications. Note that the assignment of text to numeric values (as well as the long value labels) is part of the variable's specifications, thus, it can be copied, moved, or deleted along with the variable. Also, if data are moved between variables (e.g., when blocks of data are moved or copied), their text data assignment changes accordingly and becomes consistent with the assignment in the variable to which they were copied. In other words, all text information is part of the variable, and this information can be moved to another variable only by copying its text information (by using one of the options in the *Text Values Manager* dialog).

Example. If you copy the three numeric values *1*, *1*, and *2* from one column (variable) in the spreadsheet to another column where *1=LOW* and *2=MEDIUM*, then those values (*1, 1, 2*) will now (in the new column) appear as *LOW, LOW, MEDIUM*.

This is also illustrated below, where moving a block of values to a new variable (from *ADVERT* to *MEASUR3*) affects also values outside the block in the new variable by assigning to them new text identities.

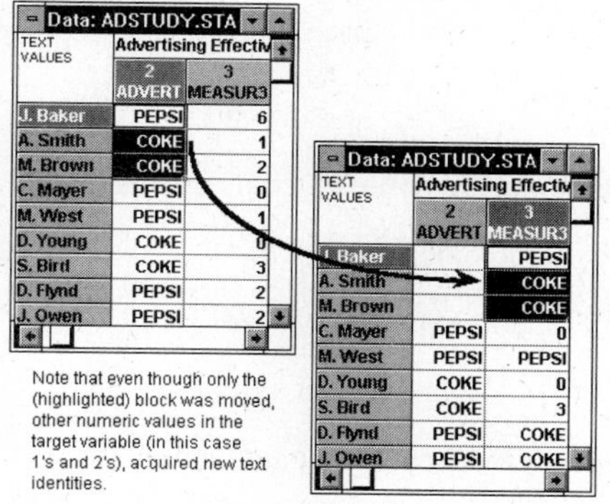

Note that even though only the (highlighted) block was moved, other numeric values in the target variable (in this case 1's and 2's), acquired new text identities.

Reviewing text values. In addition to the *Text Values Manager* (see above), text values can be reviewed in the *Variable Values* window.

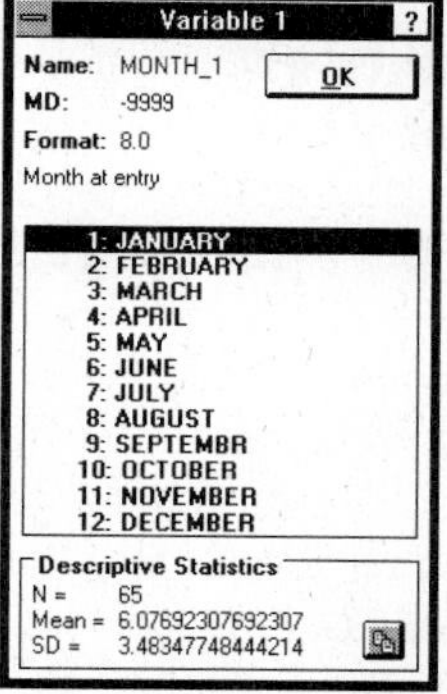

This window is accessible by clicking on the *Values/Stats* button in the *Spreadsheet Edit (Current) Specs* dialog, by selecting the *Quick Stats Graphs - Values of* option from the right-mouse-button flying menu, or by zooming on a variable in the *View Variable Specs* dialog (see *Spreadsheet Window*, Chapter 3).

Other *STATISTICA* Data Files

***Megafile Manager* data files.** The *Megafile Manager* program is accessible from the *Data Management* module. However, the specific features and applications of *Megafile Manager* are addressed in Volume III. For a brief overview of this program, see page 1329.

Other files. Many other types of information can be saved in *STATISTICA* and the file name extension is used to designated the type of information which is saved. Whenever you open or save a file in *STATISTICA*, you can either accept the default file name extension or use a different one.

The default *STATISTICA* file name extensions are given below.

- Spreadsheet (*STATISTICA* system data files, includes data, variable names, long labels, formulas, and links, case names, text values, variable specifications, file notes, and other information) file name extension: **.sta.*
- Scrollsheet (*STATISTICA* output windows, includes the formatted output table) file name extension: **.scr.*
- Graph (includes graphs, graph customizations, embedded graphic objects, links, and graph data) file name extension: **.stg.*
- User-defined graph specifications (representing customized *Stats Graphs* which have been added to the *Graphs* pull-down menu) file name extension: **.sug.*
- *R*ich *T*ext *F*ormat (such as RTF files created or used in the *Text/output Window*, see Chapter 4) file name extension: **.rtf.*
- All other non-RTF text supplementary files saved in ASCII format (e.g., multiple case selection conditions, data recoding specifications, data verification conditions, editable sequences of keystrokes, etc.) file name extension: **.txt.*
- *STATISTICA BASIC* file name extension: **.stb.*
- *STATISTICA* Command Language (*SCL*) file name extension: **.scl.*
- *Megafile Manager* (see Volume III of the manual) data file name extension: **.mfm.*

- *MML* (*Megafile Manager Language*) program file name extension: **.mml.*
- Graph axis (single or multiple) definition file name extension: **.axd.*
- Case selection conditions file name extension: **.sel.*
- *Auto Task Buttons* (including lists of *SCL* programs, *STATISTICA BASIC* programs, *Quick Open* files, and editable sequences of keystrokes) file name extension: **.atb.*
- Macro (recorded in *STATISTICA*) file name extension: **.stm.*
- *SEPATH* (*PATH1* language) program file name extension: **.cmd*
- *STATISTICA Electronic Manual* file name extension: **.hlp*
- *STATISTICA* configuration files (including the global system configuration file and specific files such as for quality control charts, contour-/surface definitions, etc.) file name extension: **.ini*
- Color palette selection file name extension: **.pal*

The following is a list of file name extensions for data and graphics files exchanged by *STATISTICA* with other applications:

- CSS (and *STATISTICA/DOS*) data file name extension: **.css*
- CSS (and *STATISTICA/DOS*) graph file name extension: **.csg*
- Windows graphics metafile file name extension: **.wmf*
- Windows device-independent bitmap graphics file name extension: **.bmp*
- Excel worksheet file name extension: **.xls*
- Lotus, Symphony, and QuattroPro worksheet file name extensions (e.g., **.wk1*, **.wk3*): **.wk?*, **.wr?*, **.wq?*
- dBASE, FoxPro file name extension: **.dbf*
- Access file name extension: **.mdb*
- Paradox file name extension: **.db*
- SPSS portable file name extension: **.por*
- ASCII (free format text) file name extension: **.txt* or **.fre*
- ASCII (fixed format text) file name extension: **.fix*

STATISTICA Matrix File Format

The *STATISTICA* standard data files described in the previous sections are the basic type of files used to store data in *STATISTICA*. In addition, *STATISTICA* matrix data (e.g., correlation, covariance, similarity, dissimilarity, distance, and other matrices) may be saved and retrieved for future processing. All modules of *STATISTICA* which calculate correlation matrices (or similarities, dissimilarities, etc.) can save them in the *STATISTICA* matrix file format (e.g., *Basic Statistics and Tables*, *Regression*, *Cluster Analysis*, *Factor Analysis*, *Canonical Analysis*, etc.). Also, correlation matrices can be saved in every module of *STATISTICA* via the *Quick Basic Stats* facilities (use option *Quick Basic Stats - More* from the *File* pull-down menu; see Chapter 10 for additional details).

You may also create a matrix data file manually, by entering data into the spreadsheet according to the following rules:

- The number of cases (rows) = the number of variables (columns) + 4.

- The matrix must be a square matrix and the case names should be the same as the variable names.
- The last four cases contain the following case names (shown below in italics) and information:

  Means: The mean of each variable is given in this row; this case can be left empty (i.e., do not enter anything in this row) for *Similarities* and *Dissimilarities* matrices.

  Std.Dev.: The standard deviation of each variable is given in this row; this case can be left empty (i.e., do not enter anything in this row) for *Similarities* and *Dissimilarities* matrices.

  No Cases: This required number is the number of cases from which the matrix was produced, not the number of cases (rows of data) in this matrix file.

  Matrix: This required number represents the type of matrix file; 1 = *Correlation*, 2 = *Similarities*, 3 = *Dissimilarities* and 4 = *Covariance*.

The following is an example correlation matrix data file (note the type of matrix indicated in the last row, *1* means correlation matrix) calculated from 100 observations:

Data: CORR_MTX.STA 10v * 14c

This is an example correlation matrix file.

Case	1 WORK_1	2 WORK_2	3 WORK_3	4 HOBBY_1	5 HOBBY_2	6 HOME_1	7 HOME_2	8 HOME_3
WORK_1	1.00000	.64740	.65262	.59812	.52110	.14282	.14514	.13779
WORK_2	.64740	1.00000	.73189	.68855	.69778	.14337	.18185	.23598
WORK_3	.65262	.73189	1.00000	.63695	.63003	.16363	.23830	.25465
HOBBY_1	.59812	.68855	.63695	1.00000	.80469	.53638	.63431	.58284
HOBBY_2	.52110	.69778	.63003	.80469	1.00000	.50591	.49591	.48235
HOME_1	.14282	.14337	.16363	.53638	.50591	1.00000	.65774	.59003
HOME_2	.14514	.18185	.23830	.63431	.49591	.65774	1.00000	.73065
HOME_3	.13779	.23598	.25465	.58284	.48235	.59003	.73065	1.00000
MISCEL_1	.61135	.70863	.69789	.90447	.81101	.49842	.64364	.58587
MISCEL_2	.54894	.68479	.67063	.84320	.75577	.42471	.59340	.51775
Means	97.02958	98.16886	98.94298	98.02522	100.1081	99.50832	101.6029	101.3717
Std.Dev.	15.52089	11.26746	12.48538	15.93673	19.94109	11.97813	11.06155	12.73475
No.Cases	100.0000							
Matrix	1.00000							

Types of Matrices

Correlation [value of last case (*Matrix*): 1]. Square correlation matrices are symmetrical and contain the correlation coefficients for all pairs of specified variables. You can create correlation matrices by saving correlations in the appropriate dialogs (for example, see the option *Save Correlation Matrix* in the *Multiple Regression - Reviewing Descriptive Statistics* dialog, Chapter 12). You can also manually create a correlation matrix by entering the correlations into a regular spreadsheet and including in the file the last four cases as described above.

Similarities [value of last case (*Matrix*): 2]. Similarities between objects (e.g., variables) are expressed in this matrix. You can manually create this type of matrix file by entering the correlations into a regular spreadsheet and including in the file, the last four cases as described above. Similarities matrices can be used in *Multidimensional Scaling* analyses (see Volume III).

Dissimilarities [value of last case (*Matrix*): 3]. The dissimilarities (distances) between objects (e.g., variables) are expressed in this matrix. You can create this matrix manually or it can be created for you by using the *Save Distance Matrix* option in the *Cluster Analysis - Joining Results* dialog (see Volume III). Dissimilarities matrices can also be used in *Multidimensional Scaling* analyses (see Volume III).

Covariances [value of last case (*Matrix*): 4]. Square covariance matrices contain the covariances for all pairs of specified variables on the off-diagonal and the variances for each variable on the diagonal of the matrix. Covariance matrices can be saved in the *Structural Equation Modeling* module (see Volume III), or you can manually create a covariance matrix by entering the covariances into a regular spreadsheet and including in the file the last four cases as described above.

Saving the Matrix File

Once the matrix values have been entered following the guidelines described above, the data may be saved as a standard *STATISTICA* data file (file name extension **.sta*) by selecting the option *Save As* from the *File* pull-down menu.

Multiple-Group Correlation Matrices Files

Some procedures (e.g., *Structural Equation Modeling*, see Volume III) support multiple correlation matrices (i.e., correlations "by group") as input, where each individual correlation matrix represents a different subset of observations (group). Such matrices can be requested from the *More...* dialog of *Quick Basic Stats* (see Chapter 10). When you press the *Save* button, the *Save Matrix As* dialog will open in which you can specify a name under which the matrix will be saved. If a grouping variable was previously selected, then multiple correlation matrices (i.e., correlations "by group") will be produced and saved in a single file.

Data: CORR_MTX.STA 4v * 16c

NUMERIC VALUES	1 MEASUR1	2 MEASUR2	3 MEASUR3	4 MEASUR4
MEASUR1	1.00000	-.17992	-.23335	.11451
MEASUR2	-.17992	1.00000	-.14362	.06526
MEASUR3	-.23335	-.14362	1.00000	-.14452
MEASUR4	.11451	.06526	-.14452	1.00000
Means	6.28571	4.64286	4.32143	5.46429
St.Dev.	2.08801	2.97165	2.93199	2.98741
No.Cases	28.00000			
Matrix	1.00000			
MEASUR1	1.00000	.20463	.00592	.33463
MEASUR2	.20463	1.00000	.06622	-.09973
MEASUR3	.00592	.06622	1.00000	.02721
MEASUR4	.33463	-.09973	.02721	1.00000
Means	5.40909	4.40909	3.90909	5.59091
St.Dev.	2.64861	2.83950	2.48633	2.23945
No.Cases	22.00000			
Matrix	1.00000			

The multiple correlation matrix file shown above was produced from the data file *Adstudy.sta* using *Gender* as a grouping variable. For more information, please refer to Chapter 10.

EXAMPLE

Overview

This example will illustrate some elementary data base management operations. It is assumed that you have read the *Introductory Overview* and *Data File Format* sections of this chapter which introduce elementary data base management concepts and explain the general features of *STATISTICA* data files.

Starting the *Data Management* Module

Start the program by clicking on the *STATISTICA Data Management* icon (alternatively, you can click on the *STATISTICA* icon to open the *Module Switcher* and then select the *Data Management* option).

The program will open and the last-used data file and the *Data Management* startup panel will appear.

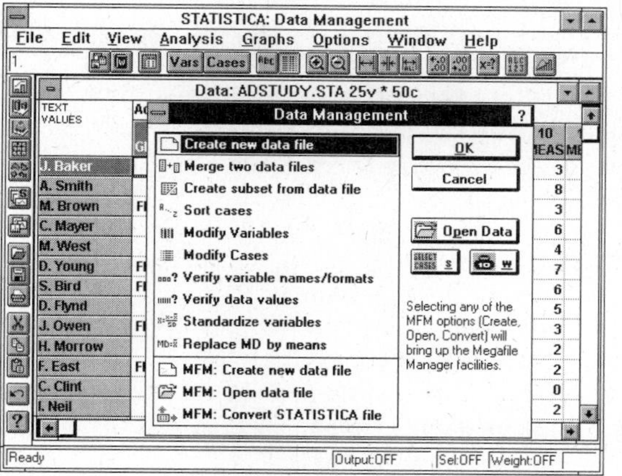

Note that, unless you are using *Quick STATISTICA*, the last-used *Megafile Manager* data file will also be opened when you start the *Data Management* module (see Volume III).

Creating a New Data File

In the *Data Management* startup panel (see above), select the option *Create new data file* to open the *Create New File* dialog.

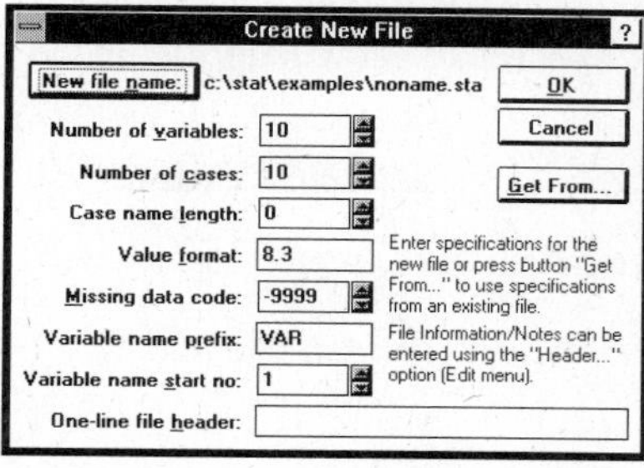

First, enter a new name for the file. Click on the *New file name* button and in the resulting *New Data: Specify File Name* dialog, enter a file name (e.g., *Myfile*; and alternatively a different path) under which to store the data. The default file name extension for *STATISTICA* data files is **.sta*. Now, follow the steps outlined below in order to create a file with 25 cases, 10 variables, and 8-character case names:

Step 1. Change the default *Number of cases* from *10* to *25*.

Step 2. Change the default *Case name length* from *0* to *8*.

Step 3. In the *One-line file header* edit field, enter an (optional) one-line file comment (e.g., *This is my first STATISTICA data file*).

StatSoft

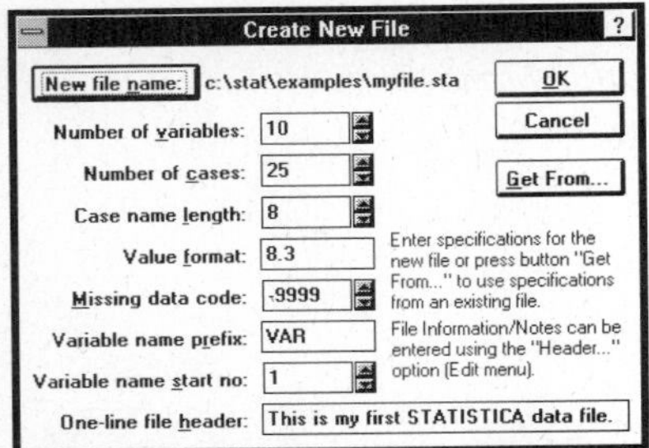

Accept all other defaults in this dialog (e.g., *Value format*, *Missing data code*, etc.), and click *OK* to create the new file (a spreadsheet will appear on the screen).

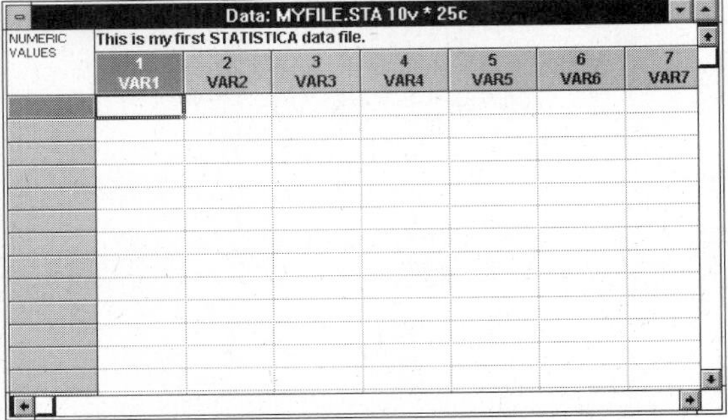

Entering data. The file is now empty (technically speaking, it is now filled with *missing data* values). To begin entering data, click with the mouse in the first cell (the one at the intersection of the first row the column labeled *VAR1*). That cell will be highlighted, indicating that it is now active for editing.

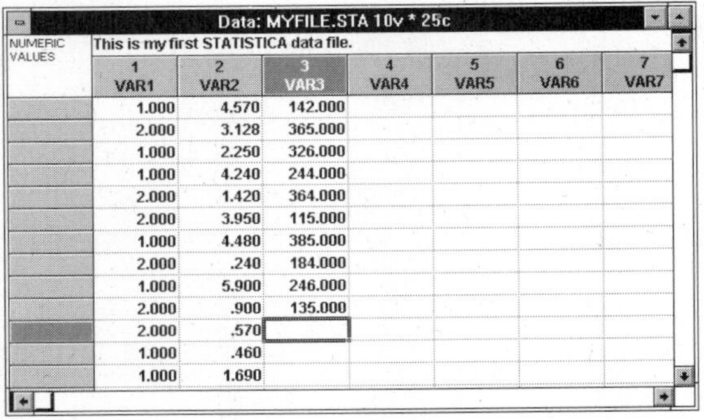
Data: MYFILE.STA 10v * 25c

This is my first STATISTICA data file.

1 VAR1	2 VAR2	3 VAR3	4 VAR4	5 VAR5	6 VAR6	7 VAR7
1.000	4.570	142.000				
2.000	3.128	365.000				
1.000	2.250	326.000				
1.000	4.240	244.000				
2.000	1.420	364.000				
2.000	3.950	115.000				
1.000	4.480	385.000				
2.000	.240	184.000				
1.000	5.900	246.000				
2.000	.900	135.000				
2.000	.570					
1.000	.460					
1.000	1.690					

When you begin typing, the highlight will disappear, and the cell will be shown with a solid outline and a vertical bar indicating your current cursor position. To store a value in the cell, type the value (e.g. *1*) and press *Enter*. The active cell will then advance to the next row (next case). Type the value for that cell and press *Enter*. When you reach the bottom of the column and type a value in that cell, pressing *Enter* will move the active cell to the first row of the next column.

Automatic advancement of the cursor. If you want to enter the data *by case*, after entering each value, you need to press *Enter* and then a cursor key. You can speed up (simplify) data entry by customizing the cursor movement. Select the *General* option from the *Options* pull-down menu to open the *STATISTICA Defaults: General* dialog.

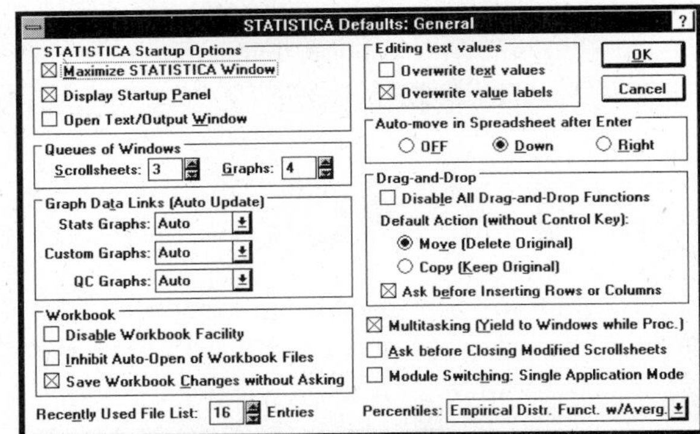

If you prefer to enter data by case (across rows) rather than by variable (*Down*), then set the *Right* option (*Auto-move in Spreadsheet after Enter*) in the *STATISTICA Defaults: General* dialog. Now, when you press *Enter*, the highlight will move to the next variable (to the right) rather than to the next case.

Variable names. When a new file is created, the variables are assigned default names of *VAR1*, *VAR2*, etc. You can customize the variable names by editing them in the *Spreadsheet Edit (Current) Specs* dialog (shown below).

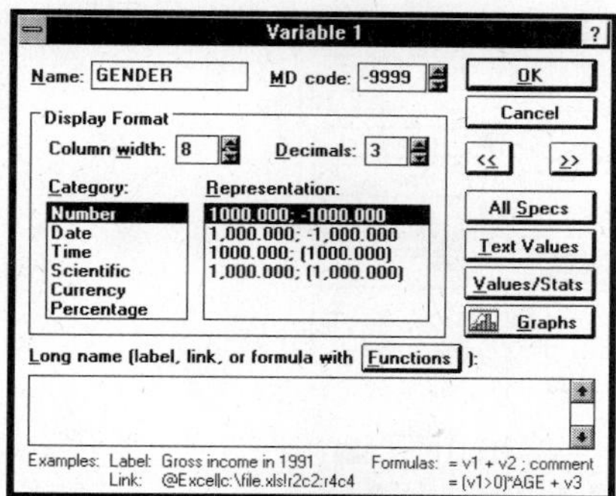

To change the first variable name to *Gender*, double-click with the mouse in that variable name cell. The *Spreadsheet Edit (Current) Specs* dialog for that variable will appear (see above). In the *Name* field of this dialog, type the variable name *Gender*.

From this same dialog, you may also change the display format of the variable, and enter a longer descriptive name or comment for the variable. Click in the field titled *Long Name* and type a longer descriptive name, e.g., *This is the respondent's gender*. This same field can also be used to enter a formula for computing values of the variable (see below and page 1338) or Dynamic Data Exchange (*DDE*) links (see page 1341).

Spreadsheet formulas. Instead of entering a descriptive label in the *Long Name* field of the *Spreadsheet Edit (Current) Specs* dialog (see above and page 1338), you could enter a formula to "define" (compute) values for the current variable. Following the Excel convention, such formulas must start with an equal sign as the first character (as shown in the example below).

When *STATISTICA* recalculates the variable for which this formula was entered, its values would be replaced by the arithmetic average of the values in variables number 2 and 3 for each case. When you enter a label that begins with an equal sign, *STATISTICA* will assume that it is a formula (instead of a descriptive label).

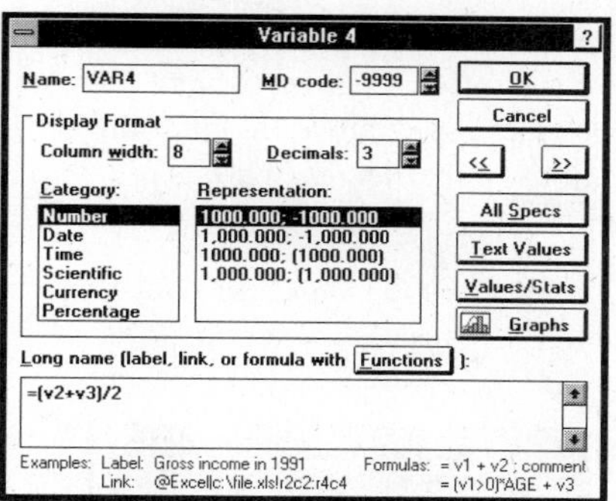

When you click *OK* to close the *Spreadsheet Edit (Current) Specs* dialog, *STATISTICA* will verify the syntax of the equation for formal correctness, and if it is interpretable, then inquire whether you wish to recalculate the variable according to the new formula.

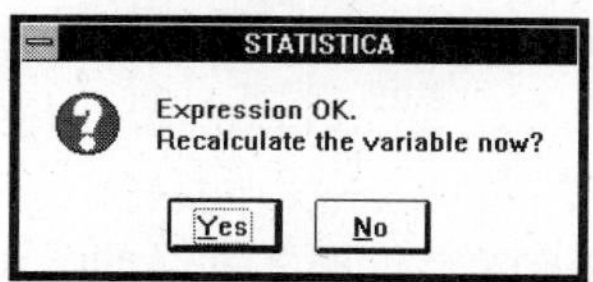

You may choose to recalculate this variable now (*Yes*) or defer recalculation for the moment (*No*). (You may later request recalculation of the variable, or all variables from the spreadsheet via the *Recalculate* spreadsheet toolbar button x=? in the toolbar.) A complete description of spreadsheet formulas may be found on page 1338.

Recoding data. Values of variables can be recoded using the designated recoding facility available from the spreadsheet *Edit-Variables* pull-down menu (or the spreadsheet Vars toolbar button) of any module of *STATISTICA*.

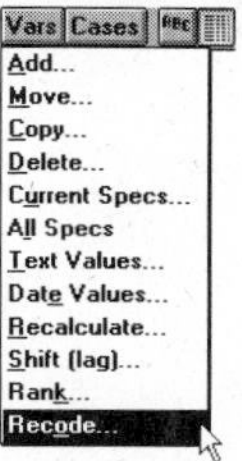

For example, in order to recode all negative values of variable number *9* into *1*'s, all zeros into *2*'s, and all positive values into *3*'s, you would enter the following conditions in the *Recode Values of Variable* dialog:

Category 1 Include if: `v9<0` *New Value 1:* `1`
Category 2 Include if: `v9=0` *New Value 2:* `2`
Category 3 Include if: `v9>0` *New Value 3:* `3`

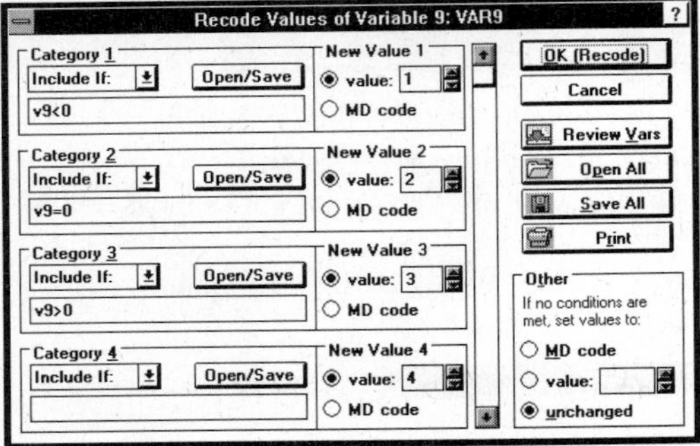

When you click *OK* in this dialog, you will be asked if you want to recode the variable now or later and (if you have not previously saved the recode conditions) whether you want to save the recode conditions. Note that you can enter up to 16 recoding conditions in this dialog. Much more elaborate recoding of data can be performed using *STATISTICA BASIC* (see page 1354 in this example section), which features designated recoding functions and supports recodes of practically unlimited complexity.

Data verification. The interactive data verification and cleaning facility provided in the *Data Management* module can be used to verify data integrity (logical consistency) and completeness.

Category 1 Include if: `v1=1 or v1=2`

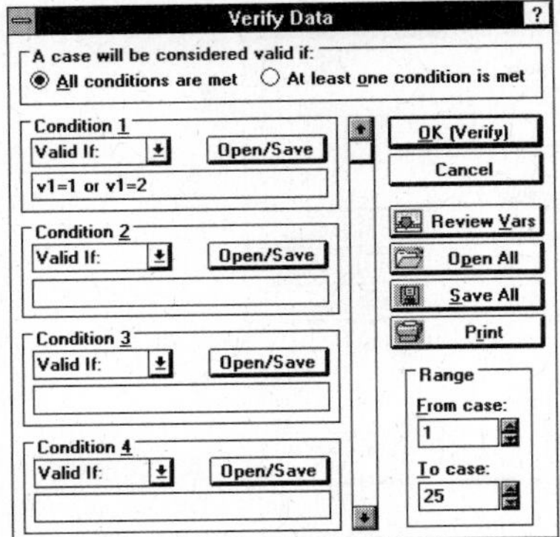

For the example shown above, assume that the allowed values of variable 1 are only *1* and *2*. To verify the integrity of the data, open the *Verify Data* dialog by clicking on the *Verify Data Values* option from the *Analysis* pull-down menu or the *Data Management* startup panel. Then enter the verification condition as shown in the illustration above.

After you specify the verification condition(s), press *OK (Verify)* and the data set (or the selected range) will be tested sequentially (one case at a time) for its consistency with the set of conditions which you have specified. When a case is found which does not meet the conditions, then the respective row of data in the spreadsheet will be brought up and highlighted and the *Data Verification* dialog will open allowing you to either ignore the inconsistency (and continue or stop the verification) or edit (correct) the case.

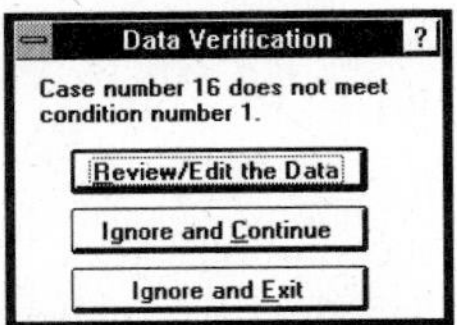

Note that you can enter up to 16 verification conditions. For more information on these dialogs, see page 1366.

Text values. Assume that the first variable, which you named *Gender* above, contains only values of 1

(representing males) and 2 (representing females). To make the display easier to read, you can assign text (alphanumeric) equivalents to these two numbers. The quickest way to assign text equivalents is to enter a text value directly over a numeric value in the spreadsheet. For example, type the value '*MALE*' over the numeric value of *1*. When you click *Enter*, all values of *1* will automatically display the text equivalent '*MALE*'.

Text values and their text/numeric value assignments can also be entered and managed (rearranged, sorted, etc.) in the *Text Values Manager*.

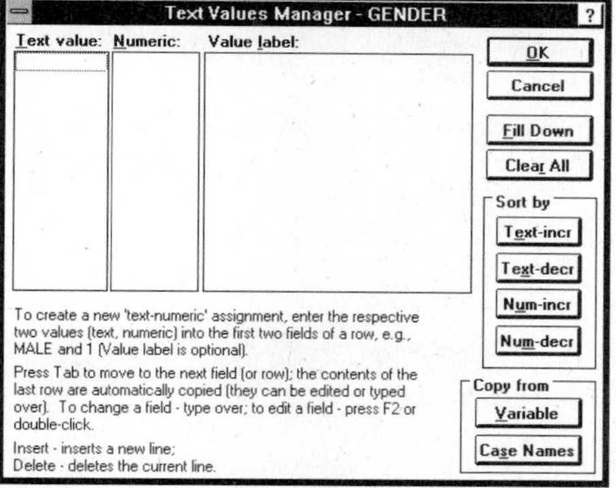

To enter the new text values into the *Text Values Manager*, call up this dialog either by clicking on the *Text Values* button in the *Spreadsheet Edit (Current) Specs* dialog, clicking on the spreadsheet toolbar button, or by selecting the *Variables - Text Values* option from the *Edit* pull-down menu. Since there are currently no text values assigned for this variable, the columns are initially blank.

In the column labeled *Text Value*, type the value *male* (you can use either upper or lower case letters) and in the corresponding *Numeric* column, type the value *1*. In the second row, type *female* in the *Text* column and *2* in the *Numeric* column.

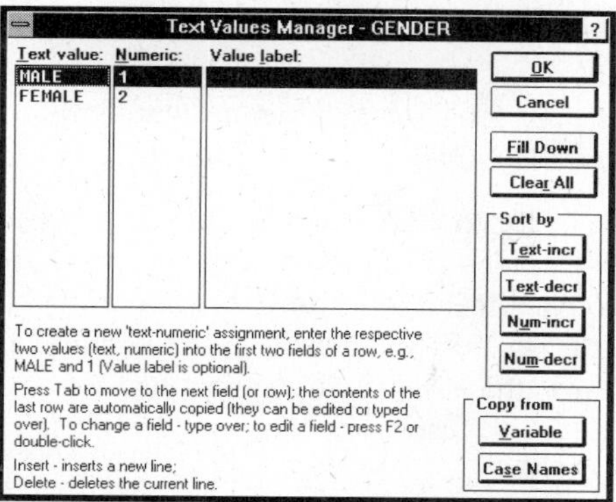

Click *OK* or press *Enter* to accept these settings and return to the spreadsheet.

Data: MYFILE.STA 10v * 25c

This is my first STATISTICA data file.

NUMERIC VALUES	1 GENDER	2 VAR2	3 VAR3
	MALE	4.570	142.000
	FEMALE	3.128	365.000
	MALE	2.250	326.000
	MALE	4.240	244.000
	FEMALE	1.420	364.000
	FEMALE	3.950	115.000
	MALE	4.480	385.000
	FEMALE	.240	184.000
	MALE	5.900	246.000

In the column for variable *Gender* the text value *MALE* (all in upper case, regardless of the way you entered it) is automatically filled in for all values of *1*, and *FEMALE* is filled in for all values of *2*.

Managing case names. When setting up this data file, an 8-character wide column of case names was requested (if you created a file without case names, simply drag the border of the first column to right, so as to make it wider). So far, it is empty, however, you can enter case names using the *Case Name Manager* dialog. You can access this dialog by double-clicking on the *Case Name* area of the spreadsheet, or by selecting the *Cases - Names* option on the *Edit* pull-down menu.

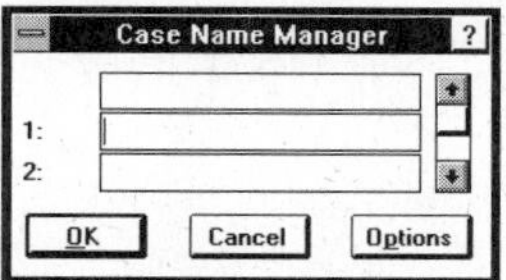

StatSoft

In this dialog, you can enter case names directly into the edit fields or use the values of another variable as the case names (click on the *Options* button to open the *Case Names Options* dialog, see below).

Although typically the case name column contains unique texts that identify records of data (entered or imported from another application), often it is handy to place in it text values of a variable, so that those values appear in the *STATISTICA* output that is by default labeled with case names (e.g., a time series graph).

For this example, copy the values of variable *1* (*Gender*) to the case names by setting the *Get from - variable* check box and then entering the variable name *Gender* in the respective edit field.

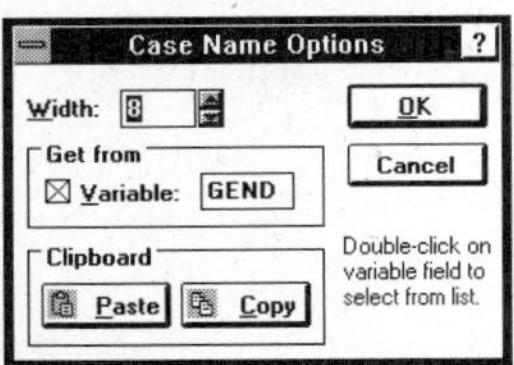

Case names can be edited by double-clicking with the mouse on the desired case name to reopen the *Case Name Manager* dialog with that case name in the edit field.

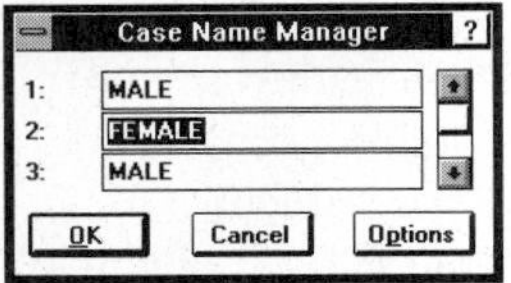

Using *STATISTICA BASIC* for Data Transformations

In addition to directly entering values from the keyboard, you may also use spreadsheet formulas or the integrated value recoding facilities to define values for a variable as described above.

The vast majority of standard data transformations and data recoding in *STATISTICA* may be accomplished in this way. However, sometimes you may need to perform more elaborate data transformations (e.g., repeat a set of complex formulas in a loop for a number of variables, set up complex conditional statements, or perform an extensive set of user-defined recodes). This can be accomplished via *STATISTICA BASIC*, a programming language (similar to *BASIC*) that is available in all modules of *STATISTICA*.

STATISTICA BASIC's window can be quickly accessed from the spreadsheet *Analysis* pull-down menu. Once you select this option, a new *STATISTICA BASIC* window will open and the toolbar will provide options specific to this program.

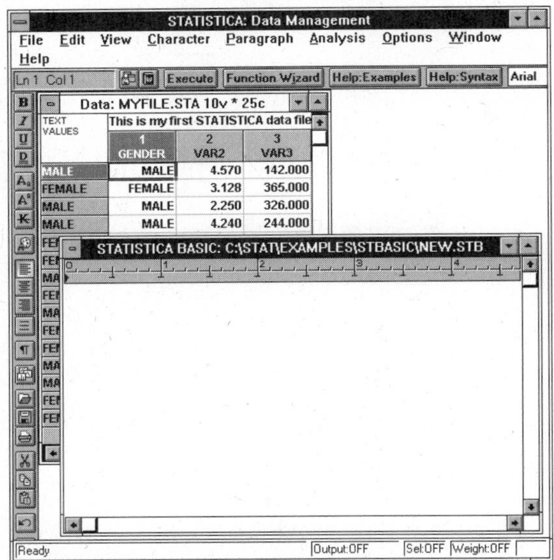

The **Function Wizard** button can be used to bring up a flexible facility that will help you select and enter specific functions (see the end of this section, page 1356).

Also, two help reference buttons are available on the *STATISTICA BASIC* window toolbar: **Help:Examples** and **Help:Syntax**. Now press the **Help:Syntax** button on the toolbar and a help window will appear containing a summary of *STATISTICA BASIC* options and syntax.

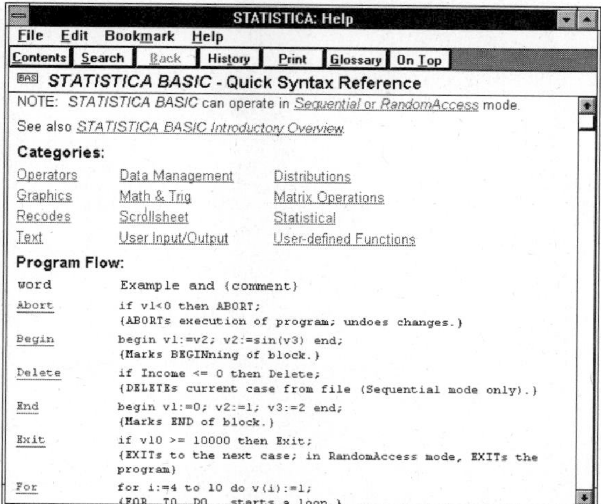

An additional help window, *STATISTICA BASIC Examples* (see below), also selectable from the toolbar **Help:Examples** button , contains brief sample programs.

Note that in order to keep these *Help* windows displayed (for quick reference) while you use the *STATISTICA BASIC* program, click on the *Always on Top* button on the *Help* button bar.

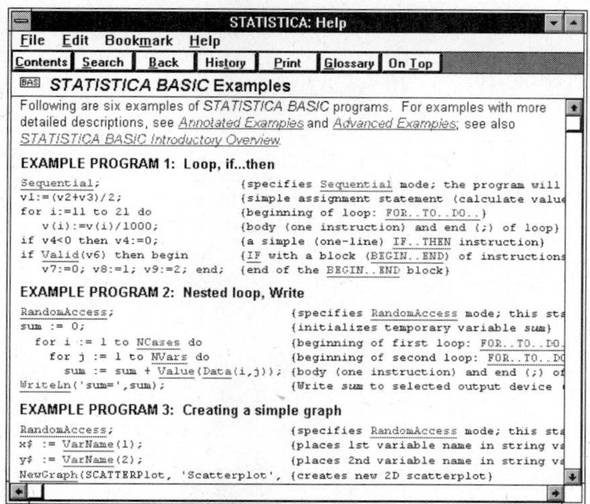

Enter a simple formula into the *STATISTICA BASIC* program editor. For example, add 100 to each value of variable number 3, and execute the formula in a loop for all cases (*NCases* is a reserved variable that stores the number of cases in the current data file; all data reside in a predefined array *DATA(case, variable)*).

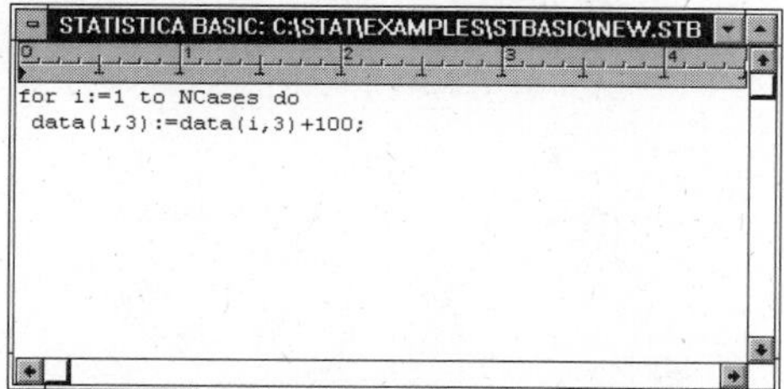

Note that in all value assignment statements, *STATISTICA BASIC* uses the " := " convention (instead of " = "); the simple equal sign is used only in logical expressions.

Now run the program by pressing the **Execute** button. After the program execution is completed, the contents of the spreadsheet will automatically be updated.

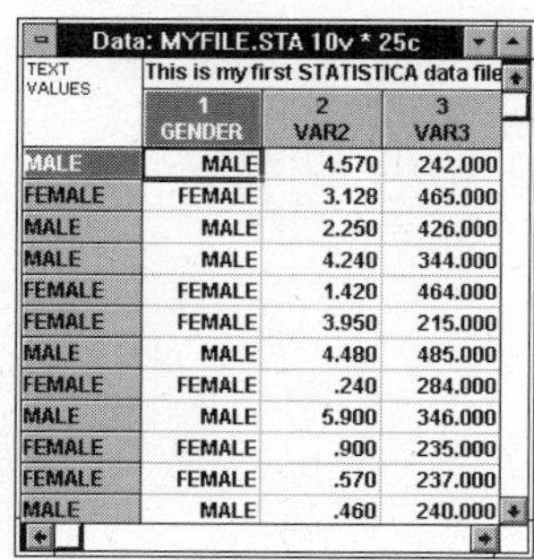

	1 GENDER	2 VAR2	3 VAR3
MALE	MALE	4.570	242.000
FEMALE	FEMALE	3.128	465.000
MALE	MALE	2.250	426.000
MALE	MALE	4.240	344.000
FEMALE	FEMALE	1.420	464.000
FEMALE	FEMALE	3.950	215.000
MALE	MALE	4.480	485.000
FEMALE	FEMALE	.240	284.000
MALE	MALE	5.900	346.000
FEMALE	FEMALE	.900	235.000
FEMALE	FEMALE	.570	237.000
MALE	MALE	.460	240.000

The *STATISTICA BASIC* program may be saved via the *Save as* option from the *File* pull-down menu. The default file name extension for *STATISTICA BASIC* programs is **.stb*. The *STATISTICA BASIC* program files are stored in the standard text format.

STATISTICA BASIC is a powerful program development tool, capable of producing advanced applications with graphs, Scrollsheets, user-interface, matrix operations, etc. *STATISTICA BASIC* allows you to organize your program into functions and subroutines, and you can also call

external functions residing in *DLL*'s (*Dynamic Link Libraries*).

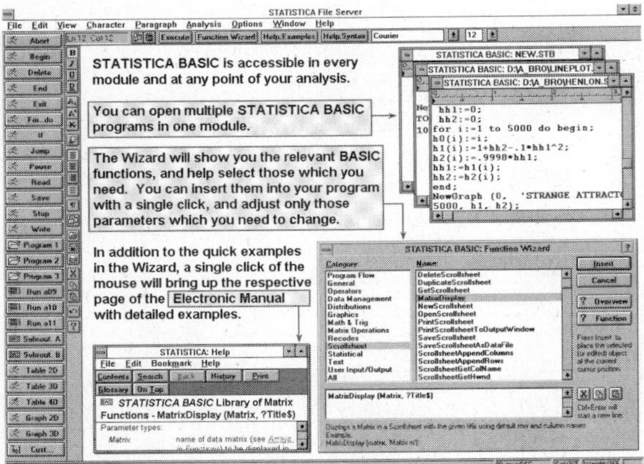

A flexible wizard (shown above) is provided to show the relevant *STATISTICA BASIC* functions, and help select those which you need. You can *Insert* them into your program with a single click, and adjust only those parameters which you need to change.

For the most complete description of all available options and facilities related to *STATISTICA BASIC*, refer to the *Electronic Manual*.

DIALOGS AND OPTIONS

Startup Panel

The *Data Management* startup panel lists all of the options available in this module.

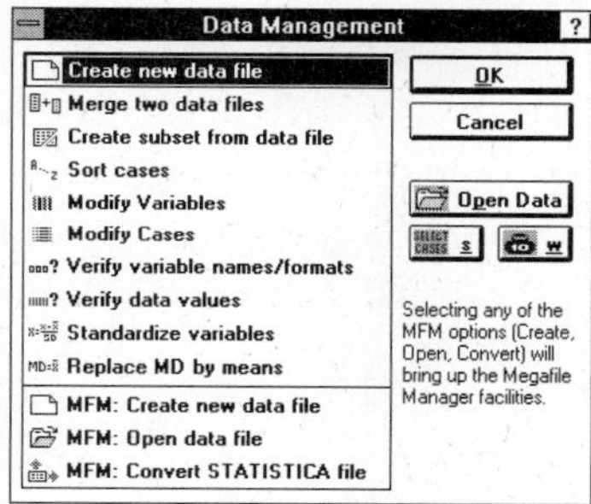

Each of these options will be described in detail below.

Create New Data File

A quick facility to create new data files is included in the *File* menu of every module (it creates a new file with default settings that can later be modified by the user). The facility to create new data files included in the *Data Management* module offers additional options (e.g., global options to automatically create variable names following user-defined criteria). For example (see also the *Examples* section of this chapter):

Step 1. Select the *New Data* option from the *File* pull-down menu to open the *Create New File* dialog.

Step 2. Specify in this dialog the new file name and path (click on the *New File* button), the file dimensions (number of cases and variables), and value format, as well as other information necessary to build the data file (each of the options are described below). Note that all specifications of the file (entered in this dialog) can be modified after the file is created.

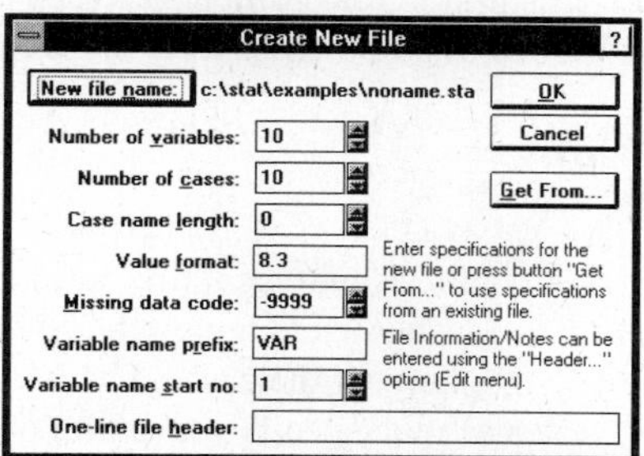

Step 3. Click on the *OK* button to open a spreadsheet in which you can enter data into the newly created file.

New File Name

Click on this button to open the *New Data: Specify File Name* dialog in which you can designate the file name for the new data file.

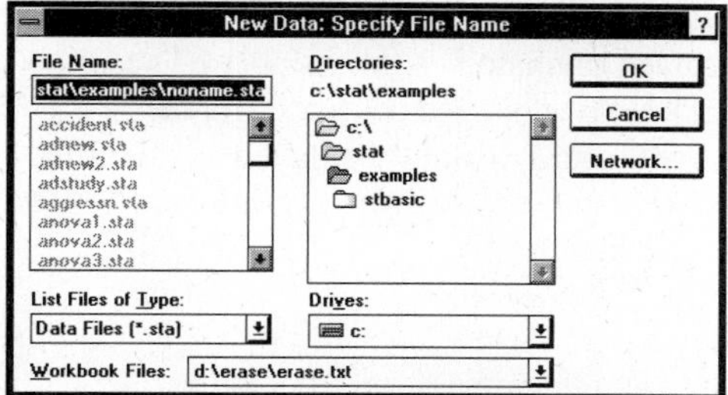

Number of Variables

Specify the number of variables to be included in the new data file. 4,092 variables may be included in one *STATISTICA* data file. (Files with up to 32,000 variables may be created and maintained in *STATISTICA*'s *Megafile Manager*, see Volume III.)

Number of Cases

Enter the number of cases to be included when creating the data file. *STATISTICA* imposes practically no limit on the number of cases in one file (up to 2,140,000,000 cases may be specified).

Case Name Length

STATISTICA data files may contain (optional) case names of up to 20 characters in length. Specify the case name length here (if the case name length varies from case to case, then specify the length of the longest case name).

Value Format

A default display width format of up to 30 characters may be defined in the form *X.Y*, where *X* is the total width, and *Y* is the number of digits following the decimal point (the default format, *8.3*, will display a width of eight characters, with the decimal point three digits to the left, e.g., *1234.567*). The format affects only the way in which values are displayed in the spreadsheet editor and does not affect the internal storage precision of the number. The value format can later be changed so that different variables may contain values displayed in scientific notation, text, dates, times, currency values, etc. (see page 1335 for details).

Missing Data Code

Set the initial value (default *-9999*) which will be used to represent "missing data" for all variables here. This value may be changed for individual variables in the *Spreadsheet Edit (Current) Specs* dialog (see page 1334). Note that *STATISTICA* displays a blank cell in the spreadsheet wherever missing data occurs.

Variable Name Prefix

Specify the variable name prefix here (all variable names in this data file will have this prefix). The variable name prefix which is defined here will have a sequential number added to the end (i.e., *VAR1*, *VAR2*, *VAR3*, etc.; the last character(s) in the prefix will be replaced by the number if necessary, to maintain the overall length of 8 characters).

Variable Name Start Number

Enter the starting number for the variable name prefixes (see above). You may want to start with a number other than 1 if you intend to merge this file with another *STATISTICA* file.

One-Line File Header

Enter one line (up to 77 characters) of comment about the file here. The *One-Line File Header* is saved as part of the file and is printed along with the spreadsheet data file when the *File Info/Notes* option is selected in the *Print Data* dialog, or along with the output of analyses when either a *Short*, *Medium* or *Long* report style is selected in the *Page/Output Setup* dialog. You can edit this file header and add a file comment (notes), in the *Data File, Notes and Workbook Info* dialog (see page 1333), accessible by double-clicking on the title area of the spreadsheet, or by pressing the Workbook toolbar button .

Get From

Click on this button to open the *Select File to Get Specs From* dialog in which you can designate the file with the complete set of all variable specifications (number of variables and cases, variable names, formats, and MD codes) of an existing *STATISTICA* data file in order to use them for the newly created file.

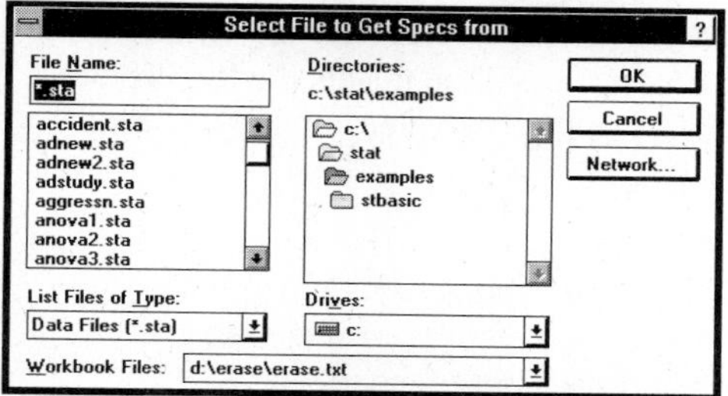

Note that the variable specifications obtained from the designated file will override all other specifications entered in this dialog.

Merge Two Data Files

There are many circumstances when you may need to merge data files. For example, you may need to append data from additional subjects to the end ("bottom") of an existing data file (i.e., merge it with another file that contains the same variables: *Merge Cases*, page 1361). You could also perform more tests (create additional variables) on cases from an existing data file. A file containing those new variables would be appended at the end ("right side") of the existing data file (i.e., merged with another file that contains the same cases: *Merge Variables*, see below). You may also merge the numeric/text value assignments from two files (*Merge Text Values*, page 1361).

Example. To merge two *STATISTICA* data files, follow the steps outlined below.

Step 1. Click on the *Merge* option from either the startup panel or the *Analysis* pull-down menu.

Step 2. Select one of the merging options (e.g., the *Merge Variables* option) and click on the *2nd File* button to select the file with the variables that will be added after the current file's variables. Click *OK* to exit this dialog and open either the *Merge Variables* or *Merge Text Values* dialog (in the case of *Merge Cases*, there is no intermediate dialog).

Step 3. Select the *Mode* of merging the variables and, in the case of *Merge Variables*, the way that you want *STATISTICA* to handle *Unmatched Cases*. Click *OK* to process the *Merge*.

When you select the *Merge Two Data Files* option, the *Merge Files* dialog will open.

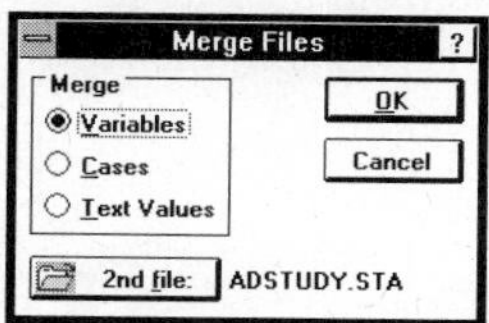

You will need to specify the type of merge that you want as well as the file to be merged with the current file.

Merge

Select one of three merging options. Each merging option is discussed in detail below.

2nd File

Click on this button to open the *Select Second File* dialog from which you can select a file to merge with the current file.

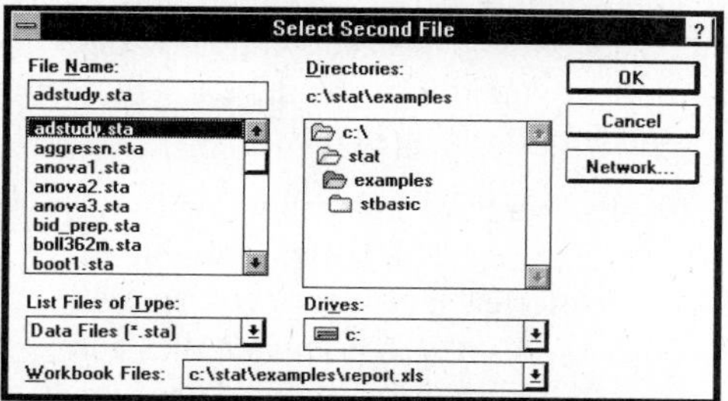

Please note that you cannot merge a file to itself (i.e., you cannot enter the current file as the second *STATISTICA* file name). If you wish to "double" the

file, use the *Save As* option from the *File* pull-down menu to create a second copy of the file.

Merge Variables

When you select the *Merge Variables* option from the *Merge Files* dialog, *STATISTICA* will add the second file's variables after the variables of the first file (see the *Introductory Overview*, page 1325). The following options (available from the *Merge Variables* dialog) are used to align (match) the cases of the second file with those of the first.

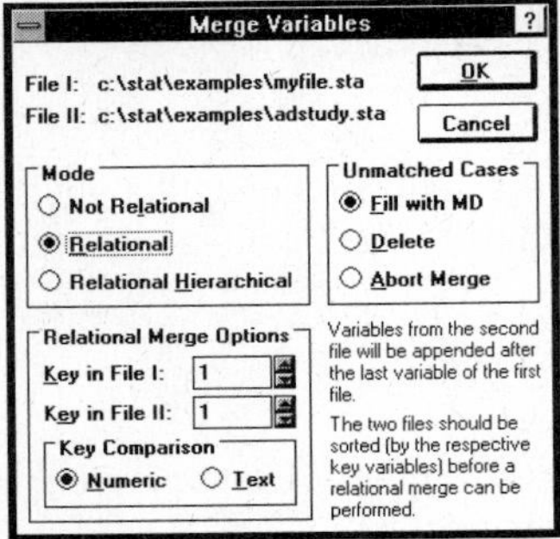

Mode

If the number and order of cases in the two data files are not precisely the same (i.e., if at least one case is missing in the second data file or there is one case that has no equivalent in the first file), then all subsequent data would be merged with the wrong cases. In order to avoid this problem, you will need to specify a mode of merging here.

When relationally merging cases from two files, you need to specify a *key* (case identifier) variable in each data set; then for each case the program will check the values of this key in both data files and merge the cases only if their respective keys match.

Not relational. Variables of the second file are simply added alongside those of the first when this mode is selected (this is the default mode).

Relational. When you select this mode, the cases from the second file will be matched with those of the first file, based on the values of a specified *key* (see below).

Relational hierarchical. This mode differs from the simple relational mode (see above) in the handling of multiple records with the same key value in either the primary or secondary file.

In the standard relational mode (see above), successive records with identical key values will be merged. If there are uneven numbers of records with identical key values in the two files, missing data are added to "pad" the file with the lesser number of records.

In contrast, in the *Relational hierarchical* mode the file is padded with the values found in the last identical key record that was matched. For example:

Standard *Relational Merge*, unmatched cases filled with missing data:

File 1		File 2		Merged File			
Key1	Var1	Key2	Var2	Key1	Var1	Key2	Var2
1	1	1	1	1	1	1	1
2	4	1	2	Miss	Miss	1	2
2	5	1	3	Miss	Miss	1	3
3	2	2	4	2	4	2	4
3	3	2	5	2	5	2	5
				3	2	Miss	Miss
				3	3	Miss	Miss

Hierarchical Relational Merge, unmatched cases filled with missing data:

Merged File			
Key1	Var1	Key2	Var2
1	1	1	1
1	1	1	2
1	1	1	3
2	4	2	4
2	5	2	5
3	2	Miss	Miss
3	3	Miss	Miss

Note that the sequence of cases is not changed during merging, therefore, each file should be sorted (see *Sort Data*, page 1362) in order of its key variable before merging.

Relational Merge Options

When you choose either the *Relational Merge* or *Relational Hierarchical Merge* option, you will need to specify a key variable for each file in order to merge the two files. *STATISTICA* will expect the two files to be sorted (see *Sort Data*, page 1362) by their respective key variables before a relational merge can be performed.

Key in file 1. Enter here the number of the variable to be used as the key in the first file.

Key in file 2. Enter here the number of the variable to be used as the key in the second file.

Key comparison (numeric or text). Choose to match the key variables in the two files based on their *numeric* or text (*text*) values.

Unmatched Cases

Select one of three ways of dealing with unmatched cases when the two files are merged. Unmatched cases may result from unequal numbers of cases in the merged files, or because some of the cases do not meet the *Relational merge* criteria (see above).

Fill with MD. Unfilled variables in unmatched cases are padded with missing data when you select this option.

Abort merge. The presence of unmatched cases in either file will cause an error message to be displayed and the merge procedure to be abandoned.

Delete. Cases from either file which cannot be matched will be removed from the merged file if you select this option.

Merge Cases

Select this option from the *Merge Files* dialog when you want to merge cases from the second file after the cases of the first file (see the *Introductory Overview*, page 1325). The following two notes will apply when you choose to merge cases.

- The number of variables in the two files must be equal.
- The lists of text values (and value labels) of the two files will be concatenated. If a variable in the second file has numeric values with different text values or value labels than those in the first file, the text values and value labels of the first file will be used.

Merge Text Values

Select the *Merge Text Values* option from the *Merge Files* dialog when you want to merge text values (and value labels) from the second file with those of the current data file. Note that only the text values of variables with the same name in both files will be merged. If two variables (from the two files) share the same name but you do not want to merge their text values, then temporarily change the name of the variable in one of the files until the merge procedure is completed. Selecting this option will open the *Merge Text Values* dialog from which you can choose the mode of merging text values.

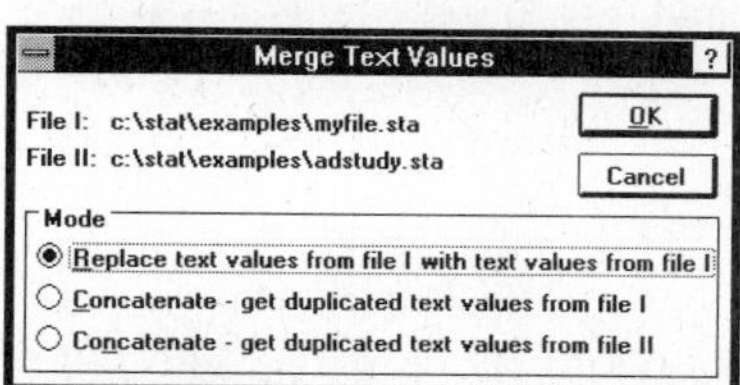

Mode

Choose one of these options for merging text values.

Replace text values from file I with text values from file II. Replace all text value lists in the first file with those from the second.

Concatenate - get duplicated text values from file I. Combine the text value lists from the

second file with those of the first, and if any duplicated text values are detected, then *STATISTICA* will use the text values from the first file.

Concatenate - get duplicated text values from file II. Combine the text value lists from the second file with those of the first, and if any duplicated text values are detected, then *STATISTICA* will use the text values from the second file.

Subset

Unlike the *Case Selection Conditions* (see Chapter 3) which allow you to temporarily limit the data set (to be analyzed) to a subset, use this *Data Management* option to extract a section (subset) of the current file to be stored under a new name. When you select this option from either the *Analysis* pull-down menu or the *Data Management* startup panel, the *Create a Subset* dialog will open.

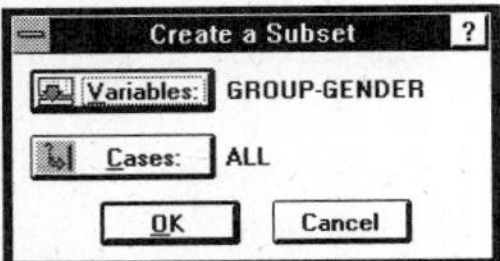

After you have created this subset file, you will need to save it under a different file name using the *Save As* option from the *File* pull-down menu.

Variables

Click on this button to bring up the *Select Variables* dialog from which you may select the variables to be included in the subset file.

Cases

Click on this button to open the *Case Selection Conditions* dialog in which you may enter conditions defining the selection of cases to be included in the subset file (see Chapter 1).

Sort Data

STATISTICA performs hierarchical (nested) sorting on the basis of user-specified key variables (i.e., if two cases have identical values in a given key, the values of the next key are used to determine ranking). When you select the *Sort* from the *Analysis* pull-down menu (or the *Sort Cases* option from the *Data Management* startup panel), the *Sort Options* dialog will open.

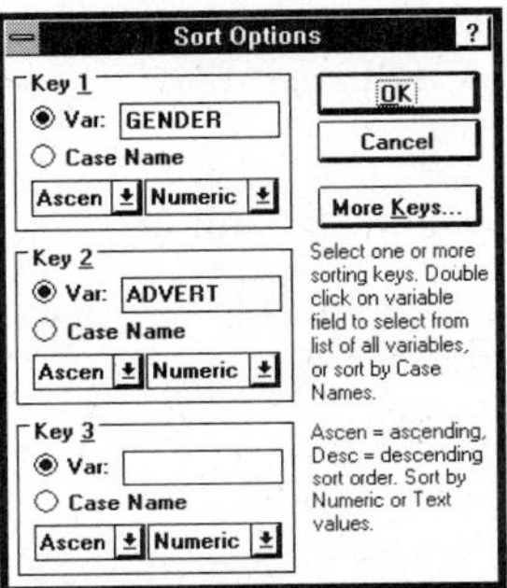

Example. In this example, use the examples data file *Adstudy.sta* and sort the data file by two key variables (*Gender* and *Advert*).

Step 1. After opening the *Sort Options* dialog (see above), enter *Gender* as the first key variable to sort by (*Key 1*) and *Advert* as the second key variable (*Key 2*).

Step 2. Specify, for each of the key variables, whether you want to sort in ascending or descending order for numeric or text values. For this example, accept the default selections of *Ascending* and *Numeric*.

Step 3. Click *OK* to proceed with the sorting operation.

You can choose up to seven key variables by which to sort in this dialog. Each key variable has the same set of options (described below).

Variable

Type in the key variable name or double-click on this window to open the *Select Variable* dialog. The *Select Variable* dialog will display a list of variables from which you can select the desired key variable.

Case Name

Select this option to sort the data by case names. Note that you will also need to set the *Sorting Mode* to *Text* (see below) when you select this option.

Sorting Order

Choose to use the *Ascending* or *Descending* sort order.

Sorting Mode

Sort either by *Numeric* or *Text* values of the key variable. When sorting based on *Text* values, if some numeric codes do not have text equivalents, then *STATISTICA* assumes that *Text* is smaller than *Numeric* (i.e., when sorting in ascending order, all text values will be at the top, followed by the numeric values without text equivalents).

More Keys

When this dialog first opens, only three keys are displayed. If you need to enter more keys than this, click on the *More Keys* button to increase the number of displayed keys.

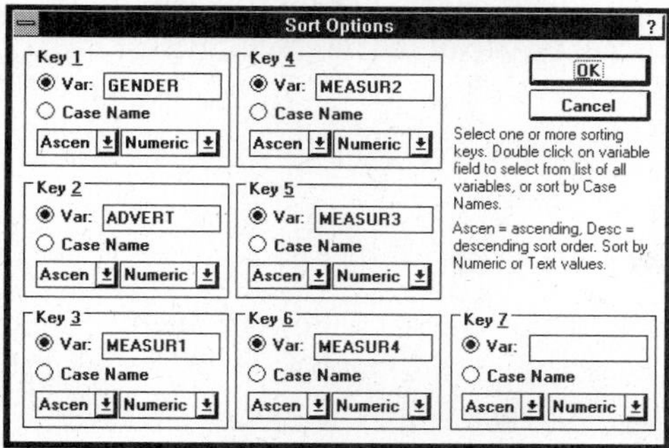

Now you can enter up to seven (the maximum) keys for sorting.

Modify Variables

Some of the most common data management operations on variables are available in the *Modify Variables* dialog (accessible from the *Data Management* startup panel).

The same operations are available when you select the *Modify Variables* option from the *Analysis* pull-down menu (a menu with these options will also open from the spreadsheet **Vars** toolbar button).

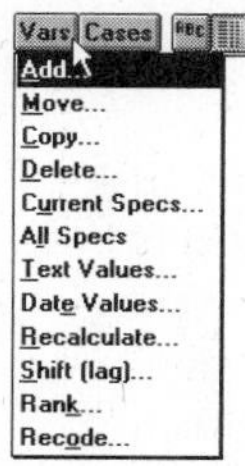

Note that this pop-up menu is available in the spreadsheet window of every module and from the spreadsheet flying menu accessible by pressing the right-mouse-button. Each of these options is explained in detail in the *Spreadsheet Window* chapter (Chapter 3).

Modify Cases

Some of the most common data management operations on cases are available in the *Modify Cases* dialog (accessible from the *Data Management* startup panel).

The same operations are available when you select the *Modify Cases* option from the *Analysis* pull-down menu (a menu with these options will also open from the spreadsheet Cases toolbar button).

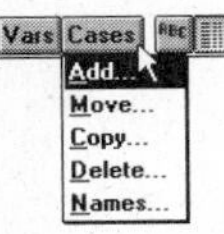

Note that this pop-up menu is available in the spreadsheet window of every module and from the spreadsheet flying menu accessible by pressing the right-mouse-button. Each of these options is explained in detail in the *Spreadsheet Window* chapter (Chapter 3).

Verify Variable Names/Format

This verification facility may be used to check for (and adjust) the "fit" of column *Formats* (see below) to the data, to check for duplicated column names, or to check their compliance with selected standards (e.g., *STATISTICA*, dBASE, SPSS). When you select this option from the *Analysis* pull-down menu or the *Data Management* startup panel, the *Verify* dialog will open.

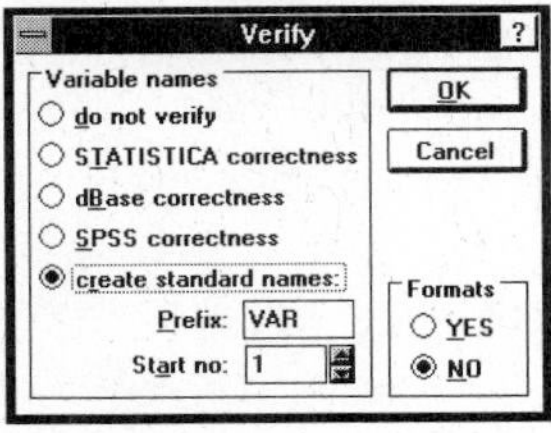

Variable Names

This option will check the correctness of the variables names according to the requirements of *STATISTICA*, dBASE, or SPSS, or it will create standard names. Select one of the options described below. If an invalid or duplicated name is found, a *Name Verification* dialog will open (see page 1365) allowing you to correct the name (either of the two names can be edited if a duplicate is found, see below).

Do not verify. Select this option if you are interested in only verifying variable formats.

***STATISTICA* correctness.** This option is used to check all variable names for duplications, either for compliance with the requirements of *STATISTICA BASIC*, or prior to exporting the file.

dBASE correctness. When selected, this option checks for compliance with the requirements of dBASE. All variables must have names which may contain the letters *A-Z*, *a-z*, the digits *0-9*, and the underscore (_). Each variable name must begin with a letter, and all variable names must be unique (which may be checked by using the *STATISTICA Correctness* option above).

SPSS correctness. When selected, this option checks for agreement with the requirements of SPSS. All variables must have names which may contain the letters *A-Z*, *a-z*, the digits *0-9*, underscore (_), period (.), @, #, and $. Each variable name must begin with either a letter, $, or @, and cannot be one of the reserved SPSS keywords (*ALL*, *AND*, *BY*, *EQ*, *GE*, *GT*, *LE*, *LT*, *NE*, *NOT*, *OR*, *TO*, and *WITH*).

Create Standard Names

When selected, this option assigns "standard" names (a prefix plus a sequential number) to all variables through the following options.

Prefix. Specify a five-letter prefix for standard variable names.

Start number. Select the starting value for the numeric portion of the names (useful when you intend to merge the file with another *STATISTICA* file).

Formats

When you select *YES*, *STATISTICA* will examine all specified variables to determine whether the variable formats are an appropriate "fit" to the data values. For example, the value *1234.5* would not "fit" in a column whose format is *2.1*.

Also, if the format is longer than any of the values in the column (e.g., the value 12.34 in a variable with a *15.7* format) the format length will be adjusted to the actual length of the longest value (however, the number of decimal places remains unchanged).

Duplicate Names

If duplicate names are encountered while verifying the correctness of variable names in the *Verify* dialog (see above), then the *Name Verification* dialog will open allowing the duplicated names to be edited.

Variable 2 - Variable 1

The duplicate variable names will be listed in an edit field next to their variable number. You can edit either or both of the names.

Accept

Click this button to accept the edited variable names and proceed with the verification process.

Break

Clicking this button will stop the verification process and return to *Data Management* (all changes to names up to this point will be saved).

Undo All

Click this button to stop the verification procedure and undo all changes made during verification.

Incorrect Variable Name

If incorrect names are encountered while verifying the correctness of variable names in the *Verify* dialog (see above), then the *Name Verification* dialog will open allowing the incorrect names to be edited.

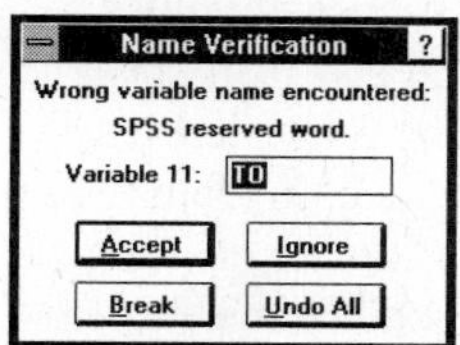

Variable Name

The incorrect variable name will be listed in an edit field next to its variable number. You can edit the name here.

Ignore

Click this button if you want to leave the variable name as it appears (uncorrected).

Accept

Click this button to accept the edited variable name and proceed to the next incorrect name.

Break

Clicking this button will stop the verification process and return to *Data Management* (all changes to names up to this point will be saved).

Undo All

Click this button to stop the verification procedure and undo all changes made during verification.

Verify Data

Once the data (entered or imported) are already in the file, you may need to verify their integrity (logical consistency) and completeness. Although some types of errors in the data may never be detected, there are many ways to perform data verification based on general criteria that the data are expected to meet.

For example, the verification can be as simple as checking whether values in a variable are "legal" (e.g., only *1* and *2* might be allowed for *Gender*) or whether they fall within allowed ranges of values (e.g., *Age* must be more than *0* and less than *200*). It can also be as complex as checking multiple logical conditions that some values must meet in relation to other values (a relatively simple example of conditional verification: if a person is a male *or* less than a certain age, then the number of pregnancies for that person cannot be more than zero). In order to apply these conditions, you would specify (for example):

Invalid if:
```
(v1='MALE' or AGE<14)
and PREGN<>0
```

STATISTICA provides such a verification facility when you select the *Verify Data* option from the *Analysis* pull-down menu (the *Verify Data* dialog will open).

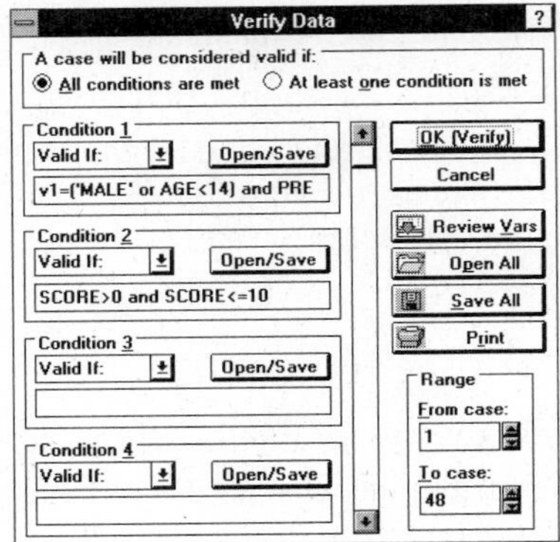

After you specify the verification conditions (following the conventions described below), click *OK* and the data set (or the selected range) will be tested sequentially (one case at a time) for its consistency with the conditions you specified. When a case is found which does not meet the conditions, then the respective row of data in the spreadsheet will be highlighted and the *Data Verification* dialog (see below) will open allowing you to either ignore it (and continue or stop the verification) or edit (correct) the case. After you edit the case, press the *Cont* (continue) button in the lower left corner of the screen to continue the verification.

A Case Will be Considered Valid if:

Select one of the two options described below to define when a case will be considered valid.

All conditions are met. When you select this option, a case will be considered correct only if all of the conditions (defined below) are met.

At least one condition is met. When you select this option, a case will be considered correct if at least one of the defined conditions (see below) is met.

Condition

Define a list of up to 16 different *Verification Conditions* as the criteria of correctness.

Verification syntax summary. For more information and examples on selection (verification) conditions, see *Case Selection Conditions*, Chapter 3.

- Refer to variables either by their numbers (e.g., *v1 = 1*) or their names (e.g., *Gender = 1*); note that you can type variable names in either upper or lower case letters (i.e., *GENDER* is equivalent to *gender*).
- Enclose text values of a variable in single quotation marks (e.g., *v1 = 'MALE'*); note that the case is ignored by the interpreter and you can type text values in either upper or lower case letters (i.e., *'Yes'* is equivalent to *'YES'*).
- Use parentheses to specify complex logical conditions, in order to change the default precedence of operators.
- Logical Operators:

`=`	- equal
`# , <>, ><`	- not equal
`<`	- less than
`>`	- greater than
`<=`	- less than or equal to
`>=`	- greater than or equal to
`NOT, ~`	- logical NOT
`AND, &`	- logical AND
`OR, !`	- logical OR

Valid/Invalid If

Select whether the value will be considered *Valid* or *Invalid if* the verification condition is met.

Open/Save

Clicking this button will open the *Case Selection Conditions* dialog (see Chapter 3). Unlike the *Open All* and *Save All* options (see below) which apply to files containing complete sets of verification conditions, this option either opens a previous (single) case selection condition (file name extension **.sel*) to be used as a component of the current set of conditions or saves the current component verification condition (use the *Open All* and *Save All* options to open/save the entire set, see below).

Edit Field

Enter the case selection condition that will be used as verification criteria in this edit window (e.g., *v1 = 1 and v2 = 'MALE' or v3 = 2 and v4 = 'YES'*). For more information on valid case selection conditions, see the *Case Selection Conditions* dialog (see Chapter 3).

Review Variables

Click on this button to open the *Single Variable List* dialog in which you can review the variable names and numbers.

Open All

When you click on this button, the *Open Verify Conditions File* dialog will open from which you can select a file with multiple case selection conditions (including all options specified in this dialog) and open them for use as verification conditions. Conditions used for *Recoding* variables (see page 1324), *Frequency* and *Graph* categorizations (see *Basic Statistics and Tables*, Chapter 9, and Volume II of the manual, respectively), and all other facilities in *STATISTICA* which allow you to define multiple case selection conditions, are compatible with the conditions that can be specified here. You can use this option to open those previously saved selection conditions for use here.

Save All

When you click on this button, the *Save Verify Conditions File* dialog will open from which you can specify the file to save these verification conditions in. These selection conditions are compatible with the conditions used for *Recoding* variables (see page 1324), *Frequency* and *Graph* categorizations (see *Basic Statistics and Tables*, Chapter 9 and Volume II, respectively), and all other facilities in *STATISTICA* which allow you to define multiple case selection conditions. The recode conditions that you save via this option can then be used as selection conditions for these other *STATISTICA* applications.

Range

Define the range of values to be verified (*From Case* number, *To Case* number).

Data Verification

During the verification process (see the *Verify Data* dialog, above), when a case is found which does not meet the specified conditions, the respective row (case) of the spreadsheet will be highlighted and the *Data Verification* dialog will open, displaying the following options:

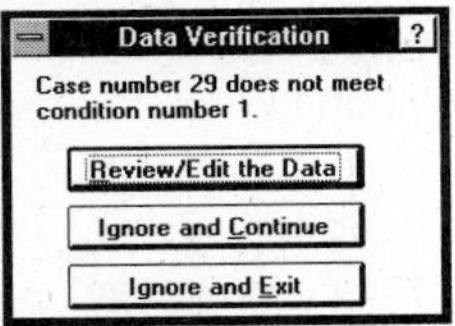

Review/Edit the Data

When you click on this option, you will be allowed to edit the data that did not meet the condition(s) before continuing the verification process. In order to continue, click on the floating *Continue* button:

on the bottom of the *STATISTICA* window.

Ignore and Continue

Clicking this button will ignore the case that did not meet the condition(s) and continue checking the next case.

Ignore and Exit

Clicking this button will ignore the case that did not meet the condition(s), stop the verification process, and exit to the *Verify Data* dialog (see above).

Data Standardization

Options to standardize values in a selected (highlighted) block are available from the spreadsheet flying menu (accessible by pressing the right-mouse-button).

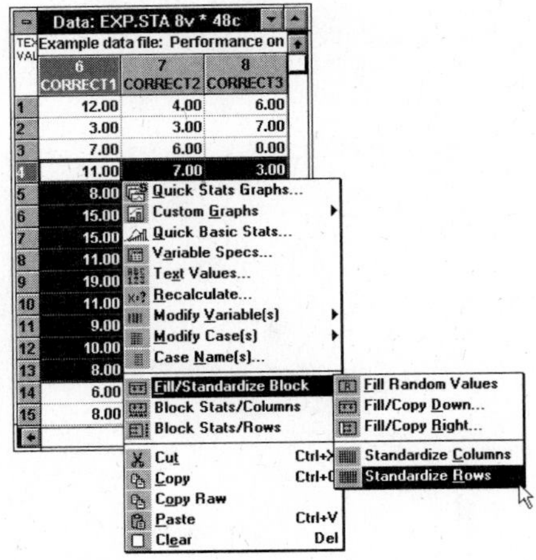

These flexible options allow you to standardize arbitrarily selected subsets of values and to perform

the standardization not only within variables (i.e., by column) but also by row.

The standardization procedure in the *Data Management* module is different in that it works not on the highlighted block of data in the spreadsheet but on all values of the selected variable(s), and while processing the data from these selected variable(s) it takes into account the currently specified case selection conditions and case weights.

In standardization, all values of selected variables are replaced by standardized values which are computed as follows:

```
Std.Score = (Raw Score-Mean)/Std.Dev.
```

In this formula, the standard deviation (*Std.Dev.*) is computed as the sum of squared deviations divided by *n-1*. When you select this option from the *Analysis* pull-down menu or from the *Data Management* startup panel, the *Standardization of Values* dialog will open from which you can select the variable to be standardized.

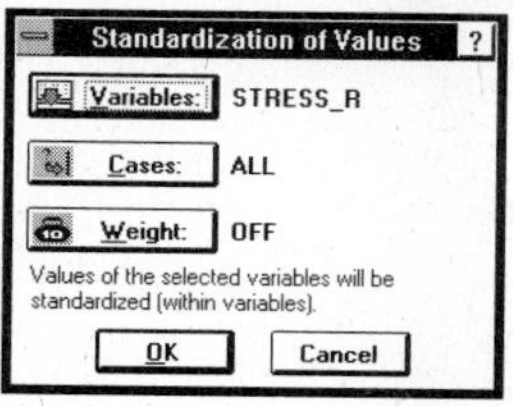

If the standardized variable has any text values, then the corresponding numeric values (assigned to the text values) will be adjusted accordingly (otherwise, after standardization, most values would "lose" their alphanumeric components). The first six significant digits will be used as numeric equivalents of text values.

Variables

By default, all variables in the file will be standardized. If desired, standardization can be performed on only selected variables. When you click on this button, the *Select Variables* dialog will open from which you can select the variables to be standardized.

Cases

By default, all cases are used in computing means and standard deviations for each variable. If desired, case selection conditions may be used, in which instance the mean and standard deviation will be computed for only the selected cases, and only those cases will be standardized. This allows you to perform a subset standardization; e.g., you can standardize values once for "*Males*" and then for "*Females*" to obtain standardized scores according to their respective (different) group means and standard deviations. When you click on this button, the *Case Selection Conditions* dialog (see Chapter 3) will open from which you can specify new case selection conditions or open existing conditions.

Weight

By default, each (selected) case contributes equally to the computation of the variable means and standard deviations. You can select a weighting variable by clicking this button to open the *Define Weight* dialog. By specifying one variable as containing weights, the influence of each case can be varied by an amount proportional to the value of the *weight* variable for the case. (Although *STATISTICA* actually uses a faster algorithm, this system can be interpreted as reading each case a number of times that is equivalent to the current value of its weight.)

Missing Data Replacement

This option will permanently replace missing data values for selected variables with the means of those variables (when applicable, this option is also available in many *STATISTICA* modules as one of the missing data handling options and is then temporary, i.e., will apply only to the current

analysis). When you select this option, the *Missing Data Replacement* dialog will open.

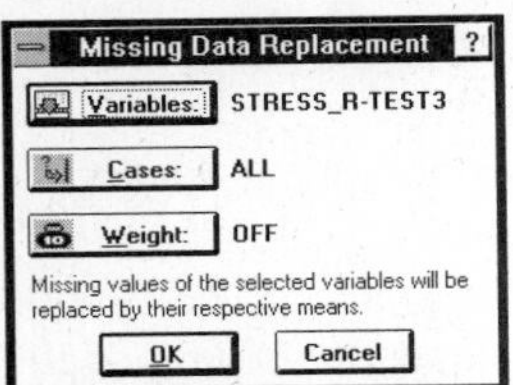

Variables

By default, all variables in the file will be included in missing data replacement. If desired, replacement can be performed on only selected variables. When you click on this button, the *Select Variables* dialog will open from which you can select specific variables.

Cases

By default, all cases are used in computing means for each variable. If desired, case selection conditions may be used, in which instance, the mean will be computed for only the selected cases, and only those cases will have their missing data replaced. When you click on this button, the *Case Selection Conditions* dialog (see Chapter 3) will open from which you can specify new case selection conditions or open existing conditions.

Weight

By default, each (selected) case contributes equally to the computation of the variable means. You can select a weighting variable by clicking this button to open the *Define Weight* dialog.

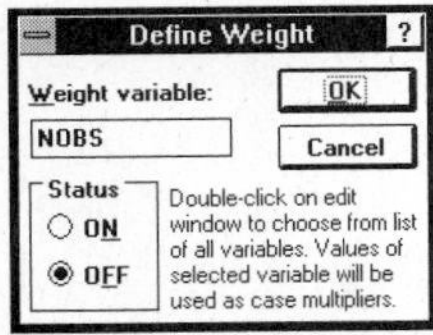

By specifying one variable as containing weights, the influence of each case can be varied by an amount proportional to the value of the *weight* variable for the case. (Although *STATISTICA* actually uses a faster algorithm, this system can be interpreted as reading each case a number of times that is equivalent to the current value of its weight.)

MEGAFILE MANAGER FACILITIES IN THE DATA MANAGEMENT MODULE

The following *Megafile Manager* facilities are available from the *Data Management* startup panel (see page 1357), *File* pull-down menu, or *Analysis* pull-down menu. Note that these facilities are not available in Quick *STATISTICA* for Windows.

For an overview of *Megafile Manager*, please refer to page 1329 earlier in this chapter. A comprehensive reference to *Megafile Manager* (and its programming language *MML*) is included in Volume III.

Create New MFM Data

You can create new *Megafile Manager* files with the *Create New File* dialog (accessible from the *New MFM Data* option in the *File* pull-down menu, or via the *MFM: Create New Data* option from the *Analysis* pull-down menu or the *Data Management* startup panel).

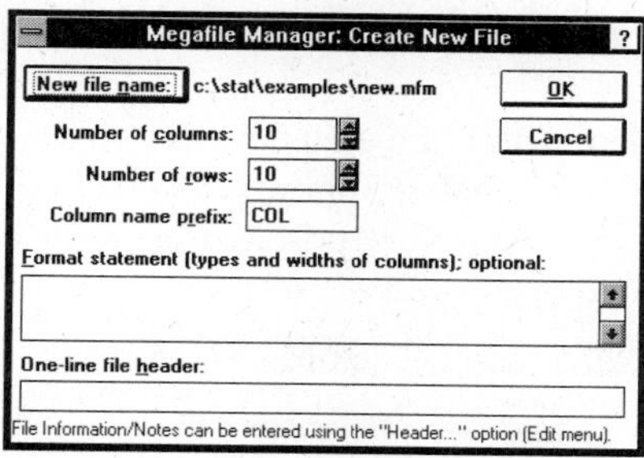

Example. Follow the steps outlined below to create a new *Megafile Manager* file.

Step 1. Select the *New MFM Data* option from the *File* pull-down menu to open the *Megafile Manager: Create New File* dialog (see above).

Step 2. Specify in this dialog the new file name and path (click on the *New file name* button), the file dimensions (number of rows and columns), and optionally the format (types and width of columns; if you omit this information, columns of type *Real* will be created), as well as other information necessary to build the data file (each of the options are described below). Note that all specifications of the file (entered in this dialog) can be modified after the file is created (see Volume III).

Step 3. Click on the *OK* button to open a *Megafile Manager* spreadsheet in which you can enter data into the newly created file.

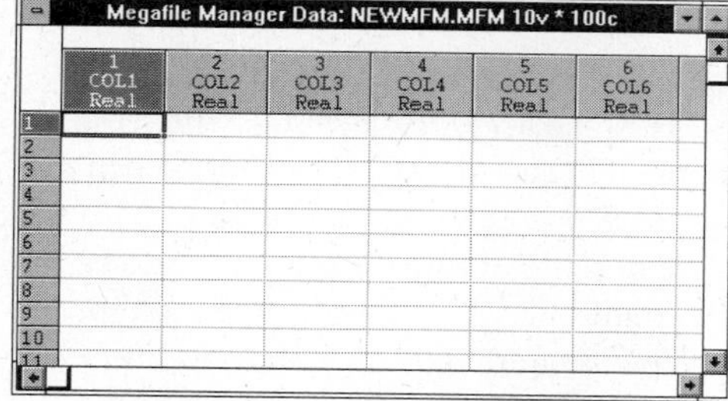

New File Name

Click on this button to open the *New Data*: *Specify File Name* dialog in which you can designate the file name for the new *Megafile Manager* file.

Number of Columns

Specify the number of columns to be included in the new data file. Up to 32,000 columns may be created and maintained in *Megafile Manager*.

Number of Rows

Enter the number of rows to be included when creating the data file. *STATISTICA* imposes

practically no limit on the number of rows in one file (up to 2.14 billion rows may be specified).

Column Name Prefix

Specify the column name prefix here (all column names in this data file will have this prefix). The column name prefix which is defined here will have a sequential number added to the end (i.e., *COL1*, *COL2*, *COL3*, etc.).

Format Statement

The (optional) format statement is a set of instructions for creating the structure of the new *Megafile Manager* file (later, you can double-click on a column title in the *Megafile Manager* spreadsheet to open the *Column Specs* dialog in which you can change the format for that particular column, see Volume III).

This option explicitly defines for *STATISTICA* the exact contents of the *Megafile Manager* file. The format statement is entered as a list of formats in the form *nXm*, where *n* is an integer multiplier indicating the number of times the format is to be repeated (no multiplier = 1); *X* is the column type (see the next paragraph); *m* is the column width [e.g., *10A8* means 10 text value (alphanumeric) fields, each 8 characters long].

Column Type Specifiers

The following column type specifiers are supported (for more information, please refer to Volume III):

A - Text (Alphanumeric)

F - Float (also *R* - Real, equivalent to *Real 4B* in the *Column Specs* dialog)

D - Double Float (also *DR* - Double Real, equivalent to *Real 8B* in the *Column Specs* dialog)

I - Integer (also *NI* - Normal Integer, equivalent to *Int 2B* in the *Column Specs* dialog)

S - Short Integer (also *SI*, equivalent to *Int 1B* in the *Column Specs* dialog)

LI - Long Integer (also *J*, equivalent to *Int 4B* in the *Column Specs* dialog)

L - Logical

For example, the format statement *2a15 i3 f5* defines four columns: the first two columns contain text (symbol *a*), 15 characters in display width; the third column contains *integer* values (symbol *i*) of display width 3; the fourth *float* column (symbol *f*) contains values 5 characters in display width. For more information on column types and widths in *Megafile Manager*, see Volume III.

One-Line File Header

Enter one line (up to 77 characters) of comment about the file here. Longer comments and notes can be entered in the *File Information/Notes* area of the *Data File Header and Info* dialog (see *Spreadsheet Window*, Chapter 3).

Open *Megafile Manager* Data

Selecting this option will bring up the *Open Megafile Manager File* dialog from which you can select a *Megafile Manager* file (file with the extension **.mfm*) to open.

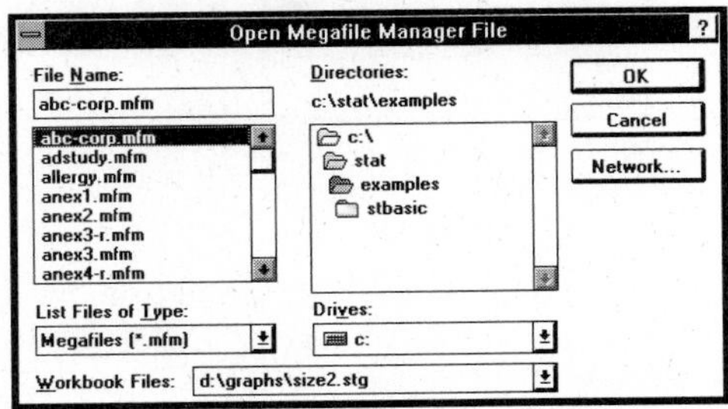

Megafile Manager files contain data values and also labels and formats, headers and notes, and other information. In order to open a non-*Megafile Manager* format file (e.g., Excel, Lotus, Quattro, dBASE, Paradox, ASCII, and others) use the *Import* option in the *File* pull-down menu (see Volume III).

MFM: Convert *STATISTICA* File

This option is accessible from the *File* pull-down menu (click on the *Make MFM Data* option), or via the *MFM: Convert STATISTICA file* option from the *Analysis* pull-down menu or the *Data Management* startup panel. Selecting either of these options will allow you to quickly open the *Save Exported File As* dialog in order to export (or convert) a *STATISTICA* data file to a *Megafile Manager* file.

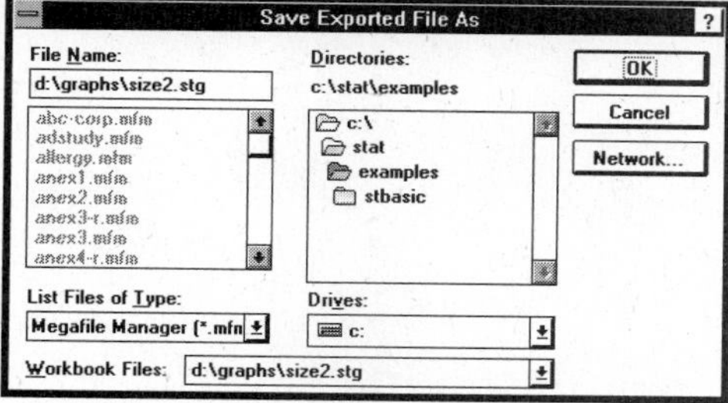

For more information on exporting a *STATISTICA* file to *Megafile Manager*, see *Export to Megafile Manager*, page 1391.

StatSoft

IMPORTING AND EXPORTING DATA

Importing Data

Data file import/export facilities are accessible in every module of *STATISTICA* (in the pull-down menu *File*); also, the *ODBC* (Open Data Base Connectivity) interface accessible in every module from the same menu offers access to a wide variety foreign files (including mainframe data base management files). For more information, see Chapter 3 (or the *Electronic Manual*). The additional import/export facilities offered in the *Data Management* module (by selecting the *More...* option in the *Import* or *Export* submenus):

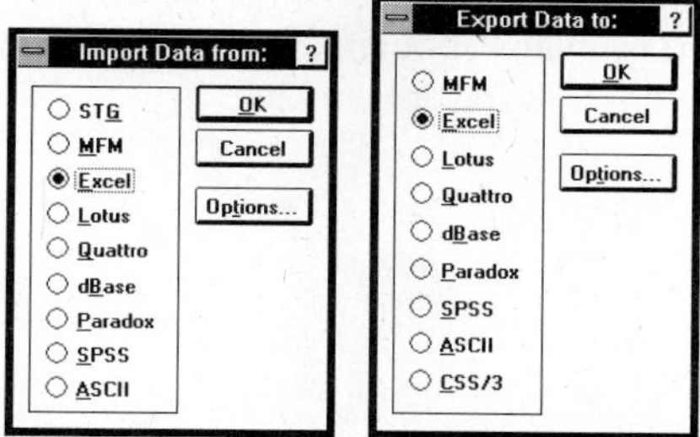

offer some additional options for specialized data transfers. Most importantly, they offer options to exchange *STATISTICA* double notation (text/numeric) and labeled values with applications that do not support labeled or double notation values. Specifically, options are provided to "mark" and split (while exporting) and merge (while importing) numeric and text data values and their labels. Also, these facilities support some of the less commonly used (and inaccessible via *ODBC*) file formats, such as the SPSS *PFF* (*Portable File Format*) files, also compatible with SAS, or STG graphics files.

Example. Importing is a very simple operation; in the *STATISTICA Data Management* module, select the *Import-More* option from the *File* pull-down menu, then follow the steps outlined below.

Step 1. Select the file name in the *Select File to Import* dialog (change the *List Files of Types* setting if necessary to show the desired file name).

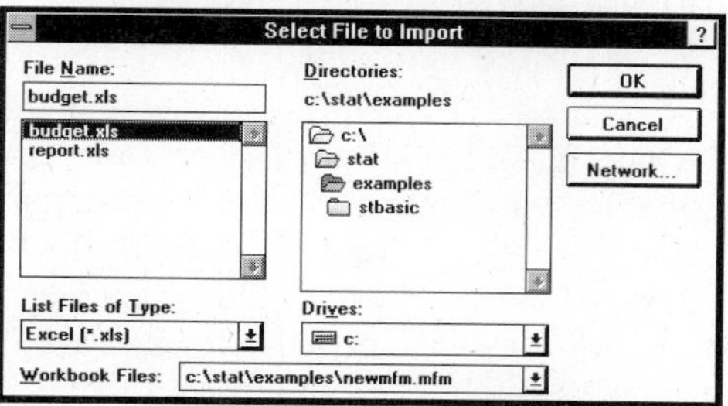

Step 2. Confirm or change the type of file to be imported in the *Import Data from* dialog.

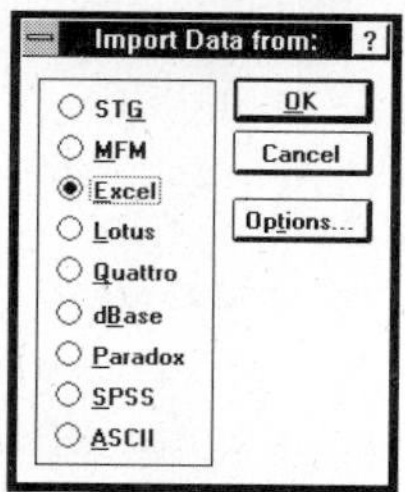

Step 3. Click on the *OK* button in the latter dialog to import and store the data in the *STATISTICA* data file (spreadsheet) format.

Each of these import options represents a group of formats (e.g., *Lotus* can import files from Lotus version 1A, 2, 3, Symphony, Lotus 1-2-3 for Windows, etc.). When importing files, *STATISTICA* will use the column/field/variable names of the source file. If an imported name is longer than eight characters, the first eight characters will be used as the *STATISTICA* variable name. See below for more detailed information on each of the import formats.

Click on the *Options* button to open a dialog that will contain importing options specific to the import format that you choose in this dialog.

Import STG File

STG files are *STATISTICA* graphics files. After you select an *STG Graph File* from the *Select File to Import* dialog, the *Import Data From* dialog will open (by default, STG will be selected). Click on the *OK* button in this dialog to import the STG file that you select.

Each of the plots in the STG file will be imported as a pair of variables containing the *X* and *Y* values for each plot or as a triplet of variables containing the *X*, *Y*, and *Z* values for each plot. If the plots were not labeled in the graph, then the default names for the imported variables will be *Plot1X*, *Plot1Y*, *Plot2X*, *Plot2Y*, etc., for 2D graphs and *Plot1X*, *Plot1Y*, *Plot1Z, Plot2X*, *Plot2Y*, *Plot2Z*, etc., for 3D graphs. If legends for the plots were entered into the STG file, then they will be used to create names for the variables within the plot. If all imported plots do not contain the same number of values, then the shorter plots will be padded with missing data. The first line of the graph title will become the *STATISTICA* data file one-line header.

Import *Megafile Manager* File

STATISTICA imports various types of data from *Megafile Manager* (see Volume III), including numeric, text, and logical data. After selecting a *Megafile Manager* (MFM) file from the *Select File to Import* dialog, the *Import Data From* dialog will open (by default, MFM will be selected). Click on the *Options* button to bring up the *MFM Import Options* dialog.

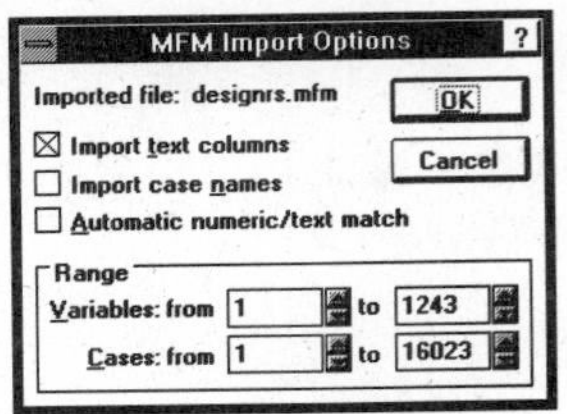

Import Text Columns

When you select this option, unpaired text columns (columns to which a numeric column has not been matched, see below) will be imported into *STATISTICA* "double variables" by assigning a numeric code (consecutive integer) for each unique text value. If the column width is greater than 8, then the remainder of the text is truncated.

If you de-select this option, then *STATISTICA* will not import unpaired text columns (i.e., text columns with no numeric equivalent columns). De-selecting this option may result in fewer variables.

Import Case Names

When you select this option, case names will be imported from the first column of the *Megafile Manager* file. If this variable contains numeric values instead of text, then the case names will be created as "text images" of these values.

Automatic Numeric-Text Match

This option determines whether *Megafile Manager* columns will be automatically combined to become *STATISTICA* "double variables" with numeric and text values (see page 1317), and optional value labels.

If you select this option, then *STATISTICA* will combine *Megafile Manager* columns to become *STATISTICA* "double variables" based on pairing a

numeric column with one or two text columns with related names, according to the following rules:

- A numeric column can be matched with one or two immediately following text columns, which will become the optional text values and value labels for the *STATISTICA* variable.
- The first of the text columns may be up to 8 characters long and will become the text values for the *STATISTICA* variable; its column name must be the same as the numeric column name (with a *$* added to the end if the numeric column name is less than 8 characters, or if the name is 8 characters long, the second character should be replaced by a *$*). (Please note that if this *$* column is wider than 8 characters, it will be disregarded, and no text values will be imported.)
- The second of the text columns will become the value labels; its column name must be the same as the numeric column name with an @ added to the end (if the numeric column name is less than 8 characters - if the name is 8 characters long, the second character should be replaced by @).

A one-to-one correspondence between the numeric and text values in these columns must exist: each numeric value must be paired with only one unique text string in the text column(s). *STATISTICA* will check for this correspondence during the process of creating the *STATISTICA* file, and if more than one text value is found to be paired with a given numeric value, then a warning will be issued. *STATISTICA* also imports the *Megafile Manager* long column names (as *STATISTICA* long variable names), as well as the one-line file header and the *Megafile Manager* file notes. The pairs or triplets of *Megafile Manager* columns which meet the conditions described above are automatically generated when you export a *STATISTICA* data file to *Megafile Manager*.

Range

By default, all cases and variables in the *Megafile Manager* file will be imported. This option permits selection of a specific range of cases and/or variables to be imported. Note that if you are importing case names (see above), and the specified range of variables includes column 1 (which contains the case names), the effective range to be imported will begin with column 2.

Variables. Specify the range of variables to be imported (*From* which variable, *To* which variable, inclusive).

Cases. Specify the range of cases to be imported (*From* which case, *To* which case, inclusive).

Import SPSS File

STATISTICA can import SPSS Portable files with this option. SPSS variable names will become *STATISTICA* variable names, and SPSS long variable names (up to 128 characters long) will become *STATISTICA* long variable names. When you click on the *Options* button in the *Import Data From* dialog, the *SPSS Import Options* dialog will open.

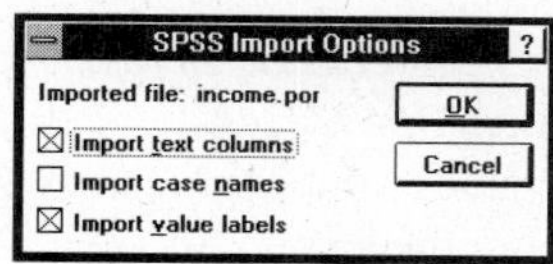

Import Text Columns

This option controls the importing of text (string) variables from SPSS. When you select this option, SPSS text variables are converted into *STATISTICA* "double variables" by assigning each text value a consecutive numeric integer value. Text values longer than eight characters will be truncated and only the first eight characters will be used as text values. When you de-select this option, *STATISTICA* will not import the SPSS text variables.

Import Case Names

Case names may be imported from the first variable of the SPSS file. If this variable contains numeric values instead of text, the case names will be created as "text images" of these values.

Import Value Labels

When you select this option, *STATISTICA* will import the SPSS value labels (up to 40 characters). In the case of numeric SPSS variables with value labels, the program will also create text equivalents (see pages 1317 and 1352) for the numeric values out of the first 8 characters of the value label.

Missing Values

Note that missing data in SPSS variables may be defined in different ways:

- If a single MD value has been assigned in a variable, then that MD value will be used as the MD code in the *STATISTICA* variable.
- If a range of values have been defined as MD for a variable in SPSS, then *STATISTICA* imports the actual data values (to maximize the information extracted from the source file), and assigns the first value from the list of MD values as the MD code in the *STATISTICA* data file.

Import Excel File

STATISTICA can import numeric and text values as well as dates from Excel. Text entries are automatically converted to text values in *STATISTICA*'s "double notation." If the text string is longer than eight characters in Excel, then *STATISTICA* will only use the first eight characters as the text value. Date values of variables imported from Excel are imported in Julian format (the number of days since Jan. 1, 1900; e.g., 24,858 instead of 1/21/1968); if you want the dates to appear not in a numeric (Julian) format but in a standard date format, change the variable display format in the *Spreadsheet Edit (Current) Specs* dialog from *Decimal* to *Date*. (See *Dates* or *Date Operations*, Chapter 1, for more information on using dates in *STATISTICA*.)

Please note that *STATISTICA* will automatically convert the Excel spreadsheet into a "data base" at the point of import, therefore it is not necessary to save the Excel file as a "data base" before importing it. Several importing options are available via the *Excel Import Options* dialog.

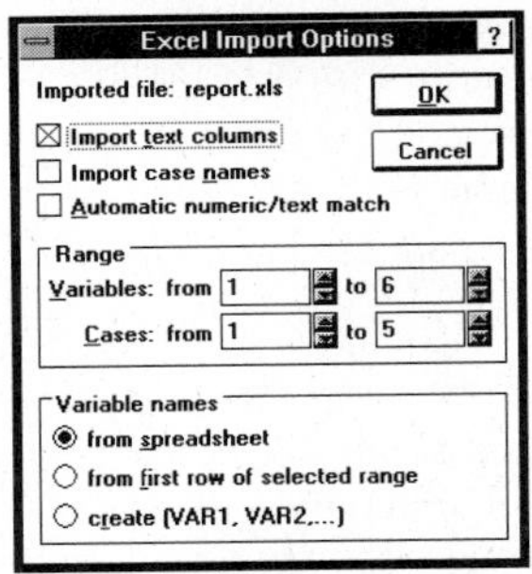

Import Text Columns

When you select this option, *STATISTICA* converts unpaired text columns (columns to which a numeric column has not been matched, see below) into *STATISTICA* "double variables" by assigning each unique text value a consecutive numeric integer value. If you de-select this option, the *STATISTICA* will not import unpaired text columns.

Import Case Names

Case names may be imported from the first column of the specified range in the Excel file. If this variable contains numeric values instead of text, then the case names will be created as "text images" of these values.

Automatic Numeric-Text Match

This option determines whether Excel columns will be automatically combined to become *STATISTICA* "double variables" with numeric and text values, and optional value labels. If you select this option, then *STATISTICA* will combine Excel columns to become *STATISTICA* "double variables" based on pairing a numeric column with one or two text columns with related names according to the following rules (note that this method of naming columns occurs by default when exporting data files from *Data Management* to Excel):

- A numeric column can be matched with one or two immediately following text columns, which will become the optional text values and value labels for the *STATISTICA* variable.
- The first of the text columns may be up to 8 characters long and will become the text values for the *STATISTICA* variable; its column name must be the same as the numeric column name (with a *$* added to the end if the numeric column name is less than 8 characters, or if the name is 8 characters long, the second character should be replaced by a *$*). (Please note that if this *$* column is wider than 8 characters, it will be disregarded, and no text values will be imported.)
- The second of the text columns will become the value labels; its column name must be the same as the numeric column name with an @ added to the end (if the numeric column name is less than 8 characters - if the name is 8 characters long, the second character should be replaced by @).

A one-to-one correspondence between the numeric and text values in the columns must exist: each numeric value must be paired with only one unique text string in the text column(s). *STATISTICA* will check for this correspondence during the process of creating the *STATISTICA* file, and if more than one text value is found to be paired with a given numeric value, then a warning will be issued.

Range

By default, the entire active area of the spreadsheet is imported. This option permits selection of a specific range of cases and/or variables to be imported.

Variables. Specify the range of variables to be imported (*From* which variable, *To* which variable, inclusive).

Cases. Specify the range of cases to be imported (*From* which case, *To* which case, inclusive).

Variable Names

This option specifies the source in Excel for *STATISTICA* variable names.

From spreadsheet. When you select this option, *STATISTICA* will use the Excel column designators (A, B, C, etc.) as *STATISTICA* variable names.

From first row of selected range. Select this option to use the labels from the first row of the specified import range (see above). If any label is longer than eight characters, it will be truncated and only the first eight characters will be used as the variable name.

Create (*VAR1*, *VAR2*, . . .). This option will result in the use of a combination of the prefix *VAR* and a sequential number (e.g., *VAR1*, *VAR2*, etc.) as variable names in the imported file.

Note that in addition to the file import operation, Excel data can be accessed by *STATISTICA* via dynamic links (*DDE*, see *Paste Link*, Chapter 1), as well as the Clipboard (*STATISTICA* recognizes the Excel Clipboard format and will properly interpret "formatted" values such as *$100* or *2,000*).

Import Lotus File

STATISTICA can import worksheets from Lotus 1-2-3 Release 1A (*Lotus/1*), Release 2.01/2.2 (*Lotus/2*), Release 3 (*Lotus/3*), and Lotus for Windows (*123w*), as well as Symphony (*Symph*). Due to their 3-dimensional structure, 1-2-3/3 and Lotus for Windows files are imported with each page placed in a successive set of variables in the *STATISTICA* file. Date values of variables imported from Lotus are imported in Julian format (the number of days since Jan. 1, 1900; e.g., 24,858 instead of 1/21/1968); if you want the dates to appear not in a numeric (Julian) format but in a standard date format, change the variable display format in the *Spreadsheet Edit (Current) Specs* dialog from *Decimal* to *Date* (see Chapter 3). After you select a Lotus file from the *Select File to Import* dialog, the *Import Data From* dialog will open (by default, Lotus will be selected). Now, in this dialog, click on the *Options* button to bring up the *Lotus Import Options* dialog (the same dialog is used for each version of Lotus that you are importing).

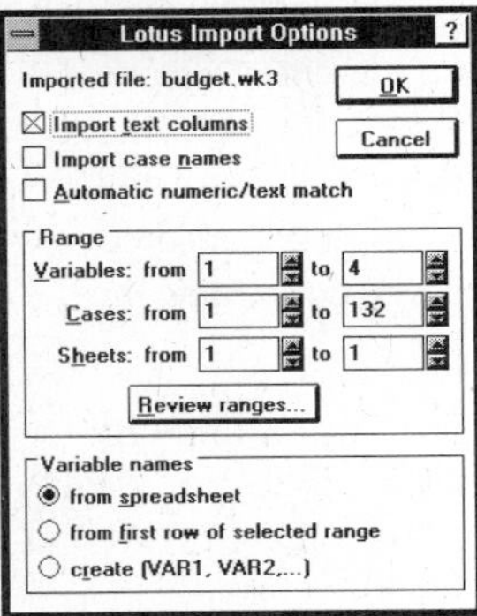

Import Text Columns

When you select this option, *STATISTICA* will automatically convert unpaired text values (labels to which no numeric value has been matched, see below) into *STATISTICA* "double variables" by assigning each text value a consecutive numeric integer value. If you de-select this option, *STATISTICA* will not import unpaired labels.

Import Case Names

At the user's option, case names may be imported from the first column of the specified range in the Lotus file. If this variable contains numeric values instead of text, the case names will be created as "text images" of these values.

Automatic Numeric-Text Match

This option determines whether Lotus 1-2-3 labels will be automatically combined to become *STATISTICA* "double variables" with numeric and text values, and optional value labels. When you select this option, then *STATISTICA* will combine Lotus columns to become *STATISTICA* "double variables" based on pairing a numeric column with one or two text columns with related names, according to the following rules (note that this method of naming columns occurs by default when exporting *STATISTICA* data files to Lotus):

- A numeric column can be matched with one or two immediately following text columns, which will become the optional text values and value labels for the *STATISTICA* variable.
- The first of the text columns may be up to 8 characters long and will become the text values for the *STATISTICA* variable; its column name must be the same as the numeric column name (with a *$* added to the end if the numeric column name is less than 8 characters, or if the

name is 8 characters long, the second character should be replaced by a *$*). (Please note that if this *$* column is wider than 8 characters, it will be disregarded, and no text values will be imported.)

- The second of the text columns will become the value labels; its column name must be the same as the numeric column name with an @ added to the end (if the numeric column name is less than 8 characters - if the name is 8 characters long, the second character should be replaced by @).

A one-to-one correspondence between the numeric and text values in the columns must exist: each numeric value must be paired with only one unique text string in the text column(s). *STATISTICA* will check for this correspondence during the process of creating the *STATISTICA* file, and if more than one text value is found to be paired with a given numeric value, then a warning will be issued.

Range

By default, the entire active area of the worksheet is imported. A portion of the worksheet can be selected by defining the range (see below).

Variables. Specify the range of variables to be imported (*From* which variable, *To* which variable, inclusive).

Cases. Specify the range of cases to be imported (*From* which case, *To* which case, inclusive).

Sheets. This option is only available if a Lotus 1-2-3 Release 3 or Lotus for Windows file is being imported (otherwise the option is dimmed). By default, all sheets are imported, however you can select specific sheets to be imported using this option (*From* which sheet, *To* which sheet, inclusive).

Review ranges. Click on this button to open the *Review Ranges* window from which you can select a named range from a listing of all of the named ranges in the selected file (see below).

Variable Names

This option specifies the source for names of variables.

From spreadsheet. Use Lotus 1-2-3 column designators (*A*, *B*, *C*, etc.) as *STATISTICA* variable names (Lotus 1-2-3 Release 3 uses names *A:A*, *A:B*, *B:A*, *B:B*, etc.; they will appear in *STATISTICA* as *A_A*, *A_B*, *B_A*, *B_B*) when you select this option. This option is especially useful in working with Release 3 files which may eventually be exported (using Lotus' column designators will preserve the identification of variables originating in different sheets).

From first row of selected range. *STATISTICA* will use labels from the first row of the specified range when you select this option. If any label is longer than eight characters, only the first eight characters of the label will be used as the *STATISTICA* variable name.

Create (*VAR1*, *VAR2*, . . .). This option will result in the use of a combination of the prefix *VAR* and a sequential number (e.g., *VAR1*, *VAR2*, etc.) as variable names in the imported file.

Note that in addition to the file import operation, Lotus data can be accessed by *STATISTICA* via dynamic links (*DDE*, see the description of *Paste Link* in Chapter 1), as well as the Clipboard (*STATISTICA* recognizes the Lotus Clipboard format and will properly interpret "formatted" values such as *$100* or *2,000*).

Import Lotus - Review Ranges

In Lotus, you can define "named ranges" of data in order to define distinctive sections of the worksheet. Clicking the *Review Ranges* button in the

STATISTICA Lotus Import Options dialog will bring up a list box of defined ranges for the Lotus worksheet that you want to import.

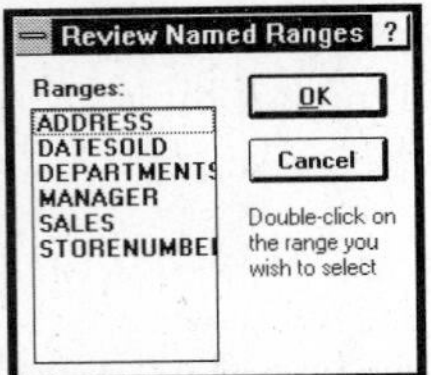

Now, instead of importing the whole Lotus worksheet (which might include column headings and other text), you can import only a subset of data by selecting the named worksheet range (highlight the range name and click the *OK* button).

Import Quattro File

STATISTICA can import worksheets from Quattro Pro (the DOS and Windows versions; see the note about importing Quattro for Windows at the end of this section). In the *Import Data from* dialog, click on the *Options* button to bring up the *Quattro Import Options* dialog.

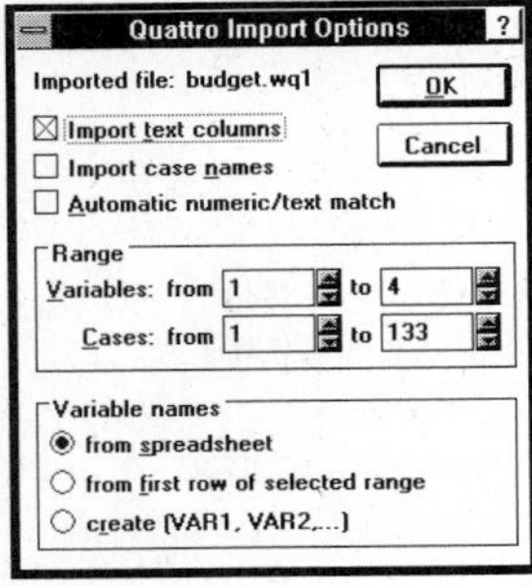

Import Text Columns

When you select this option, *STATISTICA* will automatically convert unpaired text values (labels to which no numeric value has been matched, see below) into *STATISTICA* "double variables" by assigning each text value a consecutive numeric integer value. If you de-select this option, *STATISTICA* will not import unpaired labels.

Import Case Names

At the user's option, case names may be imported from the first column of the specified range in the Quattro file. If this variable contains numeric values instead of text, then the case names will be created as "text images" of these values.

Automatic Numeric-Text Match

This option determines whether Quattro labels will be automatically combined to become *STATISTICA* "double variables" with numeric and text values, and optional value labels. When you select this option, then *STATISTICA* will combine Quattro columns to become *STATISTICA* "double variables" based on pairing a numeric column with one or two text columns with related names, according to the following rules (note that this method of naming columns occurs by default when exporting data files from *Data Management* to Quattro).

- A numeric column can be matched with one or two immediately following text columns, which will become the optional text values and value labels for the *STATISTICA* variable.

- The first of the text columns may be up to 8 characters long and will become the text values for the *STATISTICA* variable; its column name must be the same as the numeric column name (with a *$* added to the end if the numeric column name is less than 8 characters, or if the name is 8 characters long, the second character should be replaced by a *$*). (Please note that if this *$* column is wider than 8 characters, it will be disregarded, and no text values will be imported.)

- The second of the text columns will become the value labels; its column name must be the same as the numeric column name with an @ added to the end (if the numeric column name is less than 8 characters - if the name is 8 characters long, the second character should be replaced by @).

A one-to-one correspondence between the numeric and text values in the columns must exist: each numeric value must be paired with only one unique text string in the text column(s). *STATISTICA* will check for this correspondence during the process of creating the *STATISTICA* file, and if more than one text value is found to be paired with a given numeric value, then a warning will be issued.

Range

By default, the entire active area of the worksheet is imported. A portion of the worksheet can be selected by defining the range (see below).

Variables. Specify the range of variables to be imported (*From* which variable, *To* which variable, inclusive).

Cases. Specify the range of cases to be imported (*From* which case, *To* which case, inclusive).

Variable Names

This option specifies the source for names of variables.

From spreadsheet. Use Quattro column designators (*A*, *B*, *C*, etc.) as *STATISTICA* variable names.

From first row of selected range. *STATISTICA* will use labels from the first row of the specified range when you select this option. If any label is longer than eight characters, only the first eight characters of the label will be used as the *STATISTICA* variable name.

Create (*VAR1*, *VAR2*, . . .). This option will result in the use of a combination of the prefix *VAR* and a sequential number (e.g., *VAR1*, *VAR2*, etc.) as variable names in the imported file.

Note that in addition to the file import operation, Quattro for Windows data can be accessed by *STATISTICA* via dynamic links (*DDE*, see *Paste Link*, Chapter 1), as well as the Clipboard (*STATISTICA* recognizes the Quattro for Windows Clipboard format and will properly interpret "formatted" values such as *$100* or *2,000*).

Import Paradox File

STATISTICA can import data files from Paradox. When you click on the *Options* button in the *Import File from* dialog, the *Paradox Import Options* dialog will open.

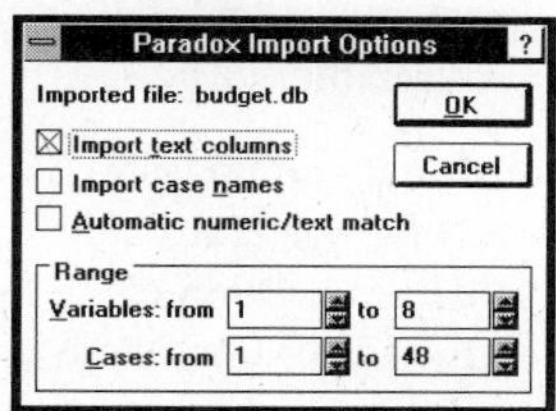

Import Text Columns

When you select this option, *STATISTICA* will automatically convert unpaired text values (labels to which no numeric value has been matched, see below) into *STATISTICA* "double variables" by assigning each text value a consecutive numeric integer value. If you de-select this option, *STATISTICA* will not import unpaired labels.

Import Case Names

At the user's option, case names may be imported from the first column of the specified range in the

Paradox file. If this variable contains numeric values instead of text, the case names will be created as "text images" of these values.

Automatic Numeric-Text Match

This option determines whether Paradox labels will be automatically combined to become *STATISTICA* "double variables" with numeric and text values, and optional value labels. When you select this option, then *STATISTICA* will combine Paradox columns to become *STATISTICA* "double variables" based on pairing a numeric column with one or two text columns with related names, according to the following rules (note that this method of naming columns occurs by default when exporting data files from *Data Management* to Paradox).

- A numeric column can be matched with one or two immediately following text columns, which will become the optional text values and value labels for the *STATISTICA* variable.
- The first of the text columns may be up to 8 characters long and will become the text values for the *STATISTICA* variable; its column name must be the same as the numeric column name (with a $ added to the end if the numeric column name is less than 8 characters, or if the name is 8 characters long, the second character should be replaced by a $). (Please note that if this $ column is wider than 8 characters, it will be disregarded, and no text values will be imported.)
- The second of the text columns will become the value labels; its column name must be the same as the numeric column name with an @ added to the end (if the numeric column name is less than 8 characters - if the name is 8 characters long, the second character should be replaced by @).

A one-to-one correspondence between the numeric and text values in these columns must exist: each numeric value must be paired with only one unique text string in the text column(s). *STATISTICA* will check for this correspondence during the process of creating the *STATISTICA* file, and if more than one text value is found to be paired with a given numeric value, then a warning will be issued.

Range

By default, the entire active area of the data file is imported. A portion of the data file can be selected by defining the range (see below).

Variables. Specify the range of variables to be imported (*From* which variable, *To* which variable, inclusive).

Cases. Specify the range of cases to be imported (*From* which case, *To* which case, inclusive).

Import dBASE File

STATISTICA can import data files from dBASE. dBASE files contain a flag within each record indicating whether the record is to be read or not; *STATISTICA* will ignore all records marked as having been deleted.

After you select a dBASE file from the *Select File to Import* dialog, the *Import Data from* dialog will open (by default, dBASE will be selected). Click on the *Options* button to bring up the *dBASE Import Options* dialog (the same dialog is used for either version of dBASE that you are importing).

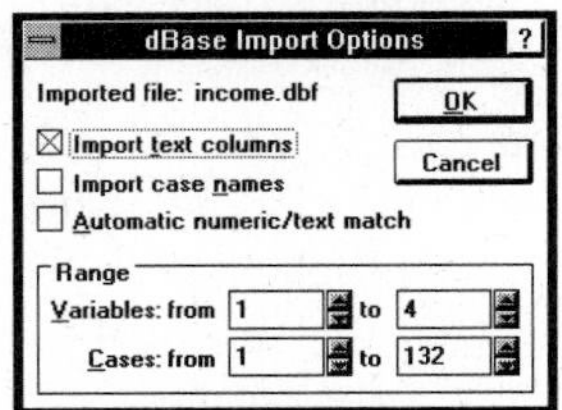

Import Text Columns

STATISTICA will convert unpaired text fields (fields to which a numeric field has not been matched) into *STATISTICA* "double variables" by assigning each alphanumeric value a consecutive numeric integer value when you select this option. If this option is de-selected, then the *STATISTICA* ignores (does not import) unpaired text fields.

Import Case Names

Case names may be imported from the first field of the dBASE file when you select this option. If this field contains numeric values instead of text, then the case names will be created as "text images" of these values.

Automatic Numeric-Text Match

This option determines whether dBASE labels will be automatically combined to become *STATISTICA* "double variables" with numeric and text values, and optional value labels. When you select this option, then *STATISTICA* will combine dBASE fields to become *STATISTICA* "double variables" based on pairing a numeric field with one or two text fields with related names, according to the following rules (note that this method of naming fields occurs by default when exporting data files from *Data Management* to dBASE).

- A numeric field can be matched with one or two immediately following text fields which will become the optional text values and value labels for the *STATISTICA* variable.
- The first of the text fields may be up to 8 characters long and will become the text values for the *STATISTICA* variable; its field name must be the same as the numeric field name (with a *$* added to the end if the numeric field name is less than 8 characters, or if the name is 8 characters long, the second character should be replaced by a *$*). (Please note that if this *$* field is wider than 8 characters, it will be disregarded, and no text values will be imported.)
- The second of the text fields will become the value labels; its field name must be the same as the numeric field name with an @ added to the end (if the numeric field name is less than 8 characters - if the name is 8 characters long, the second character should be replaced by @).

A one-to-one correspondence between the numeric and text values in these fields must exist: each numeric value must be paired with only one unique text string in the text field(s). *STATISTICA* will check for this correspondence during the process of creating the *STATISTICA* file, and if more than one text value is found to be paired with a given numeric value, then a warning will be issued.

Range

By default, the entire active area of the data file is imported. A portion of the data file can be selected by defining the range (see below).

Variables. Specify the range of variables to be imported (*From* which variable, *To* which variable, inclusive).

Cases. Specify the range of cases to be imported (*From* which case, *To* which case, inclusive).

Import ASCII File

STATISTICA can import both ASCII free (delimited) and ASCII fixed (undelimited) files. Each type of ASCII file has its own dialog of options. See below for more information on these options.

Import ASCII Free File

Unlike the ASCII fixed (undelimited) file format import option (see page 1388), the free (or delimited) file format option does not assume that the data for each variable in the ASCII file are located in specific (fixed) columns. Instead, the program will assume that delimiters or separators (e.g., commas, blanks) are used in the ASCII file to separate the different values (variables) for each case. The specific separators that will be recognized by the program can be customized in the *ASCII Free Separators* dialog (see page 1388).

When you click on the *Option* button in the *Import Data From - ASCII Free* dialog, the *ASCII Import Options* dialog will open.

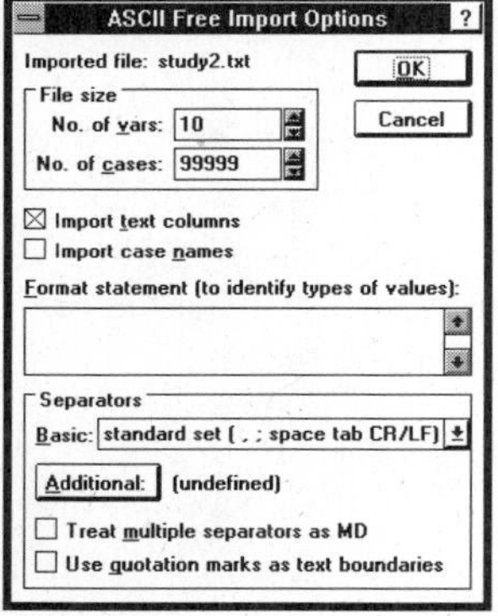

File Size

As in ASCII fixed format files, the number of variables must be accurately specified.

Number of variables. Specify the number of variables in the ASCII file.

Number of cases. Specify the number of cases in the ASCII file. If you are uncertain about the exact number of cases, you may overestimate (*STATISTICA* will detect the actual length of the file during import). Note that each line in the ASCII source file may be up to 4,000 characters in length. This limit only applies to the individual line length and not the total length of a "case" of data: Each imported case may be represented by many lines of data in the source file.

Import Text Columns

Selecting this option converts text fields into *STATISTICA* "double variables" by assigning to each text value a consecutive numeric integer value. Text values longer than eight characters will be truncated and only the first eight characters will be used as text values. De-selecting this option will cause *STATISTICA* to ignore (will not import) text variables.

Import Case Names

Case names may be obtained from the first field of each record in the ASCII file. If this variable contains more than 20 characters, only the first 20 will be used as the case name. If this field contains numeric values instead of text, the case names will be created as "text images" of these values.

Format Statement

This option explicitly defines for *STATISTICA* the exact contents of the input ASCII file. (This is an important distinction: the format statement is a set of instructions for interpreting the structure of the input file, not a definition of the *STATISTICA* variables to be created.) The format statement is entered as a list of formats in the form *nX* where *n* is an integer multiplier indicating the number of times the format is to be repeated (no multiplier = 1) and *X* is the column type (e.g., *40F* means 40 fields containing numeric [here float] values).

Column Type Specifiers

The following column type specifiers are supported:

A - Text (Alphanumeric)

F - Float (also *R* - Real)

D - Double Float (also *DR* - Double Real)

I - Integer (also *NI* - Normal Integer; range: -32,768 to 32,767)

S - Short Integer (also *SI*; range: -128 to 127)

LI - Long Integer (also *J*; range: -2,147,483,648 to 2,147,483,647)

L - Logical

The format specified as *logical* is expected to contain text designators of *true* and *false*. The following three conventions will be recognized by *STATISTICA* when the data are imported:

TRUE or *FALSE* if the field length is 5 or more.

YES or *NO* if it is 3 or 4 characters long.

Y, *N*, or *T*, *F* respectively, if it is 1 character long.

Values of *TRUE* or *YES* will be imported as *1*, *FALSE* or *NO* will be imported as *0*.

Text fields (type *A*) must also include a length value from 1 to 255 immediately following the letter *A*, indicating the maximum possible length of text in this field.

The slash character (/) may be used to indicate that the remainder of the current line in the input file should be ignored (i.e., skip to the next line in the input file). If the multiplier precedes a list of formats enclosed in parentheses, then the list of formats within the parentheses will be repeated the number of times specified by the multiplier.

For example: *2(2L a5)* is equivalent to *L L A5 L L A5* and specifies two *Logical* variables followed by a *Text* variable that can hold up to five characters, then two more *Logical* variables and a final *Text* variable (again up to five characters).

Separators

With this option, you will be able to define the characters used in the input file as delimiters. (The final list of separators to be used will be the combination of the set of selected *Basic* and any *Additional* separators.)

Basic. Select the type of delimiter used in the input file from four predefined sets of separators (*CR* stands for carriage return, *LF* stands for line feed, and *FF* stands for form feed).

Standard set. This set includes: a comma (,), semicolon (;),*<space>*, *<tab>*, *<CR\LF>*.

Undefined. This setting means that *STATISTICA* will not use a predefined set (see *Additional* button, below).

Blank Characters. This set includes: *<space>*, *<tab>*, *<FF>*, *<LF>*, and *<CR\LF>*.

Non-Numeric. This set includes all characters but: *0-9*, period (.), minus (-), and plus (+).

Additional. Click on this button to bring up the *ASCII Free Separators* dialog (see page 1388) from which you can select the delimiter(s).

Treat multiple separators as MD. When you select this option, *STATISTICA* will interpret each pair of adjacent separators as an occurrence of missing data (an absent value) and will place the default missing data value (-9999) in the position between the adjacent separators. If this option is de-selected, then multiple separator characters are treated as one separator, and missing data must be explicitly coded into the ASCII file as a unique value (for instance *-9999*). This option is particularly useful if, for instance, individual values in the data file are separated by spaces, with a variable number of spaces between values. If *spaces*

are used as separators, then each pair of *spaces* would be seen as an occurrence of missing data, and the resulting file would be full of missing values.

Use quotation marks as text boundaries. Select this option if double (") or single (') quotation marks were used as text boundaries and the specified separator characters appear within the values of text variables in the input file (e.g., *"John Jones, Ph.D."*, uses the comma both as part of the text and as a separator after it). In this case, when *STATISTICA* imports the data, the quotation marks will be recognized only as boundaries around the text values, keeping the text values and the embedded separator characters together (the quotation marks will not be included as part of the imported text values).

Note that if a text string is to contain quotation marks as part of the string itself (e.g., as in the titles of books such as *"Moby Dick"*), then two methods may be used to import them:

- Select this option and enclose the entire text string within the alternate quotation mark (opposite of the embedded one); e.g., *'William Shakespeare, "King Lear", Act 2, Scene 1'* will be imported as *William Shakespeare, "King Lear", Act 2, Scene 1.*
- Select this option and then double the quotation mark wherever it is to be preserved; e.g., *"William Shakespeare's ""King Lear"", ""Macbeth"" and ""Hamlet"""* will be imported as *William Shakespeare's "King Lear", "Macbeth" and "Hamlet".*

If this option is de-selected, then the character will be interpreted as a separator and not as a part of the text value and the quotation marks will be imported as part of the text; e.g., *'William Shakespeare, "King Lear", Act 2, Scene 1'* will be imported as *'William Shakespeare* in one column, *"King Lear"* in another column, *Act 2* in different column and *Scene 1'* in another column.

Import ASCII Free - Separators

The *ASCII Free Separators* dialog will open whenever you want to choose an undefined character as a delimiter when importing ASCII free format files (click on the *Additional* button in the *Import ASCII Free Options* dialog).

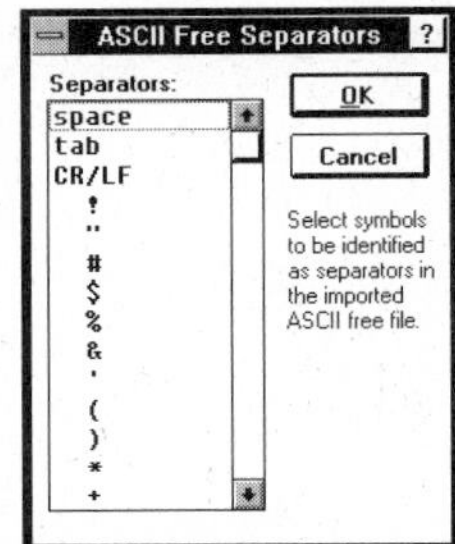

This dialog contains a list box of characters from which you can choose. The characters or symbols listed in this dialog are as follows (*CR/LF* stands for carriage return/line feed):

<space> <tab> <CR/LF>

! " # $ % & ') * (, [\ + - .

0 1 2 3 4 5 6 7 8 9

] ^ _ / : ; < = > ? @ ` { | } ~

Upper case alphabet (i.e., *A B C . . . Z*)

Lower case alphabet (i.e., *a b c . . . z*)

Note that if you want to import numeric values, you should not specify any of the numbers (i.e., *0* through *9*) or the "+", "-", or "." as separators.

Import ASCII Fixed File

Unlike the ASCII free (delimited) file format import option (see page 1386), the fixed (or undelimited) file format option assumes that the data for each variable in the ASCII file are located in specific

(fixed) columns, and that the location for each variable is the same for all cases (e.g., the values for variable *Gender* can be found in columns 3 through 4, for each case in the data file).

After you select an ASCII fixed (fixed-format) file from the *Select File to Import* dialog, the *Import Data from* dialog will open. By default, ASCII will be selected and if the file name extension is **.fix*, then *Fix* will automatically be checked as the ASCII version. If *STATISTICA* is unable to recognize (from the file name extension) that the file is an ASCII fixed file, then the *Free* ASCII version will be selected and you will need to change the version to *Fix*. When you click on the *Options* button in the *Select File to Import* dialog, the *ASCII Fixed Import Options* dialog will open.

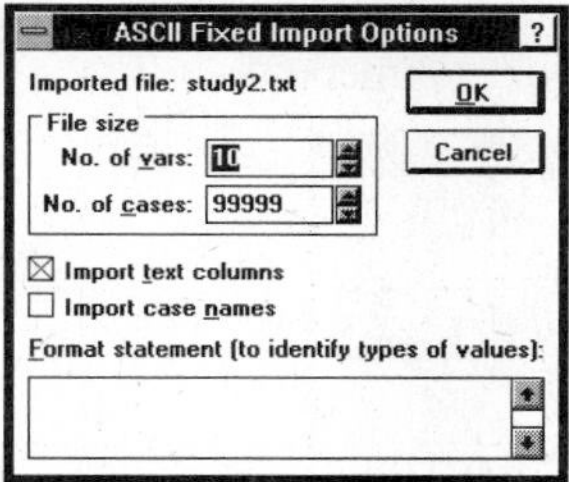

The options available in this dialog are described below.

File Size

As in ASCII free format files (see page 1386), in order for *STATISTICA* to properly interpret the file, the number of variables and cases must be accurately specified.

Number of variables. Specify the number of variables in the ASCII file here.

Number of cases. Specify the number of cases in the ASCII file here. If you are uncertain about the exact number of cases, you may overestimate (*STATISTICA* will detect the actual length of the file during import). Note that each line in the ASCII source file may be up to 4,000 characters in length. This limit only applies to the individual line length and not the total length of a "case" of data: each imported case may be represented by many lines of data in the source file.

Import Text Columns

Selecting this option converts text fields into *STATISTICA* "double variables" by assigning to each text value a consecutive numeric integer value. Text values longer than eight characters will be truncated and only the first eight characters will be used as text values. De-selecting this option will cause *STATISTICA* to ignore (will not import) text variables.

Import Case Names

Case names may be obtained from the first field of each record in the ASCII file. If this field contains more than 20 characters, then only the first 20 will be used as the case name. If this field contains numeric values instead of text, then the case names will be created as "text images" of these values.

Format Statement

This option explicitly defines for *STATISTICA* the exact contents of the input ASCII file. (This is an important distinction: the format statement is a set of instructions for interpreting the structure of the input file, not a definition of the *STATISTICA* variables to be created.) The format statement is entered as a list of formats in the form *nXm*, where *n* is an integer multiplier indicating the number of times the format is to be repeated (no multiplier = 1); *X* is the column type; *m* is the column width (e.g., *10A8* means 10 text value (alphanumeric) fields, each 8 characters long).

Column Type Specifiers

The following column type specifiers are supported:

A - Text (Alphanumeric)

F - Float (also *R* - Real)

D - Double Float (also *DR* - Double Real)

I - Integer (also *NI* - Normal Integer; range: -32,768 to 32,767)

S - Short Integer (also *SI*; range: -128 to 127)

LI - Long Integer (also *J*; range: -2,147,483,648 to 2,147,483,647)

L - Logical

T - "Jump to" specifier (see below)

The format specified as *logical* is expected to contain text designators of *true* and *false*. The following three conventions will be recognized by *STATISTICA* when the data are imported:

TRUE or *FALSE* if the field length is 5 or more.

YES or *NO* if it is 3 or 4 characters long.

Y, *N*, or *T*, *F* respectively, if it is 1 character long.

Values of *TRUE* or *YES* will be imported as *1*, *FALSE* or *NO* will be imported as *0*.

The additional specifier *Tx* is available to instruct *STATISTICA* to jump to character number *x* in the current line in the input file (i.e., to skip to that position). This may be used to jump over unwanted characters, or to return to an earlier character (if *x* specifies a character position which has already been read). The slash character (/) may be used to indicate that the remainder of the line should be ignored (i.e., skip to the next line in the input file). Example: *10I3 A8 T55 3I5 /* specifies the import of 14 values: ten 3-digit integers, followed by an 8-character text string, then skip to the 55th character in the record, import three 5-digit integers and ignore the rest of the record. If the multiplier precedes a list of formats enclosed in parentheses, the list will be repeated as many times as specified in the multiplier (e.g., *10(2A3,I5)*).

Exporting Data

Data file import/export facilities are accessible in every module of *STATISTICA* (in the pull-down menu *File*); also, the *ODBC* (Open Data Base Connectivity) interface accessible in every module from the same menu offers access to a wide variety foreign files (including mainframe data base management files). For more information, see Chapter 3 (or the *Electronic Manual*). The additional import/export facilities offered in the *Data Management* module (by selecting the *More...* option in the *Import* or *Export* submenus):

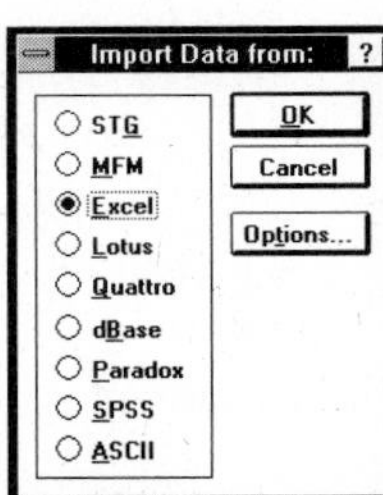

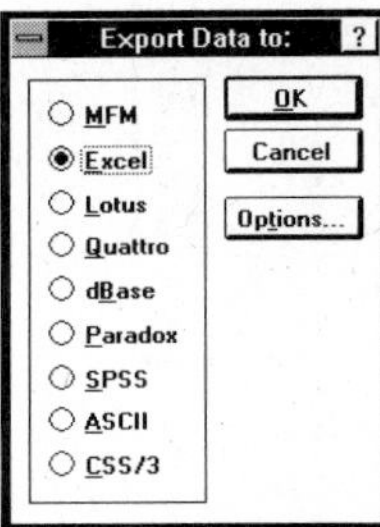

offer some additional options for specialized data transfers. Most importantly, they offer options to exchange *STATISTICA* double notation (text/numeric) and labeled values with applications that do not support labeled or double notation values. Specifically, options are provided to "mark" and split (while exporting) and merge (while importing) numeric and text data values and their labels. Also, these facilities support some of the less commonly used (and inaccessible via *ODBC*) file formats, such as the SPSS *PFF* (*Portable File Format*) files, also compatible with SAS, or STG graphics files.

Example. To export a *STATISTICA* file, follow the steps outlined below.

Step 1. Select the *Export Data* option from the *File* pull-down menu to open the *Export Data to* dialog.

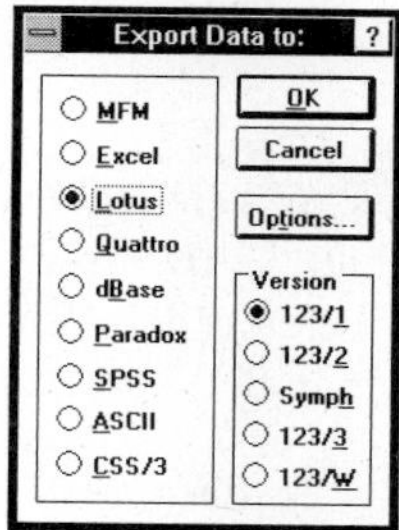

Step 2. Select one of the export options as the type of file into which the data will be exported (for example, *Lotus*). You may click on the *Options* button to select from the several exporting options, described below.

Step 3. Click the *OK* button in the latter dialog to export and store the file in the desired format.

Export File to *Megafile Manager*

You may export data sets to *STATISTICA*'s *Megafile Manager*. When you select this option from the *Export Data to* dialog, the *MFM Export Options* dialog will open.

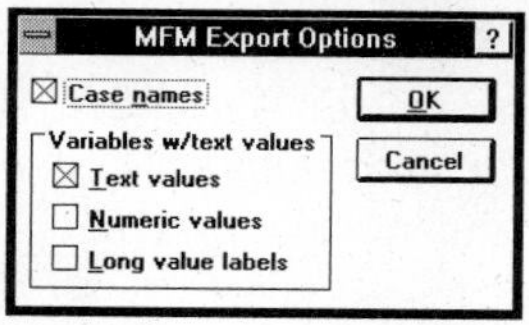

During export, *STATISTICA* long variable names (if they exist) will become *Megafile Manager* column long names, and the *STATISTICA* file header is exported as the *Megafile Manager* one-line file header.

Case Names

Select this option to export the case names as the first column of the *Megafile Manager* file.

Variables with Text Values

STATISTICA "double variables" (numeric/text) may be expanded at the user's option to become up to three *Megafile Manager* columns [representing the numeric values, text values, and (optional) value labels of the *STATISTICA* variable] with names related to the original *STATISTICA* variable. The following options govern the creation of these columns, allowing the resulting pairs or triplets of columns in *Megafile Manager* to be converted back (i.e., "compressed") into individual *STATISTICA* variables (when the file is imported by *STATISTICA*). If all of these options are de-selected, then only those *STATISTICA* variables which do not have text values will be exported.

Text values. If you select this option, then for "double notation" variables, *STATISTICA* will create text columns of alphanumeric values for that variable. When this column is created, *STATISTICA* uses the variable name of the "double notation" variable and adds a *$* to the name in the following manner:

- If the *STATISTICA* variable name is shorter than eight characters, then the *Megafile Manager* text column name will have a *$* added to the end;
- If the name is eight characters long, then the second character will be changed to a *$* (this is done to avoid later conflicts with the requirements of *Megafile Manager* regarding duplicated column names).

Numeric values. When selected, this option creates columns of numeric values associated with the text values columns created from the above option. When this variable is exported to *Megafile*

Manager, *STATISTICA* will use the same variable name as before. If this option is de-selected, then only numeric values from non-"double variables" (i.e., variables without text values) will be present in the exported file.

Long value labels. This option controls the creation of a text columns of variable value labels. When you select this option, *STATISTICA* will create a third column of text values representing the *Long Value Labels* for a variable. When this column is created, *STATISTICA* uses the variable name of the "double notation" variable and adds an @ to the name in the following manner:

- If the variable name is shorter than eight characters, then the name of the *Megafile Manager* text column will have an @ added to the end;
- If the name of the *STATISTICA* variable is eight characters long, then the second character will be changed to an @.

Note that if *only* the text values or labels are exported, then the resulting column in the MFM file will have the original *STATISTICA* variable name, rather than using the $ or @ conventions.

Export File to Excel

Excel files may contain up to 256 columns and 16,384 rows. If the current *STATISTICA* file is larger than this, then you can create *Subsets* of the file and export each of those subsets separately (see page 1362). When you select the *Excel* option from the *Export Data to* dialog, the *Excel Export Options* dialog will open.

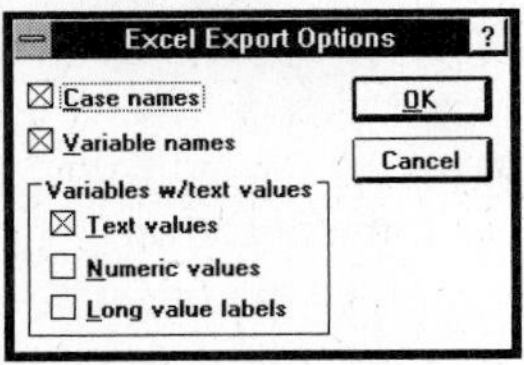

Case Names

Select this option to export the case names to the first column of the Excel file.

Variable Names

When this option is selected, *STATISTICA* will export the variable names into the first row of the Excel spreadsheet. If this option is de-selected, then variable names will not be included in the Excel file.

Variables with Text Values

STATISTICA "double variables" (numeric/text) may be expanded at the user's option to become up to three Excel columns [representing the numeric values, text values, and (optional) value labels of the *STATISTICA* variable] with names related to the original *STATISTICA* variable. The following options govern the creation of these columns, allowing the resulting pairs or triplets of columns in Excel to be converted back (i.e., "compressed") into individual *STATISTICA* variables (when the file is imported by *STATISTICA*). If all of these options are de-selected, then only those *STATISTICA* variables which do not have text values will be exported.

Text values. If you select this option, then for "double notation" variables, *STATISTICA* will create text columns of alphanumeric values for that variable. When this column is created, *STATISTICA* uses the variable name of the "double notation" variable and adds a $ to the name in the following manner:

- If the *STATISTICA* variable name is shorter than eight characters, then the Excel text column name will have a $ added to the end;
- If the name is eight characters long, then the second character will be changed to a $ (this is done to facilitate recombining the numeric and text data if the file is imported once again).

Numeric values. When selected, this option creates columns of numeric values associated with the text values columns created from the above option. If this option is de-selected, then only numeric values from non-"double variables" (i.e., variables without text values) will be present in the exported file.

Long value labels. This option controls the creation of a text columns of variable value labels. When you select this option, *STATISTICA* will create a third column of text values representing the *Long Value Labels* for a variable. When this column is created, *STATISTICA* uses the variable name of the "double notation" variable and adds an @ to the name in the following manner:

- If the variable name is shorter than eight characters, then the name of the Excel text column will have an @ added to the end;
- If the name of the *STATISTICA* variable is eight characters long, then the second character will be changed to an @.

Note that if only the text values of value labels are exported, then the resulting column in the Excel file will have the original *STATISTICA* variable name, rather than using the *$* or @ conventions.

Export File to Lotus

STATISTICA can export to Lotus 1-2-3 Release 1A, 2.01/2.2, Release 3, Lotus for Windows, and Symphony format files via the *Lotus Export Options* dialog (accessible by clicking on the *Options* button in the *Export Data to - Lotus* dialog).

Lotus 1-2-3 Release 2.01/2.2, and Release 3 files may contain up to 256 columns and 8,192 rows. If the current *STATISTICA* file is larger than this, then you can create *Subsets* of the file and export each of those subsets separately (see page 1362).

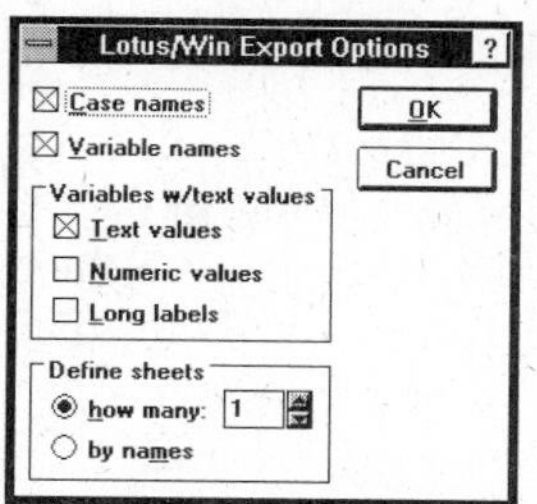

The following options are available in the *Lotus Export Options* dialog.

Option *Define Sheets* (Lotus 1-2-3 Release 3 and Lotus 1-2-3/w only)

Export options for Lotus 1-2-3 Release 1A and 2/2.2, Release 3, and Lotus for Windows are given below. The options are the same for each version with the exception of Lotus 1-2-3 Release 3 and Lotus for Windows, which has the following new option:

How many. By default, all variables in the *STATISTICA* file are exported as one worksheet. If desired, *STATISTICA* variables may be equally divided among a specified number of worksheets. You can specify that number here.

By names. Alternatively, the *STATISTICA* variables may be assigned to specific worksheets *by names*: variables named *A_A* through *A_IV* will be placed in worksheet *A*, variables *B_A* through *B_IV* in worksheet *B*, etc. (This will be the case if the option *From Spreadsheet* was selected when originally importing variable names from a Release 3 or Lotus for Windows worksheet, see page 1380.)

The following options are common to all Lotus versions.

Case Names

Select this option to export the case names to the first column of the Lotus file.

Variable Names

When this option is selected, *STATISTICA* will export the variable names into the first row of the Lotus spreadsheet. If this option is de-selected, then variable names will not be included in the Lotus file.

Variables with Text Values

STATISTICA "double variables" (numeric/text) may be expanded at the user's option to become up to three Lotus columns [representing the numeric values, text values, and (optional) value labels of the *STATISTICA* variable] with names related to the original *STATISTICA* variable. The following options govern the creation of these columns allowing the resulting pairs or triplets of columns in Lotus to be converted back (i.e., "compressed") into individual *STATISTICA* variables (when the file is imported by *STATISTICA*). If all of these options are de-selected, then only those *STATISTICA* variables which do not have text values will be exported.

Text values. If you select this option, then for "double notation" variables, *STATISTICA* will create text columns of alphanumeric values for that variable. When this column is created, *STATISTICA* uses the variable name of the "double notation" variable and adds a *$* to the name in the following manner:

- If the *STATISTICA* variable name is shorter than eight characters, then the Lotus text column name will have a *$* added to the end;
- If the name is eight characters long, then the second character will be changed to a *$* (this is done to facilitate recombining the numeric and text data if the file is imported once again).

Numeric values. When selected, this option creates columns of numeric values associated with the text values columns created from the above option. If this option is de-selected, then only numeric values from non-"double variables" (i.e., variables without text values) will be present in the exported file.

Long value labels. This option controls the creation of a text columns of variable value labels. When you select this option, *STATISTICA* will create a third column of text values representing the *Long Value Labels* for a variable. When this column is created, *STATISTICA* uses the variable name of the "double notation" variable and adds an @ to the name in the following manner:

- If the variable name is shorter than eight characters, then the name of the Lotus text column will have an @ added to the end;
- If the name of the *STATISTICA* variable is eight characters long, then the second character will be changed to an @.

As when exporting to *Megafile Manager* (see page 1391), if only the text values of value labels are exported, the resulting column in the Lotus file will have the original *STATISTICA* variable name, rather than using the *$* or @ conventions.

Export File to Quattro

You may export *STATISTICA* files to Quattro. When you select the *Quattro* option from the *Export Data to* dialog, the *Quattro Export Options* dialog will open.

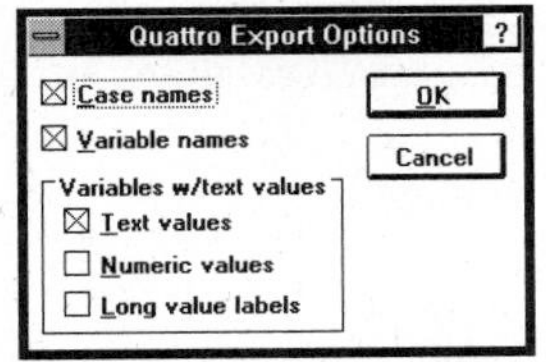

Case Names

Select this option to export the case names to the first column of the Quattro file.

Variable Names

When this option is selected, *STATISTICA* will export the variable names into the first row of the Quattro spreadsheet. If this option is de-selected, then variable names will not be included in the Quattro file.

Variable with Text Values

STATISTICA "double variables" (numeric/text) may be expanded at the user's option to become up to three Quattro columns [representing the numeric values, text values, and (optional) value labels of the *STATISTICA* variable] with names related to the original *STATISTICA* variable.

The following options govern the creation of these columns allowing the resulting pairs or triplets of columns in Quattro to be converted back (i.e., "compressed") into individual *STATISTICA* variables (when the file is imported by *STATISTICA*). If all of these options are de-selected, then only those *STATISTICA* variables which do not have text values will be exported.

Text values. If you select this option, then for "double notation" variables, *STATISTICA* will create text columns of alphanumeric values for that variable. When this column is created, *STATISTICA* uses the variable name of the "double notation" variable and adds a *$* to the name in the following manner:

- If the *STATISTICA* variable name is shorter than eight characters, then the Excel text column name will have a *$* added to the end;
- If the name is eight characters long, then the second character will be changed to a *$* (this is done to facilitate recombining the numeric and text data if the file is imported once again).

Numeric values. When selected, this option creates columns of numeric values associated with the text values columns created from the above option. If this option is de-selected, then only numeric values from non-"double variables" (i.e., variables without text values) will be present in the exported file.

Long value labels. This option controls the creation of a text column of variable value labels. When you select this option, *STATISTICA* will create a third column of text values representing the *Long Value Labels* for a variable. When this column is created, *STATISTICA* uses the variable name of the "double notation" variable and adds an @ to the name in the following manner:

- If the variable name is shorter than eight characters, then the name of the Quattro text column will have an @ added to the end;
- If the name of the *STATISTICA* variable is eight characters long, then the second character will be changed to an @.

Note that if only the text values of value labels are exported, then the resulting column in the Quattro file will have the original *STATISTICA* variable name, rather than using the *$* or @ conventions.

Export File to dBASE

STATISTICA exports to dBASE file formats. dBASE III+ files are limited to 128 fields and dBASE IV to 255 fields. If the current *STATISTICA* file is larger than this, then you can create *Subsets* of the file (see page 1362) and export each of those subsets separately. When you select the *dBASE* option from the *Export Data to* dialog, the *dBASE (III+* or *IV) Export Options* dialog will open (the dialog is the same for each version of dBASE).

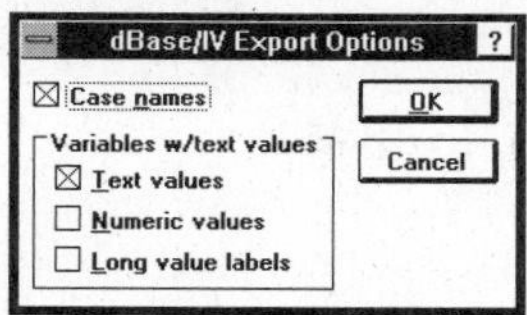

StatSoft

Case Names

Select this option to export the case names as the first field of the dBASE file.

Variables with Text Values

STATISTICA "double variables" (numeric/text) may be expanded at the user's option to become up to three dBASE fields [representing the numeric values, text values, and (optional) value labels of the *STATISTICA* variable] with names related to the original *STATISTICA* variable.

The following options govern the creation of these fields, allowing the resulting pairs or triplets of fields in dBASE to be converted back (i.e., "compressed") into individual *STATISTICA* variables (when the file is imported by *STATISTICA*). If all of these options are de-selected, then only those *STATISTICA* variables which do not have text values will be exported.

Text values. If you select this option, then for "double notation" variables, *STATISTICA* will create text fields of alphanumeric values for that variable. When this field is created, *STATISTICA* uses the variable name of the "double notation" variable and adds a *$* to the name in the following manner:

- If the *STATISTICA* variable name is shorter than eight characters, then the dBASE text field name will have a *$* added to the end;
- If the name is eight characters long, then the second character will be changed to a *$* (this is done to facilitate recombining the numeric and text data if the file is imported once again).

Numeric values. When selected, this option creates fields of numeric values associated with the text values fields created from the above option. When this variable is exported to dBASE *STATISTICA* will use the same variable name as before. If this option is de-selected, then only numeric values from non-"double variables" (i.e., variables without text values) will be present in the exported file.

Long value labels. This option controls the creation of a text field of variable value labels. When you select this option, *STATISTICA* will create a third field of text values representing the *Long Value Labels* for a variable. When this column is created, *STATISTICA* uses the variable name of the "double notation" variable and adds a "@" to the name in the following manner:

- If the variable name is shorter than eight characters, then the name of the dBASE text field will have a "@" added to the end;
- If the name of the *STATISTICA* variable is eight characters long, then the second character will be changed to a "@".

Notes

Names of text variables. If *only* the text values or labels are exported, then the resulting field in the dBASE file will have the original *STATISTICA* variable name, rather than using the *$* or @ conventions.

Numeric value format. Although the values of variables in *STATISTICA* are always stored internally in extended precision, when you export to dBASE (III+ or IV), only the portion included in the displayed format of those values will be exported.

For example, a value may be stored in *STATISTICA* as *7.3926541009725183*, however, if the value is displayed as *7.39*, then that displayed value of *7.39* is exported. In order to export the value in higher precision, change the display format for that variable via the *Spreadsheet Edit (Current) Specs* dialog (see *Spreadsheet Window*, Chapter 3).

Export File to Paradox

STATISTICA exports to Paradox file formats. When you select the *Paradox* option from the *Export Data to* dialog, the *Paradox Export Options* dialog will open.

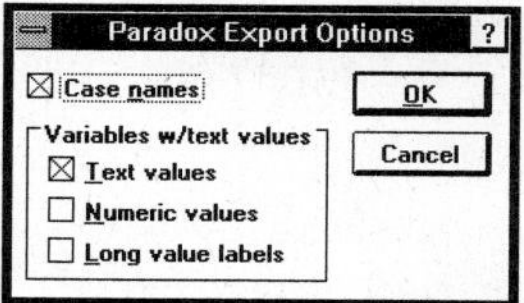

Case Names

Select this option to export the case names as the first field of the Paradox file.

Variables with Text Values

STATISTICA "double variables" (numeric/text) may be expanded at the user's option to become up to three Paradox columns [representing the numeric values, text values, and (optional) value labels of the *STATISTICA* variable] with names related to the original *STATISTICA* variable. The following options govern the creation of these columns allowing the resulting pairs or triplets of columns in Paradox to be converted back (i.e., "compressed") into individual *STATISTICA* variables (when the file is imported by *STATISTICA*). If all of these options are de-selected, then only those *STATISTICA* variables which do not have text values will be exported.

Text values. If you select this option, then for "double notation" variables, *STATISTICA* will create text columns of alphanumeric values for that variable. When this column is created, *STATISTICA* uses the variable name of the "double notation" variable and adds a *$* to the name in the following manner:

- If the *STATISTICA* variable name is shorter than eight characters, then the Paradox text column name will have a *$* added to the end;
- If the name is eight characters long, then the second character will be changed to a *$* (this is done to facilitate recombining the numeric and text data if the file is imported once again).

Numeric values. When selected, this option creates columns of numeric values associated with the text values columns created from the above option. When this variable is exported to Paradox, *STATISTICA* will use the same variable name as before. If this option is de-selected, then only numeric values from non-"double variables" (i.e., variables without text values) will be present in the exported file.

Long value labels. This option controls the creation of a text column of variable value labels. When you select this option, *STATISTICA* will create a third column of text values representing the *Long Value Labels* for a variable. When this column is created, *STATISTICA* uses the variable name of the "double notation" variable and adds an @ to the name in the following manner:

- If the variable name is shorter than eight characters, then the name of the Paradox text column will have an @ added to the end;
- If the name of the *STATISTICA* variable is eight characters long, then the second character will be changed to an @.

Note that if *only* the text values or labels are exported, then the resulting column in the Paradox file will have the original *STATISTICA* variable name, rather than using the *$* or @ conventions.

Export File to SPSS

This option exports to the SPSS Portable File Format (also compatible with SAS). *STATISTICA*

value labels are used as SPSS value labels. SPSS variable names may be up to eight characters long, must begin either with an uppercase letter (A to Z), or the characters *$* or *@*, and may also contain digits and underscore (_).

Certain names are reserved as keywords and may not be used as variable names, including *ALL*, *AND*, *BY*, *EQ*, *GE*, *GT*, *LE*, *LT*, *NE*, *NOT*, *OR*, *TO*, and *WITH*. (You may use the option *Verify Names/Formats* from the *Analysis* pull-down menu to check variable names for compliance with the requirements of SPSS, see page 1364.) When you select the *SPSS* option from the *Export Data to* dialog, the *SPSS Export Options* dialog will open.

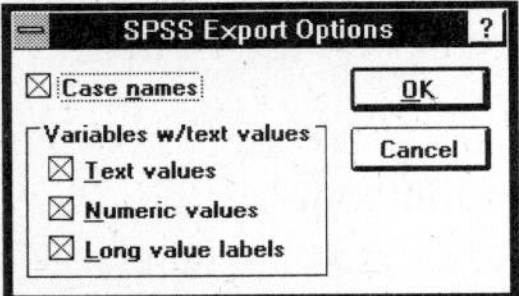

Case Names

Select this option to export the case names as text to the first variable in the SPSS file.

Variables with Text Values

The various components of *STATISTICA*'s "double variables" may be exported to SPSS using the options listed below.

Text values. Select this option to request the export of the alphanumeric values of "double variables" as SPSS text variables.

Numeric values. Select this option to request the export of the numeric values of "double variables" as SPSS numeric variables.

Long value labels. When you select this option, *STATISTICA* value labels will be exported, either as SPSS value labels or as text variables (see below). The following combinations of the above selected options are possible:

- *Text/Numeric*: This combination creates *Numeric* SPSS variables with *Text* as value labels.
- *Text/Labels*: Choose this combination to create *Text* SPSS variables with *Long Value Labels* as value labels.
- *Numeric/Labels*: This combination creates *Numeric* SPSS variables with *Long Value Labels* as value labels.
- If all three options are selected (*Text/Numeric-/Labels*), then two columns will be created: *Numeric*, and *Text* columns with *Long Value Labels* as value labels.
- If only one option is selected, then the appropriate type of variable (numeric or text) will be created.
- If all options are de-selected, then only those *STATISTICA* variables which do not contain text values will be exported.

Export File to ASCII Free Format

STATISTICA can export to ASCII free (delimited) format files. Unlike the ASCII fixed (undelimited) file format export option (see page 1400), the free (or delimited) file format option will not place the data for each variable in the ASCII file in specific (fixed) columns. Instead, the program will use delimiters or separators (e.g., commas, blanks; see *Separators* below) to separate the numbers (values for each variable for each case) in the ASCII file.

If you choose instead to export to ASCII fixed format files (see page 1400), then values which are shorter than the format are padded with blanks so that the absolute position of each value is "fixed" within the line in the output file. Free format (delimited) ASCII files are created without padding values to fill out variable formats since user-

specified characters are used to separate or delimit successive values.

When you select the *ASCII Free* option from the *Export Data to* dialog, the *ASCII Free Export Options* dialog will open.

Case Names

When you select this option, case names will be exported as the first variable in the file.

Variable with Text Values

These options will allow you to export only the *Text* and/or *Numeric* components of *STATISTICA* "double variables." If both options are selected, then a column will be created for the text values of the "double variable" and another column will be created for the numeric values of that variable. If both options are de-selected, then only those *STATISTICA* variables which do not contain text values will be exported.

Text values. Select this option if you want to export the text values of a *STATISTICA* "double variable."

Numeric values. Select this option if you want to export the numeric values of a *STATISTICA* "double variable."

Line Length

The number of variables per line in the output file is determined by the specified line length. Enter the length of the line in the ASCII file here (values can be from 80 to 4,000). If the specified line length is insufficient to contain all variables, then the line will be broken after the last complete variable (i.e., a variable will not be divided across lines). If unbroken records are desired (i.e., each record occupies only one line in the output file), specify a line length no less than the sum of all variable formats.

Separators

Field separator. Click on this button to bring up the *ASCII Free Separator* dialog (see below) from which you can select a single character to be used to separate successive values in the output file [by default, a "," (comma) will be used as the field separator]. The numeric characters *0* through *9*, period (decimal point), "+" and "-" are not permitted as delimiters.

Row separator. The *Row Separator* serves to indicate the end of each of the original rows (cases) of data (one row of data may extend across several lines of the output file). Click on this button to bring up the *ASCII Free Separator* dialog (see below) from which you can select a single character to be used to indicate the completion of each row of data in the output file [by default, a "," (comma) will be used as the row separator]. The numeric characters *0* through *9*, period (decimal point), "+" and "-" are not allowed as row separators. Note that if the length of the row in the *STATISTICA* file is longer than the specified output *Line Length* (see above), then the row will extend across one or more lines in the output file.

Export to ASCII Free - Separators

The *ASCII Free Separators* dialog will open whenever you want to choose field or row separators when exporting *ASCII Free Format Files* (see above).

This dialog contains a list box of characters from which you can choose. The characters or symbols listed in this dialog are as follows (*CR/LF* stands for carriage return/line feed):

<space> <tab> <CR/LF>

! “ # $ % & ') * (, [\ + - .

0 1 2 3 4 5 6 7 8 9

] ^ _ / : ; < = > ? @ ` { | } ~

Upper case alphabet (i.e., *A B C . . . Z*)

Lower case alphabet (i.e., *a b c . . . z*)

Note that if you want to export numeric values, you should not specify any of the numbers (i.e., *0* through *9*) or the “+”, “-”, or “.” as separators.

Export File to ASCII Fixed Format

Unlike ASCII free format files (see page 1398), fixed format (undelimited) ASCII files will be created using the current variable formats (values which are shorter than the format are padded with blanks so that the absolute position of each value is “fixed” within the line in the output file). When you select the *ASCII fixed* option from the *Export Data to* dialog, the *ASCII Fixed Export Options* dialog will open.

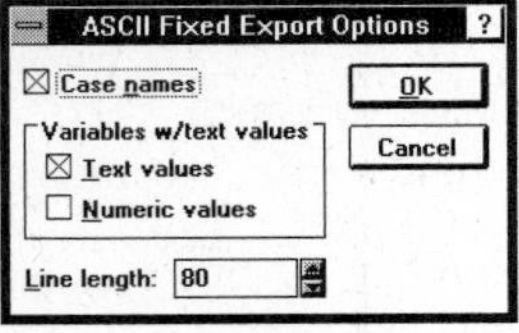

Case Names

When you select this option, case names will be exported as the first variable in the file.

Variable with Text Values

These options will allow you to export only the *Text* and/or *Numeric* components of *STATISTICA* “double variables.” If both options are selected, then a column will be created for the text values of the “double variable” and another column will be created for the numeric values of that variable. If both options are de-selected, then only those *STATISTICA* variables which do not contain text values will be exported.

Text values. Select this option if you want to export the text values of a *STATISTICA* “double variable.”

Numeric values. Select this option if you want to export the numeric values of a *STATISTICA* “double variable.”

Line Length

The number of variables per line in the output file is determined by the specified line length. Enter the length of the line in the ASCII file here (values can be from 80 to 4,000). If the specified line length is insufficient to contain all variables, then the line will be broken after the last complete variable (i.e., a variable will not be divided across lines). If unbroken records are desired (i.e., each record occupies only one line in the output file), specify a line length no less than the sum of all variable formats.

Export File to CSS/3

You can export data from *STATISTICA* for Windows to the CSS/3 (i.e., CSS:*STATISTICA* or

STATISTICA/DOS) format. These DOS files support most of the format specifications and conventions of *STATISTICA* for Windows and all of them are automatically transferred when you use this export option with the following exceptions:

- If the current long variable names are longer than 40 characters (the limit in the DOS version format), then they are truncated to 40 characters;
- Display formats (e.g., date, time, scientific notation, with commas, etc.) are not supported in the DOS version;
- The Workbook information is not supported in the DOS version;
- The file notes/comments are not supported in the DOS version (only the one-line file header is exported);
- The file size is limited to 300 variables;
- The information about the spreadsheet color, style, and fonts is not exported.

INDEX

A

C

D

StatSoft

Chapter 8:

ELEMENTARY CONCEPTS IN STATISTICS

Table of Contents

Chapter 8:

ELEMENTARY CONCEPTS IN STATISTICS

OVERVIEW OF ELEMENTARY CONCEPTS IN STATISTICS

This introduction will briefly discuss those elementary statistical concepts that provide the necessary foundations for more specialized expertise in any area of statistical data analysis. The selected topics illustrate the basic assumptions of most statistical methods and/or have been demonstrated in research to be necessary components of one's general understanding of the "quantitative nature" of reality (Nisbett, et al., 1987).

Because of space limitations, the focus will be mostly on the functional aspects of the concepts discussed and the presentation will be very short. Further information on each of those concepts can be found in the *Introductory Overview* and *Examples* sections of this manual and in statistical textbooks. Recommended introductory textbooks are: Kachigan (1986) and Runyon and Haber (1976); for a more advanced discussion of elementary theory and assumptions of statistics, see the classic books by Hays (1988), and Kendall and Stuart (1979).

What are Variables?

Variables are things that you measure, control, or manipulate in research. They differ in many respects, most notably in the role they are given in your research and in the type of measures that can be applied to them.

Correlational vs. Experimental Research

Most empirical research belongs clearly to one of these two general categories. In *correlational* research you do not (or at least try not to) influence any variables, but only measure them and look for relations (correlations) between some set of variables, such as blood pressure and cholesterol level. In *experimental* research, you manipulate some variables and then measure the effects of this manipulation on other variables. For example, a researcher might artificially increase blood pressure and then record cholesterol level. Data analysis in experimental research also comes down to calculating "correlations" between variables, specifically, those manipulated and those affected by the manipulation. However, experimental data may potentially provide qualitatively better information: Only experimental data can conclusively demonstrate causal relations between variables. For example, if you found that whenever you change variable *A* then variable *B* changes, then you can conclude that "*A* influences *B*." Data from *correlational* research can only be "interpreted" in causal terms based on some theories that you have, but correlational data cannot conclusively prove causality.

Dependent vs. Independent Variables

Independent variables are those that are manipulated, whereas *dependent* variables are only measured or registered. This distinction appears terminologically confusing to many because, as some students say, "all variables depend on something." However, once you get used to this distinction, it becomes indispensable. The terms *dependent* and *independent* variable apply mostly to experimental research where some variables are manipulated, and in this sense they are "independent" from the initial reaction patterns, features, intentions, etc. of the subjects. Some other variables are expected to be "dependent" on the manipulation or experimental conditions. That is to

say, they depend on "what the subject will do" in response. Somewhat contrary to the nature of this distinction, these terms are also used in studies where you do not literally manipulate independent variables, but only assign subjects to "experimental groups" based on some pre-existing properties of the subjects. For example, if in an experiment, males are compared with females regarding their white cell count (WCC), *Gender* could be called the *independent* variable and *WCC* the *dependent* variable.

Measurement Scales

Variables differ in "how well" they can be measured, i.e., in how much measurable information their measurement scale can provide. There is obviously some measurement error involved in every measurement, which determines the "amount of information" that you can obtain. Another factor that determines the amount of information that can be provided by a variable is its "type of measurement scale." Specifically, variables are classified as (a) *nominal*, (b) *ordinal*, (c) *interval* or (d) *ratio*.

(a) *Nominal* variables allow for only *qualitative classification*. That is, they can be measured only in terms of whether the individual items belong to some distinctively different categories, but you cannot quantify or even rank order those categories. For example, all you can say is that 2 individuals are different in terms of variable A (e.g., they are of different race), but you cannot say which one "has more" of the quality represented by the variable. Typical examples of *nominal* variables are gender, race, color, city, etc.

(b) *Ordinal* variables allow you to rank order the items you measure in terms of which has less and which has more of the quality represented by the variable, but still they do not allow you to say "how much more." A typical example of an ordinal variable is the socioeconomic status of families. For example, you know that *upper-middle* is higher than *middle* but you cannot say that it is, for example, 18% higher. Also, this very distinction between *nominal*, *ordinal*, and *interval* scales itself represents a good example of an ordinal variable. For example, you can say that *nominal* measurement provides less information than *ordinal* measurement, but you cannot say "how much less" or how this difference compares to the difference between *ordinal* and *interval* scales.

(c) *Interval* variables allow you not only to rank order the items that are measured, but also to quantify and compare the sizes of differences between them. For example, temperature, as measured in degrees Fahrenheit or Celsius, constitutes an interval scale. For example, you can say that a temperature of 40 degrees is higher than a temperature of 30 degrees, and that an increase from 20 to 40 degrees is twice as much as an increase from 30 to 40 degrees.

(d) *Ratio* variables are very similar to interval variables; in addition to all the properties of interval variables, they feature an identifiable *absolute zero point*, thus they allow for statements such as x is two times more than y. Typical examples of ratio scales are measures of time or space. For example, as the Kelvin temperature scale is a ratio scale, not only can you say that a temperature of 200 degrees is higher than one of 100 degrees, you can correctly state that it is twice as high. Interval scales do not have the ratio property. Most statistical data analysis procedures do not distinguish between the interval and ratio properties of the measurement scales.

Relations between Variables

Regardless of their type, two or more variables are related if in a sample of observations the values of those variables are distributed in a consistent manner. In other words, variables are related if their values systematically correspond to each other for these

observations. For example, *Gender* and *WCC* would be considered to be related if most males had high *WCC* and most females low *WCC*, or vice versa; *Height* is related to *Weight* because typically tall individuals are heavier than short ones; *IQ* is related to the *Number of Errors* in a test, if people with higher IQ's make fewer errors.

Why Relations between Variables are Important

Generally speaking, the ultimate goal of every research or scientific analysis is finding relations between variables. The philosophy of science teaches that there is no other way of representing "meaning" except in terms of relations between some quantities or qualities; either way involves relations between variables. Thus, the advancement of science must always involve finding new relations between variables. Correlational research involves measuring such relations in the most straightforward manner. However, experimental research is not any different in this respect. For example, the above mentioned experiment comparing *WCC* in males and females can be described as looking for a correlation between two variables: *Gender* and *WCC*. Statistics does nothing else but help one evaluate relations between variables. Actually, all of the hundreds of procedures that are described in this manual can be interpreted in terms of evaluating various kinds of inter-variable relations.

Two Basic Features of Every Relation between Variables

The two most elementary formal properties of every relation between variables are the relation's (a) magnitude (or "size") and (b) its reliability (or "truthfulness").

(a) *Magnitude (or "size").* The *magnitude* is much easier to understand and measure than *reliability*. For example, if every male in your sample was found to have a higher *WCC* than any female in the sample, then you could say that the magnitude of the relation between the two variables (*Gender* and *WCC*) is very high in your sample. In other words, you could predict one based on the other (at least among the members of your sample).

(b) *Reliability (or "truthfulness").* The *reliability* of a relation is a much less intuitive concept, but still extremely important. It pertains to the "representativeness" of the result found in your specific sample for the entire population. In other words, it says how probable it is that a similar relation would be found if the experiment was replicated with other samples drawn from the same population. Remember that one is almost never "ultimately" interested only in what is going on in the sample; one is interested in the sample only to the extent that it can provide information about the population. If your study meets some specific criteria (to be mentioned later), then the reliability of a relation between variables observed in your sample can be quantitatively estimated and represented using a standard measure (technically called *p*-level or statistical *significance level*, see the next paragraph).

What is "Statistical Significance" (*p*-level)?

The statistical significance of a result is an estimated measure of the degree to which it is "true" (in the sense of "representative of the population"). More technically, the value of the *p*-level represents a decreasing index of the reliability of a result. The higher the *p*-level, the less you can believe that the observed relation between variables in the sample is a reliable indicator of the relation between the respective variables in the population. Specifically, the *p*-level represents the probability of error that is involved in accepting your observed result as valid, that is, as "representative of the population." For example, a *p*-level of *.05* (i.e., $^1/_{20}$) indicates that

there is a 5% probability that the relation between the variables found in your sample is a "fluke." In other words, assuming that in the population there was no relation between those variables whatsoever, and you were repeating experiments like this one after another, you could expect that approximately in every 20 replications of the experiment there would be one in which the relation between the variables in question would be as strong or stronger than in this one. In many areas of research, the *p*-level of .05 is customarily treated as a "border-line acceptable" error level.

How to Determine Whether a Result is Really Significant

There is no way to avoid arbitrariness in the final decision as to what level of significance will be treated as really "significant." That is, the selection of some level of significance, up to which the results will be rejected as invalid, is arbitrary. In practice, the final decision usually depends on whether the outcome was predicted *a priori* or only found *post hoc* in the course of many analyses and comparisons performed on the data set, on the total amount of consistent supportive evidence in the entire data set, and on "traditions" existing in the particular area of research.

Typically, in many sciences, results that yield $p \leq .05$ are considered borderline statistically *significant*, but remember that this level of *significance* still involves a pretty high probability of error (5%). Results that are significant at the $p \leq .01$ level are commonly considered statistically *significant*, and $p \leq .005$ or $p \leq .001$ levels are often called *"highly" significant*. But remember that those classifications represent nothing else but arbitrary conventions that are only informally based on general research experience.

Statistical Significance and the Number of Analyses Performed

Needless to say, the more analyses you perform on a data set, the more results will meet "by chance" the conventional significance level. For example, if you calculate correlations between ten variables (i.e., 45 different correlation coefficients), then you should expect to find by chance that about two (i.e., one in every 20) correlation coefficients are significant at the $p \leq .05$ level, even if the values of the variables were totally random and those variables do not correlate in the population.

Some statistical methods that involve many comparisons, and thus a good chance for such errors, include some "correction" or adjustment for the total number of comparisons. However, many statistical methods (especially simple exploratory data analyses) do not offer any straightforward remedies to this problem. Therefore, it is up to the researcher to carefully evaluate the reliability of unexpected findings. Many examples in this manual offer specific advice on how to do this; relevant information can also be found in most research methods textbooks.

Strength vs. Reliability of a Relation between Variables

It was said before that strength and reliability are two different features of relationships between variables. However, they are not totally independent. In general, in a sample of a particular size, the larger the magnitude of the relation between variables, the more reliable the relation (see the next paragraph).

Why Stronger Relations between Variables are More Significant

Assuming that there is no relation between the respective variables in the population, the most likely

outcome would also be finding no relation between those variables in the research sample. Thus, the stronger the relation found in the sample, the less likely it is that there is no corresponding relation in the population. As you see, the magnitude and significance of a relation appear to be closely related, and you could calculate the significance from the magnitude and vice-versa; however, this is true only if the sample size is kept constant, because a relation of a given strength could be either highly significant or not significant at all, depending on the sample size (see the next paragraph).

Why the Significance of a Relation between Variables Depends on the Size of the Sample

If there are very few observations, then there are also respectively few possible combinations of the values of the variables, and thus the probability of obtaining by chance a combination of those values indicative of a strong relation is relatively high. Consider the following illustration. If you are interested in two variables (*Gender*: male/female and *WCC*: high/low) and there are only four subjects in your sample (two males and two females), then the probability that you will find, purely by chance, a 100% relation between the two variables can be as high as one-eighth. Specifically, there is a one-in-eight chance that both males will have a high *WCC* and both females a low *WCC*, or vice versa. Now consider the probability of obtaining such a perfect match by chance if your sample consisted of 100 subjects; the probability of obtaining such an outcome by chance would be practically zero.

Consider a more general example. Imagine a theoretical population in which the average value of *WCC* in males and females is exactly the same. Needless to say, if you start replicating a simple experiment by drawing pairs of samples (of males and females) of a particular size from this population and calculating the difference between the average *WCC* in each pair of samples, most of the experiments will yield results close to 0. However, from time to time, a pair of samples will be drawn where the difference between males and females will be quite different from 0. How often will it happen? The smaller the sample size in each experiment, the more likely it is that you will obtain such erroneous results, which in this case would be results indicative of the existence of a relation between gender and *WCC* obtained from a population in which such a relation does not exist.

Example: "Baby Boys to Baby Girls Ratio"

Consider the following example adapted from research on statistical reasoning (Nisbett, et al., 1987). There are two hospitals: In the first one, 120 babies are born every day, in the other, only 12. On average, the ratio of baby boys to baby girls born every day in each hospital is 50/50. However, one day, in one of those hospitals twice as many baby girls were born as baby boys. In which hospital was this more likely to happen?

The answer is obvious for a statistician, but as research shows, not so obvious for a lay person: It is much more likely to happen in the small hospital. The reason for this is that technically speaking, the probability of a random deviation of a particular size (from the population mean), decreases with the increase in the sample size.

Why Small Relations can be Proven Significant only in Large Samples

The examples in the previous paragraphs indicate that if a relationship between variables in question is "objectively" (i.e., in the population) small, then there is no way to identify such a relation in a study unless the research sample is correspondingly large. Even if your sample is in fact "perfectly representative" the effect will not be statistically significant if the sample is small. Analogously, if a relation in question is "objectively" very large (i.e., in the population), then

it can be found to be highly significant even in a study based on a very small sample. Consider the following additional illustration. If a coin is slightly asymmetrical, and when tossed is somewhat more likely to produce heads than tails (e.g., 60% vs. 40%), then ten tosses would not be sufficient to convince anyone that the coin is asymmetrical, even if the outcome obtained (six heads and four tails) was perfectly representative of the bias of the coin. However, is it so that 10 tosses is not enough to prove anything? No, if the effect in question were large enough, then ten tosses could be quite enough. For instance, imagine now that the coin is so asymmetrical that no matter how you toss it, the outcome will be heads. If you tossed such a coin ten times and each toss produced heads, most people would consider it sufficient evidence that something is "wrong" with the coin. In other words, it would be considered convincing evidence that in the theoretical population of an infinite number of tosses of this coin there would be more heads than tails. Thus, if a relation is large, then it can be found to be significant even in a small sample.

Can *No Relation* be a Significant Result?

The smaller the relation between variables, the larger the sample size that is necessary to prove it significant. For example, imagine how many tosses would be necessary to prove that a coin is asymmetrical if its bias were only .000001%! Thus, the necessary minimum sample size increases as the magnitude of the effect to be demonstrated decreases. When the magnitude of the effect approaches 0, the necessary sample size to conclusively prove it approaches infinity. That is to say, if there is almost no relation between two variables, then the sample size must be almost equal to the population size, which is assumed to be infinitely large. Statistical significance represents the probability that a similar outcome would be obtained if you tested the entire population. Thus, everything that would be found after testing the entire population would be, by definition, significant at the highest possible level, and this also includes all "no relation" results.

How to Measure the Magnitude (Strength) of Relations between Variables

There are very many measures of the magnitude of relationships between variables which have been developed by statisticians; the choice of a specific measure in given circumstances depends on the number of variables involved, measurement scales used, nature of the relations, etc. Almost all of them, however, follow one general principle: they attempt to somehow evaluate the observed relation by comparing it to the "maximum imaginable relation" between those specific variables.

Technically speaking, a common way to perform such evaluations is to look at how differentiated are the values of the variables, and then calculate what part of this "overall available differentiation" is accounted for by instances when that differentiation is "common" in the two (or more) variables in question.

Speaking less technically, you compare "what is common in those variables" to "what potentially could have been common if the variables were perfectly related." Consider a simple illustration. Say that in your sample, the average index of *WCC* is 100 in males and 102 in females. Thus, you could say that on average, the deviation of each individual score from the grand mean (101) contains a component due to the gender of the subject; the size of this component is 1. That value, in a sense, represents some measure of relation between *Gender* and *WCC*. However, this value is a very poor measure, because it does not tell you how relatively large this component is, given the "overall differentiation" of *WCC* scores. Consider two extreme possibilities:

(a) If all *WCC* scores of males were exactly equal to 100, and those of females equal to 102, then all

deviations from the grand mean in your sample would be entirely accounted for by gender. You would say that in your sample, gender is perfectly correlated with *WCC*, that is, 100% of the observed differences between subjects regarding their *WCC* is accounted for by their gender.

(b) If *WCC* scores were in the range of 0-1000, the same difference (of 2) between the average *WCC* of males and females found in the study would account for such a small part of the overall differentiation of scores that most likely it would be considered negligible. For example, one more subject taken into account could change, or even reverse the direction of the difference. Therefore, every good measure of relations between variables must take into account the overall differentiation of individual scores in the sample and evaluate the relation in terms of (relatively) how much of this differentiation is accounted for by the relation in question.

Common General Format of Most Statistical Tests

Because the ultimate goal of most statistical tests is to evaluate relations between variables, most statistical tests follow the general format that was explained in the previous paragraph. Technically speaking, they represent a ratio of some measure of the differentiation common in the variables in question to the overall differentiation of those variables. For example, they represent a ratio of the part of the overall differentiation of the *WCC* scores that can be accounted for by gender to the overall differentiation of the *WCC* scores. This ratio is usually called a ratio of *explained* variation to *total* variation.

In statistics, the term *explained variation* does not necessarily imply that you "conceptually understand" it. It is used only to denote the *common variation* in the variables in question, that is, the part of variation in one variable that is "explained" by the specific values of the other variable, and vice versa.

How the Level of Statistical Significance is Calculated

Suppose you have already calculated a measure of a relation between two variables (as explained above). The next question is "how significant is this relation?" For example, is 40% of the explained variance between the two variables enough to consider the relation significant? The answer is "it depends." Specifically, the significance depends mostly on the sample size. As explained before, in very large samples, even very small relations between variables will be significant, whereas in very small samples even very large relations cannot be considered reliable (significant). Thus, in order to determine the level of statistical significance, you need a function that represents the relationship between "magnitude" and "significance" of relations between two variables, depending on the sample size. The function you need would tell you exactly "how likely it is to obtain a relation of a given magnitude (or larger) from a sample of a given size, assuming that there is no such relation between those variables in the population." In other words, that function would give you the significance (*p*) level, and it would tell you the probability of error involved in rejecting the idea that the relation in question does not exist in the population. This "alternative" hypothesis (that there is no relation in the population) is usually called the *null hypothesis*. It would be ideal if the probability function was linear, and for example, only had different slopes for different sample sizes. Unfortunately, the function is more complex, and is not always exactly the same; however, in most cases you know its shape and can use it to determine the significance levels for your findings in samples of a particular size. Most of those functions are related to a general type of function which is called *normal*.

Why the "Normal Distribution" is Important

The "Normal distribution" is important because in most cases, it well approximates the function that was introduced in the previous paragraph. The distribution of many test statistics is normal or follows some form that can be derived from the Normal distribution.

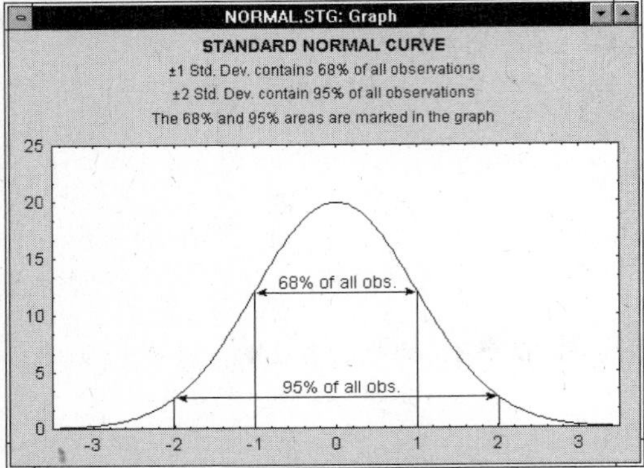

In this sense, philosophically speaking, the Normal distribution represents one of the empirically verified elementary "truths about the general nature of reality," and its status can be compared to one of the fundamental laws of natural sciences. The exact shape of the Normal distribution (the characteristic "bell curve") is defined by a function which has only two parameters: the *mean* and the *standard deviation*.

A characteristic property of the Normal distribution is that 68% of all of its observations fall within a range of ±1 standard deviation from the mean, and a range of ±2 standard deviations includes 95% of the scores. In other words, in a Normal distribution, observations that have a standardized value of less than -2 or more than +2 have a relative frequency of 5% or less. (Standardized value means that a value is expressed in terms of its difference from the mean, divided by the standard deviation.)

Illustration of how the Normal Distribution is Used in Statistical Reasoning (Induction)

Recall the example discussed on page 1413, where pairs of samples of males and females were drawn from a population in which the average value of *WCC* in males and females was exactly the same. Although the most likely outcome of such experiments (one pair of samples per experiment) was that the difference between the average *WCC* in males and females in each pair is close to zero, from time to time, a pair of samples will be drawn where the difference between males and females is quite different from 0. How often does it happen? If the sample size is large enough, the results of such replications are "normally distributed," and thus knowing the shape of the normal curve, you can precisely calculate the probability of obtaining "by chance" outcomes representing various levels of deviation from the hypothetical population mean of 0. If such a calculated probability is so low that it meets the previously accepted criterion of statistical significance (see page 1412), then you have only one choice: conclude that your result gives a better approximation of what is going on in the population than does the "null hypothesis." Remember that the null hypothesis was considered only for "technical reasons" as a benchmark against which your empirical result was evaluated.

Are all Test Statistics Normally Distributed?

Not all, but most of them are either based on the normal distribution directly or on distributions that are related to, and can be derived from the normal distribution, such as *t*, *F*, or *Chi-square*. Typically, those tests require that the variables analyzed are themselves normally distributed in the population, that is, they meet the so-called "normality assumption." Many observed variables are actually normally distributed, which is another reason why the

normal distribution represents a "general feature" of empirical reality. The problem may occur when one tries to use a normal distribution-based test to analyze data from variables that are themselves not normally distributed (see tests of normality in the *Nonparametrics and Distributions* or *ANOVA-/MANOVA* modules). In such cases you have two general choices. First, you can use some alternative "nonparametric" test (or so-called "distribution-free test," see Chapter 11 in this volume, *Nonparametrics and Distributions*); but this is often inconvenient because such tests are typically less powerful and less flexible in terms of types of conclusions that they can provide. Alternatively, in many cases you can still use the normal distribution-based test only if you make sure that the size of your samples is large enough. The latter option is based on an extremely important principle which is largely responsible for the popularity of tests that are based on the normal function. Namely, as the sample size increases, the shape of the sampling distribution (i.e., distribution of a statistic from the sample) approaches normal shape, even if the distribution of the variable in question is not normal. This principle is called the *central limit theorem.*

How Does One Know the Consequences of Violating the Normality Assumption?

Although many of the statements made in the preceding paragraphs can be proven mathematically, some of them do not have theoretical proofs and can be demonstrated only empirically, via so-called Monte-Carlo experiments. In these experiments, large numbers of samples are generated by a computer following predesigned specifications and the results from such samples are analyzed using a variety of tests. This way you can empirically evaluate the type and magnitude of errors or biases to which you are exposed when certain theoretical assumptions of the tests you are using are not met by your data. Specifically, Monte-Carlo studies were used extensively with normal distribution-based tests to determine how sensitive they are to violations of the normality assumption. The general conclusion from these studies is that the consequences of such violations are less severe than previously thought. Although these conclusions should not entirely discourage anyone from being concerned about the normality assumption, they have increased the overall popularity of the distribution-dependent statistical tests in all areas of research.

INDEX

Chapter 9:

BASIC STATISTICS AND TABLES

Table of Contents

The *Detailed Table of Contents* follows on the next page.

Detailed Table of Contents

StatSoft®

StatSoft®

STATISTICA

STATISTICA

Chapter 9:

BASIC STATISTICS AND TABLES

INTRODUCTORY OVERVIEW

The statistics included in this module are conventionally called *basic statistics* and are often discussed as a group because they are often used as a group in the initial, exploratory phase of data analysis. In fact, they include tests that serve different purposes. Each of the basic statistics methods available in this module will be discussed in this introduction (in the discussion, it will be assumed that the reader is familiar with the concepts introduced in the previous chapter, *Elementary Concepts*, Chapter 8). Further information can be found in the *Examples* section (page 1461) and in statistical textbooks. Recommended introductory textbooks are: Kachigan (1986), and Runyon and Haber (1976); for a more advanced discussion of elementary theory of basic statistics, see the classic books by Hays (1988), and Kendall and Stuart (1979).

Descriptive Statistics

Overview

Purpose (and the arrangement of data).

Descriptive statistics are calculated separately for each variable, and they provide such basic information as the mean, minimum and maximum values, different measures of variation, as well as data about the shape of the distribution of the variable. For example, the following data set contains indices of white cell counts (variable *WCC*) and cholesterol levels (variable *Cholest*) collected for each of five persons (*case 1* through *case 5*). Three types of descriptive statistics (mean, minimum, and maximum) were calculated for each of the two variables (i.e., "columns" of data).

```
                    WCC        CHOLEST
                    ---        -------
case 1              111           220
case 2              112           201
case 3              110           185
case 4              115           170
case 5              109           230
--------------------------------------
        mean        111.4         201.2
        minimum     109.0         170.0
        maximum     115.0         220.0
```

Those and other statistics are reviewed below (see also the *Statistics* dialog, page 1510, for a complete listing). For the descriptive statistics procedure, you can select all variables in the current data set, and a sequential table of "descriptives" for the consecutive variables will be generated (one row per variable).

Descriptive Statistics (wcc.sta)

BASIC STATS	Mean	Confid. -95.000%	Confid. +95.000%	Variance	Std.Dev.	Standard Error
WCC	111.4000	108.5415	114.2585	5.3000	2.30217	1.02956
CHOLEST	201.2000	170.6667	231.7333	604.7000	24.59065	10.99727

The measures of variation include the standard deviation and the standard error (the standard error is the standard deviation of the sampling distribution of a mean; see below). Numerous tests of whether the distribution of variables follows the normal distribution are also provided (refer to the *Statistics* dialog, page 1500, for a complete description of all procedures).

"True" mean and confidence interval.

Probably the most often-used descriptive statistic is the mean. The mean is a particularly informative measure of the "central tendency" of the variable if it is reported along with its confidence intervals. As mentioned earlier, usually you are interested in statistics (such as the mean) from your sample only to the extent to which you can infer information about the population. The *confidence intervals* for the mean give a range of values around the mean where you expect the "true" (population) mean is

located (with a given level of certainty, see also *Elementary Concepts*, Chapter 8).

In the *Basic Statistics and Tables* module you can request confidence intervals for any *p*-level; for example, if the mean in your sample is 23, and the lower and upper limits of the *p*=.05 confidence interval are 19 and 27 respectively, then you can conclude that there is a 95% probability that the population mean is greater than 19 and lower than 27. If you set the *p*-level to a smaller value, then the interval would become wider thereby increasing the "certainty" of the estimate, and vice versa; as you know from the weather forecast, the more "vague" the prediction (i.e., wider the confidence interval), the more likely it will materialize.

Note that the width of the confidence interval depends on the sample size and on the variation of data values. The larger the sample size, the more reliable its mean. The larger the variation, the less reliable the mean (see also *Elementary Concepts*, Chapter 8). The calculation of confidence intervals is based on the assumption that the variable is normally distributed in the population. The estimate may not be valid if this assumption is not met, unless the sample size is large, say *n*=100 or more.

Shape of the distribution; normality. An important aspect of the "description" of a variable is the shape of its distribution, which tells you the frequency of values from different ranges of the variable. Typically a researcher is interested in how well the distribution can be approximated by the normal distribution (see also *Elementary Concepts*, Chapter 8). Simple descriptive statistics can provide some information relevant to this issue.

For example, if the *skewness* (which measures the deviation of the distribution from symmetry) is clearly different from 0, then that distribution is asymmetrical, while normal distributions are perfectly symmetrical. If the *kurtosis* (which measures "peakedness" of the distribution) is clearly different from 0, then the distribution is either flatter or more peaked than normal; the kurtosis of the normal distribution is 0.

More precise information can be obtained by performing one of the *tests of normality* to determine the probability that the sample came from a normally distributed population of observations (e.g., the Kolmogorov-Smirnov test, or the Shapiro-Wilks' *W* test). However, none of these tests can entirely substitute for a visual examination of the data using a histogram (i.e., a graph that shows the frequency distribution of a variable).

As in all modules of *STATISTICA*, histograms can be generated directly from a Scrollsheet containing descriptive statistics by pointing to the desired variable (with cursor keys or the mouse), clicking on the right-mouse-button, and selecting the *Quick Stats Graph* option *Histogram/Normal* from the flying menu.

The resulting graph allows you to evaluate the normality of the empirical distribution because it also shows the normal curve superimposed over the histogram. It also allows you to examine various aspects of the distribution *qualitatively*.

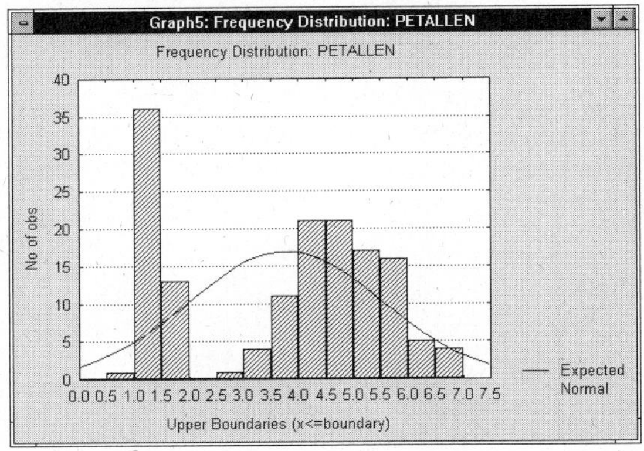

For example, the distribution could be bimodal (have 2 peaks, see the histogram above). This might suggest that the sample is not homogeneous but possibly its elements came from two different populations, each more or less normally distributed. In such cases, in order to understand the nature of

the variable in question, you should look for a way to quantitatively identify the two sub-samples.

Other descriptive statistics. The *Basic Statistics and Tables* module includes a selection of the most often-used descriptive statistics. An additional set of ordinal descriptive statistics and some less frequently-used ones (e.g., harmonic means, etc.) are also included in the *Nonparametrics and Distributions* module; in that module a variety of non-normal distributions can also be fit to the data. More specialized descriptive statistics are included in other modules of *STATISTICA*.

Quick basic statistics. In addition, basic descriptive statistics (optionally broken down by a grouping variable) are available in every module of *STATISTICA* via the *Quick Basic Stats* options, accessible via the *Analysis* pull-down menu, or via the *Quick Basic Stats* toolbar button. These options are described in Chapter 10.

Block statistics. You can compute summary descriptive statistics (including quartiles) and graphs for the values in any Scrollsheet (or the data spreadsheet) via the *Block Stats* (*Rows* or *Columns*) options, accessible via the *Edit* pull-down menu or the right mouse button flying menu. First highlight the desired block of data in the Scrollsheet or the data spreadsheet, and then select the desired *Block Stats/Rows* or *Block Stats/Columns* option.

Correlations

Overview

Purpose (What is correlation?). Correlation is a measure of the relation between two or more variables. The measurement scales used should be at least interval scales (see *Elementary Concepts*, Chapter 8), but other correlation coefficients are available to handle other types of data (e.g., see *Nonparametrics and Distributions*, Chapter 11). Correlation coefficients can range from –1.00 to +1.00. The value of –1.00 represents a perfect *negative* correlation while a value of +1.00 represents a perfect *positive* correlation. A value of 0.00 represents a lack of correlation.

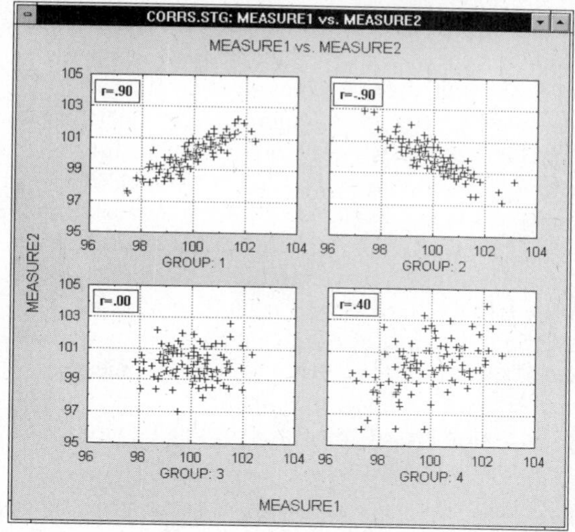

The most widely-used type of correlation coefficient is *Pearson r*, also called *linear* or *product-moment* correlation. It is the basic type of correlation that is offered in the *Basic Statistics and Tables* module. More specialized correlations are included in other modules, as explained later.

Arrangement of data. You can correlate any variables in your data set. For example, the following data set contains indices of white cell counts (variable *WCC*) and cholesterol levels (variable *Cholest*) collected for each of five persons (*case 1* through *case 5*). The correlation between these two variables (i.e., "columns" of data) is given below.

	WCC	CHOLEST
case 1	111	220
case 2	112	201
case 3	110	185
case 4	115	170
case 5	109	230
	r = -.73	

If the selected variables contain nominal data (see *Elementary Concepts*, Chapter 8), you need to use a

special type of correlation, such as those included in the *Crosstabulation tables* procedures of the *Basic Statistics and Tables* module, page 1446).

Simple linear correlation (Pearson r). Pearson correlation (hereafter called *correlation*), assumes that the two variables are measured on at least interval scales (see *Elementary Concepts*, Chapter 8), and it determines the extent to which values of the two variables are "proportional" to each other. The value of correlation (i.e., correlation coefficient) does not depend on the specific measurement units used; for example, the correlation between height and weight will be identical regardless of whether *inches and pounds*, or *centimeters and kilograms* are used as measurement units. *Proportional* means *linearly related*; that is, the correlation is high if it can be "summarized" by a straight line (sloped upwards or downwards).

This line is called the *regression line* or *least squares line*, because it is determined such that the sum of the *squared* distances of all the data points from the line is the lowest possible. Note that the concept of *squared* distances will have important functional consequences on how the value of the correlation coefficient reacts to various specific arrangements of data (e.g., so-called outliers, as you will later see).

Regression line. The slope of the regression line is indicative of the magnitude (strength) of the correlation such that if the correlation is very strongly negative or very strongly positive, the slope is about 45° or "diagonal" in the respective direction (given equivalent scaling of the two axes), and if there is no correlation, then the line runs horizontally, as on the next example scatterplot.

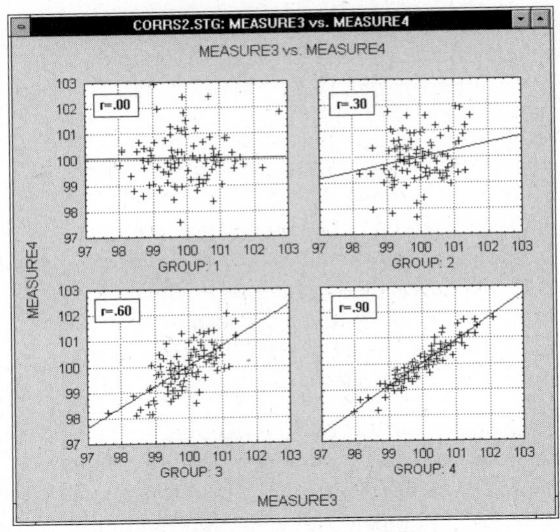

How to interpret the value of correlations. As mentioned before, the correlation coefficient (r) represents the linear relationship between two variables. If the correlation coefficient is squared, then the resulting value (r^2, the coefficient of determination) will represent the proportion of common variation in the two variables (i.e., the "strength" or "magnitude" of the relationship). In order to evaluate the correlation between variables, it is important to know this "magnitude" or "strength" as well as the *significance* of the correlation (see *Elementary Concepts*, Chapter 8).

Significance of correlations. The significance level calculated for each correlation is a primary source of information about the reliability of the correlation. In order to facilitate identifying those coefficients that are significant at some desired level, the *Correlation Matrices* dialog in *Basic Statistics and Tables* (page 1512) provides an option to have *STATISTICA* highlight or mark significant correlations with a different color.

As explained before (see *Elementary Concepts*, Chapter 8), the significance of a correlation coefficient of a particular magnitude will change depending on the size of the sample from which it was computed. The test of significance is based on

the assumption that the distribution of the residual values (i.e., the deviations from the regression line) for the dependent variable *y* follows the normal distribution, and that the variability of the residual values is the same for all values of the independent variable *x*.

Monte Carlo studies suggest that meeting those assumptions closely is not absolutely crucial if your sample size is not very small and when the departure from normality is not very large. There are, however, much more common and serious threats to the validity of information that a correlation coefficient can provide; they are briefly discussed in the following paragraphs.

Outliers. Outliers are atypical (by definition), infrequent observations. Because of the way in which the regression line is determined (especially the fact that it is based on minimizing not the sum of simple distances but the sum of *squares of distances* of data points from the line), outliers can have a profound influence on the slope of the regression line and consequently on the value of the correlation coefficient. A single outlier is capable of considerably changing the slope of the regression line and, consequently, the value of the correlation.

Typically, it is believed that outliers represent a random error that one would like to be able to control. Unfortunately, there is no widely accepted method to remove outliers automatically (however, see the next paragraph), thus what you are left with is to identify any outliers by examining a *scatterplot* of each important correlation. Note that the graphics procedures on the *Correlation Matrices* dialog (page 1512) and graphics editing facilities offer numerous ways to experiment with the interactive removal of outliers ("brushing"), to allow you to instantly see their influence on the regression line, see below.

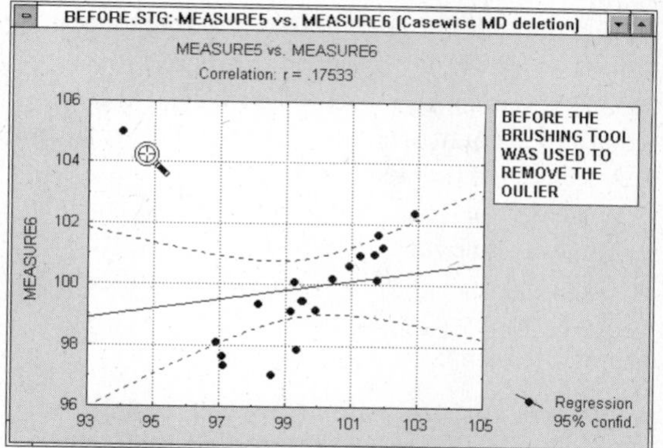

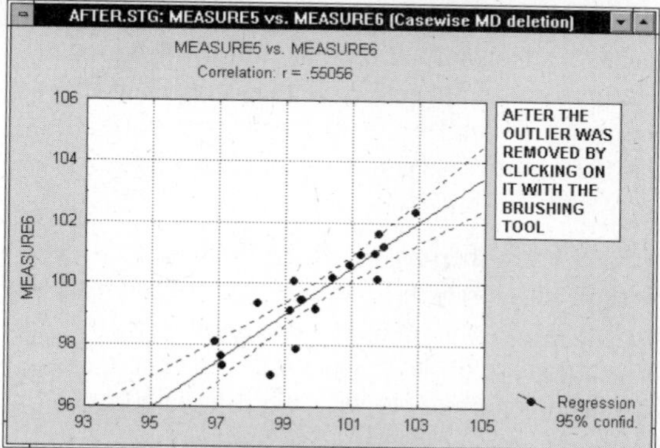

Needless to say, outliers may not only artificially increase the value of a correlation coefficient, but they can also decrease the value of a "legitimate" correlation (as shown in the illustration above).

Quantitative approach to outliers. Some researchers use quantitative methods to exclude outliers. For example, they exclude observations that are outside the range of ±2 standard deviations (or even ±1.5 s.d.'s) around the group or design cell mean. In some areas of research, such "cleaning" of the data is absolutely necessary. For example, in cognitive psychology research on reaction times, even if almost all scores in an experiment are in the range of 300-700 *milliseconds*, just a few "distracted reactions" of 10-15 *seconds* will completely change the overall picture.

Unfortunately, defining an outlier is subjective (as it should be), and the decisions concerning how to identify them must be made on an individual basis (taking into account specific experimental paradigms and/or "accepted practice" and general research experience in the respective area). It should also be noted that in some rare cases, the relative frequency of outliers across a number of groups or cells of a design can be subjected to analysis and provide interpretable results.

For example, outliers could be indicative of the occurrence of a phenomenon that is qualitatively different than the typical pattern observed or expected in the sample; thus the relative frequency of outliers could provide evidence of a relative frequency of departure from the process or phenomenon that is typical for the majority of cases in a group.

Correlations in non-homogeneous groups. A lack of homogeneity in the sample from which a correlation was calculated can be another factor that biases the value of the correlation. Imagine a case where a correlation coefficient is calculated from data points which came from two different experimental groups but this fact is ignored when the correlation is calculated. Assume that the experimental manipulation in one of the groups increased the values of both correlated variables and thus the data from each group form a distinctive "cloud" in the scatterplot.

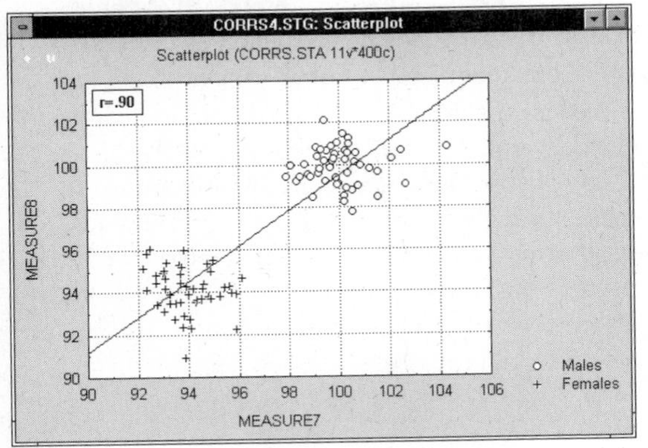

In such cases, a high correlation may result that is entirely due to the arrangement of the two groups, but which does not represent the "true" relation between the two variables, which may practically be equal to 0 (as could be seen if you looked at each group separately).

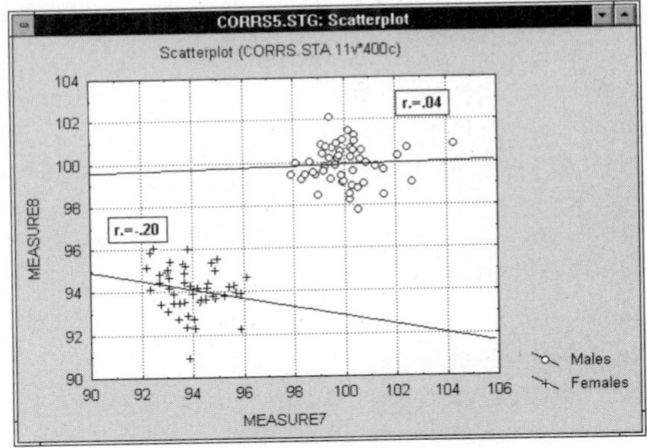

If you suspect the influence of such a phenomenon on your correlations and know how to identify such "subsets" of data, try to run the correlations separately in each subset of observations.

For example, you could use the *Breakdowns* procedure (see page 1442), *Quick Basic Stats* with the categorical variable option (see Chapter 10), or the *Categorized Scatterplot*s procedure (page 1509). Alternatively, you can also use one of the many flexible graphical facilities offered in the *Stats Graphs* menu (see the pull-down menu *Graphs*) to examine correlations using EDA (exploratory data analysis) techniques. For example, the first of the two graphs shown above was produced using the *Stats Graph - 2D Scatterplots* procedure. This method allows you to identify the subsets visually, but treats all data points as a single set and functions fitted in those graphs are based on all data points in this set. The second graph, however, was produced using the *Stats Graph - Categorized Scatterplot* procedure. This method allows you to categorize the data according to some pre-defined or user-defined criteria, in this case, according to gender; using the *Overlaid* option, functions are fitted in those graphs based on the data points within the predefined subsets.

If you do not know how to identify the hypothetical subsets, try to examine the data with some of the exploratory multivariate techniques offered in *STATISTICA* (e.g., *Cluster Analysis*, see Volume III).

Nonlinear relations between variables. Another potential source of problems with the linear (*Pearson r*) correlation is the shape of the relation. As mentioned before, *Pearson r* measures a relation between two variables only to the extent to which it is linear; deviations from linearity will increase the total sum of squared distances from the regression line even if they represent a "true" and very close relationship between two variables.

The possibility of such non-linear relationships is another reason why examining scatterplots is a necessary step in evaluating every correlation.

For example, the following extremely strong correlation between the two variables is not well described by the linear function.

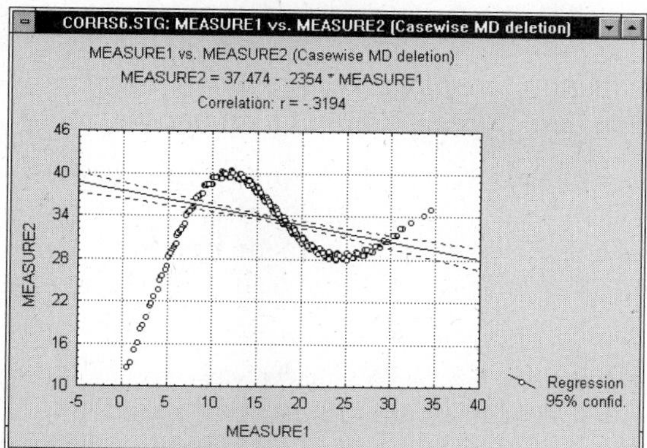

However, a fifth order polynomial function can produce a very close fit.

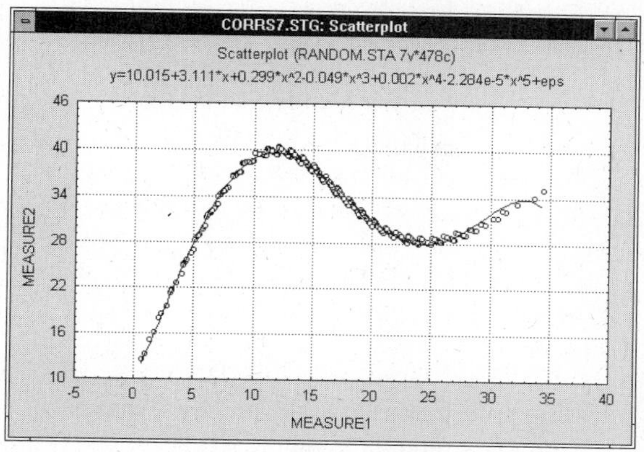

Measuring nonlinear relations. What do you do if a correlation is strong but clearly nonlinear (as concluded from examining scatterplots)? Unfortunately, there is no simple answer to this question, because there is no easy-to-use equivalent of *Pearson r* that is capable of handling nonlinear relations. If the curve is monotonous (continuously decreasing or increasing), you could try to transform one or both of the variables to remove the curvilinearity and then recalculate the correlation.

For example, a typical transformation used in such cases is the logarithmic function which will "squeeze" together the values at one end of the range (to explore this possibility you could first try to switch the scale from linear to logarithmic in the scatterplot *General Layout* dialog; double-click on the graph background to access that dialog).

Another option available if the relation is monotonous is to try a nonparametric correlation (e.g., Spearman *R*, see *Nonparametrics and Distributions*, Chapter 11) which is sensitive only to the ordinal arrangement of values; thus, by definition, it ignores monotonous curvilinearity. However, nonparametric correlations are generally less sensitive, and sometimes this method will not produce any gains. Unfortunately, the two most precise methods are not easy to use and require a good deal of "experimentation" with the data:

(a) Try to identify the specific function that best describes the curve. (A convenient facility to explore various fits is provided by the interactive *User-defined Function* dialog accessible by clicking on the *Custom Function* button in the graphics *Plot Layout* dialog, accessible by clicking on the graph background with the right-mouse-button and then selecting the *Change Plot Layout(s)* option from the flying menu.) After a function has been found, you can test its "goodness of fit" to your data using procedures available in the *Nonlinear Estimation* module (Volume III).

(b) Alternatively, you could experiment with dividing one of the variables into a number of segments (e.g., 4 or 5) of an equal width, treat this new variable as a grouping variable and then run an analysis of variance on the data (i.e., *Recode* the variable, see *Toolbars and Status Bar*, Chapter 2; see also Chapter 3 for a description for the *Recode Values* dialog).

Exploratory examination of correlation matrices. A common first step of many data analyses that involve more than a very few variables is to run a correlation matrix of all variables and then examine it for expected (and unexpected) significant relations. When this is done, you need to be aware of the general nature of statistical significance (see *Elementary Concepts*, Chapter 8). Specifically, if you run many tests (in this case, many correlations), then significant results will be found "surprisingly often" due to pure chance.

For example, by definition, a coefficient significant at the .05 level will occur by chance once in every 20 coefficients. There is no "automatic" way to weed out the "true" correlations. Thus, you should treat all results that were not predicted or planned with particular caution and look for their consistency with other results; ultimately, though, the most conclusive (although costly) control for such a randomness factor is to replicate the study. This issue is general and it pertains to all analyses that involve "multiple comparisons and statistical significance." This problem is also briefly discussed in the context of *post hoc comparisons of means* (page 1532) and the *Breakdowns* procedure (page 1442).

Casewise vs. pairwise deletion of missing data. The default way of deleting missing data while calculating a correlation matrix is to exclude all cases that have missing data in at least one of the selected variables, that is, by *casewise deletion* of missing data. Only this way will you get a "true" correlation matrix, where all correlations are obtained from the *same* set of observations. However, if missing data are randomly distributed across cases, you could easily end up with no "valid" cases in the data set, because each of them will have at least one missing data element in some variable.

The most common solution used in such instances is to use *pairwise deletion* of missing data in correlation matrices, where a correlation between each pair of variables is calculated from all cases that have valid data on those two variables. In many instances there is nothing wrong with that method, especially when the total percentage of missing data is low, say 10%, and they are relatively randomly distributed between cases and variables. However, it may sometimes lead to serious problems.

For example, a systematic bias may result from a "hidden" systematic distribution of missing data, causing different correlation coefficients in the same correlation matrix to be based on different subsets of subjects (as illustrated below).

The following correlation matrix was computed with pairwise deletion of missing data.

Correlations (corrs.sta)

BASIC STATS — Pairwise Deletion of MD's, min N = 24

Variable	VAR1	VAR2	VAR3	VAR4	VAR5
VAR1	1.00	-.15	.50	.45	-.03
VAR2	-.15	1.00	.37	.35	.15
VAR3	.50	.37	1.00	.02	.23
VAR4	.45	.35	.02	1.00	.08
VAR5	-.03	.15	.23	.08	1.00

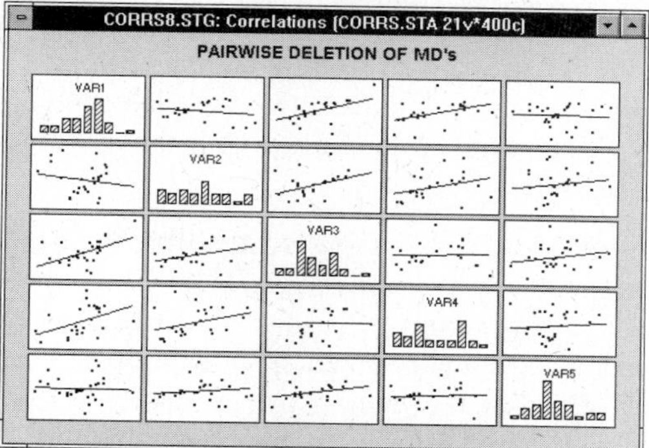

The correlation matrix shown below was computed from the same data using casewise deletion of missing data.

Correlations (corrs.sta)

BASIC STATS — Casewise Deletion of MD's, N=13

Variable	VAR1	VAR2	VAR3	VAR4	VAR5
VAR1	1.00	.72	.90	.96	.67
VAR2	.72	1.00	.90	.62	.97
VAR3	.90	.90	1.00	.86	.86
VAR4	.96	.62	.86	1.00	.56
VAR5	.67	.97	.86	.56	1.00

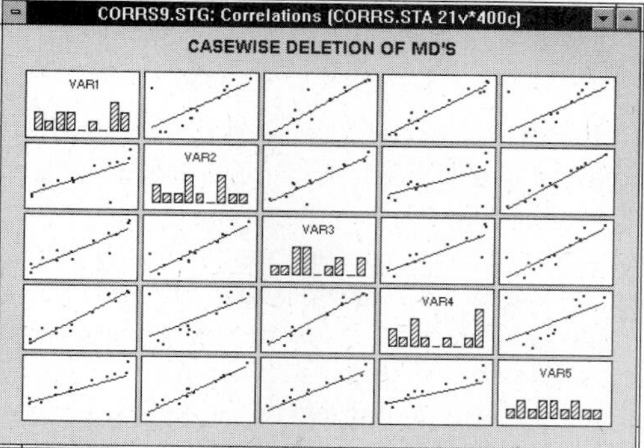

In addition to the possibly biased conclusions that you could derive from such "pairwise calculated" correlation matrices, real problems may occur when you subject such matrices to another analysis (e.g., *Multiple Regression*, *Factor Analysis*, or *Cluster Analysis*) that expects a "true correlation matrix," with a certain level of consistency and "transitivity" between different coefficients. Such a correlation matrix may turn out to be not a "true" correlation matrix, and the other program will either be unable to process it, or will give erroneous results. Thus, if you are using the pairwise method of deleting the missing data, be sure to examine the distribution of missing data across the cells of the matrix for possible systematic "patterns." The *Missing and Out of Range Data Plots* option (one of the *Stats 2D Graphs* option) is particularly useful for this purpose (see Volume II for details).

How to identify biases caused by pairwise deletion of missing data. The *Correlation Matrices* procedure will produce Scrollsheets with *n*'s, means and standard deviations calculated separately for "each variable with each variable," that is, based on subsets of values included in the calculation of individual correlation coefficients. If the pairwise deletion of missing data does not introduce any systematic bias to the correlation matrix, then all those pairwise descriptive statistics should be very similar to the analogous statistics computed for casewise (i.e., listwise) deletion of missing data. However, if they differ, then there are good reasons to suspect a bias.

For example, if the mean (or standard deviation) of the values of variable A that were taken into account in calculating its correlation with variable B is much lower than the mean (or standard deviation) of those values of variable A that were used in calculating its correlation with variable C, then you would have good reason to suspect that those two correlations (A-B and A-C) are based on different subsets of data, and thus, that there is a bias in the correlation matrix caused by a non-random distribution of missing data.

Pairwise deletion of missing data vs. mean substitution. Another common method to avoid losing data due to casewise deletion is the *mean substitution* of missing data (replacing all missing data in a variable by the mean of that variable). This way of handling missing data can be requested in many modules; you can also use this method to permanently "remove" the missing data from your data set (via the *Data Management* module, see

Chapter 7). Mean substitution offers some advantages and some disadvantages as compared to pairwise deletion. Its main advantage is that it produces "internally consistent" sets of results ("true" correlation matrices). The main disadvantages are:

(a) *Mean substitution* artificially decreases the variation of scores, and this decrease in individual variables is proportional to the number of missing data (i.e., the more missing data, the more "perfectly average scores" will be artificially added to the data set).

(b) Because it substitutes missing data with artificially created "average" data points, *mean substitution* may decrease the values of very strong correlations.

Spurious correlations. Although you cannot prove causal relations based on correlation coefficients (see *Elementary Concepts*, Chapter 8), you can still identify *spurious* correlations, that is, correlations that are due mostly to the influences of "other" variables.

For example, there is a correlation between the total amount of losses in a fire and the number of firemen that were putting out the fire; however, what this correlation does not indicate is that if you call fewer firemen, then you would lower the losses. There is a third variable (the initial *size* of the fire) that influences both the amount of losses and the number of firemen. If you "control" for this variable (e.g., consider only fires of a fixed size), then the correlation will either disappear or perhaps even change its sign.

The main problem with spurious correlations is that you typically do not know what the "hidden" agent is. However, in cases when you know where to look, you can use *partial correlations* that control for (*partial out*) the influence of specified variables. In *STATISTICA*, partial correlation procedures are included as part of the *Multiple Regression* module (see Chapter 12).

Note that there are advanced methods for analyzing correlation matrices in terms of hypothesized patterns of (causal) relations between variables (see *Structural Equation Modeling and Path Analysis, SEPATH*, Volume III).

Are correlation coefficients "additive?" No, they are not. For example, an average of correlation coefficients in a number of samples does not represent an "average correlation" in all those samples. Because the value of the correlation coefficient is not a linear function of the magnitude of the relation between the variables, correlation coefficients cannot simply be averaged. In cases when you need to average correlations, they first have to be converted into additive measures.

For example, before averaging, you can square them to obtain *coefficients of determination* which are additive (as explained before in this section), or convert them into *Fisher z values*, which are also additive (an *r*-to-*Z* transformation procedure is available via the *Probability calculator* option from the startup panel, see *Quick Basic Stats*, Chapter 10, for details).

How to determine whether two correlation coefficients are significantly different. A test is available that will evaluate the significance of differences between two correlation coefficients in two samples (see the *Other significance tests*, page 1456). The outcome of this test depends not only on the size of the raw difference between the two coefficients but also on the size of the samples and on the size of the coefficients themselves. Consistent with the previously discussed principle, the larger the sample size, the smaller the effect that can be proven significant in that sample. In general, due to the fact that the reliability of the correlation coefficient increases with its absolute value, relatively small differences between large correlation coefficients can be significant. For example, a difference of .10 between two correlations may not be significant if the two coefficients are .15 and .25, although in the same

sample, the same difference of .10 can be significant if the two coefficients are .80 and .90.

Other correlation coefficients. There are many other types of correlation coefficients, and they are included in other modules of *STATISTICA*. A variety of *nonparametric* correlations are included in the *Nonparametrics and Distributions* module; such correlation coefficients are also computed by the *Crosstabulation Tables* procedure of this module (page 1446), *partial correlations* are included in the *Multiple Regression* module, various *autocorrelations* (i.e., correlations between a variable and itself lagged by a specified lag) are included in the *Time Series and Forecasting* module (other, more specialized measures of relations between variables or groups of variables are included in many other modules). Options to compute standard (Pearson product-moment) correlations are also available in many other modules (e.g., *Multiple Regression, Factor Analysis, Data Management/Megafile Manager*). Tetrachoric correlations can be calculated in the *Reliability/Item Analysis* module. Various measures of distances can be computed in the *Cluster Analysis* module, and measures of relations between categorical (nominal) variables are available in the *Crosstabulation* procedure of the *Basic Statistics and Tables* module (see page 1540). Finally, as mentioned before, there are advanced methods for analyzing correlation matrices in terms of hypothesized patterns of (causal) relations between variables (see *Structural Equation Modeling and Path Analysis, SEPATH*, Volume III).

t-Test for Independent Samples

Overview

Purpose, assumptions. The *t*-test is the most commonly used method to evaluate the differences in means between two groups. For example, the *t*-test can be used to test for a difference in test scores between a group of patients who were given a drug and a control group who received a placebo. Theoretically, the *t*-test can be used even if the sample sizes are very small (e.g., as small as 10; some researchers claim that even smaller *n*'s are acceptable), as long as the variables are normally distributed (within the groups) and the variation of scores in the two groups is not reliably different (see also *Elementary Concepts*, Chapter 8).

As mentioned before, the normality assumption can be evaluated by looking at the distribution of the data (via histograms) or by performing a normality test (via the *Descriptive Statistics* procedure, see page 1500). The equality of variances assumption can be verified with the *F* test (which is included in the *t*-test output), or you can use the more robust *Levene's test* procedure. If these conditions are not met, then you can evaluate the differences in means between two groups using one of the nonparametric alternatives to the *t*-test (see *Nonparametrics and Distributions*, Chapter 11).

The *p*-level reported with a *t*-test represents the probability of error involved in accepting the research hypothesis about the existence of a difference. Technically speaking, this is the probability of error associated with rejecting the hypothesis of no difference between the two categories of observations (corresponding to the groups) in the population when, in fact, the hypothesis is true.

Some researchers suggest that if the difference is in the predicted direction, you can consider only one half (one "tail") of the probability distribution and thus divide the standard *p*-level reported with a *t*-test (a "two-tailed" probability) by two. Others, however, suggest that you should always report the standard, two-tailed *t*-test probability. For more information, see the textbooks recommended on page 1429.

Arrangement of data. In order to perform the *t*-test for independent samples, one independent (*grouping*) variable (e.g., *Gender*: *male/female*) and

at least one dependent variable (e.g., a test score) are required. The means of the dependent variable will be compared between selected groups based on the specified values (*grouping codes*, e.g., *male* and *female*) of the independent variable.

The following data set can be analyzed with a *t*-test comparing the average *WCC* score in *males* and *females*.

```
          GENDER  WCC
          ------  ---
case 1     male   111
case 2     male   110
case 3     male   109
case 4   female   102
case 5   female   104
-------------------------------
      mean WCC in males   = 110
      mean WCC in females = 103
```

If you specified not one, but a list of dependent variables, then a series of *t*-tests will be performed (one for each dependent variable).

Alternative arrangement of data. Sometimes, the data are already arranged (e.g., as in a spreadsheet) such that each column or variable in the file represents one group:

```
         Male  Female
         ----  ------
case 1   111    102
case 2   110    104
case 3   109
```

Note: in this nonstandard arrangement of data, all scores represent the same variable *WCC*.

Note that the *Independent t-test* procedure of the *Basic Statistics and Tables* module can also compute *t*-tests for data arranged in this manner. However, it should be stressed that this arrangement is atypical and generally not recommended when creating large data files. Practically all data analysis software, including *STATISTICA*, usually assumes data to be arranged as shown earlier. The earlier arrangement allows you to identify each individual respondent or subject in the data file; thus, when there are multiple dependent variables of interest, various multivariate methods can be applied which rely on the (within-group) correlation matrices of variables.

***t*-test graphs.** In the *t*-test analysis, comparisons of means and measures of variation in the two groups can be visualized in *box and whisker* plots that can be called directly from the results Scrollsheet by simply pointing to a selected *t*-test (using cursor keys or the mouse).

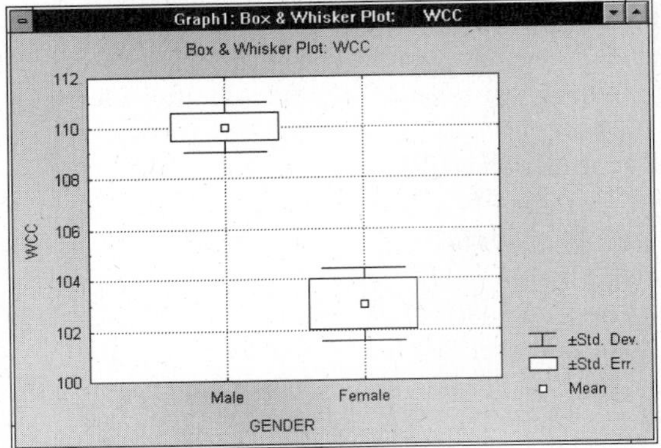

Various graphs of the distribution of scores by group can also be requested directly from the *t-test for independent samples* dialog. These graphs help you to quickly evaluate and "intuitively visualize" the strength of the relation between the grouping and dependent variable.

More complex group comparisons. It often happens in research practice that you need to compare more than two groups (e.g., *drug 1*, *drug 2*, and *placebo*), or compare groups created by more than one independent variable while controlling for the separate influence of each of them (e.g., *Gender*, type of *Drug*, and size of *Dose*). In these cases, you need to analyze the data using *Analysis of Variance* (see *ANOVA/MANOVA*, Chapter 13), which can be considered to be a generalization of the *t*-test. In fact, for a single-factor two group comparison, ANOVA will give results identical to a *t*-test [$t^2(df) = F(1,df)$]. However, when the design is more complex, ANOVA offers numerous advantages that *t*-tests cannot provide (even if you run a series of *t*-tests comparing various cells of the design, see Chapter 13).

Also, there are advanced methods for comparing groups in terms of means, variances, and covariances of underlying constructs which are

defined by multiple measurements. Refer to the *Structural Equation Modeling and Path Analysis (SEPATH)* module for details (Volume III).

t-Test for Dependent Samples

Overview

Within-group variation. As explained before (see *Elementary Concepts*, Chapter 8), the size of a relation between two variables, such as the one measured by a difference in means between two groups, depends to a large extent on the differentiation of values *within* the group. Depending on how differentiated the values are in each group, a given "raw difference" in group means will indicate either a stronger or weaker relationship between the independent (*grouping*) and dependent variable.

For example, if the mean *WCC* (White Cell Count) was 102 in males and 104 in females, then this difference of "only" 2 points would be extremely important if all values for males fell within a range of 101 to 103, and all scores for females fell within a range of 103 to 105; for example, you would be able to predict *WCC* pretty well based on gender. However, if the same difference of 2 was obtained from very differentiated scores (e.g., if their range was 0-200), then you would consider the difference entirely negligible. That is to say, reduction of the *within-group variation* increases the sensitivity of the test.

Purpose. The *t*-test for dependent samples helps you to take advantage of one specific type of design in which an important source of *within-group variation* (or *error*) can be easily identified and excluded from the analysis. Specifically, if two groups of observations (that are to be compared) are based on the same sample of cases (subjects) who were tested *twice* (e.g., *before* and *after* a treatment), then a considerable part of the within-group variation in both groups of scores can be attributed to the initial individual differences between subjects. Note that, in a sense, this fact is not much different than in cases when the two groups are entirely independent (see *t*-test for independent samples, page 1439), where individual differences also contribute to the *error variance*; but in the case of independent samples, you cannot do anything about it because you cannot identify (or "subtract") the variation due to individual differences in subjects. However, if the same sample is tested twice, then you can easily identify (or "subtract") this variation. Specifically, instead of treating each group separately and analyzing raw scores, you can look only at the differences between the two measures (e.g., "pre-test" and "post test") in each subject. By subtracting the first score from the second for each subject and then analyzing only those "pure (paired) differences," you will exclude the entire part of the variation in your data set that results from unequal base levels of individual subjects. This is precisely what is being done in the *t*-test for dependent samples, and, as compared to the *t*-test for independent samples, it always produces "better" results (i.e., it is always more sensitive).

Assumptions. The theoretical assumptions of the *t*-test for independent samples (see page 1439) also apply to the dependent samples test; that is, the paired differences should be normally distributed. If these assumptions are clearly not met, then one of the nonparametric alternative tests should be used (see the *Nonparametrics and Distributions* module).

Arrangement of data. Technically, you can apply the *t*-test for dependent samples to any two variables in the data set and the selection of variables is identical to that used for correlations (see *Correlation Matrices*, page 1512). However, applying this test will make very little sense if the values of the two variables in the data set are not logically and methodologically comparable. For example, if you compare the average *WCC* in a sample of patients before and after a treatment, but using a different counting method or different units

in the second measurement, then a highly significant *t*-test value could be obtained due to an artifact, that is, to the change of units of measurement. The following example data set can be analyzed using the *t*-test for dependent samples.

```
          WCC     WCC
        before   after
        ------   -----
case 1   111.9     113
case 2     109     110
case 3     143     144
case 4     101     102
case 5      80      80.9
...        ...     ...
----------------------------
   average change between WCC
   "before" and "after" = 1
```

The average difference between the two conditions is relatively small (*d=1*) as compared to the differentiation (range) of the raw scores (from 80 to 143, in the first sample). However, the *t*-test for dependent samples analysis is performed only on the paired differences, "ignoring" the raw scores and their potential differentiation. Thus, the size of this particular difference of *1* will be compared not to the differentiation of raw scores but to the differentiation of the *individual difference scores*, which is relatively small: *0.2* (from *0.9* in case number 5 to *1.1* in case number 1). Compared to that variability, the difference of *1* is extremely large and can yield a highly significant *t* value.

Matrices of *t*-tests. *t*-tests for dependent samples can be calculated for long lists of variables, and reviewed in the form of matrices produced with *casewise* or *pairwise* deletion of missing data, much like the correlation matrices option (see page 1512). Thus, the precautions discussed in the context of correlations also apply to *t*-test matrices; see: (a) the issue of artifacts caused by the pairwise deletion of missing data in *t*-tests (page 1436), and (b) the issue of "randomly" significant test values (page 1436).

More complex group comparisons. If there are more than two "correlated samples" (e.g., *before treatment*, *after treatment 1*, and *after treatment 2*), then analysis of variance with *repeated measures* should be used. The repeated measures ANOVA can be considered to be a generalization of the *t*-test for dependent samples and it offers various advantages that increase the overall sensitivity of the analysis.

For example, it can simultaneously control not only for the base level of the dependent variable, but it can control for other factors and/or include in the design more than one interrelated dependent variable (MANOVA; for additional details refer to *ANOVA/MANOVA*, Chapter 13).

Also, there are advanced methods for comparing dependent samples in terms of means, variances, and covariances of underlying constructs which are defined by multiple measurements. Refer to the *Structural Equation Modeling and Path Analysis, (SEPATH)* module for details (Volume III).

Descriptive Statistics and Correlations by Groups - Breakdown

Overview

Purpose. The breakdowns program calculates descriptive statistics and correlations for *dependent* variables in each of a number of groups defined by one or more *grouping* (*independent*) variables. The concept of *grouping* or *coding* variables is also explained in the *Data Management* chapter (see Chapter 7).

Arrangement of data. In the following example data set, the dependent variable *WCC* (White Cell Count) can be broken down by 2 *independent* variables: *Gender* (values: *males* and *females*), and *Height* (values: *tall* and *short*).

```
        GENDER   HEIGHT   WCC
        ------   ------   ---
case 1    male    short   101
case 2    male     tall   110
case 3    male     tall    92
case 4  female     tall   112
case 5  female    short    95
     .       .        .     .
     .       .        .     .
```

The resulting breakdowns might look as follows (assuming that *Gender* was specified as the first independent variable, and *Height* as the second).

```
                Entire
                sample
                Mean=100
                SD=13
                N=120
      ------------------------------
      All males               All females
      Mean=99                 Mean=101
      SD=13                   SD=13
      N=60                    N=60
-----------------    ------------------
Tall/     Short/     Tall/      Short/
males     males      females    females
Mean=98   Mean=100   Mean=101   Mean=101
SD=13     SD=13      SD=13      SD=13
N=30      N=30       N=30       N=30
```

The composition of the "intermediate" level cells of the "breakdown tree" depends on the order in which independent variables are arranged. For example, in the above example, you see the means for "all males" and "all females" but you do not see the means for "all tall subjects" and "all short subjects" which would have been produced had you specified independent variable *Height* as the first grouping variable rather than the second.

Thus, ideally, in a breakdown program you should have an option to easily "reorder" independent variables and thus see different "cross-sections" of the data. The *Basic Statistics and Tables* module gives you not only the option to reorder the variables in the table, but it also allows you to compute any marginal table in which you may be interested. For example, you could easily compute the means for *Tall* and *Short* individuals.

Statistical tests in breakdowns. Breakdowns are typically used as an exploratory data analysis technique; the typical question that this technique can help answer is very simple: Are the groups created by the independent variables different regarding the dependent variable? If you are interested in differences concerning the means, then the appropriate test is the breakdowns one-way ANOVA (*F test*). If you are interested in variation differences, then you should test for homogeneity of variances. The *STATISTICA* breakdowns procedure offers the *Levene's test* of homogeneity of variance (this test has practically replaced the older and less robust *Bartlett test* and *Chi-square* test; note that a comprehensive selection of univariate and multivariate tests is also offered in the *ANOVA/MANOVA* module).

Other related data analysis techniques. Although for exploratory data analysis, breakdowns can use more than one independent (i.e., grouping) variable, the statistical procedures in breakdowns assume the existence of a single grouping factor (even if, in fact, the breakdown results from a combination of a number of grouping variables). Thus, those statistics do not reveal or even take into account any possible *interactions* between grouping variables in the design.

For example, there could be differences between the influence of one independent variable on the dependent variable at different levels of another independent variable (e.g., tall people could have lower *WCC* than short ones, but only if they are males; see the "tree" data above). You can explore such effects by examining breakdowns "visually" (in Scrollsheets and graphs) using different orders of independent variables, but the magnitude or significance of such effects cannot be estimated by the breakdown statistics (use the *ANOVA/MANOVA* module, see Chapter 13).

***Post hoc* comparison of means.** The breakdowns facility in the *Basic Statistics and Tables* module also offers all common *post hoc* tests for means comparisons. Usually, after obtaining a statistically significant *F* test from the ANOVA, one wants to know which of the means contributed to the effect (i.e., which groups are particularly different from each other). One could of course perform a series of simple *t*-tests to compare all possible pairs of means. However, as explained before, due to a potentially large number of comparisons, such a procedure would *capitalize on chance*. This means that the reported probability levels would actually overestimate the statistical significance of mean

differences. Without going into much detail, suppose you took 20 samples of 10 random numbers each, and computed 20 means. Now compare all means (i.e., perform 180 comparisons). You can expect to obtain approximately 9 differences which are significant at the 5% (1/20) level partly based on chance (see *Elementary Concepts*, Chapter 8). Then, take the group (sample) with the highest mean and compare it with that of the lowest mean. The *t*-test for independent samples will test whether or not those two means are significantly different from each other, *provided they were the only two samples taken*, and the difference will most likely be very significant. *Post hoc* comparison techniques on the other hand, specifically take into account the fact that more than two samples were taken (one can say that they involve "corrections for the number of comparisons").

The *ANOVA/MANOVA* module. The *ANOVA-/MANOVA* module offers other, more sophisticated tests to evaluate the differences between groups created by a number of independent (*grouping*) variables, such as descriptive statistics for more than one dependent variable, correlations between several dependent variables in each group, etc.

Breakdowns - Correlations by groups. In addition to obtaining the descriptive statistics by groups, the breakdowns facility in the *Basic Statistics and Tables* module also provides an option to compute within-group correlations in order to observe differences between patterns of correlations in groups. This procedure also offers options (via the *Options* button) to compute covariances and significance levels within groups as well as pairwise *n*, means, and standard deviations.

For example, using the *Correlation* facility in the *Basic Statistics and Tables* module, you can obtain a correlation of *.07* between two variables *WCC* and *Cholest*. However, in order to obtain more detailed information about the relationship between the variables, you can use the *Breakdowns & one-way ANOVA* procedure to compute the correlation between these two variables within the grouping variable *Gender* (e.g., in *male* subjects $r = .54$ and in *female* subjects $r = -.25$).

Breakdowns vs. discriminant function analysis. Breakdowns can be considered as a first step toward another type of analysis that explores differences between groups: *Discriminant function analysis* (see Volume III). Similar to breakdowns, discriminant function analysis explores the differences between groups created by values (group codes) of an independent (*grouping*) variable. However, unlike breakdowns, discriminant function analysis simultaneously analyzes more than one dependent variable and it identifies "patterns" of values of those dependent variables. Technically, it determines a linear combination of the dependent variables that best predicts the group membership.

For example, discriminant function analysis can be used to analyze differences between three groups of persons who have chosen different professions (e.g., lawyers, physicians, and engineers) in terms of various aspects of their scholastic performance in high school. One could claim that such analysis could "explain" the choice of a profession in terms of specific talents shown in high school; thus discriminant function analysis can be considered to be an "exploratory extension" of simple breakdowns. For more details concerning this procedure refer to the *Discriminant Analysis* module (see Volume III).

Breakdowns vs. frequency tables. Another related type of analysis that cannot be directly performed with breakdowns is comparisons of frequencies of cases (*n*'s) between groups. Specifically, often the *n*'s in individual cells are not equal because the assignment of subjects to those groups typically results not from an experimenter's manipulation, but from subjects' pre-existing dispositions. If, in spite of the random selection of the entire sample, the *n*'s are unequal, then it may suggest that the independent variables are related.

For example, crosstabulating levels of independent variables *Age* and *Education* most likely would not create groups of equal *n*, because education is distributed differently in different age groups. If you are interested in such comparisons, you can explore specific frequencies in the breakdowns tables, trying different orders of independent variables. However, in order to subject such differences to statistical tests, you should use the *Crosstabulation Tables* procedure which offers a variety of ways for examining crosstabulations and frequency tables, or the *Log-Linear* module (for more advanced analyses on multi-way frequency tables, see Volume III).

Graphical breakdowns. Graphs can often identify effects (both expected and unexpected) in the data more quickly and sometimes "better" than any other data analysis method. The *Results* dialog of the *Breakdown* procedure (page 1522) offers numerous graphics options to plot the means, distributions, correlations, etc. across the groups of the respective table (e.g., categorized histograms, categorized probability plots, categorized box and whisker plots).

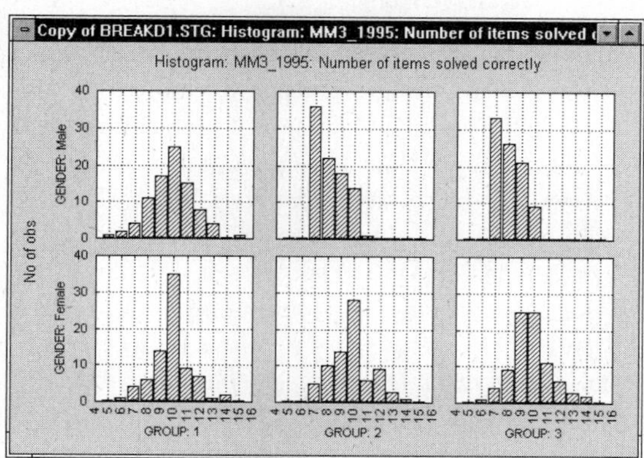

The *categorized scatterplots* option can also show differences between patterns of correlations between dependent variables across the selected groups defined by the grouping variable.

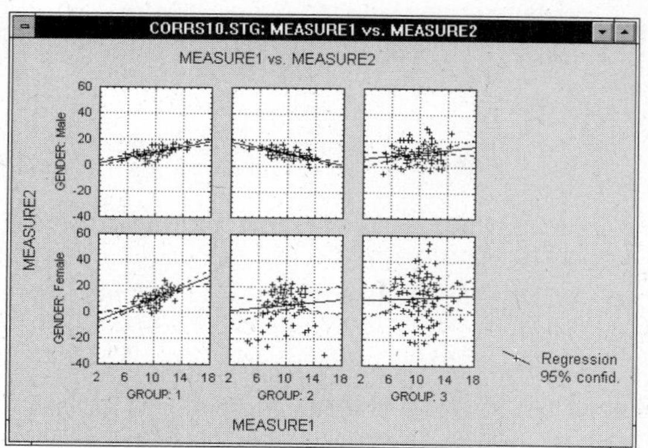

Note that more categorized graph options are available via the *Stats Graphs* procedures from the *Graphs* pull-down menu.

Path analysis for categorized data. There are advanced methods for comparing two or more groups in terms of means, variances, and covariances of variables and underlying constructs which are defined by multiple measurements. Hypotheses about the "structure" of the relationships between variables in different groups can also be tested with those methods. Refer to the *Structural Equation Modeling and Path Analysis (SEPATH)* module for details (Volume III).

Frequency Tables

Overview

Purpose. Frequency or one-way tables represent the simplest method for analyzing categorical (nominal) data (refer to *Elementary Concepts*, Chapter 8). They are often used as one of the exploratory procedures to review how different categories of values are distributed in the sample. For example, in a survey of spectator interest in different sports, you could summarize the respondents' interest in watching football in a frequency table as follows:

FOOTBALL: "Watching football" (sports.sta)

BASIC STATS	Count	Cumul. Count	Percent	Cumul. Percent
ALWAYS	39	39	39.00000	39.0000
USUALLY	16	55	16.00000	55.0000
SOMETIMS	26	81	26.00000	81.0000
NEVER	19	100	19.00000	100.0000
Missing	0	100	0.00000	100.0000

The table above shows the number, proportion, and cumulative proportion of respondents who characterized their interest in watching football as either (1) *Always interested*, (2) *Usually interested*, (3) *Sometimes interested*, or (4) *Never interested*. Of course, *STATISTICA* provides numerous options to specify the descriptive categories used in the frequency tables (e.g., "all distinctive values," intervals, user-defined subset definitions, and many others). Also, a variety of graphics options are available to visualize the distribution of the data (see the *Frequency Tables* dialog, page 1534).

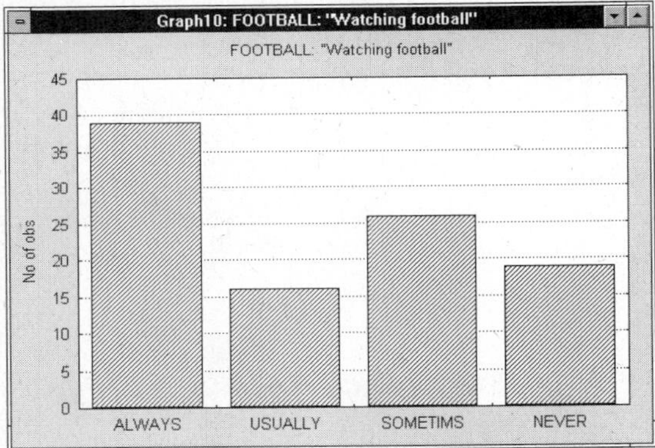

Arrangement of data. Any variable in a data set can be analyzed and presented in frequency tables. In addition to tabulation by integer codes, the user can also enter specific codes for the table, specify intervals for the frequency table, and even specify a set of (arbitrary) logical conditions which will assign specific cases to categories.

Applications. In practically every research project, a first "look" at the data usually includes frequency tables. For example, in survey research, frequency tables can show the number of males and females who participated in the survey, the number of respondents from particular ethnic and racial backgrounds, and so on. Responses on some labeled attitude measurement scales (e.g., interest in watching football) can also be nicely summarized via the frequency table. In medical research, one may tabulate the number of patients displaying specific symptoms; in industrial research one may tabulate the frequency of different causes leading to catastrophic failure of products during stress tests (e.g., which parts are actually responsible for the complete malfunction of television sets under extreme temperatures?). Customarily, if a data set includes any categorical data, then one of the first steps in the data analysis is to compute a frequency table for those categorical variables.

Crosstabulation and Stub-and-Banner Tables (Overview)

Description of Joint Frequency Distributions via Crosstabulations

Purpose and arrangement of data. Crosstabulation is a combination of two (or more) frequency tables arranged such that each cell in the resulting table represents a unique combination of specific values of crosstabulated variables. Thus, crosstabulation allows you to examine frequencies of observations that belong to specific categories on more than one variable. By examining these frequencies, you can identify relations between crosstabulated variables. Usually, only categorical (nominal) variables or variables with a relatively small number of different meaningful values should be crosstabulated. Note that in the cases where you *do* want to include a continuous variable in a crosstabulation (e.g., income), you can first *recode* it into a particular number of distinct ranges (e.g., low, medium, high; see *Toolbars and Status Bar*, Chapter 2; see also Chapter 3).

2 by 2 table. The simplest form of crosstabulation is the 2 by 2 table where two variables are "crossed," and each variable has only two distinct values. For example, suppose you conduct a simple study in which males and females are asked to choose one of two different brands of soda pop (brand *A* and brand *B*); the data file can be arranged like this:

```
          GENDER   SODA
          ------   ----
case 1      MALE     A
case 2    FEMALE     B
case 3    FEMALE     B
case 4    FEMALE     A
case 4      MALE     B
     .         .     .
     .         .     .
```

The resulting crosstabulation could look as follows.

	SODA:A	SODA:B	
GENDER: MALE	20(40%)	30(60%)	50 (50%)
GENDER: FEMALE	30(60%)	20(40%)	50 (50%)
	50(50%)	50(50%)	100(100%)

Each cell represents a unique combination of values of the two crosstabulated variables (row variable *Gender* and column variable *Soda*), and the numbers in each cell tell how many observations fall into each combination of values. In general, this table shows that more females than males chose the soda pop brand *A*, and that more males than females chose soda *B*. Thus, gender and preference for a particular brand of soda may be related (later you will see how this relationship can be measured).

Marginal frequencies. The values in the margins of the table are simply one-way (frequency) tables for all values in the table. They are important in that they help to evaluate the arrangement of frequencies in individual columns or rows. For example, the frequencies of 40% and 60% of males and females (respectively) who chose soda *A* (see the first column of the above table), would not indicate any relationship between *Gender* and *Soda* if the marginal frequencies for *Gender* were also 40% and 60%; in that case they would simply reflect the different proportions of males and females in the study. Thus, the differences between the distributions of frequencies in individual rows (or columns) and in the respective margins informs you about the relationship between the crosstabulated variables.

Column, row, and total percentages. The example in the previous paragraph demonstrates that in order to evaluate relationships between crosstabulated variables, you need to compare the proportions of marginal and individual column or row frequencies. Such comparisons are easiest to perform when the frequencies are presented as percentages.

The *Crosstabulation* procedure allows you to display the crosstabulated frequencies in Scrollsheets, along with counts, column percentages, row percentages, and total percentages.

Summary Frequency Table (cross.sta

BASIC STATS GENDER	Table Gender(2) x Soda(2) SODA A	SODA B	Row Totals
Male	20	30	50
Row %	40.00%	60.00%	
Female	30	20	50
Row %	60.00%	40.00%	
All Grps	50	50	100

A combined summary table where each cell in the table contains all of those numbers can also be produced.

Summary Frequency Table (cross.sta

BASIC STATS GENDER	Table Gender(2) x Soda(2) SODA A	SODA B	Row Totals
Male	20	30	50
Column %	40.00%	60.00%	
Row %	40.00%	60.00%	
Total %	20.00%	30.00%	50.00%
Female	30	20	50
Column %	60.00%	40.00%	
Row %	60.00%	40.00%	
Total %	30.00%	20.00%	50.00%
All Grps	50	50	100
Total %	50.00%	50.00%	

Graphical representations of crosstabulation. For analytic purposes, the individual rows or columns of a table can be represented as column graphs. However, often it is useful to visualize the entire table in a single graph. There are several

ways to do this via the *Crosstabulation Tables* procedure. A two-way table can be visualized in a *3-dimensional histogram.*

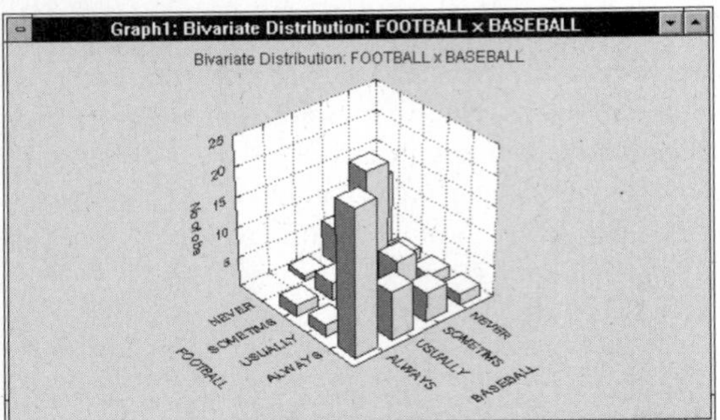

Alternatively, a *categorized histogram* can be produced, where one variable is represented by individual histograms which are drawn at each level (category) of the other variable in the crosstabulation (see below).

The advantage of the 3D histogram is that it produces an integrated picture of the entire table; the advantage of the categorized graph is that it allows you to precisely evaluate specific frequencies in each cell of the table.

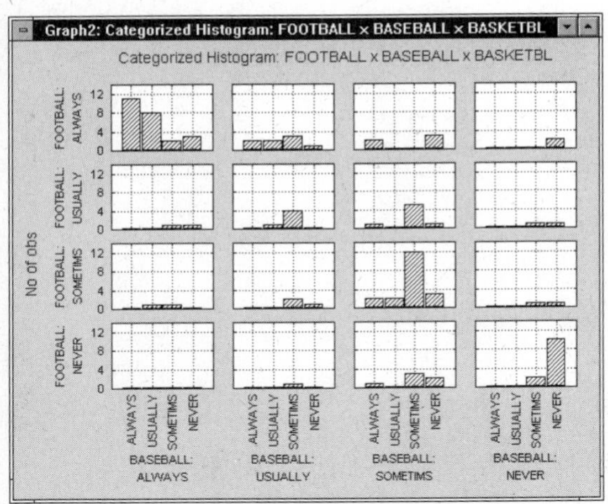

Refer to the *Crosstabulation Results* dialog (page 1542) for a complete overview of available graphics procedures. Note that when more than one table is specified, selecting one of the graphing options will produce a "cascade" of graphs for each table.

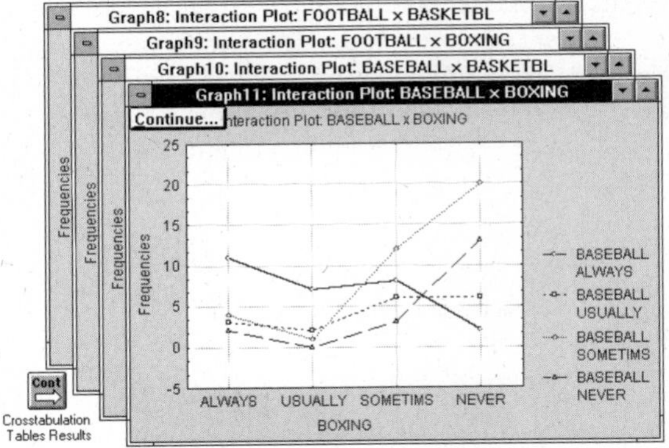

Pressing the *Continue* button (see the upper-left corner of the graph shown above) will continue the display of the sequence of graphs. Pressing the "floating" *Cont* (continue) button with the name of the dialog from which the sequence of graphs was called (see the lower-left corner of the display shown above) will interrupt the sequential display of the graphs.

Stub-and-Banner Tables

Stub-and-Banner tables, or *Banners* for short, are a way to display several two-way tables in a compressed form. This type of table is most easily explained with an illustration using the survey of sports spectators data file.

Summary Stub-and-Banner Table (sports.sta)

BASIC STATS FOOTBALL: "Watching football"	3 two-way tables BASEBALL ALWAYS	BASEBALL USUALLY	BASEBALL SOMETIMS	BASEBALL NEVER	Row Total
ALWAYS : Always interested	24	8	5	2	39
Column Percent	85.71%	47.06%	13.51%	11.11%	
USUALLY : Usually interested	2	5	7	2	16
Column Percent	7.14%	29.41%	18.92%	11.11%	
SOMETIMS: Sometimes interested	2	3	19	2	26
Column Percent	7.14%	17.65%	51.35%	11.11%	
NEVER : Never interested	0	1	6	12	19
Column Percent	0.00%	5.88%	16.22%	66.67%	
Total	28	17	37	18	100

Interpreting the banner table. The Scrollsheet above shows the two-way tables of expressed interest in *Football* by expressed interest in

Baseball, *Tennis*, and *Boxing*. The table entries represent percentages of columns, so that the percentages across rows will add up to 100 percent. For example, the number in the upper left hand corner of the Scrollsheet (*85.71*) shows that 85.71 percent of all respondents who said they are *always interested* in watching football also said that they were *always interested* in watching baseball. If you scroll the Scrollsheet further to the right, you can see that the percent of those *always interested* in watching football who were also *always interested* in watching tennis was 38.46 percent; for boxing this number is 70.0 percent.

Summary Stub-and-Banner Table (sports.sta)

BASIC STATS FOOTBALL: "Watching football"	3 two-way tables BOXING ALWAYS	BOXING USUALLY	BOXING SOMETIMS	BOXING NEVER	Row Total
ALWAYS : Always interested	14	7	12	6	39
Column Percent	70.00%	70.00%	41.38%	14.63%	
USUALLY : Usually interested	2	1	8	5	16
Column Percent	10.00%	10.00%	27.59%	12.20%	
SOMETIMS: Sometimes interested	2	1	6	17	26
Column Percent	10.00%	10.00%	20.69%	41.46%	
NEVER : Never interested	2	1	3	13	19
Column Percent	10.00%	10.00%	10.34%	31.71%	
Total	20	10	29	41	100

The percentages in the column shown after each set of variables (*Row Total*) are always relative to the total number of cases. There are many procedures in the *Crosstabulation Results* dialog that will allow you to produce different formats of banner tables; for example, you can simultaneously display the cell counts, row, column, and total percentages in the same table.

Summary Stub-and-Banner Table (sports.sta)

BASIC STATS FOOTBALL: "Watching football"	3 two-way tables TENNIS ALWAYS	TENNIS USUALLY	TENNIS SOMETIMS	TENNIS NEVER	Row Total
ALWAYS : Always interested	5	5	12	17	39
Column Percent	38.46%	35.71%	31.58%	48.57%	
Row Percent	12.82%	12.82%	30.77%	43.59%	
Table Percent	5.00%	5.00%	12.00%	17.00%	39.00%
USUALLY : Usually interested	4	2	8	2	16
Column Percent	30.77%	14.29%	21.05%	5.71%	
Row Percent	25.00%	12.50%	50.00%	12.50%	
Table Percent	4.00%	2.00%	8.00%	2.00%	16.00%
SOMETIMS: Sometimes interested	2	5	13	6	26
Column Percent	15.38%	35.71%	34.21%	17.14%	
Row Percent	7.69%	19.23%	50.00%	23.08%	
Table Percent	2.00%	5.00%	13.00%	6.00%	26.00%
NEVER : Never interested	2	2	5	10	19
Column Percent	15.38%	14.29%	13.16%	28.57%	
Row Percent	10.53%	10.53%	26.32%	52.63%	
Table Percent	2.00%	2.00%	5.00%	10.00%	19.00%
Total	13	14	38	35	100
Table Percent	13.00%	14.00%	38.00%	35.00%	100.00%

Multi-way tables with control variables. When only two variables are crosstabulated, the resulting table is called a *two-way* table. However, the general idea of crosstabulating values of variables can be generalized to more than just two variables. For example, to return to the "soda" example presented earlier (see above), a third variable could be added to the data set. This variable might contain information about the state in which the study was conducted (either *Nebraska* or *New York*).

```
        GENDER  SODA     STATE
------  ------  ----  --------
case 1    MALE     A  NEBRASKA
case 2  FEMALE     B  NEW YORK
case 3  FEMALE     B  NEBRASKA
case 4  FEMALE     A  NEBRASKA
case 5    MALE     B  NEW YORK
  .        .       .         .
  .        .       .         .
```

The crosstabulation of these variables would result in a 3-way table:

	STATE: NEW YORK SODA: A	STATE: NEW YORK SODA: B		STATE: NEBRASKA SODA: A	STATE: NEBRASKA SODA: B	
G:MALE	20	30	50	5	45	50
G:FEMALE	30	20	50	45	5	50
	50	50	100	50	50	100

Theoretically, an unlimited number of variables can be crosstabulated in a single multi-way table. However, research practice shows that it is usually difficult to examine and "understand" tables that involve more than 4 variables. (Even though the *Crosstabulation* procedure will produce tables of much greater complexity, it is recommended to analyze relationships between the factors in such tables using modeling techniques such as *Log-Linear Analysis*, Volume III.)

Graphical representations of multi-way tables. As with all analyses in *STATISTICA*, there are numerous graphics procedures available to aid in the interpretation of tables. You can produce "double categorized" histograms, 3D histograms, or line-plots that will summarize the frequencies for up

to 3 factors in a single graph, batches (cascades) of graphs are produced to summarize higher-way tables. Refer to the *Crosstabulation Results* dialog (page 1542) for further descriptions of these graphics procedures.

Statistics in Crosstabulations

Overview

Crosstabulations generally allow you to identify relationships between the crosstabulated variables. The following table illustrates an example of a very strong relationship between two variables: variable *Age* (*Adult* vs. *Child*) and variable *Cookie* preference (*A* vs. *B*).

	COOKIE: A	COOKIE: B	
AGE: ADULT	50	0	50
AGE: CHILD	0	50	50
	50	50	100

All adults chose cookie *A*, while all children chose cookie *B*. In this case there is little doubt about the reliability of the finding, because it is hardly conceivable that one would obtain such a pattern of frequencies by chance alone; that is, without the existence of a "true" difference between the cookie preferences of adults and children. However, in real-life, relations between variables are typically much weaker, and thus the question arises as to how to measure those relationships, and how to evaluate their reliability (statistical significance).

The following review includes the most common measures of relationships between *two* categorical variables; that is, measures for two-way tables. The techniques used to analyze simultaneous relations between *more than two* variables in higher-order crosstabulations are discussed in the context of the *Log-Linear Analysis* module (see Volume III).

In the *Basic Statistics and Tables* module, crosstabulation tables with up to 6 variables (6-way tables) can be generated automatically. Higher-way tables of practically unlimited order can be produced using the case selection conditions (see Chapter 3). All measures of relations between crosstabulated variables are reported for two-way tables, even if they represent only "slices" of a larger multi-way table (see the description of the *Crosstabulation Results* dialog, page 1542).

Pearson *Chi-square*. The Pearson *Chi-square* is the most common test for significance of the relationship between categorical variables. This measure is based on the fact that the *expected* frequencies in a two-way table (i.e., frequencies that you would *expect* if there was no relationship between the variables) can be computed.

For example, suppose you ask 20 males and 20 females to choose between two brands of soda pop (brands *A* and *B*). If there is no relationship between preference and gender, then you would *expect* about an equal number of choices of brand *A* and brand *B* for each sex. The *Chi-square* test becomes increasingly significant as the numbers deviate further from this expected pattern, that is, the more this pattern of choices for males and females differs.

The value of the *Chi-square* and its significance level depends on the overall number of observations and the number of cells in the table. Consistent with the principles discussed in *Elementary Concepts* (Chapter 8), relatively small deviations of the relative frequencies across cells from the expected pattern will prove significant if the number of observations is large.

The only assumption underlying the use of the *Chi-square* (other than random selection of the sample) is that the expected frequencies are not very small. The reason for this is that, actually, the *Chi-square* inherently tests the underlying *probabilities* in each cell; and when the expected cell frequencies fall, for example, below 5, those probabilities cannot be estimated with sufficient precision. For further discussion of this issue refer to Everitt (1977), Hays (1988), or Kendall and Stuart (1979).

Maximum Likelihood (M-L) *Chi-square*. The *Maximum Likelihood Chi-square* tests the same hypothesis as the Pearson *Chi-square* statistic; however, its computation is based on Maximum Likelihood theory. In practice, the M-L *Chi-square* is usually very close in magnitude to the Pearson *Chi-square* statistic. For more details about this statistic refer to Bishop, Fienberg, and Holland (1975), or Fienberg (1977); the *Log-Linear Analysis* chapter (Volume III) also discusses this statistic in greater detail.

Yates' correction. The approximation of the *Chi-square* statistic in small 2 x 2 tables can be improved by reducing the absolute value of differences between expected and observed frequencies by 0.5 before squaring (*Yates correction*). Yates' correction, which makes the estimation more conservative, is usually applied when the table contains only small observed frequencies, so that some expected frequencies become less than 10 (for further discussion of this correction, see Conover, 1974; Everitt, 1977; Hays, 1988; Kendall and Stuart, 1979; and Mantel, 1974).

Fisher exact test. This test is only available for 2 x 2 tables; it is based on the following rationale: Given the marginal frequencies in the table, and assuming that in the population the two factors in the table are not related, how likely is it to obtain cell frequencies as uneven or worse than the ones that were observed? For small *n*, this probability can be computed *exactly* by counting all possible tables that can be constructed based on the marginal frequencies. Thus, the Fisher exact test computes the *exact* probability under the null hypothesis of obtaining the current distribution of frequencies across cells, or one that is more uneven. Both one-sided and two-sided probabilities are reported.

McNemar *Chi-square*. This test is applicable in situations where the frequencies in the 2 x 2 table represent *dependent* samples. For example, in a before-after design study, you may count the number of students who fail a test of minimal math skills at the beginning of the semester and at the end of the semester. Two *Chi-square* values are reported: *A/D* and *B/C*. The *Chi-square A/D* tests the hypothesis that the frequencies in cells *A* and *D* (upper left, lower right) are identical. The *Chi-square B/C* tests the hypothesis that the frequencies in cells *B* and *C* (upper right, lower left) are identical.

Coefficient *Phi*. The *Phi-square* is a measure of correlation between two categorical variables in a 2 x 2 table. Its value can range from *0* (no relation between factors; *Chi-square = 0.0*) to *1* (perfect relation between the two factors in the table). For more details concerning this statistic, see Castellan and Siegel (1988, page 232).

Tetrachoric correlation. This statistic is also only computed for (applicable to) 2 x 2 tables. If the 2 x 2 table can be thought of as the result of two continuous variables that were (artificially) forced into two categories each, then the tetrachoric correlation coefficient will estimate the correlation between the two.

Coefficient of contingency (*C*). The coefficient of contingency is a *Chi-square* based measure of the relation between two categorical variables (proposed by Pearson, the originator of the *Chi-square* test). Its advantage over the ordinary *Chi-square* is that it is more easily interpreted, since its range is always limited to *0* through *1* (where *0* means complete independence). The disadvantage of this statistic is that its specific upper limit is "limited" by the size of the table; *C* can reach the limit of 1 only if the number of categories is unlimited (see Siegel, 1956, page 201).

Interpretation of contingency measures. An important disadvantage of measures of contingency (reviewed above) is that they do not lend themselves to clear interpretations in terms of probability or "proportion of variance," as is the case, for example, of the Pearson *r* (see *Correlations*, page 1431). There is no commonly accepted measure of relation between categories that has such a clear interpretation.

Statistics Based on Ranks

In many cases the categories used in the crosstabulation contain meaningful rank-ordering information; that is, they measure some characteristic on an *ordinal* scale (see *Elementary Concepts*, Chapter 8). Suppose you asked a sample of respondents to indicate their interest in watching different sports on a 4-point scale with the explicit labels (1) *always*, (2) *usually*, (3) *sometimes*, and (4) *never interested*. Obviously, you can assume that the response *sometimes interested* is indicative of less interest than *always interested*, and so on.

Thus, you could rank the respondents with regard to their expressed interest in, for example, watching football. When categorical variables can be interpreted in this manner, there are several additional indices that can be computed to express the relationship between variables.

Spearman *R*. Spearman *R* can be interpreted in a way similar to the regular Pearson product-moment correlation coefficient (Pearson *r*), that is, in terms of the proportion of variability accounted for, except that Spearman *R* is computed from ranks. As mentioned above, Spearman *R* assumes that the variables under consideration were measured on at least an *ordinal* (rank order) scale; that is, the individual observations (cases) can be ranked into two ordered series. Detailed discussions of the Spearman *R* statistic, its power and efficiency can be found in Gibbons (1985), Hays (1981), McNemar (1969), Siegel (1956), Siegel and Castellan (1988), Kendall (1948), Olds (1949), or Hotelling and Pabst (1936). See also *Nonparametrics and Distributions* (Chapter 11).

Kendall *tau*. Kendall *tau* is equivalent to the Spearman *R* statistic with regard to the underlying assumptions. It is also comparable in terms of its statistical power. However, Spearman *R* and Kendall *tau* are usually not identical in magnitude because their underlying logic, as well as their computational formulas are very different. Siegel and Castellan (1988) express the relationship of the two measures in terms of the inequality:

```
-1 ≤ 3*Kendall tau - 2*Spearman R ≤ 1
```

More importantly, Kendall *tau* and Spearman *R* imply different interpretations: While Spearman *R* can be thought of as the regular Pearson product-moment correlation coefficient as computed from ranks, Kendall *tau* rather represents a *probability*. Specifically, it is the difference between the probability that the observed data are in the same order for the two variables *versus* the probability that the observed data are in different orders for the two variables. See also the *Nonparametrics and Distributions* module (Chapter 11).

Two different variants of *tau* are computed, usually called tau_b and tau_c. These measures differ only with regard as to how tied ranks are handled. In most cases these values will be fairly similar, and when discrepancies occur, it is probably always safest to interpret the lowest value. Kendall (1948, 1975), Everitt (1977), and Siegel and Castellan (1988) discuss Kendall's *tau* in greater detail.

Sommers' *d*: d(X|Y), d(Y|X). Sommers' *d* is an asymmetric measure of association related to tau_b (see Siegel and Castellan, 1988, page 303-310).

***Gamma*.** The *Gamma* statistic is preferable to Spearman *R* or Kendall *tau* when the data contain many tied observations. In terms of the underlying assumptions, *Gamma* is equivalent to Spearman *R* or Kendall *tau*; in terms of its interpretation and computation, it is more similar to Kendall *tau* than Spearman *R*.

In short, *Gamma* is also a *probability*; specifically, it is computed as the difference between the probability that the rank ordering of the two variables agree minus the probability that they disagree, divided by 1 minus the probability of ties. Thus, *Gamma* is basically equivalent to Kendall *tau*, except that ties are explicitly taken into account. Detailed discussions of the *Gamma* statistic can be

found in Goodman and Kruskal (1954, 1959, 1963, 1972), Siegel (1956), and Siegel and Castellan (1988). See also the *Nonparametrics and Distributions* module (Chapter 11).

Uncertainty coefficients: S(X,Y), S(X|Y), S(Y|X). These are indices of *stochastic dependence*; the concept of *stochastic dependence* is derived from the information theory approach to the analysis of frequency tables and the user should refer to the appropriate references (see Kullback, 1959; Ku and Kullback, 1968; Ku, Varner, and Kullback, 1971; see also Bishop, Fienberg, and Holland, 1975, page 344-348). *S(Y, X)* refers to symmetrical dependence, *S(X|Y)* and *S(Y|X)* refer to asymmetrical dependence.

Multiple Responses/Dichotomies

Overview

Technically speaking, multiple response variables or multiple dichotomies are analyzed in cases when the researcher is interested not only in "simple" frequencies of events but also in some (often unstructured) qualities of these events. A typical example of such analyses is summarizing survey data where some questions are at least partially open-ended and where respondents may list one or more selections from an unlimited list of possibilities. The nature of such variables or factors in a table is best illustrated with examples. The many specific procedures for tabulating such variables are discussed in the context of the *Multiple Responses/Dichotomies* dialog (see page 1546).

Multiple Response Variables

As part of a larger market survey, suppose you asked a sample of consumers to name their three favorite soft drinks. The specific item on the questionnaire may look like this:

```
Write down your three favorite soft drinks:
1:________     2:________     3:________
```

Thus, the questionnaires returned to you will contain somewhere between 0 and 3 answers to this item. Also, a wide variety of soft drinks will most likely be named. Your goal is to summarize the responses to this item, that is, to produce a table that summarizes the percent of respondents who mentioned a respective soft drink.

The next question is how to enter the responses into a data file. Suppose 50 different soft drinks were mentioned among all of the questionnaires. You could of course set up 50 variables - one for each soft drink - and then enter a *1* for the respective respondent and variable (soft drink), if he or she mentioned the respective soft drink (and a *0* if not); for example:

```
          COKE  PEPSI  SPRITE  ....
          ----  -----  ------
case 1     0      1      0
case 2     1      1      0
case 3     0      0      1
   .       .      .      .
   .       .      .      .
```

This method of coding the responses would be very tedious and "wasteful." Note that each respondent can only give a maximum of three responses; yet 50 variables are used to code those responses. (However, if you are only interested in these three soft drinks, then this method of coding just those three variables would be satisfactory; to tabulate soft drink preferences, you could then treat the three variables as a *multiple dichotomy*; see below.)

Coding multiple response variables. Alternatively, you could set up three variables, and a coding scheme for the 50 soft drinks. Then you could enter the respective codes (or *alpha* labels) into the three variables, in the same way that respondents wrote them down in the questionnaire.

```
        Resp_1    Resp_2    Resp_3
        --------  --------  ------------
case 1  COKE      PEPSI     JOLT
case 2  SPRITE    SNAPPLE   DR PEPPER
case 3  PERRIER   GATORADE  MOUNTAIN DEW
  .       .         .         .
  .       .         .         .
  .       .         .         .
```

To produce a table of the number of respondents by soft drink, you would now treat *Resp1* to *Resp3* as a *multiple response variable*. That table could look like this:

```
N=500              Prcnt.of  Prcnt.of
Category  Count Responses Cases
--------- ----- --------- --------
COKE         44      5.23     8.80
PEPSI        43      5.11     8.60
MOUNTAIN     81      9.62    16.20
PEPPER       74      8.79    14.80
 ...        ...       ...      ...
--------- ----- --------- --------
Total
Responses   842    100.00   168.40
```

Interpreting the multiple response frequency table. The total number of respondents was $n=500$. Note that the counts in the first column of the table do not add up to 500, but rather to 842. That is the total number of *responses*; since each respondent could make up to 3 responses (write down three names of soft drinks), the total number of responses is naturally greater than the number of respondents.

For example, referring back to the sample listing of the data file shown above, the first case (*Coke*, *Pepsi*, *Jolt*) "contributes" three times to the frequency table, once to the category *Coke*, once to the category *Pepsi*, and once to the category *Jolt*. The second and third columns in the table above report the percentages relative to the number of responses (second column) as well as respondents (third column). Thus, the entry *8.80* in the first row and last column in the table above means that 8.8% of all respondents mentioned *Coke* either as their first, second, or third soft drink preference.

Repeated identical responses. Unlike some other popular programs for computing tables for multiple response variables, the *Crosstabulation* procedure in the *Basic Statistics and Tables* module will, by default, ignore multiple identical responses. For example, suppose a respondent lists as his/her three preferences *Jolt*, *Jolt*, *Jolt*. *STATISTICA* will count that case only once, and consequently that person will only contribute once to the *Jolt* category in the frequency table (as well as crosstabulation tables; see below).

Multiple Dichotomies

Suppose in the above example you were only interested in *Coke*, *Pepsi*, and *Sprite*. As pointed out earlier, one way to code the data in that case would be as follows:

```
          COKE  PEPSI  SPRITE  ....
          ----  -----  ------
case 1            1
case 2     1      1
case 3                   1
 ...      ...    ...    ...
```

In other words, one variable was created for each soft drink, then a value of *1* was entered into the respective variable whenever the respective drink was mentioned by the respective respondent. Note that each variable represents a *dichotomy*; that is, only "*1*"s and "*not 1*"s are allowed (you could have entered *1*'s and *0*'s, but to save typing, you can also simply leave the *0*'s blank or missing). When tabulating these variables, you would like to obtain a summary table very similar to the one shown earlier for multiple response variables; that is, you would like to compute the number and percent of respondents (and responses) for each soft drink. In a sense, you "compact" the three variables *Coke*, *Pepsi*, and *Sprite* into a single variable (*Soft Drink*) consisting of *multiple dichotomies*.

Crosstabulation of Multiple Responses/Dichotomies

The *Crosstabulation* procedure of the *Basic Statistics and Tables* module allows you to specify simple categorical variables (e.g., *Gender: male* or *female*), multiple response variables, and multiple dichotomies. All of these types of variables can then be used in crosstabulation tables. For example, you could crosstabulate a multiple dichotomy for *Soft Drink* (coded as described in the previous paragraph) with a multiple response variable *Favorite Fast Foods* (with many categories such as *Hamburgers*, *Pizza*, etc.), by the simple categorical variable *Gender*.

As in the frequency table, the percentages and marginal totals in that table can be computed from the total number of respondents as well as the total number of responses. For example, consider the following hypothetical respondent:

Gender	Coke	Pepsi	Sprite	Food1	Food2
FEMALE	1	1		FISH	PIZZA

This *female* respondent mentioned *Coke* and *Pepsi* as her favorite drinks, and *Fish* and *Pizza* as her favorite fast foods. In the complete crosstabulation table she will be counted in the following cells of the table:

		Food				Total No.of Resp.
Gender	Drink	HAM-BURG.	FISH	PIZZA	...	
FEMALE	COKE		X	X		2
	PEPSI		X	X		2
	SPRITE					
MALE	COKE					
	PEPSI					
	SPRITE					

This female respondent will "contribute" to (i.e., be counted in) the crosstabulation table a total of 4 times. In addition, she will be counted twice in the *Female--Coke* marginal frequency column if that column is requested to represent the total number of responses; if the user requests the marginal totals to be computed as the total number of respondents, then this respondent will only be counted once.

Paired Crosstabulation of Multiple Response Variables

A unique procedure for tabulating multiple response variables is to treat the variables in two or more multiple response variables as matched pairs. Again, this method is best illustrated with a simple example. Suppose you conducted a survey of past and present home ownership. You asked the respondents to describe their last three (including the present) homes that they purchased. Naturally, for some respondents the present home is the first and only home; others have owned more than one home in the past. For each home, the respondents were asked to write down the number of rooms in the respective house, and the number of occupants. Here is how the data for one respondent (say case number *112*) may be entered into a data file:

Case no.	Rooms 1	2	3	No.Occ. 1	2	3
112	3	3	4	2	3	5

This respondent owned three homes; the first had 3 rooms, the second also had 3 rooms, and the third had 4 rooms. The family apparently also grew; there were 2 occupants in the first home, 3 in the second, and 5 in the third.

Now suppose you wanted to crosstabulate the number of rooms by the number of occupants for all respondents. One way to do so is to prepare three different two-way tables; one for each home. You can also treat the two factors in this study (*Number of Rooms*, *Number of Occupants*) as multiple response variables. However, it would obviously not make any sense to count the example respondent *112* shown above in cell *3 Rooms - 5 Occupants* of the crosstabulation table (which you would, if you simply treated the two factors as ordinary multiple response variables). In other words, you want to ignore the combination of occupants in the third home with the number of rooms in the first home. Rather, you would like to count these variables in *pairs*; you would like to consider the number of rooms in the first home together with the number of occupants in the first home, the number of rooms in the second home with the number of occupants in the second home, and so on. This is exactly what will be accomplished if you asked for a *paired* crosstabulation of these multiple response variables.

A Final Comment

When preparing complex crosstabulation tables with multiple responses/dichotomies, it is sometimes difficult (in our experience) to "keep track" of exactly how the cases in the file are counted. The best way to verify that one understands the way in which the respective tables are constructed is to

crosstabulate some simple example data, and then to trace how each case is counted. The example section (page 1461) employs this method to illustrate how data are counted for tables involving multiple response variables and multiple dichotomies.

Other Significance Tests

Significance Testing

The *Elementary Concepts* chapter (Chapter 8) describes the logic behind statistical significance testing. To summarize, suppose you have two groups - 50 males and 50 females - and you measure the height of each person in the sample. Your goal is to test whether or not males are taller than females in the population from which the sample was obtained (e.g., among college students). The appropriate statistical test here would be the *t-test for independent samples* (see page 1439). Without going into computational details, the *t* statistic is basically the mean difference between the two groups, standardized by the variability in the data.

Now suppose you have replicated the study over and over and have repeatedly taken samples of 50 males and 50 females from the population, measured their heights, and computed a *t* statistic for each replication. After replicating the study 1,000 times or so, you could plot a distribution of the *t* statistic over the 1,000 "experiments;" this distribution is called a *sampling distribution*. Luckily, given some assumptions about the nature and distribution of the variables of interest (*Height* in this case), you can infer what that sampling distribution will be without having to replicate the study 1,000 times. In this case, if *Height* is normally distributed in the population and if there is no difference in the means or in the variability of males and females, then you can look up the percentage points of the *t* distribution in a table, or via the *Probability Calculator* procedure (see *Quick Basic Stats*, Chapter 10)

To continue with the simple example above, if after just one sample from the population, a *t* value is obtained that is highly "unusual" or improbable (e.g., $p<.01$), then you conclude (after making sure that the variability in the two groups is about the same) that the assumption of equal means must not be true. Thus you reject the hypothesis that females are as tall as males.

The options available via the *Other significance tests* option from the startup panel allow you to perform the most common types of statistical significance testing, namely, to test for differences (between independent samples) in means, correlations, and percentages. The user can type in the respective statistics (i.e., means, correlation coefficients, or percentages) and other relevant specifications (e.g., sample sizes), and the program will compute the statistical significance of the difference. For details regarding the available tests refer to the description of the *Other significance tests* dialog (page 1551). (Note that *STATISTICA* also includes a comprehensive general *Probability Calculator* for evaluating the distribution functions for various continuous distributions, including *F*, *t*, *Chi-square*, *Weibull*, etc.; refer to *Quick Basic Stats*, Chapter 10, for details.)

PROGRAM OVERVIEW

The *Basic Statistics and Tables* module provides several methods of analyzing, tabulating, or testing data. Very large analysis designs can be processed; for example, correlation matrices up to (technically) 4,092 x 4,092, computed with pairwise deletion of missing data can be produced. Note that matrices of virtually unlimited size (up to 32,000 x 32,000) can be computed in *Megafile Manager* (see Volume III). As in all other modules of *STATISTICA*, all results in the *Basic Statistics and Tables* module can be interactively converted into graphs without leaving the output Scrollsheets.

For example, by clicking on a result in the Scrollsheet with the right-mouse-button, you can "pop-up" a corresponding frequency histogram with fitted normal curve, a scatterplot with regression line and confidence intervals, or a box and whisker plot. You can create a variety of categorized multi-plots to graphically view breakdowns, categorical scatterplots, 2D and 3D scatterplots, as well as matrix scatterplots, categorized box and whisker plots, and many other exploratory and hypothesis-testing graphical methods. A large variety of complementary plots are available via the *Stats Graphs* procedures from the *Graphs* pull-down menu. A brief overview of the procedures available in the *Basic Statistics and Tables* module is given below.

Descriptive Statistics

The *Descriptive Statistics* procedures allow you to compute summary statistics such as means, medians, standard deviations, user-specified confidence limits for the means, skewness, kurtosis, and their standard errors, etc. Other descriptive statistics (ordinal statistics, mode, user-specified percentiles, harmonic and geometric means, etc.), as well as a comprehensive selection of distribution fitting procedures are available in the *Nonparametrics and Distributions* module (Chapter 11) and the *Process Analysis* module (Volume IV). A wide variety of continuous distributions can also be fit to data via the *Stats 2D Graphs - Histograms*, *Quantile-Quantile*, and *Probability-Probability* plots options (see Volume II).

More specialized descriptive statistics are available in the *Time Series and Forecasting* (Volume III), *Survival Analysis* (Volume III), and other modules. For example, the *Time Series and Forecasting* module contains specialized statistics for describing data collected over time and the *Survival Analysis* module contains statistics to describe censored data.

Note that basic descriptive statistics (including medians and quartiles) can be computed in every module of *STATISTICA* via the *Quick Basic Stats* options, accessible via the *Analysis* pull-down menu or the *Quick Basic Stats* toolbar button (for details, see Chapter 10); detailed descriptive statistics (and graphs) for selected blocks of data in any Scrollsheet or the data spreadsheet can be computed via the *Block Stats* (*Rows* or *Columns*) options, accessible via the *Edit* pull-down menu or the right mouse button flying menu (see *Spreadsheet Window*, Chapter 3).

Computation of median and quartiles (25'th, 50'th, and 75'th percentile). When the distribution of values cannot be exactly divided into halves and quartiles, then there are different ways to compute the respective median and quartile values (and percentiles). The specific method of computation for those values can be configured "system-wide" via the *STATISTICA Defaults: General* dialog (see Chapter 3; this dialog is accessible via the *Options* pull-down menu option *General*).

Correlations

This procedure allows you to compute Pearson product-moment correlations. The *Basic Statistics and Tables* module can compute square and rectangular correlation matrices, as well as expanded format correlation matrices with pairwise *n* and significance levels. The significance of differences between correlation coefficients can be tested via the *Other significance tests* options (see below).

There are many other types of correlation coefficients, and they are included in other modules of *STATISTICA*. A variety of *nonparametric* correlations (e.g., Spearman *R*, Kendall *tau*, *Gamma*, etc.) are included in the *Nonparametrics and Distributions* module; such correlation coefficients are also computed by the *Crosstabulation Tables* procedure of this module (page 1446), *partial correlations* are included in the *Multiple Regression* module (Volume III), and various *autocorrelations* (i.e., correlations between a variable and itself lagged by a specified lag) are included in the *Time Series and Forecasting* module (Volume III).

Options to compute standard (Pearson product-moment) correlations are also available in many other modules (e.g., *Multiple Regression*, *Factor Analysis*, *Megafile* Manager; see Volume III). Note that correlation matrices, optionally broken down by a grouping variable, can also be computed in every module of *STATISTICA* via the *Quick Basic Stats* options, accessible via the *Analysis* pull-down menu or the *Quick Basic Stats* toolbar button (for details, see Chapter 10).

Tetrachoric correlations can be calculated in the *Reliability/Item Analysis* module (Volume III). Various measures of distances can be computed in the *Cluster Analysis* module (Volume III) and measures of relations between categorical (nominal) variables are available in the *Crosstabulation* procedure of the *Basic Statistics and Tables* module (see page 1540).

The *Nonlinear Estimation* module (Volume III) contains various pre-defined nonlinear regression models for analyzing categorical dependent variables (probit and logit analysis); the user can also specify any arbitrary type of regression equation in that module. The *Survival Analysis* (Volume III) module contains specialized regression routines for handling survival and failure time data (option *Regression Models* in the startup panel); some of these routines are nonparametric (parameter-free) in nature (e.g., Cox proportional hazard regression). Advanced methods for analyzing correlation matrices in terms of hypothesized patterns of (causal) relations between variables are available in the *Structural Equation Modeling and Path Analysis (SEPATH)* module (Volume III).

t-Test for Independent Samples

This procedure allows you to compare means for two groups (within a variable); the significance of the difference between a group mean and a population or expected mean can be tested via the *Other significance tests* option (see below; that option can also be used to test differences between proportions). Note that various nonparametric tests for comparing groups are also available in the *Nonparametrics and Distributions* module (Chapter 11); methods for comparing groups of (partially) censored observations are available in the *Survival Analysis* module.

t-Test for Dependent Samples

This procedure allows you to compare means among variables, measured in the same sample of cases (subjects, individuals; *dependent* samples). Note that various nonparametric tests for comparing variables are also available in the *Nonparametrics and Distributions* (Chapter 11).

Breakdown: Descriptive Statistics and Correlations by Groups

This procedure will compute various descriptive statistics (e.g., means, standard deviations, correlations, etc.) broken down by one or more categorical variables (e.g., by *Gender* and *Region*). The program will also perform a one-way ANOVA on selected variables, and it is particularly suited for analyzing single-factor designs with very many groups (e.g., with more than 200 groups; such as some designs used in agricultural research).

Note that you can compute various descriptive statistics (including medians and quartiles) as well as correlation matrices, broken down by a grouping variable, in every module of *STATISTICA* via the *Quick Basic Stats* options, accessible via the *Analysis* pull-down menu or the *Quick Basic Stats* toolbar button (for details, see Chapter 10).

Frequency Tables

This procedure allows you to compute frequency tables (and histograms). Frequency tables report the frequency distributions of cases across categories (numeric or alphanumeric values and their long labels) of a variable. *STATISTICA* provides various options for determining the categories for the frequency table (e.g., integer intervals, specific codes, etc.). The user can also tabulate the data according to custom-defined categorization conditions that can be specified in terms of logical expressions. Note that frequency tables can also be computed via the *Quick Basic Stats* options (optionally broken down by a grouping variable), accessible via the *Analysis* pull-down menu or the *Quick Basic Stats* toolbar button (for details, see Chapter 10).

Crosstabulation and Stub-and-Banner Tables

These procedures allow you to crosstabulate data (up to 6-way tables; higher-way tables can be produced by using selection conditions) and produce various types of crosstabulation tables. A wide variety of statistics are also available (e.g., Pearson and maximum likelihood *Chi-square*, *Phi-square*, *Gamma*, etc.). Note that the *Log-Linear* module will also tabulate multi-way crosstabulation tables and perform log-linear analyses on such tables.

Multiple Responses /Dichotomies

The *Basic Statistics and Tables* module offers comprehensive facilities to produce summary tables for multiple response variables as well as multiple dichotomies. Usually, categorical variables or factors divide the sample into exclusive groups, for example, into *males* and *females*. Obviously, only a single categorical variable is necessary to code the gender of the subjects in the data file. However, in some areas of research, the categories of interest are not mutually exclusive.

For example, in a marketing research survey, respondents may be asked to list their top three preferences for soft drinks. A total of, for example, 60 different soft drinks may be mentioned in the survey, which can be coded accordingly in three categorical variables (first three preferences). In this case, the categories are not mutually exclusive: A person may mention three different soft drinks as his or her favorite. Such categorical variables are called *multiple response* variables (*multiple dichotomies* are similar in nature), and they can be easily analyzed with the *Basic Statistics and Tables* module.

Other Significance Tests

Use this procedure to compute the statistical significance of differences between two independent samples (groups) in means, correlation coefficients, and percentages. Both one-sided and two-sided tests can be performed.

Alternative Procedures

Detailed descriptive statistics (including correlation matrices) can be computed in every module of *STATISTICA* via the *Quick Basic Stats* options (accessible from the *Analysis* pull-down menu, or by clicking on the respective toolbar button; see also Chapter 10). The *Quick Basic Stats* options also allow you to compute statistics broken down by a grouping variable. Summary descriptive statistics (including quartiles) and graphs for the values in any Scrollsheet (or the data spreadsheet) can be computed via the *Block Stats* (*Rows* or *Columns*) options, accessible via the *Edit* pull-down menu or the right mouse button flying menu. Descriptive graphs and categorized graphs are available in every module of *STATISTICA* via the *Stats 2D Graphs*, *Stats 3D Graphs*, and *Stats Categorized Graphs* options (see Volume II). Nonparametric descriptive statistics, tests for comparing variables, samples, or for evaluating correlations between variables can be computed via the *Nonparametrics and Distributions* module (see Chapter 11), and, for censored data, via the *Survival Analysis* module (see Volume III).

EXAMPLES

Example 1: Introductory Step-by-Step Illustration of How to Use *STATISTICA*

This example is based on the data file *Adstudy.sta* that is included on the *STATISTICA* disks.

Installation and Startup of the Program

If you have not yet installed *STATISTICA*, please follow the instructions outlined below:

> To install *STATISTICA* while running Windows, insert Disk 1 in drive A: and from the *File* menu, select *Run*. Type *A:SETUP* (you may use *B:SETUP* if appropriate for your system) and follow the instructions of the installation program. *STATISTICA* includes a complete on-line *electronic manual* (press F1 at any point to access context-sensitive documentation).

When you first install *STATISTICA*, the *Setup* program creates a group of applications on your desktop called *STATISTICA*, and sets up icons for the *Module Switcher* (see the icon *STATISTICA*, the first icon in the group, below), the *Basic Statistics and Tables* module, and some other programs (e.g., *Help, Setup*; you can install icons for other frequently used modules too, using the *New - Program Item* option from the *Program Manager File* pull-down menu).

Starting the *Basic Statistics and Tables* module. Start the program by clicking on the *Basic Statistics and Tables* icon in the *STATISTICA* program group, or by clicking on the *STATISTICA* icon and selecting the *Basic Statistics/Tables* procedure from the *Module Switcher* (which will open, see below).

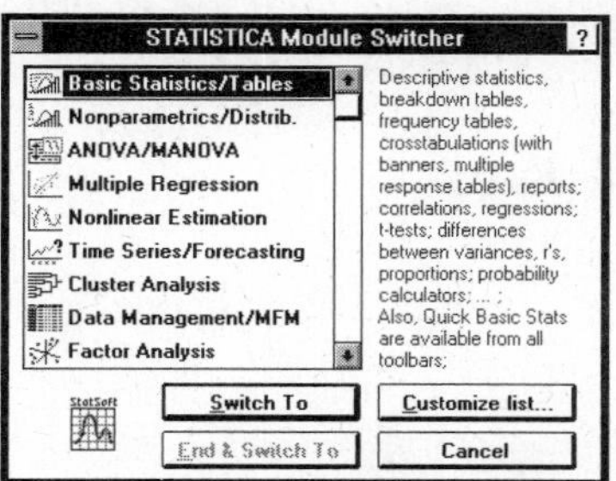

The program will open (full-screen) and the last-used data file (*Adstudy.sta* if you use the program for the first time) and the *Basic Statistics and Tables* startup panel will appear.

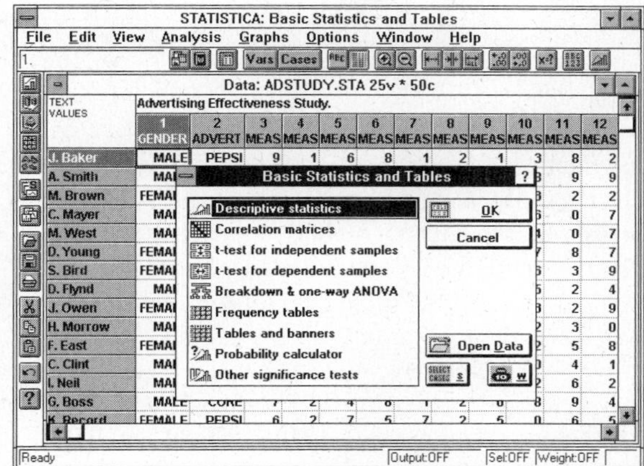

Customizing the appearance of *STATISTICA*. Practically every aspect of the appearance of *STATISTICA* can be customized. The *General Conventions* chapter (Chapter 1) contains detailed descriptions of the many customization options. For example, you can instruct *STATISTICA* to open in the "windowed" (and not full-screen) mode, to suppress the startup panel, or to automatically open the report (text/graphics) window (see the *Options* pull-down menu, option *General*).

The settings that you may want to change at this point (i.e., the first time that you are using *STATISTICA*) pertain to the colors and layout used by the program for various aspects of the display. From the *Options* pull-down menu, select option *Display* to bring up the *STATISTICA Defaults: Display* dialog.

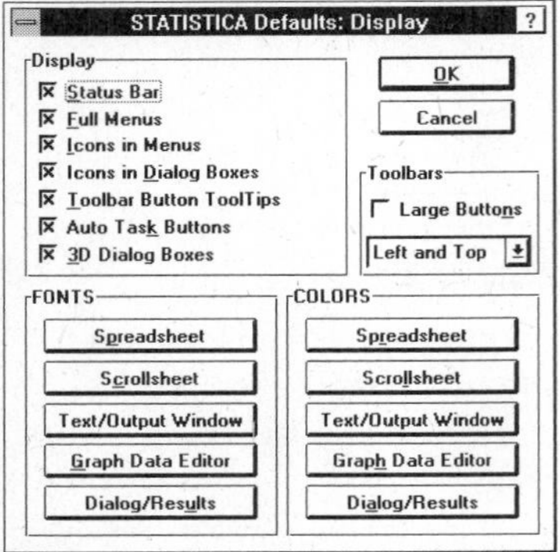

The choices that you make from this dialog will be applied "system-wide," that is, they will apply to all of your analyses with *STATISTICA*, and will remain in effect even after you turn off the computer (the chosen settings are remembered in file *Statist.ini*; please refer to Chapter 1 for details). If you are using a small display set to a high-resolution mode, you may want to set the *Large Buttons* option; this will cause the toolbar buttons to become twice as large. Also, you may want to choose the optimal layout for the toolbars, given the size of your computer screen, in the *Toolbars* area of the dialog. By default, the toolbars will be displayed at the *Left and Top* of the screen. Finally, you may want to adjust the colors, fonts, and font sizes that will be used in the various displays, Scrollsheets, spreadsheets, text windows, etc., so as to make the display most readable given the size and resolution of your computer screen. After you have made the desired customization choices, click *OK* to continue.

Selecting a data file. The current data file is displayed in a spreadsheet. If *Adstudy.sta* is not currently displayed, you can open it by selecting the *Open Data* option from the *File* pull-down menu (or by clicking on the *Open Data* spreadsheet toolbar button) and selecting the data file *Adstudy.sta* in the *Open Data File* dialog (by default, in the *Examples* subdirectory).

The subdirectory *Examples* contains example data files used in this manual to illustrate the operation of *STATISTICA*.

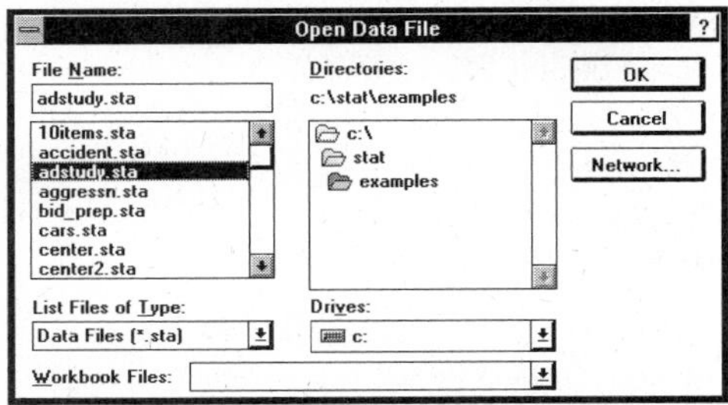

The data file *Adstudy.sta* contains 25 variables and 50 cases. These (fictitious) data were collected in an advertising study where male and female respondents evaluated two advertisements. Respondents' gender was coded in variable 1 (*Gender*: *1=male*, *2=female*). Each respondent was randomly assigned to view one of the two ads (*Advert*: *1=Coke®*, *2=Pepsi®*). They were then asked to rate the appeal of the respective ad on 23 different scales (*Measur1* to *Measur23*). On each of these scales, the respondents could give answers between 0 and 9.

Data spreadsheet. When a data file is opened, it is displayed in a spreadsheet. Also, most output produced by *STATISTICA* is displayed in dynamic, spreadsheet-like tables called Scrollsheets. However, the data spreadsheet is somewhat different from all output Scrollsheets in that it offers specific data management facilities (see *Spreadsheet Window*, Chapter 3).

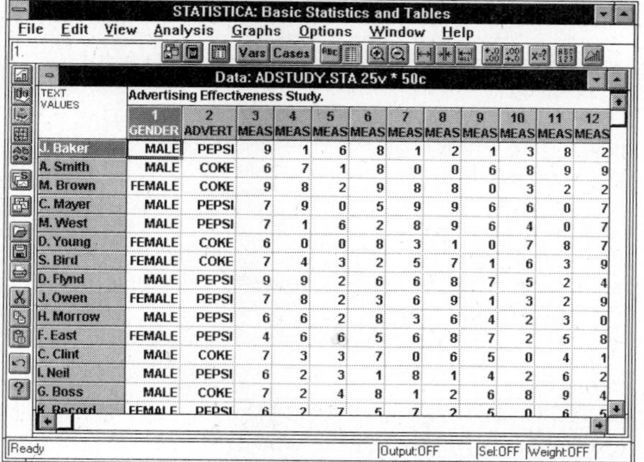

Correlations

First, check whether ratings on individual scales are correlated (in other words, whether some scales measured the "same thing"). In the *Basic Statistics and Tables* startup panel, select the *Correlation matrices* procedure and click *OK* (or you can simply double-click on the *Correlation matrices* procedure).

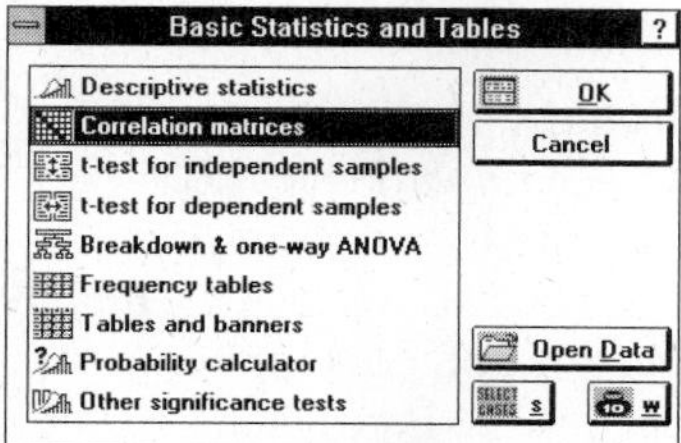

After selecting this procedure, the *Pearson Product-Moment Correlation* dialog will open.

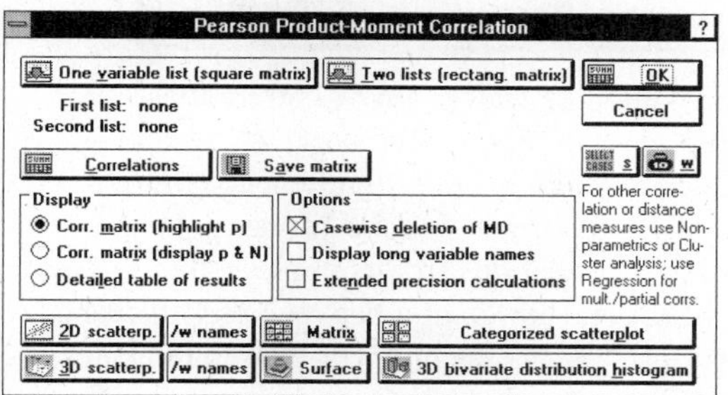

You can select variables either in one list (i.e., a square matrix) or in two lists (rectangular matrix). For this example, click on the *One variable list (square matrix)* button and the standard variable selection dialog will open.

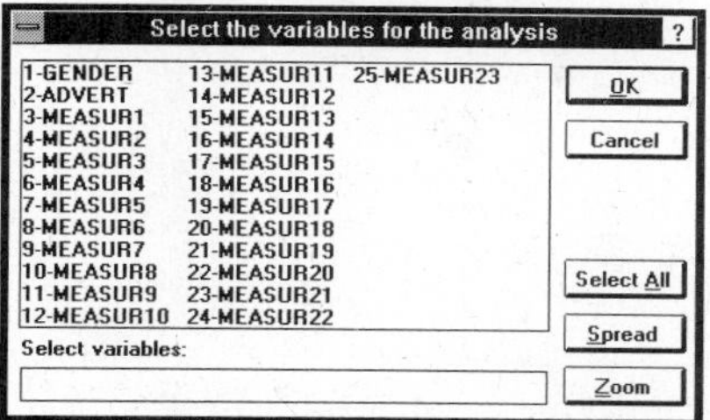

Reviewing and selecting variables. Note that if you have "explored" the data spreadsheet before and selected (i.e., highlighted) a block, then the variables highlighted in the block will automatically be selected. The variable selection window supports various ways of selecting variables and it offers various shortcuts and options to review the contents of the data file. For example, you can press the *Spread* button to "expand" the variable list to review their long labels, formulas or links;

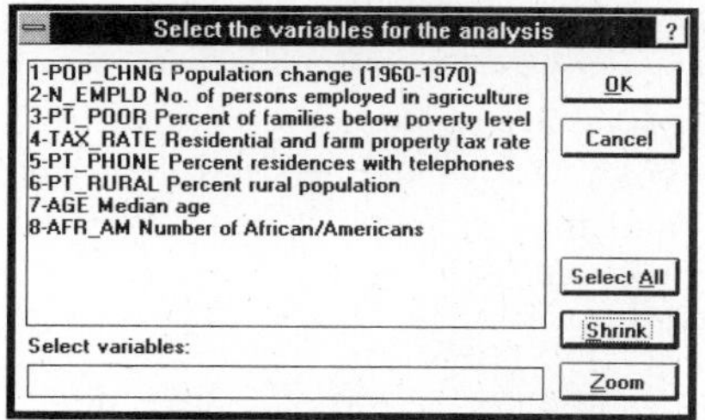

or you can *Zoom* in on a variable by pressing the *Zoom* button to review a sorted list of all its values and descriptive statistics for the variable. Note that pressing the *Copy* button on the bottom of the dialog will copy the descriptive statistics to the Clipboard.

StatSoft

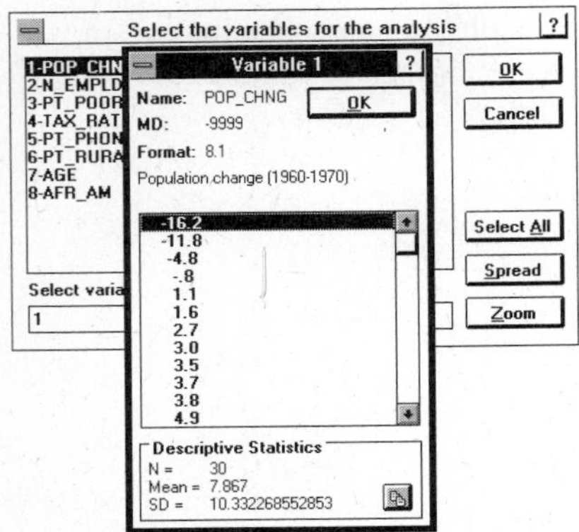

Variables can be selected in the following ways. You can:

- Click on the *Select All* button in order to select all of the variables listed in this dialog,
- Drag the mouse to highlight the specific range of variables that you want to select,
- Enter the variable numbers or ranges of numbers in the edit field below the listing (or an * in order to select all variables), or
- Select discontinuous lists of variables by holding down on the CTRL key while highlighting variables (continuous lists can be selected by holding down on the SHIFT key, and then clicking on the first and last elements in the continuous block of variables that is to be selected).

Note that specific variables can be de-selected by holding down the CTRL key and clicking on the variable. For this example, select all variables in the data file and click *OK* to return to the *Pearson Product-Correlation Correlation* dialog.

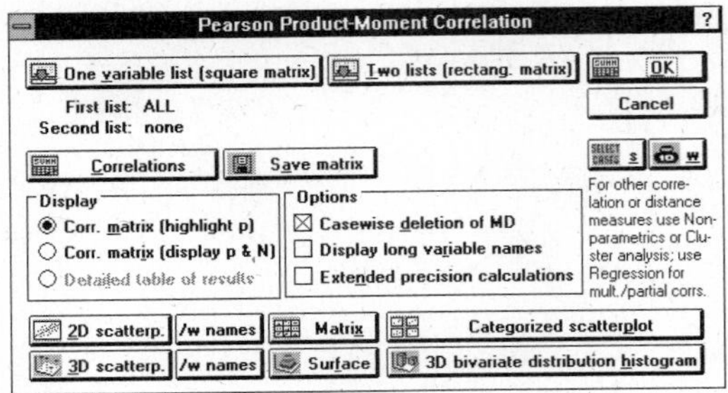

Several procedures are available in this dialog (see page 1512); however, for this example, simply click *OK* to accept the default selections and bring up a Scrollsheet with the correlations.

Correlations (adstudy.sta)

Continue...

Marked correlations are significant at p < .05000
N=50 (Casewise deletion of missing data)

Variable	GENDER	ADVERT	MEASUR 1	MEASUR 2	MEASUR 3	MEASUR 4	MEASUR 5	MEASUR 6
GENDER	1.00	-.17	-.19	-.04	-.08	.02	.26	.05
ADVERT	-.17	1.00	-.03	.13	-.03	.11	-.28	-.15
MEASUR1	-.19	-.03	1.00	.01	-.11	.19	.04	-.01
MEASUR2	-.04	.13	.01	1.00	-.06	.01	.08	.15
MEASUR3	-.08	-.03	-.11	-.06	1.00	-.09	-.21	.14
MEASUR4	.02	.11	.19	.01	-.09	1.00	.10	-.16
MEASUR5	.26	-.28	.04	.08	-.21	.10	1.00	.23
MEASUR6	.05	-.15	-.01	.15	.14	-.16	.23	1.00
MEASUR7	-.37	.05	-.12	.05	.04	.01	-.05	.12
MEASUR8	-.04	-.02	-.02	-.08	-.19	.01	-.19	-.33
MEASUR9	-.15	.38	-.12	-.21	.21	.10	-.47	-.27
MEASUR10	.04	.03	-.15	.05	-.09	-.24	-.07	.13

Highlighting significant correlations. You can specify the significance (*alpha*) level (*.05*, by default) used to highlight significant correlation coefficients in the Scrollsheet. To change the *alpha* level, click on the *Options* Scrollsheet toolbar button to open the *Alpha Level* dialog. Enter in this dialog the significance level *.001* and click *OK*.

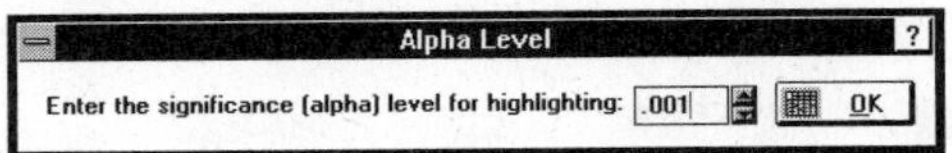

After exiting this dialog, a new correlations Scrollsheet will be produced in which all correlations that meet this significance criterion will be highlighted. It will now be very easy to spot these high correlations (for example in this Scrollsheet, the correlation between *Measur5* and *Measur9* is *-.47*). This high correlation indicates that those two rating scales may measure similar

aspects of the viewers' perception of the advertisement (although one is a decreasing and the other an increasing measure of that aspect). Two options on the *Pearson Product-Moment Correlation* dialog will allow you to produce Scrollsheets with the correlation coefficients and also more detailed statistics (e.g., *p* value, pairwise *n*, r^2 *t* value, etc.). When you select the *Corr. matrix (display p & N)* option, then along with the correlation coefficients, the *p* value and pairwise *n* will also be displayed.

Correlations (adstudy.sta)

Continue...

Marked correlations are significant at p < .00100
N=50 (Casewise deletion of missing data)

Variable	MEASUR5	MEASUR6	MEASUR7	MEASUR8	MEASUR9	MEASUR10
GENDER	.2608	.0474	-.3672	-.0412	-.1539	.0443
	p=.067	p=.744	p=.009	p=.776	p=.286	p=.760
ADVERT	-.2783	-.1520	.0458	-.0225	.3768	.0316
	p=.050	p=.292	p=.752	p=.877	p=.007	p=.828
MEASUR1	.0354	-.0137	-.1164	-.0227	-.1194	-.1505
	p=.807	p=.925	p=.421	p=.875	p=.409	p=.297
MEASUR2	.0780	.1482	.0458	-.0842	-.2142	.0547
	p=.590	p=.304	p=.752	p=.561	p=.135	p=.706
MEASUR3	-.2124	.1392	.0371	-.1868	.2062	-.0922
	p=.139	p=.335	p=.798	p=.194	p=.151	p=.524
MEASUR4	.0963	-.1623	.0087	.0090	.0953	-.2374
	p=.506	p=.260	p=.952	p=.951	p=.510	p=.097
MEASUR5	1.0000	.2276	-.0518	-.1948	-.4672	-.0663
	p= ---	p=.112	p=.721	p=.175	p=.001	p=.647

The *Detailed table of results* option in the *Pearson Product-Moment Correlation* dialog is only available if 20 or fewer variables have been selected for the analysis, since a large amount of information is automatically produced for each correlation. When you select this option, a Scrollsheet will be displayed, containing relevant descriptive statistics, the correlation coefficient, *p* value and pairwise *n*, as well as the slopes and intercepts of the regression equations for each variable in the correlation.

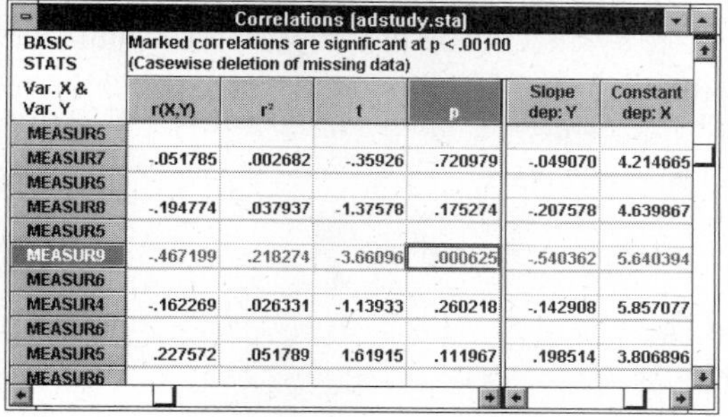

Correlations (adstudy.sta)

BASIC STATS

Marked correlations are significant at p < .00100
(Casewise deletion of missing data)

Var. X & Var. Y	r(X,Y)	r²	t	p	Slope dep: Y	Constant dep: X
MEASUR5						
MEASUR7	-.051785	.002682	-.35926	.720979	-.049070	4.214665
MEASUR5						
MEASUR8	-.194774	.037937	-1.37578	.175274	-.207578	4.639867
MEASUR5						
MEASUR9	-.467199	.218274	-3.66096	.000625	-.540362	5.640394
MEASUR6						
MEASUR4	-.162269	.026331	-1.13933	.260218	-.142908	5.857077
MEASUR6						
MEASUR5	.227572	.051789	1.61915	.111967	.198514	3.806896
MEASUR6						

This option should be used to examine only specific correlations (and not for exploratory data analysis), because 22 Scrollsheet-cells are occupied for each correlation coefficient in this format; thus, a 20x20 correlation matrix will produce a Scrollsheet with 8,800 cells. As you can see above, the correlation for *Measur5* and *Measur9* is really very significant (*p=.0006*), which means that the error associated with accepting this result is only 6 in 10,000. Technically speaking, if one would draw samples of the current sample size at random from a population in which those two variables are *not* correlated, then only six times in every 10,000 drawings would a sample be obtained in which the correlation was -.47 or stronger (i.e., in this case, more negative, see *Elementary Concepts*, Chapter 8).

Producing graphs from a Scrollsheet. In order to visualize the correlation between variables, you may want to view the correlations graphically. Click on the respective correlation coefficient (*-.47*) with the right-mouse-button and a flying menu will open.

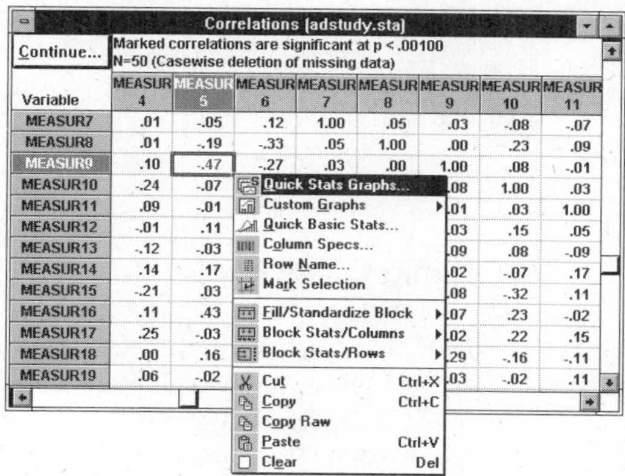

Correlations (adstudy.sta)

Continue...

Marked correlations are significant at p < .00100
N=50 (Casewise deletion of missing data)

Variable	MEASUR 4	MEASUR 5	MEASUR 6	MEASUR 7	MEASUR 8	MEASUR 9	MEASUR 10	MEASUR 11
MEASUR7	.01	-.05	.12	1.00	.05	.03	-.08	-.07
MEASUR8	.01	-.19	-.33	.05	1.00	.00	.23	.09
MEASUR9	.10	-.47	-.27	.03	.00	1.00	.08	-.01
MEASUR10	-.24	-.07				08	1.00	.03
MEASUR11	.09	-.01				01	.03	1.00
MEASUR12	-.01	.11				03	.15	.05
MEASUR13	-.12	-.03				09	.08	-.09
MEASUR14	.14	.17				02	-.07	.17
MEASUR15	-.21	.03				08	-.32	.11
MEASUR16	.11	.43				07	.23	-.02
MEASUR17	.25	-.03				02	.22	.15
MEASUR18	.00	.16				29	-.16	-.11
MEASUR19	.06	-.02				03	-.02	.11

Now, in this menu, click on the *Quick Stats Graphs* option and select the *Scatterplot/conf* option from the resulting flying-menu.

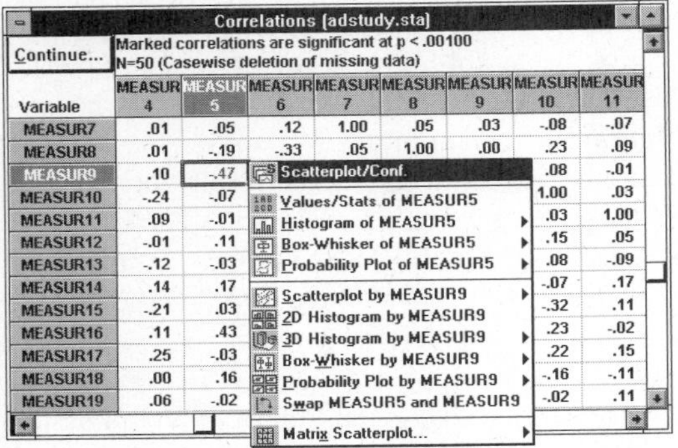

The default graph for this Scrollsheet (a scatterplot of the selected correlation coefficient with regression line, 95% confidence bands and the regression equation in the title) will appear.

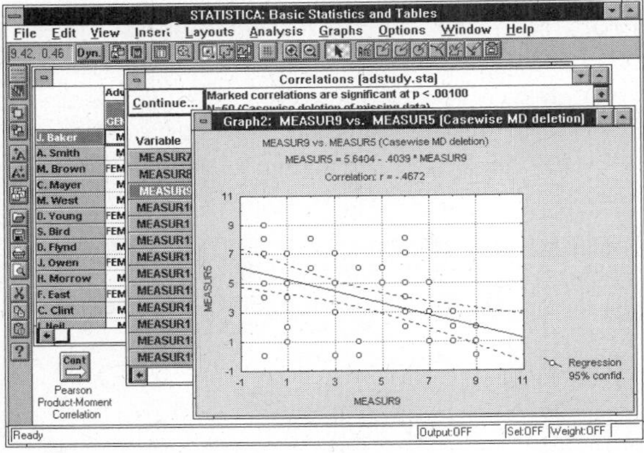

Graph customization. Note that now, when the focus is on the graph window (see above), the toolbar has changed. The graphics toolbar (which accompanies all graph windows) looks different than the toolbars for the data spreadsheet and results Scrollsheets (which are more similar to each other). It contains a variety of graph customization and drawing tools. All of those options are also available from pull-down menus (e.g., in case you wish to record them into keyboard macros). Most of them are also available from the pop-up flying menus available by clicking on specific parts of the graph. If you click anywhere on the empty space outside the graph axes, a menu of global options will appear.

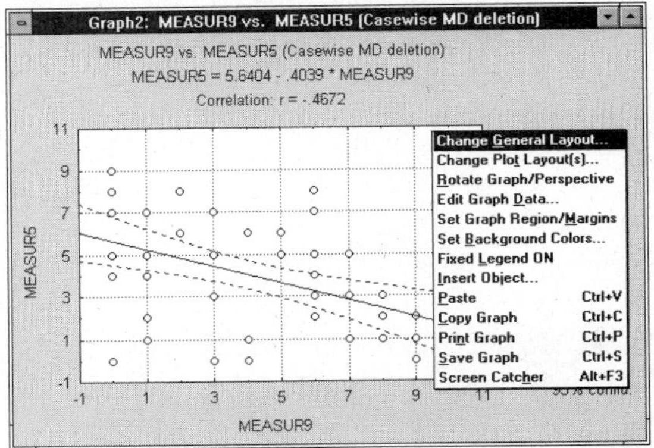

Most of the general graph layout customization features are accessible from the *General Layout* dialog (see the first option of the flying menu, above).

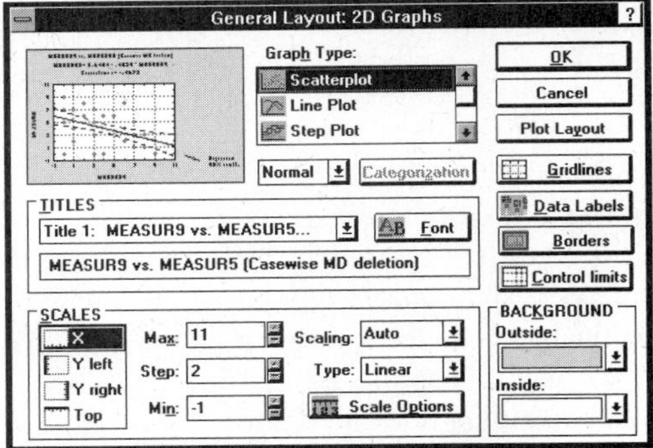

However, most of the individual components of the graph can be customized by selecting specific options from their individual flying menus, accessible by clicking on the graph component (e.g., legend, title, scale value, etc.) with the right-mouse-button (see *Options Common to all Graphs*, Volume II, for more details). The screen shot below illustrates the general conventions for using the mouse to customize graphs.

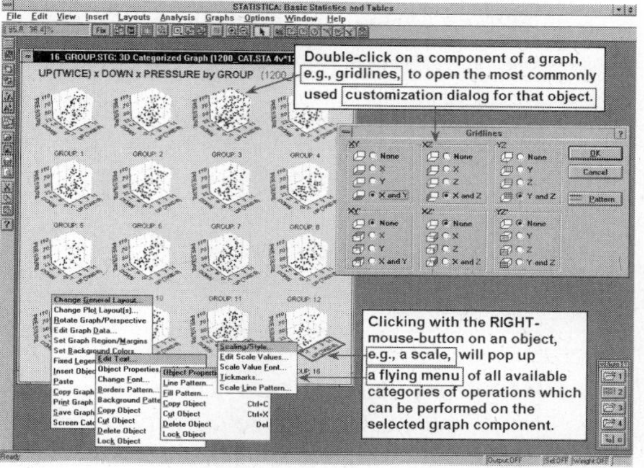

Differences between Means (*t*-Test)

In the next step of the analysis, the possibility of differences in response patterns between males and females will be examined. Specifically, males may use some rating scales in a different way, resulting in higher or lower ratings on some scales. The *t*-test for independent samples will be used to identify such potential differences. The sample of males and females will be compared regarding their average ratings on each scale. Return to the *Basic Statistics and Tables* startup panel and click on the *t-test for Independent Samples* procedure in order to open the *T-Tests for Independent Samples (Groups)* dialog.

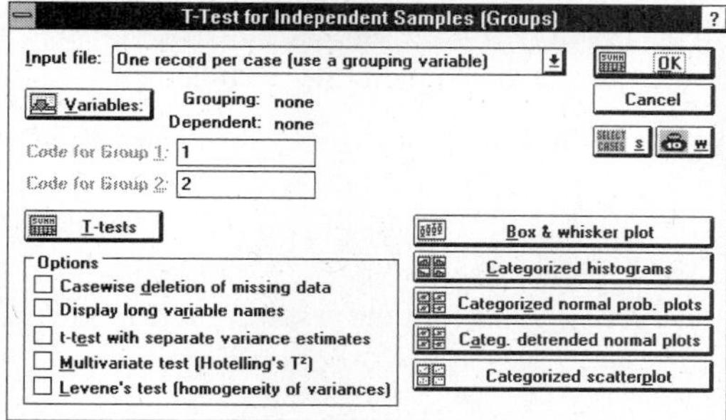

Selecting the independent (grouping) and dependent variables. Click on the *Variables* button to open the standard variable selection dialog. Here, you can select both the independent (grouping) and dependent variables for the analysis. For this example, select (highlight) variable *Gender* as the independent variable and variables 3 through 25 (the variables containing the responses) as the dependent variables.

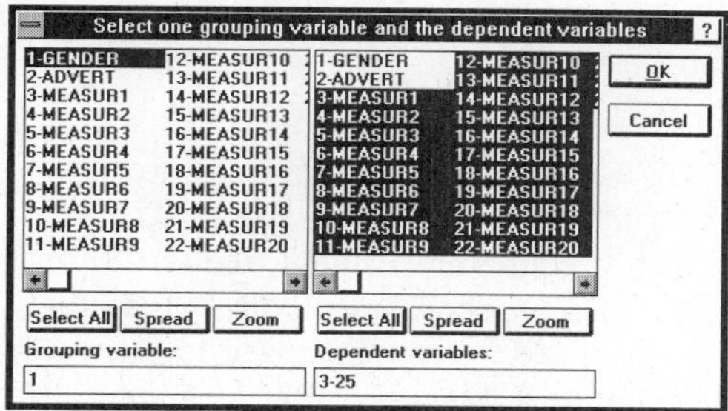

Click *OK* in this dialog to return to the *T-Tests for Independent Samples (Groups)* dialog where your selections will be displayed.

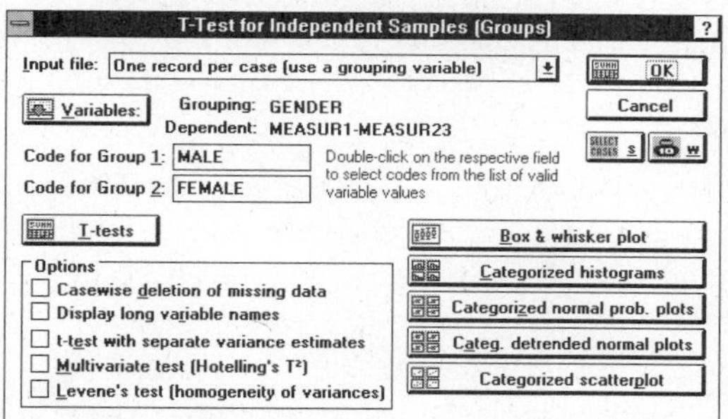

Once you have made the grouping variable selection, *STATISTICA* will automatically propose the codes used in that variable to identify the groups to be compared (in this cases the codes are *Male* and *Female*). You can double-click on either of these edit fields to bring up the *Variable Values* window (see *Spreadsheet Window*, Chapter 3) in which you can review and select the codes for each group. To quickly select a value from the list (and exit the dialog), double-click on the desired value.

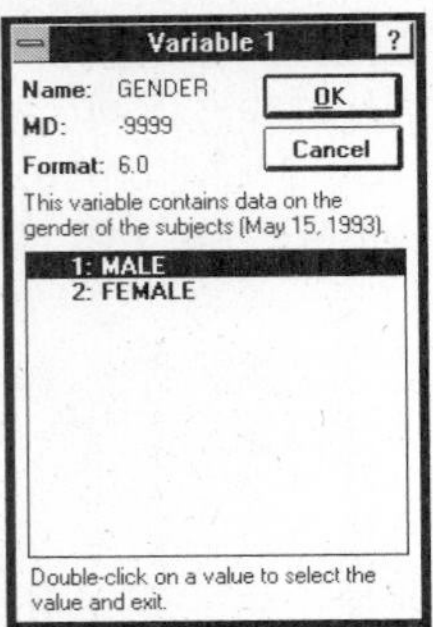

Now, click *OK* to bring up the Scrollsheet of results.

Grouping: GENDER: This variable contains data on the gender
Continue...
Group 1: MALE
Group 2: FEMALE

Variable	Mean MALE	Mean FEMALE	t-value	df	p	Valid N MALE	Valid N FEMALE
MEASUR1	6.285714	5.409091	1.30945	48	.196615	28	22
MEASUR2	4.642857	4.409091	.28152	48	.779520	28	22
MEASUR3	4.321429	3.909091	.52707	48	.600572	28	22
MEASUR4	5.464286	5.590909	-.16547	48	.869267	28	22
MEASUR5	3.357143	4.727273	-1.87198	48	.067309	28	22
MEASUR6	4.714286	5.000000	-.32910	48	.743511	28	22
MEASUR7	5.464286	3.636364	2.73550	48	.008703	28	22
MEASUR8	3.821429	3.590909	.28554	48	.776461	28	22
MEASUR9	4.571429	3.636364	1.07920	48	.285892	28	22

Many other procedures are available in the *T-Tests for Independent Samples (Groups)* dialog (each of these procedures are discussed on page 1516). Before performing the analysis, you can graphically view the distribution of the variables via the graphics procedures in this dialog. For example, click on the *Box and Whisker Plot* button to produce a cascade of box and whisker plots categorized by the grouping variable, one plot for each of the dependent variables selected (see also *t-test graph*, below).

Similarly, click on the *Categorized Histograms* button to produce a cascade of categorized (by the grouping variable) histograms (see also, page 1469).

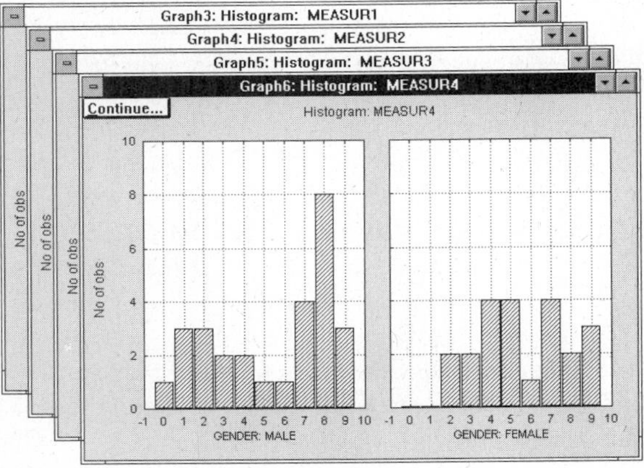

Categorized normal probability plots, detrended normal probability plots, and scatterplots are also available to review the distribution of the variable within each group.

Reviewing the *t*-test output. The quickest way to explore the table is to examine the fifth column (p-levels) and look for p values that are less than the conventional significance level of *.05* (see *Elementary Concepts*, Chapter 8). For the vast majority of dependent variables, the means in the two groups (*Males* and *Females*) are very similar. The only variable for which the t-test meets the conventional significance level of *.05* is *Measur7* for which the p-level is equal to *.0087*. A look at the columns containing the means (see the first two columns) reveals that males used much higher ratings on that scale (*5.46*) than females (*3.63*). The possibility that this difference was obtained by chance cannot be entirely excluded, although assuming that the test is valid (see below), it appears unlikely, because a difference at that significance level is expected to occur by chance (approximately) 9 times per 1,000 (thus, less than only 1 time per 100). This result will be examined further, but first, look at the default graph from the Scrollsheet.

***t*-test graph.** The default graph for this Scrollsheet is the *Box Plot*. To produce this graph, click with the right-mouse-button anywhere on the row of the respective dependent variable (for example, the mean for *Measur7*). From the resulting flying menu, select the *Quick Stats Graphs* option *Box Plot*. Next, select the *Mean/SE/SD* option in the *Box Plot Type* dialog and click *OK* to produce the plot.

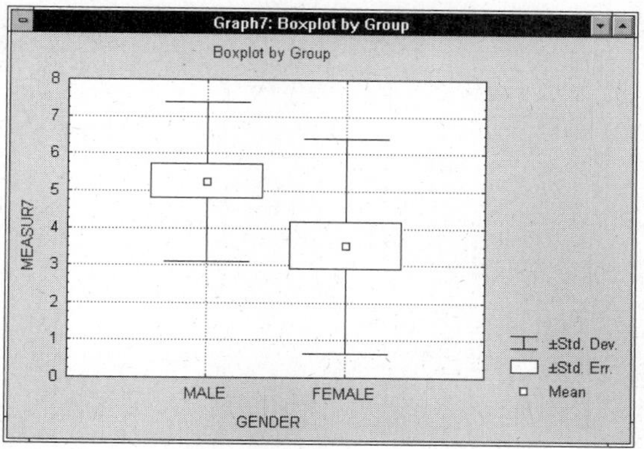

The difference appears large as compared to the variation of scores (see the "whiskers"). However, the graph also shows something unexpected: The variation in the group of females appears much larger than in males. If the variation of scores within the two groups is in fact reliably different, then one of the theoretical assumptions of the *t*-test is not met (see the *Introductory Overview*, page 1439), and you should treat the difference between the means with particular caution. Also, differences in variation are typically correlated with the means, that is, variation is usually higher in groups with higher means. However, something opposite appears to be happening in the current case. In situations like this one, experienced researchers would suspect that the distribution of *Measur7* might not be normal (in males, females, or both). However, first look at the test of variances to see whether the difference visible on the graph is reliable.

Test of difference between variances. Now, return to the results Scrollsheet and scroll to the right until the *F* test results are visible. The *F* test does in fact meet the conventional significance level of *.05*, which suggests that the variances of *Measur7* in *Males* and *Females* are reliably different. However, the difference between the variances is relatively close to the borderline significance level (the obtained *p*-level is *.029*).

Grouping: GENDER: This variable contains data on the gender

Continue...

Group 1: MALE
Group 2: FEMALE

Variable	Valid N MALE	Valid N FEMALE	Std.Dev. MALE	Std.Dev. FEMALE	F-ratio varianes	p varianes
MEASUR1	28	22	2.088011	2.648613	1.609058	.243145
MEASUR2	28	22	2.971647	2.839502	1.095242	.840625
MEASUR3	28	22	2.931989	2.486326	1.390620	.442073
MEASUR4	28	22	2.987407	2.239453	1.779528	.179048
MEASUR5	28	22	2.831232	2.186143	1.677234	.227482
MEASUR6	28	22	3.125251	2.943920	1.126984	.787578
MEASUR7	28	22	1.835497	2.870962	2.446515	.029731
MEASUR8	28	22	2.708745	2.986622	1.215694	.625190
MEASUR9	28	22	3.155578	2.887501	1.194300	.683320

Most researchers would not consider this fact alone to be sufficient to entirely discard the validity of the *t*-test for the difference between the means, given the relatively high significance level of that difference (*p = .0087*). Now, look at the distribution of *Measur7* as categorized by the independent variable *Gender*.

Categorized histogram. Now, click on the results Scrollsheet with the right-mouse-button and select the *Quick Stats Graphs* option *2D Histogram by Gender*. An intermediate dialog will open in which you can select the codes for the grouping variable.

For this example, click *OK* in this dialog to automatically accept the two codes for male and female respondents and produce the categorized histogram.

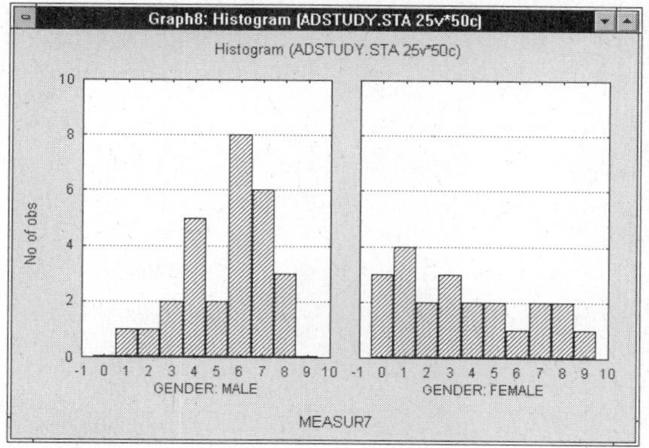

StatSoft

Examining Distributions (Descriptive Statistics)

Now, return to the *Basic Statistics and Tables* startup panel and click on the *Descriptive Statistics* procedure to open the *Descriptive Statistics* dialog. In this dialog, click on the *Variables* button and select all variables in the data file. When you click *OK* in the variable selection window, the *Descriptive Statistics* dialog will look as follows:

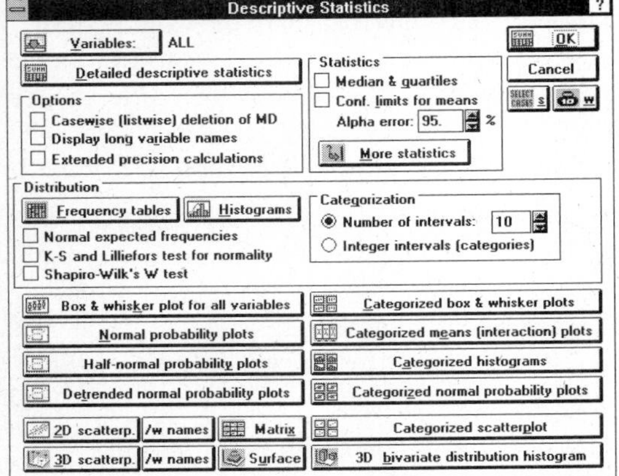

This dialog allows you to produce Scrollsheets with many types of descriptive statistics as well as frequency tables. You can also produce many types of graphs to help visualize the distributions of the selected variables.

By default, the *Descriptive Statistics* Scrollsheets will contain the mean, valid *n*, standard deviation, and minimum and maximum values of the selected variables. Click on the *More Statistics* button in the dialog to open the *Statistics* dialog in which you can select the types of statistics to be calculated (see page 1510).

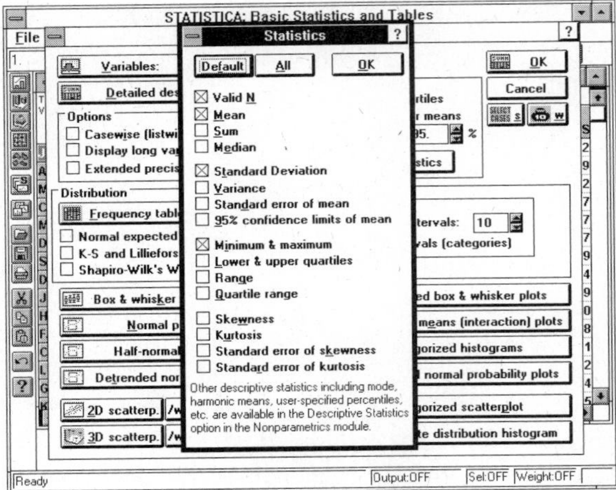

For this example, accept the default selection of statistics and click on the *Detailed Descriptive Statistics* button to produce the Scrollsheet of results.

Descriptive Statistics (adstudy.sta)

Continue...	Valid N	Mean	Minimum	Maximum	Std.Dev.
GENDER	50	1.440000	1.000000	2.000000	.501427
ADVERT	50	1.460000	1.000000	2.000000	.503457
MEASUR1	50	5.900000	0.000000	9.000000	2.366863
MEASUR2	50	4.540000	0.000000	9.000000	2.887058
MEASUR3	50	4.140000	0.000000	9.000000	2.725615
MEASUR4	50	5.520000	0.000000	9.000000	2.659139
MEASUR5	50	3.960000	0.000000	9.000000	2.633846
MEASUR6	50	4.840000	0.000000	9.000000	3.019393
MEASUR7	50	4.660000	0.000000	9.000000	2.495792
MEASUR8	50	3.720000	0.000000	9.000000	2.806988
MEASUR9	50	4.160000	0.000000	9.000000	3.046309
MEASUR10	50	3.940000	0.000000	9.000000	3.053335

The default graph for this Scrollsheet is the histogram with the normal curve superimposed over it. This graph is useful as a visual check of normality. To produce the graph, click with the right-mouse-button on the Scrollsheet (for example, on the mean of *Measur7*), and select the *Quick Stats Graph* option *Histogram/Normal* from the flying menu.

You can produce similar histograms by clicking on the *Histogram* button in the *Distributions* section of this dialog. This section allows you to examine the frequency distributions for each of the selected variables (one Scrollsheet or histogram will be produced for each variable). Specific quantitative

tests of normality as well as categorization options are also available in this dialog (see also, page 1500).

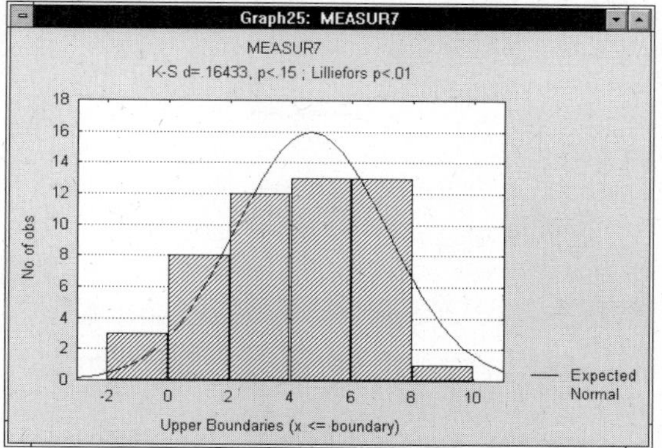

Graphics procedures. The *Descriptive Statistics* dialog offers many graphics procedures to visualize the distributions of, or correlations between variables. For example, click on the *2D Scatterplot/with names* button to produce a visual representation of the correlation between two selected variables.

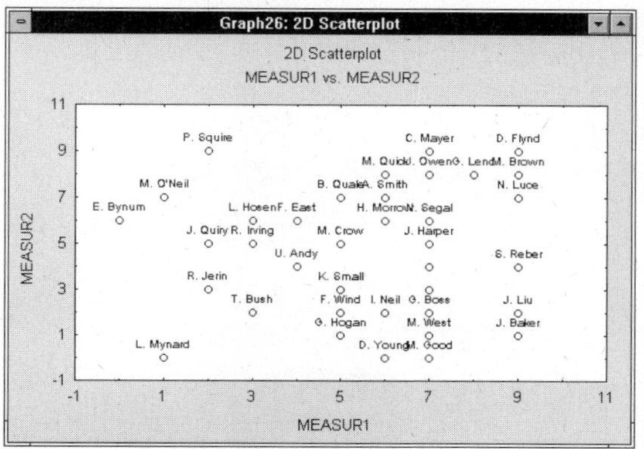

The */with names* option places case names next to the respective points in the scatterplot. You can produce a matrix of scatterplots between selected variables by clicking on the *Matrix* button.

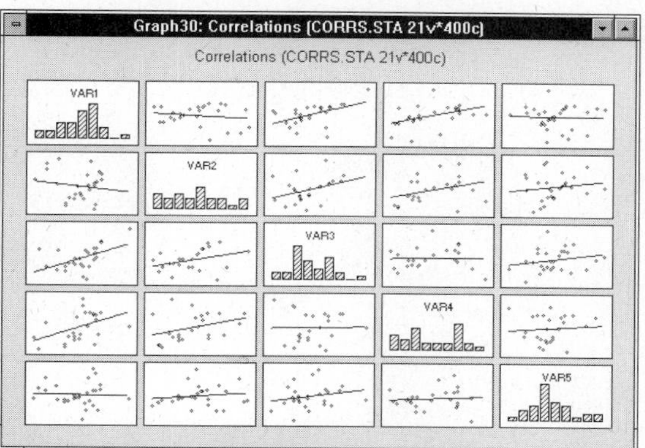

The *Surface* button in this dialog will produce a 3-dimensional (by default, quadratic) surface of the values of selected variables.

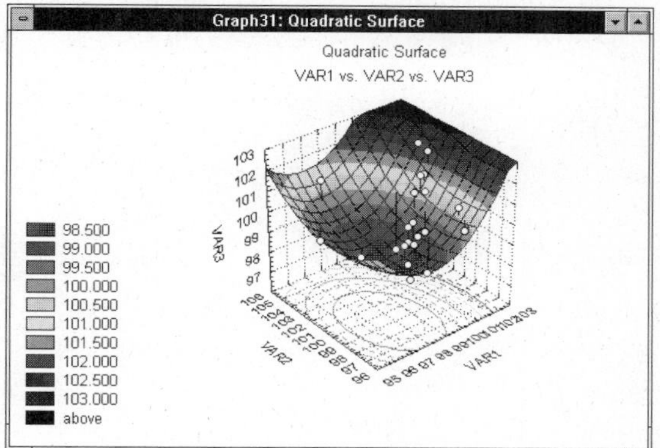

Categorized box and whisker plots, histograms, scatterplots, and probability plots are also available.

Finally, you can produce a *3D bivariate distribution histogram* in order to examine the bivariate distribution of selected variables.

StatSoft

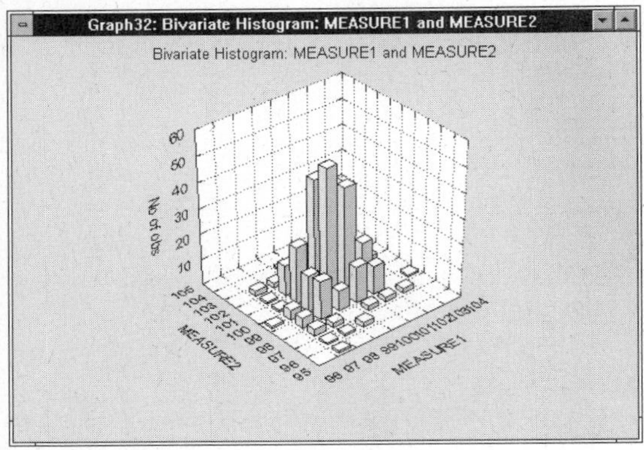

This graph is typically used for descriptive or exploratory (and not analytic) purposes; however, sometimes it is useful to examine bivariate normality of distributions.

Example 2: Breakdowns and One-Way ANOVA

Overview

You can also compute various descriptive statistics (e.g., means, standard deviations, correlations, etc.) broken down by one or more categorical variables (e.g., by *Gender* and *Region*) as well as perform a one-way Analysis of Variance via the *Breakdowns and One-way ANOVA* procedure accessible from the *Basic Statistics and Tables* startup panel. The examples data file *Adstudy.sta* will be used for this example. After clicking on the *Breakdowns and One-way ANOVA* procedure in the startup panel, click on the *Variables* button in the resulting *Descriptive Statistics and Correlations by Groups (Breakdowns)* dialog, and select the two grouping variables *Gender* (subject's gender, *male* and *female*) and *Advert* (type of advertisement shown to the subjects; *Coke* and *Pepsi*).

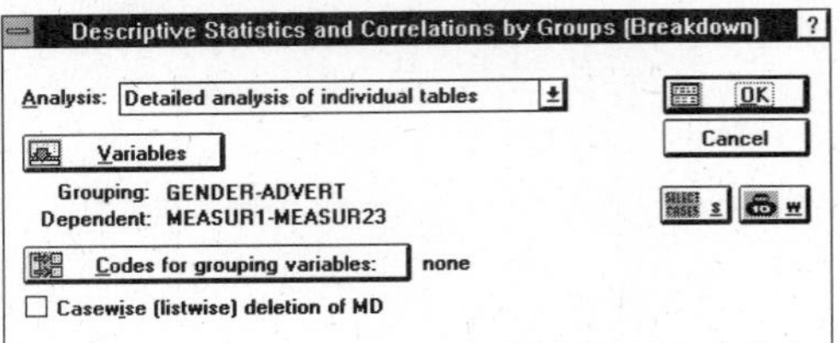

Click on the *Codes for grouping variables* button and select both of the codes for each of the grouping variables in the *Select codes for indep. vars (factors):* dialog.

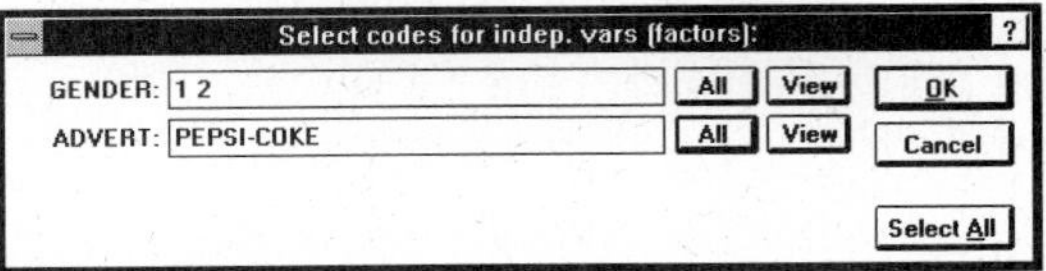

To select all codes for a variable, you can either enter the code numbers in the respective edit field, click on the respective *All* button, or place an * in the respective edit field. Clicking on the *Select All* button in this dialog will select all codes for each of the variables listed. Pressing *OK* without specifying any values is equivalent to selecting all values of all variables. Click *OK* in this and the *Descriptive Statistics and Correlations by Groups (Breakdowns)* dialog to open the *Descriptive Statistics and Correlations by Groups - Results* dialog.

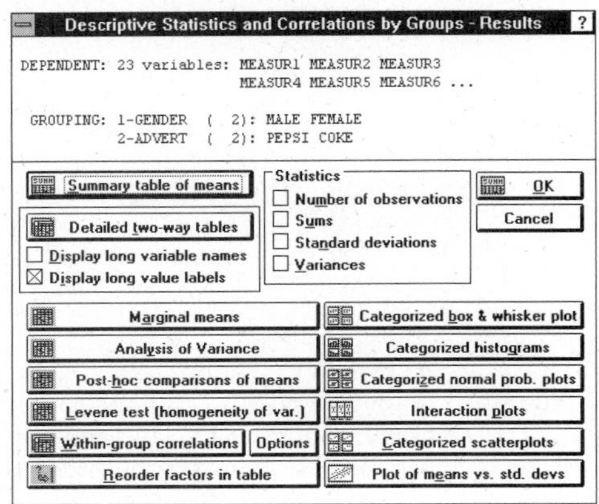

The *Descriptive Statistics and Correlations by Groups - Results* dialog provides various options

and procedures for analyzing the data within groups, in order to obtain a better understanding of the differences between categories of the grouping variables.

Summary Table of Means

You can select the desired statistics to be displayed in the *Summary table of means* or *Detailed two-way tables*. For this example, select each of the four statistics options. In the case of *Detailed two-way tables*, you can also choose to display the long variable names and long value labels, if there are any in the data file. Now, click on the *Detailed two-way tables* button to display that Scrollsheet.

Summary Table of Means (adstudy.sta)

Continue...

N=50 (No missing data in dep. var. list)

GENDER ADVERT	MEASUR1 Means	MEASUR1 N	MEASUR1 Sum	MEASUR1 Std.Dev.	MEASUR1 Variance	MEASU Means
MALE	6.285714	28	176.0000	2.088011	4.35979	4.6428
PEPSI	6.538462	13	85.0000	2.331501	5.43590	4.4615
COKE	6.066667	15	91.0000	1.907379	3.63810	4.8000
FEMALE	5.409091	22	119.0000	2.648613	7.01515	4.4090
PEPSI	5.428571	14	76.0000	2.243428	5.03297	3.9285
COKE	5.375000	8	43.0000	3.420004	11.69643	5.2500
All Groups	5.900000	50	295.0000	2.366863	5.60204	4.5400

The above Scrollsheet shows the selected descriptive statistics for the variables as broken down by the specified groups (scroll the Scrollsheet to view the results for the rest of the variables). For example, looking at the means within each group in this Scrollsheet, you can see that there is a slight difference between the means for *males* and *females* for variable *Measur1*. Now, examine the means within the *male* and *female* groups for variable *Measur1*; you can see that there is very little difference between the groups *Pepsi* and *Coke* within either gender; thus, the gender groups appear to be homogenous in this respect.

One-Way ANOVA and *Post Hoc* Comparisons of Means

You can easily test the significance of these differences via the *Analysis of Variance* button in the results dialog. Click on this button to bring up the Scrollsheet with the results of the univariate analysis of variance for each dependent variable.

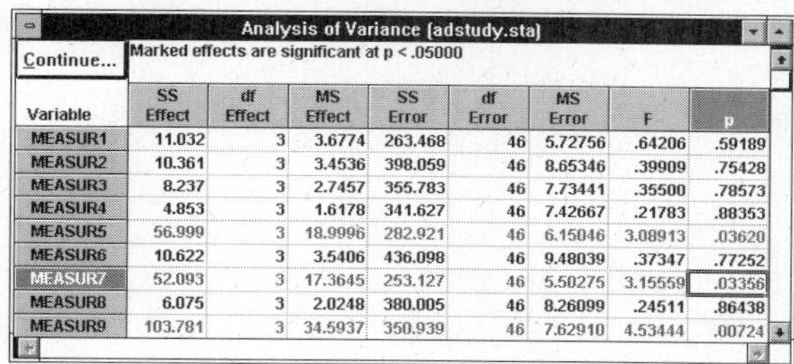

Analysis of Variance (adstudy.sta)

Continue...

Marked effects are significant at p < .05000

Variable	SS Effect	df Effect	MS Effect	SS Error	df Error	MS Error	F	p
MEASUR1	11.032	3	3.6774	263.468	46	5.72756	.64206	.59189
MEASUR2	10.361	3	3.4536	398.059	46	8.65346	.39909	.75428
MEASUR3	8.237	3	2.7457	355.783	46	7.73441	.35500	.78573
MEASUR4	4.853	3	1.6178	341.627	46	7.42667	.21783	.88353
MEASUR5	56.999	3	18.9996	282.921	46	6.15046	3.08913	.03620
MEASUR6	10.622	3	3.5406	436.098	46	9.48039	.37347	.77252
MEASUR7	52.093	3	17.3645	253.127	46	5.50275	3.15559	.03356
MEASUR8	6.075	3	2.0248	380.005	46	8.26099	.24511	.86438
MEASUR9	103.781	3	34.5937	350.939	46	7.62910	4.53444	.00724

The one-way *Analysis of Variance* procedure gave statistically significant results ($p<.05$; for information on selecting the significance level to be highlighted, see page 1464) for *Measur5*, *Measur7*, and *Measur9*. These significant results indicate that the means across the groups are different in magnitude. Now, return to the results dialog and click on the *Post hoc comparison of means* button in order to identify the significant differences between individual groups (means). When you select this option, you will first need to select the variable(s) for the comparisons. For this example, select variable *Measur7*.

When you click *OK* in the variable selection dialog, the *Post Hoc Comparisons of Means* dialog will open.

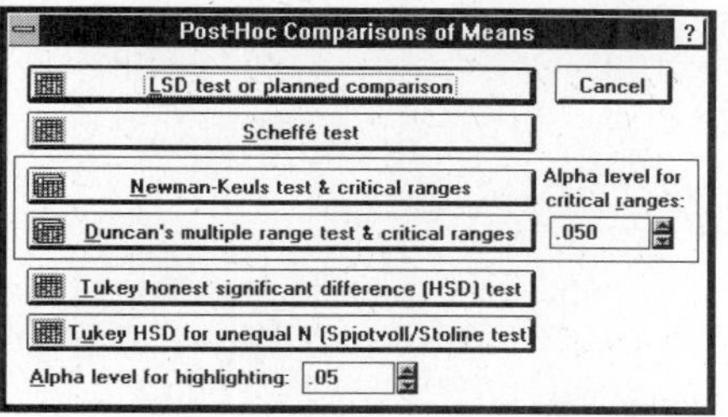

Here, you can choose from among several *post hoc* tests (each of these tests are discussed on page 1532); however, for this example, click on the *LSD test or planned comparison* button.

LSD Test; Variable: MEASUR7 (adstudy.sta)

BASIC STATS — Marked differences are significant at p <

GENDER	ADVERT		{1} M=5.0769	{2} M=5.8000	{3} M=4.0714	{4} M=2.8750
MALE	PEPSI	{1}		.420149	.271547	.042277
MALE	COKE	{2}	.420149		.053365	.006554
FEMALE	PEPSI	{3}	.271547	.053365		.255767
FEMALE	COKE	{4}	.042277	.006554	.255767	

The *LSD* test is equivalent to the *t*-test for independent samples, based on the *n* in the groups involved in the comparison. The *t*-test for independent samples results from *Example 1* (see page 1468) showed that there was a significant difference between the responses for *males* and *females* for *Measur7*. Using the *Breakdowns and One-way ANOVA* procedure, you can see from the *LSD* test that a significant difference occurs only when the subjects are shown the *Coke* advertisement.

Graphical presentation of results. These differences can be viewed graphically via the many graphic options in the *Descriptive Statistics and Correlations by Groups - Results* dialog.

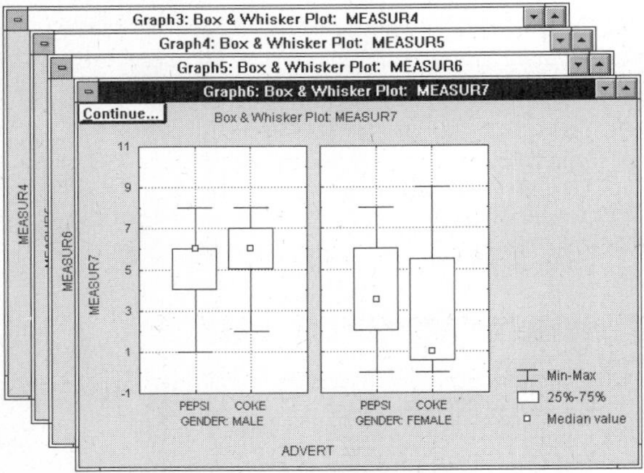

For example, to compare the distributions of the selected variables within the specified groups, click on the *Categorized Box & Whisker Plot* button and select the *Median/Quartile/Range* option from the *Box-Whisker Type* dialog. When you click *OK* in this dialog, a cascade of box and whisker plots will be produced. As you can see in the above box and whisker plot for variable *Measur7*, there does appear to be a difference in the distribution of values for the *female-Coke* group as compared to the *male-Coke* group.

Within-Group Correlations

Now look at the correlations between variables within the specified groups. Return to the *Descriptive Statistics and Correlations by Groups - Results* dialog and click on the *Within-groups Correlations* button. Note that various options are available which can be displayed along with the correlation matrices by clicking on the *Options* button next to the *Within-groups Correlations* button in this dialog (see page 1530).

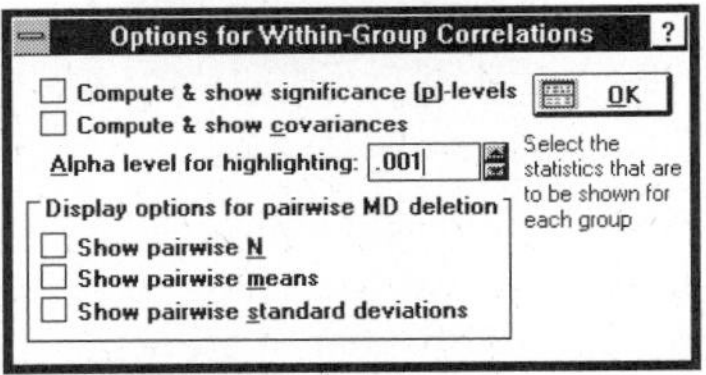

For this example, change the *Alpha level for highlighting* to *.001* and click *OK* to return to the *Descriptive Statistics and Correlations by Groups - Results* dialog. Click on the *Within-group correlations* button and the *Select a group or all groups* dialog will open in which you can select one group (or *all groups*) for the correlation matrices.

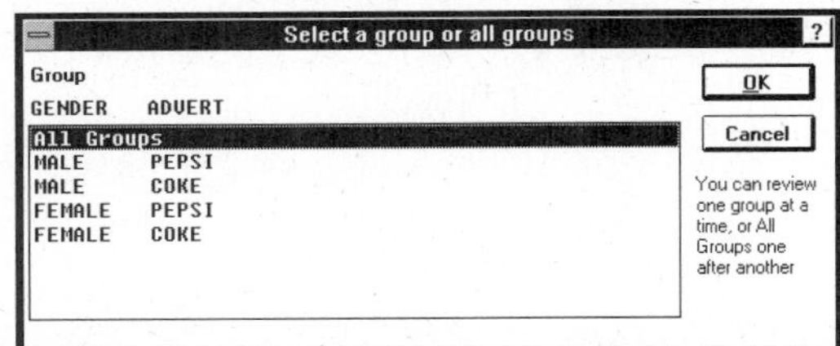

In *Example 1* (see page 1463), a correlation matrix was produced in which the correlation between variables *Measur5* and *Measur9* ($r = -.47$) was highly significant ($p<.001$). The *Breakdowns and One-way ANOVA* procedure will allow you to explore this significant correlation further by computing correlations *within* the specified grouping variables. Now, in the *Select a group or all groups* dialog, double-click on the *All Groups* option to produce a cascade of four correlation matrix Scrollsheets.

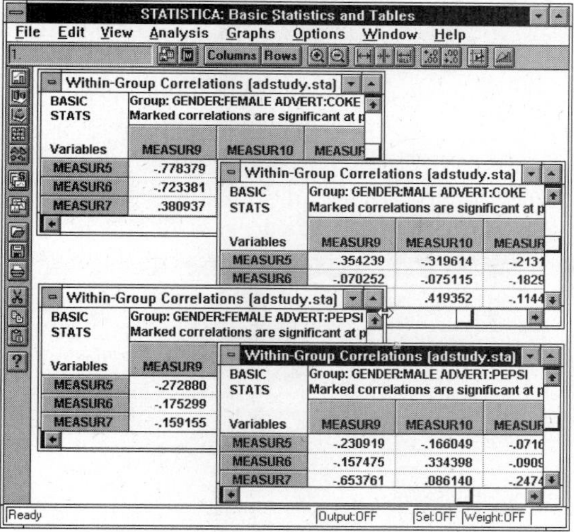

As you can see above, the results reveal that the pattern of correlations is differentiated across the groups (e.g., the correlation is very high in the *Female/Coke* group and much lower in the other three groups). None of the correlations between *Measur5* and *Measur9* were significant at the *.001* level; however, if you were to change the *alpha* level to *.05* via the *Options* button in the results dialog and click again on the *Within-group correlations* button, you would find that the correlation between *Measur5* and *Measur9* is significant at that level ($p=.02$) for the group defined by *Female* gender and *Coke* advertisement. None of the other correlations were significant at the *.05* level.

Note that the *Other significance tests* facility (see page 1551) can be used to test differences *between* correlation coefficients.

Categorized scatterplots. The within-group correlations can be graphically presented using the *Categorized Scatterplot* option in the *Descriptive Statistics and Correlations by Groups - Results* dialog. When you click on this button, you will be prompted to select the variables for the analysis (a cascade of categorized scatterplots will be produced if more than one variable is selected in a list). Select *Measur5* in the first list and *Measur9* in the second list and click *OK* to produce the plot.

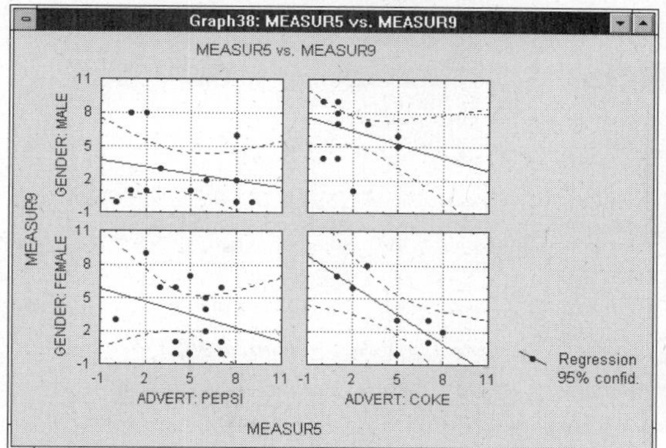

The above categorized scatterplot clearly shows the strong negative correlation between *Measur5* and *Measur9* for the group *Female/Coke*.

Example 3: Frequency Tables

Overview

The following example is based on a (fictitious) data set summarizing the results of an opinion survey. Suppose you own several "sports bars" in your city. In each bar you have two or three big-screen televisions on which you show various sporting events. Because you cannot show all possible sporting events that are simultaneously available on TV, you would like to learn in which sports your customers are most interested. Therefore, a survey was conducted in which 100 customers (who were randomly chosen at different times in different bars), were asked to express their interest in watching various types of sports on television. Specifically, each respondent was given a list of 14 sports and then asked to indicate their interest in watching the respective sport using a 4-point scale. The four points on that scale were labeled (1) *Always interested,* (2) *Usually interested*, (3) *Sometimes interested*, and (4) *Never interested.* Shown below in the variable specification Scrollsheet (accessible by clicking on the *All Specs* spreadsheet toolbar button) is a listing of the fourteen sports included in the survey.

Variables: SPORTS.STA 14v * 100c

	Name	MD Code	Format	Long Name (la
1	FOOTBALL	-9999	8.0	"Watching football"
2	BASEBALL	-9999	8.0	"Watching baseball"
3	BASKETBL	-9999	8.0	"Watching basketball"
4	BOXING	-9999	8.0	"Watching boxing"
5	GYMNASTK	-9999	8.0	"Watching gymnastics"
6	SWIMMING	-9999	8.0	"Watching swimming or diving"
7	ICE_SK	-9999	8.0	"Watching ice skating"
8	HORSE_R	-9999	8.0	"Watching horse racing"
9	TENNIS	-9999	8.0	"Watching tennis"
10	TRACK	-9999	8.0	"Watching track & field events"
11	SKIING	-9999	8.0	"Watching skiing competitions"
12	AUTO_R	-9999	8.0	"Watching auto racing"
13	MARATHON	-9999	8.0	"Watching marathon runs"
14	WRESTLNG	-9999	8.0	"Watching professional wrestling"

Data file. The responses were recorded in the examples data file *Sports.sta*. Each variable in that file represents one sport (see above), and each row represents the responses from a single subject. For each sport, the interest expressed by the subjects was recorded on a 4 point scale, and text values were entered to identify the responses.

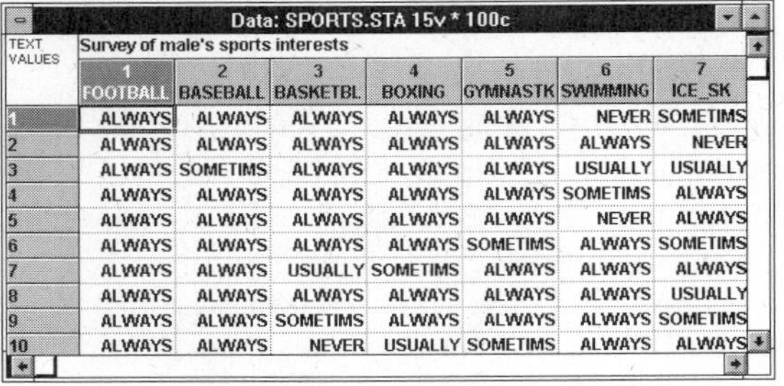

Data: SPORTS.STA 15v * 100c

TEXT VALUES — Survey of male's sports interests

	1 FOOTBALL	2 BASEBALL	3 BASKETBL	4 BOXING	5 GYMNASTK	6 SWIMMING	7 ICE_SK
1	ALWAYS	ALWAYS	ALWAYS	ALWAYS	ALWAYS	NEVER	SOMETIMS
2	ALWAYS	ALWAYS	ALWAYS	ALWAYS	ALWAYS	ALWAYS	NEVER
3	ALWAYS	SOMETIMS	ALWAYS	ALWAYS	ALWAYS	USUALLY	USUALLY
4	ALWAYS	ALWAYS	ALWAYS	ALWAYS	ALWAYS	SOMETIMS	ALWAYS
5	ALWAYS	ALWAYS	ALWAYS	ALWAYS	ALWAYS	NEVER	ALWAYS
6	ALWAYS	ALWAYS	ALWAYS	ALWAYS	SOMETIMS	ALWAYS	SOMETIMS
7	ALWAYS	ALWAYS	USUALLY	SOMETIMS	ALWAYS	ALWAYS	ALWAYS
8	ALWAYS	ALWAYS	ALWAYS	ALWAYS	ALWAYS	ALWAYS	USUALLY
9	ALWAYS	ALWAYS	SOMETIMS	ALWAYS	ALWAYS	ALWAYS	SOMETIMS
10	ALWAYS	ALWAYS	NEVER	USUALLY	SOMETIMS	ALWAYS	ALWAYS

You can click on the *Spreadsheet View Text Values* button on the spreadsheet toolbar in order to toggle between viewing the numeric equivalents of the text values and the text values in the spreadsheet.

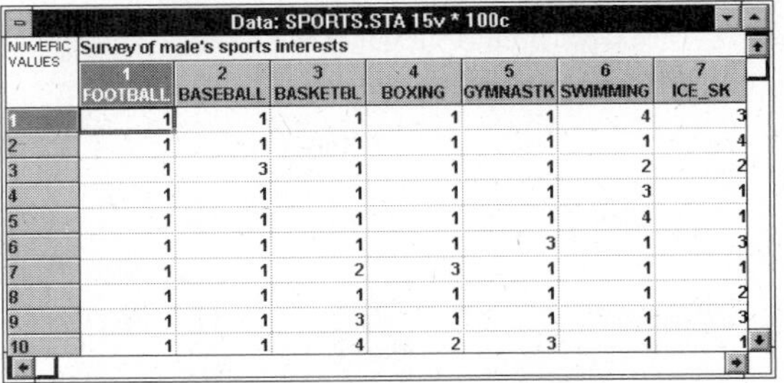

Data: SPORTS.STA 15v * 100c

NUMERIC VALUES — Survey of male's sports interests

	1 FOOTBALL	2 BASEBALL	3 BASKETBL	4 BOXING	5 GYMNASTK	6 SWIMMING	7 ICE_SK
1	1	1	1	1	1	4	3
2	1	1	1	1	1	1	4
3	1	3	1	1	1	2	2
4	1	1	1	1	1	3	1
5	1	1	1	1	1	4	1
6	1	1	1	1	3	1	3
7	1	1	2	3	1	1	1
8	1	1	1	1	1	1	2
9	1	1	3	1	1	1	3
10	1	1	4	2	3	1	1

Note that you can also switch to the value label display mode (i.e., see value labels, notes, or comments assigned to specific values) by clicking on the *Spreadsheet View Text Values* button while holding down the CTRL key.

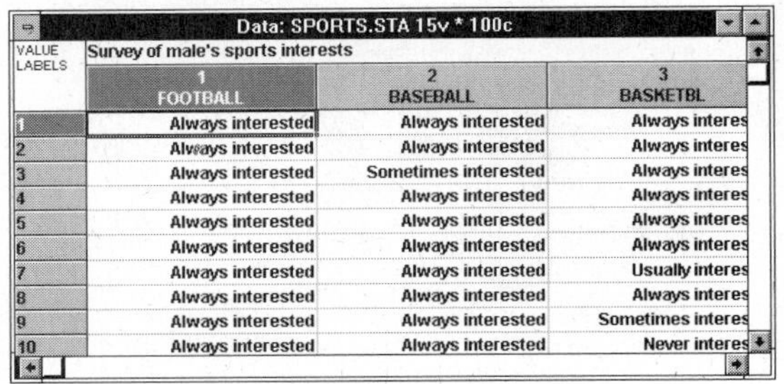

Data: SPORTS.STA 15v * 100c

VALUE LABELS — Survey of male's sports interests

	1 FOOTBALL	2 BASEBALL	3 BASKETBL
1	Always interested	Always interested	Always interes
2	Always interested	Always interested	Always interes
3	Always interested	Sometimes interested	Always interes
4	Always interested	Always interested	Always interes
5	Always interested	Always interested	Always interes
6	Always interested	Always interested	Always interes
7	Always interested	Always interested	Usually interes
8	Always interested	Always interested	Always interes
9	Always interested	Always interested	Sometimes interes
10	Always interested	Always interested	Never interes

Frequency Tables

You can first look at the interest generated by the more popular sports, that is, football, baseball, and basketball. From the *Basic Statistics and Tables* startup panel, select the procedure *Frequency Tables* to open the *Frequency Tables* dialog. In this dialog, click on the *Variables* button and select the first three variables (i.e., *Football*, *Baseball*, *Basketbl*). The *Frequency Tables* dialog will appear as follows:

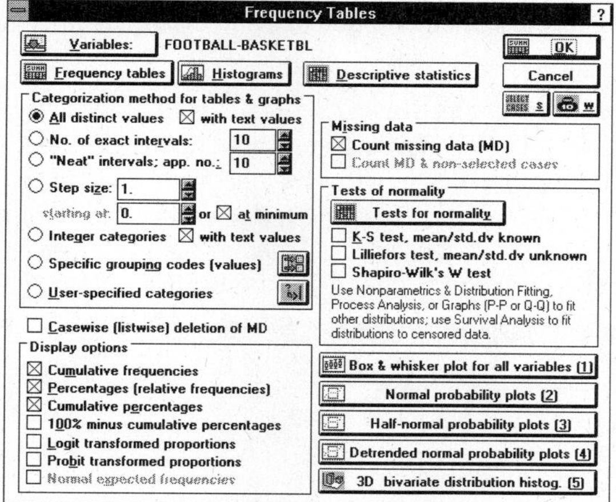

This dialog offers many options which will modify the display and categorization of the frequency tables as well as tests for normality and various graphical ways to visually inspect variables for normality. Each of these options are discussed on page 1534. For this example, accept the default categorization method (i.e., *All distinct values*, *with text values*) and display options (i.e., *Cumulative frequencies*, *Percentages (relative frequencies)*, and *Cumulative percentages*) as shown in the dialog above. Now, click on the *Frequency tables* button to display a cascade of Scrollsheets, one for each variable selected.

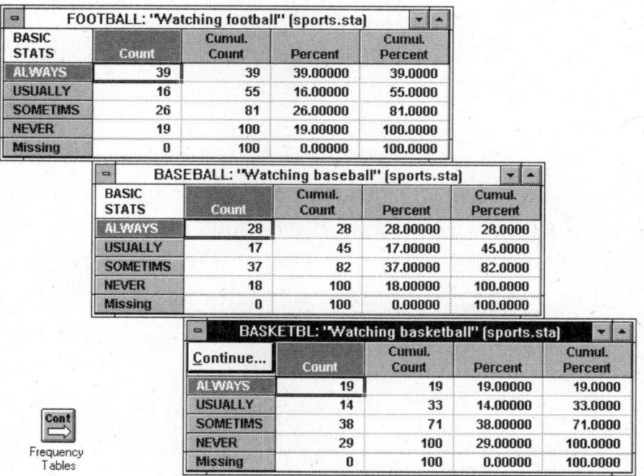

FOOTBALL: "Watching football" (sports.sta)

BASIC STATS	Count	Cumul. Count	Percent	Cumul. Percent
ALWAYS	39	39	39.00000	39.0000
USUALLY	16	55	16.00000	55.0000
SOMETIMS	26	81	26.00000	81.0000
NEVER	19	100	19.00000	100.0000
Missing	0	100	0.00000	100.0000

BASEBALL: "Watching baseball" (sports.sta)

BASIC STATS	Count	Cumul. Count	Percent	Cumul. Percent
ALWAYS	28	28	28.00000	28.0000
USUALLY	17	45	17.00000	45.0000
SOMETIMS	37	82	37.00000	82.0000
NEVER	18	100	18.00000	100.0000
Missing	0	100	0.00000	100.0000

BASKETBL: "Watching basketball" (sports.sta)

Continue...	Count	Cumul. Count	Percent	Cumul. Percent
ALWAYS	19	19	19.00000	19.0000
USUALLY	14	33	14.00000	33.0000
SOMETIMS	38	71	38.00000	71.0000
NEVER	29	100	29.00000	100.0000
Missing	0	100	0.00000	100.0000

Frequency Tables

As you can see in the Scrollsheet for variable *Football*, 39% of the respondents say they are *always interested* in watching football; 16% say they are *usually interested*, etc. Overall, 81% of the respondents fall into the categories *always*, *usually*, and *sometimes* interested combined; only 19% say they are *never* interested.

Producing histograms. Note that informative histograms of all selected variables can easily be produced by returning to the *Frequency Tables* dialog and clicking on the *Histogram* button. A cascade of histograms will be produced, one for each selected variable.

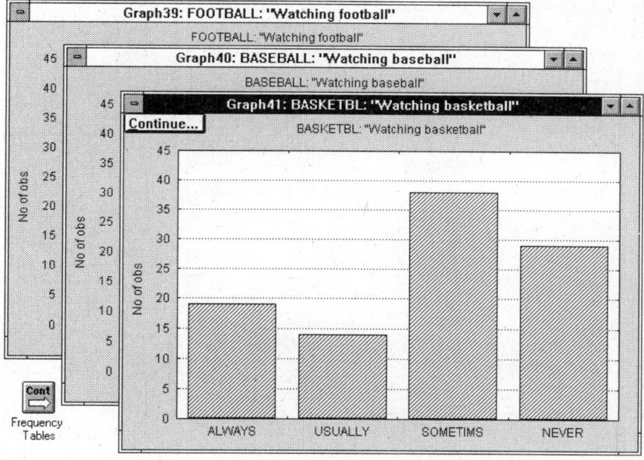

Now look at the Scrollsheet for variable 2 (*Baseball*). You can select it from the *Window* pull-down menu in order to bring it to the front of the window.

BASEBALL: "Watching baseball" (sports.sta)

BASIC STATS	Count	Cumul. Count	Percent	Cumul. Percent
ALWAYS	28	28	28.00000	28.0000
USUALLY	17	45	17.00000	45.0000
SOMETIMS	37	82	37.00000	82.0000
NEVER	18	100	18.00000	100.0000
Missing	0	100	0.00000	100.0000

Here, you can see that the majority of the respondents (37%) are only sometimes interested in watching baseball. However, 28% of the respondents still say they are always interested.

Printing tables in batch. In *STATISTICA*, you can print (or save to a file) the output from analyses

either automatically (i.e., the contents of each displayed Scrollsheet will be directed to the printer and/or the *Text/output Window*) or manually (i.e., the user selects which Scrollsheets or parts of Scrollsheets will be printed). Before you can print the results of analyses, you will first need to specify the output destination (i.e., *File*, *Printer*, *Off*, and/or *Window*) in the *Page/Output Setup* dialog (select the *Page/Output Setup* option from the *File* pull-down menu, the *Print* option from the *Options* pull-down menu, or double-click on the *Output* field on the Status Bar; see Chapter 3 for a description of this dialog).

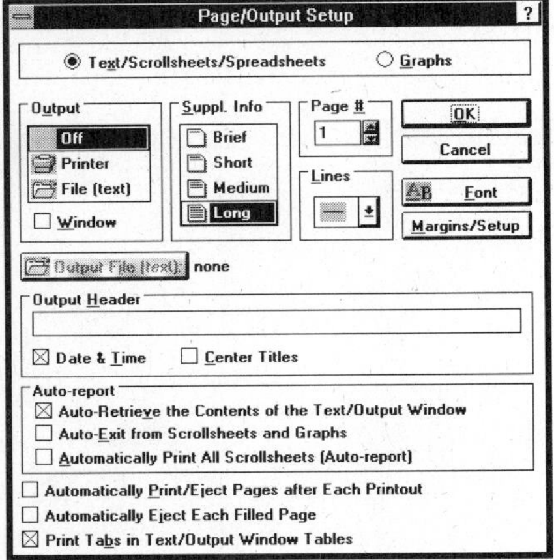

While you are in this dialog, select the amount of supplementary information to be printed along with the Scrollsheets (i.e., the report format: *Brief*, *Short*, *Medium*, or *Long*). Each of these four report formats are described in Chapter 3 (in the context of the *Page/Output Setup* dialog). If *Automatically Print All Scrollsheets* is selected in *Page/Output Setup* dialog, then in addition to the supplementary information (the amount depends on the current report format setting in the same dialog), all output from analyses will automatically be printed either to the printer or to the output file (as well as to the *Text/output Window* if it is selected, see the check box in the upper left part of the dialog). This mode of printing is useful when you want to maintain a complete log of all output displayed during the course of the analysis.

Graphics procedures. Practically all of these results can be displayed graphically via the graphics procedures available in this dialog. First click on the *Box & whisker plot for all variables* button and in the resulting dialog, select *Mean/SE/SD* as the box-whisker type and click *OK* to produce the graph.

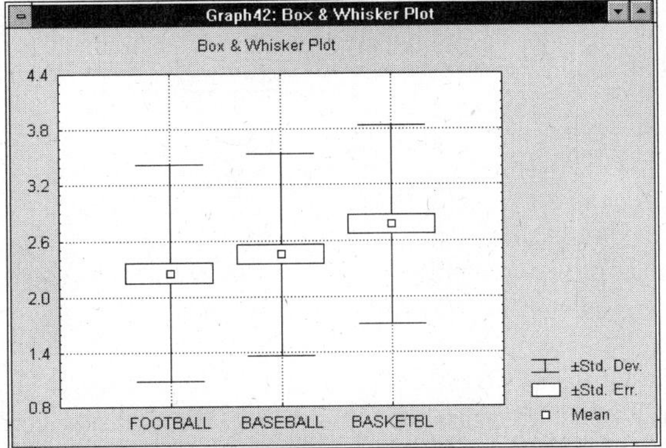

The variability in responses for each of these variables appears to be similar; however, there seems to be a greater interest in watching football as indicated by the smaller mean response for that variable (remember that *1* indicated greatest interest and *4* indicated the least interest). This can also be seen when you compare the frequency tables for these three variables.

Now look at the *3D Bivariate distribution histogram*. When you click on this button, you will be prompted to select the variables for this plot. For this example, select variables *Football* and *Baseball* and click *OK*. (Note that if you select more than one variable in a list, then cascades of 3D histograms will be produced, one for each pair of variables selected.). From a visual inspection of this bivariate distribution (shown below), it appears that there is a correlation between the responses given for variables *Football* and *Baseball*. Indeed, if you were to perform a correlation analysis, you would see that there is a Spearman correlation of *.6785*

between these two variables which would indicate that subjects who prefer watching football also prefer to watch baseball.

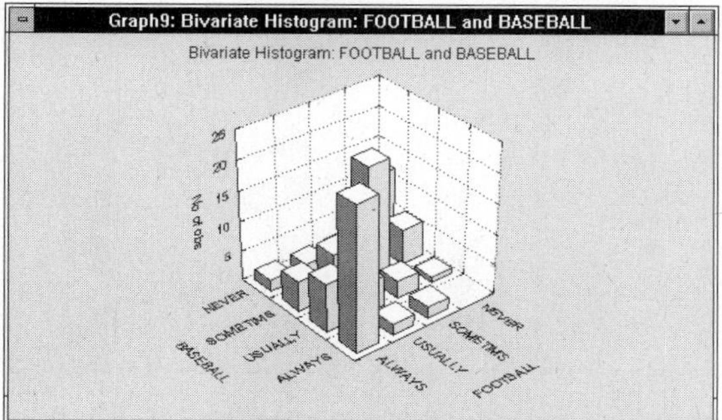

Printing graphs in batch. When you select the *Automatically Print all Graphs* option in the *Page/Output Setup* dialog (see Chapter 3), *STATISTICA* will automatically print to the printer or the text output window (or save to an output file if the *Print to File* option is checked in the *Print Graph* dialog, see Volume II) graphs as they are created.

Summary. From this analysis so far, you have learned that, not surprisingly, football and baseball are at the top of the list of spectator sports in the sample. The next question of interest would be to find out what the overlap between sports is. For example, if your clientele consists of a certain percentage of sports "nuts" who would watch any football, baseball, or basketball game, then perhaps you could only show one of those games at a time and reserve your other TV screen for something entirely different, such as tennis or marathons. However, you would first like to know how much of an overlap there is between sports, and which sports would attract an audience that is *different* from the one that likes to watch football.

Example 4: Stub-and-Banner Tables

Overview

Stub-and-banner tables are an economical way to report several two-way tables simultaneously. To continue the analysis of the above example, it is desired to learn whether the same respondents in the survey who expressed the greatest interest in football also expressed the greatest interest in baseball and basketball. As mentioned earlier, if this is the case, then perhaps it would be sufficient to show one of those sports on one TV screen, and show something entirely different on the other; this way you may attract a new and different clientele. To examine the overlap between sports, that is, the extent to which respondents' interest in football is correlated with that in other sports, compute a stub-and-banner table.

Specifying the Analysis

The data file used in this example is *Sports.sta*. The setup of this data file is described in the previous example (see page 1472). From the *Basic Statistics and Tables* startup panel, select the procedure *Tables and banners* and the *Specify table* dialog will open.

Layout of the table. The stub-and-banner table basically consists of a number of two-way tables put together. The best way to illustrate how these tables are constructed is to review a typical stub-and-banner table. Therefore, in the *Specify Table* dialog, click on the *Specify table* button under the heading *Stub-and-banners table*, and you will be prompted to select the variables for the table.

For this example, select variable *1-Football* as the *column* variable (in the second list) and variables *2-Baseball* through *14-Wrestling* as the *row* variables.

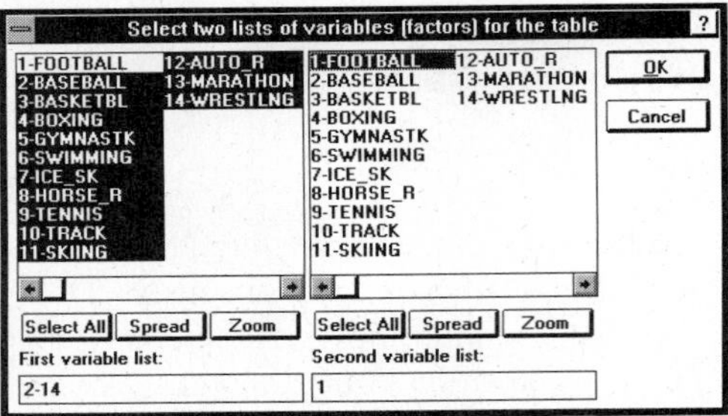

Now, the *Specify Tables* dialog will look like this:

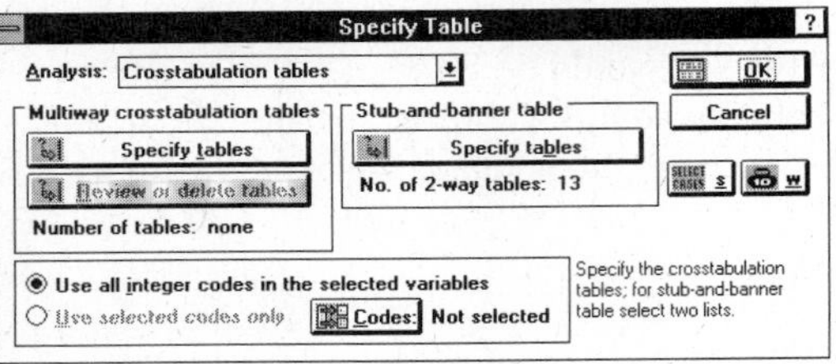

Click *OK* in this dialog to open the *Crosstabulation Tables Results* dialog.

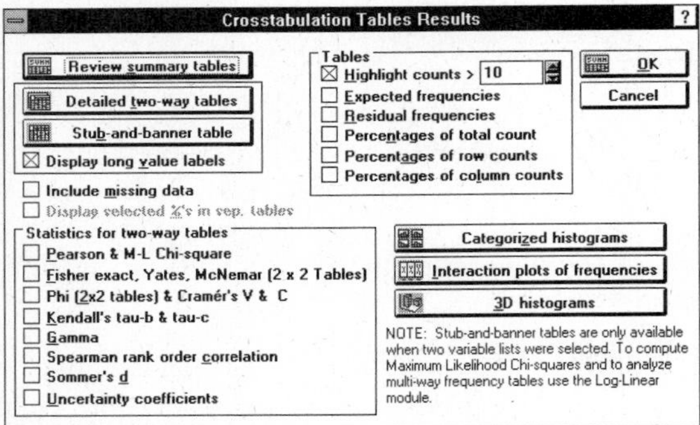

In this dialog, click on the *Stub-and-banners* button to produce the Scrollsheet of results.

Summary Stub-and-Banner Table (sports.sta)

BASIC STATS — Marked cells have counts > 10 (Marginal summaries are not marked)

Factor	FOOTBALL ALWAYS	FOOTBALL USUALLY	FOOTBALL SOMETIMS	FOOTBALL NEVER	Row Total
BASEBALL: ALWAYS	24	2	*	0	28
BASEBALL: USUALLY	8	5	3	1	17
BASEBALL: SOMETIMS	5	7	19	6	37
BASEBALL: NEVER	2	2	2	12	18
BASEBALL: Total	39	16	26	19	100
BASKETBL: ALWAYS	15	1	2	1	19
BASKETBL: USUALLY	10	1	3	0	14
BASKETBL: SOMETIMS	5	11	16	6	38
BASKETBL: NEVER	9	3	5	12	29
BASKETBL: Total	39	16	26	19	100
BOXING : ALWAYS	14	2	2	2	20
BOXING : USUALLY	7	1	1	1	10
BOXING : SOMETIMS	12	8	6	3	29
BOXING : NEVER	6	5	17	13	41
BOXING : Total	39	16	26	19	100
GYMNASTK: ALWAYS	14	0	2	2	18

Reading the Table

Again, you can think of this table as a combination of different two-way tables. For example, the first four rows of the table show the frequencies in the two-way tables of *Football* by *Baseball*. Put another way, you can see the (joint) distribution of the 100 respondents across the 4*4=16 cells created by the crosstabulation of respondents' interest in watching football by their interest in watching baseball. Now try different ways of expressing the results.

Raw frequencies. By default, the stub-and-banner table will contain raw frequencies, as shown above. Thus, you can see that 24 (out of the 100 respondents) reported being *always interested* in watching football and *always interested* in watching baseball. Looking at the first three rows of the right-most column, you can see that of those respondents who say they are *never* interested in watching football, only 7 (*0+1+6*) report being interested in baseball *always* (*0*), *usually* (*1*), or *sometimes* (*2*). Therefore, it looks like the two sports, football and baseball, to a large extent appeal to the same people.

Percentages. Now, return to the *Crosstabulation Tables Results* dialog. This dialog contains procedures which allow you to express the entries in the table in terms of column percentages, row percentages, or total percentages. You can also elect to include expected and/or residual frequencies in

the stub-and-banner table. For now, select the *Percentages of row counts* option and click once again on the *Stub-and-banner table* button.

Summary Stub-and-Banner Table (sports.sta)

BASIC STATS — Marked cells have counts > 10 (Marginal summaries are not marked)

Factor	FOOTBALL ALWAYS	FOOTBALL USUALLY	FOOTBALL SOMETIMS	FOOTBALL NEVER	Row Total
BASEBALL: ALWAYS	24	2	2	0	28
Row Percent	85.71%	7.14%	7.14%	0.00%	
BASEBALL: USUALLY	8	5	3	1	17
Row Percent	47.06%	29.41%	17.65%	5.88%	
BASEBALL: SOMETIMS	5	7	19	6	37
Row Percent	13.51%	18.92%	51.35%	16.22%	
BASEBALL: NEVER	2	2	2	12	18
Row Percent	11.11%	11.11%	11.11%	66.67%	
BASEBALL: Total	39	16	26	19	100
Table Percent	39.00%	16.00%	26.00%	19.00%	100.00%

When you select the *Percentages of row counts* option, the *Display selected %'s in separate tables* option will become available. Because so much information can be included in one table, selecting this option will place the row percentages in a separate Scrollsheet from the raw frequencies.

Now, look at the first row in the above Scrollsheet. You can see that of those respondents who said they are *always interested* in baseball (all respondents in the first row), *85.71%* say they are *always interested* in football as well.

Finding a sport unrelated to football. Now, look at the total percentages in order to find a sport that is not related to football. Return to the *Crosstabulation Tables Results* dialog and select the *Percentages of total count* option (for simplicity, de-select the *Percentages of row count* option). Once again, click on the *Stub-and-banner table* button to produce the Scrollsheet with these counts.

Summary Stub-and-Banner Table (sports.sta)

BASIC STATS — Marked cells have counts > 10 (Marginal summaries are not marked)

Factor	FOOTBALL ALWAYS	FOOTBALL USUALLY	FOOTBALL SOMETIMS	FOOTBALL NEVER	Row Total
GYMNASTK: ALWAYS	14	0	2	2	18
Table Percent	14.00%	0.00%	2.00%	2.00%	18.00%
GYMNASTK: USUALLY	8	1	5	2	16
Table Percent	8.00%	1.00%	5.00%	2.00%	16.00%
GYMNASTK: SOMETIMS	12	10	10	8	40
Table Percent	12.00%	10.00%	10.00%	8.00%	40.00%
GYMNASTK: NEVER	5	5	9	7	26
Table Percent	5.00%	5.00%	9.00%	7.00%	26.00%
GYMNASTK: Total	39	16	26	19	100
Table Percent	39.00%	16.00%	26.00%	19.00%	100.00%

Scroll the Scrollsheet down until you can view the counts for *Gymnastk* (see above). The entries in this table are now total percentages. Thus 14 percent of all respondents report to be always interested in football and *always interested* in gymnastics. Only 7 percent of the respondents say that they are *never interested* in football and *never interested* in gymnastics. At the same time, 12 percent (*2+2+8*) of the respondents say that they are never interested in football, but either *always* (*2%*), *usually* (*2%*), or *sometimes* (*8%*) interested in gymnastics. Thus, gymnastics would seem to be a nice programming alternative (for the second large-screen TV in your bars) to football, baseball, or basketball, and may attract at least some different customers.

Statistics

The *Introductory Overview* section of this chapter reviews some of the statistics commonly used to express contingency or relationships between two categorical variables (see page 1450). Look now at some of those statistics which are listed in the *Crosstabulation Tables Results* dialog. The most commonly used statistic of contingency between two categorical variables is the *Chi-square* test, therefore, select the *Pearson & M-L Chi-square* option.

A measure of correlation, similar to the Pearson *r*, is the *Spearman R*, or *Rs*. This measure assumes that the values for the variables contain at least rank order information. This assumption is reasonable in this example since a person who reports to be *always interested* in watching football is probably more of a football fan than a person who reports being only *usually interested*. Also in this dialog, select the option *Spearman rank order correlation*. The *Crosstabulation Tables Results* dialog will appear as shown below:

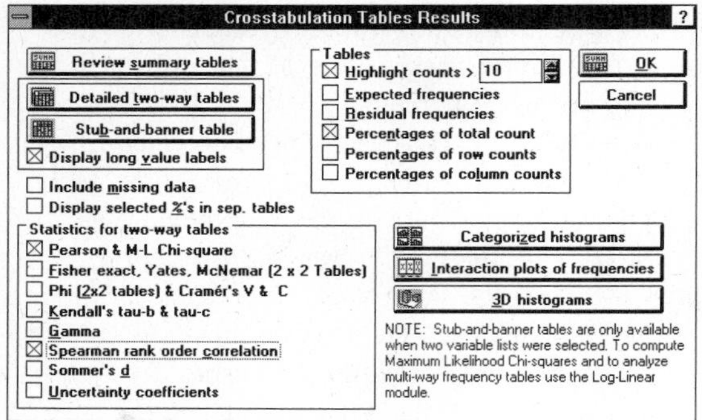

Selecting a table. Now that the statistics selections have been made, click on the *Detailed two-way tables* button in order to select the tables for the analysis. The *Select the tables you want to review* dialog will open in which all available two-way tables will be listed.

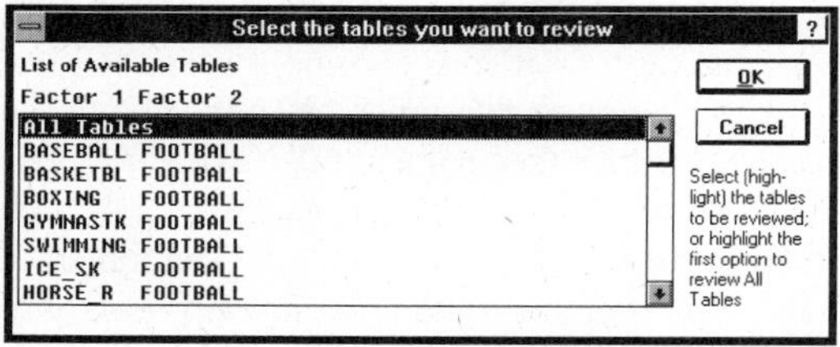

You can select the desired tables from this list or use the *All tables* option to produce a cascade of two-way tables. For this example, select the *Baseball Football* table and click *OK* in this dialog. Two Scrollsheets will be produced for each table selected.

The first Scrollsheet contains the observed (raw) frequencies and any other selections made in the *Tables* options of the *Crosstabulation Tables Results* dialog (e.g., *Percentages of total count*).

2 x 2 Summary Table: Observed Frequencies (sports.sta)

BASIC STATS BASEBALL: "Watching baseball"	FOOTBALL ALWAYS	FOOTBALL USUALLY	FOOTBALL SOMETIMS	FOOTBALL NEVER	Row Totals
Marked cells have counts > 10					
ALWAYS : Always interested	24	2	2	0	28
Total Perce	24.00%	2.00%	2.00%	0.00%	28.00%
USUALLY : Usually interested	8	5	3	1	17
Total Perce	8.00%	5.00%	3.00%	1.00%	17.00%
SOMETIMS: Sometimes interest	5	7	19	6	37
Total Perce	5.00%	7.00%	19.00%	6.00%	37.00%
NEVER : Never interested	2	2	2	12	18
Total Perce	2.00%	2.00%	2.00%	12.00%	18.00%
Column Totals	39	16	26	19	100
Total Perce	39.00%	16.00%	26.00%	19.00%	100.00%

The second Scrollsheet contains the *Chi-square* tests and *Spearman* correlation results.

Statistics: BASEBALL(4) x FOOTBALL(4) (sports.sta)

BASIC STATS	Chi-square	df	p
Pearson Chi-square	72.95470	df=9	p=.00000
M-L Chi-square	69.78099	df=9	p=.00000
Spearman Rank R	.6785191	t=9.1440	p=.00000

The Pearson *Chi-square* value for this two-way table is *72.95*, which is highly statistically significant (refer to *Elementary Concepts*, Chapter 8, for an explanation of significance testing). The *Spearman R* is equal to *0.6785*, reflecting the substantial correlation between interest in football and baseball in this sample.

Note that in addition to all methods mentioned before, you can graphically view the two-way table results by clicking on the *Interaction plots of frequencies* button in the *Crosstabulation Tables Results* dialog. When you click on this button, the *Select the tables you want to review* dialog will open. Select the *Baseball Football* table and click *OK* to produce the interaction plot.

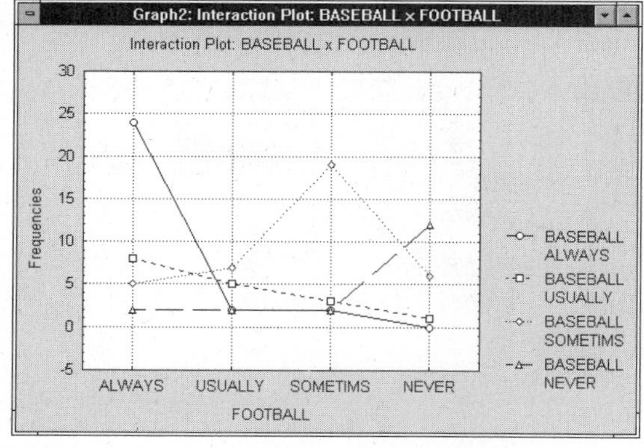

StatSoft

You can also use the *Categorized Histograms* option,

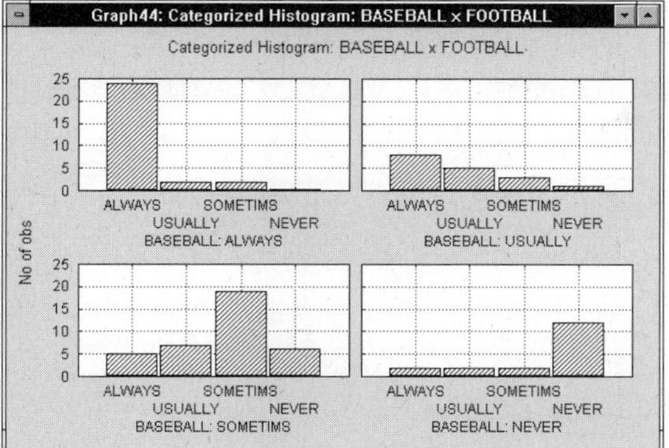

or the *3D Histograms* option,

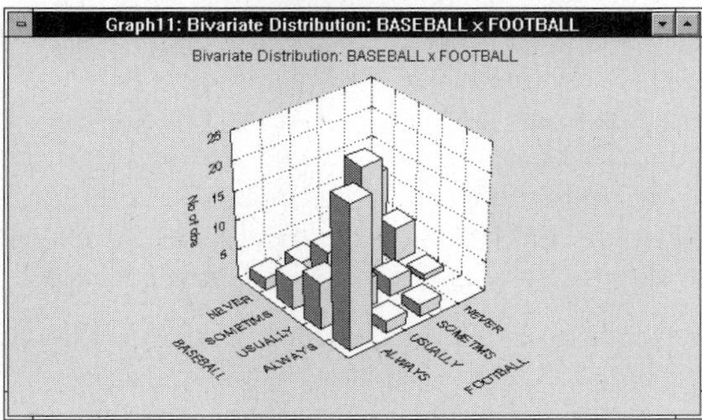

(from the *Crosstabulation and Tables Results* dialog) to visually inspect the frequencies of the selected two-way tables.

Reviewing other tables. Return to the *Crosstabulation Tables Results* dialog and click on the *Detailed two-way tables* button again. Now select the table *Gymnastk Football* and click *OK*. (The same statistics will be computed for this table since you did not make any new selections among those options.)

Statistics: GYMNASTK(4) x FOOTBALL(4) (sports.sta)

BASIC STATS	Chi-square	df	p
Pearson Chi-square	21.18554	df=9	p=.01187
M-L Chi-square	23.50668	df=9	p=.00516
Spearman Rank R	.3328759	t=3.4946	p=.00071

There is still a relationship between reported interest for football and gymnastics. However, it is not nearly as strong (the *Spearman R* is computed as *0.33*). The fact that even this variable (*Gymnastk*) is significantly related to football suggests that many of the respondents (sampled from within the sports bars) are indeed generally interested in watching all kinds of sports.

Summary

The major results of this analysis are (1) that most of the respondents in the survey were interested in watching *all* major sports, that is, football, baseball, and basketball, and (2) that showing gymnastics from time to time may appeal to at least some respondents who explicitly are not interested in watching football.

Example 5: Crosstabulation Tables

Overview

Even though some tentative conclusions have been reached concerning the sports survey (see the previous example), some higher-order tables will now be reviewed. Specifically, the percentage of respondents who are true "sports nuts" will be determined. That is, the number of respondents who say they are *always interested* in watching football *and* baseball *and* basketball will be computed. In contrast, the table of *Football* by *Baseball* by *Skiing* will also be computed.

Specifying the Analysis

In the *Basic Statistics and Tables* startup panel, select the procedure *Tables and Banners*. To specify the table, click on the *Specify tables* button in the *Multi-way crosstabulation tables* section of the *Specify Tables* dialog, and a standard variable selection dialog will open.

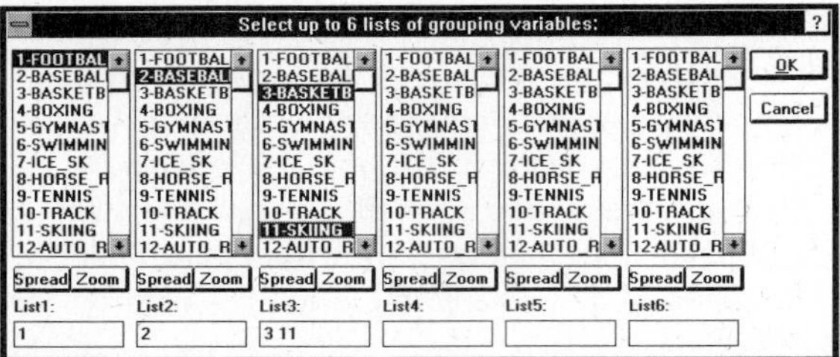

You can select one or more variables in each of the six lists to create multi-way tables. However, for this example, two tables will be specified: *Football* by *Baseball* by *Basketbl* and *Football* by *Baseball* by *Skiing*. In the variable selection dialog, select variable *Football* in the first list, variable *Baseball* in the second list, and variables *Basketbl* and *Skiing* in the third list. Selecting the variables in this way will create two tables in which the levels of *Basketbl* are used to "slice" one of the tables and of *Skiing* to "slice" the other table. In other words, each combination of levels of *Football* and *Baseball* will be reviewed at each level of *Basketbl* (or *Skiing*). The *Specify Table* dialog will now appear as follows:

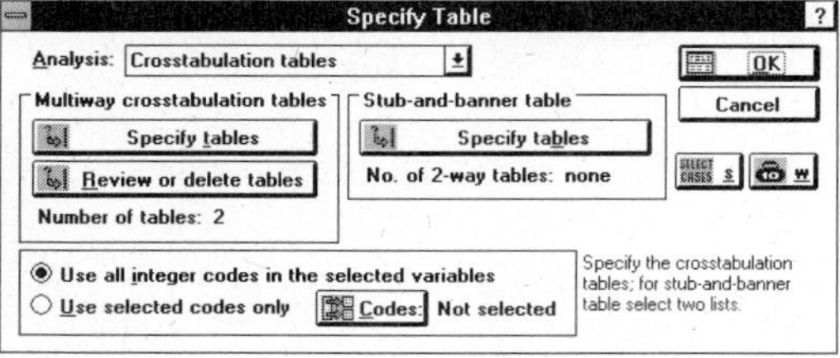

Once you have made your table selections, the *Review or delete tables* button will become available (i.e., undimmed). Click on this button to open the *Select tables to be deleted* dialog.

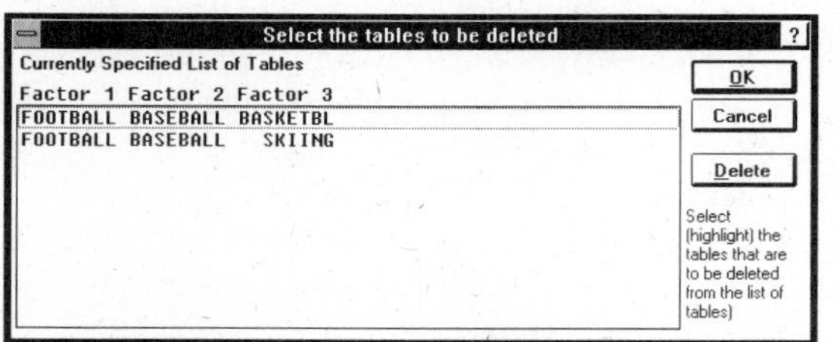

Here, you can review the tables that were selected and, if desired, delete specific tables from the list. Now, click *OK* in the *Specify Tables* dialog to open the *Crosstabulation Tables Results* dialog.

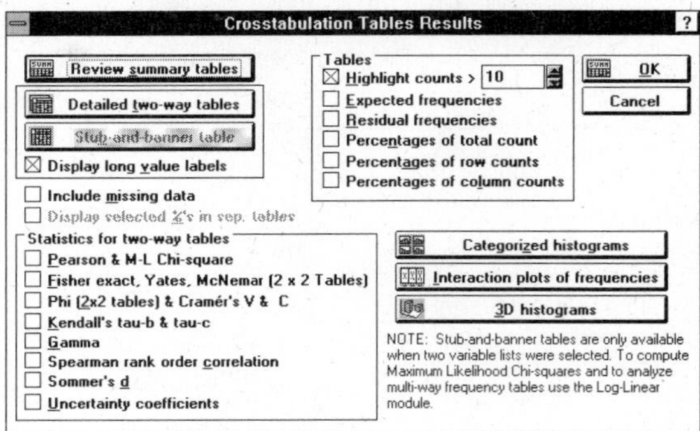

This is the same dialog as in the Stub-and-banner tables example, except the *Stub-and-banner tables* button is now dimmed. Once again, select the desired table entries (e.g., *Percentages of row counts*, *Percentages of total count*, etc.) and statistics to be computed (e.g., *Chi-square* tests, correlations, etc.) by clicking on either the *Review summary tables* or *Detailed two-way tables* buttons.

In either case, an intermediate dialog will open in which you can select a table from among the previously selected tables. When you select *All tables*, then a cascade of Scrollsheets will be produced for each of the tables listed in this dialog.

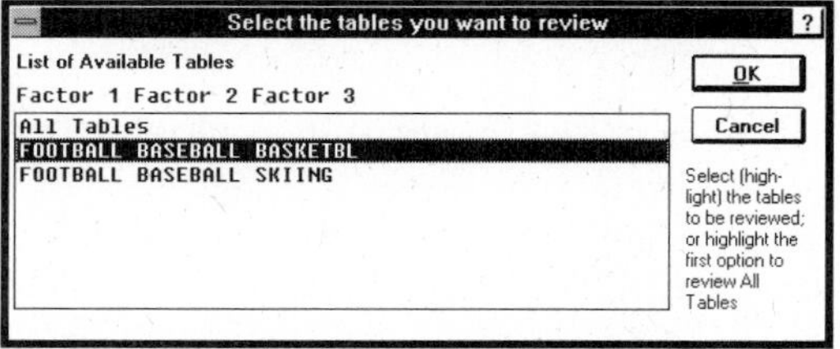

For this example click on the *Review summary tables* button and select the *Football Baseball Basketbl* table (see *Example 3*, above, for an example of the *Detailed two-way tables* procedure).

Summary Frequency Table (sports.sta)

BASIC STATS — Marked cells have counts > 10 (Marginal summaries are not marked)

FOOTBALL	BASEBALL	BASKETBL ALWAYS	BASKETBL USUALLY	BASKETBL SOMETIMS	BASKETBL NEVER	Row Totals
ALWAYS	ALWAYS	11	8	2	3	24
ALWAYS	USUALLY	2	2	3	1	8
ALWAYS	SOMETIMS	2	0	0	3	5
ALWAYS	NEVER	0	0	0	2	2
	Total	15	10	5	9	39
USUALLY	ALWAYS	0	0	1	1	2
USUALLY	USUALLY	0	1	4	0	5
USUALLY	SOMETIMS	1	0	5	1	7
USUALLY	NEVER	0	0	1	1	2
	Total	1	1	11	3	16
SOMETIMS	ALWAYS	0	1	1	0	2
SOMETIMS	USUALLY	0	0	2	1	3
SOMETIMS	SOMETIMS	2	2	12	3	19
SOMETIMS	NEVER	0	0	1	1	2
	Total	2	3	16	5	26
NEVER	ALWAYS	0	0	0	0	0

As you can see, 11 respondents from the sample of 100 said that they are *always interested* in football, baseball, and basketball. Now, return to the *Crosstabulation Tables Results* dialog, click once again on the *Review summary tables* button and select the table *Football Baseball Skiing*.

Summary Frequency Table (sports.sta)

BASIC STATS — Marked cells have counts > 10 (Marginal summaries are not marked)

FOOTBALL	BASEBALL	SKIING ALWAYS	SKIING USUALLY	SKIING SOMETIMS	SKIING NEVER	Row Totals
ALWAYS	ALWAYS	5	3	9	7	24
ALWAYS	USUALLY	1	0	2	5	8
ALWAYS	SOMETIMS	1	1	2	1	5
ALWAYS	NEVER	0	1	0	1	2
	Total	7	5	13	14	39
USUALLY	ALWAYS	0	0	2	0	2
USUALLY	USUALLY	0	1	2	2	5
USUALLY	SOMETIMS	0	1	4	2	7
USUALLY	NEVER	0	0	2	0	2
	Total	0	2	10	4	16
SOMETIMS	ALWAYS	1	0	1	0	2
SOMETIMS	USUALLY	0	0	1	2	3
SOMETIMS	SOMETIMS	3	2	8	6	19
SOMETIMS	NEVER	0	0	2	0	2
	Total	4	2	12	8	26
NEVER	ALWAYS	0	0	0	0	0

There were only 5 respondents who said that they are *always interested* in watching football, baseball, and skiing.

Graphical presentation of crosstabulations. The crosstabulation results can be represented graphically via the *Categorized histograms*, *Interaction plots of frequencies*, and *3D histograms* buttons in this dialog. As in the other crosstabulation options from the results dialog, the *Select the tables that you want to review* dialog will open when you select one of the graphic options. For each of these graph options, select the *Football Baseball Basketbl* table. The *Categorized histogram* for the *Football Baseball Basketbl* table is shown below.

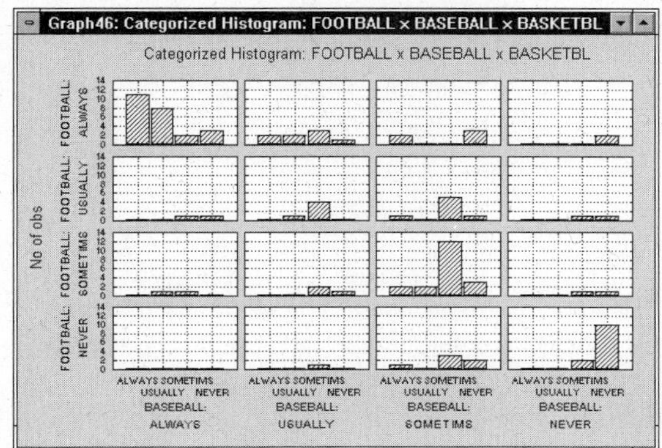

When you click on the *Interaction plots of frequencies* button for the *Football Baseball Basketbl* table, the following graph is produced.

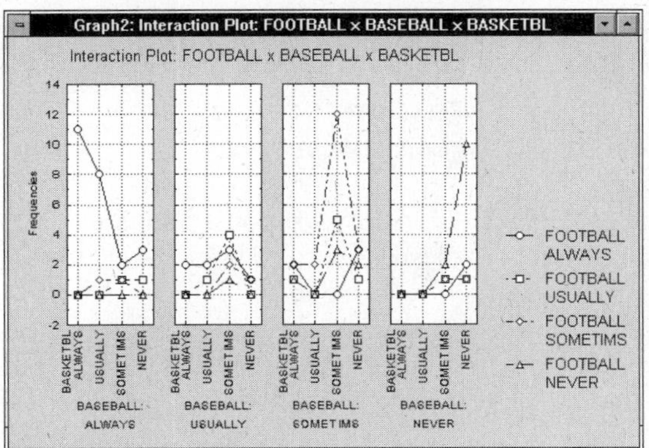

When you select the *3D histograms* option, a cascade of 3D bivariate histograms will be produced (one for each level or subtable of *Football*).

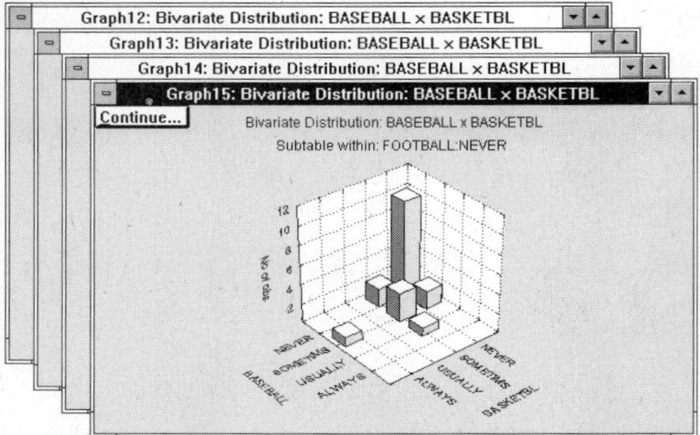

Summary

To summarize this analysis, you can conclude that 11 of the 100 respondents in the sample reported to be always interested in watching football, baseball, and basketball. Thus, it is probably fair to say that about 10% of the clientele in your sports bars are basically devoted general sports fans who watch all major popular sports.

Example 6: Tabulating Multiple Responses and Dichotomies

The general idea of multiple response variables and multiple dichotomies is described in the *Overview* section (page 1453). If you are entirely unfamiliar with such variables, it is recommended that you review that section before continuing with this example. This example will illustrate how the need to use such variables often arises in survey research, and how they can be analyzed with the *Basic Statistics and Tables* module of *STATISTICA*.

An example data file with the results of a fictitious survey is included in the *Examples* subdirectory to demonstrate the three types of variables that can be tabulated:

- Simple categorical variables,
- Multiple response variables, and
- Multiple dichotomies.

Simple frequency tables will first be computed in order to show how these three types of variables can be summarized; then cross-tabulation tables involving these variables will be examined.

Description of Data File

Suppose you conducted a survey of consumer preferences of young adults. Specifically, you were interested in young consumers' (1) preferences for different types of fast-food (favorite fast-food), (2) preferences for different types of automobiles, and (3) actual (self-reported) past patronage of specific fast-food restaurants. In addition, you recorded the respondents' gender. These preferences were measured and entered into the data file *Fastfood.sta*. Each variable in this data file is identified and described below:

Gender (simple categorical variable). The respondent's gender was simply recorded and entered as a categorical variable (*Gender)* into the data file (i.e., *Male*, *Female*).

Favorite fast-food (multiple response variable). The questionnaire that was used for this study asked the respondents to select their favorite (up to) three choices of commonly available fast-foods from a list of 8 different types. The 8 different types of fast-food which were presented to the respondents were:

(1) *Hamburger*

(2) *Sandwiches*

(3) *Chicken*

(4) *Pizza*

(5) *Mexican fast-food*

(6) *Chinese fast-food*

(7) *Seafood*

(8) *other ethnic or regionally popular fast-food*

The three choices that each respondent made were entered into the data file as a multiple response variable, that is, their first choice was entered into variable *Food_1* (first preference or favorite fast-food), their second choice (if available) was entered into variable *Food_2*, and their third choice into variable *Food_3*.

In the analysis, you could treat variable *Food_1* as a simple categorical variable, and ask the question: What is the number (proportion) of respondents that mentioned the respective type of fast-food as their *favorite*? However, you would also be interested in how many respondents mentioned a particular type of fast-food as *any one* of their three favorite fast-foods. This question requires that you treat variables *Food_1* through *Food_3* as a multiple response variable; for example, if you want to count the number of respondents who chose *Hamburgers* as either their first, second, or third preference. This will be clarified further when the frequency table for this variable is discussed.

Favorite car (multiple response variable). Here, each subject was asked to write down the three most desirable cars (make and model) that they would like to own (if money were no object). These responses (specific brands and models) were coded into four categories:

(1) *Domestic sports car*

(2) *Domestic sedan*

(3) *Foreign sports car*

(4) *Foreign sedan*

Like the *favorite fast-food* variable (see above), this variable was entered as a multiple response variable, that is, the respondents preferences were entered into variables *Car_1* through *Car_3*. Note, however, that in this case, the subjects could repeat the same answer three times (e.g., they could mention 3 sports cars as their three most desirable cars). In the *fast-food* case above, multiple identical responses were not allowed (i.e., ignored).

For example, if a respondent identified as her three favorite fast-foods *Hamburger, Hamburger*, and *Hamburger*, then *Hamburger* was only entered once as that respondent's favorite food (in variable *Food_1*), and the respective cells for variables *Food_2* and *Food_3* were left blank.

Recent patronage of specific hamburger restaurants (multiple dichotomy). Finally, the subjects were asked to indicate which of four different (specific) local fast-food hamburger restaurants they had visited in the two weeks prior to the survey. In this case, the data was entered such that a variable was included in the file for each specific restaurant. The four variables, *Burger_1* through *Burger_4*, represented the following four different local restaurants:

(1) *Burger Meister*

(2) *Bill's Best Burgers*

(3) *Hamburger Heaven*

(4) *Bigger Burger*

If a respondent reported to have eaten at one or more of these restaurants recently, then a *1* was entered into the respective column; if not, then it was left blank. Thus, this is a multiple dichotomy, and it is desired to tabulate the number (or proportion) of respondents that report to have eaten at each of the four restaurants in the study.

Note that you could also have entered this variable as a multiple response variable. In that case, you would have had to create up to four variables (e.g., *Eat_1* through *Eat_4*) and then entered the names of the restaurants (e.g., *Burger_1*, *Burger_2, ...*) as the values into the columns of the spreadsheet (similar to the *favorite car* and *favorite fast-food* variables, above).

Listing of data file. Shown below is a listing of the first few cases in the data file *Fastfood.sta*. (Note that due to the number of variables in the file, the second-half of the data file is shown below the first spreadsheet.)

Data: FASTFOOD.STA 11v * 200c

Fast food and fast cars: Survey of adolescent consumer preferences

	1 GENDER	2 FOOD_1	3 FOOD_2	4 FOOD_3	5 CAR_1	6 CAR_2	7 CAR_3
1	FEMALE	PIZZA	SEAFOOD		DOM_SEDN	DOM_SPRT	DOM_SPRT
2	MALE	SEAFOOD	PIZZA	HAMBURGR	FOR_SPRT	DOM_SPRT	FOR_SPRT
3	MALE	PIZZA	OTHER	MEXICAN	DOM_SEDN	DOM_SEDN	FOR_SEDN
4	MALE	SEAFOOD	MEXICAN	SANDWICH	DOM_SPRT	FOR_SPRT	FOR_SPRT
5	FEMALE	HAMBURGR	CHINESE		FOR_SPRT	DOM_SPRT	DOM_SEDN

Data: FASTFOOD.STA 11v * 200c

Fast food and fast cars: Survey of adolescent consum

	8 BURGER_1	9 BURGER_2	10 BURGER_3	11 BURGER_4
1	YES		YES	
2		YES		
3	YES			YES
4		YES		
5		YES	YES	YES

To illustrate how each subject's responses were entered into this data file, look at the first subject (case) in the spreadsheet above. The first subject was a woman, so the value *Female* was entered in the variable *Gender*. As her most favorite fast-food, she chose *Pizza* (entered into variable *Food_1*), as her second favorite fast-food she chose *Seafood* (entered into variable *Food_2*), and she chose no other type of fast-food, so the value for variable *Food_3* was left blank (i.e., missing).

The three cars that she mentioned were coded as (1) *domestic sedan*, (2) *domestic sports car*, and (3) again as *domestic sports* car in the variables *Car_1*, *Car_2*, and *Car_3*, respectively. Finally, she responded that she ate at *Burger_1* (*Burger Meister*) and *Burger_3* (*Hamburger Heaven*) within the last two weeks, so values of *Yes* were entered for those respective variables and the values for the other two *Burger* variables were left to missing.

Overall, there were 200 respondents in the study.

Specifying the Simple Categorical and Multiple Response Variables

Now, begin the analysis by computing simple frequency tables for the simple categorical variable *Gender* and the multiple response variables in the study. Because some respondents have missing data for all variables *Burger_1* through *Burger_4* (i.e., they have not eaten in any of the four restaurants during the previous two weeks), that table will be specified separately later. By default, the cases with all missing data in the *Burger* variables will be excluded from the analysis, and frequency counts will be obtained only for those subjects who have eaten in at least one of the four restaurants. Alternatively, you could also set the *Include missing data as an additional category* check box below. After opening the *Basic Statistics and Tables* module, select the *Tables and Banners* option on the startup panel (see page 1499). On the resulting *Specify table* dialog, select the option *Tables for multiple response items* from the *Analysis* combo box in order to open the *Multiple Response Tables* dialog. The *Multiple Response Tables* dialog allows you to specify all three types of categorical variables, that is, simple categorical variables (such as *Gender* in this example), multiple response variables (such as *Food_1* through *Food_3* or *Car_1* through *Car_3*), and multiple dichotomies (such as *Burger_1* through *Burger 4*).

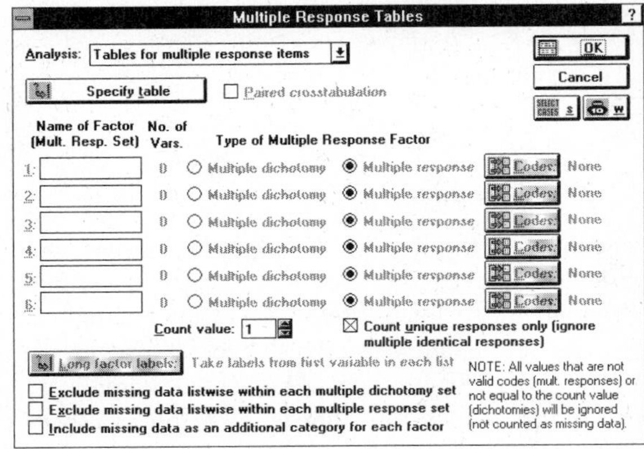

Click on the *Specify table* button in this dialog to specify the respective variables, as shown below:

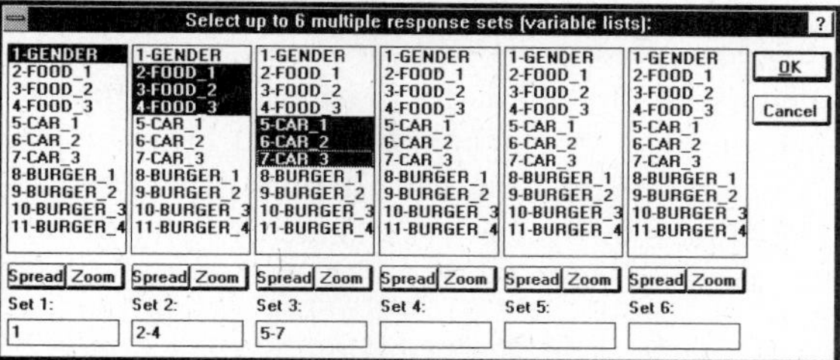

As you can see, up to 6 multiple factors (simple categorical variables, multiple responses or dichotomies) can be specified for a single table. In the first column only variable *Gender* is selected; the program will automatically interpret single variables (multiple response sets with only one variable) as simple categorical variables. In the second column variables *Food_1* through *Food_3* are selected, and in the third variables *Car_1* through *Car_3* are selected. In this preliminary analysis, the simple frequency tables for all factors will be reviewed (as mentioned above, the frequency table for the multiple dichotomy factors *Burger_1* through *Burger_4* will be examined later). Now click *OK* to finalize these selections and display them in the *Multiple Response Tables* dialog.

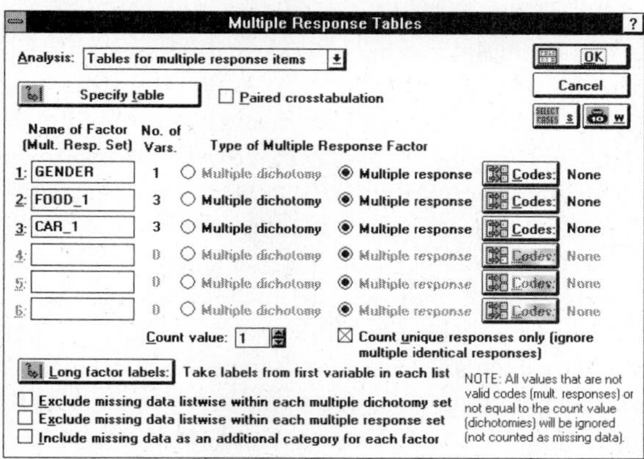

Naming conventions. In the left-most column on this dialog, you will see the default names for the factors in the analysis. The term *factor* is used here because a multiple response variable such as *food preference* in this example, consists of several variables (in the data file). Note that by default the name (both short and long) for each factor will be taken from the first variable in the respective list. Also, the text values will be taken from that variable (for an explanation of the dual numeric/text value notation used in *STATISTICA*, refer to the description of the *Text Values Manager* in Chapter 3; see also *Data Management*, Chapter 7).

If you want to change the names of the factors, click on the *Long factor labels* button to open the *Long Factor Labels for Multiple Response Sets* dialog. Here, you can enter the desired short and long names that will be used to identify the factors in subsequent tables.

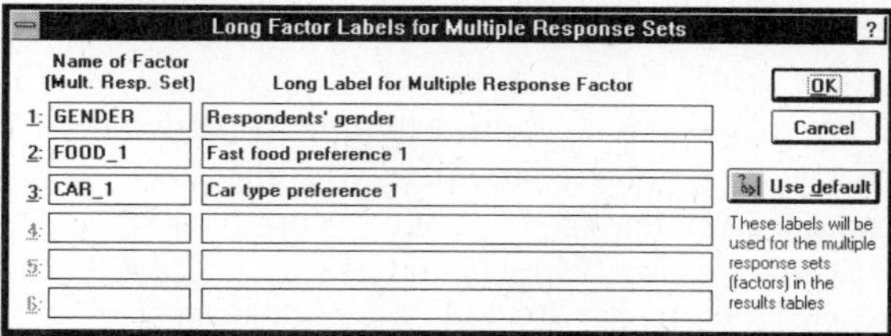

For this example, change the names of the multiple response factors slightly, so that they will more accurately reflect their meaning: *Food: Favorite 3 fast-foods*, and *Car: Favorite types of car.*

Defining factors. The radio buttons next to each factor identify its type. For the first variable -- *Gender* -- there is no choice of radio buttons since that variable is a simple categorical variable. For the second and third factors, set the *Multiple response* radio buttons. As you can see, you can now select the codes that were used in the file to identify the different categories for the respective factor, that is, the codes that were used to identify *Male* and *Female* respondents (variable *Gender)*, the different fast-foods in variables *Food_1* through *Food_3*, and the different types of cars in *Car_1* through *Car_3*. If you do not explicitly define those codes (by simply clicking *OK* and accepting defaults), then they will automatically be taken from the first

variable in each set (factor), that is, the program will identify all codes in the respective variable. This will usually identify all codes that were used in that factor, but occasionally, it may happen that a particular code is not used in the first variable of a set, but only in the second or third. In that case, simply accepting the default will not identify that code. Thus it is always advisable to enter all codes (categories) that one wants to use in the tables explicitly. After clicking on any of the *Codes* buttons, you can enter the codes for all factors.

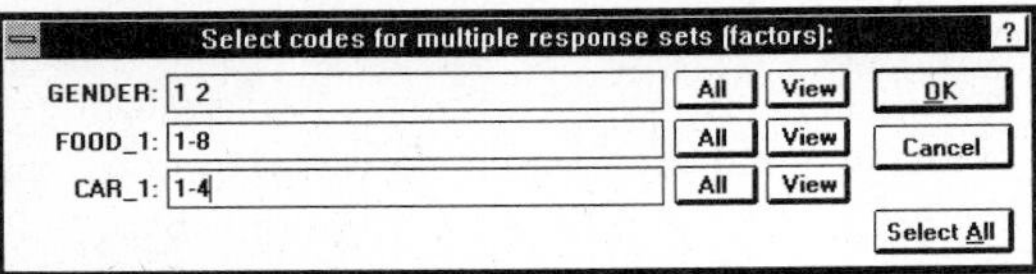

Now click *OK* to close the code selection dialog.

Other options. Before proceeding, look at some of the other options on the *Multiple Response Tables* dialog. The *Paired crosstabulation* check box will cause the program to "match up" multiple response factors with equal numbers of levels, and treat them as paired variables. Paired crosstabulation is described in greater detail in the *Overview* section (see page 1455).

The check boxes below the *Long factor labels* button in the *Multiple Response Tables* dialog control the manner in which missing data values (i.e., blank cells in the data file) are processed. For example, by default when processing a multiple dichotomy factor, the program will count the number of responses equal to the *Count value*, and ignore all others. Alternatively, one can also treat missing data (no response at all) different from a valid data point that is not equal to the *Count value.* Specifically, missing data can be excluded *listwise*, that is, all cases (respondents) are excluded from the analysis if they show missing data in any of the variables included in the multiple dichotomy set. The second check box -- *Exclude missing data listwise within each multiple response set* -- works analogously, that is, it will cause cases to be excluded *listwise* from the analysis if they have missing data for any of the variables in the multiple response set. The last check box (*Include missing data as an additional category...*) determines whether or not a separate category for missing data will be included in the frequency and cross-tabulation tables. If this check box is set then the tabulation routines will treat (count) missing data as just another category of the respective factors.

Finally, there is the *Count unique responses only ...* check box. This check box pertains to the manner in which multiple identical responses are treated in multiple response variables. In this example, the *Car* factor is made up of three variables with codes that identify the types of automobile that the respondents identified as their most desirable three cars to own. Thus, it is possible that a subject selected three foreign sports cars as his or her favorite three cars, which would then result in identical codes (*For_Sprt*) in each of the three variables *Car_1* through *Car_3*. The setting of this check box determines whether such multiple identical responses will be counted or ignored, that is, whether a subject naming three foreign sports cars will be counted three times (if the *Count unique responses only...* check box is not set) or only once (if it is set).

In this example, it is not of interest whether all three of a subjects' most favorite cars are of a specific type (thereby inflating the numbers by such multiple identical responses); therefore, it makes the most sense to set this check box (that is to accept the default) in order to determine the number of respondents who, for example, name a domestic sedan as one of their favorite three cars. Note that the variables making up the *Food* factor only contain mutually exclusive categories, since the respondents were explicitly not allowed to identify the same item (e.g., *Hamburger, Hamburger,* and *Hamburger*) as their favorite three fast-foods. Instead, the subjects had to choose from among eight fast-foods, without repeating a choice. Therefore, for factor *Food*, it does not matter whether or not this check box is set.

Reviewing Frequency Tables for Multiple Response Factors

Click *OK* in the *Multiple Response Tables* dialog in order to proceed with the analysis and open the *Multiple Response Tables Results* dialog.

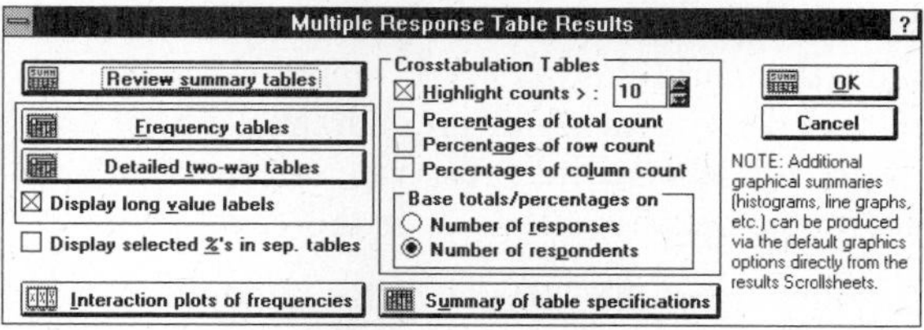

For now, only the simple tabulation of *Frequency tables* will be reviewed (the crosstabulation tables that can be selected from this dialog will be reviewed later, see page 1493). Set the *Highlight counts* edit field on the results dialog to 100 (so that all frequency counts greater than 100 will be highlighted in the Scrollsheet), and then click on the *Frequency tables* button. The interpretation of the frequency table for *Gender* is straightforward; the frequency tables for the other two variables are shown in the Scrollsheets below.

Frequencies (Identical resp. were ignored) (fastfood.sta)

BASIC STATS N=200 Category	FOOD : Favorite 3 fast-foods (Multiple Response Variable) Count	Prcnt.of Responses	Prcnt.of Cases
HAMBURGR: Hamburger	114	21.84	57.00
SANDWICH: Sandwiches	49	9.39	24.50
CHICKEN : Chicken	46	8.81	23.00
PIZZA : Pizza	138	26.44	69.00
MEXICAN : Mexican fast food	42	8.05	21.00
CHINESE : Chinese fast food	45	8.62	22.50
SEAFOOD : Seafood	46	8.81	23.00
OTHER : Other ethnic/regional	42	8.05	21.00
Total Responses	522	100.00	261.00

Frequencies (Identical resp. were ignored) (fastfood.sta)

BASIC STATS N=200 Category	CAR : Favorite types of car (Multiple Response Variable) Count	Prcnt.of Responses	Prcnt.of Cases
DOM_SPRT: Domestic sports car	123	29.29	61.50
DOM_SEDN: Domestic sedan	76	18.10	38.00
FOR_SPRT: Foreign sports car	157	37.38	78.50
FOR_SEDN: Foreign sedan	64	15.24	32.00
Total Responses	420	100.00	210.00

First look at the frequency table for the factor *Food.* Overall, there were 200 respondents in the study (*N=200* is shown in the upper left-hand corner of the Scrollsheet). The *Count* column of the Scrollsheet shows the number of respondents who mentioned the respective type of food as one of their favorite three types of fast-food. Remember that only unique responses were counted (see above) and thus, each respondent can only be counted once in this column. Therefore, you can conclude that *Pizza* was the most popular fast-food, mentioned either as the first, second, or third favorite by 138 respondents, *Hamburger* was the second most popular choice (114). All other categories of fast-food were mention by only about 40 to 50 of the respondents.

The second column of the Scrollsheet expresses the raw counts relative to the number of total responses, that is, the total of the first column. So you can say that of all fast-food preferences volunteered by the respondents (remember that some only mentioned one or two), 26.44% (100*138/522) of the expressed preferences identified *Pizza.* In a sense, this column treats as the unit of analysis each fast-food preference mentioned by the respondents (and not the respondents themselves). By contrast, the third column of the Scrollsheet shows the percentage of respondents who mentioned the respective fast-foods as either their first, second, or third preference. Here you can see that *Pizza* was identified as a favorite food by 69% (100*138/200) of all respondents.

The interpretation of the frequency table for the *Car* factor is analogous. Foreign sports cars were mentioned by 157 respondents as one of their first three choices (again, remember that only unique responses are counted, thus, each respondent can only be counted once in each category); domestic sports cars were mentioned by 123 respondents. The second column shows a 37.38% response for foreign sports cars; this number is not readily interpretable in this case since only unique responses were counted. Thus, if a respondent identified three foreign sports cars as his or her favorite cars then he or she would only be counted once in this table. The numbers in the third column (*Percent of cases*) are

more informative; for example, 78.5% of all respondents identified a foreign sports car as one of the three most desirable cars to own.

Specifying a Multiple Dichotomy Factor

Now, return to the *Multiple Response Tables* specification dialog (click *Cancel* on the *Results* dialog) to specify the multiple dichotomy variable in this survey (patronage of particular restaurants). Click on the *Specify table* button, deselect the previously selected variables and specify *Burger_1* through *Burger_4* as the variables for the first set.

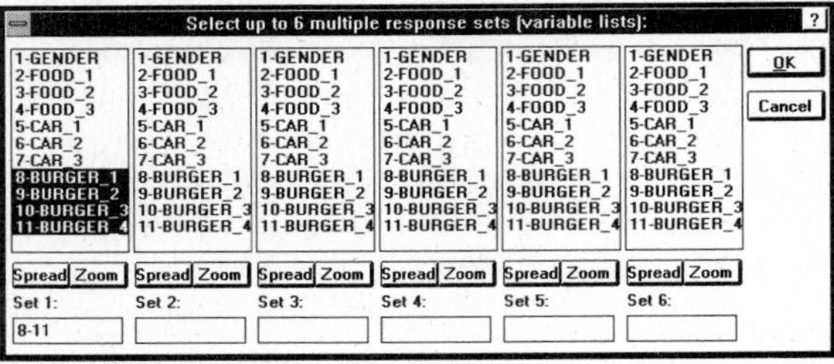

Next, set the *Multiple dichotomy* radio button next to the first factor in the *Multiple Response Tables* dialog. As before, you can use the *Long factor labels* option to enter a more appropriate name for this factor. For example, you may call this factor *Patron: Recently patronized restaurants.*

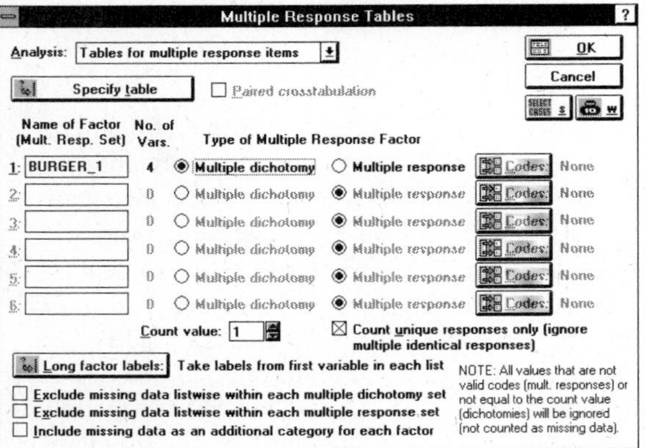

You still need to specify the code that was used in the multiple dichotomy factor *Patron* to identify whether or not a respondent had eaten at the respective restaurant during the two weeks prior to the survey. Specify this code in the *Count value* edit box below the listing of the factors. Since code number *1* (the numeric equivalent to the value *Yes*; see *Data Management*, Chapter 7, for a discussion of text/numeric equivalents of values of variables) was used to identify which restaurant had been visited by the respective respondent, you can simply accept the default code given in this edit box.

Remember that the way in which a multiple dichotomy variable (factor) is interpreted by the program is that it will treat the different variables in the set as levels (categories) of the respective multiple dichotomy factor, and then count the number of entries in those variables (categories) that are equal to the code number. All values that are not equal to the code number will be treated the same, that is, they will be ignored. Thus, you may use more "sophisticated" coding schemes for multiple dichotomies than the simple 1-0 (or nothing, i.e., missing) coding used in this example.

For example, you could have used a separate code (other than 1) to indicate that the respondent reported to have "never even considered eating there." You could enter code *2* in variables *Burger_1* through *Burger_4* to identify such strong negative responses towards the respective restaurants, and by specifying that code in the *Count value* edit field, you could tabulate those responses as well. Thus, by using different code values a multiple dichotomy can be used to identify multiple mutually exclusive responses.

Missing data. There are some respondents who have not eaten in any of the four hamburger restaurants during the two weeks prior to the survey; in the data spreadsheet, those cases show blanks (missing values) for all four variables *Burger_1* through *Burger_4*. By default, those cases will be excluded from the tabulation.

Alternatively, you could *Include missing data as an additional category* (set that check box). In that case, the resulting frequency table would show an additional fifth category labeled *Missing*, reporting the number of respondents who did not visit any of the four restaurants.

In this example, it is desired to tabulate only those respondents who visited at least one hamburger restaurant, in order to see how this "market segment of hamburger-eaters" is divided among the restaurants (see below). Click *OK* to proceed to the *Multiple Response Tables Results* dialog.

Reviewing the Frequency Table for a Multiple Dichotomy

On the *Results* dialog, select once again the *Frequency tables* option. The interpretation of the numbers reported in this table is analogous to that for multiple response variables.

Frequencies (Identical resp. were ignored) (fastfood.sta)

BASIC STATS N=157 Category	BURGER_1: Burger Meister (Multiple Dichotomy; count value: 1) Count	Prcnt.of Responses	Prcnt.of Cases
BURGER_1: Burger Meister	60	24.19	38.22
BURGER_2: Bill's Best Burgers	68	27.42	43.31
BURGER_3: Hamburger Heaven	61	24.60	38.85
BURGER_4: Bigger Burger	59	23.79	37.58
Total Responses	248	100.00	157.96

Overall, 157 respondents had eaten in one of the four restaurants in this survey (*n=157*); 60 respondents had eaten at *Burger Meister,* 68 had eaten at *Bill's Best Burgers*, and so on. The values in the second column (*Percent of responses)* express these counts relative to the total number of times that any one of the four restaurants was mentioned.

Assume that the four (fictitious) restaurants have pretty much cornered the hamburger fast-food marked in the survey city, and that the 157 respondents (out of the 200) more or less represent the total market of young adults who eat at fast-food hamburger places. In that case the values in the second column represent the market shares for the four restaurants.

For example, of all the hamburger places patronized by the respondents in the two weeks prior to the survey, *Burger Meister* was frequented in 24.19% of the cases, *Bill's Best Burger* in 27.42% of the cases, and so on. The third column (*Percent of cases*) reports the percent of respondents who had eaten in the past two weeks at the respective restaurants.

Remember that these percentages are expressed relative to the *n* of 157, that is, relative to the number of respondents who had eaten in at least one of the four restaurants. Therefore you can, for example, say that 38.22% of those respondents who had eaten in any one of the four hamburger restaurants ate at *Burger Meister*, 43.31% ate at *Bill's Best Burger*, etc.

Note that it is very easy to produce line plots or histograms of the frequencies or percentages via the *Custom graphs* options of the Scrollsheet.

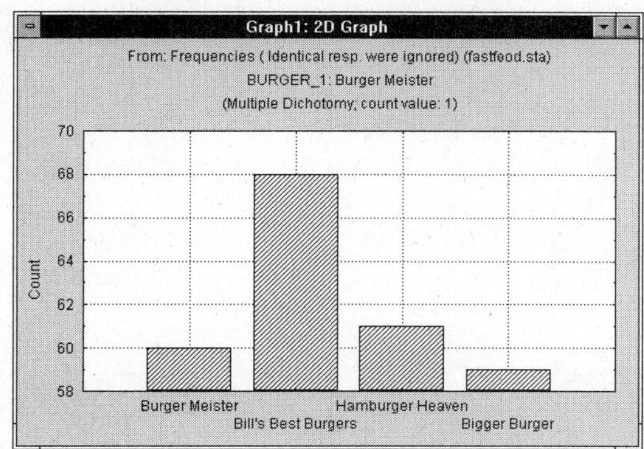

For more information about *Custom graphs*, please refer to Volume II (*Custom 2D Graphs*).

Crosstabulating Multiple Responses and Dichotomies

Now look at some crosstabulation tables involving multiple response variables and multiple dichotomies. *Cancel* the *Results* dialog in order to return to the *Multiple Response Tables* dialog. First look at the crosstabulation table of *Gender* by *Car*,

that is, examine the interest in different types of cars expressed by *Males* and *Females*. Click on the *Specify table* button and in the resulting dialog, select *Gender* as the only variable for the first set, and variables *Car_1* through *Car_3* as the variables for the second set.

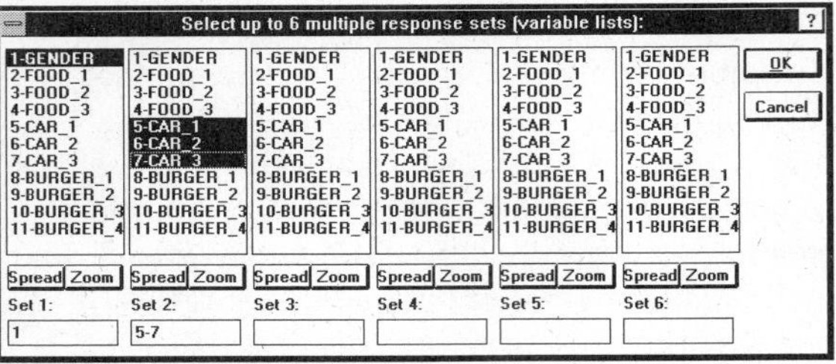

Click *OK* in this dialog to return to the *Multiple Response Tables* dialog. Next, specify the codes that were used for the *Cars* factor to identify the four different types of automobiles. Also, you may want to change the description of the *Car* factor, that is, the short and long factor labels which by default are taken from the first variable in the multiple response set (*Car_1*), via the *Long factor labels:* button.

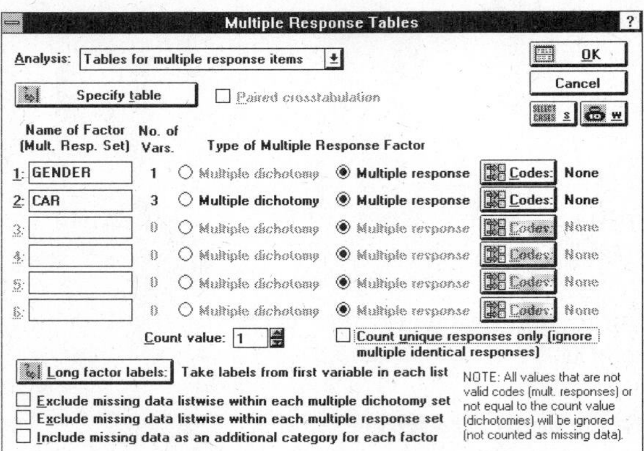

For this table, de-select the *Count unique responses only..* check box. Remember that the purpose of the box is to exclude multiple identical responses from the crosstabulation table. In this instance however, you may want to include those responses. The resulting crosstabulation table will show the total number of different types of cars identified as either the first, second, or third most desirable car, broken down by the categorical variable *Gender*. Now click *OK* to proceed to the *Multiple Response Tables Results* dialog.

For now, do not set any of the *Percent* options (check boxes) but simply request the *Summary* two-way table to produce the following Scrollsheet.

Summary Table for all Multiple Response Items (fastfoo

Totals/percentages based on number of respondents
Multiple identical responses were counted

N=200 GENDER	CAR DOM_SPRT	CAR DOM_SEDN	CAR FOR_SPRT	CAR FOR_SEDN	Row Totals
MALE	141	73	217	61	164
FEMALE	30	14	54	10	36
All Grps	171	87	271	71	200

The default *Quick Stats Graph* for this Scrollsheet is the *3D Histogram.* To produce this graph, click on the Scrollsheet with the right-mouse-button and select the *3D Histogram* option from the flying menu.

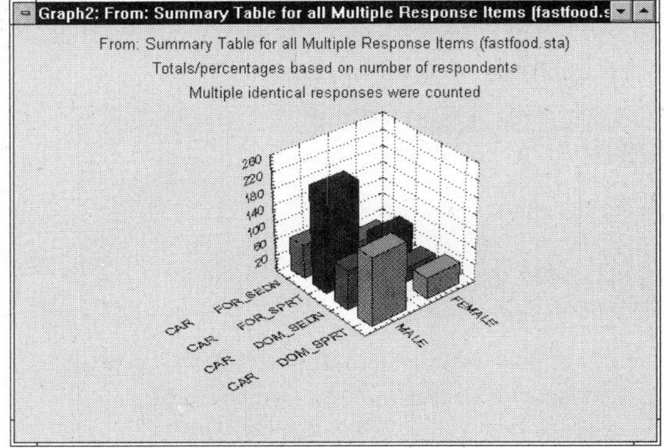

Looking at the above Scrollsheet, it is apparent that both males and females mentioned foreign and domestic sports cars more often than sedans. The difference in the total number of cars mentioned by males and females can be attributed to the greatly different number of male and female respondents in the sample (if you look at the frequency table for *Gender* you will see that there were only 36 females).

Instead of the 3D histogram, the frequencies in this table can also be expressed in a line plot. Return to

the results dialog and select the *Interaction plot* option.

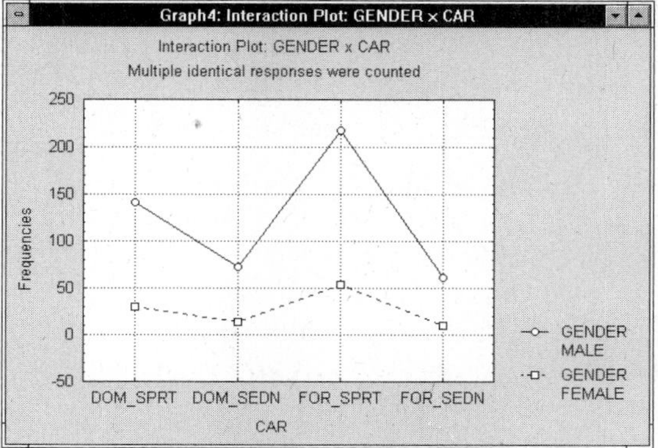

Here, it appears that differential preference for sports cars is more pronounced among males than among females (i.e., the line for males appears more jagged).

Relative Frequencies: Percentage of Responses vs. Respondents

Since each subject gave three responses, it is desired to first look at the percentages expressed in terms of the number of responses (total, row, and column). Therefore, set the *Number of responses* radio button, then check all *Percentage* check boxes in the *Multiple Response Tables Results* dialog, and again click on the *Summary* button to produce the following Scrollsheet.

Summary Table for all Multiple Response Items (fastfood.sta)

BASIC STATS N=200 GENDER	Totals/percentages based on number of responses Multiple identical responses were counted CAR DOM_SPRT	CAR DOM_SEDN	CAR FOR_SPRT	CAR FOR_SEDN	Row Totals
MALE	141	73	217	61	492
Column %	82.46%	83.91%	80.07%	85.92%	
Row %	28.66%	14.84%	44.11%	12.40%	
Table %	23.50%	12.17%	36.17%	10.17%	82.00%
FEMALE	30	14	54	10	108
Column %	17.54%	16.09%	19.93%	14.08%	
Row %	27.78%	12.96%	50.00%	9.26%	
Table %	5.00%	2.33%	9.00%	1.67%	18.00%
All Grps	171	87	271	71	600
Table %	28.50%	14.50%	45.17%	11.83%	100.00%

Each respondent named three cars; thus, the total number of responses is 600. The *Table* percentages express the frequencies relative to that total.

For example, 141 domestic sports cars were named by males, which is equivalent to 23.5% (100*141/600) of all responses. The *Row* percentages pertain to the relative frequency with regard to all responses in the respective row. So for example, the 141 domestic sports cars mentioned by males represents 28.66% (100*141/492) of all cars named by males. Accordingly, the *Column* percentages represent the relative frequencies with regard to the total number of responses in that column: Of all domestic sports cars that were named, 82.46% (100*141/171) were named by males.

Because the *Count unique responses only* check box on the *Multiple Response Tables* dialog was de-selected, it makes little sense to express the percentages in terms of the number of respondents. Remember that in the two-way table shown above some subjects are counted more than once in a single cell -- if they, for example, mentioned more than one foreign sports car.

If you set the *Count unique responses only* check box on the *Multiple Response Tables* dialog and then on the *Multiple Response Table Results* dialog, set the *Number of respondents* radio button, then the summary table would look like this:

Summary Table for all Multiple Response Items (fastfood.sta)

BASIC STATS N=200 GENDER	Totals/percentages based on number of respondents Multiple identical responses were ignored CAR DOM_SPRT	CAR DOM_SEDN	CAR FOR_SPRT	CAR FOR_SEDN	Row Totals
MALE	100	63	127	56	164
Column %	81.30%	82.89%	80.89%	87.50%	
Row %	60.98%	38.41%	77.44%	34.15%	
Table %	50.00%	31.50%	63.50%	28.00%	82.00%
FEMALE	23	13	30	8	36
Column %	18.70%	17.11%	19.11%	12.50%	
Row %	63.89%	36.11%	83.33%	22.22%	
Table %	11.50%	6.50%	15.00%	4.00%	18.00%
All Grps	123	76	157	64	200
Table %	61.50%	38.00%	78.50%	32.00%	100.00%

The interpretation of the percentages in this table is now different from the previous Scrollsheet. For example, 100 males mentioned a domestic sports car

as either their first, second, or third choice for a car they would like to own. The respondents counted in that cell represent 50% (100*100/200) of all respondents; they represent 81.3% (100*100/123) of all respondents (male and female) who mentioned a domestic sports car as either their first, second, or third choice, and they represent 60.98% (100*100/164) of all male subjects.

Reviewing a Three-Way Table

Finally, you can determine whether there are preferences for different hamburger restaurants among male and female respondents, if they mention a particular type of favorite food. In other words, crosstabulate *Gender* by *Food* by *Patron*.

Return to the *Multiple Response Tables* dialog and specify those three factors as before, that is, *Gender* as a simple (single) categorical variable, *Food* as a multiple response variable, and *Patron* as a multiple dichotomy.

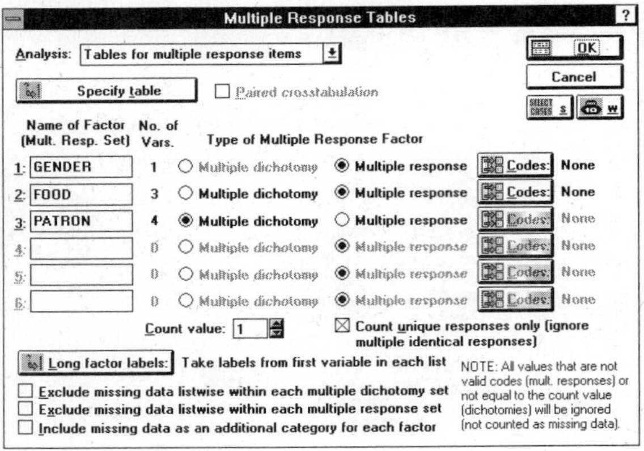

Click *OK* in this dialog and then specify on the *Results* dialog (1) *Percentage of row count*, (2) *Base totals/percentages on number of respondents*, and (3) *Display selected %'s in separate tables*.

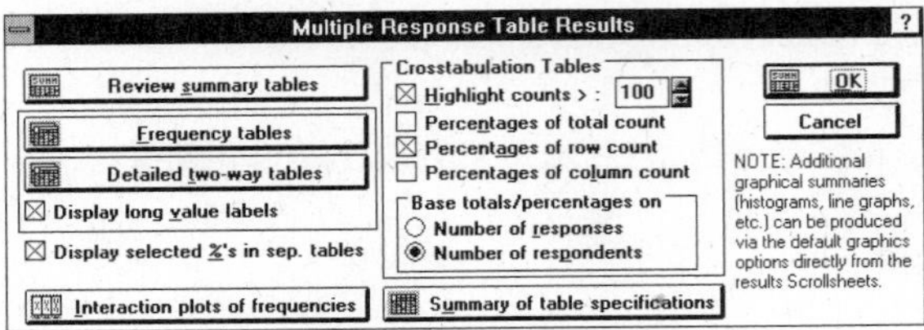

These choices will allow you to review the three-way table, one two-way table at a time, first for males and then for females. Moreover, the percentage tables (of row counts of numbers of respondents) will be displayed in separate tables. Click on the *Detailed two-way tables* button to display the percentage tables.

% of Row Totals (Totals are no. of respondents) (fastfood.sta)

BASIC STATS — Subtable within: GENDER:MALE

FOOD : Favorite 3 fast-foods	PATRON BURGER_1	PATRON BURGER_2	PATRON BURGER_3	PATRON BURGER_4	Row Totals
HAMBURGR: Hamburger	30.66667	48.00000	38.66667	36.00000	56.8182
SANDWICH: Sandwiches	43.24324	40.54054	29.72973	48.64865	28.0303
CHICKEN : Chicken	40.62500	43.75000	34.37500	25.00000	24.2424
PIZZA : Pizza	39.13043	39.13043	36.95652	36.95652	69.6970
MEXICAN : Mexican fast food	48.27586	41.37931	41.37931	37.93103	21.9697
CHINESE : Chinese fast food	31.03448	44.82759	27.58621	41.37931	21.9697
SEAFOOD : Seafood	33.33333	48.14815	33.33333	33.33333	20.4545
OTHER : Other ethnic/regional	41.37931	37.93103	34.48276	37.93103	21.9697
Column Totals	37.87879	42.42424	35.60606	37.12121	100.0000

% of Row Totals (Totals are no. of respondents) (fastfood.sta)

BASIC STATS — Subtable within: GENDER:FEMALE

FOOD : Favorite 3 fast-foods	PATRON BURGER_1	PATRON BURGER_2	PATRON BURGER_3	PATRON BURGER_4	Row Totals
HAMBURGR: Hamburger	36.36364	54.54545	45.45455	54.54545	44.0000
SANDWICH: Sandwiches	60.00000	60.00000	40.00000	0.00000	20.0000
CHICKEN : Chicken	33.33333	33.33333	66.66667	33.33333	12.0000
PIZZA : Pizza	43.75000	43.75000	62.50000	43.75000	64.0000
MEXICAN : Mexican fast food	33.33333	50.00000	50.00000	50.00000	24.0000
CHINESE : Chinese fast food	37.50000	62.50000	87.50000	37.50000	32.0000
SEAFOOD : Seafood	22.22222	44.44444	55.55556	44.44444	36.0000
OTHER : Other ethnic/regional	75.00000	0.00000	50.00000	75.00000	16.0000
Column Totals	40.00000	48.00000	56.00000	40.00000	100.0000

Look at the two-way *Food* by *Patron* table for males: 30.67% of all male respondents who listed *Hamburger* as either their most favorite, second favorite, or third favorite fast-food had eaten at *Burger Meister* in the two weeks prior to the survey; 48.00% had eaten at *Bill's Best Burgers*, and so on.

After reviewing the percentages in this table, it appears that male subjects, regardless of stated fast-food preference, generally were more likely to have eaten at *Bill's Best Burgers* recently (with the exception of the *Mexican* food row). In the sub-table for females, no such simple pattern is apparent

(however, note that those percentages are based on few observations, i.e., 36 females).

These two-way percentage tables can also be summarized via 3D histograms available from the Scrollsheet *Quick Stats Graphs* option (click on the Scrollsheet with the right-mouse-button and select the *3D Histograms* option from the flying menu).

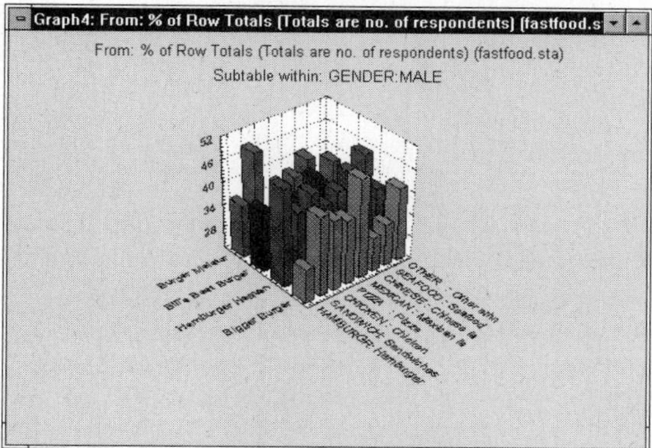

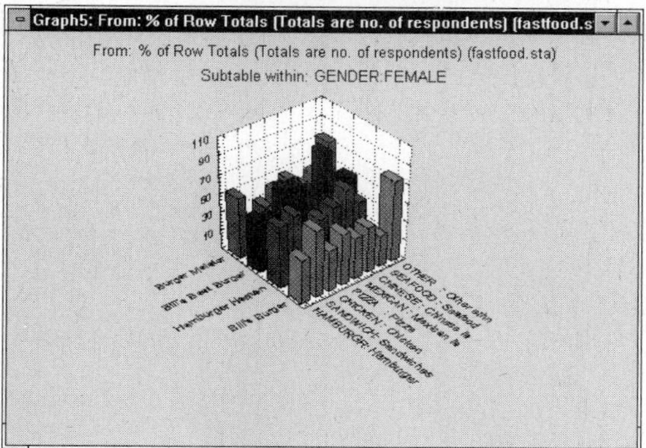

Concluding Remark

If you are not familiar with multiple response variables and dichotomies (factors), it may at first seem somewhat complicated to interpret the frequency or crosstabulation tables of such variables. As stated in the *Overview* section (page 1453), the best way to verify that one understands the way in which the respective tables are constructed is to crosstabulate some simple example data, and then to trace how each case is counted.

DIALOGS, OPTIONS, STATISTICS

Startup Panel

When you open the *Basic Statistics and Tables* module, the startup panel will appear.

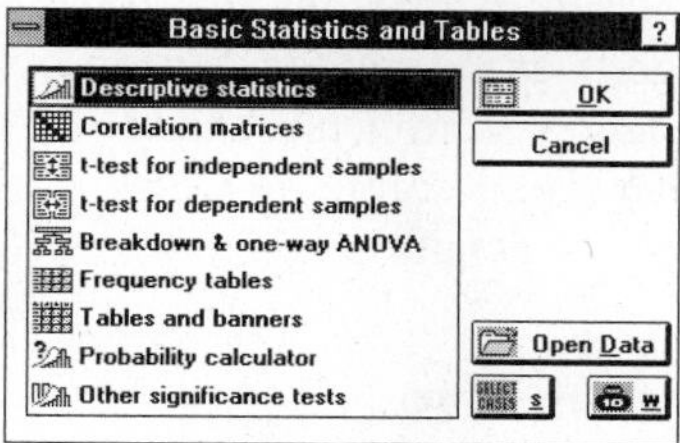

You can choose from the following analytic procedures in this module.

Descriptive Statistics

Use this procedure to produce descriptive summary statistics, simple frequency tables, and summary graphs. The available statistics are further described in the context of the *Descriptive Statistics* dialog (page 1500) and the *Statistics* dialog (page 1510).

Correlation Matrices

Use this procedure to compute *Pearson product-moment correlations* (*Pearson r*). *STATISTICA* can compute square and rectangular matrices, using *pairwise* or *casewise* deletion of missing data. Numerous accompanying statistics (including significance levels, means, standard deviations, regression equations, etc.) can also be computed. Various 2D and 3D graphs can be created in order to visualize the relationships among variables. For further details concerning available procedures refer to the *Correlation matrices* dialog (page 1512). Additional nonparametric alternatives to the Pearson product-moment are available for crosstabulation tables (see the description of the *Crosstabulation Results* dialog, page 1542, or the brief description of statistics, page 1429), as well as via the *Nonparametrics and Distributions* module.

t-Test for Independent Samples

Use this procedure to compute the *t*-tests *for independent samples or groups* (for example, to compare the responses of male and female respondents to a question on a survey). It is recommended that the data file be arranged so that each case represents one individual, identified by a grouping variable. Alternatively, *STATISTICA* can also compute *t*-tests if the data were entered such that each column (variable) in the data file represents the data for one group. Various graphs are available to aid in the interpretation of results (see the description of the *t*-test for independent samples dialog, page 1516). The significance of the difference between a group mean and a population or expected mean can be tested when you select the *Other significance tests* option from the startup panel (see below); that option can also be used to test differences between proportions. Nonparametric alternatives to the *t*-test for independent samples are also available in the *Nonparametrics and Distributions* module (see Chapter 11).

t-Test for Dependent Samples

Use this procedure to compute *t-tests for dependent or correlated samples* (for example, to compare the responses from the *same* persons to a question on a survey before and after an election). Both individual *t*-tests as well as matrices of *t*-tests can be computed. Various graphs are available to aid in the interpretation of results (see the description of the *t*-test for dependent samples dialog, page 1521). Nonparametric alternatives to the *t*-test for dependent samples are also available in the *Nonparametrics and Distributions* module.

Breakdown: Descriptive Statistics and Correlations by Groups

Use this procedure to compute various descriptive statistics (e.g., means, standard deviations, etc.) and correlations broken down by groups (e.g., by gender and age group). This procedure also allows the user to perform complete one-way *ANOVA's* and provides tests of the homogeneity of variances and *post hoc* tests of mean differences. Refer to the *Breakdown Results* and the *Post hoc Comparison* dialogs (pages 1522 and 1532, respectively) for a more detailed description of the available statistics.

Frequency Tables

Use this procedure to compute and review the distribution of variables. Frequency tables can be computed for categorical variables, variables containing integer values, or for continuous variables. The user can also define categories for frequency counts by specifying logical selection (categorization) conditions for assigning cases to categories. A number of tests for the normal distribution are also available.

For a description of available procedures refer to the *Frequency Tables* dialog (page 1534). Additional distribution fitting methods (for non-normal distributions) are available in the *Nonparametrics and Distributions* module and the *Survival Analysis* module.

Tables and Banners

Use this procedure to compute multi-way crosstabulation tables. *STATISTICA* will compute various statistics for the crosstabulations as well as a wide variety of 2D and 3D graphical summaries (see the description of the *Crosstabulation Results* dialog, page 1542). Comprehensive facilities are provided to analyze not only simple categorical variables, but also multiple response and multiple dichotomy variables (see pages 1453 and 1546).

Other Significance Tests

This procedure will bring up a probability calculator for computing statistical tests for comparing means, correlations, percentages, etc. (see page 1551 for details). Note that *STATISTICA* also includes a comprehensive general *Probability Calculator* for evaluating the distribution functions for various continuous distributions, including *F*, *t*, *Chi-square*, *Weibull*, etc.; the *Probability Calculator* also allows you to compute the significance level for Pearson product moment correlation coefficients, and to convert them into Fisher *z* values; refer to *Quick Basic Stats*, Chapter 10, for details.

Descriptive Statistics

A general discussion of descriptive statistics is provided in the overview section (page 1429). When you click on the *Descriptive Statistics* procedure in the startup panel (see above), the *Descriptive Statistics* dialog will open.

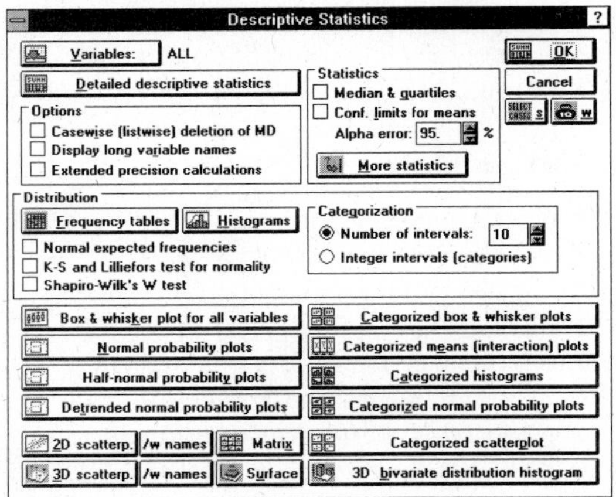

This dialog includes options to specify the variables (and optionally, the categorization) and review the results.

Variables

This option will bring up the standard variable selection dialog in which you can select the variables for the analysis.

Detailed Descriptive Statistics

This option will open a Scrollsheet with the descriptive statistics for all of the previously selected variables.

Descriptive Statistics (poverty.sta)

BASIC STATS	Valid N	Mean	Minimum	Maximum	Std.Dev.
POP_CHNG	30	7.87	-16.2000	40.0	10.33
N_EMPLD	30	1548.67	160.0000	11500.0	2038.39
PT_POOR	30	23.01	13.2000	40.5	6.43
TAX_RATE	30	.72	.4000	1.1	.20
PT_PHONE	30	74.83	48.0000	87.0	10.01
PT_RURAL	30	70.73	5.9000	100.0	24.02
AGE	30	30.28	23.3000	35.9	2.88
AFR_AM	30	11655.00	2.0000	266159.0	48289.92

You can request specific descriptive statistics in the *Statistics* dialog via the *More Statistics* button.

Options

Casewise (listwise) deletion of MD. If casewise deletion of missing data is selected, then *STATISTICA* will ignore all cases that have missing data for *any* of the variables selected in the list. If this check box is not selected, then all valid data points will be included in the analyses for the respective variables (pairwise deletion of missing data, resulting possibly in unequal *valid n* per variable).

Display long variable names. If this check box is set, then long variable names (if any were specified) will be displayed along with the short names in the first column of the Scrollsheet.

Descriptive Statistics (poverty.sta)

BASIC STATS	Valid N	Mean
POP_CHNG: Population change (1960-1970)	30	7.87
N_EMPLD: No. of persons employed in agriculture	30	1548.67
PT_POOR: Percent of families below poverty level	30	23.01
TAX_RATE: Residential and farm property tax rate	30	.72
PT_PHONE: Percent residences with telephones	30	74.83
PT_RURAL: Percent rural population	30	70.73
AGE: Median age	30	30.28
AFR_AM: Number of African/Americans	30	11655.00

If no long variable names have been specified for any of the selected variables, then the setting of this check box will have no effect.

Extended precision calculations. *STATISTICA* employs proprietary extended precision algorithms in order to minimize round-off error in the computations. This option should be selected if the variables in the analysis show extremely small *relative* variances (variance divided by the mean), for example, if all values for a variable range between 10,000.000001 and 10,000.000002. Note that there is a difference between small variance and small *relative* variance (e.g., the *relative* variance of values in the range of .0000000000000001 to .0000000000000002 is not small). For extremely large data files with many thousands of cases, the computations may be somewhat slower when this check box is set.

Statistics

Note that additional descriptive statistics (*mode*, *harmonic mean*, *geometric mean*, *average deviation*, etc.) are available in the *Nonparametrics and Distributions* module.

Median & quartiles. If checked, the *Detailed descriptive statistics* Scrollsheet will contain the *median* (50th percentile) and *quartiles* (25th and 75th percentiles) for all variables. The *median* is defined as the value that divides the distribution of all values in half; that is, 50% of all values for the respective variable will fall below the median and 50% will be greater than the median. The 25th and 75th percentiles (*quartiles)* are defined accordingly. (Note that user-specified percentiles can be

computed in the *Nonparametrics and Distributions* module.)

When the distribution of values cannot be exactly divided into halves and quartiles, then there are different ways to compute the respective median and quartile values (and percentiles). The specific method of computation for those values can be configured "system-wide" via the *STATISTICA Defaults: General* dialog (see Chapter 3; this dialog is accessible via the *Options* pull-down menu option *General*).

Confidence limits for the mean. The idea of *confidence limits* for the mean is introduced in the *Introductory Overview* section, page 1429. This option will compute the respective (*alpha*) confidence limits around the means, for the specified *Alpha Error* level.

More statistics. This button will bring up a dialog (see page 1510) for selecting additional descriptive statistics that are to be reported in the *Detailed Descriptive Statistics* Scrollsheet. Available statistics are: valid *n*, mean, sum, median, standard deviation, variance, standard error of the mean, 95% confidence limits of the mean, minimum, maximum, lower and upper quartiles, range, quartile range, skewness, kurtosis, and the standard errors of the skewness and kurtosis (additional statistics are available in the *Nonparametrics and Distributions* module).

Distribution

Frequency tables. This option will bring up a cascade of Scrollsheets with the frequency distributions for the selected variables (one Scrollsheet per variable). The manner in which the selected variables will be categorized depends on the selections made in the *Categorization* box (to the right): The full range of values in the selected variables can be divided into a specific *Number of intervals* (use this method if the selected variables have continuous non-integer values). Alternatively, *STATISTICA* can use *Integer intervals (categories)*; if this option is chosen then: (1) all non-integer values will be ignored, and (2) tests of normality (see below) will not be available.

Note that an extensive selection of categorization methods and frequency table statistics are available if you choose the *Frequency Tables* procedure from the *Basic Statistics and Tables* startup panel (page 1499).

Histograms. This option will produce a cascade of histograms, analogous to the *Frequency tables* procedure. If *Normal expected frequencies* (see below) is selected then the histograms will also display the normal curve, superimposed over the observed frequencies.

Normal expected frequencies. This check box is only available (active) if the *Number of intervals* button is set in the *Categorization* box. If selected, subsequent Scrollsheets will contain the expected normal frequencies (cumulative frequencies and relative frequencies) for each category. The *Histograms* option will display the normal curve superimposed over the observed frequencies.

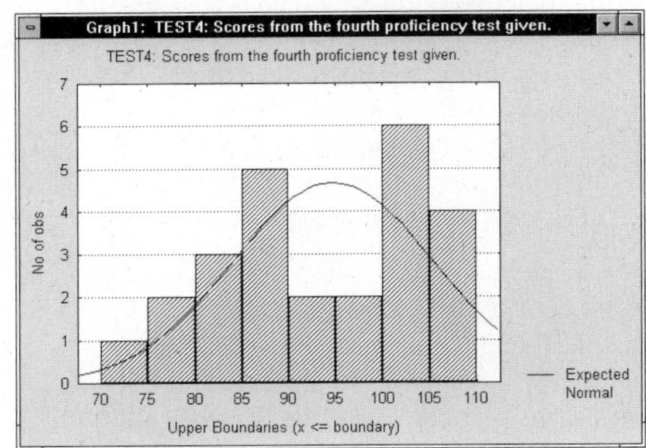

Note that the option to produce frequency histograms available from the *Quick Stats Graphs* menu (accessible by clicking with the right-mouse-button on the Scrollsheet and selecting the *Quick Stats Graphs* option from the flying menu, see Volume II) uses a somewhat different graph layout

and the description of the fitted function in the title of the graph (see below) contains information on the mean and standard deviation of the variable (in this case 94.68 and 10.676, respectively).

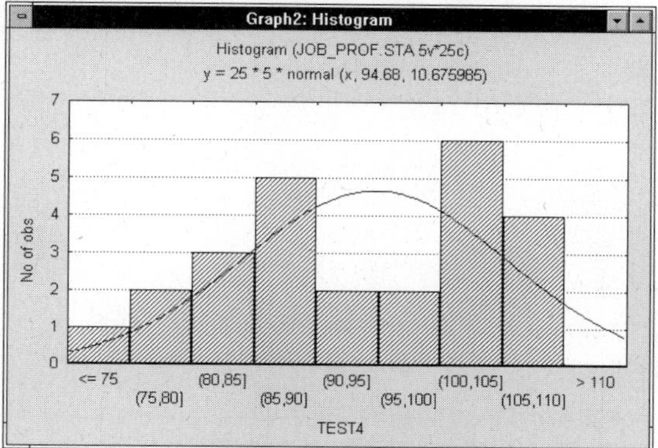

You can also produce histograms via the *Stats Graphs* options accessible from the spreadsheet or Scrollsheet *Graphs* pull-down menu at any point of the analysis and offering numerous additional analytic and graph layout options (e.g., a selection of five types of categorization definition methods and a wide selection of fitted distributions).

A wide variety of non-normal distributions can be fit to observed data in the *Nonparametrics and Distributions* module (see Chapter 7), the *Process Analysis* module (see Volume IV), and via the *Stats 2D Graphs - Histograms* options (see Volume II); specialized distributions for survival and reliability studies are available in the *Survival Analysis* module.

Kolmogorov-Smirnov test for normality. This check box is only available (active) if the *Number of intervals* button is set in the *Categorization* box (to the right). If selected, subsequent frequency Scrollsheets will include the results of the Kolmogorov-Smirnov one-sample test of normality. If the *D* statistic is significant, then the hypothesis that the respective distribution is normal should be rejected. Two probability (significance) values will be reported for each Kolmogorov-Smirnov *D*: The first is based on the probability values as tabulated by Massey (1951); those probability values pertain to cases when the mean and standard deviation of the normal distribution are known *a priori* and *not* estimated from the data. However, these parameters are typically computed from the actual data. In this case, the test for normality involves a complex conditional hypothesis ("how likely is it to obtain a *D* statistic of this magnitude or greater, contingent upon the mean and standard deviation computed from the data"), and the *Lilliefors* probabilities should be interpreted (Lilliefors, 1967). Note that, in recent years, the Shapiro-Wilks' *W* test (see below) has become the preferred test of normality because of its good power properties as compared to a wide range of alternative tests (see Shapiro, Wilk, and Chen, 1968).

Shapiro-Wilks' *W* test. This check box is only available (active) if the *Number of intervals* button is set in the *Categorization* box (to the right). If selected, subsequent frequency Scrollsheets will include the results of the Shapiro-Wilks' *W* test of normality. If the *W* statistic is significant, then the hypothesis that the respective distribution is normal should be rejected.

The Shapiro-Wilks' *W* test is the preferred test of normality because of its good power properties as compared to a wide range of alternative tests (see Shapiro, Wilk, and Chen, 1968). The algorithm implemented in *STATISTICA* employs an extension to the test described by Royston (1982), which allows it to be applied to samples with up to 2000 observations; if there are more than 2000 observations, then this test cannot be performed.

Categorization

The procedures selected in this box will only affect the frequency tables and histograms produced via the procedures in the *Distribution* box (to the left). The *Descriptive Statistics* option has only two modes of categorizing the values of selected variables for the frequency table; a number of

additional options, graphs, and statistics are available via the *Frequency tables* procedure (on the startup panel, page 1499).

Number of intervals. If this radio button is set, then subsequent Frequency tables Scrollsheets or Histograms will divide the range of values for the selected variables into approximately the requested number of intervals. This option is appropriate when the variables to be tabulated are continuous in nature. The tests of normality (see above) are only available if this option is chosen. Note that the actual number of categories that will be produced may sometimes differ from the number of intervals requested. *STATISTICA* will produce "neat" intervals; that is, interval boundaries and widths with the last digit being 1, 2, or 5 (e.g., 10.5, 11.0, 11.5, etc.). Such "simple" or "neat" intervals are more easily interpreted than interval boundaries defined by many significant digits (e.g., 10.12423, 10.13533, etc.). Full control over the method of categorization of variables is available via the *Frequency tables* procedure (see page 1499).

Integer intervals. Choose this method of categorization if the variables to be tabulated can be interpreted as integer categories, or contain only integer values. If this method is chosen, all non-integer values will be ignored when producing frequency tables or histograms via the *Distribution* procedures (to the right); the choice of categorization in this box will not affect other computations (e.g., of detailed descriptive statistics).

Box and Whisker Plot for All Variables

This option will produce a box and whisker plot for the selected variables.

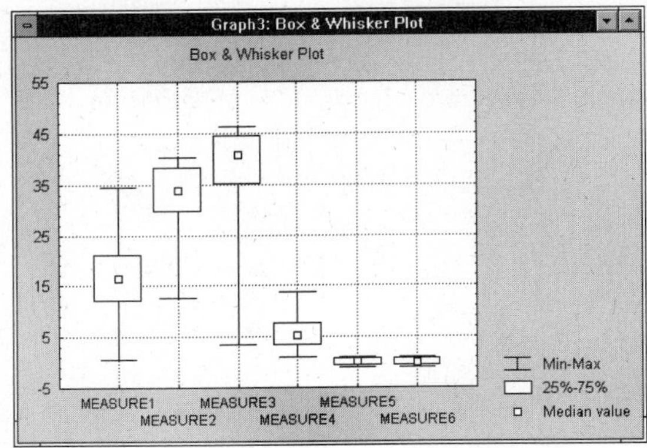

The box and whisker plot will summarize each variable by three components:

(1) A central line to indicate central tendency or location (the *median* in the plot above);

(2) A box to indicate variability around this central tendency (the *25th* and *75th percentiles* in the plot above);

(3) Whiskers around the box to indicate the range of the variable (the *Min-Max* data values in the plot above).

After clicking on this button, the *Box-Whisker Type* dialog will open.

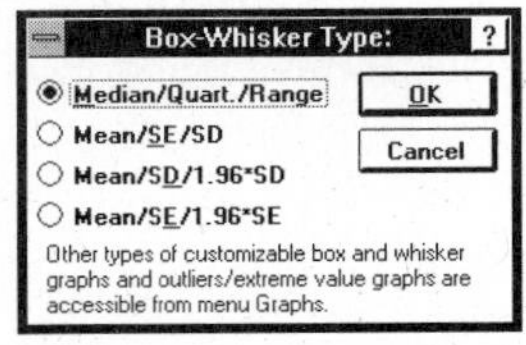

Here, you can choose to plot for each variable: (1) medians (central line), quartiles (box), and ranges (whiskers); (2) Means, standard errors of the means, and standard deviations; (3) Means, standard deviations, and 1.96 times the standard deviations (95% normal confidence interval for individual observations around the mean); (4) Means, standard errors of the means, and 1.96 times the standard errors of the means (95% normal confidence interval for means).

If you select to compute for the box-whisker plot the median and the quartiles, those values will be computed according to the setting of the *Percentiles* option on the *STATISTICA Defaults: General* dialog (choose option *General* on the *Options* pull-down menu). For computational details, refer to the description of this dialog in Chapter 3 (see also Appendix I).

You can also produce box and whisker plots via the *Stats Graphs* options accessible from the spreadsheet or Scrollsheet *Graphs* pull-down menu at any point of the analysis and offering numerous additional analytic and graph layout options.

Normal Probability Plots

This option will produce a cascade of normal probability plots for the selected variables, one plot per selected variable.

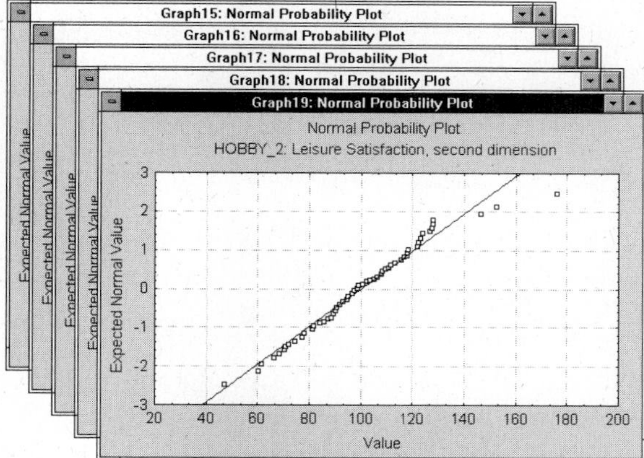

The standard normal probability plot is constructed as follows. First, the deviations from the respective means (*residuals*) are rank ordered. From these ranks, z values (i.e., standardized values of the normal distribution) can be computed *based on the assumption* that the data come from a normal distribution. These z values are Y-axis in the plot. If the observed residuals (plotted on the X-axis) are normally distributed, then all values should fall onto a straight line (marked *Normal Expected* in the plot). If the residuals are not normally distributed, then they will deviate from the line.

Outliers may also become evident in this plot. If there is a general lack of fit, and the data seem to form a clear pattern (e.g., an *S* shape) around the line, then the dependent variable may have to be transformed in some way (e.g., a log transformation to "pull in" the tail of the distribution, etc., see *Spreadsheet Edit (Current) Specs* (Chapter 3, or *STATISTICA BASIC*, Volume V).

Probability plots for non-normal distributions. Note that probability plots can also be produced for a wide variety of continuous non-normal distributions (e.g., Weibull, log-normal, Beta, exponential, etc.) via the *Probability - Probability Plots* option on the *Stats 2D Graphs* menu (accessible from the *Graphs* pull-down menu, or by clicking on the *Graphs Gallery* button). *Quantile - Quantile Plots* are also available as a *Stats 2D Graphs* option. For details refer to the description of *Stats 2D Graphs* in Volume II.

Half-Normal Probability Plots

This option will produce a cascade of half-normal probability plots for the selected variables, one plot per selected variable.

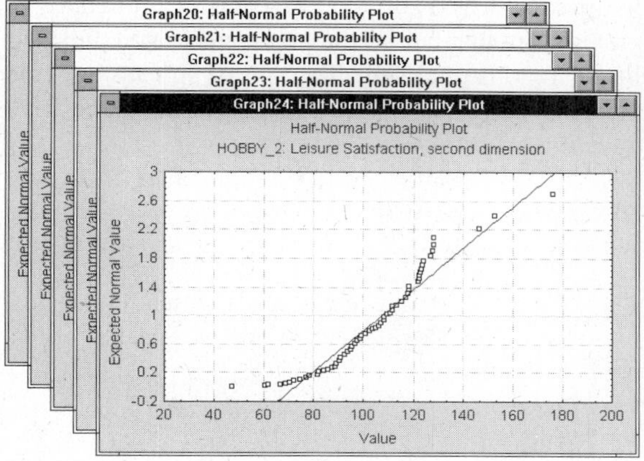

The half-normal probability plot is constructed in the same way as the standard normal probability plot, except that only the positive half of the normal curve is considered. Consequently, only positive normal values will be plotted on the *Y*-axis. This plot is used when one wants to ignore the sign of the residual, that is, when one is mostly interested in the distribution of absolute residuals, regardless of sign.

Detrended Normal Probability Plots

This option will produce a cascade of detrended normal probability plots for the selected variables, one plot per selected variable.

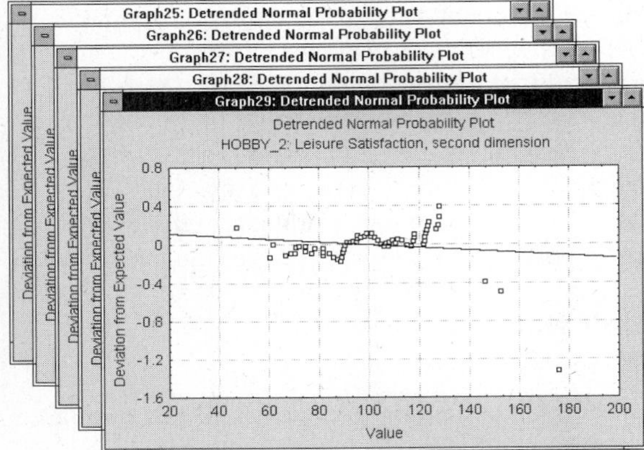

The detrended normal probability plot is constructed in the same way as the standard normal probability plot, except that before the plot is generated, the linear trend is removed. This often "spreads out" the plot, thereby allowing the user to detect patterns of deviations more easily.

2D Scatterplot (/with Names)

This option will produce a cascade of scatterplots for selected pairs of variables, one plot per variable pair.

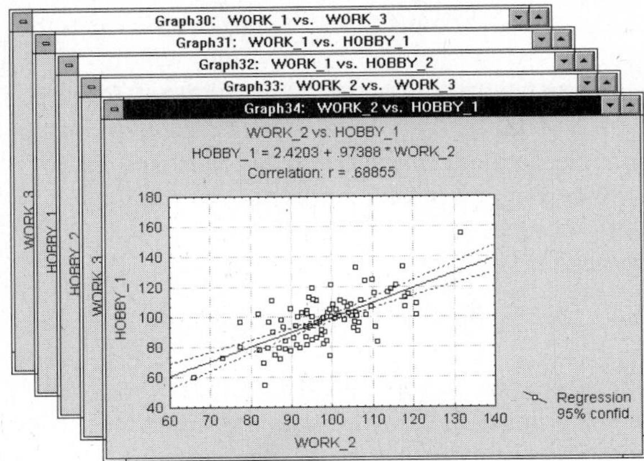

If the *2D scatterplot* option is chosen (see plot above), then the plot will show the regression line and the standard error of the predicted values (as error lines) in the scatterplot.

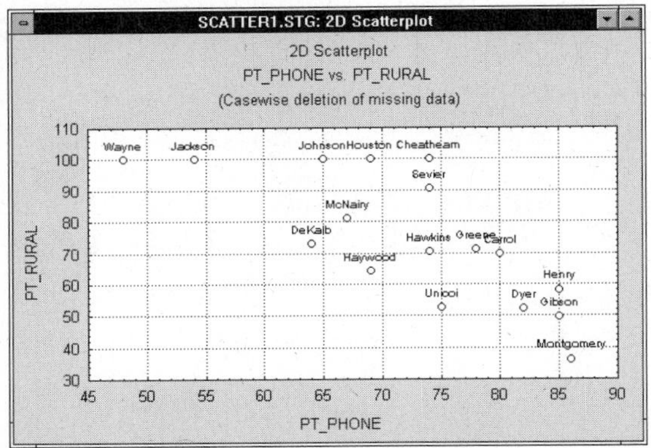

If the */w names* button is used (see plot above), then the scatterplot will not contain those lines but will identify the points in the scatterplot with the case numbers or names (if case names are specified in the respective data file).

Matrix

This option will produce a scatterplot matrix for the selected variables.

3D Scatterplot (/with Names)

This option will produce a 3D scatterplot for a selected triplet of variables.

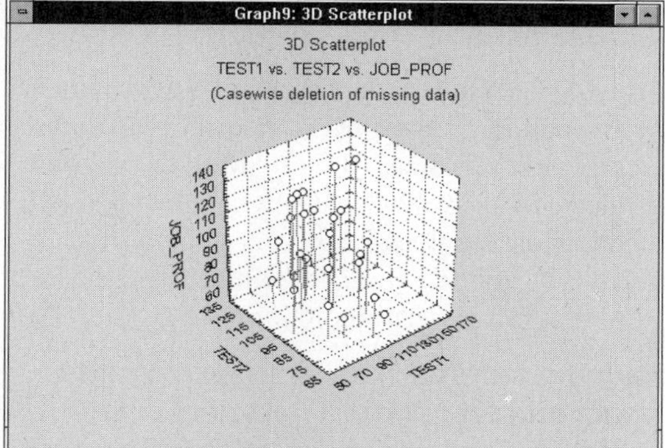

If the */w names* button is used, then the points in the scatterplot will be identified by the case numbers or names (if case names are specified in the respective data file).

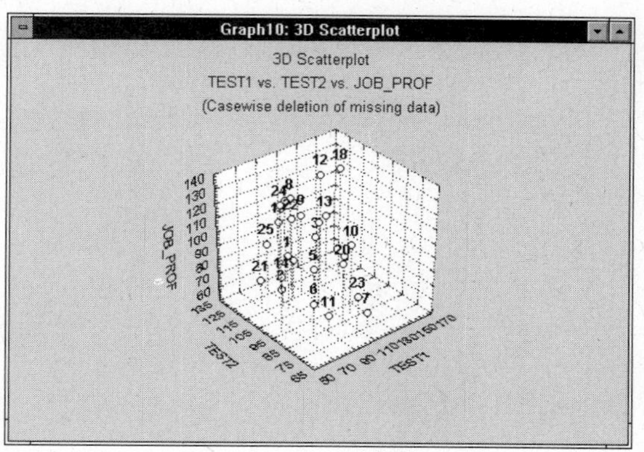

Surface

This option will produce a 3D scatterplot for a selected triplet of variables, and fit a quadratic surface to the data.

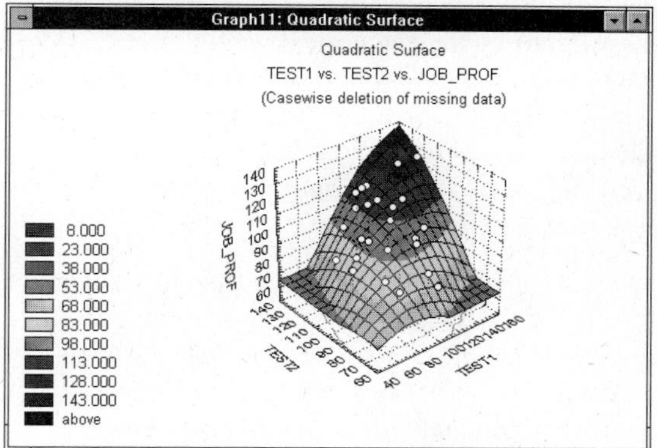

Individual data points are shown in the plot in relation to the quadratic fit of the surface; this exploratory technique is sometimes useful to identify "hidden" aspects of relations between multiple variables (for more details, e.g., how to fit other types of surfaces, see Volume II).

Categorized Box and Whisker Plots

This option will produce a cascade of categorized box and whisker plots for the selected variables, one plot per selected variable.

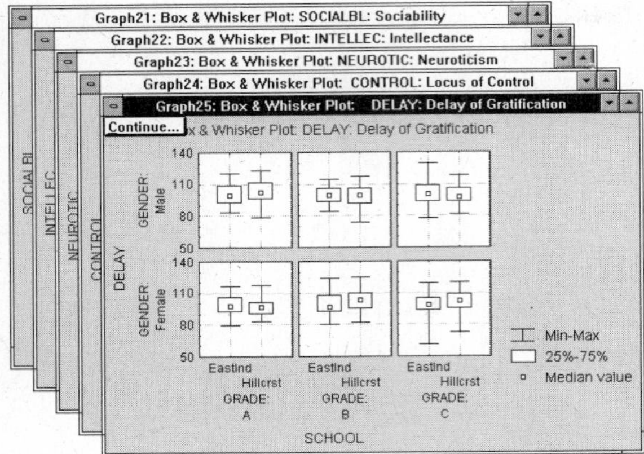

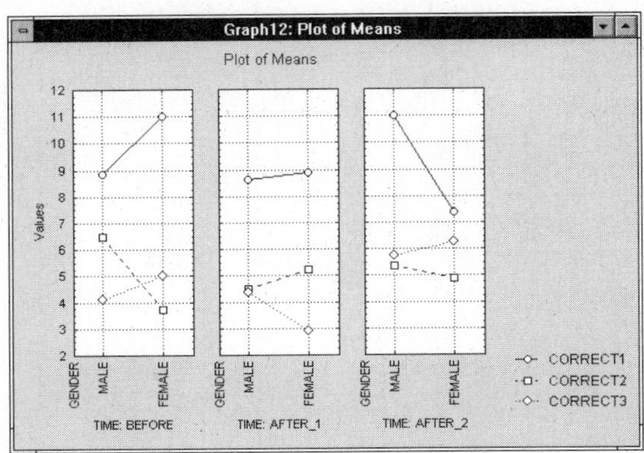

After clicking on this button, the user is first prompted to select up to three categorical variables (e.g., *Gender*, *Ethnic Origin*). For each selected variable (via the *Variables* button), *STATISTICA* will produce a box and whisker plot broken down (categorized) by the categorical variables (e.g., separately for males and females for each ethnic group). Note that more complex *Breakdown* analyses are available via the *Breakdown: Descriptive statistics by groups* procedure on the startup panel (page 1499).

You can also produce categorized box and whisker plots via the *Stats Graphs* options accessible from the spreadsheet or Scrollsheet *Graphs* pull-down menu at any point of the analysis and offering numerous additional analytic and graph layout options.

Categorized Means (Interaction) Plots

This option will produce a standard interaction plot of means by one, two, or three categorical variables (e.g., by *Gender* and *Ethnic Origin*).

After selecting this option, the user is prompted to select the categorization variables. Overall, the interaction plot can show the means broken down by three categories. (Note that cascades of interaction plots to show higher-way interactions can be produced via the *Breakdown: Descriptive statistics by groups* procedure, see page 1522.)

If one ("dependent") variable was selected via the *Variable* option, then the user can specify up to three categorization variables. If more than one variable was selected via the *Variable* option, then up to two categorization variables can be selected; the different (dependent) variables will be represented by different line patterns (colors) in the graph.

Assigning factors to aspects (axes) of the interaction plot. This dialog allows you to control the assignment of grouping variables (factors) to the line patterns, upper *X*-axis, and lower *X*-axis.

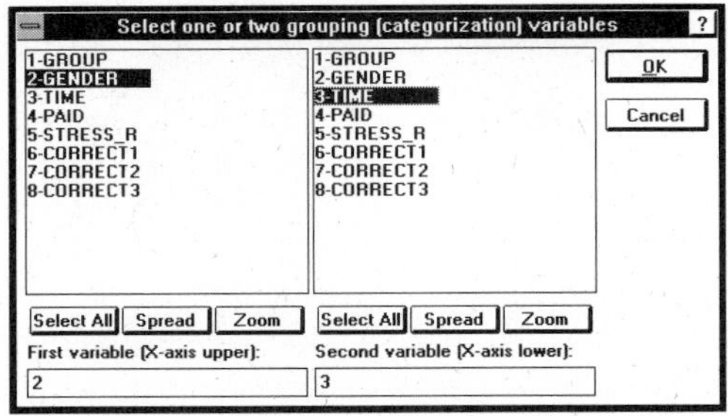

If more than three factors need to be plotted, the plot is produced in "chunks" within the levels of the other (not-selected) factors.

Categorized Histograms

This option will produce a cascade of categorized histograms for the selected variables, one plot per selected variable.

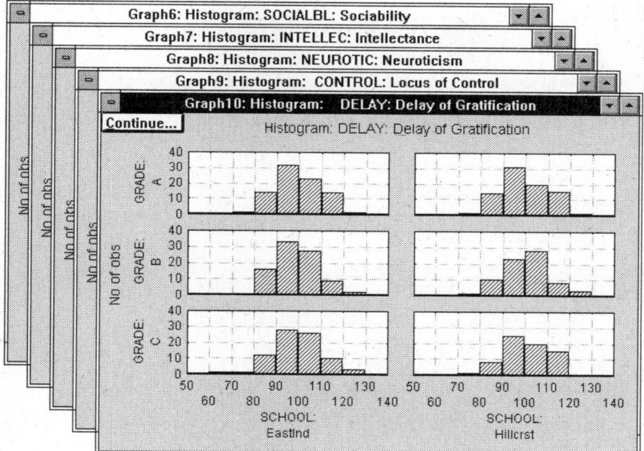

After clicking on this button (or the *Categorized Normal Probability Plots* button, see below), you will be prompted to select up to two categorical variables (e.g., *Gender*, *Ethnic Origin*). For each selected (via the *Variables* button) variable, *STATISTICA* will then produce a histogram, broken down (categorized) by the categorical variables (e.g., separately for males and females for each ethnic group). Note that more complex *Breakdown* analyses and graphs are available via the *Breakdown: Descriptive statistics by groups* procedure on the startup panel (page 1499).

You can also produce categorized histograms via the *Stats Graphs* options accessible from the spreadsheet or Scrollsheet *Graphs* pull-down menu at any point of the analysis and offering numerous additional analytic and graph layout options.

Categorized Normal Probability Plots

This option will produce a cascade of categorized normal probability plots for the selected variables, one plot per selected variable.

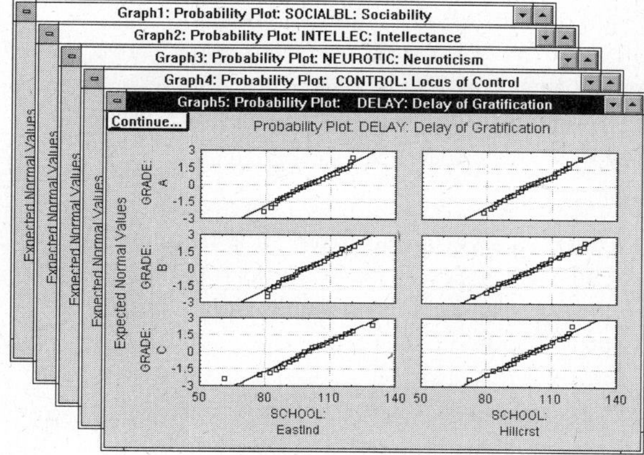

Categorized Scatterplots

This option will produce a cascade of categorized scatterplots for selected pairs of variables, one plot per pair.

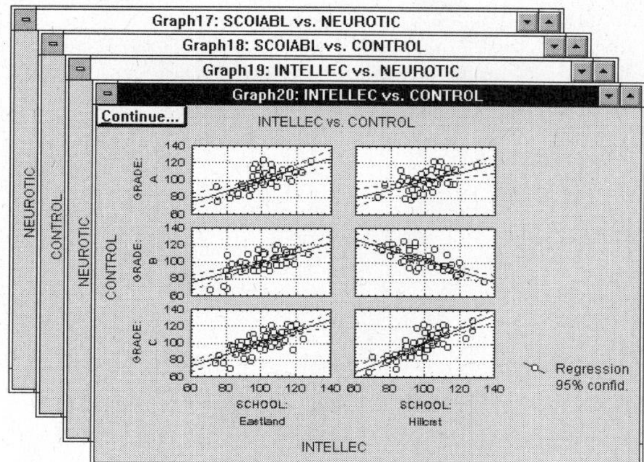

After clicking on this button, the user is first prompted to select two lists of variables (from among those originally selected via the *Variables* button). Scatterplots will be produced for each

variable in the first list with each variable in the second list. Next the user will be prompted to select up to two categorical variables (e.g., *Gender*, *Ethnic Origin*). *STATISTICA* will then produce a cascade of scatterplots broken down (categorized) by the categorical variables (e.g., separately for males and females for each ethnic group). Note that more complex *Breakdown* analyses and graphs are available via the *Breakdown: Descriptive statistics by groups* procedure on the startup panel (page 1499).

You can also produce categorized scatterplots via the *Stats Graphs* options accessible from the spreadsheet or Scrollsheet *Graphs* pull-down menu at any point of the analysis and offering numerous additional analytic and graph layout options.

3D Bivariate Distribution Histograms

This option will produce a cascade of 3D histograms for selected pairs of variables, one plot per pair.

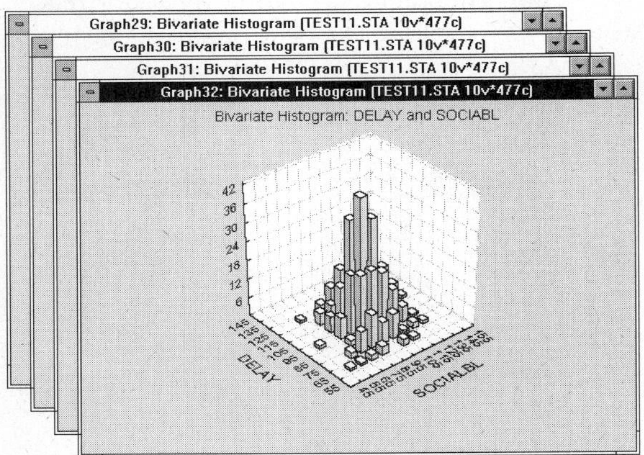

After clicking on this button, the user will first be prompted to select two lists of variables (from among those originally selected via the *Variables* button). 3D histograms will be produced for each variable in the first list with each variable in the second list.

Statistics Dialog

The options selected in this dialog will determine which statistics will be computed when the user selects *Detailed descriptive statistics* from the *Descriptive Statistics* dialog (see page 1500).

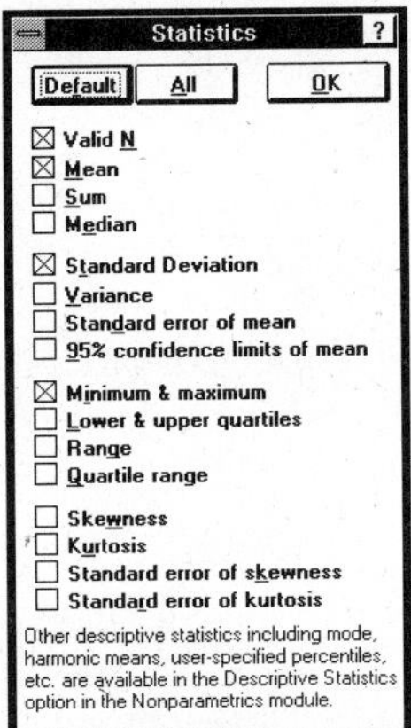

Refer to the *Introductory Overview* section (page 1429) for a discussion of the most common descriptive statistics and their interpretation.

Computation of median and quartiles (25'th, 50'th, and 75'th percentile). When the distribution of values cannot be exactly divided into halves and quartiles, then there are different ways to compute the respective median and quartile values (and percentiles). The specific method of computation for those values can be configured "system-wide" via the *STATISTICA Defaults: General* dialog (see the description of this dialog in Chapter 3; this dialog is accessible via the *Options* pull-down menu option *General*).

Default

This option will reset the selection of descriptive statistics in this dialog to the default selection; the default statistics are: *Valid n*, *Mean*, *Standard Deviation*, and *Minimum & Maximum*.

All

This option will automatically select all available statistics.

Valid *n*

Set this check box to compute the number of valid cases for each selected variable.

Mean

Set this check box to compute the means.

Sum

Set this check box to compute the sums of values of selected variables.

Median

Set this check box to compute the medians. The median (or 50th percentile) is defined as the value that divides the distribution of all values in half; that is, 50% of all values for a respective variable will fall below the median, and 50% will be greater than the median. Note that the specific computational procedure that is used to determine the median can be configured "system-wide" via the *STATISTICA Defaults: General* dialog (see the description of this dialog in Chapter 3; this dialog is accessible via the *Options* pull-down menu option *General*).

Standard Deviation

Set this check box to compute the standard deviations. The standard deviation is computed as the square root of the sum of squared deviations (from the mean) divided by *n-1*.

Variance

Set this check box to compute the variances. The variance of a variable is computed as the sum of squared deviations (from the mean) divided by *n-1*.

Standard Error of the Mean

The standard error of the mean is computed as the standard deviation divided by the square root of *n*.

95% Confidence Limits of the Mean

The confidence limits of the mean are computed based on the respective critical *t* values. Refer to the *Introductory Overview* section (page 1429) for a basic discussion of confidence limits. Note that you can change the default (95%) confidence level via the *Alpha Error* option in the *Descriptive Statistics* dialog (see page 1502).

Minimum and Maximum

Set this check box to compute the minima and maxima.

Lower and Upper Quartiles

Set this check box to compute the 25th and 75th percentile (lower and upper quartile, respectively; user-specified percentiles can be computed via the *Nonparametrics and Distributions* module). Note that the specific computational procedure that is used to determine the quartile values can be configured "system-wide" via the *STATISTICA Defaults: General* dialog (see the description of this dialog in Chapter 3; this dialog is accessible via the *Options* pull-down menu option *General*).

Range

Set this check box to compute ranges (maximum minus minimum).

Quartile Range

The quartile range is computed as the upper quartile value (75th percentile) minus the lower quartile value (25th percentile).

Skewness

The skewness is a measure of the symmetry of the distribution of values. If the distribution is symmetrical, then the skewness is equal to zero.

Kurtosis

The kurtosis is a measure of "peakedness" of the distribution of values. If the distribution follows the standard normal distribution, then the value of the kurtosis is zero.

Standard Error of Skewness

Set this check box to compute the standard error of the skewness.

Standard Error of Kurtosis

Set this check box to compute the standard error of the kurtosis.

Other Statistics

Other specialized descriptive statistics (including the mode, harmonic mean, geometric mean, and others) are available in the *Nonparametrics and Distributions* module (see Chapter 11).

Correlation Matrices

A general discussion of correlation matrices is provided in the *Introductory Overview*, page 1431.

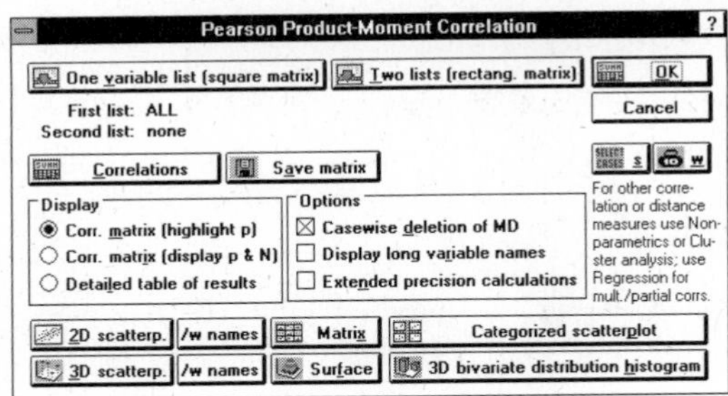

One Variable List (Square Matrix)

This option will bring up the standard single variable list selection dialog. Use this option to compute a square matrix of correlations. Note that such matrices can be saved (via the *Save matrix* button, see below) in the special *STATISTICA* "matrix input data format" (see *Data Management*, Chapter 7) for further analysis with other modules (e.g., *Multiple Regression*, *Factor Analysis*, *Structural Equation Modeling*). Matrices up to (technically) 4,092 x 4,092 can be produced in this module; correlation matrices of virtually unlimited size (up to 32,000 x 32,000) can be computed in *Megafile Manager* (see Volume III).

Two Lists (Rectangular Matrix)

This option will bring up the standard two-variable list selection dialog. Use this option to compute a rectangular matrix of correlations for two lists. Note that rectangular correlation matrices cannot be used as "matrix input" for further analyses (they can be saved only as regular Scrollsheet output).

Correlations

This button will bring up the results Scrollsheet for the currently selected variables. The computation of correlations and the display format of results depend on the current settings in the *Display* and *Options* boxes (see below).

Save Matrix

Use this option to save *Square Matrices* of correlations (see above) in a file. When you click on this button, the *Save Matrix As* dialog will open in which you can specify a name under which to store the matrix. For information about the format of *STATISTICA*'s statistical matrix files, please refer to Chapter 7, *Data Management*.

Display Options

Correlation matrix (highlight *p*). If this radio button is set, then clicking on the *Correlations* button (see above) will produce a matrix of correlation coefficients.

Correlations (10items.sta)

BASIC STATS — Marked correlations are significant at p < .05000
N=100 (Casewise deletion of missing data)

Variable	ITEM 1	ITEM 2	ITEM 3	ITEM 4	ITEM 5	ITEM 6	ITEM 7	ITEM 8	ITEM 9	ITEM 10
ITEM1	1.00	.58	.49	.43	.04	.14	.54	.38	.40	.50
ITEM2	.58	1.00	.46	.36	-.03	.12	.57	.55	.44	.47
ITEM3	.49	.46	1.00	.36	.11	.05	.47	.38	.35	.29
ITEM4	.43	.36	.36	1.00	.06	-.04	.27	.35	.42	.37
ITEM5	.04	-.03	.11	.06	1.00	.03	.01	.13	-.04	.01
ITEM6	.14	.12	.05	-.04	.03	1.00	.14	.10	.07	.09
ITEM7	.54	.57	.47	.27	.01	.14	1.00	.44	.29	.43
ITEM8	.38	.55	.38	.35	.13	.10	.44	1.00	.41	.51
ITEM9	.40	.44	.35	.42	-.04	.07	.29	.41	1.00	.41
ITEM10	.50	.47	.29	.37	.01	.09	.43	.51	.41	1.00

The significant correlations will be highlighted in the Scrollsheet; use the *Options* button on the Scrollsheet toolbar to change the default *p* (*alpha*) level (default *p* = *.05*).

Correlation matrix (display *p* & *n*). If this radio button is set, then clicking on the *Correlations* button (see above) will produce an augmented summary correlation matrix; that is, each cell in the matrix will not only contain the respective correlation coefficient but also the *p*-level and valid *n* (if the *Casewise deletion of missing data* check box is *not* set).

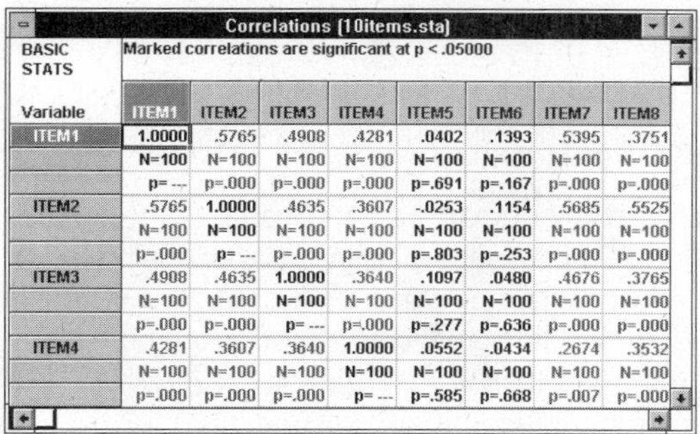

Correlations (10items.sta)

BASIC STATS — Marked correlations are significant at p < .05000

Variable	ITEM1	ITEM2	ITEM3	ITEM4	ITEM5	ITEM6	ITEM7	ITEM8
ITEM1	1.0000	.5765	.4908	.4281	.0402	.1393	.5395	.3751
	N=100	N=100	N=100	N=100	N=100	N=100	N=100	N=100
	p= ---	p=.000	p=.000	p=.000	p=.691	p=.167	p=.000	p=.000
ITEM2	.5765	1.0000	.4635	.3607	-.0253	.1154	.5685	.5525
	N=100	N=100	N=100	N=100	N=100	N=100	N=100	N=100
	p=.000	p= ---	p=.000	p=.000	p=.803	p=.253	p=.000	p=.000
ITEM3	.4908	.4635	1.0000	.3640	.1097	.0480	.4676	.3765
	N=100	N=100	N=100	N=100	N=100	N=100	N=100	N=100
	p=.000	p=.000	p= ---	p=.000	p=.277	p=.636	p=.000	p=.000
ITEM4	.4281	.3607	.3640	1.0000	.0552	-.0434	.2674	.3532
	N=100	N=100	N=100	N=100	N=100	N=100	N=100	N=100
	p=.000	p=.000	p=.000	p= ---	p=.585	p=.668	p=.007	p=.000

Again, significant correlations (cells in the matrix) will be highlighted in the Scrollsheet, and you can use the *Options* button on the Scrollsheet toolbar to change the default *p* (*alpha*) level.

Detailed table of results. If this radio button is set, then clicking on the *Correlations* button (see above) will produce a detailed table of results (*not* in matrix format). This table will report not only the correlation coefficients but also the pairwise means, pairwise standard deviations, *r-square*, *t* value, *p* value, sample size, regression weights, and regression intercepts.

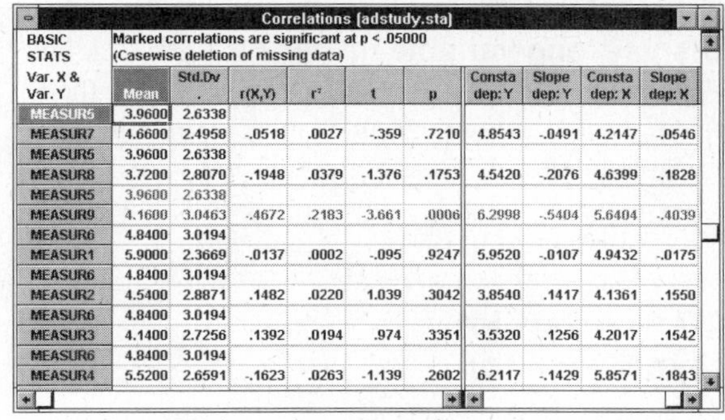

Correlations (adstudy.sta)

BASIC STATS — Marked correlations are significant at p < .05000
(Casewise deletion of missing data)

Var. X & Var. Y	Mean	Std.Dv.	r(X,Y)	r²	t	p	Consta dep: Y	Slope dep: Y	Consta dep: X	Slope dep: X
MEASUR5	3.9600	2.6338								
MEASUR7	4.6600	2.4958	-.0518	.0027	-.359	.7210	4.8543	-.0491	4.2147	-.0546
MEASUR5	3.9600	2.6338								
MEASUR8	3.7200	2.8070	-.1948	.0379	-1.376	.1753	4.5420	-.2076	4.6399	-.1828
MEASUR5	3.9600	2.6338								
MEASUR9	4.1600	3.0463	-.4672	.2183	-3.661	.0006	6.2998	-.5404	5.6404	-.4039
MEASUR6	4.8400	3.0194								
MEASUR1	5.9000	2.3669	-.0137	.0002	-.095	.9247	5.9520	-.0107	4.9432	-.0175
MEASUR6	4.8400	3.0194								
MEASUR2	4.5400	2.8871	.1482	.0220	1.039	.3042	3.8540	.1417	4.1361	.1550
MEASUR6	4.8400	3.0194								
MEASUR3	4.1400	2.7256	.1392	.0194	.974	.3351	3.5320	.1256	4.2017	.1542
MEASUR6	4.8400	3.0194								
MEASUR4	5.5200	2.6591	-.1623	.0263	-1.139	.2602	6.2117	-.1429	5.8571	-.1843

The *Detailed table of results* option in this dialog is only available if 20 or fewer variables have been selected for the analysis since a large amount of information is automatically produced for each correlation. This option should be used to examine only specific correlations (and not for exploratory data analysis), because 22 Scrollsheet-cells are occupied for each correlation coefficient in this

format; thus, a 20x20 correlation matrix will produce a Scrollsheet with 8,800 cells.

Other Options

Extended precision calculations. *STATISTICA* can employ proprietary extended precision calculations when extreme precision is necessary for "difficult" data. Set this option when one or more of the variables that are to be correlated have extremely small relative variances (e.g., the ratio of the standard deviation divided by the mean is less than .0000000000001).

Casewise deletion of missing data. If this check box is set, then only the cases that have complete (valid) data for *all* variables that are currently selected for the analysis (i.e., *casewise deletion of missing data*) will be included in the computation of the correlations. If this check box is not set (i.e., *pairwise deletion of missing data*), then each correlation will be computed from all cases that have complete (valid) data for the respective pair of variables, possibly resulting in unequal *n* for different correlations.

Display long variable names. If this check box is set then the results Scrollsheet will report in the first column the long variable labels along with the variable names. If none of the selected variables have any long variable names, this check box will have no effect.

2D Scatterplot (/with Names)

This option will produce a cascade of scatterplots for selected pairs of variables, one plot per variable pair (i.e., correlation). If the *2D scatterplot* option is chosen, then the plot will show the regression line and the 95% confidence bands for the line in the scatterplot.

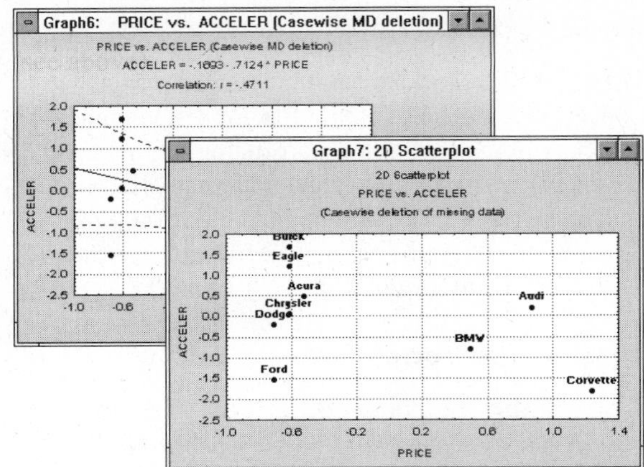

If the */w names* button is used, then the scatterplot will not contain those lines, but will identify the points in the scatterplot with the case numbers or names (if case names are specified in the respective data file).

Matrix

This option will produce a scatterplot matrix for selected variables.

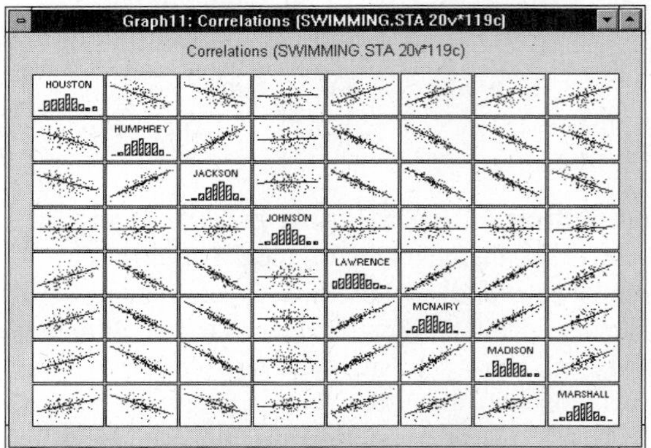

Categorized Scatterplots

This option will produce a cascade of categorized scatterplots for selected pairs of variables, one plot per pair (i.e., per correlation).

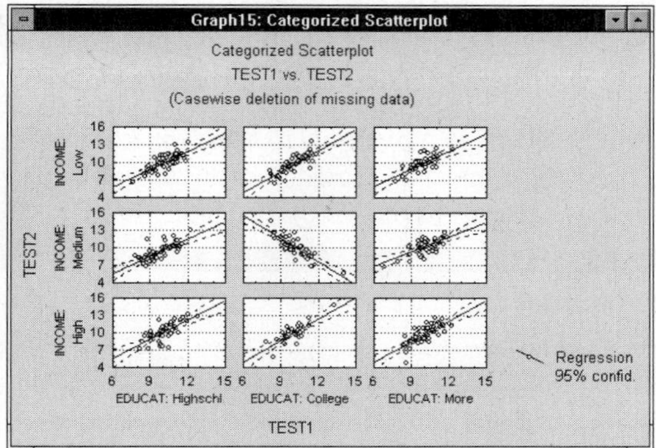

If a single list of variables was previously selected (*One variable list (square matrix)*), then you will be asked to select two lists of variables from among the previously selected variables and scatterplots will be produced for each variable in the first list with each variable in the second list. Next, you will be prompted to select up to two categorical variables (e.g., *Gender*, *Ethnic Origin*).

STATISTICA will then produce a cascade of scatterplots broken down (categorized) by the categorical variables (e.g., separately for males and females for each ethnic group). Note that more complex *Breakdown* analyses and graphs are available via the *Breakdown: Descriptive statistics by groups* procedure (see page 1522).

You can also produce categorized scatterplots via the *Stats Graphs* options accessible from the spreadsheet or Scrollsheet *Graphs* pull-down menu at any point of the analysis and offering numerous additional analytic and graph layout options.

3D Scatterplot (/with Names)

This option will produce a 3D scatterplot for a selected triplet of variables.

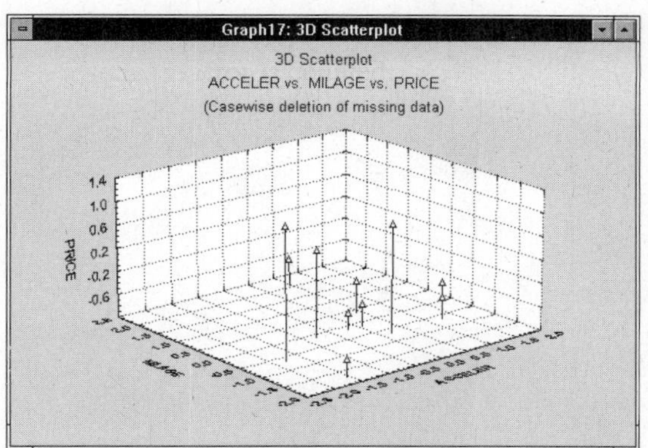

If the */w names* button is used, then the points in the scatterplot will be identified by the case numbers or names (if case names are specified in the respective data file).

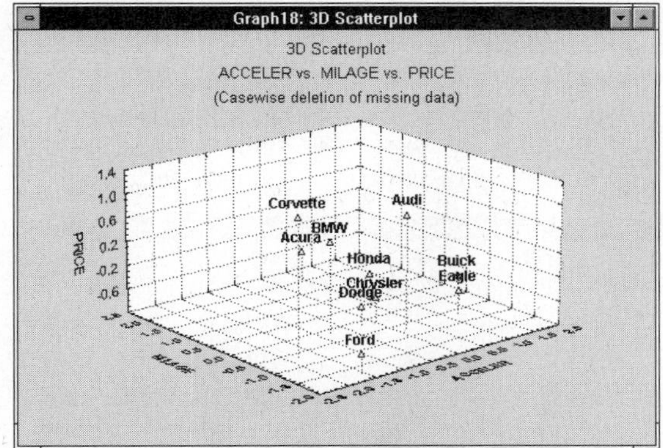

Surface Plot

This option will produce a 3D scatterplot for a selected triplet of variables, and fit a quadratic surface to the data.

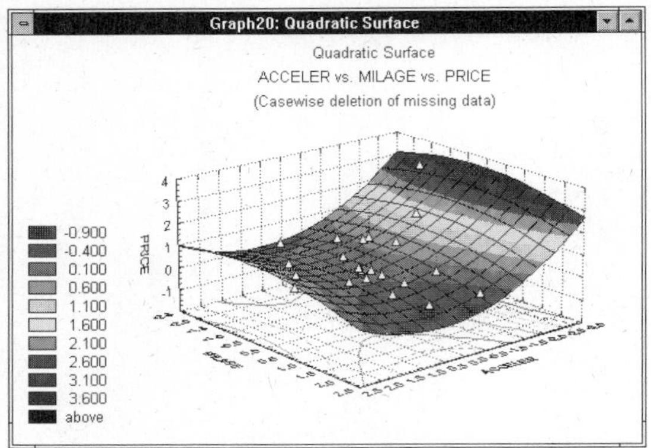

Applications for surface plots for exploratory data analysis are discussed in Volume II, *Stats 3D XYZ Graphs*.

3D Bivariate Distribution Histogram

This option will produce a cascade of 3D histograms for selected pairs of variables, one plot per pair.

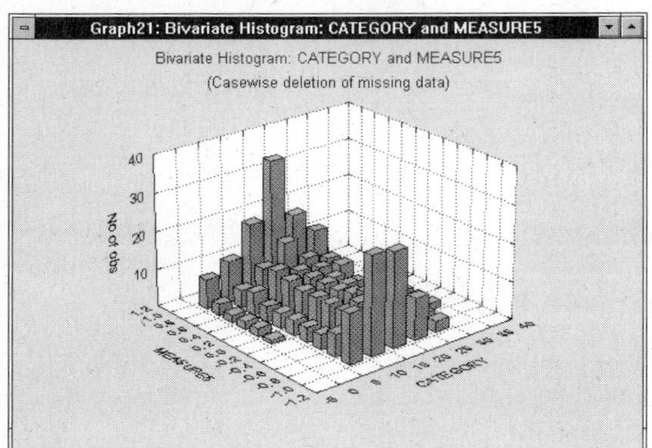

If a single list of variables was previously selected (*One variable list (square matrix)*), then you will be asked to select two lists of variables from among the previously selected variables and 3D histograms will be produced for each variable in the first list with each variable in the second list.

t-Test for Independent Samples

A general overview covering the *t*-test for independent samples is provided in the *Introductory Overview* section (page 1439).

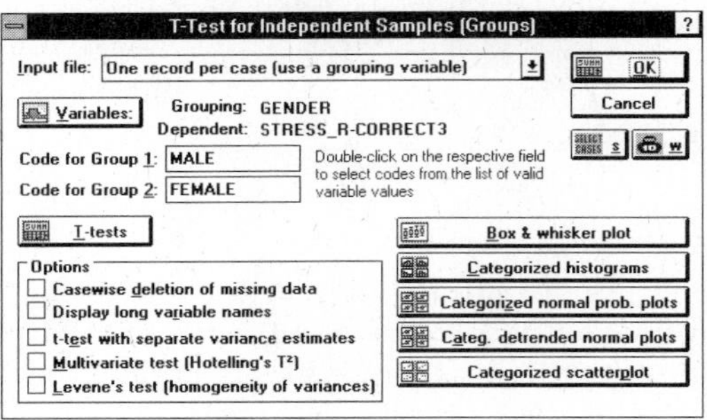

Input File

This combo box has two settings: *One record per case (use grouping variable)* and *Each variable contains the data for one group*. The appropriate setting of this box depends on the way in which the user has set up the data file for the *t*-test for independent samples (see page 1439). The default and recommended way to set up a data file is to enter data case by case, that is, to let each row in the data file represent one case (e.g., individual, respondent) and to let each column in the data file represent one variable or measurement (e.g., response to a questionnaire item). In this setup, a grouping variable (e.g., *Gender*) should be included to denote to which group each case belongs.

The default setting of this combo box (*One record per case*) expects the data to be arranged precisely in this manner. However, for simple data analyses, it is sometimes easier to enter the data so that each column in the data file (variable) represents the responses of one group (e.g., the data for all male respondents were entered into the first column of the file and the data for all female respondents were entered into the second column). If your data are arranged in this manner, set this combo switch to

Each variable contains the data for one group (see page 1519).

Variables

This option will bring up the standard two variable selection dialog. Specify one grouping variable (e.g., Gender) and a list of dependent variables for the comparison. *STATISTICA* will compute the *t*-test for all variables in the dependent variable list, comparing the two groups that are identified by the two selected group codes (see below) in the grouping variable.

Code for Group 1; Code for Group 2

Specify the two codes that identify the two groups in the grouping variable that are to be compared. If you are not sure about the codes that were used in the grouping variables to identify the groups, double-click on the edit field, and a pop-up window (see *Variable Values Window*, Chapter 3) will appear containing all integer codes and their alphanumeric equivalents found in the grouping variable in the current data file.

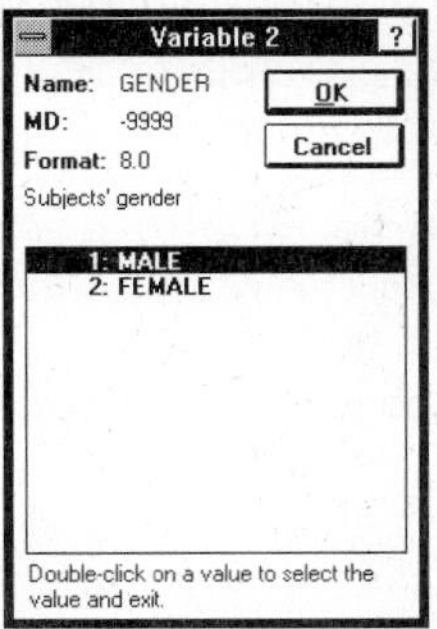

You can select a grouping code in this pop-up window (i.e., transfer it to the edit field) by double-clicking on it.

t-Tests

After clicking on this button, the *t*- tests for independent samples will be computed and displayed in a results Scrollsheet.

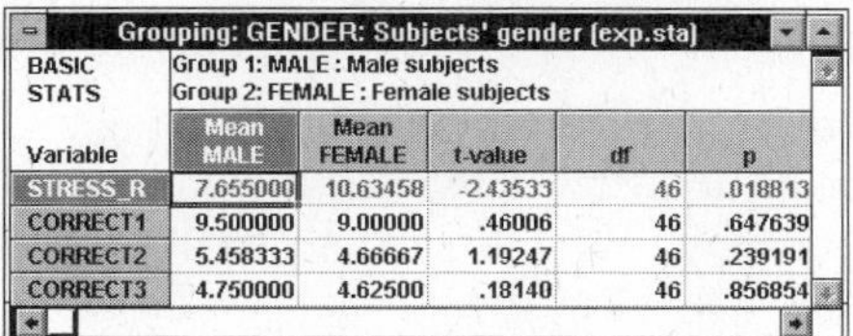

Grouping: GENDER: Subjects' gender (exp.sta)

BASIC STATS — Group 1: MALE : Male subjects; Group 2: FEMALE : Female subjects

Variable	Mean MALE	Mean FEMALE	t-value	df	p
STRESS_R	7.655000	10.63458	-2.43533	46	.018813
CORRECT1	9.500000	9.00000	.46006	46	.647639
CORRECT2	5.458333	4.66667	1.19247	46	.239191
CORRECT3	4.750000	4.62500	.18140	46	.856854

The detail and formatting of the results depends on your selections in the *Options* box below this button (see below).

Options

The selections from this group of check boxes will determine the detail and formatting of the *t*-test for independent samples results Scrollsheet.

Casewise deletion of missing data. By default, missing data will be excluded on a variable-by-variable basis (i.e., *pairwise* missing data deletion). If this check box is set, then *STATISTICA* will exclude all cases from the analysis that have missing data for *any* of the variables in the dependent variable list (i.e., *casewise* missing data deletion).

Display long variable names. If this check box is set, then the first column of the Scrollsheet will show not only the names of the respective dependent variables, but also their long variable names (if one was specified, see *Spreadsheet Edit (Current) Specs*, Chapter 3).

***t*-test with separate variance estimate.** In order to compute the *t*-test for independent samples, *STATISTICA* has to estimate the variance of the difference for the respective dependent variable. By default, this variance is estimated from the pooled (averaged) within-group variances. If the variances in the two groups are widely different, and the number of observations in each group also differs,

then the *t*-test computed in this manner may not accurately reflect the statistical significance of the difference. In that case one should use this option to compute the *t*-test with separate variance estimates and approximate degrees of freedom (see Blalock, 1972).

Multivariate test (Hotelling's T^2). Hotelling's T^2 test is a multivariate test for differences in means between two groups. This test will only be computed if more than one dependent variable was selected. Because this test is based on the within-group variance/covariance matrices for the dependent variables, it will automatically exclude missing data *casewise* from the computations. That is, this test will be computed only for cases that have complete data for all dependent variables in the selected list.

Levene's test (homogeneity of variances). The standard *t*-test for independent samples is based on the assumption that the variances in the two groups are the same (homogeneous). A powerful statistical test of this assumption is *Levene's* test. For each dependent variable, an analysis of variance is performed on the absolute deviations of values from the respective group means. If the *Levene's* test is statistically significant, then the hypothesis of homogeneous variances should be rejected. However, note that the *t*-test for independent samples is a robust test as long as the *n* per group is greater than 30; thus, a significant *Levene's* test does not necessarily call into question the validity of the *t*-test (see page 1439).

Box and Whisker Plots

This option will produce a cascade of box and whisker plots for the dependent variables; one box plot for each variable will be produced. Box and whisker plots summarize the distribution of the dependent variable for each group. For more information on this type of plot, see page 1504.

Categorized Histograms

This option (also available on the *Descriptive Statistics* dialog, see page 1500), will produce a cascade of categorized histograms (one for each dependent variable), summarizing the distribution of the respective variable in the two groups.

Categorized Normal Probability Plots

This option will produce a cascade of normal probability plots for the dependent variables, categorized by the two groups.

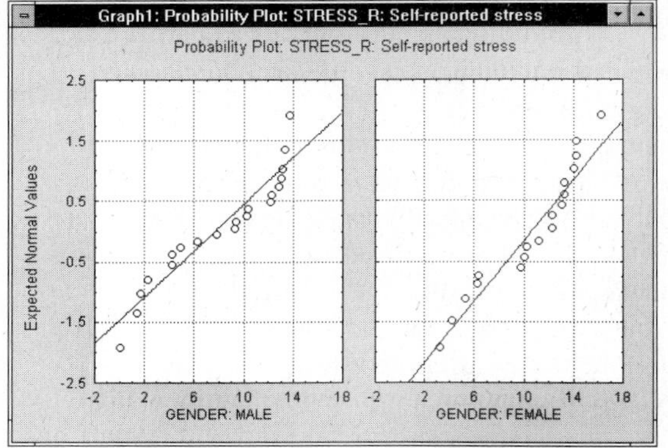

Categorized Detrended Probability Plots

This option will produce a cascade of detrended normal probability plots for the dependent variables, categorized by the two groups.

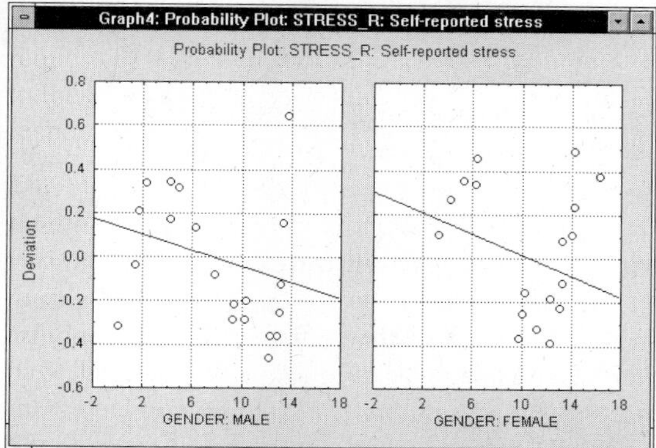

Categorized Scatterplots

This option (also available on the *Descriptive Statistics* dialog, see page 1500), will produce a cascade of categorized scatterplots for selected pairs of variables, one plot per pair.

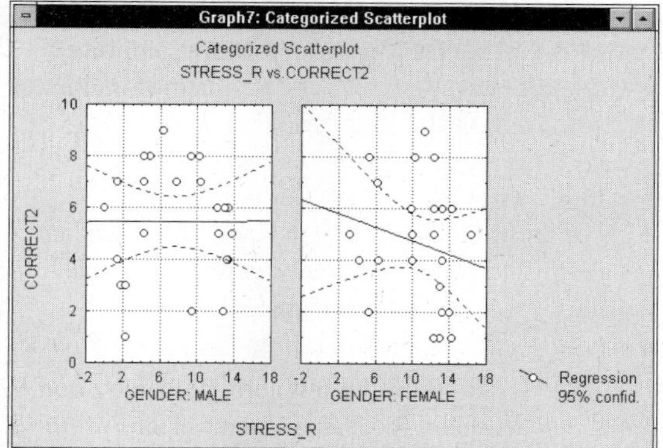

After clicking on this button, the user will be prompted to select two lists of variables (from the list of dependent variables). Scatterplots will be produced for each variable in the first list with each variable in the second list, categorized by the two groups for the *t*-test.

t-Test for Independent Samples - Compare Columns (Variables)

A general discussion of the *t*-test for independent samples is provided in the *Introductory Overview* section (page 1439). This dialog becomes available when you select the *Each variable contains the data for one group* procedure as the *Input File* (see below) in the *T-test for Independent Samples (Groups)* dialog (page 1516).

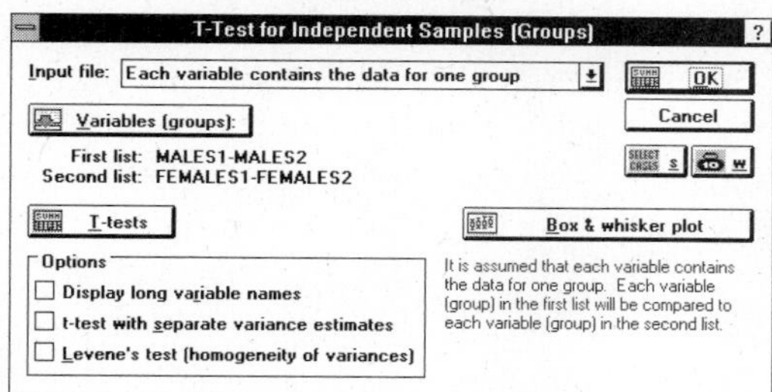

As mentioned before, this is not a standard arrangement of the data set.

Input File

This combo box has two settings: *One record per case (use grouping variable)* and *Each variable contains the data for one group*. The appropriate setting of this box depends on the way in which the user has set up the data file for the *t*-test for independent samples (see page 1439). The default and recommended way to set up a data file is to enter data case by case; that is, to let each row in the data file represent one case (individual, respondent) and to let each column in the data file represent one variable or measurement (e.g., response to a questionnaire item). In this set-up, a grouping variable (e.g., *Gender*) should be included to denote to which group each case belongs. The default first setting of this combo box expects the data to be arranged in this manner. However, for simple data analyses, it is sometimes easier to enter the data so that each column in the data file (variable)

represents the responses of one group (e.g., the data for all male respondents was entered into the first column of the file and the data for all female respondents was entered into the second column). If your data are arranged in this manner, set this combo switch to *Each variable contains the data for one group*.

Variables (Groups)

This option will bring up the standard two variable selection dialog in which you can specify two lists of variables. Since this setting of the *Input file* combo box assumes that each variable represents the data for one group, each variable (group) in the first list will be compared with each variable (group) in the second list.

t-Tests

After clicking on this button, the *t*-tests for independent samples will be computed and displayed in a results Scrollsheet.

T-test for Independent Samples (ttest.sta)

BASIC STATS — Note: Variables were treated as independent samples

Group 1 vs. Group 2	Mean Group 1	Mean Group 2	t-value	df	p
MALES1 vs. FEMALES1	9.52403	12.00413	-2.87939	60	.005516
MALES1 vs. FEMALES2	9.52403	12.73950	-3.78855	60	.000353
MALES2 vs. FEMALES1	11.94790	12.00413	-.08131	60	.935468
MALES2 vs. FEMALES2	11.94790	12.73950	-1.17125	60	.246127

The detail and formatting of the results depends on the selections that you made in the *Options* box below this button (see below).

Options

The selections from this group of check boxes will determine the detail and formatting of the *t*-test for independent samples results Scrollsheet.

Display long variable names. If this check box is set, then the first column of the Scrollsheet will show not only the names of the respective variables (groups), but also their long (variable) names (if one was specified, see *Spreadsheet Edit (Current) Specs*, Chapter 3).

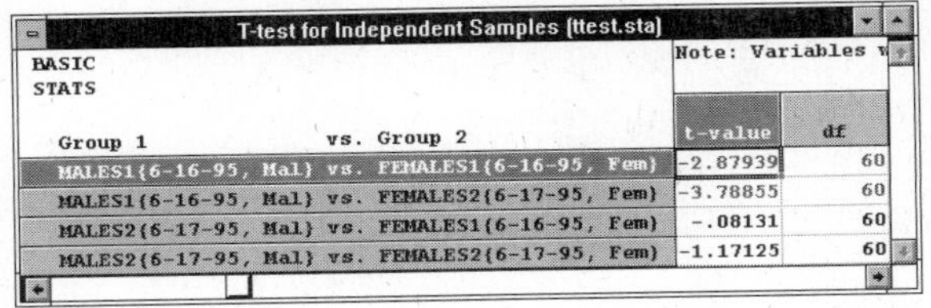

T-test for Independent Samples (ttest.sta)

BASIC STATS — Note: Variables w

Group 1 vs. Group 2	t-value	df
MALES1(6-16-95, Mal) vs. FEMALES1(6-16-95, Fem)	-2.87939	60
MALES1(6-16-95, Mal) vs. FEMALES2(6-17-95, Fem)	-3.78855	60
MALES2(6-17-95, Mal) vs. FEMALES1(6-16-95, Fem)	-.08131	60
MALES2(6-17-95, Mal) vs. FEMALES2(6-17-95, Fem)	-1.17125	60

***t*-test with separate variance estimate.** In order to compute the *t*-test for independent samples, *STATISTICA* has to estimate the variance of the difference for the respective pair of variables (groups). By default, this variance is estimated from the pooled (averaged) within-group variances. If the variances in the two groups are widely different, and the number of observations in each group also differs, then the *t*-test computed in this manner may not accurately reflect the statistical significance of the difference. In that case one should compute the *t*-test with separate variance estimates and approximated degrees of freedom (see Blalock, 1972).

Levene's test (homogeneity of variances). The standard *t*-test for independent samples is based on the assumption that the variances in the two groups are the same (homogeneous). A powerful statistical test of this assumption is *Levene's* test. For each dependent variable, an analysis of variance is performed on the absolute deviations of values from the respective group means. If the *Levene's* test is statistically significant, then the hypothesis of homogeneous variances should be rejected. However, note that the *t*-test for independent samples is a robust test as long as the *n* per group is greater than 30; thus, a significant *Levene's* test does not necessarily call into question the validity of the *t*-test (see *t-test for independent samples*, page 1439).

Box and Whisker Plots

This option will produce a cascade of box and whisker plots for the selected variables (groups). Specifically, a graph will be produced for each pair

of variables (groups) from the first list with the second list (i.e., one graph for each *t*-test). Box and whisker plots summarize the distributions within each group. For more information on *Box and Whisker* plots, see page 1504.

t-Test for Dependent Samples

A general discussion of the *t*-test for dependent samples is provided in the *Introductory Overview*, page 1441.

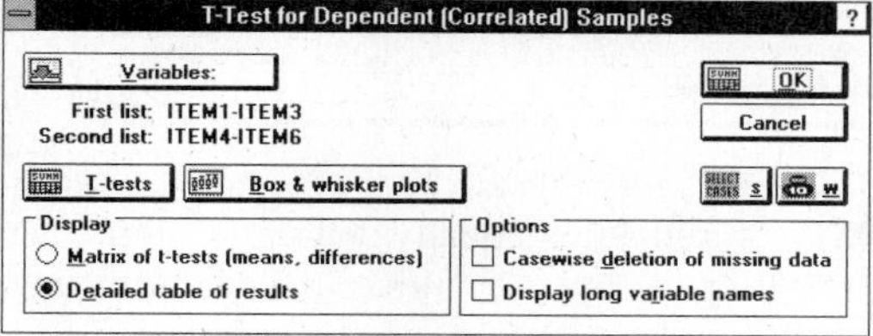

Variables

This option will bring up the standard two-variable-lists selection dialog in which you can specify two lists of variables to be analyzed. Each variable in the first list will be compared with each variable in the second list.

t-Tests

After clicking on this button, the *t*-tests for dependent samples will be computed and displayed in a results Scrollsheet.

T-test for Dependent Samples (ttest.sta)

BASIC STATS — Marked differences are significant at $p < .05000$

Variable	Mean	Std.Dv.	N	Diff.	Std.Dv Diff.	t	df	p
TEST1	9.524	3.6534						
TEST3	12.004	3.1067	31	-2.480	4.7964	-2.879	30	.0073
TEST1	9.524	3.6534						
TEST4	12.739	2.9973	31	-3.215	4.2274	-4.235	30	.0002
TEST2	11.948	2.2752						
TEST3	12.004	3.1067	31	-.056	3.9479	-.079	30	.9373
TEST2	11.948	2.2752						
TEST4	12.739	2.9973	31	-.792	3.5951	-1.226	30	.2297

The detail and formatting of the results depends on the selections that you make in the *Display* box below this button (see below).

Box and Whisker Plots

This option will produce a cascade of box and whisker plots for the selected variables (groups). Specifically, a graph will be produced for each pair of variables (groups) from the first list with the second list (i.e., one graph for each *t*-test). Box and whisker plots summarize the distributions within each group. For more information on *Box and Whisker* plots, see page 1504.

Display Options

Matrix of *t*-tests. If this button is set, then clicking on the *t-tests* button will produce a cascade of Scrollsheets reporting for each pair of variables (from the two lists) the mean difference, the *t*-value for the respective difference, and the significance level (*p*-level) for the respective *t*-value.

Detailed table of results. If this radio button is set then clicking on the *t-tests* button will produce a summary results Scrollsheet reporting for each *t*-test the means, standard deviations, valid *n*, etc.

Other Options

Casewise deletion of missing data. By default, *STATISTICA* will include in the computations all cases with valid data for the respective two variables in the comparison (i.e., *pairwise deletion of missing data*). If this check box is set, then *STATISTICA* will exclude all cases that have missing data for *any* of the variables in the two lists (i.e., *casewise deletion of missing data*).

Display long variable names. If this check box is set, then the results Scrollsheet will report in the first column the long variable names of the respective variables. If no long names were specified for any of the variables selected for the

analyses, then the setting of this check box will not effect the format of the results Scrollsheet.

Descriptive Statistics and Correlations by Groups (Breakdown)

A general discussion of the *Breakdown* procedure is provided in the *Introductory Overview*, page 1442.

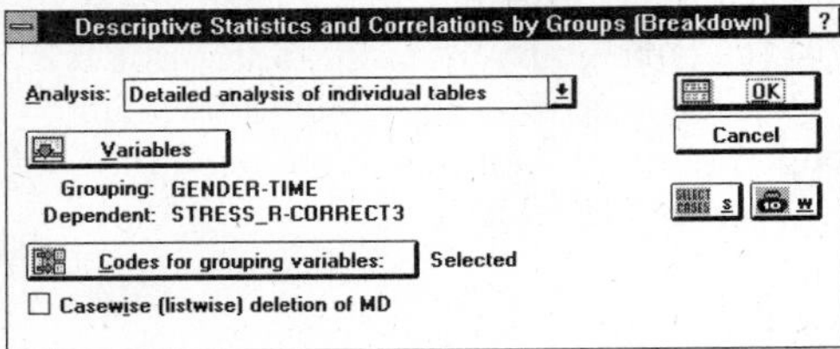

Analysis

This combo box has two settings, discussed below.

Detailed analysis of single tables. In this setting, the user can specify one set of categorical (breakdown) variables and a list of dependent variables. The *Breakdown Results* dialog then provides numerous options to examine in detail and graph various descriptive statistics and correlations broken down by groups.

Batch process (and print) lists of tables. This setting of the combo box allows the user to specify up to six lists of grouping variables and a list of dependent variables (see page 1530). *STATISTICA* will then compute breakdown tables for all possible combinations of variables from the lists of grouping variables. This option allows the user to compute a large number of breakdown tables in *batch,* that is, without requiring any further user input.

Variables

This option will bring up the standard two-variable list selection dialog in which you can select a set of up to 6 grouping (categorization) variables and a list of dependent variables.

Codes for Grouping Variables

This option will bring up a standard codes selection dialog in which you can specify the codes that were used in the grouping variables (in order to denote the group membership of each case).

If you click *OK* without selecting any codes, *STATISTICA* will automatically determine all integer codes for the grouping variables in the data file, and compute the breakdown tables accordingly.

Casewise (Listwise) Deletion of MD

If this check box is set, then all cases that have missing data in *any* of the dependent variables will be excluded from the analysis (i.e., *casewise deletion of missing data*). If this check box is not set, then cases will only be excluded from the computations for those variables, where they have missing data (i.e., *pairwise deletion of missing data*), possibly resulting in different numbers of valid cases for different dependent variables.

Descriptive Statistics and Correlations by Groups - Breakdown Results

The *Descriptive Statistics and Correlations by Groups - Results* dialog will allow you to calculate various statistics as well as graphs of the data.

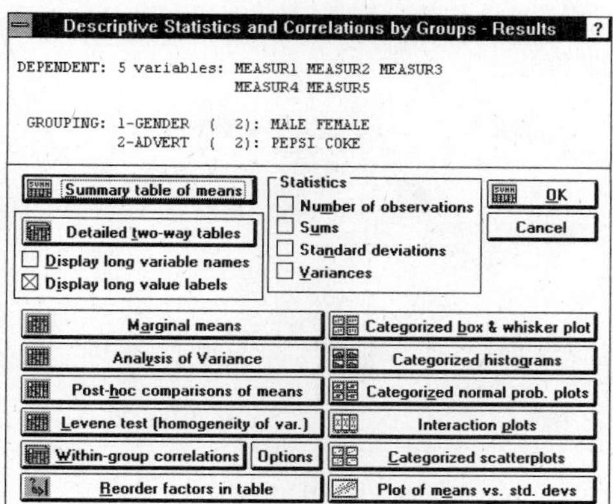

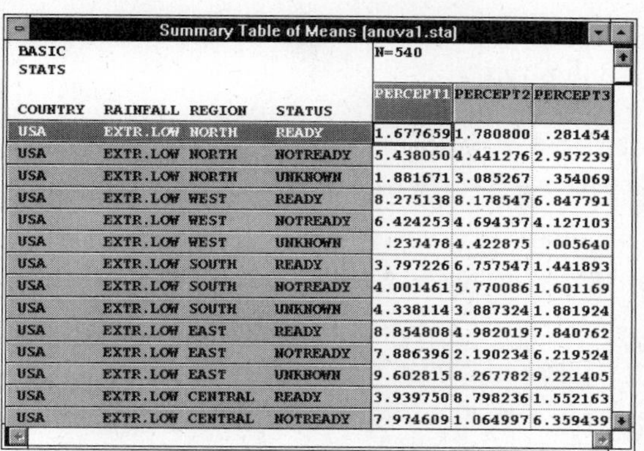

Summary Table of Means (anova1.sta)

BASIC STATS — N=540

COUNTRY	RAINFALL	REGION	STATUS	PERCEPT1	PERCEPT2	PERCEPT3
USA	EXTR.LOW	NORTH	READY	1.677659	1.780800	.281454
USA	EXTR.LOW	NORTH	NOTREADY	5.438050	4.441276	2.957239
USA	EXTR.LOW	NORTH	UNKNOWN	1.881671	3.085267	.354069
USA	EXTR.LOW	WEST	READY	8.275138	8.178547	6.847791
USA	EXTR.LOW	WEST	NOTREADY	6.424253	4.694337	4.127103
USA	EXTR.LOW	WEST	UNKNOWN	.237478	4.422875	.005640
USA	EXTR.LOW	SOUTH	READY	3.797226	6.757547	1.441893
USA	EXTR.LOW	SOUTH	NOTREADY	4.001461	5.770086	1.601169
USA	EXTR.LOW	SOUTH	UNKNOWN	4.338114	3.887324	1.881924
USA	EXTR.LOW	EAST	READY	8.854808	4.982019	7.840762
USA	EXTR.LOW	EAST	NOTREADY	7.886396	2.190234	6.219524
USA	EXTR.LOW	EAST	UNKNOWN	9.602815	8.267782	9.221405
USA	EXTR.LOW	CENTRAL	READY	3.939750	8.798236	1.552163
USA	EXTR.LOW	CENTRAL	NOTREADY	7.974609	1.064997	6.359439

A general overview of the *Breakdown* procedure is provided in the *Introductory Overview*, page 1442.

***Quick Basic Stats* options.** Note that you can compute detailed descriptive statistics (including correlations, medians, quartiles, etc.), broken down by a grouping variable, in every module of *STATISTICA* via the *Quick Basic Stats* options (see Chapter 10).

Summary Box

The summary box (in the upper part of the dialog) lists your choices for the dependent variable and grouping (independent) variables as well as the codes for the grouping variables.

Summary Table of Means

This button will bring up a summary table of descriptive statistics broken down by the grouping variables.

The statistics reported in the table depend on the selections in the *Statistics* box to the right of the button (see below).

Statistics Options

The selections in this box will determine the statistics that are reported in the results Scrollsheets when the user chooses either the *Summary table of means*, *Detailed two-way tables*, or *Marginal means* (see below).

Number of observations. Set this check box to compute the number of observations in each group.

Sums. Set this check box to compute the sums for the dependent variables for each group.

Standard deviations. Set this check box to compute the standard deviations for the dependent variables for each group. Note that the standard deviation is computed as the square roots of the sums of squared deviations (from the mean) divided by *n-1*; the resulting statistic is an estimate of the population *sigma* (this statistic can then be used to draw inferences about the variability of values in the population from which the sample was drawn).

Variances. Set this check box to compute the variances for the dependent variables for each group. The variance is computed as the sum of squared deviations (from the mean) divided by *n-1*; the

resulting variances are unbiased estimates of the population variances.

Detailed Two-Way Tables

This button will bring up a cascade of Scrollsheets with two-way tables.

Summary Table of Means (breakdn.sta)
BASIC STATS — Within: GENDER:Male

Summary Table of Means (breakdn.sta)
Continue... — Within: GENDER:Female
N=509 (No missing data in dep. var. list)

GROUP INCOME	MEASURE1	MEASURE2
G_1:1	10.15888	10.82112
Low	10.30466	9.87653
Medium	10.17503	10.53281
High	10.05024	11.69094
G_2:2	9.70705	5.85049
Low	9.38244	5.90555
Medium	9.81444	6.20157
High	10.04294	5.35387
G_3:3	10.21317	12.08388
Low	10.19843	10.62477
Medium	10.31082	14.15728
High	10.10527	11.12250
All Groups	10.03577	9.70423

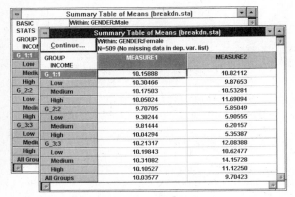

If two or less grouping variables were selected, then only a single Scrollsheet will be produced. If more than two grouping variables were selected, then the tables will be produced for the last two grouping variables, within the respective levels of the remaining (preceding) grouping variables. Use the *Reorder factors in table* option (see below) to change the order of grouping variables and therefore the order in which the two-way tables are produced. The statistics reported in the Scrollsheets depend on your selections in the *Statistics* box (see above). Additional formatting options are available via the check boxes below this button (see below). The two-way tables will not only report summary statistics within each group, but also marginal summary statistics, that is, statistics for each factor ignoring the other. User-specified marginal tables are available via the *Marginal means* option (see below).

Display long variables names. Set this check box to display the long variable labels for the grouping variables in the header of the first Scrollsheet column.

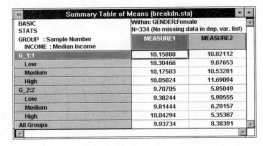

Summary Table of Means (breakdn.sta)
BASIC STATS — Within: GENDER:Female
N=334 (No missing data in dep. var. list)

GROUP : Sample Number INCOME : Median Income	MEASURE1	MEASURE2
G_1:1	10.15888	10.82112
Low	10.30466	9.87653
Medium	10.17503	10.53281
High	10.05024	11.69094
G_2:2	9.70705	5.85049
Low	9.38244	5.90555
Medium	9.81444	6.20157
High	10.04294	5.35387
All Groups	9.93734	8.38391

If no long variable labels are specified for the grouping variables in the table, then the setting of this check box is ignored.

Display long value labels. Set this check box to report long value labels for the levels of the grouping variables in the first column of the Scrollsheet.

Summary Table of Means (breakdn.sta)
BASIC STATS — Within: GEND
N=334 (No mi

GROUP : Sample Number INCOME : Median Income	MEASURE1
Sample_1: Sample 1: 6-15-95	10.15888
Low : Income less than $20,000	10.30466
Medium : Income between $20,000 and $40,000	10.17503
High : Income above $40,000	10.05024
Sample_2: Sample 2: 6-25-95	9.70705
Low : Income less than $20,000	9.38244
Medium : Income between $20,000 and $40,000	9.81444
High : Income above $40,000	10.04294
All Groups	9.93734

If no long value labels exist for the grouping variables in the two-way table, then the setting of this check box is ignored.

Marginal Means

This option allows you to compute summary statistics for the selected marginal table, that is, only for the combination of selected grouping variables, ignoring those that are not selected. For example, suppose there are three grouping variables *Gender, Age Group,* and *Ethnic Origin.* If you selected (highlighted) only *Gender* and *Ethnic Origin*, then summary statistics will be computed for the two-way

table of *Gender* by *Ethnic Origin*, ignoring (averaging over) *Age Group*.

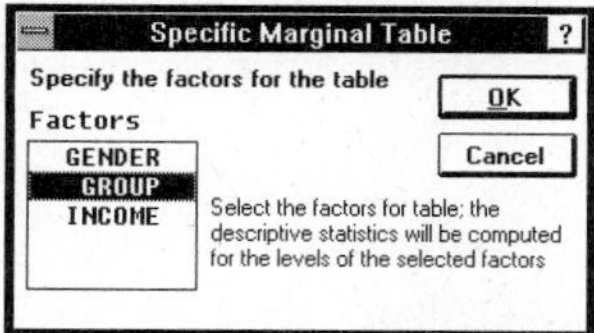

When you click *OK* in this window, the Scrollsheet containing the marginal means for the selected table will be produced.

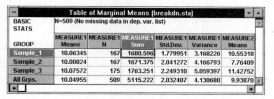

Table of Marginal Means (breakdn.sta)

BASIC STATS — N=509 (No missing data in dep. var. list)

GROUP	MEASURE1 Means	MEASURE1 N	MEASURE1 Sum	MEASURE1 Std.Dev.	MEASURE1 Variance	MEASURE2 Means
Sample_1	10.06345	167	1680.596	1.779951	3.168226	10.55318
Sample_2	10.00824	167	1671.375	2.041272	4.166793	7.76409
Sample_3	10.07572	175	1763.251	2.249310	5.059397	11.42752
All Grps.	10.04955	509	5115.222	2.032407	4.130680	9.93870

Note that the marginal means (sums, standard deviations, etc.) are not necessarily identical to the *averages* across the non-selected factors. Rather, they represent *weighted* averages taking into account unequal *n's* across groups.

To change the order of factors in the table, use the *Reorder factors in table* option (see below) before specifying the marginal table.

Analysis of Variance

This option will bring up a Scrollsheet with the results of univariate analyses of variance for each dependent variable.

Analysis of Variance (breakdn.sta)

BASIC STATS — Marked effects are significant at p < .05000

Variable	SS Effec	df Effec	MS Effec	SS Error	df Error	MS Error	F	p
MM3_1995	372.7	17	21.92	993.	491	2.023	10.838	.0000
MEASURE1	50.4	17	2.97	2048.	491	4.171	.711	.7922
MEASURE2	2305.6	17	135.62	44557.	491	90.747	1.495	.0915

If statistically significant, it can be concluded that the means across the groups are different in magnitude; you can use the *Post hoc comparisons of means* procedure (see below) to identify significant differences between individual groups (means). Use the *ANOVA/MANOVA* module to compute complete univariate and multivariate analysis of variance tables. However, note that the one-way ANOVA available from this dialog is particularly suited for quickly analyzing one-way univariate designs with very many groups.

Post Hoc Comparisons of Means

This option allows the user to compute the common *post hoc* tests for multiple comparisons of means (LSD, Scheffé, Newman-Keuls, Duncan, Tukey, Spjotvoll & Stoline). After clicking on this button, select a dependent variable for the tests; a pop-up window with available tests will then be displayed (see *Post hoc comparison of means*, page 1532).

Levene's Test (Homogeneity of Variances)

The significance tests reported by the *Analysis of Variance* procedure (see above) are based on the assumption that the variances in the different groups are the same (homogeneous). A powerful statistical test of this assumption is *Levene's* test. For each dependent variable, an analysis of variance is performed on the absolute deviations of values from the respective group means. If the *Levene's* test is statistically significant, then the hypothesis of homogeneous variances should be rejected. However, note that the *F* statistic (in ANOVA) provides a robust test for mean differences as long as (1) the *n* per group is greater than 10, and (2) the means across groups are not correlated with the standard deviations across groups. Thus, a significant *Levene's* test does not necessarily call into question the validity of the ANOVA results. The assumption of uncorrelated means and standard deviations can easily be checked by producing the *Plot of means vs. standard deviations* from this dialog (see below).

Within-Group Correlations

If more than one dependent variable was selected for the current analysis, then this option will allow you to compute the within-group correlation matrices for those variables (see page 1530). After clicking this option, you will be prompted to select the group for which to display the correlation matrix.

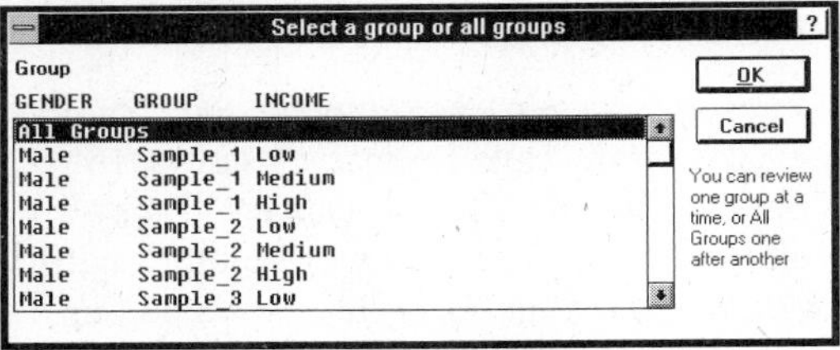

You can select one group or choose *All groups* in order to display a cascade of Scrollsheets (displaying the correlation matrices for all groups).

Options. This button will pop-up a dialog of display options for the *within-group correlation matrices* (see above).

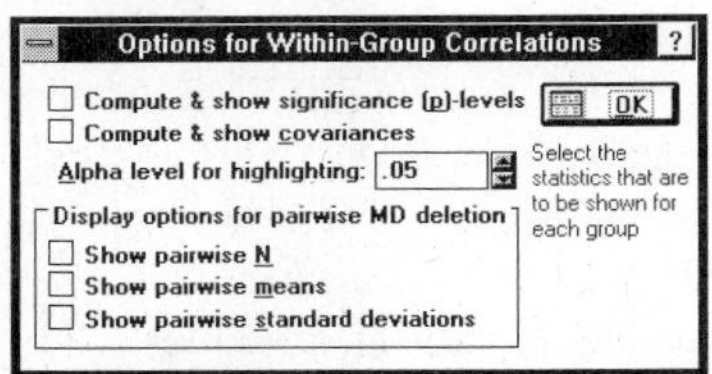

Specifically, you can determine an *alpha* (*p*) level for highlighting significant correlations, request to compute within-group covariance matrices, or report various additional statistics (e.g., pairwise *n*, means, standard deviations; see *Within-group correlations* for details, page 1530, for descriptions of each of these options).

Reorder Factors in Table

This option allows you to change the order of grouping variables for the current analysis. Note that, when reporting the within-group statistics, *STATISTICA* will cycle through the groups in the current breakdown analysis so that the factor that was selected last is the one with the fastest-changing subscript, the factor that was selected next-to-last is the one with the second-fastest changing subscript, and so on. This option allows you to change the order of selected grouping variables, and thus the order in which within-group statistics are reported.

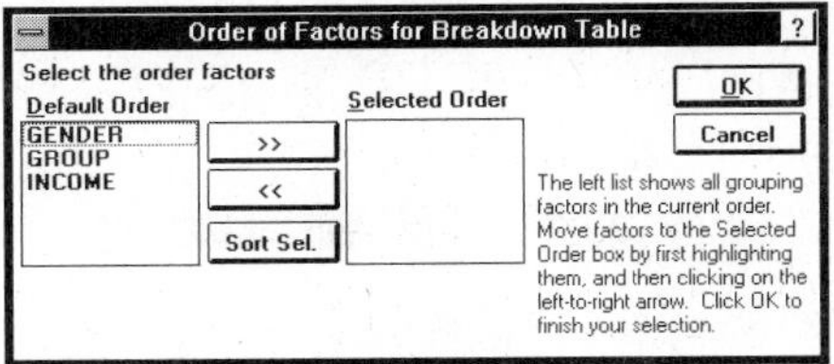

To change the order of grouping variables, move them in the desired (new order) from the left side (*Default order*) to the right (*Selected order*) and then click *OK*.

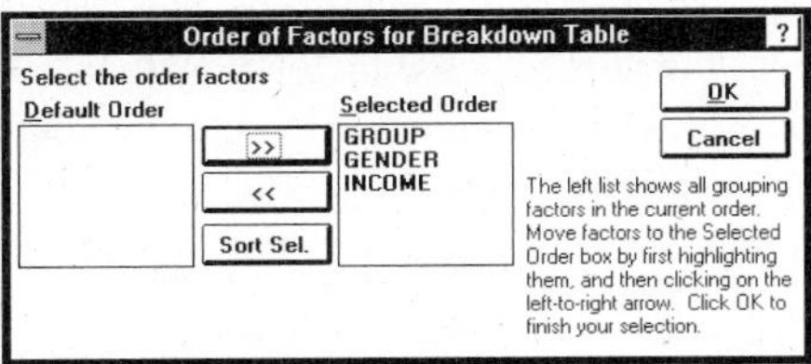

Before reordering:

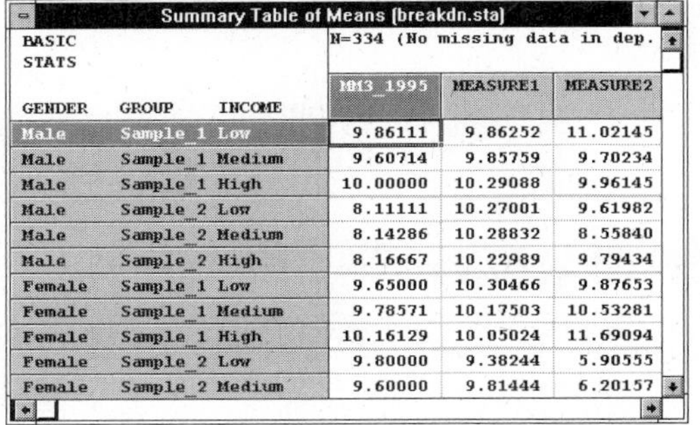

Summary Table of Means (breakdn.sta)

BASIC STATS			N=334 (No missing data in dep.		
GENDER	GROUP	INCOME	MM3_1995	MEASURE1	MEASURE2
Male	Sample_1	Low	9.86111	9.86252	11.02145
Male	Sample_1	Medium	9.60714	9.85759	9.70234
Male	Sample_1	High	10.00000	10.29088	9.96145
Male	Sample_2	Low	8.11111	10.27001	9.61982
Male	Sample_2	Medium	8.14286	10.28832	8.55840
Male	Sample_2	High	8.16667	10.22989	9.79434
Female	Sample_1	Low	9.65000	10.30466	9.87653
Female	Sample_1	Medium	9.78571	10.17503	10.53281
Female	Sample_1	High	10.16129	10.05024	11.69094
Female	Sample_2	Low	9.80000	9.38244	5.90555
Female	Sample_2	Medium	9.60000	9.81444	6.20157

After reordering:

Summary Table of Means (breakdn.sta)

BASIC STATS — N=334 (No missing data in dep.

GROUP	GENDER	INCOME	MM3_1995	MEASURE1	MEASURE2
Sample_1	Male	Low	9.86111	9.86252	11.02145
Sample_1	Male	Medium	9.60714	9.85759	9.70234
Sample_1	Male	High	10.00000	10.29088	9.96145
Sample_1	Female	Low	9.65000	10.30466	9.87653
Sample_1	Female	Medium	9.78571	10.17503	10.53281
Sample_1	Female	High	10.16129	10.05024	11.69094
Sample_2	Male	Low	8.11111	10.27001	9.61982
Sample_2	Male	Medium	8.14286	10.28832	8.55840
Sample_2	Male	High	8.16667	10.22989	9.79434
Sample_2	Female	Low	9.80000	9.38244	5.90555
Sample_2	Female	Medium	9.60000	9.81444	6.20157
Sample_2	Female	High	10.19048	10.04294	5.35387

You can return to the default order at any time by clicking on the *Sort Sel.* button in the *Order of Factors* dialog.

Categorized Box and Whisker Plots

This option will produce a cascade of categorized box and whisker plots for the dependent variables, one plot per dependent variable. For each variable *STATISTICA* will produce a box and whisker plot, broken down (categorized) by the grouping variables (e.g., separately for males and females for each ethnic group).

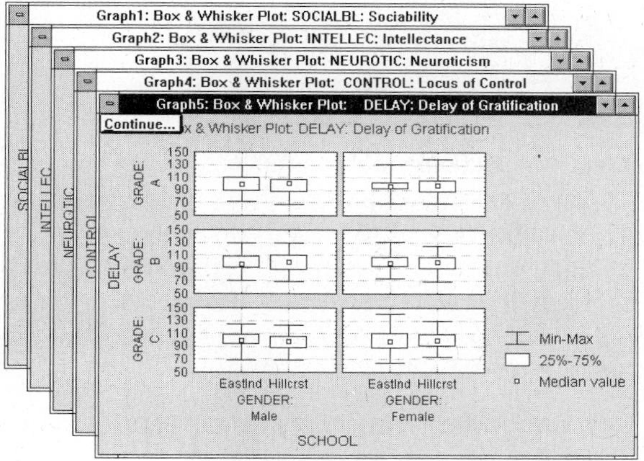

Categorized Histograms

This option will produce a cascade of categorized histograms.

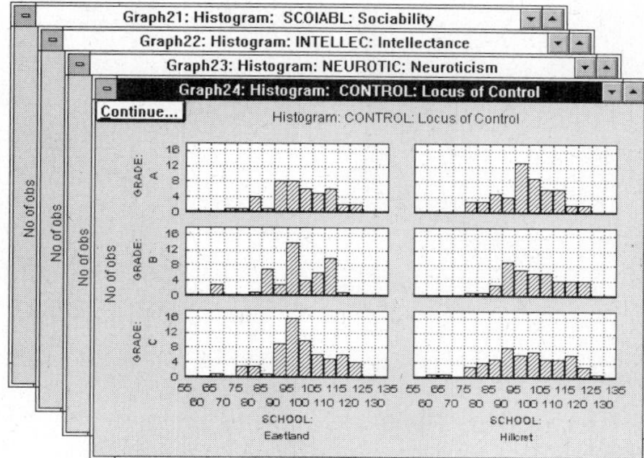

After clicking on this button you can select variables for the plot from among the list of dependent variables in the current analysis. For each selected variable, a categorized histogram will be produced, summarizing the within-group distribution of the respective variable.

Categorized Normal Probability Plots

This option will produce a cascade of normal probability plots for the selected dependent variables, categorized by the grouping variables. After clicking on this button, you will be prompted to select standard normal probability plots, half-normal plots, or detrended normal plots (see page 1500).

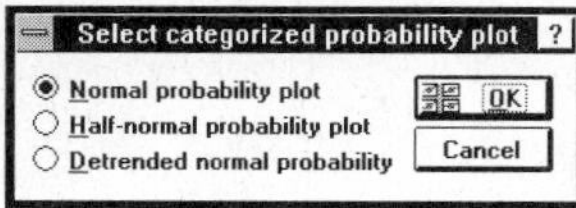

When you click *OK* in this dialog, you will then be asked to select the dependent variable(s) for the plot (if more than one dependent variable was previously

selected). Once you have made your selections, the categorized probability plot will be produced.

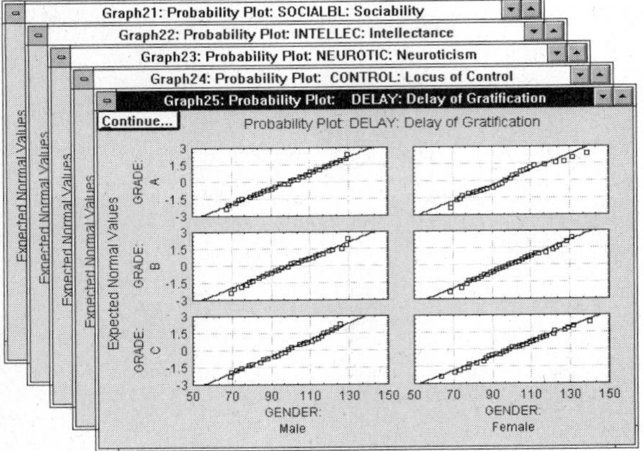

Interaction Plot

This option will produce an interaction plot of means by groups.

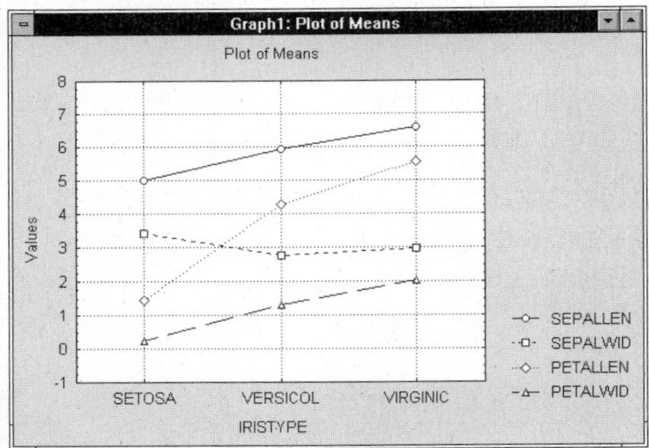

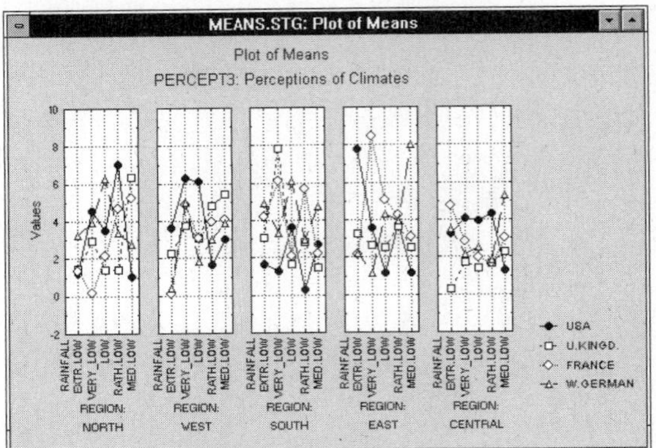

Interaction plots will be produced according to the following specifications, within the levels of any additional grouping factors.

More than one dependent variable was selected for the current analysis. In this case, when you click on the *Interaction plot* button, the resulting *Select the variables for interaction plot* dialog will display each of the previously selected dependent variables.

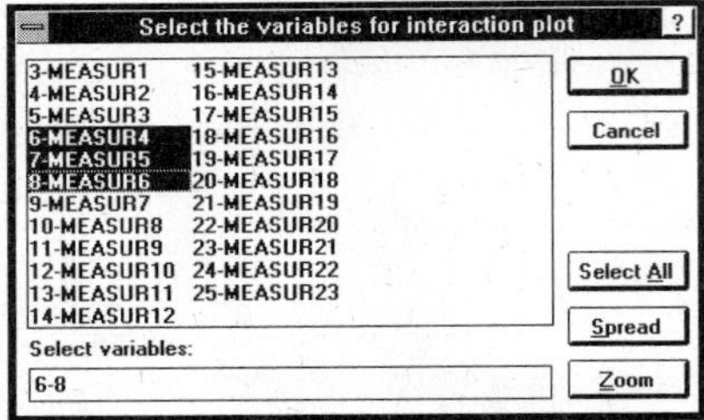

You can select only those variables that you want plotted, or click *OK* to accept the default selection (all variables in the list); each variable in the resulting interaction plots will be represented by a different line color or pattern. Clicking *OK* in this dialog will open the *Arrangement of factors* dialog (see below).

One dependent variable was selected for the current analysis. Since you have already selected the dependent variable to plot, when you click on the *Interaction plot* button, the *Arrangement of factors* dialog will open (see below). In this interaction

plot, the grouping variables will be represented by different line colors and patterns.

Arrangement of factors. Once you selected the variables (see above) to be plotted, the *Arrangement of factors* dialog will open.

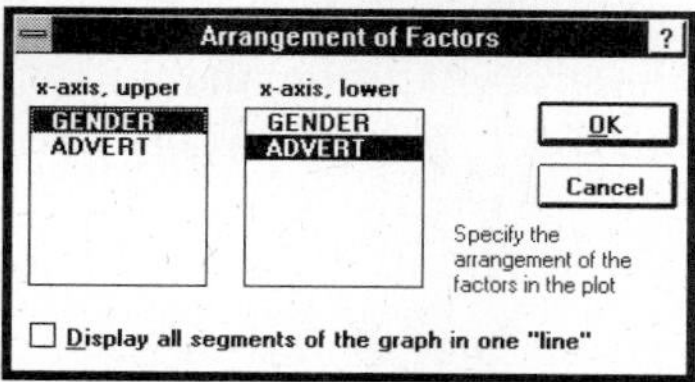

In this dialog, you can assign two (if two or more dependent variables were selected) or three (if one dependent variable was selected) grouping variables to different aspects of the interaction plot (line pattern, lower *X*-axis, upper *X*-axis).

Categorized Scatterplots

This option will produce a cascade of categorized scatterplots.

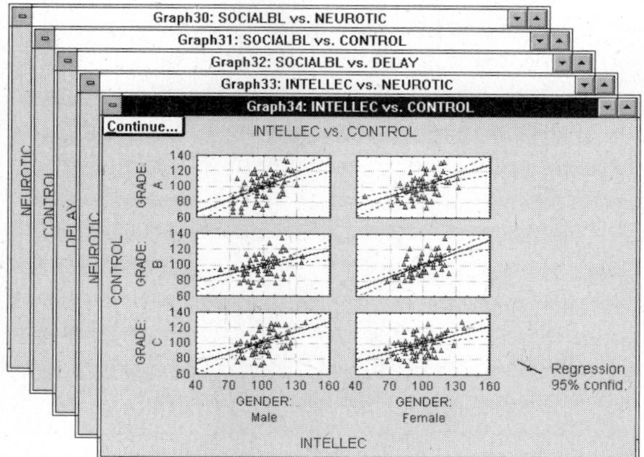

After clicking on this button you can select variables for the plot from among the list of dependent variables in the current analysis. A categorized scatterplot will be produced for each selected variable.

Plot of Means vs. Standard Deviations

This option allows you to plot the means for selected variables across groups against the respective standard deviations.

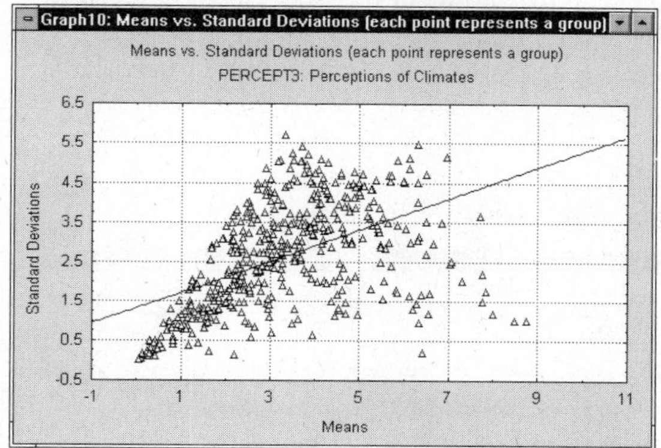

This plot is useful in order to spot potential outliers among the means that may contribute to an erroneous conclusion of statistically significant differences between means. One of the most common and most serious violations of assumptions for ANOVA is when the means are correlated with the standard deviations across groups. For example, suppose there are 5 groups of 10 observations each. If in one group, two observations are extreme outliers, then the variance in that group will be much larger and the mean will be very different (larger or smaller) from the grand mean. However, for the overall *F* test (ANOVA) the *pooled* (averaged) within-group variance is taken as an estimate of the error variance. Thus, the reliability of the outlier mean will be overestimated, and the ANOVA may erroneously yield a significant *F* statistic.

Descriptive Statistics and Correlations by Groups (Breakdown) - Lists

A general discussion of the *Breakdown* procedure is provided in the *Introductory Overview* section (page 1442). The *Descriptive Statistics and Correlations by Groups (Breakdowns) - Lists* dialog will open when you select *Batch process (and print) lists of tables* in the *Descriptive Statistics and Correlations by Groups (Breakdowns)* dialog.

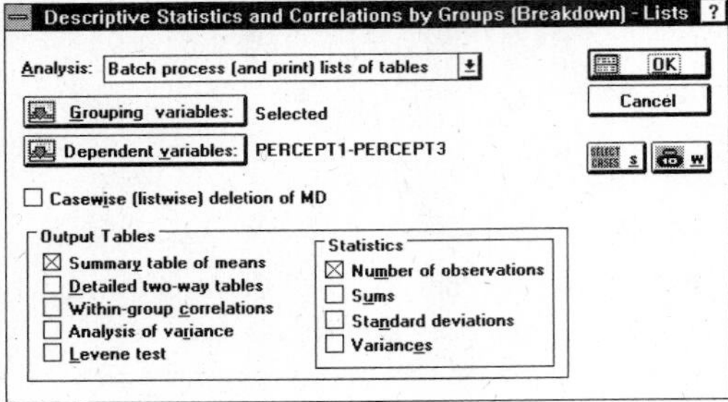

Analysis

This combo box has two settings, discussed below.

Detailed analysis of single tables. In this setting, the user can specify one set of categorical (breakdown) variables and a list of dependent variables (see page 1522). The *Breakdown Results* dialog (page 1522) then provides numerous options to examine and graph various descriptive statistics broken down by groups.

Batch process (and print) lists of tables. This setting of the combo box allows the user to specify up to six lists of grouping variables and a list of dependent variables. *STATISTICA* will then compute breakdown tables for all possible combinations of variables from the lists of grouping variables. This option allows the user to compute a large number of breakdown tables in *batch*; that is, without requiring any further user input.

Grouping Variables

This option will bring up a standard six-variable lists selection window in which you will need to select at least one list of grouping variables; breakdown tables will be computed for all possible combinations of grouping variables from the six lists. Note that *STATISTICA* will automatically take all valid integer values in the respective grouping variables to construct the tables.

Dependent Variables

This option will bring up a standard single variable list selection window in which you can select the list of dependent variables for the breakdown tables.

Casewise (Listwise) Deletion of Missing Data

If this check box is set then all cases that have missing data in *any* of the dependent variables will be excluded from the analyses (i.e., *casewise deletion of missing data*). If this check box is not set, then cases will only be excluded from the computations for those dependent variables, where they have missing data (possibly resulting in different numbers of valid cases for different dependent variables).

Output Tables

Note that in this setting of the *Analysis* combo box (i.e., *Batch process (and print) lists of tables*), a cascade of results Scrollsheets will be computed for each table (combination of grouping variables). The settings in this group of check boxes will determine the types of Scrollsheets that will be computed for each table and the detail of results for each dependent variable (*Statistics*, see below).

Summary table of means. Set this check box to display (and print if printer or disk output is selected) summary breakdown tables. The statistics

reported in the Scrollsheets depend on the selection of *Statistics* (see below).

Detailed two-way tables. Set this check box to compute Scrollsheets with two-way tables. If more than two lists of grouping variables were selected, then the tables will be produced for the last two grouping variables in the current table, within the respective levels of preceding grouping variables. The statistics that are reported in the Scrollsheets depend on your selection of *Statistics* (see below).

Within-group correlations. Set this check box to compute Scrollsheets of within-group correlation matrices for the dependent variables (see page 1530).

Analysis of variance. Set this check box to compute Scrollsheets of summary ANOVA tables for the dependent variables.

Levene's test. The significance tests reported by the *Analysis of variance* procedure (see above) is based on the assumption that the variances in the different groups are the same (homogeneous). A powerful statistical test of this assumption is *Levene's* test. For each dependent variable, an analysis of variance is performed on the absolute deviations of values from the respective group means. If the *Levene's* test is statistically significant, then the hypothesis of homogeneous variances should be rejected. However, note that the *F* statistic (in ANOVA) provides a robust test for mean differences as long as (1) the *n* per group is greater than 10, and (2) the means across groups are not correlated with the standard deviations across groups. Thus, a significant *Levene's* test does not necessarily call into question the validity of the ANOVA results.

Statistics Options

The selections in this box will determine the statistics that are reported in the *Summary tables of means* and the *Detailed two-way tables*.

Number of observations. Set this check box to compute the number of observations in each group.

Sums. Set this check box to compute the sums for the dependent variables for each group.

Standard deviations. Set this check box to compute the standard deviations for the dependent variables for each group. Note that the standard deviation is computed as the square roots of the sums of squared deviations (from the mean) divided by *n-1*; the resulting statistic is an estimate of the population *sigma* (this statistic can then be used to draw inferences about the variability of values in the population from which the sample was drawn).

Variances. Set this check box to compute the variances for the dependent variables for each group. The variance is computed as the sum of squared deviations (from the mean) divided by *n-1*; the resulting variances are unbiased estimates of the population variances.

Options for Within-Group Correlations

Your choice of options in this dialog (resulting from the *Options* button in the *Descriptive Statistics and Correlations by Groups - Results* dialog, page 1522) will determine the detail of results reported after selecting the *Within group correlations* option.

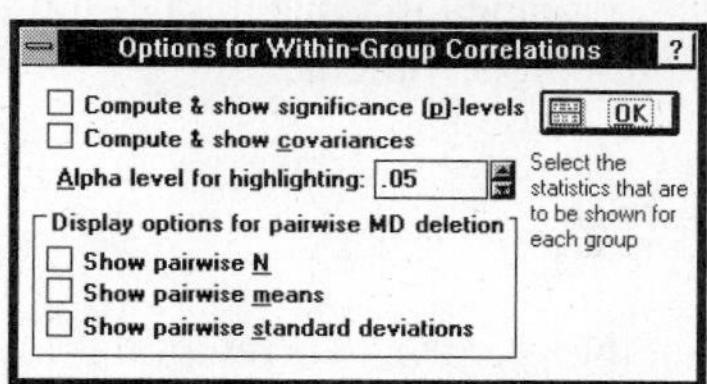

In this dialog, you can also adjust the *alpha* level for highlighting (see below).

Compute and Show Significance (*p*) Levels

If this check box is set, then for each correlation matrix, a matrix of *p* (significance) levels will be computed.

Compute and Show Covariance

If this check box is set, then for each correlation matrix, a matrix of covariances will be computed.

Display Options for Pairwise MD Deletion

The options in this box are only meaningful and available if *pairwise* deletion of missing data was selected prior to processing the data.

Show Pairwise *n*

If this check box is set, then for each correlation matrix, a matrix of valid *n* for each correlation will be displayed.

Show Pairwise Means

If this check box is set, then for each correlation matrix, a matrix of pairwise means will be displayed. For each correlation, those means will be computed from all cases that were included in the computation of the respective correlation coefficient.

Show Pairwise Standard Deviations

If this check box is set, then for each correlation matrix, a matrix of pairwise standard deviations will be displayed. For each correlation, those standard deviations will be computed from all cases that were included in the computation of the respective correlation coefficient.

Post hoc Comparison of Means

This dialog provides a choice of various *post hoc* procedures. You may refer to the *Introductory Overview* section for a discussion of the basic logic behind these tests (page 1443).

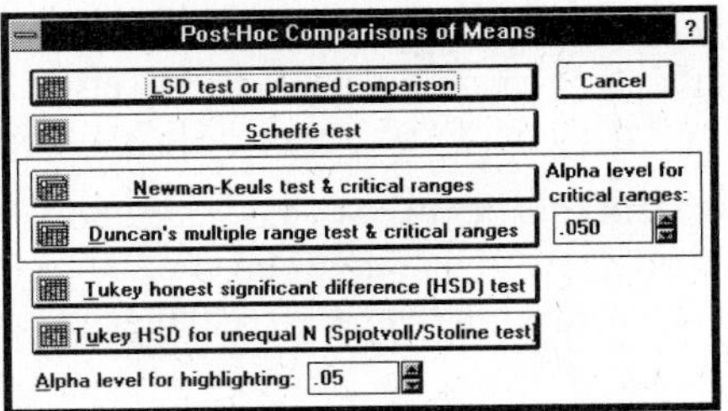

Discussions of *post hoc* procedures are also provided in Winer (1962), Hays (1988), or Milliken and Johnson (1984). In short, usually, after obtaining a statistically significant *F* test from the ANOVA, one wants to know which means contributed to the effect, that is, which groups are particularly different from each other. One could of course perform a series of simple *t*-tests to compare all possible pairs of means. However, such a procedure would *capitalize on chance*. This means that the reported probability levels would actually overestimate the statistical significance of mean differences. Without going into much detail, suppose you took 20 samples of 10 random numbers each, and computed 20 means. Then, take the group (sample) with the highest mean and compare it with that of the lowest mean. The *t-test for independent samples* will test whether or not those two means are significantly different from each other, provided that they were *the only two samples* taken. *Post hoc* comparison techniques on the other hand, specifically take into account the fact that more than two samples were taken.

LSD Test

This test is equivalent to the *t*-test for independent samples, based on the *n* in the groups involved in the

comparison. It offers the least amount of protection against the increased *alpha* error rate due to multiple *post hoc* comparisons. After choosing this option, a matrix of *p* values will be displayed in a Scrollsheet.

LSD Test; Variable: MEASUR7 (adstudy.sta)

BASIC STATS	Marked differences are significant at p < .0500(			
GENDER ADVERT	{1} M=5.0769	{2} M=5.8000	{3} M=4.0714	{4} M=2.8750
MALE PEPSI {1}		.420149	.271547	.042277
MALE COKE {2}	.420149		.053365	.006554
FEMALE PEPSI {3}	.271547	.053365		.255767
FEMALE COKE {4}	.042277	.006554	.255767	

These *p* values indicate the *post hoc* significance levels for the respective pairs of means.

Scheffé Test

This option will bring up a Scrollsheet with the *post hoc p*-levels for the Scheffé test. The Scheffé test is more conservative than the Newman-Keuls or Duncan test (see Winer, 1962).

Neuman-Keuls Test and Critical Ranges

This test is based on the *studentized* range statistic. Computationally, *STATISTICA* first sorts the means into ascending order. For each pair of means *STATISTICA* then assesses the probability under the null hypothesis (no differences between means in the population) of obtaining differences between means of this (or greater) magnitude, *given the respective number of samples*. Thus, it actually tests the significance of *ranges*, given the respective number of samples. Note that *STATISTICA* does not merely report cut-off values for *p*, but will compute the actual probabilities based on the distribution of the *studentized range* statistics.

A second Scrollsheet will display the *critical ranges* between ordered means, given the respective *alpha* level (by default $p<.05$).

Duncan Multiple Range Test and Critical Ranges

This test is based on the same logic as the Newman-Keuls procedure; however, it uses a less conservative test criterion (see, for example, Milliken and Johnson, 1984).

Tukey *HSD* (Honest Significant Difference) Test

The Tukey *HSD* (see Winer, 1971) test falls between the Newman-Keuls and Scheffé procedures with regard to conservatism.

Tukey *HSD* for Unequal Sample Sizes (Spjotvoll & Stoline Test)

This test is a generalization of the Tukey test to the case of unequal samples sizes (see Spjotvoll and Stoline, 1973, page 975).

Alpha Level for Highlighting

In all results Scrollsheets, significant differences are highlighted. Enter the desired critical *p* (*alpha*) level for highlighting into the edit field. You can later change the *alpha* level via the *Options* Scrollsheet toolbar button (see page 1552)

Frequency Tables

A general discussion of the *Frequency tables* procedure is provided in the *Introductory Overview* section (page 1445).

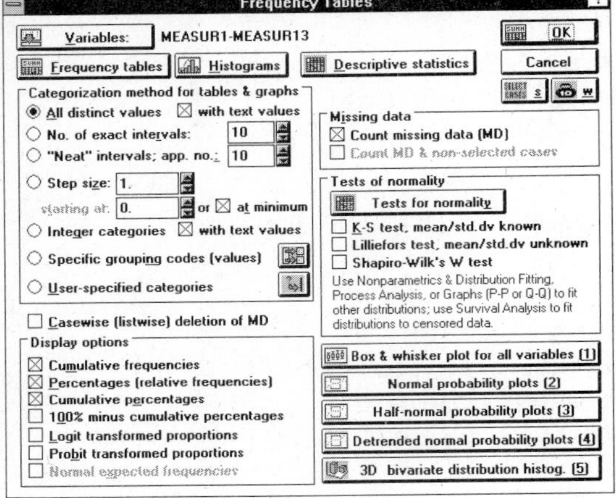

Variables

This option will bring up a standard single variable list selection window in which you can select the variables for the analyses.

Frequency Tables

This option will produce a cascade of frequency tables for the selected variables.

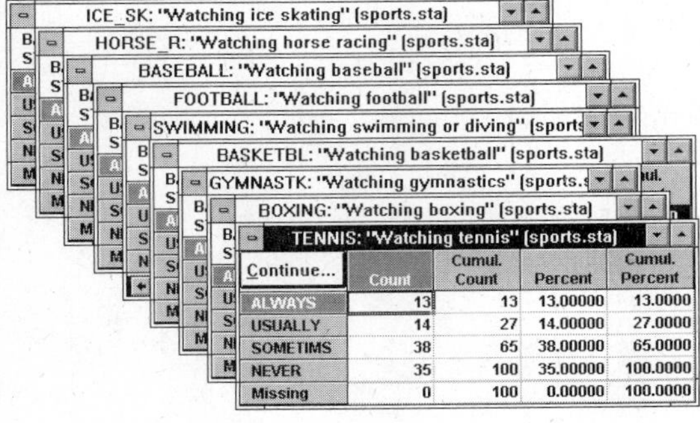

Continue...	Count	Cumul. Count	Percent	Cumul. Percent
ALWAYS	13	13	13.00000	13.0000
USUALLY	14	27	14.00000	27.0000
SOMETIMS	38	65	38.00000	65.0000
NEVER	35	100	35.00000	100.0000
Missing	0	100	0.00000	100.0000

The manner in which the variables are categorized for the frequency tables is determined by the selection of options in the *Categorization method for tables & graphs* box (see below). The options in the *Display option* box (see below) determine the different summary statistics that will be reported in the frequency tables. If any *Tests for normality* are selected (i.e., if any of the check boxes in that box are set, see below), then for each variable, an additional Scrollsheet with the results for the respective selected tests will be displayed (test for other non-normal distributions are available in the *Nonparametrics and Distributions* and the *Survival Analysis* modules).

Histograms

This option will produce a cascade of histograms for the selected variables, one histogram per variable.

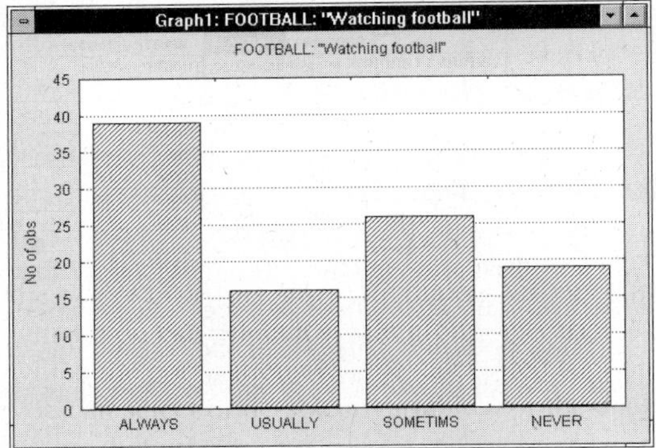

The manner in which the variables are categorized for the histograms is determined by the same settings of options as in *Frequency tables* (see above).

Descriptive Statistics

This option will produce a Scrollsheet of descriptive statistics for the selected variables. Note that the manner in which data are processed in the computation of descriptive statistics depends on the *Categorization method for tables & graphs* (see below). Specifically:

(1) If the *Step size* radio button is selected and a user-defined minimum is specified, then all cases with values less than the minimum will be ignored;

(2) If the *Integer categories* button is selected, then all non-integer values will be ignored;

(3) If the *Specific grouping codes (labels)* button is selected then all values that do not match any of the selected integer codes will be ignored;

(4) If the *User-specified intervals* button is selected, then *Descriptive statistics* are not available (because complex compound conditions can be specified to assign cases to categories, see below).

In all cases, missing data will either by deleted casewise or pairwise, depending on whether or not the *Casewise (listwise) deletion of MD* check box is set (see below).

Categorization Method for Tables and Graphs

The settings in this box will determine (1) how the currently selected variables will be categorized or tabulated for the *Frequency tables* and *Histograms*, and (2) how cases are processed for *Descriptive statistics* (see above).

All distinct values. Select this option if you want the frequencies to be based on all of the distinct values for each of the selected variables.

With text values. Select this option if you want the frequencies to be based on the distinct text values for each of the selected variables.

No. of exact intervals. If this radio button is set, then the entire range of values for each variable will be divided into the respective number of intervals.

"Neat" intervals; app. no. (approximate number). If this radio button is set, then the category or interval boundaries and step-sizes (interval ranges) for the frequency tables will be "neat;" that is, those values will be rounded to simple values with the last digit being either a 1, 2, or 5 (e.g., 10.5, 11.0, 11.5, etc.). In this manner, clean and easy to read tables can be produced; however, the tables may not always have the exact number of intervals requested in the *No. of intervals* option.

Step size. If this radio button is set, then the frequency tables (and histograms) will be based on the user-specified step sizes (interval widths).

Starting at minimum. If this check box is set, then the first inclusive interval boundary for the frequency tables will be set as equal to the minimum value for the respective variable. If this check box is not set, then the first inclusive interval boundary for the frequency tables will be set as equal to the user-defined value entered into the respective edit box.

Integer categories. If this radio button is set, then the frequency tables (and histograms) will be based on integer category (interval) boundaries and step sizes, starting with the smallest integer value found in the respective variable. All non-integer values will be ignored (in the *Frequency tables*, *Histograms*, and *Descriptive statistics* options).

With text labels. If this check box is set, then the categories in the *Frequency tables* and *Histograms* will be labeled with text values (e.g., *males*, *females*) rather than integer values (e.g., *1*, *2*), provided that text values are available for the respective variables in the current data file.

Specific grouping codes (labels). If this radio button is set, then the frequency tables (and histograms) will be based on integer categories (codes) specified by the user (via the button next to this option). All non-integer values and codes that are not selected will be ignored. If no codes are specified, all integer codes found in the data file for the respective variables will be used.

User-specified categories. This option allows the user to specify a set of up to 16 logical case selection conditions, defining how cases are to be assigned to (up to 16) categories for the *Frequency table.* These logical case selection conditions can be complex, and reference more than one variable in the data file, as well as case numbers.

For each case in the data file, the case selection conditions are processed in sequence, and a respective case is assigned to the first category where it "fits" (where the respective logical case selection condition is *true*). Click on the button next to this option to specify the case selection conditions; for a brief overview of the syntax for those case selection conditions refer to the description of the *Specifying custom-defined categories* dialog (page 1538).

Casewise (Listwise) Deletion of Missing Data

If this check box is set then cases are excluded from computations if they have missing data for *any* of the variables currently selected for the analysis (i.e., *casewise deletion of missing data*). If this check box is not set, then cases are excluded from the computations for only those variables for which they have missing data (possibly resulting in different numbers of valid cases for different variables).

Display Options

The selection of options in this box determines the statistics that are computed for each category in the *Frequency tables* (see above). Note that all percentages are computed with respect to the total number of cases reported in the table, that is, including or excluding missing data and/or out-of-range values, depending on the settings in the *Missing data* box (see below).

Cumulative frequencies. If this check box is set, then the cumulative frequencies are reported.

Percentages (relative frequencies). If this check box is set then the relative frequencies (percentages) are reported.

Cumulative percentages. If this check box is set, then the relative cumulative frequencies (cumulative percentages) are reported.

100% minus cumulative percentages. If this check box is set, then 100-minus-cumulative-percent-values are reported for each category.

Logit transformed proportions. If this check box is set, then for each category in the frequency table, the logit-transformed cumulative proportions will be reported. Specifically, the logits for a category *i* are computed from the respective cumulative proportion p_i as: $Logit_i = natural\ log(p_i/(1-p_i))$.

Probit transformed proportions. If this check box is set, then for each category in the frequency table, the probit-transformed cumulative proportions will be reported. Specifically, probits are computed as the normal values (*z*-values) associated with the probability (cumulative proportion of observations) in the respective cell.

Normal expected frequencies. If this check box is set, then for each category in the frequency table, the expected frequencies are computed based on the normal distribution.

Missing Data

Count missing data (MD). If this check box is set then an extra category for missing data will be displayed in the frequency table Scrollsheets. Also, percentages and cumulative percentages will be computed relative to the total number of cases plus the number of missing data.

Count MD & non-selected cases. If this check box is set then an extra category for non-selected (and non-missing) cases will be displayed in the frequency table Scrollsheets. Also, percentages and cumulative percentages will be computed relative to

the total number of cases plus the number of non-selected, non-missing cases. Note that this option is not available (active) if the current *Categorization method for tables & graphs* is *No. of intervals* or *Step size.., starting at minimum.* In those instances, the regular categories of the frequency table will always include all non-missing data.

Tests of Normality

If any of the following check boxes are set, then after the frequency tables for the selected variable have been displayed, additional Scrollsheets will be displayed with the requested tests of normality (one Scrollsheet per test). To display these tests only, use the *Tests for normality* button.

Tests for normality. This option will bring up the results Scrollsheets with the requested tests of normality for the selected variables.

Kolmogorov-Smirnov test, mean/std.dv known. If this check box is set, then the Kolmogorov-Smirnov one-sample test of normality will be computed. Specifically, if the Kolmogorov-Smirnov *D* statistic is significant, then the hypothesis that the respective distribution is normal should be rejected. The probability values that will be reported are based on those tabulated by Massey (1951); those probability values are valid when the mean and standard deviation of the normal distribution are known *a priori* and *not* estimated from the data. However, usually those parameters are computed from the actual data. In that case, the test for normality involves a complex conditional hypothesis ("how likely is it to obtain a *D* statistic of this magnitude or greater, contingent upon the mean and standard deviation computed from the data"), and the *Lilliefors* probabilities should be interpreted (Lilliefors, 1967).

Note that, in recent years, the Shapiro-Wilks' *W* test (see below) has become the preferred test of normality because of its good power properties as compared to a wide range of alternative tests (Shapiro, Wilk, and Chen, 1968).

Lilliefors test, mean/std.dv unknown. If this check box is set, then the Kolmogorov-Smirnov one-sample *D* statistic will be computed, and Lilliefors probabilities will be reported (see previous paragraph; see also Lilliefors, 1967).

Shapiro-Wilks' *W* test. If this check box is set, then the Shapiro-Wilks' *W* test of normality will be computed for each selected variable. If the *W* statistic is significant, then the hypothesis that the respective distribution is normal should be rejected.

The Shapiro-Wilks' *W* test is the preferred test of normality because of its good power properties as compared to a wide range of alternative tests (Shapiro, Wilk, and Chen, 1968). The algorithm implemented in *STATISTICA* employs an extension to the test described by Royston (1982), which allows it to be applied to large samples (with up to 2000 observations).

Box and Whisker Plot for all Variables

This option will produce a box and whisker plot for all of the selected variables.

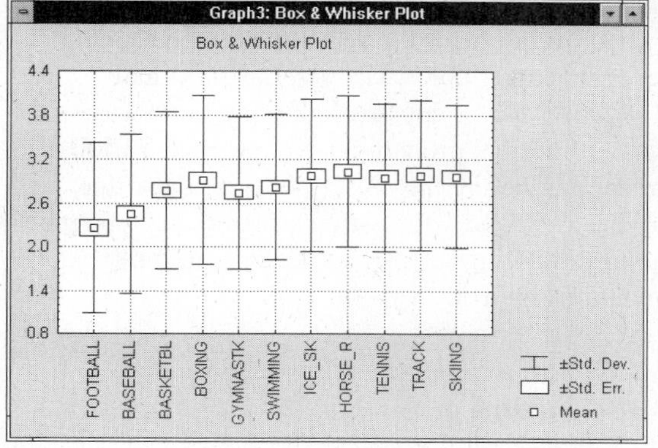

The box and whisker plot is described in the *Descriptive Statistics* dialog (page 1504).

Normal Probability Plots

This option will produce a cascade of normal probability plots for the selected variables, one plot per selected variable. The standard normal probability plot is also described in the *Descriptive Statistics* dialog (page 1504).

Half-Normal Probability Plots

This option will produce a cascade of half-normal probability plots for the selected variables, one plot per selected variable.

The half-normal probability plot is constructed in the same way as the standard normal probability plot (see page 1505), except that only the positive half of the normal curve is considered. Consequently, only positive normal values will be plotted on the *Y*-axis. This plot is used when one wants to ignore the sign of the residual; that is, when one is mostly interested in the distribution of absolute residuals, regardless of sign.

Detrended Normal Probability Plots

This option will produce a cascade of half-normal probability plots for the selected variables, one plot per selected variable. The detrended normal probability plot is constructed in the same way as the standard normal probability plot (see page 1500), except that before the plot is generated, the linear trend is removed. This often "spreads out" the plot, thereby allowing the user to detect patterns of deviations more easily.

3D Bivariate Distribution Histogram

This option will produce a cascade of 3D histograms for selected pairs of variables, one plot per pair.

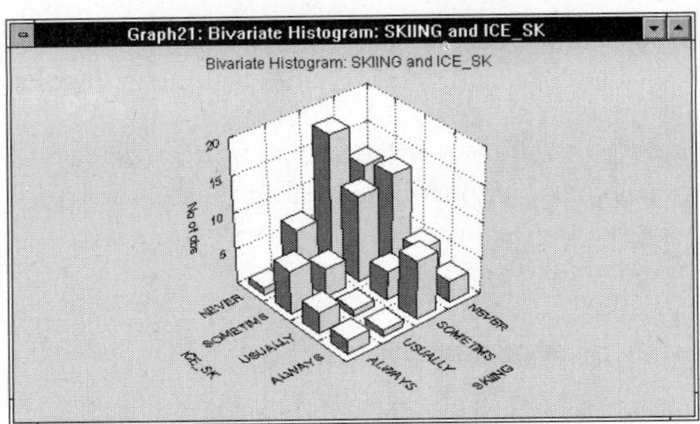

After clicking on this button, the user is first prompted to select two lists of variables (from among those originally selected via the *Variables* option). 3D histograms will be produced for each variable in the first list with each variable in the second list.

Specifying Custom-Defined Categories

This facility can be used to custom-define multiple subsets of cases by specifying logical case selection conditions. Versions of this subset definition dialog are used for different purposes throughout *STATISTICA* (e.g., in the spreadsheet data recoding facility, see *Spreadsheet Window*, Chapter 3; data verification facilities, see *Data Management*, Chapter 7; *Stats Graphs*, see Volume II), and they are compatible with each other, that is, subset definitions entered in one of them can be used in all others.

In this case, this option allows you to specify up to 16 case selection conditions that will be used in the computation of the frequency table to assign cases to categories. The selection conditions will be checked sequentially; that is, a case will be assigned to the first category where it "fits."

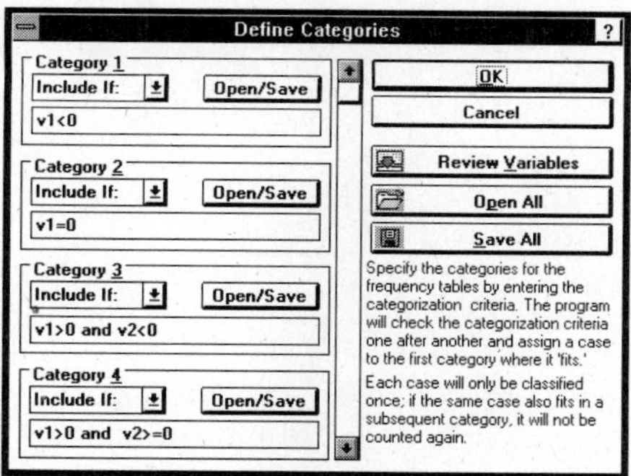

Note that you could also use other facilities provided in *STATISTICA* to create temporary or permanent custom-defined grouping variables such as the integrated spreadsheet recoding facility (see Chapter 3 for details).

For example, when you need to recode data in a way that requires that the values of the target variable are not fixed but calculated following some specific formulas (e.g., as an average of values of some other variables), use the spreadsheet formulas (see *Spreadhseet Window*, Chapter 3) or the user-defined recoding functions in the *STATISTICA BASIC* programming language.

Example

The following set of (two) case selection conditions will result in ("translate" to) two categories in the frequency table.

Category 1 Include if: `v1>=0`

Category 2 Include if: `v1<0`

The first will include all cases with values for variable 1 greater than or equal to zero; the second category will include all cases with values for variable 1 less than zero.

Category

You can define up to 16 categories by entering up to 16 case selection conditions. The selection conditions will be checked sequentially; that is, a case will be assigned to the first category where it "fits."

Include/Exclude If

When you choose *Include if* and the selection condition evaluates to true, cases (observations) that meet the condition will be assigned to the respective category (unless the same case was placed into a previous category where it also fits). *Exclude if* will assign cases to the respective category if they do not meet the specified selection condition.

Syntax of the Case Selection Condition

Specify the case selection condition in the edit field *Category* following the standard *STATISTICA Case Selection Conditions* (see Chapter 3 for details). The following is a summary of syntax conventions for the case selection conditions. The same conventions apply to all instances where user-defined case selection conditions are entered in *STATISTICA*.

- Refer to variables either by their numbers (e.g., *v1 = 1*) or their names (e.g., *Gender = 1*); note that you can type variable names in either upper or lower case letters (i.e., *'GENDER'* is equivalent to *'gender'*).
- Enclose text values of a variable in single quotation marks (e.g., *v1 = 'MALE'*); note that you can type text values in either upper or lower case letters (i.e., *'Yes'* is equivalent to *'YES'*).
- Use parentheses to specify complex logical conditions (see the example above) or change the default precedence of operators.
- Logical Operators:

`=`	- equal
`# , <>, ><`	- not equal
`<`	- less than
`>`	- greater than
`<=`	- less than or equal to
`>=`	- greater than or equal to
`NOT, ~`	- logical NOT
`AND, &`	- logical AND
`OR, !`	- logical OR

Open/Save

Use this option to open (and use for categorizing) an existing standard *STATISTICA Case Selection Condition* file (those which can be used to select/filter cases for all analyses in *STATISTICA*, see Chapter 3) as well as save the current condition in each *Category*. Clicking on the *Open/Save* button will open the *Case Selection Condition* dialog where you can edit, save or load individual case selection conditions (these are the same conditions which are used for processing subsets of cases in all procedures throughout *STATISTICA*).

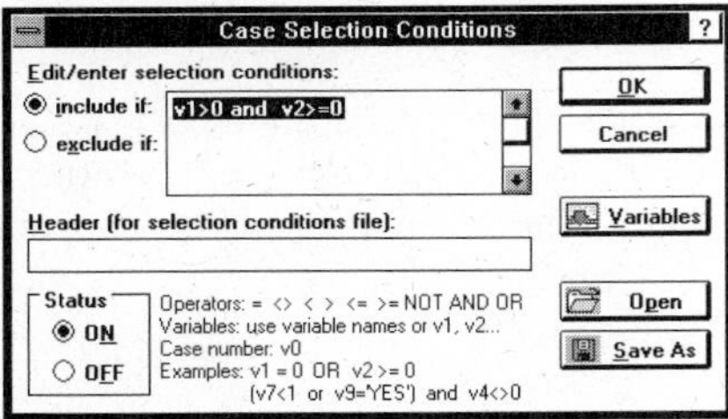

Individual case selection conditions saved in this dialog are saved under the file name extension **.sel*. These case selection conditions are then used as categorization conditions when you click *OK* in the *Case Selection Condition* dialog.

Review Vars

Clicking this button will open the *Variables* dialog from which you can view the variables in the spreadsheet.

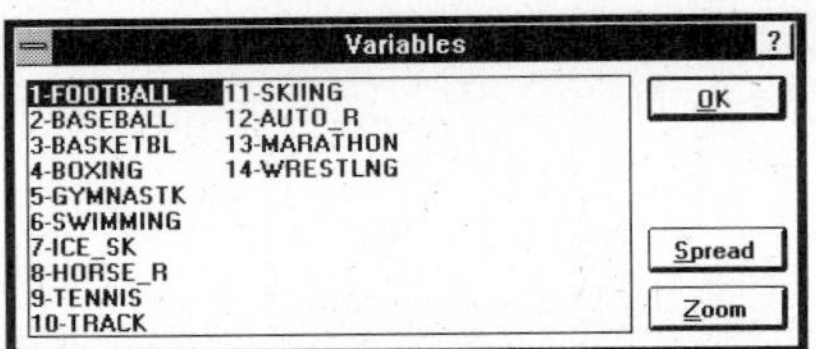

Open All

Unlike the *Open* option (click on an *Open/Save* button) which allows you to open a file containing a single case selection condition (see *Open/Save*, above), this button opens the *Open Case Selection Conditions File* dialog from which you can select a file (containing all of the case selection conditions) to open into the *Define Categories* dialog. Files opened from this dialog are text files with the file name extension **.txt*.

Save All

Unlike the *Save* option (click on an *Open/Save* button) which allows you to save individual case selection conditions (see *Open/Save*, above), this button opens the *Save Case Selection Conditions File* dialog from which you can designate a file into which the case selection conditions will be saved. This file will be saved in text file format (**.txt* extension).

Crosstabulation and Stub-and-Banner Tables

When you select *Tables and Banners* from the startup panel, the *Specify Table* dialog will open.

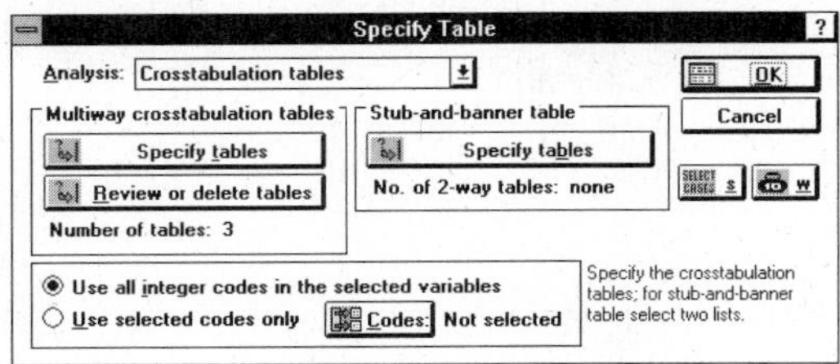

The options shown above are available when you select *Crosstabulation Tables* in the *Analysis* option (see below).

Analysis

Choose one of two settings in this combo box.

Crosstabulation tables. In this setting, *STATISTICA* expects to crosstabulate standard categorical (grouping) variables (e.g., *Gender, Ethnic Origin;* see also the *Crosstabulation & stub-and-banner tables* overview, page 1446).

Tables for multiple response items. If this setting is chosen, then the user can specify multiple response variables and multiple dichotomies (see *Multiple responses/dichotomies* overview, page 1453) in the *Multiple Response Tables* dialog (see page 1546), and compute:

(1) Frequency tables for such variables, or

(2) Compute crosstabulation tables involving such variables (e.g., ordinary categorical variables can be crosstabulated with multiple response variables/dichotomies).

Multi-Way Crosstabulation Tables

Specify tables. Use this option to select variables for a multiway crosstabulation table. After clicking on this button, a standard six-variable list selection window will open. Crosstabulation tables will be computed for all possible combinations of variables from up to six selected lists. You can repeatedly use this option to add tables or lists of tables to the total list of tables that will be computed. To review or edit the current list of selected tables use the *Review or delete tables* option (see below).

Review or delete tables. This option allows you to review and edit the current list of selected tables.

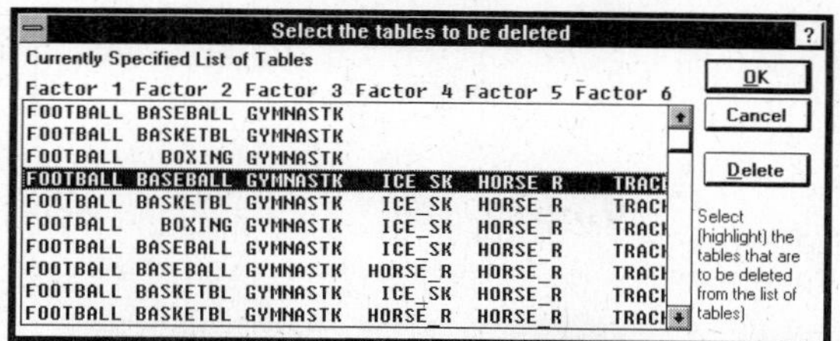

To delete tables from the currently selected list of tables, first highlight the respective tables and then click *Delete.*

Stub-and-Banner Table

Stub-and-banner tables are essentially two-way tables, except that two lists of categorical variables are crosstabulated. In the stub-and-banner results table, one list will be tabulated in the columns (horizontally) and the second list will be tabulated in the rows (vertically) of the Scrollsheet. After clicking on the *Specify tables* button, a standard two-variable list selection window will be displayed. Note that, after selecting this option, the list of crosstabulation tables will be cleared (if one has previously been selected via the *Multiway crosstabulation tables* options).

Use all Integer Codes in the Selected Variables

If this radio button is set, then all integer code values in the selected variables will be used for the crosstabulation.

Use Selected Codes Only

If this radio button is set, then the user can specify the codes that are to be used for the crosstabulation tables.

Crosstabulation Results

A general discussion of the *Crosstabulation & stub-and-banner tables* option is provided in the *Introductory Overview* section (page 1446).

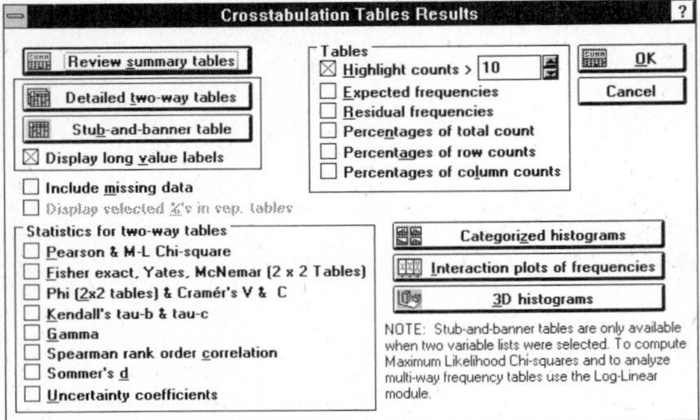

Review Summary Tables

This option will bring up summary tables for multi-way crosstabulation tables. If more than one table was specified, then a dialog will open allowing the user to select the table(s) to be displayed. In this dialog (see below), you can select the tables to be reviewed by highlighting them and then clicking *OK*.

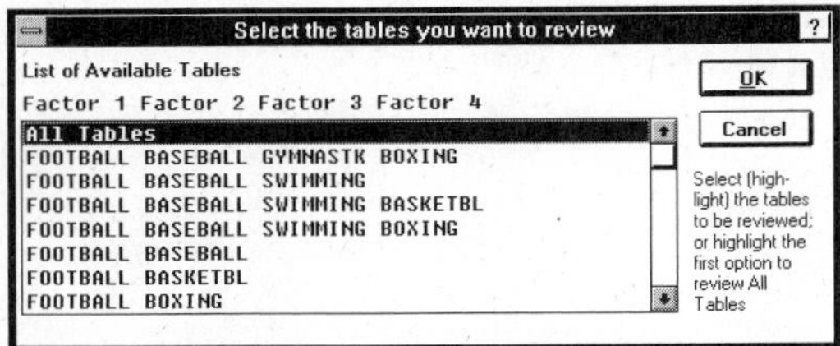

If you select *All tables*, a cascade of results tables (Scrollsheets) or graphs will be produced for all tables.

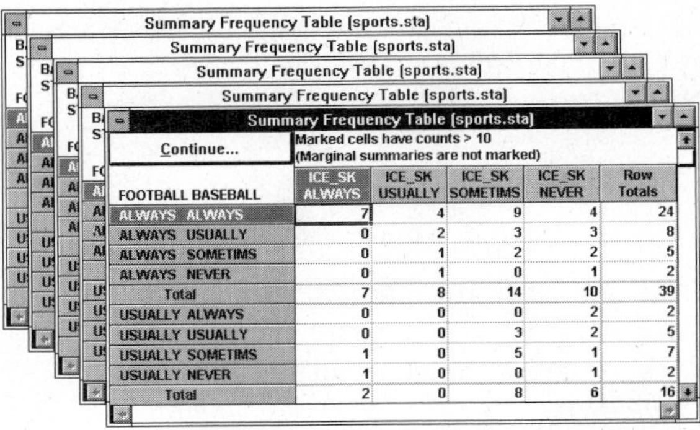

Summary Frequency Table (sports.sta)

Continue...

Marked cells have counts > 10
(Marginal summaries are not marked)

FOOTBALL BASEBALL	ICE_SK ALWAYS	ICE_SK USUALLY	ICE_SK SOMETIMS	ICE_SK NEVER	Row Totals
ALWAYS ALWAYS	7	4	9	4	24
ALWAYS USUALLY	0	2	3	3	8
ALWAYS SOMETIMS	0	1	2	2	5
ALWAYS NEVER	0	1	0	1	2
Total	7	8	14	10	39
USUALLY ALWAYS	0	0	0	2	2
USUALLY USUALLY	0	0	3	2	5
USUALLY SOMETIMS	1	0	5	1	7
USUALLY NEVER	1	0	0	1	2
Total	2	0	8	6	16

The summary crosstabulation table will report the frequencies for the entire respective table; the last variable (factor) that makes up the table will be tabulated in the columns of the Scrollsheet and all remaining variables (factors) will be tabulated in the rows. If there are more than two variables (factors) in a table, then the structure of the table will be as if several two-way tables (for the last two factors) were "glued" together one-after-another for the different levels of the remaining factors. In this manner even 6-way tables can be reviewed in a single Scrollsheet. The detail of results that are reported depends on the selections of options in the *Tables* box (see below).

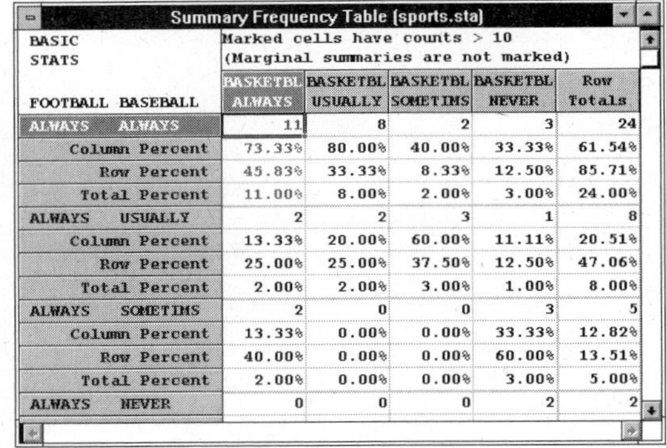

Summary Frequency Table (sports.sta)

BASIC STATS

Marked cells have counts > 10
(Marginal summaries are not marked)

FOOTBALL BASEBALL	BASKETBL ALWAYS	BASKETBL USUALLY	BASKETBL SOMETIMS	BASKETBL NEVER	Row Totals
ALWAYS ALWAYS	11	8	2	3	24
Column Percent	73.33%	80.00%	40.00%	33.33%	61.54%
Row Percent	45.83%	33.33%	8.33%	12.50%	85.71%
Total Percent	11.00%	8.00%	2.00%	3.00%	24.00%
ALWAYS USUALLY	2	2	3	1	8
Column Percent	13.33%	20.00%	60.00%	11.11%	20.51%
Row Percent	25.00%	25.00%	37.50%	12.50%	47.06%
Total Percent	2.00%	2.00%	3.00%	1.00%	8.00%
ALWAYS SOMETIMS	2	0	0	3	5
Column Percent	13.33%	0.00%	0.00%	33.33%	12.82%
Row Percent	40.00%	0.00%	0.00%	60.00%	13.51%
Total Percent	2.00%	0.00%	0.00%	3.00%	5.00%
ALWAYS NEVER	0	0	0	2	2

Note that, if *Expected frequencies* or *Residual frequencies* are requested (see below), then they will be computed simultaneously for the entire multi-way table, via *iterative proportional fitting* (e.g., see Haberman, 1972, 1974; see also the *Log-Linear Analysis* module).

Specifically, expected frequencies are computed contingent upon the single-factor marginal tables; that is, it is assumed that there are no interactions between factors in the table. For three- or higher-way tables these values will be different from those that are displayed when *Detailed two-way tables* are requested (see below), where the expected frequencies are computed based on the respective two-way tables alone.

Detailed Two-Way Tables

This option will bring up Scrollsheets with two-way tables. If more than one table was specified, then a dialog will open allowing the user to select the table(s) to be displayed. For tables with more than two variables (factors), a cascade of Scrollsheets will be produced for the last two factors in the table, within the levels of the other factors.

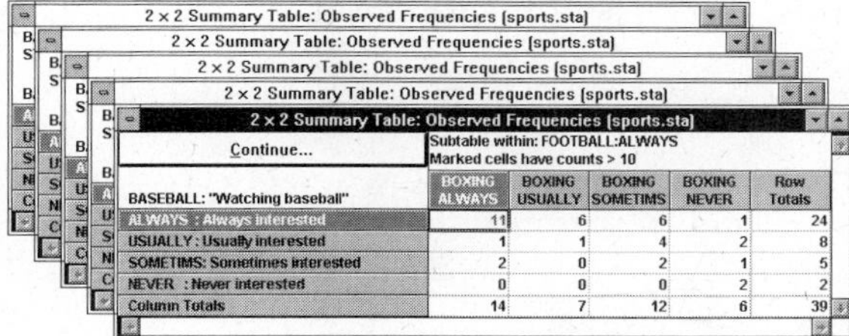
2 x 2 Summary Table: Observed Frequencies (sports.sta)

Continue...

Subtable within: FOOTBALL:ALWAYS
Marked cells have counts > 10

BASEBALL: "Watching baseball"	BOXING ALWAYS	BOXING USUALLY	BOXING SOMETIMS	BOXING NEVER	Row Totals
ALWAYS : Always interested	11	6	6	1	24
USUALLY : Usually interested	1	1	4	2	8
SOMETIMS: Sometimes interested	2	0	2	1	5
NEVER : Never interested	0	0	0	2	2
Column Totals	14	7	12	6	39

The detail of reported results depends on the choices of options in the *Statistics for two-way tables* box as well as the *Tables* box (see below). If any *Statistics for two-way tables* are selected, then a Scrollsheet with requested statistics will be computed for each two-way table.

For example, shown below is one of the Scrollsheets produced when all of the statistics options are selected (note that some of these statistics are only applicable to 2 x 2 tables).

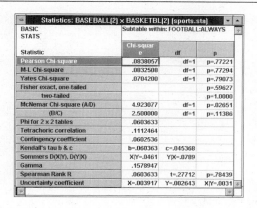

Statistics: BASEBALL(2) x BASKETBL(2) (sports.sta)

BASIC STATS — Subtable within: FOOTBALL:ALWAYS

Statistic	Chi-square	df	p
Pearson Chi-square	.0838057	df=1	p=.77221
M-L Chi-square	.0832508	df=1	p=.77294
Yates Chi-square	.0704200	df=1	p=.79073
Fisher exact, one-tailed			p=.59627
two-tailed			p=1.0000
McNemar Chi-square (A/D)	4.923077	df=1	p=.02651
(B/C)	2.500000	df=1	p=.11386
Phi for 2 x 2 tables	.0603633		
Tetrachoric correlation	.1112464		
Contingency coefficient	.0602536		
Kendall's tau b & c	b=.060363	c=.045368	
Sommers D(X|Y), D(Y|X)	X|Y=.0461	Y|X=.0789	
Gamma	.1578947		
Spearman Rank R	.0603633	t=.27712	p=.78439
Uncertainty coefficient	X=.003917	Y=.002643	X|Y=.0031

Stub-and-Banner Table

This option is only available (active) if the *Stub-and-banner tables* option was selected on the previous dialog (see *Crosstabulation & stub-and-banner tables*, page 1540). In general, stub-and-banner tables are two-way tables where one list is tabulated in the columns (horizontally) and the second list is tabulated in the rows (vertically) of the Scrollsheet.

Summary Stub-and-Banner Table (intrview.sta)

BASIC STATS — Marked cells have counts > 10 (Marginal summaries are not marked)

INTRVW_1	INTRVW_2 NO	INTRVW_2 YES	Row Total	INTRVW_3 NO	INTRVW_3 YES	Row Total
NO	3	2	5	5	0	5
Column %	60.00%	15.38%		33.33%	0.00%	
Row %	60.00%	40.00%		100.00%	0.00%	
Table %	16.67%	11.11%	27.78%	27.78%	0.00%	27.78%
YES	2	11	13	10	3	13
Column %	40.00%	84.62%		66.67%	100.00%	
Row %	15.38%	84.62%		76.92%	23.08%	
Table %	11.11%	61.11%	72.22%	55.56%	16.67%	72.22%
Total	5	13	18	15	3	18
Table %	27.78%	72.22%	100.00%	83.33%	16.67%	100.00%

The detail of reported results depends on the choices of options in the *Tables* box (see below).

Display Long Value Labels

If this check box is set then long value labels will be displayed in the first column of the two-way table results Scrollsheets.

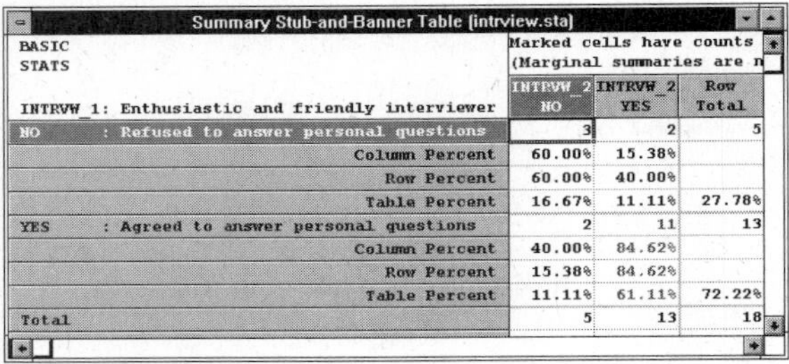

Summary Stub-and-Banner Table (intrview.sta)

BASIC STATS — Marked cells have counts (Marginal summaries are n

INTRVW_1: Enthusiastic and friendly interviewer	INTRVW_2 NO	INTRVW_2 YES	Row Total
NO : Refused to answer personal questions	3	2	5
Column Percent	60.00%	15.38%	
Row Percent	60.00%	40.00%	
Table Percent	16.67%	11.11%	27.78%
YES : Agreed to answer personal questions	2	11	13
Column Percent	40.00%	84.62%	
Row Percent	15.38%	84.62%	
Table Percent	11.11%	61.11%	72.22%
Total	5	13	18

If the respective variable (factor) tabulated in the rows of a Scrollsheet does not have any long value labels (none were specified in the data file), then the setting of this check box will be ignored. Note that value labels can be reviewed in the data spreadsheet by clicking on the *Spreadsheet View Text Values* button [ABC] while holding down the CTRL key.

Data: SPORTS.STA 15v * 100c

VALUE LABELS — Survey of male's sports interests

	1 FOOTBALL	2 BASEBALL	3 BASKETBL
1	Always interested	Always interested	Always interes
2	Always interested	Always interested	Always interes
3	Always interested	Sometimes interested	Always interes
4	Always interested	Always interested	Always interes
5	Always interested	Always interested	Always interes
6	Always interested	Always interested	Always interes
7	Always interested	Always interested	Usually interes
8	Always interested	Always interested	Always interes
9	Always interested	Always interested	Sometimes interes
10	Always interested	Always interested	Never interes

Include Missing Data

If this check box is set, then an extra category (level) for missing data is added to each variable (factor) in the table. Thus the table will show the number of missing cases crosstabulated with the other variables (factors), and all marginal frequencies and percentages will be adjusted accordingly.

Display Selected %'s in Separate Tables

This check box is only available (active) if one of the *Percentages...* options is selected in the *Tables* box (see below). By default, if percentages are requested they will be displayed in the same table together with the frequencies; thus each cell in such results Scrollsheets will consist of more than one line. If this check box is set, then the percentage tables will be displayed in separate Scrollsheets (this is desirable when you want to produce graphs of percentages from the Scrollsheets).

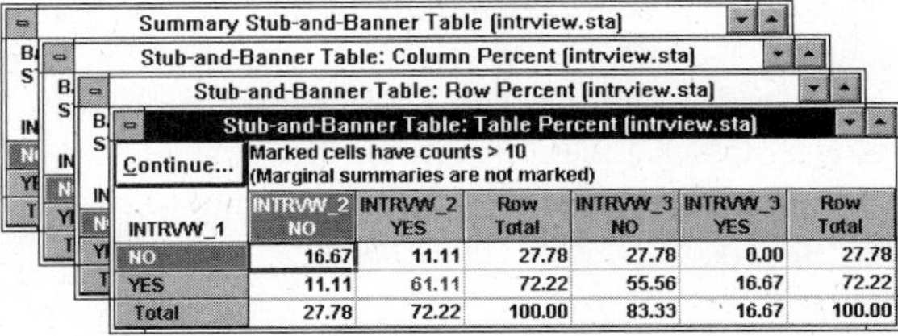

Summary Stub-and-Banner Table (intrview.sta)
Stub-and-Banner Table: Column Percent (intrview.sta)
Stub-and-Banner Table: Row Percent (intrview.sta)
Stub-and-Banner Table: Table Percent (intrview.sta)

Continue... — Marked cells have counts > 10 (Marginal summaries are not marked)

INTRVW_1	INTRVW_2 NO	INTRVW_2 YES	Row Total	INTRVW_3 NO	INTRVW_3 YES	Row Total
NO	16.67	11.11	27.78	27.78	0.00	27.78
YES	11.11	61.11	72.22	55.56	16.67	72.22
Total	27.78	72.22	100.00	83.33	16.67	100.00

Statistics for Two-Way Tables

The options selected in this box will determine the statistics that will be computed when *Detailed two-way tables* are requested. If any of these statistics are selected, a separate Scrollsheet will be displayed after each two-way table, reporting the respective statistics for that table (see above).

Tables

The selection of options in this box will determine the detail of results reported in *Summary tables* and *Detailed two-way tables*, and some apply to *Stub-and-banner tables.*

Highlight counts > ... If this check box is set, then all counts (raw frequencies) in the table that are greater than the value in the edit box will be highlighted.

Expected frequencies. If this check box is set, then for all two-way tables and summary tables, the expected frequencies are computed contingent upon complete independence of all factors in the table.

Summary Table: Expected Frequencies (sports.sta)

BASIC STATS — Marked cells have counts > 10; Pearson Chi-square: 72.9547, df=9, p=.000000

FOOTBALL	BASEBALL ALWAYS	BASEBALL USUALLY	BASEBALL SOMETIMS	BASEBALL NEVER	Row Totals
ALWAYS	10.92000	6.63000	14.43000	7.02000	39.0000
USUALLY	4.48000	2.72000	5.92000	2.88000	16.0000
SOMETIMS	7.28000	4.42000	9.62000	4.68000	26.0000
NEVER	5.32000	3.23000	7.03000	3.42000	19.0000
All Grps	28.00000	17.00000	37.00000	18.00000	100.0000

Thus, for *Detailed two-way tables*, those expected frequencies are computed based on the marginal frequencies for the two factors in the current table; for *Summary tables* with more than two variables (factors), the expected frequencies are based on the marginal frequencies of *all* factors in the table (i.e., no interactions between factors are assumed). Expected frequencies for tables with more than two factors are computed via *Iterative proportional fitting* (e.g., see Haberman, 1972, 1974; see also the *Log-Linear Analysis* module).

Residual frequencies. If this check box is set, then for all two-way tables and summary tables, the residual frequencies (observed minus *expected frequencies*; see above) will be displayed.

Summary Table: Observed minus Expected Frequencies

BASIC STATS — Marked cells have counts > 10
Pearson Chi-square: 72.9547, df=9, p=.000000

FOOTBALL	BASEBALL ALWAYS	BASEBALL USUALLY	BASEBALL SOMETIMS	BASEBALL NEVER	Row Totals
ALWAYS	13.08000	1.37000	-9.43000	-5.02000	0.000000
USUALLY	-2.48000	2.28000	1.08000	-.88000	-.000000
SOMETIMS	-5.28000	-1.42000	9.38000	-2.68000	.000000
NEVER	-5.32000	-2.23000	-1.03000	8.58000	-.000000
All Grps	-.00000	0.00000	.00000	.00000	-.000000

Percentages of total count. If this check box is set, then for each cell in the *Summary tables*, *Detailed two-way tables*, and *Stub-and-banner tables*, percentages are computed relative to the total number of cases in the current table. If the *Display selected %'s in sep. tables* option is not set, then the percentages will be shown in the same table together with the raw frequencies.

Percentages of row counts. If this check box is set, then for each cell in the *Summary tables*, *Detailed two-way tables*, and *Stub-and-banner tables*, percentages are computed relative to the total number of cases in the respective row of the current table. If the *Display selected %'s in sep. tables* option is not set, then the percentages will be shown in the same table together with the raw frequencies.

Percentages of column counts. If this check box is set, then for each cell in the *Summary tables*, *Detailed two-way tables*, and *Stub-and-banner tables*, percentages are computed relative to the total number of cases in the respective column of the current table. If the *Display selected %'s in sep. tables* option is not set, then the percentages will be shown in the same table together with the raw frequencies.

Categorized Histograms

After choosing this option, if more than one table was computed, the user can select the table(s) for the plot. *STATISTICA* will then compute the categorized histograms for the selected tables.

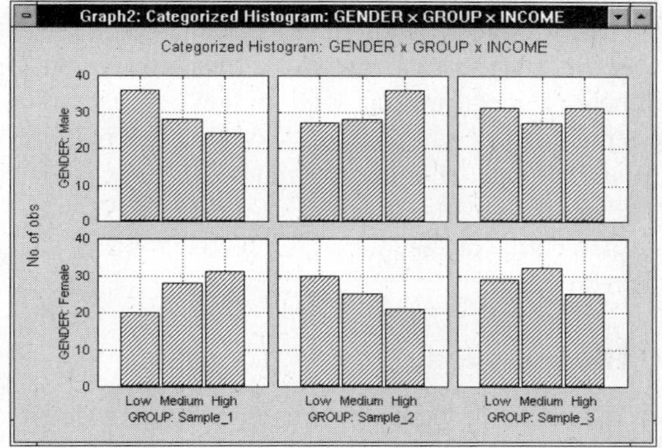

Note that each plot can summarize up to three variables (factors); that is, one categorized histogram can summarize a three-way table: The last (fastest-changing) factor will be represented by the columns in the graph; the next-to-last factor will be represented by the different histograms "tabulated" horizontally; the third factor will be represented by the different histograms "tabulated" vertically. Cascades of categorized histograms are produced for tables with more than three factors.

Interaction Plots of Frequencies

Another way of summarizing the distribution of frequencies across up to three variables (factors) is by a line graph (*interaction plot*).

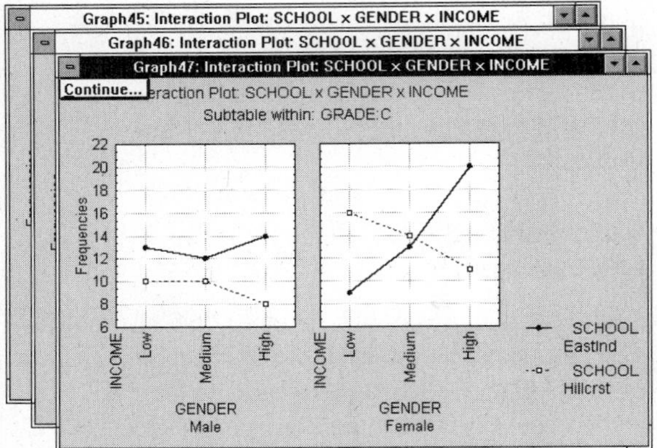

Note that if there are more than three factors in the respective table, then a cascade of interaction plots will be produced for each combination of levels of the remaining factors. After clicking on this button, if more than one table was computed, then the user can select the table(s) for the plot(s). *STATISTICA* will then compute the interaction plot(s) for the selected table(s).

3D Histograms

This option will produce 3D histograms for selected tables.

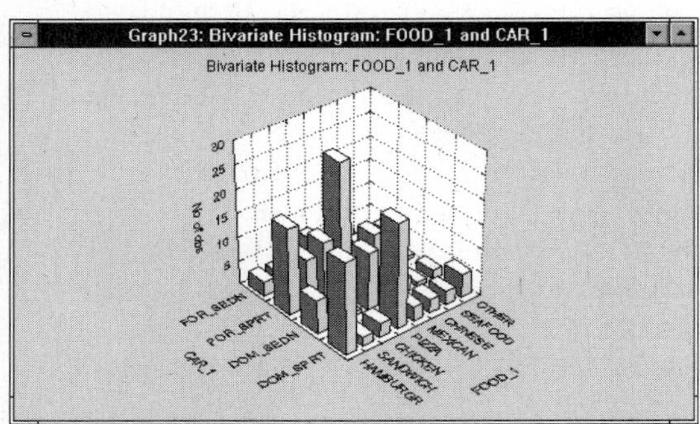

After clicking on this button, if more than one table was originally computed, the user can select the table(s) for the plot(s). Each 3D histogram will summarize the joint frequency distribution for two variables (factors); it is in a sense the graphical equivalent to the *Detailed two-way tables* option (see above).

Specifying Multiple Responses/Dichotomies

When you select *Tables and Banners* from the startup panel and you select *Tables for Multiple Response Items* in the *Analysis* combo box (see below), then the *Multiple Response Tables* dialog will open.

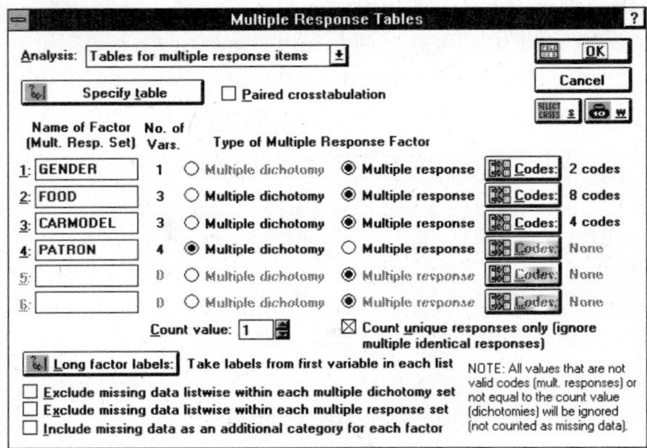

In this dialog, you can specify the design for the multiple response table analysis.

Analysis

Choose one of two settings in this combo box.

Crosstabulation tables. In this setting, *STATISTICA* expects to crosstabulate standard categorical (grouping) variables (e.g., *Gender, Ethnic Origin;* see also the *Crosstabulation & stub-and-banner tables* overview, page 1446).

Tables for multiple response items. If this setting is chosen, then the user can specify multiple response variables and multiple dichotomies (see *Multiple responses/dichotomies* overview, page 1453) in the *Multiple Response Tables* dialog, and compute:

(1) Frequency tables for such variables, or

(2) Compute crosstabulation tables involving such variables (e.g., ordinary categorical variables can be crosstabulated with multiple response variables/dichotomies).

Specify Table

This option will bring up a standard six-variable lists selection window.

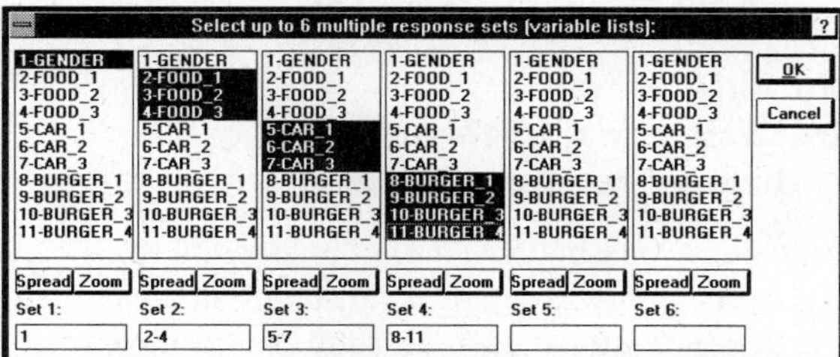

Each list will be interpreted as a single multiple response/dichotomy variable or factor. If only a single variable is chosen in a list, then the respective variable will be treated as a standard categorical (grouping) variable in the crosstabulation.

By default, (1) short and long names as well as (2) short and long alphanumeric value labels for the factors will be taken from the first variable in each list. Factor names can later be changed (see *1*, *2*, ... and *Long factor labels* below).

Paired Crosstabulation

The logic of paired crosstabulation of multiple response variables is explained in the *Paired Crosstabulation of Multiple Response Variables* overview (page 1455). This option is only applicable if there are two or more multiple response variables specified for the current table and if at least two of them consist of identical numbers of actual variables. If so, *STATISTICA* will proceed as follows:

- The number of actual variables in each multiple response factor is counted;
- Paired crosstabulation is performed on the first two or more multiple response variables with identical numbers of actual variables.

Thus, for example, if there are three multiple response factors, the first two with 2 actual variables and the third with 3, then only the first two factors will be processed as paired factors.

Name of Factor (Multiple Response Set)

By default, the names for factors are taken from the first variable in each respective list (see *Specify Table*, above). To change the names, simply enter the new name into the respective edit field.

The general logic of multiple response variables and multiple dichotomies is explained in the *Introductory Overview* section (page 1453).

Type of Multiple Response Factor

Multiple dichotomy. Set this radio button to treat the respective factor (list of actual variables) as a multiple dichotomy. Be sure that the desired *Count value* is set (by default *1*, see below). All values that do not match the count value will be ignored in the analysis.

Count value. This is the actual value that will be counted in the multiple response table; that is, *STATISTICA* will count how frequent this value is present in the different actual variables (levels) that comprise the respective multiple dichotomy.

Multiple response. Set this radio button to treat the respective factor (list of actual variables) as a multiple response variable. If no *Codes* are selected, then *STATISTICA* will automatically tabulate all integer values found in the first variable of the respective list. If there is only one variable in the list, then the respective variable will be treated

(tabulated) as an ordinary categorical (grouping) variable.

Count unique responses only (ignore multiple identical responses). If this check box is set (default), then multiple identical responses in the different actual variables comprising a respective multiple response factor will be ignored. For example, if a multiple response factor *Preferred Sport* consists of two actual variables (first preference, second preference) and a respondent listed the *same* sport for both preferences, then *STATISTICA* will only count this as one response. (In other popular programs that compute multiple response tables, this respondent would be counted twice; do not set this check box if this is what is desired for the current crosstabulation or frequency table.)

Long Factor Labels

Use this option to enter long labels for the factors.

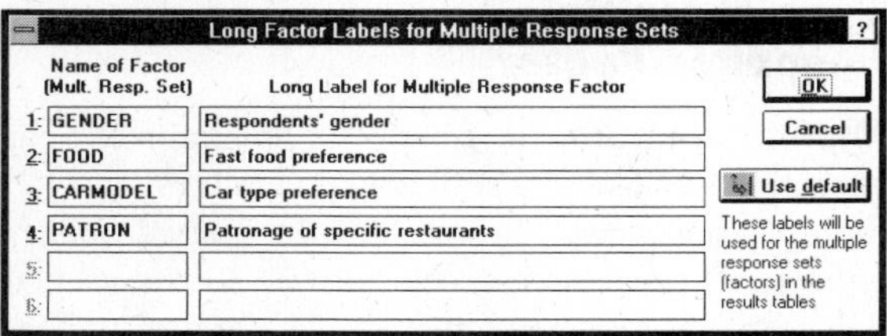

By default, *STATISTICA* will take as the short and long label for a factor the short and long variable name from the first actual variable in the respective list (if one is specified in the data file). You can change those labels by typing in the desired names into the respective edit fields. To return to the default, click on the *Set default* button.

Exclude Missing Data Listwise within Each Multiple Dichotomy Set

If this check box is set, then a case will be "declared" as missing ("no response") if it has missing data for any of the actual variables comprising the respective multiple dichotomy factor.

Exclude Missing Data Listwise within Each Multiple Response Set

If this check box is set, then a case will be "declared" as missing ("no response") if it has missing data for any of the actual variables comprising the respective multiple response factor.

Include Missing Data as an Additional Category for Each Factor

By default, missing data are ignored in the analysis. If this check box is set, *STATISTICA* will count (tabulate) missing data as an additional category (level) for each factor.

Reviewing Multiple Response/Dichotomies Tables

A general discussion of the *Crosstabulation & stub-and-banner tables* procedure is provided in the *Introductory Overview* section (page 1453).

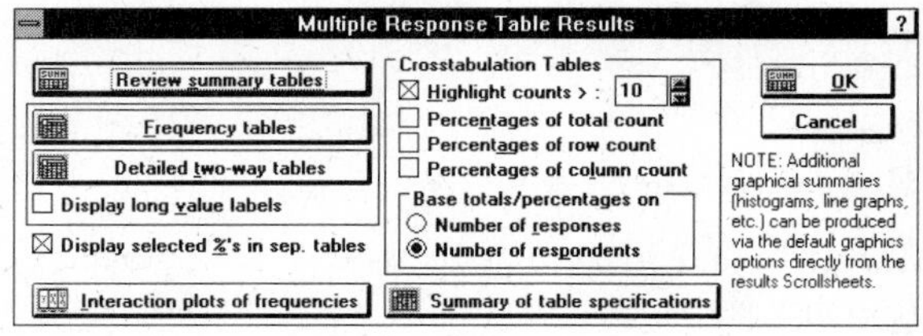

Review Summary Table

This option will bring up a summary table for multi-way crosstabulation tables. The summary crosstabulation table will report the frequencies for the entire respective table; the last factor that makes up the table will be tabulated in the columns of the

Scrollsheet, and all remaining factors will be tabulated in the rows. If there are more than two factors in a table, then the structure of the table will be as if several two-way tables (for the last two factors) were "glued" together one-after-another for the different levels of the remaining factors. In this manner even 6-way tables can be reviewed in a single Scrollsheet. The detail of results that are reported depends on the selections of options in the *Crosstabulation Tables* box (see below).

Frequency Tables

This option will bring up a cascade of frequency tables, one for each factor in the table. For each category or level of a factor, the Scrollsheet will report:

(1) The number of responses;

(2) The percentage of responses relative to the total number of responses;

(3) The percentage of responses relative to the total number of respondents (cases); that is, the percentage of respondents who gave the respective response (provided that multiple identical responses were ignored; see the option *Count unique responses only*, *Specifying multiple responses/dichotomies*, page 1546). For multiple response variables and multiple dichotomies, each respondent can give multiple responses; thus, the last column of the table will not add to 100%.

Detailed Two-Way Tables

This option will bring up Scrollsheets with two-way tables. For tables with more than two variables (factors), a cascade of Scrollsheets will be produced for the last two factors in the table, within the levels of the other factors.

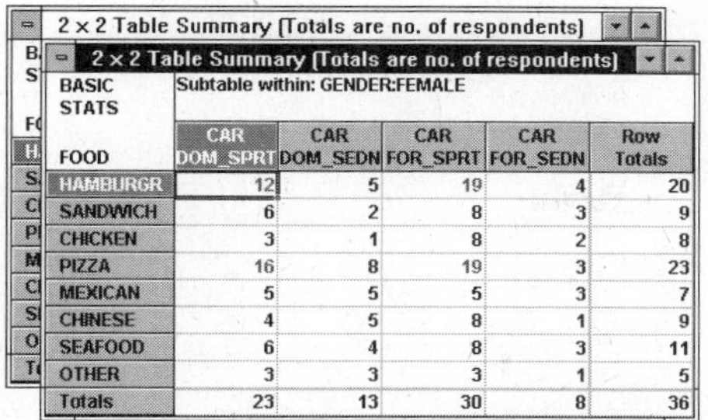

2 x 2 Table Summary (Totals are no. of respondents)

Subtable within: GENDER:FEMALE

BASIC STATS FOOD	CAR DOM_SPRT	CAR DOM_SEDN	CAR FOR_SPRT	CAR FOR_SEDN	Row Totals
HAMBURGR	12	5	19	4	20
SANDWICH	6	2	8	3	9
CHICKEN	3	1	8	2	8
PIZZA	16	8	19	3	23
MEXICAN	5	5	5	3	7
CHINESE	4	5	8	1	9
SEAFOOD	6	4	8	3	11
OTHER	3	3	3	1	5
Totals	23	13	30	8	36

The detail of reported results depends on the choices of options in the *Crosstabulation Tables* box (and the options described below).

Display Long Value Labels

If this check box is set then long value labels will be displayed in the first column of the two-way table results Scrollsheets.

Display Selected %'s in Separate Tables

This check box is only available (active) if one of the *Percentages...* options is selected in the *Crosstabulation Tables* box (see below). By default, if percentages are requested they will be displayed in the same table together with the frequencies; thus each cell in such results Scrollsheets will consist of more than one line. If this check box is set, then the percentage tables will be displayed in separate Scrollsheets (this is desirable when you want to produce graphs of percentages from the Scrollsheets).

Interaction Plots of Frequencies

One way to summarize the distribution of frequencies across up to three variables (factors) in a single graph is via a line graph (*interaction plot*).

StatSoft

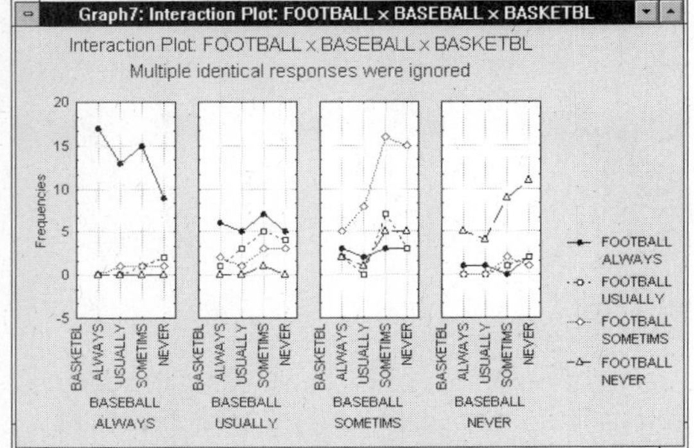

In each graph, the last (fastest changing) factor will be represented by different line patterns and colors; the next-to-last factor will be represented by "upper-x" labels; the last factor will be represented by "lower x" labels. If there are more than three factors in the respective table, a cascade of interaction plots will be produced for each combination of levels of the remaining factors.

Crosstabulation Tables

The selection of options in this box will determine the detail of results reported in the *Summary tables* and *Detailed two-way tables* (see above).

Highlight counts > ... If this check box is set, then all counts (raw frequencies) in the table that are greater than the value in the edit box will be highlighted.

Percentages of total count. If this check box is set, then for each cell in the *Summary tables* and *Detailed two-way tables*, percentages are computed relative to the total number of responses or respondents in the current table. If the *Display selected %'s in sep. tables* is not set, then the percentages will be shown in the same table together with the raw frequencies.

Percentages of row counts. If this check box is set, then for each cell in the *Summary tables* and *Detailed two-way tables*, percentages are computed relative to the total number of responses or respondents in the row of the current table. If the *Display selected %'s in sep. tables* is not set, then the percentages will be shown in the same table together with the raw frequencies.

Percentages of column counts. If this check box is set, then for each cell in the summary tables and detailed two-way tables, percentages are computed relative to the total number of responses or respondents in the column of the current table. If the *Display selected %'s in sep. tables* is not set, then the percentages will be shown in the same table together with the raw frequencies.

Base totals/percentages on ... For multiple response variables and multiple dichotomies, a single respondent (case) may contribute more than one answer and be counted more than once. The setting of these radio buttons will determine whether the totals and percentages reported in the tables will be based on the total number of responses or the total number of respondents (cases) that contributed to the respective marginal frequency (provided that multiple identical responses were ignored; see the option *Count unique responses only* in the *Specifying multiple responses/dichotomies* dialog, page 1546).

Number of responses. If this radio button is set, then the frequencies reported in the margins of the tables will be based on the number of responses. Thus, they will be the sum of the respective reported (i.e., in that row or column) cell frequencies. If percentages were requested, they will be computed with reference to those marginal frequencies.

Number of respondents. If this radio button is set, then the frequencies reported in the margins of the tables will be based on the number of respondents (cases) that "contributed" to or were counted in the respective column or row (or two-way table, for total frequencies). For multiple response variables and multiple dichotomies, those marginal frequencies will usually *not* be identical to the sum of the respective reported (i.e., in that row, column, or two-

way table) cell frequencies. If percentages were requested, then they will be computed with reference to these marginal frequencies of number of respondents.

This option is not available if *Paired cross-tabulation* was requested for multiple response variables (see *Specifying multiple responses-/dichotomies*, page 1546; see also the *Paired Cross-tabulation of Multiple Response Variables* section, page 1455).

Summary of Table Specifications

This option will bring up a Scrollsheet with the summary specifications for the factors in the current table. For each factor, the Scrollsheet will report:

(1) The name of the factor and the number of levels;

(2) The type of factor (ordinary categorical variable, multiple response, multiple dichotomy);

(3) The names of all actual variables comprising the multiple responses and dichotomies.

Other Significance Tests

When you select the *Other significance tests* option from the startup panel, you will be able to test hypotheses using the options described below.

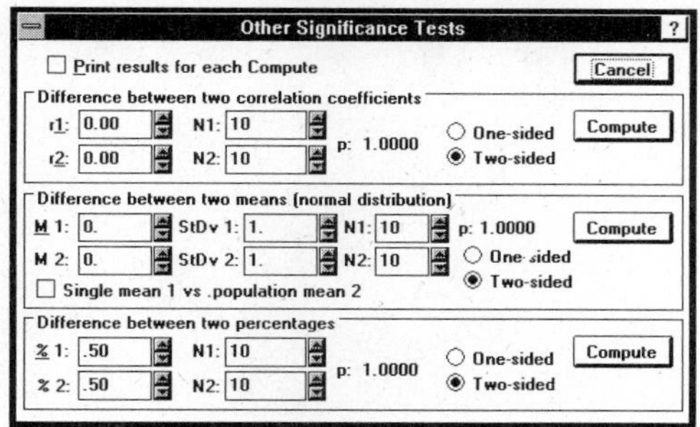

Note that *STATISTICA* also includes a comprehensive general *Probability Calculator* for evaluating the distribution functions for various continuous distributions, including *F*, *t*, *Chi-square*, *Weibull*, etc; the *Probability Calculator* also allows you to compute the significance level for Pearson product moment correlation coefficients, and to convert them into Fisher *z* values; refer to *Quick Basic Stats*, Chapter 10, for details.

Print Results for Each Compute

Set this check box if you want to automatically print (or send to printer file, whichever output destination you selected in the *Page/Output Setup* dialog, see Chapter 3) the results of the selected probability computations.

Difference between Two Correlation Coefficients

The options in this box allow you to compare the statistical significance of differences between two Pearson *r*'s. Both *One-sided* and *Two-sided* tests can be performed.

Difference between Two Means (Normal Distribution)

These options allow you to compute:

(1) The significance level for the difference between two means computed from two samples;

(2) The significance level for the difference between one mean computed from a sample and a population mean (if the *Single mean 1 vs. population mean 2* check box is set).

The *p*-level is computed based on the *t*-value for the respective comparison; both *One-sided* and *Two-sided* tests can be performed.

Differences between Two Percentages

These options allow you to compute the significance level for the difference between two percentages; both *One-sided* and *Two-sided* tests can be performed. The *p*-level is computed based on the *t*-value for the respective comparison:

$$|t| = \sqrt{[(N_1*N_2)/(N_1+N_2)]}*|p_1-p_2|/\sqrt{(p*q)}$$

where

p is equal to $(p_1*N_1+p_2*N_2)/(N_1+N_2)$

q is equal to $(1-p)$.

Highlighting Significant Results

When statistically significant results (*p<alpha*) are highlighted in the current Scrollsheet, the *Options* button will appear on the Scrollsheet toolbar. You can request a different threshold *p*-level by clicking on the *Options* button to open the *Alpha level* dialog.

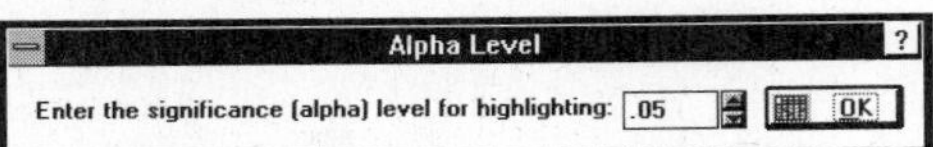

When you enter the desired new *alpha* level, a new Scrollsheet will be prepared with highlights reflecting the new significance criterion. The general logic of significance testing is described in the *Elementary Concepts* chapter (Chapter 8).

INDEX

A

B

C

D

STATISTICA

StatSoft

StatSoft

U

W

Y

Chapter 10:

QUICK BASIC STATS

Table of Contents

The *Detailed Table of Contents* follows on the next page.

Detailed Table of Contents

StatSoft

StatSoft

Chapter 10:

QUICK BASIC STATS

INTRODUCTORY OVERVIEW

The *Quick Basic Stats* options are available from either the spreadsheet or Scrollsheet right-mouse-button flying menu, from the *Analysis* pull-down menu of any module of *STATISTICA*, or from the toolbar button. *Quick Basic Statistics* can be used at any point of your data analysis (e.g., to provide supplementary information when you review output from any *STATISTICA* module).

Data: IRISDAT.STA 5v * 150c

Fisher (1936) iris data: length & width of sepals and petals,

#	1 SEPALLEN	2 SEPALWID	3 PETALLEN	4 PETALWID	5 IRISTYPE
1	5.0	3.3			
2	6.4	2.8			
3	6.5	2.8			
4	6.7	3.1			
5	6.3	2.8			
6	4.6	3.4			
7	6.9	3.1			
8	6.2	2.2			
9	5.9	3.2			
10	4.6	3.6	1.0	.2	SETOSA
11	6.1	3.0	4.6	1.4	VERSICOL

Descriptives of PETALLEN-PETALWID
Correlations of PETALLEN-PETALWID
Frequencies of PETALLEN-PETALWID
Descriptives by...
Correlations by...
Frequencies by...
Probability Calculator...
More...

These procedures include a selection of basic statistics which can be performed on long lists of variables (e.g., correlation indices for *all* variables in the data set), and all analyses can be performed *by groups*, for every value (i.e., code) of a selected grouping variable.

Also, the *Quick Basic Stats* menus include access to a flexible *Probability Calculator* (see page 1579 for details).

"Quick" Selection of Variables in *Quick Basic Stats*

One of the main advantages of *Quick Basic Stats* is that usually they do not require that you select the variables for the analysis via the standard variable selection dialogs – instead, the variables are automatically chosen from the block currently highlighted in the spreadsheet or Scrollsheet. *STATISTICA* will prompt you to select variables only if the block does not contain a sufficient number of variables or if a grouping variable is required. (Note that if *Quick Basic Stats* are called from the pull-down menu *Analysis*, then the variables to be analyzed are selected via subsequent variable selection dialogs.)

In all spreadsheets (and those Scrollsheets which involve only one list of variables rather than two lists or one grouping variable and a list) the flying menu will have the following format:

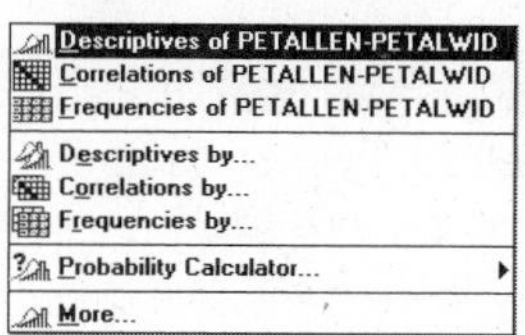

If you select any of the analyses involving a grouping variable (*by...*), *STATISTICA* will open the standard *Select Variable* dialog from which you may select the desired grouping variable. If Scrollsheets have a matrix format, or a format where the cursor position may indicate two variables rather than one, then predefined analyses *by groups* are available from the *Quick Basic Stats* menu (and *STATISTICA* will not ask you for the selection of the "*by...*" variable for the analysis).

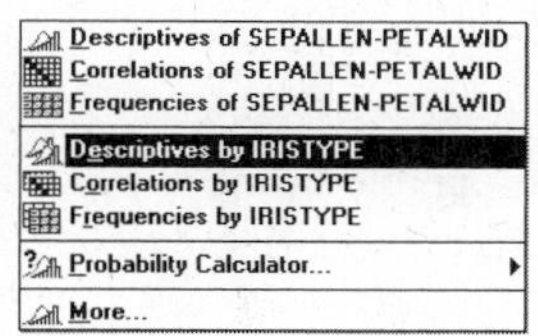

StatSoft

If no variables are indicated by the current cursor position, then selecting any of the *Quick Basic Stats* will prompt you to select the variable(s) from a list.

As the *Quick Basic Statistics* are computed, *STATISTICA* will take into account the current case selection and weighting conditions for the variables being analyzed (case selection and weighting conditions may also be changed from the *Quick Basic Statistics - Extended Options* dialog, see page 1570).

See also *Block Stats* (Chapter 3) which produce descriptive statistics and statistical graphs for data in the currently highlighted block.

DESCRIPTIVE STATISTICS VIA *QUICK BASIC STATS*

Overview

STATISTICA will compute a wide selection of descriptive statistics for the selected variables in the current data set when you select *Descriptive Statistics* from the *Analysis - Quick Basic Stats* menu or the *Descriptive Statistics of ...* or *Descriptive Statistics by ...* options from the right-mouse-button flying menu. Use the *Quick Basic Statistics - Extended Options* dialog (accessible via the *Quick Basic Stats - More...* option, see page 1570) to customize the computations, for example, to select casewise deletion of missing data, the display of long variable names, the computation of medians and quartiles, etc. (the choices that you make on that dialog will remain in effect the next time that you compute *Quick Basic Stats* without going through the *Extended Options* dialog).

A sequential table of "descriptives" for the consecutive variables will be generated (one row per variable) for each level of a grouping variable (if one is selected).

Descriptive Statistics (adstudy.sta)

Continue...	Valid N	Mean	Confid. -95.000%	Confid. 95.000	Sum	Minimum	Maximum
MEASUR2	50	4.5400	3.7195	5.3605	227.00	0.00	9.0000
MEASUR3	50	4.1400	3.3654	4.9146	207.00	0.00	9.0000
MEASUR4	50	5.5200	4.7643	6.2757	276.00	0.00	9.0000
MEASUR5	50	3.9600	3.2115	4.7085	198.00	0.00	9.0000
MEASUR6	50	4.8400	3.9819	5.6981	242.00	0.00	9.0000
MEASUR7	50	4.6600	3.9507	5.3693	233.00	0.00	9.0000
MEASUR8	50	3.7200	2.9223	4.5177	186.00	0.00	9.0000
MEASUR9	50	4.1600	3.2942	5.0258	208.00	0.00	9.0000

Additionally, if a grouping variable was selected, then a Scrollsheet of the descriptive statistics will be produced for each level of the grouping variable.

The descriptive statistics which are computed when you select any of these options are:

- valid *n*;
- mean;
- confidence limits of the mean;
- sum;
- minimum;
- maximum;
- range;
- variance;
- standard deviation;
- standard error of the mean;
- skewness;
- kurtosis;
- standard errors of the skewness and kurtosis.
- medians and quartiles, if previously selected via the *Extended Options* dialog

For more information on computing these statistics, see *Appendix II* of this volume. Note that the specific method of computation for the median and the quartiles can be configured in the *STATISTICA Defaults: General* dialog, accessible from the *Options* pull-down menu; see also the *Spreadsheet Window*, Chapter 3).

Customizing the computations via the *Quick Basic Stats - Extended Options* dialog. The *Extended Options* dialog (accessible via the *Quick*

Basic Stats - More... option, see page 1570) provides additional statistical options. Also, the choices that you make on that dialog will remain in effect the next time that you compute *Quick Basic Stats* without going through the *Extended Options* dialog.

For example, you can compute medians and quartiles via this dialog. Additionally, casewise deletion of missing data can be requested and long variable names can be included in the output Scrollsheets by setting a global option in the *Quick Basic Stats - Extended Options* dialog.

Descriptive Statistics (from the *Analysis* Pull-down Menu)

When you first select this option from the *Analysis* pull-down menu, the *Select Variables (and optional grouping variable)* dialog will open in which you can select the variables (up to 4,096 variables can be selected) for the analysis and (optionally) a single grouping variable by which the descriptive statistics will be calculated.

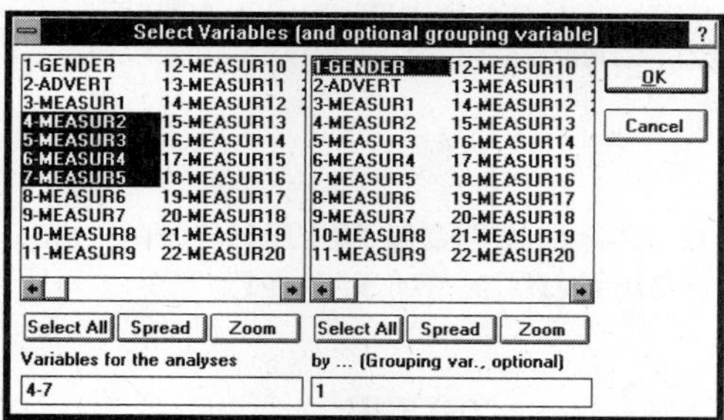

If you do not select a grouping variable, then clicking *OK* in this dialog will produce the descriptive statistics Scrollsheet.

If you select a grouping variable, then clicking *OK* in this dialog will bring up the *Select codes for grouping variable* dialog in which you can select the codes (i.e., groups) by which the descriptive statistics will be calculated.

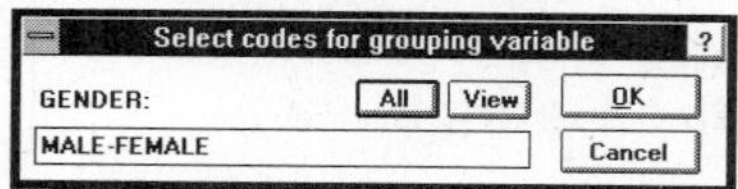

After selecting the desired codes for the groups, the *Select a group* dialog will open.

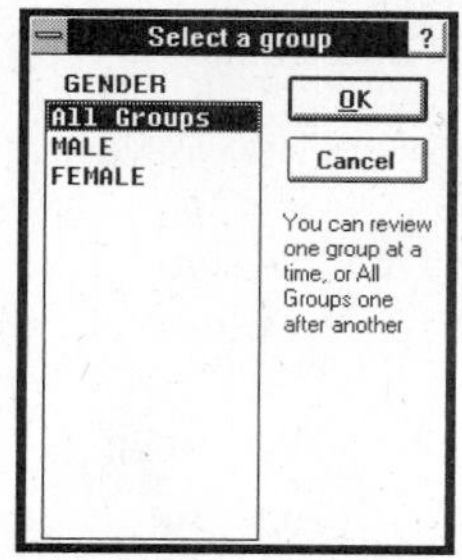

In this dialog, you can choose to display the series of descriptive statistics Scrollsheets for all groups (press *OK* to select this default option) or only for specific groups (one Scrollsheet per group). Click *OK* to complete the analysis.

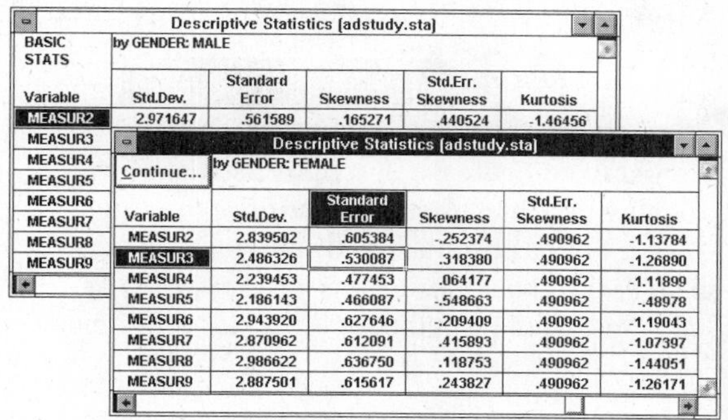

Variable	Std.Dev.	Standard Error	Skewness	Std.Err. Skewness	Kurtosis
MEASUR2	2.839502	.605384	-.252374	.490962	-1.13784
MEASUR3	2.486326	.530087	.318380	.490962	-1.26890
MEASUR4	2.239453	.477453	.064177	.490962	-1.11899
MEASUR5	2.186143	.466087	-.548663	.490962	-.48978
MEASUR6	2.943920	.627646	-.209409	.490962	-1.19043
MEASUR7	2.870962	.612091	.415893	.490962	-1.07397
MEASUR8	2.986622	.636750	.118753	.490962	-1.44051
MEASUR9	2.887501	.615617	.243827	.490962	-1.26171

Customizing the computations. Use the *Quick Basic Statistics - Extended Options* dialog (accessible via the *Quick Basic Stats - More...* option, see page 1570) to customize the computations, for example, to select casewise deletion of missing data, the display of long variable names, the computation of medians and quartiles, etc. (the choices that you make on that dialog will remain in effect the next time that you compute *Quick Basic Stats* without going through the *Extended Options* dialog).

Descriptives of ... (from the Flying Menu)

If you want to compute some descriptive statistics for selected variables without having to go through some intermediate dialogs (e.g., for selecting variables or codes), use the *Quick Basic Stats - Descriptive of* ... option from the right-mouse-button flying menu.

When you select this option, *STATISTICA* will compute the descriptive statistics for the values of the currently highlighted variable(s) in the spreadsheet without prompting you for any other information.

Data: ADSTUDY.STA 25v * 50c

Advertising Effectiveness Study.

Case	1 GENDER	2 ADVERT	3 MEASUR1	4 MEASUR2	5 MEASUR3	6 MEASUR4	7 MEASUR5
J. Baker	MALE	PEPSI				8	1
A. Smith	MALE	COKE				8	0
M. Brown	FEMALE	COKE				9	8
C. Mayer	MALE	PEPSI				5	9
M. West	MALE	PEPSI				2	8
D. Young	FEMALE	COKE				8	3
S. Bird	FEMALE	COKE				2	5
D. Flynd	MALE	PEPSI				6	6
J. Owen	FEMALE	PEPSI				3	6
H. Morrow	MALE	PEPSI	6	6	2	8	3
F. East	FEMALE	PEPSI	4	6	6	5	6

Descriptives of MEASUR1-MEASUR4
Correlations of MEASUR1-MEASUR4
Frequencies of MEASUR1-MEASUR4
Descriptives by...
Correlations by...
Frequencies by...
Probability Calculator
More...

In order to compute the descriptive statistics by a grouping variable, use the *Descriptive by* ... or *More* ... options from the right-mouse-button flying menu or the *Quick Basic Stats - Descriptive Statistics* option from the *Analysis* pull-down menu.

Descriptives by ... (from the Flying Menu)

This *Quick Basic Stats* option will allow you to calculate descriptive statistics for the values of the currently highlighted variable(s) as categorized by the levels of a grouping variable. When you select this option from the spreadsheet right-mouse-button flying menu, the *Select codes for grouping variable* dialog will open in which you can select the codes (i.e., groups) by which the descriptive statistics will be calculated (optionally, you can select or de-select variables for the analysis in this dialog; up to 4,096 variables can be selected). Clicking *OK* in this dialog will bring up the *Select a group* dialog. In this dialog, you can choose to display the series of descriptive statistics Scrollsheets for all groups (press *OK* to select this default option) or only for specific groups (one Scrollsheet per group). Click *OK* to complete the analysis.

If you click on a Scrollsheet with the right-mouse-button and a grouping variable or a secondary variable was used in the analysis, then that grouping variable will automatically be selected and displayed in the *Quick Basic Stats* flying menu.

Grouping: GENDER: This variable contains data on the gender

BASIC STATS — Group 1: MALE; Group 2: FEMALE

Variable	Mean MALE	Mean FEMALE	t-value	df	p
MEASUR1			1.30945	48	.196615
MEASUR2			.28152	48	.779520
MEASUR3			.52707	48	.600572
MEASUR4			-.16547	48	.869267
MEASUR5			-1.87198	48	.067309

Descriptives of MEASUR1
Correlations...
Frequencies of MEASUR1
Descriptives by GENDER
Correlations by GENDER
Frequencies by GENDER
Probability Calculator
More...

In this case, selecting this option will bring up the *Select a group* dialog in which you can choose to display the descriptive statistics Scrollsheets for all groups or only for specific groups (one Scrollsheet per group). Click *OK* in this dialog to complete the analysis.

CORRELATION MATRICES VIA *QUICK BASIC STATS*

Overview

STATISTICA will compute correlations between the selected variables for each level of a grouping variable (if one is selected) when you select either the *Correlation Matrices* option from the *Analysis - Quick Basic Stats* menu or the *Correlations of* ... or *Correlations by* ... options from the right-mouse-button flying menu.

Correlations, Casewise MD deletion, N=100 (10items.sta)

Variable	ITEM1	ITEM2	ITEM3	ITEM4	ITEM5	ITEM6
ITEM1	1.00	.58	.49	.43	.04	.14
ITEM2	.58	1.00	.46	.36	-.03	.12
ITEM3	.49	.46	1.00	.36	.11	.05
ITEM4	.43	.36	.36	1.00	.06	-.04
ITEM5	.04	-.03	.11	.06	1.00	.03
ITEM6	.14	.12	.05	-.04	.03	1.00

The size of the correlation matrix is restricted only by the amount of memory in your computer.

Customizing the computations via the *Quick Basic Stats - Extended Options* dialog. The *Extended Options* dialog (accessible via the *Quick Basic Stats - More...* option, see page 1570) allows you to choose between casewise or pairwise deletion of missing data (by default, correlation matrices will be computed with casewise deletion of missing data). Additionally, you can display *p*-levels in the correlation Scrollsheet by selecting the *p-levels* option. Long variable names can be included in the output Scrollsheets by setting a global option in this dialog. Note that the choices that you make on the *Extended Options* dialog will remain in effect the next time that you compute *Quick Basic Stats - Correlation Matrices* without going through the *Extended Options* dialog.

Correlation Matrices (from the *Analysis* Pull-down Menu)

When you first select this option from the *Analysis* pull-down menu, the *Select Variables (and optional grouping variable)* dialog will open in which you can select the variables for the analysis and (optionally) a grouping variable by which the correlations will be calculated.

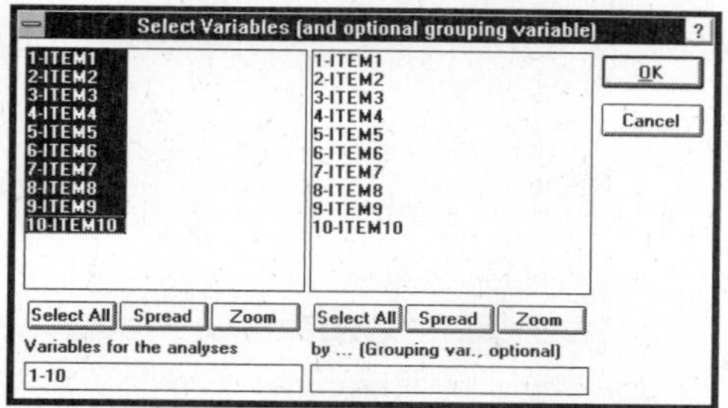

If you do not select a grouping variable, then clicking *OK* in this dialog will display the correlation matrix in a Scrollsheet.

Correlations, Casewise MD deletion, N=100 (10items.sta)

Variable	ITEM1	ITEM2	ITEM3	ITEM4	ITEM5	ITEM6	ITEM7	ITEM8	ITEM9	ITEM10
ITEM1	1.00	.58	.49	.43	.04	.14	.54	.38	.40	.50
ITEM2	.58	1.00	.46	.36	-.03	.12	.57	.55	.44	.47
ITEM3	.49	.46	1.00	.36	.11	.05	.47	.38	.35	.29
ITEM4	.43	.36	.36	1.00	.06	-.04	.27	.35	.42	.37
ITEM5	.04	-.03	.11	.06	1.00	.03	.01	.13	-.04	.01
ITEM6	.14	.12	.05	-.04	.03	1.00	.14	.10	.07	.09
ITEM7	.54	.57	.47	.27	.01	.14	1.00	.44	.29	.43
ITEM8	.38	.55	.38	.35	.13	.10	.44	1.00	.41	.51
ITEM9	.40	.44	.35	.42	-.04	.07	.29	.41	1.00	.41
ITEM10	.50	.47	.29	.37	.01	.09	.43	.51	.41	1.00

If you select a grouping variable, then clicking *OK* in this dialog will bring up the *Select codes for grouping variable* dialog in which you can select the codes (i.e., groups) by which the correlations will be calculated.

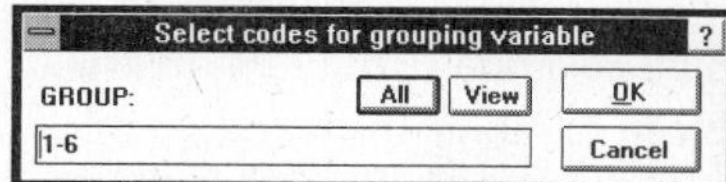

After selecting the desired codes for the groups, the *Select a group* dialog will open.

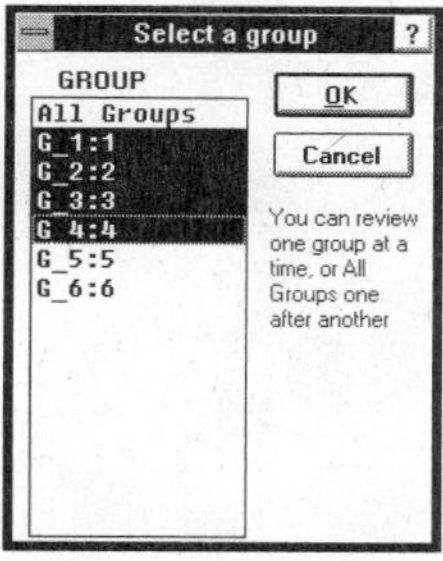

In this dialog, you can choose to display the correlation matrices for all groups or only for

specific groups (one Scrollsheet per group). Click *OK* to complete the analysis.

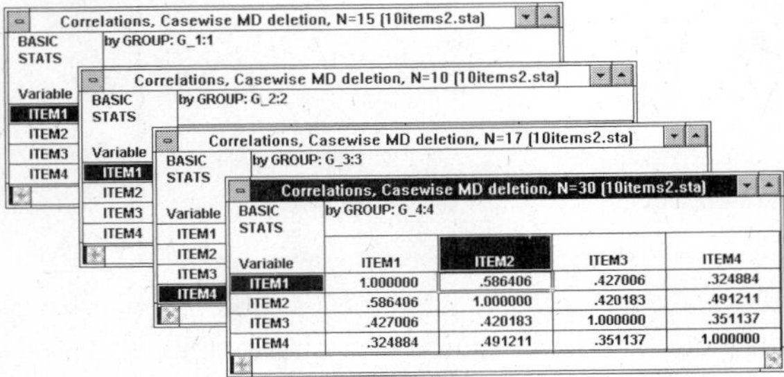

Correlations, Casewise MD deletion, N=30 (10items2.sta)

BASIC STATS — by GROUP: G_4:4

Variable	ITEM1	ITEM2	ITEM3	ITEM4
ITEM1	1.000000	.586406	.427006	.324884
ITEM2	.586406	1.000000	.420183	.491211
ITEM3	.427006	.420183	1.000000	.351137
ITEM4	.324884	.491211	.351137	1.000000

Customizing the computations. Use the *Quick Basic Statistics - Extended Options* dialog (accessible via the *Quick Basic Stats - More...* option, see page 1570) to customize the computations, for example, to select pairwise deletion of missing data, the display of long variable names, etc. (the choices that you make on that dialog will remain in effect the next time that you compute *Quick Basic Stats - Correlation Matrices* without going through the *Extended Options* dialog).

Correlations of ... (from the Flying Menu)

If you want to compute a square correlation matrix without having to select variables from an intermediate dialog, then select this *Quick Basic Stats* option from the right-mouse-button flying menu to compute correlations between the currently highlighted variables.

In order to compute the correlations by a grouping variable, use the *Correlations by ...* or *More ...* options from the right-mouse-button flying menu or the *Quick Basic Stats - Correlation Matrices* option from the *Analysis* pull-down menu. To compute a rectangular correlation matrix, use the *Correlation Matrices* option in the *Basic Statistics and Tables* module of *STATISTICA*.

Correlations by ... (from the Flying Menu)

This *Quick Basic Stats* option (called from the right-mouse-button flying menu) will allow you to produce a square matrix of correlations between the currently highlighted variable(s) as categorized by the levels of a grouping variable. When you select this option from the spreadsheet right-mouse-button flying menu,

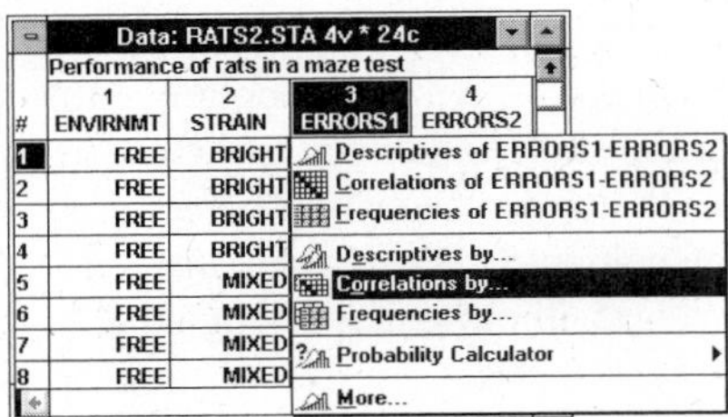

the *Select grouping Variable* dialog will open in which you can select a single grouping variable by which the correlations will be calculated (optionally, you can select or de-select variables for the analysis in this dialog).

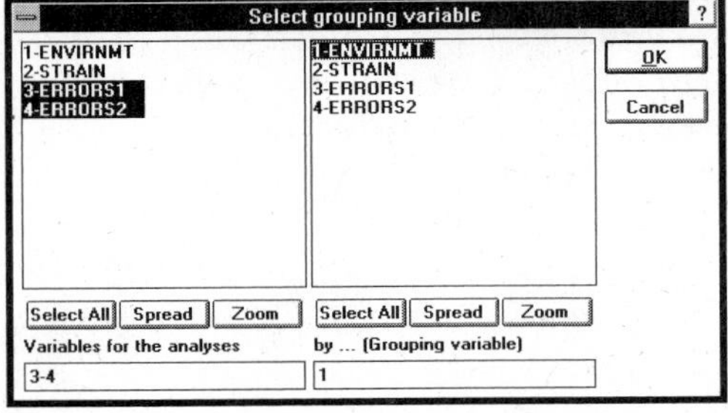

Clicking *OK* in this dialog will bring up the *Select a group* dialog. In this dialog, you can choose to display the descriptive statistics Scrollsheets for all

groups or only for specific groups (one Scrollsheet per group).

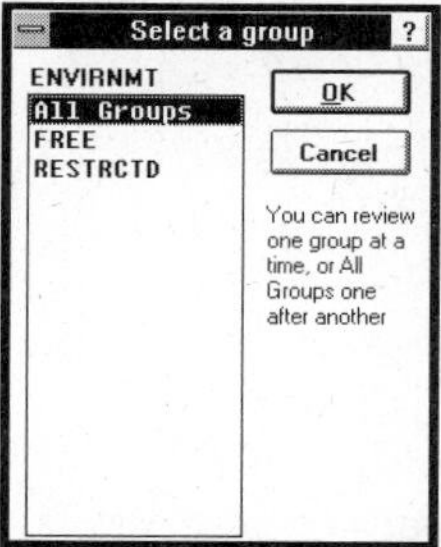

Click *OK* to complete the analysis.

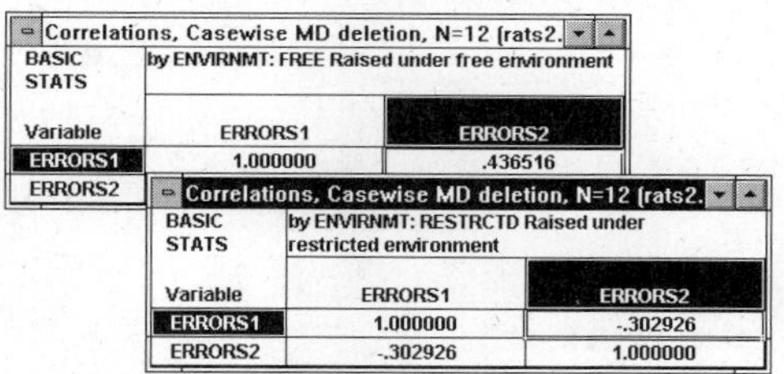

If you click on a Scrollsheet with the right-mouse-button and a grouping variable or a secondary variable was used in the analysis, then that grouping variable will automatically be selected and displayed in the *Quick Basic Stats* flying menu.

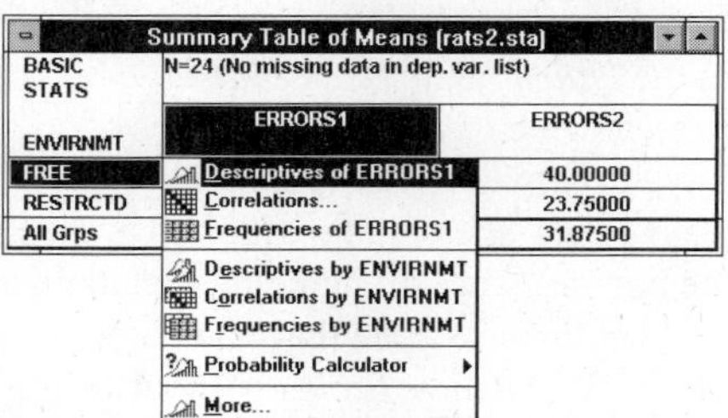

In this case, selecting this option will bring up the *Select a group* dialog in which you can choose to display the correlations for all groups or only for specific groups (one Scrollsheet per group). Click *OK* in this dialog to complete the analysis.

FREQUENCY TABLES VIA *QUICK BASIC STATS*

Overview

STATISTICA will compute a cascade of frequency tables for the selected variables, one Scrollsheet per variable for each level of a grouping variable (if one is selected) when you select either the *Frequency Tables* option from the *Analysis - Quick Basic Stats* menu or the *Frequencies of ...* or *Frequencies by ...* options from the right-mouse-button flying menu.

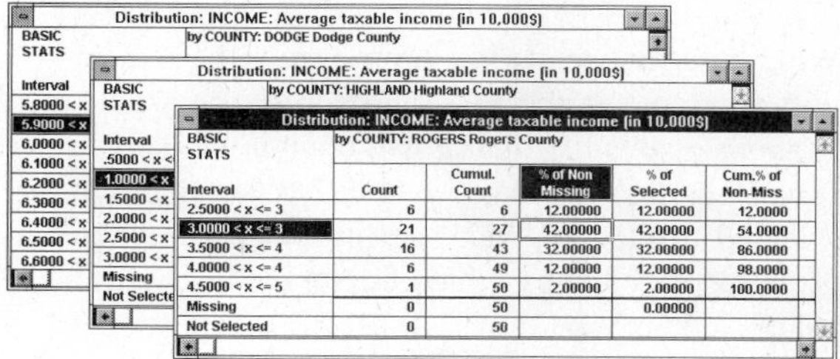

The summary statistics which are computed for the selected values (e.g., the highlighted block of values) in each category when you select any of these *Frequency* options are:

- count;
- cumulative count;
- percent of non-missing values;
- percent of selected values;
- cumulative percent of non-missing values;
- 100 - percent of non-missing values;
- cumulative percent of selected values;
- 100 - percent of selected values.

Customizing the computations via the *Quick Basic Stats - Extended Options* dialog. To compute normal expected frequencies and other statistics, use the options in the *Quick Basic Stats - Extended Options* dialog (accessible by selecting the *More...* option in the *Quick Basic Stats* menu, see page 1570). Long variable names can be included in

the output and casewise deletion of missing data can be requested by selecting the appropriate options in the *Quick Basic Stats - Extended Options* dialog (see page 1570). Note that the choices that you make on the *Extended Options* dialog will remain in effect the next time that you compute *Quick Basic Stats - Frequency Tables* without going through the *Extended Options* dialog.

Frequency Tables (from the Analysis Pull-down Menu)

When you first select this option from the *Analysis* pull-down menu, the *Select Variables (and optional grouping variable)* dialog will open in which you can select the variables (up to 4,096 variables can be selected) for the analysis and (optionally) a single grouping variable by which the frequencies will be calculated.

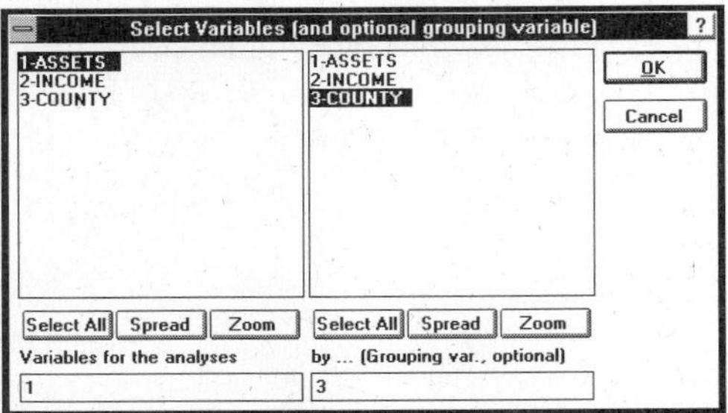

If you do not select a grouping variable, then clicking *OK* in this dialog will display the frequency Scrollsheets. If you select a grouping variable, then clicking *OK* in this dialog will bring up the *Select codes for grouping variable* dialog in which you can select the codes (i.e., groups) by which the frequencies will be calculated.

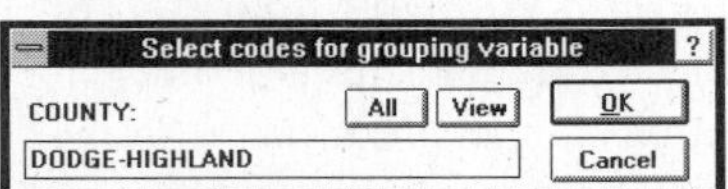

After selecting the desired codes for the groups, the *Select a group* dialog will open.

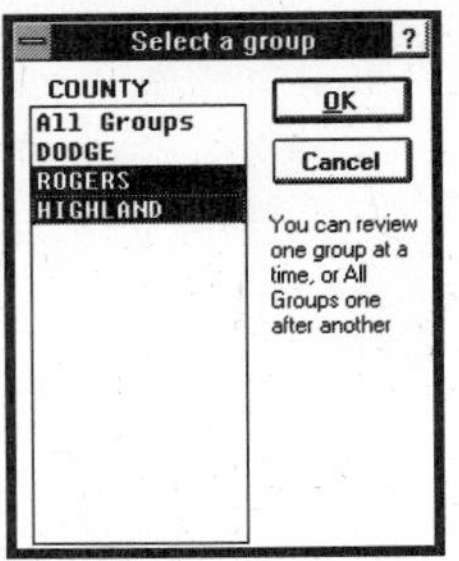

In this dialog, you can choose to display the frequency Scrollsheets for all groups or only for specific groups (one Scrollsheet per group). Click *OK* to complete the analysis.

Distribution: ASSETS: Sum of all assets (in 100,000$)

BASIC STATS — by COUNTY: ROGERS Rogers County

Interval	% of Selected	Cum.% of Non-Miss	100-%Non Missing	Cum.% of Selected	100-%of Selected
1.8000 < x <= 2.0000	2.00000	2.0000	100.0000	2.0000	100.0000
2.0000 < x <= 2.					
2.2000 < x <= 2.					
2.4000 < x <= 2.					
2.6000 < x <= 2.					
2.8000 < x <= 3.					
3.0000 < x <= 3.					
3.2000 < x <= 3.					
Missing					
Not Selected					

Distribution: ASSETS: Sum of all assets (in 100,000$)

BASIC STATS — by COUNTY: HIGHLAND Highland County

Interval	Count	Cumul. Count	% of Non Missing	% of Selected
2.2000 < x <= 2.4000	1	1	2.27273	2.27273
2.4000 < x <= 2.6000	6	7	13.63636	13.63636
2.6000 < x <= 2.8000	9	16	20.45455	20.45455
2.8000 < x <= 3.0000	13	29	29.54545	29.54545
3.0000 < x <= 3.2000	7	36	15.90909	15.90909
3.2000 < x <= 3.4000	5	41	11.36364	11.36364
3.4000 < x <= 3.6000	1	42	2.27273	2.27273
3.6000 < x <= 3.8000	2	44	4.54545	4.54545
Missing	0	44		0.00000
Not Selected	0	44		

Customizing the computations. Use the *Quick Basic Statistics - Extended Options* dialog (accessible via the *Quick Basic Stats - More...* option, see page 1570) to customize the computations, for example, to select casewise deletion of missing data, the display of long variable names, etc. (the choices that you make on that dialog will remain in effect the next time that you compute *Quick Basic Stats - Frequency Tables* without going through the *Extended Options* dialog).

Frequencies of ... (from the Flying Menu)

If you want to compute the summary statistics without having to select variables from an intermediate dialog, then select this *Quick Basic Stats* option from the right-mouse-button flying

menu to compute frequency tables for the highlighted variable(s).

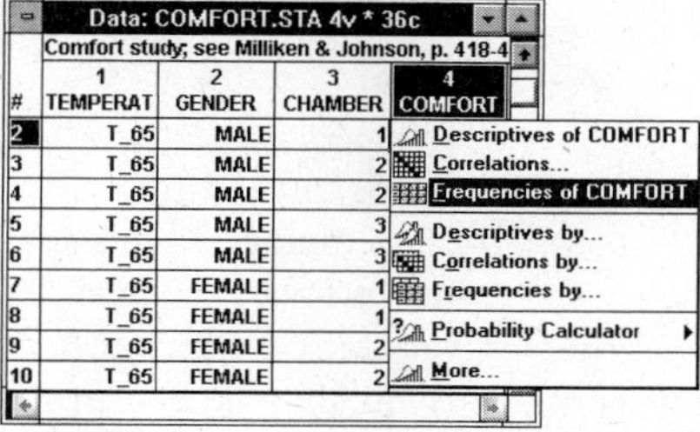

Selecting this *Quick Basic Stats* option will display frequency Scrollsheets of the values of the currently highlighted variable(s), one Scrollsheet per variable. In order to compute the frequencies by a grouping variable, use the *Frequencies by ...* or *More ...* options from the right-mouse-button flying menu or the *Quick Basic Stats - Frequency Tables* option from the *Analysis* pull-down menu.

Frequencies by ... (from the Flying Menu)

This *Quick Basic Stats* option (from the right-mouse-button flying menu) will allow you to calculate frequencies for the values of the currently highlighted variable(s) as categorized by the levels of a grouping variable.

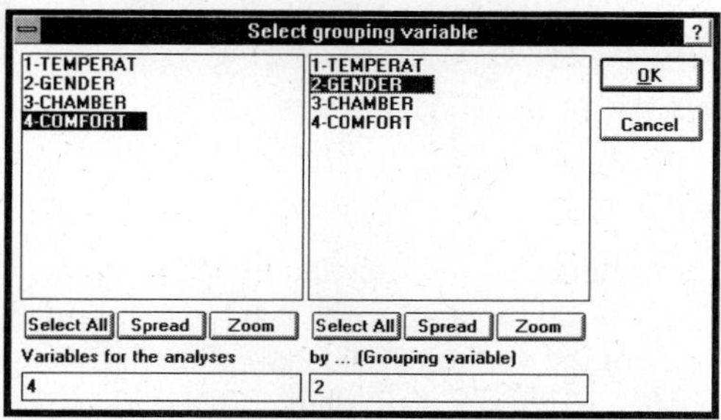

When you select this option from the spreadsheet right-mouse-button flying menu, the *Select grouping variable* dialog will open in which you can select a single grouping variable by which the frequencies will be calculated (optionally, you can select or de-select variables for the analysis in this dialog; up to 4,096 variables can be selected).

Clicking *OK* in this dialog will bring up the *Select a group* dialog. In this dialog, you can choose to display the frequency tables for all groups or only for specific groups (one Scrollsheet per group).

Click *OK* to complete the analysis.

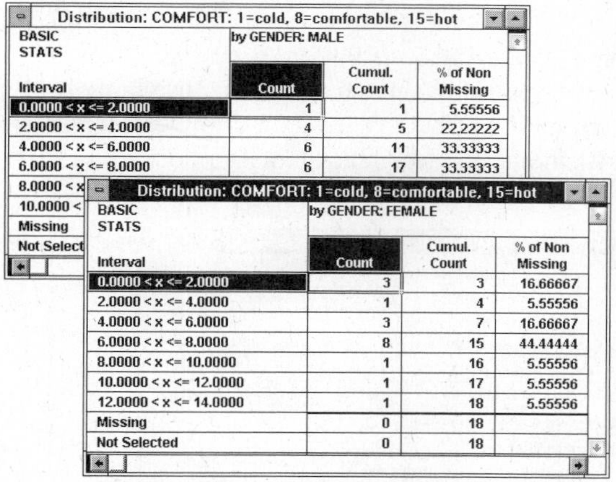

Distribution: COMFORT: 1=cold, 8=comfortable, 15=hot

BASIC STATS — by GENDER: MALE

Interval	Count	Cumul. Count	% of Non Missing
0.0000 < x <= 2.0000	1	1	5.55556
2.0000 < x <= 4.0000	4	5	22.22222
4.0000 < x <= 6.0000	6	11	33.33333
6.0000 < x <= 8.0000	6	17	33.33333
8.0000 < x			
10.0000 <			
Missing			
Not Select			

Distribution: COMFORT: 1=cold, 8=comfortable, 15=hot

BASIC STATS — by GENDER: FEMALE

Interval	Count	Cumul. Count	% of Non Missing
0.0000 < x <= 2.0000	3	3	16.66667
2.0000 < x <= 4.0000	1	4	5.55556
4.0000 < x <= 6.0000	3	7	16.66667
6.0000 < x <= 8.0000	8	15	44.44444
8.0000 < x <= 10.0000	1	16	5.55556
10.0000 < x <= 12.0000	1	17	5.55556
12.0000 < x <= 14.0000	1	18	5.55556
Missing	0	18	
Not Selected	0	18	

If you click on a Scrollsheet with the right-mouse-button and a grouping variable or a secondary variable was used in the analysis, then that grouping variable will automatically be selected and displayed in the *Quick Basic Stats* flying menu.

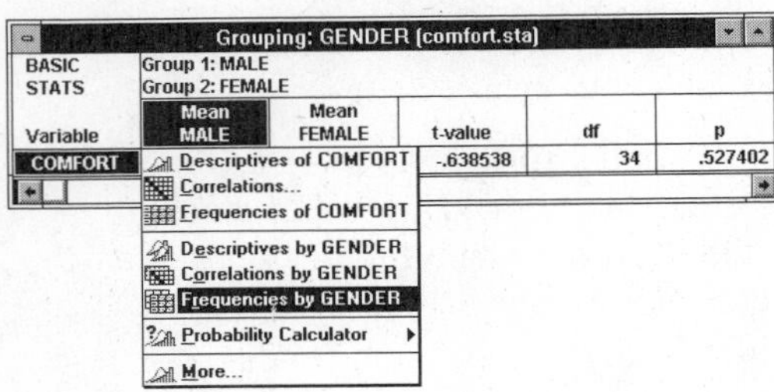

In this case, selecting this option will bring up the *Select a group* dialog in which you can choose to display the frequency tables for all groups or only for specific groups (one Scrollsheet per group). Click *OK* in this dialog to complete the analysis.

QUICK BASIC STATS EXTENDED OPTIONS

This *Quick Basic Stats* option (accessible from the *Analysis* pull-down menu or right-mouse-button flying menu) offers extended descriptive statistics, correlations, and frequency tables options as well as some graphing options.

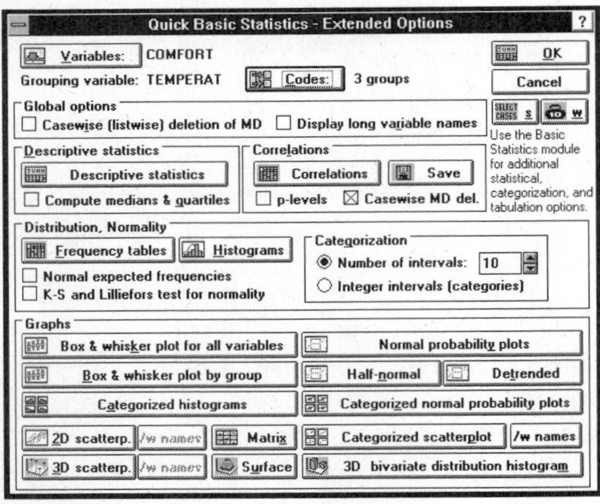

Note that the choices that you make on this dialog will remain in effect the next time that you compute *Quick Basic Stats* without going through the *Extended Options* dialog (e.g., via the *Analysis* pull-down menu). Each of these options are described below.

Variables

Click on this button to open the *Select Variables (and optional grouping variable)* dialog. In this dialog you can select the variables for the analysis and (optionally) a grouping variable by which the analysis will be performed. (Note that the name of the grouping variable will be displayed below this button.)

Codes

Click on this button to open the *Select codes for grouping variable* dialog in which you can select the codes (i.e., groups) by which the desired analysis will be performed.

Global Options

With the exception of casewise deletion of missing data for correlations (which is specified independently of this option, see *Correlations*, below), the following two options apply globally to all of the other options described in this dialog.

Casewise (Listwise) Deletion of Missing Data

If casewise deletion of missing data is selected, then *STATISTICA* will ignore all cases that have missing data for *any* of the variables selected in the list. If this check box is not selected, then all valid data points will be included in the analyses for each respective pair of variables (pairwise deletion of missing data, possibly resulting in unequal *valid n* per variable).

Display Long Variable Names

If this check box is set, then long variable names (if any were specified, see *Spreadsheet Edit (Current) Specs*, Chapter 3, *Spreadsheet Window*) will be displayed along with the short names in the first column or the title of the Scrollsheet. If no long variable names have been specified for any of the selected variables, then the setting of this check box will have no effect.

Descriptive Statistics

These options allow you to compute specific descriptive statistics for the selected variables (up to 4,096 variables can be selected). A sequential table of "descriptives" for the consecutive variables will be generated (one row per variable) for each level of a grouping variable (if one is selected).

For a listing of the descriptive statistics that are computed when you select this option, see page 1562. In order to compute the medians and quartiles, select the *Compute medians & quartiles* option (see below).

Compute Medians & Quartiles

If checked, then in addition to the statistics listed on page 1562, the descriptive statistics Scrollsheets will contain the median (50th percentile), quartiles (25th and 75th percentiles), and *quartile range* for all variables.

Descriptive Statistics (normal.sta)

Variable	Lower Quartile	Upper Quartile	Range	Quartile Range	Variance	Std.Dev.
VAR1	9.28892	10.89056	6.22797	1.601640	1.12968	1.062865
VAR2	.49501	2.00381	13.47208	1.508797	3.32044	1.822206
VAR3	2.23596	2.36642	.62590	.130454	.01116	.105625
VAR4	28.31051	35.93976	30.13782	7.629252	25.69439	5.068963

The median is defined as the value that divides the distribution of all values in half; that is, 50% of all values for the respective variable (within the respective group) will fall below the median and 50% will be greater than the median. The 25th and 75th percentiles (quartiles) are defined accordingly.

Percentiles. Note that you can also calculate percentiles in the *Basic Statistics & Tables* module and user-specified percentiles can be calculated in the *Nonparametrics* module or via *STATISTICA BASIC*. For all modules, you can specify the method of computing percentiles in the *STATISTICA Defaults: General* dialog (see Chapter 3).

Correlations

These options allow you to compute correlations between the selected variables for each level of a grouping variable (if one is selected). The size of the correlation matrix is restricted only by the amount of memory in your computer.

Save

Use this option to first compute the correlation matrix (without displaying it) and then save it in a file. When you click on this button, the *Save Matrix As* dialog will open in which you can specify a name under which the matrix will be saved. If a grouping variable was previously selected, then multiple correlation matrices (i.e., correlations "by group") will be produced and saved in a single file (for use in such procedures as *Structural Equation Modeling*, see Volume III, which can use multiple correlation matrices for input).

p-levels

Set this checkbox in order to display the *p*-level along with the correlation coefficient in the Scrollsheet.

Correlations, Casewise MD deletion, N=300 (normal.sta)

Variable	VAR1	VAR2	VAR3	VAR4
VAR1	--	-.110929	.075735	.999432
		p=.0550	p=.1915	p=0.000
VAR2	-.110929	--	-.120741	-.110909
	p=.0550		p=.0370	p=.0550
VAR3	.075735	-.120741	--	.079178
	p=.1915	p=.0370		p=.1719
VAR4	.999432	-.110909	.079178	--
	p=0.000	p=.0550	p=.1719	

Note that the significance levels reported in correlation matrices for individual coefficients should be interpreted with caution (for example, at *alpha=.05*, one can expect by chance correlations to be significant for 5% of the pairs of variables).

Casewise MD Deletion

Unlike the *Casewise (listwise) deletion of MD* option (which is a global option), this option applies only to *Correlations*. If this check box is set, then only the cases that have complete (valid) data for *all* variables that are currently selected for the analysis (i.e., *casewise deletion of missing data*) will be included in the computation of the correlations.

If this check box is not set (i.e., *pairwise deletion of missing data*), then each correlation will be computed from all cases that have complete (valid) data for the respective pair of variables, possibly resulting in unequal *n* for different correlations.

Distribution, Normality

These options will compute a cascade of frequency tables for the selected variables, one Scrollsheet per variable for each level of a grouping variable (if one is selected). You can select the method of categorization for this option via the *Categorization* box in the dialog (see below). For more information on these and other options, see *Frequency Tables - Overview* (page 1567).

Frequency Tables

When you click on this button, the *Select a group* dialog will open. In this dialog, you can choose to compute frequency tables for all groups or only for specific groups (one Scrollsheet per group). Click *OK* in this dialog to complete the analysis.

Distribution: VAR3 (normal.sta)

Interval	Count	Cumul. Count	% of Non Missing	% of Selected
1.9000 < x <= 2.0000	1	1	.33333	.33333
2.0000 < x <= 2.1000	12	13	4.00000	4.00000
2.1000 < x <= 2.2000	41	54	13.66667	13.66667
2.2000 < x <= 2.3000	82	136	27.33333	27.33333
2.3000 < x <= 2.4000	111	247	37.00000	37.00000
2.4000 < x <= 2.5000	49	296	16.33333	16.33333
2.5000 < x <= 2.6000	4	300	1.33333	1.33333
Missing	0	300		0.00000
Not Selected	0	300		

Histograms

When you click on this button, the *Select a group* dialog will open. In this dialog, you can choose to compute frequency histograms for all groups or only for specific groups (one Scrollsheet per group). Click *OK* in this dialog to display the histograms.

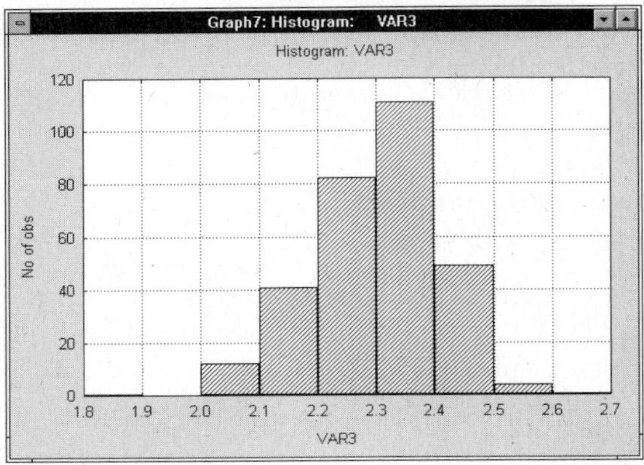

Many other types of histograms are available via the *Stats Graphs* options [accessible from the pull-down menu *Graphs* and the *Graph Gallery* (click on the toolbar button)].

Normal Expected Frequencies

If this check box is set then for each category in the frequency table, the expected frequencies are computed based on the normal distribution.

K-S and Lilliefors Test

If this check box is set, then the Kolmogorov-Smirnov one-sample *D* statistic will be computed and Lilliefors probabilities will be reported (see Lilliefors, 1976).

Distribution: VAR3 (normal.sta)

BASIC STATS Interval	K-S d=.0537 , p> .20; Lilliefors p<.05 Count	Cumul. Count	% of Non Missing	% of Selected
1.9000 < x <= 2.0000	1	1	.33333	.33333
2.0000 < x <= 2.1000	12	13	4.00000	4.00000
2.1000 < x <= 2.2000	41	54	13.66667	13.66667
2.2000 < x <= 2.3000	82	136	27.33333	27.33333
2.3000 < x <= 2.4000	111	247	37.00000	37.00000
2.4000 < x <= 2.5000	49	296	16.33333	16.33333
2.5000 < x <= 2.6000	4	300	1.33333	1.33333
Missing	0	300		0.00000
Not Selected	0	300		

If the Kolmogorov-Smirnov *D* statistic is significant, then the hypothesis that the respective distribution is normal should be rejected. The probability values that will be reported are based on those tabulated by Massey (1951); those probability values are valid when the mean and standard deviation of the normal distribution are known *a priori* and *not* estimated from the data. However, usually those parameters are computed from the actual data. In that case, the test for normality involves a complex conditional hypothesis ("how likely is it to obtain a *D* statistic of this magnitude or greater, contingent upon the mean and standard deviation computed from the data"), and thus the *Lilliefors* probabilities should be interpreted (Lilliefors, 1967; see also the *STATISTICA BASIC* program *Lillief.stb*, which will perform Monte Carlo replications, and tabulate the critical Lilliefors values).

Categorization

The options selected in this box will only affect the frequency tables and histograms produced via the options in the *Distribution, Normality* box (to the left). This categorization option has only two modes of categorizing the values of selected variables for the frequency table; a number of additional options, graphs, and statistics are available via the *Frequency Tables* option (on the *Basic Statistics and Tables* startup panel, see Chapter 9). You can also use the *Recode* option (accessible via the *Edit - Variables* pull-down menu option in the spreadsheet window) which allows you to categorize data (i.e., create values for a grouping variable) based on user-defined criteria of practically unlimited complexity.

Number of Intervals

If this radio button is set, then the range of values for the selected variables will be divided into approximately the requested number of intervals when subsequent *Frequency tables* Scrollsheets or *Histograms* are requested. This option is appropriate when the variables to be tabulated are continuous in nature. The tests of normality (*Normal expected frequencies* and *K-S and Lilliefors test*, see above) are only available if this option is chosen.

Note that the actual number of categories that will be produced may sometimes differ from the number of intervals requested. *STATISTICA* will produce "neat" intervals; that is, interval boundaries and widths with the last digit being *1*, *2*, or *5* (e.g., *10.5*, *11.0*, *11.5*, etc.). Such "simple" or "neat" intervals are more easily interpreted than interval boundaries defined by many significant digits (e.g., *10.12423*, *10.13533*, etc.). Full control over the method of categorization of variables is available via the *Basic Statistics and Tables - Frequency tables* option (see Chapter 9).

Integer Intervals

Chose this method of categorization if the variables to be tabulated can be interpreted as integer categories, or contain only integer values. If this method is chosen, all non-integer values will be ignored when producing *Frequency tables* or *Histograms* via the *Distribution, Normality* option; the choice of *Categorization* in this box will not affect other computations (e.g., of *Descriptive Statistics*).

Note that you can also use the *Recode* option (accessible via the *Edit - Variables* pull-down menu option in the spreadsheet window) which allows you to categorize data (i.e., create values for a grouping variable) based on user-defined criteria of practically unlimited complexity.

Graph Options

Box & Whisker Plot for All Variables

This option will produce a box and whisker plot for the selected variables by group (if a grouping variable was selected), one graph for each group.

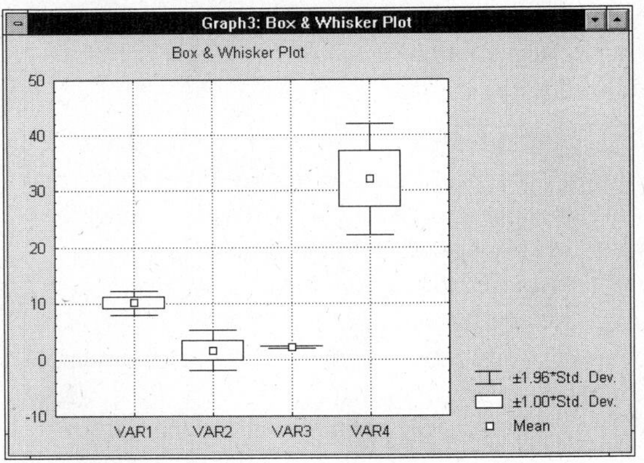

This box and whisker plot will summarize each variable by three components:

(1) A central line to indicate central tendency or location;

(2) A box to indicate variability around this central tendency;

(3) Whiskers around the box to indicate the range of the variable.

After clicking on this button you can choose to plot for each variable:

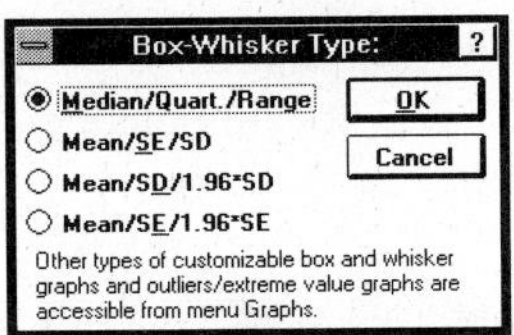

(1) Medians (central line), quartiles (box), and ranges (whiskers; you can specify the method of computing medians/quartiles in the *STATISTICA Defaults: General* dialog);

(2) Means, standard errors of the means, and standard deviations;

(3) Means, standard deviations, and 1.96 times the standard deviations (95% normal confidence interval for individual observations around the mean);

(4) Means, standard errors of the means, and 1.96 times the standard errors of the means (95% normal confidence interval for means).

Many other types of box-whisker plots are available via the *Stats Graphs* options [accessible from the pull-down menu *Graphs* and the *Graph Gallery* (click on the toolbar button)].

Box & Whisker Plot by Group

This option will produce a box and whisker plot for each selected variable categorized by each of the groups in the previously selected grouping variable, one graph per variable. (If a grouping variable has

not been previously selected, you will be prompted to select one when you click on this button.)

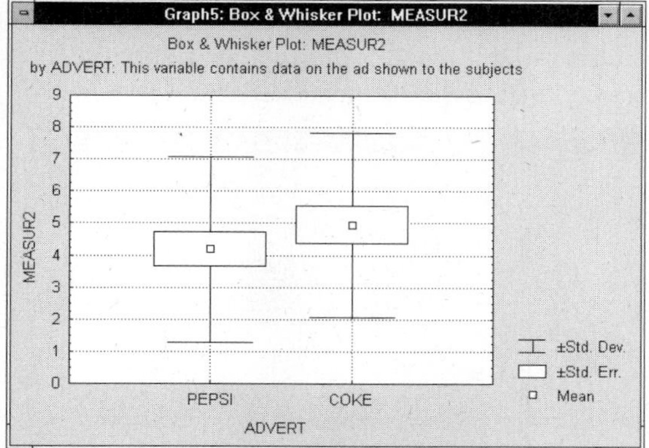

This box and whisker plot will summarize each group by three components:

(1) A central line to indicate central tendency or location;

(2) A box to indicate variability around this central tendency;

(3) Whiskers around the box to indicate the range of the variable.

After clicking on this button you can choose to plot for each variable:

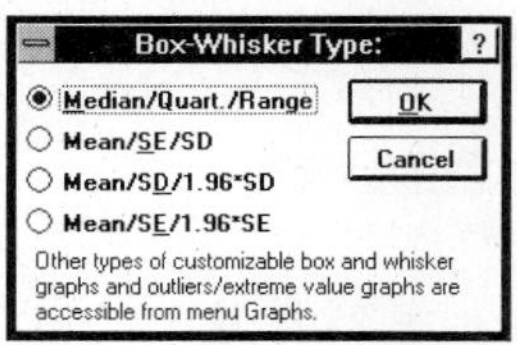

(1) Medians (central line), quartiles (box), and ranges (whiskers; you can specify the method of computing medians/quartiles in the *STATISTICA Defaults: General* dialog);

(2) Means, standard errors of the means, and standard deviations;

(3) Means, standard deviations, and 1.96 times the standard deviations (95% normal confidence interval for individual observations around the mean);

(4) Means, standard errors of the means, and 1.96 times the standard errors of the means (95% normal confidence interval for means).

Categorized Histograms

This option will produce a cascade of categorized histograms for the selected variables, one plot per variable. For each selected variable, *STATISTICA* will produce a histogram, broken down (categorized) by the levels of the grouping variable (e.g., separately for males and females).

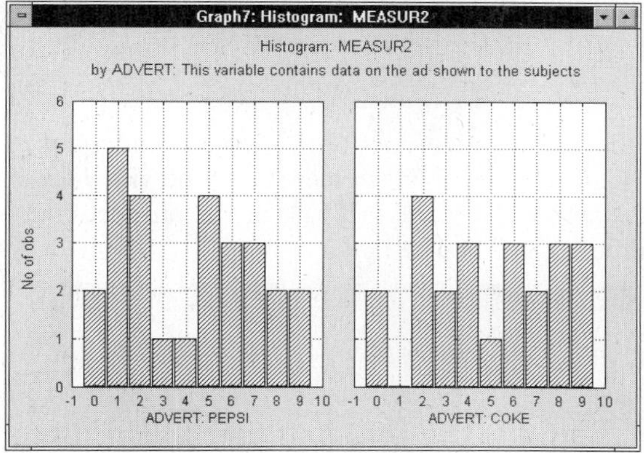

If a grouping variable has not been previously selected, you will be prompted to select one when you click on this button.

Categorized histograms are also available via the *Stats Graphs* options [accessible from the pull-down menu *Graphs* and the *Graph Gallery* (click on the toolbar button)].

2D Scatterplot (/with names)

This option will produce a cascade of scatterplots for selected pairs of variables and for each selected level of the grouping variable. (If a grouping variable has not been previously selected, you will

StatSoft

be prompted to select one when you click on this button.)

If the *2D scatterplot* option is chosen, then the plot will show the regression line and the 95% confidence interval bands for the regression line.

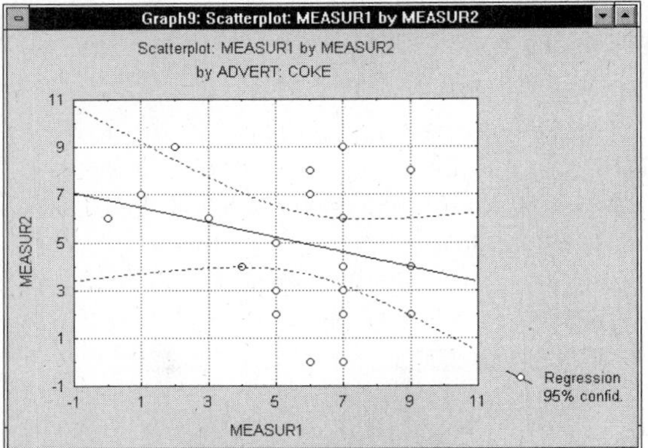

If the */w names* button is used, then the scatterplot will identify the points in the scatterplot with the case numbers or names (if case names are specified in the respective data file).

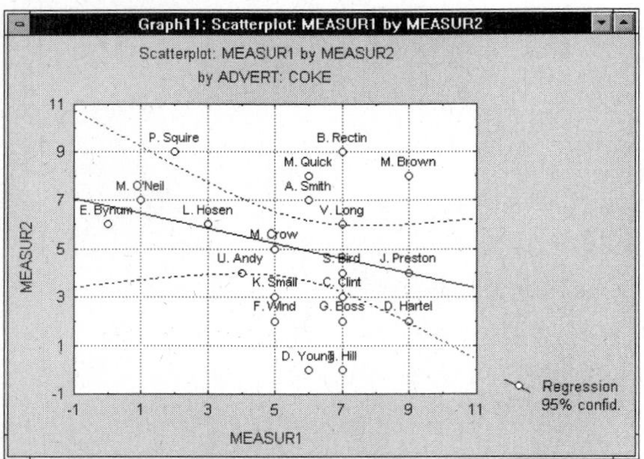

Many other types of scatterplots are available via the *Stats Graphs* options [accessible from the pull-down menu *Graphs* and the *Graph Gallery* (click on the toolbar button)].

Matrix (2D Scatterplot)

This option will produce a scatterplot matrix for the selected variables, one scatterplot matrix for each selected level of the grouping variable.

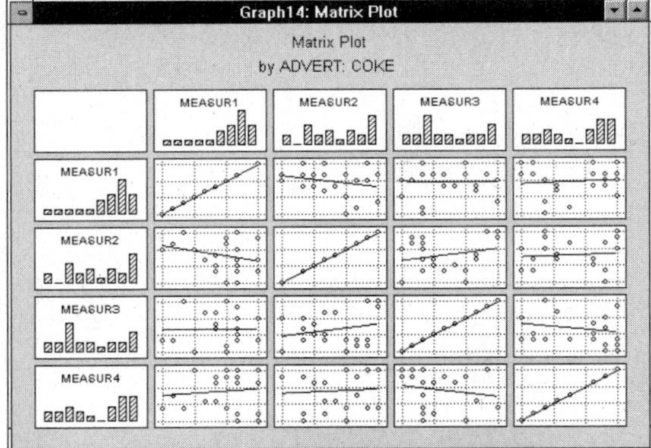

Matrix scatterplots are also available via the *Stats Graphs* options [accessible from the pull-down menu *Graphs* and the *Graph Gallery* (click on the toolbar button)].

3D Scatterplot (/with names)

This option will produce a 3D scatterplot for a selected triplet of variables and for each selected level of the grouping variable.

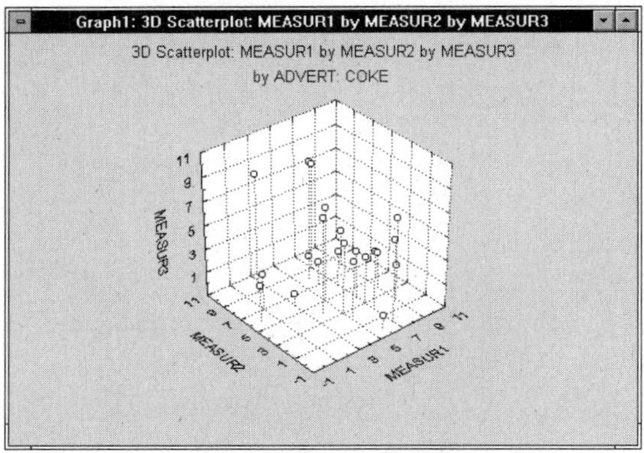

StatSoft

If a grouping variable has not been previously selected, you will be prompted to select one when you click on this button. If the */w names* button is used, then the points in the scatterplot will be identified by the case numbers or names (if case names are specified in the respective data file).

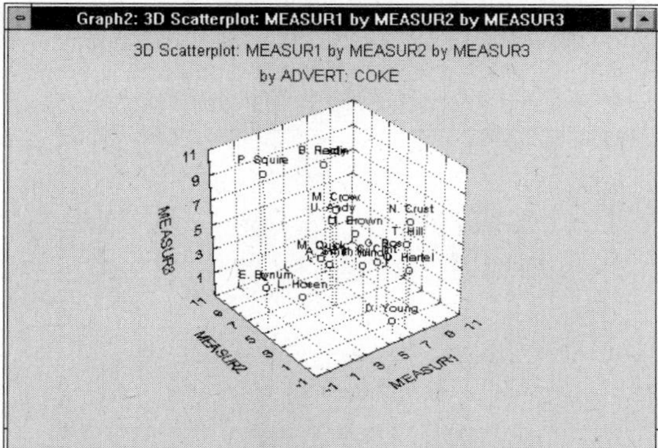

See also, *Stats Graphs* [accessible from the pull-down menu *Graphs* and the *Graph Gallery* (click on the toolbar button)].

Surface

This option will produce a 3D scatterplot for a selected triplet of variables and for each selected level of the grouping variable and fit a least squares surface to the data.

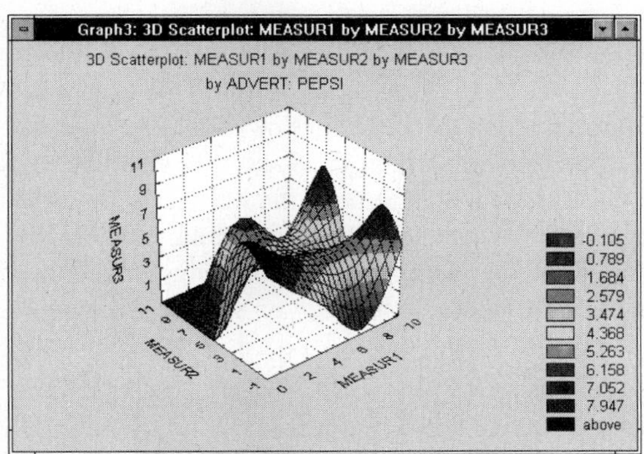

See also, *Stats Graphs* [accessible from the pull-down menu *Graphs* and the *Graph Gallery* (click on the toolbar button)].

Normal Probability Plots

This option will produce a cascade of normal probability plots for the selected variables by group (if a grouping variable was selected), one plot per selected variable per group.

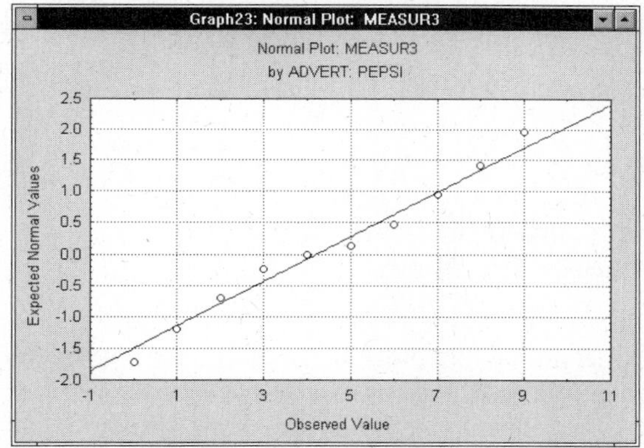

See also, *Stats Graphs* [accessible from the pull-down menu *Graphs* and the *Graph Gallery* (click on the toolbar button)].

Half-normal Probability Plots

This option will produce a cascade of half-normal probability plots for the selected variables by group (if a grouping variable was selected), one plot per selected variable per group.

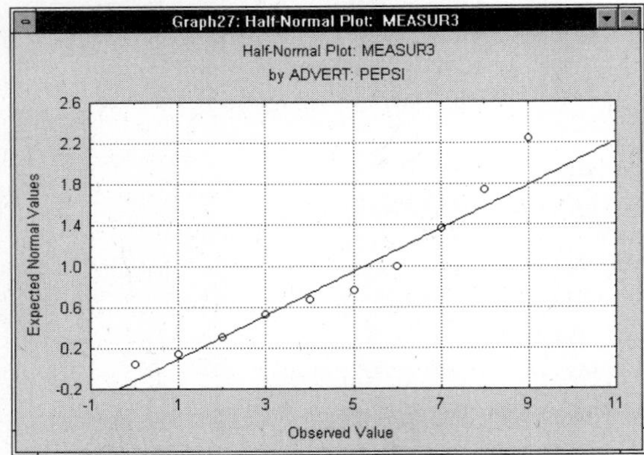

See also, *Stats Graphs* [accessible from the pull-down menu *Graphs* and the *Graph Gallery* (click on the toolbar button)].

Detrended Normal Probability Plots

This option will produce a cascade of detrended normal probability plots for the selected variables by group (if a grouping variable was selected), one plot per selected variable per group.

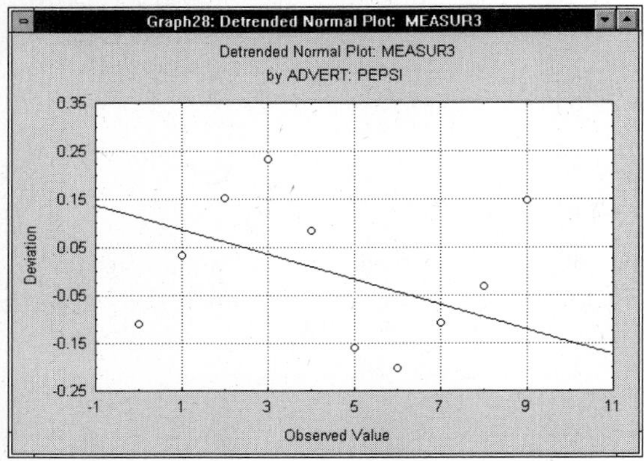

See also, *Stats Graphs* [accessible from the pull-down menu *Graphs* and the *Graph Gallery* (click on the toolbar button)].

Categorized Normal Probability Plots

This option will produce a cascade of normal probability plots for the selected variables (one plot per variable), categorized by the levels of the grouping variable.

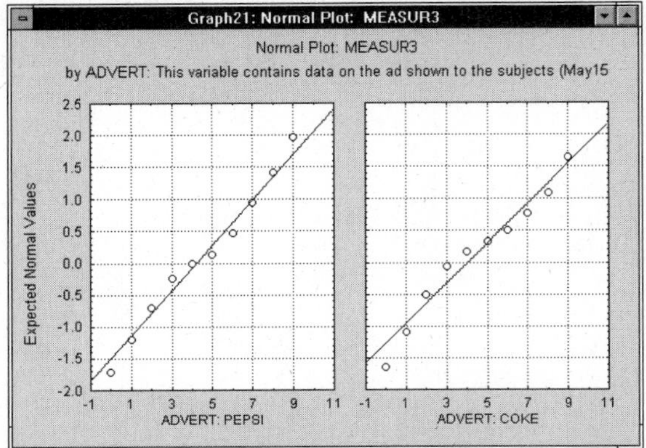

If a grouping variable has not been previously selected, you will be prompted to select one when you click on this button. See also, *Stats Graphs* [accessible from the pull-down menu *Graphs* and the *Graph Gallery* (click on the toolbar button)].

Categorized Scatterplots

This option will produce a cascade of categorized scatterplots for selected pairs of variables, one plot per pair. After clicking on this button, the user will be prompted to select two lists of variables (from the list of dependent variables). Scatterplots will be produced for each variable in the first list with each variable in the second list, categorized by the levels of the grouping variable. (If a grouping variable has not been previously selected, you will be prompted to select one when you click on this button.)

If the */w names* button is used, then the scatterplot will identify the points in the categorized scatterplot with the case numbers or names (if case names are specified in the respective data file).

3D Bivariate Distribution Histogram

This option will produce a cascade of 3D histograms for selected pairs of variables by group (if a grouping variable was selected).

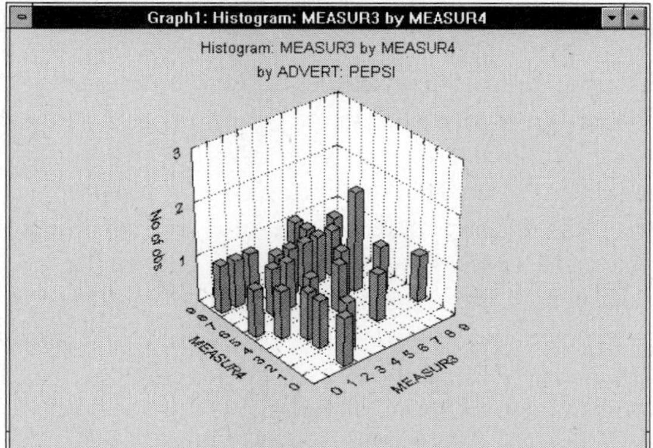

After clicking on this button, the user is first prompted to select the groups by which the 3D histogram will be produced. Once selected, you will then be prompted to select two lists of variables (from among those originally selected via the *Variables* option). 3D histograms will be produced for each variable in the first list with each variable in the second list for each previously selected level of the grouping variable.

Note that in order to produce histograms, normal probability plots, or box plots representing the distribution of the values in cases (and not variables), use the *Block Stats Graphs* options available from the flying menu, *Graphs* pull-down menu, or in the *Graphs Gallery* (instead of transposing your data file; see Chapter 3, *Spreadsheet Window*).

PROBABILITY CALCULATOR

When you select the *Quick Basic Stats - Probability Calculator* option from either the *Analysis* pull-down menu, right-mouse-button flying menu, or the toolbar button menu, you can choose to open the *Probability Distribution Calculator* (select *Chi*^{2}, *F*, *Z*, or *More...* from the extended menu) or *Pearson Product Moment Correlation Distribution* dialog (select *Corr* from the extended menu).

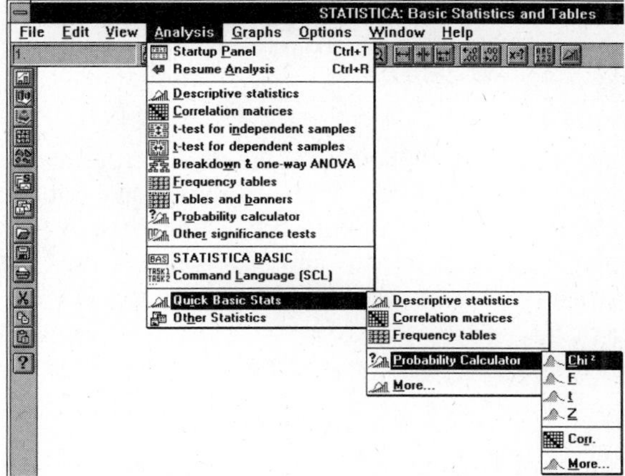

The *Probability Distribution Calculator* and *Pearson Product Moment Correlation Distribution* dialogs are discussed below.

Probability Distribution Calculator

Introductory Overview

The *Probability Distribution Calculator* facility allows you to compute, for various theoretical distributions and parameters (e.g., *F*, *df 1*, *df 2*), either (1) the upper or lower tail areas, given a user-specified variate value (two-sided probability values can be computed for symmetrical distributions; e.g.,

the normal distribution), or (2) the critical values, given a user-specified probability value.

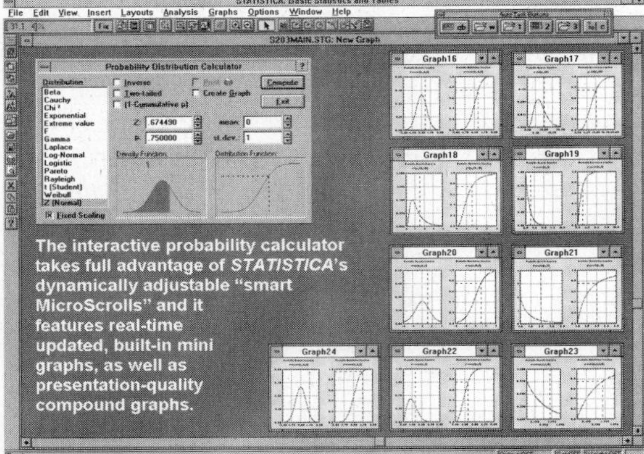

The interactive probability calculator takes full advantage of STATISTICA's dynamically adjustable "smart MicroScrolls" and it features real-time updated, built-in mini graphs, as well as presentation-quality compound graphs.

One of the useful functions of the *Probability Distribution Calculator* facility is to compute critical values for statistical significance testing, or to compute *p*-levels (significance levels), given the variate values of a particular distribution (usually *F*, *t*, or *z*). The *Elementary Concepts* chapter (Chapter 8) describes the logic behind statistical significance testing.

Distributions

The following distributions are available in this dialog. For more information on the probability distribution function as well as the specific parameters for each distribution, see *Appendix I*.

- *Beta*
- Cauchy
- *Chi-square*
- Exponential
- Extreme Value
- *F*
- *Gamma*
- Laplace
- Logistic
- Lognormal
- Pareto
- Rayleigh
- *t* (Student)
- Weibull
- *Z* (Normal)

Fixed Scaling

This option affects the scaling of the (continuously updated) graph depicted in the two icons at the bottom of the dialog, and the graphs that are produced if you select the option *Create Graph*. When this option is selected, the program will use a fixed scale for the graphs, and as you change the parameters of the respective distribution, you can observe the changes in the graph relative to the same fixed scales. Note that for extreme parameter settings, this may result in the graphs "running-off the screen." To avoid this, deselect the *Fixed Scale* option, which causes the program to recompute the optimum scaling for the graphs for each parameter setting, resulting in optimum resolution.

Fixed Scale: ON

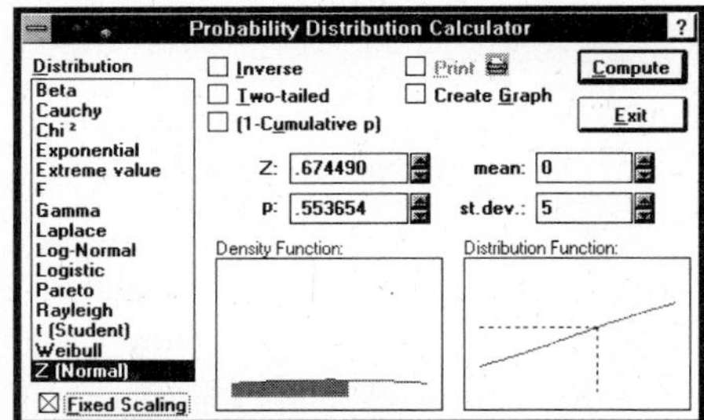

Fixed Scale: OFF

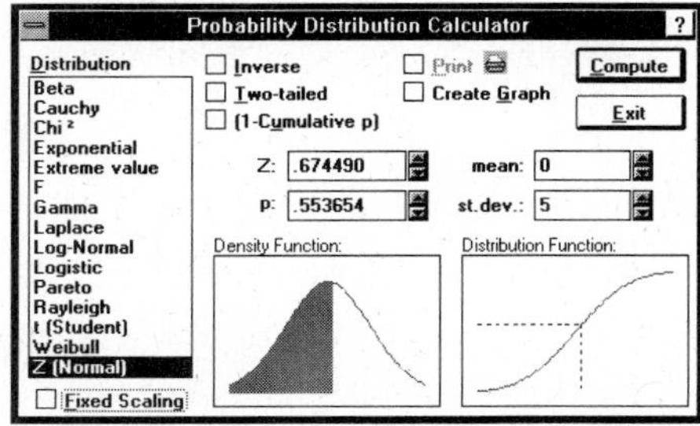

However, for some distributions, this will give the appearance that the shapes of the functions are not changing in response to different parameter settings; this happens, for example, when you change the *st.dev.* (standard deviation) parameter for the normal (*z*) distribution, while the *Fixed Scale* option is deselected.

Inverse

When set, this option allows you to compute the inverse of the integral; that is, you can enter a desired significance level and *STATISTICA* will compute the critical value of the respective statistic. Note that if you change the value of *p* in the respective edit field, then this option will automatically be selected.

Two-Tailed

This option allows you to specify a two-tailed (set the check box) or one-tailed test. This option is only available for symmetric distributions.

(1-Cumulative *p*)

Set this check box in order to compute the critical value for the specified distribution based on a (1-cumulative *p*) value or the (1-cumulative *p*) value based on a specified critical value.

Distribution Variate

This edit field displays the current variate value for the selected distribution. When you edit this value (either manually or with the *MicroScrolls*), *STATISTICA* will compute the associated *p* value for the distribution with the distribution parameters. For more information on the specific distribution or parameters for the distribution, see *Appendix I.*

p-Value

This edit field displays the *p*-value computed from the specified variate value and degrees of freedom or you can enter a desired *p*-value and compute the critical value for the specified degrees of freedom.

Distribution Parameters

Specific parameters are displayed for each distribution. If the distribution parameters are changed, then the *p*-value will be recomputed based on the respective variate value (see above). For more information on the parameters for each distribution in this dialog, see *Appendix I.*

Print

Set this check box if you want to print (send to the printer, file, and/or *Text/output Window* whichever output destination you selected in the *Page/Output Setup* dialog, see Chapter 3) the *p*-value and critical value for the specified distribution and parameters. These values will be printed when you click on the *Compute* button, and not when you change the parameters with the *MicroScrolls*. Therefore, you can edit the parameters using the *MicroScrolls* and review the results in the edit fields in the dialog, then when you are ready, click on the *Compute* button to print the resulting values. In order to print the graphs created when you select the *Create Graph* option, you can use the *Print Graph* option or the graphics window *Print Graph* toolbar button to print the selected graphs, or if the *Automatically Print All Graphs* option was previously selected (in the *Page/Output Setup* dialog), then the graphs will automatically be printed when they are created.

Create Graph

Set this option if you would like the probability density function and cumulative distribution function graphs for the specified distribution and parameters to be placed in a compound graph (see Volume II for more information on compound graphs).

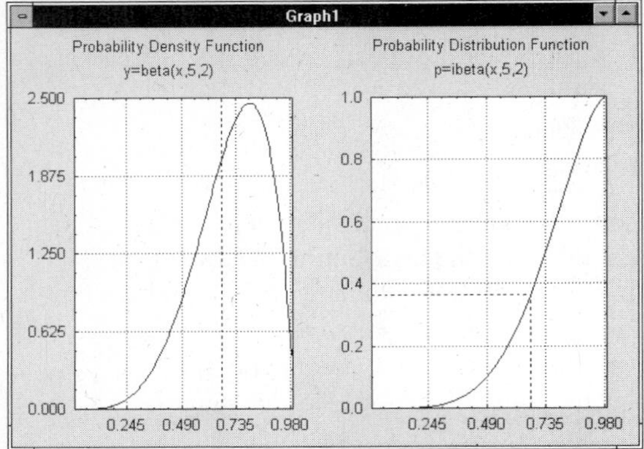

The graph will be created when you click on the *Compute* button, and not when you change the parameters with the *MicroScrolls*. Therefore, you can edit the parameters using the *MicroScrolls* and review the results in the graph icons in the dialog, then when you are ready, click on the *Compute* button to create the desired graph. In order to print the graphs created when you select the *Create Graph* option, you can use the *Print Graph* option or the graphics window *Print Graph* toolbar button to print the selected graphs, or if the *Automatically Print All Graphs* option was previously selected (in the *Page/Output Setup* dialog), then the graphs will automatically be printed when they are created.

Compute

Clicking on this button will enter the value currently edited in an edit box (if *MicroScrolls* are not used) and will compute the *p*-value or critical value for the specified distribution based on the distribution's parameters and (when the respective options are checked):

- *Print* the resulting critical value and *p*-value to the printer, file, and/or *Text/output Window* (whichever output destination you selected in the *Page/Output Setup* dialog);
- *Create* a compound graph containing the probability density function and cumulative distribution function for the specified distribution and parameters.

Pearson Product Moment Correlation Distribution

Introductory Overview

The most widely-used type of correlation coefficient is *Pearson r*, also called *linear* or *product-moment* correlation. It is the basic type of correlation that is offered in *Quick Basic Stats* (in every module) and the *Basic Statistics and Tables* module (see Chapter 9 for an overview of correlations). Using non-technical language, one can say that the correlation coefficient determines the extent to which values of two variables are "proportional" to each other. The value of the correlation (i.e., correlation coefficient) does not depend on the specific measurement units used; for example, the correlation between height and weight will be identical regardless of whether *inches and pounds*, or *centimeters and kilograms* are used as measurement units. *Proportional* means *linearly related*; that is, the correlation is high if it can be approximated by a straight line (sloped upwards or downwards). This line is called the *regression line* or *least squares line*, because it is determined such that the sum of the *squared* distances of all the data points from the line is the lowest possible. The Pearson product moment correlation coefficient is calculated as follows:

$$r_{12} = \Sigma(Y_{i1}\text{-Y-bar}_1)*(Y_{i2}\text{-Y-bar}_2) / [\Sigma(Y_{i1}\text{-Y-bar}_1)^2 * \Sigma(Y_{i2}\text{-Y-bar}_2)^2]^{1/2}$$

The *Pearson Product Moment Correlation Distribution* dialog allows you to compute the *p* value for a given correlation coefficient or you can enter a desired *p* value and determine the correlation coefficient (based on a specified sample size). The test of significance is based on the assumption that the distribution of the residual values (i.e., the deviations from the regression line) for the

dependent variable *y* follows the normal distribution, and that the variability of the residual values is the same for all values of the independent variable *x*.

The options available in this dialog are discussed below.

Parameters

The parameters in this dialog are *N* (the sample size), *r* (the correlation coefficient), *p* (the significance level), and Fisher *Z* (the critical value of the distribution). These parameters can be specified or computed (see below).

Two-tailed

You can choose to perform a one-tailed (de-select this option) or two-tailed (select this option) test via this option.

Compute *p* from *r*

Select this option in order to compute the *p*-level and *Z* value based on a specified correlation coefficient *r* and sample size *N*.

Compute *r* from *p*

Select this option in order to compute *r* and the *Z* value based on a specified *p*-level and sample size *N*.

Compute *r* from *Z*

Select this option in order to compute *r* and the *p*-level based on a specified *Z* value and sample size *N*.

Print

Set this check box if you want to print (send to the printer, file, and/or *Text/output Window* whichever output destination you selected in the *Page/Output Setup* dialog, see Chapter 3) the results of the computation. These values will be printed when you click on the *Compute* button, and not when you change the parameters with the *MicroScrolls*. Therefore, you can edit the parameters using the *MicroScrolls* and review the results in the edit fields in the dialog, then when you are ready, click on the *Compute* button to print the resulting values.

Compute

Click on this button to perform the computations and *Print* the results (if the *Print* check box is set (see above).

INDEX

Chapter 11:

NONPARAMETRIC STATISTICS AND DISTRIBUTION FITTING

Table of Contents

Detailed Table of Contents

Chapter 11: NONPARAMETRIC STATISTICS AND DISTRIBUTION FITTING

INTRODUCTORY OVERVIEW

General Purpose

Brief review of the idea of significance testing. To understand the idea of *nonparametric* statistics first requires a basic understanding of *parametric* statistics. The *Elementary Concepts* chapter (Chapter 8) introduces the concept of statistical significance testing based on the sampling distribution of a particular statistic (you may want to review that chapter before reading on). In short, if you have a basic knowledge of the underlying distribution of a variable, then you can make predictions about how, in repeated samples of equal size, this particular statistic will "behave," that is, how it is distributed.

For example, if you draw 100 random samples of 100 adults each from the general population, and compute the mean height in each sample, then the distribution of the means across samples will likely approximate the normal distribution (to be precise, Student's *t* distribution with 99 degrees of freedom; see below). Now imagine that you take an additional sample in a particular city ("Tallburg") where you suspect that people are taller than the average population. If the mean height in that sample falls outside the upper 95% tail area of the *t* distribution, then you conclude that, indeed, the people of Tallburg are taller than the average population.

Are most variables normally distributed? In the above example, you relied on your knowledge that in repeated samples of equal size, the means (for height) will be distributed following the *t* distribution (with a particular mean and variance). However, this will only be true if in the population the variable of interest (height in this example) is normally distributed, that is, if the distribution of people of particular heights follows the normal distribution. For many variables of interest, you simply do not know for sure that this is the case. For example, is income distributed normally in the population? -- probably not. The incidence rates of rare diseases are not normally distributed in the population, the number of car accidents is also not normally distributed, and neither are very many other variables in which a researcher might be interested.

Sample size. Another factor that often limits the applicability of tests based on the assumption that the sampling distribution is normal is the size of the sample of data available for the analysis (*sample size*; *n*). You can assume that the sampling distribution is normal even if you are not sure that the distribution of the variable in the population is normal, as long as your sample is large enough (e.g., 100 or more observations). However, if your sample is very small, then those tests can be used only if you are sure that the variable is normally distributed, and there is no way to test this assumption if the sample is small.

Problems in measurement. Applications of tests that are based on the normality assumptions are further limited by a lack of precise measurement. For example, consider a study where grade point average (*GPA*) is measured as the major variable of interest. Is an A average twice as good as a C average? Is the difference between a B and an A average comparable to the difference between a D and a C average? Somehow, the GPA is a crude measure of scholastic accomplishments that only allows one to establish a rank ordering of students from "good" students to "poor" students. This general measurement issue is usually discussed in statistics textbooks in terms of *types of measurement* or *scale of measurement* (see also *Elementary Concepts*, Chapter 8) . Without going into too much detail, most common statistical techniques such as analysis of variance (and *t*-tests), regression, etc. assume that the underlying measurements are at least of *interval* quality, meaning that equally-spaced intervals on the scale can be compared in a meaningful manner (e.g., *B* minus *A* is equal to *D* minus *C*). However, as in this example, this assumption is very often not tenable, and the data rather represent a *rank* ordering of observations (*ordinal* scale) rather than precise measurements.

Parametric and nonparametric methods. Hopefully, after this somewhat lengthy introduction, the need is evident for statistical procedures that allow you to process data of "low quality" from small samples, on variables about which nothing is known (concerning their distribution). Specifically, nonparametric methods were developed to be used in cases when the researcher knows nothing about the parameters of the variable of interest in the population (hence the name *nonparametric*).

In more technical terms, nonparametric methods do not rely on the estimation of parameters (such as the mean or the standard deviation) describing the distribution of the variable of interest in the population. Therefore, these methods are also sometimes (and more appropriately) called *parameter-free* methods or *distribution-free* methods.

Brief Overview of Nonparametric Procedures

Basically, there is at least one nonparametric equivalent for each parametric general type of test. In general, these tests fall into the following categories:

- Tests of differences between groups (independent samples);
- Tests of differences between variables (dependent samples);
- Tests of relationships between variables.

Differences between independent groups. Usually, when you have two samples that you want to compare concerning their mean value for some variable of interest, you would use the *t*-test for independent samples (in *Basic Statistics and Tables*, Chapter 9); nonparametric alternatives for this test are the *Wald-Wolfowitz runs* test, the *Mann-Whitney U* test, and the *Kolmogorov-Smirnov two-sample* test. If you have multiple groups, you would use analysis of variance (see *ANOVA/MANOVA*, Chapter 13); the nonparametric equivalents to this method are the *Kruskal-Wallis* analysis of ranks and the *Median* test.

Differences between dependent groups. If you want to compare two variables measured in the same sample, you would customarily use the *t*-test for dependent samples (in *Basic Statistics and Tables*, Chapter 9); for example, if you wanted to compare students' math skills at the beginning of the semester with their skills at the end of the semester. Nonparametric alternatives to this test are the *Sign* test and *Wilcoxon's matched pairs* test. If the variables of interest are categorical in nature (i.e., "pass" vs. "no pass"), then *McNemar's Chi-square* test is appropriate.

If there are more than two variables that were measured in the same sample, then a repeated measures ANOVA would customarily be used. Nonparametric alternatives to this method are *Friedman's two-way analysis of variance* and *Cochran Q test* (if the variable was measured in terms of categories, e.g., "passed" vs. "failed"). Cochran *Q* is particularly useful for measuring changes in frequencies (proportions) across time.

Relationships between variables. To express a relationship between two variables, one usually computes the correlation coefficient. Nonparametric equivalents to the standard correlation coefficient are *Spearman R*, *Kendall tau*, and coefficient *Gamma* (see *Nonparametric Correlation*, page 1609). If the two variables of interest are categorical in nature (e.g., "passed" vs. "failed" by "male" vs. "female") appropriate nonparametric statistics for testing the relationship between the two variables are the *Chi-square* test, the *Phi* coefficient, and the *Fisher exact* test (see *Nonparametrics and Distributions Startup Panel*, page 1599). In addition, a simultaneous test for relationships between multiple variables is available: *Kendall coefficient of concordance*. This test is often used for expressing inter-rater agreement among independent judges who are rating (ranking) the same stimuli.

Descriptive statistics. When one's data are not normally distributed, and the measurements at best contain rank order information, then computing the standard descriptive statistics (e.g., mean, standard deviation) is sometimes not the most informative way to summarize the data. For example, in the area of psychometrics it is well known that the *rated* intensity of a stimulus (e.g., perceived brightness of a light) is often a logarithmic function of the actual intensity of the stimulus (brightness as measured in objective units of *Lux*).

In this example, the simple mean rating (sum of ratings divided by the number of stimuli) is not an adequate summary of the average actual intensity of the stimuli. (In this example, one would probably rather compute the geometric mean.) The *Nonparametrics and Distributions* module will compute a wide variety of measures of location (mean, median, mode, etc.) and dispersion (variance, average deviation, quartile range, etc.) to provide the "complete picture" of one's data (see *Descriptive Statistics*, page 1603).

When to Use Which Method

It is not easy to give simple advice concerning the use of nonparametric procedures. Each nonparametric procedure has its peculiar sensitivities and blind spots. For example, the Kolmogorov-Smirnov two-sample test is not only sensitive to differences in the location of distributions (for example, differences in means) but is also greatly affected by differences in their shapes. The Wilcoxon matched pairs test assumes that one can rank order the magnitude of differences in matched observations in a meaningful manner. If this is not the case, one should rather use the Sign test. In general, if the result of a study is important (e.g., does a very expensive and painful drug therapy help people get better?), then it is always advisable to run different nonparametric tests; should discrepancies in the results occur contingent upon which test is used, one should try to understand why some tests give different results. On the other hand, nonparametric statistics are less statistically powerful (sensitive) than their parametric counterparts, and if it is important to detect even small effects (e.g., is this food additive harmful to people?) one should be very careful in the choice of a test statistic.

Large data sets and nonparametric methods. Nonparametric methods are most appropriate when the sample sizes are small. When the data set is large (e.g., $n > 100$) it often makes little sense to use nonparametric statistics at all. The *Elementary Concepts* chapter (Chapter 8) briefly discusses the idea of the *central limit theorem*. In a nutshell, when the samples become very large, then the sample means will follow the normal distribution even if the respective variable is not normally distributed in the population or is not measured very well. Thus, parametric methods, which are usually much more sensitive (i.e., have more statistical power) are in most cases appropriate for large samples. However, the tests of significance of many

of the nonparametric statistics described here are based on asymptotic (large sample) theory; therefore, meaningful tests can often not be performed if the sample sizes become too small. Please refer to the descriptions of the specific tests to learn more about their power and efficiency.

Distribution Fitting

In some research applications one can formulate hypotheses about the specific distribution of the variable of interest. For example, variables whose values are determined by an infinite number of independent random events will be distributed following the normal distribution: one can think of a person's height as being the result of many independent factors such as numerous specific genetic predispositions, early childhood diseases, nutrition, etc. As a result, height tends to be normally distributed in the US population. On the other hand, if the values of a variable are the result of very rare events, then the variable will be distributed according to the *Poisson* distribution (sometimes called the distribution of rare events). For example, industrial accidents can be thought of as the result of the intersection of a series of unfortunate (and unlikely) events, and their frequency tends to be distributed according to the Poisson distribution. These and other available distributions are described in greater detail later in this chapter.

The *Nonparametrics and Distributions* module allows you to test the goodness of fit of your data to the respective hypothesized distribution. You can also enter any set of arbitrary expected values (i.e., "make up" a hypothesized distribution) and test the fit of an observed set of values (*observed vs. expected* frequencies).

Normality assumption. Another common application where distribution fitting procedures are useful is when one wants to verify the assumption of normality before using some parametric test (see above).

Distribution Fitting via *Stats 2D Graphs* Options and the *Process Analysis* Module

Beginning with release 5 of *STATISTICA*, there are several alternative procedures available for fitting continuous distributions to data. Specifically, you can choose (categorized or non-categorized) *Quantile-Quantile* plots, *Probability-Probability* plots, or *2D Histograms* (with a line indicating the expected frequencies) from the *Graphs* pull-down menu, and then choose to produce the respective plots based on the *Normal*, *Beta*, *Extreme Value*, *Gamma*, *Geometric*, *Laplace*, *Logistic*, *Lognormal*, *Poisson*, *Rayleigh*, and *Weibull* distributions. The program will compute maximum likelihood parameter estimates for the respective distributions (see Volume II for additional details).

The *Process Analysis* module of *STATISTICA* (see Volume IV) also contains several options for fitting these distributions, and for computing tables with expected and observed frequencies. That module also has an option to fit simultaneously all of these continuous distributions to the data; the results Scrollsheet for this option contains the respective Kolmogorov-Smirnov *d-max* values, sorted in ascending order (i.e., from the best-fitting to the worst-fitting distribution).

Structure of this Chapter

This chapter of the manual is structured somewhat differently than the chapters pertaining to other statistical procedures. In a sense, the *Nonparametrics and Distributions* module is a complete statistical package all by itself, with many different procedures for different types of data and

research questions. Therefore, the reference section (starting on page 1599) which discusses each method in greater detail and compares it to other alternative methods is discussed first. After that section, examples are provided for each statistical procedure (starting on page 1619).

PROGRAM OVERVIEW

Nonparametric Statistics

The *Nonparametrics and Statistics* module contains a comprehensive set of inferential and descriptive statistics for analyzing ordinal and nominal data. Additional, more specialized techniques are also available in other modules of *STATISTICA*; refer to the *Alternative Procedures* below.

Alternatives to the *t*-test for independent samples. Available alternatives to the *t*-test for independent samples are the Wald-Wolfowitz Runs test, Mann-Whitney *U* test, and the Kolmogorov-Smirnov two sample test.

Alternatives to the *t*-test for dependent (correlated) samples. Available alternatives to the *t*-test for dependent (correlated) samples are the sign test and Wilcoxon matched pairs test.

Alternatives to between-groups ANOVA. Available alternatives to between-groups ANOVA are the Kruskal-Wallis ANOVA by ranks and the Median test.

Alternatives to within-subjects (repeated measures) ANOVA. Available alternatives are the Spearman *R*, Kendall *tau*, *Gamma*, and Kendall coefficient of concordance.

Procedures for frequency data. The *Nonparametrics and Distributions* module includes numerous statistics for analyzing 2 x 2 frequency tables: *Chi-square*, *V-square*, Fisher exact test, *Phi-square* (an alternative to correlation), and McNemar's *Chi-square* (for testing changes in frequencies); Cochran's *Q* test is an alternative to repeated measures ANOVA if the variable of interest is categorical. Note that other *STATISTICA* modules also contain many additional procedures for analyzing frequency data (see *Alternative Procedures*, below).

Descriptive statistics. The *Nonparametrics and Distributions* module will compute an extensive set of descriptive statistics including the mean, median, mode, percentiles (user-defined), geometric mean, harmonic mean, standard deviation, variance, average deviation, range, quartile range, skewness, kurtosis, etc.

Distribution Fitting

The *Nonparametrics and Distributions* module will tabulate observed data and compute the respective expected values for a variety of continuous and discrete distributions. Distribution fitting plots are available from within the summary Scrollsheets. The program will compute the *Chi-square* test and Kolmogorov-Smirnov single-sample test to evaluate the fit of the observed data to the hypothesized distribution. Continuous distributions available in this module include the normal distribution, rectangular distribution, exponential distribution, *Gamma* distribution, log-normal distribution, and *Chi-square* distribution; discrete distributions include the binomial distribution, Poisson distribution, geometric distribution, and Bernoulli distribution. The user can also evaluate the fit of the observed data to any arbitrary (user-defined) set of expected frequencies. Note that additional, specialized distributions (e.g., Weibull, Gompertz) are available in the *Survival Analysis* module (see Volume III), in the *Process Analysis* module (see Volume IV), or via the *Stats 2D Graphs - Quantile-Quantile* plots, *Probability-Probability* plots, and *Histograms* options (see Volume II; see also *Alternative Procedures*, below).

Alternative Procedures

Correlations. You can compute standard (Pearson product moment) correlations in every module of

STATISTICA via the *Quick Basic Stats* options (available from the toolbar and the *Analysis* pull-down menu; see Chapter 10 for details) as well as in many other modules (e.g., *Basic Statistics and Tables*, Chapter 9; *Multiple Regression*, Chapter 12; *Factor Analysis*, Volume III; *Megafile Manager*, Volume III). Tetrachoric correlations can be calculated in the *Reliability and Item Analysis* module (see Volume III). Various measures of distances can be computed in the *Cluster Analysis* module. Various measures of relations between categorical (nominal) variables are available in the crosstabulation part of the *Basic Statistics and Tables* module (Chapter 9).

The *Nonlinear Estimation* module (Volume III) contains various pre-defined nonlinear regression models for analyzing categorical dependent variables (probit and logit analysis); the user can also specify any arbitrary type of regression equation in that module. The *Survival Analysis* module (Volume III) contains specialized regression routines for handling survival and failure time data (option *Regression Models* in the startup panel of that module); some of these routines are also nonparametric (parameter-free) in nature (e.g., Cox proportional hazard regression).

Frequency (contingency) tables. Additional nonparametric measures of contingency between two categorical variables can be obtained from the *Basic Statistics and Tables* module (*Chi-square* tests, Kendall *tau b*, *tau c*, entropy measures, and coefficients of dependence; see Chapter 9). The *Log-Linear* module (Volume III) is a comprehensive program for analyzing multi-level, multi-way contingency tables. The *STATISTICA* package also contains an example *STATISTICA BASIC* program (file *Manthaen.stb* in the *STBASIC* subdirectory) for computing the Mantel-Haenszel test for comparing two groups (see Mantel and Haenszel, 1959; see also Lee, 1992). Refer to the comments included in file *Manthaen.stb* for additional details.

Distribution fitting. The *Survival Analysis* module (Volume III) will fit the Weibull and Gompertz distributions to observed survival or failure time data. That module will also handle incomplete (censored) observations.

The *Stats 2D Graphs* histogram options (see the pull-down menu *Graphs*) offer a variety of facilities to produce simple, cumulative, multiple, and categorized graphs of frequency distributions; available distributions include *Normal*, *Beta*, *Extreme Value*, *Gamma*, *Geometric*, *Laplace*, *Logistic*, *Lognormal*, *Poisson*, *Rayleigh*, and *Weibull* (see Appendix I for a description of these distributions). You can also produce *Quantile-Quantile* and *Probability-Probability* plots for these distributions, and thus evaluate the fit of the respective distribution to the observed data. These options are described in detail in Volume II of the manual.

The *Process Analysis* module of *STATISTICA* (see Volume IV) also contains several options for fitting these distributions, and for computing tables with expected and observed frequencies. That module also offers an option to fit simultaneously all of these continuous distributions to the data; the results Scrollsheet for this option contains the respective Kolmogorov-Smirnov *d-max* values, sorted in ascending order (i.e., from the best-fitting to the worst-fitting distribution).

DIALOGS, OPTIONS, STATISTICS

Startup Panels

The startup panel dialogs (i.e., the two layers of the startup dialog) give access to all nonparametric statistics and distribution fitting procedures included in this module.

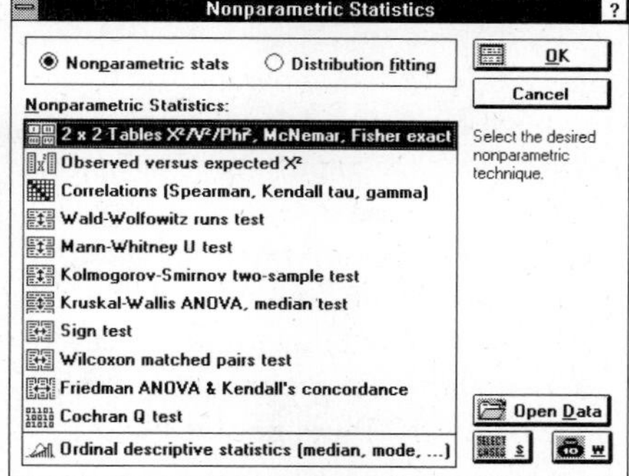

You can switch between the layers by selecting the respective radio button in the upper part of the dialog.

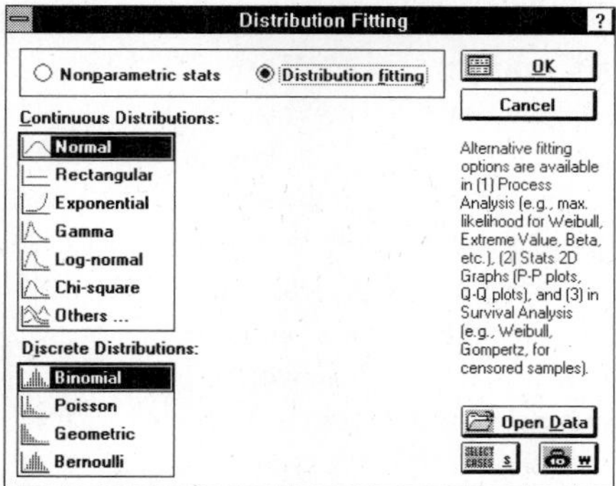

Each of these options are described in the following sections.

Startup Panel - Nonparametric Statistics

2 x 2 Tables, *Chi/V/Phi-square*, McNemar, Fisher Exact

This option will bring up a dialog that allows the user to enter frequencies into a 2 x 2 table, and to calculate various statistics to evaluate the relationship between two dichotomous variables. For more information on this option, see page 1608.

The 2 x 2 option can be used as an alternative to correlation when the two variables of interest are dichotomous. *STATISTICA* will also compute the McNemar *Chi-square* test for the significance of changes. In that case, one can think of the 2 x 2 option as an alternative to the *t*-test for dependent samples when the variable of interest is dichotomous.

Observed vs. Expected *Chi-square*

This option allows the user to evaluate the fit of data (frequencies) to any arbitrary set of expected frequencies (see also page 1609). The option will prompt the user to enter 2 variables, one containing the expected and another containing the observed frequencies. The standard *Chi-square* value is then computed.

Correlations (Spearman *R*, Kendall *tau*, *Gamma*)

This option allows the user to compute three different alternatives to the parametric Pearson product-moment correlation coefficient: Spearman *R*, Kendall *tau*, and *Gamma* (see page 1609 for descriptions of each). After selecting this option, a dialog will be displayed from which the user can select variables, and the specific type of correlation to be computed. The user can choose to compute single nonparametric correlations, or matrices of

nonparametric correlations. A scatterplot matrix for all variables can be produced by clicking on the *Matrix plot* button. The results Scrollsheet features the scatterplot as the default graph, so the user can easily graph the correlations. Note that alternative nonparametric measures of contingency between two variables are also available in *Basic Statistics and Tables*, Chapter 9.

Wald-Wolfowitz Runs Test

The Wald-Wolfowitz runs test is a nonparametric alternative to the *t*-test for independent samples (see *Basic Statistics and Tables*, Chapter 9). The option expects the data to be arranged in the same way as for the *t*-test for independent samples (see *Basic Statistics and Tables*, Chapter 9). Specifically, the data file should contain a coding variable (*independent* variable) with at least two distinct codes that uniquely identify the group membership of each case in the data file.

Choosing this option will bring up a dialog for selecting the coding variable and a dependent variable list (variables in which the two groups are to be compared), and the codes used in the coding variable for identifying the two groups (option *Codes*).

Assumptions and interpretation. The Wald-Wolfowitz runs test works as follows: Imagine that you want to compare male and female subjects on some variable. You can sort the data by that variable and look for cases when, in the sorted data, same-gender subjects are adjacent to each other. If there are no differences between male and female subjects, then the number and "lengths" of such adjacent "runs" of subjects of the same gender will be more or less random. If not, the two groups (genders in this example) are somehow different from each other.

This test assumes that the variable under consideration is continuous, and that it was measured on at least an ordinal scale (i.e., rank order). The Wald-Wolfowitz runs test assesses the hypothesis that two independent samples were drawn from two populations that differ in some respect, i.e., not just with respect to the mean, but also with respect to the general shape of the distribution. The null hypothesis is that the two samples were drawn from the same population. In this respect, this test is different from the parametric *t*-test which strictly tests for differences in locations (means) of two samples.

Mann-Whitney *U* Test

The Mann-Whitney *U* test is a nonparametric alternative to the *t*-test for independent samples (see, *Basic Statistics and Tables*, Chapter 9). The option expects the data to be arranged in the same way as for the *t*-test for independent samples. Specifically, the data file should contain a coding variable (*independent* variable) with at least two distinct codes that uniquely identify the group membership of each case in the data file. Pressing this button will bring up a dialog for selecting the coding variable and a dependent variable list (variables on which the two groups are to be compared), and the codes used in the coding variable for identifying the two groups (option *Codes*).

Assumptions and interpretation. The Mann-Whitney *U* test assumes that the variable under consideration was measured on at least an ordinal (rank order) scale. The interpretation of the test is essentially identical to the interpretation of the result of a *t*-test for independent samples, except that the *U* test is computed based on rank sums rather than means. The *U* test is the most powerful (or sensitive) nonparametric alternative to the *t*-test for independent samples; in fact, in some instances it may offer even *greater* power to reject the null hypothesis than the *t*-test.

Kolmogorov-Smirnov Two-Sample Test

The Kolmogorov-Smirnov test is another nonparametric alternative to the *t*-test for independent samples (see, *Basic Statistics and Tables*, Chapter 9). The option expects the data to be arranged in the same way as for the *t*-test for independent samples. Specifically, the data file should contain a coding variable (*independent* variable) with at least two distinct codes that uniquely identify the group membership of each case in the data file.

Choosing this option will bring up a dialog for selecting the coding variable and a dependent variable list (variables on which the two groups are to be compared), and the codes used in the coding variable for identifying the two groups (option *Codes*).

Assumptions and interpretation. The Kolmogorov-Smirnov test assesses the hypothesis that two samples were drawn from different populations. Unlike the parametric *t*-test for independent samples or the Mann-Whitney *U* test (see above), which test for differences in the location of two samples (differences in means, differences in average ranks, respectively), the Kolmogorov-Smirnov test is also sensitive to differences in the *general shapes* of the distributions in the two samples (i.e., to differences in dispersion, skewness, etc.). Thus, its interpretation is similar to that of the Wald-Wolfowitz runs test (see above).

Kruskal-Wallis ANOVA by Ranks and Median Test

These two tests are nonparametric alternatives to between-groups one-way analysis of variance. *STATISTICA* expects the data to be arranged in the same way as one would arrange a data file for an analysis with the *ANOVA/MANOVA* module. Specifically, the data file should contain a coding variable with codes to uniquely identify the group membership of each case. Up to 10 groups can be compared.

Choosing this option will bring up a dialog window for specifying the coding variable (*Variables*) and a dependent variables list (variables on which the two groups are to be compared), and the codes (*Codes*) used in the coding variable for identifying the different groups that are to be compared.

Assumptions and interpretation. The Kruskal-Wallis ANOVA by Ranks test assumes that the variable under consideration is continuous and that it was measured on at least an ordinal (rank order) scale. The test assesses the hypothesis that the different samples in the comparison were drawn from the same distribution or from distributions with the same median. Thus, the interpretation of the Kruskal-Wallis test is basically identical to that of the parametric one-way ANOVA, except that it is based on ranks rather than means.

The Median test is a "crude" version of the Kruskal-Wallis ANOVA in that it frames the computation in terms of a contingency table. Specifically, *STATISTICA* will simply count the number of cases in each sample that fall above or below the common median, and compute the *Chi-square* value for the resulting 2 x *k* samples contingency table. Under the null hypothesis (all samples come from populations with identical medians), approximately 50% of all cases in each sample are expected to fall above (or below) the common median. The Median test is particularly useful when the scale contains artificial limits, and many cases fall at either extreme of the scale ("off the scale"). In this case, the Median test is in fact the only appropriate method for comparing samples.

Sign Test

is a nonparametric alternative to the *t*-test for dependent samples (see, *Basic Statistics and Tables*, Chapter 9). The test is applicable to situations when the researcher has two measures (e.g., under two conditions) for each subject and wants to establish

that the two measurements (or conditions) are different.

After choosing this option, a dialog will be displayed from which the user can choose variables from two lists. Each variable in the first list will be compared to each variable in the second list.

Assumptions and interpretation. The only assumption required by this test is that the underlying distribution of the variable of interest is continuous; no assumptions about the nature or shape of the underlying distribution are required. The test simply computes the number of times (across subjects) that the value of the first variable (*A*) is larger than that of the second variable (*B*).

Under the null hypothesis (stating that the two variables are not different from each other) this is expected to be the case about 50% of the time. Based on the binomial distribution you can compute a z value for the observed number of cases where $A > B$, and compute the associated tail probability for that z value. For small n's (less than 20) you may prefer to use the tabulated values found in Siegel and Castellan (1988) to evaluate statistical significance.

Wilcoxon Matched Pairs Test

This test is a nonparametric alternative to the *t*-test for dependent (correlated) samples (see *Basic Statistics and Tables*, Chapter 9). Choosing this option will bring up a dialog for specifying variables from two lists. Each variable from the first list will be compared with each variable from the second list. This is the same arrangement of data that is expected for the *t*-test (dependent samples) in the *Basic Statistics and Tables* module.

Assumptions and interpretation. The procedure assumes that the variables under consideration were measured on a scale that allows the rank ordering of observations based on each variable (i.e., ordinal scale) *and* that allows rank ordering of the *differences* between variables (this type of scale is sometimes referred to as an *ordered metric scale,* see Coombs, 1950). Thus, the required assumptions for this test are more stringent than those for the Sign test (see above). However, if they are met, that is, if the magnitudes of differences (e.g., different ratings by the same individual) contain meaningful information, then this test is more powerful than the sign test. In fact, if the assumptions for the parametric *t*-test for dependent samples (interval scale) are met, then this test is almost as powerful as the *t*-test.

Friedman ANOVA & Kendall Concordance

These two tests are somewhat different in nature, however, they require similar user input. Friedman ANOVA is a nonparametric alternative to one-way repeated measures analysis of variance (see *ANOVA-/MANOVA*, Chapter 13). The Kendall concordance statistic is similar to Spearman *R* (nonparametric correlation between two variables, see above) except that it expresses the relationship between *multiple* variables.

For Friedman ANOVA, the procedure expects the data to be arranged in the same way as one would arrange a data file for a within-subjects (repeated measures) analysis of variance with the *ANOVA/MANOVA* module. Specifically, the values for each level of the repeated measures factor should be contained in a different variable. Choosing this option will bring up a dialog for specifying a list of variables.

Assumptions and interpretation: Friedman ANOVA. The Friedman ANOVA by ranks test assumes that the variables (levels) under consideration were measured on at least an ordinal (rank order) scale. The null hypothesis for the procedure is that the different columns of data (i.e., *STATISTICA* variables) contain samples drawn from the same population, or specifically, populations with identical medians. Thus, the interpretation of

results from this option is similar to that of a repeated measures ANOVA.

Assumptions and interpretation: Kendall concordance. The Kendall concordance coefficient expresses the simultaneous association (relatedness) between *k* cases (correlated samples). For example, this statistic is commonly used to assess inter-judge reliability. Basically, the concordance coefficient is the average of all Spearman *R*'s between cases; specifically:

```
avg. Spearman R = (k*concordance-1)/(k-1)
```

Thus the general assumptions of this test are identical to that of the Spearman rank order correlation (see above).

Cochran *Q* Test

The Cochran *Q* test is an extension of McNemar's *Chi-square* test for changes (see option *2 x 2 Tables ...*, above) in frequencies or proportions to *k* (more than two) dependent samples. Specifically, it tests whether several matched frequencies or proportions differ significantly among themselves. After selecting the *Cochran Q Test* option in the startup panel, you will be prompted to specify a variable list and codes that identify the two categories or levels of the dichotomous measure. The test assumes that the variables are coded as 1's and 0's, and the codes specified by the user will cause the variables to be transformed accordingly (only for this analysis, the data file itself will not be changed).

Assumptions and interpretation. The Cochran *Q* test only requires a nominal scale, or that the data have been artificially dichotomized. A typical example where the *Q* test is useful is when one wants to compare the difficulty of dichotomous questionnaire items that can either be answered right or wrong. Here, each variable in the data file would represent one item, and contain 0's (wrong) and 1's (right). If the *Q* test is significant, then you conclude that the items are of different difficulty since different items were answered correctly by more or fewer respondents.

Startup Panel - Descriptive Statistics

Choosing this option will allow the user to calculate various ordinal descriptive statistics (median, percentiles, quartiles, range, quartile range) and other descriptive statistics (mean, harmonic mean, geometric mean, standard deviation, skewness, kurtosis, variance, average deviation, sum) for selected variables. The user can also specify specific percentile values to be computed and displayed in the Scrollsheet; by default the program will compute the quartile values, that is, the 25'th and 75'th percentiles.

In addition to the standard descriptive statistics (minimum value, maximum value, mean, valid *n*) the statistics discussed below are computed for each variable.

Median

The median value is the value that "splits the sample in half," given the respective variable. Fifty percent of the cases will fall below the median, and fifty percent will fall above the median. If the median value is very different from the mean, then the distribution of data is skewed.

Computation of the median value. When the number of observations is even, or when there are tied observations, then the definition of the median in the previous paragraph does not lead to an unambiguous computational method. The method of computation for medians, quartiles, and other percentile values in *STATISTICA* can be configured "system-wide" on the *STATISTICA Defaults: General* dialog (see Chapter 3; see also *Appendix II* for computational details), accessible from the *Options* pull-down menu. Once configured, the identical computational method will be used in all

relevant places throughout the *STATISTICA* system (e.g., when computing box and whisker plots, or when computing medians and quartiles via the respective functions in *STATISTICA BASIC*; see Volume V for a description of those functions).

Mode

The mode is the value that occurs with the greatest frequency. The frequency with which the mode occurs is also displayed; if there is a tie (i.e., more than one value occurs with equal frequency), then the respective frequency column will contain the label *multiple* to indicate that more than one mode was found.

Geometric Mean

The geometric mean is the product of all scores to the power of *1/n* (one over the valid number of cases). The geometric mean is useful in instances when you know that the measurement scale is not linear. For example, in the area of psychometrics it is well known that the *rated* intensity of a stimulus (e.g., brightness of a light) is often a logarithmic function of the actual intensity of the stimulus (brightness measured in units of *Lux*). In this instance, the geometric mean is a better "summary" of ratings than the simple mean. *STATISTICA* calculates the geometric mean via the logarithm (log):

$$\log(\text{geometric mean}) = \{\Sigma[\log(x_i)]\}/n$$

where

x_i is the *i*'th score

n is the number of valid cases

Note that if a variable contains negative values or a zero (*0*), then the geometric mean cannot be calculated.

Harmonic Mean

The harmonic mean is sometimes used to average frequencies (sample sizes). The harmonic mean is calculated as:

$$HM = n/\Sigma(1/x_i)$$

where

HM is the harmonic mean

n is the number of valid cases

x_i is the score for the *i*'th valid case

If a variable contains a zero (*0*) as a valid score, then the harmonic mean cannot be calculated (since it implies division by zero).

Variance and Standard Deviation

The variance and standard deviation are standard measures of variability (see *Basic Statistics and Tables*, Chapter 9). *STATISTICA* will calculate the variance as the sum of squared deviations about the mean divided by *n-1* (not *n*). The standard deviation is calculated as the square root of this value. The *n-1* vs. *n* issue is usually of little practical importance. Technically, you most often want to estimate the variability of the *population* from which the current sample was drawn (for example, you would like to generalize your results to all males, given your random sample of males). In this case you should always use *n-1* as the divisor in the computations in order to obtain an estimate of the population standard deviation; using *n* as the divisor results in purely *descriptive* statistics *for the current sample*.

Average Deviation

The average deviation is another measure of variability. It is calculated as the sum of absolute deviations (mean for respective variable minus raw score) divided by *n* (number of valid cases).

Range

The range of a variable is also an indicator of variability. It is calculated as the largest valid score minus the smallest valid score.

Quartile Range

The quartile range of a variable is calculated as the value of the 75'th percentile minus the value of the 25'th percentile. Thus it is the width of the range about the median that includes 50% of the cases. The specific computational method for calculating this statistic can be configured by the user; for details, please refer to the description of the *Median* above.

Skewness

As implied by the term, the skewness is a measure of the extent to which the distribution of the respective variable is skewed to the left (negative value) or right (positive value), relative to the standard normal distribution (for which the skewness is *0*). The skewness is also referred to as the *third moment* of the distribution. The skewness is defined as:

$$\text{Skewness} = n*M^3/[(n-1)*(n-2)*\sigma^3]$$

where

M^3 is equal to: $\Sigma(x_i\text{-}Mean_x)^3$

σ^3 is the standard deviation (*sigma*) raised to the third power

n is the valid number of cases

Kurtosis

The kurtosis is a measure of how "wide" or "skinny" ("flat" or "peaked") the distribution is for the respective variable, relative to the standard normal distribution (for which the kurtosis is equal to *0*). It is also referred to as the *fourth moment* of the distribution. The kurtosis is defined as:

$$\text{Kurtosis} = [n*(n+1)*M^4 - 3*M^2*M^2*(n-1)]/[(n-1)*(n-2)*(n-3)*\sigma^4]$$

where

M^j is equal to: $\Sigma(x_i\text{-}Mean_x)^j$

σ^4 is the standard deviation (*sigma*) raised to the fourth power

n is the valid number of cases

Startup Panel - Distribution Fitting

General

After choosing any of the following distributions, you are prompted to specify the variable to which the chosen distribution will be fitted. Regardless of the distribution selected from this dialog, you can toggle through all other distributions of the same type (*continuous* or *discrete*) on the subsequent dialog.

After a variable has been specified, the parameters yielding the best fit for each of the respective types of distributions are computed. These parameters are displayed as default values, but user-specified values may be entered.

Distribution Fitting via Stats 2D Graphs Options. Beginning with release 5 of *STATISTICA*, there are several alternative procedures available for fitting continuous distributions to data. Specifically, you can choose (categorized or non-categorized) *Quantile-Quantile* plots, *Probability-Probability* plots, or *2D Histograms* (with a line indicating the expected frequencies) from the *Graphs* pull-down menu, and then choose to produce the respective plots based on the *Beta*, *Exponential*, *Extreme Value*, *Gamma*, *Laplace*, *Logistic*, *Lognormal*, *Rayleigh*, or *Weibull* distributions. The program will compute maximum likelihood parameter estimates for the respective distributions (see Volume II for additional details).

Normal Distribution

The normal distribution (the "bell-shaped curve" which is symmetrical about the mean) is a theoretical function commonly used in inferential statistics as an approximation to sampling distributions (see also *Elementary Concepts*, Chapter 8). In general, the normal distribution provides a good model for a random variable, when:

(1) There is a strong tendency for the variable to take a central value;

(2) Positive and negative deviations from this central value are equally likely;

(3) The frequency of deviations falls off rapidly as the deviations become larger.

As an underlying mechanism that produces the normal distribution, one may think of an infinite number of independent random (binomial) events that bring about the values of a particular variable. For example, there are probably a nearly infinite number of factors that determine a person's height (thousands of genes, nutrition, diseases, etc.). Thus, height can be expected to be normally distributed in the population. The normal distribution function is determined by the following formula:

$$f(x)=\{1/[(2*\pi)^{1/2}*\sigma]\} * e^{\{-1/2*[(x-\mu)/\sigma]^2\}}$$

where

μ is the mean

σ is the standard deviation

e is Euler's constant (2.71...)

π is the constant *Pi* (3.14...)

Rectangular Distribution

The rectangular distribution is useful for describing random variables where each value has an equal probability of occurrence; that is:

$$f(x) = a$$

where

a is a constant

Exponential Distribution

If *T* is the time between occurrences of rare events that happen on the average with a rate λ per unit of time, then *T* is distributed exponentially with parameter λ (*lambda*). Thus, the exponential distribution is frequently used to model the time interval between successive random events. Examples of variables distributed in this manner would be the gap length between cars crossing an intersection, life-times of electronic devices, or arrivals of customers at the check-out counter in a grocery store. The exponential distribution function is defined as:

$$f(x) = \lambda*e^{-\lambda x}$$

where

λ (*lambda*) is an exponential function parameter

e is Euler's constant (2.71...)

Gamma Distribution

The probability density function of the exponential distribution has a mode of zero. In many instances, it is known *a priori* that the mode of the distribution of a particular random variable of interest is not equal to zero (e.g., when modeling the distribution of the life-times of a product such as an electric light bulb, or the serving time taken at a ticket booth at a baseball game). In those cases, the *Gamma* distribution is more appropriate for describing the underlying distribution. The *Gamma* distribution is defined as:

$$f(x) = [1/(\Gamma(\alpha)*\beta^{\alpha})] * x^{\alpha-1} * e^{-x/\beta}$$

where

Γ (*gamma*) is the *Gamma* function (of argument *alpha*)

α (*alpha*) is the shape parameter

β (*beta*) is the scale parameter

e is Euler's constant (2.71...)

Lognormal Distribution

The lognormal distribution is often used in simulations of variables such as personal incomes, age at first marriage, or tolerance to poison in animals. In general, if x is a sample from a normal distribution, then $y = e^x$ is a sample from a lognormal distribution. Thus, the lognormal distribution is defined as:

$$f(x) = \{1/[x*\sigma*(2*\pi)^{1/2}]\} * e^{-\{1/[2*(\sigma^2)]\}*[\ln(x)-\mu]^2}$$

where

π is the constant *Pi* (3.14...)

σ is the estimated population standard deviation

e is Euler's constant (2.71...)

μ is the estimated population mean

Chi-square Distribution

The sum of v independent squared random variables, each distributed following the standard normal distribution, is distributed as *Chi-square* with v degrees of freedom. This distribution is most frequently used in the modeling of random variables (e.g., representing frequencies) in statistical applications. The *Chi-square* distribution is defined by:

$$f(x)=\{1/[2^{v/2}*\Gamma(v/2)]\} * x^{(v/2)-1} * e^{-x/2}$$

where

v is the degrees of freedom

e is Euler's constant (2.71...)

Γ(y) is the *Gamma* function (of argument *y*)

Binomial Distribution

The binomial distribution is useful for describing distributions of binomial events, such as the number of males and females in a random sample of companies, or the number of defective components in samples of 20 units taken from a production process. The binomial distribution is defined as:

$$f(x) = [n!/(x!*(n-x)!)]*p^x * q^{n-x}$$

where

p is the probability that the respective event will occur

q is equal to *1-p*

n is the maximum number of independent trials

Poisson Distribution

The Poisson distribution is also sometimes referred to as the distribution of rare events. Examples of Poisson distributed variables are number of accidents per person, number of sweepstakes won per person, or the number of catastrophic defects found in a production process. It is defined as:

$$f(x) = (\lambda^x * e^{-\lambda})/x!$$

where

λ (*lambda*) is the expected value of x (the mean)

e is Euler's constant (2.71...)

Geometric Distribution

If independent Bernoulli trials (see below) are made until a "success" occurs, then the total number of trials required is a geometric random variable.

The geometric distribution is defined as:

$$f(x) = p*(1-p)^{x-1}$$

where

p is the probability that a particular event (e.g., success) will occur

Bernoulli Distribution

This distribution best describes all situations where a "trial" is made resulting in either "success" or "failure," such as when tossing a coin, or when modeling the success or failure of a surgical procedure.

The Bernoulli distribution is defined as:

$$f(x) = p^x*(1-p)^{1-x}$$

where

p is the probability that a particular event (e.g., success) will occur.

2 x 2 Frequency Tables

Specify the frequencies for the *2 x 2 Table* in this dialog (see also page 1599).

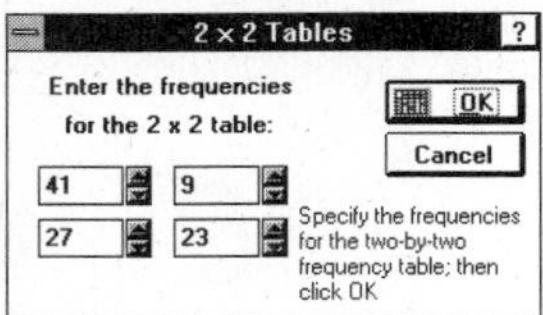

In addition to the standard Pearson *Chi-square* statistic, and the corrected *Chi-square* statistic (*V-square*, see page 1619), the following statistics will be computed (as shown in the Scrollsheet, below):

2 x 2 Table (intrview.sta)

NONPAR STATS	Column 1	Column 2	Row Totals
Frequencies, row 1	41	9	50
Percent of total	41.000%	9.000%	50.000%
Frequencies, row 2	27	23	50
Percent of total	27.000%	23.000%	50.000%
Column totals	68	32	100
Percent of total	68.000%	32.000%	
Chi-square (df=1)	9.01	p= .0027	
V-square (df=1)	8.92	p= .0028	
Yates corrected Chi-square	7.77	p= .0053	
Phi-square	.09007		
Fisher exact p, one-tailed		p= .0025	
two-tailed		p= .0049	
McNemar Chi-square (A/D)	4.52	p= .0336	
Chi-square (B/C)	8.03	p= .0046	

Yates' correction. The approximation of the *Chi-square* statistic in 2 x 2 tables with small expected frequencies can be improved by reducing the absolute value of differences between expected and observed frequencies by 0.5 before squaring (*Yates' correction*). This correction, which makes the estimation more conservative, is usually applied when the table contains only small observed frequencies, so that some expected frequencies become less than 10 (for further discussion of this correction, see Conover, 1974; Everitt, 1977; Hays, 1988; Kendall and Stuart, 1979; and Mantel, 1974).

Phi-square. The *Phi-square* is a measure of correlation between the two categorical variables in the table.

Fisher exact test. Given the marginal frequencies in the table, and assuming that in the population the two factors in the table are not related, how likely is it to obtain cell frequencies as uneven as (or more uneven than) the ones that were observed?

For small *n*, this probability can be computed *exactly* by counting all possible tables that can be constructed based on the marginal frequencies. This is the underlying rationale for the Fisher exact test. It computes the *exact* probability under the null hypothesis of obtaining the current distribution of frequencies across cells, or one that is more uneven. Both one-sided and two-sided probabilities are reported.

McNemar *Chi-square*. This test is applicable in situations where the frequencies in the 2 x 2 table represent *dependent* samples. For example, in a before-after design study, you may count the number of students who fail a test of minimal math skills at the beginning of the semester and at the end of the semester. Two *Chi-square* values are reported: *A/D* and *B/C*. The *Chi-square A/D* tests the hypothesis that the frequencies in cells *A* and *D* (upper left, lower right) are identical. The *Chi-square B/C* tests the hypothesis that the frequencies in cells *B* and *C* (upper right, lower left) are identical.

Note that *STATISTICA* also includes two designated modules (the *Tables* procedure in the *Basic Statistics and Tables* module and the *Log-Linear* module) for the analysis of frequencies and contingencies in multi-dimensional tables of practically unlimited size and complexity. The *Tables* option of the *Basic Statistics and Tables* module produces a comprehensive set of descriptive and inferential statistics; *Log-Linear* performs complete log-linear analyses of multi-way frequency tables. Your *STATISTICA* program also contains an example *STATISTICA BASIC* program (file *Manthaen.stb* in the *STBASIC* subdirectory) for computing the Mantel-Haenszel test for comparing two groups (see Mantel and Haenszel, 1959; see also Lee, 1992). Refer to the comments included in file *Manthaen.stb* for additional details.

Observed vs. Expected Frequencies

Specify two variables: one with the observed frequency counts (in the first variable list) and another with the expected frequencies (in the second variable list).

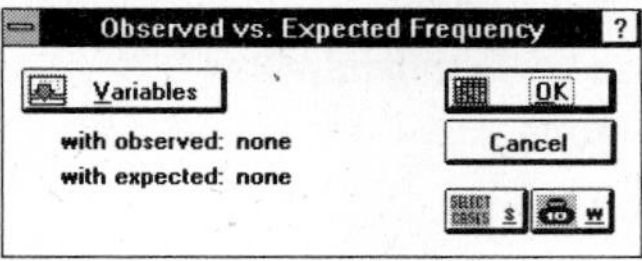

For an example of this nonparametric test, see page 1621.

Correlation Coefficients

When you select the *Correlations (Spearman, Kendall tau, Gamma)* option from the *Nonparametrics and Distributions* startup panel, the *Nonparametric Correlations* dialog will open.

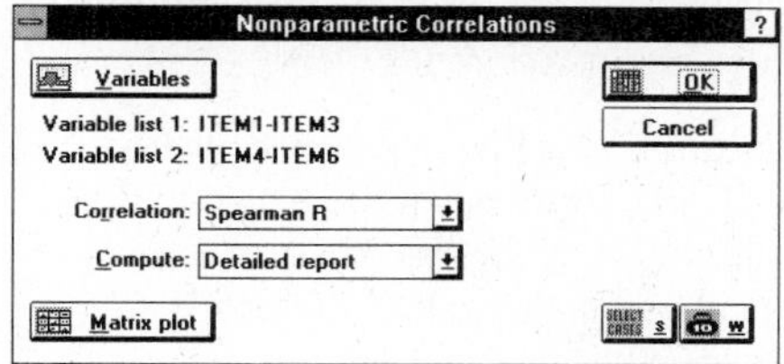

Variables

Select at least two variables for which correlations will be computed (each variable in the first list will be correlated with each variable in the second list).

Correlation

This combo box allows you to choose between the Spearman *R*, Kendall *tau*, and *Gamma* coefficients (discussed below).

Spearman *R*. Spearman *R* assumes that the variables under consideration were measured on at least an ordinal (rank order) scale, that is, that the individual observations can be ranked into two ordered series.

Kendall *tau*. Kendall *tau* is equivalent to Spearman *R* with regard to the underlying assumptions. It is also comparable in terms of its statistical power. However, Spearman *R* and Kendall *tau* are usually not identical in magnitude because their underlying logic as well as their computational formulas are very different. Siegel and Castellan (1988) express the relationship of the two measures in terms of the inequality:

-1 ≤ 3 * Kendall tau - 2 * Spearman R ≤ 1

More importantly, Kendall *tau* and Spearman *R* imply different interpretations: Spearman *R* can be thought of as the regular Pearson product moment correlation coefficient, that is, in terms of proportion of variability accounted for, except that Spearman *R* is computed from ranks.

Kendall *tau*, on the other hand, represents a *probability*; that is, it is the difference between the probability that the two variables are in the same order in the observed data *versus* the probability that the two variables are in different orders.

***Gamma*.** The *Gamma* statistic is preferable to Spearman *R* or Kendall *tau* when the data contain many tied observations. In terms of the underlying assumptions, *Gamma* is equivalent to Spearman *R* or Kendall *tau*; in terms of its interpretation and computation, it is more similar to Kendall *tau* than Spearman *R*. In short, *Gamma* is also a *probability*; specifically, it is computed as the difference between the probability that the rank ordering of the two variables agree minus the probability that they disagree, divided by 1 minus the probability of ties. Thus, *Gamma* is basically equivalent to Kendall *tau*, except that ties are explicitly taken into account.

Compute

You can choose to compute single nonparametric correlations or matrices of nonparametric correlations with the options in this combo box (described below). The results Scrollsheet features the scatterplot as the default graph, so you can easily graph the correlations.

Detailed report. Selecting this option will result not only in the correlations between the specified variables (see above), but also in the *Valid n*, *t-value*, and *p-level* for each correlation.

Spearman Rank Order Correlations (cars.sta)

NONPAR STATS — MD pairwise deleted

Pair of Variables	Valid N	Spearman R	t(N-2)	p-level
PRICE & HANDLING	22	.288513	1.34757	.192864
PRICE & MILAGE	22	-.322880	-1.52568	.142749
ACCELER & HANDLING	22	-.316321	-1.49120	.151514
ACCELER & MILAGE	22	.040194	.17990	.859041
BRAKING & HANDLING	22	-.259910	-1.20372	.242752
BRAKING & MILAGE	22	-.013672	-.06115	.951849

Matrix of two lists. This option will compute only the correlations between the variables specified in the first list against the variables specified in the second list.

Square matrix. This option will compute correlations from a single list of variables (resulting in a square matrix of correlations). Note that if you have already specified two lists of variables and then select this option, the two lists will be "stacked" to make one list of variables.

Matrix Plot

Click on this button to produce a scatterplot matrix for all selected variables.

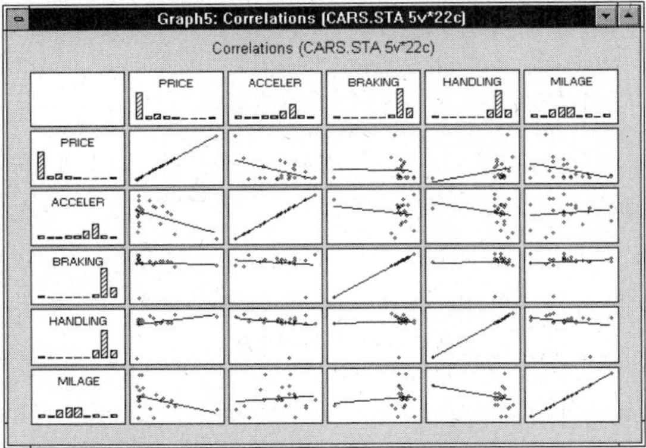

In the context of nonparametric correlations, this graph is useful to quickly examine and compare the distributions of the selected variables and shapes of relations between them (e.g., Spearman *R* can measure curvilinear relations between variables as long as they are monotonous).

Comparing Two Groups

The following nonparametric tests are available for comparing two groups (the dialog options for each of the three tests are the same and are discussed below).

Wald-Wolfowitz Runs Test
Variables
Grouping variable: GENDER
Dependent variables: MEASUR1-MEASUR3
Code for Group 1: MALE
Code for Group 2: FEMALE
Double-click on the respective field to select codes from the list of valid variable values
OK
Cancel
Box & whisker
Categorized histogram

Wald-Wolfowitz runs test. The Wald-Wolfowitz runs test works as follows: Imagine that you want to compare male and female subjects on some variable. You can sort the data by that variable and look for instances when, in the sorted data, same-gender subjects are adjacent to each other. If there are no differences between male and female subjects, then the number and "lengths" of such adjacent "runs" of subjects of the same gender will be more or less random. If not, the two groups (genders in this example) are somehow different from each other.

This test assumes that the variable under consideration is continuous, and that it was measured on at least an ordinal scale (i.e., rank order). The Wald-Wolfowitz runs test assesses the hypothesis that two independent samples were drawn from two populations that differ in some respect, i.e., not just with respect to the mean, but also with respect to the general shape of the distribution. The null hypothesis is that the two samples were drawn from the same population. In this respect, this test is different from the parametric *t*-test which strictly tests for differences in locations (means) of two samples.

Mann-Whitney *U* test. The Mann-Whitney *U* test assumes that the variable under consideration was measured on at least an ordinal (rank order) scale. The interpretation of the test is essentially identical to the interpretation of the result of a *t*-test for independent samples, except that the *U* test is computed based on rank sums rather than means.

The *U* test is the most powerful (or sensitive) nonparametric alternative to the *t*-test for independent samples; in fact, in some instances it may even offer *greater* power to reject the null hypothesis than the *t*-test.

Kolmogorov-Smirnov two-sample test. The Kolmogorov-Smirnov test assesses the hypothesis that two samples were drawn from different populations. Unlike the parametric *t*-test for independent samples or the Mann-Whitney *U* test, which test for differences in the location of two samples (differences in means, differences in average ranks, respectively), the Kolmogorov-Smirnov test is also sensitive to differences in the *general shapes* of the distributions in the two samples, i.e., to differences in dispersion, skewness, etc. Thus, its interpretation is similar to that of the Wald-Wolfowitz runs test.

Variables

Choosing this option will bring up the regular two-variable lists selection dialog. In general, the procedure expects the data to be arranged in the same way as in the *t*-test for independent samples. Specifically, the data file should contain a coding variable (*independent* or *grouping* variable) with at least two distinct codes that uniquely identify the group membership of each case in the data file. Thus, in the first list, select the variable containing the grouping codes; then in the second list, select a list of variables for the respective comparison.

Next, specify the codes that were used in the grouping variable to uniquely identify the group membership of each case. You can also double-click on the code edit field to bring up the *Variable Values Window* in order to select the appropriate grouping code.

Box and Whisker Plot

The box and whisker plot is a useful graphical method to compare the distribution of a variable in two groups. Both medians and quartiles, or means and related measures of dispersion can be plotted.

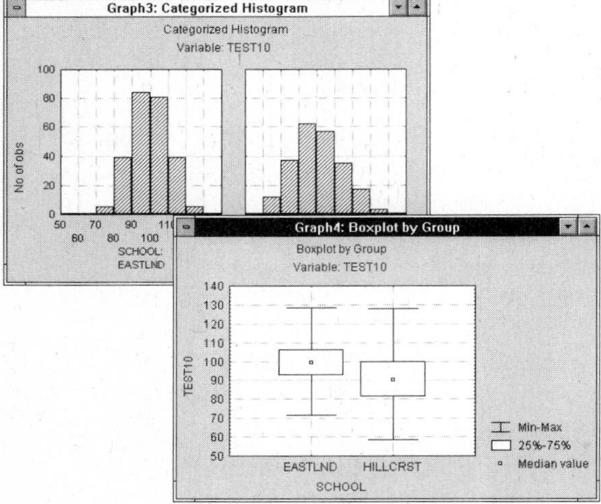

Categorized Histogram

This option will produce a categorized histogram of the distribution of a selected variable, separately for each group (as shown in the example above).

Kruskal-Wallis ANOVA & Median Test

The Kruskal-Wallis ANOVA by ranks test assumes that the variable under consideration is continuous and that it was measured on at least an ordinal (rank order) scale. This test assesses the hypothesis that the different samples in the comparison were drawn from the same distribution or from distributions with the same median. Thus, the interpretation of the Kruskal-Wallis test is basically identical to that of parametric one-way ANOVA, except that it is based on ranks rather than means.

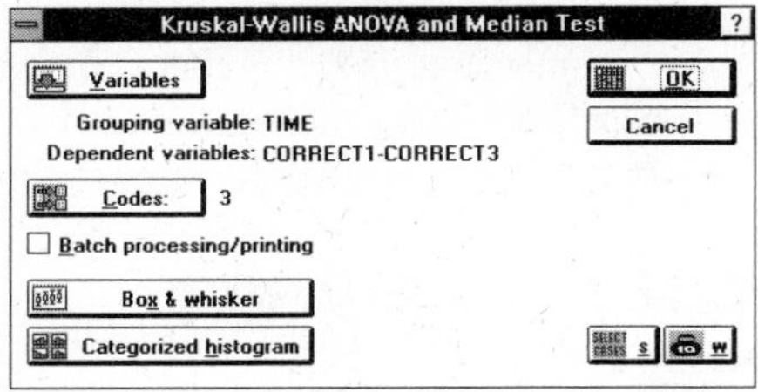

The Median test is a "crude" version of the Kruskal-Wallis ANOVA in that it frames the computation in terms of a contingency table. Specifically, the program will simply count the number of cases in each sample that fall above or below the common median, and compute the *Chi-square* value for the resulting 2 x *k* samples contingency table. Under the null hypothesis (all samples come from populations with identical medians), approximately 50% of all cases in each sample are expected to fall above (or below) the common median. The Median test is particularly useful when the scale contains artificial limits, and many cases fall at either extreme of the scale ("off the scale"). In this case, the Median test is in fact the most appropriate method for comparing samples.

Variables

Clicking on this button will bring up the regular two-variable lists selection dialog. In general, the procedure expects the data to be arranged in the same way as in the *t*-test for independent samples or between-groups ANOVA. Specifically, the data file should contain a coding variable (*independent* or *grouping* variable) with at least two distinct codes that uniquely identify the group membership of each case in the data file. Thus, in the first list, select the variable containing the grouping codes; then in the second list, select a list of variables for the respective comparison.

Codes

When you click on this button, the *Selecting Codes* dialog will open in which you can specify the codes that were used in the grouping variable (in order to uniquely identify the group membership of each case).

Batch Processing/Printing

This option is applicable if you have selected either the *Printer, Disk File*, and/or *Text/output Window* as the output destination in the *Page/Output Setup* dialog. If you set the *Batch Processing/Printing* option here, then all variables in the dependent variable list will be processed and the results printed without requiring any other user input.

Box and Whisker Plot

The box and whisker plot is a useful graphical method to compare the distribution of a variable in the different groups. Both medians and quartiles, or means and related measures of dispersion can be plotted.

Categorized Histogram

This option will produce a categorized histogram of the distribution of a selected variable, separately (categorized) for each group.

Comparing Two Variables

The following two nonparametric tests are available for comparing two variables (the dialog options for both tests are the same and are discussed below).

Sign test. The only assumption required by this test is that the underlying distribution of the variable of interest is continuous; no assumptions about the nature or shape of the underlying distribution are required. The test simply computes the number of times (across subjects) that the value of the first variable (A) is larger than that of the second variable (B). Under the null hypothesis (stating that the two variables are not different from each other) this is expected to be the case about 50% of the time. Based on the binomial distribution, you can compute a z value for the observed number of cases where $A > B$, and compute the associated tail probability for that z value. For small n's (less than 20) you may prefer to use the tabulated values found in Siegel and Castellan (1988) to evaluate statistical significance.

Wilcoxon matched pairs test. This option assumes that the variables under consideration were measured on a scale that allows the rank ordering of observations based on each variable (i.e., ordinal scale) *and* that allows rank ordering of the *differences* between variables (this type of scale is sometimes referred to as an *ordered metric scale,* see Coombs, 1950). Thus, the required assumptions for this test are more stringent than those for the Sign test. However, if they are met, that is, if the magnitudes of differences (e.g., different ratings by the same individual) contain meaningful information, then this test is more powerful than the Sign test. In fact, if the assumptions for the parametric t-test for dependent samples (interval scale) are met, then this test is almost as powerful as the t-test.

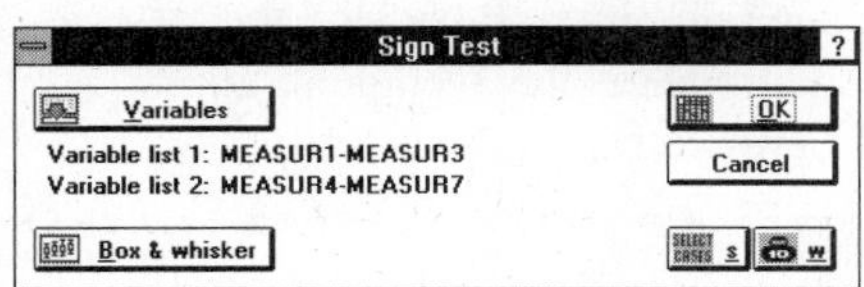

Variables

Choosing this option will bring up the standard two-variable lists selection dialog. After you select the variables in the two lists, click on the *OK* button to compare each variable in the first list against each variable in the second list.

Box and Whisker Plot

The box and whisker plot is a useful graphical method to compare the distribution of two variables. After clicking on this button, select the two variables for the plot. Both medians and quartiles, or means and related measures of dispersion can be plotted.

Friedman ANOVA & Kendall Concordance

When you compute the Friedman ANOVA, the Kendall Concordance coefficient is also computed (the dialog options for both tests are discussed below).

Friedman ANOVA. The Friedman ANOVA by ranks test assumes that the variables (levels) under consideration were measured on at least an ordinal (rank order) scale. The null hypothesis for the procedure is that the different columns of data (i.e., *STATISTICA* variables) contain samples drawn from the same population, or specifically, populations with identical medians. Thus, the interpretation of results from this procedure is similar to that of a repeated measures ANOVA.

Kendall concordance. The Kendall concordance coefficient expresses the simultaneous association (relatedness) between *k* cases (correlated samples). For example, this statistic is commonly used to assess inter-judge reliability. Basically, the concordance coefficient is the average of all Spearman *R*'s between cases; specifically:

```
average Spearman R = (k*concordance-1)/(k-1)
```

Thus the general assumptions of this test are identical to that of the Spearman rank order correlation.

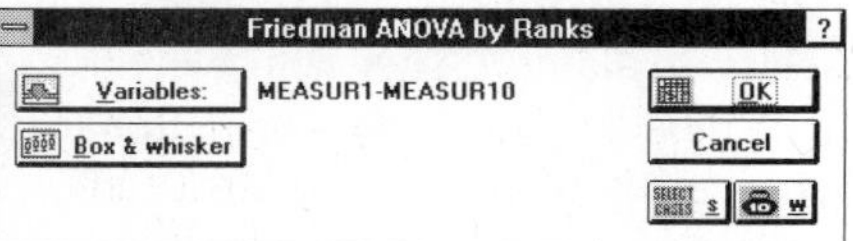

Variables

Choosing this option will bring up the standard single variable list selection dialog from which you may select the variables to be analyzed.

Box and Whisker Plot

The box and whisker plot is used to graphically compare the distribution of two or more variables. You can select to plot medians and quartiles or means and related measures of dispersion.

Cochran *Q* Test

The Cochran *Q* test is an extension of McNemar's *Chi-square* test for changes (see option *2 x 2 Tables*, page 1608) in frequencies or proportions to *k* (more than two) dependent samples. Specifically, it tests whether several matched frequencies or proportions differ significantly among themselves. The Cochran *Q* test requires only a nominal scale, or that the data have been artificially dichotomized.

A typical example where the *Q* test is useful is when one wants to compare the difficulty of dichotomous questionnaire items that can either be answered right or wrong. Here, each variable in the data file would represent one item, and contain 0's (wrong) and 1's (right). If the *Q* test is significant, then you conclude that the items are of different difficulty since different items were answered correctly by more or fewer respondents.

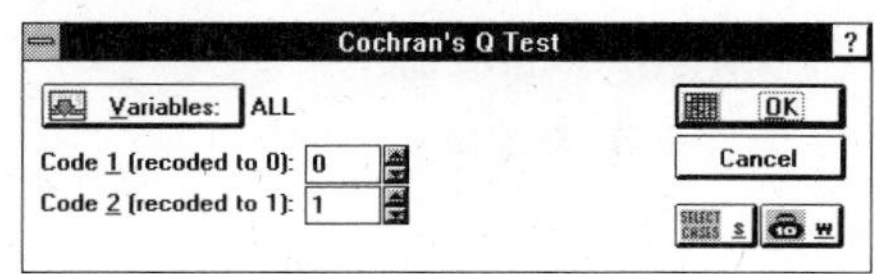

Variables

Choosing this option will bring up the standard single variable list selection dialog. Note that this

test requires that the selected variables contain two integer values or codes (see below).

Codes

The Cochran *Q* test assumes that the selected variables only contain 0's and 1's. If you used different codes, you may specify them in the edit boxes; the program will then (internally) recode those values to 0's and 1's (only temporarily; the data file will not be changed).

Descriptive Statistics

When you click on the *Ordinal Descriptive Statistics* option from the *Nonparametrics and Distributions* startup panel, the *Descriptive Statistics* dialog will open.

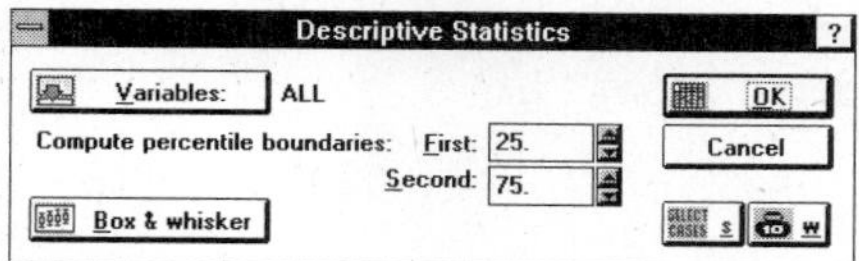

This option will allow you to compute several descriptive statistics (each of the statistics computed are explained in detail in *Startup Panel - Descriptive Statistics*, page 1603).

Variables

After clicking on this button a standard single variable list selection dialog will appear in which you can select the variables for which the statistics will be computed.

Compute Percentile Boundaries

Specify here specific percentile values to be computed and displayed in the Scrollsheet; by default the program will compute the quartile values, that is, the 25'th and 75'th percentiles.

Computation of median, quartiles, and percentile boundaries. When the number of observations is even, or when there are tied observations, then there is some ambiguity concerning the exact computation of percentile boundaries. The method of computation in *STATISTICA* can be configured "system-wide" on the *STATISTICA Defaults: General* dialog (see Chapter 3; see also *Appendix II* for computational details), accessible from the *Options* pull-down menu. Once configured, the identical computational method will be used in all relevant places throughout the *STATISTICA* system (e.g., when computing box and whisker plots, or when computing medians and quartiles via the respective functions in *STATISTICA BASIC*; see Volume V for a description of those functions).

Descriptive Statistics Computed

In addition to the standard descriptive statistics, *STATISTICA* computes several other ordinal descriptive statistics when you click *OK* in this dialog.

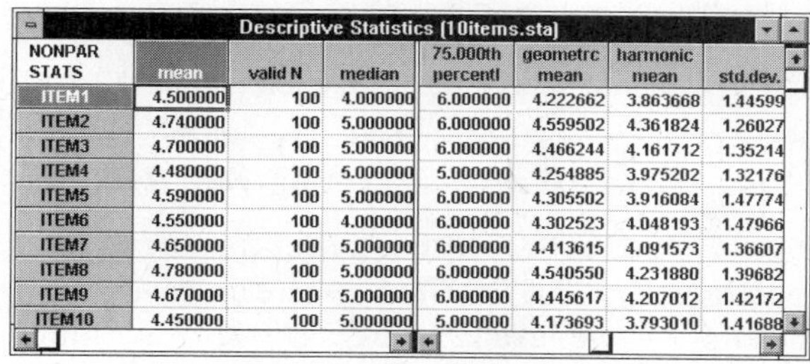

Descriptive Statistics (10items.sta)

NONPAR STATS	mean	valid N	median	75.000th percentl	geometrc mean	harmonic mean	std.dev.
ITEM1	4.500000	100	4.000000	6.000000	4.222662	3.863668	1.44599
ITEM2	4.740000	100	5.000000	6.000000	4.559502	4.361824	1.26027
ITEM3	4.700000	100	5.000000	6.000000	4.466244	4.161712	1.35214
ITEM4	4.480000	100	5.000000	5.000000	4.254885	3.975202	1.32176
ITEM5	4.590000	100	5.000000	6.000000	4.305502	3.916084	1.47774
ITEM6	4.550000	100	4.000000	6.000000	4.302523	4.048193	1.47966
ITEM7	4.650000	100	5.000000	6.000000	4.413615	4.091573	1.36607
ITEM8	4.780000	100	5.000000	6.000000	4.540550	4.231880	1.39682
ITEM9	4.670000	100	5.000000	6.000000	4.445617	4.207012	1.42172
ITEM10	4.450000	100	5.000000	5.000000	4.173693	3.793010	1.41688

For a complete list and descriptions of each of the descriptive statistics computed, see *Startup Panel - Descriptive Statistics*, page 1603.

Distribution Fitting

When you click on the distribution of interest in the *Nonparametrics and Distributions* startup panel, the appropriate distribution fitting dialog (continuous or discrete) will open.

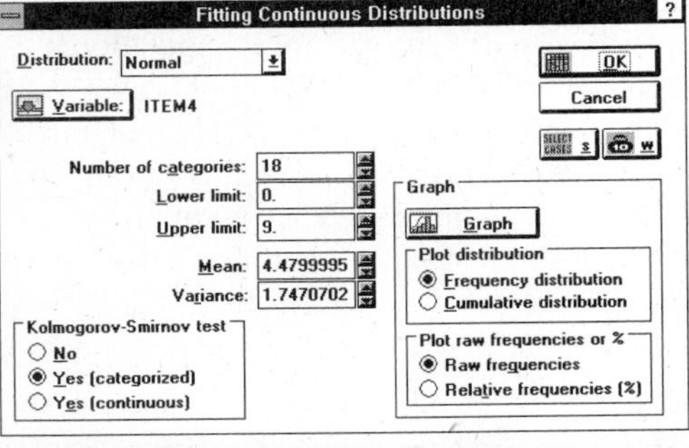

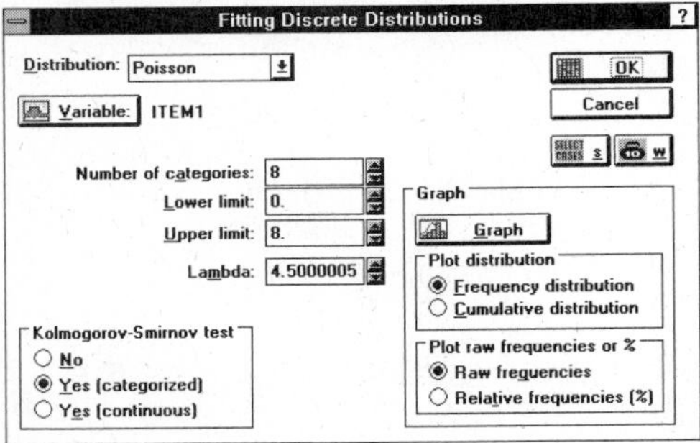

Each of the available distributions are discussed in *Startup Panel - Distribution Fitting*, page 1605.

Other distribution fitting procedures available in *STATISTICA*. There are several other procedures available in *STATISTICA* for fitting continuous distributions. The *Survival Analysis* module will fit the Weibull and Gompertz distributions to observed survival or failure time data. That module will also handle incomplete (censored) observations.

The *Stats 2D Graphs* histogram options (see the pull-down menu *Graphs*) offer a variety of facilities to produce simple, cumulative, multiple, and categorized graphs of frequency distributions; available distributions include *Normal*, *Beta*, *Extreme Value*, *Gamma*, *Geometric*, *Laplace*, *Logistic*, *Lognormal*, *Poisson*, *Rayleigh*, and *Weibull* (see Appendix I for a description of these distributions). You can also produce *Quantile-Quantile* and *Probability-Probability* plots for these distributions, and thus evaluate the fit of the respective distribution to the observed data. These options are described in detail in Volume II of the manual.

The *Process Analysis* module of *STATISTICA* (see Volume IV) also contains several options for fitting the continuous distributions mentioned in the previous paragraph, and for computing tables with expected and observed frequencies. That module also has an option to fit simultaneously all of these continuous distributions to the data; the results Scrollsheet for this option contains the respective Kolmogorov-Smirnov *d-max* values, sorted in ascending order (i.e., from the best-fitting to the worst-fitting distribution).

Variable

To fit a distribution to a variable, first specify the variable to which the chosen distribution will be fitted, by clicking on the *Variable* button.

Distribution

Once you have specified the variable of interest, you can then switch between fitting the different distributions (of the same type, i.e., *continuous* or *discrete*) via the *Distribution* combo box. After a variable has been specified, the parameters yielding the best fit for each of the respective types of distributions are computed. These parameters are displayed as default values, but user-specified values may be entered.

Controlling the Number of Categories

The way in which the frequency distribution is computed (and the histogram of observed data is drawn) can be controlled by the user. Use the option *No. of Categories* to specify the number of categories in the frequency table or histogram, and use the *Lower limit* or *Upper limit* fields to control the lower and upper limits, respectively. Note that, where appropriate, the program will re-define the most extreme categories into open-ended classes.

Chi-square Test of Goodness of Fit

By default, the program will compute the *Chi-square* test based on the observed and expected frequencies. Categories where the expected frequency is less than 5 are collapsed to form larger categories. If this test is significant, you reject the hypothesis that the observed data follow the hypothesized distribution.

Kolmogorov-Smirnov One-Sample Test

This test can be computed either from the tabulated values (which is faster; set the *Kolmogorov-Smirnov categorized* radio button) or based on the raw data (which is slower; set the *Continuous distribution* button).

Kolmogorov-Smirnov categorized. In this case (categorized), the program will compute the *d-max* statistic from the tabulated data in the Scrollsheet. If the Kolmogorov-Smirnov test is statistically significant, you reject the hypothesis that the observed data follow the hypothesized distribution (however, see the note on *Lilliefors probabilities* below!).

Continuous distribution. In this case, the program will "step" through the sorted observed data and compute the cumulative expected frequency at each point; the Kolmogorov *d-max* statistic is the largest absolute difference between the cumulative observed and expected distribution.

A-priori knowledge of parameters, Lilliefors probabilities. The significance level reported in the results Scrollsheet for the Kolmogorov-Smirnov *d-max* statistic is based on the probability values tabulated by Massey (1951). These probability values pertain to the case when the parameters of the respective theoretical distribution are known *a priori* and *not* estimated from the data. However, in practice these parameters are typically computed from the actual data. Thus, when fitting, for example, the normal distribution, the test for normality in this case involves a complex conditional hypothesis ("how likely is it to obtain a *d-max* statistic of this magnitude or greater, contingent upon the mean and standard deviation computed from the data"), and for the case of the normal distribution, the so-called *Lilliefors* probabilities should be interpreted (Lilliefors, 1967).

For other distributions, one should interpret with caution the standard significance level based on the critical values tabulated by Massey (1951), because they will most likely cause you to underestimate the lack of fit of the respective distribution to the data (i.e., the standard *p* level may be non-significant, when, in fact, the respective distribution does not fit the data very well, given that the parameters for the distribution where estimated from the observed data).

If you are interested in examining the "behavior" of the *d-max* statistic for different distributions, based on Monte-Carlo methods, you may study the *STATISTICA BASIC* example program *Lillief.stb*, which will perform Monte-Carlo replications, and tabulate the critical Lilliefors values for the normal distribution. That program can easily be modified to accommodate other distributions (see also Volume V of the manual).

Graph

If no variables have been selected, click on the *Graph* button to select the variables. After the variables have been selected, clicking on the graph button will produce a graph specified by the following options:

Plot distribution. Choose to plot the *Frequency Distributions* or the *Cumulative Distribution* by selecting the appropriate radio button.

Plot raw Frequency or %. When you choose to plot the *Frequency Distributions* (see above), you will be able to select between plotting the *Raw Frequencies* or *Relative Frequencies (%)* with this option.

EXAMPLES

Example 1: 2 x 2 Tables

After choosing the *2 x 2 Tables* $X^2/V^2/Phi^2$*, McNemar, Fisher Exact Test* option from the *Nonparametrics and Distributions* startup panel, a dialog will be displayed in which the user is prompted to enter frequencies into the four cells of a 2 x 2 contingency table.

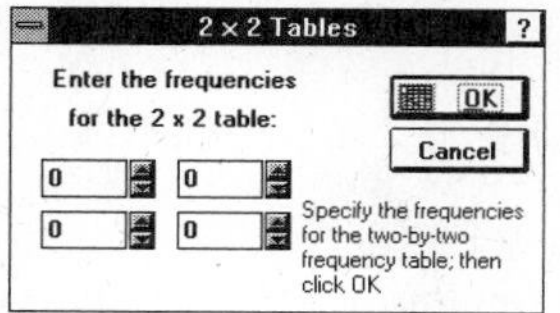

Chi-square, V-square. Suppose that you are considering whether to introduce a new formula for a successful soft drink. Before finally deciding on the new formula, you conducted a survey in which you asked male and female respondents to express their preference for either the old or new soft drink. Assume that out of 50 males, 41 prefer the new formula over the old formula; out of 50 females, only 27 prefer the new formula. You would enter these data as follows:

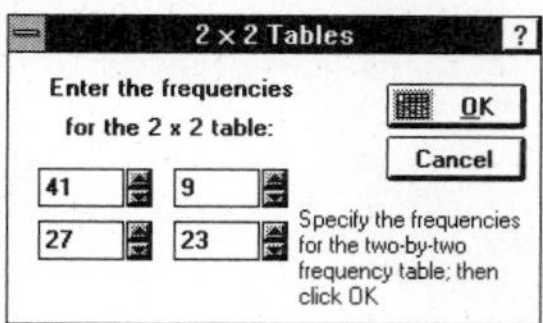

Now, click *OK* to display a Scrollsheet of results (see the next column).

The *Chi-square* value for these numbers (*9.01*) is highly significant (refer to *Elementary Statistics*, Chapter 8, for an explanation of the basic idea of statistical significance testing). Thus, the preferences expressed by males are significantly different from those of females (apparently, the new formula is mostly preferred by males). The *V-square* statistic is a *Chi-square* corrected for sample size (Kendall and Stuart, 1979; see also Rhoades and Overall, 1982). If the frequencies in the table are rather small (e.g., less than 10 on the average), one should probably rely on the *V-square* statistic rather than *Chi-square*.

2 x 2 Table (10items.sta)

Continue...	Column 1	Column 2	Row Totals
Frequencies, row 1	41	9	50
Percent of total	41.000%	9.000%	50.000%
Frequencies, row 2	27	23	50
Percent of total	27.000%	23.000%	50.000%
Column totals	68	32	100
Percent of total	68.000%	32.000%	
Chi-square (df=1)	9.01	p= .0027	
V-square (df=1)	8.92	p= .0028	
Yates corrected Chi-square	7.77	p= .0053	
Phi-square	.09007		
Fisher exact p, one-tailed		p= .0025	
two-tailed		p= .0049	
McNemar Chi-square (A/D)	4.52	p= .0336	

The rationale behind the *V-square* statistic (and other corrections for small *n*) is as follows: Imagine that you observe 3 and 7 in one row of the 2 x 2 table. Then the probability of an observation falling into the first cell can be estimated as 30%, and, likewise, the probability of an observation falling into the second cell as 70%. However, you could equally well estimate those probabilities as 34% and 66%, respectively; the observed data would still be perfectly consistent. In other words, with low *n*, there is a great uncertainty regarding the estimation of underlying probabilities (and expected values), and the *V-square* adjusts for this uncertainty. The *V-square* statistic will, therefore, always be smaller than the *Chi-square*.

Phi-square. Another way of looking at the example above is to say that *Gender* is correlated with *Preference*. This correlation is expressed via *Phi-square*.

Fisher exact test. Given the marginal frequencies (i.e., *50, 50,* 68, and 32 in the this example), and assuming that in the population, males and females do not differ in their preferences, how likely is it to

obtain cell frequencies as uneven or worse than the ones you found in this study? For small *n*, this probability can be computed *exactly* by counting all possible tables that can be constructed based on the marginal frequencies. This is the underlying rationale for the Fisher exact test. It computes the *exact* probability under the null hypothesis of obtaining the current distribution of frequencies across cells, or one that is more uneven. Both one-sided and two-sided probabilities are reported.

McNemar *Chi-square*. This test is applicable in situations where the frequencies in the 2 x 2 table represent *dependent* samples. For example, in a before-after design study, you may count the number of students who fail a test of minimal math skills at the beginning of the semester and at the end of the semester. Two *Chi-square* values are reported: *A/D* and *B/C*. The *Chi-square A/D* tests the hypothesis that the frequencies in cells *A* and *D* (upper-left, lower-right) are identical. The *Chi-square B/C* tests the hypothesis that the frequencies in cells *B* and *C* (upper-right, lower-left) are identical.

Note that *STATISTICA* also includes two designated modules (*Basic Statistics and Tables* and *Log-Linear*) for the analysis of frequencies and contingencies in multidimensional tables of practically unlimited size and complexity. The *Tables* option of the *Basic Statistics and Tables* module produces a comprehensive set of descriptive and inferential statistics (including Kendall tau_b, tau_c, *Gamma*, concordance coefficients, entropy measures, and other coefficients of dependence); the *Log-Linear* module performs complete log-linear analyses of multi-way frequency tables.

Example 2: Sign Test

The Sign test is a nonparametric alternative to the *t*-test for dependent samples (see *Basic Statistics and Tables*, Chapter 9). For a discussion of the logic and assumptions of this test, or for a comparison with the Wilcoxon matched pairs test, refer to page 1602.

The following example is based on a study by Dodd (1979). When processing speech, one actually pays a lot of attention to visual cues as well; specifically, one can understand (*encode*) spoken words much more readily when the face of the person talking can be seen. In a sense, all people are "lip readers," at least to some extent. Dodd tried to find out whether infants as young as only 10 to 16 weeks old are already aware of the relationship between spoken words and the corresponding movements of the lips (of the speaker). For that purpose, Dodd placed the infants in a room so that they could watch a person behind a window reading normal speech. This speech was either delivered directly into the room (*synchronous* condition) or it was delayed by 400 milliseconds (*asynchronous* condition). The dependent variable was the amount of time that the infant watched the face behind the window. No hypotheses were formulated regarding the specific condition that should elicit the most attention (the asynchronous speech could be more interesting because it is novel, or it could draw attention away from the face because the face does not seem to be the source of the speech).

The results of this study are contained in the example data file *Synchron.sta*. Below is a listing of the data file; note that a two-letter identifier for each subject was entered as the case name.

Data: SYNCHRON.STA 2

NUMERIC VALUES	Sensitivity of infants to	
	1 IN_SYNC	2 OUT_SYNC
DC	20.3	50.4
MK	17.0	87.0
VH	6.5	25.1
JM	25.0	28.5
SB	5.4	26.9
MM	29.2	36.6
RH	2.9	1.0
DJ	6.6	43.8
JD	15.8	44.2
ZC	8.3	10.4
CW	34.0	29.9
AF	8.0	27.7

Specifying the analysis. The sign test is a nonparametric alternative to the *t*-test for dependent samples. Since the same infants are listening to speech under two different conditions, this test is appropriate here. For details concerning the assumptions of this and alternative procedures, also see pages 1601, 1602, and 1629. After starting the *Nonparametrics and Distributions* module, open the data file *Synchron.sta*. Then click on the *Sign Test* option in the startup panel. You can simultaneously perform this test on lists of variables (i.e., lists of pairs); however, there are only two variables of interest in this example. Thus, click on the *Variables* button and select variables *In_sync* and *Out_sync* for this test.

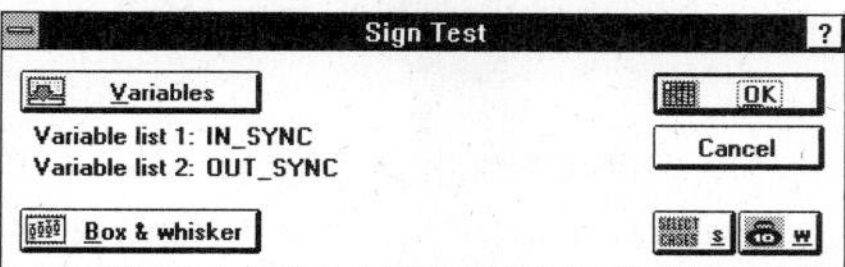

Now, click *OK* to begin the analysis. Below is the Scrollsheet of the results.

Sign Test (synchron.sta)

Continue...	No. of Non-ties	Percent v < V	Z	p-level
IN_SYNC & OUT_SYNC	12	83.33334	2.020726	.043308

The *p*-level for the sign test is significant at the *.05* level (refer to *Elementary Concepts*, Chapter 8, for a discussion of "statistical significance"). Thus, you can conclude that even at this early age, infants can already discriminate between speech that is synchronized with the movement of lips and unsynchronized speech; the term "read my lips" seems to capture a lot of truth about how one learns to understand language.

The default graph for this test is the *Box Plot*. You can produce this plot in one of two ways. Either click on the *Box & Whisker* button in the *Sign Test* dialog or click on the Scrollsheet with the right-mouse-button and select the *Quick Stats Graphs* option *Box Plot*. When you select either option, you will first be asked to select the variables for the plot. For this example, select both variables. Next, you will need to select the type of statistics to be plotted in the *Box-Whisker Type* dialog (shown below).

Select the *Median/Quart./Range* option in this dialog and click *OK* to produce the graph.

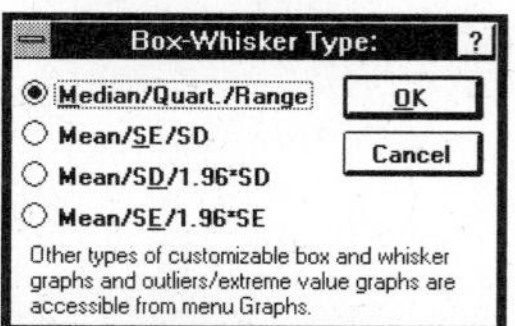

Here, the box plot will indicate, for each variable, the median, quartile range (25th and 75th percentile), and range (minimum and maximum).

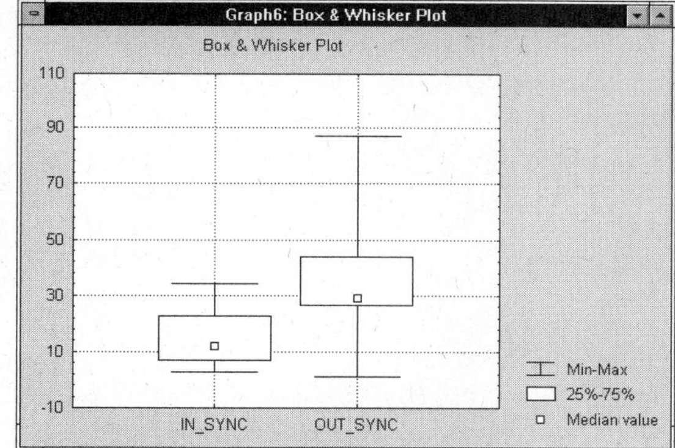

This plot indicates that apparently, the out-of-sync speech resulted in higher median attention as well as in greater variability for this variable.

Example 3: Observed vs. Expected *Chi-square*

The following example is based on a (fictitious) data set of traffic accidents on a particularly treacherous highway (the data for this example are contained in the example data file *Accident.sta*). The data are recorded for each month of the year, for two years: 1983 and 1985.

Data: ACCIDENT.STA 2v *

NUMERIC VALUES — Number of accidents ov

	1 Y_1983	2 Y_1985
January	125	85
February	150	80
March	80	85
April	50	40
May	40	45
June	43	40
July	80	42
August	75	43
September	80	50
October	65	36
November	50	78
December	95	83

Imagine that a considerable amount of money had been spent in 1984 to improve the safety of traffic on that highway. If these improvements were in vain (the null hypothesis), then the number and distribution of traffic accidents in 1985 can be expected to be the same as in 1983 (provided that the overall amount and nature of traffic has not changed). Thus, the data for 1983 will serve as the expected values here, and the data for 1985 will serve as the observed values.

Specifying the analysis. After starting the *Nonparametrics and Distributions* module, open the data file *Accident.sta* and select the option *Observed vs. expected Chi-square* from the startup panel. In the resulting *Observed vs. Expected Frequency* dialog, click on the *Variables* button and select variable *Y_1985* as the variable with the observed frequencies and variable *Y_1983* as the variable with the expected frequencies.

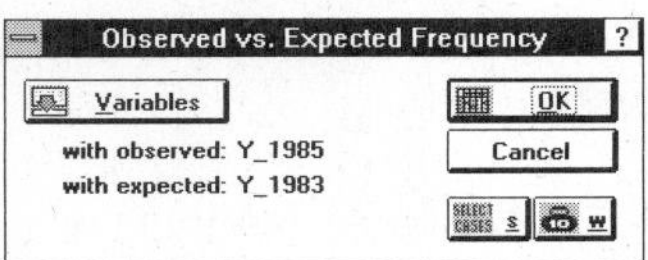

Once you click *OK* in the variable selection dialog, a Scrollsheet with the results of the analysis will be displayed.

Observed vs. Expected Frequencies (accident.sta)

NONPAR STATS — Chi-Square = 121.7010 df = 11 p < .000000
NOTE: Unequal sums of obs. & exp. frequen

Case	observed Y_1985	expected Y_1983	O - E	(O-E)**2 /E
January	85.0000	125.0000	-40.000	12.8000
February	80.0000	150.0000	-70.000	32.6667
March	85.0000	80.0000	5.000	.3125
April	40.0000	50.0000	-10.000	2.0000
May	45.0000	40.0000	5.000	.6250
June	40.0000	43.0000	-3.000	.2093
July	42.0000	80.0000	-38.000	18.0500
August	43.0000	75.0000	-32.000	13.6533
September	50.0000	80.0000	-30.000	11.2500
October	36.0000	65.0000	-29.000	12.9385
November	78.0000	50.0000	28.000	15.6800
December	83.0000	95.0000	-12.000	1.5158
Sum	707.0000	933.0000	-226.000	121.7010

Apparently, there has been a highly significant drop in the number of traffic accidents between 1983 and 1985.

Note that the Scrollsheet contains the totals across months at the bottom (*Sum*); the differences between the observed and the expected values are displayed in the third column, and the squared differences divided by the expected values (components of *Chi-square*) are displayed in the fourth column of the Scrollsheet.

Example 4: Correlations

A discussion and comparison of the different nonparametric correlation coefficients (Spearman *R*, Kendall *tau*, and *Gamma*) available in the *Nonparametrics and Distributions* module is provided on page 1609. The following example is based on a data set (contained in the example data file *Striving.sta*) reported by Siegel and Castellan (1988, page 238).

Twelve students completed two questionnaires designed to measure (1) authoritarianism and (2) striving for social status. Authoritarianism (Adorno et al., 1950) is a psychological concept; in short, highly authoritarian people tend to be rigid and believe in authority ("law and order").

Data: STRIVING.STA — Correlation between authoritarianism and striving

	1 AUTHORIT	2 STRIVING
1	82	42
2	98	46
3	87	39
4	40	37
5	116	65
6	113	88
7	111	86
8	83	56
9	85	62
10	126	92
11	106	54
12	117	81

The purpose of the study was to find out whether these two variables are correlated.

Specifying the analysis. In the startup panel of the *Nonparametrics and Distributions* module, select the *Correlations (Spearman, Kendall tau, Gamma)*. In the resulting dialog, click on the variables button and select variable *Authorit* as the first variable and variable *Striving* as the second variable.

Note that the *Nonparametrics and Distributions* module will also compute matrices of correlations, either of single lists (i.e., square matrices, select the *Square matrix* option in the *Compute* combo box) or two different lists of variables (select the *Matrix of two lists* option in the *Compute* combo box). For this example, accept the default selections of *Spearman R* and *Detailed report*.

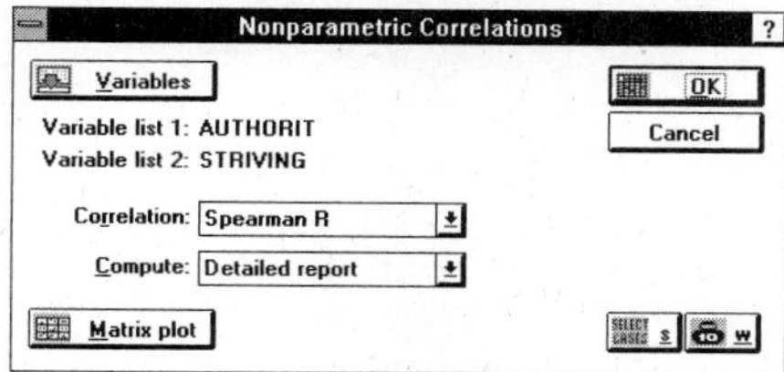

Results. Now, click *OK* and the Scrollsheet with results will be displayed.

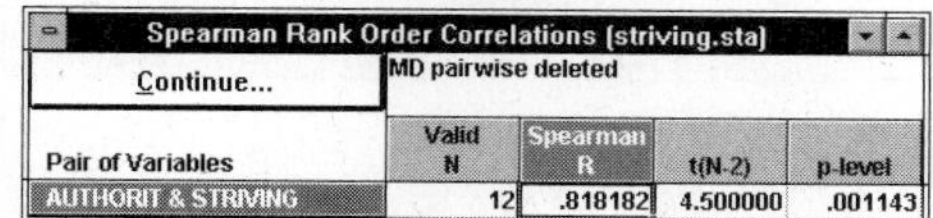

Spearman Rank Order Correlations (striving.sta)

MD pairwise deleted

Pair of Variables	Valid N	Spearman R	t(N-2)	p-level
AUTHORIT & STRIVING	12	.818182	4.500000	.001143

The correlation between the two scales is highly significant (see *Elementary Concepts*, Chapter 8, for a discussion of statistical significance testing), and you can conclude that highly authoritarian individuals probably also seek to strive towards social status (provided that the questionnaires are valid).

You can visualize the correlation by displaying the default graph in one of two ways. You can either click on the *Matrix plot* button in the *Nonparametrics Correlation* dialog (after you have selected the variables for the analysis) or you can click on the results Scrollsheet with the right-mouse-button and select the *Quick Stats Graphs* option *Scatterplot/Conf.*

The parametric correlation (Pearson product-moment correlation) between the two scales ($r = .77$) is shown in the title area of the scatterplot (see below). Interestingly, this correlation is lower than the Spearman rank order correlation (Spearman R is $.82$).

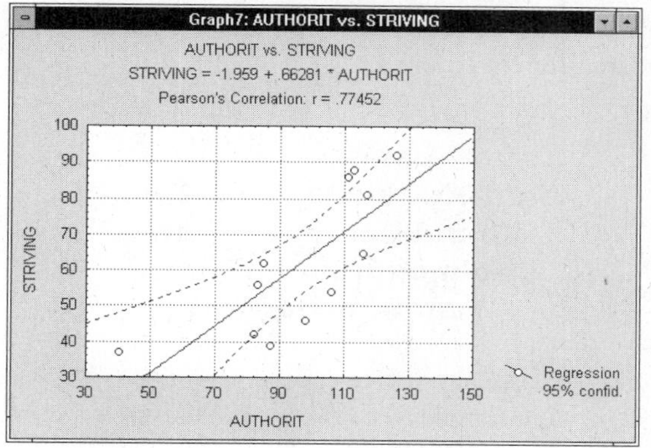

If the sample size was larger in this instance, one could conclude that treating the information in the data as ranks actually improves the estimate of the relationship between the variables by "blocking out" random variability and dampening the effects of outliers.

Kendall *tau* and *Gamma*. For comparison, return to the *Nonparametrics Correlation* dialog and

select the *Kendall tau* option and again to select the *Gamma* option. Kendall *tau* and *Gamma* are both computed as *.67*.

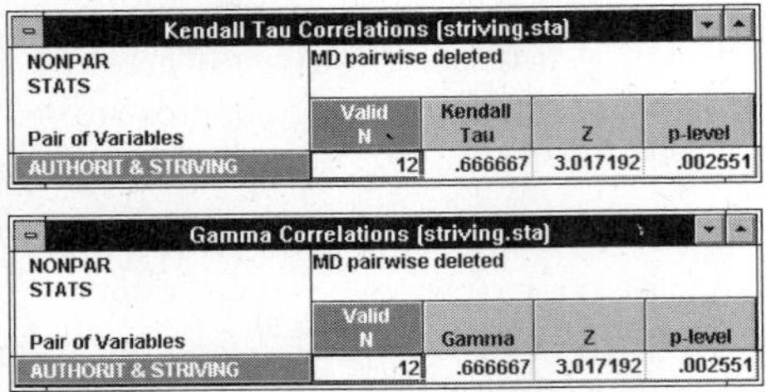

Kendall Tau Correlations (striving.sta)

NONPAR STATS — MD pairwise deleted

Pair of Variables	Valid N	Kendall Tau	Z	p-level
AUTHORIT & STRIVING	12	.666667	3.017192	.002551

Gamma Correlations (striving.sta)

NONPAR STATS — MD pairwise deleted

Pair of Variables	Valid N	Gamma	Z	p-level
AUTHORIT & STRIVING	12	.666667	3.017192	.002551

As discussed in detail earlier (see the description of the opening panel on page 1609), these two measures are indeed closely related to each other, but different from Spearman *R*. Spearman *R* can be thought of as the regular Pearson product moment correlation coefficient, that is, in terms of proportion of variability accounted for, except that Spearman *R* is computed from ranks. Kendall *tau* and *Gamma* on the other hand, rather represent *probabilities*, that is, the difference between the probability that in the observed data the two variables are in the same order *versus* the probability that the two variables are in different orders.

Example 5: Wald-Wolfowitz Runs Test, Mann-Whitney *U* Test, Kolmogorov-Smirnov Two-Sample Test

These tests are alternatives to the *t*-test for independent samples (see *Basic Statistics and Tables*, Chapter 9). Refer to pages 1600 and 1601 for a discussion of the logic and assumptions of these tests. This example is based on a study of gender differences in aggressiveness of four-year-old boys and girls (Siegel, 1956, page 138). These data are contained in the data file *Aggressn.sta*.

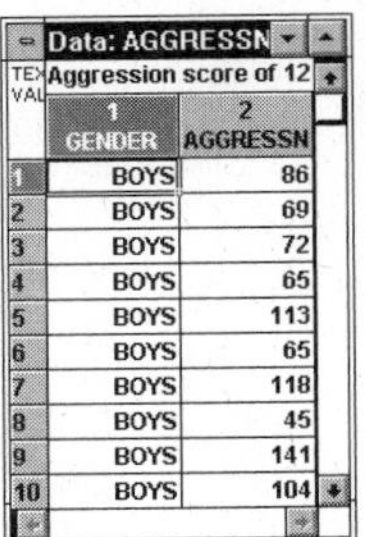

Data: AGGRESSN — Aggression score of 12

	1 GENDER	2 AGGRESSN
1	BOYS	86
2	BOYS	69
3	BOYS	72
4	BOYS	65
5	BOYS	113
6	BOYS	65
7	BOYS	118
8	BOYS	45
9	BOYS	141
10	BOYS	104

Twelve boys and 12 girls were observed during two 15-minute play sessions; each child's aggressiveness was scored (in terms of frequency and degree) during those sessions and a combined single aggressiveness index was derived for each child.

Specifying the analysis. After opening the *Nonparametrics and Distributions* module, click on either the *Wald-Wolfowitz runs test* option, the *Mann-Whitney U test*, or the *Kolmogorov-Smirnov two-sample test* (the dialogs are basically the same for all three tests). Next, click on the *Variables* button and select variable *Gender* as the independent variable, and variable *Aggressn* as the dependent variable. The codes that were used to uniquely identify the subjects' gender will automatically be selected by the program once the variables have been identified.

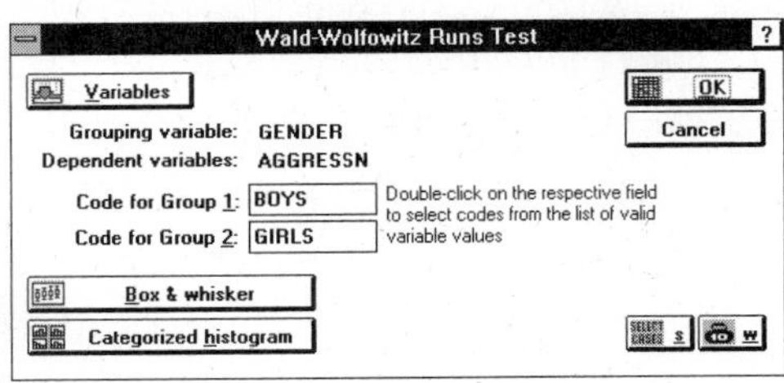

Now, click *OK* to perform the analysis.

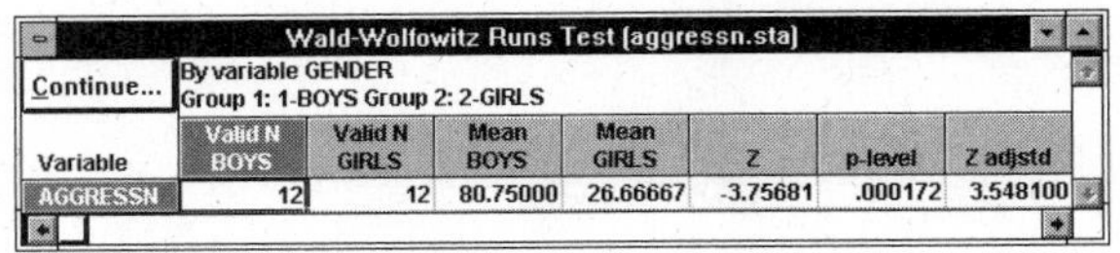

Wald-Wolfowitz Runs Test (aggressn.sta)

By variable GENDER
Group 1: 1-BOYS Group 2: 2-GIRLS

Variable	Valid N BOYS	Valid N GIRLS	Mean BOYS	Mean GIRLS	Z	p-level	Z adjstd
AGGRESSN	12	12	80.75000	26.66667	-3.75681	.000172	3.548100

The difference between boys and girls in this study with respect to aggressiveness is highly significant (see *Elementary Statistics*, Chapter 8, for a

discussion of statistical significance testing), regardless of which test was used.

The default graph for these tests is the box plot. You can display the default graph in one of two ways. You can either click on the *Box & Whisker* button in the dialog (after you have selected the variables for the analysis) or you can click on the results Scrollsheet with the right-mouse-button and select the *Quick Stats Graphs* option *Box plot*. When you select this option, you will need to select the type of statistics to be plotted in the *Box-Whisker Type* dialog.

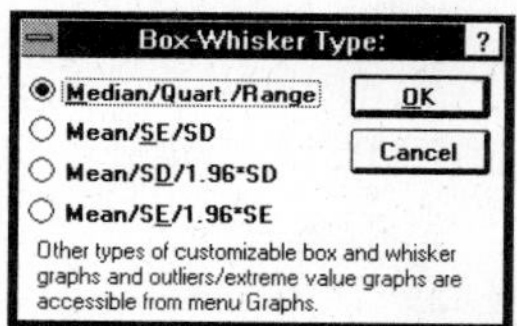

For this example, select the *Median/Quart./Range* option in this dialog and click *OK* to produce the graph. Here, the box plot will indicate, for the dependent variable, the median, quartiles (25th and 75th percentiles), and range (minimum and maximum) for each category of the grouping variable.

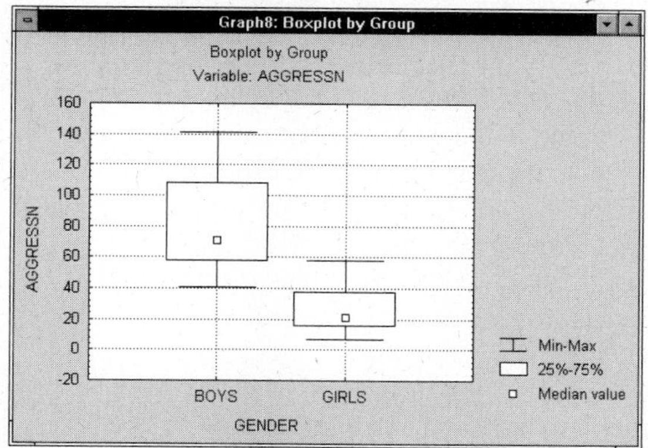

It is apparent from this plot (and the one below) that boys were more aggressive than girls. In order to view the distribution of the dependent variable as categorized by the grouping variable, click on the *Categorized histogram* button in the dialog.

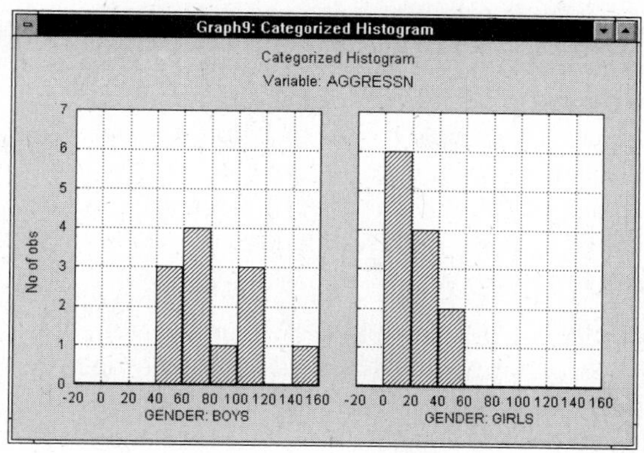

Example 6: Kruskal-Wallis ANOVA & Median Test

These tests are alternatives to one-way between-groups analysis of variance (ANOVA, see the *ANOVA/MANOVA* chapter, Chapter 13). Refer to page 1601 for a discussion of the logic and assumptions of these tests.

The present example is based on a (fictitious) data set reported in Hays (1981, page 592). The data set (included in the *Examples* directory) is in the file *Kruskal.sta* and is shown below.

Data: KRUSKAL.S

Correct choice of rewa

	1 CONDITN	2 PERFRMNC
8	FORM	15
9	FORM	14
10	FORM	10
11	FORM	8
12	FORM	14
13	COLOR	31
14	COLOR	7
15	COLOR	9
16	COLOR	11
17	COLOR	16

These data were obtained from small children who were randomly assigned to one of three experimental groups (treatments). Each child was shown a series of pairs of stimuli. Their task was to choose one of those stimuli, and, if it was the "correct" one, they received a reward. In one group, the relevant

dimension that the children had to detect in order to make correct choices was form (group *1-Form*), in a second group the relevant dimension was color (group *2-Color*), and in the third group, the relevant dimension was size (*3-Size*). The dependent variable was the number of trials that these children required to detect the relevant dimension that was being rewarded.

Specifying the analysis. After opening the *Nonparametrics and Distributions* module, open the data file *Kruskal.sta*. Then, in the startup panel, select the *Kruskal-Wallis ANOVA, Median test* option to open the *Kruskal-Wallis ANOVA and Median Test* dialog.

In this dialog, click on the *Variables* button and select variable *Conditn* as the independent variable and variable *Perfrmnc* as the dependent variable. Now, click on the *Codes* button and in that dialog, select all codes for the independent variable (click on the *All* button). The *Kruskal-Wallis ANOVA and Median Test* dialog will appear as follows:

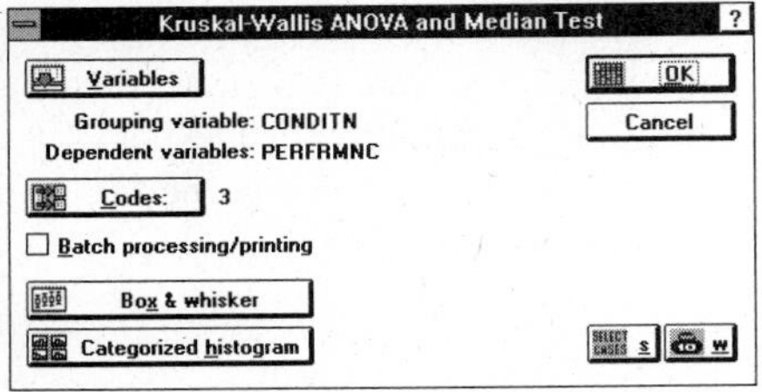

Results of Kruskal-Wallis ANOVA. Click *OK* in the above dialog to begin the analysis. The results of the Kruskal-Wallis ANOVA by ranks will be displayed first, and then the Median Test results will be displayed in a Scrollsheet.

Kruskal-Wallis ANOVA by Ranks (kruskal.sta)

NONPAR STATS — Independent (grouping) variable: CONDITN
Kruskal-Wallis test: H (2, N= 36) = 13.84438 p =.0010

Depend.: PERFRMNC	Code	Valid N	Sum of Ranks
FORM	1	12	139.0000
COLOR	2	12	200.0000
SIZE	3	12	327.0000

The Kruskal-Wallis test is highly significant. Thus, you can conclude that the performances of the different experimental groups were significantly different from each other. Remember that the Kruskal-Wallis test is basically an analysis of variance performed on ranks. The sum of ranks is displayed in the rightmost column of the Scrollsheet. The highest rank sum (worst performance) appears in the *Size* condition, that is, in the condition where children were rewarded for identifying size as the critical discriminating dimension; the lowest rank sum (best performance) appears in the *Form* condition.

Results of Median test. The Median test is displayed right after you exit from the Kruskal-Wallis results Scrollsheet.

Median Test, Overall Median = 19.50000 (kruskal.sta)

NONPAR STATS — Independent (grouping) variable: CONDITN
Chi-Square = 8.666667, df = 2, p = .0131

Dependent: PERFRMNC	FORM	COLOR	SIZE	Total
<= Median: observed	9.00000	7.00000	2.00000	18.00000
expected	6.00000	6.00000	6.00000	
obs.-exp.	3.00000	1.00000	-4.00000	
> Median: observed	3.00000	5.00000	10.00000	18.00000
expected	6.00000	6.00000	6.00000	
obs.-exp.	-3.00000	-1.00000	4.00000	
Total: observed	12.00000	12.00000	12.00000	36.00000

The Median test is also significant, however, less so. Remember that the Median test is more "crude" and less sensitive than the Kruskal-Wallis ANOVA (see the discussion on page 1601). The Scrollsheet shows the number of cases (children) in each experimental condition that fall below (or are equal to) the common median and the number of cases that fall above the common median. Again, the greatest number of subjects with above-median number of trials (below-median performance) are in experimental condition *Size*; the greatest number of subjects with below-median number of trials (above-median performance) are in experimental condition *Form*. Thus, this test confirms that the *Form* dimension was most easily recognized by the subjects, and the *Size* dimension was least easily recognized.

Graphical representation of results. The default graph for this Scrollsheet is the box plot (click with the right-mouse-button on the Scrollsheet

and select the *Quick Stats Graphs* option *Box plot*). However, you can also produce this plot by clicking on the *Box & Whisker* button in the *Kruskal-Wallis ANOVA and Median Test* dialog. When you select the box plot option, you will first need to specify the variable to be plotted. Next, you will be prompted to select the statistics for the box plot.

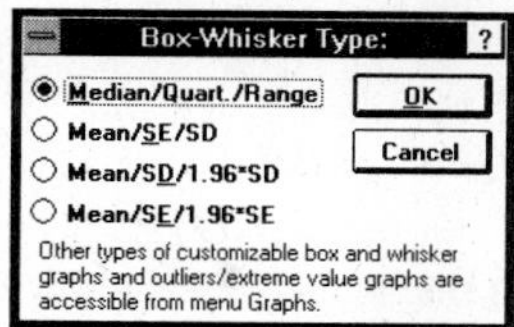

For this example, select the *Median/Quart./Range* option. Click *OK* to produce the plot.

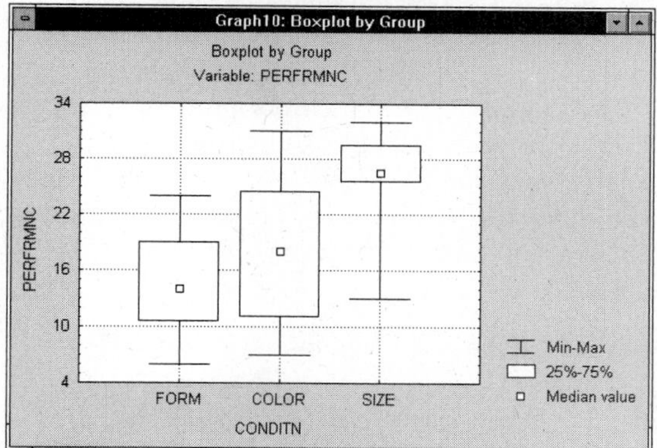

Again, it appears that performance in the *Form* condition was better than in any other condition; the median number of trials in that condition is lower than in any other condition.

Another way to look at the distribution of the dependent variable within each condition is with the *Categorized Histogram* option. Click on this button in the *Kruskal-Wallis ANOVA and Median Test* dialog to produce this graph. This graph again confirms that the performance in the *Form* category is "better" (i.e., the distribution is slightly skewed to the left) than in the other two conditions; performance clearly appears to be worst in the *Size* condition.

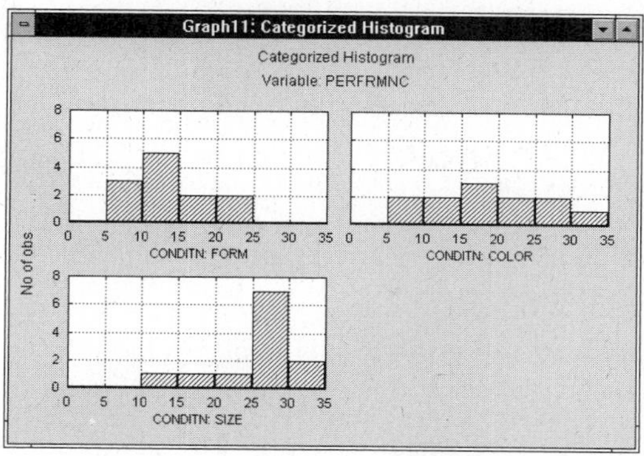

Thus you can conclude that children most easily identified the *Form* dimension when it was rewarded.

Example 7: Friedman ANOVA & Kendall Concordance

Friedman's ANOVA by ranks is an alternative to one-way within-subjects (repeated measures) analysis of variance (see *ANOVA/MANOVA*, Chapter 13). This test compares variables that were measured in dependent samples (repeated measures). Kendall coefficient of concordance essentially denotes the average rank order correlation between the cases. For a discussion of the logic and assumptions of these tests, refer to page 1602.

Data: MOTHERS.STA 20v * 13c

NUMERIC VALUES	Ranking of mothers by 13 judges					
	1 MOTH_1	2 MOTH_2	3 MOTH_3	4 MOTH_4	5 MOTH_5	6 MOTH_6
H. Smith	1.000	2.000	3.000	4.000	5.000	6.000
B. Jones	5.000	1.000	16.000	8.000	9.000	2.000
T. Hill	3.000	2.000	7.000	5.000	14.000	9.000
W. Miller	8.000	3.000	10.000	11.000	4.000	2.000
B. Robertson	2.000	1.000	15.000	8.000	14.000	4.000
C. Hansson	16.000	17.000	5.000	13.000	15.000	11.000
S. Mann	12.000	9.000	14.000	6.000	7.000	2.000
F. Jordan	11.000	2.000	13.000	10.000	7.000	3.000
B. Frank	9.000	2.000	15.000	6.000	5.000	7.000
W. Weiner	2.000	4.000	16.000	3.000	10.000	6.000
W. Kink	11.000	14.000	12.000	8.000	7.000	2.000
R. Clark	8.000	1.000	13.000	3.000	5.000	2.000
L. Evans	5.000	3.000	13.000	2.000	8.000	1.000

The following example is based on a data set reported by Siegel (1956, page 233). Twenty

mothers and their deaf children attended a seminar to receive training in how to deal with and care for their children. At the end of the seminar, the 13 staff members ranked the 20 mothers regarding how likely it was that the respective mother would raise her child in a way that would be detrimental to the child's development. The data set is contained in the file *Mothers.sta*.

Purpose of the analysis. The purpose of this analysis is twofold:

(1) To determine whether there are any significant differences between mothers with regard to their ability to raise their children, as judged by the staff members. This question can be answered by the Friedman ANOVA by ranks.

(2) Can the judges be trusted? Put another way, are the judges' ratings in agreement (i.e., correlated)? If not, then you cannot place much faith in the staffs' assessments of the mothers' likely child rearing abilities. This hypothesis (that the judges are in agreement more than what would be expected by chance) will be assessed via Kendall concordance coefficient.

Specifying the analysis. In the *Nonparametrics and Distributions* startup panel, select the *Friedman ANOVA & Kendall Concordance* option. Click on the *Variables* button in the resulting dialog and select all 20 variables (mothers).

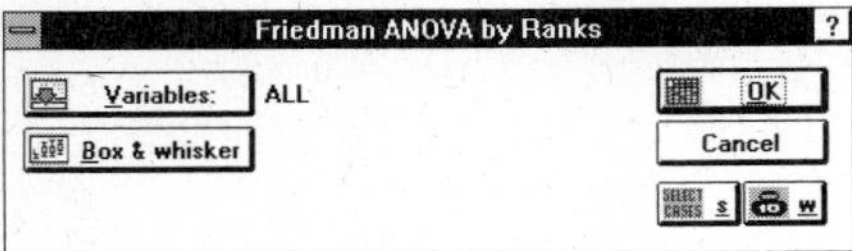

Now, click *OK* in this dialog and a Scrollsheet of results will be displayed. As you can see, there are highly significant differences between mothers. In addition, the staff members show substantial agreement in their judgments -- Kendall concordance coefficient is equal to *.57* (average rank order correlations is *.53*; refer to page 1614 for the precise relationship between these two measures).

Friedman ANOVA and Kendall Coeff. of Concordance (mothers.sta)

ANOVA Chi Sqr. (N = 13, df = 19) = 139.9814 p < .00000
Coeff. of Concordance = .56673 Aver. rank r = .53062

Variable	Average Rank	Sum of Ranks	Mean	Std.Dev.
MOTH_1	7.26923	94.5000	7.15385	4.597937
MOTH_2	4.69231	61.0000	4.69231	5.266001
MOTH_3	11.92308	155.0000	11.69231	4.230536
MOTH_4	6.69231	87.0000	6.69231	3.351234
MOTH_5	8.57692	111.5000	8.46154	3.755338
MOTH_6	4.38462	57.0000	4.38462	3.150092
MOTH_7	8.00000	104.0000	7.92308	3.988766
MOTH_8	11.07692	144.0000	10.92308	3.475187

The default plot for this Scrollsheet is the box plot. You can produce this plot either by clicking on the *Box & Whisker* button in the *Friedman ANOVA by Ranks* dialog or by clicking on the Scrollsheet with the right-mouse-button and selecting the *Quick Stats Graphs* option *Box Plot*.

When you click on the button or select the *Quick Stats Graphs* option, you will first be asked to select the variables for the plot. For this example, select all 20 variables. Next, you will be prompted to select the statistics for the box plot; select the *Median/Quart./Range* option in order to display the medians, quartile ranges (25th and 75th percentiles), and ranges (minima and maxima) of the variables in the plot.

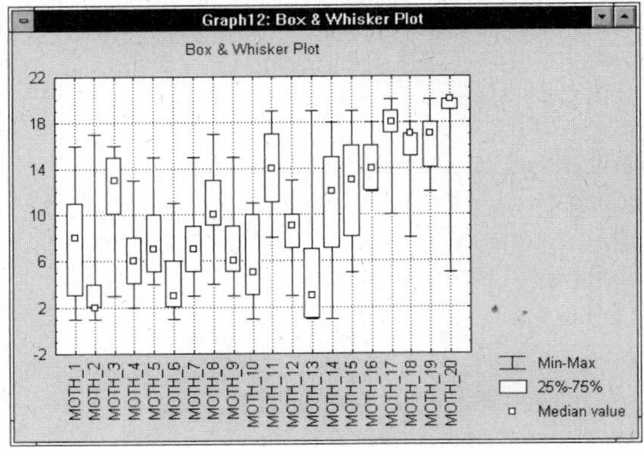

If you actually knew the names of the mothers participating in the seminar, this graph would give you an indication of who, according to the judgments of the staff, is least likely to be successful in providing her deaf child with the optimum care.

Example 8: Wilcoxon Matched Pairs Test

The Wilcoxon matched pairs test is a nonparametric alternative to the *t*-test for dependent samples (see *Basic Statistics and Tables*, Chapter 9). It will test the hypothesis that the scores for two variables were drawn from the same distribution. For a discussion of the logic and assumptions of this test, or for a comparison with the sign test, refer to page 1602.

For this example, use the same data set (*Synchron.sta*), based on a study by Dodd (1979), that was used in the *Sign Test* example (see page 1620). When processing speech, one actually pays a lot of attention to visual cues as well; specifically, one can understand (*encode*) spoken words much more readily when the face of the person talking can be seen. In a sense, all people are "lip readers," at least to some extent. Dodd tried to find out whether infants as young as only 10 to 16 weeks old are already aware of the relationship between spoken words and the corresponding movements of the lips (of the speaker). For that purpose, Dodd placed the infants in a room so that they could watch a person behind a window reading normal speech. This speech was either delivered directly into the room (*synchronous* condition) or it was delayed by 400 milliseconds (*asynchronous* condition). The dependent variable was the amount of time that the infant watched the face behind the window. No hypotheses were formulated regarding the specific condition that should elicit the most attention (the asynchronous speech could be more interesting because it is novel, or it could draw attention away from the face because the face does not seem to be the source of the speech). File *Synchron.sta* contains the results of the study. Note that a two-letter identifier for each subject was entered as the case name.

Specifying the analysis. The Wilcoxon matched pairs test is a nonparametric alternative to the *t*-test for dependent samples. Since you have the same infants listening to speech under two different conditions, this test is appropriate here. After starting the module, open the data file *Synchron.sta*. Then click on the *Wilcoxon matched pairs test* option in the startup panel. You can simultaneously perform this test on lists of variables (i.e., lists of pairs); however, you only have two variables of interest in this example. Thus, click on the *Variables* button and select variables 1 (*In_sync*) and 2 (*Out_sync*) for this test.

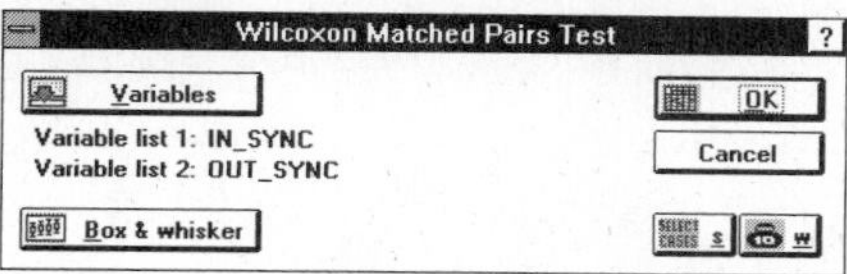

Now, click *OK* in this dialog and the results Scrollsheet will be displayed.

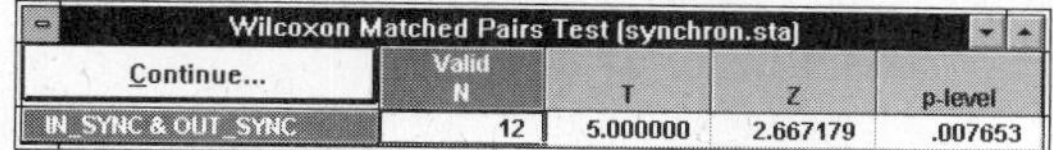

Wilcoxon Matched Pairs Test (synchron.sta)

Continue...	Valid N	T	Z	p-level
IN_SYNC & OUT_SYNC	12	5.000000	2.667179	.007653

Results. The Wilcoxon test is significant at the *.01* level (refer to the *Elementary Statistics* chapter, Chapter 8, for a discussion of "statistical significance"), which is more significant than the sign test was on the same data (see page 1602 for a comparison of these tests). This reflects the fact that the sign test only uses information about the sign of the difference between the two variables, while the Wilcoxon test also takes the relative *magnitude* of those differences into account; thus the Wilcoxon test is more sensitive than the sign test. From the results you can conclude that even at this age, infants can already discriminate between speech that is synchronized with the movement of the lips and unsynchronized speech; the term "read my lips" seems to capture a lot of truth about how one learns to understand language.

The default graph for this test is the box plot (via the *Box & Whisker* button on the *Wilcoxon Matched Pairs Test* dialog, or the Scrollsheet right-mouse button flying menu *Quick Stats Graphs* option *box*

plot). Once again, after selecting the variables for the plot, select *Mean/SE/SD* from the *Box-Whisker Type* dialog to produce the following plot.

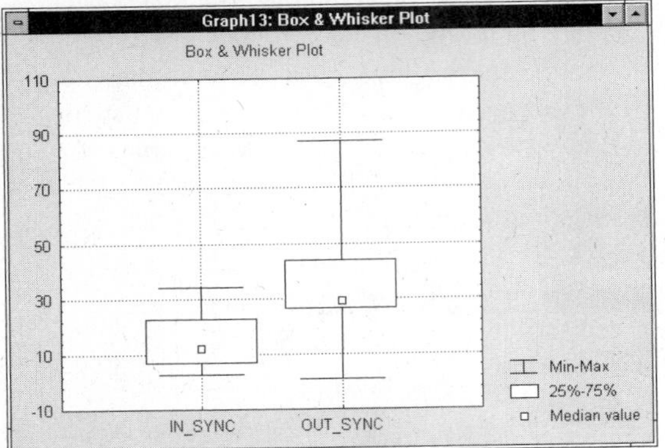

Apparently, the out-of-sync speech resulted in higher mean attention as well as greater variability on this variable.

Example 9: Cochran Q Test

The Cochran *Q* test is an extension of McNemar's *Chi-square* test (see page 1609) to more than two dependent samples. This test can also be considered to be an alternative to one-way within-subjects (repeated measures) analysis of variance (ANOVA; see *ANOVA/MANOVA*, Chapter 13) when the dependent variable is dichotomous in nature. This test is also applicable when one wants to test changes in proportions at different times in the same sample. For a discussion of the logic and assumptions of this test, see page 1614.

The following example is based on a (fictitious) data set reported in Siegel and Castellan (1988, page 173). Suppose that you are interested in investigating the effect of interviewing style on the number of respondents who agree to answer personal questions in face-to-face surveys. For example, it is always most difficult to get responses concerning personal finances or health in this type of survey, and you might want to learn whether interviewing style improves the response rate (non-refusals) to such personal questions. For that purpose, you could train an interviewer to conduct the interview in either (1) an enthusiastic manner, being friendly and showing interest (*Interview 1*), (2) a very reserved and formal manner (*Interview 2*), or (3) in a disinterested and abrupt manner (*Interview 3*). You could then select 18 sets of three households that are carefully matched in their responses to previous surveys, and randomly assign the three households in each set to one of the interviewing styles. As the dependent variable, you record whether the respective interviewee does (*1-Yes*) or does not (*0-No*) answer the personal questions. The results of this study are recorded in the data file *Interview.sta*.

Specifying the analysis. After starting the *Nonparametrics and Distributions* module, open the data file *Interview.sta* and then click on the *Cochran Q Test* option on the startup panel. In the resulting dialog, specify the variables to be compared (click on the *Variables* button), in this case, select all 3 variables (*Intrvw_1*, *Intrvw_2*, and *Intrvw_3*).

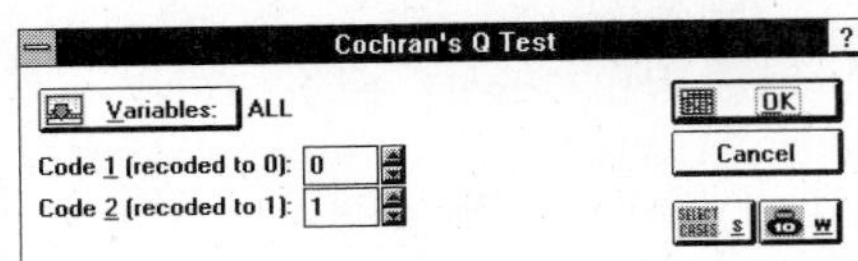

Click *OK* to begin the analysis and the results will be displayed.

Cochran's Q Test (intrview.sta)

Number of valid cases: 18
Q = 16.66667, df = 2, p < .000241

Variable	Sum	Percent 0's	Percent 1's
INTRVW_1	13.00000	27.77778	72.22222
INTRVW_2	13.00000	27.77778	72.22222
INTRVW_3	3.00000	83.33334	16.66667

Results. The *Q* test is highly significant. The right-most column shows the percent of households that disclosed personal information (*Percent 1's*). Interestingly, there is no difference in the effectiveness of the interested, enthusiastic style (variable *Intrvw_1*) and the formal, courteous style

(*Intrvw_2*), so interviewer interest does not seems to matter. However, refusals increased when the interviewer acted disinterested and abrupt (*Intrvw_3*). A quick visual summary of these results can be obtained by producing the default plot for this Scrollsheet, that is, the box plot. Select from the right-mouse-button flying menu *Quick Stats Graphs* the option *Box Plot*. After selecting the variables for the plot, select *Mean/SE/SD* from the *Box-Whisker Type* dialog to produce the following plot.

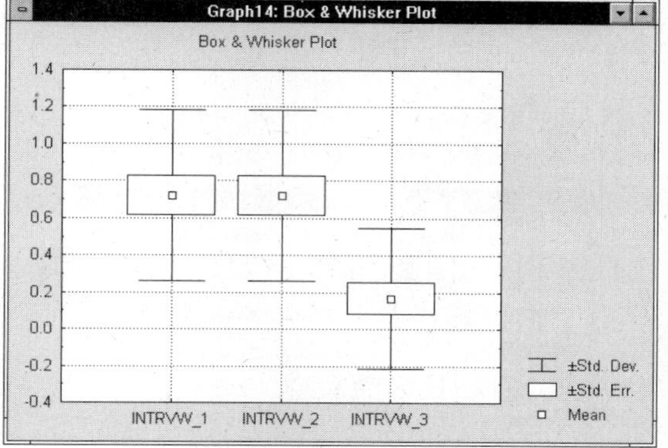

Example 10: Descriptive Statistics

This option provides a wide range of descriptive statistics that may be of particular interest if one suspects that the data for some variables are not normally distributed, and perhaps were measured on an ordinal (rank order) scale. For a discussion of these statistics and how they are computed, refer to page 1603.

For this example, use the data file *Irisdat.sta*. This file contains data reported by Fisher (1936). It contains the lengths and widths of sepals (*Sepallen, Sepalwid*) and petals *(Petallen, Petalwid*) for 50 flowers of three types of iris.

Specifying the analysis. After starting the *Nonparametrics and Distributions* module, open the data file *Irisdat.sta*. Now, click on the *Ordinal descriptive statistics* option in the startup panel and in the resulting *Descriptive Statistics* dialog, click on the *Variables* button. Variable *5-Iristype* is a coding variable to identify the type of iris, therefore, select only variables *1-4* in the variable selection dialog.

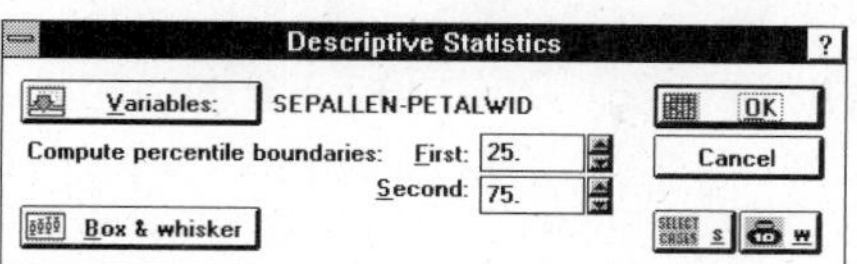

Now, click *OK* in this dialog to bring up a Scrollsheet with the results.

Descriptive Statistics (irisdat.sta)

Continue...	mean	valid N	median	mode	freq-cy of mode	minimum	maximum
SEPALLEN	5.843333	150	5.800000	5.000000	10	4.300000	7.900000
SEPALWID	3.057333	150	3.000000	3.000000	26	2.000000	4.400000
PETALLEN	3.758000	150	4.350000	multiple	--	1.000000	6.900000
PETALWID	1.199333	150	1.300000	.2000000	29	.100000	2.500000

The default plot for this Scrollsheet is a histogram of the frequency distribution with the normal curve superimposed..

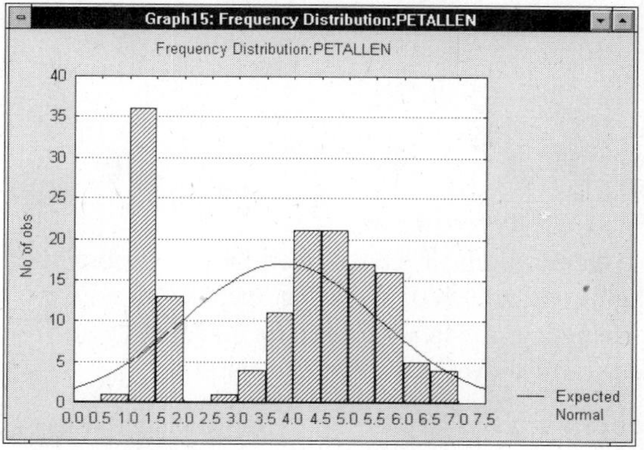

This plot is very useful for identifying deviations from the normal distribution. To produce the plot for variable *Petallen*, click on that Scrollsheet row with the right-mouse-button and select the *Quick Stats Graphs* option *Histogram/Normal*. The histogram shows that variable *Petallen* is indeed multi-modal (as indicated in the results Scrollsheet); it appears as if one group of observations forms a cluster on the left side of the plot.

Example 11: Distribution Fitting

The distribution fitting options allow you to evaluate the fit of observed data to some theoretical distributions. Refer to page 1605 for descriptions of the available distributions. Also note that the *Survival Analysis* module contains specialized routines for fitting censored (incomplete) survival or failure time data to the Weibull and Gompertz distribution. The data file used for this example is *Irisdat.sta* (shown below). This file contains data reported by Fisher (1936) on the lengths and widths of sepals (*Sepallen*, *Sepalwid*) and petals (*Petallen*, *Petalwid*) for 50 flowers of three types of iris. A discriminant function analysis of this data set is also described in the *Discriminant Analysis* chapter (Volume III).

Data: IRISDAT.STA 5v * 150c

Fisher (1936) iris data: length & width of sepals and petals,

	1 SEPALLEN	2 SEPALWID	3 PETALLEN	4 PETALWID	5 IRISTYPE
1	5.0	3.3	1.4	.2	SETOSA
2	6.4	2.8	5.6	2.2	VIRGINIC
3	6.5	2.8	4.6	1.5	VERSICOL
4	6.7	3.1	5.6	2.4	VIRGINIC
5	6.3	2.8	5.1	1.5	VIRGINIC
6	4.6	3.4	1.4	.3	SETOSA
7	6.9	3.1	5.1	2.3	VIRGINIC
8	6.2	2.2	4.5	1.5	VERSICOL
9	5.9	3.2	4.8	1.8	VERSICOL
10	4.6	3.6	1.0	.2	SETOSA

The distributions of the four variables describing the lengths and widths of sepals and petals will now be examined. Specifically, it is expected that those measures follow the normal distribution.

Specifying the analysis. After starting the *Nonparametrics and Distributions* module, open the data file *Irisdat.sta* and select the *Continuous distribution: Normal* option in the startup panel. In the resulting dialog, click on the *Variables* button and select variable *Sepallen*. At this point, the data file will be processed and the dialog will show the computed mean and variance as the default values for the *Mean* and *Variance* options. You can also adjust the *Number of categories* and the *Lower* and *Upper limits* for the computation of the frequency distribution. The *Fitting Continuous Distributions* dialog will now appear as follows.

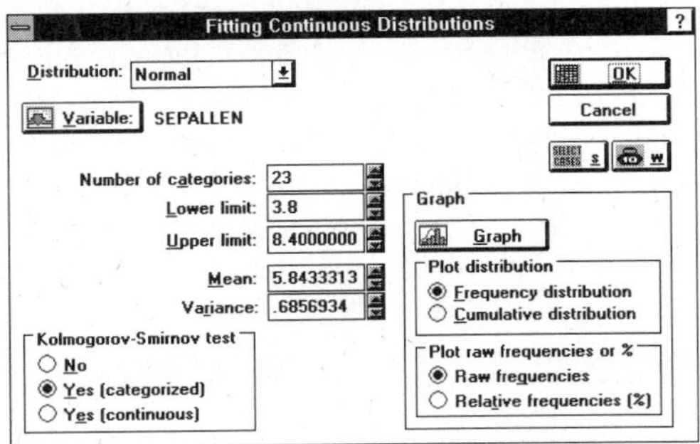

Accept all of the default selections in this dialog and click *OK* to compute the frequency distribution.

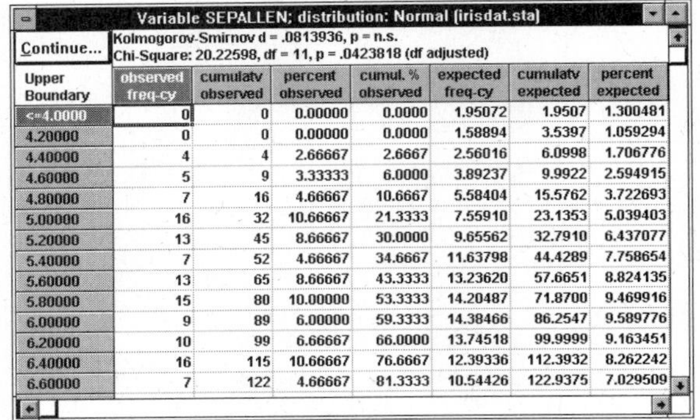

Variable SEPALLEN; distribution: Normal (irisdat.sta)

Kolmogorov-Smirnov d = .0813936, p = n.s.
Chi-Square: 20.22598, df = 11, p = .0423818 (df adjusted)

Upper Boundary	observed freq-cy	cumulatv observed	percent observed	cumul. % observed	expected freq-cy	cumulatv expected	percent expected
<=4.0000	0	0	0.00000	0.0000	1.95072	1.9507	1.300481
4.20000	0	0	0.00000	0.0000	1.58894	3.5397	1.059294
4.40000	4	4	2.66667	2.6667	2.56016	6.0998	1.706776
4.60000	5	9	3.33333	6.0000	3.89237	9.9922	2.594915
4.80000	7	16	4.66667	10.6667	5.58404	15.5762	3.722693
5.00000	16	32	10.66667	21.3333	7.55910	23.1353	5.039403
5.20000	13	45	8.66667	30.0000	9.65562	32.7910	6.437077
5.40000	7	52	4.66667	34.6667	11.63798	44.4289	7.758654
5.60000	13	65	8.66667	43.3333	13.23620	57.6651	8.824135
5.80000	15	80	10.00000	53.3333	14.20487	71.8700	9.469916
6.00000	9	89	6.00000	59.3333	14.38466	86.2547	9.589776
6.20000	10	99	6.66667	66.0000	13.74518	99.9999	9.163451
6.40000	16	115	10.66667	76.6667	12.39336	112.3932	8.262242
6.60000	7	122	4.66667	81.3333	10.54426	122.9375	7.029509

Test statistics. The *Chi-square* value is significant at the *.05* level ($p = .042$). Thus, based on the *Chi-square* test, you would conclude that the distribution deviates significantly from the standard normal distribution. However, the Kolmogorov-Smirnov test is not significant (however, see the note in the *Dialogs, Options, Statistics* section on Lilliefors probabilities, page 1617). This pattern of results is not uncommon because the Kolmogorov-Smirnov test is not as much a *precise* procedure as it is a technique to detect gross deviations from some assumed distribution. Often, the *Chi-square* value is greatly affected by the way in which the distribution is "sliced up," that is, by the number of categories, minimum, and maximum values that the user chooses. For example, if you slice the distribution

for *Sepallen* into only 10 pieces (set the *Number of categories* option to *10*), rather than the default *23* categories, then the resulting *Chi-square* value is only marginally significant at the *.07* level.

Variable SEPALLEN; distribution: Normal (irisdat.sta)

NONPAR STATS — Kolmogorov-Smirnov d = .0617852, p = n.s.
Chi-Square: 8.627198, df = 4, p = .0711498 (df adjusted)

Upper Boundary	observed freq-cy	cumulatv observed	percent observed	cumul. % observed	expected freq-cy	cumulatv expected	percent expected
<=4.2600	0	0	0.00000	0.0000	4.18991	4.1899	2.79327
4.72000	11	11	7.33333	7.3333	8.92888	13.1188	5.95258
5.18000	30	41	20.00000	27.3333	18.61343	31.7322	12.40896
5.64000	24	65	16.00000	43.3333	28.72008	60.4523	19.14672
6.10000	30	95	20.00000	63.3333	32.80342	93.2557	21.86895
6.56000	25	120	16.66667	80.0000	27.73582	120.9915	18.49055
7.02000	18	138	12.00000	92.0000	17.35935	138.3509	11.57290
7.48000	6	144	4.00000	96.0000	8.04170	146.3926	5.36114
7.94000	6	150	4.00000	100.0000	2.75682	149.1494	1.83788
Infinity	0	150	0.00000	100.0000	.85059	150.0000	.56706

Of much greater importance is how the general shape of the observed distribution approximates the hypothesized normal distribution.

Now, return to the *Fitting Continuous Distributions* dialog. Under the *Graphs* options, you can choose to plot a histogram of the *Frequency* or *Cumulative* distributions with the *Raw* or *Relative* frequencies. For the default number of categories (*23*), accept the default graph selections and click on the *Graph* button to produce the frequency histogram for this variable.

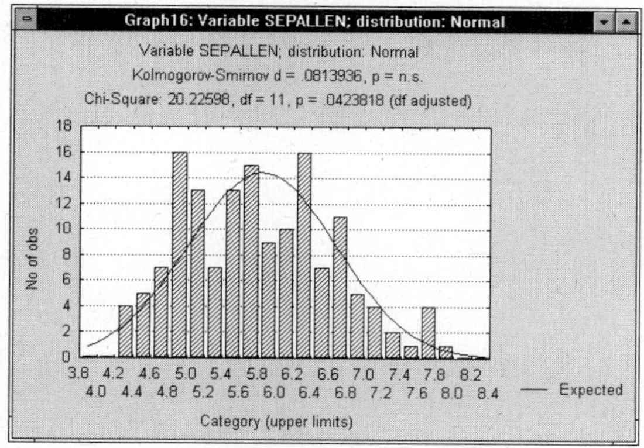

It seems that the distribution of *Sepallen* is bimodal, that is, it appears to have two "peaks." Also, a major lack of fit exists on the left side of the observed distribution where the first peak occurs. Thus you would conclude from the analysis that the continuous normal distribution probably does not provide an adequate model for the observed distribution.

StatSoft

NOTES AND TECHNICAL INFORMATION

Tied Ranks

In all methods that are based on ranks, the program will adjust for tied ranks using procedures discussed in Siegel (1956) and Siegel and Castellan (1988).

Significance Tests for Samples of Small Size

If the sample size is very small (e.g., n = 10 or less) significance levels for those tests that use z approximations should be treated as rough estimates only. Refer to Hays (1981), Siegel (1956), and Siegel and Castellan (1988) for detailed discussions of these z approximations.

Fitting the Weibull and Gompertz Distribution to Censored Data

These distributions are commonly used in biomedical as well as engineering research as theoretical distributions for failure times (time to failure) or survival times (time to death). An additional special problem in those areas of research is the issue of incomplete or censored observations, for example, patients who survived until after the study was terminated, or parts that did not fail at all. Those observations obviously contain valuable information (patient *X* survived over 3 years) but they are not complete (how long *did* patient *X* survive?). Because of these special issues involved in fitting the Weibull and Gompertz distribution to survival or failure times, fitting options for complete or censored data sets are available in the *Survival Analysis* module of *STATISTICA*.

Distribution Fitting via *Stats 2D Graphs* Options and the *Process Analysis* Module

There are several alternative procedures available in *STATISTICA* for fitting continuous distributions to data. Specifically, you can choose (categorized or non-categorized) *Quantile-Quantile* plots, *Probability-Probability* plots, or *2D Histograms* (with a line indicating the expected frequencies) from the *Graphs Gallery* or the *Graphs* pull-down menu, and then choose to produce the respective plots based on the *Normal*, *Beta*, *Extreme Value*, *Gamma*, *Geometric*, *Laplace*, *Logistic*, *Lognormal*, *Poisson*, *Rayleigh*, and *Weibull* distributions. The program will compute maximum likelihood parameter estimates for the respective distributions (see Volume II for additional details).

The *Process Analysis* module of *STATISTICA* (see Volume IV) also contains several options for fitting these distributions, and for computing tables with expected and observed frequencies. That module also has an option to fit simultaneously all of these continuous distributions to the data; the results Scrollsheet for this option contains the respective Kolmogorov-Smirnov *d-max* values, sorted in ascending order (i.e., from the best-fitting to the worst-fitting distribution).

INDEX

N

O

P

Q

R

S

T

V

W

Y

Chapter 12: MULTIPLE REGRESSION

Table of Contents

Detailed Table of Contents

StatSoft®

STATISTICA

Chapter 12: MULTIPLE REGRESSION

INTRODUCTORY OVERVIEW

General Purpose

The general purpose of multiple regression is to analyze the relationship between several independent or predictor variables and a dependent or criterion variable. For example, a real estate agent might record for each listing, the size of the house (in square feet), the number of bedrooms, the average income in the respective neighborhood according to census data, and a subjective rating of appeal of the house.

Once this information has been compiled for various houses it would be interesting to see whether and how these measures relate to the price for which a house is sold. For example, one might learn that the number of bedrooms is a better predictor of the price for which a house sells in a particular neighborhood than how "pretty" the house is (subjective rating). One may also detect "outliers," that is, houses that should really sell for more, given their location and characteristics.

Personnel professionals customarily use multiple regression procedures to determine equitable compensation. One can determine a number of factors or dimensions such as "amount of responsibility" (*Resp*) or "number of people to supervise" (*No_Super*) that one believes to contribute to the value of a job. The personnel analyst then usually conducts a salary survey among comparable companies in the market, recording the salaries and respective characteristics (i.e., values on dimensions) for different positions. This information can be used in a multiple regression analysis to build a regression equation of the form:

```
Salary = .5*Resp + .8*No_Super
```

Once this so-called regression line has been determined, the analyst can now easily construct a graph of the expected (predicted) salaries and the actual salaries of job incumbents in the company. Thus, the analyst is able to determine which position is underpaid (below the regression line) or overpaid (above the regression line), or paid equitably.

In the social and natural sciences multiple regression procedures are very widely used in research. In general, multiple regression allows the researcher to ask (and hopefully answer) the general question "what is the best predictor of ...".

For example, educational researchers might want to learn what are the best predictors of success in high-school. Psychologists may want to determine which personality variable best predicts social adjustment. Sociologists may want to find out which of the multiple social indicators best predict whether or not a new immigrant group will adapt and be absorbed into society.

Computational Approach

The general computational problem that needs to be solved in multiple regression analysis is to fit a straight line to a number of points.

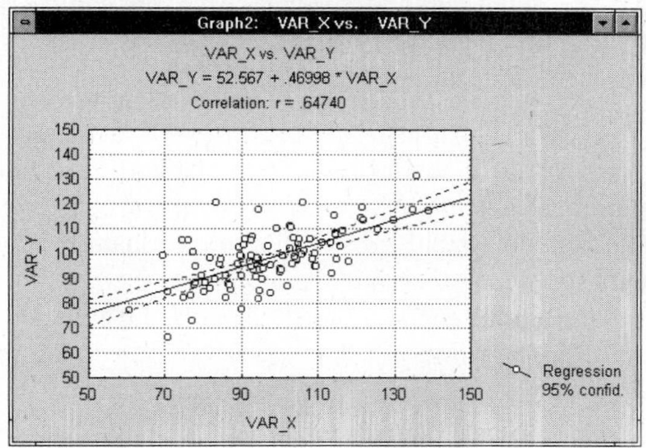

StatSoft

In the simplest case -- one dependent and one independent variable -- one can visualize this in a scatterplot.

Linear least squares. In the scatterplot, there is an independent or *X* variable, and a dependent or *Y* variable. These variables may, for example, represent IQ (intelligence as measured by a test) and school achievement (grade point average; GPA), respectively. Each point in the plot represents one student, that is, the respective student's IQ and GPA.

The goal of linear regression procedures is to fit a line through the points. Specifically, the program will compute a line so that the squared deviations of the observed points from that line are minimized. Thus, this general procedure is sometimes also referred to as *least squares* estimation.

The regression equation. A line in a two dimensional or two-variable space is defined by the equation $Y=a+b*X$; in full text: the *Y* variable can be expressed in terms of a constant (*a*) and a slope (*b*) times the *X* variable. The constant is also referred to as the *intercept*, and the slope as the *regression coefficient* or *B coefficient*. For example, GPA may best be predicted as $1+.02*IQ$. Thus, knowing that a student has an *IQ* of 130 would lead you to predict that her GPA would be 3.6 (since, 1+.02*130=3.6).

In the multivariate case, when there is more than one independent variable, the regression line cannot be visualized in the two dimensional space, but can be computed just as easily (via the *Multiple Regression* module; the computations are actually quite complex).

For example, if in addition to *IQ* you had other predictors of achievement (e.g., *Motivation*, *Self-discipline*), you could construct a linear equation containing all those variables. In general then, multiple regression procedures will estimate a linear equation of the form:

$$Y = a + b_1*X_1 + b_2*X_2 +...+ b_p*X_p$$

Unique prediction and partial correlation. Note that in this equation, the regression coefficients (or *B* coefficients) represent the *independent* contributions of each independent variable to the prediction of the dependent variable. Another way to express this fact is to say that, for example, variable X_1 is correlated with the *Y* variable, after controlling for all other independent variables. This type of correlation is also referred to as a *partial correlation*. Perhaps the following example will clarify this issue.

One would probably find a significant negative correlation between hair length and height in the population (i.e., short people have longer hair). At first this may seem odd; however, if you were to add the variable *Gender* into the multiple regression equation, this correlation would probably disappear. This is because women, on the average, have longer hair than men; they also are shorter on the average than men. Thus, after you remove this gender difference by entering *Gender* into the equation, the relationship between hair length and height disappears because hair length does *not* make any unique contribution to the prediction of height, above and beyond what it shares in the prediction with variable *Gender*. Put another way, after controlling for the variable *Gender*, the partial correlation between hair length and height is zero.

Predicted and residual scores. The regression line expresses the best prediction of the dependent variable (*Y*), given the independent variables (*X*). However, nature is rarely (if ever) perfectly predictable, and usually there is substantial variation of the observed points around the fitted regression line (as in the scatterplot shown earlier). The deviation of a particular point from the regression line (its predicted value) is called the *residual* value.

Residual variance and *R-square*. The smaller the variability of the residual values around the regression line relative to the overall variability, the better is the prediction.

For example, if there is no relationship between the *X* and *Y* variables, then the ratio of the residual variability of the *Y* variable to the original variance is equal to 1.0. If *X* and *Y* are perfectly related, then there is no residual variance and the ratio of variance would be 0.0. In most cases, the ratio would fall somewhere between these extremes, that is, between 0.0 and 1.0. 1.0 minus this ratio is referred to as *R-square* or the *coefficient of determination*.

This value is immediately interpretable in the following manner. If you have an *R-square* of 0.4, then you know that the variability of the *Y* values around the regression line is 1-0.4 times the original variance; in other words, 40% of the original variability has been explained, and 60% residual variability is left. Ideally, you would like to explain most if not all of the original variability. The *R-square* value is an indicator of how well the model fits the data (e.g., an *R-square* close to 1.0 indicates that the model accounts for almost all of the variability in the respective variables).

Interpreting the multiple correlation coefficient *R*. Customarily, the degree to which two or more predictors (independent or *X* variables) are related to the dependent (*Y*) variable is expressed in the multiple correlation coefficient *R*. In multiple regression, *R* can assume values between 0 and 1.

To interpret the direction of the relationship between variables, one looks at the signs (plus or minus) of the regression or *B* coefficients. If a *B* coefficient is positive, then the relationship of this variable with the dependent variable is positive (e.g., the greater the IQ the better the grade point average); if the *B* coefficient is negative, then the relationship is negative (e.g., the lower the class size the better the average test scores). Of course, if the *B* coefficient is equal to 0, then there is no relationship between the variables.

Assumptions, Limitations, and Practical Considerations

Assumption of linearity. First of all, as is evident in the name multiple *linear* regression, it is assumed that the relationship between variables is linear. In practice this assumption can virtually never be confirmed; fortunately, multiple regression procedures are not greatly affected by minor deviations from this assumption. However, as a rule, it is prudent to *always* look at bivariate scatterplots of the variables of interest.

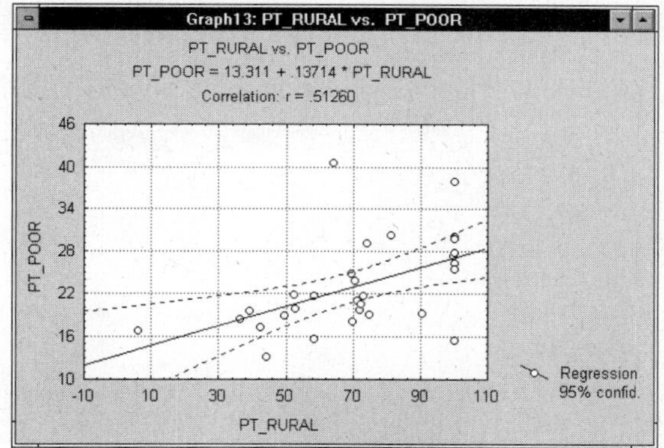

In the *Multiple Regression* module, these plots are readily available from anywhere within the program by simply requesting the Scrollsheet with the correlation matrix, and then displaying the customized graph (scatterplot) for the respective highlighted cell. If curvature in the relationships is evident, one may consider either transforming the variables (via *STATISTICA BASIC* or *Spreadsheet Formulas*, see Chapter 3), or explicitly allowing for nonlinear components.

The *Multiple Regression* module's *Fixed Nonlinear* option allows you to fit various nonlinear components, that is, to test explicitly for the significance of a nonlinear component in the relationship between two or more variables (other nonlinear regression options are available in the *Nonlinear Estimation* module; see Volume III).

Normality assumption. It is assumed in multiple regression that the residuals (prediced minus observed values) are distributed normally (i.e., follow the normal distribution). Again, even though most tests (specifically the *F*-test) are quite robust with regard to violations of this assumption, it is *always* a good idea, before drawing final conclusions, to review the distributions of the major variables of interest. In *Multiple Regression* one can produce a histogram (with the normal curve superimposed) from within the descriptive statistics Scrollsheet that is available at all times in the program. Also, the user can produce histograms for the residuals as well as normal probability plots, in order to inspect the distribution of the residual values.

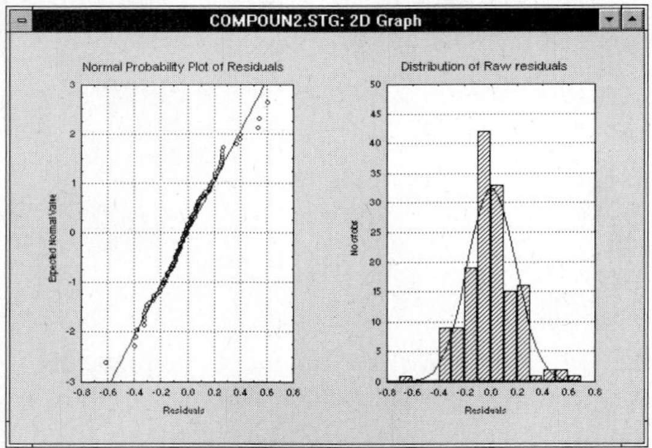

Limitations. The major conceptual limitation of all regression techniques is that one can only ascertain *relationships*, but never be sure about underlying *causal* mechanisms. For example, one would find a strong positive relationship (correlation) between the damage that a fire does and the number of firemen involved in fighting the blaze. Do you conclude that the firemen cause the damage? Of course, the most likely explanation of this correlation is that the size of the fire (an external variable that you forgot to include in your study) caused the damage as well as the involvement of a certain number of firemen (i.e., the bigger the fire, the more firemen are called to fight the blaze). Even though this example is fairly obvious, in real correlational research, alternative causal explanations are often not considered.

Choice of the number of variables. Multiple regression is a seductive technique: "plug in" as many predictor variables as you can think of and usually at least a few of them will come out significant. This is because one is capitalizing on chance when simply including as many variables as one can think of as predictors of some other variable of interest. This problem is compounded when, in addition, the number of observations is relatively low. Intuitively, it is clear that one can hardly draw conclusions from an analysis of 100 questionnaire items based on 10 respondents. Most authors recommend that one should have at least 10 to 20 times as many observations (cases, respondents) as one has variables, otherwise the estimates of the regression line are probably very unstable and unlikely to replicate if one were to do the study over.

Multicollinearity and matrix ill-conditioning. This is a common problem in many correlational analyses. Imagine that you have two predictors (*X* variables) of a person's height: (1) weight in pounds and (2) weight in ounces. Obviously, the two predictors are completely redundant; weight is one and the same variable, regardless of whether it is measured in pounds or ounces. Trying to decide which one of the two measures is a better predictor of height would be rather silly; however, this is exactly what one would try to do if one were to perform a multiple regression analysis with height as the dependent (*Y*) variable and the two measures of weight as the independent (*X*) variables. *STATISTICA* would issue a *matrix ill-conditioned* message to let the user know that he or she is trying to do the impossible. When there are very many variables involved, it is often not immediately apparent that this problem exists, and it may only manifest itself after several variables have already been entered into the regression equation. Nevertheless, when this problem occurs, it means that at least one of the predictor variables is

(practically) completely redundant with other predictors. The *Multiple Regression* module contains many statistical indicators of this type of redundancy (tolerances, semi-partial *R*, etc., see *Multiple Regression Results*, page 1670) as well as some remedies (e.g., *Ridge regression*).

The importance of residual analysis. Even though most assumptions of multiple regression cannot be tested explicitly, gross violations can be detected and should be dealt with appropriately. In particular, outliers (i.e., extreme cases) can seriously bias the results by "pulling" or "pushing" the regression line in a particular direction, thereby leading to biased regression coefficients. Often, excluding just a single extreme case can yield a completely different set of results. Therefore, one of the design goals for the *Multiple Regression* module was to make residual analyses as readily available as possible to the user so that violations of assumptions that threaten the validity of results can easily be identified.

PROGRAM OVERVIEW

With this module, the user can perform linear multiple regression, forward or backward stepwise regression, enter or remove variables in blocks (hierarchical analysis), perform ridge regression analyses, and perform *fixed nonlinear* regression (e.g., fit polynomial equations). The *Multiple Regression* module will also perform extensive residual analyses. The user can compute predicted and residual scores (including deleted residuals, standardized predicted and residual scores, Mahalanobis distances, Cook's distances, etc.), and calculate the Durbin-Watson statistic and the serial correlation of residuals. Residuals and predicted scores may be saved for further analysis with other modules.

All analyses can be performed with or without an intercept in the regression equation (the intercept may be forced to zero; regression through the origin); adjusted sums of squares and *R-square* values can be computed for models without an intercept (based on the variability around the mean, and not the origin). Raw data files or correlation matrices may be used as input for this module. In addition to the standard multiple regression output, the user can review the standardized and non-standardized regression coefficients, their standard errors and statistical significance, partial correlations, part correlations (semi-partial correlations), tolerances, the correlations and covariances of regression weights, the inverse of the correlation matrix of independent variables, and a summary of stepwise regression (forward, backward, or in blocks) analyses.

Also, after the regression equation has been estimated, the user can interactively compute the predicted value for any set of independent variable values. The correlation matrix can be calculated with pairwise or casewise deletion of missing data, or missing data may automatically be substituted by the respective means. The correlation matrix can be saved for later analyses with other *STATISTICA* modules.

In addition to the standard batch and macro processing options available in all modules of *STATISTICA*, the *Multiple Regression* module contains an internal batch option allowing the user to specify a list of dependent variables that will be processed consecutively with the same regression design.

Plots. Numerous statistical graphs are available for evaluating the regression model. The distribution of residuals can be visualized via normal, half-normal, and detrended normal probability plots and histograms; predicted values, residuals, deleted residuals, Mahalanobis distances, etc. can be simultaneously visualized in icon plots; various types of scatterplots are available for displaying the residuals versus the predicted values, squared residuals versus predicted values, deleted residuals versus residuals, etc.

Alternative procedures. The *Factor Analysis* module (see Volume III) will also perform multiple regression analyses for large problems (up to 300 variables); regression problems of practically unlimited size can be solved via the *STATISTICA BASIC* example program *Regressn.stb* (in the *STBASIC* subdirectory). A general (linear or nonlinear) multiple regression procedure is provided in the *Nonlinear Estimation* module, where the user can estimate any arbitrary regression function, using least squares estimation or any other arbitrary loss function (e.g., absolute deviations, weighted least squares, etc.). If one has multiple dependent as well as independent variables, then canonical analysis (see *Canonical Correlation*, Volume III) is appropriate. To test specific *a priori* hypotheses about the structure of a correlation matrix, and the relationships between variables or underlying latent constructs (e.g., to perform a path analysis), use the

Structural Equation Modeling and Path Analysis (SEPATH) module (see Volume III). If the dependent variable is measured in terms of categories (e.g., applicant passed vs. did not pass exam), then one may use the *Discriminant Analysis* module (finding the best predictors that discriminate between people who pass or fail the examination). If the dependent variable is truly categorical in nature (e.g., the phenotype is either male or female; you want to predict the *underlying probability* of obtaining one or the other phenotype), then the *probit* or *logit* regression models may be more appropriate (see *Nonlinear Estimation*, Volume III). If the data set includes incomplete (or censored) observations (e.g., as in the analysis of failure or survival times), use the different regression models available in the *Survival Analysis* module. The *Time Series* module contains procedures for detecting auto-correlations (correlation of a variable with itself, measured at different points in time) and it also includes a comprehensive set of procedures for analyzing lagged correlations. Finally, there are several *STATISTICA BASIC* example programs (in the *STBASIC* subdirectory) for addressing specific regression problems (e.g., weighted least squares, two-stage least squares, Cox-Box and Box-Tidwell transformations, etc.; see page 1685 for details).

EXAMPLES

Example 1: Standard Regression Analysis

Data File

The following example is based on the data file *Poverty.sta* that is included with your *STATISTICA* program. Below is a partial listing of that file:

Data: POVERTY.STA 8v * 30c

NUMERIC VALUES	1 POP_CHNG	2 N_EMPLD	3 PT_POOR	4 TAX_RATE	5 PT_PHONE	6 PT_RURAL	7 AGE	8 AFR_AM
	Predictors of poverty							
Benton	13.7	400	19.0	1.09	82	75.	33.5	360
Cannon	-.8	710	26.2	1.01	66	100	32.8	193
Carrol	9.6	1610	18.1	.40	80	70.	33.4	3080
Cheatheam	40.0	500	15.4	.93	74	100	27.8	592
Cumberland	8.4	640	29.0	.92	65	74	27.9	2
DeKalb	3.5	920	21.6	.59	64	73.	33.2	230
Dyer	3.0	1890	21.9	.63	82	52.	30.8	3978
Gibson	7.1	3040	18.9	.49	85	50.	32.4	9816
Greene	13.0	2730	21.1	.71	78	71.	29.2	1137
Hawkins	10.7	1850	23.8	.93	74	71.	28.7	992
Haywood	-16.2	2920	40.5	.51	69	64.	25.1	10723
Henry	6.6	1070	21.6	.80	85	58.	35.9	3129
Houston	21.9	160	25.4	.74	69	100	31.4	338
Humphreys	17.8	380	19.7	.44	83	72	30.1	516
Jackson	-11.8	1140	38.0	.81	54	100	34.1	12
Johnson	7.5	690	30.1	1.05	65	100	30.5	104

The data are based on a comparison of 1960 and 1970 Census figures for a random selection of 30 counties. The names of the counties were entered as case names.

The following information for each variable is given in the *View (All) Variable Specs* Scrollsheet (accessible by clicking on the *All Specs* button on the spreadsheet toolbar or by selecting *Variables - All Specs* from the spreadsheet window *Edit* pull-down menu; see Chapter 3, *Spreadsheet Window*):

Variables: POVERTY.STA 8v * 30c

	Name	MD Code	Format	Long Name (label, fo
1	POP_CHNG	-9999	8.1	Population change (1960-1970)
2	N_EMPLD	-9999	7.0	No. of persons employed in agriculture
3	PT_POOR	-9999	7.1	Percent of families below poverty level
4	TAX_RATE	-9999	8.2	Residential and farm property tax rate
5	PT_PHONE	-9999	8.0	Percent residences with telephones
6	PT_RURAL	-9999	8.0	Percent rural population
7	AGE	-9999	5.1	Median age
8	AFR_AM	-9999	6.0	Number of African/Americans

Research Question

Now, analyze the correlates of poverty, that is, the variables that best predict the percent of families below the poverty line in a county. Thus, you will treat variable *3* (*Pt_Poor*) as the dependent or criterion variable, and all other variables as the independent or predictor variables.

Starting the Analysis

When you start the *Multiple Regression* module, the *Multiple Regression* startup panel will open. You can specify the regression equation by clicking on the *Variables* button and selecting *Pt_Poor* as the dependent variable and all of the other variables in the data file as the independent variables. Also, set the *Perform default analysis* and *Review descr. stats, corr matrix* check boxes. When you check these boxes, *STATISTICA* will perform a standard (i.e., not stepwise) regression analysis.

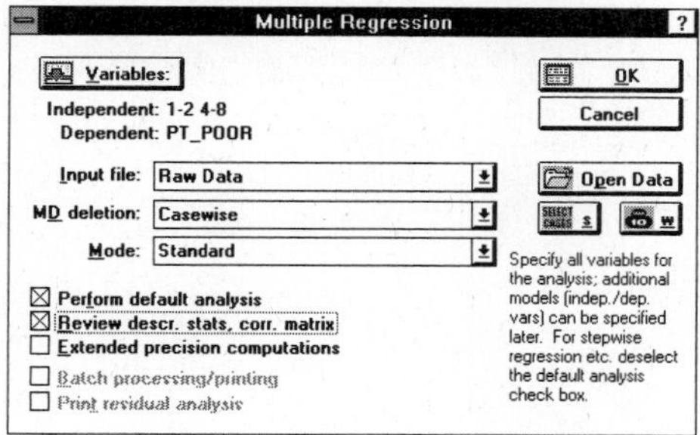

Now, click *OK* in this dialog and the *Review Descriptive Statistics* dialog will open.

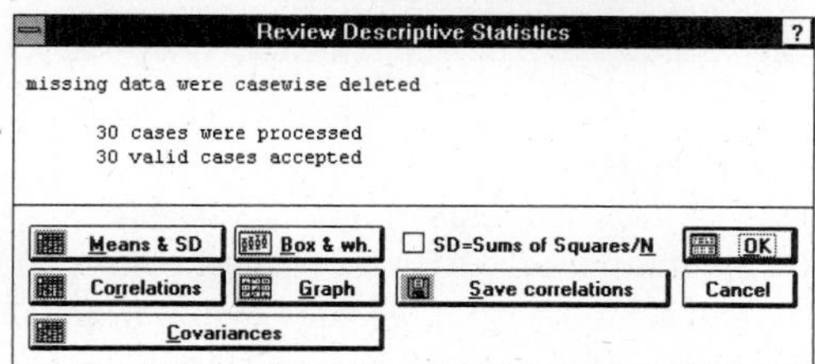

Here, you can review the means and standard deviations, correlations, and covariances between variables. Note that this dialog is also available

from basically all subsequent *Multiple Regression* dialogs, so you can always go back to look at the descriptive statistics for specific variables. Also, as in all other Scrollsheets, there are numerous graphs available from the right-mouse-button flying menu.

Distribution of variables. First examine the distribution of the dependent variable *Pt_Poor* across counties. Click on the *Means & SD* button to display this Scrollsheet.

Means and Standard Deviations (poverty.s

Continue...	mean	St.dev.	N
POP_CHNG	7.87	10.33	30
N_EMPLD	1548.67	2038.39	30
TAX_RATE	.72	.20	30
PT_PHONE	74.83	10.01	30
PT_RURAL	70.73	24.02	30
AGE	30.28	2.88	30
AFR_AM	11655.00	48289.92	30
PT_POOR	23.01	6.43	30

Now, click with the right-mouse-button on the variable *Pt_Poor* and select the *Quick Stats Graphs* option *Histogram/Normal* to bring up the following default histogram.

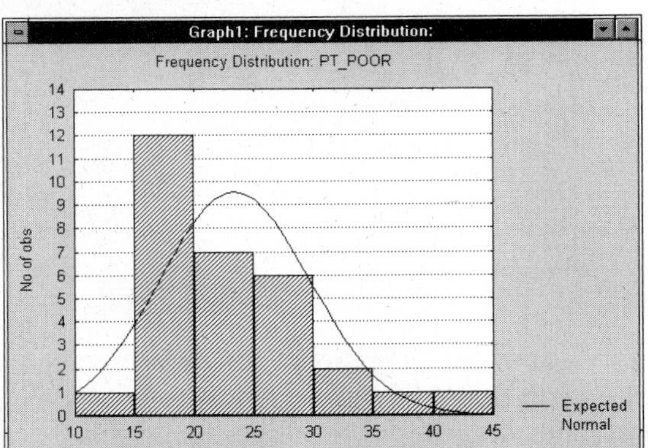

Using the *Stats Graphs* option *Stats 2D Graphs - Histograms* from the *Graphs* pull-down menu, you can produce the following histogram of variable *Pt_Poor* with more intervals (in the resulting *Stats Graphs* dialog, set the *# of Categories* option in the *Categories* box to *16*). As you can see below, the distribution for this variable deviates somewhat from the normal distribution. Correlation coefficients can become substantially inflated or deflated if extreme outliers are present in the data. However, even though two counties (the two right-most columns) have a higher percentage of families below the poverty level than what would be expected according to the normal distribution, they still seem to be sufficiently "within range."

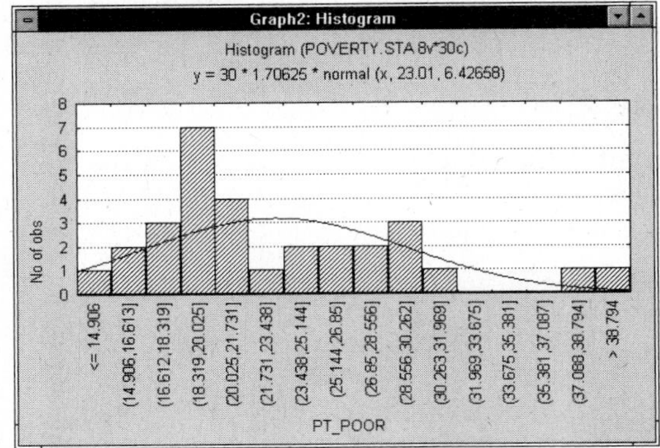

This decision is somewhat subjective; a rule of thumb is that one needs to be concerned if an observation (or observations) falls outside the mean ± 3 times the standard deviation. In that case, it is wise to repeat critical analyses with and without the outlier(s) to ensure that they did not seriously affect the pattern of intercorrelations. You can also view the distribution of this variable by clicking on the *Box and whisker* button in the *Review Descriptive Statistics* dialog and selecting the variable *Pt_Poor*. Next, select the *Median/Quartile/Range* option, then click *OK* to produce the box and whisker plot.

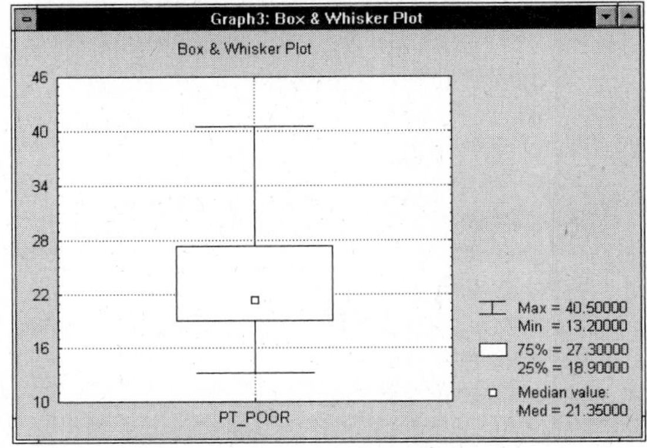

StatSoft

(Note that the specific method of computation for the median and the quartiles can be configured "system-wide" in the *STATISTICA Defaults: General* dialog; see Chapter 3.)

Scatterplots. If one has *a priori* hypotheses about the relationship between specific variables at this point it may be instructive to plot the respective scatterplot.

For example, look at the relationship between population change and the percent of families below poverty level. It seems reasonable to predict that poverty will lead to outward migration; thus, there should be a negative correlation between the percent below poverty level and population change.

Return to the *Review Descriptive Statistics* dialog and click on the *Correlations* button to display the Scrollsheet with the correlation matrix.

Correlations (poverty.sta)

Continue...	POP_CHNG	N_EMPLD	TAX_RATE	PT_PHONE	PT_RURAL	AGE	AFR_AM	PT_POOR
POP_CHNG	1.00	.04	.13	.38	-.02	-.15	.12	-.65
N_EMPLD	.04	1.00	.10	.36	-.66	-.36	.94	-.17
TAX_RATE	.13	.10	1.00	-.04	.02	-.05	.23	.01
PT_PHONE	.38	.36	-.04	1.00	-.75	-.08	.27	-.73
PT_RURAL	-.02	-.66	.02	-.75	1.00	.31	-.56	.51
AGE	-.15	-.36	-.05	-.08	.31	1.00	-.35	.02
AFR_AM	.12	.94	.23	.27	-.56	-.35	1.00	-.19
PT_POOR	-.65	-.17	.01	-.73	.51	.02	-.19	1.00

With the right-mouse-button, click on the correlation between *Pop_Chng* and *Pt_Poor* and select the *Quick Stats Graphs - Scatterplot/Conf* option to produce the default scatterplot.

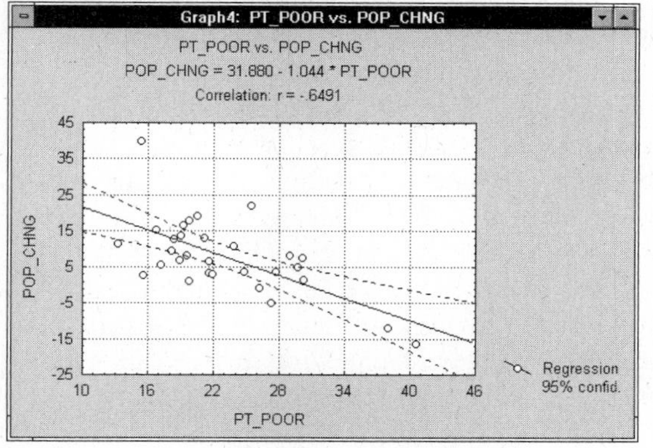

This scatterplot illustrates the substantial negative correlation (-.65) between the two variables. It also shows the 95% confidence limits for the regression line, that is, you can be 95% certain that the actual regression line in the population falls within the limits defined by the two curved, dashed lines.

The correlations between variables can also be displayed in a matrix scatterplot. A matrix scatterplot of selected variables can be produced by clicking on the *Graph* button in the *Review Descriptive Statistics* dialog, and then selecting the desired variables. In the case of the matrix scatterplot shown below, all variables were selected.

Graph5: Correlations (POVERTY.STA 8v*30c)

Correlations (POVERTY.STA 8v*30c)

POP_CHNG N_EMPLD TAX_RATE PT_PHONE PT_RURAL AGE AFR_AM PT_POOR

Specifying the Multiple Regression

If the *Perform default analysis* option on the startup panel is selected (a default setting), then all you have to do is click *OK* in the *Review Descriptive Statistics* dialog to perform the regression analysis and go to the results dialog. A standard regression (which includes the intercept) will be performed.

Reviewing Results

The *Multiple Regression Results* dialog is displayed below. Overall, the multiple regression equation is highly significant (refer to *Elementary Concepts*, Chapter 8, for a discussion of statistical significance

testing). Thus, given the independent variables, you can "predict" poverty better than what would be expected by pure chance alone.

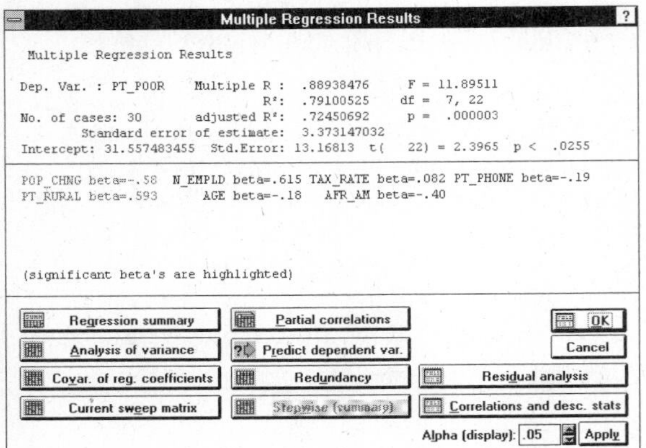

Regression coefficients. In order to learn which of the independent variables contribute most to the prediction of poverty, examine the regression (or *B*) coefficients. Click on the *Regression summary* button to bring up a Scrollsheet with those coefficients.

Regression Summary for Dependent Variable: PT_POOR

MULTIPLE REGRESS. R= .88938476 R²= .79100525 Adjusted R²= .72450692
F(7,22)=11.895 p<.00000 Std.Error of estimate: 3.3731

N=30	BETA	St. Err. of BETA	B	St. Err. of B	t(22)	p-level
Intercpt			31.55748	13.16813	2.39651	.025487
POP_CHNG	-.578434	.136127	-.35978	.08467	-4.24924	.000328
N_EMPLD	.614602	.352958	.00194	.00111	1.74129	.095601
TAX_RATE	.082054	.106579	2.60150	3.37904	.76989	.449552
PT_PHONE	-.192963	.209013	-.12392	.13423	-.92321	.365914
PT_RURAL	.592775	.230528	.15859	.06167	2.57138	.017413
AGE	-.176649	.114227	-.39352	.25446	-1.54647	.136256
AFR_AM	-.396321	.341287	-.00005	.00005	-1.16125	.257984

This Scrollsheet shows the standardized regression coefficients (*Beta*) and the raw regression coefficients (*B*). The *Beta* coefficients are the coefficients you would have obtained had you first standardized all of your variables to a mean of *0* and a standard deviation of *1*. Thus, the magnitude of these *Beta* coefficients allow you to compare the relative contribution of each independent variable in the prediction of the dependent variable. As is evident in the Scrollsheet shown above, variables *Pop_Chng*, *Pt_Rural*, and *N_Empld* are the most important predictors of poverty; of those, only the first two variables are statistically significant. The regression coefficient for *Pop_Chng* is negative; the less the population increased, the greater the number of families who lived below the poverty level in the respective county. The regression weight for *Pt_Rural* is positive; the greater the percent of rural population, the greater the poverty level.

Partial correlations. Another way of looking at the unique contributions of each independent variable to the prediction of the dependent variable is to compute the partial and semi-partial correlations (click on the *Partial correlations* button in the results dialog, see below). Partial correlations are the correlations between the respective independent variable adjusted by all other variables, and the dependent variable adjusted by all other variables. Thus, it is the correlation between the residuals, after adjusting for all independent variables. The partial correlation represents the unique contribution of the respective independent variable to the prediction of the dependent variable.

Variables currently in the Equation; DV: PT_POOR

MULTIPLE REGRESS.	Beta in	Partial Cor.	Semipart Cor.	Tolernce	R-square	t(22)	p-level
POP_CHNG	-.578434	-.671393	-.414159	.512657	.487343	-4.24924	.000328
N_EMPLD	.614602	.348034	.169718	.076255	.923745	1.74129	.095601
TAX_RATE	.082054	.161974	.075039	.836319	.163681	.76989	.449552
PT_PHONE	-.192963	-.193123	-.089982	.217453	.782547	-.92321	.365914
PT_RURAL	.592775	.480720	.250624	.178758	.821242	2.57138	.017413
AGE	-.176649	-.313128	-.150730	.728071	.271929	-1.54647	.136256
AFR_AM	-.396321	-.240324	-.113184	.081559	.918441	-1.16125	.257984

The semi-partial correlation is the correlation of the respective independent variable adjusted by all other variables, with the raw (unadjusted) dependent variable. Thus, the semi-partial correlation is the correlation of the residuals for the respective independent variable after adjusting for all other variables, and the unadjusted raw scores for the dependent variable. Put another way, the squared semi-partial correlation is an indicator of the percent of *Total* variance uniquely accounted for by the respective independent variable, while the squared partial correlation is an indicator of the percent of *residual* variance accounted for after adjusting the dependent variable for all other independent variables.

In this example, the partial and semi-partial correlations are relatively similar. However, sometimes their magnitude can differ greatly (the semi-partial correlation is always lower). If the semi-partial correlation is very small, but the partial correlation is relatively large, then the respective variable may predict a unique "chunk" of variability in the dependent variable (that is not accounted for in the other variables). However, in terms of practical significance, this chunk may be tiny and represent only a very small proportion of the total variability (see, for example, Lindeman, Merenda, and Gold, 1980; Morrison, 1967; Neter, Wasserman, and Kutner, 1985; Pedhazur, 1973; or Stevens, 1986).

Residual Analysis

After fitting a regression equation, one should always examine the predicted and residual scores. For example, extreme outliers may seriously bias results and lead to erroneous conclusions. From the *Multiple Regression Results* dialog, click on the *Residual analysis* button to proceed to the *Residual Analysis* dialog.

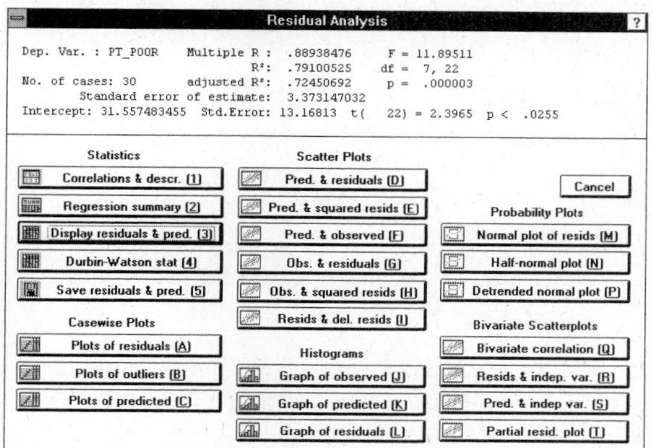

Casewise plot of residuals. This section in the dialog gives you a choice of various residuals for a casewise plot. Usually, one should at least examine the pattern of the raw or standardized residuals to identify any extreme outliers.

For this example, click on the *Plots of residuals* button and select *Raw residuals* from the resulting *Select residual for casewise plot* dialog.

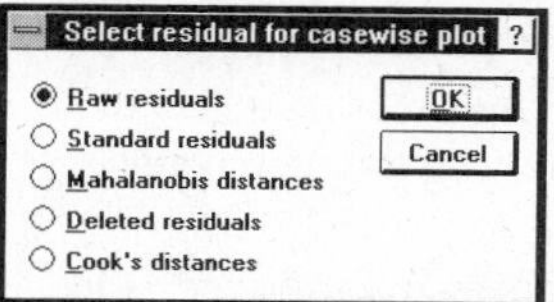

When you click *OK* in the above dialog, the following Scrollsheet with a casewise diagram will open:

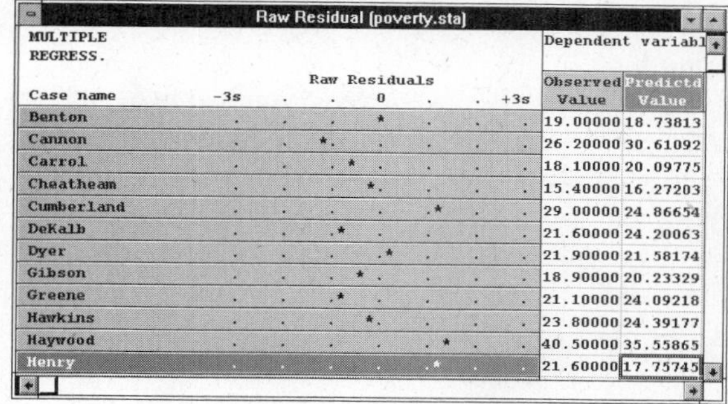

Case name	Observed Value	Predictd Value
Benton	19.00000	18.73813
Cannon	26.20000	30.61092
Carrol	18.10000	20.09775
Cheatheam	15.40000	16.27203
Cumberland	29.00000	24.86654
DeKalb	21.60000	24.20063
Dyer	21.90000	21.58174
Gibson	18.90000	20.23329
Greene	21.10000	24.09218
Hawkins	23.80000	24.39177
Haywood	40.50000	35.55865
Henry	21.60000	17.75745

The scale used in the casewise plot in the left-most column is in terms of *sigma*, that is, the standard deviation of residuals. If one or several cases fall outside of the ± 3 times *sigma* limits, one should probably exclude the respective cases (which is easily accomplished via selection conditions) and run the analysis over to make sure that key results were not biased by these outliers.

Casewise plot of outliers. A quick way to identify outliers is to use the *Plot of outliers* option. You may either plot all standard residuals that fall outside the ± 2-5 times *sigma* limits or plot the 100 most extreme cases.

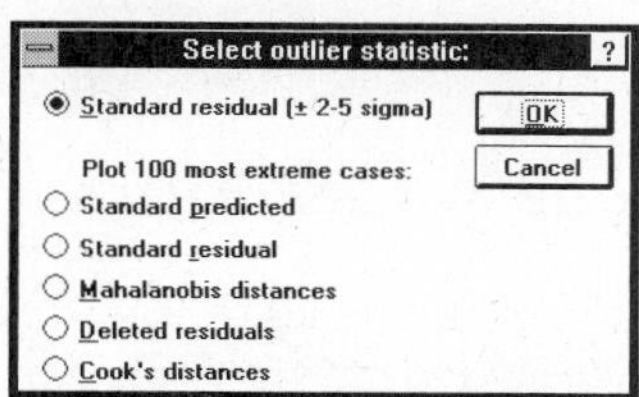

When you select the *Standard residual (± 2-5 times sigma)* option, no outliers will be detected in the current example.

Mahalanobis distances. Most statistics textbooks devote some discussion to the issue of outliers and residuals concerning the dependent variable. However, the role of outliers in the *independent* variable list is often overlooked. On the independent variable side, you have a list of variables that participate with different weights (the regression coefficients) in the prediction of the dependent variable. One can think of the independent variables as defining a multidimensional space in which each observation can be located. For example, if you had two independent variables with equal regression coefficients, then you could construct a scatterplot of those two variables, and place each observation in that plot. You could then plot one point for the mean on both variables and compute the distances of each observation from this mean (now called *centroid*) in the two-dimensional space; this is the conceptual idea behind the computation of the *Mahalanobis distances*. Now, look at those distances -- sorted by size -- to identify extreme cases on the independent variable side. Click on the *Plot of outliers* button and then select *Mahalanobis distances* from the *Select Outlier Statistic* dialog. The resultant plot will show the Mahalanobis distances sorted in descending order.

Mahalanobis distances: PT_POOR (poverty.sta)

MULTIPLE REGRESS.

Case name	Mahalanobis distances (.513 … 27.9)	Sorted Observed Value
Shelby	*	16.80000
Wayne	*	27.70000
Haywood	*	40.50000
Cheatheam	*	15.40000
Morgan	*	27.30000
Montgomery	*	18.40000
Greene	*	21.10000
Jackson	*	38.00000
Unicoi	*	19.80000
Gibson	*	18.90000
DeKalb	*	21.60000

Note that Shelby county (in the first line) appears somewhat extreme as compared to the other counties in the plot. If you look at the raw data you will find that, indeed, Shelby county is by far the largest county in the data file with many more persons employed in agriculture (variable *N_Empld*) and a much larger population of African/Americans. Probably, it would have been wise to express those numbers in percentages rather than in absolute numbers, and in that case, the Mahalanobis distance of Shelby county from the other counties in the sample would probably not have been as large. As it stands, however, Shelby county is clearly an outlier. Now, click on the plot of Mahalanobis distances Scrollsheet with the right-mouse-button and select the *Quick Stats Graphs* option *Icon Plot of Cases*.

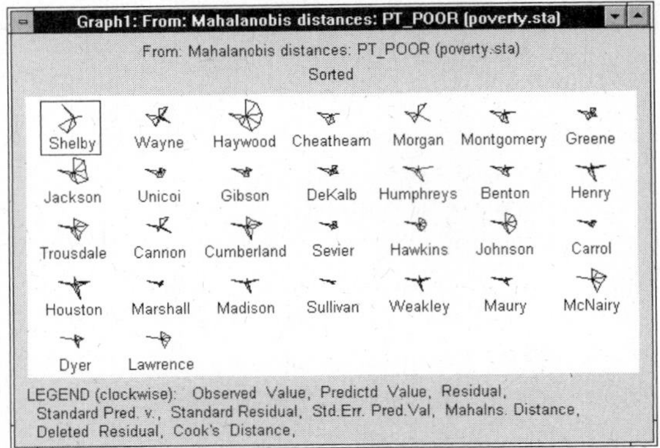

The resulting icon plot displays an icon for each case analyzed. Individual components of each icon are represented by specific regression results for that case (given in the legend, e.g., observed value, predicted value, residual, etc.). The icon plot helps to visualize the differences between the different cases (in this case, counties).

Deleted residuals. Another very important statistic that allows one to evaluate the seriousness of the outlier problem is the *deleted residual*. This is the standardized residual for the respective case that one would obtain if the case were excluded from the analysis. Remember that the multiple regression procedure fits a straight line to express the relationship between the dependent and independent variables. If one case is clearly an outlier (as is

Shelby county in this data), then there is a tendency for the regression line to be "pulled" by this outlier so as to account for it as much as possible. As a result, if the respective case were excluded, a completely different line (and *B* coefficients) would emerge. Therefore, if the deleted residual is grossly different from the standardized residual, you have reason to believe that the regression analysis is seriously biased by the respective case. In this example, the deleted residual for *Shelby* county is an outlier that seriously affects the analysis. You can plot the residuals against the deleted residuals via the option *Resids & del resids*, which will produce a scatterplot of these values. The scatterplot below clearly shows the outlier.

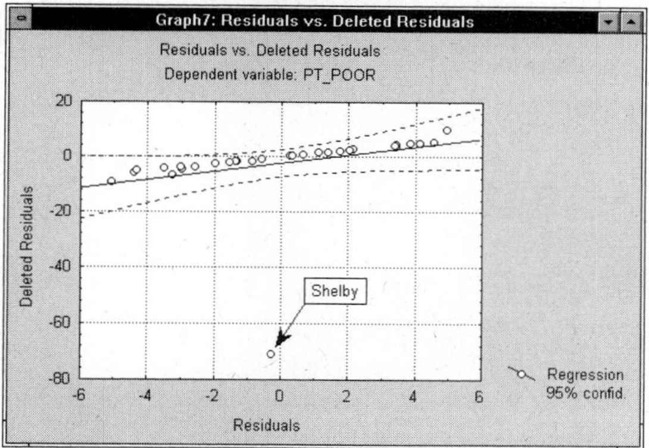

STATISTICA provides an interactive outlier removal tool (the *Brushing Tool* on the graphics toolbar; see Volume II for details) in order to experiment with the removal of outliers and allow you to instantly see their influence on the regression line. When the tool is activated, the cursor changes to a cross-hair, and the *Brushing* dialog will be displayed next to the graph (see below). You can (temporarily) interactively eliminate individual data points from the graph by setting (1) the *Auto Update* checkbox and (2) the *Turn OFF* radio button in the *Action* box; then click on the point that is to be removed with the cross-hair.

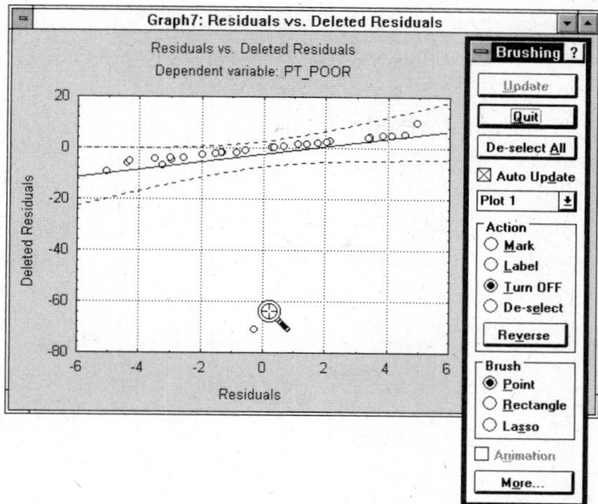

Clicking on a point will now automatically remove it (temporarily) from the graph, mark it (highlight it) in the *Graph Data Editor* so that you can examine the data, and recalculate the fit (see the graph below).

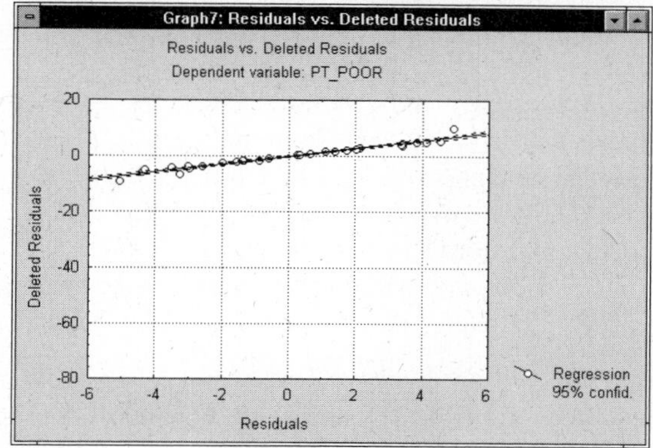

Note that you can "put back" the removed point(s) by clicking on the *De-select All* button on the *Brushing* dialog.

Normal probability plots. There are many additional graphs available from the *Residual Analysis* dialog, and each of them is briefly discussed beginning on page 1680. Most of them are more or less straightforward in their interpretation; however, the normal probability plots will be commented on here.

As previously mentioned, multiple linear regression assumes *linear* relationships between the variables in the equation, and a *normal* distribution of residuals. If these assumptions are violated, your final conclusion may not be accurate. The normal probability plot of residuals will give you an indication of whether or not gross violations of the assumptions have occurred. Click on the *Normal plot of resid.* button to bring up this plot.

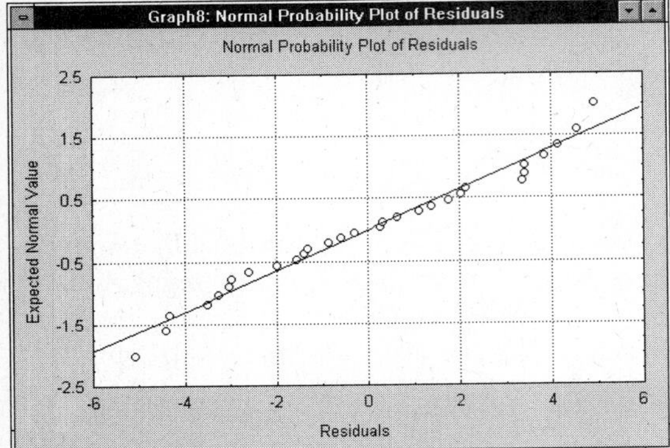

This plot is constructed as follows. First the residuals are rank ordered. From these ranks, z values can be computed (i.e., standard values of the normal distribution) *based on the assumption* that the data come from a normal distribution. These z values are plotted on the Y-axis in the plot (see the *Notes* section, page 1683, for additional details).

If the observed residuals (plotted on the X-axis) are normally distributed, then all values should fall onto a straight line in the plot; in this plot, all points follow the line very closely. If the residuals are not normally distributed, then they will deviate from the line. Outliers may also become evident in this plot.

If there is a general lack of fit, and the data seem to form a clear pattern (e.g., an S shape) around the line, then the dependent variable may have to be transformed in some way (e.g., a log transformation to "pull in" the tail of the distribution, etc.; see also the brief discussion of Box-Cox and Box-Tidwell transformations in the *Notes* section, page 1686). A discussion of such techniques is beyond the scope of this manual (Neter, Wasserman, and Kutner, 1985, page 134, present an excellent discussion of transformations as remedies for non-normality and non-linearity); however, too often researchers simply accept their data at face value without ever checking for the appropriateness of their assumptions, leading to erroneous conclusions. For that reason, one design goal of the *Multiple Regression* module was to make residual (graphical) analysis as easy and accessible as possible.

Example 2: Stepwise Regression Analysis

Data File

The following example is based on the examples data file *Job_prof.sta* (from Neter, Wasserman, and Kutner, 1989, page 473) which is shown in the spreadsheet below.

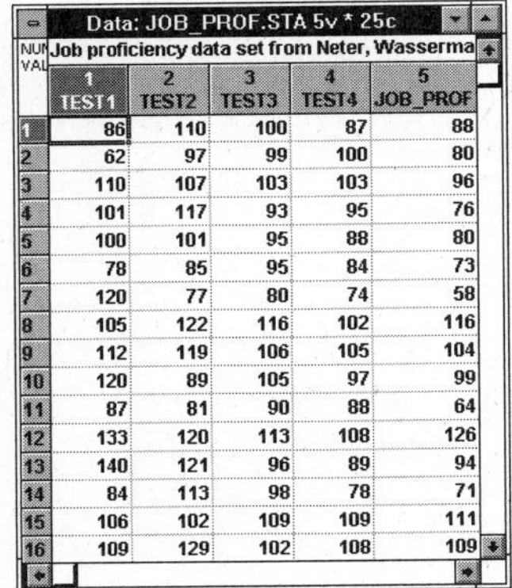

Data: JOB_PROF.STA 5v * 25c

Job proficiency data set from Neter, Wasserma

	1 TEST1	2 TEST2	3 TEST3	4 TEST4	5 JOB_PROF
1	86	110	100	87	88
2	62	97	99	100	80
3	110	107	103	103	96
4	101	117	93	95	76
5	100	101	95	88	80
6	78	85	95	84	73
7	120	77	80	74	58
8	105	122	116	102	116
9	112	119	106	105	104
10	120	89	105	97	99
11	87	81	90	88	64
12	133	120	113	108	126
13	140	121	96	89	94
14	84	113	98	78	71
15	106	102	109	109	111
16	109	129	102	108	109

The first four variables (*Test1-Test4*) represent four different aptitude tests that were administered to each of the 25 applicants for entry-level clerical positions in a company. Regardless of their test scores, all 25 applicants were hired. Once their probationary period had expired, each of these employees were evaluated and given a job proficiency rating (variable *Job_prof*).

Research Question

Using stepwise regression, the variables (or subset of variables) which best predict job proficiency will be analyzed. Thus, the dependent variable will be *Job_prof* and variables *Test1-Test4* will be the independent variables.

Starting the Analysis

After starting the *Multiple Regression* module, open the data file *Job_prof.sta*. In the *Multiple Regression* startup panel, click on the *Variables* button and specify variable *Job_prof* as the dependent variable and variables *Test1-Test4* as the independent variables.

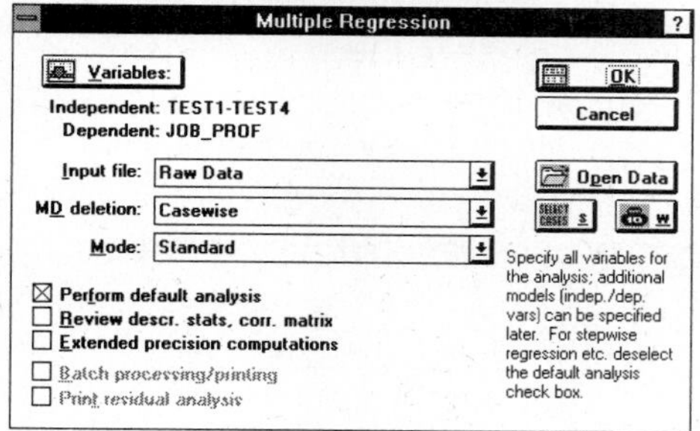

Next, de-select the *Perform default analysis* check box and click *OK* in this dialog to go to the *Model Definition* dialog.

Specifying the Stepwise Regression

You can choose to analyze the data using a *Standard*, *Forward stepwise*, or *Backward stepwise* regression method. The popular *Forward stepwise* method evaluates the independent variables at each step, adding or deleting them from the model based on user-specified criteria (for more information, see Neter, Wasserman, and Kutner, 1989, and the *Notes* section, page 1684). Therefore, the forward stepwise regression will be used to analyze the data for this example.

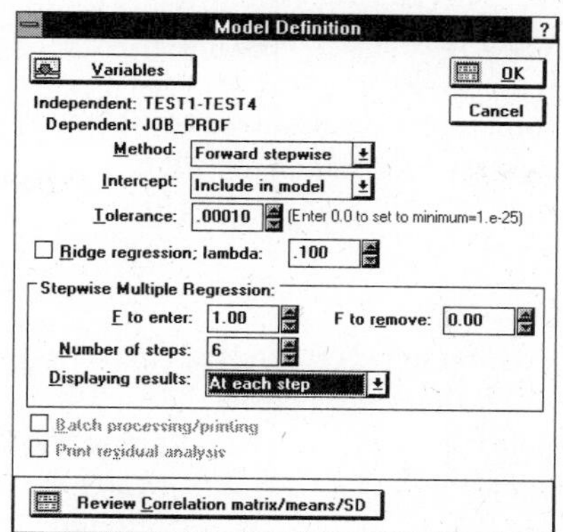

In the *Model Definition* dialog, click on the *Method* combo box and select *Forward stepwise*. The intercept will be included in the model, therefore, set the *Intercept* option to *Include in model*. Now, the *Stepwise Multiple Regression* options will become available, You can change the *F to enter* and *F to remove* values here, however, for this example, accept the default values of *1.0* and *0*, respectively. In order to view the results at each step of the analysis, select *At each step* in the *Displaying results* combo box. Now, accept all other defaults in this dialog and click *OK* to begin the forward stepwise regression.

Step 0

First, the results dialog will be displayed for step 0, when no variables have been entered in the model.

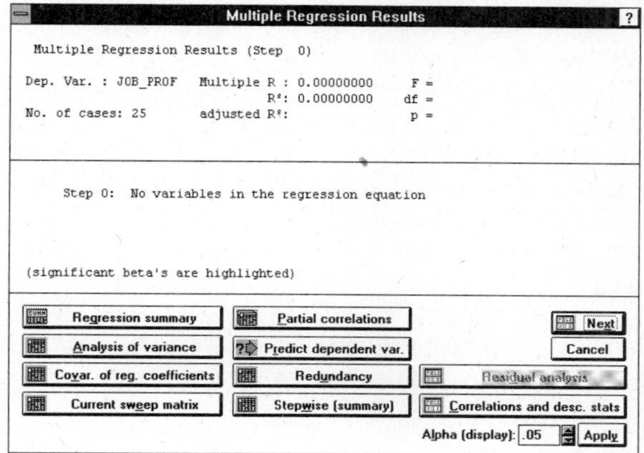

You can, at this point, review the descriptive statistics (click on the *Correlations and descr.* button) or correlations for the variables not included in the model (click on the *Partial correlations* button).

Step 1

Click on the *Next* button to proceed to the next step in the analysis. In the first step, each of the independent variables are evaluated individually and the variable which has the largest *F* value greater than or equal to the *F to enter* value is entered into the regression equation.

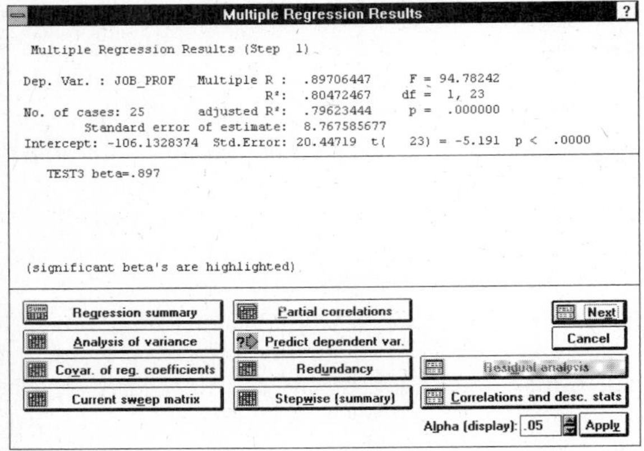

Here, variable *Test3* met the *F to enter* criteria (F>1.0) and was added to the model. Click on the *Stepwise (summary)* button to display a Scrollsheet with a summary of the steps so far in the analysis.

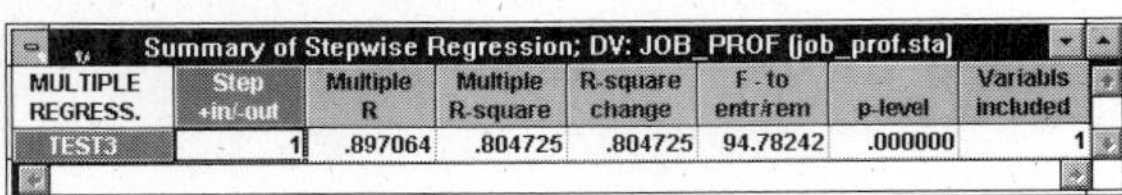

Summary of Stepwise Regression; DV: JOB_PROF (job_prof.sta)

MULTIPLE REGRESS.	Step +in/-out	Multiple R	Multiple R-square	R-square change	F - to entr/rem	p-level	Variabls included
TEST3	1	.897064	.804725	.804725	94.78242	.000000	1

Click on the *Next* button in the *Multiple Regression Results* dialog to proceed to the next step.

Step 2

Now, in subsequent steps when a variable is added to the model (based on the *F to enter* criteria), the forward stepwise regression method will examine the variables included in the model, and, based on the *F to remove* criteria, will determine whether any variables already in the model should be removed.

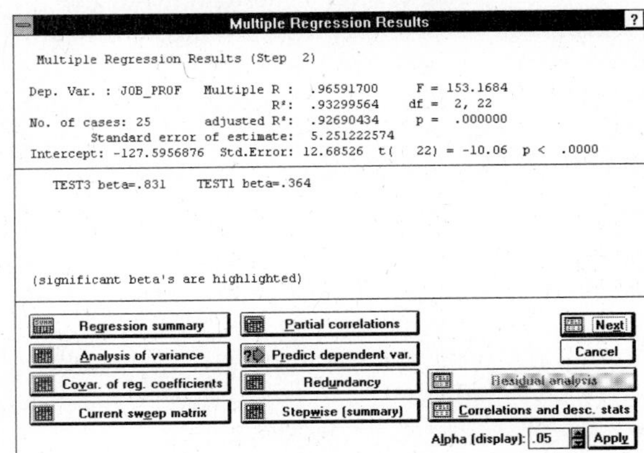

In this step, variable *Test1* is entered into the model. Clicking on the *Stepwise (summary)* button will produce the following Scrollsheet of summary data.

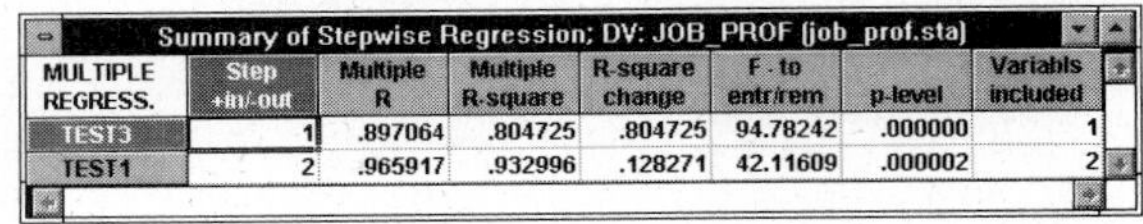

Summary of Stepwise Regression; DV: JOB_PROF (job_prof.sta)

MULTIPLE REGRESS.	Step +in/-out	Multiple R	Multiple R-square	R-square change	F - to entr/rem	p-level	Variabls included
TEST3	1	.897064	.804725	.804725	94.78242	.000000	1
TEST1	2	.965917	.932996	.128271	42.11609	.000002	2

Once again, click on the *Next* button in the *Multiple Regression Results* dialog to proceed to step 3 in the forward stepwise analysis.

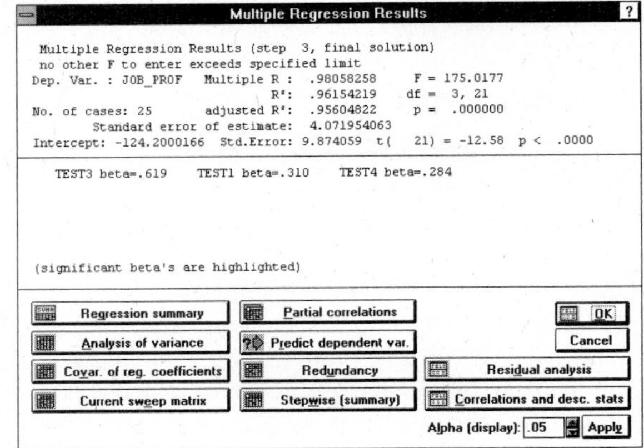

Step 3 (Final Solution)

There are two variables remaining to evaluate (*Test2* and *Test4*). For this step, the largest *F* value was given by *Test4*, therefore, it was added to the model. When *Test2* was evaluated, the *F* value was less than the *F to enter* value of *1.0*, therefore, it was not entered into the model.

The *Stepwise (summary)* Scrollsheet now summarizes the variables which were entered into and kept in the model.

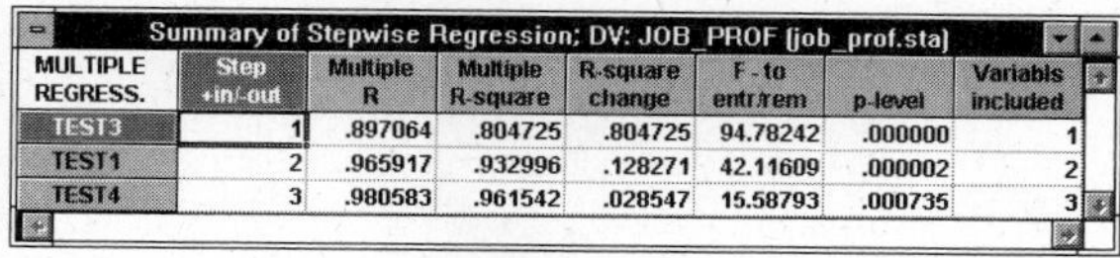

Summary of Stepwise Regression; DV: JOB_PROF (job_prof.sta)

MULTIPLE REGRESS.	Step +in/-out	Multiple R	Multiple R-square	R-square change	F - to entr/rem	p-level	Variabls included
TEST3	1	.897064	.804725	.804725	94.78242	.000000	1
TEST1	2	.965917	.932996	.128271	42.11609	.000002	2
TEST4	3	.980583	.961542	.028547	15.58793	.000735	3

Now, according to the *Forward stepwise regression* procedure, the subset of aptitude tests (independent variables) which best predicts the job proficiency score (dependent variable) contains *Test3*, *Test1*, and *Test4*. Therefore, the regression equation appears as follows:

$$y = B_0+B_1*X_3+B_2*X_1+B_3*X_4$$

To obtain the regression coefficients from the regression summary Scrollsheet, click on the *Regression summary* button.

Regression Summary for Dependent Variable: JOB_PROF

MULTIPLE REGRESS. R= .98058258 R²= .96154219 Adjusted R²= .95604822
F(3,21)=175.02 p<.00000 Std.Error of estimate: 4.0720

N=25	BETA	St. Err. of BETA	B	St. Err. of B	t(21)	p-level
Intercpt			-124.200	9.874059	-12.5784	.000000
TEST3	.618670	.069224	1.357	.151832	8.9373	.000000
TEST1	.309670	.045646	.296	.043679	6.7841	.000001
TEST4	.284405	.072035	.517	.131054	3.9482	.000735

The final regression equation is:

$$y = -124.200+1.357*X_3+0.296*X_1+0.517*X_4$$

DIALOGS, OPTIONS, STATISTICS

Startup Panel

When you first start the *Multiple Regression* module, the *Multiple Regression Startup Panel* will open from which you can designate the variables for the analysis, type of data file, and other options (see below).

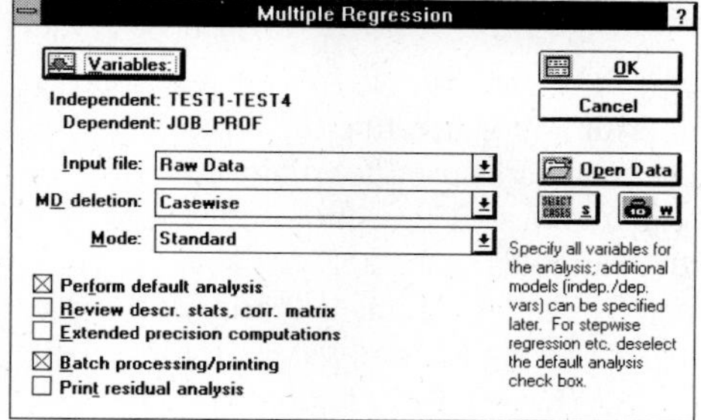

Variables

Clicking on this button will bring up the standard variable selection dialog in which you can select the variables that will be used in the regression analysis (a correlation matrix will be calculated for all variables that are selected).

Input

Select either raw data input or a correlation matrix previously created via *Multiple Regression*, the *Quick Basic Stats* options (see Chapter 10), another *STATISTICA* module (e.g., *Basic Statistics and Tables*, Chapter 9; *Factor Analysis*, Volume III; *Canonical Analysis*, Volume III; or *Reliability and Item Analysis*, Volume III), or by entering matrix data into the spreadsheet (see *STATISTICA Matrix File Format*, Chapter 7).

Missing Data Deletion

This switch is only active if a raw data file has been specified as the input data (see above). Missing data can be deleted *casewise*; substituted by *means*, or deleted *pairwise* by selecting the appropriate option from the combo box.

Casewise deletion of missing data. If this option is selected, then only cases that do not contain any missing data for any of the variables selected for the analysis will be included in the analysis.

Mean substitution. If this option is selected, then missing data will be replaced by the means for the respective variables (for this analysis only, not in the data file).

Pairwise deletion of missing data. If this option is requested, then cases will be excluded from the calculation of correlations involving variables for which they have missing data. In subsequent analyses, all tests of statistical significance in that instance will be based on the smallest number of valid cases found in any of the selected variables.

Mode

In this combo box, the user can select either a *standard* or *fixed nonlinear* regression.

Standard regression mode. In the default *standard* setting, the standard correlation matrix of all selected variables will be computed.

Fixed nonlinear regression. When you select this mode, the startup panel will appear as follows:

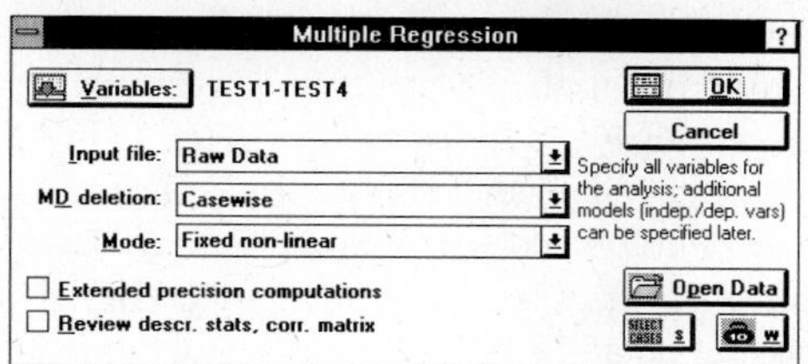

This mode will allow you to select various transformations of the independent variables (see *Fixed Nonlinear Regression*, page 1665); thus, new variables will be created (in memory) as transformations of the raw data and included in the overall correlation matrix. A common application of this technique is to estimate the linear, squared, cubic, etc. components of the relationship of an independent variable with the dependent variable. Note that *STATISTICA* also includes the module *Nonlinear Estimation* (Volume III) for estimating nonlinear regression models of any complexity (including predefined models such as *probit*, *logit*, discontinuous regression models, etc.).

Perform Default Analysis

When you select this option and then click *OK* in the startup panel, the program will accept the default selections (i.e., a *Standard* regression model which includes the intercept) in the *Model Definition* dialog and proceed to the *Regression Results* dialog. If this option is de-selected, then when you click *OK* in the startup panel, the *Model Definition* dialog will open in which you can select the type of regression analysis (i.e., stepwise, ridge, etc.) as well as other options.

Review Descriptive Statistics, Correlation Matrix

Select this check box in order to open the *Review Descriptive Statistics* dialog (page 1665) after you leave the startup panel. Although the *Review Descriptive Statistics* dialog is available at every point in the analysis, when you select this option from the startup panel, the descriptive statistics will be based on *pairwise n* if *Pairwise MD deletion* is selected in the startup panel. Thus, if you select *Pairwise MD deletion* and you would like to review the descriptive statistics based on this method of deleting missing data, then you should select the *Review Descriptive Statistics* option at this point in the analysis (of course, you can also always compute descriptive statistics, using pairwise deletion of missing data, via the *Quick Basic Stats* options; see Chapter 10). In the *Review Descriptive Statistics* dialog, you can review detailed descriptive statistics (and pairwise *n*, if *Pairwise deletion of missing data* was requested, see above) for the selected variables. In order to continue the analysis and open the *Model Definition* dialog, click *OK* in the *Review Descriptive Statistics* dialog.

Extended Precision Computations

Select this check box in order to use the extended precision algorithm in generating the input correlation matrix that is used for multiple regression calculations. This option should be selected if the variables in the analysis show extremely small *relative* variances (variance divided by the mean), for example, if all values for a variable range between 10000.000001 and 10000.000002. Note that there is a difference between small variance and small *relative* variance (e.g., the *relative* variance of values in the range of .0000000000000001 to .0000000000000002 is not small). For extremely large data files with many thousands of cases, the computations may be somewhat slower when this check box is set. The default double precision calculations performed in *Multiple Regression* feature precision optimizations and offer superior accuracy, and for almost all data sets obtained from measurements (i.e., not artificially created), will produce results identical to those which can be obtained by using the extended precision option.

Batch Processing and Printing

This option is only available if *Perform Default Analysis* is checked (see above) and either the *printer*, *disk file*, and/or *Text/output Window* is

currently selected in the *Page/Output Setup* dialog (click on the *Output* field on the status bar to open this dialog). The selection of the *Batch Processing/Printing* option affects the way in which the regression output is printed. The default setting of the option is *interactive processing* (i.e., *Batch Processing/Printing* is de-selected). In this mode you can determine (interactively) which Scrollsheets to print. In the *Batch Processing/Printing* mode, the resulting Scrollsheets will automatically be printed, sent to the printer file, and/or sent to the *Text/output Window* (whichever you have selected in the *Page/Output Setup* dialog). If this option is checked, the program will perform the specified regression analysis (or set of analyses if more than one dependent variable was specified), "print" the results, and return to the dialog entitled *Defining Multiple Regression.*

Print Residual Analysis

This option is only available if *Perform Default Analysis* is checked (see above) and either the *printer*, *disk file*, and/or *text/output* is currently selected in the *Page/Output Setup* dialog and *Batch processing/printing* was selected (see above). If this option is checked, the default printed output will include the Scrollsheet with various residual statistics for each case.

Fixed Nonlinear Regression

The *Non-linear Components Regression* dialog is only available after the mode switch in the startup panel was set to *Fixed Nonlinear*. When you click *OK* in the resulting startup panel, then this dialog will open.

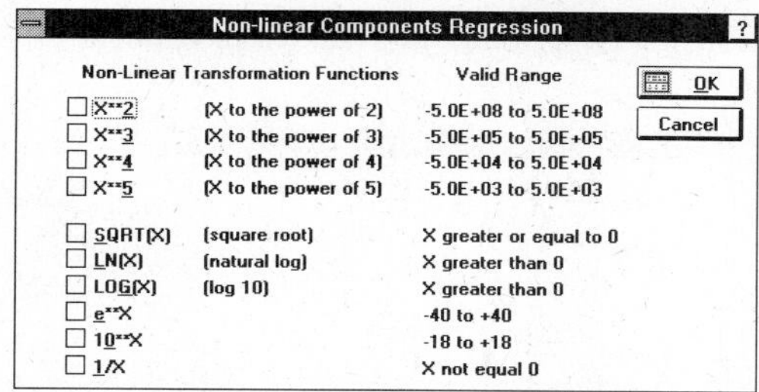

This dialog allows you to specify nonlinear transformations of the previously selected variables. Selected transformations are marked by a "check" in the check box next to the respective function. The available transformations and their valid ranges (for data values) are listed above. You can select more than one transformation.

For each selected variable, new temporary variables will be created (in memory, the actual data file will not be changed), containing the results of the respective transformations (a new variable will be created for each selected transformation for each selected variable). The new variable names will be a combination of the respective original variable number and the chosen transformation, e.g., *V4**2*, *10**V7*, etc.

The default *missing value* code (-9999) will be assigned to the new (transformed) variables for a case if:

(a) The original (un-transformed) variable contains a missing value for the same case;

(b) The value for the case does not fall within the valid range.

Review Descriptive Statistics

This intermediate dialog in the regression analysis will allow you to review specific descriptive statistics on the previously selected variables (and any transformed variables) including the table of

StatSoft

pairwise *n* (if *Pairwise MD deletion* was selected in the startup panel).

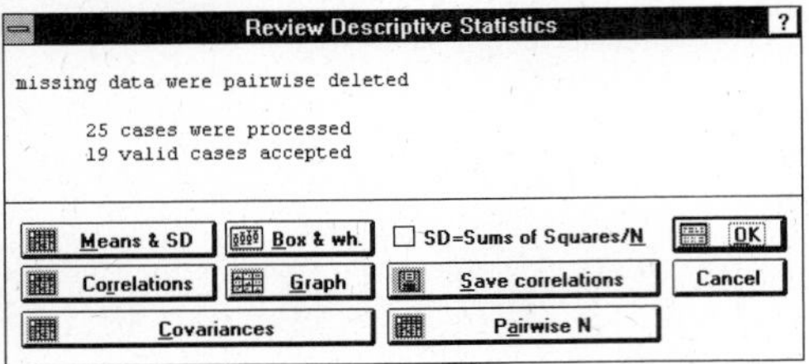

Means and Standard Deviations

This option will bring up a Scrollsheet with means and standard deviations. The mean of the sample is an unbiased *estimate* of the population mean. By default the standard deviation is computed as the square root of the sum of squared deviations about the mean (SS) divided by *n*-1. The resulting statistic is an estimate of the population *sigma* (this statistic can then be used to draw inferences about the variability of values in the population from which the sample was drawn).

You can use the *SD = Sums of Squares/n* option (see below) to compute the standard deviation as the SS divided by *n*. This resultant statistic is a *description* of the standard deviation *in this sample* (no inferences should be drawn from this statistic about the population from which the sample came).

The default graph for this Scrollsheet is a histogram (frequency distribution) of the chosen variable, with the normal distribution superimposed (this option is not available for *Fixed Non-linear Regression*, page 1665). This plot can be very useful as a quick check of whether the assumption of normality has been violated by the respective variable.

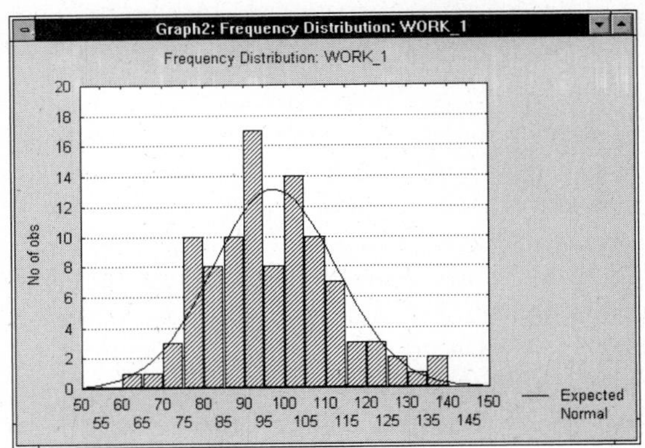

Box and Whisker Plot

This option allows you to produce a box and whisker plot (showing medians and quartiles, means and standard deviations, etc.) for the selected variables.

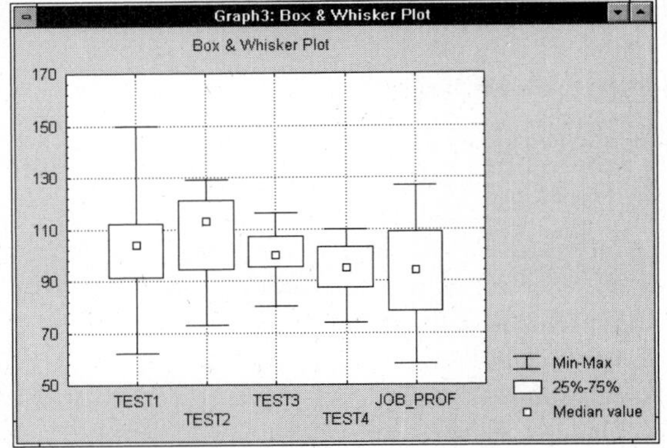

Correlations

This option will bring up a Scrollsheet with correlations. The default graph for this Scrollsheet is a scatterplot of the respective two variables. The plot will indicate the regression line as well as the 95% confidence limits for the regression line.

Matrix Plot

This option will bring up a matrix scatterplot for the variables selected for the analysis.

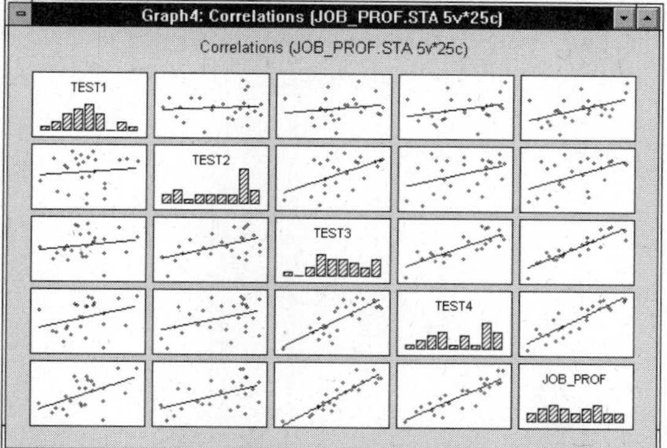

Covariances

This option will bring up a Scrollsheet with covariances. The default graph for this Scrollsheet is a scatterplot of the respective two variables. The plot will indicate the regression line as well as the 95% confidence limits for the regression line.

Save Correlation Matrix

When you click on this button, the *Save Matrix As* dialog will open in which you can save the correlation matrix as a standard *STATISTICA* matrix file (see *Matrix File Format*, Chapter 7).

Pairwise *n*

This option is only available if *raw data input* and *pairwise deletion of missing data* was selected in the startup panel. This option will bring up a Scrollsheet with the number of valid cases for each pair of variables in the correlation matrix.

SD=Sums of Squares/*n*

This check box affects the way in which the standard deviations (*Means and standard deviations)* and variances/covariances (option *Covariances*) are computed. If this box is checked, the resultant statistics are *descriptions* of the standard deviation, variance, and covariance in *this sample* (see *Means and Standard Deviations*, above). The setting of this switch only affects the respective values in the Scrollsheets; it does not affect any subsequent computations.

Defining the Regression Analysis

Select the independent and dependent variables for the multiple regression analysis in the *Model Definition* dialog.

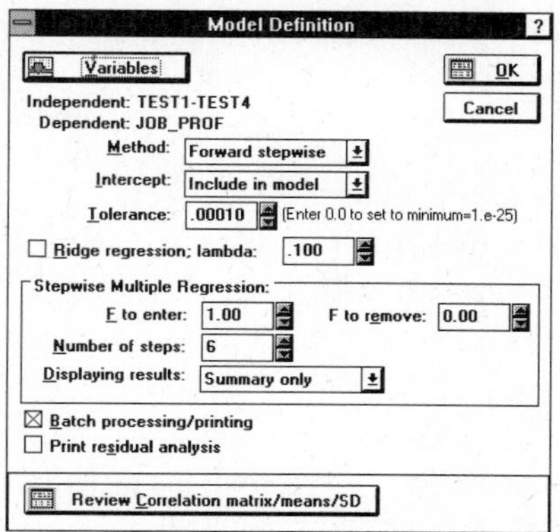

If multiple dependent variables are selected, then the program will cycle through the dependent variables list one by one.

Variables

Choosing this option will bring up the standard two-variable selection dialog in which you can select the dependent and independent variables. If more than one dependent variable is selected, then regression analyses will be performed consecutively for each variable in the dependent variable list.

Method

This option allows you to choose the type of regression analysis.

Standard regression. When you select this option, all variables will be entered into the regression equation in one single block or step.

Forward stepwise regression. When you select this option, the independent variables will be individually added or deleted from the model at each step of the regression (depending on your choice of *F to enter* or *F to remove*, see below) until the "best" regression model is obtained.

Backward stepwise regression. When you select this option, the independent variables will be removed from the regression equation one at a time (depending on your choice of *F to enter* or *F to remove*, see below) until the "best" regression model is obtained.

Stepwise Regression in Blocks (Hierarchical Regression)

The *Multiple Regression* module automatically keeps track of successive analyses. When the *standard* regression method is selected, the program will automatically calculate and evaluate the *R-square* increase or decrease in consecutive analyses of the same dependent variable.

For example, in the *Multiple Regression* startup panel, select all of the independent variables of interest and de-select the *Perform default analysis* option (e.g., for the example data file *Job_prof.sta*, select the dependent variable *Job_prof* and the independent variables *Test1-Test4*). Click *OK* to go to the *Model Definition* dialog. Now, in this dialog, click on the *Variables* button and select the subset of variables that you are interested in evaluating (e.g., *Test1-Test2*).

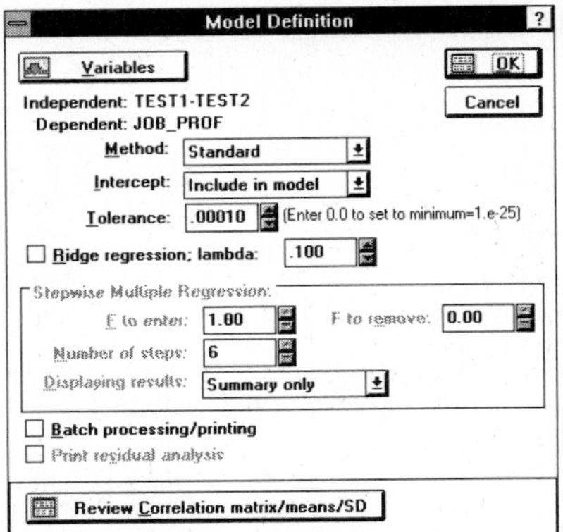

Now, click *OK* and in the resulting *Multiple Regression Results* dialog, click *Cancel* to return to the *Model Definition* dialog. Once again, click on the *Variables* button and this time, select (along with the previously-selected independent variables) additional independent variables (e.g., *Test1-Test4*).

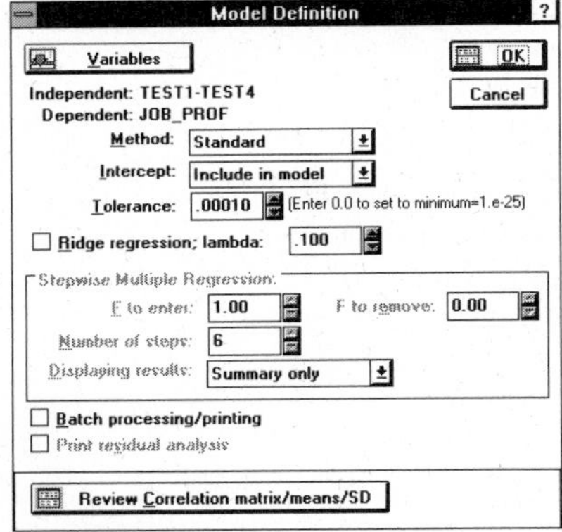

Click *OK* to go to the *Multiple Regression Results* dialog. The program will automatically calculate and evaluate the incremental change in the *R-square* due to the additional variables (e.g., *Test3* and *Test4*). Click on the *Stepwise (summary)* button to bring up a Scrollsheet with this value.

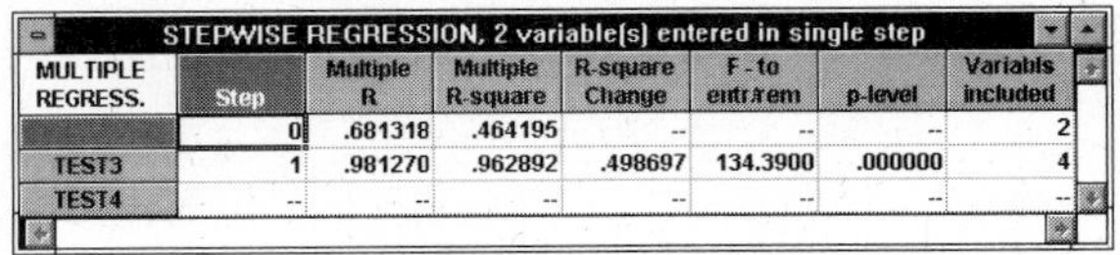

STEPWISE REGRESSION, 2 variable(s) entered in single step

MULTIPLE REGRESS.	Step	Multiple R	Multiple R-square	R-square Change	F - to entr/rem	p-level	Variabls included
	0	.681318	.464195	--	--	--	2
TEST3	1	.981270	.962892	.498697	134.3900	.000000	4
TEST4	--	--	--	--	--	--	--

Intercept

This option allows you to specify a regression equation *with* an intercept (select *Include in model*) or *without* an intercept (intercept forced to zero, regression through the origin, select *Set to zero*). Regression without the intercept is often used in analyses of economic data in cases when, by definition, the regression line describing the relationship between some variables would be predicted to have a zero intercept.

For example, if one were to correlate tax revenues with gross national product (GNP) then it is obvious that, if there is zero GNP, there is zero tax revenue. However, in the majority of applications (in particular in the social and natural sciences) variables of interest are measured on more or less arbitrary scales where the zero points have no special meaning. Therefore, the default setting of the *intercept* combo box is *Include in model*.

Tolerance

The tolerance of a variable is defined as 1 minus the squared multiple correlation of this variable with all other independent variables in the regression equation. Therefore, the smaller the tolerance of a variable, the more redundant is its contribution to the regression (i.e., it is redundant with the contribution of other independent variables). If the tolerance of any of the variables in the regression equation is equal to zero (or very close to zero) then the regression equation cannot be evaluated (the matrix is said to be ill-conditioned, and it cannot be inverted).

This option allows you to specify the minimum tolerance that is considered acceptable by *STATISTICA*. The minimum value that can be specified here is $1.00E^{-25}$ (i.e., a number with 24 zeros past the decimal point). However, it is not recommended to reset this switch to such an extremely low value. If the tolerance of a variable about to be entered into the regression equation is less than the default tolerance value (*.0001*) it means that this variable is 99 percent redundant with (identical to) the variables already in the equation. Forcing very redundant variables into the regression equation is not only questionable in terms of relevance of results, but the resultant estimates (regression coefficients) will become increasingly unreliable.

F to Enter, F to Remove

These options are only available if *Forward* or *Backward Stepwise* regression was selected (see above). The *F to enter* value that you specify here determines how significant the contribution of a variable to the regression has to be in order for it to be *added* to the equation. The *F to remove* value that you specify here determines how "insignificant" the contribution of a variable in the regression equation has to be in order for it to be *removed* from the regression equation.

If it is desirable in *Forward Stepwise* regression to force all (or almost all) variables into the equation (one at a time), then the *F to enter* value should be set to its minimum (*0.0001*), and the *F to remove* value should be set to its minimum (*0.0*; the *F to remove* must always be less than the *F to enter*).

If it is desired in *Backward Stepwise* regression to remove all variables from the equation (one at a time), then the *F to enter* value should be set to a very large value (e.g., 999) and the *F to remove* value should be set to a value of similar magnitude (e.g., 998; remember that the *F to remove* value must always be less than the *F to enter* value).

Number of Steps

This option is only available if *Forward Stepwise* or *Backward Stepwise* regression was selected (see above). This option allows the user to select the maximum number of steps that *STATISTICA* will perform before displaying the final results of the stepwise regression analysis.

Displaying Results

This option affects the display of results from stepwise (*Forward* or *Backward*) multiple regression analyses. You can elect to review only the final (summary) results of the stepwise regression analysis (select *Summary Only*) or you may review the results after each step of the analysis (select *At Each Step*).

Ridge Regression

Ridge regression analysis is used when the independent variables are highly intercorrelated, and stable estimates for the regression coefficients cannot be obtained via ordinary least squares methods (see Hoerl, 1962; Schmidt and Muller, 1978; Rozeboom, 1979). Specifically, a constant (*lambda*) will be added to the diagonal of the correlation matrix, which is then re-standardized so that all diagonal elements are equal to 1.0 (and the off-diagonal elements are divided by the constant).

In other words, ridge regression artificially decreases the correlation coefficients so that more stable (yet biased) estimates (*beta coefficients*) can be computed. Note that the standard errors for *B* and *beta* are calculated using the formulas for standard regression. After selecting this option, you will need to enter a value for *lambda*.

Batch Processing and Printing

This option is only available if *printer*, *disk file*, and/or *Text/output Window* is currently selected in the *Page/Output Setup* dialog (click on the *Output* field on the status bar to open this dialog). The selection of the *Batch Processing/Printing* option affects the way in which the regression output is printed.

The default setting of this option is *interactive processing* (i.e., *Batch Processing/Printing* is de-selected). In this mode you can determine (interactively) which Scrollsheets to print. In the *Batch Processing/Printing* mode, the resulting Scrollsheets will automatically be printed, sent to the printer file, and/or sent to the *Text/output Window* (whichever you have selected in the *Page/Output Setup* dialog).

If this option is checked the program will perform the specified regression analysis (or set of analyses if more than one dependent variable was specified), "print" the results, and return to the dialog entitled *Model Definition*. This option is particularly useful when one wants to print the results of a stepwise regression after each step for several dependent variables.

Print Residual Analysis

This option is only available if *printer*, *disk file*, and/or *Text/output* is currently selected in the *Page/Output Setup* dialog and *Batch processing/printing* was selected (see above). If this option is checked, the default printed output will include the Scrollsheet with various residual statistics for each case.

Review Correlation Matrix/Means/SD

Click on this button to return to the *Review Descriptive Statistics* dialog from which you can choose to review the means and standard deviations, the correlation matrix and the covariance matrix, or choose to save the correlation matrix in a standard *STATISTICA* matrix file.

Multiple Regression Results

The *Multiple Regression Results* dialog shows the summary of results for the current regression analysis and offers several options to review specific results.

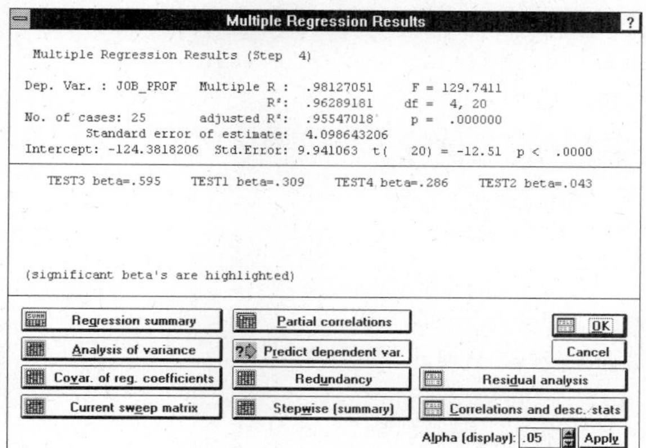

Summary Box

The following information is summarized in this area of the dialog:

Dep. Var. The name of the dependent variable is given here.

No. of cases. The minimum valid sample size (*n*) is displayed here (depending on the *Missing Data Deletion* option that you selected).

Multiple *R*. This is the coefficient of multiple correlation (between the independent variables and the dependent variable).

***R-square*.** This coefficient of multiple determination measures the reduction in the total variation of the dependent variable due to the (multiple) independent variables.

R-square = 1 - (Residual SS/Total SS)

Adjusted *R-square*. The *R-square* is adjusted by dividing the error sum of squares and total sums of square by their respective degrees of freedom.

R-square(adjusted) =
1-[(Residual SS/df)/(Total SS/df)]

Standard error of the estimate. This statistic measures the dispersion of the observed values about the regression line.

Intercept. If you selected a regression analysis which includes the intercept (see *Defining the Regression Analysis*), then the value for the intercept will be displayed here.

Std. Error. This is the standard error of the intercept.

***t*(df) and *p*-value.** The *t*-value and resulting *p*-value are used to test the hypothesis that the intercept is equal to 0.

***F*, df, and *p*-value:** The *F*-value and resulting *p*-value is used as an overall *F* test of the relationship between the dependent variable and the independent variables. Here:

F = Regression MS/Residual MS

Model Box

Statistically significant regression coefficients (*beta* coefficients) for the variables in the analysis are highlighted in this box. The criterion for determining statistical significance (*alpha* level) can be changed from the *.05* default (see below).

Regression Summary

This option will bring up a Scrollsheet with the standardized (*beta*) and non-standardized (*B*) regression coefficients (weights), their standard error, and statistical significance.

Regression Summary for Dependent Variable: JOB_PROF

MULTIPLE REGRESS.	R= .98127051 R²= .96289181 Adjusted R²= .95547018 F(4,20)=129.74 p<.00000 Std.Error of estimate: 4.0986					
N=25	BETA	St. Err. of BETA	B	St. Err. of B	t(20)	p-level
Intercpt			-124.382	9.941063	-12.5119	.000000
TEST3	.595438	.074813	1.306	.164091	7.9591	.000000
TEST1	.309042	.045951	.296	.043971	6.7254	.000002
TEST4	.285723	.072524	.520	.131943	3.9397	.000810
TEST2	.042992	.050408	.048	.056617	.8529	.403826

The summary statistics for the regression analysis (e.g., *R*, *R-square*, etc.) will be displayed in the headers of the Scrollsheet.

Analysis of Variance

Clicking on this button will bring up a Scrollsheet with a complete Analysis of Variance table for the current regression equation.

Analysis of Variance; DV: JOB_PROF (job_prof.sta)

MULTIPLE REGRESS.	Sums of Squares	df	Mean Squares	F	p-level
Regress.	8718.022	4	2179.506	129.7412	.000000
Residual	335.978	20	16.799		
Total	9054.000				

ANOVA, Adjusted for Mean

This option is only available if the current regression model does not include an intercept. In that case, you can compute the multiple R-square value either based on the variability around the origin (zero), or based on the variability around the mean. The default R-square value reported in the Summary Box pertains to the former, that is, it is the proportion of variability of the dependent variable around 0 (zero) that is accounted for by the predictor variables. If you click on this button, then the program will compute the ANOVA table, including the sums of squares and R-square value, based on the proportion of variability around the mean for the dependent variable, explained by the predictor variables. For various alternative ways for computing the R-square value, refer to Kvålseth (1985).

Covariances of Weights

This option will bring up (1) a Scrollsheet with the correlations of the regression coefficients

Correlations of Regression Weights B; DV: JOB_PROF

MULTIPLE REGRESS.	TEST1	TEST2	TEST3	TEST4
TEST1	1.000000	-.016015	.123918	-.302527
TEST2	-.016015	1.000000	-.364106	.021309
TEST3	.123918	-.364106	1.000000	-.731972
TEST4	-.302527	.021309	-.731972	1.000000

and (2) a Scrollsheet with the variances (on the diagonal) and covariances of the regression coefficients.

Covariances of Regression Weights B; DV: JOB_PROF

MULTIPLE REGRESS.	TEST1	TEST2	TEST3	TEST4
TEST1	.001933	-.000040	.000894	-.001755
TEST2	-.000040	.003206	-.003383	.000159
TEST3	.000894	-.003383	.026926	-.015848
TEST4	-.001755	.000159	-.015848	.017409

Current Sweep Matrix

This option will bring up a Scrollsheet with the current sweep matrix.

Current Status of Sweep Matrix; DV: JOB_PROF (job_prof.sta)

MULTIPLE REGRESS.	TEST1	TEST2	TEST3	TEST4	JOB_PROF
TEST1	-1.13804	.01999	-.22960	.54338	.309042
TEST2	.01999	-1.36951	.74006	-.04199	.042992
TEST3	-.22960	.74006	-3.01655	2.14047	.595438
TEST4	.54338	-.04199	2.14047	-2.83478	.285723
JOB_PROF	.30904	.04299	.59544	.28572	.037108

Matrix inversion in *Multiple Regression* is accomplished via sweeping. The sweep matrix of all independent variables that are currently in the regression equation is also -1 times the inverse of the correlation matrix of those variables (that is, the sign of each element in the matrix is reversed). The diagonal elements for those variables that are not in the equation can be interpreted as the (*1 - R-square*) values, treating the respective variable as the dependent variable, and using all current independent variables.

Partial Correlations

Clicking on this button will bring up Scrollsheets with:

(1) The *beta in* (standard regression coefficient for the respective variable if it were to enter into the regression equation as an independent variable);

(2) The *partial* correlation (between the respective variable and the dependent variable, after controlling for all other independent variables in the equation);

(3) The *semi-partial* (part) *correlation* (the correlation between the *unadjusted* dependent variable with the respective variable after controlling for all independent variables in the equation);

(4) The *tolerance* for the respective variable (defined as 1 minus the squared multiple correlation between the respective variable and all independent variables in the regression equation);

(5) The *minimum tolerance* (the smallest tolerance among all independent variables in the equation if the respective variable were to be entered as an additional independent variable);

(6) The *t*-value associated with these statistics for the respective variable; and,

(7) The statistical significance of the *t*-value.

These statistics will first be displayed separately for variables not currently in the regression equation, and then for the variables *in* the regression equation (if any).

Stepwise Summary

This option will only appear on the *Multiple Regression Results* dialog if (1) the user has selected *forward* or *backward stepwise* regression, or (2) if in the previous *standard* regression analysis the same dependent variable was analyzed and the independent variable list in the previous analysis was a subset of the current independent variable list or vice versa (see page 1668). Thus, in the latter case, the user may evaluate the change in *R-square* caused by removing or entering several variables in a single step (hierarchical analysis). For example, if in the first analysis, variables 1 through 5 were selected as independent variables, and in the subsequent analysis with *the same dependent variable* the user specified variables 1 through 3 as the independent variables, then choosing this option will bring up a Scrollsheet with *R-square*, the *R-square* change, *F to remove*, and the number of variables removed in the single step (two in this example). If *forward* or *backward stepwise* regression was specified, the Scrollsheet will contain the *R-square* increment (or decrease) at each step.

Predict Dependent Variable

This option will bring up a data entry window that allows you to enter values for each independent variable in the regression equation and to calculate the predicted value for the dependent variable based on the current regression equation.

Redundancy

This option will bring up a Scrollsheet with various indicators of the redundancy of independent variables (currently included or not included in the equation). Specifically, for each variable, the Scrollsheet will show:

(1) the *tolerance* (defined as *1 - R-square* for the respective variable with all other variables currently in the equation),

(2) the *R-square* (between the current variable and all other variables in the regression equation),

(3) the *partial correlation* (between the respective variable and the dependent variable, after controlling for all other independent variables in the equation), and

(4) the *semi-partial* (part) *correlation* (the correlation between the *unadjusted* dependent variable with the respective variable after controlling for all independent variables in the equation).

Correlations and Descriptive Statistics

This button will bring up the *Review Descriptive Statistics* dialog (page 1665). From this dialog you can choose to review the means and standard deviations, the correlation matrix and the covariance

matrix, or choose to save the correlation matrix in a standard *STATISTICA* matrix file.

Alpha (Display)

The default value for *alpha* is *.05*. This value is used as a "cut-off" for statistical significance (i.e., if the *p*-value is less than *alpha*, then the effect is highlighted in the Scrollsheet to indicate significance). In this dialog, you can edit this "cut-off" value ($.0001 < \alpha < .5$) and then click on the *Apply* button to immediately apply this change to the next copy of the current Scrollsheet.

Predicting Dependent Variable Values

When you click on the *Predict dependent var* button in the *Multiple Regression Results* dialog, the *Specify Values for Independent Variables* dialog will open.

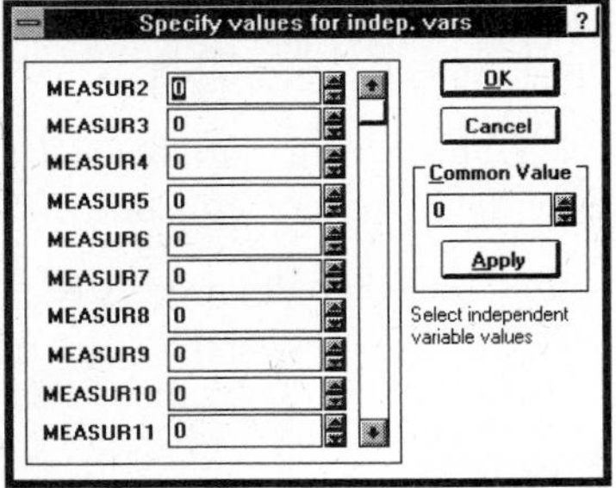

You can enter specific values for the independent variables in this dialog, in order to predict the value of the dependent variable. Enter the values individually for each variable in the current regression equation or enter one common value (click on the *Apply* button to transfer this value to each variable). *STATISTICA* will then compute the value for the dependent variable, given the current regression equation.

Residual Analysis

This dialog is only available if you choose *Raw Data File* as the type of data input.

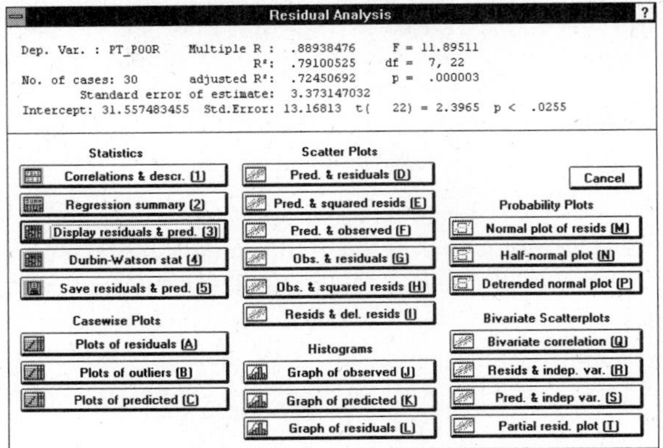

Here, you can choose from several summary statistics and graphics options.

Correlations and Descriptive Statistics

This option will bring up the *Review Descriptive Statistics* dialog (page 1665) from which you can choose to review the means and standard deviations, the correlation matrix and the covariance matrix, or choose to save the correlation matrix in a standard *STATISTICA* matrix file.

Regression Summary

Click on this button to bring up a Scrollsheet with the standardized (*beta*) and non-standardized (*B*) regression coefficients, their standard errors, and statistical significance's. The summary statistics for the regression analysis (e.g., *R*, *R-square*, etc.) will be displayed in the headers of the Scrollsheet.

Display Residuals

This option will bring up a Scrollsheet with various statistics (types of residuals) for each observation. The default graph for this Scrollsheet is the

integrated icon plot (see page 1656). To produce this graph, click on the Scrollsheet with the right-mouse-button and select the *Quick Stats Graphs* option *Icon Plot of Cases*.

Observed value. This is the observed value for the dependent variable.

Predicted value. This is the predicted value given the current regression equation.

Residual value. This is the observed value minus the predicted value.

Standard predicted value. This is the standardized predicted value of the dependent variable.

Standard residual value. This is the standardized residual value (observed minus predicted divided by the square root of the residual mean square).

Standard error of predicted value. This is the standard error of the unstandardized predicted value.

Mahalanobis distance. One can think of the independent variables (in the equation) as defining a multidimensional space in which each observation can be plotted. Also, one can plot a point representing the means for all independent variables. This "mean point" in the multidimensional space is also called the *centroid*.

The Mahalanobis distance is the distance of a case from the centroid in the multidimensional space, defined by the correlated independent variables (if the independent variables are uncorrelated, it is the same as the simple Euclidean distance). Thus, this measure provides an indication of whether or not an observation is an outlier with respect to the independent variable values.

Deleted residual. The deleted residual is the standardized residual value for the respective case, had it *not* been included in the regression analysis, that is, if one would exclude this case from all computations. If the deleted residual differs greatly from the respective standardized residual value, then this case is possibly an outlier because its exclusion changed the regression equation.

Cook's distance. This is another measure of the impact of the respective case on the regression equation. It indicates the difference between the computed *B* values and the values one would have obtained, had the respective case been excluded. All distances should be of about equal magnitude; if not, then there is reason to believe that the respective case(s) biased the estimation of the regression coefficients.

Remedies for outliers. The purpose of all of these statistics is to identify outliers. Remember that particularly with small *n* (less than 100), multiple regression estimates (the *B* coefficients) are not very stable. In other words, single extreme observations can greatly influence the final estimates. Therefore, it is advisable always to review these statistics (using these or the following options), and to repeat crucial analyses after discarding any outliers.

Another alternative is to repeat crucial analyses using *absolute deviations* rather than *least squares* regression, thereby "dampening" the effect of outliers. The *Nonlinear Estimation* module (see Volume III) allows you to estimate such models.

Durbin-Watson Statistic

The Durbin-Watson statistic is useful for evaluating the presence or absence of a serial correlation of residuals (i.e., whether or not residuals for adjacent cases are correlated, indicating that the observations or cases in the data file are not independent).

Note that all statistical significance tests in multiple regression assume that the data consist of a random sample of independent observations. If this is not the case, then the estimates (*B* coefficients) may be more unstable than the significance levels would lead one to believe.

Intuitively, it should be clear that, for example, giving the same questionnaire to the same person 100 times will yield less information about the general population than administering that questionnaire to a random sample of 100 different individuals, who complete the questionnaire only once. In the former case, observations are not independent of each other (the same respondent will give similar responses in repeated questionnaires), while in the latter case, the observations are independent (different people). After clicking on this button, a Scrollsheet will be displayed with the Durbin-Watson *D* statistic and the serial correlation (correlation of adjacent residuals).

Save Residuals

This option is useful if one wants to save predicted and/or residual scores for further analyses with other *STATISTICA* modules. Click on this button to open the *Save Pred/Resid As* dialog in which you can select the file name under which the file will be saved. Next, a variable selection window will appear, allowing you to select additional variables to be saved together with the predicted and residual values.

Note that all values shown in the Scrollsheet will be saved along with the residuals.

Plots of Residuals

After clicking on this button, a dialog will appear from which you can choose the specific residual for the plot (see below). Available residual values are *raw residuals*, *standard residuals*, *Mahalanobis distances*, *deleted residuals*, and *Cook's distances*. These statistics are explained above (see the option *Display residuals*).

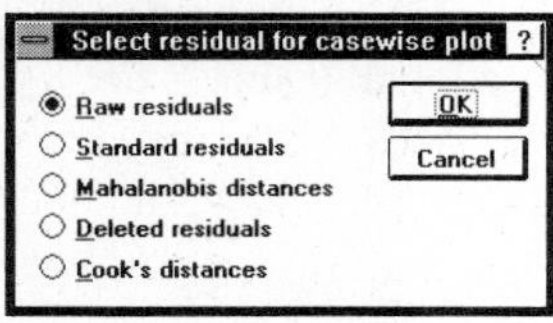

After selecting the desired residual for the plot, a Scrollsheet will come up in which the selected values are plotted in the left-most column.

Raw Residual (poverty.sta)

MULTIPLE REGRESS.

Case name	Raw Residuals (-3s . . 0 . . +3s)	Dependent Observed Value
Benton		19.00000
Cannon		26.20000
Carrol		18.10000
Cheatheam		15.40000
Cumberland		29.00000
DeKalb		21.60000
Dyer		21.90000
Gibson		18.90000
Greene		21.10000
Hawkins		23.80000
Haywood		40.50000
Henry		21.60000
Houston		25.40000
Humphreys		19.70000
Jackson		38.00000
Johnson		30.10000
Lawrence		24.80000

At the same time, *all* residual statistics are computed and can be reviewed (in the subsequent columns of the Scrollsheet).

Plots of Outliers

After clicking on this button, a dialog will open that will allow you to choose to: (1) plot only cases for which the absolute standard residual value is greater than +2, or (2) plot the 100 most extreme cases, sorted in descending order of magnitude, of either the *standard predicted* values, *standard residuals*, *Mahalanobis distances*, *deleted residuals*, or *Cook's distances* (for explanations of these statistics see above under option *Display residuals*).

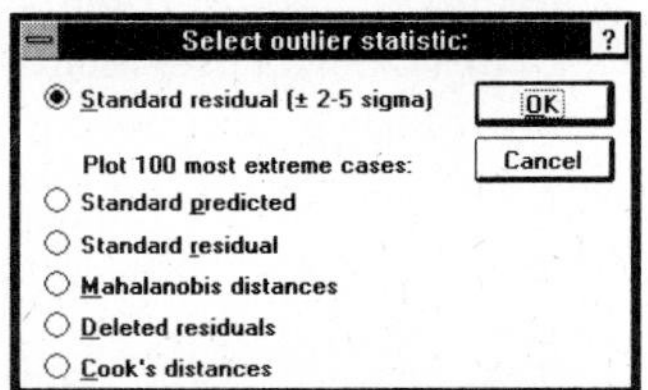

Thus, this option allows you to identify outliers in even very large data files, since only the most extreme cases are plotted. In the Scrollsheet the

selected values are plotted in the left-most column; at the same time, *all* residual statistics are computed and can be reviewed (in the subsequent columns of the Scrollsheet).

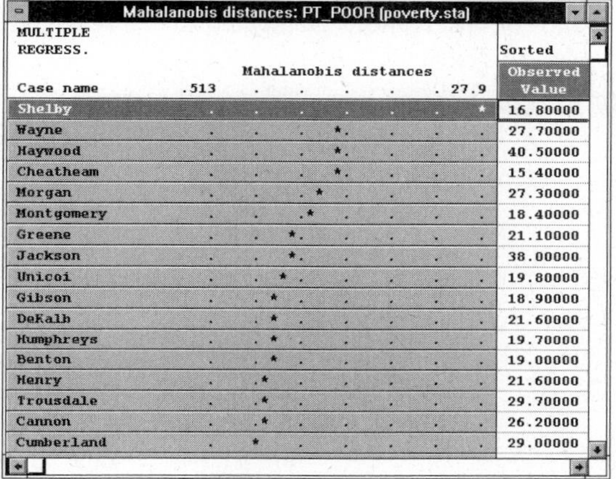

Mahalanobis distances: PT_POOR (poverty.sta)

MULTIPLE REGRESS. — Mahalanobis distances (.513 … 27.9)

Case name	Sorted Observed Value
Shelby	16.80000
Wayne	27.70000
Haywood	40.50000
Cheatheam	15.40000
Morgan	27.30000
Montgomery	18.40000
Greene	21.10000
Jackson	38.00000
Unicoi	19.80000
Gibson	18.90000
DeKalb	21.60000
Humphreys	19.70000
Benton	19.00000
Henry	21.60000
Trousdale	29.70000
Cannon	26.20000
Cumberland	29.00000

Plots of Predicted

After clicking on this button you can choose to plot the *raw predicted* or the *standard predicted* values.

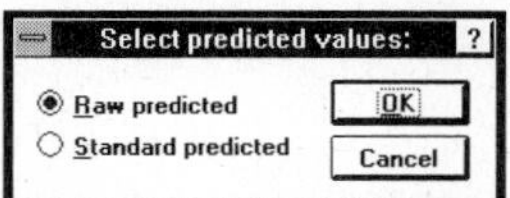

In the Scrollsheet the selected values are plotted in the left-most column; at the same time, *all* residual statistics are computed and can be reviewed (in the subsequent columns of the Scrollsheet).

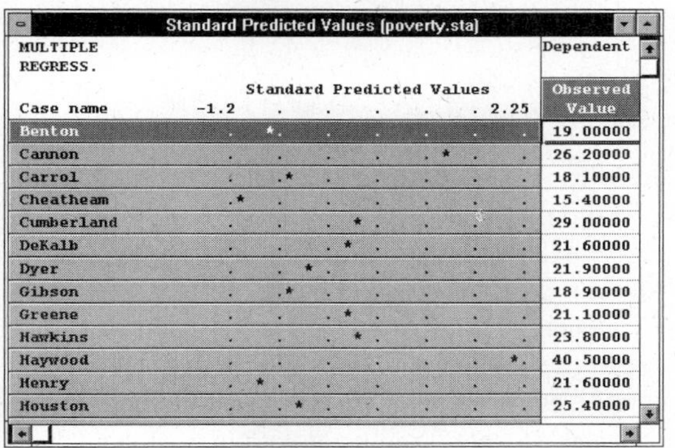

Standard Predicted Values (poverty.sta)

MULTIPLE REGRESS. — Standard Predicted Values (-1.2 … 2.25)

Case name	Dependent Observed Value
Benton	19.00000
Cannon	26.20000
Carrol	18.10000
Cheatheam	15.40000
Cumberland	29.00000
DeKalb	21.60000
Dyer	21.90000
Gibson	18.90000
Greene	21.10000
Hawkins	23.80000
Haywood	40.50000
Henry	21.60000
Houston	25.40000

Predicted and Residuals

This option will bring up a scatterplot of the raw predicted values (on the *X*-axis) versus the raw residuals (on the *Y*-axis).

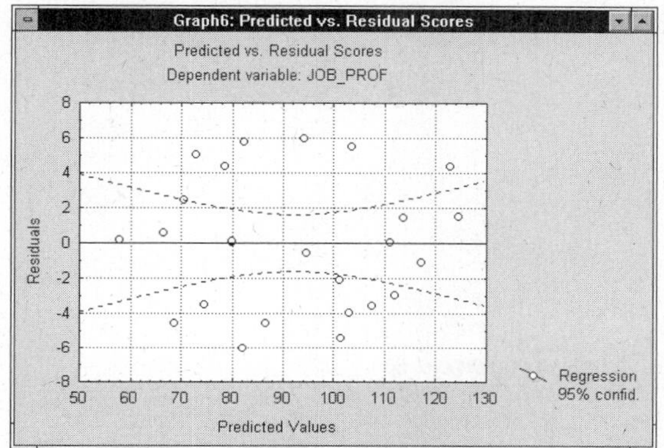

This plot is very useful for testing the assumption of *linearity* regarding the relationship between the independent variables and dependent variable. Specifically, if the relationship is linear, then the residual scores can be expected to form a homogeneous "cloud" around the center line. However, if non-linearity is present, then peculiar patterns may emerge.

For example, if the true relationship between variables is curvilinear rather than linear, the residuals may form an inverted *U* around the center line, indicating that predictions are consistently too high on the extreme ends of the scale, but too low in the central region of the scale. In that case, one may try to include second or third order polynomial transformations of the original independent variables in the regression (that is, X^2, X^3, etc.). This can easily be accomplished via the *fixed nonlinear* regression option (see page 1665).

Predicted and Squared Residuals

This option will bring up a scatterplot of the raw predicted values (on the *X*-axis) versus the squared raw residuals (on the *Y*-axis).

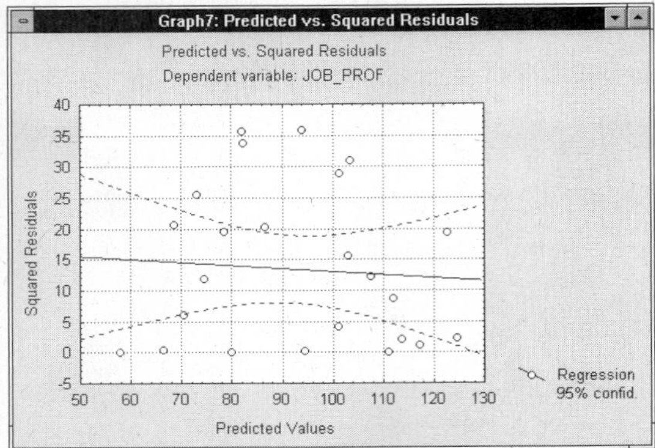

Predicted and Observed Values

This option allows you to plot a scatterplot of the predicted versus the observed values.

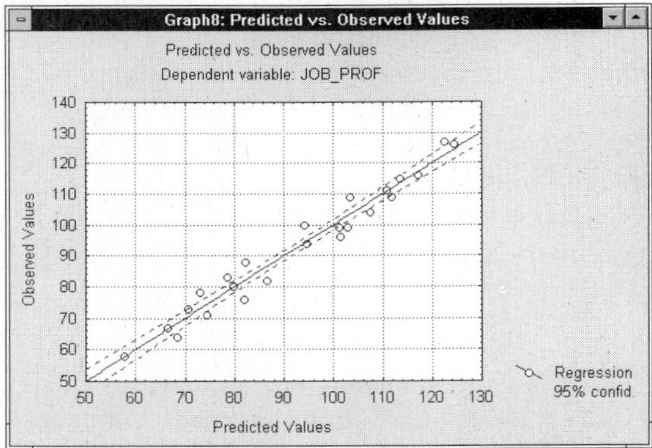

This plot is particularly useful for identifying potential clusters of cases that are not well predicted. For example, if one were to analyze job performance data (using some employment test as the predictor variable), it could happen that the test predicts success well for the majority of employees, but that there is a distinct group of employees for whom the prediction based on the employment test is consistently too low (a common problem in tests that rely heavily on verbal skills), and who would be unfairly discriminated against if the test were to be used as the sole criterion for selection.

Observed and Residual Values, and Observed and Squared Residual Values

These plots are also very useful for detecting outliers or groups of observations that are consistently over- or under-predicted (see above).

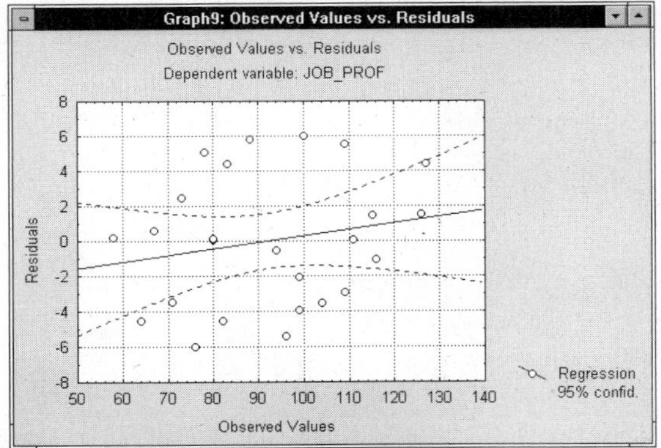

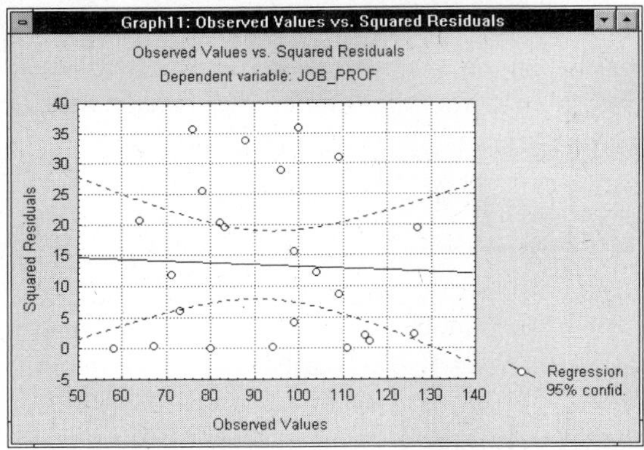

Residuals and Deleted Residuals

Deleted residuals are the standardized residuals that one would obtain if the respective case would be excluded from the estimation of the multiple regression (i.e., the computation of the regression coefficients). Thus, if there are large discrepancies between the deleted residuals and the regular standardized residuals, then one can conclude that the regression coefficients are not very stable, that

is, they are greatly affected by the exclusion of single cases (see also the discussion of the *Display residuals* option, above).

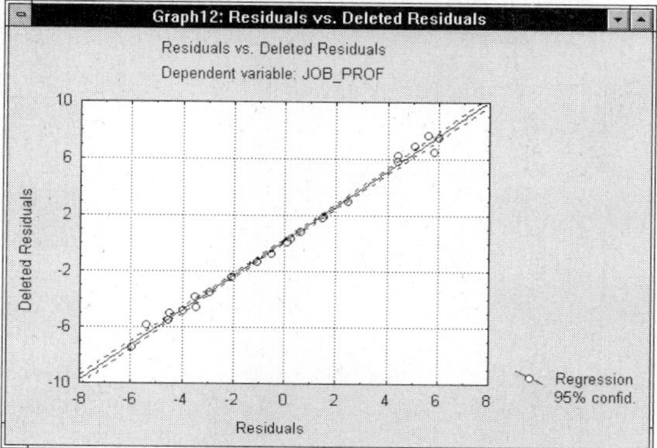

Histogram of Observed

This option will bring up a histogram (frequency distribution) of the observed values for the dependent variable and superimpose the expected normal distribution values over this plot.

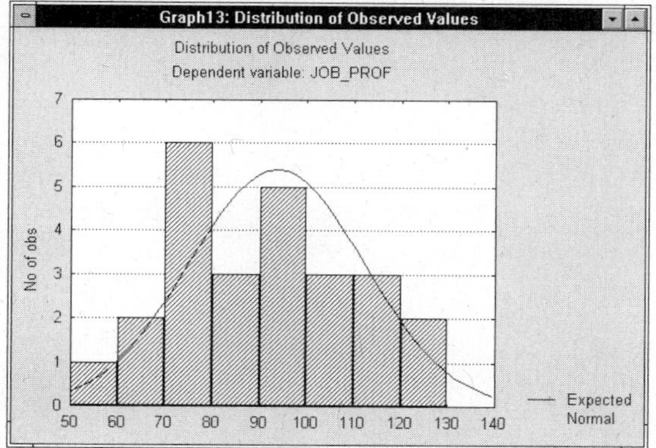

Histograms of Predicted

After clicking on this button you can choose to plot a histogram of the *raw* (unstandardized) *predicted* values or the *standardized predicted* values in the *Select Predicted Values* dialog.

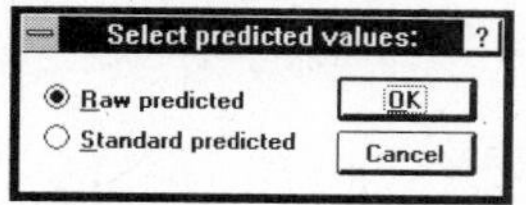

When you click *OK* in this dialog the respective graph will be produced.

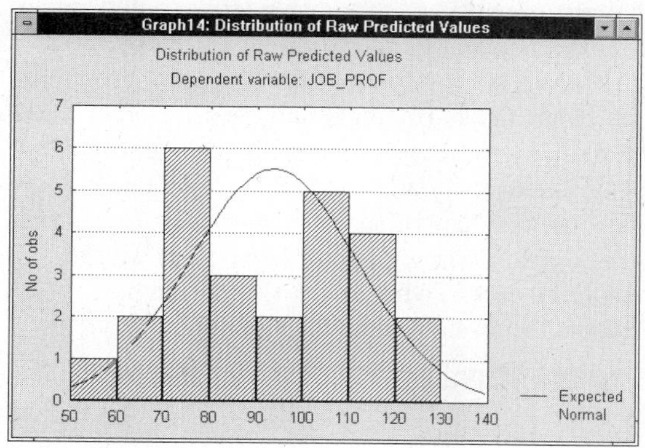

Histograms of Residuals

After clicking on this button, a submenu will appear from which you can choose the specific residual for the histogram. Available residual values are *raw residuals*, *standard residuals*, *Mahalanobis distances*, *deleted residuals*, and *Cook's distances*. (These statistics are briefly explained in the above option, *Display residuals*, page 1674).

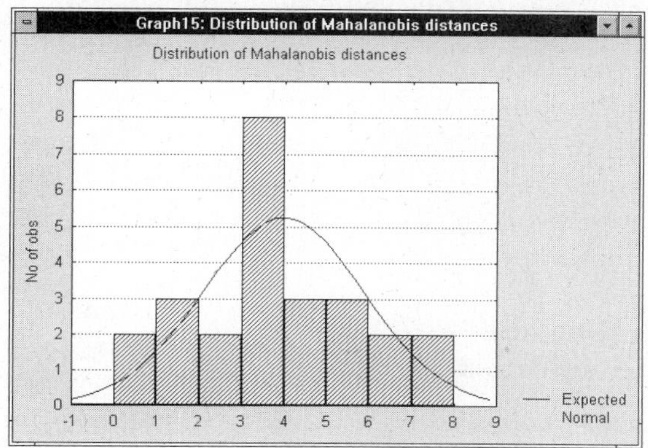

Normal Plot of Residuals

Multiple regression assumes that the residual values (observed minus predicted values) are normally distributed, and that the regression function (the relationship between the independent and dependent variables) is linear in nature. If any of these assumptions is grossly violated, then the regression coefficients (*B* coefficients) may be affected (inflated or deflated) and the statistical significance tests inflated or deflated. If "all is well," one can expect the residual values to be normally distributed. *Normal probability plots* provide a quick way to visually inspect to what extent the pattern of residuals follows a normal distribution.

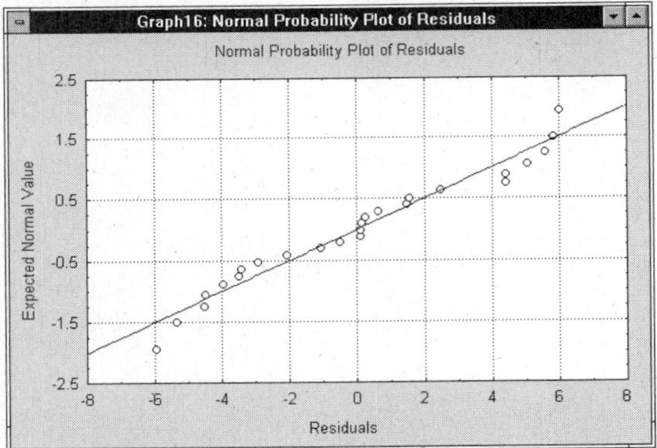

If the residuals are not normally distributed, they will deviate from the line. Outliers may also become evident in this plot. If there is a general lack of fit, and the data seem to form a clear pattern (e.g., an *S* shape) around the line, then the dependent variable may have to be transformed in some way (e.g., a log transformation to "pull in" the tail of the distribution, etc.).

Half-normal Plot of Residuals

The *half-normal probability plot* is constructed in the same way as the standard normal probability plot, except that only the positive half of the normal curve is considered. Consequently, only positive normal values will be plotted on the *Y*-axis.

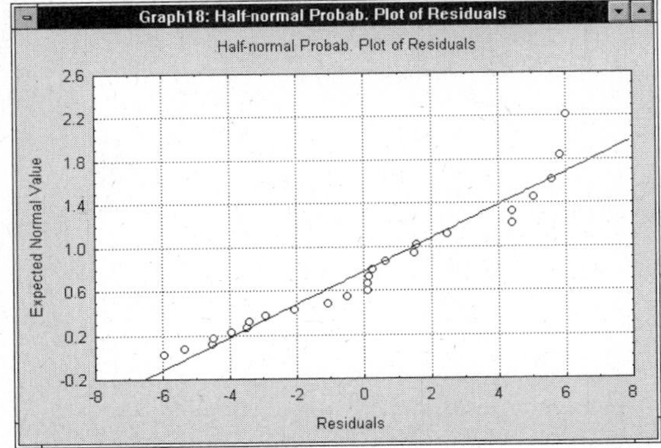

This plot is basically used when one wants to ignore the sign of the residual, that is, when one is mostly interested in the distribution of absolute residuals, regardless of sign.

Detrended Normal Plot of Residuals

The *detrended normal probability plot* is constructed in the same way as the standard normal probability plot, except that, before the plot is produced, the linear trend is removed. This often "spreads out" the plot, thereby allowing the user to detect patterns of deviations more easily.

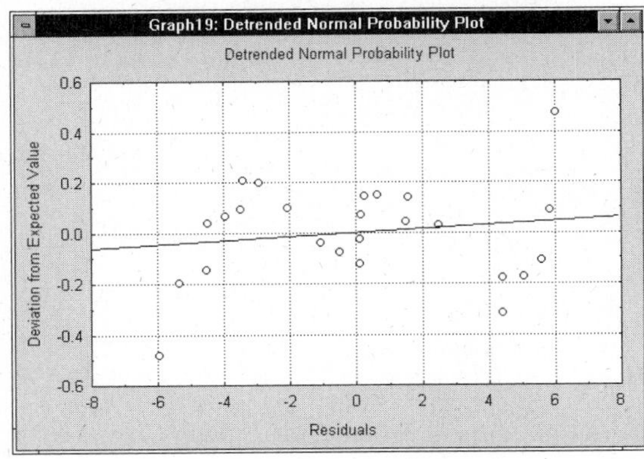

Bivariate Correlation

This option allows you to produce a scatterplot of any two variables in the data file, regardless of whether or not they are included in the regression analysis.

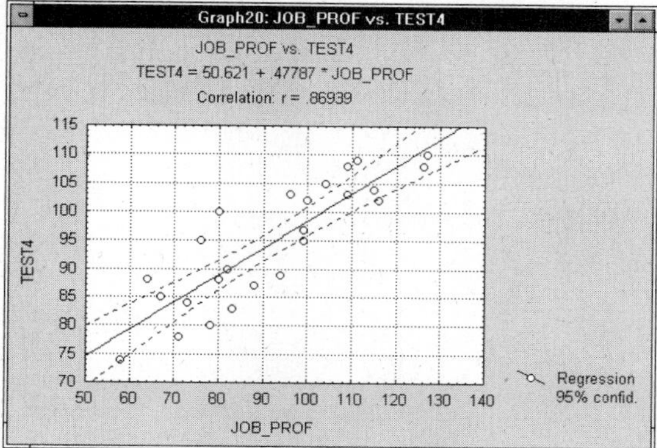

Residual and Independent Variable

This option allows you to produce a scatterplot of various residual values (for the dependent variable) with any variable in the data file, regardless of whether or not it was included in the regression analysis. After clicking on this button, the *Select Residual for Casewise Plot* dialog will appear in which you can choose the specific residual for the scatterplot.

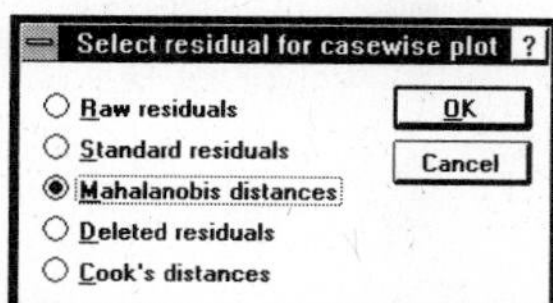

Available residual values are *raw residuals*, *standard residuals*, *Mahalanobis distances*, *deleted residuals*, and *Cook's distances*. These statistics are briefly explained above in the D*isplay residuals* option.

Next, you will be prompted to enter the other variable for the plot. This option allows you to explore the relationship between the residualized dependent variable and other variables in your data file.

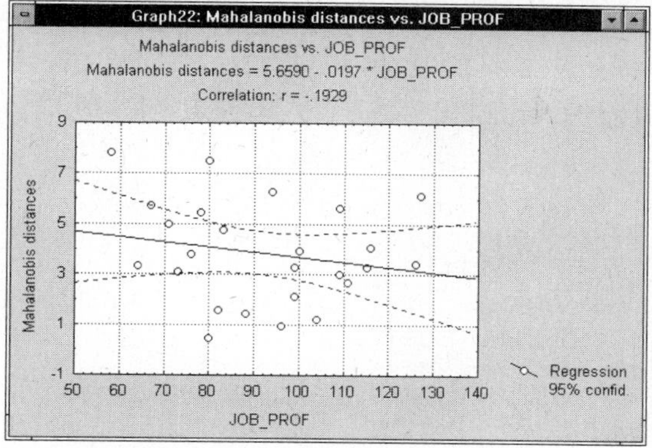

Predicted and Independent Variable

This option allows you to produce a scatterplot of various residual values with any variable in the data file, regardless of whether or not the respective variable was included in the regression analysis. After clicking on this button, a dialog will come up from which you can elect to plot either raw predicted or standardized predicted values. Next you will be prompted to select the variable for the plot.

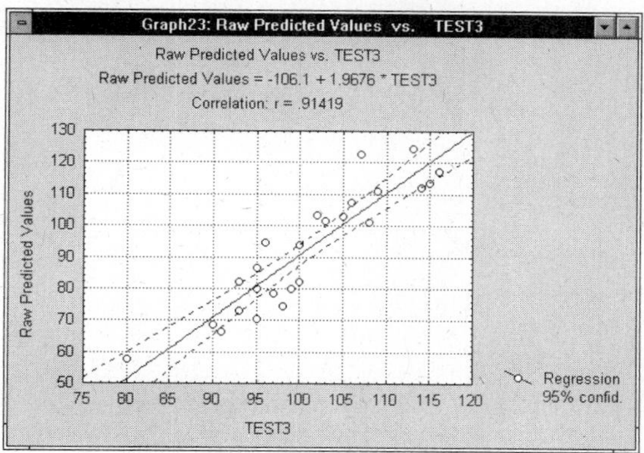

Partial Residual Plot

This option allows you to produce a *partial residual* plot for any variable currently in the regression equation. After clicking on this button you are prompted to select one independent variable from among those currently in the regression equation.

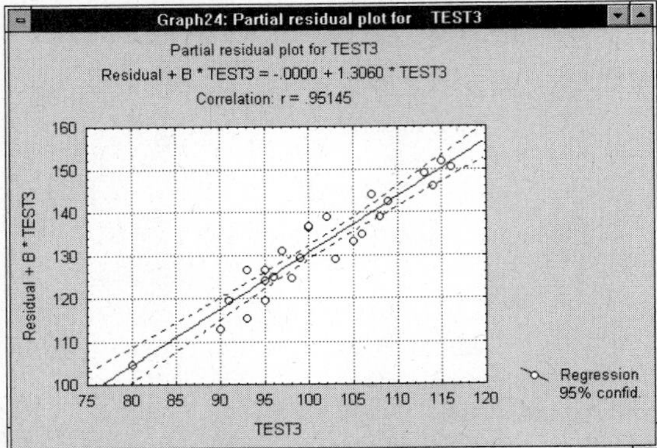

In a partial residual plot, the residual plus the contribution of the respective independent variable to the regression (i.e., $residual+b_i*x_{ii}$) is plotted against the values for that independent variable. This plot is discussed in detail by Larsen and McCleary (1972).

NOTES

Raw Data Input, Missing Data Deletion

If a raw data file is used for input, the *Multiple Regression* module will first calculate the correlation matrix. Missing data can be deleted *casewise*, *pairwise*, or missing data may be *substituted by means* (see *Elementary Concepts*, Chapter 8).

If *pairwise* deletion of missing data is requested, then subsequent regression analysis and significance tests will be calculated based on the degrees of freedom (*df*) derived from the smallest number of valid cases that occurred among the selected variables (the number of valid cases for each pair of selected variables may be reviewed). Therefore, the results of the regression analyses using pairwise deletion of missing data should be interpreted with caution because they are only approximations based on the smallest number of valid cases.

If *casewise* deletion of missing data is selected, the calculation of the correlation matrix will be faster and the test statistics (e.g., *R-square*, *F*) calculated in subsequent multiple regression analyses with be more accurate.

Matrix Input

If a correlation matrix is chosen for input into the *Multiple Regression* module, the submatrix of selected variables will be extracted from the chosen correlation matrix. Obviously, predicted and residual scores cannot be calculated if a correlation matrix is used for input.

The input correlation matrix file must be stored in *STATISTICA* matrix file format. Those files can be created in every module of *STATISTICA* via the *Quick Basic Stats* options (see Chapter 10); several modules of *STATISTICA* also have designated options to produce those files (e.g., *Basic Statistics and Tables*, *Multiple Regression*, *Factor Analysis*, *Canonical Analysis*, *Reliability*), or the user can create those files directly by typing them into the data spreadsheet (see *Matrix File Format*, Chapter 7).

Internal Batch Processing Option

In addition to the batch processing language (*SCL*) and macro capabilities available in all modules of *STATISTICA*, the *Multiple Regression* module also offers an internal batch processing option. The user can specify up to 99 dependent variables on the *Define Model* dialog (clicking on the *Variables* button will bring up the variable selection dialog). If a dependent variable *list* is specified, the program will cycle through the list, performing the multiple regression analysis (according to the current specifications) for one dependent variable at a time. The results of several analyses specified in this manner may be printed continuously (without requiring any user input) by specifying the printer as the output in the *Page/Output Setup* dialog and setting the *Batch processing and printing* option in the *Multiple Regression* startup panel.

Using Pairwise Deletion of Missing Data

It is advisable to use caution when interpreting the results of a multiple regression analysis using the pairwise deletion of missing data option. Theoretically, a case (observation) should not be taken into account if it has missing data for any of the variables involved in the multiple regression analysis. The *Multiple Regression* module will perform the regression analysis treating the correlation matrix (that was calculated using

pairwise deletion of missing data) as if it were based on only complete cases (i.e., without any missing data; the *Multiple Regression* module will use the minimum number of cases for any of the variables in the regression equation to determine the degrees of freedom for significance tests and to estimate the *Sums of Squares*). It is always advisable to compare the results using pairwise deletion of missing data with the results obtained using casewise deletion of missing data or mean substitution of missing data to detect major discrepancies.

Specifying *F to Enter/Remove* in Stepwise Regression

In stepwise regression, a variable is entered into the regression equation if its *F* value is greater than the specified minimum value (i.e., the *F to enter* specified on the *Model Definition* dialog), and a variable is removed from the regression equation if its *F* value is less than the specified minimum value (i.e., the *F to remove* value on the *Model Definition* dialog). Therefore, the *F to enter* value must always be specified greater than the *F to remove* value; otherwise, a variable would be entered and removed in an endless loop. The *Multiple Regression* module will issue an error message if the user violates this rule.

If *backward stepwise* regression is requested in the *Model Definition* dialog, then the program will first enter all variables into the regression equation (step 0) and then check for the variable with the lowest *F to remove* value. Variables will then be removed in consecutive steps until no variable in the regression equation has an *F to remove* value less than the one that was specified. Therefore, if one wants to remove *all* variables, one at a time, from the regression equation, one should specify a very large *F to enter* value (e.g., *999*) and a very large *F to remove* value (e.g., *998*; remember that the *F to remove* value must always be less than the *F to enter* value).

If *forward stepwise* regression is specified, then at each step, the program will check the list of independent variables that are not yet in the regression equation and enter the variable with the largest *F to enter* value. Stepping will terminate when no *F to enter* value for any independent variable (that is not yet in the regression equation) exceeds the specified *F to enter* limit. Therefore, if one wants to enter, one by one, *all* independent variables into the regression equation, a very small *F to enter* should be specified (e.g., *0.0001*) and the *F to remove* should be set to zero (enter *0.0*).

Entering Variables in Blocks (Hierarchical Analysis)

The *forward* and *backward stepwise* regression options will cause variables to be entered or removed one at a time. Often, one wants to assess the combined effect of several variables that are entered into a regression equation in a single step or in a succession of steps. The necessary statistics to do this are automatically calculated by the *Multiple Regression* module if the independent variable list is properly specified on the *Model Definition* dialog.

When *standard* multiple regression is selected, the program will always compare the variables that were selected for a particular analysis with those that were specified in the previous analysis. First, the program will check whether the same dependent variable is being analyzed. If not, the incremental increase or decrease in the *R-square* from the previous analysis of course cannot be interpreted. Next, the program will check (1) whether the independent variable list is a subset of the independent variable list previously specified (i.e., variables were removed), or (2) whether the previously specified independent variable list is a subset of the list that is currently specified (i.e., variables were entered). If either of these two conditions is met (in addition to the

analysis of a common dependent variable), then the *Multiple Regression* module will calculate the incremental increase or decrease in *R-square* and related statistics (accessible via the *Stepwise Summary* button on the *Multiple Regression Results* dialog; for a brief example, refer to page 1668).

Matrix Ill-Conditioning

A correlation matrix is said to be ill-conditioned if there is linear dependency among the variables. For example, if one of the independent variables specified for the regression is the sum of two other independent variables, then the multiple regression analysis cannot be performed. In practice, matrix ill-conditioning occurs when one tries to use several independent variables that are highly intercorrelated.

There are two possible solutions that you may want to try if this problem occurs. First, use forward stepwise multiple regression to enter variables one by one. This will allow you to monitor the unique contribution of independent variables to the prediction, as they are moved into the regression equation. The *Redundancy* option on the *Multiple Regression Results* dialog is particularly useful in this regard. For each independent variable, it will compute the *R-square* value with all other variables currently in the regression equation, *1-R-square* (the *Tolerance*), and the *partial* and *semi-partial* (part) correlations. These statistics allow one to identify variables that are excessively redundant with other predictors.

Ridge Regression

The second possibility is to perform a *ridge regression* (select the *Ridge regression* option in the *Model Definition* dialog, page 1670). In ridge regression (see Hoerl, 1962), the user is asked to specify a value for *lambda*. This value is then added to the diagonal of the correlation matrix; in effect the correlations are artificially decreased. Although the resulting estimates are not unbiased, they may actually be accurate and robust (see Schmidt and Muller, 1978, for a discussion; see also Rozeboom, 1979, for a critical appraisal of this method).

Some Useful *STATISTICA BASIC* Programs

The *STATISTICA* system includes several *STATISTICA BASIC* example programs (in subdirectory *STBASIC*) that are useful for solving certain regression problems.

Extremely Large Multiple Regression Problems

Program *Regressn.stb* will perform a multiple regression analysis with very many predictor variables (the arrays used in the computations are dynamically dimensioned inside the program, so the size of the problem that can be analyzed is only limited by the amount of memory available on your system). Regression models with and without an intercept can be evaluated, and the program also will compute residual statistics and plots.

Weighted Least Squares Estimation

The program *Wls.stb* will perform weighted least squares analyses and compute various alternative R-square statistics (see Kvålseth, 1985). Instead of the iterative derivative-free estimation method described in the *Nonlinear Estimation* chapter (Volume III), program *Wls.stb* uses matrix algebra expressions (e.g., see Neter, Wassermann, and Kutner, 1985) to estimate the weighted least squares parameters. Thus, for large data files program *Wls.stb* is more efficient, and often much faster.

Two-Stage Least Squares Estimation

Program *2stls.stb* provides an example for 2-stage least squares regression. That program can easily be expanded or tailored to, for example, perform iteratively reweighted least squares analysis.

Box-Cox and Box-Tidwell Transformations

Often, when the residuals from an ordinary least squares analysis do not follow the normal distribution, one can apply certain transformations of the independent or dependent variables to correct the problem. A family of simple power transformations for positive response values *y* can be expressed as:

$$z = y^{\lambda}, \quad \lambda \neq 0$$
$$= \text{natural log}(y), \quad \lambda = 0$$

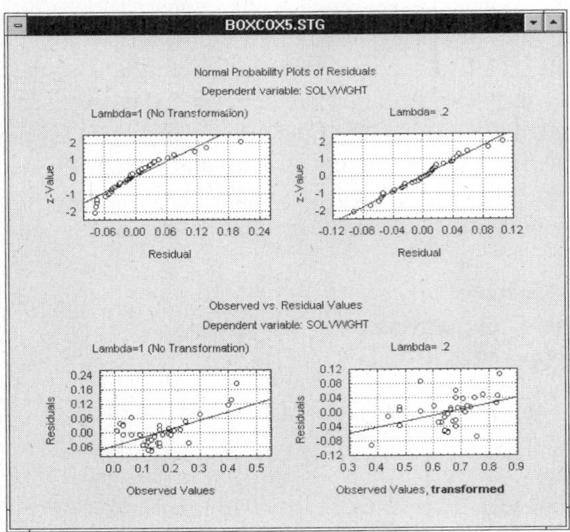

Note that for $\lambda = 1$ (*lambda =1*) no transformation is performed; for $\lambda = -1$ the result of the transformation is the reciprocal of *y*, for $\lambda = \frac{1}{2}$ the result of the transformation is the square root of y. Thus, various common transformations of the dependent variable can be expressed in this general form.

Program *Boxcox.stb* will compute the maximum likelihood estimate for *lambda* for the *Box-Cox* transformation of the dependent variable (Box and Cox, 1964; see also Mason, Gunst, and Hess, 1989), and allows you to construct graphs of the error sums of squares as a function of different values for *lambda*.

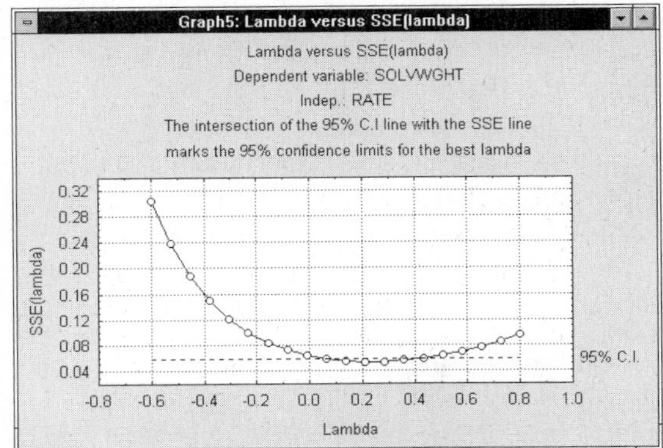

The same type of power-transformation can be applied to the predictor (independent) variables in a linear regression problem. Program *Boxtid.stb* will compute the *lambda* parameters for this so-called *Box-Tidwell* transformation for the independent variables (see Mason, Gunst, and Hess, 1989).

TECHNICAL INFORMATION

General

The *Multiple Regression* routine consists of two major parts. The first part calculates a correlation matrix (or extracts a correlation matrix if matrix input is selected) according to the user's specifications (i.e., missing data, selection conditions, etc.). The second part performs the actual multiple regression analyses.

Calculating Multiple Regression, Matrix Inversion

Matrix inversion is accomplished via sweeping (see Dempster, 1969, page 62). The regression coefficients, residual *Sums of Squares*, tolerances, and partial correlations are also calculated as part of the sweeping operation (see also Jennrich, 1977).

Statistical Significance Tests

The standard formulas are used for calculating the *F*-value associated with the multiple *R*, and for the *t*-values associated with the regression coefficients (e.g., see Cooley and Lohnes, 1971; Darlington, 1990; Lindeman, Merenda, and Gold, 1980; Morrison, 1967; Neter, Wasserman, and Kutner, 1985; Pedhazur, 1973; Stevens, 1986; Younger, 1985).

Residuals

The *standard error* of a residual score is computed as the square root of:

$$[1-1/n-(X_{raw}-X_{mean})*C^{-1}*(X_{raw}-X_{mean})']*RMS$$

where

X_{raw} is the vector of raw data for the independent variables

X_{mean} is the vector of means for the independent variables

C^{-1} is the inverse of the matrix of crossproducts of deviations for the independent variables

n is the number of valid cases

RMS is the residual mean square

The terms *1/n* and X_{mean} are dropped if there is no intercept (regression forced through the origin).

The *standardized residuals* are obtained by dividing each residual by its standard error.

The *Mahalanobis distance* is the distance of a case from the centroid of all cases in the space defined by the independent variables. It is computed as:

$$(n-1)*(X_{raw}-X_{mean})*C^{-1}*(X_{raw}-X_{mean})'$$

where

X_{raw} is the vector of raw data for the independent variables

X_{mean} is the vector of means for the independent variables

C^{-1} is the inverse of the matrix of crossproducts of deviations for the independent variables

n is the number of valid cases

The terms *1/n* and X_{mean} are dropped if there is no intercept (regression forced through the origin). Refer to the *Examples* section of this chapter for an example of how Mahalanobis distances can aid in the detection of outliers.

The *deleted residual* is the residual which would have been obtained had the case not been included in the estimation of the regression equation. It is calculated by dividing the ordinary residual by:

$$1-(1/n)-(X_{raw}-X_{mean})*C^{-1}*(X_{raw}-X_{mean})'$$

where

x_{raw} is the vector of raw data for the independent variables

x_{mean} is the vector of means for the independent variables

C^{-1} is the inverse of the matrix of crossproducts of deviations for the independent variables

n is the number of valid cases

The terms *1/n* and X_{mean} are dropped if there is no intercept (regression forced through the origin). Refer to the *Example* section of this chapter for an illustration of how deleted residuals can aid in the detection of outliers.

Cook's distance (Cook, 1977) is useful for assessing the changes that would result in all residuals if the respective case were to be omitted from the regression analysis. It is defined as:

$$\{DR^2 * [1/n + MD/(n-1)]\}/[(No.Vars + 1)*RSM]$$

where

DR is the *deleted residual*

MD is the Mahalanobis distance

RSM is the residual mean square

If there is no intercept, *n-1* is replaced by *n*, the term *1/n* is dropped, and the term *+1* (adding 1 to the number of independent variables) is dropped.

Computations for Normal Probability Plots

The following formulas are used to convert the ranks (computed from the residuals) into expected normal probability values, that is, the respective normal *z* values.

Normal probability plot. The normal probability value z_j for the *j*'th value (rank) in a variable with *n* observations is computed as:

$$z_j = \Phi^{-1} [(3*j-1)/(3*N+1)]$$

where Φ^{-1} is the inverse normal cumulative distribution function (converting the normal probability *p* into the normal value *z*).

Half-normal probability plot. Here, the half-normal probability value z_j for the *j*'th value (rank) in a variable with *n* observations is computed as:

$$z_j = \Phi^{-1} [(3*N+3*j-1)/(6*N+1)]$$

where Φ^{-1} is again the inverse normal cumulative distribution function.

Detrended normal probability plot. In this plot each value (x_j) is standardized by subtracting the *mean* and dividing by the respective standard deviation (*s*). The detrended normal probability value z_j for the *j*'th value (rank) in a variable with *n* observations is computed as:

$$z_j = \Phi^{-1} [(3*j-1)/(3*N+1)] - (x_j-mean)/s$$

where Φ^{-1} is again the inverse normal cumulative distribution function.

INDEX

StatSoft

Chapter 13:
ANOVA/MANOVA

Table of Contents

Detailed
Table Contents

StatSoft

StatSoft

Chapter 13: ANOVA/MANOVA

INTRODUCTORY OVERVIEW

The following discussions are a "primer" on the basic logic, assumptions, and terminology of analysis of variance techniques. To learn how to specify particular designs in the *ANOVA/MANOVA* module, refer to the appropriate section (between-group designs, see page 1763, repeated measures designs, see page 1768) where the general conventions for specifying designs are explained. For detailed examples of selected common designs, refer to the *Examples* section, page 1719.

The basic ideas on which analysis of variance (ANOVA) is based will first be reviewed, then the analysis of covariance (ANCOVA) and multivariate analysis of variance (and covariance; MANOVA and MANCOVA) designs will be introduced. After briefly discussing the importance of contrast analysis and *post hoc* testing, the assumptions on which the various ANOVA techniques are based will be considered. Finally, the reasons why using the multivariate approach to repeated measures is preferable over the traditional univariate approach will be explained.

Basic Ideas

The purpose of analysis of variance. In general, the purpose of analysis of variance (ANOVA) is to test for significant differences between means. The *Elementary Concepts* chapter (Chapter 8) provides a brief introduction into the basics of statistical significance testing. If you are only comparing two means, then ANOVA will give the same results as the *t*-test for independent samples (if you are comparing two different groups of cases or observations), or the *t*-test for dependent samples (if you are comparing two variables in one set of cases or observations). If you are not familiar with those tests you may at this point want to "brush up" on your knowledge about those tests by reading the introduction to the *Basic Statistics and Tables* chapter (Chapter 9).

Why the name *analysis of variance*? It may seem odd to you that a procedure that compares means is called analysis of *variance*. However, this name is derived from the fact that in order to test for statistical significance between means, the variances are actually compared (i.e., analyzed).

The Partitioning of Sums of Squares

At the heart of ANOVA is the fact that variances can be divided up, that is, partitioned. Remember that the variance is computed as the sum of squared deviations from the overall mean, divided by *n-1* (sample size minus one). Thus, given a certain *n*, the variance is a function of the sums of (deviation) squares, or *SS* for short. Partitioning of variance works as follows. Consider the following data set:

	Group 1	Group 2
Observation 1	2	6
Observation 2	3	7
Observation 3	1	5
Mean	2	6
Sums of Squares (SS)	2	2
Overall Mean	4	
Total Sums of Squares	28	

The means for the two groups are quite different (*2* and *6*, respectively). The sums of squares *within* each group are equal to *2*. Adding them together, you get *4*. If you now repeat these computations, *ignoring* group membership, that is, if you compute the total *SS* based on the overall mean, you get the number *28*. In other words, computing the variance (sums of squares) based on the within-group variability yields a much smaller estimate of

variance than computing it based on the total variability (the overall mean). The reason for this in the above example is of course that there is a large difference between means, and it is this difference that accounts for the difference in the *SS*. In fact, if you were to perform an ANOVA on the above data, you would get the following result:

MAIN EFFECT: GROUP (aov.sta)

GENERAL MANOVA	1-GROUP				
Univar. Test	Sum of Squares	df	Mean Square	F	p-level
Effect	24.00000	1	24.00000	24.00000	.008050
Error	4.00000	4	1.00000		

As you can see, in the above Scrollsheet, the total *SS* (*28*) was partitioned into the *SS* due to *within*-group variability (*2+2 = 4*; see the second row of the Scrollsheet) and variability due to differences between means (*28-(2+2) = 24*; see the first row of the Scrollsheet).

SS error and SS effect. The within-group variability (*SS*) is usually referred to as *Error* variance. This term denotes the fact that you cannot readily explain or account for it in the current design. However, the *SS Effect* can be explained. Namely, it is due to the differences in means between the groups. Put another way, group membership *explains* this variability because you know that it is due to the differences in means.

Significance testing. The basic idea of statistical significance testing is discussed in the *Elementary Concepts* chapter (Chapter 8). The *Elementary Concepts* chapter also explains why very many statistical tests represent ratios of explained to unexplained variability. ANOVA is a good example of this. Here, the crucial test is based on a comparison of the variance due to the between-groups variability (called *Mean Square Effect*, or MS_{effect}) with the within-group variability (called *Mean Square Error*, or MS_{error}). Under the null hypothesis (that there are no mean differences between groups in the population), you would still expect some minor random fluctuation in the means for the two groups when taking small samples (as in this example). Therefore, under the null hypothesis, the variance estimated based on within-group variability should be about the same as the variance due to between-groups variability. You can compare those two estimates of variance via the *F* test, which tests whether the ratio of the two variance estimates is significantly greater than 1. In the above example, that test is highly significant, and you would in fact conclude that the means for the two groups are significantly different from each other.

Summary of the basic logic of ANOVA. To summarize the discussion up to this point, the purpose of analysis of variance is to test differences in means (for groups or variables) for statistical significance. This is accomplished by analyzing the variance, that is, by partitioning the total variance into the component that is due to true random error (i.e., within-group *SS*) and the components that are due to differences between means. These latter variance components are then tested for statistical significance, and, if significant, you reject the null hypothesis of no differences between means, and accept the alternative hypothesis that the means (in the population) are different from each other.

Dependent and independent variables. The variables that are measured (e.g., a test score) are called *dependent* variables. The variables that are manipulated or controlled (e.g., a teaching method or some other criterion used to divide observations into groups that are compared) are called *factors* or *independent* variables. For more information on this important distinction, refer to the *Elementary Concepts* chapter (Chapter 8).

Multi-Factor ANOVA

In the simple example above, it may have occurred to you that you could have simply computed a *t*-test for independent samples using the options in the *Basic Statistics and Tables* module to arrive at the same conclusion. And, indeed, you would get the identical result if you were to compare the two

groups using this test. However, ANOVA is a much more flexible and powerful technique that can be applied to much more complex research issues.

Multiple factors. The world is complex and multivariate in nature, and instances when a single variable completely explains a phenomenon are rare. For example, when trying to explore how to grow a bigger tomato, you would need to consider factors that have to do with the plants' genetic makeup, soil conditions, lighting, temperature, etc. Thus, in a typical experiment, many factors are taken into account. One important reason for using ANOVA methods rather than multiple two-group studies analyzed via *t*-tests, is that the former method is more *efficient*, and with fewer observations you can gain more information. This statement will be expanded on in the following paragraphs.

Controlling for factors. Suppose that in the above two-group example you introduce another grouping factor, for example, *Gender*. Imagine that in each group you have 3 males and 3 females. You could summarize this design in a 2 by 2 table:

```
                 Experimental   Experimental
                   Group 1        Group 2
---------------------------------------------
Males                 2              6
                      3              7
                      1              5
                    -----          -----
          Mean        2              6
---------------------------------------------
Females               4              8
                      5              9
                      3              7
                    -----          -----
          Mean        4              8
---------------------------------------------
```

Before performing any computations, it appears that the total variance can be partitioned into at least 3 sources:

(1) error (within-group) variability,

(2) variability due to experimental group membership, and

(3) variability due to gender.

(Note that there is an additional source -- *interaction* -- that will be discussed shortly.) What would have happened had you not included *gender* as a factor in the study but rather computed a simple *t*-test? If you compute the *SS* ignoring the *gender* factor (use the within-group means *ignoring* or *collapsing across gender*; the result is *SS* = 10+10 = 20), you will see that the resulting within-group *SS* is larger than it is when you include *gender* (use the within-group, within-gender means to compute those *SS*; they will be equal to 2 in each group, thus the combined *SS*-within is equal to 2+2+2+2 = 8). This difference is due to the fact that the means for *males* are systematically lower than those for *females*, and this difference in means adds variability if you ignore this factor. Controlling for error variance increases the sensitivity (power) of a test.

This example demonstrates another principal of ANOVA that makes it preferable over simple two-group *t*-test studies: In ANOVA you can test each factor while controlling for all others; this is actually the reason why ANOVA is more statistically powerful (i.e., you need fewer observations to find a significant effect) than the simple *t*-test.

Interaction Effects

There is another advantage of using ANOVA over simple *t*-tests: ANOVA allows you to detect *interaction* effects between variables, and, therefore, to test more complex hypotheses about the investigated reality. Consider another example to illustrate this point.

Main effects, two-way interaction. Imagine that you have a sample of highly achievement-oriented students and another of achievement "avoiders." You now create two random halves in each sample, and give one half of each sample a challenging test, the other an easy test. You measure how hard the students work on the test. The means of this (fictitious) study are as follows:

Test	Achievement-oriented	Achievement-avoiders
Challenging	10	5
Easy	5	10

How can these results be summarized? Is it appropriate to conclude that (1) challenging tests make students work harder, and (2) achievement-oriented students work harder than achievement-avoiders? None of these statements captures the essence of this clearly systematic pattern of means. The appropriate way to summarize the result would be to say that challenging tests make only achievement-oriented students work harder, while easy tests make only achievement-avoiders work harder. In other words, the type of achievement orientation and test difficulty *interact* in their effect on effort; specifically, this is an example of a *two-way interaction* between achievement orientation and test difficulty. Note that statements 1 and 2 above describe the *main effects*.

Higher-order interactions. While the previous two-way interaction can be put into words relatively easily, higher order interactions are increasingly difficult to verbalize. Imagine that you had included factor *Gender* in the achievement study above, and had obtained the following pattern of means:

FEMALES

Test	Achievement-oriented	Achievement-avoiders
Challenging	10	5
Easy	5	10

MALES

Test	Achievement-oriented	Achievement-avoiders
Challenging	1	6
Easy	6	1

How could you now summarize the results of this study? The *ANOVA/MANOVA* module allows you to produce graphs of means for all effects with basically a single click of the mouse; those graphs greatly facilitate the interpretation of complex effects.

The pattern shown in the graph below represents a *three-way* interaction between factors.

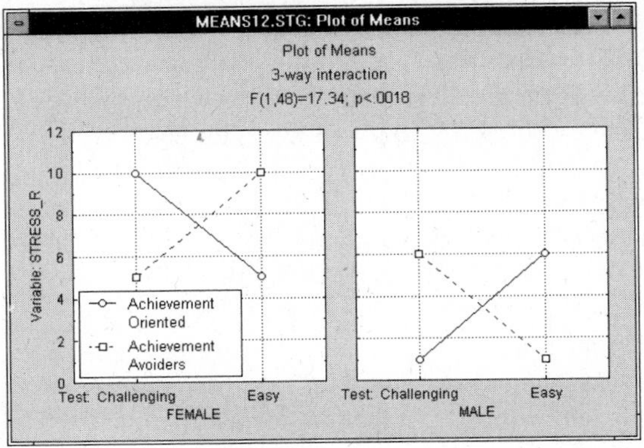

You may summarize this pattern by saying that for females there is a two-way interaction between achievement-orientation type and test difficulty: achievement-oriented females work harder on challenging tests than on easy tests, achievement-avoiding females work harder on easy tests than on difficult tests. For males, this interaction is reversed. As you can see, the description of the interaction has become much more involved.

A general way to express interactions. A general way to express all interactions is to say that an effect is modified (qualified) by another effect. Try to express the two-way interaction in the above example this way. The main effect for test difficulty is modified by achievement orientation. For the three-way interaction in the previous paragraph, you may summarize that the two-way interaction between test difficulty and achievement orientation is modified (qualified) by *Gender*. If you have a four-way interaction, you may say that the three-way interaction is modified by the fourth variable, that is, that there are different types of interactions in the different levels of the fourth variable. As it turns out, in many areas of research, five- or higher-way interactions are not that uncommon.

Complex Designs

Numerous examples of complex designs (e.g., between-group designs, see page 1763, repeated measures designs, see page 1768) are discussed later, therefore, a review of the basic "building blocks" of these complex designs will now be discussed.

Between-Groups and Repeated Measures

When you want to compare two groups, you would use the *t*-test for independent samples (in the *Basic Statistics and Tables* module); when you want to compare two variables given the same subjects (observations), you would use the *t*-test for dependent samples. This distinction -- dependent and independent samples -- is important for ANOVA as well. Basically, if you have repeated measurements of the same variable (under different conditions or at different points in time) *on the same subjects*, then the factor is a *repeated measures factor* (also called a *within-subjects factor*, because to estimate its significance the within-subjects *SS* is computed). If you compare different groups of subjects (e.g., males and females; three strains of bacteria, etc.), then the factor is referred to as a *between-groups factor*. The computations of significance tests are different for these different types of factors; however, the logic of computations and interpretations is the same.

Between-within designs. In many instances, experiments call for the inclusion of between-groups *and* repeated measures factors. For example, you may measure math skills in male and female students (*Gender*, a between-groups factor) at the beginning and the end of the semester. The two measurements *on each student* would constitute a within-subjects (repeated measures) factor. The interpretation of main effects and interactions is not affected by whether a factor is between-groups or repeated measures, and both factors may obviously interact with each other (e.g., females improve over the semester while males deteriorate).

Incomplete (Nested) Designs

There are instances where you may decide to ignore interaction effects. This happens when (1) you know that in the population the interaction effect is negligible, or (2) when a complete *factorial* design cannot be used for economic reasons. Imagine a study where you want to evaluate the effect of four fuel additives on gas mileage. For this test, a company has provided you with four cars and four drivers. A complete *factorial* experiment, that is, one in which each combination of driver, additive, and car appears at least once, would require 4 x 4 x 4 = 64 individual test conditions (groups). However, you may not have the resources (time) to run all of these conditions; moreover, it seems unlikely that the type of driver would interact with the fuel additive to an extent that would be of practical relevance. Given these considerations, one could actually run a *Latin square* design and "get away" with only 16 individual groups (the four additives are denoted by letters *A*, *B*, *C*, and *D*):

	Car 1	Car 2	Car 3	Car 4
Driver 1	A	B	C	D
Driver 2	B	C	D	A
Driver 3	C	D	A	B
Driver 4	D	A	B	C

Latin square designs are described in most textbooks on experimental methods (e.g., Hays, 1988; Lindman, 1974; Milliken and Johnson, 1984; Winer, 1962), and so the details of how they are constructed will not be discussed here. Suffice it to say that this design is *incomplete* insofar as not all combinations of factor levels occur in the design. For example, Driver 1 will only drive Car 1 with additive A, while Driver 3 will drive that car with additive C. In a sense, the levels of the *additives* factor (*A*, *B*, *C*, and *D*) are placed into the cells of the *car* by *driver*

matrix like "eggs into a nest." This mnemonic device is sometimes useful for remembering the nature of *nested* designs. The *ANOVA/MANOVA* module will easily analyze these types of designs (see page 1774).

Analysis of Covariance (ANCOVA)

General Idea

The *Basic Ideas* section (page 1697) discussed briefly the idea of "controlling" for factors and how the inclusion of additional factors can reduce the error *SS* and increase the statistical power (sensitivity) of the design. This idea can be extended to continuous variables, and when such continuous variables are included as factors in the design they are called *covariates*.

Fixed Covariates

Suppose that you want to compare the math skills of students who were randomly assigned to one of two alternative textbooks. Imagine that you also have data about the general intelligence (IQ) for each student in the study. You would suspect that general intelligence is related to math skills, and you can use this information to make your test more sensitive. Specifically, imagine that in each one of the two groups you can compute the correlation coefficient (see *Basic Statistics and Tables*, Chapter 9) between IQ and math skills. Remember that once you have computed the correlation coefficient you can estimate the amount of variance in math skills that is accounted for by IQ, and the amount of (residual) variance that you cannot explain with IQ (refer also to the *Elementary Concepts* and *Basic Statistics and Tables* chapters, Chapters 8 and 9, respectively). You may use this residual variance in the ANOVA as an estimate of the true error *SS after* controlling for IQ. If the correlation between IQ and math skills is substantial, then a large reduction in the error *SS* may be achieved.

Effect of a covariate on the *F* test. In the *F* test to evaluate the statistical significance of between-groups differences, the ratio of the between-groups variance (MS_{effect}) over the error variance (MS_{error}) is computed. If the MS_{error} becomes smaller, due to the explanatory power of IQ, then the overall *F* value will become larger.

Multiple covariates. The logic described above for the case of a single covariate (IQ) can easily be extended to the case of multiple covariates. For example, in addition to IQ, you might include measures of motivation, spatial reasoning, etc., and instead of a simple correlation, compute the multiple correlation coefficient (see *Multiple Regression*, Chapter 12).

When the *F* value gets smaller. In some studies with covariates it happens that the *F* value actually becomes smaller (less significant) after including covariates in the design. This is usually an indication that the covariates are not only correlated with the dependent variable (e.g., math skills), but also with the between-groups factors (e.g., the two different textbooks). For example, imagine that you measured IQ at the end of the semester, after the students in the different experimental groups had used the respective textbook for almost one year. It is possible that, even though students were initially randomly assigned to one of the two textbooks, the different books were so different that *both* math skills *and* IQ improved differentially in the two groups. In that case, the covariate will not only partition variance away from the error variance, but also from the variance due to the between-groups factor. Put another way, after controlling for the differences in IQ that were produced by the two textbooks, the math skills are not that different. Put in yet a third way, by "eliminating" the effects of IQ, you have inadvertently eliminated the true effect of the textbooks on students' math skills.

Adjusted means. When the latter case happens, that is, when the covariate is affected by the between-groups factor, then it is appropriate to

compute *adjusted means*. These are the means that one would get after removing all differences that can be accounted for by the covariate.

Interactions between covariates and factors. Just as you can test for interactions between factors, you can also test for the interactions between covariates and between-groups factors. Specifically, imagine that one of the textbooks is particularly suited for intelligent students, while the other actually bores those students but challenges the less intelligent ones. As a result, you may find a positive correlation in the first group (the more intelligent, the better the performance), but a zero or slightly negative correlation in the second group (the more intelligent the student, the less likely he or she is to acquire math skills from the particular textbook). In some older statistics textbooks this condition is discussed as a case where the assumptions for analysis of covariance are violated (see *Assumptions and Effects of Violating Assumptions*, page 1710). However, because the *ANOVA/MANOVA* module uses a very general approach to analysis of covariance, you can specifically estimate the statistical significance of interactions between factors and covariates.

Changing Covariates

While fixed covariates are commonly discussed in textbooks on ANOVA, changing covariates are discussed less frequently. In general, when you have repeated measures, you are interested in testing the differences in repeated measurements on the same subjects. Thus you are actually interested in evaluating the significance of *changes*. If you have a covariate that is also measured at each point when the dependent variable is measured, then you can compute the correlation between the changes in the covariate and the changes in the dependent variable.

For example, you could study math anxiety and math skills at the beginning and at the end of the semester. It would be interesting to see whether any changes in math anxiety over the semester correlate with changes in math skills.

The *ANOVA/MANOVA* module of *STATISTICA* will automatically evaluate the statistical significance of changing covariates when the design allows it.

Multivariate Designs: MANOVA/MANCOVA

Between-Groups Designs

All examples discussed so far have involved only one dependent variable. Even though the computations become increasingly complex, the *logic* and *nature* of the computations do not change when there is more than one dependent variable at a time.

For example, you may conduct a study where you try two different textbooks, and you are interested in the students' improvements in math *and* physics. In that case, you have two dependent variables, and your hypothesis is that both together are affected by the difference in textbooks. You could now perform a multivariate analysis of variance (MANOVA) to test this hypothesis. Instead of a univariate F value, you would obtain a multivariate F value (Wilks' *lambda*) based on a comparison of the error variance-/covariance matrix and the effect variance-/covariance matrix.

The "covariance" here is included because the two measures are probably correlated and this correlation must be taken into account when performing the significance test. Obviously, if you were to take the *same* measure twice, then you would really not learn anything new. If you take a correlated measure, you gain *some* new information, but the new variable will also contain redundant information that is expressed in the covariance between the variables.

Interpreting results. If the overall multivariate test is significant, you conclude that the respective effect (e.g., textbook) is significant. However, your next question would of course be whether only math skills improved, only physics skills improved, or both. In fact, after obtaining a significant multivariate test for a particular main effect or interaction, customarily one would examine the univariate *F* test for each variable to interpret the respective effect. In other words, one would identify the specific dependent variables that contributed to the significant overall effect.

Repeated Measures Designs

If you were to measure math and physics skills at the beginning of the semester and again at the end of the semester, you would have a multivariate repeated measure. Again, the logic of significance testing in such designs is simply an extension of the univariate case (see page 1701). Note that MANOVA methods are also commonly used to test the significance of *univariate* repeated measures factors with more than two levels; this application will be discussed later in this section.

Sum Scores vs. MANOVA

Even experienced users of ANOVA and MANOVA techniques are often puzzled by the differences in results that sometimes occur when performing a MANOVA on, for example, three variables as compared to a univariate ANOVA on the *sum* of the three variables.

The logic underlying the *summing* of variables is that each variable contains some "true" value of the variable in question, as well as some random measurement error. Therefore, by summing up variables, the measurement error will sum to approximately 0 across all measurements, and the sum score will become more and more reliable (increasingly equal to the sum of true scores). In fact, under these circumstances, ANOVA on sums is appropriate and represents a very sensitive (powerful) method. However, if the dependent variable is truly multi-dimensional in nature, then summing is inappropriate.

For example, suppose that the dependent measure consists of four indicators of *success in society*, and each indicator represents a completely independent way in which a person could "make it" in life (e.g., successful professional, successful entrepreneur, successful homemaker, etc.). Now, summing up the scores on those variables would be like adding apples to oranges, and the resulting sum score will not be a reliable indicator of a single underlying dimension. Thus, one should treat such data as multivariate indicators of success in a MANOVA.

Contrast Analysis and *Post Hoc* Tests

Why Compare Individual Sets of Means?

Usually, experimental hypotheses are stated in terms that are more specific than simply main effects or interactions. You may have the *specific* hypothesis that a particular textbook will improve math skills in males, but not in females, while another book would be about equally effective for both genders, but less effective overall for males. Now generally, you are predicting an interaction here: the effectiveness of the book is modified (qualified) by the student's gender. However, you have a particular prediction concerning the *nature* of the interaction: you expect a significant difference between genders for one book, but not the other. This type of specific prediction is usually tested via contrast analysis.

Contrast Analysis

Briefly, contrast analysis allows you to test the statistical significance of predicted specific

differences in particular parts of your complex design. It is a major and indispensable component of the analysis of every complex ANOVA design. The *ANOVA/MANOVA* module has a uniquely flexible contrast analysis facility that allows the user to specify and analyze practically any type of desired comparison (see page 1763 for a description of how to specify contrasts).

Post Hoc Comparisons

Sometimes you find effects in your experiment that were not expected. Even though in most cases a creative experimenter will be able to explain almost any pattern of means, it would not be appropriate to analyze and evaluate that pattern as if one had predicted it all along. The problem here is one of capitalizing on chance when performing multiple tests *post hoc*, that is, without *a priori* hypotheses. To illustrate this point, consider the following "experiment." Imagine you were to write down a number between 1 and 10 on 100 pieces of paper. You then put all of those pieces into a hat and draw 20 samples (of pieces of paper) of 5 observations each, and compute the means (from the numbers written on the pieces of paper) for each group. How likely do you think it is that you will find two sample means that are significantly different from each other? It is very likely! Selecting the extreme means obtained from 20 samples is very different from taking only 2 samples from the hat in the first place, which is what the test via the contrast analysis implies. Without going into further detail, there are several so-called *post hoc* tests that are explicitly based on the first scenario (taking the extremes from 20 samples), that is, they are based on the assumption that you have chosen for your comparison, the most extreme (different) means out of *k* total means in the design. Those tests apply "corrections" that are designed to offset the advantage of *post hoc* selection of the most extreme comparisons. The *ANOVA/MANOVA* module offers a wide selection of those tests. Whenever one finds unexpected results in an experiment one should use those *post hoc* procedures to test their statistical significance.

Type I, II, III, and IV Sums of Squares

Multiple Regression and ANOVA

There is a close relationship between the multiple regression method and analysis of variance. In fact, both are special cases of the general linear model. For a detailed discussion of the linear model, you should refer to the references provided in the *Technical Notes* section (page 1797). In short, practically all experimental designs can be analyzed via multiple regression. Consider the following simple 2 x 2 between-groups design.

DV	A	B	AxB
3	1	1	1
4	1	1	1
4	1	-1	-1
5	1	-1	-1
6	-1	1	-1
6	-1	1	-1
3	-1	-1	1
2	-1	-1	1

Columns *A* and *B* contain the codes that identify the levels of factors *A* and *B*; the column denoted as *AxB* contains the product of the two columns *A* and *B*. You can analyze these data via multiple regression; specify variable *DV* as the dependent variable, and variables *A* through *AxB* as the independent variables. The significance tests for the regression coefficients will be identical to those computed via ANOVA for the main effects (*A* and *B*) and the interaction (*AxB*).

Unbalanced and Balanced Designs

If you compute the correlation matrix for all variables for the example data shown above, you will notice that the main effects (*A* and *B*) and interaction (*AxB*) are all uncorrelated. This property of the effects is usually also referred to as

orthogonality, that is, effects *A* and *B* are said to be *orthogonal* or *independent* of each other. Because all effects in the design shown above are orthogonal to each other, the design is said to be *balanced.*

Balanced designs have some "nice" properties; specifically, the computations to analyze such designs are quite simple. For example, all you would have to do is compute the simple correlations between the effects and the dependent variable. Since the effects are orthogonal, partial correlations (i.e., the full *multiple* regression) do not have to be computed. However, in real life, research designs are not always balanced.

Consider the following data set with unequal numbers of observations in different cells.

```
              Factor B
Factor   ------------------
  A        B1           B2
---------------------------
 A1       3            4, 5
 A2       6, 6, 7      2
```

If you again coded these data as before, and compute the correlation matrix for all variables, you would find that the factors in the design are now correlated with each other. Thus, the factors in the design are no longer orthogonal, and the design is said to be *unbalanced.* Note that the correlation among the factors is entirely due to the different frequencies of the 1's and -1's in the effect columns of the data matrix. Put another way, experimental designs with unequal cell sizes (or non-proportional cell sizes to be exact) will be unbalanced, that is, the main effects and interactions will be confounded. Thus, in order to evaluate the statistical significance of effects, you have to compute the complete multiple regression. In fact, there are several strategies that one can follow.

Type I, II, III, and IV Sums of Squares

Type I, and III sums of squares. In general, you can test the significance of partial correlations, in effect controlling for other effects, or you can enter the variables in a stepwise fashion, controlling for all other factors that were previously entered and ignoring those that have not yet been entered. In essence, this is the difference between *Type III* and *Type I* sums of squares (the terminology was introduced in SAS, e.g., see SAS, 1982; detailed discussions can also be found in Searle, 1987, page 461; Woodward, Bonett, and Brecht, 1990, page 216; or Milliken and Johnson, 1984, page 138).

Type II sums of squares. Another "intermediate" strategy would be to control for all other main effects when testing a particular main effect, for all main effects and two-way interactions when testing a particular two-way interaction, for all main effects, two-way interactions, and three-way interactions when testing a particular three-way interaction, and so on. Sums of squares for effects computed in this manner are called *Type II* sums of squares. Thus, *Type II* sums of squares control for all effects of the same or lower order while ignoring all effects of higher order.

Type IV sums of squares. Finally, for some special designs with missing cells (incomplete designs), one can also compute so-called *Type IV* sums of squares. This method will be discussed later in the context of incomplete (missing cells) designs.

Interpreting Type I, II, and III Hypothesis

Type III sums of squares are most easily interpreted. Remember that *Type III* sums of squares are tests of effects after controlling for all other effects. For example, after finding a statistically significant *Type III* effect for factor *A*, one can say that after controlling for all other effects (factors) in the experimental design, there is a unique significant effect for factor *A* as reported by the *ANOVA-/MANOVA* module, and interpret the effect accordingly. Probably, in 99% of all ANOVA applications, this is the type of test that the researcher is interested in. This, incidentally, is also the type of sums of squares that is usually computed

by default in the *ANOVA/MANOVA* module regardless of whether or not the *Regression Approach* option was selected (the default approach taken in the *ANOVA/MANOVA* module is discussed below).

Significant effects based on *Type I*, or *Type II* sums of squares cannot be interpreted as easily. One best consider such results in the context of stepwise multiple regression (e.g., as discussed in Chapter 12). If, using *Type I* sums of squares, a main effect *B* is significant (after *A* was already entered into the model, but before the *AxB* interaction was added), one should conclude that there is a significant main effect for factor *B*, provided that there is no interaction between *A* and *B*. (Of course, if the *Type III* test for factor *B* is also significant, the you can conclude that there is a significant unique main effect for *B*, after controlling for all other factors and their interactions.)

In terms of marginal means, *Type I* and *Type II* hypotheses usually have no simple interpretation. That is to say, one cannot interpret significant effects by looking simply at the marginal means. Rather, the reported *p* values pertain to complex hypotheses that combine means and sample sizes. For example, the *Type II* hypothesis for factor *A* in the simple 2 x 2 example shown earlier (page 1706) would be (see Woodward, Bonett, and Brecht, 1990, page 219):

$$\Sigma(n_{ij}-n_{ji}{}^2/n_{.j})*u_{ij} = \Sigma\Sigma n_{ij}*n_{i'j}/n_{.j}*u_{i'j}$$

where

n_{ij} are the cell *n*'s

u_{ij} are the cell means

. (dot) (e.g., $n_{.j}$) refer to the respective marginal elements (e.g., marginal *n*'s or marginal means)

Without going into further detail (for a thorough discussion, see Milliken and Johnson, 1984, Chapter 10), it is clear that this is not a simple hypothesis, and in most cases, not one that is of particular interest to the researcher. However, there are cases when *Type I* hypotheses may be of interest.

The Default Computational Approach in the ANOVA/MANOVA Module

By default, when the *Regression Approach* check box (see the startup panel of the *ANOVA/MANOVA* module, page 1737) is not checked, then the *ANOVA/MANOVA* module uses the *Cell Means ANOVA Model*. Specifically, the sums of squares for the different effects in the design are computed for linear combinations of the cell means. For complete factorial designs, this yields sums of squares that are identical to those discussed earlier as *Type III*. However, with the *Planned comparison* option (in the *ANOVA Results* dialog, see page 1742), the user can test hypotheses about any weighted or unweighted linear combination of cell means. In this manner, the user can test not only *Type III* hypotheses, but any type of hypothesis (including *Type IV*). This general approach proves particularly useful when analyzing designs with missing cells (so-called incomplete designs), as will be demonstrated in the *Notes, Part II* section (page 1783).

For complete designs, this approach is useful when one wants to analyze weighted marginal means. For example, suppose in the simple 2 x 2 design shown earlier (page 1706), you wanted to compare the weighted (across the levels of factor *B*) marginal means for factor *A*. This can sometimes be useful when the distribution of cases across the cells in the design was not pre-arranged by the experimenter, but is the result of a true probability sample, and thus represents the distribution of observations across the levels of factor *B* in the population.

For example, suppose you had a factor *Age* in a study of widows. A probability sample of respondents was taken and grouped into 2 groups: younger than 40 and older than 40 (factor *B*). A

second factor in the design could be whether or not the widows participated in a social support group offered by your agency (suppose that some widows were randomly selected for the program while others served as controls; factor *A*). In this case, the distribution of subjects across the two age groups represents the actual age distribution of widows in the population from which you extracted the sample. To evaluate the effectiveness of the social support group for widows of *all ages*, it would be appropriate to weight the means for the two age groups by the respective numbers of observations.

Planned Comparisons

The general procedure for constructing and entering the contrast coefficients for planned comparisons is described in the *Notes, Part I* section, page 1763. Note that the contrast coefficients do not have to add up to 0 (zero). Instead, the program will automatically adjust the coefficients so that the respective hypothesis is not confounded by the grand mean.

To illustrate this, return to the simple 2 x 2 example design discussed earlier. Recall that the cell *n*'s for the four cells of the unbalanced design were 1, 2, 3, and 1. Suppose you wanted to compare the weighted marginal means for factor *A*; that is, weighted by the cell frequencies across the levels of factor *B*. You could enter the contrast coefficients:

```
1  2 -3 -1
```

Note that these coefficients do not add to zero. The program will re-adjust the coefficients so that they will add to zero but retain their relative magnitudes, that is:

```
1/3  2/3 -3/4 -1/4
```

This contrast will compare the weighted means for factor *A*.

Hypotheses about the grand mean. The only time when the program will not perform this adjustment is when the sign of all coefficients is positive, in which case the respective hypothesis is about the grand mean. For example, the hypothesis that the unweighted grand mean is equal to 0 can be tested via:

```
1  1  1  1
```

The hypothesis that the weighted grand mean is equal to 0 can be tested via:

```
1  2  3  1
```

In neither case will the program perform any adjustments to the contrast coefficients.

Analyzing Designs with Missing Cells (Incomplete Designs)

Factorial designs that contain some missing cells (treatment combinations where there are no observations) are said to be incomplete. In such designs, some factors are usually not orthogonal, and some interactions cannot be computed. In general, there is no one best method to analyze such designs.

Regression Approach

In some older programs, which basically analyze ANOVA designs via multiple regression, the default way of handling incomplete designs is to code the factors in the design in the usual manner (as if the design were complete), and then to perform the multiple regression analysis for those dummy-coded factors that can be estimated. Unfortunately, this method will yield results that are very difficult, if not impossible, to interpret because it is not clear how each effect translates in terms of linear combinations of means. Consider the following simple example:

Factor A	Factor B: B1	Factor B: B2
A1	3	4, 5
A2	6, 6, 7	Missing

If you were to perform a multiple regression of the form *Dependent variable = Intercept + Factor A +*

Factor B, the actual hypotheses being tested in terms of linear combinations of means would be:

```
Factor A: Cell A1,B1 = Cell A2,B1
Factor B: Cell A1,B1 = Cell A1,B2
```

While this case is simple, when the design is more complicated it is virtually impossible to determine what exactly is being tested.

Cell Means ANOVA Approach; Type IV Hypotheses

The approach that is recommended, and which seems to be preferred in the literature on this subject, is to test meaningful (with regard to the research question) *a priori* hypotheses about the means observed in the cells of the design. Detailed discussions of this approach can be found in Dodge (1985), Heiberger (1989), Milliken and Johnson (1984), Searle (1987), or Woodward, Bonett, and Brecht (1990). The sums of squares associated with hypotheses about linear combinations of means in incomplete designs, testing the estimable portions of effects, are also called *Type IV* sums of squares.

Automatic generation of Type IV hypotheses. When a multi-factorial design contains a complex pattern of missing cells it can be quite challenging to identify orthogonal (independent) hypotheses that test something equivalent to main effects or interactions. Algorithmic (computer) strategies (based on the generalized inverse of the design matrix) have been developed to generate the appropriate weights for such comparisons; unfortunately, the resulting hypotheses are not unique. Instead, they depend on the order in which the effects were specified, and they rarely allow for simple interpretation. Therefore, it is recommended that you carefully study the pattern of missing cells in the design, and then formulate *Type IV* hypotheses that are most meaningful given the research question at hand. Then, test those hypotheses using the *Planned comparison* option from the *Results* dialog (page 1742). The easiest way to specify planned comparisons in this case is to request to enter contrast *vectors* for all factors *together* on the *Planned comparisons options* dialog; the dialog that will appear after you then request *Planned comparisons* will show all groups in the current design, and mark those that are missing.

Missing Cells and the Specific Effect Option

There are several types of designs in which the pattern of missing cells is not haphazard, but rather carefully planned to allow for simple tests of main effects which are not confounded by other effects. For example, *Latin Squares* designs (see pages 1701 and 1776) are often used to evaluate main effects for several factors with many levels; if complete designs were used for that purpose, then the number of necessary cells in the design would quickly get out of hand.

For example, consider a 4 x 4 x 4 x 4 factorial design which would require 256 cells; at the same time one can use a *Greco Latin Square* design to estimate main effects from only 16 cells in the design (the *Experimental Design* chapter, Volume IV, also discusses such designs in detail). In general, incomplete designs in which main effects (and some interactions) can be estimated from simple linear combinations of means are said to be *balanced incomplete designs*.

When designs are balanced, the standard (default) method of generating the contrasts (weights) for the main effects and interactions will produce an analysis of variance table in which the sums of squares for the respective effects are not confounded with each other. The *Specific effect* option on the *Results* dialog (page 1742) will generate such default contrasts assigning zeros to the cells that are missing in the design. To inform the user regarding the specific hypothesis that is being tested, a

Scrollsheet with the actual weights will be displayed right after an effect was requested (via option *Specific effect*). However, note that the sums of squares computed for the respective effect are only orthogonal (independent) to other main effect (or interaction) hypotheses if the design is balanced! Otherwise one should use the *Planned comparison* option to test meaningful comparisons between means.

Missing Cells and the Pooled Effect/Error Option

When the *Regression approach* option in the startup panel of the *ANOVA/MANOVA* module is not selected (default setting, see page 1737), then the cell means model will be used to compute the sums of squares for the effects. If the design is unbalanced, and one pools effects that are not orthogonal (see discussion under *Missing Cells and the Specific Effect* option above), then the resulting pooled sums of squares may consist of non-orthogonal (or overlapping) components. The results are then basically not interpretable (note that the sums of squares for effects that are to be pooled are computed successively, not simultaneously). Therefore, be careful in your choice and implementation of a complex incomplete experimental design.

There are many textbooks that offer detailed discussions of different types of designs (e.g., Dodge, 1985; Heiberger, 1989; Lindman, 1974; Milliken and Johnson, 1984; Searle, 1987; Woodward and Bonett, 1990), and such advice is beyond the scope of this manual. However, later in this chapter, the analysis of various types of incomplete designs will be illustrated (12 representative examples from textbooks on advanced ANOVA designs will be discussed; see the section *Notes, Part II*, page 1783).

Assumptions and Effects of Violating Assumptions

Deviation from Normal Distribution

Assumptions. It is assumed that the dependent variable is measured on at least an interval scale level (see the *Elementary Concepts* chapter, Chapter 8). Moreover, the dependent variable should be normally distributed within groups. The *ANOVA-/MANOVA* module contains extensive diagnostic graphics as well as statistics to test the validity of this assumption.

Effects of violations. Overall, the *F* test is remarkably robust to deviations from normality (see Lindman, 1974, for a summary). If the kurtosis (see *Basic Statistics and Tables*, Chapter 9) is greater than 0, then the *F* tends to be too small and you cannot reject the null hypothesis even though it is incorrect. The opposite is the case when the kurtosis is less than 0. The skewness of the distribution usually does not have a sizable effect on the *F* statistic.

If the *n* per cell is fairly large, then deviations from normality do not matter much at all because of the *central limit theorem*, according to which the sampling distribution of the mean approximates the normal distribution, regardless of the distribution of the variable in the population. A detailed discussion of the robustness of the *F* statistic can be found in Box and Anderson (1955), or Lindman (1974).

Homogeneity of Variances

Assumptions. It is assumed that the variances in the different groups of the design are identical; this assumption is called the *homogeneity of variances* assumption. Remember that at the beginning of this section you computed the error variance (*SS* error) by adding up the sums of squares within each group.

If the variances in the two groups are different from each other, then adding the two together is not appropriate, and will not yield an estimate of the common within-group variance (since no common variance exists). The *ANOVA/MANOVA* module contains a wide variety of statistical tests to detect violations of this assumption.

Effects of violations. Lindman (1974, page 33) shows that the *F* statistic is quite robust against violations of this assumption (*heterogeneity* of variances; see also Box, 1954a, 1954b; Hsu, 1938).

Special case: correlated means and variances. However, one instance when the *F* statistic is *very misleading* is when the means are correlated with variances across cells of the design. The *ANOVA/MANOVA* module allows you to plot a scatterplot of variances or standard deviations against the means to detect such correlations. The reason why this is a "dangerous" violation is the following: Imagine that you have 8 cells in the design, 7 with about equal means but one with a much higher mean. The *F* statistic may suggest to you a statistically significant effect. However, suppose that there also is a much larger variance in the cell with the highest mean, that is, the means and the variances are correlated across cells (the higher the mean the larger the variance). In that case, the high mean in the one cell is actually quite unreliable, as is indicated by the large variance. However, because the overall *F* statistic is based on a *pooled* within-cell variance estimate, the high mean is identified as significantly different from the others, when in fact it is not at all significantly different if one based the test on the within-cell variance in that cell alone.

This pattern -- a high mean and a large variance in one cell -- frequently occurs when there are *outliers* present in the data. One or two extreme cases in a cell with only 10 cases can greatly bias the mean, and will dramatically increase the variance.

Homogeneity of Variances and Covariances

Assumptions. In multivariate designs, with multiple dependent measures, the homogeneity of variances assumption described earlier also applies. However, since there are multiple dependent variables, it is also required that their intercorrelations (covariances) are homogeneous across the cells of the design. The *ANOVA-/MANOVA* module offers various specific tests of this assumption.

Effects of violations. The multivariate equivalent of the *F* test is Wilks' *lambda*. Not much is known about the robustness of Wilks' *lambda* to violations of this assumption. However, because the interpretation of MANOVA results usually rests on the interpretation of significant *univariate* effects (after the overall test is significant), the above discussion concerning univariate ANOVA basically applies, and important significant univariate effects should be carefully scrutinized.

Special case: ANCOVA. A special serious violation of the homogeneity of variances-/covariances assumption may occur when covariates are involved in the design. Specifically, if the correlations of the covariates with the dependent measure(s) are very different in different cells of the design, gross misinterpretations of results may occur. Remember that in ANCOVA, you in essence perform a regression analysis within each cell to partition out the variance component due to the covariates. The homogeneity of variances-/covariances assumption implies that you perform this regression analysis subject to the constraint that all regression equations (slopes) across the cells of the design are the same. If this is not the case, serious biases may occur. The *ANOVA/MANOVA* module provides specific tests of this assumption, and it is advisable to look at those tests to ensure that the regression equations in different cells are approximately the same.

Sphericity and Compound Symmetry: Reasons for Using the Multivariate Approach to Repeated Measures ANOVA

In repeated measures ANOVA containing repeated measures factors with more than two levels, additional special assumptions enter the picture: the compound symmetry assumption and the assumption of sphericity. Because these assumptions rarely hold (see below), the MANOVA approach to repeated measures ANOVA has gained popularity in recent years (both tests are automatically computed in the *ANOVA/MANOVA* module).

Compound symmetry assumption. The compound symmetry assumption requires that the variances (pooled within-group) and covariances (across subjects) of the different repeated measures are homogeneous (identical). This is a sufficient condition for the univariate *F* test for repeated measures to be valid (i.e., for the reported *F* values to actually follow the *F* distribution). However, it is not a necessary condition.

Sphericity assumption. The sphericity assumption is a necessary and sufficient condition for the *F* test to be valid; it states that the within-subject "model" consists of independent (orthogonal) components. The nature of these assumptions, and the effects of violations are usually not well-described in ANOVA textbooks; this matter is addressed in the following paragraphs and an explanation of what it means when the results of the univariate approach differ from the multivariate approach to repeated measures ANOVA will also be given.

The necessity of independent hypotheses. One general way of looking at ANOVA is to consider it a *model fitting* procedure. In a sense you bring to your data a set of *a priori* hypotheses; you then partition the variance (test main effects, interactions) to test those hypotheses. Computationally, this approach translates into generating a set of contrasts (comparisons between means in the design) that specify the main effect and interaction hypotheses. However, if these contrasts are not independent of each other, then the partitioning of variances runs afoul. For example, if two contrasts *A* and *B* are identical to each other and you partition out their components from the total variance, then you take the same thing out twice. Intuitively, specifying the two (*not* independent) hypotheses "the mean in Cell 1 is higher than the mean in Cell 2" *and* "the mean in Cell 1 is higher than the mean in Cell 2" is silly and simply makes no sense. Thus, hypotheses must be independent of each other, or *orthogonal*.

Independent hypotheses in repeated measures. The general algorithm implemented in the *ANOVA/MANOVA* module will attempt to generate, for each effect, a set of independent (orthogonal) contrasts (see the *Technical Notes* section, page 1797). In repeated measures ANOVA, these contrasts specify a set of hypotheses about *differences* between the levels of the repeated measures factor. However, if these differences are correlated across subjects, then the resulting contrasts are no longer independent. For example, in a study where you measured learning at three times during the experimental session, it may happen that the changes from time 1 to time 2 are negatively correlated with the changes from time 2 to time 3: subjects who learn most of the material between time 1 and time 2 improve less from time 2 to time 3. In fact, in most instances where a repeated measures ANOVA is used, one would probably suspect that the changes across levels are correlated across subjects. However, when this happens, the compound symmetry and sphericity assumptions have been violated, and independent contrasts cannot be computed.

Effects of violations and remedies. When the compound symmetry or sphericity assumptions have been violated, the univariate ANOVA table will give erroneous results. Before multivariate procedures

were well understood, various approximations were introduced to compensate for the violations (e.g., Greenhouse and Geisser, 1959; Huynh and Feldt, 1970), and these techniques are still widely used (therefore, the *ANOVA/MANOVA* module provides those methods).

MANOVA approach to repeated measures. To summarize, the problem of compound symmetry and sphericity pertains to the fact that multiple contrasts involved in testing repeated measures effects (with more than two levels) are not independent of each other. However, they do not need to be independent of each other if you use *multivariate* criteria to simultaneously test the statistical significance of the two or more repeated measures contrasts. This "insight" is the reason why MANOVA methods are increasingly applied to test the significance of univariate repeated measures factors with more than two levels. This approach is wholeheartedly endorsed because it simply bypasses the assumption of compound symmetry and sphericity altogether.

Cases when the MANOVA approach cannot be used. There are instances (designs) when the MANOVA approach cannot be applied; specifically, when there are few subjects in the design and many levels on the repeated measures factor, there may not be enough degrees of freedom to perform the multivariate analysis. For example, if you have 12 subjects and $p = 4$ repeated measures factors, each at $k = 3$ levels, then the four-way interaction would "consume" $(k\text{-}1)^p = 2^4 = 16$ degrees of freedom. However, you have only 12 subjects, so in this instance the multivariate test cannot be performed. The *ANOVA/MANOVA* module will detect those instances and only compute the univariate tests.

Differences in univariate and multivariate results. Anyone whose research involves extensive repeated measures designs has seen cases when the univariate approach to repeated measures ANOVA gives clearly different results from the multivariate approach. To repeat the point, this means that the differences between the levels of the respective repeated measures factors are in some way correlated across subjects. Sometimes, this insight by itself is of considerable interest.

MANOVA and Structural Equation Modeling

In recent years, structural equation modeling has become increasingly popular as an alternative to multivariate analysis of variance (e.g., see, for example, Bagozzi and Yi, 1989; Bagozzi, Yi, and Singh, 1991; Cole, Maxwell, Arvey, and Salas, 1993). This approach allows you to test explicit hypotheses not only about means in different groups, but also about differences in the structure of the correlation matrices of dependent variables. For example, you can relax the homogeneity of variances/covariances assumption, and explicitly include in the model different error variances and covariances in each group. The *Structural Equation Modeling and Path Analysis (SEPATH)* module of *STATISTICA* (see Volume III) allows you to perform these types of analyses, and examples of how to test these so-called models for structured means in multiple groups are discussed in that chapter.

StatSoft

PROGRAM OVERVIEW

The *ANOVA/MANOVA* module is a general univariate and multivariate analysis of variance and covariance program. The program will handle designs with fixed and random effects, perform between-groups as well as repeated measures analyses of variance with either single or multiple dependent variables, and will evaluate the effects of fixed (static) and changing covariates. In addition, the program will perform user-specified contrast analyses of any complexity, *post hoc* contrast analysis, and discriminant function analyses.

By default, the *ANOVA/MANOVA* module will use the *Means-Model* approach to ANOVA, but the user can choose to compute *Type I* (sequential, following a default or user-specified order), *Type II*, or *Type III* sums of squares; *Type IV* hypotheses for incomplete designs can also be tested.

Extensive graphics options are available to aid the analysis (such as automatic plots of interactions, within-group distributions of variables, within-group correlations, etc.).

ANOVA/MANOVA Features

Standard results. The *ANOVA/MANOVA* module can analyze multifactor between-groups and/or within-subjects designs with single (ANOVA) or multiple (MANOVA) dependent variables. The program will automatically compute all effects (simultaneously) and display the results in an interactive Scrollsheet; from that Scrollsheet, the user can examine marginal means or plots of all effects and interactions.

Fixed and random effects. The program will automatically handle fixed and random effects (as requested by the user).

Incomplete designs, customized error terms. The *ANOVA/MANOVA* module will routinely analyze most standard incomplete designs (nested designs, Latin squares, Greco-Latin squares, designs with single observations per cell, randomized block designs, etc.). In addition, the user can build customized (pooled) error terms for the analysis of variance.

Testing assumptions. A wide variety of graphs are available for testing the assumptions of ANOVA/MANOVA: plots of distributions, stem and leaf plots, plots of correlations, plot of means vs. standard deviations or variances, normal and half-normal probability plots, half-normal plot of within-cell correlations, etc. A wide range of statistical procedures are also provided for testing assumptions; Cochran C, Hartley test, Bartlett test, Levene's test, Box M, Sen and Puri's nonparametric test, Kolmogorov-Smirnov test, Mauchley's sphericity test, etc.

Specialized output. The program will compute the Greenhouse-Geisser and Huynh-Feldt adjustments for repeated measure factors with more than two levels; the univariate as well as multivariate results for those repeated measures factors will also be automatically computed. The user can examine the sums of squares (*SS*) matrices (hypothesis, error) and, when appropriate, the program will perform a full canonical analysis and compute the canonical roots, eigenvalues, percent of variance accounted for by each root, and the standardized and non-standardized discriminant functions (note that the *Discriminant Analysis* module, Volume III, offers full-featured stepwise discriminant function analysis).

Covariates

Fixed and changing covariates. The user can specify multiple covariates in conjunction with any type of design. In repeated measures designs, the *ANOVA/MANOVA* module supports both fixed (static) covariates that do not change across the

levels of the repeated measures factors, as well as changing covariates that were measured at each level of the repeated measures factors.

Statistical tests. The parallelism hypothesis (interaction of covariates with between-groups factors) can be tested specifically. Full univariate and multivariate regression results will be computed, and the adjusted means can be displayed or plotted.

Contrast Analysis

***A priori* contrasts.** Contrasts of any complexity can be specified for all aspects of the design: for between-groups factors, within-subjects repeated measures factors, and multiple dependent variables. A flexible edit window is provided for entering and editing of contrast coefficients; those windows also allow the user to enter automatically (with a single click of the mouse) sets of polynomial contrasts, deviation contrasts, difference contrasts, Helmert contrasts, simple contrasts, and repeated contrasts. Sets of contrast coefficients can also be entered for all between or within-subject factors simultaneously. This feature is particularly useful for analyzing unbalanced designs with missing cells (incomplete designs); for that purpose, missing cells will automatically be flagged by the contrast coefficient editor.

***Post hoc* analysis.** Available *post hoc* tests include the *LSD* (*L*east *S*ignificant *D*ifference test), Newman-Keuls test (and critical ranges), Duncan multiple range test (and critical ranges), Scheffé test, Tukey *HSD* (*H*onest *S*ignificant *D*ifference test), and the Spjotvoll and Stoline *HSD* test. *Post hoc* tests can be performed on the marginal means for main effects or interaction effects; they can be performed on effects involving between-groups factors, repeated measures factors, or both.

Graphs

As in all other *STATISTICA* modules, the *ANOVA-/MANOVA* module contains a wide variety of specialized graphs and plots. Normal probability plots, histograms, and stem-and-leaf diagrams are provided for testing distributional assumptions. A selection of categorized plots (for multiple levels or cells of the current design) is available including categorized normal probability plots, histograms, box and whisker plots, scatterplots, and others. To test for the independence of cell means from cell variances, scatterplots of means against standard deviations, variances, and standard errors can be produced. To test for the homogeneity of covariances across cells, a normal probability plot of the z-transformed within-group correlations can be computed. Finally, to aid with the interpretation of results, line plots of means can easily be produced; for those plots, the user has full control over the layout (ordering of factors) and can include only selected dependent variables and/or covariates.

Alternative Procedures

For some special applications, the following alternatives may be considered. In the area of industrial and quality control research, specialized design methods have been developed (e.g., response surface designs, Latin squares, Plackett-Burman screening designs, 2^{k-p} designs, 3^{k-p} and Box-Behnken designs, Taguchi orthogonal arrays, designs for mixtures, etc.). Such designs can be generated and analyzed with the *Experimental Design* module (see Volume IV). If the primary goal of a study is to identify the variables that discriminate between groups, use discriminant function analysis (see Volume III, *Discriminant Function Analysis*). The *Nonparametrics and Distributions* module (see Chapter 11) contains various nonparametric alternatives to compare groups or variables (repeated measures). If the data set contains censored observations (survival times, failure times), use the *Survival Analysis* module (see Volume III) to compare groups. To test complex hypotheses concerning differential between-groups linear or nonlinear regression models, use the

Nonlinear Estimation module. To test hypotheses about structured means in different groups use the *Structural Equation Modeling and Path Analysis (SEPATH)* module (see Volume III). Finally, to write your own customized analysis procedures, you can use the *STATISTICA BASIC* programming language which includes a complete library of matrix algebra functions (including functions for computing the inverse and generalized inverse of a matrix, orthonormalization, singular value decomposition, etc.). An example program, *Manova.stb* (in the *STBASIC* subdirectory), is provided to show how a multivariate analysis of variance (MANOVA) can be computed with a few lines of code by using the available matrix functions.

EXAMPLES

Example 1: A 2 x 3 Between-Groups ANOVA Design

Data File

This section will begin with a simple analysis of a 2 x 3 complete factorial between-groups design. This example is based on a fictitious data set reported in Lindman (1974).

Suppose that you have conducted an experiment to address the *nature* vs. *nurture* question; specifically, you test the performance of different rats in the "T-maze." The T-maze is a simple maze, and the rat's task is to learn to run straight to the food placed in a particular location, without errors. Three strains of rats whose general ability to solve the T-maze can be described as *bright*, *mixed*, and *dull*, were used. From each of these strains you rear 4 animals in a *free* (stimulating) environment, and 4 animals in a *restricted* environment. The dependent measure is the number of errors made by each rat while running the T-maze problem.

The data for this study are contained in the *STATISTICA* example data file *Rats.sta*; a portion of this file is shown below.

Data: RATS.STA 3v * 24c

Performance of rats in a maze test

	1 ENVIRNMT	2 STRAIN	3 ERRORS
1	FREE	BRIGHT	26.000
2	FREE	BRIGHT	14.000
3	FREE	BRIGHT	41.000
4	FREE	BRIGHT	16.000
5	FREE	MIXED	41.000
6	FREE	MIXED	82.000
7	FREE	MIXED	26.000
8	FREE	MIXED	86.000
9	FREE	DULL	36.000
10	FREE	DULL	87.000
11	FREE	DULL	39.000
12	FREE	DULL	99.000
13	RESTRCTD	BRIGHT	51.000
14	RESTRCTD	BRIGHT	35.000

After starting the *ANOVA/MANOVA* module, open the data file *Rats.sta*.

Specifying the Analysis

When you open the *ANOVA/MANOVA* module, the *General ANOVA/MANOVA* startup panel will open in which you can enter the specifications for the design.

Independent and dependent variables. The *ANOVA/MANOVA* module classifies variables as either independent, dependent, or covariates (refer to the *Elementary Concepts* chapter, Chapter 8, for more on this distinction); covariates will be used in the next example. Independent variables are those under the experimenter's control. You may also refer to those variables as *grouping* variables, *coding* variables, or *between-groups* factors. These variables contain the codes that were used to uniquely identify to which group in the experiment the respective case belongs.

In the data file *Rats.sta,* the codes *1-free* and *2-restricted* were used in the independent variable *Envirnmt* to denote whether the respective rat belongs to the group of rats that were raised in the free or restricted environment, respectively. The codes used for the second independent variable -- *Strain* -- are *1-bright*, *2-mixed*, and *3-dull*. The dependent variable in an experiment is the one that *depends* on or is affected by the independent variables; in this study this would be the variable *Errors*, which contains the number of errors made by the respective rat running the maze.

Specifying the design. This is a 2 (*Environment*) by 3 (*Strain*) between-groups experimental design. The variables *Envirnmt* and *Strain* are the independent variables, variable *Errors* is the dependent variable. Specify these variables via the *Variables* button on the startup panel. Next, specify the codes that were used to uniquely identify the groups; click on the *Codes* button and either enter each of the codes for each variable, click on the *All* button for a variable to enter all of the codes

for that variable, or click on the *Select all* button to select all of the codes for all of the variables in this dialog.

The *General ANOVA/MANOVA* startup panel will now look like this:

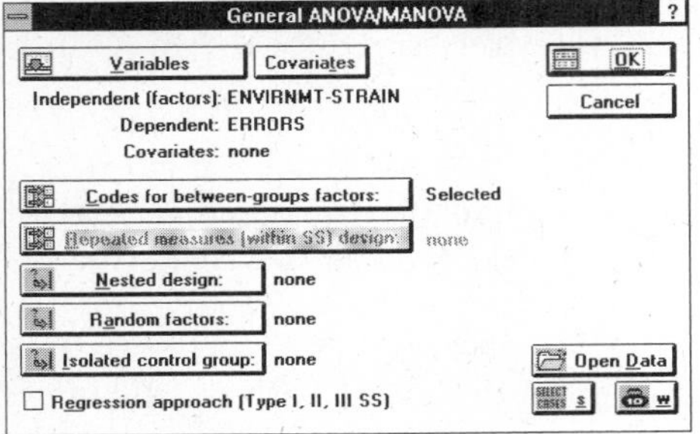

Reviewing Results

Click *OK* in the startup panel to begin the analysis. When complete, the *ANOVA Results* dialog will open.

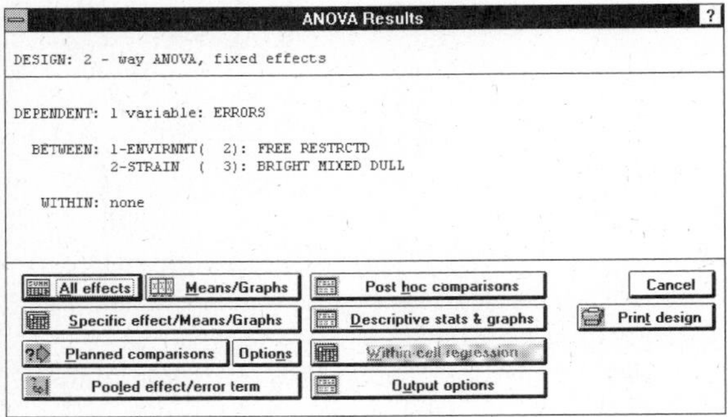

This dialog includes a summary of the design, and offers a number of output options. For now, click on the *All effects* button to display the table of all effects in a Scrollsheet.

Summary of all Effects; design: (rats.sta)

1-ENVIRNMT, 2-STRAIN

Effect	df Effect	MS Effect	df Error	MS Error	F	p-level
1	1	5551.042	18	953.3750	5.822516	.026705
2	2	3969.875	18	953.3750	4.164022	.032635
12	2	8.042	18	953.3750	.008435	.991604

Summary ANOVA table. This table summarizes the main results of the analysis. Note that significant effects (*p<.05*) in this table are highlighted in this Scrollsheet. You can adjust the significance criterion (for highlighting) by clicking on the *Options* toolbar button and entering the desired *alpha* level. Both of the main effects (*Envirnmt* and *Strain*) are statistically significant (*p<.05*) while the interaction is not (*p>.05*).

Reviewing marginal means. The marginal means for the *Envirnmt* main effect will now be reviewed. (Note that the marginal means are calculated as unweighted means.) First, click on the *Means/graphs* button in the *ANOVA Results* dialog to open the *Table of All Effects* dialog.

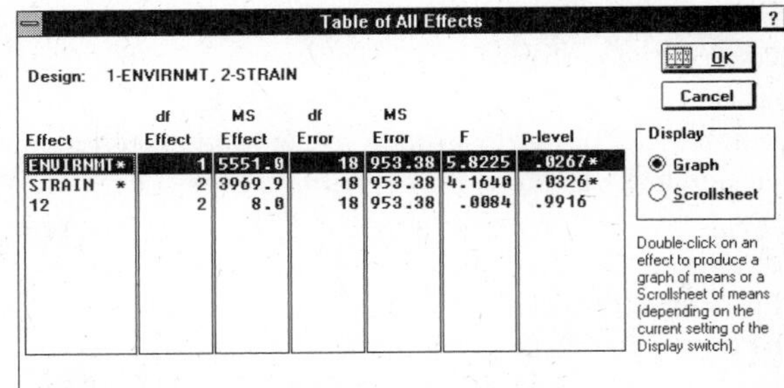

Table of All Effects

Design: 1-ENVIRNMT, 2-STRAIN

Effect	df Effect	MS Effect	df Error	MS Error	F	p-level
ENVIRNMT*	1	5551.0	18	953.38	5.8225	.0267*
STRAIN *	2	3969.9	18	953.38	4.1640	.0326*
12	2	8.0	18	953.38	.0084	.9916

In this dialog, highlight the *Envirnmt* main effect and set the *Display* option to *Scrollsheet* (see above), then click *OK* to produce a Scrollsheet with the table of marginal means for the highlighted effect.

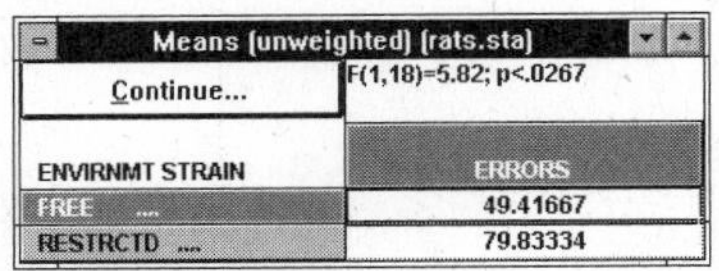

Means (unweighted) (rats.sta)

F(1,18)=5.82; p<.0267

ENVIRNMT STRAIN	ERRORS
FREE	49.41667
RESTRCTD	79.83334

The default graph for *all* Scrollsheets with marginal means is the means plot. In this case, the plot is rather simple. To produce this plot of the two means for the *free* and *restricted* environment, return to the *Table of All Effects* dialog (click on the continue button on the Scrollsheet) and change the *Display* option to *Graphs*, and again click *OK*.

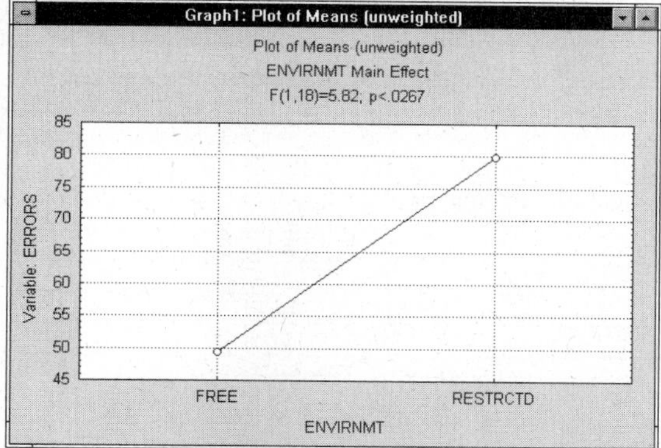

It appears that rats that were raised in the more restricted environment made more errors than the rats raised in the free environment. Now, look at all of the means simultaneously, that is, at the plot of the interaction of *Environmt* by *Strain*.

Reviewing the interaction plot. Once again, return to the *Table of All Effects* dialog and this time highlight the interaction effect. When you click *OK*, the following dialog will appear:

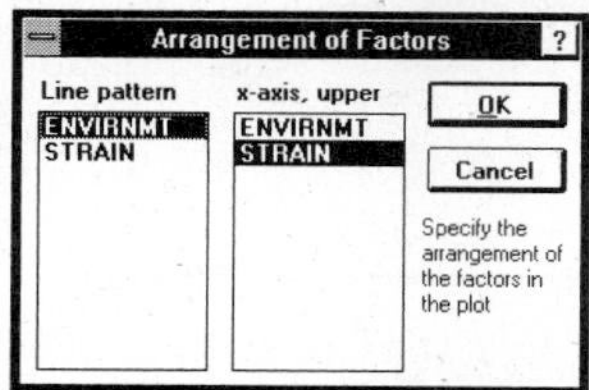

As you can see, you have full control over the order in which the factors in the interaction will be plotted. For this example, accept the default selection (see above) and the graph of means will appear.

The graph below nicely summarizes the results of this study, that is, the two main effects pattern. The rats raised in the restricted environment (dashed line) made more errors than those raised in the free environment (solid line). At the same time, the *dull* rats made the most errors, followed by the *mixed* rats, and the *bright* rats made the fewest number of errors.

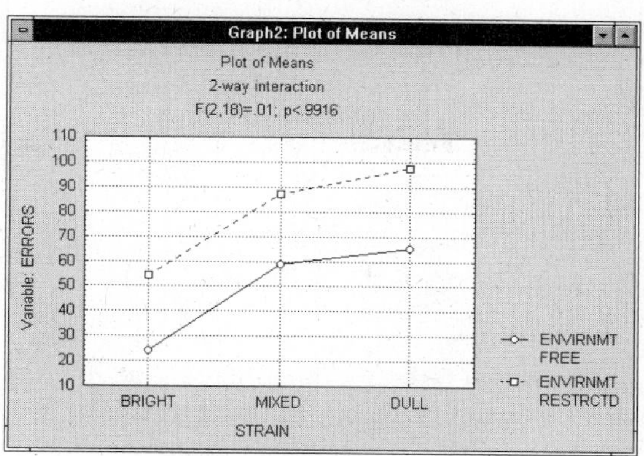

Post Hoc Comparisons of Means

In the previous plot, one might ask whether the mixed strain of rats were significantly different from the dull and the bright strain. However, no *a priori* hypotheses about this question were specified, therefore, you should use *post hoc* comparisons to test the mean differences between strains of rats (refer to the *Introductory Overview*, page 1705, for an explanation of the logic of *post hoc* tests).

Specifying *post hoc* tests. After returning to the *ANOVA Results* dialog, click on the *Post hoc comparison* button. An intermediate dialog will open allowing you to select the effects for the *post hoc* tests.

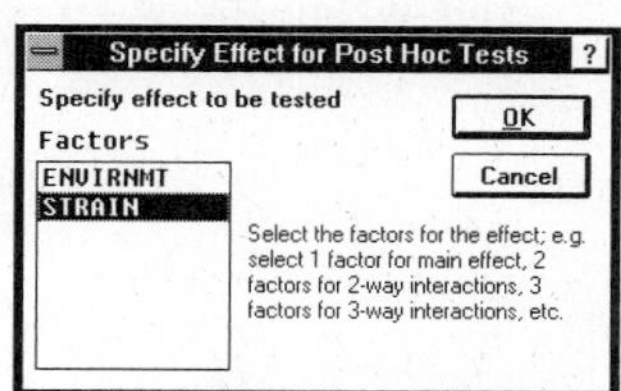

For this example, select the effect *Strain* in order to compare the (unweighted) marginal means for that effect.

Choosing a test. Now, click *OK* in this dialog and the *Post hoc Comparison of Means* dialog will open.

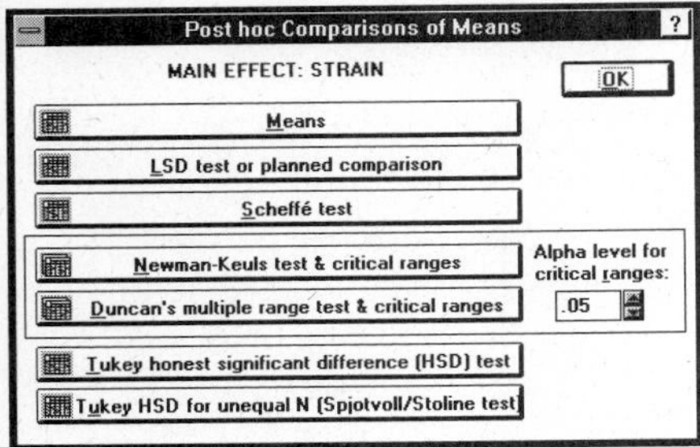

The different *post hoc* tests on this dialog all "protect" you to some extent against capitalizing on chance (due to the *post hoc* nature of the comparisons, see page 1705). All tests allow you to compare means under the assumption that you bring no *a priori* hypotheses to the study. These tests are discussed in greater detail on page 1748. For now, simply click on the *Scheffé test* button.

Scheffe test; variable ERRORS (rats.sta)

GENERAL MANOVA — Probabilities for Post Hoc Tests — MAIN EFFECT: STRAIN

ENVIRNMT	STRAIN	{1} 39.37500	{2} 73.00000	{3} 81.50000
....	BRIGHT {1}		.121814	.044361
....	MIXED {2}	.121814		.860446
....	DULL {3}	.044361	.860446	

This Scrollsheet shows the statistical significance of the differences between all pairs of means. As you can see, only the difference between group 1 (*bright*) and group 3 (*dull*) reaches statistical significance at the *p<.05* level. Thus, you would conclude that the dull strain of rats made significantly more errors than the bright strain of rats, while the mixed strain of rats is not significantly different from either.

Testing Assumptions

The *Introductory Overview* section discussed the assumptions underlying the use of ANOVA techniques (see page 1710). Now, review the data in terms of these assumptions. Return to the *ANOVA Results* dialog and click on the *Descriptive stats & graphs* button. The resulting *Descriptive Statistics & Graphs* dialog offers many different tests and graphs; some are applicable only to more complex designs. These options are described on page 1749.

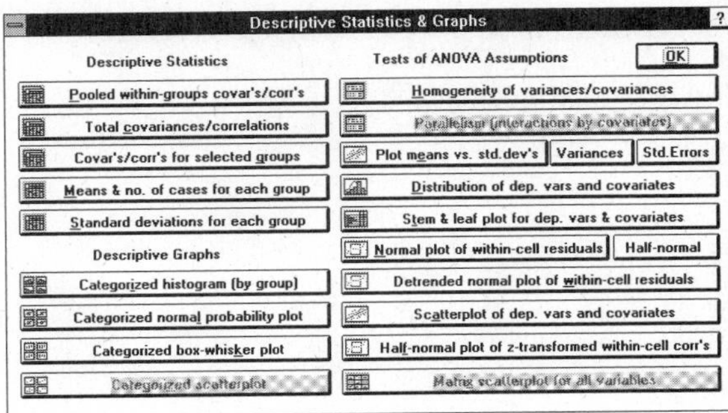

Distribution of dependent variable. ANOVA assumes that the distribution of the dependent variable (within groups) follows the normal distribution. To see how the dependent variable is distributed, click on the *Distribution of dep. vars & covariates* button to select the frequency distribution. You can view the distribution for all groups combined, or for only a selected group by selecting the group in the *Select Groups* dialog.

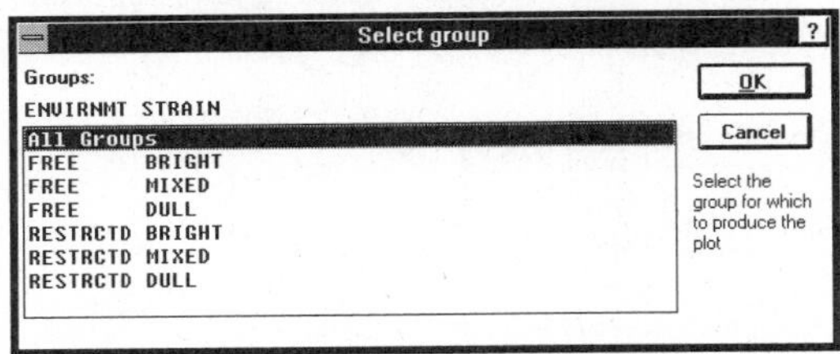

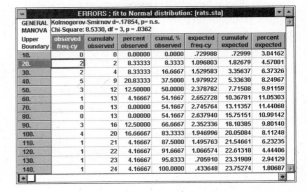

For this example, click *OK* to accept the default selection of *All Groups*, and a Scrollsheet and histogram of the frequencies will be produced.

ERRORS ; fit to Normal distribution: (rats.sta)

GENERAL MANOVA — Kolmogorov-Smirnov d=.17854, p= n.s. — Chi-Square: 8.5330, df = 3, p = .0362

Upper Boundary	observed freq-cy	cumulatv observed	percent observed	cumul. % observed	expected freq-cy	cumulatv expected	percent expected
10.	0	0	0.00000	0.0000	.729988	.72999	3.04162
20.	2	2	8.33333	8.3333	1.096803	1.82679	4.57001
30.	2	4	8.33333	16.6667	1.529583	3.35637	6.37326
40.	5	9	20.83333	37.5000	1.979922	5.33630	8.24967
50.	3	12	12.50000	50.0000	2.378782	7.71508	9.91159
60.	1	13	4.16667	54.1667	2.652728	10.36781	11.05303
70.	0	13	0.00000	54.1667	2.745764	13.11357	11.44068
80.	0	13	0.00000	54.1667	2.637940	15.75151	10.99142
90.	3	16	12.50000	66.6667	2.352336	18.10385	9.80140
100.	4	20	16.66667	83.3333	1.946996	20.05084	8.11248
110.	1	21	4.16667	87.5000	1.495763	21.54661	6.23235
120.	1	22	4.16667	91.6667	1.066574	22.61318	4.44406
130.	1	23	4.16667	95.8333	.705910	23.31909	2.94129
140.	1	24	4.16667	100.0000	.433648	23.75274	1.80687

The Scrollsheet shows the frequency distribution for variable *Error*. Apparently, it is not exactly normally distributed across all groups; the *Chi-square* test of normality is significant at the *.05* level. However, the normality assumption pertains to the *within-group* distributions, not the overall distribution, so at this point, you do not have to be too concerned. Moreover, as was discussed in the introduction (page 1710), small violations of the normality assumption usually do not adversely bias the *F* test.

Now, look at the histogram of the distribution.

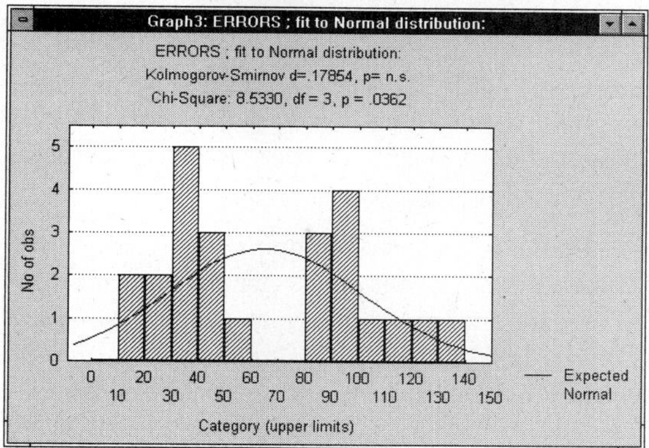

It appears as if the distribution across groups is multi-modal, that is to say, it has more than one "peak." You could have anticipated that, given the fact that strong main effects were found. If you want to test the homogeneity assumption more thoroughly, you could now look at the distributions within individual groups. Instead, a potentially more serious violation of the ANOVA assumptions will be tested.

Correlation between mean and standard deviation. As mentioned in the introduction (see page 1710), deviation from normality is not the major "enemy;" the most likely "trap" to fall into is to base one's interpretations of an effect on an "extreme" cell in the design with much greater than average variability. Put another way, when the means and the standard deviations are correlated across cells of the design, then the performance (*alpha* error rate) of the *F* test deteriorates greatly, and you may reject the null hypothesis with *p<.05* when the real *p* value is possibly as high as *.50*!

Now, look at the correlation between the 6 means and standard deviations in this design. You can elect to plot the means vs. either the standard deviations, the variances, or the standard errors of the means by clicking on the appropriate button (*Plot means vs. std dev's*, *variances*, *std. errors*, respectively) in the *Descriptive Statistics & Graphs* dialog. For this example, click on the *Plot means vs. std dev's* button.

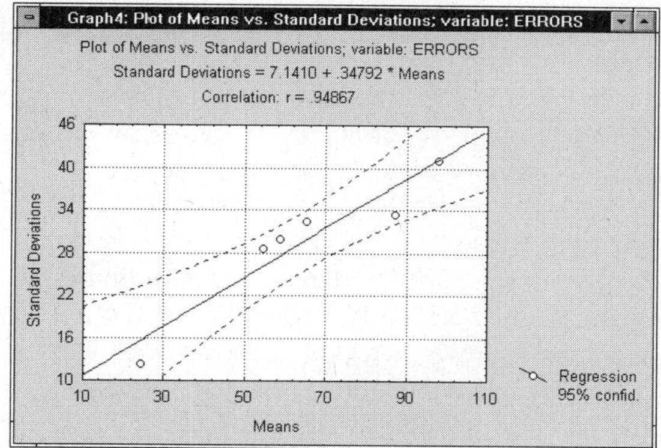

Indeed, the means and standard deviations appear substantially correlated in this design. If an important decision were riding on this study, one would be well advised to double-check the significant main effects pattern by using for example, some nonparametric procedure (see the *Nonparametrics and Distributions* chapter, Chapter 11) that does not depend on raw scores (and variances) but rather on ranks. In any event, you should view these results with caution.

Homogeneity of variances. Now, look also at the homogeneity of variance tests. Click on the *Homogeneity of variances/covariances* button in the *Descriptive Statistics & Graphs* dialog and an intermediate dialog of available procedures will open.

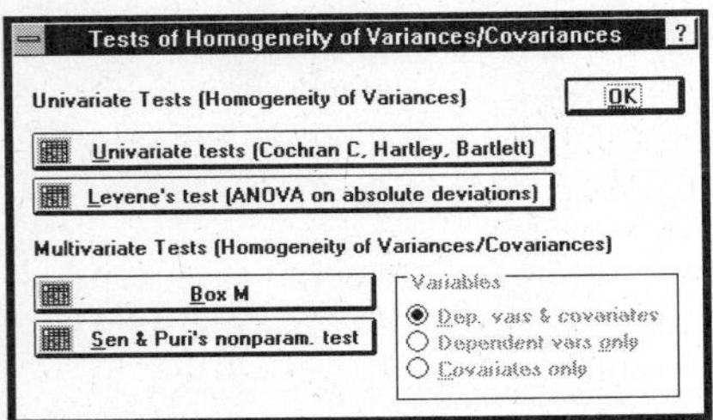

You may try a *Univariate test* to compute the standard homogeneity of variances test, or the *Levene's test*, but neither will yield statistically significant results.

Summary

Besides illustrating the major functional aspects of the *ANOVA/MANOVA* module, this analysis has demonstrated how important it is to be able to graph data easily (e.g., to produce the scatterplot of means vs. standard deviations). Had you relied on nothing else but the *F* tests of significance and the standard tests of homogeneity of variances, you would not have caught the potentially serious violation of assumptions that was detected in the scatterplot of means vs. standard deviations. As it stands, you would probably conclude that the effects of environment and genetic factors (*Strain*) both seem to have an (additive) effect on performance in the T maze. However, the data should be further analyzed using nonparametric methods to ensure that the statistical significance (*p*) levels from the ANOVA are not inflated.

Example 2: A 2 (Between) x 3 x 3 (Repeated Measures) ANOVA Design

Overview

The following example will demonstrate how to set up a repeated measures design with more than one repeated measures factor. How contrast analyses can aid in the interpretation of interaction effects will also be shown. The issue of *sphericity* will be illustrated when the alternative multivariate test of the key interaction is not statistically significant, while the conventional univariate test indicates significance. The results from the Greenhouse-Geisser and Huynh-Feldt adjustments will be compared to the multivariate test. And finally, the nature and cause of the violation of the sphericity assumption will be explained.

Research Problem

Overview. This example is based on a (fictitious) data set reported in Winer (1962, page 324). Suppose you are interested in learning how *meaningful* versus *white* (non-meaningful) background noise over time affects people's ability to perform a fine-tuning task.

For example, operators of complex industrial machinery (e.g., nuclear power plants) constantly need to read (and process) various gauges and adjust machines (dials) accordingly. It would be interesting to learn how people's performance on this task is affected by white noise (which sounds like the hiss you hear when tuning your radio in between stations) as compared to meaningful background noise (if you tune the radio to an actual station).

This will be simulated in an experiment in which subjects are required to adjust one of three different dials whenever the respective gauge indicates a significant deviation from specification. Some subjects will perform this task under *white* background noise conditions, while others will perform it under *meaningful* background noise (e.g., a radio news program). The dependent measure is the number of errors that the subjects make (failure to set a dial properly within a short tolerance period) during three consecutive 10-minute time intervals.

Summary of design. The resulting design is a 2 (*Noise* condition) by 3 (*Time* periods of 10 minutes each) by 3 (*Dials*; the three dials) analysis of

variance. The last two factors are *within-subject* or *repeated measures* factors because they represent repeated measurements on the same subject; the first factor is a *between-groups* factor because subjects will be randomly assigned to work under one or the other noise condition.

Setup of the data file. The setup of a data file for repeated measures analysis is straightforward: The between-groups factor (*Noise* condition) can be specified as before, that is, a variable is set up containing the codes that uniquely identify to which experimental condition each subject belongs. Each repeated measurement is then put into a different variable.

It may be convenient to order those variables in a meaningful manner, but no special order is necessary because the *ANOVA/MANOVA* module allows you great flexibility in specifying the levels of the repeated measures factors. In this example data file, there are 6 subjects (3 in each group), and the order of variables are arranged so that for each successive time period the measurements for each dial are placed next to each other. Below is a listing of the data file *Dials.sta*.

Data: DIALS.STA 10v * 6c

Example data file for repeated measures ANOVA

	1 NOISE	2 TIM1_DL1	3 TIM1_DL2	4 TIM1_DL3	5 TIM2_DL1	8 TIM3_DL1	9 TIM3_DL2	10 TIM3_DL3
1	MEANGFLL	45	53	60	40	28	37	46
2	MEANGFLL	35	41	50	30	25	32	41
3	MEANGFLL	60	65	75	58	40	47	50
4	WHITE	50	48	61	25	16	23	35
5	WHITE	42	45	55	30	22	27	37

Specifying the Design

After starting the *ANOVA/MANOVA* module, open the data file *Dials.sta*. Click on the *Variables* button in the *General ANOVA/MANOVA* startup panel to select variable *1* (*Noise*) as the independent variable, and variables *2-10* (*Tim1_Dl1* to *Tim3_Dl3*) as the dependent/repeated measures variables. Next, click on the *Codes* button and select the codes (*1-White* and *2-Meangfl*) for the independent variable.

Specifying the repeated measures factors. Repeated measures factors in the *ANOVA/MANOVA* module are always specified in the following manner. First, you tell the program *how many* repeated measures factors there are; next, you name those factors and specify their levels. The program will later divide the dependent variable list by cycling through the specified levels for each repeated measures factor, and assign successive variables from the dependent variable list to the levels of the repeated measures factors. When cycling through the levels of the repeated measures factors, the fastest changing "subscript" is that of the last specified factor, the next-to-the-last specified factor, and so on. See also pages 1739 and 1768, for more information on how to specify repeated measures designs in the *ANOVA/MANOVA* module.

In this example, there are two repeated measures factors: (1) the three successive 10 minute *time* periods, and (2) the three *dials*. To specify these factors, click on the *Repeated measures (within SS) design* button and in the resulting *Specify within-subjects (repeated measures) factors* dialog, specify the repeated measures factors and their levels.

When you look at the data file, the slowest changing subscript in the list of variables is that specifying the levels of the *Time* factor. To clarify the term "subscript," look back at the spreadsheet of the data file, and while moving your finger over the list beginning with variable *Tim1_Dl1* say out loud "one two three one two three one two three." Each "one" in this case points to a variable that contains data for the first dial (*Dl1*), each "two" for the second dial (*Dl2*), and each "three" for the third dial (*Dl3*). Thus, the fastest changing subscript is that of factor *Dial*, and you must specify that factor last. Consequently, factor *Time* must be specified first.

When you click on the *Repeated measures (within SS) design* button in the *General ANOVA/MANOVA* startup panel, the *Specify within subjects (repeated measures) factors* dialog will open. Enter in this dialog the factor names and number of levels for the

repeated measures design. For this example, enter *3* as the number of levels and *Time* as the first repeated measures factor; likewise, enter *3* as the number of levels for the second repeated measures factor *Dials*.

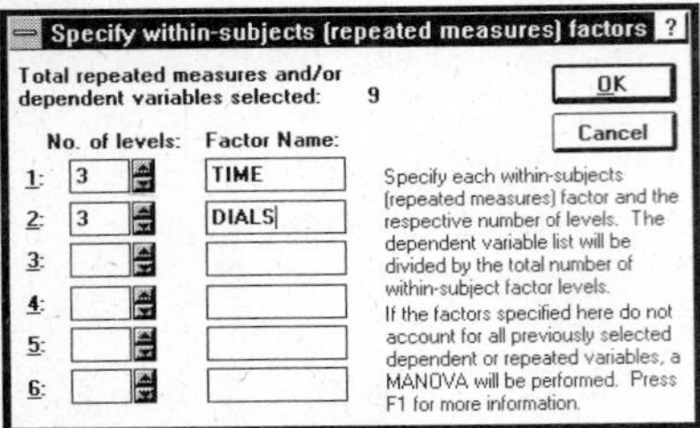

You have now specified the within-subject (repeated measures) part of the design; click *OK* in this dialog to return to the startup panel.

Reviewing Results

Now, click *OK* in the startup panel to begin the analysis and the *ANOVA Results* dialog will open.

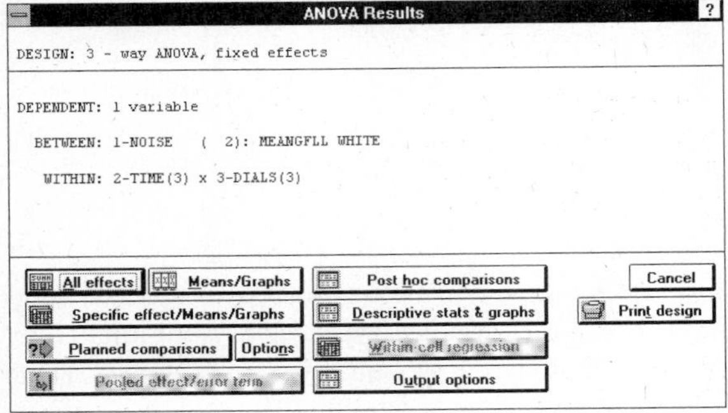

The table of all effects will first be examined.

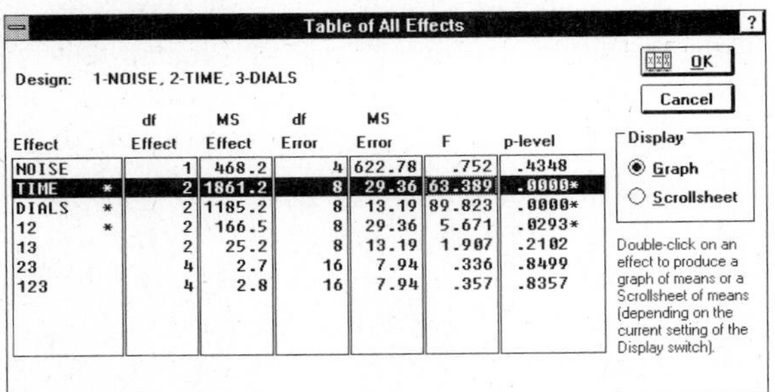

Table of All Effects

Design: 1-NOISE, 2-TIME, 3-DIALS

Effect		df Effect	MS Effect	df Error	MS Error	F	p-level
NOISE		1	468.2	4	622.78	.752	.4348
TIME	*	2	1861.2	8	29.36	63.389	.0000*
DIALS	*	2	1185.2	8	13.19	89.823	.0000*
12	*	2	166.5	8	29.36	5.671	.0293*
13		2	25.2	8	13.19	1.907	.2102
23		4	2.7	16	7.94	.336	.8499
123		4	2.8	16	7.94	.357	.8357

OK

Cancel

Display
- Graph
- Scrollsheet

Double-click on an effect to produce a graph of means or a Scrollsheet of means (depending on the current setting of the Display switch).

Click on the *Means/graphs* button to view the ANOVA table. There are three significant effects (with an * by the *p*-level) in this analysis: the main effect for *Time*, the main effect for *Dials*, and the interaction between *Noise* and *Time*. Now, look at the highest-order interaction. First, move the highlight in this dialog over the *12* (factor *1* by factor *2*) interaction, then set the *Display* option to *Scrollsheet*. Click *OK* to display the Scrollsheet of marginal means for this effect.

Means (dials.sta)

Continue...

F(2,8)=5.67; p<.0293

NOISE	TIME	DIALS	Depend. Var.1
MEANGFLL	1	....	53.77778
MEANGFLL	2	....	49.44444
MEANGFLL	3	....	38.44444
WHITE	1	....	54.88889
WHITE	2	....	39.55556
WHITE	3	....	29.55556

The easiest (and sometimes it seems only) way to understand interactions is to plot them. Therefore, click on the *Continue* button in the Scrollsheet to return to the *Table of All Effects* dialog and set the *Display* option to *Graphs*. Now, click *OK* and the *Arrangement of Factors* dialog will open.

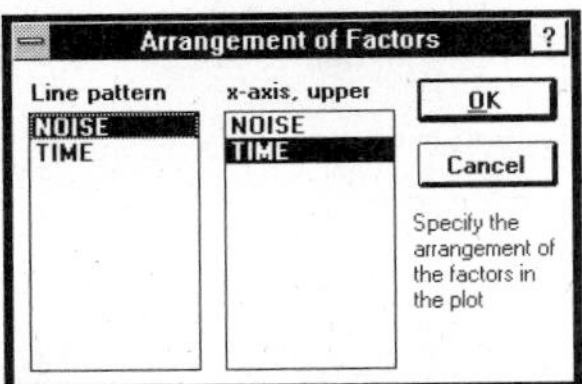

Here you can rearrange the factors for the plot, however, for this example, just click *OK* and accept the default selections.

It appears that in both *Noise* conditions, subjects' performance improved, that is, they made fewer errors in successive 10-minute trials. However, the two lines denoting the two *Noise* conditions diverge starting at time period 2 (*level_2*). It seems that subjects did better (made fewer errors) in the *white* noise condition than in the *meaningful* noise condition at times 2 and 3, but not at time 1.

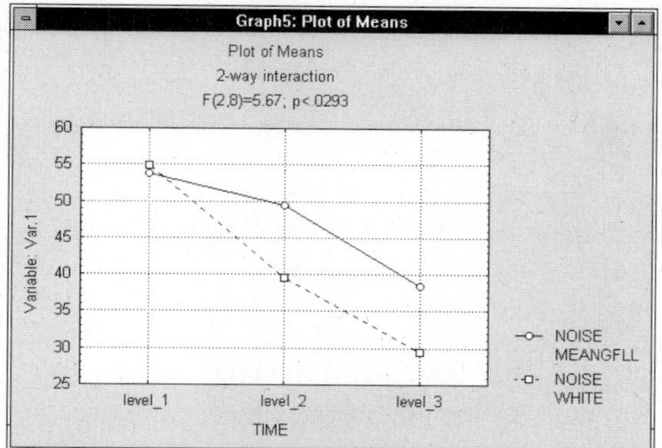

The main effect. You may want to plot the main effect for factor *Dials* in the same manner. This effect simply shows that for some reason, subjects made more errors adjusting the third dial than the second dial, and more errors adjusting the second dial than the first dial. This effect reflects the differences between the different dials used in the experiment, but it is not of particular theoretical interest in this study. Therefore, now turn to the interaction effect.

Exploring the interaction: Contrast analysis. Explore the interaction further by performing a contrast analysis. Return to the *ANOVA Results* dialog and click on the *Planned comparisons* button. The general conventions for specifying contrasts are explained in detail starting on pages 1704, and in the *Notes* section (*Part I*) starting on page 1763. For now, just remember that contrasts are specified in terms of patterns of positive and negative integers that, in a sense, serve as weights. Cells that are assigned integers of different sign are compared (contrasted) in the analysis.

Specifying the contrast. Note that complex contrasts can also be entered in one long string of contrasts coefficients (instead of separately for each factor, see below), by clicking on the *Options* button (next to the *Planned comparisons* button) on the *ANOVA Results* dialog and selecting the *Enter contrasts for factors together* option.

For this example, the difference between the two noise conditions, separately at times 2 and 3, will be evaluated. When you click on the *Planned comparisons* button the *Specify Contrasts for this Factor* dialog will open. In this dialog, first specify a contrast for factor *Noise*, thus enter *1* and *-1*, respectively (in order to contrast the first level with the second level). Note that instead of typing the values of contrast coefficients, you can use the *Quick Fill* facility which allows you to enter the coefficients (into individual cells or entire columns) by pressing the respective buttons.

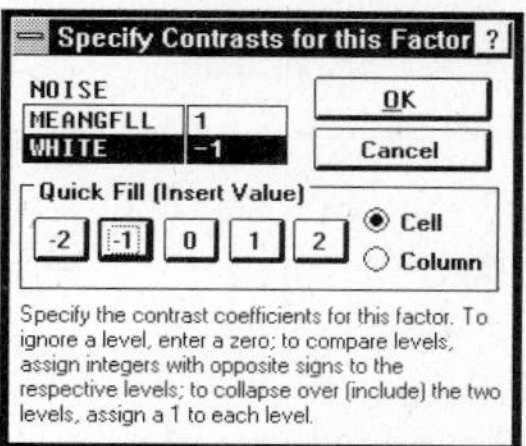

Click *OK* and the following dialog will open listing each of the repeated measures factors.

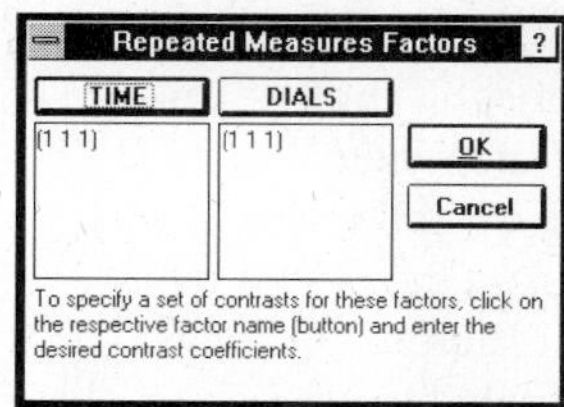

In order to enter the contrast for the factor *Time*, click on the *Time* button.

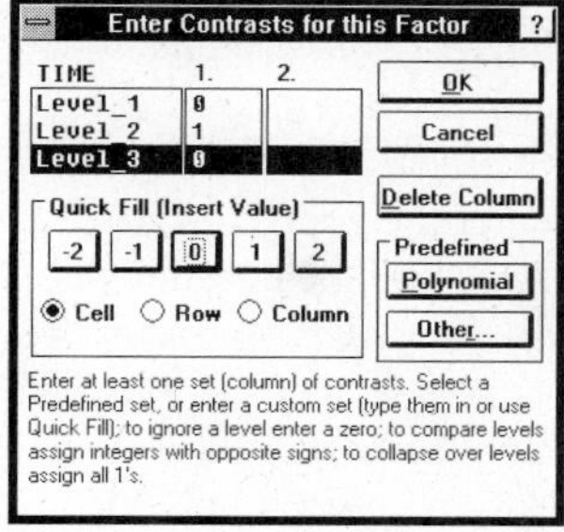

Then enter the coefficients *0*, *1*, and *0*, respectively, in the *Enter Contrasts for this Factor* dialog. (Note

that you can use the *Quick Fill* facility, as explained above.) Click *OK* to return to the *Repeated Measures Factors* dialog and similarly click on the *Dials* button. Enter *1*, *1*, and *1* as the coefficients for this factor. In this manner, you will collapse across all levels of this factor. Because these are the default coefficients, you may also simply click *OK* in the *Enter Contrasts for this Factor* dialog. Now, click *OK* in the *Repeated Measures* dialog to view the Scrollsheet.

Planned Comparison (dials.sta)

GENERAL MANOVA — 1-NOISE, 2-TIME, 3-DIALS

Univar. Test	Sum of Squares	df	Mean Square	F	p-level
Effect	440.0555	1	440.0555	1.910977	.239027
Error	921.1111	4	230.2778		

Apparently, the difference between the two means (*White* vs. *Meaningful* noise) at time 2 is not statistically significant. You may also want to try the comparison between those two groups at time 3 (for factor *Time* enter the coefficients *0*, *0*, *1*; all other specifications are the same). That comparison is not significant either.

Specifying a partial interaction contrast. As it turns out, you cannot say that different types of noise led to significantly different numbers of errors at time 2 or 3. However, the overall interaction is significant, and, looking back at the plot of the interaction, it looks like the differential changes from time 1 to time 2 are mainly responsible for this interaction. The significance of the interaction between *Noise* and *Time* (ignoring the third level of *Time*, i.e., time 3) will now be tested. To do this, once again, click on the *Planned comparisons* button and specify the contrast coefficients *1* and *-1* for the *Noise* variable in the *Specify Contrasts for this Factor* dialog. Next, enter the coefficients *1*, *-1*. *0*, respectively, for factor *Time* and the coefficients *1*, *1*, *1* for factor *Dials* in the *Repeated Measures Factors* dialog (see above). As you can see, the first two levels of factor *Noise* and the first two levels of factor *Time* are being contrasted. Now, click *OK* to view the Scrollsheet.

Planned Comparison (dials.sta)

GENERAL MANOVA — 1-NOISE, 2-TIME, 3-DIALS

Univar. Test	Sum of Squares	df	Mean Square	F	p-level
Effect	272.2500	1	272.2500	17.75543	.013546
Error	61.3333	4	15.3333		

This contrast is significant. It indeed looks as though the significant two-way interaction between *Noise* and *Time* can be traced to the differential changes (improvements) in the number of errors from time 1 to time 2 in the *White* noise condition as compared to the *Meaningful* condition; subjects in the former condition improved their performance more than subjects in the latter condition.

Multivariate Approach

In the introduction, the special assumptions of univariate repeated measures ANOVA was discussed (see page 1710). In some scientific disciplines, the multivariate approach to repeated measures ANOVA with more than two levels has quickly become the only accepted way of analyzing these types of designs. This is because the multivariate approach does not rest on the assumption of *sphericity* or *compound symmetry* (refer to page 1712).

In short, univariate repeated measures ANOVA assumes that the *changes* across levels are uncorrelated across subjects. This assumption is highly suspect in most cases. In the present example, it is quite conceivable that subjects who improved a lot from time *1* to time *2* reached a ceiling in their accuracy, and improved *less* from time *2* to time *3*. Given the suspicion that the sphericity assumption for univariate ANOVA has been violated, look at the multivariate statistics.

Requesting the interaction effect. From the results dialog, click on the *Specific effect/means* button to open the *Testing a Specific Effect* dialog in which you can examine a specific effect in detail. In this dialog, highlight factors *Noise* and *Time* in order to look at that interaction effect.

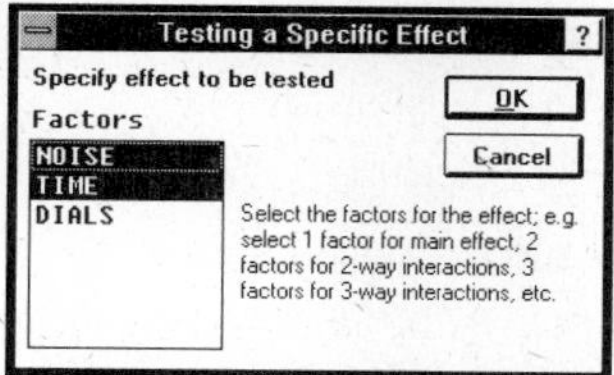

First the univariate results will be displayed in a Scrollsheet.

INTERACTION: 1 × 2 (dials.sta)

GENERAL MANOVA	1-NOISE, 2-TIME, 3-DIALS				
Univar. Test	Sum of Squares	df	Mean Square	F	p-level
Effect	333.0000	2	166.5000	5.670766	.029268
Error	234.8889	8	29.3611		

As before, the univariate F test is significant (it is of course identical to the one in the summary table requested via the *All effects* button). Now, review the multivariate results.

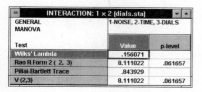

INTERACTION: 1 × 2 (dials.sta)

GENERAL MANOVA	1-NOISE, 2-TIME, 3-DIALS	
Test	Value	p-level
Wilks' Lambda	.156071	
Rao R Form 2 (2, 3)	8.111022	.061657
Pillai-Bartlett Trace	.843929	
V (2,3)	8.111022	.061657

There are different multivariate test criteria; in this case, *Wilks' Lambda*, *Rao R*, *Pillai-Bartlett Trace*, and *V* agree: the interaction is not significant at the *.05* level! Thus, here you have a case where the violation of the sphericity assumption led to an erroneous acceptance of the interaction effect as being statistically significant.

Technical note: Identifying the source of the violation. If you are content with putting the sphericity issue to rest, you may skip this paragraph and continue on with the next paragraph. Otherwise, without going into much detail, there is a way to identify where the sphericity assumption was violated.

Namely, you can request to see the pooled within-group variance/covariance matrix of differences (on the *ANOVA Results* dialog, click on the *Output options* button and in the resulting dialog, check the *Display sum of squares matrices* option). Then click on the *Planned comparisons* button to specify two independent contrasts for factor *Time*; for example, you might want to enter (1) *-2*, *1*, *1* and (2) *0*, *1*, *-1*. Set all other contrast coefficients for all other factors to *1*.

Two independent hypotheses that comprise the main effect for *Time* have been specified here. The first contrast compares time *1* with time *2* and *3* combined; the second contrast tests time *2* against time *3*. The *SSCP: Error* (error sums of squares and cross-product) matrix (containing the variances and covariances of difference scores) will look as follows:

SSCP: Error (dials.sta)

GENERAL MANOVA	1	2
1	146.5556	-81.5988
2	-81.5988	88.3333

The off-diagonal element in this matrix is equal to *-81.6*. To compute the actual correlations between the two contrasts, take the off-diagonal element and divide it by the square root of the product of the respective diagonal elements, i.e.,

-81.6/√(146.6*88.33) = -.72.

Thus, the two sets of contrast coefficients are correlated at *-.72*. The F test is only valid if the sphericity assumption holds, that is, if this correlation is zero. The negative sign of the correlation shows that the greater the change from time *1* to time *2* and *3* combined (contrast 1 above), the *smaller* is the change from time *2* to time *3* (contrast 2 above). This proves the initial suspicion that those subjects who improved early had less room to improve later on.

Adjusted univariate tests. Before the multivariate approach gained popularity, some authors proposed corrections for the univariate F to adjust for violations, notably the Greenhouse-Geisser correction (Greenhouse and Geisser, 1958, 1959) and the Huynh-Feldt correction (Huynh and Feldt, 1976).

Note that these corrections represent approximations, and the multivariate approach should be used instead whenever possible. However, in some scientific disciplines, these corrections are still commonly used. To compute those corrections, return to the *ANOVA Results* dialog and click on the *Output options* button.

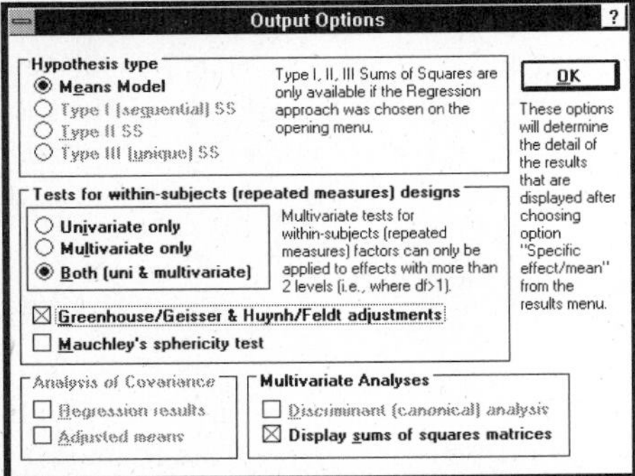

Requesting Greenhouse-Geisser and Huynh-Feldt corrections. The above dialog contains numerous specialized output options, some of which are not applicable to this design (therefore they have been dimmed). Select the *Greenhouse-Geisser & Huynh-Feldt adjustments* option and then click *OK* in this dialog. Now, click on the *Specific effect/means/graphs* button in the *ANOVA Results* dialog and highlight factors *Noise* and *Time*. When you click *OK* in this dialog, a Scrollsheet of *epsilon* factors will first be displayed.

Greenhouse/Geisser & Huynh/Feldt Epsilon (dials.s

GENERAL MANOVA	INTERACTION: 1 x 2 Epsilon
Greenhouse-Geisser Epsilon	.647598
Huynh-Feldt Epsilon	1.000000
Lower-bound Epsilon	.500000

Reviewing results. The Scrollsheet above shows the adjustment factors for the univariate tests. Specifically, these are correction factors for the degrees of freedom; the respective *epsilon* values are used to multiply the degrees of freedom of the respective Mean Squares for the effect and the error. The regular (significant) univariate *F* test is displayed with 2 degrees of freedom for the effect, and 8 degrees of freedom in the error term. The Scrollsheet with the adjusted *F* tests is displayed below.

As you can see below, the Greenhouse-Geisser adjustment does a "good job" of protecting against erroneously accepting the interaction as statistically significant at the *.05* level. In fact, the *p*-level for that test (*.063*) is very similar to that for the multivariate test (*p* = *.062*). The Huynh-Feldt adjustment does not help much in this case.

Univariate Test with Adjusted Degrees of Freedom (dial

GENERAL MANOVA — F = 5.670766, INTERACTION: 1 x 2

Univar. Test	Unadjstd	Greenhs. Geisser	Huynh Feldt	Lower Bound
Epsilon		.647598	1.000000	.500000
df 1	2.000000	1.295195	2.000000	1.000000
df 2	8.000000	5.180781	8.000000	4.000000
p-level	.029268	.063060	.029268	.075879

Summary

To summarize the analysis of this example, an interaction between *Noise* and *Time* emerged between time *1* and time *2* (the first and the second 10-minute segment) subjects in the white noise condition improved more (made fewer errors) than subjects in the meaningful noise condition. However, the differences in the number of errors (between groups) are not statistically significant at any time. Further analyses revealed a serious violation of the sphericity assumption, casting doubt on the initial conclusions. The multivariate test of the interaction between *Noise* and *Time*, as well as the Greenhouse-Geisser adjusted univariate test, failed to reach statistical significance at the *.05* level. This example has demonstrated the advantages of using the multivariate approach to repeated measures ANOVA with more than two levels (on the repeated measures).

Example 3: Multivariate ANOVA with Covariates: MANCOVA

Overview

A multivariate analysis of variance design with multiple (fixed) covariates will be specified in this example. The parallelism hypothesis will be tested and the standard multivariate results will be computed.

Data File

This example is based on a data set reported by Finn (1974). Four groups of 12 subjects each were asked to sort a list of 50 words (each printed on one card) into a specified number of categories.

The experimental groups differed with regard to the *instructions* they received concerning the number of categories represented in the word lists, and the actual number of categories in the word lists (as "built" into them by the experimenter). Specifically, the four groups differed as follows:

(1) subjects in group 1 were told to sort the word list into 5 major categories, each containing 2 sub-categories (condition *M5_S2*);

(2) subjects in group 2 were instructed to sort the same words into 10 major categories, and no sub-categories were mentioned (condition *M10_S0*);

(3) subjects in group 3 were told to sort the same word list into 5 major categories, and no sub-categories were mentioned (*M5_S0*);

(4) subjects in group 4 were instructed in the same manner as subjects in group 3, however, the word list did not contain any salient or intended (by the experimenter) structure (Control group; *M5_S0_C*).

The major dependent variables were (1) the number of words recalled after six trials of sorting and (2) the percentage of categories -- intended by the experimenter -- recreated by the subjects in their sorts. The amount of time (in seconds) that subjects spent on their 2nd, 4th, and 6th sorting trials was recorded and served as covariates in the design.

These data are contained in the example data file *Mancova.sta*. A portion of that file is reproduced below.

Data: MANCOVA.STA 6v * 48c

TEXT VALUES: Study of recall for words and word categories as a function of instru

	1 GROUP	2 WORDS	3 CATS	4 TIME2	5 TIME4	6 TIME6
1	M5_S2	50	100	83	77	75
2	M5_S2	36	100	136	106	116
3	M5_S2	31	90	144	111	115
4	M5_S2	35	90	133	102	91
5	M5_S2	43	100	201	125	147
6	M5_S2	49	100	161	164	129
7	M5_S2	31	90	178	169	135
8	M5_S2	33	90	338	129	103
9	M5_S2	36	100	112	91	86

Variable 1 (*Group*) contains the codes that identify to which experimental group each subject belongs; variable 2 (*Words*) contains the number of words recalled; variable 3 (*Cats*) contains the percent of intended categories reproduced by subjects; variables 4 through 6 (*Time2* to *Time6*) contain the amount of time spent by the respective subject on the 2nd, 4th, and 6th sorting trial, respectively.

Specifying the Design

After starting the *ANOVA/MANOVA* module, open the data file *Mancova.sta*. In the *General ANOVA-/MANOVA* startup panel, click on the *Covariates* button and specify variable 1 (*Group*) as the independent variable, variables 2 and 3 (*Words* and *Cats*) as the dependent variables, and variables 4, 5, and 6 (*Time2*, *Time4*, *Time6*) as the covariates in this design. Next, select the codes used in the independent variable (click on the *Codes for between groups factor* button and in the resulting dialog click on the *All* button to specify all four codes which identify the groups *M5_S2*, *M10_S0*, *M5_S0*, and *M5_S0_C*,). The design is now fully specified.

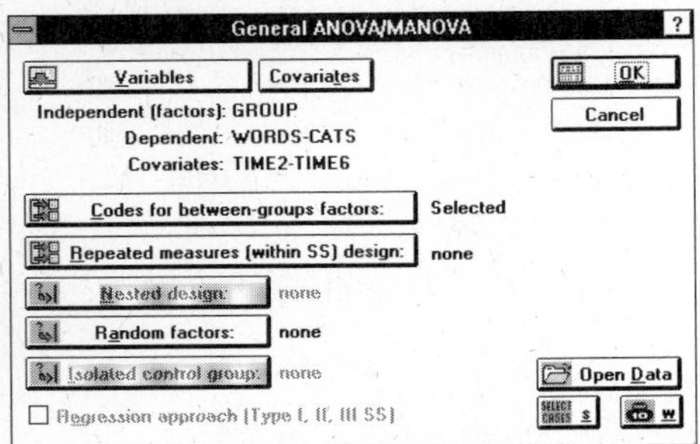

Reviewing the Results

After clicking *OK* in the startup panel, the *ANOVA Results* dialog will open.

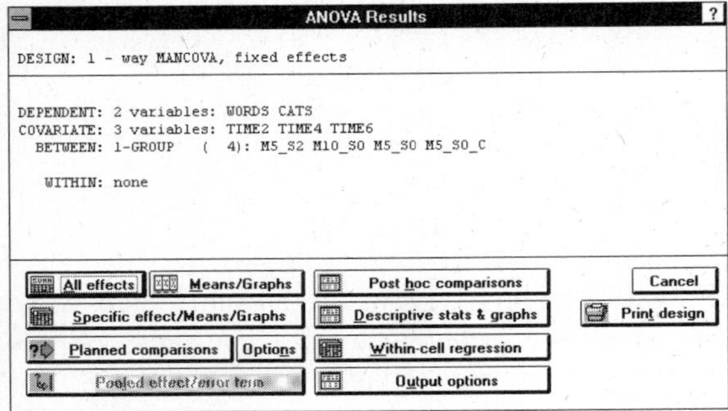

There is only one factor in this design (in addition to the covariates); thus you should examine that effect in detail rather than use the *All effects* option.

First, open the *Output Options* dialog (click on the *Output options* button) and select *Regression results* (to compute the results of the regression analysis for the covariates), *Discriminant (canonical) analysis* (to compute the discriminant analysis), and *Adjusted means* (to compute the adjusted means).

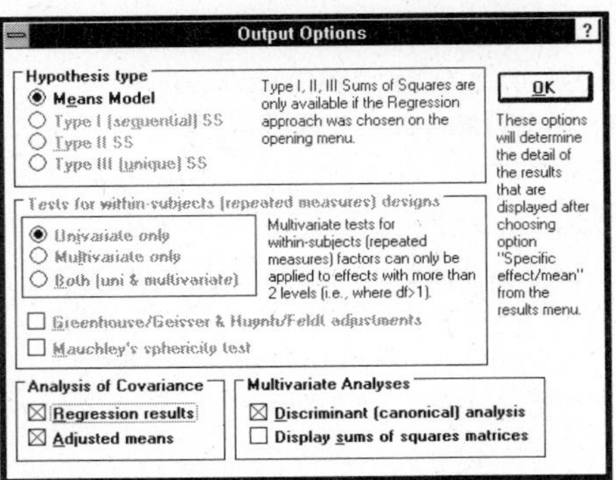

Now, click *OK* and return to the *ANOVA Results* dialog. Click on the *Specific effects/means/graphs* button and the *Regression Results (Covariates)* dialog will open.

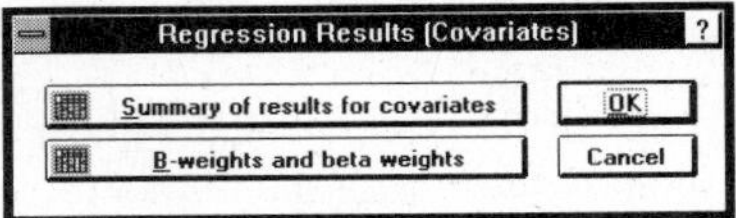

Regression results (covariates). Because there are multiple dependent variables, you can perform a summary test of whether or not the canonical correlation (within-groups) between all dependent variables and all covariates is significant. Click on the *Summary of results for covariates* button to select that test.

Multivariate Tests (mancova.sta)

Continue...

Test	Within-Cells Regression 3 Covariates Value	p-level
Wilks' Lambda	.908427	
Rao R Form 1 (6, 80)	.655897	.685266
Pillai-Bartlett Trace	.092792	
V (6,82)	.664932	.678103

The overall test is not significant. Thus, you can conclude that, overall, the covariates are not related to the dependent variables. At this point, you could return to the *Regression Results* dialog (click on the *Continue* button in the Scrollsheet) and select the *B-weights and beta weights* option to review the univariate tests (these would be the multiple correlation results for each dependent variable). However, since the overall test is not significant, you can skip this step.

Univariate tests. After returning to the *Regression Results* dialog, click *OK* to bring up a Scrollsheet with the univariate *F* tests for each dependent variable.

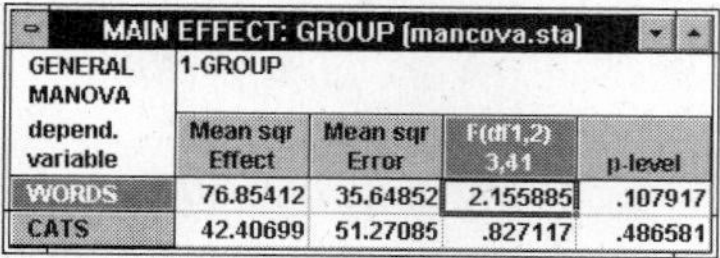

MAIN EFFECT: GROUP (mancova.sta)

GENERAL MANOVA	1-GROUP			
depend. variable	Mean sqr Effect	Mean sqr Error	F(df1,2) 3,41	p-level
WORDS	76.85412	35.64852	2.155885	.107917
CATS	42.40699	51.27085	.827117	.486581

None of the univariate tests reaches statistical significance; only the result for the number of words recalled (*Words*) approaches marginal significance (at the *.10* level).

Multivariate tests. The multivariate tests are significant. The two common tests displayed here (*Rao's R* and *V*) are significant at the $p<.03$ level.

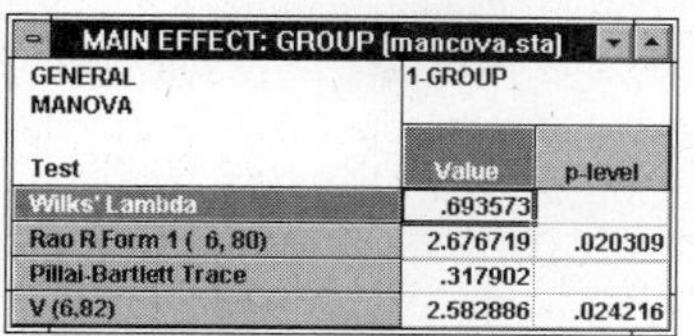

MAIN EFFECT: GROUP (mancova.sta)

GENERAL MANOVA	1-GROUP	
Test	Value	p-level
Wilks' Lambda	.693573	
Rao R Form 1 (6, 80)	2.676719	.020309
Pillai-Bartlett Trace	.317902	
V (6,82)	2.582886	.024216

Canonical analysis. Now, review the Scrollsheet with the discriminant function analysis results. The *ANOVA/MANOVA* module will cycle through all canonical roots. For each root, the standardized as well as unstandardized discriminant function parameters are displayed.

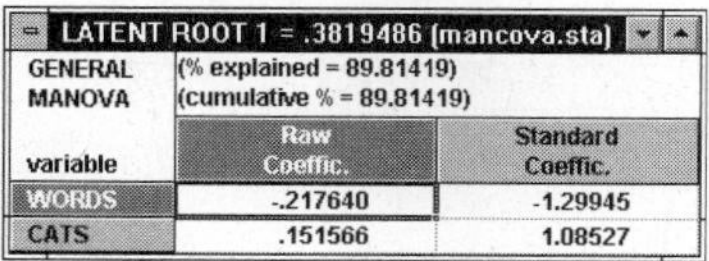

LATENT ROOT 1 = .3819486 (mancova.sta)

GENERAL MANOVA	(% explained = 89.81419) (cumulative % = 89.81419)	
variable	Raw Coeffic.	Standard Coeffic.
WORDS	-.217640	-1.29945
CATS	.151566	1.08527

The first root accounts for almost 90% of the *common* variance. Common variance here refers to the variability of the dependent variables that can be explained by the between-groups factors. thus, you can remember from this analysis that the first canonical root extracted appears to explain the majority of all variability that makes up the significant multivariate effects for factor *Group*. In addition, the sign of the discriminant function coefficient for variable *Words* is negative, and for variable *Cats* is positive. This means that the two variables have opposite signs in the linear function that maximizes the variance explained by the main effect. This information will be used later to interpret the plot of canonical means (see below). For now, review the Scrollsheet with the parameters for the second root. The second root only accounts for 10% of the common variance.

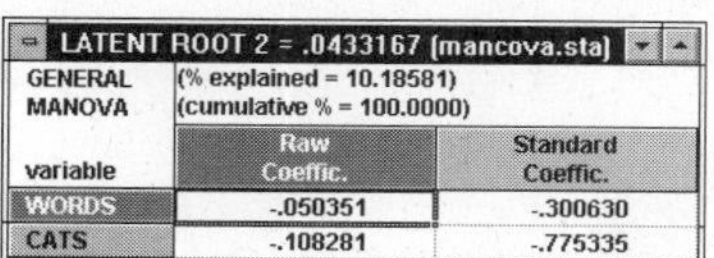

LATENT ROOT 2 = .0433167 (mancova.sta)

GENERAL MANOVA	(% explained = 10.18581) (cumulative % = 100.0000)	
variable	Raw Coeffic.	Standard Coeffic.
WORDS	-.050351	-.300630
CATS	-.108281	-.775335

Reviewing the means. Now proceed to the table of means.

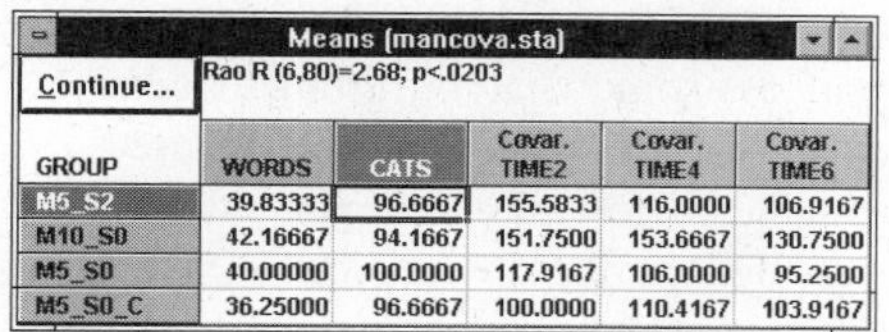

Means (mancova.sta)

Continue... Rao R (6,80)=2.68; p<.0203

GROUP	WORDS	CATS	Covar. TIME2	Covar. TIME4	Covar. TIME6
M5_S2	39.83333	96.6667	155.5833	116.0000	106.9167
M10_S0	42.16667	94.1667	151.7500	153.6667	130.7500
M5_S0	40.00000	100.0000	117.9167	106.0000	95.2500
M5_S0_C	36.25000	96.6667	100.0000	110.4167	103.9167

As in all Scrollsheets of marginal means in the *ANOVA/MANOVA* module, you may plot one or several of these variables by clicking with the right-mouse-button and selecting the *Quick Stats Graphs* option. Then in the resulting flying menu, select the *Means Plot* option.

Plotting the means. When you click on the *Means plots* option in the flying menu, you can elect to plot the dependent variables as well as the covariates in the *Select Variables for Plot* dialog.

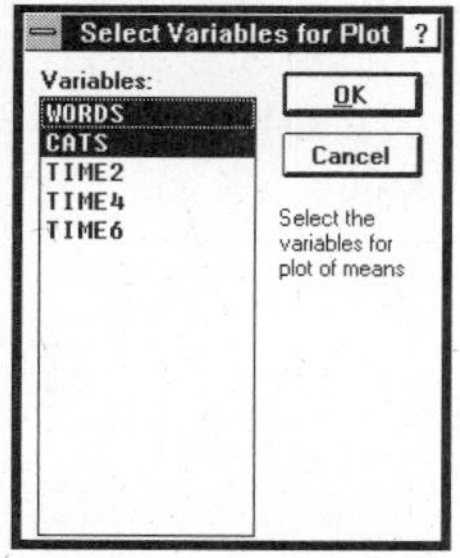

For this example, select only variables *Words* and *Cats* by highlighting them in this dialog. Now, click *OK* to produce the plot.

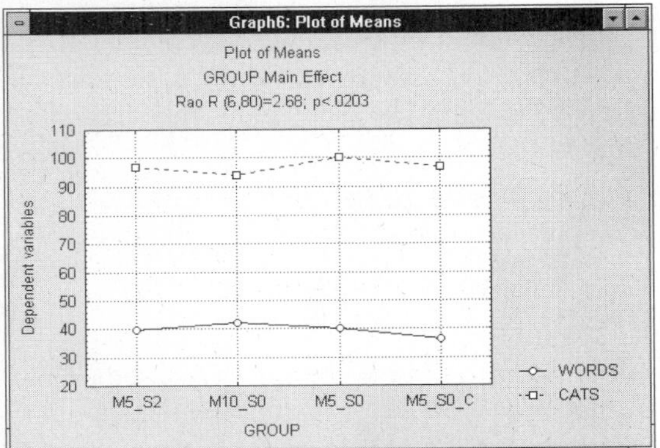

The resulting plot is somewhat unfortunate because variable *Cats* and variable *Words* were measured with different scales. However, it appears that group 2 (*M10_S0*) recalled the most words but the least number of categories; a clear pattern regarding the other groups is not immediately apparent. Now, return to the Scrollsheet of means and click on the *Continue* button to display the Scrollsheet of *adjusted* means. These are the means for the dependent variables, adjusted for the covariates. You may want to produce a plot of these means, following the same steps as in the previous Scrollsheet (i.e., click on the Scrollsheet with the right-mouse-button, etc.). The plot will look very similar to that of the unadjusted means.

Reviewing means for discriminant function. Now, click on the *Continue* button in the adjusted means Scrollsheet to bring up the Scrollsheet with the means for the discriminant function.

Means on Discriminant Functions (mancova.sta)

Continue... Rao R (6,80)=2.68; p<.0203

GROUP	Discrim. Funct.1	Discrim. Funct.2
M5_S2	5.982027	-12.4729
M10_S0	5.095286	-12.3197
M5_S0	6.450972	-12.8422
M5_S0_C	6.761903	-12.2924

Remember that the first function accounted for most of the common variance, that is, of the common (to both *Words* and *Cats*) variability due to the significant main effect. Plot the means for that function by clicking on the Scrollsheet with the right-mouse-button and again selecting the *Quick Stats Graphs* option. Now, select *Means Plots* from the flying menu and the *Select Variables for Plot* dialog will open. Select the first discriminant function (*Funct.1*) in this dialog and click *OK*.

Here, a clearer pattern emerges (see below). Apparently, group 2 (*M10_S0*) has the lowest value on the function, while the control group (*M5_S0_C*) has the highest mean; the other two fall in between. Remember that this first discriminant function was defined by a negative weight for variable *Words*, and a positive weight for variables *Cats*. Thus, a low value on this first discriminant function means that *more* words were recalled and *fewer* categories recreated; in general, this plot is consistent with the plot of means produced above.

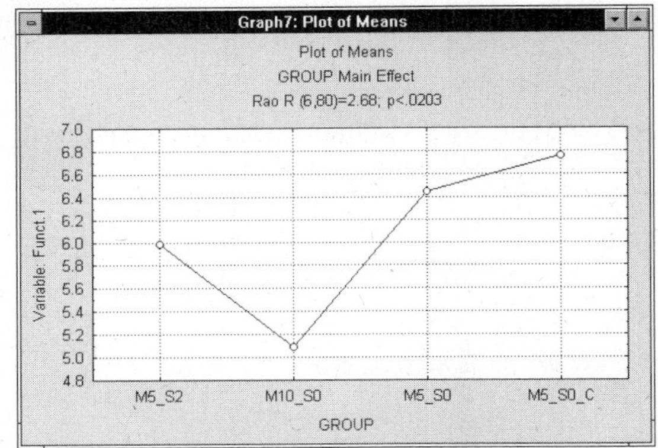

Conclusion. From the analysis so far, you can conclude that there is a significant main effect for the manipulation in this experiment: In particular, subjects in group 2 (*M10_S0*) who were instructed to sort the word list into 10 categories (no sub-categories), recalled more words than other subjects, but fewer categories. The covariates do not appear to be related to the dependent measure. At this point you might want to continue with contrast analyses to explore the significant main effect further.

However, for now, return to the *ANOVA Results* dialog to consider the effect of the covariates.

Testing the Parallelism Hypothesis

One of the assumptions of the standard analysis of covariance is that the regression lines have equal slopes (are parallel) in each group, or, put another way, that there are no interactions that involve the covariates. In the multivariate case (multiple dependent variables) the assumption is that the regression *planes* are parallel. You can specifically test this assumption. Click on the *Descriptive stats & graphs* button in the *ANOVA Results* dialog to bring up the *Descriptive Statistics & Graphs* dialog. In this dialog, click on the *Parallelism (interactions by covariates)* button and a Scrollsheet with the univariate tests for each dependent variable will be first be displayed.

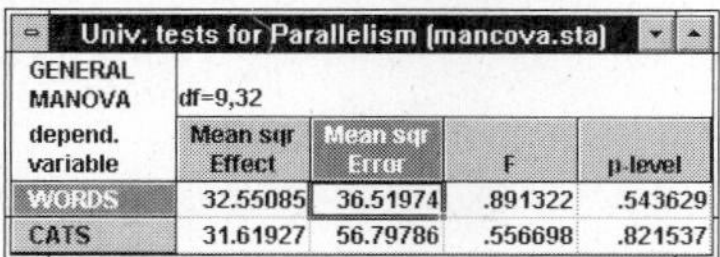

Univ. tests for Parallelism (mancova.sta)

GENERAL MANOVA depend. variable	df=9,32 Mean sqr Effect	Mean sqr Error	F	p-level
WORDS	32.55085	36.51974	.891322	.543629
CATS	31.61927	56.79786	.556698	.821537

Then, a Scrollsheet with the multivariate results will be displayed.

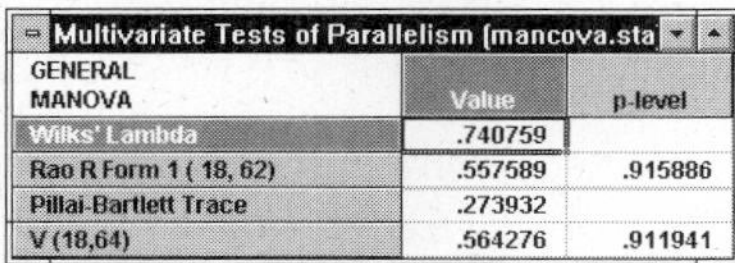

Multivariate Tests of Parallelism (mancova.sta

GENERAL MANOVA	Value	p-level
Wilks' Lambda	.740759	
Rao R Form 1 (18, 62)	.557589	.915886
Pillai-Bartlett Trace	.273932	
V (18,64)	.564276	.911941

None of these tests are significant, so there is no reason to reject the hypothesis of parallel regression planes.

StatSoft

DIALOGS, OPTIONS, STATISTICS

Startup Panel

When you first open the *ANOVA/MANOVA* module, the *General ANOVA/MANOVA* dialog will open.

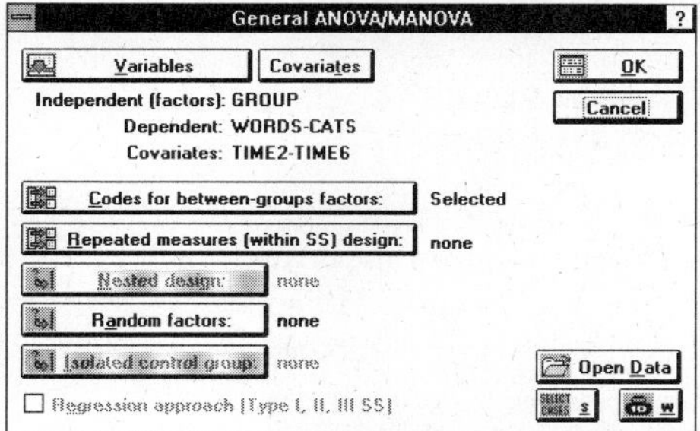

Between-groups design. In order to specify a between-groups design in this dialog, at least one dependent variable must be selected, at least one independent or grouping variable must be selected, and at least two independent variable codes must be specified (via the *Codes* option) for each between-groups factor (note that if you do not explicitly specify the codes, by default, the program will use as codes all values encountered in the specified independent variables).

Repeated measures design. In order to specify a repeated measures factor design in this opening dialog, at least two dependent variables must be selected, and the repeated measures factor has to be identified via the *Repeated measures (within SS) design* option. Multiple dependent variables that cannot be interpreted (by the program, given the design you specified) as levels of repeated measures factors are interpreted as multiple dependent variables in a MANOVA design (this will occur if, for example you select two or more dependent variables and do not define them as repeated measures, or whenever you select more dependent variables than can be accounted for by the currently defined repeated measure factors and their levels).

Designs with missing cells. The *ANOVA-/MANOVA* module will automatically handle designs with empty cells. To analyze *Latin squares*, *Greco-Latin squares*, or other balanced incomplete designs, simply specify them as if they were complete factorial designs. Then use the option *Pooled effect-/error* on the *Results* dialog to build the appropriate error term for testing the effects. Designs with complex patterns of missing cells should be analyzed via specific planned comparisons.

Variables (Independent and Dependent)

Choosing this option will bring up a dialog for selecting a list of independent variables (between-groups factors) and a list of dependent variables.

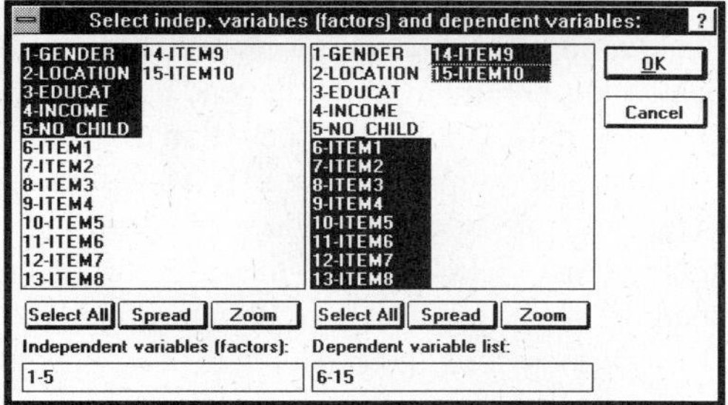

Independent (or grouping) variables are the variables that contain codes that uniquely identify to which group (cell) in the between-groups design a case belongs. Up to 8 independent variables can be specified; if the design has no between-groups factors, leave the first list blank. If a repeated measures analysis is desired, specify as dependent variables *all* variables that contain the data for the different levels of the repeated measures factor(s). The assignment of variables to levels of the repeated measures factor(s) is determined by *the order in which dependent variables appear in the dependent variable list*, not by the order in which variables were entered into the file.

Covariates

After choosing this option a standard three-variable-lists selection dialog will be displayed. The first two lists allow you to select the independent or grouping variables and dependent variables (as described under option *Variables* above). The third list is for covariates in the design (see page 1702).

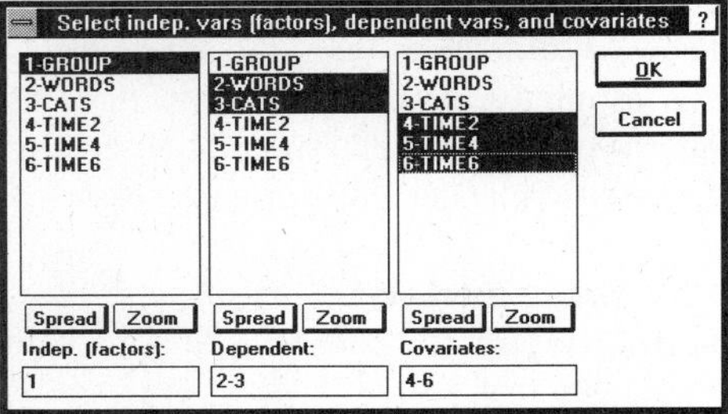

At this point select all covariates, regardless of whether they represent fixed (static) covariates (each covariate was measured once for each subject) or changing covariates (each covariate was measured at each repeated measurement of the dependent variable). If the number of covariates is an even multiple of the total number of levels in the within-subjects (repeated measures) design, then upon exiting this dialog by clicking *OK*, the user will be asked whether the covariates are to be interpreted as changing covariates or as fixed covariates.

Codes for Between-Groups Factors

Clicking on this button will bring up the independent variable codes selection dialog. Independent variable codes are the code numbers or names (text codes) that were entered for the independent variables in order to uniquely identify the group membership of each case (e.g., a *1* or *Male* was entered if a subject was male, a *2* or *Female* was entered if a subject was female). You may also refer to the *Examples* section (page 1719) to see how codes are used to specify the between-groups ANOVA design.

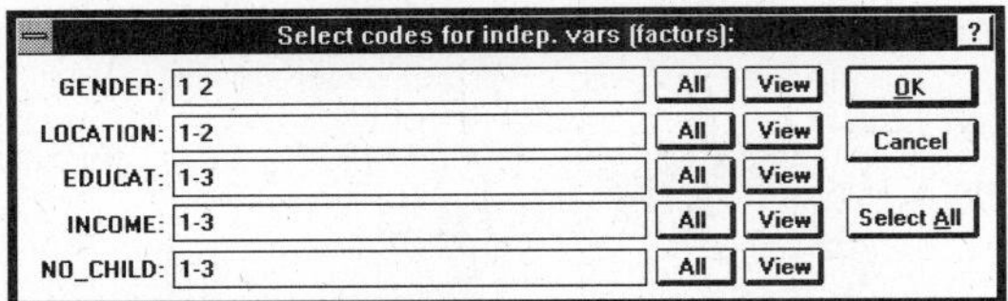

If you do not explicitly specify codes for the independent variables, but simply click *OK* to continue on from the startup panel, the program will automatically use all codes in the respective independent variables.

Repeated Measures (Within-SS) Design

This option allows you to specify the *within-subjects* or repeated measures part of the design. After choosing this option, a dialog will come up for specifying repeated measures factors.

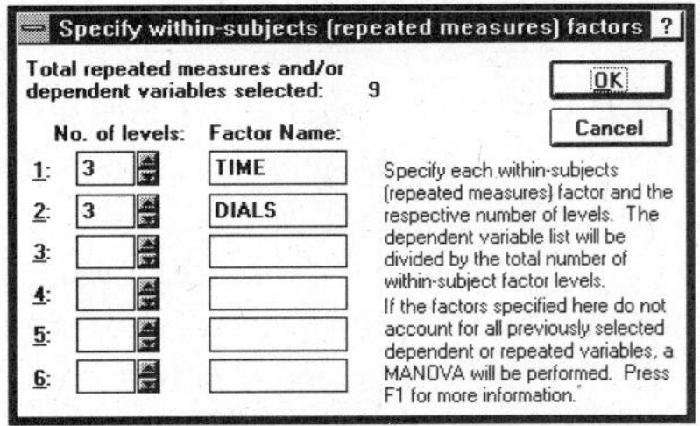

For each repeated measures factor, specify a name up to 8 characters long, and the number of levels that the factor contains. For more information on specifying a repeated measures design see *Specifying Repeated Measures Designs*, page 1739; for examples, see page 1768.

Nested Design

This option allows the user to specify nested designs. In nested designs, the levels of a factor are nested within the levels of another factor. For example, if one were to administer four different tests to four high school classes (i.e., a between-groups factor with 4 levels), and two of those four classes are in high school A, whereas the other two classes are in high school B, then the levels of the

first factor (4 different tests) would be nested in the second factor (2 different high schools).

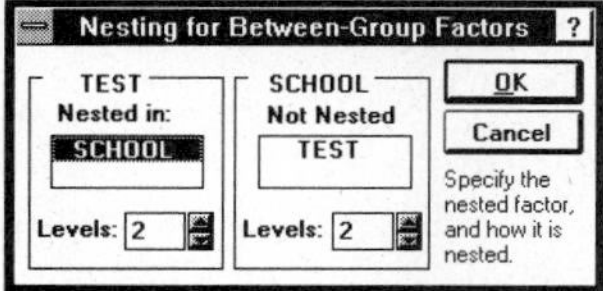

Note that not all nested designs must be (or, in fact, can be) set up via this option (see below).

After choosing this option, the *Nesting for Between-group Factors* dialog will open (see above) in which the user can select:

(1) the nested factors,

(2) the factors in which they are nested, and

(3) the number of levels the respective factors have within the factors in which they are nested.

Repeated measures factors can only be nested in other repeated measures factors, and between-groups factors can only be nested in other between-groups factors.

Random Factors

After choosing this option, the user can select the factors in the design that are to be treated as random factors.

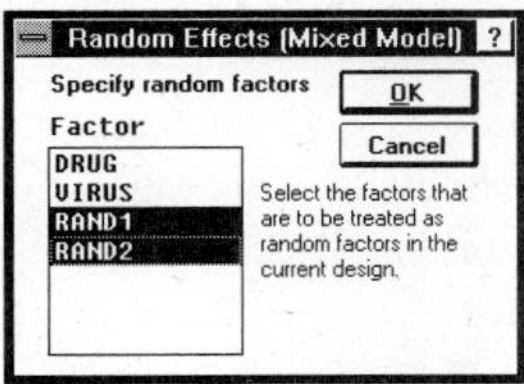

For more information about selecting random factors see *Random Effects (mixed models)*, page 1778.

Isolated Control Group

This option allows the user to specify an independent variable code that identifies an isolated control group (or "hanging" control group).

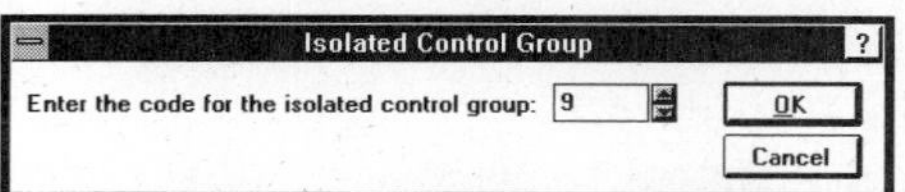

For more information on specifying the isolated control group, see *Specifying the Isolated Control Group*, page 1766.

Regression Approach

If the *Regression approach* check box is set, then the program will perform additional computations while reading the data, and the user can later request to test all effects, specific hypotheses, or pooled effects, using *Type I*, *II*, or *III* sums of squares. (These options are described later in this chapter, see pages 1742, 1746, and 1756, respectively.)

Specifying Repeated Measures Designs

To specify a repeated measures factor, enter a label and the number of levels for the factor (see also page 1768). The program will interpret the variables in the dependent variable list as levels of the repeated measures factors. Thus, the number of dependent variables must be evenly divisible by the total number of repeated measures factors. If there are more (twice or three times as many) dependent variables than levels for the repeated measures factors, then adjacent variables in the dependent variable list will be interpreted as multiple dependent measures in a (multivariate) repeated measures MANOVA.

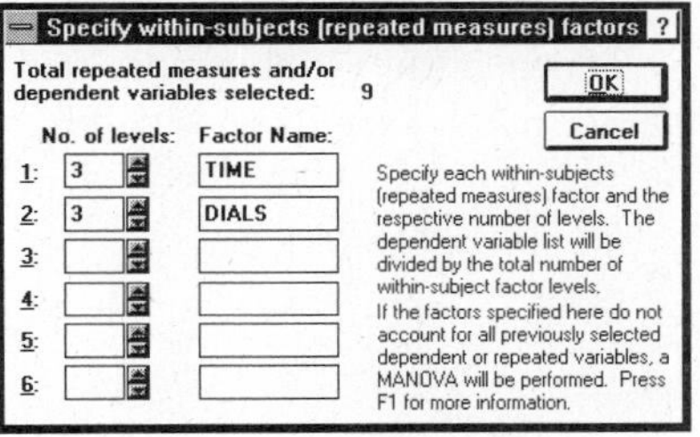

Specifying More than One Repeated Measures Factor

If a design contains more than one repeated measures factor, the order in which they are specified will determine the assignment of dependent variables to levels of the repeated measures factors. The program will "cycle" through the dependent variable list, assigning variables to subsequent levels of the repeated measures factor. Specifically, the fastest-moving (changing) levels are those of the repeated measures factor which was specified *last*, the next-fastest moving (changing) levels are those of the repeated measures factor which was specified *next to last*, and so on. If one or more *changing* covariates were specified (covariates that were measured at each level of the repeated measures factors), the list of covariates will be assigned to levels of the repeated measures factors in the same manner.

Example. If 12 dependent variables were selected, and the user wants to specify a 2 x 2 x 3 repeated measures design, then the assignment of variables to levels should be as follows:

Repeated measures factor	levels of repeated measures factors											
First	1	1	1	1	1	1	2	2	2	2	2	2
Second	1	1	1	2	2	2	1	1	1	2	2	2
Third	1	2	3	1	2	3	1	2	3	1	2	3
Dep.Var.	1	2	3	4	5	6	7	8	9	10	11	12

Note that the numbers in the last row of the example table above represent the consecutive numbers of variables in the list of dependent variables specified by the user, and not the numbers of those variables in the data file (e.g., the number *1* above may represent variable number *256* in the data file).

Multivariate Repeated Measures Designs

If, in the above example, the dependent variable list had consisted of 24 rather than 12 dependent variables, a 2 x 2 x 3 *multivariate* analysis of variance (MANOVA) with repeated measures would be performed (with two dependent variables at each level of the repeated measures factors).

When cycling through the dependent variable list, the fastest changing levels (i.e., adjacent variables in the dependent variable list) always represent the multiple dependent variables. Refer to Example 2 (page 1724) and *Specifying Repeated Measures Designs* (page 1768), for detailed explanations of how the program assigns variables from the dependent variable list to levels of repeated measures factors (see also page 1739).

Specifying Code for Isolated ("Hanging") Control Group

Specify here the code that is used in the independent (grouping) variables to identify the cases that belong to the isolated ("hanging") control group.

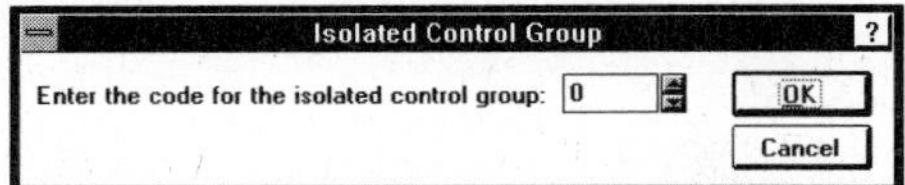

Experimental designs are usually completely crossed (factorial designs), that is, each level of each factor appears with each level of all others. For example, in a 2 (types of drug) x 2 (types of virus) design, each type of drug would be used with each type of virus. However, in order to establish an appropriate control group (e.g., a group of healthy animals that were not exposed to any virus or drug) experimental designs sometimes require the addition of a single group, i.e., an *isolated control group* (or "hanging" control group).

The *ANOVA/MANOVA* module expects that the isolated control group is identified by *one common code value* in *all* independent (or grouping) variables. Valid code values that may be entered are integer values in the range from -999 to +999. Later in the computations of the sums of squares, the *ANOVA/MANOVA* module will take the isolated control group into account in the calculation of the error sums of squares.

Specific comparisons involving the isolated control group can be specified via the *Planned comparisons* option on the results dialog. Refer to the *Specifying Codes for Isolated ("Hanging") Control Group* section (page 1766) for a more detailed discussion of how to analyze isolated control group designs.

Specifying Nested Designs

Specify the nested factors in the *Nesting For Between-Groups Factors* dialog.

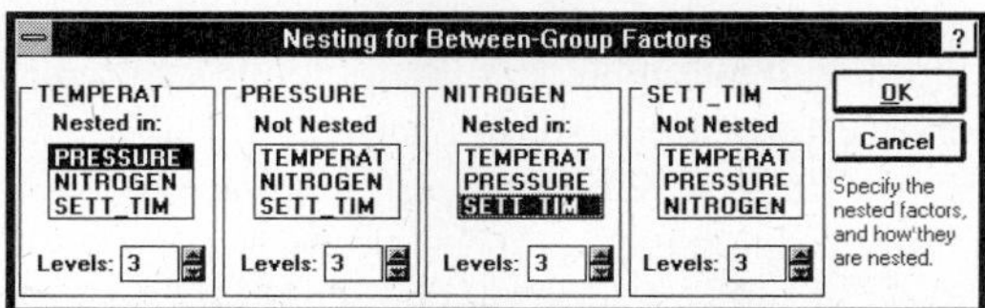

When you open this dialog, several columns will be displayed (one for each factor) with a factor name at the top and the remaining factors listed below. To specify a nested factor:

(1) Go to the column with the name of the factor (at the top of the column) that you want to designate as the nested variable;

(2) In this column, select the factor(s) in which this factor is nested by clicking on the factor names to highlight them. The column will now refer to the first factor (listed at the top of the column) as "nested in" the selected factor(s);

(3) Specify the number of levels of this factor within each of the factor(s) in which it is nested;

(4) Repeat this process for each of the nested factors (in their respective columns).

Nested Designs

In nested designs the levels of a factor are nested within the levels of another factor. For example, if one were to administer four different tests to four high school classes (i.e., a between-groups factor with 4 levels), and two of those four classes are in high school A, whereas the other two classes are in high school B, then the levels of the first factor (4 different tests) would be nested in the second factor (2 different high schools).

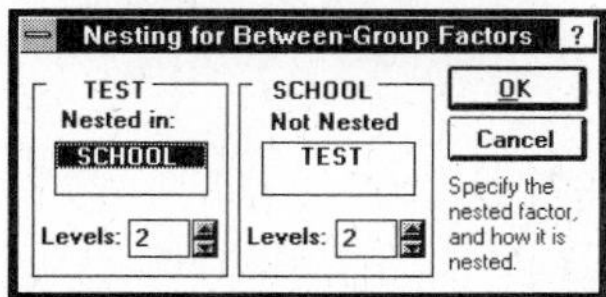

Specifying Random Factors (Effects)

Select the factors that are to be treated as random factors in the design, in the *Random Effects (Mixed Model)* dialog.

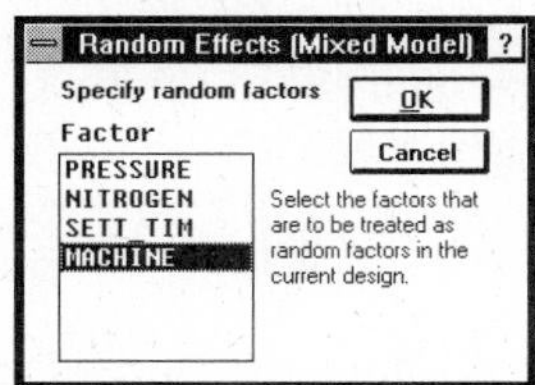

Fixed and random effects differ in that the levels for fixed effects are especially selected or "fixed" by the researcher (e.g., manipulation in an experiment), whereas the levels for random effects are selected by the researcher via some *random* selection procedure from a population of possible levels (e.g., three different schools in which an experiment was conducted).

Designs with Multiple Random Effects

If an ANOVA design contains several random factors or random and repeated measures factors, the sums of squares (and *F* values) for some effects are not determined, and they cannot be estimated.

Fixed vs. Changing Covariates

If the number of covariates selected in a design is evenly divisible by the total number of levels of the repeated measures factors, then the list of variables selected as covariates can be treated as fixed or changing covariates.

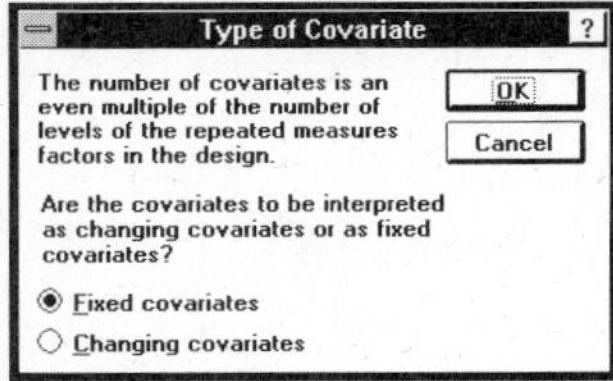

Changing Covariates

While fixed covariates are commonly discussed in textbooks on ANOVA, changing covariates are discussed less frequently. In general, when you have repeated measures, you are interested in testing the differences in repeated measurements on the same subjects. Thus you are actually interested in evaluating the significance of *changes*. If you have a covariate that is also measured at each point when the dependent variable is measured, then you can compute the correlation between the changes in the covariate and the changes in the dependent variable. For example, you could study math anxiety and math skills at the beginning and at the end of the semester. It would be interesting to see whether any changes in math anxiety over the semester correlate with changes in math skills.

Results Dialog

After you make your selections and click *OK* in the *General ANOVA* startup panel, the *ANOVA Results* dialog will open.

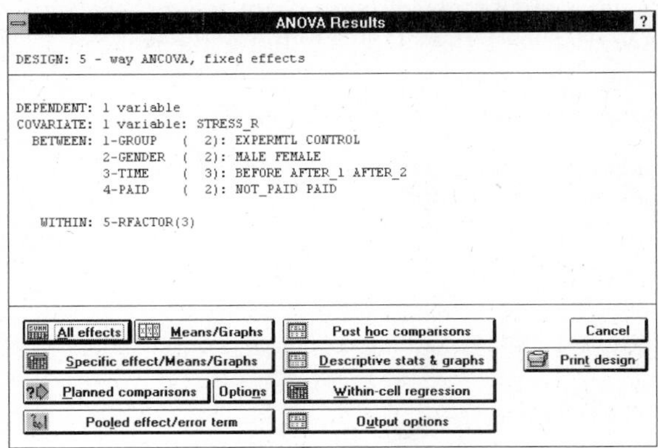

In this dialog you can choose from several options to review specific results.

Table of All Effects

This option will automatically compute the complete table of all effects and display a summary Scrollsheet. In that Scrollsheet, significant effects will by highlighted; the *alpha*-level criterion for highlighting can be changed via the *Options* Scrollsheet toolbar button.

Means/Graphs

This option will also automatically compute the complete table of all effects. A dialog will subsequently be displayed allowing you to select specific effects and to display either a plot of means (interaction) or a Scrollsheet of means. This option is the quickest way to explore patterns of significant effects from complex ANOVA designs. (For more information, see page 1746.)

Specific Effect /Means/Graphs

Click on this button to open a dialog where you can select the effect that you want to examine more closely. You can choose the results reported here by clicking on the *Output options* button (see below) to specify the detail of results to be reported. The rules for specifying effects are given on page 1746.

Planned Comparisons

This option allows you to test specific contrasts (*contrast analysis*). The type of contrasts (separate or together) that you choose in the *Options for Planned Comparisons Facility* dialog (accessible from the *Options* button, see below) determines which contrast dialog will open when you click on the *Planned Comparisons* button. If *Separate Contrasts* is selected, then after you click on this button, you will be prompted to enter the contrast coefficients factor by factor in the *Specify Contrasts* dialog. If you elected to enter the contrasts *Together*, then you will be prompted to enter the contrast coefficients for the factors in the *Contrasts for Between-Group (Within-Subjects) Factors* dialog. The general logic and rules for "building" contrasts are described on page 1763 for both between-group designs as well as repeated measures designs; the dialogs used to specify contrasts are described on page 1758.

Options

When you click on this button, the *Option for Planned Comparisons Facility* dialog will open in which you can select the manner in which contrasts will be entered in the *Planned Comparison* option, above. Contrasts can be entered separately for each factor (choose *Enter Contrasts Separately for Each Factor*), or for all factors combined (*together*, as a contrast *vector*; choose *Enter Contrasts for Factors Together*); in multivariate designs the user can also choose to enter contrasts for the dependent variables. For more information, see page 1758.

Pooled Effect/Error

After choosing this option, the user can specify effects that are to be pooled together, and effects that are to be pooled into the error term in the *Pooled Effects & Error Terms* dialog. This option is particularly useful for testing effects in incomplete designs (see page 1756).

Post Hoc Comparisons

After choosing this option, the *Specify Effect for Post hoc Tests* dialog will open, prompting the user to specify the effect for which to perform the *Post hoc* tests. The conventions for specifying effects in this window are identical to those for specifying effects after choosing option *Specific effect/means-/graphs* (above). The *post hoc* tests will be performed on the marginal means for the respective effect. Available *post hoc* tests are the *LSD* (Least Significant Difference) test, the Newman-Keuls test, the Duncan multiple range test, the Scheffé test, the Tukey *HSD* (Honest Significant Difference) test, and the Spjotvoll and Stoline *HSD* test. These tests can be chosen from the *Post hoc Comparisons of Means* dialog that will be displayed after specifying the effect. For more information, see page 1748.

Descriptive Statistics and Graphs

This option will bring up the *Descriptive Statistics & Graphs* dialog with a wide variety of options for computing descriptive statistics, for testing ANOVA assumptions, and for plotting various aspects of the data. For more information, see page 1749.

Within-Cell Regression

This option will perform a regression analysis for the covariates. Results can be viewed for each dependent variable separately (univariate), or for all dependent variables simultaneously (multivariate). Note that this option will *always* perform the

analyses separately for each variable in the dependent variable list, even if those variables represent levels of a repeated measures factor. If, in a repeated measures design, you want to review the results for a dependent variable that is actually comprised of many levels, use the *Output options* (see below) to request *Regression results;* then use option *Specific effect/means/graphs* (above) to look at the effect of interest (see also page 1746).

Output Options

This option will bring up the *Output Options* dialog for selecting the specific output options that are to be displayed when examining a specific effect via option *Specific effect/means/graphs*, above. Note that not all options here may be applicable to your specific design, and the settings of those options will be ignored (see also *Output Options* below).

Print Design

Click on this button to print the *ANOVA/MANOVA* design either to the printer or output file (as specified in the *Page/Output Setup* dialog).

Output Options

The selections on this dialog will determine the detail of the results displayed when examining specific effects via option *Specific effect/means-/graphs* on the results dialog.

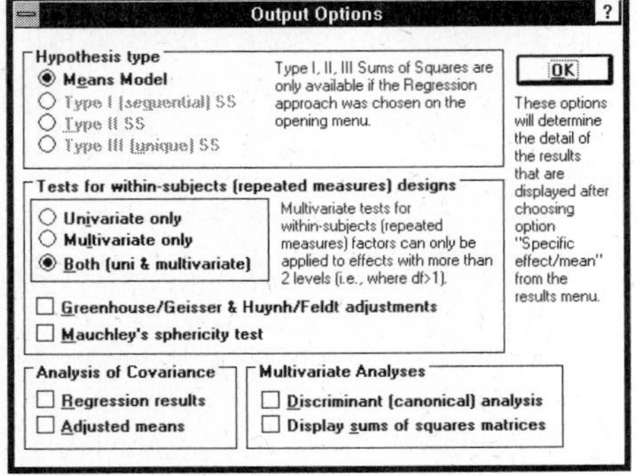

Note that not all options on this dialog are applicable to all designs.

Hypothesis Type

Select the type of hypothesis for the analysis (see below).

Means model. By default, when the R*egression approach* check box on the startup panel is not set, then the *ANOVA/MANOVA* module uses the *Cell Means ANOVA Model*. Specifically, the sums of squares for the different effects in the design are computed for linear combinations of the cell means. For complete factorial designs, this yields sums of squares that are identical to those discussed below as *Type III*. However, with the *Planned comparison* option in the *ANOVA Results* dialog, the user can test hypotheses about any weighted or unweighted linear combination of cell means. In this manner, the user can test not only *Type III* hypotheses, but any type of hypothesis (including *Type IV*). This general approach proves particularly useful when analyzing designs with missing cells (so-called incomplete designs). For more information, see page 1709.

Type I, II, and III hypotheses. These options are only available if the R*egression approach* check box on the startup panel was set. In general, you can test the significance of partial correlations, in effect controlling for other effects, or you can enter the variables in a stepwise fashion, controlling for all other factors that were previously entered and ignoring those that have not yet been entered. In essence, this is the difference between *Type III* and *Type I* Sums of Squares. For more information, see page 1706.

Another "intermediate" strategy would be to control for all other main effects when testing a particular main effect, for all main effects and two-way interactions when testing a particular two-way interaction, for all main effects, two-way interactions, and three-way interactions when testing a particular three-way interaction, and so on. Sums

of squares for effects computed in this manner are called *Type II* sums of squares. Thus, *Type II* sums of squares control for all effects of the same or lower order, while ignoring all effects of higher order. For more information, see page 1706.

Tests for Within-Subjects (Repeated Measures) Designs

These options are only applicable to designs containing repeated measures factors with more than two levels. The *Introductory Overview* section discusses the advantage of multivariate tests of effects involving those factors over the traditional univariate approach (page 1712). Briefly, an important assumption underlying the use of univariate test statistics for repeated measures factors with more than two levels is the so-called *compound symmetry* assumption. This assumption, which is frequently violated, is not implied by the multivariate approach. Set the respective radio buttons to compute the *univariate only* tests, the *multivariate only* tests, or *both* (default).

Greenhouse-Geisser & Huynh-Feldt. The purpose of these tests is to adjust the univariate results of repeated measures ANOVA (for factors with more than two levels) for violations of the *compound symmetry* assumption. This assumption, as well as these tests, are discussed in the *Introductory Overview* section (page 1712).

Mauchley's sphericity test. This test is only applicable to designs with repeated measures factors with more than two levels. The *sphericity* assumption is related to the *compound symmetry* assumption; both are concerned with the conditions under which the univariate approach to repeated measures ANOVA yields valid statistical significance tests. These assumptions are discussed in the *Introductory Overview* section (page 1712).

The Mauchley test of sphericity evaluates the hypothesis that the sphericity assumption holds (null hypothesis); if the test is significant, then reject the hypothesis of sphericity and declare the assumption violated. However, Monte Carlo studies (Rogan, Keselman, and Mendoza, 1979; Keselman, Rogan, Mendoza, and Breen, 1980) have shown the Mauchley test to be very sensitive to departures from multivariate normality; yet, even minor (non-significant) violations of the sphericity assumption can lead to erroneous conclusions in the ANOVA (see Bock, 1975; Box, 1954; Kirk, 1982). Therefore, the user is advised to always compute the multivariate statistics for repeated measures, just in case.

Analysis of Covariance

The following two options are only applicable when the design contains covariates and (in the case of *Adjusted Means*) between-groups factors.

Regression results. This option controls whether or not the regression results for the covariates are reported (click on this option in order to include regression results in the output).

Adjusted means. This option controls whether or not the adjusted means (adjusted for covariates) will be reported (click on this option in order to include adjusted means in the output).

Multivariate Analysis

The following two options are available when performing multivariate analysis.

Discriminant analysis. In multivariate designs with between-groups factors, a discriminant function analysis can be performed (see also *Discriminant Analysis*, Volume III for details concerning this procedure). This check box controls whether or not these results are reported. If requested, the program will compute the linear combination of dependent variables that results in the best discrimination between groups. The maximum number of those linear combinations (or *roots*) that can be computed

is equal to the minimum of (1) the number of groups minus one, or (2) the number of dependent variables.

Display sums of squares matrices. When this check box is set, the sums of squares matrices for the hypothesis and the error are displayed. When the design is between-groups multivariate in nature (multiple dependent variables), the rows and columns of these matrices contain the hypothesis or error *SS* for each dependent variable in the diagonal, and the respective sums of cross-products in the off-diagonal locations.

If the design is univariate but contains repeated measures factors with more than two levels, then when evaluating hypotheses involving those repeated measures, these matrices will contain the respective sums of squares and cross-products (*SSCP*) for the within-subject model.

Testing Specific Effects

Specify the effect that you wish to examine more closely. You can click on the *Output options* button to specify the detail of results that will be reported for the effect that you select here.

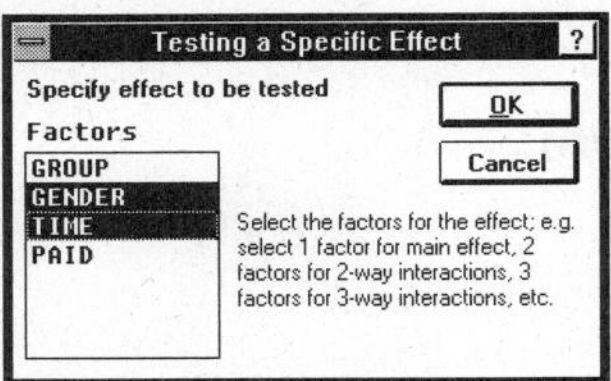

The rules for specifying effects are straightforward:

- To examine a main effect, select (highlight) the respective factor;
- To examine an interaction between two factors, highlight the respective two factors;
- To examine three-way interactions, select the three respective factors, and so on.

Note that you can select a discontinuous set of variables by holding down the CTRL key while clicking on the desired variables with the left-mouse-button.

Results for Covariates (Regression Results)

This dialog is only available if the design contains covariates and will be displayed when either of the following two cases occur:

(1) If the user chooses *Within-cell Regression* from the results dialog;

(2) If the user chooses *Regression Results* from the *Output Options* dialog, and then examines a *specific effect* (via the *Specific effect/means-/graphs* option).

Covariates and repeated measures. The results displayed in the two instances described above will be different if the design includes repeated measures factors. If the user chooses the option *Within-cell Regression* from the results dialog, then the displayed regression results pertain to the regression of the covariates on each variable in the dependent variable list, even though they specify *levels* of a repeated measures factor. In the second case (via *Specific Effect*), the regression results pertain to regression of the covariates on the logical respective dependent variable. If the covariates are *fixed* (*static*), then this logical dependent variable is always the *sum* across all levels of all repeated measures factors. If the covariates are *changing* covariates, then the regression results pertain to the regression of the respective orthonormal effect/error matrices for the covariates on the orthonormal effect/error matrices for the dependent variables.

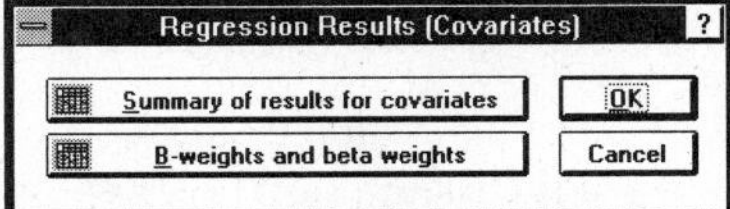

Summary of Results for Covariates

If there is only one dependent variable in the design, the univariate ANOVA table for all covariates will be displayed. In the multivariate case, the respective multivariate tests will be displayed.

B-weights and *beta* Weights

This option allows the user to review the raw and standardized regression coefficients (*B*- and *beta* weights, respectively) and their statistical significance, for each covariate and for each dependent variable.

Selecting Effects for Means (Interaction) Plots or Means Scrollsheets

When you click on the *Means/Graphs* button in the results dialog, the *Table of all Effects* dialog will open in which you can select the variables or their interactions to be included in either a plot of means or Scrollsheet of means (click on the *Graph* or *Scrollsheet* radio button in the *Display* option).

Table of All Effects

Design: 1-GROUP, 2-GENDER, 3-TIME, 4-PAID, 5-RFACTOR1

Effect	df Effect	MS Effect	df Error	MS Error	F	p-level
GROUP	1	16.47	23	3.8644	4.261	.0504
GENDER	1	.12	23	3.8644	.030	.8640
TIME	2	.85	23	3.8644	.220	.8044
PAID	1	5.47	23	3.8644	1.416	.2462
RFACTOR1*	1	421.78	24	4.9792	84.710	.0000*
12 *	1	17.63	23	3.8644	4.561	.0436*
13 *	2	21.14	23	3.8644	5.469	.0114*
23 *	2	19.36	23	3.8644	5.010	.0156*
14	1	1.50	23	3.8644	.388	.5394
24	1	3.87	23	3.8644	1.001	.3274

OK

Cancel

Display

Graph

Scrollsheet

Double-click on an effect to produce a graph of means or a Scrollsheet of means (depending on the current setting of the Display switch).

This dialog gives a summary of the analysis of variance so that you can decide which effect to look at; for example, you may only want to look at the significant effects which are marked with an asterisk (*). To select the desired main effect or interaction, click on the variable name or interaction to highlight it and then click *OK* to display or plot the means.

Display

Scrollsheet. When you select this option and click *OK* in this dialog, a Scrollsheet of the means of the highlighted interaction or main effect will come up.

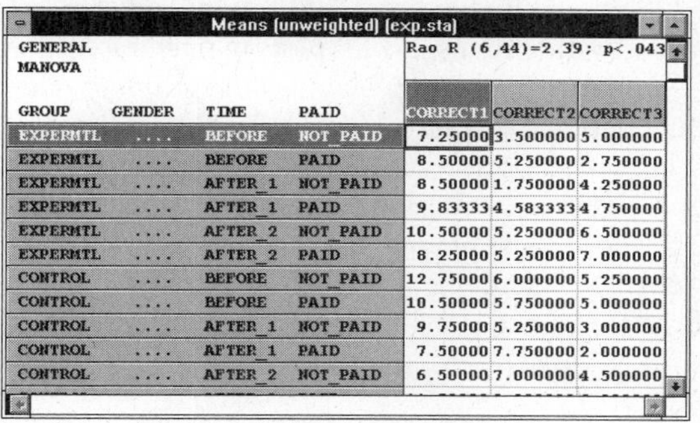

Means (unweighted) (exp.sta)

GENERAL MANOVA — Rao R (6,44)=2.39; p<.043

GROUP	GENDER	TIME	PAID	CORRECT1	CORRECT2	CORRECT3
EXPERMTL	....	BEFORE	NOT_PAID	7.25000	3.500000	5.000000
EXPERMTL	....	BEFORE	PAID	8.50000	5.250000	2.750000
EXPERMTL	....	AFTER_1	NOT_PAID	8.50000	1.750000	4.250000
EXPERMTL	....	AFTER_1	PAID	9.83333	4.583333	4.750000
EXPERMTL	....	AFTER_2	NOT_PAID	10.50000	5.250000	6.500000
EXPERMTL	....	AFTER_2	PAID	8.25000	5.250000	7.000000
CONTROL	....	BEFORE	NOT_PAID	12.75000	6.000000	5.250000
CONTROL	....	BEFORE	PAID	10.50000	5.750000	5.000000
CONTROL	....	AFTER_1	NOT_PAID	9.75000	5.250000	3.000000
CONTROL	....	AFTER_1	PAID	7.50000	7.750000	2.000000
CONTROL	....	AFTER_2	NOT_PAID	6.50000	7.000000	4.500000

Graphs. When you select this option and click *OK* in this dialog, a graph of the means of the highlighted interaction or main effect will be displayed.

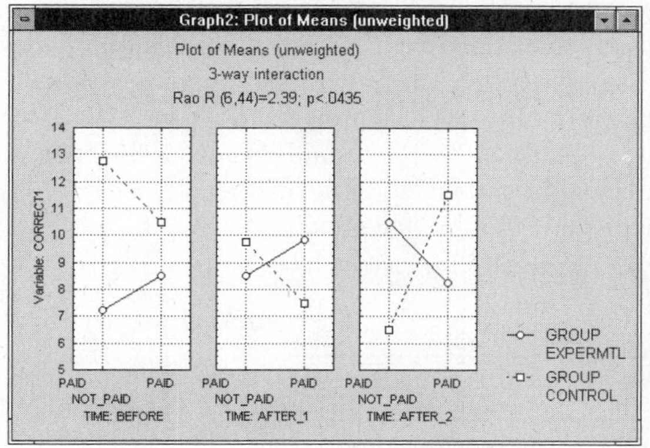

Assignment of Factors to Axes of the Plot

When plotting interactions (see *Means/Graphs*, above), you can control the assignment of design factors to the line patterns, upper *X*-axis, and lower *X*-axis in the *Arrangement of Factors* dialog.

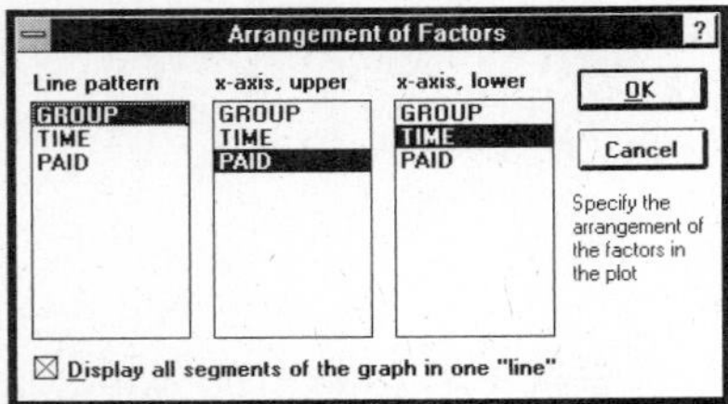

For a 3-way or higher order interaction, you also have the option to display all plots in one graph (select the *Display all segments of the graph in one "line"* option to display the plots side by side in one row) or not (de-select this option to display the plots in more than one row). However, if more than three factors need to be plotted, then the plot is produced in "chunks" within the levels of the other (not-selected) factors.

Post Hoc Comparisons

This dialog provides a choice of various *post hoc* procedures. You may refer to the *Introductory Overview* section (page 1705) for a discussion of the basic logic behind these tests. Discussions of *post hoc* procedures are also provided in Winer (1962), Hays (1988), or Milliken and Johnson (1984). The tests will be computed for the marginal means involved in the selected effect.

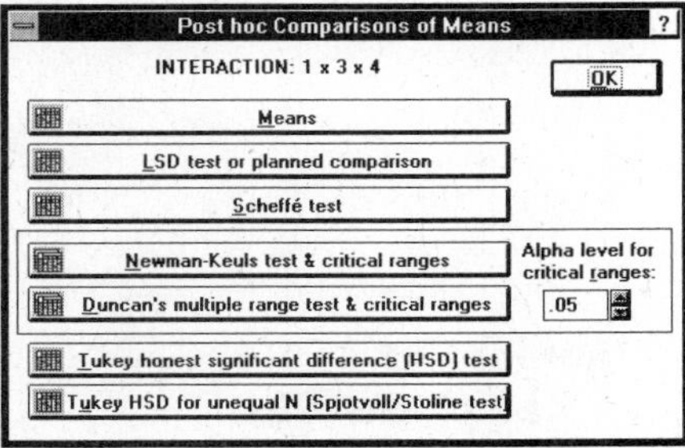

For example, if a main effect was specified, then the *post hoc* tests are performed on the marginal means for each level of the respective factor. If the *post hoc* test was requested for a 2 x 2 interaction effect then the *post hoc* tests will be performed on the four means of the 2 x 2 table that make up the interaction.

Choice of error term. The *post hoc* tests are performed based on the error terms from the respective overall analysis. Thus, *post hoc* tests for both repeated measures as well as between-groups factors can be performed.

Means

This option will bring up a Scrollsheet with the marginal means for the respective effect. As in all other Scrollsheets of marginal means in the *ANOVA-/MANOVA* module, these means can be plotted via the *Quick Stats Graphs* options from the right-mouse-button flying menu.

LSD Test or Planned Comparison

This test is equivalent to the *t*-test for independent or dependent samples (see also *Basic Statistics and Tables*, Chapter 9), based on the *n* in the respective cells of the design involved in the comparison. It offers the least amount of protection against the increased *alpha* error rate due to multiple *post hoc* comparisons. After choosing this option, a matrix of *p*-values will be displayed in a Scrollsheet. These *p*-values indicate the *post hoc* significance levels for the respective pairs of means.

Scheffé Test

This option will bring up a Scrollsheet with the *post hoc p*-levels for the Scheffé test. The Scheffé test is usually more conservative than the Newman-Keuls or Duncan test (see Winer, 1962).

Newman-Keuls Test and Critical Ranges

This test is based on the *studentized* range statistic. Computationally, the program first sorts the means into ascending order. For each pair of means the program then assesses the probability under the null

hypothesis (no differences between means in the population) of obtaining differences between means of this (or greater) magnitude, *given the respective number of samples*. Thus, it actually tests the significance of *ranges*, given the respective number of samples. Note that *ANOVA/MANOVA* does not merely report cut-off values for *p*, but will compute the actual probabilities based on the distribution of the *studentized range* statistics.

After exiting from the Scrollsheet which displays the matrix of *p*-values for pairs of means, the program will compute the *critical ranges* between ordered means, given the respective *alpha* level (by default $p<.05$). You can change this *alpha* level using the *Alpha Level for Critical Ranges* option.

Duncan Multiple Range Test and Critical Ranges

This test is based on the same logic as the Newman-Keuls procedure; however, it uses a less conservative test criterion (see, for example, Milliken and Johnson, 1984).

Tukey HSD (Honest Significant Difference) Test

The Tukey *HSD* test falls between the Newman-Keuls and Scheffé procedures with regard to conservatism.

Tukey HSD for Unequal Sample Sizes (Spjotvoll and Stoline test)

This test is a generalization of Tukey's test to the case of unequal samples sizes (see Spjotvoll and Stoline, 1973, page 975).

Descriptive Statistics and Tests of ANOVA Assumptions

When you click on the *Descriptive Stats & Graphs* button in the ANOVA/MANOVA results dialog, the *Descriptive Statistics & Graphs* dialog will open.

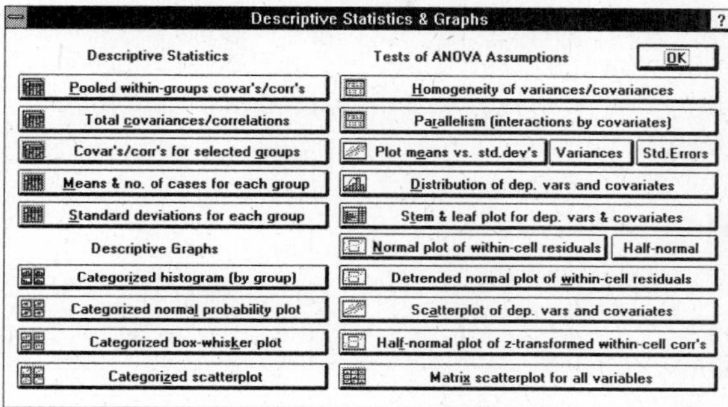

Descriptive Statistics

The following options are available under the *Descriptive Statistics* heading in this dialog.

Pooled within-groups covariances & correlations. Via this option you can display the pooled within-group variance/covariance matrix and the correlation matrix of dependent variables and covariates. First, the covariance matrix will be displayed, then the pooled within-group correlation matrix will be displayed.

Total covariances & correlations. This option will display the total variance/covariance matrix and correlation matrix of dependent variables and covariates.

Covariances & correlations for selected groups. This option is useful for examining the variance/covariance matrices for selected groups (cells in the between-groups design). After choosing this option the list of cells in the between-groups design will be displayed. From that list select the group for which to display the variance/covariance and correlation matrix of dependent variables and covariates.

Means & number of cases. This option will bring up a Scrollsheet of means for each dependent variable and covariate, and the number of cases (*valid n*) for each cell of the between-groups design. The overall means and total *n* are also reported.

Standard deviations. This option will bring up a Scrollsheet of standard deviations for each dependent variable and covariate and the number of cases (*valid n*) for each cell of the between-groups design. The overall standard deviations and total *n* are also reported.

Descriptive Graphs

The following options allow you to plot specific descriptive graphs. After you click on any of these options, a dialog window will be displayed prompting you to select the "effect" for which to produce the plot. The plot will be categorized by the selected factors, *collapsing* across those that were not selected.

Categorized histogram (by group). This option allows you to visually examine the distribution of values of the currently highlighted variable broken down (categorized) by the levels of the previously selected grouping factor(s).

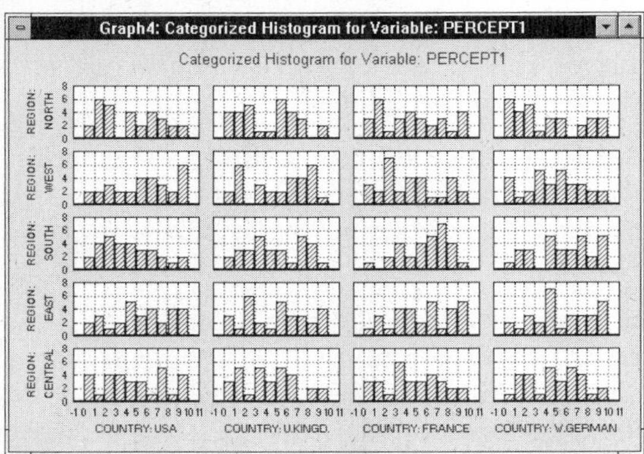

Categorized normal probability plot. When you click on this button, a plot displaying separate probability plots for each category of the previously selected grouping factor will be produced.

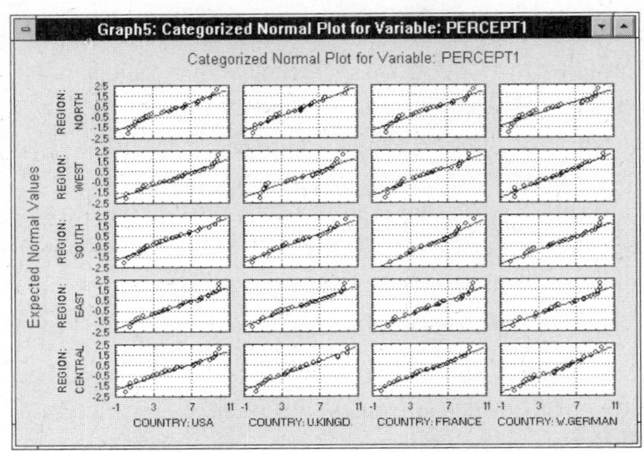

These categorized probability plots visualize the normality of the distribution of the currently selected factor categorized by the grouping factor. The assumption of normality (the data follow a normal distribution) is a very important assumption in statistics (see *Elementary Concepts*, Chapter 8), and normal probability plots are often used to visually verify this assumption.

Categorized box-whisker plot. You can choose one of four types of categorized box and whisker plots to represent the distribution of categorized values of the selected factor.

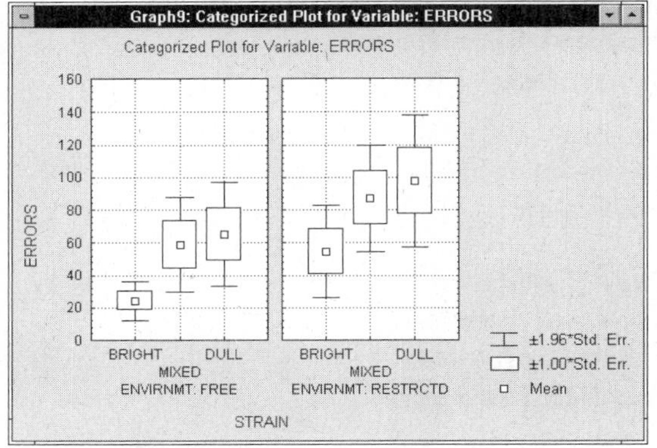

The box plots resulting from this option represent the selected factor's central tendency and variability for each category of the previously selected grouping factor(s). As measures of central tendency, you can choose between plotting the means and

medians of the values in each category and for each, their respective measures of variability; standard deviations or standard errors, and ranges in the *Box and Whisker Plot Type* dialog. (Note that the specific method of computation for the median and the quartiles can be configured via the *STATISTICA Defaults: General* dialog, accessible by selecting option *General* from the *Options* pull-down menu; see Chapter 3 for additional details; see also *Appendix II* for computational details.)

Categorized scatterplot. Click on this button in order to plot the values of one factor against the values of another, categorized by the levels of the grouping factor(s).

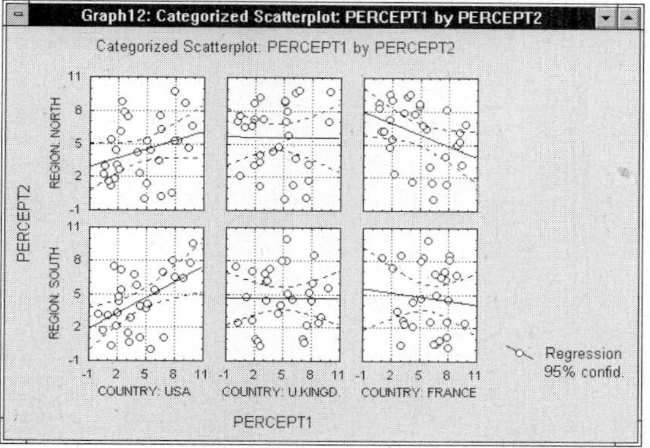

The *Categorized Scatterplot* visualizes a relationship between two variables *X* and *Y* (e.g., weight and height). Individual data points are represented in two-dimensional space, where axes represent the variables. The two coordinates (*X* and *Y*) that determine the location of each point correspond to its specific values on the two variables.

Tests of ANOVA Assumptions

The following options are available for testing specific assumptions. For more general discussion of these assumptions, see the *Assumptions and the Effects of Violating Assumptions* section (page 1710).

Homogeneity of variances/covariances. One of the assumptions of univariate ANOVA is that the variances are equal (homogeneous) across the cells of the between-groups design. In the multivariate case (MANOVA), this assumption applies to the variance/covariance matrix of dependent variables (and covariates).

Those assumptions, and the effect of their violation, are discussed in the *Introductory Overview* (page 1710). After choosing this option the *Tests of Homogeneity of Variances/Covariances* dialog will be displayed from which the user can choose a specific univariate (*Cochran C*, *Hartley*, *Bartlett*, or *Levene's test*) or multivariate (*Box M* or *Sen & Puri's Nonparametric test*) test.

Parallelism of regression lines/planes (interactions by covariates). One of the common assumptions of analysis of covariance is that the regression models in each cell of the between-groups design are equal. With this option, this assumption can be specifically tested. Basically, the test amounts to comparing the residual variance-/covariance matrices within each cell based on a common regression model (common *beta* coefficients) with the within-cell residual matrix based on separate models.

If there is more than one between-group factor, then the user can specify which factor(s) to ignore (i.e., which cells in the design to constrain to identical regression models), and which factors to include (for which cells in the design to allow for separate regression models). Put another way, the user can specifically test *interactions* of the covariates with the between-groups factors.

After choosing this option, if there is more than one between-groups factor in the design, an effects specification window will open. As the default, the highest order between-groups interaction is specified. Accepting this default will result in the test of whether or not there are differences in the regression lines or planes across any of the cells of the between-groups design. If there are multiple

dependent variables, both the univariate results (for each dependent variable) as well as the multivariate results (for all variables simultaneously) are reported.

Plot of means versus standard deviations-/variances/standard errors. These options allow you to plot the means for the dependent variables against the respective measure of variability (select either *standard deviations*, *variances*, or *standard errors*), across the between-groups cells of the design.

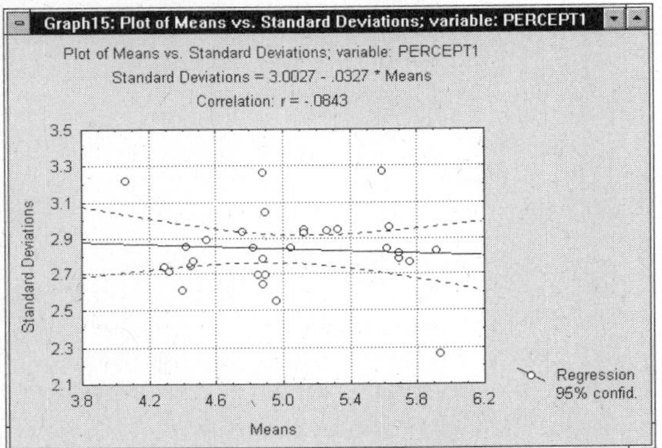

The section on *Assumptions and the Effects of Violating Assumptions* (page 1710) discusses how the overall F tests in the ANOVA table can be very misleading if the means are correlated with the variances. Briefly, if extreme (large or small) means occur in cells with larger variances, then there are usually outliers present in those cells. As a result, the confidence limits of the respective means would be much larger if estimated from those cells alone, while the overall ANOVA result makes those means appear more reliable, leading to statistically significant results. This happens quite often in actual research, and one is well-advised to produce this plot before accepting critical results. If the means *are* correlated with the variability across the cells of the design, one can:

(1) try to identify outliers and exclude them from the analysis,

(2) use nonparametric tests, or

(3) use transformations (such as a *log* transformation) on the data to "pull in the long tails" of the distributions with the larger variances.

Distribution of dep. variables and covariates. This option allows you to produce a histogram for the selected dependent variables and covariates, either for selected groups or all groups combined. First, a Scrollsheet with the observed distribution will be displayed; the expected frequencies under the normal distribution will also be reported in that Scrollsheet.

SEPALLEN; fit to Normal distribution: (irisdat.sta)

GENERAL MANOVA — Kolmogorov-Smirnov d=.06097, p= n.s.
Chi-Square: 15.653, df = 5, p = .0079

Upper Boundary	observed freq-cy	cumulatv observed	percent observed	cumulatv expected	percent expected	cumul. % expected	observd-expected
4.0	0	0	0.00000	1.6063	1.07087	1.07087	-1.60630
4.5	5	5	3.33333	7.5295	3.94883	5.01969	-.92324
5.0	27	32	18.00000	22.8546	10.21670	15.23639	11.67495
5.5	27	59	18.00000	50.6842	18.55308	33.78947	-.82962
6.0	30	89	20.00000	86.1636	23.65292	57.44239	-5.47938
6.5	31	120	20.66667	117.9213	21.17184	78.61423	-.75776
7.0	18	138	12.00000	137.8790	13.30511	91.91934	-1.95766
7.5	6	144	4.00000	146.6829	5.86928	97.78861	-2.80391
8.0	6	150	4.00000	149.4082	1.81688	99.60549	3.27469

In addition, the *Kolmogorov-Smirnov one-sample test* and the *Chi-square Goodness of fit test* will be reported.

Next the plot of the histogram will be displayed with the normal curve superimposed over the observed data.

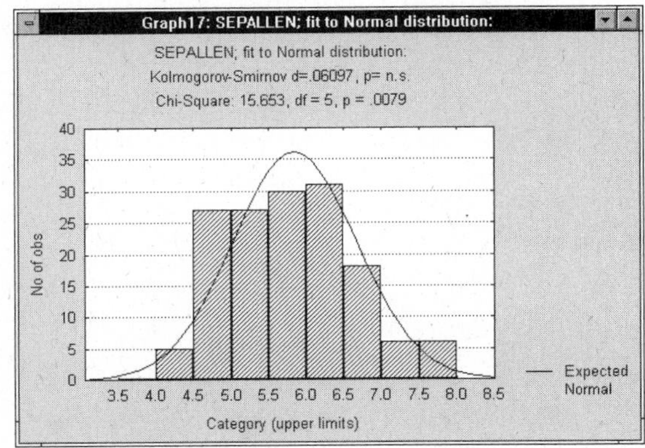

StatSoft

Usually only severe deviations from normality pose problems for the validity of the *F* statistic. Lindman (1974, page 32) discusses the impact of deviations from the normal distribution with regard to the *Kurtosis* of the distribution; after reviewing evidence from Monte-Carlo research, he concludes that the *F* statistic is quite robust in this respect. However, "odd" systematic shapes in this plot may be very useful for identifying outliers or multi-modality in the distribution.

Stem & leaf plot for dep. vars & covariates. This is an alternative to the histogram (above). Like the histogram, the stem and leaf plot can be produced for selected variables, either for selected groups only, or for all groups combined.

Stem and Leaf Plot (irisdat.sta)

GENERAL
MANOVA

stem°leaf (leaf unit=1.000000, e.g., 6°5 = 6.500000)	SEPALLEN one leaf=1 class n	percen-tiles
4°3444	4	
4°566667788888999999	18	
5°000000000011111111122223444444	30	25%
5°5555555666666777777778888888999	31	median
6°00000011111122223333333334444444	32	75%
6°5555566777777778889999	22	
7°0122234	7	
7°677779	6	
8°	0	

In this plot, each *stem* represents an interval, just like in a regular histogram. However, unlike in the histogram where a vertical "bar" is plotted to indicate the number of cases that fall into the respective interval, here the actual values are plotted as *leaves* of the stem.

Normal and half-normal probability plots. These options allow you to plot the within-cell deviations from the respective cell means in a *normal* probability plot (click on the *Normal plot of within-cell residuals* button), *half-normal* probability plot (click on the *Half-normal* button), or a *detrended half-normal* probability plot (click on the *Detrended normal plot of within-cell residuals* button).

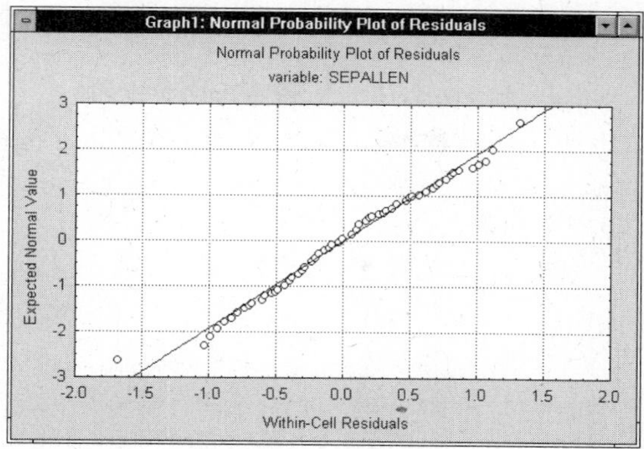

These options provide another "visual" check of whether or not the normality assumption is violated.

Scatterplot of dep. vars and covariates. This option allows you to compute scatterplots between any two dependent variables or covariates.

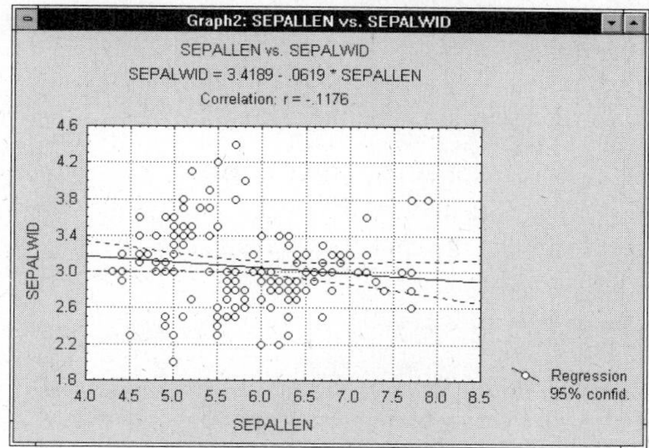

These plots can be produced for all groups (between-groups cells in the design) combined, or for selected groups only. The program will first prompt you to select the two variables for the plot, and then ask you to specify whether to produce the plot for a specific group or all groups combined.

Half-normal prob. plot of z-transformed within-cell correlations. This option is only available if there are multiple dependent variables or covariates in the design. It is useful for exploring the distribution of the within-cell (group) correlations between variables.

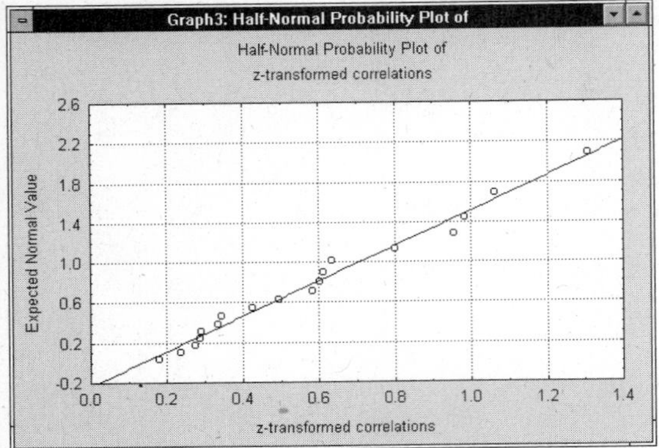

If the correlations are homogeneous across groups in the population (a MANOVA assumption), then you would expect the correlations to be normally distributed across the samples in this study.

Because correlation coefficients generally do not follow the normal distribution, the *z*-transformed correlations are used for the plot instead. The half-normal probability plot is constructed from those *z*-transformed within-cell correlations.

Matrix scatterplot for all variables. This option will bring up a matrix scatterplot for all dependent variables and covariates in the current design.

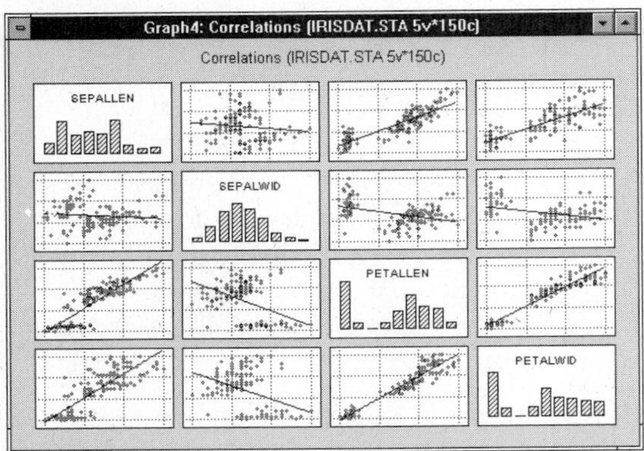

Selecting a Group for the Scrollsheet or Plot

This window lists all groups in the current between-group design. Select a group by clicking on it.

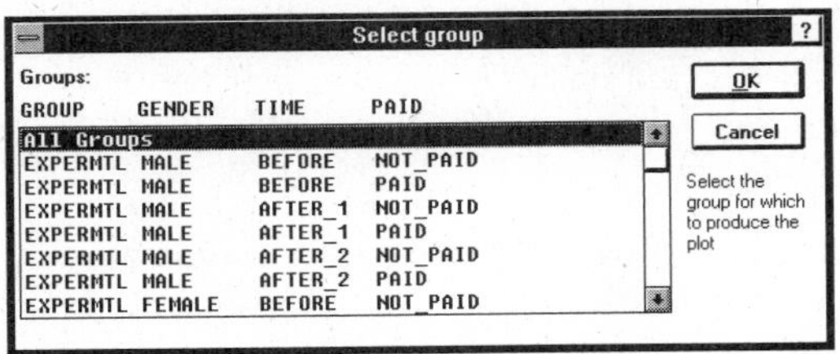

If you select the *All Groups* option, then the Scrollsheet or plot will be produced for all groups combined.

Tests of Homogeneity of Variances

One of the assumptions of univariate ANOVA is that the variances are equal (homogeneous) across the cells of the between-groups design. In the multivariate case (MANOVA), this assumption applies to the variance/covariance matrix of dependent variables (and covariates). Those assumptions, and the effect of their violation, are discussed in the *Introductory Overview* (page 1710).

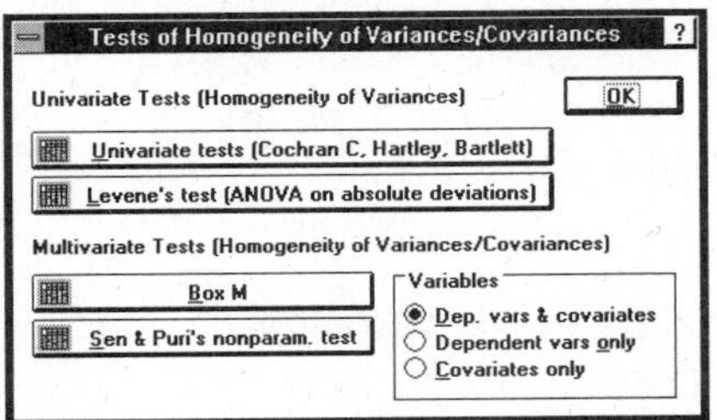

Univariate tests. This option will bring up a Scrollsheet with the *Hartley F-max* statistic, *Cochran C* statistic, and the *Bartlett Chi-square* test (with appropriate degrees of freedom and *p*-level). All of these statistics test the homogeneity of

variances assumption in the univariate case. If there are multiple dependent variables or covariates, the tests are displayed for each dependent variable and for each covariate. All of these tests are described in most standard ANOVA textbooks (e.g., see Winer, 1962, page 94). As described in the *Introductory Overview* (page 1710), the consequences of even quite major violations of the homogeneity of variances assumption are not that critical. Lindman (1974, page 33) summarizes the results of various studies of this issue, and shows that only under the most severe violations do you need to be concerned about the validity of the *F* statistic. It is, however, very important to examine any correlations between the means and the variances (or standard deviations; use option *Plot of Means versus standard deviations...* to look at those correlations).

Levene's test. *Levene's* test for the homogeneity of variances amounts to performing a one-way ANOVA on the absolute deviation scores (from the respective cell means). The logic of this test is that the greater the variance in a cell, the larger are the absolute deviations from the respective cell mean. This test is discussed in Milliken and Johnson (1984).

Multivariate Test Options

Box M. This is a multivariate test of the homogeneity of variances and covariances for multiple dependent variables or covariates. Use the *Variables* radio buttons to specify whether or not to include the covariates in this test. The Box M test is very sensitive to deviations from the normal distribution and its results should be viewed with some skepticism. If this test is significant, then it means that the variance/covariance matrices in the different between-group cells in the design are significantly different from each other (see Anderson, 1958). In that case, one should probably examine the within-group variance/covariance matrices for any *major* heterogeneity problems; however, violations of this homogeneity of variances/covariances assumption usually do not seriously threaten the validity of the multivariate results.

Sen & Puri's nonparametric test. This nonparametric alternative to the Box M test (Sen and Puri, 1968) has recently gained in popularity. In essence, the test is based only on the rank-order information in the data, and therefore it is not affected by deviations from the normal distribution. However, it is also not a very sensitive test.

Compress/Spread Stem and Leaf Plot

This option affects the number of intervals that is created for the stem and leaf plot. When you click on the *Stem & leaf plot for dep. vars & covariates* button in the *Descriptive Statistics and Graphs* dialog, a stem and leaf plot will be produced.

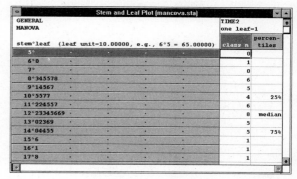

Stem and Leaf Plot (mancova.sta)

GENERAL MANOVA	TIME2 one leaf=1	
stem°leaf (leaf unit=10.00000, e.g., 6°5 = 65.00000)	class n	percen-tiles
5°	0	
6°0	1	
7°	0	
8°345578	6	
9°14567	5	
10°5577	4	25%
11°224557	6	
12°23345669	8	median
13°02369	5	
14°04455	5	75%
15°6	1	
16°1	1	
17°8	1	

When you click on the *Options* toolbar button and select the *Compress/spread plot* option, the stem and leaf plot will be compressed into fewer intervals (or if it has already been compressed, it will be expanded back to the original number of intervals). The stem and leaf plot shown below is a "compressed" version of the above plot.

StatSoft

Stem and Leaf Plot (mancova.sta)

GENERAL
MANOVA

stem°leaf (leaf unit=100.0000, e.g., 6°5 = 650.0000)	TIME2 one leaf=1 class n	percen-tiles
0°688888899999	12	
1°0000111112222222233333344444	28	median
1°5678	4	
2°02	2	
2°	0	
3°13	2	
3°	0	
min = 60.00000 max = 338.0000	48	

Pooled Effects & Error Terms

This dialog allows the user to build customized effects or error terms. In some cases, a researcher may want to perform a summary test of all main effects. Another common practice is to *pool* into the error term higher order interactions that are of little theoretical or practical interest. Via this method, a wide variety of incomplete designs (including Latin squares) can be analyzed (see below). Note that only effect and error terms involving between-groups factors can be pooled.

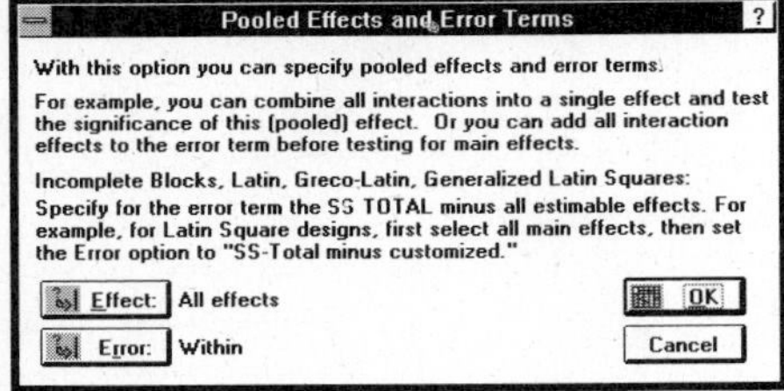

Effect

After clicking on this button, the *Between-Group Effect* dialog (see below) will open with all between-groups effects in the design. Select all effects that are to be pooled together in this dialog and then click *OK*.

Error

This button actually represents a switch with three settings: *Within*, *Customized*, and *SS-Total minus customized*.

Within. In the first setting, the standard within-group error term is used to test the pooled effect selected via option *Effect*. Click *OK* in this dialog (once you have selected the pooled effects) to complete the test.

Customized. In order to define a customized (pooled) error term, click on the *Error* button (while it is still on the *Within* setting) to open the *Between-Group Effect* dialog. Select in this dialog, the effects to be pooled into the error term (e.g., a 3-way interaction and the within error terms) just as in option *Effect* above, and after closing this window, the *Error* switch will be set to *Customized*. Click *OK* in this dialog to complete the test using the pooled error term.

SS-Total minus customized. Once you have selected the variables to pool into the customized error term in the *Between-Group Effect* dialog, click *OK* to exit the dialog and then click on the *Error* button to change the setting to *SS-Total minus customized*. In that setting, the error term used in the analysis is the total sums of squares minus the sums of squares attributable to the effects pooled into the customized error term (as selected in the previous setting of the switch). This latter setting of the switch is particularly useful for analyzing Latin square type designs or randomized block designs (see below).

Latin squares. To analyze a (univariate or multivariate) Latin square, Greco-Latin square, Hyper-Greco Latin square, etc., first define the design as if it were a full factorial design. Next bring up the *Pooled Effects and Error Terms* dialog and select the desired main effect to be tested (via option *Effect*). As the error term, select the sums of squares total minus all main effects (click on the *Error* button, select all effects, click on the *Error* button again to change the error term to *SS-Total minus customized*). This will result in the appropriate significance tests for the main effects.

Note that a comprehensive implementation of Latin, Greco-Latin, and Hyper-Greco Latin square designs is also available in the *Experimental Design* module (Volume IV).

Specifying Pooled Effects (Combining Effects)

Select the effects that are to be pooled together (combined).

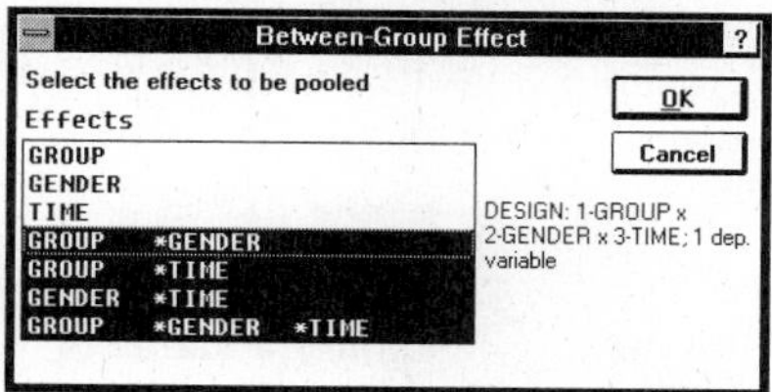

Highlight an effect in this dialog by clicking on it; highlight a group of effects by moving the mouse over them while holding down the left-mouse-button. To select/deselect individual effects press the CTRL key and click on the respective effect.

Order of Effects of Sequential (Type I) Sums of Squares

Type I sums of squares test effects sequentially, in a way similar to stepwise multiple regression (see page 1705; see also *Multiple Regression*, Chapter 12). All effects that were previously entered into the model are controlled for, and all effects not yet entered into the model are ignored.

When you select *Type I Sums of Squares* in the *Output Options* dialog and then click on the *All Effects* button in the results dialog, the *Order of Effects for Type I Sums of Squares* dialog will open.

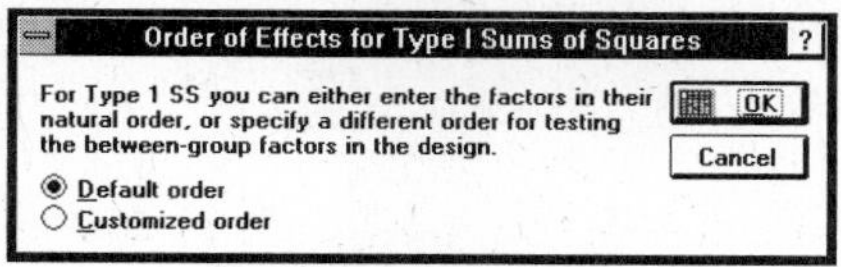

You can elect to test the effects in the default order (click on the *Default* radio button) or in a customized order (click on the *Customized* radio button, see the next section).

Reordering Effects for Type I Sums of Squares

When you elect to customize the order of effects for *Type I* sums of squares in the *Order of Effects for Type I Sums of Squares* dialog (see above), the *Order of Effects of Type I Hypothesis* dialog will open.

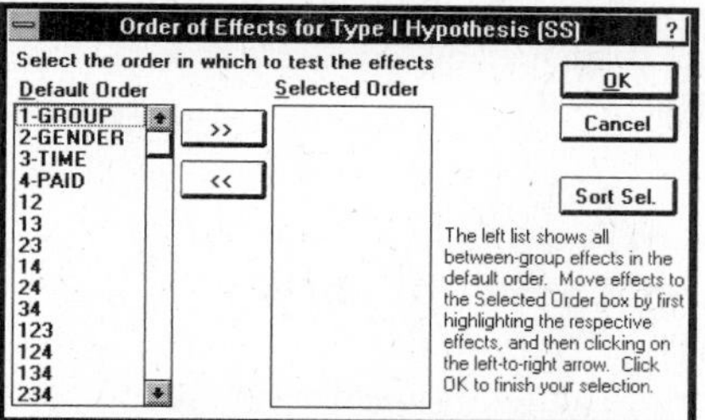

In this dialog, you can specify the order in which the effects are to be tested (entered into the model). The left column show the effects in the default order. You can select single or multiple effects in that column in the standard manner, that is, by clicking on them. Then click on the >> button to append the selected effects to the right column, which shows the order in which the effects will be tested (entered into the model). If you make a mistake, you can also move effects out of the right column.

You do not have to select all effects into the right column. After you click *OK*, all effects that were not selected will automatically be tested last, in the default order. You can click on the *Sort Sel.* button to sort the list of effects in the right column according to the default order.

Alpha Level for Table of All Effects

Enter the *alpha* error probability that is to be used for highlighting effects in the table of all effects.

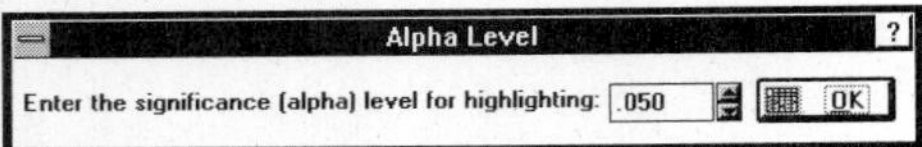

The default value for *alpha* is .05. This value is used as a "cut-off" for statistical significance (i.e., if the *p*-value is less than *alpha*, then the effect is highlighted in the Scrollsheet to indicate significance). In this dialog, you can edit this "cut-off" value ($.0001 < \alpha < .5$) and then click *OK* to immediately apply this change to the next copy of the current Scrollsheet.

Plots of Means/Interactions and Tables of Means

In order to produce a plot of means (interaction plot) or Scrollsheet of means (depending on the setting of the *Display* radio buttons), first select either a main effect or interaction by highlighting it (clicking on it). Then click *OK* to exit this dialog and display the Scrollsheet or graph.

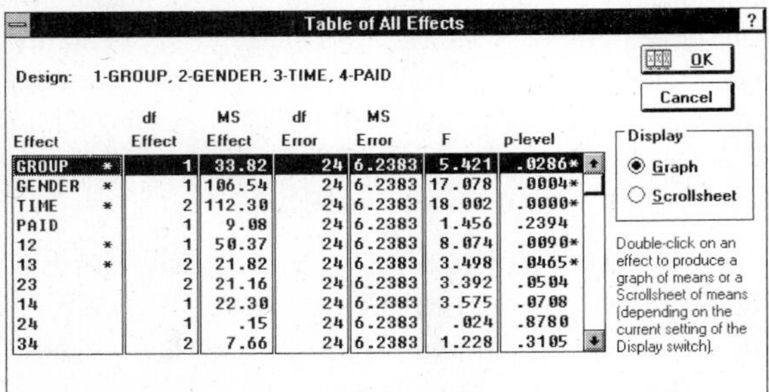

Table of All Effects

Design: 1-GROUP, 2-GENDER, 3-TIME, 4-PAID

Effect	df Effect	MS Effect	df Error	MS Error	F	p-level
GROUP *	1	33.82	24	6.2383	5.421	.0286*
GENDER *	1	106.54	24	6.2383	17.078	.0004*
TIME *	2	112.30	24	6.2383	18.002	.0000*
PAID	1	9.08	24	6.2383	1.456	.2394
12 *	1	50.37	24	6.2383	8.074	.0090*
13 *	2	21.82	24	6.2383	3.498	.0465*
23	2	21.16	24	6.2383	3.392	.0504
14	1	22.30	24	6.2383	3.575	.0708
24	1	.15	24	6.2383	.024	.8780
34	2	7.66	24	6.2383	1.228	.3105

You will return to this dialog after pressing *Continue* on the Scrollsheet or graph of the selected effect.

Options for Planned Comparison Facility

Contrasts can be entered separately for each factor, or for all factors combined (*together*, as a contrast *vector*); in multivariate designs the user can also choose to enter contrasts for the dependent variables.

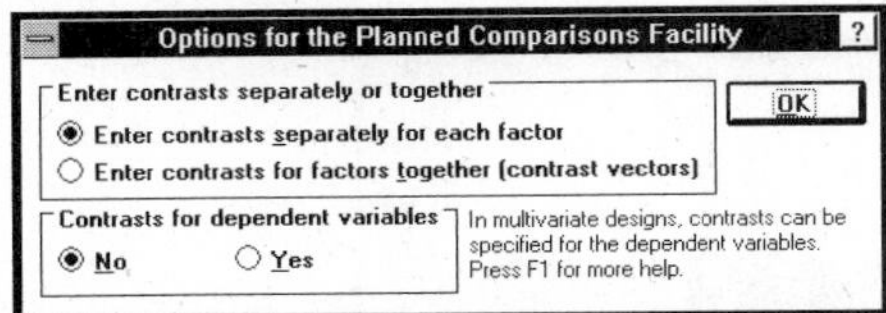

To learn more about the logic and interpretation of contrast analysis refer to the *Introductory Overview* section (page 1704); examples of how to specify contrasts are also discussed in the *Notes* section (page 1763), for between-group designs as well as repeated measures designs.

Entering Contrasts for Each Factor Separately

When you choose to enter contrasts for factors separately in the *Options for the Planned Comparison Facility* dialog (see above), and then click on the *Planned comparisons* button in the results dialog, the *Specify Contrasts* dialog will open. To specify a contrast for an effect in this intermediate dialog, first click on the desired effect and then enter the respective contrast coefficients in the *Entering Contrasts for this Factor* dialog. The currently specified set(s) of contrasts are listed under each factor.

Specify Contrasts

GROUP | GENDER | TIME | PAID

(1 1) | (1 1) | (1 1 1) | (1 1)

OK

Cancel

To specify a set of contrasts for these factors, click on the respective factor name (button) and enter the desired contrast coefficients.

To learn more about the logic and interpretation of contrast analysis refer to the *Introductory Overview* section (page 1704); examples of how to specify contrasts are also discussed in the *Notes* section (page 1763), for between-group designs as well as repeated measures designs.

Specifying a Set of Contrasts

When you click on the factor name button in the *Specify Contrasts* dialog (see above), the *Enter Contrasts for this Factor* dialog will open in which you can specify the contrast coefficients for the previously selected factor.

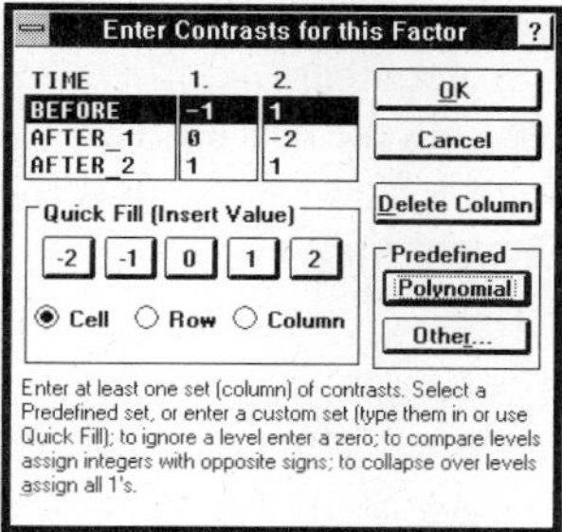

The general rules for generating contrast coefficients are given below (to learn more about the logic and interpretation of contrast analysis refer to the *Introductory Overview* section, page 1704, and the *Notes* section, page 1763).

(1) The contrast must have as many coefficients as there are levels for the respective factor.

(2) Levels that are to be omitted in the contrast are assigned a 0 (zero).

(3) Levels that are to be compared *against each other* are assigned positive or negative integer values; however, it is important that the sum of such contrasts is *equal to zero*.

(4) Levels that are to be collapsed are assigned identical integer values (e.g., all 1's).

If the highlighted factor has more than two levels, then several predefined sets of contrasts are also available, including contrast coefficients for testing orthogonal polynomials (trend analysis).

The size and layout of the *Enter Contrasts for this Factor* dialog depends on the number of levels in the respective factor (the maximum number of sets of contrast coefficients is *k-1*, where *k* is the number of levels in the current factor). For factors with many levels, you can scroll across both levels and sets of contrasts coefficients.

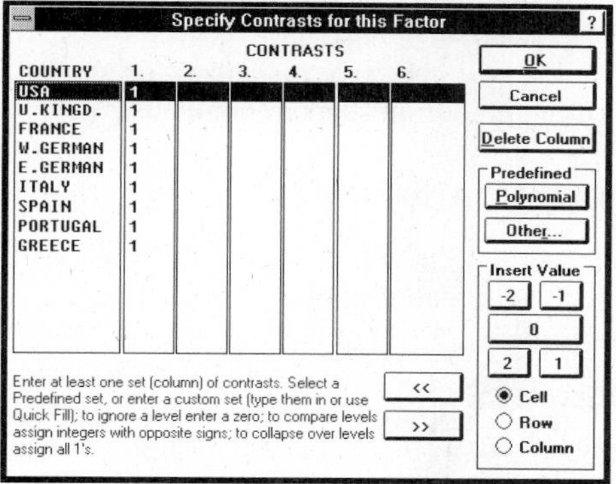

Quick Fill

The *Quick Fill* option allows you to quickly enter contrast coefficients. When you select *Cell* and click on one of the number buttons, the coefficient in the cell for the highlighted variable will be replaced by that number (i.e., only that cell will be replaced).

If you select *Column*, then clicking on one of the number buttons will replace the coefficients for all of the variables with the selected number (i.e., the entire column of contrast coefficients will be replaced with this number).

If you select *Row*, then clicking on one of the number buttons will replace all of the coefficients for a variable with the selected number (i.e., the entire row of contrast coefficients will be replaced with this number).

Predefined Contrasts

If desired, you can click on either the *Polynomial* or *Other* buttons under this option in order to select a predefined contrast (see the next section).

Predefined Types of Contrasts

When you click on either the *Polynomial* or *Other* buttons in the *Specify Contrasts for this Factor* dialog (see the previous section), then the respective *Polynomial Coefficients* dialog or *Predefined Contrasts* dialog will open from which you can select one of the predefined sets of contrasts.

Polynomial Coefficients

Select in this dialog, the degree of polynomial (up to a fifth order polynomial, if applicable) for the contrast coefficients.

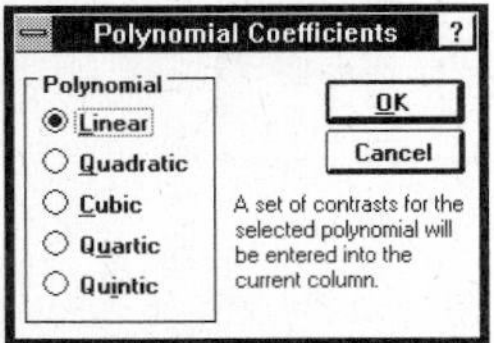

For more information on the polynomial contrast analysis, see the *Notes* section, page 1781.

Predefined Contrasts

You can choose from several predefined contrasts in this dialog.

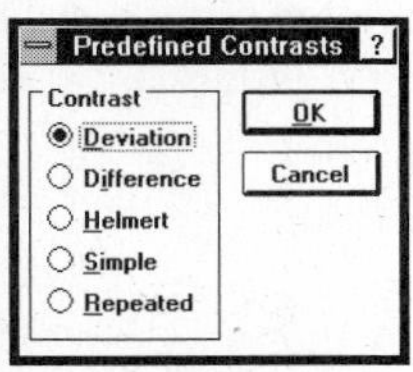

Deviation. This type of contrast compares the deviations from the grand mean of the dependent variable. For example, for a factor with 3 levels, the following matrix of contrasts would be created:

```
 2 -1 -1
-1  2 -1
```

Difference. This type of contrast compares the levels of a variable with the mean of the preceding levels of that variable. For example for a factor with 3 levels, the following matrix of contrasts would be created:

```
-1  1  0
-1 -1  2
```

Helmert. This is the Helmert contrast matrix (Kirk, 1982). For example for a factor with 3 levels, the following matrix of contrasts would be created:

```
 2 -1 -1
 0  1 -1
```

Simple. This type of contrast compares a preceding level of a variable with the last level of that variable. For example for a factor with 3 levels, the following matrix of contrasts would be created:

```
 1  0 -1
 0  1 -1
```

Repeated. This type of contrast compares adjacent levels of a variable. For example for a factor with 3 levels, the following matrix of contrasts would be created:

```
 1 -1  0
 0  1 -1
```

Specifying Contrast Vectors

When you choose to enter contrasts for factors together in the *Options for the Planned Comparison Facility* dialog (see above), and then click on the *Planned comparisons* button in the *Results* dialog, the *Contrasts for Between-Group Factors* dialog will open. Here, you can enter the desired contrast coefficients for the respective combination of treatment levels (cells of the between-group or within-subject design). Note that in this dialog, if there are missing cells in the between-group design, then asterisks are shown next to the respective rows. Only 0's may be entered for those cells.

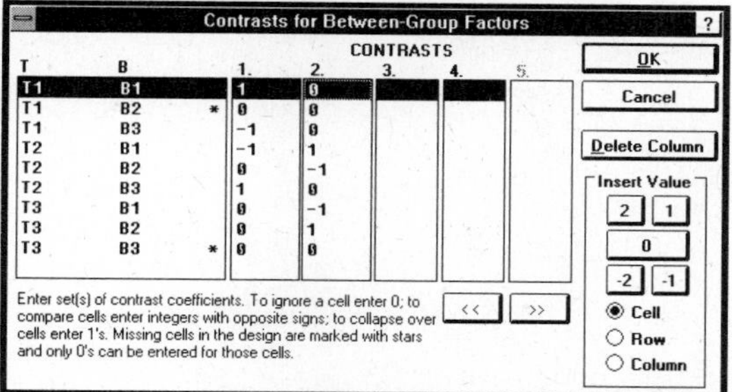
Contrasts for Between-Group Factors
CONTRASTS
OK
Cancel
Delete Column
Insert Value
Cell
Row
Column
Enter set(s) of contrast coefficients. To ignore a cell enter 0; to compare cells enter integers with opposite signs; to collapse over cells enter 1's. Missing cells in the design are marked with stars and only 0's can be entered for those cells.

The general rules for generating contrast coefficients are given above. To learn more about the logic and interpretation of contrast analysis refer to the *Introductory Overview* section (page 1704) and the *Notes* section (page 1763).

NOTES, PART I: EXAMPLE ANALYSES OF COMMON TYPES OF DESIGNS

Specifying Univariate and Multivariate Between-Groups Designs

One-way Between-Groups ANOVA and Contrast Analysis

Summary. *Between-groups* designs are ANOVA designs with several distinct groups of subjects (or observations). For example, one may use three different algebra textbooks, one in each of three classes, and subsequently measure students' performance on a standardized algebra test. The three classes would then represent three distinct groups, and if one wanted to compare their performance, a one-way between-groups analysis of variance would be specified.

Each group in this design was "exposed" to a different algebra textbook; thus, the type of algebra book used represents the *between-groups* factor. Because three different textbooks were used, this between-groups factor contains three levels.

Setting up the data file. When entering the data for this study, the user must create a data file with *at least two variables*. One variable should contain students' scores on the standardized algebra test. This variable is referred to as the *dependent variable*. Another variable that needs to be included in the data file should contain code numbers or text codes that uniquely identify the group membership of each case in the data file; this variable is referred to as the *independent* or *grouping* variable.

For example, one may assign the text value *Book_1* to a student if he or she was in the class in which the first algebra textbook was used; one may assign the text value *Book_2* if the respective student was in the class in which the second algebra textbook was used, and one may assign the text value *Book_3* if the student participated in the class in which the third algebra textbook was used. The resulting data file may look like this:

```
Independent      Dependent
variable         variable
-----------      ---------
  Book_1            23
  Book_3            48
  Book_3            26
  Book_2            27
  Book_1            43
  Book_1            39
  Book_2            30
  ...               ...
```

In this example, the grouping variable contains only the three different text codes that the user entered in order to code the between-groups factor. If a data file contains cases with numeric or text values for the grouping variable that were not specified in the list of valid codes, those cases are excluded from the analysis.

Note that when entering data into the file, it is not necessary to enter the subjects (cases) in any particular order.

Analyzing the design. In order to analyze these data, one would first click on the *Variables* button from the *General ANOVA/MANOVA* startup panel (page 1737), and specify as the between-groups factor or *independent variable* the variable number *1*. Then, variable *2* would be specified as the dependent variable. Next, one would specify (via the *Codes* button) the independent variable codes as entered in the data file.

Note that it is not necessary to explicitly enter into the codes window all integer codes representing the text values; you could also simply click *OK* at this point and let the program select all codes by default. After clicking *OK* the program will process the data and display the results dialog.

Testing planned comparisons. *Planned comparisons* are useful if one wants to compare specific groups in the design. The program expects the user to enter a *set of contrasts* that identifies the

desired comparisons. If, in the present example, one wants to compare the group taught with the first algebra textbook (i.e., group 1) with the group that was taught with the third algebra textbook (i.e., group 3) and ignore group 2 in this particular comparison, one set of contrasts would be entered, namely *1*, *0*, and *-1*.

Rules for generating contrasts. The rules for generating these contrasts are as follows:

(1) The contrast must have as many coefficients as there are levels for the respective factor.

(2) Groups to be omitted in the contrast are given a coefficient of *0* (zero).

(3) Groups that are to be compared *against each other* are assigned positive or negative integer values, respectively; however, it is important that the sum of such contrast coefficients is *equal to zero*.

(4) Groups that are to be collapsed in the contrast are assigned identical integer values (e.g., *1*).

For example, if one wanted to compare group 1 with groups 2 and 3 combined, the proper set of contrast coefficients would be *2*, *-1*, *-1*. If one wanted to compare group 2 against groups 1 and 3 combined, the proper contrast would be *1*, -*2*, and *1*. If one wanted to compare group 2 with group 3 (ignoring group 1), the proper contrast would be *0*, *1*, and *-1*.

Multivariate analysis of variance. The discussion so far has been restricted to univariate analysis of variance. However, if one selects multiple dependent variables on the *ANOVA-/MANOVA* dialog, then a multivariate analysis of variance will automatically be performed (unless the multiple dependent variables are specified to be levels of repeated measures factors).

For example, if in the previous example students' algebra ability had been measured with three tests rather than just one, the data file could look like this:

```
Independent     Dependent  variables
variable            1      2      3
-----------     ------------------
   Book_1          23     24     28
   Book_3          48     43     40
   Book_3          26     38     21
   Book_2          27     29     35
   Book_1          43     42     42
   Book_1          39     40     31
   Book_2          30     29     27
   ...             ...    ...    ...
```

In order to perform a multivariate analysis of variance (MANOVA) of the three test scores, enter *all three variables* into the dependent variable list. When subsequently testing the main effect or planned comparisons, both multivariate test results (for all dependent variables simultaneously) and the results of the univariate tests (testing one variable at a time) will be calculated.

The manner in which planned comparison*s* are specified is basically identical to the univariate case. However, when entering contrast coefficients for a planned comparison, the user also has the option to enter contrasts for the dependent variables. Click on the O*ptions* button next to the *Planned comparisons* button (see the results dialog, page 1742) and select *Contrasts for dependent variables*; the program will then allow you to specify contrasts for the dependent variables. For example, the user may choose to ignore some of the dependent variables in the comparison by assigning *0*'s (zeros) to them when specifying the contrast.

Multi-way Between-Groups ANOVA and Contrast Analysis

Summary. When an analysis of variance design contains more than one between-groups factor, the design is referred to as a *multi-way* or *multi-factor between-groups* design. For example, one may try three different algebra textbooks (between-groups factor number 1) and, in addition, evaluate gender differences (between-groups factor number 2). The dependent variable would be students' scores on a standardized algebra test.

Setting up the data file. In addition to the dependent variable (scores on the standardized

algebra test), *two independent* or *grouping* variables must be included in the data file. One independent or grouping variable should contain code numbers or text values that uniquely identify to which textbook group the respective subject belongs (i.e., which algebra textbook was used to teach the respective student); the other independent or grouping variable should contain code numbers or text values that uniquely identify the respective student's gender. The data file may look like this:

```
Independent variables    Dependent
  Text      Gender       variable
---------------------    ---------
  Book_1    Male            23
  Book_3    Female          48
  Book_3    Male            26
  Book_2    Female          27
  Book_1    Male            43
  Book_1    Male            39
  Book_2    Female          30
  ...       ...             ...
```

The first variable (column) contains the values *Book_1*, *Book_2*, and *Book_3*. This variable is the independent or grouping variable that uniquely identifies which algebra textbook was used. The second variable (column) contains only the values *Male* and *Female*. This variable is the independent or grouping variable that uniquely identifies students' gender. The third variable (column) contains students' scores on the standardized algebra test.

Specifying the design. The design that needs to be specified is a 3 (textbook) by 2 (gender) between-groups analysis of variance design. From the *ANOVA/MANOVA* startup panel (page 1737), specify variables 1 and 2 as the independent variables (between-groups factors), and variable 3 as the dependent variable.

Testing main effects and interactions. In this design, there are three effects that can be tested: The interaction effect between students' gender and the type of textbook used, the main effect for textbook, and the main effect for students' gender. If you use option *All effects* or *Means/Graphs* from the results dialog (page 1742), all effects will be computed. If you want to examine the effects in detail, use option *Specific effect/means* from the results dialog and specify the desired effect.

Testing planned comparisons. Planned comparisons are specified in exactly the same manner as in one-way between-groups ANOVA. However, instead of specifying a set of contrasts for just one factor, one has to specify sets of contrasts for each factor in the design.

In addition to the rules for specifying contrasts that were introduced in the discussion of one-way between-groups ANOVA designs (page 1764), it is also possible (and often necessary) to enter contrast coefficients that do not sum to zero (0). For example, in order to specify a set of contrasts that is equivalent to the test of the main effect of students' gender, one could enter the following set of contrasts:

For factor 1 (type of algebra text):

```
1    1    1
```

For factor 2 (gender):

```
1   -1
```

Thus, all levels of the first factor (type of algebra textbook) are given the same weight, whereas the contrast coefficients for the second factor contrasts males versus females.

There are many specific comparisons that may be "composed." For example, if one wants to test the main effect for the type of algebra text, but *only for males* (level 1 of the gender factor), one may enter the following set of contrasts:

For factor 1 (type of algebra text) the following two contrasts:

```
1    0   -1
0    1   -1
```

For factor 2 (gender):

```
1    0
```

The resulting *Specify Contrasts* dialog would look as follows:

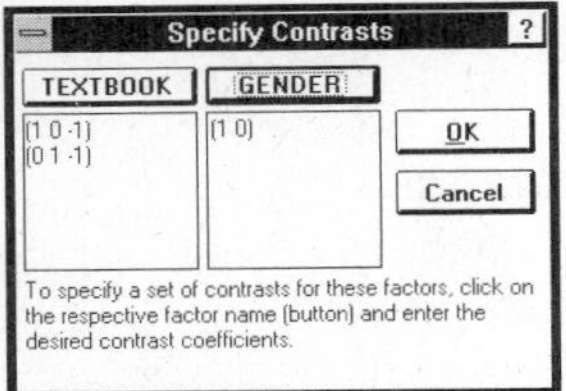

For factor 1, two independent contrasts were entered that will be tested *simultaneously*. These two contrasts represent an exhaustive set of contrasts, i.e., they simultaneously compare all levels of factor 1 (omnibus set of contrasts). For factor 2, one contrast was entered that assigns a zero to the second level of the gender factor (females). Thus, females will be ignored, and the resulting analysis is a test of the main effect of textbook, *for males only*.

In a similar manner, more complex contrasts may be specified in higher order (three-way, four-way, etc.) designs (e.g., interactions within one level of another variable). It is recommended to refer to a specialized ANOVA textbook (e.g., Lindman, 1974; Keppel, 1973; Winer, 1962, 1971) for more information on how to specify complex contrasts via contrast coefficients (e.g., simple effects, linear and nonlinear effects and interactions). Note that the dialog window for entering contrast coefficients also contains options for specifying appropriate predefined contrasts; of particular interest are the *Polynomial* contrasts (page 1760) which let you test linear and nonlinear trends across the levels of the respective factor.

Multivariate multi-way between-groups ANOVA (MANOVA). The specifications for a multi-way between-groups ANOVA with multiple dependent variables (MANOVA) are identical to those necessary for a univariate analysis. Independent or grouping variables must be specified which contain code numbers to uniquely identify the group membership of each case in the data file. If more than one dependent variable is specified for the dependent variable list, a multivariate analysis of variance will automatically be performed (unless the dependent variables can be interpreted as the levels of repeated measures factors). By default, univariate tests are also performed for each dependent variable in the list.

The manner in which planned comparisons are specified is basically identical to the univariate case. However, when entering contrast coefficients for a planned comparison, the user also has the option to enter contrasts for the dependent variables. Click on the O*ptions* button next to the *Planned comparisons* button (see the results dialog, page 1742) and select *Contrasts for dependent variables*; *STATISTICA* will then allow you to specify contrasts for the dependent variables. For example, the user may choose to ignore some of the dependent variables in the comparison by assigning *0*'s (zeros) to them when specifying the contrast.

Isolated ("Hanging") Control Group

Sometimes, experimental designs require the inclusion of control groups that did not receive any treatment. For example, imagine an experimental test of the effectiveness of two different drugs (factor 1) for treating infections with two different strains of a particular virus (factor 2). In the experiment, two groups of laboratory animals were infected with one of the two types of viruses, and treated with one of the two drugs. The primary dependent variable is the animals' performance on a learning task, e.g., after how many trials the animal learns to distinguish reliably between different geometric shapes.

In this experiment it may be desirable to compare the performance of the animals in the different experimental conditions with the performance of animals that were not affected with any virus and not exposed to any drug. Without this comparison, the experiment could be described as a 2 (type of drug) by 2 (strain of virus) experimental design. Adding to the experimental design a group of animals that were not exposed to any level of any of the independent variables means adding an *isolated* or *hanging control group*. The resulting design could be described as a 2 by 2 design with a "hanging control group."

Setting up the data file. The file containing the data from the experiment in this example should be arranged as follows (note that, for simplicity, the text values are not used in the coding variable):

```
Independent variables    Dependent
     Drug    Virus       variable
---------------------    ---------
       1        1            45
       2        1            29
       9        9            35
       2        2            38
       2        1            20
       9        9            26
       1        1            25
       2        1            39
       1        2            37
       1        2            34
       9        9            25
```

The first variable (column) contains the codes that identify which one of two drugs was administered (codes *1* and *2*). The second variable (column) contains codes that identify with which one of the two viruses the respective animal had been infected (codes *1* and *2*). *Both variables* also contain the code number *9*. This is the code number that was entered for both independent variables to indicate that the respective case "belongs" to the isolated control group.

In general, an isolated control group must be identified by *one unique code number* that is entered for *all independent variables* in order to identify that a case belongs to the isolated control group.

Specifying the design. When specifying this example design on the *ANOVA/MANOVA* startup panel (page 1737), one would first specify the 2 by 2 between-groups design as usual. As the independent variable codes, *1* and *2* would be entered. Then click on the *Isolated control group* button to specify the code number that was used to uniquely identify the cases that belong to the isolated control group (i.e., *9* in this example) is entered.

The test of main effects and interactions will proceed as usual, i.e., as if a simple 2 by 2 ANOVA design was specified. However, the sum of squares for the error term (and the degrees of freedom for the error term) will be estimated based on the four experimental groups in the design *and* the isolated control group (i.e., pooled within-group variance across *all* groups).

In order to see the mean(s) for the isolated control group, use the *Specific effect* option on the results dialog (page 1742) and select the test of the highest order interaction between the factors (i.e., the two-way interaction in the present example); after exiting the Scrollsheet with the means for the part of the design that is completely crossed, the program will display the mean(s) for the isolated control group.

Planned comparisons. To evaluate differences between the isolated control group and the other groups in the design, one must enter an appropriate set of contrast *vectors;* that is, rather than entering contrasts factor by factor separately, you must enter contrast coefficients for all groups *together.* Click on the *Options* button next to the *Planned comparison* button (see the results dialog, page 1742), and on the subsequent dialog set the *Together (contrast vectors)* radio button. Then select *Planned comparisons*; the isolated control group is referred to (i.e., "weighted") by the last contrast coefficient that is entered.

For example, if in the present example one wanted to compare the isolated control group with *all* other groups in the experimental design, the proper set of contrasts (entered as one vector or set, i.e., all coefficients are entered together) would be:

```
Factor 1, level:         1    1    2    2
Factor 2, level:         1    2    1    2
                         -------------
Enter these
Contrast Coefficients:   1    1    1    1    -4
```

If one wanted to compare the performance of animals that were treated with the first drug (level 1 of the first independent variable) with the

performance of animals in the isolated group, the set of coefficients would look like this:

```
Factor 1, level:            1    1    2    2
Factor 2, level:            1    2    1    2
                            -------------
Enter these
Contrast Coefficients: 1    1    0    0    -2
```

If one wanted to compare the performance of animals that were infected with the first virus (level 1 of the second independent variable) and treated with the second drug (level 2 of the first independent variable) to the performance of animals in the isolated control group, the set of coefficients would look like this:

```
Factor 1, level:            1    1    2    2
Factor 2, level:            1    2    1    2
                            -------------
Enter these
Contrast Coefficients: 0    0    1    0    -1
```

In general, when entering a set of contrasts all at once, the program will assign contrast coefficients to subsequent levels of factors; the fastest moving (changing) levels are those of the last factor that was specified, the second fastest moving (changing) levels are those of the next to the last factor, and so on. The coefficient that refers to the isolated control group is always entered as the last one.

Specifying Within-Subjects (Repeated Measures) Univariate and Multivariate Designs

One-way Within-Subjects (Repeated Measures) ANOVA

Often, one wants to administer the same test to the same subjects repeatedly over a period of time or under different circumstances. In essence, one is interested in examining differences *within* each subject, for example, subjects' improvement over time. Such designs are referred to as *within-subjects* designs or *repeated measures* designs.

For example, imagine that one wants to monitor the improvement of students' algebra skills over three months of instruction. A standardized algebra test is administered after one month (level 1 of the repeated measures factor), and comparable tests are administered after two months (level 2 of the repeated measures factor) and after three months (level 3 of the repeated measures factor). Thus, the repeated measures factor (*Time*) has three levels.

Setting up the data file. In order to analyze such a data set, one needs to perform a within-subjects (or repeated measures) analysis of variance. First, a data file should be created that contains the test scores for all subjects; this file should be arranged as follows:

	Test administered after		
	1 Month	2 Months	3 Months
Case 1	24	26	28
Case 2	30	30	32
Case 3	30	29	28
Case 4	30	29	34
Case 5	35	36	32
...	...	...	...

The first variable (column) contains subjects' scores on the algebra test after one month of instruction, the second variable (column 2) contains the respective subjects' scores on the algebra test after two months of instruction, and variable 3 (column 3) contains the respective subjects' scores after three months of instruction.

Specifying the design. In order to analyze this data set, one would first specify variables *1* to *3* as the dependent variable list (leave the independent variable list empty). Next, one needs to specify the repeated measures design. After clicking on the repeated measures button, specify one repeated measures factor with three levels (the default in this case).

Testing effects. Effects involving repeated measures factors are tested in exactly the same manner as in between-groups ANOVA. If a repeated measures factor has more than two levels, then there are two alternative ways of assessing the significance of effects involving that factor. The traditional way (see Winer, 1962, 1971) is to perform a univariate test; however, in recent years it has become common practice to use multivariate analysis of variance to analyze such designs. The advantage of the latter approach is discussed in the *Introductory Overview* section (pages 1701 and 1768); in short, the multivariate approach requires less restrictive assumptions. In practice, the two approaches usually yield similar results, *unless* the changes (differences) across the levels are correlated with each other across subjects. In this example, this would be the case if students' *improvement* from 1 to 2 months is correlated with their improvement from 2 to 3 months.

In any event, it is prudent to carefully evaluate the univariate *and* multivariate solutions. The second example in this chapter (page 1724) presents data where the univariate and multivariate approach to repeated measures ANOVA yield discrepant results; that example also discusses how to locate the source of the discrepancy.

Testing planned comparisons. The user can test planned comparisons between particular levels of the repeated measures factor in exactly the same manner as one would test planned comparisons in between-groups designs. After choosing *Planned comparisons* from the results dialog, the user is asked to enter a set of contrast coefficients.

The rules for generating contrast coefficients are as follows.

(1) The contrast must have as many coefficients as there are levels for the respective factor.

(2) Levels that are to be omitted in the contrast are assigned a coefficient of *0* (zero).

(3) Levels that are to be compared *against each other* are assigned positive or negative integer values; however, it is important that the sum of such contrasts is *equal to zero.*

(4) Levels that are to be collapsed are assigned identical integer values (e.g., *1*).

Referring back to the example, if one wanted to compare the students' performance on the algebra test after one month of instruction with their performance after three months of instructions, the following contrast coefficients would be appropriate:

```
1     0     -1
```

If one wanted to compare subjects' performance after three months of instruction with their performance after one and two months of instruction combined, one would enter the coefficients:

```
-1    -1     2
```

Example 2 in the *Examples* section (page 1724) provides an illustration of how to specify and interpret contrast coefficients.

One-way Within-Subjects (Repeated Measures) ANOVA with Multiple Dependent Measures (MANOVA)

If, in the example described above, one had administered two different tests of algebra skills at each time, it would be appropriate to perform a *multivariate* analysis of variance with repeated measures.

Setting up the data file. The data file could be arranged like this:

Test administered after					
1 Month		2 Months		3 Months	
Test		Test		Test	
1	2	1	2	1	2
24	30	26	34	28	28
30	32	30	28	32	34
30	27	29	28	28	33
30	28	29	26	34	35
35	25	36	27	32	36
..	..	..	..	..	..

In this example, the first variable (first column) contains the data for the first test that was administered after one month of instruction, the second variable (second column) contains the respective subjects' scores on the second test that was administered after one month of instruction.

The third variable contains the respective subjects' scores on the first test after two months of instruction, the fourth variable contains subjects' scores on the second test after two months of instruction, etc.

Specifying the design. In order to analyze these data as a one-way repeated measures MANOVA design with multiple dependent variables (two tests), all variables (i.e., *1-6*) would be selected into the dependent variable list (via the *Variables* button on the startup panel, page 1737). Then the *Repeated measures (within SS) design* would be specified as before, i.e., one repeated measures factor with three levels.

In general, *STATISTICA* will cycle through the list of dependent variables and attempt to divide it evenly. The assignment of variables to levels of the repeated measures factor is determined by *the order in which dependent variables appear in the dependent variable list*, not by the order in which variables were entered into the file. For example, imagine that the data in the above example were entered into a data file in the following manner:

Test 1			Test 2		
Test administered after month			Test administered after month		
1	2	3	1	2	3
24	26	28	30	34	28
30	30	32	32	28	34
30	29	28	27	28	33
30	29	34	28	26	35
35	36	32	25	27	36
..	..	..	..	..	..

In this case, the data were entered such that the first variable contains the scores for the first test after one month of instruction, the second variable contains the scores for the first test after two months of instruction, the third variable contains the scores for the first test after three months of instruction, the fourth variable contains the scores for the second test after one month of instruction, the fifth variable contains the scores for the second test after two months of instruction, and the sixth variable contains the scores for the second test after three months of instruction. When specifying the dependent variable list, the variables have to be "reordered," i.e., the user should enter *1 4 2 5 3 6* as the dependent variable list, in exactly this order. The *within-subjects design* can then be specified as before.

Multi-Way Within-Subjects (Repeated Measures) ANOVA Designs

Summary. In experimental designs, it is not uncommon to include more than one repeated measures factor. *Example 2* in the *Example* section (page 1724) describes such a study. For example, in a memory experiment one may compare subjects' recall of words that were presented at the beginning of a list of words, in the middle of the list, and at the end of the list (first repeated measures factor with three levels); in addition, the words either contained four letters or five letters (second repeated measures factor with two levels); finally, the words were either meaningful words in the English language, or were not meaningful (third repeated measures factor with two levels). The resultant design is a 3 (position of words) by 2 (length of words) by 2 (meaningful vs. nonsense words) ANOVA design where all factors are repeated measures factors.

Setting up the data file. Now, assume that the data were entered into a file as follows:

Rep. measures factor:	Level:											
1 (Position)	1				2				3			
2 (Length)	1		2		1		2		1		2	
3 (Meaning)	1	2	1	2	1	2	1	2	1	2	1	2
Subject 1	9	4	3	4	3	4	5	4	3	4	5	4
Subject 2	7	4	3	4	6	4	3	7	6	5	4	3
Subject 3	6	5	7	8	7	6	8	5	6	4	5	2
.	.	.	.	.	.	.	.	.	.	.	.	.
.	.	.	.	.	.	.	.	.	.	.	.	.
.	.	.	.	.	.	.	.	.	.	.	.	.

The first variable in the data file contains the data for the first level of all repeated measures factors. The second variable contains the data for the second level of the third repeated measures factor, and the

first levels of the first and second repeated measures factors, and so on.

Specifying the design. In order to specify the design for the example data, one would first select all variables into the dependent variable list, in exactly the same order in which the variables appear in the file (in this example the variables do not have to be reordered); i.e., enter *1-12* into the dependent variable list selection window. Then specify the *Repeated measures (within SS) design* as follows: Specify three repeated measures factors. First specify the factor *Position* with 3 levels, then specify the factor *Length* with 2 levels, and then specify the factor *Meaning* with 2 levels.

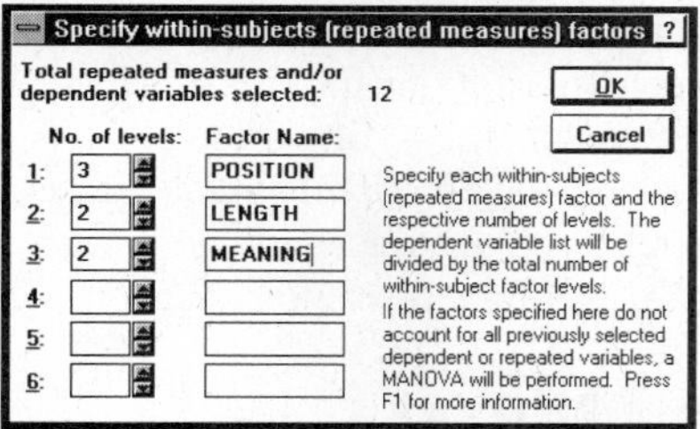

In general, the program will assign variables to levels of the repeated measures factors in the following manner: The program will "cycle" through the list of dependent variables and assign the variables to consecutive levels of the repeated measures factors. In this procedure, the fastest "moving" (changing) levels are those of the repeated measures factor that was specified *last*; the next-fastest moving (changing) levels are those of the factor that was specified *next to the last*, and so on.

When the program cycles through the list of dependent variables, the assignment of variables to levels is determined by the order in which dependent variables appear in the list of dependent variables (*not* by the order in which variables appear in the file).

For example, if a 2 x 2 x 3 repeated measures ANOVA is specified, the program would assign consecutive variables from the dependent variable list to levels of repeated measures factors in the following manner:

Rep. measures factor:	Level:											
1st Factor:	1						2					
2nd Factor:	1			2			1			2		
3rd Factor:	1	2	3	1	2	3	1	2	3	1	2	3
Position in the dependent var. list:	1	2	3	4	5	6	7	8	9	10	11	12

Note that the last row of numbers refers to the *position* of the respective dependent variable in the list of dependent variables (not the position of the variable in the file). Thus, when specifying complex multi-way within-subjects designs, there are two things that determine how variables are assigned to levels of the repeated measures factors: (1) the order in which repeated measures factors are specified, and (2) the order in which dependent variables are specified in the dependent variable list.

Examining specific effects. Specific effects (option *Specific effect/means* on the results dialog) are specified in the usual manner. Referring back to the example, in order to specify the three-way interaction between all three factors, click on the *Specific effect/means* button and select all three factors. In order to specify the two-way interaction between the first and the third factor, select those two factors. In order to test the main effect for the second factor, only select the second factor, and so on. Again, the user has the choice of computing the multivariate or univariate test (or both) when evaluating effects that involve repeated measures factors with more than two levels (use *Output options* to determine the detail of reported results).

Testing planned comparisons. Planned comparisons can be performed in exactly the same manner as in between-groups designs, that is, the program expects the user to enter a set of contrast coefficients. It is usually easier to enter these contrasts separately for each factor rather than together for all effects.

In general, the same rules introduced for the one-way repeated measures ANOVA apply when specifying contrasts for multi-way repeated measures designs. However, in addition it is admissible (and often necessary) to enter contrast coefficients for a factor that do not sum to zero (*0*). Referring back to the example of a 3 x 2 x 2 repeated measures design, if one wanted to evaluate the interaction of the second and third factor, but only for the first level of the first factor, the following coefficients would be entered:

```
Factor 1 (Position):  1  0  0
Factor 2 (Length)  :  1 -1
Factor 3 (Meaning) :  1 -1
```

The contrasts would appear as follows:

Repeated Measures Factors

POSITION	LENGTH	MEANING
[1 0 0]	[1 -1]	[1 -1]

OK

Cancel

To specify a set of contrasts for these factors, click on the respective factor name (button) and enter the desired contrast coefficients.

In this case, the second and third level of the first repeated measures factor will be ignored, and the interaction between factors 2 and 3 will be evaluated only within level 1 of the first repeated measures factor. If one wanted to evaluate the main effect for *Meaning* (third factor) within the first level of the first repeated measures factor, the following set of coefficients should be entered:

```
Factor 1 (Position):  1  0  0
Factor 2 (Length)  :  1  1
Factor 3 (Meaning) :  1 -1
```

Again, the second and third level of the first repeated measures factor will be ignored. Both the first and second level of the second repeated measures factor will be "weighted" equally, i.e., not contrasted against each other, while the two levels of the third repeated measures factor will be compared.

If one wanted to evaluate the interaction of the first two factors within the first level of the third factor, the appropriate set of coefficients would be:

```
Factor 1 (Position):  1  0 -1
               and :  0  1 -1
Factor 2 (Length)  :  1 -1
Factor 3 (Meaning) :  1  0
```

Note that in this set of contrasts, one has to specify two sets of coefficients (an omnibus set of contrasts) for the first repeated measures factor because the first factor contains three levels, allowing for two independent comparisons. A detailed discussion of contrast analysis and the issue of independence (orthogonality) is beyond the scope of this introduction. The user should refer to an ANOVA textbook (e.g., Lindman, 1978; Winer, 1962, 1971) for more information on how to set up contrasts to test specific hypotheses (e.g., linear and nonlinear trends, with equal or unequal spacing, etc.). Note that the dialog window for entering contrast coefficients also contains options for specifying appropriate predefined contrasts; of particular interest are often the so-called *Polynomial* contrasts (page 1760) which let you test linear and nonlinear trends across the levels of the respective factor.

Multivariate (MANOVA) Multi-Way Within-Subjects (Repeated Measures) Designs

As described earlier, the program will "cycle" through the list of dependent variables in order to assign dependent variables to levels of the repeated measures factor. If there are more variables in the dependent variable list than the total number of levels of the repeated measures factors, a multivariate analysis of variance will automatically be performed (see also page 1739). The program will assign the appropriate number of dependent variables to consecutive levels of the repeated measures factors. The number of dependent variables assigned is equal to the quotient of the number of variables specified in the dependent variable list divided by the product of the number of levels for all repeated measures factors.

For example, if one wants to specify a 2 x 3 repeated measures ANOVA with 2 dependent variables, then

the program would assign consecutive variables in the dependent variable list as follows:

Repeated measures factor:	level:											
First:	1						2					
Second:	1		2		3		1		2		3	
Dep. Var.	1	2	1	2	1	2	1	2	1	2	1	2
Position in the dependent variable list:	1	2	3	4	5	6	7	8	9	10	11\12	

Again, note that what is important is the *position* of the dependent variables in the list of dependent variables, *not* their position in the data file.

Between-Within Univariate (ANOVA) and Multivariate (MANOVA) Designs

Summary. In experimental research it is very common to administer different treatments to different groups of subjects (between-groups factors), and then to monitor a dependent variable over time or under different circumstances (within-subjects or repeated measures factor). This type of design combines repeated measures factors and between-groups factors into a single design.

For example, a researcher may infect laboratory animals with two types of viruses (between-groups factor 1 with 2 levels) and then administer two different drugs (between-groups factor 2 with 2 levels). Then the researcher may monitor the animals' activity levels 1 day after the drugs were administered, after 2 days, and after 3 days (repeated measures factor *Time* with 3 levels). The resulting design is 2 x 2 x 3 ANOVA design, where the third factor is a repeated measures factor.

Setting up the data file. To specify this design, the user must separately specify the between-groups part of the design and the within-subjects part of the design. For example, imagine that data were entered into a data file as follows:

	Variable:				
	1	2	3	4	5
Case 1	1	1	23	34	32
Case 2	1	2	40	43	45
Case 3	2	2	23	24	23
Case 4	2	1	54	34	54
Case 5	1	2	23	24	25
Case 6	2	1	34	23	34
.	.	.	.	.	.
.	.	.	.	.	.
.	.	.	.	.	.

The first two variables (columns) are the independent or grouping variables that uniquely identify to which experimental group the respective case (laboratory animal) "belongs" (to simplify matters, integer codes rather than text values are shown here). Variables 3 to 5 contain the dependent variables, i.e., the activity measures that were obtained after one, two, and three days. Thus, variable 3 contains the data for the first level of the repeated measures factor, variable 4 contains the data for the second level of the repeated measures factor, and variable 5 contains the data for the third level of the repeated measures factor.

Specifying the design. In order to specify the 2 x 2 x 3 between-within design, use the *Variables* button (on the startup panel, page 1737) to select variables 1 and 2 as the independent variables, and variables 3, 4, and 5 as the dependent variables. Next, select the independent variable codes for the independent variables; in this example, the codes 1 and 2 were used to specify with which virus the respective animal had been infected (independent variable 1), and with which drug it had been treated (independent variable 2).

The between-groups part of the ANOVA design is now completely specified. Next specify the *Repeated measures (within SS)* part of the design, that is, specify one repeated measures factor (you may call it *Time*) with 3 levels.

In general, one can specify between-within ANOVA designs of any complexity by separately specifying

the between-groups part of the design and the within-subjects part of the design.

Examining specific effects and testing planned comparisons. On the results dialog you may select specific effects (*Specific effect/means*) and *Planned comparisons* in exactly the same manner as in multi-way between-groups designs or in within-subjects designs. Between-groups factors and within-subjects (repeated measures) factors are listed consecutively.

Multiple Dependent Measures (MANOVA)

The *ANOVA/MANOVA* module will automatically perform a multivariate analysis of variance when multiple dependent variables are specified (i.e., dependent variables that are not levels of repeated measures factors). For example, if the user-specified a between-groups design with three dependent variables, a multivariate analysis of variance (MANOVA) with three dependent variables would automatically be performed. However, if in addition, a within-subjects factor with three levels is specified, then a univariate analysis of variance would be performed because the three dependent variables would be interpreted as representing the levels of the repeated measures factor. If six dependent variables were specified, then once again a multivariate analysis of variance would be performed, with 2 dependent variables for each level of the repeated measures factor.

In general, the *ANOVA/MANOVA* module will divide the number of dependent variables that are specified by the product of numbers of levels of all repeated measures factors. If the result of this division is greater than 1, then a multivariate analysis of variance is performed (if the result of the division is not an integer value, then an error message will be displayed).

For example, if a design is specified with 2 repeated measures factors, the first with 3 levels and the second with 2 levels, then at least 6 dependent variables must be specified (since there is a total of 2 x 3 = 6 levels). However, if the user specifies 12 dependent variables, then the program will perform a multivariate analysis of variance with 2 dependent variables (since 12 divided by 6 is equal to 2). In all other respects, the analysis of designs with multiple dependent variables (i.e., calculation of major effects and planned comparisons) proceeds in exactly the same manner as in the univariate case. However, when entering contrast coefficients for a planned comparison, the user also has the option of entering contrasts for the dependent variables. For example, the user may choose to ignore some of the dependent variables in the comparison by assigning *0*'s (zeros) to them when specifying the contrast. In order to specify contrasts for the dependent variables, set the respective button on the *Planned comparisons Options* dialog. Refer to page 1739 for more detailed examples of how to specify multivariate repeated measures designs.

Nested Designs

Simple Between-Groups Nested Designs

In some studies it is not feasible to implement a complete factorial design, i.e., a design where each level of each factor co-occurs with each level of all others. For example, suppose one wanted to evaluate the effects of 4 different fertilizers (between-groups factor 1 with 4 levels) on the growth of corn. Imagine that the researcher used two fertilizers on each one of two different fields (between-groups factor 2 with 2 levels). The resulting design would be a 4 (*Fertilizer*) by 2 (*Field*) design; however, because only two levels of the first factor occur within each of the two levels of the second factor, the design is actually a 4 (nested within factor 2) by 2 design. In general, designs are

nested when only some levels of a factor occur within the levels of another factor. In a sense, the levels of one factor are "placed" within the levels of the other factor like "eggs into a nest," hence the name "nested" design. To return to the example, the data for this design may be entered as follows:

Fertilizer	Field	Growth (dependent variable)
1	1	24
1	1	34
2	1	25
2	1	28
3	2	45
3	2	42
4	2	33
4	2	31

Now, assume that the researcher took two samples of corn from each field and measured their size (on some arbitrary scale). Each row in the data set represents the data for one of those samples. The first variable (column) contains code numbers that uniquely identify what fertilizer was used for the respective corn sample, therefore this is an independent or grouping variable. The second variable (columns) contains codes that uniquely identify the field from which the respective corn sample was taken; thus this is the second independent or grouping variable. Note that levels 1 and 2 of the first between-groups factor (*Fertilizer*) only appear *within* the first level (i.e., within level 1) of the second factor (*Field*), whereas levels 3 and 4 of the first factor only appear *within* level 2 of the second factor. Therefore, the first factor (*Fertilizer*) is nested within the second factor (*Field*).

Specifying the design. In order to specify this design, first select the dependent variable (variable 3) and the independent or grouping variables (variables 1 and 2) as usual in the startup panel (page 1737). When specifying the code values that were used to indicate the four levels of the first between-groups factor, enter *1-4*, i.e., specify the four values that were actually used in the data file. Next, click on the *Nested design* button. For each factor, specify (1) whether or not the factor is nested, (2) in which other factors the respective factor is nested, and (3) how many levels the respective factor has within the factors in which it is nested. In this example, the first factor is nested in only one other factor; namely, it is nested in factor 2. There are 2 levels of the first factor within each level of the second factor; therefore, enter *2* in the respective field.

Testing main effects and interactions. Because of nesting, interactions of the nested factor with the factor(s) in which it is nested cannot be evaluated. Thus, in the present example one cannot test the hypothesis that the type of fertilizer and the particular field interact in their effect on the size of corn. It is simply impossible to determine, based on the current study, to what size the corn would have grown on field 1 (i.e., level 1 of the *Field* factor) had the third and fourth fertilizer (i.e., level 3 and level 4 of the *Fertilizer* factor) been used.

Simple Within-Subjects (Repeated Measures) Designs

In some instances, one may want to analyze designs where a repeated measures factor is nested in other repeated measures factors. For example, one may administer to subjects 4 different memory tests (repeated measures factor 1 with 4 levels) over 2 days (repeated measures factor 2 with 2 levels). If 2 memory tests were administered on the first day, and the 2 remaining tests on the second day, one may consider the 4 levels of the first repeated measures factor to be nested in the 2 levels of the second repeated measures factor. In the present example, the data file may be arranged as follows:

Repeated measures factor:				
Factor 1 (Test), level	1	2	3	4
Factor 2 (Day) , level	1	1	2	2
Case 1	23	24	23	25
Case 2	25	23	25	28
Case 3	29	38	37	29
Case 4	48	47	48	47
...	..	..	..	..

The first variable (column) contains the data for the first level of the first repeated measures factor and

the first level of the second repeated measures factor. The second variable (column) contains the data for the second level of the first repeated measures factor and the first level of the second repeated measures factor, and so on. Note that in this example, levels 1 and 2 of the first repeated measures factor are only paired with level 1 of the second repeated measures factor, while levels 3 and 4 of the first repeated measures factor are only paired with level 2 of the second repeated measures factor; thus this design is a nested repeated measures design.

In order to specify this design (in the startup panel, page 1737), first enter all variables into the dependent variable list in the same order in which they appear in the data file, i.e., enter *1-4* into the dependent variable list selection dialog. Next specify the *Repeated measures (within SS) design.* First, specify the first repeated measures factor (*Test*), however, specify that this factor contains 2 levels; then specify the second repeated measures factor (*Day*) to contain 2 levels. At this point the program "does not know yet" that there are going to be nested factors. Consequently, it expects the number of variables to divide evenly by the total number of levels. If one were to specify the first factor as having 4 levels and the second factor with 2 levels, the program would expect to find at least 8 variables (total number of levels: 2 x 4 = 8) in the dependent variable list. Next, specify the nesting: The first repeated measures factor is nested within the second repeated measures factor, and it contains 2 levels within each level of the second factor.

Testing main effects and interactions. Testing for main effects and interactions in nested repeated measures designs is done in exactly the same manner as if a complete factorial within-subjects design had been analyzed. However, note that interactions between nested factors and the factors in which they are nested cannot be evaluated.

In the present example, it is simply impossible to know how subjects would have performed on the first and second memory test (levels 1 and 2 of the first repeated measures factor) had they been administered on the second day (i.e., level 2 of the second repeated measures factor); this study does not provide the information necessary to estimate such interaction.

Between-within designs. In designs that contain both between-groups and within-subjects (repeated measures) factors, one may specify nesting of factors both in the between-groups part of the design and the within-subjects part of the design. Note that between-groups factors can only be nested in other between-groups factors, and that within-subjects (repeated measures) factors can only be nested in other repeated measures factors.

Latin Squares, Greco-Latin Squares, Generalized Latin Squares

A general class of balanced nested designs are the Latin squares (see for example Hays, 1988; Lindman, 1974; Milliken and Johnson, 1984; Winer, 1962). An example of a Latin square design is also discussed in the *Introductory Overview* section (page 1701). In nested designs, the combination of treatment levels is arranged so as to yield unconfounded main effect estimates with a minimum number of observations. To analyze these types of designs, use the *Pooled effect/error term* option from the results dialog.

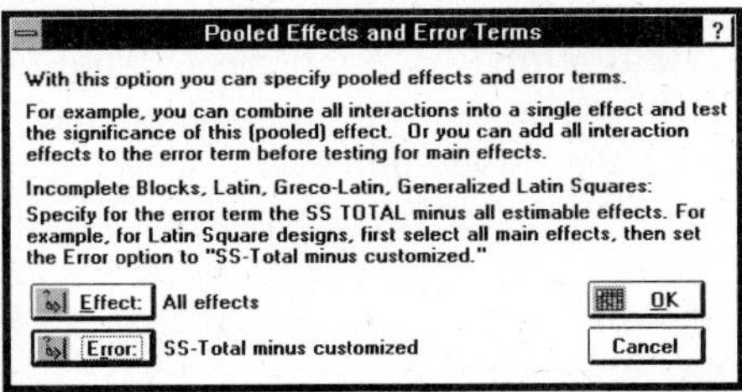

First select the desired *Effect* in the *Pooled Effects and Error Terms* dialog (or leave the default *All effects*). Next click on the *Error* button and pool all main effects into the error term; then click on the

Error button again to set this switch to *SS Total minus customized*. In this manner the selected effect will be evaluated against the *SS* total minus the *SS* due to all effects that can be estimated.

Other Special Designs

Designs with Cell *n* of 1

In some instances the observations for the study are not easy to come by, and costs are associated with obtaining an observation. Economic aspects then have to be weighed against design aspects. One way to design economical experiments is to select only single observations for different cells in the design. If the design is a full factorial design with an *n* of 1 in each cell, then estimating the sums of squares for all effects exhausts the degrees of freedom, and no *SS* error can be computed.

To analyze such designs, first compute the complete table of all effects; of course, because no *SS*-error can be computed, no *F* tests can be computed either. Then examine the reported Means Squares (*MS*; *SS* divided by the respective degrees of freedom). Their size is an estimate of the size of the respective effect. Use that information to decide which effects to pool into the error term (the small, non-significant effects). Usually, one discards higher order interactions in these types of designs. Finally, use the *Pooled effect/error* option on the results dialog to "build" the chosen error term and to test the statistical significance of effects. However, remember that the statistical significance tests here are not to be taken too "literally" because this procedure capitalizes on chance (only small effects are pooled into the error).

Randomized Block Designs

Sometimes, experiments with an *n* of 1 are designed deliberately in order to reduce the *SS* error, yielding a more sensitive ANOVA design. Specifically, the observations in the design can be arranged in blocks, in a manner that allows computation of an unconfounded main effect estimate of the blocking factor. The error term is then reduced by the *SS* due to the blocking factor.

Example. Suppose you want to test the yield of different varieties of wheat under three types of fertilizer. You have four different fields available for your research, and decide to treat them as an additional blocking factor in the design. The design could be summarized as follows:

		Field (Block)			
Fertilizer	Variety	I	II	III	IV
1	A	10.2	10.1	11.1	12.3
	B	11.1	9.8	8.6	9.4
	C	.	.	.	.
	D	.	.	.	.
2	A	.	.	.	.
	B	.	.	.	.
	C	.	.	.	.
	D	.	.	.	.
3	A	.	.	.	.
	B	.	.	.	.
	C	.	.	.	.
	D	.	.	.	.

In this example, the effect of the blocking variable itself is not of interest, that is, any significant differences between fields are of no theoretical interest. However, by estimating the *SS* due to the blocking factor (*Field*), you may be able to reduce the error variance, allowing for more sensitive tests for the effect of *Fertilizer*, *Variety*, and the interaction between the two. Also note that in this type of design one also decides to ignore any interactions of the blocking variable with the variables of interest.

Setting up the data file. The data file for this experiment is set up in the same way as one would set up the file from a regular full factorial between-groups experiment. The file should contain three grouping variables (*Fertilizer*, *Variety*, and *Field*) with codes that uniquely identify to which cell in the design each case belongs. The fourth variable in the file would be the dependent variable (*Yield*).

Specifying and analyzing the design. One would specify this design as if it were a regular full factorial design. When testing for the statistical significance of the effects of interest, use the *Pooled effect/error* option to build the appropriate error term for the test. Remember that the effects of interest are the main effects for *Fertilizer* and *Variety*, and the interaction between the two. In addition, the main effect for the blocking variable (*Field*) can be estimated. To specify the error term, first select to pool *all* of these effects together, and then click on the *Error* button again to set this switch to *SS-Total minus customized.*

Random Effects

Some research questions require the assessment of the significance of random effects. For example, one may want to test the hypothesis that there are significant differences in students' algebra skills across different high schools in the state (i.e., the high school factor would represent a random effect). Note that if one's hypothesis were more specific (e.g., algebra skills in rural high schools are better than in urban schools), then the high school factor would be a fixed effect. However, the hypothesis as it stands requires that one draw a *random sample of high schools* from the population of high schools in the state. Then a sample of students within each selected high school would be tested. Thus, each level of the high school factor (i.e., each high school that was selected into the random sample of high schools) does not represent a distinct level of the factor, but instead represents one possible level chosen from a population of levels, and one is interested in *generalizing* from the chosen levels to the population of levels (i.e., the hypothesis pertains to *any differences* between high schools in the state).

As a rule of thumb, a factor should probably be treated as a random factor if one would not choose the same levels of the factor for a replication of the study. In the present example, if you wanted to replicate the study, you would not test students in exactly the same high schools; rather, you would draw a new sample of high schools, that is, a new sample of levels of the high school factor. Thus, the high school factor is a random effect.

On the other hand, if you wanted to replicate a learning experiment where subjects had to memorize lists of either 10 words or 20 words (level 1 and level 2, respectively, of a between-groups factor) you would again expose subjects to exactly the same levels, i.e., to lists of 10 words or lists of 20 words. Thus, this factor is a fixed effect.

Please refer to ANOVA textbooks (e.g., Lindman, 1974; Winer, 1962, 1971) if you are not familiar with the distinction between fixed and random effects.

Comparing Experiments

Another example of when one may specify a factor as random is in comparisons across different experiments. Sometimes, one may want to compare the results of different experiments that used identical designs. In that case, it is advisable to treat the between-groups factor "Experiment" as a random effect, because one is interested in drawing inferences about the entire "population of experiments" that could have been performed.

Specifying the Design

In order to specify a random factor, first specify all (between-groups and within-subjects) factors. Then click on *Random factors* on the startup panel and select the factors in the design that should be treated as random factors.

Tests of Main Effects and Interactions

Main effects that are completely crossed with random effects have as their error term the interaction of the respective fixed factor with the random factor.

Technically, planned comparisons cannot be evaluated in designs with random effects (see Kirk, 1982). If you try to do so, the *ANOVA/MANOVA* module will issue a warning message to this effect and then proceed as if the design contained no random effects.

Fixed (Static) and Changing Covariates in Between-Groups and Within-Subjects Designs

In general, covariates represent continuous factors in the design. They are usually included in order to reduce the *SS* error term, resulting in a more sensitive design.

Fixed Covariates

The most common application of covariates is in between-groups designs, in cases when one has continuous variables that are likely to be correlated with the dependent variable of interest. For example, before beginning a special math training course, the IQ (Intelligence Quotient) of all participating students can be measured. Students are then randomly assigned to one of two courses, and their improvement in that course is measured as the major dependent variable of interest.

In this study one might suspect that the large differences in intelligence among participating students contributes a lot of "random" variability to the dependent measure. In fact, this variability (due to differences in intelligence) may be so large that it will "mask" the differential effectiveness of the two training courses. In that case, one could specify the IQ measure as the covariate. If related to students' improvements in the math course, the covariate may significantly reduce the error variance.

Adjusted means. When the covariate is not only correlated with the dependent variable *within* each group in the design, but also correlated with the between-groups factors themselves, then you need to adjust the means before interpreting any effects. A covariate can be correlated with the between-groups factors if it is affected by them.

For example, if in the above study you were to have measured IQ *after* the math training courses, then it is conceivable that the covariate (IQ) could have been affected by the different courses. In those cases, you will see that the inclusion of the covariate will not only affect the *SS* error term in the analysis but also *SS* effect terms for the between-groups factors. Also, the adjusted means (computed by the *ANOVA/MANOVA* module if requested via *Output options* on the results dialog, see page 1742) will be different from the raw observed means. When this happens, the inclusion of a covariate sometimes actually *decreases* the statistical significance of effects.

Contrast analysis. Many textbooks on ANOVA are somewhat "evasive" on the issue of contrast analysis in designs with covariates. In the *ANOVA-/MANOVA* module, simply specify contrasts as usual; because of the general computational approach used in the program, the results of contrast analyses automatically take into account the covariates. Note that, in effect, the contrast analysis is performed on the adjusted means.

Changing Covariates

These types of covariates can only occur in repeated measures designs (see pages 1701 and 1768). The general idea of changing covariates can be illustrated as follows: Imagine that, in a repeated measures design, you measure a covariate at each point of repeated measurement of the dependent variable. You can now ask two questions: (1) overall, is the covariate related to the dependent variable; and (2) are the *changes* in the covariate across the repeated measurements related to the *changes* in the dependent variable? The first question amounts to an analysis equivalent to that of fixed covariates. The second question requires that the *SS* for the

repeated measures design be adjusted by the respective covariates.

Computational approach. The *ANOVA-/MANOVA* module employs the general linear model approach to ANOVA. The adjustment of within-subjects effects for covariates is handled practically automatically. After the respective within-subjects hypothesis and error matrices have been computed, and before the final results statistics are computed, the hypothesis and error matrices are adjusted by the covariates. However, this procedure is multivariate by its very nature, and one should definitely rely on the multivariate test for repeated measures (and covariates) with more than two levels.

Note that the regression results for the changing covariates are only reported when requesting those results via *Output options* from the results dialog (page 1742), and then examining a *specific effect* involving the repeated measures factor. If you choose the option *Within-cell regression*, the within-cell (group) regression analyses are performed by treating each level of the repeated measures factor as a dependent variable.

Between-groups and within-subjects ANOVA. If the design contains between-groups as well as repeated measures factors, the results for the covariates regarding the between-groups model are the same as if you had analyzed the sum scores across all levels of the repeated measures factor.

Specifying changing covariates. The logic of specifying changing covariates follows exactly that of specifying repeated measures factors (see pages 1701 and 1768). The program will cycle through the list of covariates (entered via option *Covariates* on the startup panel) and assign the successive levels of repeated measures factors to the variables. As is the case when specifying repeated measures factors, the fastest-changing levels are those of the repeated measures factor specified last; the next-fastest changing levels are those of the repeated measures factor specified next to the last, etc. If there are multiple changing covariates, then the fastest-changing factor is the covariate number ("adjacent" variables in the list of covariates will be treated as "belonging" to different covariates).

For example, suppose you had two tests that were measured at three times (month 1, 2, and 3), and you wanted to specify the two tests as changing covariates. Imagine the data for the covariates were entered in the file as follows:

```
         Test administered after
------------------------------------
1 Month        2 Months        3 Months
--------       --------        --------
  Test           Test            Test
 1     2        1     2         1     2
--    --       --    --        --    --
24    30       26    34        28    28
30    32       30    28        32    34
30    27       29    28        28    33
30    28       29    26        34    35
35    25       36    27        32    36
..    ..       ..    ..        ..    ..
```

Specify the list of covariates in this order. (Of course, you also need to specify the within-subjects model as a single factor, three-level repeated measures design.) Upon exiting the startup panel, you will be prompted to specify whether this list represents a set of fixed covariates or changing covariates.

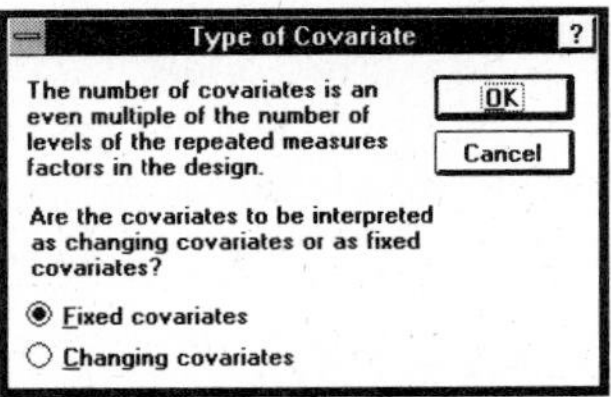

If you select *Changing*, then the list of covariates will be interpreted as intended, that is, in this example, as two changing covariates. Note that the question concerning the nature of the covariate will only appear if the number of specified covariates can be divided evenly by the total number of repeated measurements; otherwise, the list of covariates can of course not be interpreted in any other way but as fixed covariates.

Polynomial Contrast Analysis

Because the user may specify contrast coefficients for all factors in a design, it is very easy to test for polynomial (linear, nonlinear) trends (main effects, interactions) across levels of factors. *STATISTICA* provides a fast and easy way to specify the polynomial contrast by selecting one from a dialog. When you select the *Planned Comparisons* option in the results dialog, you can click on the *Polynomial* button in the *Specify Contrasts for this Factor* dialog and select a predefined polynomial contrast.

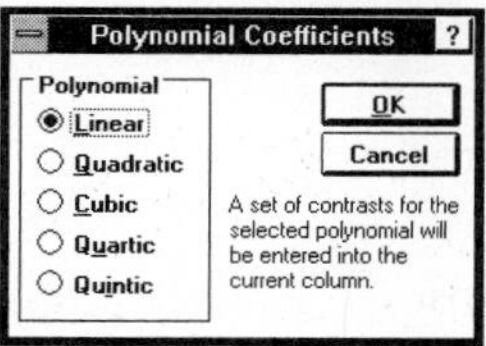

Presented below is a table of contrast coefficients that may be used for factors with up to 10 levels.

Lev-els	Poly-nomial	Coefficients									
3	Linear	-1	0	1							
	Quadratic	1	-2	1							
4	Linear	-3	-1	1	3						
	Quadratic	1	-1	-1	1						
	Cubic	-1	3	-3	1						
5	Linear	-2	-1	0	1	2					
	Quadratic	2	-1	-2	-1	2					
	Cubic	-1	2	0	-2	1					
	Quartic	1	-4	6	-4	1					
6	Linear	-5	-3	-1	1	3	5				
	Quadratic	5	-1	-4	-4	-1	5				
	Cubic	-5	7	4	-4	-7	5				
	Quartic	1	-3	2	2	-3	1				
	Quintic	-1	5	-10	10	-5	1				
7	Linear	-3	-2	-1	0	1	2	3			
	Quadratic	5	0	-3	-4	-3	0	5			
	Cubic	-1	1	1	0	-1	-1	1			
	Quartic	3	-7	1	6	1	-7	3			
	Quintic	-1	4	-5	0	5	-4	1			
8	Linear	-7	-5	-3	-1	1	3	5	7		
	Quadratic	7	1	-3	-5	-5	-3	1	7		
	Cubic	-7	5	7	3	-3	-7	-5	7		
	Quartic	7	-13	-3	9	9	-3	-13	7		
	Quintic	-7	23	-17	-15	15	17	-23	7		
9	Linear	-4	-3	-2	-1	0	1	2	3	4	
	Quadratic	28	7	-8	-17	-20	-17	-8	7	28	
	Cubic	-14	7	13	9	0	-9	-13	-7	14	
	Quartic	14	-21	-11	9	18	9	-11	-21	14	
	Quintic	-4	11	-4	-9	0	9	4	-11	4	
10	Linear	-9	-7	-5	-3	-1	1	3	5	7	9
	Quadratic	6	2	-1	-3	-4	-4	-3	-1	2	6
	Cubic	-42	14	35	31	12	-12	-31	-35	-14	42
	Quartic	18	-22	-17	3	18	18	3	-17	-22	18
	Quintic	-6	14	-1	-11	-6	6	11	1	-14	6

If you desire, you may enter these polynomial contrast coefficients in any combination with other sets of contrasts in complex contrast analyses. For example, tests for polynomial trends can be performed for a selected subset of a design or they can be included as part of a complex polynomial interaction comparison.

NOTES, PART II: EXAMPLE ANALYSES OF UNBALANCED AND INCOMPLETE ANOVA DESIGNS

The following examples will illustrate how to analyze different unbalanced and incomplete designs. Excellent sources that discuss the issues involved in the analyses of such designs are Dodge (1985), Lindman (1974), Milliken and Johnson (1984), and Searle (1987), and you are strongly encouraged to consult those sources before designing complex experiments.

Example 1: Unbalanced Designs and Type I and II Sums of Squares

Milliken and Johnson (1984, page 129) discuss in some detail the analysis of a 2 x 3 unbalanced between-group design. The data file *Twoway.sta* is shown in the spreadsheet below.

Data: TWOWAY.

Unbalanced two-way d

	1 T	2 B	3 DV
1	T1	B1	19
2	T1	B1	20
3	T1	B1	21
4	T1	B2	24
5	T1	B2	26
6	T1	B3	22
7	T1	B3	25
8	T1	B3	25
9	T2	B1	25
10	T2	B1	27
11	T2	B2	21
12	T2	B2	24
13	T2	B2	24
14	T2	B3	31
15	T2	B3	32
16	T2	B3	33

This design is unbalanced because cells *T1,B2* and *T2,B1* have two observations (cases), while the remaining cells have 3 observations. In Chapter 10 of their book, Milliken and Johnson discuss the computation and interpretation of *Type I*, *II*, and *III* sums of squares for the factors and their interactions.

To obtain the results reported in Milliken and Johnson, first open the data file *Twoway.sta* and specify variables *T* and *B* as the independent variables, and variable *DV* as the dependent variable. Also, set the *Regression Approach* option on the *ANOVA* results dialog.

Now, click *OK* to begin the analysis (*STATISTICA* will automatically select the codes for the independent variables). To compute the *Type I* analysis of variance table, click on the *Output options* button and in the resulting dialog select the *Type I (sequential SS)* option.

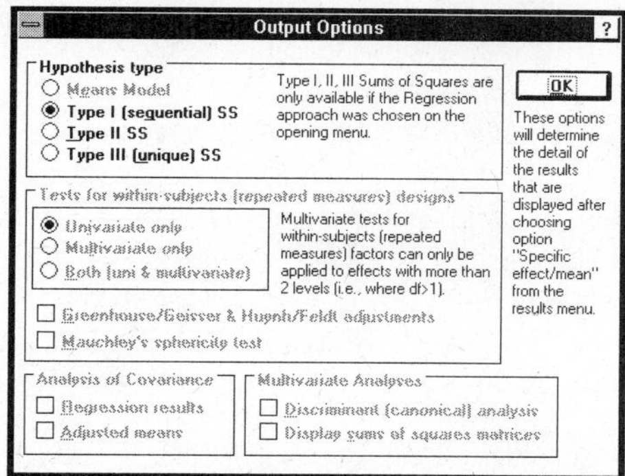

Click *OK* in this dialog and then in the *ANOVA* results dialog, click on the *All effects* button. The *Order of Effects for Type I Sums of Squares* dialog will open in which you can select the order of the between-group factors in the design. For this example, select the *Default order*.

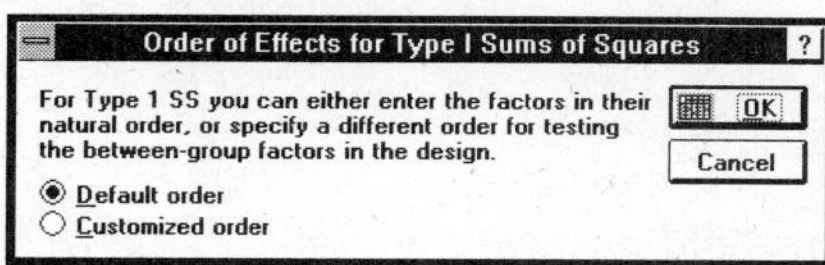

Click *OK* to display the *Type I* analysis of variance table of all effects.

StatSoft

Summary of all Effects (Type I SS); design: (twoway.sta)

GENERAL MANOVA — 1-T, 2-B

Effect	df Effect	MS Effect	df Error	MS Error	F	p-level
1	1	76.56250	10	2.000000	38.28125	.000103
2	2	45.37212	10	2.000000	22.68606	.000192
12	2	35.81538	10	2.000000	17.90769	.000495

Type I sums of squares and the option *Specific effect/means/graphs*. When you use the *Specific effect/means/graphs* option in the *ANOVA Results* dialog after requesting a *Type I* analysis, then the respective effect is (logically) entered into the model after all lower-order effects were entered, but before any other effect of the same or higher order was entered. Thus, the respective effect is tested after controlling for all lower-order effects, and ignoring all effects of the same or higher order.

Example 2: A Simple Nested Design

Now consider a simple nested design. Lindman (1974, page 167) discusses a two-way nested design where factor *A* has three levels, and factor *B* has six levels, with two levels each nested in each level of factor *A*.

The structure of this design can be summarized as follows (the X's indicate the observed treatment combinations):

```
Factor B          Factor A
                  1    2    3
-------------------------------
   1              x
   2              x
   3                   x
   4                   x
   5                        x
   6                        x
```

As you can see, there are actually only 6 experimental groups in this design, while the full factorial design would require 18 groups. In this design, you can estimate the main effects for the two factors, which will be unconfounded if there is no interaction between the factors (something you must *assume* since you can only explicitly test the interaction in a complete design).

The data presented in Lindman were entered into the data file *Nested3.sta*, and are shown below.

Data: NESTED3.STA 3v * 18 — A simple nested design: See Linden

	1 A	2 B	3 DV
1	A1	B1	20
2	A1	B1	18
3	A1	B1	14
4	A1	B2	19
5	A1	B2	20
6	A1	B2	20
7	A2	B3	14
8	A2	B3	18
9	A2	B3	14
10	A2	B4	12

To analyze this design, in the *General ANOVA* startup panel, select variables *A* and *B* as the independent variables, and variable *DV* as the dependent variable. Then click on the *Codes* button and select the codes for the independent variables (*1-3* and *1-6*, respectively). Next, specify the nesting (click on the *Nested design* button) and select factor *B* to be nested in *1* other factor, namely factor *1*, where it has 2 levels at each level of that factor.

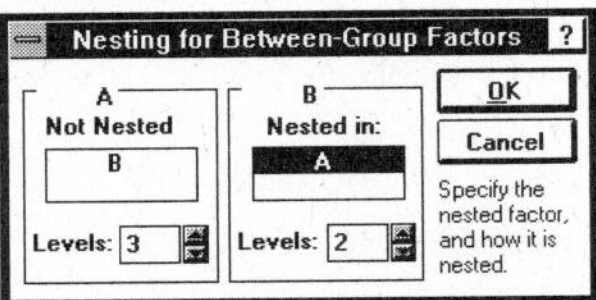

Then click *OK* in this and the *General ANOVA* dialog to begin the analysis. In the *ANOVA Results* dialog, click on the *All effects* button to review the complete analysis of variance table.

Summary of all Effects; design: (nested3.sta)

GENERAL MANOVA — 1-A, 2-B

Effect	df Effect	MS Effect	df Error	MS Error	F	p-level
1	2	114.6667	12	4.888889	23.45455	.000071
2	3	46.8333	12	4.888889	9.57955	.001656
12	--	--	--	--	--	--

These results are reported and discussed on page 172 of Lindman (1974).

Example 3: A 3-way Nested Design

Now consider a three-way nested design. Milliken and Johnson (1984, page 418) present an example of such a design (given in the example data file *Comfort.sta*, shown below).

Data: COMFORT.STA 4v * 36c

Comfort study; see Milliken & Johnson, p. 418-4

	1 TEMPERAT	2 GENDER	3 CHAMBER	4 COMFORT
1	T_65	MALE	1	5
2	T_65	MALE	1	4
3	T_65	MALE	2	5
4	T_65	MALE	2	4
5	T_65	MALE	3	4
6	T_65	MALE	3	2
7	T_65	FEMALE	1	1
8	T_65	FEMALE	1	2
9	T_65	FEMALE	2	5
10	T_65	FEMALE	2	5

In this experiment, male and female subjects were randomly assigned to one of 9 environmental chambers; the 9 environmental chambers, in turn were assigned to 3 levels of a temperature factor. Thus, in this design, *Chamber* is nested in *Temperature*, and subjects are nested in chambers. The data file is shown above. The structure of this design can be summarized as follows (the X's indicate the observed treatment combinations):

Temper-ature	Gender	Chamber 1	2	3	4	5	6	7	8	9
65	male	x	x	x						
	female	x	x	x						
70	male				x	x	x			
	female				x	x	x			
75	male							x	x	x
	female							x	x	x

To analyze this design, first open the data file *Comfort.sta*. Then, click on the *Variables* button and select variables *Temperat*, *Gender*, and *Chamber* as the independent variables, and variable *Comfort* as the dependent variable. Next, click on the *Codes* button and select the codes for the independent variables, that is *1-3* for *Temperat*, *1 2* for *Gender*, and *1-9* for *Chamber*.

Now, specify the nesting by clicking on the *Nested design* button and identify *Chamber* as being nested in *Temperat* with 3 levels at each level of that factor.

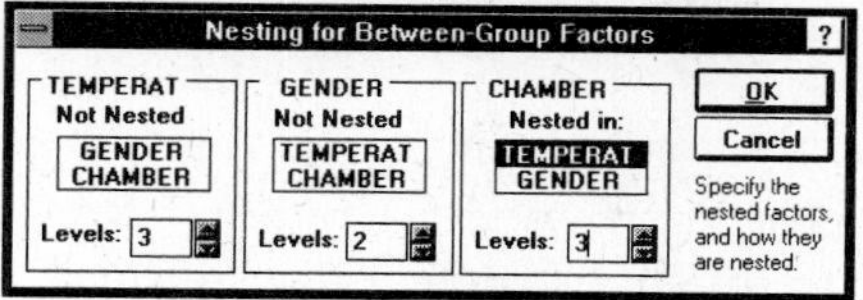

Click *OK* in this and the *General ANOVA* startup panel to begin the analysis. To produce the results as shown in Milliken and Johnson (1984, page 419), use the *Pooled effect/error* option in the *ANOVA Results* dialog to bring up the *Pooled Effects and Error Terms* dialog.

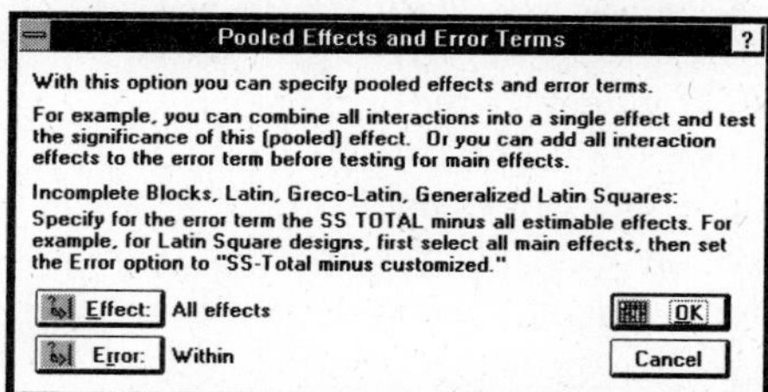

In this dialog, click on the *Error* button and pool the *Gender* by *Chamber* interaction into the error term (i.e., add the *23* interaction to the *Within* error).

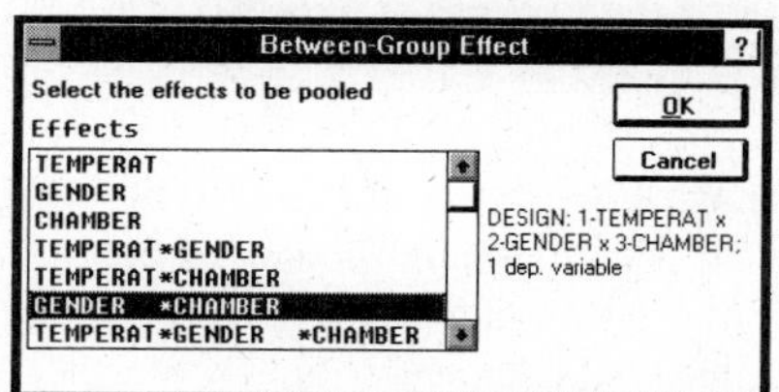

When you click *OK* in this dialog, the text next to the *Error* button in the *Pooled Effects and Error Terms* dialog will now say "*Customized*." Click *OK* to estimate the sums of squares for all effects.

Summary of all Effects; design: (comfort.sta)

GENERAL MANOVA — 1-TEMPERAT, 2-GENDER, 3-CHAMBER — Customized Error Term

Effect	df Effect	MS Effect	df Error	MS Error	F	p-level
1	2	79.19444	6	2.027778	39.05479	.000363
2	1	3.36111	6	2.027778	1.65753	.245365
3	6	11.08333	6	2.027778	5.46575	.028943
12	2	7.86111	6	2.027778	3.87671	.083027
13	--	--	--	--	--	--
23	--	--	--	--	--	--
123	--	--	--	--	--	--

When analyzing nested designs, it is important that you understand the specific nature of the particular design. As Milliken and Johnson discuss, in this particular instance, there really are two error terms. First there is the *Subjects* within *Chambers* term; in the Scrollsheet shown above the mean square for this error is shown in the *MS Error* column. This error term would be appropriate for testing the effect of the *Chamber* factor. However, in order to test the effect of *Temperat* (temperature), the more appropriate error term is that of *Chamber* within *Temperat*. Thus, you should use the *Pooled effect/error* option again, but this time test the individual effects against the appropriate error term.

Example 4: Analyzing a Repeated Measures Design as a Nested Design with a Random Effect

Lindman (1974, page 173) shows an interesting example of a nested design, where the nested factor is random. Each of 9 subjects was asked to learn four lists of nonsense syllables under one of three instructions. Thus, there are three factors: Factor *A* with four levels, represents the four lists of nonsense syllables, factor *B* with 3 levels represents the three different types of instruction, and factor *C* with 9 levels represents the 9 subjects.

Note that factor *C* (subjects) is nested within factor *B* (three subjects each listened to one of the three instructions). Shown below are the data from Lindman (1974) as they were recorded in the example data file *Nested2.sta.*

Data: NESTED2.S

Nested design: See Lind

	1 A	2 B	3 C	4 DV
1	A1	B1	C1	8
2	A2	B1	C1	15
3	A3	B1	C1	12
4	A4	B1	C1	17
5	A1	B1	C2	20
6	A2	B1	C2	24
7	A3	B1	C2	16
8	A4	B1	C2	20
9	A1	B1	C3	14
10	A2	B1	C3	20
11	A3	B1	C3	19
12	A4	B1	C3	20
13	A1	B2	C4	21
14	A2	B2	C4	18
15	A3	B2	C4	17
16	A4	B2	C4	28
17	A1	B2	C5	23

The structure of the experiment can be summarized as follows (the X's indicate the observed treatment combinations):

```
                                Subject
Factor  Factor   -------------------------
  A       B      1  2  3  4  5  6  7  8  9
------------------------------------------
 A1       B1     x  x  x
          B2              x  x  x
          B3                       x  x  x
 A2       B1     x  x  x
          B2              x  x  x
          B3                       x  x  x
 A3       B1     x  x  x
          B2              x  x  x
          B3                       x  x  x
 A4       B1     x  x  x
          B2              x  x  x
          B3                       x  x  x
```

To analyze this design, first open the data file *Nested2.sta*. Specify as the independent variables *A*, *B*, and *C*, and variable *DV* as the dependent variable. Then specify the codes for the independent variables (*1-4*, *1-3*, and *1-9*, respectively).

As you can see in the schematic representation of the design shown above, factor *C* (subjects) is nested in the levels of factor *B*. Specify this nesting by clicking on the *Nested design* button and identify factor *C* as being nested in factor *B* and that it has *3* levels at each level of that factor).

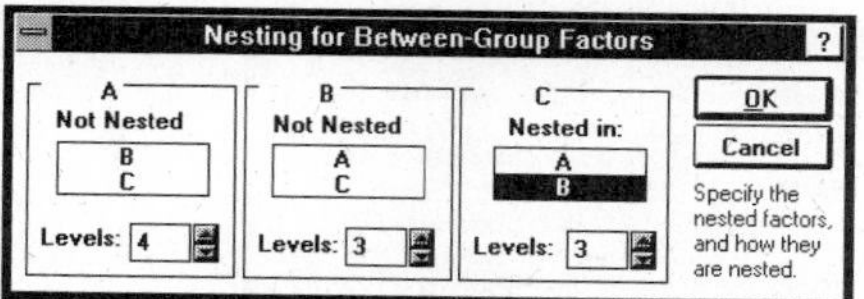

Fixed and random effects in experiments are discussed on page 1778 of this chapter. In short, when levels of a factor are sampled from a population of levels to which you want to generalize any findings, then the respective factor should be considered to be random. In this example, the subjects factor *C* (nested in factor *B*) should be considered to be random, because one usually wants to generalize the findings to the population from which the subjects were recruited. Therefore, next specify factor *C* as a random factor via the *Random factors* button.

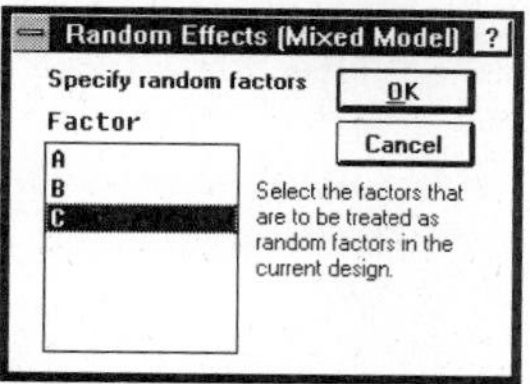

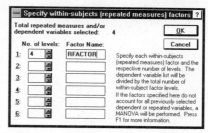

Now click *OK* in this and the *General ANOVA* startup panel to begin the analysis. In the *ANOVA Results* dialog, click on the *All effects* button to produce the summary ANOVA table as presented in Lindman (1974, page 178).

Summary of all Effects; design: (nested2.sta)

GENERAL MANOVA — 1-A, 2-B, 3-C

Effect	df Effect	MS Effect	df Error	MS Error	F	p-level
1	3	86.4444	18	8.52778	10.13681	.000390
2	2	365.0833	6	44.30556	8.24013	.019013
3	6	44.3056	0	0.00000	--	--
12	6	11.1944	18	8.52778	1.31270	.301608
13	18	8.5278	0	0.00000	--	--
23	--	--	--	--	--	--
123	--	--	--	--	--	--

Analyzing the design as a repeated measures design. As you may have wondered already, the design described above actually looks like a repeated measures design. Indeed, you could consider factor *A* (the four lists of nonsense syllables) as a repeated measures factor, since each subject was asked to learn all four of them; factor *B* would be a between-group factor since different subjects listened to different instructions. Thus, the data could be entered into a file as follows:

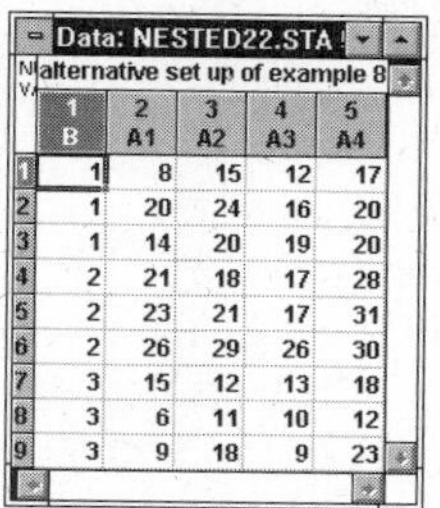

Data: NESTED22.STA

alternative set up of example 8

	1 B	2 A1	3 A2	4 A3	5 A4
1	1	8	15	12	17
2	1	20	24	16	20
3	1	14	20	19	20
4	2	21	18	17	28
5	2	23	21	17	31
6	2	26	29	26	30
7	3	15	12	13	18
8	3	6	11	10	12
9	3	9	18	9	23

To analyze this data set as a repeated measures design, click on the *Variables* button and select variable *B* as the independent variable and variables *A1* through *A4* as the dependent variables. Next specify a repeated measures factor (click on the *Within-subjects design* button) with *4* levels.

Specify within-subjects (repeated measures) factors

Total repeated measures and/or dependent variables selected: 4

No. of levels: Factor Name:
1: 4 RFACTOR
2:
3:
4:
5:
6:

OK
Cancel

Specify each within-subjects (repeated measures) factor and the respective number of levels. The dependent variable list will be divided by the total number of within-subject factor levels.
If the factors specified here do not account for all previously selected dependent or repeated variables, a MANOVA will be performed. Press F1 for more information.

Click *OK* in this and the *General ANOVA* startup panel to go to the *ANOVA Results* dialog. Here, click on the *All effects* button to display the table of all effects shown below.

Summary of all Effects; design: (nested22.sta)

GENERAL MANOVA — 1-B, 2-RFACTOR

Effect	df Effect	MS Effect	df Error	MS Error	F	p-level
1	2	365.0833	6	44.30556	8.24013	.019013
2	3	86.4444	18	8.52778	10.13681	.000390
12	6	11.1944	18	8.52778	1.31270	.301608

As you can see, the results are identical to those shown earlier.

Example 5: Split-plot Designs

The general type of design discussed in the previous example is sometimes also referred to as a split-plot design, because of its common use in agricultural research. Suppose one wants to study the effectiveness of four different fertility regimes (factor *A*) on two varieties of wheat (factor *B*). The researcher divides a field into two blocks, each with four whole plots. Each of the four fertilizers is then randomly assigned to one whole plot within each block. Each plot is then again divided into two sub-plots, and the two wheat varieties randomly assigned to one of the halves. An example of this design is presented in Milliken and Johnson (1984, page 297). The data were entered into the example data file *Splitplt.sta*, shown below.

Data: SPLITPLT.STA 4v * 16c

Split-plot design: Data from Milliken & Johnson,

	1 FERTILTY	2 VARIETY	3 BLOCK	4 YIELD
1	A1	B1	1	35.4
2	A1	B2	1	37.9
3	A2	B1	1	36.7
4	A2	B2	1	38.2
5	A3	B1	1	34.8
6	A3	B2	1	36.4
7	A4	B1	1	39.5
8	A4	B2	1	40.0
9	A1	B1	2	41.6
10	A1	B2	2	40.3

To produce the analysis of variance table presented in Milliken and Johnson (page 299), first specify this design as a regular between-group design. Click on the *Variables* button in the *General ANOVA* startup panel and select variables *Fertility*, *Variety*, and *Block* as the independent variables, and variable *Yield* as the dependent variable; then specify the respective codes for the independent variables. Click *OK* to process the data. The appropriate error term for the *Fertility* factor in this design is the interaction between factors *Fertility* and *Block* (since the experimental units here are really the plots; see Milliken and Johnson, 1984, page 297, for a detailed discussion of this design). Thus, click on the *Pooled effect/error* button in the *ANOVA Results* dialog to bring up the *Pooled Effects and Error Terms* dialog.

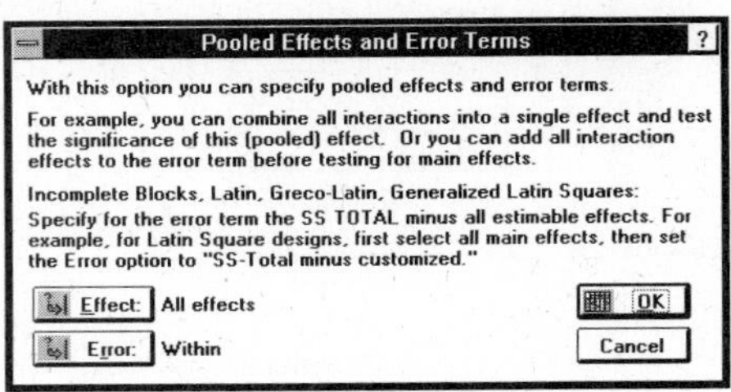

Now, click on the *Effect* button and select *Fertility* as the effect to be tested. Next, click on the *Errors* button and specify the *Fertility* by *Block* (*13*) interaction as the error term used to test the specified effect. Shown below is the resulting ANOVA table.

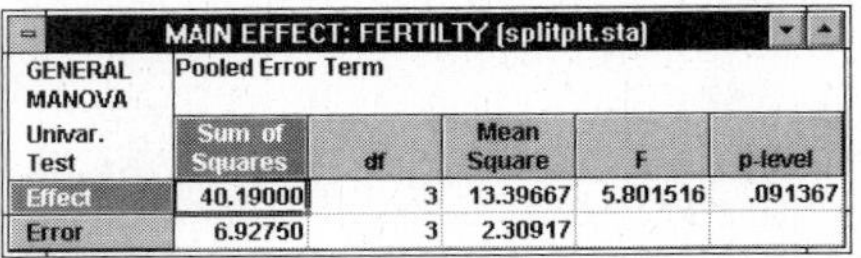

MAIN EFFECT: FERTILTY (splitplt.sta)

GENERAL MANOVA — Pooled Error Term

Univar. Test	Sum of Squares	df	Mean Square	F	p-level
Effect	40.19000	3	13.39667	5.801516	.091367
Error	6.92750	3	2.30917		

The *Variety* factor as well as the *Variety* by *Fertilizer* interaction involve comparisons between subplots. Therefore, these effects should be tested against the variability due to subplots, that is, against the *Variety* by *Block* and the three-way interaction combined.

Once again, click on the *Pooled effect/error* button and in the resulting *Pooled Effects and Error Terms* dialog, click on the *Effect* button and select *Variety* as the effect to be tested.

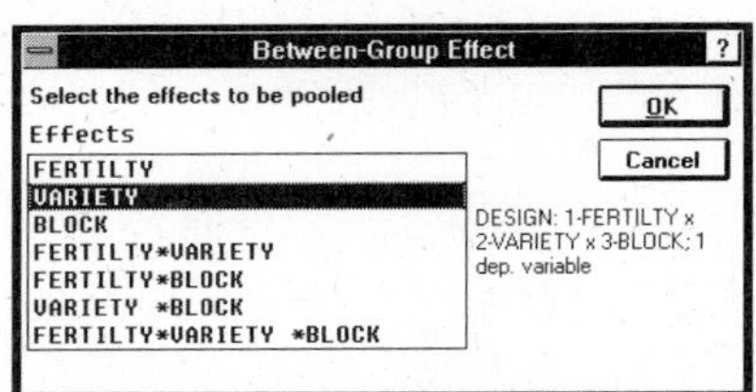

Click on the *Error* button and select the two-way interaction *Variety* by *Block* and the three-way interaction *Fertility* by *Variety* by *Block* as the pooled error term.

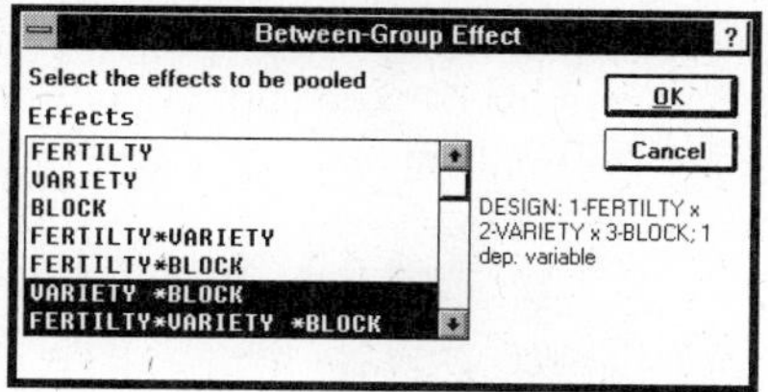

Shown below is the resulting ANOVA table.

MAIN EFFECT: VARIETY (splitplt.sta)

GENERAL MANOVA — Pooled Error Term

Univar. Test	Sum of Squares	df	Mean Square	F	p-level
Effect	2.250000	1	2.250000	1.067616	.359860
Error	8.430000	4	2.107500		

Example 6: Strip-plot Designs

The strip-plot design is similar to the split-plot design. A detailed discussion of the design is beyond the scope of this example; you should refer to Milliken and Johnson (1984, page 321). The example discussed there involves an experiment on the relationship between two irrigation methods and three levels of nitrogen on the yield of wheat. The example data were entered into the data file *Irrigat.sta*.

Data: IRRIGAT.STA 4v * 24c

Strip-plot design: Irrigation data from Milliken &

	1 REPLICAT	2 IRRIGAT	3 NITROGEN	4 DV
1	1	I1	N1	55
2	1	I1	N3	69
3	1	I1	N2	62
4	1	I2	N1	71
5	1	I2	N3	78
6	1	I2	N2	77
7	2	I1	N2	70
8	2	I1	N3	79
9	2	I1	N1	63
10	2	I2	N2	78
11	2	I2	N3	80
12	2	I2	N1	77
13	3	I2	N3	81
14	3	I2	N1	77
15	3	I2	N2	79
16	3	I1	N3	77
17	3	I1	N1	63

You can easily compute the analysis of variance table presented in Milliken and Johnson on page 320; all variance components are automatically computed by the *ANOVA/MANOVA* module when you select the *All effects* option. Note that there is a typographical error in the table presented in Milliken and Johnson; specifically the sums of squares for factor *Irrigation* are 570.4 (and not 507.4). Other than that, via the *Pooled effect/error* button, you can produce all results presented there.

Summary of all Effects; design: (irrigat.sta)

GENERAL MANOVA — 1-REPLICAT, 2-IRRIGAT, 3-NITROGEN

Effect	df Effect	MS Effect	df Error	MS Error	F	p-level
1	3	41.1528	0	0.00	--	--
2	1	570.3750	0	0.00	--	--
3	2	169.5417	0	0.00	--	--
12	3	10.9306	0	0.00	--	--
13	6	2.8194	0	0.00	--	--
23	2	47.3750	0	0.00	--	--
123	6	1.4306	0	0.00	--	--

Example 7: Split-plot Designs with Unequal Numbers of Subplots

All examples of nested designs presented so far are "nicely" balanced, that is, as you could see, unconfounded estimates for effects were easily obtained. Because their interpretation is straightforward, in practice, one is well advised to stay with such balanced designs whenever possible. Unbalanced nested designs are rarely discussed in the literature, however, real-world constraints sometimes may force one to deal with such data.

Milliken and Johnson (1984, page 385) discuss an example of such a data set. Five patients suffering from depression were randomly assigned to one of two treatment conditions (*Treatment*: *Placebo* vs. *Drug*). They were then examined after one week and after five weeks; the dependent variable was the patients' depression score during those examinations. Two patients did not return for the second examination. Here are the data:

Patient	Treatment	Week 1	Week 2
1	Placebo	24	18
2	Placebo	22	--
3	Drug	25	22
4	Drug	23	--
5	Drug	26	24

While incomplete designs with more-or-less random empty cells can generally be analyzed with contrast analysis (see below), a different technique will be illustrated here. Specifically, when entering the data file, three "dummy variables" (with codes that uniquely identify comparisons between subjects within each treatment condition) were added. Shown below in the data file *Depresse.sta*.

Data: DEPRESSE.STA 7v * 8c

Example of an unbalanced nested design; see Milliken & Johnson, p. 385

	1 PATIENT	2 TREATMNT	3 WEEK	4 SCORE	5 P_INTRT1	6 P_INTRT2	7 P_INTRT3
1	1	PLACEBO	1	24	1	0	0
2	1	PLACEBO	2	18	1	0	0
3	2	PLACEBO	1	22	-1	0	0
4	3	DRUG	1	25	0	1	1
5	3	DRUG	2	22	0	1	1
6	4	DRUG	1	23	0	-1	0
7	5	DRUG	1	26	0	0	-1
8	5	DRUG	2	24	0	0	-1

As you can see, variable *5* (*P_IntrT1*) identifies the comparison between patient 1 and patient 2 (within the *Placebo* treatment condition); variables *6* and *7* (*P_IntrT2* and *P_IntrT3*) identify the two possible comparisons between subjects 3, 4, and 5 (within the *Drug* treatment condition).

To produce the ANOVA table with all variance components presented on page 394 in Milliken and Johnson, simply use those coded variables as covariates and specify the design as a simple 2 (*Treatment*) x 2 (*Week*) between-group analysis of covariance (see page 1731 for an example of a design with covariates).

Note that the construction of significance tests for this design is not straight-forward, and you should refer to Milliken and Johnson for details.

Example 8: Youden Square Designs

The strategy from Example 7 (see above) will now be illustrated with another example. The Youden square design is sometimes used to balance the effect of position of a treatment in a sequence, so as not to confound two other factors of interest. Here is an example of a 4 x 4 Youden square with three factors *A*, *B*, and *C*; the numbers in parentheses are data from an example in Lindman (1974, page 209):

```
      B1     B2     B3     B4
      ------ ------ ------ ------
C1    A1(15) A2( 7) A3(14) A4( 8)
C2    A2(17) A3( 6) A4( 8) A1( 7)
C3    A3(22) A4(14) A1(11) A2(15)
```

As you can see, factor *A* is "rotated" in its position with respect to factor *B*. To analyze these data, three dummy-variables were created with codes that specify the three comparisons between the 4 groups of factor *A* (see data file *Youden.sta*). Those dummy variables were then treated as covariates, and the design was specified as a complete 4 (*B*) x 3 (*C*) analysis of covariance.

Here is the table of all effects, with the *B* x *C* interaction as the error term (see also the results table in Lindman, page 209):

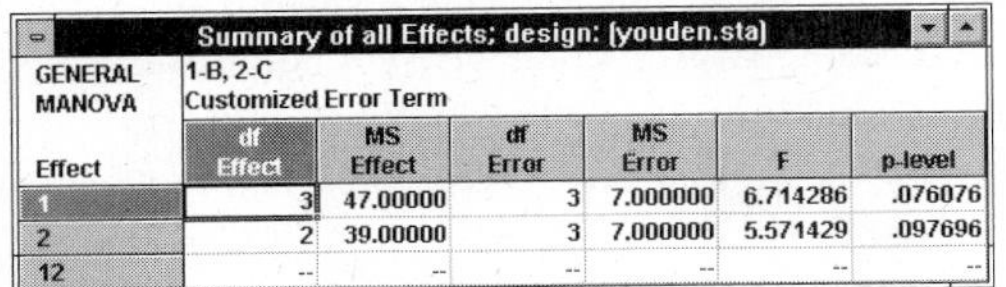

Summary of all Effects; design: (youden.sta)

GENERAL MANOVA — 1-B, 2-C — Customized Error Term

Effect	df Effect	MS Effect	df Error	MS Error	F	p-level
1	3	47.00000	3	7.000000	6.714286	.076076
2	2	39.00000	3	7.000000	5.571429	.097696
12	--	--	--	--	--	--

Note that, in order to test the significance of factor *A*, you can request the *Within cell regression* option from the *ANOVA Results* dialog.

Designs with Missing Cells

The following examples will discuss experimental designs that are really "supposed" to be complete, but which for some reason contain one or more missing cells. Unlike the designs discussed so far, the pattern of missing cells in such designs is not in some way planned (e.g., in order to be able to readily test main effects), but instead is haphazard. It is often not easy to determine how main effects and interactions should be estimated in such design.

As was discussed earlier (see page 1709), in those cases, one should carefully study the pattern of

observed and missing cells and formulate specific hypotheses (in terms of comparisons between cell means) that approximate the hypotheses of interest as closely as possible. A detailed discussion of how to construct such comparisons is beyond the scope of this chapter; in-depth discussions are presented in Dodge (1985), Milliken and Johnson (1984), and Searle (1987).

Example 9: A 3 x 3 Design with Missing Cells

Milliken and Johnson (1984, page 173) present the following example of a 3 x 3 design with missing cells and unequal numbers of observations per (observed) cell. Here are the data:

Factor T	Factor B: B1	B2	B3
T1	2,6	missing	8,6
T2	3	14	12,9
T3	6	9	missing

For this discussion, the cells are numbered by rows (missing cells are indicated by parentheses):

Factor T	Factor B: B1	B2	B3
T1	Cell 1	(Cell 2)	Cell 3
T2	Cell 4	Cell 5	Cell 6
T3	Cell 7	Cell 8	(Cell 9)

As you can see, cells 2 and 9 are missing in this design; how can the main effects and interactions be estimated? Begin with factor *T*. In order not to confound the main effect estimate with the interaction, you must make sure that you are comparing means across the levels of *T* within the same levels of factor *B*. One way (and not the only one) to accomplish this is to, in a sense, break down the design into two complete factorial experiments:

Design 1:

T	B: B1	B3
T1	Cell 1	Cell 3
T2	Cell 4	Cell 6

Design 2:

T	B: B1	B2
T1	Cell 4	Cell 5
T2	Cell 7	Cell 8

Within each one of these designs, you can now construct your comparisons for testing the main effects and interactions in the usual manner. For factor *T* this can be accomplished by comparing (a) Cell 1 + Cell 3 vs. Cell 4 + Cell 6 and (b) Cell 4 + Cell 5 vs. Cell 7 + Cell 8.

Using the same logic, in order to test the *B* main effect, you can compare (a) Cell 1 + Cell 4 vs. Cell 3 + Cell 6 and (b) Cell 4 + Cell 7 vs. Cell 5 + Cell 8. Finally, the interaction can be estimated by comparing (a) Cell 1 + Cell 6 vs. Cell 4 + Cell 3, and (b) Cell 4 + Cell 8 vs. Cell 7 + Cell 5.

Example 2 (page 1727) uses contrast analyses and this is discussed on pages 1704 and 1763. Note that in this case, the contrast should be entered as one long vector (click on the *Options* button in the *ANOVA Results* dialog and select the *Enter contrasts for factors together* option). The data shown above were entered into the example data file *Two_miss.sta*. Shown below are the contrast coefficients for the interactions.

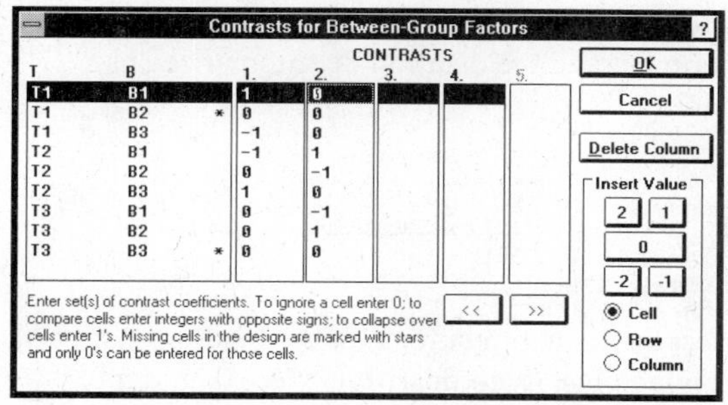

When you click *OK* in the above dialog, the following Scrollsheet will appear.

Planned Comparison (two_miss.sta)

GENERAL MANOVA	1-T, 2-B				
Univar. Test	Sum of Squares	df	Mean Square	F	p-level
Effect	18.77778	2	9.388889	1.942529	.287621
Error	14.50000	3	4.833333		

Example 10: Weighted Means Analysis of a Nested Design with Unequal *n*

This example was taken from Searle (1987, page 62) and the data were entered into the example data file *Opinion.sta* (shown below).

Data: OPINION.STA 3v * 12c — Searle, p 62

	1 COURSE	2 SECTION	3 DV
1	ENGLISH	1	5
2	ENGLISH	2	8
3	ENGLISH	2	10
4	ENGLISH	2	9
5	GEOLOGY	3	8
6	GEOLOGY	3	10
7	GEOLOGY	4	6
8	GEOLOGY	4	2
9	GEOLOGY	4	1
10	GEOLOGY	4	3
11	GEOLOGY	5	3
12	GEOLOGY	5	7

Even though this is a nested design, the nesting is not planned by the experimenter but occurred "naturally" in the data. Specifically, the data describe a two-way nested classification of student opinions concerning computers. There were two classes -- *English* and *Geology* (factor *Course*) -- with different numbers of sections (taught by different teachers): *English* had two sections, *Geology* had 3 sections. The structure of the experiment and the data can be summarized as follows:

	Section				
Course	**1**	**2**	**3**	**4**	**5**
English	5	8,10,9			
Geology			8,10	6,2,1,3	3,7

To test the main effect for *Course*, Searle constructs a weighted means comparison. Note that in this example, the uneven distribution of the cell *n*'s (1, 3, 2, 4, 2, going from left to right in the table above) was not due to the experimenter's choice, but rather a true reflection of the actual distribution of students across courses and sections. Since the experimenter would like to generalize the results to the entire student population, in this case it may be meaningful to look at the weighted means for the *Course* factor rather than the unweighted means.

To compute the respective sums of squares as reported in Searle (1987, page 71) first specify the design as if it were complete. Then, enter the following contrasts for factor *Course*, using the cell *n*'s as weights:

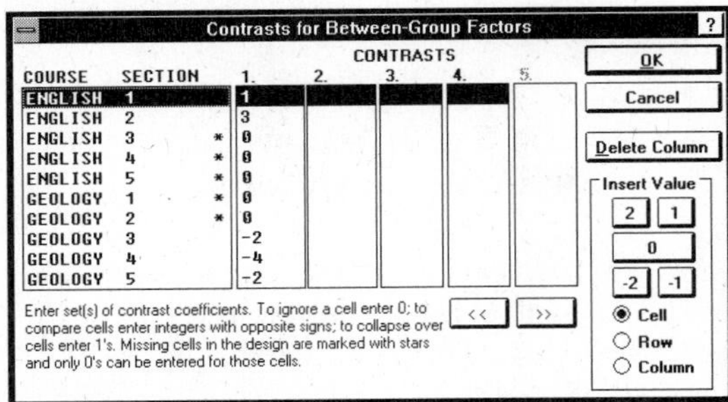

Note that the contrast coefficients do not add to zero in this case. The *ANOVA/MANOVA* module will automatically adjust the contrast coefficients so that they will add to zero (unless the coefficients consist of only positive integers, in which case the hypothesis is about the grand mean).

Shown below is the result of this comparison:

Planned Comparison (opinion.sta)

GENERAL MANOVA — 1-COURSE, 2-SECTION

Univar. Test	Sum of Squares	df	Mean Square	F	p-level
Effect	24.00000	1	24.00000	6.461538	.038554
Error	26.00000	7	3.71429		

Note that the grand mean, and the main effect for the *Section* factor (as reported in Searle, page 71) can be tested analogously.

Example 11: A 4 x 11 Nested Design with Unequal Numbers of Levels

Here is another example of a nested design, where the nesting is not "neat," that is, where the number of levels nested in another factor is not even. Again,

such designs can best be analyzed via contrast analysis.

Milliken and Johnson (1984, page 415) present an example data set, comparing 11 insecticides produced by four different companies.

Company	Product 1	2	3	4	5	6	7	8	9	10	11
A	x	x	x								
B				x	x						
C						x	x				
D								x	x	x	x

One company makes three insecticides, others two, and one makes four. The design can be summarized as shown above (the X's indicate the observed treatment combinations).

The data reported in Milliken and Johnson are contained in the example data file *Insect.sta*. Note that the main effect for *Company* can be estimated in the usual manner. However, in order to test the *Product* factor, you must use planned comparisons. Specifically, you can construct two contrasts to compare the three products manufactured by company *A*, one contrast each for the products manufactured by companies *B* and *C*, and three contrasts for the four products manufactured by company *D*, for a total of 7 contrasts.

To do this, first click on the *Options* button in the *ANOVA Results* dialog and select the *Enter contrasts for factors together* option. Then, click on the *Planned comparisons* button and in the resulting dialog enter the appropriate contrast coefficients.

Note that missing cells in the design are marked with stars and only *0*'s can be entered in those cells. Shown below is the Scrollsheet with the results of a simultaneous test of all 7 contrasts:

Planned Comparison (insect.sta)

GENERAL MANOVA — 1-COMPANY, 2-PRODUCT

Univar. Test	Sum of Squares	df	Mean Square	F	p-level
Effect	1500.583	7	214.3690	3.742952	.008098
Error	1260.000	22	57.2727		

Note that these results are slightly different than those reported in Milliken and Johnson (on page 422); somehow the analysis reported there is not consistent, and a typographical error must have found its way into the analysis somewhere (e.g., compare the mean reported on page 417 for the last group with the data reported on page 415).

Example 12: A Complex Design with Many Missing Cells (Testing Type IV Hypothesis)

Milliken and Johnson (1984, page 202) discuss a complex example of a design with many missing cells. The design contains 3 factors: *Group* (2 levels; whether or not subject received food stamps), *Age* (classified into three groups), and *Race* (*black*, *hispanic*, *white*). The dependent variable is a change score from pre-training to post-training on a nutrition test.

The distribution of missing cells and the cell *n*'s can be summarized as follows:

Age	Group (Foodstamps)	Race: Black	Hispanic	White
1	No			3
	Yes	2		2
2	No	7		8
	Yes			8
3	No	6	2	20
	Yes	4	1	31
4	No	1		
	Yes	1		11

Now, consider the main effect for *Race*. In Example 9, a strategy of constructing a set of comparisons for a particular effect that is balanced across the factors not involved in the effect was briefly discussed. To do this, one should examine the distribution of observed and missing cells and attempt to extract "sub-designs" that are complete with regard to the factor of interest.

The *Race* factor has 3 levels. You can extract the following two complete sub-designs (as before, the entries in the table represent the cell *n*'s):

StatSoft

Sub-design 1:

Age	Group (Foodstamps)	Race: Black	White
1	Yes	2	2
2	No	7	8
3	No	6	20
	Yes	4	31
4	Yes	1	11

Sub-design 2:

Age	Group (Foodstamps)	Race: Hispanic	White
3	No	2	20
	Yes	1	31

Given these two sub-designs, the usual main effect contrasts can now be constructed for the *Race* factor (see also Table 17.3 in Milliken and Johnson, 1984, page 204). Shown below are the two contrasts that were entered after clicking on the *Planned comparison* button in the *ANOVA Results* dialog (the data are in the example data file *Food.sta*; first click on the *Options* button in the *ANOVA Results* dialog and select the *Enter contrasts for factors together* option, then enter the complete vectors of contrast coefficients shown below):

Contrasts for Between-Group Factors

AGE	GROUP	RACE	1.	2.	3.	4.	5.
1	NO	BLACK *	0	0			
1	NO	HISPANIC*	0	0			
1	NO	WHITE	0	0			
1	YES	BLACK	1	0			
1	YES	HISPANIC*	0	0			
1	YES	WHITE	-1	0			
2	NO	BLACK	1	0			
2	NO	HISPANIC*	0	0			
2	NO	WHITE	-1	0			
2	YES	BLACK *	0	0			
2	YES	HISPANIC*	0	0			

CONTRASTS — OK — Cancel — Delete Column — Insert Value: 2, 1, 0, -2, -1 — Cell, Row, Column — << >>

Enter set(s) of contrast coefficients. To ignore a cell enter 0; to compare cells enter integers with opposite signs; to collapse over cells enter 1's. Missing cells in the design are marked with stars and only 0's can be entered for those cells.

The complete set of contrast coefficients are listed below:

```
Contrast 1:
0 0 0 1 0 -1 1 0 -1 0 0 0
1 0 -1 1 0 -1 0 0 0 1 0 -1

Contrast 2:
0 0 0 0 0 0 0 0 0 0 0 0
0 1 -1 0 1 -1 0 0 0 0 0 0
```

When you click *OK* in this dialog, the following analysis of variance table will be displayed.

Planned Comparison (food.sta)

GENERAL MANOVA	Sum of Squares	df	Mean Square	F	p-level
Effect	11.677	2	5.83851	.204433	.815478
Error	2627.472	92	28.55948		

Now, consider the *Race* by *Group* interaction. Looking back at the distribution of observed cells shown above, it is clear that the only complete sub-design that can be extracted with regard to this interaction is for *Age = 3*. The two sub-designs are (the respective contrast coefficients for the interaction contrast are added in parentheses):

Sub-design 1:

Age	Group (Foodstamps)	Race: Black	White
3	No	6(+1)	20(-1)
	Yes	4(-1)	31(+1)

Sub-design 2:

Age	Group (Foodstamps)	Race: Hispanic	White
3	No	2(+1)	20(-1)
	Yes	1(-1)	31(+1)

Note that in the table presented in Milliken and Johnson (1984, page 204), there is a typographical error in the first hypothesis listed for the *Group* by *Race* interaction (a positive weight should be assigned to the last mean). Click on the *Planned Comparisons* button and enter the respective contrasts (shown below) in the *Contrasts for Between-Groups Factors* dialog.

```
Contrast 1:
0 0 0 0 0 0 0 0 0 0 0 0
1 0 -1 -1 0 1 0 0 0 0 0 0

Contrast 2:
0 0 0 0 0 0 0 0 0 0 0 0
0 1 -1 0 -1 1 0 0 0 0 0 0
```

When you click *OK* in the *Contrasts for Between-Groups Factors* dialog, the following analysis of variance table will be displayed.

Planned Comparison (food.sta)

GENERAL MANOVA	Sum of Squares	df	Mean Square	F	p-level
Effect	113.703	2	56.85172	1.990643	.142449
Error	2627.472	92	28.55948		

These results are identical to those reported for the *Type IV* analysis in Milliken and Johnson (Table 17.2, page 203). In a sense, the analysis is presented here as if the design were a one-way ANOVA design in which certain specific hypotheses about differences between means were tested. Along those lines it may be useful to look at the comparisons between all means. This can be accomplished by

clicking on the *post hoc* button from the *ANOVA Results* dialog and then specifying the *123* interaction.

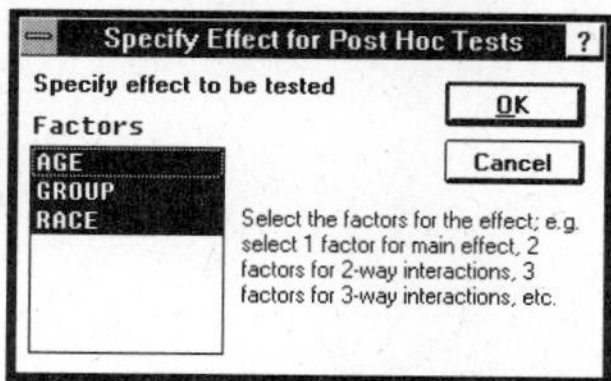

Click *OK*, and in the resulting *Post hoc Comparisons of Means* dialog, click on the *LSD test or planned comparison* option.

Shown below is the results Scrollsheet (see also Milliken and Johnson, table 17.5, page 206; note that the order of factors was rearranged for the Scrollsheet below, to make the order of means in the table equivalent to that reported in Milliken and Johnson):

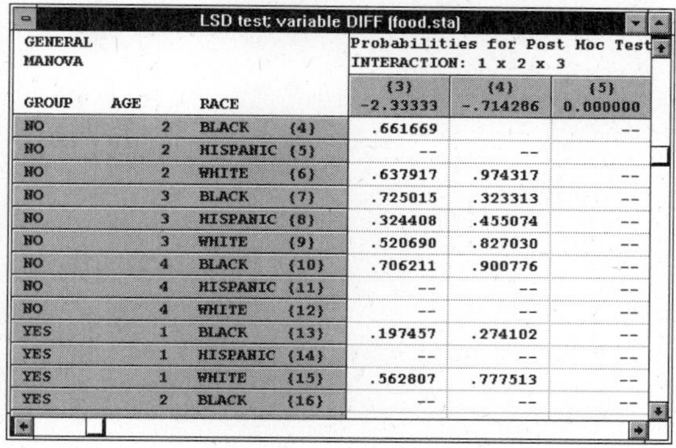

LSD test; variable DIFF (food.sta)

GENERAL MANOVA — Probabilities for Post Hoc Tests, INTERACTION: 1 x 2 x 3

GROUP	AGE	RACE		{3} -2.33333	{4} -.714286	{5} 0.000000
NO	2	BLACK	{4}	.661669		--
NO	2	HISPANIC	{5}	--	--	
NO	2	WHITE	{6}	.637917	.974317	--
NO	3	BLACK	{7}	.725015	.323313	--
NO	3	HISPANIC	{8}	.324408	.455074	--
NO	3	WHITE	{9}	.520690	.827030	--
NO	4	BLACK	{10}	.706211	.900776	--
NO	4	HISPANIC	{11}	--	--	--
NO	4	WHITE	{12}	--	--	--
YES	1	BLACK	{13}	.197457	.274102	--
YES	1	HISPANIC	{14}	--	--	--
YES	1	WHITE	{15}	.562807	.777513	--
YES	2	BLACK	{16}	--	--	--

TECHNICAL NOTES

Computational Procedures

ANOVA/MANOVA is an implementation of the general linear model (see Bock, 1975; Finn, 1974, 1977; Hays, 1981; Lindeman, Merenda, and Gold, 1980). The program will first compute the within-cell variance/covariance matrix of dependent variables (and covariates, see below). The design matrix of main effects and interactions (or the matrix of contrasts coefficients) is first orthonormalized (see Bjorck, 1967), and then used to compute the sums of squares hypothesis (from the cell means) and sums of squares error (from the within-cell variance/covariance matrix). If the design contains covariates, they are appended to the within-cell variance/covariance matrix of dependent variables and treated as such; before the computation of the statistical tests, the hypothesis and error matrices are reduced (adjusted by covariates) via sweeping (Dempster, 1969). These procedures are described in detail by Finn (1974, 1977).

Detailed treatments of this model can be found in numerous sources. A few examples are Bock (1975); Finn (1974); Hocking and Speed (1975); Morrison (1967); Timm (1975), and Timm and Carlson (1973, 1975).

Multivariate Analysis of Variance via *STATISTICA BASIC* Matrix Functions Library

You can write your own customized analysis procedures using the *STATISTICA BASIC* programming language which includes a complete library of matrix algebra functions (including functions for computing the inverse and generalized inverse of a matrix, orthonormalization, singular value decomposition, etc.). An example program, *Manova.stb* (in the *STBASIC* subdirectory), is provided to show how a multivariate analysis of variance (MANOVA) can be computed with a few lines of code by using the available matrix functions.

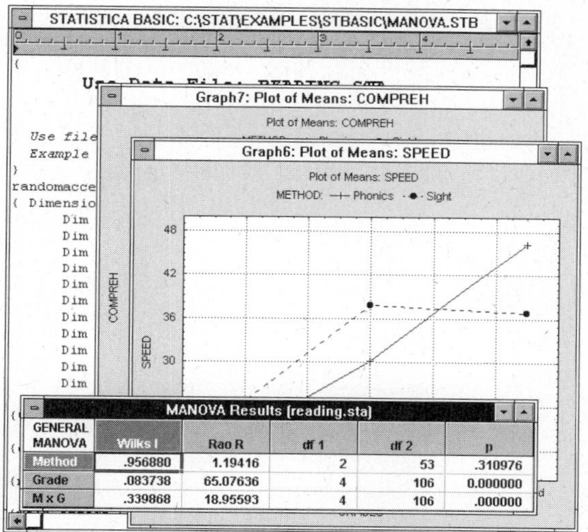

There are several other *STATISTICA BASIC* example programs included in the *STBASIC* subdirectory, for example programs to determine a Box-Cox or Box-Tidwell transformation of the dependent variable (*Boxcox.stb* and *Boxtid.stb*, respectively), to perform weighted least squares estimation (*Wls.stb*), two-stage least squares estimation (*2stls.sta*), etc. These programs are described in detail in comments included in the code.

MANOVA and Structural Equation Modeling

In recent years, structural equation modeling has become increasingly popular as an alternative to multivariate analysis of variance (e.g., see, for example, Bagozzi and Yi, 1989; Bagozzi, Yi, and Singh, 1991; Cole, Maxwell, Arvey, and Salas, 1993). This approach allows you to test explicit

hypotheses not only about means in different groups, but also about differences in the structure of the correlation matrices of dependent variables. For example, you can relax the homogeneity of variances/covariances assumption, and explicitly include in the model different error variances and covariances in each group. The *Structural Equation Modeling and Path Analysis (SEPATH)* module of *STATISTICA* (see Volume III) allows you to perform these types of analyses, and examples of how to test these so-called models for structured means in multiple groups are discussed in that chapter.

INDEX

A

B

StatSoft

C

D

E

F

G

H

I

L

M

N

O

P

R

S

T

U

W

Y

Appendices:

Table of Contents

The *Detailed Table of Contents* follows on the next page.

Detailed Table of Contents

STATISTICA

Appendices:

APPENDIX I: DISTRIBUTION FUNCTIONS

STATISTICA provides a broad selection of predefined distribution functions, their integrals and inverse distribution functions that can be used in spreadsheet formulas (see Chapter 3, *Spreadsheet Window*), the *Probability Distribution Calculator* (see Chapter 10, *Quick Basic Stats*), *Graphics* (see Volume II), *STATISTICA BASIC* (see the *Electronic Manual*), and other user-defined functions. The distribution functions available in *STATISTICA* are described below.

Generating Random Numbers that Follow Specific Distributions

Using the uniform random number generator and the inverse distribution functions available in *STATISTICA BASIC* (see the *Electronic Manual*) or the spreadsheet formulas (see Chapter 3), you can generate random numbers that follow any of the distributions described below. For example, the spreadsheet formula:

```
= vweibull(rnd(1), 1, 2, 0)
```

will produce random numbers that follow the Weibull distribution with scale parameter *1*, shape parameter *2*, and location parameter 0. For additional details, see Evans, Hastings, and Peacock (1993, pages 23-24).

Beta Distribution

The *Beta* distribution has the probability density function:

$$f(x) = \Gamma(\nu+\omega)/[\Gamma(\nu)\Gamma(\omega)]*[x^{\nu-1} * (1-x)^{\omega-1}]$$

$$0 \le x \le 1,\ \nu > 0,\ \omega > 0$$

where

Γ (*gamma*) is the *Gamma* function

ν, ω are the *Shape* parameters

θ is the *Threshold* (*Location*) parameter

Threshold (location, θ) and sigma (σ). The standardized *beta* distribution has a valid range from 0 to 1. However, in some cases (e.g., in *Process Analysis* and *Stats Graphs Quantile-Quantile Plots*) the user may specify a lower threshold (location) parameter and a scale parameter (*sigma*); the program will then fit the *beta* distribution to the standardized variate computed as:

```
(x-location)/sigma
```

Note that the *location* parameter must be less than the smallest observed value, and that *location* + *sigma* must be greater than the largest observed value.

Beta Distribution for Spreadsheet Formulas, *STATISTICA BASIC*, and User-defined Functions

For spreadsheet formulas, *STATISTICA BASIC*, and user-defined functions, the *Location* parameter θ is equal to *0* and the *Scale* parameter σ is equal to *1*. Therefore, you only need to specify the *Shape* parameters of the distribution. For the *Beta* distribution, use *beta(x,ν,ω)*; for the *Beta* integral, use *ibeta(x,ν,ω)*; for the inverse *Beta* distribution, use *vbeta(x,ν,ω)*. For example, you could specify the following spreadsheet formula

```
= beta(v5,5,9)
```

to put the probability density values for the values in *v5* into the current variable.

Beta Distribution for the *Probability Distribution Calculator*

For the *Probability Distribution Calculator*, the *Location* parameter θ is equal to *0* and the *Scale* parameter σ is equal to *1*. Therefore, you only need to specify the *Shape* parameters (ν and ω, respectively) of the distribution. Note that you can change the values of these parameters by either manually editing them in the respecitve edit fields (you will need to click on the *Compute* button to complete the calculations) or by using the micro scrolls to incrementally change the values in the edit fields. (When you use the micro scrolls to change a value, *STATISTICA* will automatically recompute the other values.) If one or both of these parameters are changed, then the *p*-value will be recomputed based on the respective variate value.

Beta Distribution for *Quantile-Quantile* Plots

In *Quantile-Quantile* (*Q-Q*) plots (see Volume II), the standardized *Beta* distribution with *Shape* parameters ν and ω will be used to find the best-fitting distribution function. The *Shape* parameters can be specified in one of two ways in the *Stats Graphs Quantile-Quantile Plots* dialog:

(1) Enter user-defined values for *Shape1* and *Shape2* (ν and ω, respectively) and de-select the *Compute parameters from* option.

(2) Estimate the *Shape1* and *Shape2* parameters (ν and ω, respectively) by selecting the *Compute parameters from* option and entering user-defined *Threshold* (θ) and *Scale* (σ) parameters.

For more information on *Q-Q* plots, see Volume II, or the *Electronic Manual*. In general if the points in the *Q-Q* plot form a straight line, then the respective family of distributions (*Beta* distribution with the respective ν and ω parameters in this case) provides a good fit to the data; in that case, the intercept and slope of the fitted line can be interpreted as graphical estimates of the *Threshold* (θ) and *Scale* (σ) parameters, respectively.

Beta Distribution for *Probability-Probability* Plots

You can use the *Probability-Probability* (or *P-P*) plot to determine how well the *Beta* distribution fits the observed data. In order to create this plot, the theoretical distribution function must be completely specified. Therefore, the parameters for the distribution must either be defined by the user or computed from the data. You can specify the distribution parameters in the following manners:

De-select *Compute from data*. When you de-select this option in the dialog, you will need to specify the two *Shape* parameters ν and ω as well as the *Threshold* and *Scale* parameters θ and σ, respectively.

Select *Compute from data*. When you select this option and specify the *Threshold* and *Scale* parameters (θ and σ, respectively), *STATISTICA* will estimate both *Shape* parameters ν and ω from the data.

In general, if the observed points follow the *Beta* distribution with the respective parameters, then they will fall onto the straight line in the *P-P* plot. Note that you can use the *Quantile-Quantile* plot to obtain the parameter estimates (for the best fitting distribution from a family of distributions) to enter here. For more information on *Q-Q* and *P-P* plots, see Volume II, or the *Electronic Manual*.

Binomial Distribution

The Binomial distribution has the probability function:

$f(x) = \{n!/[x!*(n-x)!]\} * p^x * q^{n-x}$

$0 < p < 1,\ x = 0, 1, ..., n$

where

p is the probability of success at each trial

q is equal to *1-p*

n is the number of independent trials

Binomial Distribution in Spreadsheet Formulas, *STATISTICA BASIC*, and User-defined Functions

For the Binomial distribution use *binom(x,p,n)*; for the Binomial integral, use *ibinom(x,p,n)*. For example, you could specify the following spreadsheet formula,

```
= binom(v2,.5,200)
```

to transform the values of variable 2.

Cauchy Distribution

The Cauchy distribution has the probability density function:

$f(x) = 1/ \theta*\pi*\{1+[(x-\eta)/ \theta]^2\}$

$0 < \theta$

where

η is the *Location* parameter (median)

θ is the *Scale* parameter

π is the constant *Pi* (3.14...)

The cumulative distribution function is:

$F(x) = 1/2 + 1/\pi*\arctan[(x-\eta)/ \theta]$

Cauchy Distribution in Spreadsheet Formulas, *STATISTICA BASIC*, and User-defined Functions

For the Cauchy distribution use *cauchy(x,η,θ)*; for the Cauchy integral, use *icauchy(x,η,θ)*; for the inverse Cauchy distribution, use *vcauchy(x,η,θ)*. For example the *STATISTICA BASIC* statement

```
v1 := cauchy(v2,25,10);
```

will transform the values of variable 2 and place the probability density values for the Cauchy distribution in variable 1.

Cauchy Distribution for the *Probability Distribution Calculator*

You can specify the *Location* and *Scale* parameters (η and θ, respectively) for the Cauchy distribution in the *Probability Distribution Calculator* (accessible from the *Analysis - Quick Basic Stats - Probability Calculator* option).

Note that you can change the values of the parameters by either manually editing them in the respecitve edit field (you will need to click on the *Compute* button to complete the calculations) or by using the micro scrolls to incrementally change the values in the edit fields. (When you use the micro scrolls to change a value, *STATISTICA* will automatically recompute the other values.) If one or both of these parameters are changed, then the *p*-value will be recomputed based on the respective variate value.

Chi-square Distribution

The *Chi-square* distribution has the probability density function:

$$f(x)=\{1/[2^{\nu/2}*\Gamma(\nu/2)]\}*[x^{(\nu/2)-1}*e^{-x/2}]$$

$\nu = 1, 2, \ldots, \quad 0 < x$

where

ν is the degrees of freedom

e is Euler's constant (2.72...)

Γ (*gamma*) is the *Gamma* function

x is interpreted as the value of *Chi-square*

Chi-square Distribution in Spreadsheet Formulas, *STATISTICA BASIC*, and User-defined Functions

For the *Chi-square* distribution use *chi2(x,ν)*; for the *Chi-square* integral, use *ichi2(x,ν)*; for the inverse *Chi-square* distribution, use *vchi2(x,ν)*. For example, via the *Current Specs* dialog (see Chapter 3, *Spreadsheet Window*), the spreadsheet formula

```
= chi2(v1,20)
```

will put the probability density values for the values of variable 1 into the current variable.

Chi-square Distribution for the *Probability Distribution Calculator*

You can specify the *Shape* parameter, ν (*df*) for the *Chi-square* distribution in the *Probability Distribution Calculator* (accessible from the *Analysis - Quick Basic Stats - Probability Calculator* option). Note that you can change the value of the parameter by either manually editing it in the edit field (you will need to click on the *Compute* button to complete the calculations) or by using the micro scrolls to incrementally change the value in the edit field. (When you use the micro scrolls to change the parameter value, *STATISTICA* will automatically recompute the other values.) If this parameter is changed, then the *p*-value will be recomputed based on the respective variate value.

Exponential Distribution

The Exponential distribution has the probability density function:

$$f(x) = \lambda*e^{[-\lambda(x-\theta)]}$$

$0 < \lambda, \quad \theta < x$

where

θ is the *Threshold* (*Location*) parameter

λ (*lambda*) is the *Scale* parameter (an alternative parameterization is $\lambda = 1/b$)

e is Euler's constant (2.72...)

The cumulative distribution function is (for θ=0):

$$F(x) = 0 \qquad x\le 0$$
$$\quad = 1 - e^{-\lambda x} \qquad x>0$$

The inverse distribution function (of probability α) is (for θ=0):

$$-1/\lambda*\log(1-\alpha)$$

Exponential Distribution in Spreadsheet Formulas, *STATISTICA BASIC*, and User-defined Functions

For spreadsheet formulas, *STATISTICA BASIC*, and user-defined functions, the *Location* parameter θ is equal to *0*. Therefore, you only need to specify the *Scale* parameter (λ) of the distribution. For the Exponential distribution use, *expon(x,λ)*; for the Exponential integral, use *iexpon(x,λ);* for the inverse Exponential distribution, use *vexpon(x,λ)*. For example, you could specify the following user-defined function (e.g., in the *2D Custom Function Plot*),

```
expon(x,2)
```

to plot the exponential distribution for a pre-specified range of *x* values.

Exponential Distribution for the *Probability Distribution Calculator*

For the *Probability Distribution Calculator*, the *Location* parameter θ is equal to *0*. Therefore, you only need to specify the *Scale* parameter (λ) of the distribution. Note that you can change the value of the parameter by either manually editing it in the edit field (you will need to click on the *Compute* button to complete the calculations) or by using the micro scrolls to incrementally change the value in the edit field. (When you use the micro scrolls to change the parameter, *STATISTICA* will automatically recompute the other values.) If this parameter is changed, then the *p*-value will be recomputed based on the respective variate value.

Exponential Distribution for *Quantile-Quantile* Plots

In *Quantile-Quantile* (*Q-Q*) plots (see Volume II, or the *Electronic Manual*), the standardized Exponential distribution will be used to find the best-fitting distribution. It is not necessary to specify any parameters for this plot.

In general, if the points in the *Q-Q* plot form a straight line, then the respective family of distributions (Exponential distribution) provides a good fit to the data; in that case, the intercept and slope of the fitted line can be interpreted as graphical estimates of the *Threshold* (θ) and *Scale* (λ) parameters, respectively.

Exponential Distribution for *Probability-Probability* Plots

You can use the *Probability-Probability* (or *P-P*) plot to determine how well the Exponential distribution fits the observed data. In order to create this plot, the theoretical distribution function must be completely specified. Therefore, the parameters for the distribution must either be defined by the user or computed from the data. You can specify the distribution parameters in the following manners:

De-select *Compute from data*. When you de-select this option, you will need to specify the *Scale* and *Threshold* parameters (λ and θ, respectively).

Select *Compute from data*. When you select this option and specify the *Threshold* parameter θ, *STATISTICA* will estimate the *Scale* parameter λ from the data.

In general, if the observed points follow the Exponential distribution with the respective parameters, then they will fall onto the straight line in the *P-P* plot.

Note that you can use the *Quantile-Quantile* plot to obtain the parameter estimates (for the best fitting distribution from a family of distributions) to enter here.

For more information on *Q-Q* and *P-P* plots, see Volume II, or the *Electronic Manual*.

Extreme Value (Gumbel) Distribution

The Extreme Value (Type I, Gumbel) distribution has the probability density function:

$$f(x) = 1/b * e^{-(x-a)/b} * e^{-e^{-(x-a)/b}}$$

$$-\infty < x < \infty, \quad 0 < b$$

where

a is the *Location* parameter

b is the *Scale* parameter

e is Euler's constant (2.72...)

The cumulative distribution function is:

$$F(x) = e^{-e^{-(x-a)/b}}$$

The inverse distribution function (of probability α) is:

```
a-[b*loglog(1/α)]
```

This distribution is also sometimes referred to as the distribution of the largest extreme.

Extreme Value Distribution in Spreadsheet Formulas, *STATISTICA BASIC*, and User-defined Functions

For the Extreme *Value* distribution, use *extreme(x,a,b)*; for the Extreme Value integral, use *iextreme(x,a,b)*; for the inverse Extreme Value distribution, use *vextreme(x,a,b)*. For example, the following spreadsheet formula

```
= extreme(v1,-1,1)
```

will put the probability density values for the values in *v1* into the current variable.

Extreme Value Distribution for the *Probability Distribution Calculator*

You can specify the *Location* and *Scale* parameters (*a* and *b*, respectively) for the Extreme Value distribution in the *Probability Distribution Calculator* (accessible from the *Analysis - Quick Basic Stats - Probability Calculator* option). Note that you can change the values of the parameters by either manually editing them in the respecitve edit field (you will need to click on the *Compute* button to complete the calculations) or by using the micro scrolls to incrementally change the values in the edit fields. (When you use the micro scrolls to change a value, *STATISTICA* will automatically recompute the other values.) If one or both of these parameters are changed, then the *p*-value will be recomputed based on the respective variate value.

Extreme Value Distribution for *Quantile-Quantile* Plots

In *Quantile-Quantile* (*Q-Q*) plots (see Volume II, or the *Electronic Manual*), the standardized Extreme Value distribution will be used to find the best-fitting distribution. It is not necessary to specify any parameters for this plot.

In general, if the points in the *Q-Q* plot form a straight line, then the respective family of distributions (Extreme Value distribution) provides a good fit to the data; in that case, the intercept and slope of the fitted line can be interpreted as graphical estimates of the *Threshold* (*a*) and *Scale* (*b*) parameters, respectively.

Extreme Value Distribution for *Probability-Probability* Plots

You can use the *Probability-Probability* (or *P-P*) plot to determine how well the Extreme Value distribution fits the observed data. In order to create this plot, the theoretical distribution function must be completely specified. Therefore, the parameters for the distribution must either be defined by the user or computed from the data. You can specify the distribution parameters in the following manners:

De-select *Compute from data*. When you de-select this option, you will need to specify the *Threshold* and *Scale* parameters (*a* and *b*, respectively).

Select *Compute from data*. When you select this option, *STATISTICA* will estimate the *Threshold* parameter *a* and the *Scale* parameter *b* from the data.

In general, if the observed points follow the Extreme Value distribution with the respective parameters, then they will fall onto the straight line in the *P-P* plot. Note that you can use the *Quantile-Quantile* plot to obtain the parameter estimates (for the best fitting distribution from a family of distributions) to enter here.

For more information on *Q-Q* and *P-P* plots, see Volume II or the *Electronic Manual*.

F Distribution

The *F* distribution has the probability density function:

$$f(x) = \{\Gamma[(\nu+\omega)/2]*(\nu/\omega)^{\nu/2}*x^{(\nu-2)/2}\}/\{\Gamma(\nu/2)*\Gamma(\omega/2)[1+(\nu/\omega)*x]^{(\nu+\omega)/2}\}$$

$0 \le x < \infty$

$\nu = 1,2,\ldots,\ \omega = 1,2,\ldots$

where

ν, ω are the degrees of freedom

Γ (*gamma*) is the *Gamma* function

F Distribution in Spreadsheet Formulas, *STATISTICA BASIC*, and User-defined Functions

Spreadsheet formulas and user-defined functions. For the *F* distribution, use *F(x,ν,ω)*; for the *F* integral, use *iF(x,ν,ω)*; for the inverse *F* distribution, use *vF(x,ν,ω)*.

For example, the following spreadsheet formula

```
= F(v3,5,10)
```

will put the probability density values for the values in *v3* into the current variable.

***STATISTICA BASIC*.** For the *F* distribution, use *FDistr(x,ν,ω)*. Because *if* is already used as a *STATISTICA BASIC* function, for the *F* integral use *iFDistr(x,ν,ω)*. For the inverse *F* distribution, use *vFDistr(x,ν,ω)*.

For example, the following *STATISTICA BASIC* statement

```
v10 := FDistr(v3,5,10);
```

will transform the values of *v3* and place the probability density values for the *F* distribution into *v10*.

F Distribution for the *Probability Distribution Calculator*

You can specify the *Shape* parameters (ν, and ω, or *df1* and *df2*, respectively) for the *F* distribution in the *Probability Distribution Calculator* (accessible from the *Analysis - Quick Basic Stats - Probability Calculator* option). Note that you can change the values of the parameters by either manually editing them in the respecitve edit field (you will need to click on the *Compute* button to complete the calculations) or by using the micro scrolls to incrementally change the values in the edit fields. (When you use the micro scrolls to change a value, *STATISTICA* will automatically recompute the other values.) If one or both of these parameters are changed, then the *p*-value will be recomputed based on the respective variate value.

Gamma Distribution

The *Gamma* distribution has the probability density function:

$$f(x) = \{1/[\Gamma(c)b]\}*[(x-\theta)/b]^{c-1}*e^{[-(x-\theta)/b]}$$

$0 \le x$

where

Γ (*gamma*) is the *Gamma* function

θ is the *Threshold* (*Location*) parameter

c is the *Shape* parameter

b is the *Scale* parameter

e is Euler's constant (2.72...)

Gamma Distribution in Spreadsheet Formulas, *STATISTICA BASIC*, and User-defined Functions

For spreadsheet formulas, *STATISTICA BASIC*, and user-defined functions, the *Threshold* parameter θ is equal to *0* and the *Scale* parameter *b* is equal to *1*. Therefore, you only need to specify the *Shape* parameter (*c*) of the distribution.

For the *Gamma* distribution, use *gamma(x,c)*; for *Gamma* integral, use *igamma(x,c)*; for inverse *Gamma* distribution, use *vgamma(x,c)*. For example, the following spreadsheet formula

```
= gamma(v10,5)
```

will put the probability density values for the values in *v10* into the current variable.

Gamma Distribution for the *Probability Distribution Calculator*

For the *Probability Distribution Calculator*, the *Threshold* parameter θ is equal to *0* and the *Scale* parameter *b* is equal to *1*. Therefore, you only need to specify the *Shape* parameter (*c*) of the distribution. Note that you can change the value of this parameter by either manually editing it in the respective edit field (you will need to click on the *Compute* button to complete the calculations) or by using the micro scrolls to incrementally change the value in the edit field. (When you use the micro scrolls to change a value, *STATISTICA* will automatically recompute the other values.) If this parameter is changed, then the *p*-value will be recomputed based on the respective variate value.

Gamma Distribution for *Quantile-Quantile* Plots

The standardized *Gamma* distribution with *Shape* parameter *c* will be used to find the best-fitting distribution function. The *Shape* parameter can be specified in one of two ways:

(1) Enter a user-defined value for the *Shape* parameter and de-select the *Compute parameters from* option.

(2) Estimate the *Shape* parameter by selecting the *Compute parameters from* option and entering a user-defined *Threshold* parameter.

In general, if the points in the *Q-Q* plot form a straight line, then the respective family of distributions (*Gamma* distribution with the *Shape* parameter *c* in this case) provides a good fit to the data; in that case, the intercept and slope of the fitted line can be interpreted as graphical estimates of the *Threshold* (θ) and *Scale* (*b*) parameters, respectively.

Gamma Distribution for *Probability-Probability* Plots

You can use the *Probability-Probability* (or *P-P*) plot to determine how well the *Gamma* distribution fits the observed data. In order to create this plot, the theoretical distribution function must be completely specified. Therefore, the parameters for the distribution must either be defined by the user or computed from the data. You can specify the distribution parameters in the following manners:

De-select *Compute from data*. When you de-select this option, you will need to specify the *Shape* and *Scale* parameters (*c* and *b*, respectively) as well as the *Threshold* parameter θ.

Select *Compute from data*. When you select this option and specify the *Threshold* parameter θ,

STATISTICA will estimate both the *Shape* and *Scale* parameters (*c* and *b*, respectively) from the data.

In general, if the observed points follow the *Gamma* distribution with the respective parameters, then they will fall onto the straight line in the *P-P* plot. Note that you can use the *Quantile-Quantile* plot to obtain the parameter estimates (for the best fitting distribution from a family of distributions) to enter here.

For more information on *Q-Q* and *P-P* plots, see Volume II, or the *Electronic Manual*.

Geometric Distribution

The geometric distribution has the probability function:

$$f(x) = p*(1-p)^{x-1}$$

$$0 < p < 1, \quad x = 1, 2, \ldots$$

where

p is the probability that a particular event (e.g., success) will occur

Geometric Distribution in Spreadsheet Formulas, *STATISTICA BASIC*, and User-defined Functions

For the Geometric distribution, use *geom(x,p)*; for the Geometric integral, use *igeom(x,p)* (the inverse Geometric distribution function is not available here). For example, the *STATISTICA BASIC* formula

```
v7 := geom(v1,.5);
```

will transform the values of *v1* and place the probability density values for the Geometric distribution into *v7*.

Laplace Distribution

The Laplace distribution has the probability density function:

$$f(x) = 1/(2b) * e^{-|x-a|/b}$$

$$-\infty < x < \infty, \quad 0 < b$$

where

a is the mean of the distribution

b is the *Scale* parameter

e is Euler's constant (2.72...)

The cumulative distribution function is:

$$F(x) = 1/2 * e^{-(a-x)/b} \qquad x < a$$

$$= 1 - \{1/2 * e^{-(x-a)/b} \qquad x \geq a$$

Laplace Distribution in Spreadsheet Formulas, *STATISTICA BASIC*, and User-defined Functions

For the Laplace distribution, use *laplace(x,a,b)*; for the Laplace integral, use *ilaplace(x,a,b)*; for the inverse Laplace distribution, use *vlaplace(x,a,b)*. For example, the following function

```
laplace(x,-2,5)
```

can be entered as a user-defined function in the *2D Custom Function Plot* dialog in order to produce a graph of the Laplace distribution for the specified range of *x* values.

Laplace Distribution for the *Probability Distribution Calculator*

You can specify the *Location* and *Scale* parameters (*a* and *b*, respectively) for the Laplace distribution in the *Probability Distribution Calculator* (accessible from the *Analysis - Quick Basic Stats - Probability Calculator* option). Note that you can change the values of the parameters by either manually editing them in the respecitve edit field (you will need to click on the *Compute* button to complete the calculations) or by using the micro scrolls to incrementally change the values in the edit fields. (When you use the micro scrolls to change a value, *STATISTICA* will automatically recompute the other values.) If one or both of these parameters are changed, then the *p*-value will be recomputed based on the respective variate value.

Logistic Distribution

The logistic distribution has the probability density function:

$$f(x) = (1/b)*e^{-(x-a)/b} * [1+e^{-(x-a)/b}]^{-2}$$

$-\infty < x < \infty, \ 0 < b$

where

a is the mean of the distribution

b is the *Scale* parameter

e is Euler's constant (2.72...)

The cumulative distribution function is:

$$F(x) = \{1 + e^{[-(x-a)/b]}\}^{-1}$$

The invese distribution function (of probability α) is:

$$a-b * \log(1/\alpha - 1)$$

Logistic Distribution in Spreadsheet Formulas, *STATISTICA BASIC*, and User-defined Functions

For the Logistic distribution, use *logis(x,a,b)*; for the logistic integral, use *ilogis(x,a,b)*; for the inverse logistic distribution, use *vlogis(x,a,b)*. For example, the following spreadsheet formula

```
= logis(v0,-4,15)
```

will put the probability density values for the values in *v0* (the case numbers) into the current variable.

Logistic Distribution for the *Probability Distribution Calculator*

You can specify the *Location* and *Scale* parameters (*a* and *b*, respectively) for the Logistic distribution in the *Probability Distribution Calculator* (accessible from the *Analysis - Quick Basic Stats - Probability Calculator* option).

Note that you can change the values of the parameters by either manually editing them in the respecitve edit field (you will need to click on the *Compute* button to complete the calculations) or by using the micro scrolls to incrementally change the values in the edit fields. (When you use the micro scrolls to change a value, *STATISTICA* will automatically recompute the other values.)

If one or both of these parameters are changed, then the *p*-value will be recomputed based on the respective variate value.

Lognormal Distribution

The Lognormal distribution has the probability density function:

$$f(x)=1/[(x-\theta)\sigma(2\pi)^{1/2}]*e^{-[\log(x-\theta)-\mu]^2/2\sigma^2}$$

$\theta < x < \infty, \ 0 < \mu, \ 0 < \sigma$

where

μ is the *Scale* parameter

σ is the *Shape* parameter

θ is the *Threshold* (*Location*) parameter

e is Euler's constant (2.72...)

Lognormal Distribution in Spreadsheet Formulas, *STATISTICA BASIC*, and User-defined Functions

For spreadsheet formulas, *STATISTICA BASIC*, and user-defined functions, the *Threshold* parameter θ is equal to *0*. Therefore, you only need to specify the *Scale* and *Shape* parameters (μ and σ, respectively) of the distribution.

For the Lognormal distribution, use *lognorm(x,μ,σ)*; for the Lognormal integral, use *ilognorm(x,μ,σ)*; for the inverse Lognormal distribution, use *vlognorm(x,μ,σ)*.

For example, the following spreadsheet formula

```
= lognorm(v12,0,1)
```

will put the probability density values for the values in *v12* into the current variable.

Lognormal Distribution for the *Probability Distribution Calculator*

For the *Probability Distribution Calculator*, the *Threshold* parameter θ is equal to *0*. Therefore, you only need to specify the *Scale* and *Shape* parameters (μ and σ, respectively) of the distribution. Note that you can change the value of these parameters by either manually editing them in the respecitve edit fields (you will need to click on the *Compute* button to complete the calculations) or by using the micro scrolls to incrementally change the values in the edit fields. (When you use the micro scrolls to change a value, *STATISTICA* will automatically recompute the other values.) If one or both of these parameters are changed, then the *p*-value will be recomputed based on the respective variate value.

Lognormal Distribution for *Quantile-Quantile* Plots

The standardized Lognormal distribution with *Shape* parameter σ will be used to find the best-fitting distribution function. The *Shape* parameter σ can be specified in one of two ways:

(1) Enter a user-defined value for the *Shape* parameter σ and de-select the *Compute parameters from* option.

(2) Estimate the *Shape* parameter σ by selecting the *Compute parameters from* option and entering a user-defined *Threshold* parameter θ.

In general, if the points in the *Q-Q* plot form a straight line, then the respective family of distributions (Lognormal distribution with the *Shape* parameter σ in this case) provides a good fit to the data; in that case, the intercept and slope of the fitted line can be interpreted as graphical estimates of the *Threshold* (θ) and *Scale* (μ) parameters, respectively.

Lognormal Distribution for *Probability-Probability* Plots

You can use the *Probability-Probability* (or *P-P*) plot to determine how well the Lognormal distribution fits the observed data. In order to create this plot, the theoretical distribution function must be completely specified. Therefore, the parameters for the distribution must either be defined by the user or computed from the data. You can specify the distribution parameters in the following manners:

De-select *Compute from data*. When you de-select this option, you will need to specify the *Shape* and *Scale* parameters (σ and μ, respectively) as well as the *Threshold* parameter θ.

Select *Compute from data*. When you select this option and specify the *Threshold* parameter θ, *STATISTICA* will estimate both the *Shape* and *Scale* parameters (σ and μ, respectively) from the data.

In general, if the observed points follow the Lognormal distribution with the respective parameters, then they will fall onto the straight line in the *P-P* plot. Note that you can use the *Quantile-Quantile* plot to obtain the parameter estimates (for the best fitting distribution from a family of distributions) to enter here.

For more information on *Q-Q* and *P-P* plots, see Volume II, or the *Electronic Manual*.

Normal Distribution

The Normal distribution has the probability density function:

$$f(x) = 1/[\sigma(2\pi)^{1/2}] * e^{\{-1/2[(x-\mu)/\sigma]^2\}}$$

$$-\infty < x < \infty,\ 0 < \sigma$$

where

μ is the mean

σ is the standard deviation

e is Euler's constant (2.72...)

π is the constant *Pi* (3.14...)

Normal Distribution in Spreadsheet Formulas, *STATISTICA BASIC*, and User-defined Functions

Spreadsheet formulas and user-defined functions. For the Normal distribution, use *normal(x,μ,σ)*; for the Normal integral, use *inormal(x,μ,σ)*; for the inverse Normal distribution, use *vnormal(x,μ,σ)*.

For example, the following spreadsheet formula

```
= Normal(v2,0,1)
```

will put the probability density values for the values in *v2* into the current variable.

***STATISTICA BASIC*.** Because *normal* is already used as a *STATISTICA BASIC* function, for the Normal distribution, use *dnormal(x,μ,σ)*. For the Normal integral, use *inormal(x,μ,σ)*; for the inverse Normal distribution, use *vnormal(x,μ,σ)*.

For example, the *STATISTICA BASIC* formula

```
v25 := dnormal(v15,10,5);
```

will transform the values of *v15* and place the probability density values for the Normal distribution into *v25*.

Normal Distribution for the *Probability Distribution Calculator*

You can specify the mean and standard deviation parameters (μ and σ , respectively) for the Normal distribution in the *Probability Distribution Calculator* (accessible from the *Analysis - Quick Basic Stats - Probability Calculator* option). Note that you can change the values of the parameters by either manually editing them in the respecitve edit field (you will need to click on the *Compute* button to complete the calculations) or by using the micro scrolls to incrementally change the values in the edit fields. (When you use the micro scrolls to change a value, *STATISTICA* will automatically recompute the other values.) If one or both of these parameters are changed, then the *p*-value will be recomputed based on the respective variate value.

Normal Distribution for *Quantile-Quantile* Plots

In *Quantile-Quantile* (*Q-Q*) plots, the standardized Normal distribution will be used to find the best-fitting distribution. It is not necessary to specify any parameters for this plot.

In general, if the points in the *Q-Q* plot form a straight line, then the respective family of distributions (Normal distribution) provides a good fit to the data; in that case, the intercept and slope of the fitted line can be interpreted as graphical estimates of the mean (μ) and standard deviation (σ) parameters, respectively.

Normal Distribution for *Probability-Probability* Plots

You can use the *Probability-Probability* (or *P-P*) plot to determine how well the Normal distribution fits the observed data. In order to create this plot, the theoretical distribution function must be completely specified. Therefore, the parameters for the distribution must either be defined by the user or computed from the data. You can specify the distribution parameters in the following manners:

De-select *Compute from data*. When you de-select this option, you will need to specify both the *Mu* (μ) and *Sigma* (σ) parameters.

Select *Compute from data*. When you select this option, *STATISTICA* will estimate *Mu* (μ) and *Sigma* (σ) from the data.

In general, if the observed points follow the Normal distribution with the respective parameters, then they will fall onto the straight line in the *P-P* plot. Note that you can use the *Quantile-Quantile* plot to obtain the parameter estimates (for the best fitting distribution from a family of distributions) to enter here.

For more information on *Q-Q* and *P-P* plots, see Volume II, or the *Electronic Manual*.

Pareto Distribution

The Pareto distribution has the probability density function:

$f(x) = c/x^{c+1}$

$1 \leq x,\ c < 0$

where

c is the *Shape* parameter of the distribution

The cumulative distribution function is:

$F(x) = 1 - x^{-c}$

The inverse distribution function (of probability α) is:

$(1-\alpha)^{c}$

Pareto Distribution in Spreadsheet Formulas, *STATISTICA BASIC*, and User-defined Functions

For the Pareto distribution, use *pareto(x,c)*; for the Pareto integral, use *ipareto(x,c)*; for the inverse Pareto distribution, use *vpareto(x,c)*. For example, the following spreadsheet formula

```
= pareto(v1,1)
```

will put the probability density values for the values in *v1* into the current variable.

Pareto Distribution for the *Probability Distribution Calculator*

You can specify the *Shape* parameter (*c*) for the Pareto distribution in the *Probability Distribution Calculator* (accessible from the *Analysis - Quick Basic Stats - Probability Calculator* option). Note that you can change the value of the parameter by either manually editing it in the respecitve edit field (you will need to click on the *Compute* button to complete the calculations) or by using the micro

scrolls to incrementally change the value in the edit fields. (When you use the micro scrolls to change a value, *STATISTICA* will automatically recompute the other values.) If this parameter is changed, then the *p*-value will be recomputed based on the respective variate value.

Poisson Distribution

The Poisson distribution has the probability function:

$$f(x) = (\lambda^x * e^{-\lambda})/x!$$

$$0 < \lambda,\ x = 0,\ 1,\ ...$$

where

λ (*lambda*) is the expected value of *x* (the mean)

e is Euler's constant (2.72...)

Poisson Distribution in Spreadsheet Formulas, *STATISTICA BASIC*, and User-defined Functions

Spreadsheet formulas and user-defined functions. For the Poisson distribution, use *poisson(x,λ)*; for the Poisson integral, use *ipoisson(x,λ)*. The inverse Poisson function is not available for this distribution.

For example, the following function

```
poisson(x,25)
```

can be entered as a user-defined function in the *2D Custom Function Plot* dialog in order to produce a graph of the Poisson distribution for the specified range of *x* values.

***STATISTICA BASIC*.** Because *poisson* is already used as a *STATISTICA BASIC* function, for the Poisson distribution, use *dpoisson(x,λ)*. For the Poisson integral, use *ipoisson(x,λ)*.

For example, the *STATISTICA BASIC* formula

```
v4 := dpoisson(v1,2);
```

will transform the values of *v1* and place the probability density values for the Poisson distribution into *v4*.

Rayleigh Distribution

The Rayleigh distribution has the probability density function:

$$f(x) = (x-\theta)/b^2 * e^{-[(x-\theta)^2/(2b^2)]}$$

$$\theta \le x < \infty,\ b > 0$$

where

b is the *Scale* parameter

θ is the *Threshold* (*Location*) parameter

e is Euler's constant (2.72...)

The cumulative distribution function is (for θ=0):

$$F(x) = 1 - e^{-(x^2/(2b^2))}$$

The inverse distribution function (of probability α) is (for θ=0):

$$\{-2b^2[\log(1-\alpha)]\}^{1/2}$$

Rayleigh Distribution in Spreadsheet Formulas, *STATISTICA BASIC*, and User-defined Functions

For spreadsheet formulas, *STATISTICA BASIC*, and user-defined functions, the *Threshold* parameter θ is equal to *0*. Therefore, you only need to specify the *Scale* parameter *b* of the distribution. For the Rayleigh distribution, use *rayleigh(x,b)*; for the Rayleigh integral, use *irayleigh(x,b)*; for the inverse Rayleigh distribution, use *vrayleigh(x,b)*.

For example, the following spreadsheet formula

```
= rayleigh(v2,4)
```

will put the probability density values for the values in *v2* into the current variable.

Rayleigh Distribution for the *Probability Distribution Calculator*

For the *Probability Distribution Calculator*, the *Threshold* parameter θ is equal to *0*. Therefore, you only need to specify the *Scale* parameter (*b*) of the distribution. Note that you can change the value of this parameter by either manually editing it in the respecitve edit field (you will need to click on the *Compute* button to complete the calculations) or by using the micro scrolls to incrementally change the value in the edit field. (When you use the micro scrolls to change a value, *STATISTICA* will automatically recompute the other values.) If this parameter is changed, then the *p*-value will be recomputed based on the respective variate value.

Rayleigh Distribution for *Quantile-Quantile* Plots

In *Quantile-Quantile* (*Q-Q*) plots (see Volume II, or the *Electronic Manual*), the standardized Rayleigh distribution will be used to find the best-fitting distribution. It is not necessary to specify any parameters for this plot.

In general, if the points in the *Q-Q* plot form a straight line, then the respective family of distributions (Rayleigh distribution) provides a good fit to the data; in that case, the intercept and slope of the fitted line can be interpreted as graphical estimates of the *Threshold* (θ) and *Scale* (*b*) parameters, respectively.

Rayleigh Distribution for *Probability-Probability* Plots

You can use the *Probability-Probability* (or *P-P*) plot to determine how well the Rayleigh distribution fits the observed data. In order to create this plot, the theoretical distribution function must be completely specified. Therefore, the parameters for the distribution must either be defined by the user or computed from the data. You can specify the distribution parameters in the following manners:

De-select *Compute from data*. When you de-select this option, you will need to specify the *Scale* parameter *b* as well as the *Threshold* parameter θ.

Select *Compute from data*. When you select this option and specify the *Threshold* parameter θ, *STATISTICA* will estimate the *Scale* parameter *b* from the data.

In general, if the observed points follow the Rayleigh distribution with the respective parameters, then they will fall onto the straight line in the *P-P* plot. Note that you can use the *Quantile-Quantile* plot to obtain the parameter estimates (for the best fitting distribution from a family of distributions) to enter here.

For more information on *Q-Q* and *P-P* plots, see Volume II, or the *Electronic Manual*.

Student's *t* Distribution

The Student's *t* distribution has the probability density function:

$$f(x) = \Gamma[(\nu+1)/2] / \Gamma(\nu/2) * (\nu*\pi)^{-1/2} * [1+(x^2/\nu)]^{-(\nu+1)/2}$$

$$\nu = 1,2,...$$

where

ν is the degrees of freedom

Γ (*gamma*) is the *Gamma* function

π is the constant *Pi* (3.14...)

The cumulative distribution function for the Student's *t* distribution depends on whether *v* is odd or even and is completely described in Evans, Hastings, and Peacock, 1993.

Student's *t* Distribution in Spreadsheet Formulas, *STATISTICA BASIC*, and User-defined Functions

For the Student's *t* distribution, use *student(x,df)*; for the Student's *t* integral, use *istudent(x,df)*; for the inverse Student's *t* distribution, use *vstudent(x,df)*. For example, the following spreadsheet formula

```
= student(v4,25)
```

will put the probability density values for the values in *v4* into the current variable.

```
= pareto(v1,1)
```

will put the probability density values for the values in *v1* into the current variable.

Student's *t* Distribution for the *Probability Distribution Calculator*

You can specify the *Shape* parameter (ν) for the Student's *t* distribution in the *Probability Distribution Calculator* (accessible from the *Analysis - Quick Basic Stats - Probability Calculator* option). Note that you can change the value of the parameter by either manually editing it in the respecitve edit field (you will need to click on the *Compute* button to complete the calculations) or by using the micro scrolls to incrementally change the value in the edit field. (When you use the micro scrolls to change a value, *STATISTICA* will automatically recompute the other values.) If this parameter is changed, then the *p*-value will be recomputed based on the respective variate value.

Weibull Distribution

The Weibull distribution has the probability density function:

$$f(x) = c/b*[(x-\theta)/b]^{c-1} * e^{-[(x-\theta)/b]^c}$$

$$x \geq \theta,\ 0 < b,\ 0 < c$$

where

b is the *Scale* parameter of the distribution

c is the *Shape* parameter of the distribution

θ is the *Threshold* (*Location*) parameter of the distribution

e is Euler's constant (2.72...)

The inverse distribution function (of probability α) is:

$$b\{\log[1/(1-\alpha)]\}^{1/c}$$

Weibull Distribution in Spreadsheet Formulas, *STATISTICA BASIC*, and User-defined Functions

For the Weibull distribution, use *weibull(x,b,c,θ)*; for the Weibull integral, use *iweibull(x,b,c,θ)*; for the inverse Weibull distribution, use *vweibull(x,b,c,θ)*. For example, the following function

```
weibull(x,1,3,1)
```

can be entered as a user-defined function in the *2D Custom Function Plot* dialog in order to produce a graph of the Weibull distribution for the specified range of *x* values.

Weibull Distribution for the *Probability Distribution Calculator*

For the *Probability Distribution Calculator*, the *Threshold* parameter θ is equal to *0*. Therefore, you only need to specify the *Scale* and *Shape* parameters (*b* and *c*, respectively) of the distribution. Note that you can change the values of these parameters by either manually editing them in the respecitve edit fields (you will need to click on the *Compute* button to complete the calculations) or by using the micro scrolls to incrementally change the values in the edit fields. (When you use the micro scrolls to change a value, *STATISTICA* will automatically recompute the other values.) If one or both of these parameters are changed, then the *p*-value will be recomputed based on the respective variate value.

Weibull Distribution for *Quantile-Quantile* Plots

The standardized Weibull distribution with *Shape* parameter *c* will be used to find the best-fitting distribution function. The *Shape* parameter *c* can be specified in one of two ways:

(1) Enter a user-defined value for the *Shape* parameter *c* and de-select the *Compute parameters from* option.

(2) Estimate the *Shape* parameter *c* by selecting the *Compute parameters from* option and entering a user-defined *Threshold* parameter θ.

In general, if the points in the *Q-Q* plot form a straight line, then the respective family of distributions (Weibull distribution with *Shape* parameter *c* in this case) provides a good fit to the data; in that case, the intercept and slope of the fitted line can be interpreted as graphical estimates of the *Threshold* (θ) and *Scale* (*b*) parameters, respectively.

Weibull Distribution for *Probability-Probability* Plots

You can use the *Probability-Probability* (or *P-P*) plot to determine how well the Weibull distribution fits the observed data. In order to create this plot, the theoretical distribution function must be completely specified. Therefore, the parameters for the distribution must either be defined by the user or computed from the data. You can specify the distribution parameters in the following manners:

De-select *Compute from data*. When you de-select this option, you will need to specify the *Shape* and *Scale* parameters (*b* and *c*, respectively) as well as the *Threshold* parameter θ.

Select *Compute from data*. When you select this option and specify the *Threshold* parameter θ, *STATISTICA* will estimate both the *Shape* and *Scale* parameters (*b* and *c*, respectively) from the data.

In general, if the observed points follow the Weibull distribution with the respective parameters, then they will fall onto the straight line in the *P-P* plot. Note that you can use the *Quantile-Quantile* plot to obtain the parameter estimates (for the best fitting distribution from a family of distributions) to enter here.

For more information on *Q-Q* and *P-P* plots, see Volume II, or the *Electronic Manual*.

APPENDIX II: SUMMARY STATISTICS

The following summary statistics are given when you select the *Quick Basic Stats - Descriptives* option (see Chapter 10).

Valid *n*

This is the sample size resulting from all valid (i.e., non-missing) data points in the respective variable. Missing data can be treated on one of the following ways in *STATISTICA*:

Casewise Deletion of Missing Data

When casewise deletion of missing data is selected (e.g., set the *Casewise (listwise) deletion of MD* checkbox in the *Quick Basic Stats - Extended Options* dialog), then only cases that do not contain any missing data for any of the variables selected for the analysis will be included in the analysis. In the case of correlations, all correlations are calculated by excluding cases that have missing data for any of the selected variables (all correlations are based on the same set of data).

Pairwise Deletion of Missing Data

If pairwise deletion of missing data is selected (e.g., the *Casewise (listwise) deletion of MD* checkbox is not set in the *Quick Basic Stats - Extended Options* dialog), then all valid data points will be included in the analyses for the respective variables, possibly resulting in unequal *valid n* per variable.

Mean Substitution of Missing Data

When you select *Mean Substitution*, the missing data will be replaced by the means for the respective variables during an analysis. (This option is available in selected modules only; note that you can also replace missing data with the mean via the option *Replace Missing Data* from the *Analysis* pull-down menu in the *Data Management* module.)

Sum

This value is the sum of the non-missing values of the respective variable.

$\text{sum} = \Sigma x_i \quad \text{for } i = 1 \text{ to } n$

Minimum

This is the minimum value of the respective variable.

Maximum

This is the maximum value of the respective variable.

Mean

The mean is a particularly informative measure of the "central tendency" of the variable if it is reported along with its confidence intervals (see below). Usually we are interested in statistics (such as the mean) from a sample only to the extent to which they are informative about the population. The larger the sample size, the more reliable its mean. The larger the variation of data values, the less reliable the mean (see also *Elementary Concepts*, Chapter 8).

$\text{Mean} = (\Sigma x_i)/n$

where

n is the sample size.

Confidence Limits of the Mean

The *confidence intervals* for the mean give us a range of values around the mean where we expect the "true" (population) mean is located (with a given level of certainty, see also *Elementary Concepts*, Chapter 8).

For example, if the mean in your sample is 23, and the lower and upper limits of the p=.95 confidence interval are 19 and 27 respectively, then you can conclude that there is a 95% probability that the population mean is greater than 19 and lower than 27. If you set the p-level to a smaller value (e.g., as in the *Basic Statistics and Tables* module), then the interval would become wider thereby increasing the "certainty" of the estimate, and vice versa; as we all know from the weather forecast, the more "vague" the prediction (i.e., wider the confidence interval), the more likely it will materialize.

Note that the width of the confidence interval depends on the sample size and on the variation of data values. The calculation of confidence intervals is based on the assumption that the variable is normally distributed in the population. This estimate may not be valid if this assumption is not met, unless the sample size is large, say n = 100 or more.

Range

This value is computed by subtracting the minimum value from the maximum value for the respective variable.

Percentiles

From the *STATISTICA Defaults: General* dialog (see Chapter 3) you may select from among six methods for computing percentile values, including medians (50th percentile) and quartiles (25th and 75th percentiles). The method that you select there will apply to every place in the *STATISTICA* program where medians, quartiles, or percentiles are computed, for example, to the computation of:

- percentiles in the *Nonparametrics & Distributions* module;
- medians and quartiles in the *Basic Statistics & Tables* module;
- medians and quartiles in *2D Box Plots*;
- medians and quartiles in box-whisker plots in *Reproducibility and Repeatability* studies;
- medians and quartiles in box-whisker plots in *Discriminant Analysis*, *Reliability and Item Analysis*, *Basic Statistics*, *Multiple Regression*, and all other modules of *STATISTICA* that offer box-whisker plots as an option from the dialog.

For the following methods, let n be the number of cases, and p be the percentile value divided by 100 (e.g., *50/100* = *.5* for the median). Then, the available choices for computing percentiles are:

Weighted Average at X_{np} Method

This is the weighted average centered at X_{np}. Express np (n times p) as $np=j+g$ where j is the integer part of np, and g is the fractional part of np; then compute:

$$\text{PercentileValue} = (1-g)x_j + gx_{j+1}$$

Note that X_0 in the above computation is replaced by X_1 (e.g., if $j = 0$, then the above formula would be $(1-g)x_1 + gx_{(0+1)}$).

Example. To illustrate this method of computing percentiles, consider the following sorted data:

```
1, 2, 4, 7, 8, 9, 10, 12, 13
```

Here, $n = 9$ and let $p = .25$ (the 25th percentile). Express *np* (*n* times *p*) as:

```
np = 9*.25 = 2.25 = j + g
```

therefore, $j = 2$ and $g = .25$. Now compute the 25th percentile as:

$$\text{25th Percentile} = (1-.25)x_2 + .25x_3 = (.75)2 + (.25)4 = 2.5$$

Weighted Average at $X_{(n+1)p}$ Method

This is the weighted average centered at $X_{(n+1)p}$. Express $(n+1)p$ as $(n+1)p=j+g$ where j is the integer part of $(n+1)p$, and g is the fractional part of $(n+1)p$; then compute:

$$\text{PercentileValue} = (1-g)x_j + gx_{j+1}$$

Note that X_{n+1} in the above computation is replaced by X_n (e.g., if $j = n$, then the above formula would be $(1-g)x_n + gx_n$).

Example. To illustrate this method of computing percentiles, consider the following sorted data:

```
1, 2, 4, 7, 8, 9, 10, 12, 13
```

Here, $n = 9$ and let $p = .25$ (the 25th percentile). Express $(n+1)p$ as:

```
(n+1)p = 10*.25 = 2.5 = j + g
```

therefore, $j = 2$ and $g = .5$. Now compute the 25th percentile as:

$$\text{25th Percentile} = (1-.5)x_2 + .5x_3 = (.5)2 + (.5)4 = 3.0$$

Empirical Distribution Function Method

Express *np* (*n* times *p*) as $np=j+g$ where j is the integer part of *np*, and g is the fractional part of *np*; then choose the percentile value as:

$$\text{PercentileValue} = x_j \quad \text{if } g=0$$

$$\text{PercentileValue} = x_{j+1} \quad \text{if } g>0$$

Example. To illustrate this method of computing percentiles, consider the following sorted data:

```
1, 2, 4, 7, 8, 9, 10, 12, 13
```

Here, $n = 9$ and let $p = .25$ (the 25th percentile). Express *np* (*n* times *p*) as:

```
np = 9*.25 = 2.25 = j + g
```

therefore, $j = 2$ and $g = .25$. Now, since $g>0$, compute the 25th percentile as:

$$\text{25th Percentile} = x_3 = 4.0$$

Empirical Distribution Function with Averaging Method

Express *np* (*n* times *p*) as $np=j+g$ where j is the integer part of *np*, and g is the fractional part of *np*; then compute the percentile value as:

$$\text{PercentileValue} = (x_j + x_{j+1})/2 \quad \text{if } g=0$$

$$\text{PercentileValue} = x_{j+1} \quad \text{if } g>0$$

Example. To illustrate this method of computing percentiles, consider the following sorted data:

```
1, 2, 4, 7, 8, 9, 10, 12, 13
```

Here, $n = 9$ and let $p = .25$ (the 25th percentile). Express *np* (*n* times *p*) as:

```
np = 9*.25 = 2.25 = j + g
```

therefore, $j = 2$ and $g = .25$. Now, since $g>0$, compute the 25th percentile as:

$$25th\ Percentile = x_3 = 4.0$$

Empirical Distribution Function with Interpolation (MS Excel) Method

Express *(n-1)p* (*(n-1)* times *p*) as *(n-1)p=j+g* where *j* is the integer part of *(n-1)p*, and *g* is the fractional part of *(n-1)p*; then compute the percentile value as:

$$PercentileValue = x_{j+1} \quad \text{if } g=0$$

$$PercentileValue = x_{j+1} + g(x_{j+2} - x_{j+1}) \quad \text{if } g>0$$

Example. To illustrate this method of computing percentiles, consider the following sorted data:

`1, 2, 4, 7, 8, 9, 10, 12, 13`

Here, $n = 9$ and let $p = .25$ (the 25th percentile). Express *(n-1)p* as:

$$(n-1)p = 8*.25 = 2.0 = j + g$$

therefore, $j = 2$ and $g = 0$. Now, since g=0, compute the 25th percentile as:

$$25th\ Percentile = x_3 = 4.0$$

Closest Observation Method

This is the observation closest to *np*. Compute *j* as the integer part of *np+1/2*, then compute:

$$PercentileValue = x_j$$

Example. To illustrate this method of computing percentiles, consider the following sorted data:

`1, 2, 4, 7, 8, 9, 10, 12, 13`

Here, $n = 9$ and let $p = .25$ (the 25th percentile). Express *np* as:

$$np + 1/2 = (9*.25) + .5 = 2.75 = j + g$$

therefore, $j = 2$. Now, compute the 25th percentile as:

$$25th\ Percentile = x_2 = 2.0$$

Variance

The sample estimate of the population variance is computed as:

$$s^2 = \Sigma(x_i - xbar)^2 / n-1$$

where

xbar is the sample mean

n is the sample size.

Standard Error of the Mean

The standard error is the standard deviation of a mean and is computed as:

$$std.err. = \sqrt{(s^2/n)}$$

where

s^2 is the sample standard deviation

n is the sample size.

Kurtosis

Kurtosis measures the "peakedness" of a distribution. If the kurtosis is clearly different than 0, then the distribution is either flatter or more peaked than normal; the kurtosis of the normal distribution is 0. Kurtosis is computed as:

$$Kurtosis = [n*(n+1)*M_4 - 3*M_2*M_2*(n-1)] / [(n-1)*(n-2)*(n-3)*\sigma^4]$$

where

M_j is equal to: $\Sigma(x_i\text{-}Meanx)^j$

σ^4 is the standard deviation (*sigma*) raised to the fourth power

n is the valid number of cases.

Standard Error of Kurtosis

The standard error of kurtosis is computed as:

$$Std.Err. = \{[4*(n^2-1)*SE(S)^2]/[(n-3)*(n+5)]\}^{1/2}$$

where

SE(S) is equal to the standard error of skewness (see below)

n is the valid number of cases.

Skewness

Skewness measures the deviation of the distribution from symmetry. If the skewness is clearly different from 0, then that distribution is asymmetrical, while normal distributions are perfectly symmetrical.

$$Skewness = n*M_3/(n-1)*(n-2)*\sigma^3$$

where

M^j is equal to: $\sum(x_i\text{-}Meanx)^j$

σ^3 is the standard deviation (*sigma*) raised to the third power

n is the valid number of cases.

Standard Error of Skewness

The standard error of skewness is computed as:

$$Std.Err.=\{[6n*(n-1)]/[(n-2)*(n+1)*(n+3)]\}^{1/2}$$

where

n is the valid number of cases.

INDEX

B

C

D

E

F

G

K

L

M

N

P

REFERENCES

Abraham, B., & Ledolter, J. (1983). *Statistical methods for forecasting*. New York: Wiley.

Adorno, T. W., Frenkel-Brunswik, E., Levinson, D. J., & Sanford, R. N. (1950). *The authoritarian personality*. New York: Harper.

Akaike, H. (1973). Information theory and an extension of the maximum likelihood principle. In B. N. Petrov and F. Csaki (Eds.), *Second International Symposium on Information Theory*. Budapest: Akademiai Kiado.

Akaike, H. (1983). Information measures and model selection. *Bulletin of the International Statistical Institute: Proceedings of the 44th Session, Volume 1*. Pages 277-290.

Aldrich, J. H., & Nelson, F. D. (1984). *Linear probability, logit, and probit models*. Beverly Hills, CA: Sage Publications.

Almon, S. (1965). The distributed lag between capital appropriations and expenditures. *Econometrica*, *33*, 178-196.

American Supplier Institute (1984-1988). *Proceedings of Supplier Symposia on Taguchi Methods*. (April, 1984; November, 1984; October, 1985; October, 1986; October, 1987; October, 1988), Dearborn, MI: American Supplier Institute.

Anderson, O. D. (1976). *Time series analysis and forecasting*. London: Butterworths.

Anderson, S. B., & Maier, M. H. (1963). 34,000 pupils and how they grew. *Journal of Teacher Education*, *14*, 212-216.

Anderson, T. W. (1958). *An introduction to multivariate statistical analysis*. New York: Wiley.

Anderson, T. W., & Rubin, H. (1956). Statistical inference in factor analysis. *Proceedings of the Third Berkeley Symposium on Mathematical Statistics and Probability*. Berkeley: The University of California Press.

Andrews, D. F. (1972). Plots of high-dimensional data. *Biometrics*, *28*, 125-136.

AT&T (1956). *Statistical quality control handbook, Select code 700-444*. Indianapolis, AT&T Technologies.

Auble, D. (1953). Extended tables for the Mann-Whitney statistic. *Bulletin of the Institute of Educational Research, Indiana University*, *1*, No. 2.

Bagozzi, R. P., & Yi, Y. (1989). On the use of structural equation models in experimental design. *Journal of Marketing Research*, *26*, 271-284.

Bagozzi, R. P., Yi, Y., & Singh, S. (1991). On the use of structural equation models in experimental designs: Two extensions. *International Journal of Research in Marketing*, *8*, 125-140.

Bails, D. G., & Peppers, L. C. (1982). *Business fluctuations: Forecasting techniques and applications*. Englewood Cliffs, NJ: Prentice-Hall.

Bain, L. J. (1978). *Statistical analysis of reliability and life-testing models*. New York: Decker.

Baird, J. C. (1970). *Psychophysical analysis of visual space*. New York: Pergamon Press.

Baird, J. C., & Noma, E. (1978). *Fundamentals of scaling and psychophysics*. New York: Wiley.

Barcikowski, R., & Stevens, J. P. (1975). A Monte Carlo study of the stability of canonical correlations, canonical weights, and canonical variate-variable correlations. *Multivariate Behavioral Research*, *10*, 353-364.

Barker, T. B. (1986). Quality engineering by design: Taguchi's philosophy. *Quality Progress*, *19*, 32-42.

Barlow, R. E., & Proschan, F. (1975). *Statistical theory of reliability and life testing*. New York: Holt, Rinehart, & Winston.

Barnard, G. A. (1959). Control charts and stochastic processes. *Journal of the Royal Statistical Society*, Ser. B, *21*, 239.

Bartholomew, D. J. (1984). The foundations of factor analysis. *Biometrika*, *71*, 221-232.

Bates, D. M., & Watts, D. G. (1988). *Nonlinear regression analysis and its applications.* New York: Wiley.

Bayne, C. K., & Rubin, I. B. (1986). *Practical experimental designs and optimization methods for chemists.* Deerfield Beach, FL: VCH Publishers.

Becker, R. A., Denby, L., McGill, R., & Wilks, A. R. (1986). Datacryptanalysis: A case study. *Proceedings of the Section on Statistical Graphics, American Statistical Association*, 92-97.

Bendat, J. S. (1990). *Nonlinear system analysis and identification from random data.* New York: Wiley.

Bentler, P. M, & Bonett, D. G. (1980). Significance tests and goodness of fit in the analysis of covariance structures. *Psychological Bulletin*, *88*, 588-606.

Bentler, P. M. (1986). Structural modeling and Psychometrika: A historical perspective on growth and achievements. *Psychometrika*, *51*, 35-51.

Bentler, P. M. (1989). *EQS Structural equations program manual.* Los Angeles, CA: BMDP Statistical Software.

Bentler, P. M., & Weeks, D. G. (1979). Interrelations among models for the analysis of moment structures. *Multivariate Behavioral Research*, *14*, 169-185.

Bentler, P. M., & Weeks, D. G. (1980). Linear structural equations with latent variables. *Psychometrika*, *45*, 289-308.

Berkson, J., & Gage, R. R. (1950). The calculation of survival rates for cancer. *Proceedings of Staff Meetings, Mayo Clinic*, *25*, 250.

Bhote, K. R. (1988). *World class quality.* New York: AMA Membership Publications.

Binns, B., & Clark, N. (1986). The graphic designer's use of visual syntax. *Proceedings of the Section on Statistical Graphics, American Statistical Association*, 36-41.

Birnbaum, Z. W. (1952). Numerical tabulation of the distribution of Kolmogorov's statistic for finite sample values. *Journal of the American Statistical Association*, *47*, 425-441.

Birnbaum, Z. W. (1953). Distribution-free tests of fit for continuous distribution functions. *Annals of Mathematical Statistics*, *24*, 1-8.

Bishop, Y. M. M., Fienberg, S. E., & Holland, P. W. (1975). *Discrete multivariate analysis.* Cambridge, MA: MIT Press.

Bjorck, A. (1967). Solving linear least squares problems by Gram-Schmidt orthonormalization. *Bit*, *7*, 1-21.

Blackman, R. B., & Tukey, J. (1958). *The measurement of power spectral from the point of view of communication engineering.* New York: Dover.

Blackwelder, R. A. (1966). *Taxonomy: A text and reference book.* New York: Wiley.

Blalock, H. M. (1972). *Social statistics* (2nd ed.). New York: McGraw-Hill.

Bloomfield, P. (1976). *Fourier analysis of time series: An introduction*. New York: Wiley.

Bock, R. D. (1963). Programming univariate and multivariate analysis of variance. *Technometrics*, *5*, 95-117.

Bock, R. D. (1975). *Multivariate statistical methods in behavioral research*. New York: McGraw-Hill.

Bolch, B.W., & Huang, C. J. (1974). *Multivariate statistical methods for business and economics*. Englewood Cliffs, NJ: Prentice-Hall.

Bollen, K. A. (1989). *Structural equations with latent variables.* New York: John Wiley & Sons.

Borg, I., & Lingoes, J. (1987). *Multidimensional similarity structure analysis*. New York: Springer.

Borg, I., & Shye, S. (in press). *Facet Theory*. Newbury Park: Sage.

Bowker, A. G. (1948). A test for symmetry in contingency tables. *Journal of the American Statistical Association*, *43*, 572-574.

Box, G. E. P. (1954a). Some theorems on quadratic forms applied in the study of analysis of variance problems: I. Effect of inequality of variances in the one-way classification. *Annals of Mathematical Statistics*, *25*, 290-302.

Box, G. E. P. (1954b). Some theorems on quadratic forms applied in the study of analysis of variance problems: II. Effect of inequality of variances and of correlation of errors in the two-way classification. *Annals of Mathematical Statistics*, *25*, 484-498.

Box, G. E. P., & Anderson, S. L. (1955). Permutation theory in the derivation of robust criteria and the study of departures from assumptions. *Journal of the Royal Statistical Society*, *17*, 1-34.

Box, G. E. P., & Behnken, D. W. (1960). Some new three level designs for the study of quantitative variables. *Technometrics*, *2*, 455-475.

Box, G. E. P., & Cox, D. R. (1964). An analysis of transformations. *Journal of the Royal Statistical Society*, *26*, 211-253.

Box, G. E. P., & Cox, D. R. (1964). An analysis of transformations. *Journal of the Royal Statistical Society, B26*, 211-234.

Box, G. E. P., & Draper, N. R. (1987). *Empirical model-building and response surfaces.* New York: Wiley.

Box, G. E. P., & Jenkins, G. M. (1970). *Time series analysis*. San Francisco: Holden Day.

Box, G. E. P., & Jenkins, G. M. (1976). *Time series analysis: Forecasting and control*. San Francisco: Holden-Day.

Box, G. E. P., & Tidwell, P. W. (1962). Transformation of the independent variables. *Technometrics*, *4*, 531-550.

Box, G. E. P., Hunter, W. G., & Hunter, S. J. (1978). *Statistics for experimenters: An introduction to design, data analysis, and model building*. New York: Wiley.

Brenner, J. L., et al. (1968). Difference equations in forecasting formulas. *Management Science*, *14*, 141-159.

Brent, R. F. (1973). *Algorithms for minimization without derivatives.* Englewood Cliffs, NJ: Prentice-Hall.

Breslow, N. E. (1970). A generalized Kruskal-Wallis test for comparing *K* samples subject to unequal pattern of censorship. *Biometrika*, *57*, 579-594.

Breslow, N. E. (1974). Covariance analysis of censored survival data. *Biometrics*, *30*, 89-99.

Brigham, E. O. (1974). *The fast Fourier transform.* Englewood Cliffs, NJ: Prentice-Hall.

Brillinger, D. R. (1975). *Time series: Data analysis and theory*. New York: Holt, Rinehart. & Winston.

Brown, D. T. (1959). A note on approximations to discrete probability distributions. *Information and Control*, *2*, 386-392.

Brown, R. G. (1959). *Statistical forecasting for inventory control*. New York: McGraw-Hill.

Browne, M. W. (1968). A comparison of factor analytic techniques. *Psychometrika*, *33*, 267-334.

Browne, M. W. (1974). Generalized least squares estimators in the analysis of covariance structures. *South African Statistical Journal*, *8*, 1-24.

Browne, M. W. (1982). Covariance Structures. In D. M. Hawkins (Ed.) *Topics in Applied Multivariate Analysis.* Cambridge, MA: Cambridge University Press.

Browne, M. W. (1984). Asymptotically distribution free methods for the analysis of covariance structures. *British Journal of Mathematical and Statistical Psychology*, *37*, 62-83.

Browne, M. W., & Cudeck, R. (1990). Single sample cross-validation indices for covariance structures. *Multivariate Behavioral Research*, *24*, 445-455.

Browne, M. W., & Cudeck, R. (1992). Alternative ways of assessing model fit. In K. A. Bollen and J. S. Long (Eds.), *Testing structural equation models.* Beverly Hills, CA: Sage.

Browne, M. W., & DuToit, S. H. C. (1982). *AUFIT* (Version 1). A computer programme for the automated fitting of nonstandard models for means and covariances. Research Finding WS-27. Pretoria, South Africa: Human Sciences Research Council.

Browne, M. W., & DuToit, S. H. C. (1987). *Automated fitting of nonstandard models*. Report WS-39. Pretoria, South Africa: Human Sciences Research Council.

Browne, M. W., & DuToit, S. H. C. (1992). Automated fitting of nonstandard models. *Multivariate Behavioral Research*, *27*, 269-300.

Browne, M. W., & Mels, G. (1992). *RAMONA User's Guide.* The Ohio State University: Department of Psychology.

Browne, M. W., & Shapiro, A. (1989). *Invariance of covariance structures under groups of transformations*. Research Report 89/4. Pretoria, South Africa: University of South Africa Department of Statistics.

Browne, M. W., & Shapiro, A. (1991). Invariance of covariance structures under groups of transformations. *Metrika*, *38*, 335-345.

Buffa, E. S. (1972). *Operations management: Problems and models* (3rd. ed.). New York: Wiley.

Buja, A., & Tukey, P. A. (Eds.) (1991). *Computing and Graphics in Statistics.* New York: Springer-Verlag.

Buja, A., Fowlkes, E. B., Keramidas, E. M., Kettenring, J. R., Lee, J. C., Swayne, D. F., & Tukey, P. A. (1986). Discovering features of multivariate data through statistical graphics. *Proceedings of the Section on Statistical Graphics, American Statistical Association*, 98-103.

Burman, J. P. (1979). Seasonal adjustment - a survey. *Forecasting, Studies in Management Science*, *12*, 45-57.

Burns, L. S., & Harman, A. J. (1966). *The complex metropolis, Part V of profile of the Los Angeles metropolis: Its people and its homes.* Los Angeles: University of Chicago Press.

Campbell D. T., & Fiske, D. W. (1959). Convergent and discriminant validation by the multitrait-multimethod matrix. *Psychological Bulletin*, *56*, 81-105

Carmines, E. G., & Zeller, R. A. (1980). *Reliability and validity assessment*. Beverly Hills, CA: Sage Publications.

Carroll, J. D., & Wish, M. (1974). Multidimensional perceptual models and measurement methods. In E. C. Carterette and M. P. Friedman (Eds.), *Handbook of perception*. (Vol. 2, pp. 391-447). New York: Academic Press.

Cattell, R. B. (1966). The scree test for the number of factors. *Multivariate Behavioral Research*, *1*, 245-276.

Cattell, R. B., & Jaspers, J. A. (1967). A general plasmode for factor analytic exercises and research. *Multivariate Behavioral Research Monographs*.

Chambers, J. M., Cleveland, W. S., Kleiner, B., & Tukey, P. A. (1983). *Graphical methods for data analysis*. Bellmont, CA: Wadsworth.

Chan, L. K., Cheng, S. W., & Spiring, F. (1988). A new measure of process capability: C_{pm}. *Journal of Quality Technology*, *20*, 162-175.

Chernoff, H. (1973). The use of faces to represent points in k-dimensional space graphically. *Journal of American Statistical Association*, *68*, 361-368.

Christ, C. (1966). *Econometric models and methods*. New York: Wiley.

Clarke, G. M., & Cooke, D. (1978). *A basic course in statistics*. London: Edward Arnold.

Cleveland, W. S. (1979). Robust locally weighted regression and smoothing scatterplots. *Journal of the American Statistical Association*, *74*, 829-836.

Cleveland, W. S. (1984). Graphs in scientific publications. *The American Statistician*, *38*, 270-280.

Cleveland, W. S. (1985). *The elements of graphing data*. Monterey, CA: Wadsworth.

Cleveland, W. S., Harris, C. S., & McGill, R. (1982). Judgements of circle sizes on statistical maps. *Journal of the American Statistical Association*, *77*, 541-547.

Cliff, N. (1983). Some cautions concerning the application of causal modeling methods. *Multivariate Behavioral Research*, *18*, 115-126.

Cochran, W. G. (1950). The comparison of percentages in matched samples. *Biometrika*, *37*, 256-266.

Cole, D. A., Maxwell, S. E., Arvey, R., & Salas, E. (1993). Multivariate group comparisons of variable systems: MANOVA and structural equation modeling. *Psychological Bulletin*, *114*, 174-184.

Conover, W. J. (1974). Some reasons for not using the Yates continuity correction on 2 x 2 contingency tables. *Journal of the American Statistical Association*, *69*, 374-376.

Cook, R. D. (1977). Detection of influential observations in linear regression. *Technometrics*, *19*, 15-18.

Cook, R. D., & Nachtsheim, C. J. (1980). A comparison of algorithms for constructing exact D-optimal designs. *Technometrics*, *22*, 315-324.

Cooke, D., Craven, A. H., & Clarke, G. M. (1982). *Basic statistical computing*. London: Edward Arnold.

Cooley, J. W., & Tukey, J. W. (1965). An algorithm for the machine computation of complex Fourier series. *Mathematics of Computation*, *19*, 297-301.

Cooley, W. W., & Lohnes, P. R. (1971). *Multivariate data analysis*. New York: Wiley.

Cooley, W. W., & Lohnes, P. R. (1976). *Evaluation research in education*. New York: Wiley.

Coombs, C. H. (1950). Psychological scaling without a unit of measurement. *Psychological Review*, *57*, 145-158.

Coombs, C. H. (1964). *A theory of data.* New York: Wiley.

Corballis, M. C., & Traub, R. E. (1970). Longitudinal factor analysis. *Psychometrika, 35*, 79-98.

Cormack, R. M. (1971). A review of classification. *Journal of the Royal Statistical Society, 134*, 321-367.

Cornell, J. A. (1990a). *How to run mixture experiments for product quality.* Milwaukee, WI: ASQC.

Cornell, J. A. (1990b). *Experiments with mixtures: designs, models, and the analysis of mixture data* (2nd ed.). New York: Wiley.

Cox, D. R. (1957). Note on grouping. *Journal of the American Statistical Association, 52*, 543-547.

Cox, D. R. (1959). The analysis of exponentially distributed life-times with two types of failures. *Journal of the Royal Statistical Society, 21*, 411-421.

Cox, D. R. (1964). Some applications of exponential ordered scores. *Journal of the Royal Statistical Society, 26*, 103-110.

Cox, D. R. (1970). *The analysis of binary data*. New York: Halsted Press.

Cox, D. R. (1972). Regression models and life tables. *Journal of the Royal Statistical Society, 34*, 187-220.

Cox, D. R., & Oakes, D. (1984). *Analysis of survival data.* New York: Chapman & Hall.

Cramer, H. (1946). *Mathematical methods in statistics*. Princeton, NJ: Princeton University Press.

Crowley, J., & Hu, M. (1977). Covariance analysis of heart transplant survival data. *Journal of the American Statistical Association, 72*, 27-36.

Cudeck, R. (1989). Analysis of correlation matrices using covariance structure models. *Psychological Bulletin, 105*, 317-327.

Cudeck, R., & Browne, M. W. (1983). Cross-validation of covariance structures. *Multivariate Behavioral Research, 18*, 147-167.

Cutler, S. J., & Ederer, F. (1958). Maximum utilization of the life table method in analyzing survival. *Journal of Chronic Diseases, 8*, 699-712.

Dahlquist, G., & Bjorck, A. (1974). *Numerical Methods.* Englewood Cliffs, NJ: Prentice-Hall.

Daniel, C. (1976). *Applications of statistics to industrial experimentation.* New York: Wiley.

Daniell, P. J. (1946). Discussion on symposium on autocorrelation in time series. *Journal of the Royal Statistical Society, Suppl. 8*, 88-90.

Darlington, R. B. (1990). *Regression and linear models.* New York: McGraw-Hill.

Darlington, R. B., Weinberg, S., & Walberg, H. (1973). Canonical variate analysis and related techniques. *Review of Educational Research, 43*, 433-454.

Davies, P. M., & Coxon, A. P. M. (1982). *Key texts in multidimensional scaling.* Exeter, NH: Heinemann Educational Books.

De Boor, C. (1978). *A practical guide to splines*. New York: Springer-Verlag.

De Gruitjer, P. N. M., & Van Der Kamp, L. J. T. (Eds.). (1976). *Advances in psychological and educational measurement*. New York: Wiley.

Deming, S. N., & Morgan, S. L. (1993). *Experimental design: A chemometric approach.* (2nd ed.). Amsterdam, The Netherlands: Elsevier Science Publishers B.V.

Deming, W. E., & Stephan, F. F. (1940). The sampling procedure of the 1940 population census. *Journal of the American Statistical Association, 35*, 615-630.

Dempster, A. P. (1969). *Elements of Continuous Multivariate Analysis*. San Francisco: Addison-Wesley.

Dempster, A. P., Laird, N. M., & Rubin, D. B. (1977). Maximum likelihood from incomplete data via the EM algorithm. *Journal of the Royal Statistical Society*, *39*, 1-38.

Dennis, J. E., & Schnabel, R. B. (1983). *Numerical methods for unconstrained optimization and nonlinear equations.* Englewood Cliffs, NJ: Prentice Hall.

Diamond, W. J. (1981). *Practical experimental design.* Belmont, CA: Wadsworth.

Dijkstra, T. K. (1990). Some properties of estimated scale invariant covariance structures. *Psychometrika*, *55*, 327-336.

Dixon, W. J. (1954). Power under normality of several non-parametric tests. *Annals of Mathematical Statistics*, *25*, 610-614.

Dixon, W. J., & Massey, F. J. (1983). *Introduction to statistical analysis* (4th ed.). New York: McGraw-Hill.

Dodd, B. (1979). Lip reading in infants: Attention to speech presented in- and out-of-synchrony. *Cognitive Psychology*, *11*, 478-484.

Dodge, Y. (1985). *Analysis of experiments with missing data*. New York: Wiley.

Dodge, Y., Fedorov, V. V., & Wynn, H. P. (1988). *Optimal design and analysis of experiments.* New York: North-Holland.

Duncan, A. J. (1974). *Quality control and industrial statistics*. Homewood, IL: Richard D. Irwin.

Duncan, O. D., Haller, A. O., & Portes, A. (1968). Peer influence on aspiration: A reinterpretation. *American Journal of Sociology*, *74*, 119-137.

Durbin, J. (1970). Testing for serial correlation in least-squares regression when some of the regressors are lagged dependent variables. *Econometrica*, *38*, 410-421.

Durbin, J., & Watson, G. S. (1951). Testing for serial correlations in least squares regression. II. *Biometrika*, *38*, 159-178.

Dykstra, O. Jr. (1971). The augmentation of experimental data to maximize |X'X|. *Technometrics*, *13*, 682-688.

Eason, E. D., & Fenton, R. G. (1974). A comparison of numerical optimization methods for engineering design. *ASME Paper 73-DET-17*.

Efron, B. (1982). *The jackknife, the bootstrap, and other resampling plans.* Philadelphia, PA: Society for Industrial and Applied Mathematics.

Elandt-Johnson, R. C., & Johnson, N. L. (1980). *Survival models and data analysis*. New York: Wiley.

Elliott, D. F., & Rao, K. R. (1982). *Fast transforms: Algorithms, analyses, applications.* New York: Academic Press.

Enslein, K., Ralston, A., & Wilf, H. S. (1977). *Statistical methods for digital computers.* New York: Wiley.

Everitt, B. S. (1977). *The analysis of contingency tables.* London: Chapman & Hall.

Everitt, B. S. (1984). *An introduction to latent variable models*. London: Chapman and Hall.

Ewan, W. D. (1963). When and how to use Cu-sum charts. *Technometrics*, *5*, 1-32.

Feigl, P., & Zelen, M. (1965). Estimation of exponential survival probabilities with concomitant information. *Biometrics*, *21*, 826-838.

Fetter, R. B. (1967). *The quality control system.* Homewood, IL: Richard D. Irwin.

Fienberg, S. E. (1977). *The analysis of cross-classified categorical data*. Cambridge, MA: MIT Press.

Finn, J. D. (1974). *A general model for multivariate analysis.* New York: Holt, Rinehart & Winston.

Finn, J. D. (1977). Multivariate analysis of variance and covariance. In K. Enslein, A. Ralston, and H. S. Wilf (Eds.), *Statistical methods for digital computers. Vol. III.* (pp. 203-264). New York: Wiley.

Finney, D. J. (1971). *Probit analysis*. Cambridge, MA: Cambridge University Press.

Fisher, R. A. (1936). The use of multiple measurements in taxonomic problems. *Annals of Eugenics*, *7*, 179-188.

Fletcher, R. (1969). *Optimization*. New York: Academic Press.

Fletcher, R., & Powell, M. J. D. (1963). A rapidly convergent descent method for minimization. *Computer Journal*, *6*, 163-168.

Fletcher, R., & Reeves, C. M. (1964). Function minimization by conjugate gradients. *Computer Journal*, *7*, 149-154.

Fomby, T.B., Hill, R.C., & Johnson, S.R. (1984). *Advanced econometric methods*. New York: Springer-Verlag.

Fraser, C., & McDonald, R. P. (1988). COSAN: Covariance structure analysis. *Multivariate Behavioral Research*, *23*, 263-265.

Friedman, M. (1937). The use of ranks to avoid the assumption of normality implicit in the analysis of variance. *Journal of the American Statistical Association*, *32*, 675-701.

Friedman, M. (1940). A comparison of alternative tests of significance for the problem of *m* rankings. *Annals of Mathematical Statistics*, *11*, 86-92.

Fries, A., & Hunter, W. G. (1980). Minimum aberration $2^{(k-p)}$ designs. *Technometrics*, *22*, 601-608.

Frost, P. A. (1975). Some properties of the Almon lag technique when one searches for degree of polynomial and lag. *Journal of the American Statistical Association*, *70*, 606-612.

Fuller, W. A. (1976). *Introduction to statistical time series*. New York: Wiley.

Gale, N., & Halperin, W. C. (1982). A case for better graphics: The unclassed choropleth map. *The American Statistician*, *36*, 330-336.

Galil, Z., & Kiefer, J. (1980). Time- and space-saving computer methods, related to Mitchell's DETMAX, for finding D-optimum designs. *Technometrics*, *22*, 301-313.

Gara, M. A., & Rosenberg, S. (1979). The identification of persons as supersets and subsets in free-response personality descriptions. *Journal of Personality and Social Psychology*, *37*, 2161-2170.

Gara, M. A., & Rosenberg, S. (1981). Linguistic factors in implicit personality theory. *Journal of Personality and Social Psychology*, *41*, 450-457.

Gardner, E. S., Jr. (1985). Exponential smoothing: The state of the art. *Journal of Forecasting*, *4*, 1-28.

Garvin, D. A. (1987). Competing on the eight dimensions of quality. *Harvard Business Review*, November/December, 101-109.

Gbur, E., Lynch, M., & Weidman, L. (1986). An analysis of nine rating criteria on 329 U. S. metropolitan areas. *Proceedings of the Section on Statistical Graphics, American Statistical Association*, 104-109.

Gedye, R. (1968). *A manager's guide to quality and reliability*. New York: Wiley.

Gehan, E. A. (1965a). A generalized Wilcoxon test for comparing arbitrarily singly-censored samples. *Biometrika*, *52*, 203-223.

Gehan, E. A. (1965b). A generalized two-sample Wilcoxon test for doubly-censored data. *Biometrika*, *52*, 650-653.

Gehan, E. A., & Siddiqui, M. M. (1973). Simple regression methods for survival time studies. *Journal of the American Statistical Association*, *68*, 848-856.

Gehan, E. A., & Thomas, D. G. (1969). The performance of some two sample tests in small samples with and without censoring. *Biometrika*, *56*, 127-132.

Gerald, C. F., & Wheatley, P. O. (1989). *Applied numerical analysis* (4th ed.). Reading, MA: Addison Wesley.

Gibbons, J. D. (1976). *Nonparametric methods for quantitative analysis.* New York: Holt, Rinehart, & Winston.

Gibbons, J. D. (1985). *Nonparametric statistical inference* (2nd ed.). New York: Marcel Dekker.

Gifi, A. (1990). *Nonlinear multivariate analysis.* New York: Wiley.

Gill, P. E., & Murray, W. (1972). Quasi-Newton methods for unconstrained optimization. *Journal of the Institute of Mathematics and its Applications*, *9*, 91-108.

Gill, P. E., & Murray, W. (1974). *Numerical methods for constrained optimization.* New York: Academic Press.

Glass, G. V., & Stanley, J. (1970). *Statistical methods in education and Psychology.* Englewood Cliffs, NJ: Prentice-Hall.

Glasser, M. (1967). Exponential survival with covariance. *Journal of the American Statistical Association*, *62*, 561-568.

Gnanadesikan, R., Roy, S., & Srivastava, J. (1971). *Analysis and design of certain quantitative multiresponse experiments.* Oxford: Pergamon Press, Ltd.

Golub, G. H., & Van Loan, C. F. (1983). *Matrix computations.* Baltimore: Johns Hopkins University Press.

Goodman, L .A., & Kruskal, W. H. (1972). Measures of association for cross-classifications IV: Simplification of asymptotic variances. *Journal of the American Statistical Association*, *67*, 415-421.

Goodman, L. A. (1954). Kolmogorov-Smirnov tests for psychological research. *Psychological Bulletin*, *51*, 160-168.

Goodman, L. A. (1971). The analysis of multidimensional contingency tables: Stepwise procedures and direct estimation methods for models building for multiple classification. *Technometrics*, *13*, 33-61.

Goodman, L. A., & Kruskal, W. H. (1954). Measures of association for cross-classifications. *Journal of the American Statistical Association*, *49*, 732-764.

Goodman, L. A., & Kruskal, W. H. (1959). Measures of association for cross-classifications II: Further discussion and references. *Journal of the American Statistical Association*, *54*, 123-163.

Goodman, L. A., & Kruskal, W. H. (1963). Measures of association for cross-classifications III: Approximate sampling theory. *Journal of the American Statistical Association*, *58*, 310-364.

Grant, E. L., & Leavenworth, R. S. (1980). *Statistical quality control* (5th ed.). New York: McGraw-Hill.

Green, P. E., & Carmone, F. J. (1970). *Multidimensional scaling and related techniques in marketing analysis.* Boston: Allyn & Bacon.

Greenhouse, S. W., & Geisser, S. (1958). Extension of Box's results on the use of the *F* distribution in multivariate analysis. *Annals of Mathematical Statistics*, *29*, 95-112.

Greenhouse, S. W., & Geisser, S. (1959). On methods in the analysis of profile data. *Psychometrika*, *24*, 95-112.

Gross, A. J., & Clark, V. A. (1975). *Survival distributions: Reliability applications in the medical sciences*. New York: Wiley.

Gruvaeus, G., & Wainer, H. (1972). Two additions to hierarchical cluster analysis. *The British Journal of Mathematical and Statistical Psychology*, *25*, 200-206.

Guttman, L. (1954). A new approach to factor analysis: the radex. In P. F. Lazarsfeld (Ed.), *Mathematical thinking in the social sciences.* New York: Columbia University Press.

Guttman, L. (1968). A general nonmetric technique for finding the smallest coordinate space for a configuration of points. *Pyrometrical*, *33*, 469-506.

Haberman, S. J. (1972). Loglinear fit for contingency tables. *Applied Statistics*, *21*, 218-225.

Haberman, S. J. (1974). *The analysis of frequency data*. Chicago: University of Chicago Press.

Hahn, G. J., & Shapiro, S. S. (1967). *Statistical models in engineering*. New York: Wiley.

Hakstian, A. R., Rogers, W. D., & Cattell, R. B. (1982). The behavior of numbers of factors rules with simulated data. *Multivariate Behavioral Research*, *17*, 193-219.

Hald, A. (1952). *Statistical theory with engineering applications.* New York: Wiley.

Harman, H. H. (1967). *Modern factor analysis.* Chicago: University of Chicago Press.

Harris, R. J. (1976). The invalidity of partitioned *U* tests in canonical correlation and multivariate analysis of variance. *Multivariate Behavioral Research*, *11*, 353-365.

Hart, K. M., & Hart, R. F. (1989). *Quantitative methods for quality improvement.* Milwaukee, WI: ASQC Quality Press.

Hartigan, J. A. (1975). *Clustering algorithms.* New York: Wiley.

Hartley, H. O. (1959). Smallest composite designs for quadratic response surfaces. *Biometrics*, *15*, 611-624.

Haviland, R. P. (1964). *Engineering reliability and long life design*. Princeton, NJ: Van Nostrand.

Hayduk, L. A. (1987). *Structural equation modelling with LISREL: Essentials and advances.* Baltimore: The Johns Hopkins University Press.

Hays, W. L. (1981). *Statistics* (3rd ed.). New York: CBS College Publishing.

Hays, W. L. (1988). *Statistics* (4th ed.). New York: CBS College Publishing.

Heiberger, R. M. (1989). *Computation for the analysis of designed experiments*. New York: Wiley.

Henley, E. J., & Kumamoto, H. (1980). *Reliability engineering and risk assessment*. New York: Prentice-Hall.

Hettmansperger, T. P. (1984). *Statistical inference based on ranks*. New York: Wiley.

Hibbs, D. (1974). Problems of statistical estimation and causal inference in dynamic time series models. In H. Costner (Ed.), *Sociological Methodology 1973/1974* (pp. 252-308). San Francisco: Jossey-Bass.

Hilton, T. L. (1969). *Growth study annotated bibliography. Princeton, NJ: Educational Testing Service Progress Report 69-11.*

Hochberg, J., & Krantz, D. H. (1986). Perceptual properties of statistical graphs. *Proceedings of the Section on Statistical Graphics, American Statistical Association*, 29-35.

Hocking, R. R., & Speed, F. M. (1975). A full rank analysis of some linear model problems. *Journal of the American Statistical Association*, *70*, 707-712.

Hoerl, A. E. (1962). Application of ridge analysis to regression problems. *Chemical Engineering Progress*, *58*, 54-59.

Hoff, J. C. (1983). *A practical guide to Box-Jenkins forecasting*. London: Lifetime Learning Publications.

Hogg, R. V., & Craig, A. T. (1970). *Introduction to mathematical statistics*. New York: Macmillan.

Holzinger, K. J., & Swineford, F. (1939). *A study in factor analysis: The stability of a bi-factor solution.* University of Chicago: Supplementary Educational Monographs, No. 48.

Hooke, R., & Jeeves, T. A. (1961). Direct search solution of numerical and statistical problems. *Journal of the Association for Computing Machinery*, *8*, 212-229.

Hotelling, H. (1947). Multivariate quality control. In Eisenhart, Hastay, and Wallis (Eds.), *Techniques of Statistical Analysis*. New York: McGraw-Hill.

Hotelling, H., & Pabst, M. R. (1936). Rank correlation and tests of significance involving no assumption of normality. *Annals of Mathematical Statistics*, *7*, 29-43.

Hsu, P. L. (1938). Contributions to the theory of Student's *t* test as applied to the problem of two samples. *Statistical Research Memoirs*, *2*, 1-24.

Huba, G. J., & Harlow, L. L. (1987). Robust structural equation models: implications for developmental psychology. *Child Development*, *58*, 147-166.

Huberty, C. J. (1975). Discriminant analysis. *Review of Educational Research*, *45*, 543-598.

Huynh, H., & Feldt, L. S. (1970). Conditions under which mean square ratios in repeated measures designs have exact *F*-distributions. *Journal of the American Statistical Association*, *65*, 1582-1589.

Ireland, C. T., & Kullback, S. (1968). Contingency tables with given marginals. *Biometrika*, *55*, 179-188.

Jaccard, J., Weber, J., & Lundmark, J. (1975). A multitrait-multimethod factor analysis of four attitude assessment procedures. *Journal of Experimental Social Psychology*, *11*, 149-154.

Jacobs, D. A. H. (Ed.). (1977). *The state of the art in numerical analysis.* London: Academic Press.

Jacoby, S. L. S., Kowalik, J. S., & Pizzo, J. T. (1972). *Iterative methods for nonlinear optimization problems.* Englewood Cliffs, NJ: Prentice-Hall.

James, L. R., Mulaik, S. A., & Brett, J. M. (1982). *Causal analysis. Assumptions, models, and data.* Beverly Hills, CA: Sage Publications.

Jardine, N., & Sibson, R. (1971). *Mathematical taxonomy.* New York: Wiley.

Jastrow, J. (1892). On the judgment of angles and position of lines. *American Journal of Psychology*, *5*, 214-248.

Jenkins, G. M., & Watts, D. G. (1968). *Spectral analysis and its applications.* San Francisco: Holden-Day.

Jennrich, R. I, & Sampson, P. F. (1968). Application of stepwise regression to non-linear estimation. *Technometrics*, *10*, 63-72.

Jennrich, R. I. (1970). An asymptotic χ^2 test for the equality of two correlation matrices. *Journal of the American Statistical Association*, *65*, 904-912.

Jennrich, R. I. (1977). Stepwise regression. In K. Enslein, A. Ralston, & H.S. Wilf (Eds.), *Statistical methods for digital computers*. New York: Wiley.

Jennrich, R. I. (1977). Stepwise discriminant analysis. In K. Enslein, A. Ralston, & H.S. Wilf (Eds.), *Statistical methods for digital computers*. New York: Wiley.

Jennrich, R. I., & Moore, R. H. (1975). Maximum likelihood estimation by means of nonlinear least squares. *Proceedings of the Statistical Computing Section*, American Statistical Association, 57-65.

Johnson, L. W., & Ries, R. D. (1982). *Numerical Analysis* (2nd ed.). Reading, MA: Addison Wesley.

Johnson, N. L. (1961). A simple theoretical approach to cumulative sum control charts. *Journal of the American Statistical Association*, *56*, 83-92.

Johnson, N. L., & Leone, F. C. (1962). Cumulative sum control charts - mathematical principles applied to their construction and use. *Industrial Quality Control*, *18*, 15-21.

Johnson, R. A. & Wichern, D. W. (1988). *Applied multivariate statistical analysis*. Englewood Cliffs, NJ: Prentice Hall.

Johnson, S. C. (1967). Hierarchical clustering schemes. *Psychometrika*, *32*, 241-254.

Johnston, J. (1972). *Econometric methods*. New York: McGraw-Hill.

Jöreskog, K. G. (1973). A general model for estimating a linear structural equation system. In A. S. Goldberger and O. D. Duncan (Eds.), *Structural Equation Models in the Social Sciences*. New York: Seminar Press.

Jöreskog, K. G. (1974). Analyzing psychological data by structural analysis of covariance matrices. In D. H. Krantz, R. C. Atkinson, R. D. Luce, and P. Suppes (Eds.), *Contemporary Developments in Mathematical Psychology, Vol. II*. New York: W. H. Freeman and Company.

Jöreskog, K. G. (1978). Structural analysis of covariance and correlation matrices. *Psychometrika*, *43*, 443-477.

Jöreskog, K. G., & Lawley, D. N. (1968). New methods in maximum likelihood factor analysis. *British Journal of Mathematical and Statistical Psychology*, *21*, 85-96.

Jöreskog, K. G., & Sörbom, D. (1979). *Advances in factor analysis and structural equation models*. Cambridge, MA: Abt Books.

Jöreskog, K. G., & Sörbom, D. (1982). Recent developments in structural equation modeling. *Journal of Marketing Research*, *19*, 404-416.

Jöreskog, K. G., & Sörbom, D. (1984). *Lisrel VI. Analysis of linear structural relationships by maximum likelihood, instrumental variables, and least squares methods*. Mooresville, Indiana: Scientific Software.

Jöreskog, K. G., & Sörbom, D. (1989). *Lisrel 7. A guide to the program and applications.* Chicago: SPSS Inc.

Judge, G. G., Griffith, W. E., Hill, R. C., Luetkepohl, H., & Lee, T. S. (1985). *The theory and practice of econometrics*. New York: Wiley.

Juran, J. M. (1960). Pareto, Lorenz, Cournot, Bernnouli, Juran and others. *Industrial Quality Control*, *17*, 25.

Juran, J. M. (1962). *Quality control handbook*. New York: McGraw-Hill.

Juran, J. M., & Gryna, F. M. (1970). *Quality planning and analysis*. New York: McGraw-Hill.

Juran, J. M., & Gryna, F. M. (1980). *Quality planning and analysis* (2nd ed.). New York: McGraw-Hill.

Juran, J. M., & Gryna, F. M. (1988). *Juran's quality control handbook* (4th ed.). New York: McGraw-Hill.

Kachigan, S. K. (1986). *Statistical analysis: An interdisciplinary introduction to univariate & multivariate methods*. New York: Redius Press.

Kackar, R. M. (1985). Off-line quality control, parameter design, and the Taguchi method. *Journal of Quality Technology, 17*, 176-188.

Kackar, R. M. (1986). Taguchi's quality philosophy: Analysis and commentary. *Quality Progress, 19*, 21-29.

Kaiser, H. F. (1958). The varimax criterion for analytic rotation in factor analysis. *Pyrometrical, 23*, 187-200.

Kaiser, H. F. (1960). The application of electronic computers to factor analysis. *Educational and Psychological Measurement, 20*, 141-151.

Kalbfleisch, J. D., & Prentice, R. L. (1980). *The statistical analysis of failure time data*. New York: Wiley.

Kane, V. E. (1986). Process capability indices. *Journal of Quality Technology, 18*, 41-52.

Kaplan, E. L., & Meier, P. (1958). Nonparametric estimation from incomplete observations. *Journal of the American Statistical Association, 53*, 457-481.

Karsten, K. G., (1925). *Charts and graphs*. New York: Prentice-Hall.

Keeves, J. P. (1972). *Educational environment and student achievement.* Melbourne: Australian Council for Educational Research.

Kendall, M. G. (1948). *Rank correlation methods.* (1st ed.). London: Griffin.

Kendall, M. G. (1975). *Rank correlation methods* (4th ed.). London: Griffin.

Kendall, M. G. (1984). *Time Series*. New York: Oxford University Press.

Kendall, M., & Ord, J. K. (1990). *Time series* (3rd ed.). London: Griffin.

Kendall, M., & Stuart, A. (1979). *The advanced theory of statistics* (Vol. 2). New York: Hafner.

Kennedy, A. D., & Gehan, E. A. (1971). Computerized simple regression methods for survival time studies. *Computer Programs in Biomedicine, 1*, 235-244.

Kennedy, W. J., & Gentle, J. E. (1980). *Statistical computing*. New York: Marcel Dekker, Inc.

Kenny, D. A. (1979). *Correlation and causality.* New York: Wiley.

Keppel, G. (1973). *Design and analysis: A researcher's handbook*. Engelwood Cliffs, NJ: Prentice-Hall.

Keppel, G. (1982). *Design and analysis: A researcher's handbook* (2nd ed.). Engelwood Cliffs, NJ: Prentice-Hall.

Keselman, H. J., Rogan, J. C., Mendoza, J. L., & Breen, L. L. (1980). Testing the validity conditions for repeated measures *F* tests. *Psychological Bulletin, 87*, 479-481.

Khuri, A. I., & Cornell, J. A. (1987). *Response surfaces: Designs and analyses*. New York: Marcel Dekker, Inc.

Kiefer, J., & Wolfowitz, J. (1960). The equivalence of two extremum problems. *Canadian Journal of Mathematics, 12*, 363-366.

Kim, J. O., & Mueller, C. W. (1978a). *Factor analysis: Statistical methods and practical issues*. Beverly Hills, CA: Sage Publications.

Kim, J. O., & Mueller, C. W. (1978b). *Introduction to factor analysis: What it is and how to do it.* Beverly Hills, CA: Sage Publications.

Kirk, D. B. (1973). On the numerical approximation of the bivariate normal (tetrachoric) correlation coefficient. *Psychometrika, 38*, 259-268.

Kirk, R. E. (1968). *Experimental design: Procedures for the behavioral sciences.* (1st ed.). Monterey, CA: Brooks/Cole.

Kirk, R. E. (1982). *Experimental design: Procedures for the behavioral sciences.* (2nd ed.). Monterey, CA: Brooks/Cole.

Kivenson, G. (1971). *Durability and reliability in engineering design*. New York: Hayden.

Klecka, W. R. (1980). *Discriminant analysis*. Beverly Hills, CA: Sage.

Klein, L. R. (1974). *A textbook of econometrics*. Englewood Cliffs, NJ: Prentice-Hall.

Kline, P. (1979). *Psychometrics and psychology*. London: Academic Press.

Kline, P. (1986). *A handbook of test construction*. New York: Methuen.

Kmenta, J. (1971). *Elements of econometrics*. New York: Macmillan.

Knuth, Donald E. (1981). *Seminumerical algorithms*. 2nd ed., Vol 2 of: *The art of computer programming*. Reading, Mass.: Addison-Wesley.

Kolata, G. (1984). The proper display of data. *Science*, *226*, 156-157.

Kolmogorov, A. (1941). Confidence limits for an unknown distribution function. *Annals of Mathematical Statistics*, *12*, 461-463.

Korin, B. P. (1969). On testing the equality of *k* covariance matrices. *Biometrika*, *56*, 216-218.

Kruskal, J. B. (1964). Nonmetric multidimensional scaling: A numerical method. *Pyrometrical*, *29*, 1-27, 115-129.

Kruskal, J. B., & Wish, M. (1978). *Multidimensional scaling*. Beverly Hills, CA: Sage Publications.

Kruskal, W. H. (1952). A nonparametric test for the several sample problem. *Annals of Mathematical Statistics*, *23*, 525-540.

Kruskal, W. H. (1975). Visions of maps and graphs. In J. Kavaliunas (Ed.), *Auto-carto II, proceedings of the international symposium on computer assisted cartography*. Washington, DC: U. S. Bureau of the Census and American Congress on Survey and Mapping.

Kruskal, W. H., & Wallis, W. A. (1952). Use of ranks in one-criterion variance analysis. *Journal of the American Statistical Association*, *47*, 583-621.

Ku, H. H., & Kullback, S. (1968). Interaction in multidimensional contingency tables: An information theoretic approach. *J. Res. Nat. Bur. Standards Sect. B*, 72, 159-199.

Ku, H. H., Varner, R. N., & Kullback, S. (1971). Analysis of multidimensional contingency tables. *Journal of the American Statistical Association*, *66*, 55-64.

Kullback, S. (1959). *Information theory and statistics*. New York: Wiley.

Kvålseth, T. O. (1985). Cautionary note about R^2. *The American Statistician*, *39*, 279-285.

Lagakos, S. W., & Kuhns, M. H. (1978). Maximum likelihood estimation for censored exponential survival data with covariates. *Applied Statistics*, *27*, 190-197.

Lance, G. N., & Williams, W. T. (1966). A general theory of classificatory sorting strategies. *Computer Journal*, *9*, 373.

Lance, G. N., & Williams, W. T. (1966). Computer programs for hierarchical polythetic classification ("symmetry analysis"). *Computer Journal*, *9*, 60.

Larsen, W. A., & McCleary, S. J. (1972). The use of partial residual plots in regression analysis. *Technometrics*, *14*, 781-790.

Lawless, J. F. (1982). *Statistical models and methods for lifetime data*. New York: Wiley.

Lawley, D. N., & Maxwell, A. E. (1971). *Factor analysis as a statistical method.* New York: American Elsevier.

Lawley, D. N., & Maxwell, A. E. (1971). *Factor analysis as a statistical method* (2nd. ed.). London: Butterworth & Company.

Lee, E. T. (1980). *Statistical methods for survival data analysis.* Belmont, CA: Lifetime Learning.

Lee, E. T., & Desu, M. M. (1972). A computer program for comparing *K* samples with right-censored data. *Computer Programs in Biomedicine*, *2*, 315-321.

Lee, E. T., Desu, M. M., & Gehan, E. A. (1975). A Monte-Carlo study of the power of some two-sample tests. *Biometrika*, *62*, 425-532.

Lee, S., & Hershberger, S. (1990). A simple rule for generating equivalent models in covariance structure modeling. *Multivariate Behavioral Research*, *25*, 313-334.

Lehmann, E. L. (1975). *Nonparametrics: Statistical methods based on ranks.* San Francisco: Holden-Day.

Lilliefors, H. W. (1967). On the Kolmogorov-Smirnov test for normality with mean and variance unknown. *Journal of the American Statistical Association, 64*, 399-402.

Lindeman, R. H., Merenda, P. F., & Gold, R. (1980). *Introduction to bivariate and multivariate analysis*. New York: Scott, Foresman, & Co.

Lindman, H. R. (1974). *Analysis of variance in complex experimental designs*. San Francisco: W. H. Freeman & Co.

Linfoot, E. H. (1957). An informational measure of correlation. *Information and Control*, *1*, 50-55.

Linn, R. L. (1968). A Monte Carlo approach to the number of factors problem. *Psychometrika*, *33*, 37-71.

Lipson, C., & Sheth, N. C. (1973). *Statistical design and analysis of engineering experiments*. New York: McGraw-Hill.

Lloyd, D. K., & Lipow, M. (1977). *Reliability: Management, methods, and mathematics.* New York: McGraw-Hill.

Loehlin, J. C. (1987). *Latent variable models: An introduction to latent, path, and structural analysis.* Hillsdale, NJ: Erlbaum.

Long, J. S. (1983a). *Confirmatory factor analysis.* Beverly Hills: Sage.

Long, J. S. (1983b). *Covariance structure models: An introduction to LISREL.* Beverly Hills: Sage.

Longley, J. W. (1967). An appraisal of least squares programs for the electronic computer from the point of view of the user. *Journal of the American Statistical Association*, *62*, 819-831.

Longley, J. W. (1984). *Least squares computations using orthogonalization methods*. New York: Marcel Dekker.

Lord, F. M. (1957). A significance test for the hypothesis that two variables measure the same trait except for errors of measurement. *Psychometrika*, *22*, 207-220.

Lorenz, M. O. (1904). Methods of measuring the concentration of wealth. *American Statistical Association Publication*, *9*, 209-219.

Lucas, J. M. (1976). The design and use of cumulative sum quality control schemes. *Journal of Quality Technology*, *8*, 45-70.

Lucas, J. M. (1982). Combined Shewhart-CUSUM quality control schemes. *Journal of Quality Technology*, *14*, 89-93.

Maddala, G. S. (1977) *Econometrics*. New York: McGraw-Hill.

Maiti, S. S., & Mukherjee, B. N. (1990). A note on the distributional properties of the Jöreskog-Sörbom fit indices. *Psychometrika*, *55*, 721-726.

Makridakis, S. G. (1983). Empirical evidence versus personal experience. *Journal of Forecasting*, *2*, 295-306.

Makridakis, S. G. (1990). *Forecasting, planning, and strategy for the 21st century.* London: Free Press.

Makridakis, S. G., & Wheelwright, S. C. (1978). *Interactive forecasting: Univariate and multivariate methods* (2nd ed.). San Francisco, CA: Holden-Day.

Makridakis, S. G., & Wheelwright, S. C. (1989). *Forecasting methods for management* (5th ed.). New York: Wiley.

Makridakis, S. G., Wheelwright, S. C., & McGee, V. E. (1983). *Forecasting: Methods and applications* (2nd ed.). New York: Wiley.

Makridakis, S., Andersen, A., Carbone, R., Fildes, R., Hibon, M., Lewandowski, R., Newton, J., Parzen, R., & Winkler, R. (1982). The accuracy of extrapolation (time series) methods: Results of a forecasting competition. *Journal of Forecasting*, *1*, 11-153.

Malinvaud, E. (1970). *Statistical methods of econometrics*. Amsterdam: North-Holland Publishing Co.

Mandel, B. J. (1969). The regression control chart. *Journal of Quality Technology*, *1*, 3-10.

Mann, H. B., & Whitney, D. R. (1947). On a test of whether one of two random variables is stochastically larger than the other. *Annals of Mathematical Statistics*, *18*, 50-60.

Mann, N. R., Schafer, R. E., & Singpurwalla, N. D. (1974). *Methods for statistical analysis of reliability and life data*. New York: Wiley.

Mantel, N. (1966). Evaluation of survival data and two new rank order statistics arising in its consideration. *Cancer Chemotherapy Reports*, *50*, 163-170.

Mantel, N. (1967). Ranking procedures for arbitrarily restricted observations. *Biometrics*, *23*, 65-78.

Mantel, N. (1974). Comment and suggestion on the Yates continuity correction. *Journal of the American Statistical Association*, *69*, 378-380.

Mantel, N., & Haenszel, W. (1959). Statistical aspects of the analysis of data from retrospective studies of disease. *Journal of the National Cancer Institute*, *22*, 719-748.

Marascuilo, L. A., & McSweeney, M. (1977). *Nonparametric and distribution free methods for the social sciences.* Monterey, CA: Brooks/Cole.

Marple, S. L., Jr. (1987). *Digital spectral analysis.* Englewood Cliffs, NJ: Prentice-Hall.

Mardia, K. V., Kent, J. T., and Bibby, J. M. (1979). *Multivariate analysis*. New York: Academic Press.

Marsaglia, G. (1962). Random variables and computers. In J. Kozenik (Ed.), *Information theory, statistical decision functions, random processes: Transactions of the Third Prague Conference*. Prague: Czechoslovak Academy of Sciences.

Mason, R. L., Gunst, R. F., & Hess, J. L. (1989). *Statistical design and analysis of experiments with applications to engineering and science.* New York: Wiley.

Massey, F. J., Jr. (1951). The Kolmogorov-Smirnov test for goodness of fit. *Journal of the American Statistical Association*, *46*, 68-78.

Matsueda, R. L., & Bielby, W. T. (1986). Statistical power in covariance structure models. In N. B. Tuma (Ed.), *Sociological methodology.* Washington, DC: American Sociological Association.

McArdle, J. J. (1978). A structural view of structural models. Paper presented at the *Winter Workshop on Latent Structure Models Applied to Developmental Data, University of Denver, December, 1978.*

McArdle, J. J., & McDonald, R. P. (1984). Some algebraic properties of the Reticular Action Model for moment structures. *British Journal of Mathematical and Statistical Psychology*, *37*, 234-251.

McCleary, R., & Hay, R. A. (1980). *Applied time series analysis for the social sciences*. Beverly Hills, CA: Sage Publications.

McDonald, R. P. (1980). A simple comprehensive model for the analysis of covariance structures. *British Journal of Mathematical and Statistical Psychology*, *31*, 59-72.

McDonald, R. P. (1989). An index of goodness-of-fit based on noncentrality. *Journal of Classification*, *6*, 97-103.

McDonald, R. P., & Hartmann, W. M. (1992). A procedure for obtaining initial value estimates in the RAM model. *Multivariate Behavioral Research*, *27*, 57-76.

McDonald, R. P., & Mulaik, S. A. (1979). Determinacy of common factors: A nontechnical review. *Psychological Bulletin*, *86*, 297-306.

McDowall, D., McCleary, R., Meidinger, E. E., & Hay, R. A. (1980). *Interrupted time series analysis*. Beverly Hills, CA: Sage Publications.

McKenzie, E. (1984). General exponential smoothing and the equivalent ARMA process. *Journal of Forecasting*, *3*, 333-344.

McKenzie, E. (1985). Comments on 'Exponential smoothing: The state of the art' by E. S. Gardner, Jr. *Journal of Forecasting*, *4*, 32-36.

McLain, D. H. (1974). Drawing contours from arbitrary data points. *The Computer Journal*, *17*, 318-324.

McLean, R. A., & Anderson, V. L. (1984). *Applied factorial and fractional designs*. New York: Marcel Dekker.

McLeod, A. I., & Sales, P. R. H. (1983). An algorithm for approximate likelihood calculation of ARMA and seasonal ARMA models. *Applied Statistics*, 211-223 (Algorithm AS).

McNemar, Q. (1947). Note on the sampling error of the difference between correlated proportions or percentages. *Psychometrika*, *12*, 153-157.

McNemar, Q. (1969). *Psychological statistics* (4th ed.). New York: Wiley.

Mels, G. (1989). *A general system for path analysis with latent variables*. M. S. Thesis: Department of Statistics, University of South Africa.

Mendoza, J. L., Markos, V. H., & Gonter, R. (1978). A new perspective on sequential testing procedures in canonical analysis: A Monte Carlo evaluation. *Multivariate Behavioral Research*, *13*, 371-382.

Meredith, W. (1964). Canonical correlation with fallible data. *Psychometrika*, *29*, 55-65.

Miller, R. (1981). *Survival analysis*. New York: Wiley.

Milligan, G. W. (1980). An examination of the effect of six types of error perturbation on fifteen clustering algorithms. *Psychometrika*, *45*, 325-342.

Milliken, G. A., & Johnson, D. E. (1984). *Analysis of messy data: Vol. I. Designed experiments*. New York: Van Nostrand Reinhold, Co.

Mitchell, T. J. (1974a). Computer construction of "D-optimal" first-order designs. *Technometrics*, *16*, 211-220.

Mitchell, T. J. (1974b). An algorithm for the construction of "D-optimal" experimental designs. *Technometrics*, *16*, 203-210.

Mittag, H. J. (1993). *Qualitätsregelkarten*. München/Wien: Hanser Verlag.

Mittag, H. J., & Rinne, H. (1993). *Statistical methods of quality assurance*. London/New York: Chapman & Hall.

Monro, D. M. (1975). Complex discrete fast Fourier transform. *Applied Statistics*, *24*, 153-160.

Monro, D. M., & Branch, J. L. (1976). The chirp discrete Fourier transform of general length. *Applied Statistics*, *26*, 351-361.

Montgomery, D. C. (1976). *Design and analysis of experiments*. New York: Wiley.

Montgomery, D. C. (1985). *Statistical quality control*. New York: Wiley.

Montgomery, D. C. (1991) *Design and analysis of experiments* (3rd ed.). New York: Wiley.

Montgomery, D. C., & Wadsworth, H. M. (1972). Some techniques for multivariate quality control applications. *Technical Conference Transactions*. Washington, DC: American Society for Quality Control.

Montgomery, D. C., Johnson, L. A., & Gardiner, J. S. (1990). *Forecasting and time series analysis* (2nd ed.). New York: McGraw-Hill.

Mood, A. M. (1954). *Introduction to the theory of statistics*. New York: McGraw Hill.

Morris, M., & Thisted, R. A. (1986). Sources of error in graphical perception: A critique and an experiment. *Proceedings of the Section on Statistical Graphics, American Statistical Association*, 43-48.

Morrison, A. S., Black, M. M., Lowe, C. R., MacMahon, B., & Yuasa, S. (1973). Some international differences in histology and survival in breast cancer. *International Journal of Cancer*, *11*, 261-267.

Morrison, D. (1967). *Multivariate statistical methods*. New York: McGraw-Hill.

Moses, L. E. (1952). Non-parametric statistics for psychological research. *Psychological Bulletin*, *49*, 122-143.

Mulaik, S. A. (1972). *The foundations of factor analysis*. New York: McGraw Hill.

Muth, J. F. (1960). Optimal properties of exponentially weighted forecasts. *Journal of the American Statistical Association*, *55*, 299-306.

Nachtsheim, C. J. (1979). *Contributions to optimal experimental design*. Ph.D. thesis, Department of Applied Statistics, University of Minnesota.

Nachtsheim, C. J. (1987). Tools for computer-aided design of experiments. *Journal of Quality Technology*, *19*, 132-160.

Nelder, J. A., & Mead, R. (1965). A Simplex method for function minimization. *Computer Journal*, *7*, 308-313.

Nelson, L. (1984). The Shewhart control chart - tests for special causes. *Journal of Quality Technology, 15*, 237-239.

Nelson, L. (1985). Interpreting Shewhart X-bar control charts. *Journal of Quality Technology, 17*, 114-116.

Nelson, W. (1982). *Applied life data analysis*. New York: Wiley.

Neter, J., Wasserman, W., & Kutner, M. H. (1985). *Applied linear statistical models: Regression, analysis of variance, and experimental designs.* Homewood, IL: Irwin.

Neter, J., Wasserman, W., & Kutner, M. H. (1989). *Applied linear regression models* (2nd ed.). Homewood, IL: Irwin.

Nisbett, R. E., Fong, G. F., Lehman, D. R., & Cheng, P. W. (1987). Teaching reasoning. *Science*, *238*, 625-631.

Noori, H. (1989). The Taguchi methods: Achieving design and output quality. *The Academy of Management Executive*, *3*, 322-326.

Nunally, J. C. (1970). *Introduction to psychological measurement*. New York: McGraw-Hill.

Nunnally, J. C. (1978). *Psychometric theory*. New York: McGraw-Hill.

Nussbaumer, H. J. (1982). *Fast Fourier transforms and convolution algorithms* (2nd ed.). New York: Springer-Verlag.

O'Brien, R. G., & Kaiser, M. K. (1985). MANOVA method for analyzing repeated measures designs: An extensive primer. *Psychological Bulletin*, *97*, 316-333.

O'Neill, R. (1971). Function minimization using a Simplex procedure. *Applied Statistics*, *3*, 79-88.

Okunade, A. A., Chang, C. F., & Evans, R. D. (1993). Comparative analysis of regression output summary statistics in common statistical packages. *The American Statistician*, *47*, 298-303.

Olds, E. G. (1949). The 5% significance levels for sums of squares of rank differences and a correction. *Annals of Mathematical Statistics*, *20*, 117-118.

Olson, C. L. (1976). On choosing a test statistic in multivariate analysis of variance. *Psychological Bulletin*, *83*, 579-586.

Ostle, B., & Malone, L. C. (1988). *Statistics in research: Basic concepts and techniques for research workers* (4th ed.). Ames, IA: Iowa State Press.

Ostrom, C. W. (1978). *Time series analysis: Regression techniques*. Beverly Hills, CA: Sage Publications.

Overall, J. E., & Speigel, D. K. (1969). Concerning least squares analysis of experimental data. *Psychological Bulletin*, *83*, 579-586.

Page, E. S. (1954). Continuous inspection schemes. *Biometrics*, *41*, 100-114.

Page, E. S. (1961). Cumulative sum charts. *Technometrics*, *3*, 1-9.

Palumbo, F. A., & Strugala, E. S. (1945). Fraction defective of battery adapter used in handie-talkie. *Industrial Quality Control*, *November*, 6-8.

Pankratz, A. (1983). *Forecasting with univariate Box-Jenkins models: Concepts and cases*. New York: Wiley.

Parzen, E. (1961). Mathematical considerations in the estimation of spectra: Comments on the discussion of Messers, Tukey, and Goodman. *Technometrics*, *3*, 167-190; 232-234.

Patil, K. D. (1975). Cochran's Q test: Exact distribution. *Journal of the American Statistical Association*, *70*, 186-189.

Peace, G. S. (1993). *Taguchi methods: A hands-on approach*. Milwaukee, WI: ASQC.

Pearson, K., (Ed.). (1968). *Tables of incomplete beta functions* (2nd ed.). Cambridge, MA: Cambridge University Press.

Pedhazur, E. J. (1973). *Multiple regression in behavioral research*. New York: Holt, Rinehart, & Winston.

Pedhazur, E. J. (1982). *Multiple regression in behavioral research* (2nd ed.). New York: Holt, Rinehart, & Winston.

Peressini, A. L., Sullivan, F. E., & Uhl, J. J., Jr. (1988). *The mathematics of nonlinear programming*. New York: Springer.

Peto, R., & Peto, J. (1972). Asymptotically efficient rank invariant procedures. *Journal of the Royal Statistical Society*, *135*, 185-207.

Phadke, M. S. (1989). *Quality engineering using robust design*. Englewood Cliffs, NJ: Prentice-Hall.

Piepel, G. F. (1988). Programs for generating extreme vertices and centroids of linearly constrained experimental regions. *Journal of Quality Technology, 20*, 125-139.

Pike, M. C. (1966). A method of analysis of certain class of experiments in carcinogenesis. *Biometrics, 22*, 142-161.

Pillai, K. C. S. (1965). On the distribution of the largest characteristic root of a matrix in multivariate analysis. *Biometrika*, *52*, 405-414.

Plackett, R. L., & Burman, J. P. (1946). The design of optimum multifactorial experiments. *Biometrika*, *34*, 255-272.

Porebski, O. R. (1966). Discriminatory and canonical analysis of technical college data. *British Journal of Mathematical and Statistical Psychology*, *19*, 215-236.

Powell, M. J. D. (1964). An efficient method for finding the minimum of a function of several variables without calculating derivatives. *Computer Journal*, *7*, 155-162.

Prentice, R. (1973). Exponential survivals with censoring and explanatory variables. *Biometrika*, *60*, 279-288.

Press, William, H., Flannery, B. P., Teukolsky, S. A., Vetterling, W. T. (1986). *Numerical recipies*. New York: Cambridge University Press.

Priestley, M. B. (1981). *Spectral analysis and time series*. New York: Academic Press.

Pyzdek, T. (1989). *What every engineer should know about quality control*. New York: Marcel Dekker.

Ralston, A., & Wilf, H.S. (Eds.). (1960). *Mathematical methods for digital computers*. New York: Wiley.

Ralston, A., & Wilf, H.S. (Eds.). (1967). *Mathematical methods for digital computers* (Vol. II). New York: Wiley.

Randles, R. H., & Wolfe, D. A. (1979). *Introduction to the theory of nonparametric statistics*. New York: Wiley.

Rao, C. R. (1951). An asymptotic expansion of the distribution of Wilks' criterion. *Bulletin of the International Statistical Institute*, *33*, 177-181.

Rao, C. R. (1965). *Linear statistical inference and its applications*. New York: Wiley.

Rhoades, H. M., & Overall, J. E. (1982). A sample size correction for Pearson chi-square in 2 x 2 contingency tables. *Psychological Bulletin*, *91*, 418-423.

Rinne, H., & Mittag, H. J. (1995). *Statistische Methoden der Qualitätssicherung (3rd. edition)*. München/Wien: Hanser Verlag.

Ripley, B. D. (1981). *Spacial statistics*. New York: Wiley.

Rogan, J. C., Keselman, J. J., & Mendoza, J. L. (1979). Analysis of repeated measurements. *British Journal of Mathematical and Statistical Psychology*, *32*, 269-286.

Rosenberg, S. (1977). New approaches to the analysis of personal constructs in person perception. In A. Landfield (Ed.), *Nebraska symposium on motivation* (Vol. 24). Lincoln, NE: University of Nebraska Press.

Rosenberg, S., & Sedlak, A. (1972). Structural representations of implicit personality theory. In L. Berkowitz (Ed.). *Advances in experimental social psychology* (Vol. 6). New York: Academic Press.

Roskam, E. E., & Lingoes, J. C. (1970). *MINISSA-I*: A Fortran IV program for the smallest space analysis of square symmetric matrices. *Behavioral Science*, *15*, 204-205.

Ross, P. J. (1988). *Taguchi techniques for quality engineering: Loss function, orthogonal experiments, parameter, and tolerance design*. Milwaukee, WI: ASQC.

Roy, J. (1958). Step-down procedure in multivariate analysis. *Annals of Mathematical Statistics*, *29*, 1177-1187.

Roy, J. (1967). *Some aspects of multivariate analysis*. New York: Wiley.

Roy, R. (1990). *A primer on the Taguchi method*. Milwaukee, WI: ASQC.

Royston, J. P. (1982). An extension of Shapiro and Wilk's W test for normality to large samples. *Applied Statistics, 31*, 115-124.

Rozeboom, W. W. (1979). Ridge regression: Bonanza or beguilement? *Psychological Bulletin*, *86*, 242-249.

Rozeboom, W. W. (1988). Factor indeterminacy: the saga continues. *British Journal of Mathematical and Statistical Psychology*, *41*, 209-226.

Runyon, R. P., & Haber, A. (1976). *Fundamentals of behavioral statistics*. Reading, MA: Addison-Wesley.

Ryan, T. P. (1989). *Statistical methods for quality improvement.* New York: Wiley.

Sandler, G. H. (1963). *System reliability engineering*. Englewood Cliffs, NJ: Prentice-Hall.

SAS Institute, Inc. (1982). *SAS user's guide: Statistics, 1982 Edition*. Cary, NC: SAS Institute, Inc.

Satorra, A., & Saris, W. E. (1985). Power of the likelihood ratio test in covariance structure analysis. *Psychometrika*, *50*, 83-90.

Saxena, K. M. L., & Alam, K. (1982). Estimation of the noncentrality parameter of a chi squared distribution. *Annals of Statistics*, *10*, 1012-1016.

Scheffé, H. (1953). A method for judging all possible contrasts in the analysis of variance. *Biometrica*, *40*, 87-104.

Scheffé, H. (1959). *The analysis of variance*. New York: Wiley.

Scheffé, H. (1963). The simplex-centroid design for experiments with mixtures. *Journal of the Royal Statistical Society*, *B25*, 235-263.

Scheffé, H., & Tukey, J. W. (1944). A formula for sample sizes for population tolerance limits. *Annals of Mathematical Statistics*, *15*, 217.

Scheines, R. (1994). Causation, indistinguishability, and regression. In F. Faulbaum, (Ed.), *SoftStat '93. Advances in statistical software 4*. Stuttgart: Gustav Fischer Verlag.

Schiffman, S. S., Reynolds, M. L., & Young, F. W. (1981). *Introduction to multidimensional scaling: Theory, methods, and applications*. New York: Academic Press.

Schmidt, P., & Muller, E. N. (1978). The problem of multicollinearity in a multistage causal alienation model: A comparison of ordinary least squares, maximum-likelihood and ridge estimators. *Quality and Quantity*, *12*, 267-297.

Schmidt, P., & Sickles, R. (1975). On the efficiency of the Almon lag technique. *International Economic Review*, *16*, 792-795.

Schmidt, P., & Waud, R. N. (1973). The Almon lag technique and the monetary versus fiscal policy debate. *Journal of the American Statistical Association*, *68*, 11-19.

Schnabel, R. B., Koontz, J. E., and Weiss, B. E. (1985). A modular system of algorithms for unconstrained minimization. *ACM Transactions on Mathematical Software*, *11*, 419-440.

Schneider, H. (1986). *Truncated and censored samples from normal distributions*. New York: Marcel Dekker.

Schönemann, P. H., & Steiger, J. H. (1976). Regression component analysis. *British Journal of Mathematical and Statistical Psychology*, *29*, 175-189.

Schrock, E. M. (1957). *Quality control and statistical methods*. New York: Reinhold Publishing.

Schwarz, G. (1978). Estimating the dimension of a model. *Annals of Statistics*, *6*, 461-464.

Scott, D. W. (1979). On optimal and data-based histograms. *Biometrika*, *66*, 605-610.

Searle, S. R. (1987). *Linear models for unbalanced data*. New York: Wiley.

Searle, S. R., Casella, G., & McCullock, C. E. (1992). *Variance components*. New York: Wiley.

Seber, G. A. F., & Wild, C. J. (1989). *Nonlinear regression.* New York: Wiley.

Sebestyen, G. S. (1962). *Decision making processes in pattern recognition.* New York: Macmillan.

Sen, P. K., & Puri, M. L. (1968). On a class of multivariate multisample rank order tests, II: Test for homogeneity of dispersion matrices. *Sankhya*, *30*, 1-22.

Shapiro, A., & Browne, M. W. (1983). On the investigation of local identifiability: A counter example. *Psychometrika*, *48*, 303-304.

Shapiro, S. S., Wilk, M. B., & Chen, H. J. (1968). A comparative study of various tests of normality. *Journal of the American Statistical Association, 63*, 1343-1372.

Shewhart, W. A. (1931). *Economic control of quality of manufactured product*. New York: D. Van Nostrand.

Shewhart, W. A. (1939). *Statistical method from the viewpoint of quality*. Washington, DC: The Graduate School Department of Agriculture.

Shirland, L. E. (1993). *Statistical quality control with microcomputer applications.* New York: Wiley.

Shiskin, J., Young, A. H., & Musgrave, J. C. (1967). *The X-11 variant of the census method II seasonal adjustment program.* Technical paper no. 15. Washington, DC: Bureau of the Census.

Shumway, R. H. (1988). *Applied statistical time series analysis.* Englewood Cliffs, NJ: Prentice Hall.

Siegel, A. E. (1956). Film-mediated fantasy aggression and strength of aggressive drive. *Child Development*, *27*, 365-378.

Siegel, S. (1956). *Nonparametric statistics for the behavioral sciences.* New York: McGraw-Hill.

Siegel, S., & Castellan, N. J. (1988). *Nonparametric statistics for the behavioral sciences* (2nd ed.) New York: McGraw-Hill.

Simkin, D., & Hastie, R. (1986). Towards an information processing view of graph perception. *Proceedings of the Section on Statistical Graphics, American Statistical Association*, 11-20.

Sinha, S. K., & Kale, B. K. (1980). *Life testing and reliability estimation*. New York: Halstead.

Smirnov, N. V. (1948). Table for estimating the goodness of fit of empirical distributions. *Annals of Mathematical Statistics*, *19*, 279-281.

Smith, D. J. (1972). *Reliability engineering*. New York: Barnes & Noble.

Smith, K. (1953). Distribution-free statistical methods and the concept of power efficiency. In L. Festinger and D. Katz (Eds.), *Research methods in the behavioral sciences* (pp. 536-577). New York: Dryden.

Sneath, P. H. A., & Sokal, R. R. (1973). *Numerical taxonomy.* San Francisco: W. H. Freeman & Co.

Snee, R. D. (1975). Experimental designs for quadratic models in constrained mixture spaces. *Technometrics*, *17*, 149-159.

Snee, R. D. (1979). Experimental designs for mixture systems with multi-component constraints. *Communications in Statistics - Theory and Methods*, *A8(4)*, 303-326.

Snee, R. D. (1985). Computer-aided design of experiments - some practical experiences. *Journal of Quality Technology*, *17*, 222-236.

Snee, R. D. (1986). An alternative approach to fitting models when re-expression of the response is useful. *Journal of Quality Technology, 18*, 211-225.

Sokal, R. R., & Mitchener, C. D. (1958). A statistical method for evaluating systematic relationships. *University of Kansas Science Bulletin*, *38*, 1409.

Sokal, R. R., & Sneath, P. H. A. (1963). *Principles of numerical taxonomy*. San Francisco: W. H. Freeman & Co.

Spirtes, P., Glymour, C., & Scheines, R. (1993). *Causation, prediction, and search.* Lecture Notes in Statistics, V. 81. New York: Springer-Verlag.

Spjotvoll, E., & Stoline, M. R. (1973). An extension of the *T*-method of multiple comparison to include the cases with unequal sample sizes. *Journal of the American Statistical Association*, *68*, 976-978.

Springer, M. D. (1979). *The algebra of random variables*. New York: Wiley.

Spruill, M. C. (1986). Computation of the maximum likelihood estimate of a noncentrality parameter. *Journal of Multivariate Analysis*, *18*, 216-224.

Steiger, J. H. (1979). Factor indeterminacy in the 1930's and in the 1970's; some interesting parallels. *Psychometrika*, *44*, 157-167.

Steiger, J. H. (1980a). Tests for comparing elements of a correlation matrix. *Psychological Bulletin*, *87*, 245-251.

Steiger, J. H. (1980b). Testing pattern hypotheses on correlation matrices: Alternative statistics and some empirical results. *Multivariate Behavioral Research*, *15*, 335-352.

Steiger, J. H. (1988). Aspects of person-machine communication in structural modeling of correlations and covariances. *Multivariate Behavioral Research*, *23*, 281-290.

Steiger, J. H. (1989). *EzPATH: A supplementary module for SYSTAT and SYGRAPH.* Evanston, IL: SYSTAT, Inc.

Steiger, J. H. (1990). Some additional thoughts on components and factors. *Multivariate Behavioral Research*, *25*, 41-45.

Steiger, J. H., & Browne, M. W. (1984). The comparison of interdependent correlations between optimal linear composites. *Psychometrika*, *49*, 11-24.

Steiger, J. H., & Hakstian, A. R. (1982). The asymptotic distribution of elements of a correlation matrix: Theory and application. *British Journal of Mathematical and Statistical Psychology*, *35*, 208-215.

Steiger, J. H., & Lind, J. C. (1980). Statistically-based tests for the number of common factors. Paper presented at the annual Spring Meeting of the Psychometric Society in Iowa City, IA. May 30, 1980.

Steiger, J. H., & Schönemann, P. H. (1978). A history of factor indeterminacy. In S. Shye, (Ed.), *Theory Construction and Data Analysis in the Social Sciences.* San Francisco: Jossey-Bass.

Steiger, J. H., Shapiro, A., & Browne, M. W. (1985). On the multivariate asymptotic distribution of sequential chi-square statistics. *Psychometrika*, *50*, 253-264.

Stelzl, I. (1986). Changing causal relationships without changing the fit: Some rules for generating equivalent LISREL models. *Multivariate Behavioral Research*, *21*, 309-331.

Stenger, F. (1973). Integration formula based on the trapezoid formula. *Journal of the Institute of Mathematics and Applications*, *12*, 103-114.

Stevens, J. (1986). *Applied multivariate statistics for the social sciences.* Hillsdale, NJ: Erlbaum.

Stevens, W. L. (1939). Distribution of groups in a sequence of alternatives. *Annals of Eugenics*, *9*, 10-17.

Stewart, D. K., & Love, W. A. (1968). A general canonical correlation index. *Psychological Bulletin*, *70*, 160-163.

Steyer, R. (1992). *Theorie causale regressionsmodelle* [Theory of causal regression models]. Stuttgart: Gustav Fischer Verlag.

Steyer, R. (1994). Principles of causal modeling: a summary of its mathematical foundations and practical steps. In F. Faulbaum, (Ed.), *SoftStat '93. Advances in statistical software 4.* Stuttgart: Gustav Fischer Verlag.

Taguchi, G. (1987). *Jikken keikakuho* (3rd ed., Vol I & II). Tokyo: Maruzen. English translation edited by D. Clausing. *System of experimental design.* New York: UNIPUB/Kraus International

Tanaka, J. S., & Huba, G. J. (1985). A fit index for covariance structure models under arbitrary GLS estimation. *British Journal of Mathematical and Statistical Psychology*, *38*, 197-201.

Tanaka, J. S., & Huba, G. J. (1989). A general coefficient of determination for covariance structure models under arbitrary GLS estimation. *British Journal of Mathematical and Statistical Psychology*, *42*, 233-239.

Tatsuoka, M. M. (1970). *Discriminant analysis.* Champaign, IL: Institute for Personality and Ability Testing.

Tatsuoka, M. M. (1971). *Multivariate analysis.* New York: Wiley.

Tatsuoka, M. M. (1976). Discriminant analysis. In P. M. Bentler, D. J. Lettieri, and G. A. Austin (Eds.), *Data analysis strategies and designs for substance abuse research.* Washington, DC: U.S. Government Printing Office.

Thorndyke, R. L., & Hagen, E. P. (1977). *Measurement and evaluation in psychology and education.* New York: Wiley.

Thurstone, L. L. (1947). *Multiple factor analysis.* Chicago: University of Chicago Press.

Timm, N. H. (1975). *Multivariate analysis with applications in education and psychology.* Monterey, CA: Brooks/Cole.

Timm, N. H., & Carlson, J. (1973). *Multivariate analysis of non-orthogonal experimental designs using a multivariate full rank model.* Paper presented at the American Statistical Association Meeting, New York.

Timm, N. H., & Carlson, J. (1975). Analysis of variance through full rank models. *Multivariate behavioral research monographs*, No. *75-1*.

Tribus, M., & Sconyi, G. (1989). An alternative view of the Taguchi approach. *Quality Progress*, *22*, 46-48.

Trivedi, P. K., & Pagan, A. R. (1979). Polynomial distributed lags: A unified treatment. *Economic Studies Quarterly*, *30*, 37-49.

Tucker, L. R., Koopman, R. F., & Linn, R. L. (1969). Evaluation of factor analytic research procedures by means of simulated correlation matrices. *Psychometrika*, *34*, 421-459.

Tufte, E. R. (1983). *The visual display of quantitative information.* Cheshire, CT: Graphics Press.

Tufte, E. R. (1990). *Envisioning information.* Cheshire, CT: Graphics Press.

Tukey, J. W. (1953). *The problem of multiple comparisons.* Unpublished manuscript, Princeton University.

Tukey, J. W. (1967). An introduction to the calculations of numerical spectrum analysis. In B. Harris (Ed.), *Spectral analysis of time series.* New York: Wiley.

Tukey, J. W. (1977). *Exploratory data analysis.* Reading, MA: Addison-Wesley.

Tukey, J. W. (1984). *The collected works of John W. Tukey.* Monterey, CA: Wadsworth.

Tukey, P. A. (1986). A data analyst's view of statistical plots. *Proceedings of the Section on Statistical Graphics, American Statistical Association*, 21-28.

Tukey, P. A., & Tukey, J. W. (1981). Graphical display of data sets in 3 or more dimensions. In V. Barnett (Ed.), *Interpreting multivariate data*. Chichester, U.K.: Wiley.

Vale, C. D., & Maurelli, V. A. (1983). Simulating multivariate nonnormal distributions. *Psychometrika*, *48*, 465-471.

Vandaele, W. (1983). *Applied time series and Box-Jenkins models*. New York: Academic Press.

Vaughn, R. C. (1974). *Quality control*. Ames, IA: Iowa State Press.

Velicer, W. F., & Jackson, D. N. (1990). Component analysis vs. factor analysis: some issues in selecting an appropriate procedure. *Multivariate Behavioral Research*, *25*, 1-28.

Velleman, P. F., & Hoaglin, D. C. (1981). *Applications, basics, and computing of exploratory data analysis*. Belmont, CA: Duxbury Press.

Wainer, H. (1995). Visual revelations. *Chance*, *8*, 48-54.

Wald, A. (1947). *Sequential analysis*. New York: Wiley.

Walker, J. S. (1991). *Fast Fourier transforms*. Boca Raton, FL: CRC Press.

Wallis, K. F. (1974). Seasonal adjustment and relations between variables. *Journal of the American Statistical Association*, *69*, 18-31.

Wang, C. M., & Gugel, H. W. (1986). High-performance graphics for exploring multivariate data. *Proceedings of the Section on Statistical Graphics, American Statistical Association*, 60-65.

Ward, J. H. (1963). Hierarchical grouping to optimize an objective function. *Journal of the American Statistical Association*, *58*, 236.

Wei, W. W. (1989). *Time series analysis: Univariate and multivariate methods*. New York: Addison-Wesley.

Welstead, S. T. (1994). *Neural network and fuzzy logic applications in C/C++*. New York: Wiley.

Wescott, M. E. (1947). Attribute charts in quality control. *Conference Papers, First Annual Convention of the American Society for Quality Control*. Chicago: John S. Swift Co.

Wheaton, B., Múthen, B., Alwin, D., & Summers G. (1977). Assessing reliability and stability in panel models. In D. R. Heise (Ed.), *Sociological Methodology*. New York: Wiley.

Wheeler, D. J., & Chambers, D.S. (1986). *Understanding statistical process control*. Knoxville, TN: Statistical Process Controls, Inc.

Wherry, R. J. (1984). *Contributions to correlational analysis*. New York: Academic Press.

Whitney, D. R. (1948). *A comparison of the power of non-parametric tests and tests based on the normal distribution under non-normal alternatives*. Unpublished doctoral dissertation, Ohio State University.

Whitney, D. R. (1951). A bivariate extension of the *U* statistic. *Annals of Mathematical Statistics*, *22*, 274-282.

Wiggins, J. S., Steiger, J. H., and Gaelick, L. (1981). Evaluating circumplexity in models of personality. *Multivariate Behavioral Research*, *16*, 263-289.

Wilcoxon, F. (1945). Individual comparisons by ranking methods. *Biometrica Bulletin*, *1*, 80-83.

Wilcoxon, F. (1947). Probability tables for individual comparisons by ranking methods. *Biometrics*, *3*, 119-122.

Wilcoxon, F. (1949). *Some rapid approximate statistical procedures.* Stamford, CT: American Cyanamid Co.

Wilde, D. J., & Beightler, C. S. (1967). *Foundations of optimization.* Englewood Cliffs, NJ: Prentice-Hall.

Wilks, S. S. (1946). *Mathematical statistics.* Princeton, NJ: Princeton University Press.

Williams, W. T., Lance, G. N., Dale, M. B., & Clifford, H. T. (1971). Controversy concerning the criteria for taxonometric strategies. *Computer Journal*, *14*, 162.

Wilson, G. A., & Martin, S. A. (1983). An empirical comparison of two methods of testing the significance of a correlation matrix. *Educational and Psychological Measurement*, *43*, 11-14.

Winer, B. J. (1962). *Statistical principles in experimental design*. New York: McGraw-Hill.

Winer, B. J. (1971). *Statistical principles in experimental design* (2nd ed.). New York: McGraw-Hill.

Wolynetz, M. S. (1979a). Maximum likelihood estimation from confined and censored normal data. *Applied Statistics*, *28*, 185-195.

Wolynetz, M. S. (1979b). Maximum likelihood estimation in a linear model from confined and censored normal data. *Applied Statistics*, *28*, 195-206.

Wonnacott, R. J., & Wonnacot, T. H. (1970). *Econometrics*. New York: Wiley.

Woodward, J. A., Bonett, D. G., & Brecht, M. L. (1990). *Introduction to linear models and experimental design*. New York: Harcourt, Brace, Jovanovich.

Woodward, J. A., & Overall, J. E. (1975). Multivariate analysis of variance by multiple regression methods. *Psychological Bulletin*, *82*, 21-32.

Woodward, J. A., & Overall, J. E. (1976). Calculation of power of the *F* test. *Educational and Psychological Measurement*, *36*, 165-168.

Woodward, J. A., Douglas, G. B., & Brecht, M. L. (1990). *Introduction to linear models and experimental design*. New York: Academic Press.

Yokoyama, Y., & Taguchi, G. (1975). *Business data analysis: Experimental regression analysis.* Tokyo: Maruzen.

Youden, W. J., & Zimmerman, P. W. (1936). Field trials with fiber pots. *Contributions from Boyce Thompson Institute, 8*, 317-331.

Young, F. W, & Hamer, R. M. (1987). *Multidimensional scaling: History, theory, and applications.* Hillsdale, NJ: Erlbaum

Young, F. W., Kent, D. P., & Kuhfeld, W. F. (1986). Visuals: Software for dynamic hyper-dimensional graphics. *Proceedings of the Section on Statistical Graphics, American Statistical Association*, 69-74.

Younger, M. S. (1985). *A first course in linear regression* (2nd ed.). Boston: Duxbury Press.

Yuen, C. K., & Fraser, D. (1979). *Digital spectral analysis*. Melbourne: CSIRO/Pitman.

Zippin, C., & Armitage, P. (1966). Use of concomitant variables and incomplete survival information in the estimation of an exponential survival parameter. *Biometrics*, *22*, 665-672.

Zupan, J. (1982). *Clustering of large data sets*. New York: Research Studies Press.

Zwick, W. R., & Velicer, W. F. (1986). Comparison of five rules for determining the number of components to retain. *Psychological Bulletin*, *99*, 432-442.

INDEX

A

B

C

D

StatSoft

E

F

G

H

I

J

K

L

StatSoft

StatSoft

N

O

P

Q

R

S

T

StatSoft

U

V

W

X

Y

Z